The Little Red Book 2011

Passenger Transport Directory for the British Isles

Editor

Ian Allan PUBLISHING

Riverdene Business Park, Molesey Road, Hersham, Surrey KT12 4RG
Tel: 01932 266600 Fax: 01932 266601

STOP PRESS · STOP PRESS · STOP PRESS · STOP PRESS · STOP PRESS · STOP PRESS · STOP PRESS

Page 77
ARRIVA PLC
The acquisition of Arriva by DB UK Holding Ltd has now been completed

Page 78
FIRSTGROUP PLC
Chief Executive: Tim O'Toole (from 1 November 2010). Sir Moir Lockhead retires in March 2011.

Page 198
RENFREWSHIRE
GIBSON DIRECT LTD
Local bus services sold to McGills Bus Service Ltd, Barrhead (see Inverclyde)

Other titles from Ian Allan Publishing

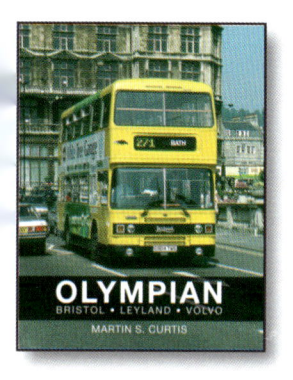

Olympian: Bristol, Leyland, Volvo

Martin Curtis

Ian Allan Publishing • Printed Paper Cased • 280 x 212mm • 96pp • 175 mono and colour illustrations • 978 0 7110 3479 2 • £18.99

- This exciting new book provides a definitive history of the Leyland Olympian, one of Britain's most significant buses.
- Written by *Bristol Lodekka* author Martin Curtis, the book contains a wealth of 175 mono and colour photographs with detailed and informative captions.
- This book will deserve a place on every enthusiast's bookshelf!

Buses Yearbook 2011

Edited by Stewart J. Brown

Ian Allan Publishing • Hardback • 235 x 172mm • 128 pages • 978 0 7110 3474 7 • £15.99

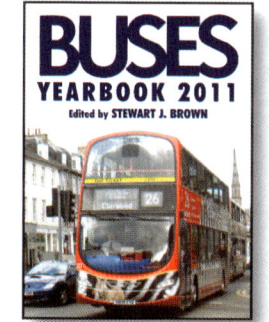

- The eagerly awaited *Buses Yearbook* has become one of the fastest selling annuals and a must have for enthusiasts nationwide.
- Author Stewart Brown has worked in the bus industry for more than 30 years and has compiled *Buses Yearbook* and its predecessor *Buses Annual* since the 1987 edition.
- The book includes a varied mix of articles and photo-features, both historic and contemporary, covering a wide range of subjects of road transport interest.

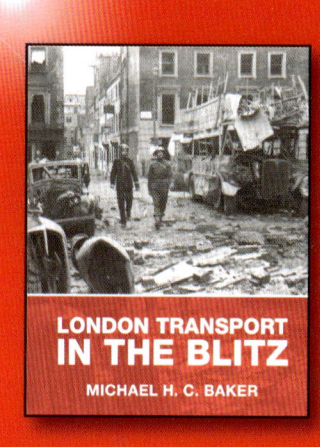

London Transport in the Blitz

Michael H.C. Baker

This fascinating story details London transport's heroic efforts to keep the capital moving during the worst onslaughts of the Luftwaffe during World War 2. Not only did Underground stations have to provide essential additional air raid shelters but buses, trains, trams and trolleybuses had to continue operating despite sustaining vast damage to vehicles and infrastructure.

This book provides an anecdotal history of London Transport during the period between 1939 and 1945. Author Michael Baker draws from personal reminiscences and stories from local newspapers to describe one of the most hellish periods in London's long history

Ian Allan Publishing • Hardback • 254 x 202mm • 160 pages • c120 mono and colour illustrations • 978 0 7110 3478 5 • £19.99

Order **today** from Ian Allan *plus*

Our specialist mail order service offering thousands of titles from hundreds of publishers.

Buy online at **www.ianallanplus.com**

Call **+44 (0) 01455 254450** (P&P charges apply)

Visit our Ian Allan Plus Showroom:
4 Watling Drive, Hinckley, Leics LE10 3EY

or visit one of our Ian Allan Book & Model Shops in:

BIRMINGHAM	CARDIFF	LONDON	MANCHESTER
12 Ethel Street	31 Royal Arcade	45/46 Lower Marsh	5 Piccadilly Station App.
Birmingham B2 4BG	Cardiff CF10 1AE	Waterloo SE1 7RG	Manchester M1 2GH
Tel: 0121 643 2496	Tel: 029 2039 0615	Tel: 020 7401 2100	Tel: 0161 237 9840

Ian Allan PUBLISHING

Britain's Leading Specialist Publisher

www.ianallanpublishing.com

Contents

Stop Press 4

List of Abbreviations 8

Index of Advertisers 8

Foreword 9

Section 1:
Trade Directory 10

Section 2:
Tendering & Regulatory
Authorities 59

Section 3:
Organisations and Societies 67

Section 4:
British Isles Operators 76

Section 5:
Index
(Trade) 220
Index
(British Isles Operators) 224

Key to Symbols in Section 4 - British Isles Operators

♿	Vehicle suitable for disabled		Seat belt-fitted Vehicle	R24	24 hour recovery service
T	Toilet-drop facilities available		Coach(es) with galley facilities		Replacement vehicle available
R	Recovery service available		Air-conditioned vehicle(s)		Vintage Coach(es) available
	Open top vehicle(s)		Coaches with toilet facilities		

Little Red Book 2011
73rd Annual Edition
Britain's longest established passenger transport directory

ISBN   978 0711 034 488

All rights reserved. No part of this book may be reproduced or transmitted in any form or by any means, electronic or mechanical, including photocopying, recording or by any information storage and retrieval system, without permission from the publisher in writing.

© Ian Allan Publishing Ltd 2010

Published by

Ian Allan PUBLISHING

Printed by Ian Allan Printing Ltd, Riverdene Business Park, Hersham, Surrey KT12 4RG.

Visit the Ian Allan Publishing web site:
www.ianallanpublishing.com

Advertising in LRB
For information regarding advertising contact:
Graham Middleton
Tel: 01780 484632
Fax: 01780 763388
E-mail:
graham.middleton@ianallanpublishing.co.uk

List of Abbreviations

Acct = Accountant
Admin = Administrative
Asst = Assistant
CEO = Chief Executive Officer
Ch = Chief
Chmn = Chairman
Co = Company
Comm Man = Commercial Manager
Cont = Controller
Dep = Deputy
Dir = Director
Eng = Engineer
Exec = Executive
Fin = Financial
Gen Man = General Manager
H&S = Health & Safety
HR = Human Relations
Insp = Inspector
Jnt = Joint
Man = Manager
Man Dir = Managing Director
Mktg = Marketing
Off = Officer
Op = Operating
Ops = Operations
Plan = Planning
Pres = President
Prin = Principal
Prop = Proprietor(s)
Ptnrs = Partner(s)
Reg Off = Registered Office
Sec = Secretary
Supt = Superintendent
Svce = Service
Traf Man = Traffic Manager
Traf Supt = Traffic Superintendent
Tran Man = Transport Manager

Index to advertisers

Airconco	19
Buses magazine	44
Eminox	29
Holdsworth Fabrics Ltd	40
Ian Allan Books	5
J & K Recovery Ltd	50
Partline	240
Rigton Insurance Services Ltd	16
Scancoin	23
The Wright Group	2

Transport Benevolent Fund **77**
2011 Little Red Book - Main Sponsor

TTS	21, 22, 26, 28, 29, 32, 37, 47, 49
Voith Turbo Ltd	32

How LRB entries are compiled

As always, our principal source of data has been the thousands of questionnaires we send out to operators, manufacturers, suppliers and other organisations. We have again made significant changes to the circulation list to try to reflect the many changes that have been happening, to omit ceased businesses, etc. Where we have not received responses, we have tried to use other publicly available sources to ensure the entries are as accurate as possible.

New entrants to the bus and coach market need not wait for LRB to make contact. If you are active in the industry, and would like to appear in the next edition of LRB (free of charge), please write to the editor of LRB at Ian Allan Publishing Ltd, Foundry Road, Stamford, Lincolnshire PE9 2PP, requesting to receive a form for the next edition.

LRB is used by a substantial number of bus and coach operators, as well as by national and local government, trade organisations, tendering authorities, group travel organisers, hotels and leisure attractions.

Foreword

Welcome to the 2011 edition of the Little Red Book, now in its 73rd year as the leading industry directory.

We have again made a huge number of amendments and updates, as well as introducing many new entries in all sections of the book. This reflects the fact that the rate of change in the industry remains continuous, and we seek to provide a directory that will be current and useful to its subscribers. Of course while we may be right up to date at the time of going to press, some things may have changed in a matter of weeks, so a reminder that you can update your LRB on a monthly basis by taking our sister publication *Buses* magazine, which will continue to have a section in each month's edition to notify updates and changes to LRB.

We remain very grateful to the large number of suppliers, authorities, organisations and operators who have taken the trouble to update and return their entries via our questionnaires. We have again been overwhelmed with the quantity returned this year. As I proposed in this column last year, we have changed our structure so that we now send out separate questionnaires for trade suppliers and for organisations and authorities; this provides more space, allowing for greater detail and supporting notes on the part of the latter. We are grateful to those authorities in particular who have enhanced their entries by adding a few words about their responsibilities, and we hope that more will take advantage of this feature next year.

The usual reminder – if there is no change to your entry, please don't worry about re-writing it all. A simple statement to the effect that there is no change will be fine, but please remember to make sure to tell us who you are!

At the time of writing, the industry finds itself surrounded by considerable uncertainty. The results of the Government's spending review are awaited with some trepidation, to the effect that if spending cuts prove to be as harsh as some have suggested, then the whole shape and extent of domestic bus operations could change.

Further far reaching implications could come with the publication, in due course, of the Competition Commission report on the industry. Both of these factors could well affect the content of this directory next year. Further changes will be inevitable as part of the normal commercial process; again at the time of writing, the sale of Arriva to German interests is under way, as is the proposed merger between Transdev and Veolia, while other major businesses are known to be for sale. But this is a resilient industry that has been known in the past for its ability to adjust and adapt to the surrounding circumstances and conditions while still providing a high quality service to its customers; we will seek to do our job by accurately recording all of the changes.

Ian Barlex, Editor

Acknowledgements

I would like to acknowledge the help and support of Paul Appleton and his team at Ian Allan – especially Debbie Walker – for their hard work and support in producing this edition. And a particular mention for Irena Cornwell, who worked very hard to liaise with the advertisers, and has now been succeeded by Graham Middleton.

I must also thank those readers and contributors who have taken the trouble to get in touch to highlight changes and amendments through the year; if you notice something that needs changing, please do not hesitate to contact me via the Stamford office.

Thanks too to Keith Shayshutt, who has kindly allowed us to use some of his photographs, and to operators who have helped with logos and illustrations.

And many thanks to all of our advertisers for their support, without which this directory would be difficult to sustain. Please give them your support and tell them you saw their advertisement in LRB. In particular, I would like to thank the Transport Benevolent Fund, main sponsor for this year's edition.

Section 1

Trade Directory

- Vehicle suppliers and dealers
- A-Z listing of suppliers and manufacturers
- Bus & Coach industry service providers

Vehicle Suppliers & Dealers
Manufacturers of full-size bus and coach chassis and integrals, bus rapid transit vehicles and light rail vehicles

Trade Directory

ALEXANDER DENNIS LTD
91 Glasgow Road,
Falkirk FK1 4JB
Tel: 01324 621672
Fax: 01324 632469
E-mail: enquiries@alexander-dennis.co.uk
Web site: www.alexander-dennis.com
Range: hybrid single-deck bus; rear-engined low-floor single-deck bus; chassis for rear-engined low-floor midibus; mid-engined coach; rear-engined coach hybrid double-deck bus; rear-engined low-floor double-deck bus (two- or three-axle); low-floor school bus.

ARRIVA BUS & COACH
Lodge Garage, Whitehall Road West,
Gomersal, Cleckheaton, West Yorkshire
BD19 4BJ
Tel: 01274 681144
Fax: 01274 651198
E-mail: whiter@arriva.co.uk
Web site: www.arrivabusandcoach.co.uk

AUTOSAN UK
UK Supplier: Blue Ribbon Coach Sales
23 Brook Road, Bomere Heath,
Shrewsbury SY4 3PU
Tel/Fax: 01939 290512
E-mail: paul.busman@btopenworld.com
Web site: www.blueribboncoachsales.com
Range: High-floor school bus, single-deck bus, single-deck coach

AYATS
UK Supplier: Blue Ribbon Coach Sales
23 Brook Road, Bomere Heath,
Shrewsbury SY4 3PU
Tel/Fax: 01939 290512
E-mail: paul.busman@btopenworld.com
Web site: www.blueribboncoachsales.com
Ireland supplier: Bartons Transport
Straffan Road, Maynooth, Co Kildare
Tel: 00 353 1 628 6026
Fax: 00 353 1 628 6722
E-mail: info@bartons-transport.ie
Models: Rear-engined integral single and double-deck coach range - up to 15m

BMC PLC
BMC House, Ibstock Road,
Coventry CV6 6JR
Tel: 02476 363003
Fax: 02476 365835
E-mail: enquiries@bmcplc.com
Web site: www.bmcplc.com
Models: integral front-engined school bus, integral front-engined midicoach, integral rear-engined 11m low-floor single-deck bus

FAST EUROPE NV
Ambachtenlaan 38c, 3001 Leuven, Belgium
Tel: 07823 772900
E-mail: roger.clode@fast-europe.eu
Web site: www.fast-europe.eu

IRISBUS (UK) LTD
Iveco House, Station Road,
Watford WD17 1SR
Tel: 01923 259660
Fax: 01923 259623
E-mail: info@irisbus.co.uk
Models: midibus, low-floor midibus, minibuses, guided bus system, low-floor rear-engined single-deck bus, rear-engined single-deck coach.

KING LONG UK LTD
Bedworth Road, Coventry CV6 6BP
Tel: 02476 363004
Fax: 02476 365835
E-mail: paul@kinglonguk.com
Web site: www.kinglonguk.com
Models: single-deck coach

MAN
UK Suppliers: MAN Bus & Coach
Frankland Road, Blagrove,
Swindon SN5 8YU
Tel: 01793 448000
Web site: www.manbusandcoach.co.uk

MAN Coach Sales Ashburton Road West,
Trafford Park, Manchester M17 1QX
Tel: 0161 848 8331
Web site: www.manbusandcoachsales.co.uk
Ireland supplier: Brian Noone Straffan Road, Maynooth, Co Kildare
Tel: 00 353 1 628 6311
Fax: 00 353 1 628 5404
Web site: www.briannooneltd.ie
Models: single-deck low-floor bus, rear-engined coach

MERCEDES-BENZ
UK Supplier: Evobus (UK) Ltd
Cross Point Business Park, Ashcroft Way,
Coventry CV2 2TU
Tel: 024 7662 6000
Web site: www.evobus.com
Models: rear-engine coach, rear-engine integral low-floor single-deck bus, rear-engine integral low-floor single-deck articulated bus

MINIS TO MIDIS LTD
MTM House, 135 Nutwell Lane,
Doncaster DN3 3JR
Tel: 01302 833203
Fax: 01302 831756
E-mail: sales@ministomidis.com
Web site: www.ministomidis.com
Models: Distributors for Mercedes-Benz coaches, Optare Coach Sales, Toyota/Caetano Optimo, Unvi bodywork

MOSELEY (PCV) LTD
Elmsall Way, Dale Lane, South Elmsall,
Pontefract WF9 2XS
Tel: 01977 609000
Fax: 01977 609900
E-mail: sales@moseleycoachsales.co.uk
Web site: www.moseleycoachsales.co.uk

NEOPLAN
UK Supplier: MAN Bus & Coach
Frankland Road, Blagrove,
Swindon SN5 8YU
Tel: 01793 448000
Web site: www.manbusandcoach.co.uk
Models: single-deck and double-deck rear-engine integral coaches

OPTARE PLC (Blackburn)
Lower Philips Road, Whitebirk Industrial Estate, Blackburn BB1 5UD
Tel: 0845 838 9901
Fax: 0845 838 9902
E-mail: info@optare.com
Web site: www.optare.com
Models: Optare Olympus, double-deck low-floor bus. Distribution for Optare Toro luxury midicoach and Optare Soroco luxury minicoach.

OPTARE PLC (Leeds)
Manston Lane, Leeds LS15 8SU
Tel: 0113 264 5182
Fax: 0113 260 6635
E-mail: info@optare.com
Web site: www.optare.com
Models: Optare Tempo, rear-engined integral low-floor single-deck city bus. Optare Versa, Optare Solo, Optare Solo SR, Optare Solo EV, rear-engined integral low-floor single-deck midibus.

PLAXTON COACH SALES
Ryton Road, Anston, Sheffield S25 4DL
Tel: 01909 551166
Fax: 01909 567994
E-mail: sales@plaxtonlimited.co.uk
Web site: www.plaxtonlimited.co.uk
Range: coaches, buses, midicoach and midibus bodies
(Part of Alexander Dennis)

SANTANDER ASSET FINANCE
Taylor Road, Trafford Park,
Manchester M41 7JQ
Tel: 0161 747 5698
Fax: 0161 275 4501
E-mail: steve.moult@hansar.co.uk
Web site: www.buses247.co.uk

SCANIA (GB) LTD
Delaware Drive, Tongwell, Milton Keynes
MK15 8HB
Tel: 01908 210210
Fax: 01908 215040
E-mail: info@scania.co.uk
Web site: www.scania.com
Range: rear-engined low-floor single-deck and double-deck bus chassis, integral low-floor single-deck bus, integral low-floor double-deck bus, rear-engined coach.

SETRA
UK Supplier: Evobus (UK) Ltd
Cross Point Business Park, Ashcroft Way,
Coventry CV2 2TU
Tel: 02476 626000
Web site: www.evobus.com, www.setra.de
Models: rear-engined integral coaches

SOLBUS (UK) LTD
16 Browning Avenue, Kettering,
Northamptonshire NN16 8NP
Tel: 01536 482049
Fax: 01536 482342
E-mail: phill@solbus-uk.com
Web site: www.solbus-uk.com

TESLA VEHICLES LIMITED
22 Larbre Crescent, Whickham,
Newcastle upon Tyne NE16 5YG
Tel: 0191 488 6258
Fax: 0191 488 9158
E-mail: info@teslavehicles.com
Web site: www.teslavehicles.com

TEMSA EUROPE
Lodge Garage, Whitehall Road West,
Gomersal, Cleckheaton, West Yorkshire
BD19 4BJ
Tel: 01274 681144
E-mail: albert.atat@temsa.com
Web site: www.temsa.com

Trade Directory

UNVI
UK Supplier: Coachtraders
Tel: 01501 744000
E-mail: info@coachtraders.co.uk
Web site: www.coachtraders.co.uk
Range: single-deck coach, midicoach, minicoach

VAN HOOL
Bernard Van Hoolstraat 58,
Lier-Koningshooikt, BE2500,
Belgium
Tel: 00 32 3 420 20 20
Fax: 00 32 3 482 33 60
E-mail: sales.bc.uk@vanhool.be
Web site: www.vanhool.be
Models: integral coaches

VDL BOVA
Web site: www.vdlbova.nl
UK Supplier: Moseley (PCV) Ltd
Elmsall Way, Dale Lane,
South Elmsall, Pontefract WF9 2XS
Tel: 01977 609000
Fax: 01977 609900
E-mail: sales@moseleycoachsales.co.uk
Web site: www.moseleycoachsales.co.uk

Moseley in the South Ltd
Summerfield Avenue,
Chelston Business Park,
Wellington TA21 9JF
Tel: 01823 653000
Fax: 01823 663502
E-mail: enquiries@moseleysouth.co.uk
Web site: www.moselesouth.co.uk
Models: Lexio, Magiq, Futura single-deck luxury coach; Synergy double-deck coach

VDL BUS INTERNATIONAL
UK Supplier: Arriva Bus & Coach
Lodge Garage, Whitehall Road West,
Gomersal, Cleckheaton, West Yorkshire
BD19 4BJ
Tel: 01274 681144
Fax: 01274 651198
E-mail: busandbusandcoach@arriva.co.uk
Web site: www.arrivabusandcoach.co.uk
Models: rear-engined low-floor single-deck bus, rear-engined low-floor double-deck bus, rear-engined coach, rear-engined three-axle single- or double-deck coach.

VOLVO BUS
Wedgnock Lane,
Warwick CV34 5YA
Tel: 01926 401777
Fax: 01926 407407
Web site: www.volvo.com
Models: rear-engined low-floor single-deck bus, rear-engined low-floor articulated single-deck bus, mid-engined coach, rear-engined integral coach, rear-engined low-floor double-deck bus.

Volvo Bus & Coach Sales Centre
Siskin Parkway East,
Middlemarch Business Park,
Coventry CV3 4PE
Tel: 02476 210250
Fax: 02476 210258
Web site: www.volvo.com
Range: New & Pre-owned buses and coaches.

BUS RAPID TRANSIT VEHICLES

IRISBUS (UK) LTD
Iveco House, Station Road,
Watford WD17 1SR
Tel: 01923 259660
Fax: 01923 259623
E-mail: info@irisbus.co.uk
Web site: www.irisbus.co.uk
Models: guided bus system

MINITRAM SYSTEMS LTD
12 Waterloo Park Estate,
Bidford on Avon B50 4JH
Tel: 07770 931274
E-mail: martinp@tdi.uk.com
Web site: www.minitram.com
Models: Rubber tyre-guided/unguided/rail 7.8m vehicle

VOLVO BUS
Wedgnock Lane,
Warwick CV34 5YA
Tel: 01926 401777
Fax: 01926 407407
Web site: www.volvobuses.volvo.co.uk, www.volvo.com
Models: rear-engined low-floor single-deck bus, rear-engined low-floor articulated single-deck bus, rear-engined low-floor double-deck bus (chassis can be equipped with guide wheels for operation on guideways).

THE WRIGHT GROUP
Fenaghy Road, Galgorm, Ballymena,
Northern Ireland BT42 1PY
Tel: 028 2564 1212
Fax: 028 2564 9703
E-mail: info@wright-bus.com
Web site: www.wright-bus.com
Models: StreetCar rapid transit vehicle (further models - see bodybuilders section).

LIGHT RAIL VEHICLES

ALSTOM TRANSPORT
Worldwide headquarters:
48 rue Albert Dhalenne,
F-93482 Saint-Ouen Cedex, France
Tel: 00 33 1 41 66 90 00
Fax: 00 33 1 41 66 96 66
Web site: www.transport.alstom.com
Models: rail vehicles including light rail vehicles, traction equipment, infrastructure and maintenance services.

BOMBARDIER TRANSPORTATION
Management Office:
1101 Parent Street, Saint-Bruno,
Quebec J3V 6E6, Canada
Tel: 00 1 450 441 20 20
Fax: 00 1 450 441 15 15
Web site: www.transportation.bombardier.com

BOMBARDIER TRANSPORTATION METROS
Litchurch Lane, Derby DE24 8AD
Tel: 01332 344666
Fax: 01332 266271
Models: light rail vehicles, trams, guided or unguided bi-mode rubber tyred electric vehicle.

MINITRAM SYSTEMS LTD
12 Waterloo Park Estate,
Bidford on Avon B50 4JH
Tel: 07770 931274
E-mail: martyinp@tdi.uk.com
Web site: www.minitram.com
Models: Rubber tyre-guided/unguided/rail 7.8m vehicle

PARRY PEOPLE MOVERS LTD
Overend Road, Cradley Heath,
Dudley B64 7DD
Tel: 01384 569553
Fax: 01384 637753
E-mail: jpmparry@aol.com
Web site: www.parrypeoplemovers.com
Models: Ultra light rail vehicles and trams

TRAM POWER LTD
99 Stanley Road, Bootle,
Liverpool L20 7DA

Web site: www.trampower.co.uk/CityClass.html
Models: Articulated lightweight low-cost tram

BODYBUILDERS (LARGE VEHICLES)

ALEXANDER DENNIS LTD
91 Glasgow Road, Falkirk FK1 4JB
Tel: 01324 621 672
Fax: 01324 632 269
E-mail: enquiries@alexander-dennis.com
Web site: www.alexander-dennis.com

BEULAS
UK Supplier: Base Ltd
57 Clydesdale Place,
Moss Side Industrial Estate,
Leyland PR26 7QS
Tel: 01772 425355
Fax: 01772 425748
Web site: www.basecoachsales.co.uk

CAETANO (UK) LTD
Mill Lane, Heather, Coalville LE67 2QE
Tel: 01530 263333
Fax: 01530 263379
E-mail: enquiries@caetano.co.uk
Web site: www.caetano.co.uk
Models: single-deck coach

EXPRESS COACH REPAIRS LTD
Outgang Lane, Pickering,
North Yorkshire YO18 7JA
Tel: 01751 475 215
E-mail: info@expresscoachrepairs.co.uk
Web site: www.expresscoachrepairs.co.uk

IRIZAR
UK spares supplier:
Tramontana Chapelknowe Road,
Carfin, Motherwell ML1 5LE
Tel: 01698 861790
Fax: 01698 860778
E-mail: wdt90@tiscali.co.uk
Web site: tramontanacoach.co.uk

KING LONG UK LTD
Bedworth Road, Coventry CV6 6BP
Tel: 02476 363004
Fax: 02476 365835
E-mail: paul@kinglonguk.com
Web site: www.kinglonguk.com
Models: single-deck coach

LAWTON SERVICES LTD
Knutsford Road, Church Lawton,
Stoke-on-Trent ST7 3DN
Tel: 01270 882056
Fax: 01270 883014
E-mail: andrea@lawtonservices.co.uk
Web site: www.lawtonservices.co.uk

LEICESTER CARRIAGE BUILDERS
Marlow Road, Leicester
LE3 2BQ
Tel: 01162 824 270
Fax: 01162 630 554
E-mail: lcbo116@yahoo.co.uk
Web site: www.leicestercarriagebuilders.co.uk

MARCOPOLO
UK Supplier: Base Ltd
57 Clydesdale Place, Moss Side Industrial Estate, Leyland PR26 7QS
Tel: 01772 425355
Fax: 01772 425748
Web site: www.basecoachsales.co.uk

MCV BUS AND COACH LTD
Sterling Place, Elean Business Park,
Sutton, Ely CB6 2QE
Tel: 01353 773000
Fax: 01353 773001

E-mail: enquiries@mcvbus.com
Web site: www.mcv-eg.com

NEOPLAN
UK Supplier: MAN Bus & Coach UK
Frankland Road, Blagrove,
Swindon SN5 8YU
Tel: 01793 448000
Web site: www.manbusandcoach.co.uk
Models: single-deck coach, also integral coach.

NOGE
UK Supplier: MAN Bus & Coach UK
Frankland Road, Blagrove
Swindon SN5 8YU
Tel: 01793 448000
Web site: www.manbusandcoach.co.uk
Ireland supplier:
Brian Noone Straffan Road, Maynooth,
Co Kildare
Tel: 00 353 1 628 6311
Fax: 00 353 1 628 5404
Models: two-axle and three-axle integral coach bodies.

OPTARE PLC (Blackburn)
Lower Philips Road, Whitebirk Industrial Estate, Blackburn BB1 5UD
Tel: 0845 838 9901
Fax: 0845 838 9902
E-mail: info@optare.com
Web site: www.optare.com
Models: Optare Olympus, double-deck low-floor bus. Plus distribution for Optare Toro luxury midicoach and Optare Soroco luxury minicoach.

OPTARE PLC (Leeds)
Manston Lane, Leeds LS15 8SU
Tel: 0113 264 5182
Fax: 0113 260 6635
E-mail: info@optare.com
Web site: www.optare.com
Models: Optare Tempo, rear-engined integral low-floor single-deck city bus. Optare Versa, Optare Solo, Optare Solo SR, Optare Solo EV, rear-engined integral low-floor single-deck midibus.

PLAXTON
Plaxton Park, Cayton Low Road,
Eastfield, Scarborough YO11 3BY
Tel: 01723 581500
Fax: 01723 581479
E-mail: sales@plaxtonlimited.co.uk
Web site: www.plaxtonlimited.co.uk
Range: coaches, buses, midicoach and midibus bodies
(Part of Alexander Dennis)

PLAXTON COACH SALES CENTRE
Ryton Road, Anston,
Sheffield S25 4DL
Tel: 01909 551166
Fax: 01909 567994
E-mail: sales@plaxtonlimited.co.uk
Web site: www.plaxtonlimited.co.uk
(Part of Alexander Dennis)

SUNSUNDEGUI
UK Importer:
Volvo Bus & Coach Sales Centre
Siskin Parkway East,
Middlemarch Business Park, Coventry CV3 4PE
Tel: 02476 210250
Fax: 02476 210258
Web site: www.volvo.com
UK Service: Tramontana Chapelknowe Road, Carfin, Motherwell ML1 5LE
Tel: 01698 861790
Fax: 01698 860778
E-mail: wdt90@tiscali.co.uk
Web site: tramontanacoach.co.uk

TESLA VEHICLES LIMITED
22 Larbre Crescent, Whickham,
Newcastle upon Tyne NE16 5YG
Tel: 0191 488 6258
Fax: 0191 488 9158
E-mail: info@teslavehicles.com
Web site: www.teslavehicles.com

UNVI
UK Supplier: Coachtraders
Tel: 01501 744000
E-mail: info@coachtraders.co.uk
Web site: www.coachtraders.co.uk
Range: single-deck coach, midicoach, minicoach

VAN HOOL
Bernard Van Hoolstraat 58, Lier-Koningshooikt, 2500, Belgium
Tel: 00 32 3 420 20 20
Fax: 00 32 3 482 33 60
E-mail: sales.bc.uk@vanhool.be
Web site: www.vanhool.be
Models: coach bodies

VDL BERKHOF
UK Supplier: Arriva Bus & Coach Lodge Garage, Whitehall Road West, Gomersal, Cleckheaton BD19 4BJ
Tel: 01274 681144
Fax: 01274 651198
E-mail: busandcoachsales@arriva.co.uk
Web site: www.arrivabusandcoach.co.uk
Models: rear-engined three-axle or two-axle single-deck coach.

VDL JONCKHEERE
UK Importer:
Volvo Bus & Coach Sales Centre
Siskin Parkway East,
Middlemarch Business Park,
Coventry CV3 4PE
Tel: 02476 210250
Fax: 02476 210258
Web site: www.volvo.com
UK Service:
Tramontana Chapelknowe Road, Carfin, Motherwell ML1 5LE
Tel: 01698 861790
Fax: 01698 860778
E-mail: wdt90@tiscali.co.uk
Web site: tramontanacoach.co.uk

VOLVO BUS
Wedgnock Lane, Warwick CV34 5YA
Tel: 01926 401777
Fax: 01926 407407
Web site: www.volvo.com
Models: rear-engined low-floor single-deck bus, rear-engined low-floor articulated single-deck bus, mid-engined coach, rear-engined integral coach, rear-engined low-floor double-deck bus.

Volvo Bus & Coach Sales Centre
Siskin Parkway East, Middlemarch Business Park, Coventry CV3 4PE
Tel: 02476 210250
Fax: 02476 210258
Web site: www.volvo.com
Range: New & Pre-owned buses and coaches.

THE WRIGHT GROUP
Fenaghy Road, Galgorm, Ballymena,
Northern Ireland BT42 1PY
Tel: 028 2564 1212 **Fax:** 028 2564 9703
E-mail: info@wright-bus.com
Web site: www.wright-bus.com
www.the-wright-group.com
Models: double-deck low-floor bus body, single-deck low-floor articulated bus body, FTR advanced bus rapid transit vehicle, single-deck low-floor bus, single-deck low entry coach, single-deck low-floor midibus.

CHASSIS AND INTEGRAL VEHICLES (SMALL VEHICLES - UNDER 9M)

ALEXANDER DENNIS LTD
91 Glasgow Road, Falkirk FK1 4JB
Tel: 01324 621 672
Fax: 01324 632 269
E-mail: enquiries@alexander-dennis.com
Web: www.alexander-dennis.com

AVID VEHICLES LTD
Unit 8, Arcot Court, Nelson Road, Nelson Park, Cramlington NE23 1BB
Tel: 01670 707 040
Fax: 01670 715 230
E-mail: sales@avidvehicles.com
Web site: www.avidvehicles.com

BLUE BIRD VEHICLES LTD
Unit 7, Plaxton Park, Cayton Low Road, Eastfield, Scarborough YO11 3BY
Tel: 01723 860800
Fax: 01723 585235
E-mail: info@bluebirdvehicles.com
Web site: www.bluebirdvehicles.com

FORD MOTOR COMPANY
Ford Motor Co Ltd, Eagle Way, Brentwood CM13 3BW
Tel: 08457 111 888
Web site:
www.ford.co.uk/Commercialvehicles/Transit Minibus
Models: Transit, complete minibus or chassis-cowl.

IRISBUS (UK) LTD
Iveco House, Station Road,
Watford WD17 1SR
Tel: 01923 259660
Fax: 01923 259623
E-mail: info@irisbus.co.uk
Web site: www.irisbus.co.uk

JOHN BRADSHAW LTD
New Lane, Stibbington,
Peterborough PE8 6LW
Tel: 01780 781801
Web site: www.john-bradshaw.co.uk
Models: Electric minibus/taxi

KING LONG UK LTD
Bedworth Road, Coventry CV6 6BP
Tel: 02476 363004 **Fax:** 02476 365835
E-mail: paul@kinglonguk.com
Web site: www.kinglonguk.com
Models: single-deck coach

LEICESTER CARRIAGE BUILDERS
Marlow Road, Leicester LE3 2BQ
Tel: 0116 282 4270
Fax: 0116 263 0554
E-mail: rick.johnson@midlandsco-op.com
Web site:
www.leicestercarriagebuilders.co.uk

MERCEDES-BENZ
UK Supplier: Evobus (UK) Ltd
Cross Point Business Park, Ashcroft Way, Coventry CV2 2TU
Tel: 02476 626000
Web site: www.evobus.com
Models: Complete low-floor minibus or chassis cowl

MINIS TO MIDIS LTD
MTM House, 135 Nutwell Lane,
Doncaster DN3 3JR
Tel: 01302 833203
Fax: 01302 831756
E-mail: sales@ministomidis.com
Web site: www.ministomidis.com
Models: Distributors for Mercedes-Benz coaches, Optare Coach Sales, Toyota/Caetano Optimo, Unvi bodywork.

The Little Red Book 2011 - in association with **tbf** Transport Benevolent Fund

MINITRAM SYSTEMS LTD
12 Waterloo Park Estate, Bidford on Avon B50 4JH
Tel: 07770 931274
E-mail: martinp@tdi.uk.com
Web site: www.minitram.com
Models: Rubber tyre-guided/unguided/rail 7.8m vehicle

MISTRAL BUS & COACH PLC
Booths Hall, Chelford Road, Knutsford, Cheshire WA16 8QZ
Tel: 01565 621 881
Fax: 01565 621 882
E-mail: sales@mistral-group.com
Web site: www.mistral-group.com

MOSELEY (PCV) LTD
Elmsall Way, Dale Lane, South Elmsall, Pontefract WF9 2XS
Tel: 01977 609000
Fax: 01977 609900
E-mail: sales@moseleycoachsales.co.uk
Web site: www.moseleycoachsales.co.uk

NU-TRACK LTD
Steeple Industrial Estate, Antrim, Northern Ireland BT41 1AB
Tel: 028 94 469 550
Fax: 028 94 465 430
E-mail: enquiries@nu-track.co.uk

OPTARE PLC (Leeds)
Manston Lane, Leeds LS15 8SU
Tel: 0113 264 5182
Fax: 0113 260 6635
E-mail: info@optare.com
Web site: www.optare.com
Models: Optare Tempo, rear-engined integral low-floor single-deck city bus. Optare Versa, Optare Solo, Optare Solo SR, Optare Solo EV, rear-engined integral low-floor single-deck midibus.

PLAXTON COACH SALES CENTRE
Ryton Road, Anston, Sheffield S25 4DL
Tel: 01909 551166
Fax: 01909 567994
E-mail: sales@plaxtonlimited.co.uk
Web site: www.plaxtonlimited.co.uk
(Part of Alexander Dennis)

RENAULT UK LTD
Rivers Office Park, Denham Way, Maple Cross, Rickmansworth WD3 9YS
Tel: 01923 855500
Web site: www.renault.co.uk
Models: Complete minibus or chassis-cowl; electric vehicle.

SANTANDER ASSET FINANCE
Taylor Road, Trafford Park, Manchester M41 7JQ
Tel: 0161 747 5698
Fax: 0161 275 4501
E-mail: steve.moult@hansar.co.uk
Web site: www.buses247.co.uk

TESLA VEHICLES LIMITED
22 Larbre Crescent, Whickham, Newcastle upon Tyne NE16 5YG
Tel: 0191 488 6258
Fax: 0191 488 9158
E-mail: info@teslavehicles.com
Web site: www.teslavehicles.com

TOYOTA (GB) PLC
Great Burgh, Burgh Heath, Epsom KT18 5UX
Tel: 01737 363633
Mobile: 07785 238798
E-mail: steve.prime@tgb.toyota.co.uk
Web site: www.toyota.com
UK suppliers:
AD Coach Sales **Tel:** 01884 860767;

Holloway Commercials **Tel:** 01902 636661
Caetano (UK) Ltd **Tel:** 01530 263333
Models: Optimo midicoach, chassis cowl

VAUXHALL MOTORS LTD
Luton LU1 3YT
Tel: 020 7439 0303
Vauxhall Mobility: 0800 731 5267
Web site: www.vauxhall.co.uk
Models: Complete minibus or chassis-cowl.

VOLKSWAGEN COMMERCIAL VEHICLES
Yeomans Drive, Blakelands, Milton Keynes MK14 5AN
Web site: www.volkswagen-vans.co.uk
Models: Complete minibus or chassis-cowl.

BODYBUILDERS (SMALL VEHICLES), MINIBUS CONVERSIONS

ADVANCED VEHICLE BUILDERS
Upper Mantle Close, Clay Cross S45 9NU
Tel: 01246 250022
Fax: 01246 250016
E-mail: info@minibus.co.uk

ALEXANDER DENNIS LTD
91 Glasgow Road, Falkirk FK1 4JB
Tel: 01324 621 672
Fax: 01324 632 269
E-mail: enquiries@alexander-dennis.com
Web site: www.alexander-dennis.com

AVID VEHICLES LTD
Unit 8, Arcot Court, Nelson Road, Nelson Park, Cramlington NE23 1BB
Tel: 01670 707 040
Fax: 01670 715 230
E-mail: sales@avidvehicles.com
Web site: www.avidvehicles.com

BLUE BIRD VEHICLES LTD
Unit 7, Plaxton Park, Cayton Low Road, Eastfield, Scarborough YO11 3BY
Tel: 01723 860800
Fax: 01723 585235
E-mail: info@bluebirdvehicles.com
Web site: www.bluebirdvehicles.com

BURNT TREE VEHICLE SOLUTIONS
Burnt Tree House, Knights Way, Battlefield Enterprise Park, Harlescott Lane, Shrewsbury SY1 3JE
Tel: 01743 457650
Web site: www.burnt-tree.co.uk

CHASSIS DEVELOPMENTS
Grovebury Road, Leighton Buzzard LU7 8SL
Tel: 01525 374151
Web site: www.chassisdevelopments.co.uk

CONCEPT COACHCRAFT
Far Cromwell Road, Bredbury, Stockport SK6 2SE
Tel: 0161 406 9322
Fax: 0161 406 9588
E-mail: sales@conceptcoachcraft.com
Web site: www.conceptcoachcraft.com

COURTSIDE CONVERSIONS LTD
1 Woodward Road, Howden Industrial Estate, Tiverton EX16 5HW
Tel: 01884 256048
Fax: 01884 256087
E-mail: courtsidesales@aol.com
Web site: www.courtsideconversions.com

CVI (COMMERCIAL VEHICLE INNOVATION)
Moorfoot View, Bilston, Edinburgh EH25 9SL
Tel: 0131 473 9300
Web site: www.c-v-i.co.uk

EXCEL CONVERSIONS LTD
Excel House, Durham Lane, Armthorpe, Doncaster DN3 3FE
Tel: 01302 835388
Fax: 01302 835389
E-mail: sales@excelconversions.co.uk
Web site: www.excelconversions.co.uk

EXPRESS COACH REPAIRS LTD
Outgang Lane, Pickering, North Yorkshire YO18 7JA
Tel: 01751 475 215
E-mail: info@expresscoachrepairs.co.uk
Web site: www.expresscoachrepairs.co.uk

GM COACHWORK LTD
Teign Valley, Trusham, Newton Abbot TQ13 0NX
Tel: 01626 853050
Fax: 01626 855066
E-mail: david.vadght@gmcoachwork.co.uk
Web site: www.gmcoachwork.co.uk

INDCAR SA
Poligono Industrial Torres Pujals, E-17401 Arbucies (Girona), Spain
Web site: www.indcar.com
UK Supplier:
Base Ltd 57 Clydesdale Place, Moss Side Industrial Estate, Leyland PR26 7QS
Tel: 01772 425355
Fax: 01772 425748
Web site: www.basecoachsales.co.uk

JDC - JOHN DENNIS COACHBUILDERS
25 Westfield Road, Guildford GU1 1RR
Tel: 01483 501457
Web site: www.jdcbus.co.uk

JUBILEE AUTOMOTIVE GROUP
Woden Road South, Wednesbury WS10 0NQ
Tel: 0121 502 2252
Fax: 0121 502 2258
E-mail: sales@jubileeauto.com

LAWTON SERVICES LTD
Knutsford Road, Church Lawton, Stoke-on-Trent ST7 3DN
Tel: 01270 882056
Fax: 01270 883014
E-mail: andrea@lawtonservices.co.uk
Web site: www.lawtonservices.co.uk

LEICESTER CARRIAGE BUILDERS
Marlow Road, Leicester LE3 2BQ
Tel: 0116 282 4270
Fax: 0116 263 0554
E-mail: lcb0116@yahoo.co.uk
Web site: www.leicestercarriagebuilders.co.uk

MCV BUS AND COACH LTD
Sterling Place, Elean Business Park, Sutton, Ely CB6 2QE
Tel: 01353 773000
Fax: 01353 773001
Web site: www.mcv-eg.com

MELLOR COACHCRAFT
Miall Street, Rochdale OL11 1HY
Tel: 01706 860610
Fax: 01706 860402
E-mail: mcsales@woodall-nicholson.co.uk
Web site: www.woodall-nicholson.co.uk

MINIBUS OPTIONS LTD
Bingswood Industrial Estate, Whaley Bridge, High Peak SK23 7LY
Tel: 01663 735355
Fax: 01663 735352
E-mail: info@minibusoptions.co.uk
Web site: www.minibusoptions.co.uk

NU-TRACK LTD
Steeple Industrial Estate, Antrim, Northern Ireland BT41 1AB
Tel: 028 9446 9550
Fax: 028 9446 5430
E-mail: enquiries@nu-track.co.uk

OPTARE PLC (Leeds)
Manston Lane, Leeds LS15 8SU
Tel: 0113 264 5182
Fax: 0113 260 6635
E-mail: info@optare.com
Web site: www.optare.com

PLAXTON LIMITED
Plaxton Park, Cayton Low Road, Eastfield, Scarborough YO11 3BY
Tel: 01723 581500
Fax: 01723 581479
E-mail: sales@plaxtonlimited.co.uk
Web site: www.plaxtonlimited.co.uk
Range: coaches; midicoach and midibus bodies.
(Part of Alexander Dennis)

PLAXTON COACH SALES CENTRE
Ryton Road, Anston, Sheffield S25 4DL
Tel: 01909 551166
Fax: 01909 567994
E-mail: sales@plaxtonlimited.co.uk
Web site: www.plaxtonlimited.co.uk
(Part of Alexander Dennis)

PVS MANUFACTURING LTD
8 Ardboe Business Park, Kilmascally Road, Ardboe, Dungannon, Northern Ireland BT71 5BP
Tel: 028 8673 6969
Fax: 028 8673 7178
E-mail: mail@pvsltd.com
Web site: www.conversionspecialists.com

STANFORD COACH WORKS
Mobility House, Stanhope Industrial Park, Wharf Road, Stanford-le-Hope SS17 0EH
Tel: 01375 676088
Fax: 01375 677999
E-mail: sales@stanfordcoachworks.co.uk
Web site: www.stanfordcoachworks.co.uk
Range: mini- and midibuses, mini- and midicoaches

TESLA VEHICLES LIMITED
22 Larbre Crescent, Whickham, Newcastle upon Tyne NE16 5YG
Tel: 0191 488 6258
Fax: 0191 488 9158
E-mail: info@teslavehicles.com
Web site: www.teslavehicles.com

TREKA BUS LTD
Archer Road, Armytage Industrial Estate, Brighouse, West Yorkshire HD6 1XF
Tel: 01484 726641
Fax: 01484 717144

UNVI
UK Supplier: Coachtraders
Tel: 01501 744000
E-mail: info@coachtraders.co.uk
Web site: www.coachtraders.co.uk
Range: single-deck coach, midicoach, minicoach

WILKER GROUP
Frederick Street, Clara, Co Offaly, Republic of Ireland
Tel: 00 353 506 31010
E-mail: info@wilkergroup.com
UK subsidiary
Sandy Lane, Ettiley Heath, Sandbach CW11 3NG
Tel: 01270 705999
E-mail: info.uk@wilkergroup.com
Range: low-floor mini- and midibuses, mini- and midicoaches

DEALERS

AD COACH SALES
Newbridge Coach Depot, Witheridge EX16 8PY
Tel: 01884 860767
E-mail: enquiries@adcoachsales.co.uk
Web site: www.adcoachsales.co.uk

ALEXANDER DENNIS LTD
91 Glasgow Road, Falkirk FK1 4JB
Tel: 01324 621 672
Fax: 01324 632 269
E-mail: enquiries@alexander-dennis.com
Web site: www.alexander-dennis.com

ALLIED VEHICLES LTD
230 Balmore Road, Glasgow G22 6LJ
Tel: 0800 916 3046
E-mail: info@alliedvechicles.co.uk
Web site: www.alliedvechicles.co.uk/bus

ARRIVA BUS AND COACH
Lodge Garage, Whitehall Road West, Gomersal, Cleckheaton, West Yorkshire BD19 4BJ
Tel: 01274 681144
Fax: 01274 651198
E-mail: whiter@arriva.co.uk
Web site: www.arrivabusandcoach.co.uk

B.A.S.E. LTD
57 Clydesdale Place, Moss Side Industrial Estate, Leyland PR26 7QS
Tel: 01772 425355
Fax: 01772 425748
Web site: www.basecoachsales.co.uk

BLYTHSWOOD MOTORS LTD
1175 Argyle Street, Glasgow G3 8TQ
Tel: 0141 221 3165
Fax: 0141 221 3172
E-mail: blythswoodmotors@aol.com
Web site: www.blythswoodmotors.co.uk

BOB VALE COACH SALES LTD
Eastfield House, Amesbury Road, Thruxton, Andover, Hampshire SP11 8ED
Tel: 01264 773000
Fax: 01264 774833
E-mail: bobvalecoachsale@btconnect.com
Web site: www.bobvalecoachsales.com

BRIAN NOONE
Straffan Road, Maynooth, Co Kildare, Republic of Ireland
Tel: 00 353 1 628 6311
Fax: 00 353 1 628 5404
Web site: www.briannooneltd.ie

BRISTOL BUS & COACH SALES
6/7 Freestone Road, St Philips, Bristol BS2 0QN
Tel: 0117 971 0251
Fax: 0117 972 3121
E-mail: simon.munden@bristolbusandcoach.co.uk
Web site: www.bristolbusandcoach.co.uk

BRITISH BUS SALES – MIKE NASH
PO Box 534, Dorking RH5 5XB
Tel: 07836 656692
E-mail: nashionalbus1@btconnect.com
Web site: www.britishbussales.co.uk

CAETANO (UK) LTD
Mill Lane, Heather, Coalville LE67 2QE
Tel: 01530 263333
Fax: 01530 263379
E-mail: enquiries@caetano.co.uk
Web site: www.caetano.co.uk
Models: single-deck coach, single-deck low-floor midibus.

CONNAUGHT PSV
8 Mosham Close, Blaxton, Doncaster DN9 3BB
Tel: 01302 770863
Fax: 01302 771666
E-mail: steve@connaughtpsv.co.uk
Web site: www.connaughtpsv.co.uk

DAWSONRENTALS BUS AND COACH LTD
Delaware Drive, Tongwell, Milton Keynes MK15 8JH
Tel: 01908 218111
Fax: 01908 610156
E-mail: info@dawsongroup.co.uk
Web site: www.dawsongroup.co.uk

ENSIGN BUS CO LTD
Juliette Close, Purfleet Industrial Park, Purfleet RM15 4YF
Tel: 01708 865656
Fax: 01708 864340
E-mail: sales@ensignbus.com
Web site: www.ensignbus.com

EVOBUS (UK) LTD
Cross Point Business Park, Ashcroft Way, Coventry CV2 2TU
Tel: 02476 626000
Fax: 02476 626034
Web site: www.evobus.com

DAVID FISHWICK VEHICLE SALES
North Valley, Byron Road, Colne, Lancashire BB8 0RF
Tel: 0800 294 9474
E-mail: matthew@davidfishwick.net
Web site: www.davidfishwick.com

FLEET AUCTION GROUP
Brindley Road, Stephenson Industrial park, Coalville LE67 3HG
Tel: 01530 833535
E-mail: fleet.master@btinternet.com
Web site: www.fleetauctiongroup.com

FURROWS COMMERCIAL VEHICLES
Haybridge Road, Wellington, Telford TF1 2FF
Tel: 01952 640156
Fax: 01952 640178
Web site: www.furrowscommercials.co.uk

GM COACHWORK LTD
Teign Valley, Trusham, Newton Abbot TQ13 0NX
Tel: 01626 853050
Fax: 01626 855066
E-mail: david.vadght@gmcoachwork.co.uk
Web site: www.gmcoachwork.co.uk

IAN GORDON COMMERCIALS
Schawkirk Garage, Stair, Ayrshire KA5 5JA
Tel: 01292 591764
Fax: 01292 591484
E-mail: mail@iangordoncommercials.com
Web site: www.iangordoncommercials.com

THOMAS HARDIE COMMERCIALS LTD
Newstet Road, Knowsley Industrial Park, Liverpool L33 7TJ
Tel: 0151 549 3000
E-mail: info@thardie.co.uk

HEATONS MOTOR CO
53 Bickershaw Lane, Abram, Wigan WN2 5PL
Tel: 01942 864222
E-mail: info@heatonsmotorco.co.uk
Web site: www.heatonsmotorco.co.uk

The Little Red Book 2011 - in association with *tbf* Transport Benevolent Fund

Trade Directory

B & D HOLT LTD
Cuthbert Street, Bolton BL3 3SD
Tel: 01204 650999
Fax: 01204 665300
E-mail: bevholt@bdholt.co.uk
Web site: www.bdholt.co.uk

IRISH COMMERCIALS (SALES)
Naas, Co Kildare, Republic of Ireland
Tel: 00 353 45 879881
Fax: 00 353 45 875462
E-mail: info@irishcomms.ie
Web site: www.irishcomms.ie

KING LONG UK LTD
Bedworth Road, Coventry CV6 6BP
Tel: 02476 363004
Fax: 02476 365835
E-mail: paul@kinglonguk.com
Web site: www.kinglonguk.com
Models: single-deck coach

LVD
Leinster Vehicle Distributors Ltd,
Urlingford, Co Kilkenny, Republic of Ireland
Tel: 00 353 56 31189/88 3 1899
Web site: www.lvd.ie

THE LONDON BUS EXPORT CO
PO Box 12, Chepstow NP16 5UZ
Tel: 01291 689 741
Fax: 01291 689 361
E-mail: lonbusco@globalnet.co.uk
Web site: www.london-bus.co.uk

LOUGHSHORE AUTOS LTD
26 Killycanavan Road, Ardboe,
Dungannon BT71 5BP
Tel: 028 8673 7225
Fax: 028 8673 5882
E-mail: michael@loughshoreautosltd.com
Web site: www.loughshoreautosltd.com

MASS SPECIAL ENGINEERING LTD
ston, Sheffield S25 4SD
Tel: 01909 550480
Fax: 01909 550486

NIGEL McCREE COACH SALES
8 Tamworth Close, Shepshed,
Loughborough, Leicestershire
LE12 9NE
Tel: 01509 502695
E-mail: nigel@nigelmccree.com
Web site: www.nigelmccree.com

MINIS TO MIDIS LTD
MTM House, 135 Nutwell Lane,
Doncaster DN3 3JR
Tel: 01302 833203
Fax: 01302 831756
E-mail: sales@ministomidis.com
Web site: www.ministomidis.com

MISTRAL BUS & COACH PLC
Booths Hall, Chelford Road, Knutsford,
Cheshire WA16 8QZ
Tel: 01565 621881
Fax: 01565 621882
E-mail: sales@mistral-group.com
Web site: www.mistral-group.com

MOSELEY (PCV) LTD
Elmsall Way, Dale Lane, South Elmsall,
Pontefract WF9 2XS
Tel: 01977 609000
Fax: 01977 609900
E-mail: sales@moseleycoachsales.co.uk
Web site: www.moseleycoachsales.co.uk

MOSELEY IN THE SOUTH LTD
Summerfield Avenue, Chelston Business
Park, Wellington TA21 9JF
Tel: 01823 653000
Fax: 01823 663502

E-mail: enquiries@moseleysouth.co.uk
Web site: www.moseleysouth.co.uk

MOSELEY DISTRIBUTORS LTD
Rydenmains, Condoratt Road, Glenmavis,
Airdrie ML6 0PP
Tel: 01236 750501/2
Fax: 01236 750503/4
E-mail: enquiries@moseleydistributors.co.uk
Web site: www.moseleydistributors.co.uk

NEXT BUS LTD
Vincients Road, Bumpers Farm Industrial
Estate, Chippenham SN14 6QA
Tel: 01249 462462
Fax: 01249 448844
E-mail: sales@next-bus.co.uk
Web site: www.next-bus.co.uk

OPTARE PLC (Leeds)
Manston Lane, Leeds LS15 8SU
Tel: 0113 264 5182
Fax: 0113 260 6635
E-mail: info@optare.com
Web site: www.optare.com

OWENS OF OSWESTRY BMC
Unit 3, Four Crosses Business Park,
Llanymynech SY22 6ST
Tel: 01691 652126
Fax: 01691 831142
E-mail: sales@owens-bmc.co.uk
Web site: www.owens-bmc.co.uk

PEMBRIDGE VEHICLE MANAGEMENT
Autopia House, Llantarnam Road,
Cwmbran NP44 3BB
Tel: 01633 485858
Fax: 01633 866333
E-mail: sales@minibussales.co.uk
Web site: www.minibussales.co.uk

Fleet Insurances

RIGTON Insurance Services Ltd
Chartered Insurance Brokers

We offer you a wealth of expertise gained over 35 years, qualified and knowledgeable staff and a personal and professional service

Call us today on **01943 879 539**
or email our us at
enquiries@rigtoninsurance.co.uk

For a full range of our services and to find out more, please visit our website:
www.rigtoninsurance.co.uk

RIGTON CHARTERED INSURANCE BROKERS

- Coach, Mini bus, Bus and Haulage insurance
- Mini-fleets
- Preserved vehicle insurances
- Conversion to fleets from individual policies
- Breakdown 'Gold' Cover
- Heavy vehicles
- Liability cover

Proud members of the
COACH TOURISM COUNCIL
Promoting Travel and Tourism by Coach

Rigton Insurance Services Limited are Authorised and Regulated by the Financial Services Authority

H W PICKRELL
Gardiners Lane North, Crays Hill,
Billericay CM11 2XE
Tel: 01268 521033
Fax: 01268 284951
Web site: www.hwpickrell.co.uk

PLAXTON COACH SALES CENTRE
Crossroads, Anston, Sheffield S25 4DL
Tel: 01909 551166
Fax: 01909 567994
E-mail: sales@plaxtonlimited.co.uk
Web site: www.plaxtonlimited.co.uk
(Part of Alexander Dennis)

SANTANDER ASSET FINANCE
Taylor Road, Trafford Park,
Manchester M41 7JQ
Tel: 0161 747 5698
Fax: 0161 275 4501
E-mail: steve.moult@hansar.co.uk
Web site: www.buses247.co.uk

SOUTHDOWN PSV LTD
Silverwood, Snow Hill,
Copthorne RH10 3EN
Tel: 01342 715222
Fax: 01342 719619
E-mail: bussales@southdownpsv.co.uk
Web site: www.southdownpsv.co.uk

STAFFORD BUS CENTRE
Unit 27, Moorfields Industrial Estate,
Cotes Heath ST21 6QY
Tel: 01782 791774
Fax: 01782 791721
E-mail: mail@staffordbuscentre.com
Web site: www.staffordbuscentre.com

STEPHENSONS OF ESSEX
Riverside Industrial Estate, South Street,
Rochford SS4 1BS
Tel: 01702 541511
Fax: 01702 549461
E-mail: sales@stephensonsofessex.com
Web site: www.stephensonsofessex.com

STOKE TRUCK & BUS CENTRE
Bute Street, Fenton,
Stoke-on-Trent ST4 3PS
Tel: 01782 598310
Fax: 01782 598674
Web site: www.bmcstoke.co.uk

TAYLOR COACH SALES
102 Beck Road, Isleham,
Ely CB7 5QP
Tel (mobile): 07850 241848
Tel: 01638 780010
Fax: 01638 780011
E-mail: taylorscoach@live.co.uk
Web site: www.taylorscoachsales.co.uk

TOYOTA (GB) PLC
Great Burgh, Burgh Heath,
Epsom KT18 5UX
Tel: 01737 363633
Fax: 01737 367713
E-mail: steve.prime@tgb.toyota.co.uk
Web site: www.toyota.com
UK suppliers:
AD Coach Sales Tel: 01884 860767;
Holloway Commercials Tel: 01902 636661
Caetano (UK) Ltd Tel: 01530 263333

TRAMONTANA
Chapelknowe Road, Carfin,
Motherwell ML1 5LE
Tel: 01698 861790
Fax: 01698 860778
E-mail: wdt90@tiscali.co.uk
Web site: www.tramontanacoach.co.uk

UK BUS DISMANTLERS LTD
Streamhall Garage,
Linton Trading Estate, Bromyard,
Herefordshire, HR7 4QT
Tel: 01885 488 448
Fax: 01885 482 127
E-mail: wactonbus@yahoo.co.uk
Web site: www.uk-bus.co.uk

USED COACH SALES
The Red House, Underbridge Lane,
Higher Walton, Warrington
WA4 5QR
Tel: 01925 210202
Web site: www.usedcoachsales.co.uk

VENTURA BUS + COACH SALES
Unit 39, Hobbs Industrial Estate,
Newchapel, Lingfield RH7 6HN
Tel: 01342 835206
Fax: 01342 835813
E-mail: info@venturasales.co.uk
Web site: www.venturasales.co.uk

VOLVO BUS & COACH SALES CENTRE
Siskin Parkway East,
Middlemarch Business Park,
Coventry CV3 4PE
Tel: 02476 210250
Fax: 02476 210258
Web site: www.volvo.com
Range: New & Pre-owned buses and coaches.

WACTON COACH SALES & SERVICES
Linton Trading Estate, Bromyard,
Herefordshire HR7 4QL
Tel: 01885 482782
Fax: 01885 482127

WEALDEN PSV LTD
The Bus Garage,
64 Whetsted Road,
Five Oak Green, Tonbridge,
Kent TN12 6RT
Tel: 01892 833830
Fax: 01892 836977
E-mail: sales@wealdenpsv.co.uk
Web site: www.wealdenpsv.co.uk

ALAN WHITE COACH SALES
135 Nutwell Lane,
Doncaster DN3 3JR
Tel: 01302 833203
Fax: 01302 831756
E-mail: sales@alanwhitecoachsales.com
Web site: www.alanwhitecoachsales.com

TREVOR WIGLEY & SONS BUS LTD
Passenger Vehicle Dismantling/Spares
Works: Boulder Bridge Lane,
off Shaw Lane,
Barnsley S71 3HJ
Correspondence:
148 Royston Road, Cudworth,
Barnsley S72 8BN
Tel: 01226 713636
Fax: 01226 700199
E-mail: wigleys@btintenet.com
Web site: www.twigley.com

DREW WILSON COACH SALES
2/3, 179 Finnieston Street,
Glasgow G3 8HE
Tel: 0141 248 5524
E-mail: enquiries@drewwilson.co.uk
Web site: www.drewwilson.co.uk

YORKSHIRE BUS & COACH SALES
254A West Ella Road,
West Ella, Hull HU10 7SF
Tel: 01482 653302
Fax: 01482 653302
E-mail: craig.porteous@virgin.net

Advertising in the

The Little Red Book
2011
Passenger Transport Directory for the British Isles

For information regarding advertising contact:

Graham Middleton
Tel: 01780 484632
Fax: 01780 763388
E-mail:
graham.middleton@ianallanpublishing.co.uk

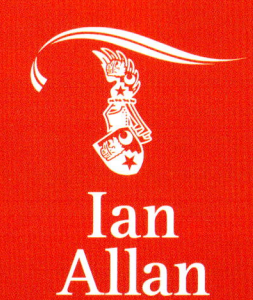

Ian Allan

Riverdene Business Park,
Molesey Road, Hersham,
Surrey KT12 4RG
Tel: 01932 266600
Fax: 01932 266601

The Little Red Book 2011 - in association with *tbf* Transport Benevolent Fund

A-Z Listing of Bus, Coach & Tram Suppliers

LIST OF CATEGORIES

Air Conditioning/Ventilation
Audio/Video Systems
Badges – Drivers/Conductors
Batteries
Bicycle carriers
Body/Electrical Repairs & Refurbishing
Brakes and Brake Linings
Bus Stops/Shelters – see Shelters/Street Furniture
Cash Handling Equipment
Chassis Lubricating Systems
Clutches
Cooling Systems
Destination Indicator Equipment
Door Operating Gear
Drinks Dispensing Equipment
Driving Axles and Gears
Electrical Equipment
Electronic Control
Emission Control Devices
Engineering
Engines
Engine Oil Drain Valves
Exhaust Systems
Fans & Drive Belts
Fare Boxes
Fire Extinguishers
First Aid Equipment
Floor Coverings
Fuel, Fuel Management & Lubricants
Garage Equipment
Gearboxes
Hand Driers (In Coaches)
Hand Rails
Headrest Covers & Curtains
Heating & Ventilation Systems
Hub Odometers
In-Coach Catering Equipment
Information Displays – see Passenger Information Systems

Labels, Nameplates & Decals
Lifting Equipment
Lifts/Ramps (Passenger)
Lighting & Lighting Design
Mirrors/Mirror Arms
Oil Management Systems
Painting & Signwriting
Parts Suppliers
Passenger Information Systems
Pneumatic Valves/Cylinders
Rapid Transit/Priority Equipment
Repairs/Refurbishment – see Body/Electrical Repairs
Retarders & Speed Control Systems
Reversing Safety Systems
Roller Blinds – Passenger & Driver
Roof Lining Fabrics
Seat Belts/Restraint Systems
Seats/Seat Cushions & Seat Frames
Shelters/Street Furniture
Shock Absorbers/Suspension
Steering
Surveillance Systems
Suspension
Tachographs
Tachograph Calibrators
Tachograph Chart Analysis Service
Tickets, Ticket Machines and Ticket Systems
Timetable Display Frames
Toilet Equipment
Transmission Overhaul
Tree Guards
Tyres
Uniforms
Upholstery
Vacuum Systems
Vehicle Washing & Washers
Wheels, Wheeltrims & Covers
Windows and Windscreens

INDUSTRY SERVICE PROVIDERS

Accident Investigation
Accountancy & Audit
Advisory Services
Artwork
Breakdown & Recovery Services
Cleaning Services
Coach Driver Agencies
Coach Hire Brokers/Vehicle Rental
Coach Interchange & Parking Facilities
Computer Systems/Software
Consultants
Driver Supply
Driver Training
Exhibition/Event Organisers
Ferry Operators
Finance and Leasing
Graphic Design
Health & Safety
Hotel Agents
Insurance
Legal & Operations Advisers
Livery Design
Maps for the Bus Industry
Marketing Services
Mechanical Investigation
On-Bus Advertising
Printing and Publishing
Promotional Material
Publications – Magazines & Books
Quality Management Systems
Recruitment
Reference Books
Timetable Production
Tour Wholesalers
Training Services
Vehicle Certification
Vehicle Rental – see Coach Hire Brokers/Vehicle Rental

Air Conditioning/Ventilation

AIRCONCO
Units 10 (Head Office), 6 (Part Centre),
Middleton Trade Park, Oldham Road,
Middleton, Manchester M24 1QZ
Tel: 0845 402 4014
Fax: 0845 402 4041
E-mail: mail@airconco.carriersutrak.co.uk
Web site: www.airconco.ltd.uk

AMA LTD
Unit 17, Springmill Industrial Estate, Avening Road, Nailsworth GL6 0BH
Tel: 01453 832884
Fax: 01453 832040
E-mail: ama@ftech.co.uk

ARRIVA BUS AND COACH
Lodge Garage, Whitehall Road West, Gomersal, Cleckheaton, West Yorkshire BD9 4BJ
Tel: 01274 681144
Fax: 01274 651198
E-mail: whiter@arriva.co.uk
Web site: www.arrivabusandcoach.co.uk

BRT BEARINGS LTD
21-24 Regal Road, Wisbech, Cambridgeshire PE13 2RQ
Tel: 01945 464 097
Fax: 01945 464 523
E-mail: info@brt-group.com

CARRIER SUTRAK
15 Moat Lane, Barn Way, Towcester, Northamptonshire NN12 6AD
Tel: 01327 358192
Fax: 01327 354194
E-mail: info.suetrak@carrier.utc.com
Web site: www.suetrak.com

CLAYTON HEATERS LTD
Hunter Terrace, Fletchworth Gate, Burnsall Road, Coventry CV5 6SP
Tel: 02476 691 916
Fax: 02476 691 969
E-mail: admin@claytoncc.co.uk
Web Site: www.claytoncc.co.uk

CONSERVE (UK) LTD
Suite 7, Logistics House, Kingsthorpe Road, Northampton NN2 6LJ
Tel: 01604 710055
Fax: 01604 710065
E-mail: information@conserveuk.co.uk
Web site: www.conserveuk.co.uk

DIRECT PARTS LTD
Unit 1, Churnet Court, Churnetside Business Park, Harrison Way, Cheddleton ST13 7EF
Tel: 01538 361777
Fax: 01538 369100
E-mail: sales@direct-group.co.uk
Web site: www.direct-group.co.uk

EBERSPACHER (UK) LTD
Headlands Business Park, Salisbury Road, Ringwood BH24 3PB
Tel: 01425 480151
Fax: 01425 480152
E-mail: enquiries@eberspacher.com
Web site: www.eberspacher.com

HISPACOLD
See: Clayton Heaters above
Web Site: www.hispacold.es

M A C LTD
Unit 8, Oldends Lane Industrial Estate, Oldends Lane, Stonehouse GL10 3RQ
Tel: 01453 828781
Fax: 01453 828167
E-mail: sales@macair.uk.com
Web site: www.macair.uk.com

OPTARE PARTS DIVISION (Rotherham)
Denby Way, Hellaby, Rotherham S66 8HR
Tel: 01709 792000
Fax: 01709 792009
E-mail: parts@optare.com

OPTARE PRODUCT SUPPORT LONDON
Unit 9, Eurocourt, Olivers Close, West Thurrock RM20 3EE
Tel: 08444 123222
Fax: 01708 869920
E-mail: london.service@optare.com

OPTARE PRODUCT SUPPORT ROTHERHAM
Denby Way, Hellaby, Rotherham S66 8HR
Tel: 01709 535101
Fax: 01709 535103
E-mail: rotherham.service@optare.com

OPTARE PRODUCT SUPPORT SCOTLAND
Unit 7, Cumbernauld Business Park, Ward Park Road, Cumbernauld G67 3JZ
Tel: 01236 726738
Fax: 01236 795651
E-mail: scotland.service@optare.com

PLAXTON SERVICE
Ryton Road, Anston, Sheffield S25 4DL
Tel: 01909 551155
Fax: 01909 550050
E-mail: service@plaxtonlimited.co.uk
Web site: www.plaxtonaftercare.co.uk

SCANIA
Scania Bus & Coach (UK) Ltd, Claylands Avenue, Worksop S81 7DJ
Tel: 01909 500822.
Fax: 01909 500165
Web Site: www.scania.co.uk

WEBASTO PRODUCT UK LTD
Webasto House, White Rose Way, Doncaster Carr, South Yorkshire DN4 5JH
Tel: 01302 322232
Fax: 01302 322231
E-mail: info@webastouk.com
Web site: www.webasto.co.uk

Audio/Video Systems

AUTOSOUND LTD
4 Lister Street, Dudley Hill, Bradford BD4 9PQ
Tel: 01274 688990
Fax: 01274 651318
Web site: www.autosound.co.uk
E-mail: sales@autosound.co.uk

AVT SYSTEMS LTD
Unit 3 & 4, Tything Road, Arden Forest Trading Estate, Alcester, Warwickshire B49 6ES
Tel: 01789 400357
Fax: 01789 400359
E-mail: enquiries@avtsystems.co.uk
Web site: www.avtsystems.co.uk

CONCEPT COACHCRAFT LTD
Far Cromwell Road, Stockport, Cheshire SK6 2SE
Tel: 0161 406 9322
Fax: 0161 406 9588
E-mail: sales@conceptcoachcraft.com
Web site: www.conceptcoachcraft.com

EXPRESS COACH REPAIRS LTD
Outgang Lane, Pickering YO18 7JA
Tel: 01751 475215
Fax: 01751 475215
E-mail: info@expresscoachrepairs.co.uk
Web site: www.expresscoachrepairs.co.uk

FCAV & CO
Brooklyn House, Coleford Road, Bream, Gloucestershire GL15 6EU
Tel: 07900 572382
Fax: 01594 564556
E-mail: info@fcav.co.uk
Web site: www.fcav.co.uk

INIT GmbH – INNOVATION IN TRANSPORT
32A Stoney Street, The Lace Market, Nottingham NG1 1LL
Tel: 0870 890 4648
Fax: 0115 988 6917
E-mail: sales@init.co.uk
Web site: www.init.co.uk

KCP CAR & COMMERCIAL LTD
Unit 15, Hillside Business Park, Kempson Way, Bury St Edmunds, Suffolk IP32 7EA
Tel: 01284 750777
Fax: 01284 750773
E-mail: info@kcpcarandcommercial.co.uk
Web site: www.kcpcarandcommercial.co.uk

OPTARE PARTS DIVISION (Rotherham)
Denby Way, Hellaby, Rotherham S66 8HR
Tel: 01709 792000
Fax: 01709 792009
E-mail: parts@optare.com

PLAXTON SERVICE
Ryton Road, Anston, Sheffield S25 4DL

Trade Directory

Tel: 01909 551155
Fax: 01909 550050
E-mail: service@plaxtonlimited.co.uk
Web site: www.plaxtonaftercare.co.uk

PSV PRODUCTS
The Red House, Underbridge Lane, Higher Walton, Warrington WA4 5QR
Tel: 01925 210220
Fax: 01925 601534
E-mail: info@psvproducts.com
Web site: www.psvproducts.com

Badges - Drivers/Conductors

GSM-ABBOT BROWN
Castlegarth Works, Thirsk, YO7 1PS
Tel: 01845 522184
Fax: 01845 522206
E-mail: gsmgraphicarts@gsmgroup.co.uk
Web Site: www.gsmabbotbrown.co.uk

MARK TERRILL PSV BADGES
5 De Grey Close, Lewes BN7 2JR
Tel: 01273 474816
Fax: 01273 474816
Mobile: 07770 666159

Batteries

ARRIVA BUS AND COACH
Lodge Garage, Whitehall Road West, Gomersal, Cleckheaton, West Yorkshire BD19 4BJ
Tel: 01274 681144
Fax: 01274 651198
E-mail: whiter@arriva.co.uk
Web site: www.arrivabusandcoach.co.uk

CUMMINS UK
Rutherford Drive, Park Farm South, Wellingborough NN8 6AN
Tel: 01933 334200
Fax: 01933 334198
E-mail: cduksales@cummins.com
Web site: www.cummins-uk.com

EXPRESS COACH REPAIRS LTD
Outgang Lane, Pickering YO18 7JA
Tel: 01751 475215
Fax: 01751 475215
E-mail: info@expresscoachrepairs.co.uk
Web site: www.expresscoachrepairs.co.uk

THOMAS HARDIE COMMERCIALS LTD
Newstet Road, Knowsley Industrial Park, Liverpool L33 7TJ
Tel: 0151 549 3000
E-mail: info@thardie.co.uk

KCP CAR & COMMERCIAL LTD
Unit 15, Hillside Business Park, Kempson Way, Bury St Edmunds, Suffolk IP32 7EA
Tel: 01284 750777
Fax: 01284 750773
E-mail: info@kcpcarandcommercial.co.uk
Web site: www.kcpcarandcommercial.co.uk

MASS SPECIAL ENGINEERING LTD
Houghton Road, North Anston S25 4JJ
Tel: 01909 550480
Fax: 01909 550486

OPTARE PARTS DIVISION (Rotherham)
Denby Way, Hellaby, Rotherham S66 8HR
Tel: 01709 792000
Fax: 01709 792009
E-mail: parts@optare.com

OPTARE PRODUCT SUPPORT LONDON
Unit 9, Eurocourt, Olivers Close, West Thurrock RM20 3EE
Tel: 08444 123222
Fax: 01708 869920
E-mail: london.service@optare.com

OPTARE PRODUCT SUPPORT ROTHERHAM
Denby Way, Hellaby, Rotherham S66 8HR
Tel: 01709 535101
Fax: 01709 535103
E-mail: rotherham.service@optare.com

OPTARE PRODUCT SUPPORT SCOTLAND
Unit 7, Cumbernauld Business Park, Ward Park Road, Cumbernauld G67 3JZ
Tel: 01236 726738
Fax: 01236 795651
E-mail: scotland.service@optare.com

POWER BATTERIES (GB) LTD
Units 5-8, Canal View Business Park, Wheelhouse Road, Rugeley WS15 1UY
Tel: 01889 571100
Fax: 01889 577342
Web site: www.bannerbatteries.com

VARTA AUTOMOTIVE BATTERIES LTD
Broadwater Park, North Orbital Road, Denham UB9 5AG
Tel: 01895 838999
Fax: 01895 838981
Web site: www.varta-automotive.com

Bicycle Carriers

JES BUSCYCLE
27-33 High Street, Totton SO40 9HL
Tel: 023 8066 3535

PLAXTON SERVICE
Ryton Road, Anston, Sheffield S25 4DL
Tel: 01909 551155
Fax: 01909 550050
E-mail: service@plaxtonlimited.co.uk
Web site: www.plaxtonaftercare.co.uk

Body/Electrical Repairs & Refurbishing

AD COACH SALES
Newbridge Coach Depot, Witheridge EX16 8PY
Tel: 01884 860787
Fax: 01884 860711
E-mail: enquiries@adcoachsales.co.uk
Web site: www.adcoachsales.co.uk

ARRIVA BUS AND COACH
Lodge Garage, Whitehall Road West, Gomersal, Cleckheaton, West Yorkshire BD19 4BJ
Tel: 01274 681144
Fax: 01274 651198
E-mail: whiter@arriva.co.uk
Web Site: www.arrivabusandcoach.co.uk

BULWARK BUS & COACH ENGINEERING LTD
Unit 5, Bulwark Business Park, Bulwark, Chepstow NP16 6QZ
Tel: 01291 622326
Fax: 01291 622726
E-mail: bulwarkbusandcoach@tiscali.co.uk
Web site: www.bulwarkbusandcoach.co.uk

CARLYLE BUS & COACH LTD
Carlyle Business Park, Great Bridge Street, Swan Village, West Bromwich B70 0X4
Tel: 0121 524 1200
Fax: 0121 524 1201
E-mail: admin@carlyleplc.co.uk
Web Site: www.carlyleplc.co.uk

CHANNEL COMMERCIALS PLC
Unit 6, Cobbs Wood Industrial Estate, Brunswick Road, Ashford TN23 1EH
Tel: 01233 629272
Fax: 01233 636322
E-mail: info@ccplc.co.uk
Web site: www.channelcommercials.co.uk

CREST COACH CONVERSIONS
Unit 5, Holmeroyd Road, Bentley Moor Lane, Carcroft, Doncaster DN6 7BH
Tel: 01302 723723
Fax: 01302 724724

CROWN COACHBUILDERS LTD
32 Flemington Industrial Park, Flemington, Motherwell ML1 1SN
Tel: 01698 276087
Fax: 01698 262676
E-mail: davidgreer@hotmail.com
Web site: www.crowncoachbuilders.co.uk

EASTGATE COACH TRIMMERS
3 Thornton Road Industrial Estate, Pickering YO18 7HZ
Tel/Fax: 01751 472229
E-mail: info@eastgate-coachtrimmers.co.uk
Web site: eastgate-coachtrimmers.co.uk

EXPRESS COACH REPAIRS LTD
Outgang Lane, Pickering YO18 7JA
Tel: 01751 475215
Fax: 01751 475215
E-mail: info@expresscoachrepairs.co.uk
Web site: www.expresscoachrepairs.co.uk

GHE
Unit 30, Fort Industrial Park, Fort Parkway, Castle Bromwich B35 7AR
Tel: 0121 747 4400
Fax: 0121 747 4977
Web site: www.ghegroup.com

HANTS & DORSET TRIM LTD
Canada Road, West Wellow SO51 6DE.
Tel: 02380 644200
Fax: 02380 647802
E-mail: dclack@hdtrim.co.uk
Web site: www.hantsanddorsettrim.co.uk

THOMAS HARDIE COMMERCIALS LTD
Newstet Road, Knowsley Industrial Park, Liverpool L33 7TJ
Tel: 0151 549 3000
E-mail: info@thardie.co.uk

INVERTEC LTD
Whelford Road, Fairford GL7 4DT
Tel: 01285 713550
Fax: 01285 713548
Mobile: 07802 793828
E-mail: ian@invertec.co.uk
Web site: www.invertec.co.uk

LAWTON SERVICES LTD
Knutsford Road, Church Lawton, Stoke-on-Trent ST7 3DN
Tel: 01270 882056
Fax: 01270 883014
E-mail: andrea@lawtonservices.co.uk
Web site: www.lawtonservices.co.uk

LEICESTER CARRIAGE BUILDERS
Marlow Road, Leicester LE3 2BQ
Tel: 0116 282 4270
Fax: 0116 263 0554
E-mail: rick.johnson@midlandsco-op.com
Web site: www.leicestercarriagebuilders.co.uk

MARTYN INDUSTRIALS LTD
5 Brunel Way, Durranhill, Harraby, Carlisle CA1 3NQ
Tel: 01228 544000
Fax: 01228 544001
E-mail: enquiries@martyn-industrials.co.uk
Web site: www.martyn-industrials.com

MASS SPECIAL ENGINEERING LTD
Houghton Road, North Anston S25 4JJ
Tel: 01909 550480.
Fax: 01909 550486

Trade Directory

MCV BUS & COACH LTD
Sterling Place, Elean Business Park, Sutton, Cambridge CB6 2QE
Tel: 01353 773000
Fax: 01353 773001
E-mail: vernon.edwards@mcv-uk.com

MELLOR COACHCRAFT
Miall Street, Rochdale OL11 1HY
Tel: 01706 860610
Fax: 01706 860042
E-mail: mcsales@woodhall-nicholson.co.uk
Web site: www.woodhall-nicholson.co.uk

OPTARE PARTS DIVISION (Rotherham)
Denby Way, Hellaby, Rotherham S66 8HR
Tel: 01709 792000
Fax: 01709 792009
E-mail: parts@optare.com

OPTARE PRODUCT SUPPORT LONDON
Unit 9, Eurocourt, Olivers Close, West Thurrock RM20 3EE
Tel: 08444 123222
Fax: 01708 869920
E-mail: london.service@optare.com

OPTARE PRODUCT SUPPORT ROTHERHAM
Denby Way, Hellaby, Rotherham S66 8HR
Tel: 01709 535101
Fax: 01709 535103
E-mail: rotherham.service@optare.com

OPTARE PRODUCT SUPPORT SCOTLAND
Unit 7, Cumbernauld Business Park, Ward Park Road, Cumbernauld G67 3JZ
Tel: 01236 726738
Fax: 01236 795651
E-mail: scotland.service@optare.com

PLAXTON SERVICE
Ryton Road, Anston, Sheffield S25 4DL
Tel: 01909 551155
Fax: 01909 550050
E-mail: service@plaxtonlimited.co.uk
Web site: www.plaxtonaftercare.co.uk

RH BODYWORKS
A140 Ipswich Road, Brome, Eye IP23 8AW
Tel: 01379 870666
Fax: 01379 872106
E-mail: mike.ball@rhbodyworks.co.uk
Web site: www.rhbodyworks.co.uk

TRAMONTANA
Chapelknowe Road, Carfin, Motherwell ML1 5LE
Tel: 01698 861790
Fax: 01698 860778
E-mail: wdt90@tiscali.co.uk
Web site: www.tramontanacoach.co.uk

TRUCKALIGN CO LTD
VIP Trading Estate, Anchor & Hope Lane, London SE7 7RY
Tel: 020 8858 3781
Fax: 020 8858 3781
E-mail: tony.rodwell@dsl.pipex.com

TTS UK
Total Tool Solutions Ltd, Newhaven Business Park, Lowergate, Milnsbridge, Huddersfield HD3 4HS
Tel: 01484 642211
Fax: 01484 461002
E-mail: sales@ttsuk.com
Web site: www.ttsuk.com

VOLVO BUS AND COACH CENTRE
Parts Sales & Body Repair/Refurbishment Specialists
Byron Street Extension, Loughborough LE11 5HE
Tel: 01509 217700
Fax: 01509 238770
E-mail (Body Support): dporter@volvocoachsales.co.uk
Web site: www.volvo.com

WILKINSONS VEHICLE SOLUTIONS
62 Scalby Avenue, Scarborough YO12 6HP
Tel: 01262 603307
Fax: 01262 608208

Brakes and Brake Linings

ARRIVA BUS AND COACH
Lodge Garage, Whitehall Road West, Gomersall, Cleckheaton, West Yorkshire BD19 4BJ
Tel: 01274 681144
Fax: 01274 651198
E-mail: whiter@arriva.co.uk
Web site: www.arrivabusandcoach.co.uk

ARVIN MERITOR
Unit 21, Suttons Park Avenue, Reading RG6 1LA
Tel: 0118 935 9126
Fax: 0118 935 9138
E-mail: james.randall@arvinmeritor.com
Web site: www.arvinmeritor.com

CAPARO AP BRAKING LTD
Tachbrook Road, Leamington Spa CV31 3SF
Tel: 01926 473737.
Fax: 01926 473836
E-mail: sales.enquiries@caparoapbraking.com
Web site: www.caparoapbraking.co.uk

DIRECT PARTS LTD
Unit 1, Churnet Court, Churnetside Business Park, Harrison Way, Cheddleton ST13 7EF
Tel: 01538 361777
Fax: 01538 369100
E-mail: sales@direct-group.co.uk
Web site: www.direct-group.co.uk

IMEXPART LTD
Links 31, Willowbridge Way, Whitwood, Castleford WF10 5NP
Tel: 0845 605 0404
Fax: 01977 513412
E-mail: sales@imexpart.com
Web site: www.imexpart.com

IMPERIAL ENGINEERING
Delamare Road, Cheshunt, Hertfordshire EN8 9UD
Tel: 01992 634255
Fax: 01992 630506
E-mail: orders@imperialengineering.co.uk
Web site: www.imperialengineering.co.uk

KCP CAR & COMMERCIAL LTD
Unit 15, Hillside Business Park, Kempson Way, Bury St Edmunds, Suffolk IP32 7EA
Tel: 01284 750777
Fax: 01284 750773
E-mail: info@kcpcarandcommercial.co.uk
Web site: www.kcpcarandcommercial.co.uk

KELLETT (UK) LTD
8 Stevenson Way, Sheffield S9 3WZ
Tel: 0114 261 1122
Fax: 0114 261 1199
E-mail: sales@kellett.co.uk

KNORR-BREMSE SYSTEMS FOR COMMERCIAL VEHICLES LTD
Douglas Road, Kingswood, Bristol BS15 8NL
Tel: 0117 984 6100
Fax: 0117 984 6101
Web site: www.knorr-bremse.com

NUTEXA FRICTIONS LTD
PO Box 11, New Hall Lane, Hoylake, Wirral CH47 4DH
Tel: 0151 632 5903
Fax: 0151 632 5908
E-mail: sales@nutexafrictions.co.uk
Web Site: www.sergeant.co.uk

OPTARE PARTS DIVISION (Rotherham)
Denby Way, Hellaby, Rotherham S66 8HR
Tel: 01709 792000
Fax: 01709 792009
E-mail: parts@optare.com

OPTARE PRODUCT SUPPORT LONDON
Unit 9, Eurocourt, Olivers Close, West Thurrock RM20 3EE
Tel: 08444 123222
Fax: 01708 869920
E-mail: london.service@optare.com

OPTARE PRODUCT SUPPORT ROTHERHAM
Denby Way, Hellaby, Rotherham S66 8HR
Tel: 01709 535101
Fax: 01709 535103
E-mail: rotherham.service@optare.com

OPTARE PRODUCT SUPPORT SCOTLAND
Unit 7, Cumbernauld Business Park, Ward Park Road, Cumbernauld G67 3JZ
Tel: 01236 726738
Fax: 01236 795651
E-mail: scotland.service@optare.com

PARTLINE LTD
Dockfield Road, Shipley BD17 7AZ
Tel: 01274 531531
Fax: 01274 531088

Trade Directory

E-mail: sales@partline.co.uk
Web site: www.partline.co.uk

PLAXTON SERVICE
Ryton Road, Anston, Sheffield S25 4DL
Tel: 01909 551155
Fax: 01909 550250
E-mail: service@plaxtonlimited.co.uk
Web site: www.plaxtonaftercare.co.uk

ROADLINK INTERNATIONAL LTD
Strawberry Lane, Willenhall, West Midlands WV13 3RL
Tel: 01902 636206
Fax: 01902 631515
E-mail: sales@roadlink-international.co.uk
Web site: www.roadlink-international.co.uk

TMD FRICTION UK LTD
PO Box 18, Hunsworth Lane, Cleckheaton, West Yorkshire BD19 3UJ
Tel: 01274 854000
Fax: 01274 854001
E-mail: marketing@tmdfriction.co.uk
Web site: www.tmdfriction.co.uk

TTS UK
Total Tool Solutions Ltd, Newhaven Business Park, Lowergate, Milnsbridge, Huddersfield HD3 4HS
Tel: 01484 642211
Fax: 01484 461002
E-mail: sales@ttsuk.com
Web site: www.ttsuk.com

WABCO AUTOMOTIVE UK
Texas Street, Leeds LS27 0HQ
Tel: 0113 251 2510
Fax: 0113 251 2844
Web site: www.wabco-auto.com

Cash Handling Equipment

CUMMINS-ALLISON LTD
William H Klotz House, Colonnade Point, Central Boulevard, Prologis Park, Coventry CV6 4BU
Tel: 0800 018 6484
Fax: 024 7633 9811
E-mail: sales@cummins-allison.co.uk
Web site: www.cumminsallison.co.uk

ETMSS LTD
c/o Ground Floor, Austin House, 43 Poole Road, Westbourne, Bournemouth BH4 9DN
Tel: 0844 800 9299
E-mail: info@etmss.com
Web Site: www.etmss.com

JOHN GROVES TICKET SYSTEMS
Unit 10, North Circular Business Centre, 400 NCR, London NW10 0JG

Tel: 0208 830 1222
Fax: 0208 830 1223
E-Mail: sales@jgts.co.uk
Web site: www.jgts.co.uk

MARK TERRILL TICKET MACHINERY
5 De Grey Close, Lewes BN7 2JR
Tel: 01273 474816
Fax: 01273 474816
E-mail: mark.terrill@ukonline.co.uk

QUICK CHANGE (UK) LTD
Yew Tree Cottage, Newcastle, Monmouthshire, NP25 5NT
Tel: 01600 750650
Fax: 01600 750650
E-mail: ttservices@tiscali.co.uk
Web Site: www.ticket-machines.co.uk

SCAN COIN LTD
110 Broadway, Salford Quays M50 2UW
Tel: 0161 873 0505
Fax: 0161 873 0501
E-mail: sales@scancoin.co.uk
Web site: www.scancoin.co.uk

THOMAS AUTOMATION LTD
5 Weldon Road, Loughborough LE11 5RN
Tel: 01509 225692
Fax: 0700 600 7749
E-mail: sales@thomasa.co.uk
Web site: www.thomasa.co.uk

TICKETER
Riverside Centre, 82 Station Road, Barnes, London SW13 0LS
Tel: 0844 800 9299
E-mail: sales@ticketer.co.uk
Web site: www.ticketer.co.uk

Chassis Lubricating Systems

ARRIVA BUS AND COACH
Lodge Garage, Whitehall Road West, Gomersal, Cleckheaton, West Yorkshire BD19 4BJ
Tel: 01274 681144
Fax: 01274 651198
E-mail: whiter@arriva.co.uk
Web site: www.arrivabusandcoach.co.uk

GROENEVELD UK LTD
The Greentec Centre, Gelders Hall Road, Shepshed, Leicestershire LE12 9NH
Tel: 01509 600033
Fax: 01509 602000
E-mail: info@groeneveld.co.uk
Web site: www.groeneveld.co.uk

PLAXTON SERVICE
Ryton Road, Anston, Sheffield S25 4DL
Tel: 01909 551155
Fax: 01909 550250

E-mail: service@plaxtonlimited.co.uk
Web site: www.plaxtonaftercare.co.uk

Clutches

ARRIVA BUS AND COACH
Lodge Garage, Whitehall Road West, Gomersal, Cleckheaton, West Yorkshire BD19 4BJ
Tel: 01274 681144
Fax: 01274 651198
E-mail: whiter@arriva.co.uk
Web site: www.arrivabusandcoach.co.uk

BUSS BIZZ
Goughs Transport Depot, Morestead, Winchester SO21 1JD
Tel: 01962 715555/66.
Fax: 01962 714868.

CAPARO AP BRAKING LTD
Tachbrook Road, Leamington Spa CV31 3ER.
Tel: 01926 473737
Fax: 01926 473836
E-mail: sales@caparoapbraking.com
Web site: www.caparoapbraking.com

COACH-AID
Unit 2, Brindley Close, Tollgate Industrial Estate, Stafford ST16 3SU
Tel: 01785 222666
E-mail: workshop@coach-aid.com
Web site: www.coach-aid.com

IMEXPART LTD
Links 31, Willowbridge Way, Whitwood, Castleford WF10 5NP
Tel: 0845 605 0404
Fax: 01977 513412
E-mail: sales@imexpart.com
Web site: www.imexpart.com

KCP CAR & COMMERCIAL LTD
Unit 15, Hillside Business Park, Kempson Way, Bury St Edmunds, Suffolk IP32 7EA
Tel: 01284 750777
Fax: 01284 750773
E-mail: info@kcpcarandcommercial.co.uk
Web site: www.kcpcarandcommercial.co.uk

KELLETT (UK) LTD
8 Stevenson Way, Sheffield S9 3WZ
Tel: 0114 261 1122
Fax: 0114 261 1199
E-mail: sales@kellett.co.uk

NUTEXA FRICTIONS LTD
PO Box 11, New Hall Lane, Hoylake, Wirral CH47 4DH
Tel: 0151 632 5903
Fax: 0151 632 5908
E-mail: sales@nutexafrictions.co.uk
Web Site: www.sergeant.co.uk

OPTARE PARTS DIVISION (Rotherham)
Denby Way, Hellaby, Rotherham S66 8HR
Tel: 01709 792000
Fax: 01709 792009
E-mail: parts@optare.com

OPTARE PRODUCT SUPPORT LONDON
Unit 9, Eurocourt, Olivers Close, West Thurrock RM20 3EE
Tel: 08444 123222
Fax: 01708 869920
E-mail: london.service@optare.com

OPTARE PRODUCT SUPPORT ROTHERHAM
Denby Way, Hellaby, Rotherham S66 8HR
Tel: 01709 535101
Fax: 01709 535103
E-mail: rotherham.service@optare.com

T T S UK
Total Tool Solutions Limited
Newhaven Business Park
Lowergate
Milnsbridge
Huddersfield
HD3 4HS
T: 01484 642211
F: 01484 461002
E: sales@ttsuk.com
W: www.ttsuk.com

⟨⟨⟩⟩ SCAN COIN

AUTOMATED CASH DEPOSITING SYSTEM

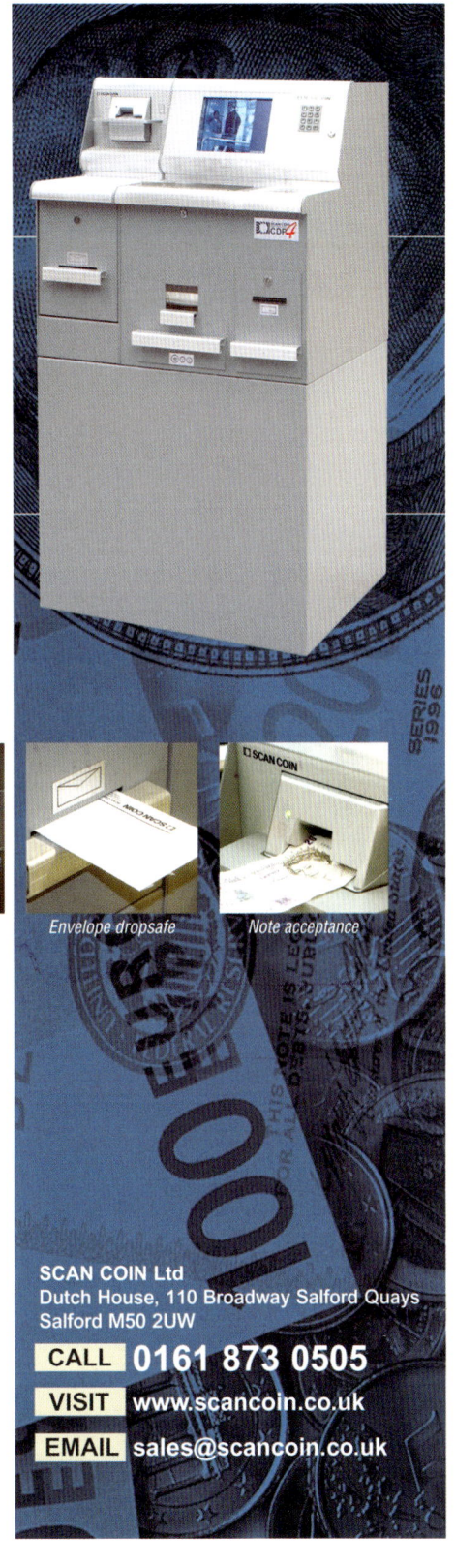

Fast and accurate processing of bank notes, coins and transport tokens plus dropsafe for depositing of non-cash items.

Safe, secure and easy to use.

Network capability  *Fast coin deposit*  *High capacity printer* *Envelope dropsafe* *Note acceptance*

- Easy to install, through-the-wall or free-standing
- Front or rear access for changing vaults and for servicing
- Fully customisable user interface
- All totals displayed on-screen
- Multiple coin acceptance and value counting
- Bank notes accepted in any direction
- Vehicle defect reporting
- Exchange rates can be programmed into the system
- Wide range of additional software available

SCAN COIN Ltd
Dutch House, 110 Broadway Salford Quays
Salford M50 2UW

CALL 0161 873 0505
VISIT www.scancoin.co.uk
EMAIL sales@scancoin.co.uk

Trade Directory

OPTARE PRODUCT SUPPORT SCOTLAND
Unit 7, Cumbernauld Business Park,
Ward Park Road, Cumbernauld G67 3JZ
Tel: 01236 726738
Fax: 01236 795651
E-mail: scotland.service@optare.com

PARTLINE LTD
Dockfield Road, Shipley BD17 7AZ
Tel: 01274 531531
Fax: 01274 531088
E-mail: sales@partline.co.uk
Web site: www.partline.co.uk

PLAXTON SERVICE
Ryton Road, Anston, Sheffield
S25 4DL
Tel: 01909 551155
Fax: 01909 550050
E-mail: service@plaxtonlimited.co.uk
Web site: www.plaxtonaftercare.co.uk

SHAWSON SUPPLY LTD
12 Station Road, Saintfield, County Down,
Northern Ireland BT24 7DU
Tel: 028 9751 0994
Fax: 028 9751 0816
E-mail: info@shawsonsupply.com
Web site: www.shawsonsupply.com

Cooling Systems

ARRIVA BUS AND COACH
Lodge Garage, Whitehall Road West,
Gomersal, Cleckheaton, West Yorkshire
BD19 4BJ
Tel: 01274 681144
Fax: 01274 651198
E-mail: whiter@arriva.co.uk
Web site: www.arrivabusandcoach.co.uk

CLAYTON HEATERS LTD
Hunter Terrace, Fletchworth Gate,
Burnsall Road, Coventry CV5 6SP
Tel: 02476 691916
Fax: 02476 691969
E-mail: admin@claytoncc.co.uk
Web Site: www.claytoncc.co.uk

DIRECT PARTS LTD
Unit 1, Churnet Court, Churnetside Business
Park, Harrison Way, Cheddleton ST13 7EF
Tel: 01538 361777
Fax: 01538 369100
E-mail: sales@direct-group.co.uk
Web site: www.direct-group.co.uk

KCP CAR & COMMERCIAL LTD
Unit 15, Hillside Business Park,
Kempson Way, Bury St Edmunds,
Suffolk IP32 7EA
Tel: 01284 750777
Fax: 01284 750773
E-mail: info@kcpcarandcommercial.co.uk
Web site: www.kcpcarandcommercial.co.uk

OPTARE PRODUCT SUPPORT LONDON
Unit 9, Eurocourt, Olivers Close, West
Thurrock RM20 3EE
Tel: 08444 123222
Fax: 01708 869920
E-mail: london.service@optare.com

OPTARE PRODUCT SUPPORT ROTHERHAM
Denby Way, Hellaby, Rotherham S66 8HR
Tel: 01709 535101
Fax: 01709 535103
E-mail: rotherham.service@optare.com

OPTARE PRODUCT SUPPORT SCOTLAND
Unit 7, Cumbernauld Business Park, Ward
Park Road, Cumbernauld G67 3JZ
Tel: 01236 726738
Fax: 01236 795651
E-mail: scotland.service@optare.com

PACET MANUFACTURING LTD
Wyebridge House, Cores End Road,
Bourne End SL8 5HH
Tel: 01628 526754
Fax: 01628 810080
E-mail: sales@pacet.co.uk
Web site: www.pacet.co.uk

PARTLINE LTD
Dockfield Road, Shipley BD17 7AZ
Tel: 01274 531531
Fax: 01274 531088
E-mail: sales@partline.co.uk
Web site: www.partline.co.uk

PLAXTON SERVICE
Ryton Road, Anston, Sheffield
S25 4DL
Tel: 01909 551155
Fax: 01909 550050
E-mail: service@plaxtonlimited.co.uk
Web site: www.plaxtonaftercare.co.uk

SILFLEX LTD
Coed Cae Lane Industrial Estate,
Pontyclun CF72 9HJ
Tel: 01443 238464
Fax: 01443 237781
E-mail: silflex@silflex.com
Web site: www.silflex.com

Destination Indicator Equipment

ARRIVA BUS AND COACH
Lodge Garage, Whitehall Road West,
Gomersal, Cleckheaton, West Yorkshire
BD19 4BJ
Tel: 01274 681144
Fax: 01274 651198
E-mail: whiter@arriva.co.uk
Web site: www.arrivabusandcoach.co.uk

HANOVER DISPLAYS LTD
Unit 24, Cliffe Industrial Estate,
Lewes BN8 6JL
Tel: 01273 477528
Fax: 01273 407766
E-mail: sales@hanoverdisplays.com
Web site: www.hanoverdisplays.com

INDICATORS INTERNATIONAL LTD
41 Aughrim Road, Magherafelt,
Northern Ireland BT45 6JX
Tel: 028 7963 2591
Fax: 028 7963 3927
E-mail: sales@indicators-int.com
Web site: www.indicators-int.com

INVERTEC LTD
Whelford Road, Fairford GL7 4DT
Tel: 01285 713550
Fax: 01285 713548
Mobile: 07802 793828
E-mail: sales@invertec.co.uk
Web site: www.invertec.co.uk

McKENNA BROTHERS LTD
McKenna House, Jubilee Road,
Middleton, Manchester M24 2LX
Tel: 0161 655 3244
Fax: 0161 655 3059
E-mail: info@mckennabrothers.co.uk
Web site: www.mckennabrothers.co.uk

NORBURY BLINDS LTD
41-45 Hanley Street, Newtown,
Birmingham B19 3SP
Tel: 0121 359 4311
Fax: 0121 359 6388
E-mail: info@norbury-blinds.com
Web site: www.norbury-blinds.com

PERCY LANE PRODUCTS LTD
Lichfield Road, Tamworth B79 7TL
Tel: 01827 63821
Fax: 01827 310159
E-mail: sales@percy-lane.co.uk
Web site: www.percy-lane.co.uk

PLAXTON SERVICE
Ryton Road, Anston, Sheffield S25 4DL
Tel: 01909 551155
Fax: 01909 550050
E-mail: service@plaxtonlimited.co.uk
Web site: www.plaxtonaftercare.co.uk

TOP GEARS
46 Fulwood Hall Lane, Fulwood,
Preston PR2 8DD
Tel/Fax: 01772 700536
E-mail: steve@pitlane-2000.com
Web site: www.pitlane-2000.com

VULTRON INTERNATIONAL LTD
Unit 2 Stadium Way, Elland Road, Leeds
LS11 0EW
Tel: 0113 387 7310
Fax: 0113 387 7317
E-mail: sales@vultron.co.uk
Web site: www.vultron.co.uk

Door Operating Gear

AIR DOOR SERVICES
The Pavilions, Holly Lane Industrial Estate,
Atherstone CV9 2QZ
Tel: 01827 11660
Fax: 01827 713577
E-mail: airdoorservices@aol.com

ARRIVA BUS AND COACH
Lodge Garage, Whitehall Road West,
Gomersal, Cleckheaton, West Yorkshire
BD19 4BJ
Tel: 01274 681144
Fax: 01274 651198
E-mail: whiter@arriva.co.uk
Web site: www.arrivabusandcoach.co.uk

CARLYLE BUS & COACH LTD
Carlyle Business Park, Great Bridge Street,
Swan Village, West Bromwich B70 0X4
Tel: 0121 524 1200
Fax: 0121 524 1201
E-mail: admin@carlyleplc.co.uk
Web Site: www.carlyleplc.co.uk

DEANS SYSTEMS (UK) LTD
PO Box 8, Borwick Drive, Grovehill,
Beverley HU17 0HQ
Tel: 01482 868111
Fax: 01482 881890
E-mail: customerservice@deanssystems.com
Web Site: www.deanssystems.com

EXPRESS COACH REPAIRS LTD
Outgang Lane, Pickering YO18 7JA
Tel: 01751 475215
Fax: 01751 475215
E-mail: info@expresscoachrepairs.co.uk
Web site: www.expresscoachrepairs.co.uk

KCP CAR & COMMERCIAL LTD
Unit 15, Hillside Business Park,
Kempson Way, Bury St Edmunds,
Suffolk IP32 7EA
Tel: 01284 750777
Fax: 01284 750773
E-mail: info@kcpcarandcommercial.co.uk
Web site: www.kcpcarandcommercial.co.uk

KELLETT (UK) LTD
8 Stevenson Way, Sheffield S9 3WZ.
Tel: 0114 261 1122
Fax: 0114 261 1199
E-mail: sales@kellett.co.uk

Trade Directory

KARIVE LIMITED
PO Box 205, Southam, Warwickshire
CV47 0ZL
Tel: 01926 813938
Fax: 01926 814898
E-mail: karive.ltd@btinternet.com
Web site: www.karive.co.uk

KNORR-BREMSE SYSTEMS FOR COMMERCIAL VEHICLES LTD
Douglas Road, Kingswood,
Bristol BS15 8NL
Tel: 0117 984 6100
Fax: 0117 984 6101
Web site: www.knorr-bremse.com

OPTARE PARTS DIVISION (Rotherham)
Denby Way, Hellaby, Rotherham S66 8HR
Tel: 01709 792000
Fax: 01709 792009
E-mail: parts@optare.com

OPTARE PRODUCT SUPPORT LONDON
Unit 9, Eurocourt, Olivers Close, West Thurrock RM20 3EE
Tel: 08444 123222
Fax: 01708 869920
E-mail: london.service@optare.com

OPTARE PRODUCT SUPPORT ROTHERHAM
Denby Way, Hellaby, Rotherham S66 8HR
Tel: 01709 535101
Fax: 01709 535103
E-mail: rotherham.service@optare.com

OPTARE PRODUCT SUPPORT SCOTLAND
Unit 7, Cumbernauld Business Park, Ward Park Road, Cumbernauld G67 3JZ
Tel: 01236 726738
Fax: 01236 795651
E-mail: scotland.service@optare.com

PETERS DOOR SYSTEMS (UK) LTD
Bradbury Drive, Springwood Industrial Estate, Braintree CM7 2ET
Tel: 01376 555255
Fax: 01376 555292
E-mail: sales@petersdoors.co.uk

PLAXTON PARTS
Ryton Road, Anston, Sheffield S25 4DL
Tel: 0844 822 6224
Fax: 01909 550050
E-mail: parts@plaxtonlimited.co.uk
Web site: www.plaxtonaftercare.co.uk

PLAXTON SERVICE
Ryton Road, Anston, Sheffield S25 4DL
Tel: 01909 551155
Fax: 01909 550050
E-mail: service@plaxtonlimited.co.uk
Web site: www.plaxtonaftercare.co.uk

PNEUMAX LTD
Unit 8, Venture Industrial Park, Fareham Road, Gosport PO13 0BA
Tel: 01329 823999
Fax: 01329 822345
E-mail: sales@pneumax.co.uk
Web site: www.pneumax.co.uk

VAPOR-STONE UK LTD
Derwent House, RTC Business Park, London Road, Derby DE24 8UP
Tel: 01332 228901
Fax: 01332 228909
Web site: www.wabtec.com

WABCO AUTOMOTIVE UK LTD
Texas Street, Morley LS27 0HQ.
Tel: 0113 251 2510
Fax: 0113 251 2844
Web site: www.wabco-auto.com

Drinks Dispensing Equipment

ARRIVA BUS AND COACH
Lodge Garage, Whitehall Road West,
Gomersal, Cleckheaton,
West Yorkshire BD19 4BJ
Tel: 01274 681144
Fax: 01274 651198
E-mail: whiter@arriva.co.uk
Web site: www.arrivabusandcoach.co.uk

BRADTECH LTD
Unit 3, Ladford Covert, Seighford,
Stafford ST18 9QL
Tel: 01785 282800
Fax: 01785 282558
E-mail: sales@bradtech.ltd.uk
Web site: www.bradtech.ltd.uk

DRINKMASTER LTD
Drinkpac House, Plymouth Road,
Liskeard PL14 3PG
Tel: 01579 342082
Fax: 01579 342591
E-mail: info@drinkmaster.co.uk
Web site: www.drinkmaster.co.uk

ELSAN LTD
Bellbrook Park, Uckfield, East Sussex TN22 1QF
Tel: 01825 748200
Fax: 01825 761212
E-mail: sales@elsan.co.uk
Web site: www.elsan.co.uk

EXPRESS COACH REPAIRS LTD
Outgang Lane, Pickering YO18 7JA
Tel: 01751 475215
Fax: 01751 475215
E-mail: info@expresscoachrepairs.co.uk
Web site: www.expresscoachrepairs.co.uk

PLAXTON PARTS
Ryton Road, Anston,
Sheffield S25 4DL
Tel: 0844 822 6224
Fax: 01909 550050
E-mail: parts@plaxtonlimited.co.uk
Web site: www.plaxtonaftercare.co.uk

PLAXTON SERVICE
Ryton Road, Anston,
Sheffield S25 4DL
Tel: 01909 551155
Fax: 01909 550050
E-mail: service@plaxtonlimited.co.uk
Web site: www.plaxtonaftercare.co.uk

PSV PRODUCTS
The Red House, Underbridge Lane, Higher Walton, Warrington WA4 5QR
Tel: 01925 210220
Fax: 01925 601534
E-mail: info@psvproducts.com
Web site: www.psvproducts.com

SHADES TECHNICS LTD
Units E3 & E4, Rd Park, Stephenson Close, Hoddesdon, Hertfordshire EN11 0BW
Tel: 01992 501683
Fax: 01992 501669
E-mail: sales@shades-technics.com
Web site: www.shades-technics.com

Driving Axles & Gears

ALBION AUTOMOTIVE LTD
South Street, Scotstoun,
Glasgow G14 0DT
Tel: 0141 434 2400
Fax: 0141 959 6362
E-mail: sales@albion_auto.co.uk
Web site: www.albion_auto.co.uk

ARRIVA BUS AND COACH
Lodge Garage, Whitehall Road West,
Gomersal, Cleckheaton,
West Yorkshire
BD19 4BJ
Tel: 01274 681144
Fax: 01274 651198
E-mail: whiter@arriva.co.uk
Web site: www.arrivabusandcoach.co.uk

ARVIN MERITOR
Unit 21, Suttons Park Avenue,
Reading RG6 1LA
Tel: 0118 935 9126
Fax: 0118 935 9138
E-mail: james.randall@arvinmeritor.com
Web site: www.arvinmeritor.com

BUSS BIZZ
Goughs Transport Depot,
Morestead, Winchester
SO21 1JD
Tel: 01962 715555/66
Fax: 01962 714868

DIRECT PARTS LTD
Unit 1, Churnet Court,
Churnetside Business Park,
Harrison Way,
Cheddleton ST13 7EF
Tel: 01538 361777
Fax: 01538 369100
E-mail: sales@direct-group.co.uk
Web site: www.direct-group.co.uk

HL SMITH TRANSMISSIONS LTD
Enterprise Business Park,
Cross Road, Albrighton,
Wolverhampton WV7 3BJ
Tel: 01902 373011
Fax: 01902 373608
Web site: www.hlsmith.co.uk

KCP CAR & COMMERCIAL LTD
Unit 15, Hillside Business Park,
Kempson Way, Bury St Edmunds,
Suffolk IP32 7EA
Tel: 01284 750777
Fax: 01284 750773
E-mail: info@kcpcarandcommercial.co.uk
Web site: www.kcpcarandcommercial.co.uk

LH GROUP SERVICES LTD
Graycar Business Park,
Barton under Needwood,
Burton-on-Trent
DE13 8EN
Tel: 01283 722600
Fax: 01283 722622
E-mail: lh@lh-group.com
Web site: www.lh-group.com

OPTARE PARTS DIVISION (Rotherham)
Denby Way, Hellaby,
Rotherham S66 8HR
Tel: 01709 792000
Fax: 01709 792009
E-mail: parts@optare.com

PARTLINE LTD
Dockfield Road,
Shipley BD17 7AZ
Tel: 01274 531531
Fax: 01274 531088
E-mail: sales@partline.co.uk
Web site: www.partline.co.uk

PLAXTON SERVICE
Ryton Road, Anston,
Sheffield S25 4DL
Tel: 01909 551155
Fax: 01909 550050
E-mail: service@plaxtonlimited.co.uk
Web site: www.plaxtonaftercare.co.uk

Trade Directory

TTS UK
Total Tool Solutions Ltd,
Newhaven Business Park, Lowergate,
Milnsbridge, Huddersfield HD3 4HS
Tel: 01484 642211
Fax: 01484 461002
E-mail: sales@ttsuk.com
Web site: www.ttsuk.com

VOR TRANSMISSIONS LTD
Little London House, St Anne's House,
Willenhall WV13 1DT
Tel: 01902 604141
Fax: 01902 603868
E-mail: sueh@vor.co.uk

ZF POWERTRAIN
Stringes Close, Willenhall WV13 1LE
Tel: 01902 366000
Fax: 01902 366504
E-mail: sales@powertrain.org.uk
Web site: www.powertrain.org.uk

Electrical Equipment

ARRIVA BUS AND COACH
Lodge Garage, Whitehall Road West,
Gomersal, Cleckheaton, West Yorkshire
BD19 4BJ
Tel: 01274 681144
Fax: 01274 651198
E-mail: whiter@arriva.co.uk
Web site: www.arrivabusandcoach.co.uk

AVT SYSTEMS LTD
Units 3 & 4 Tything Road, Arden Forest
Industrial Estate, Alcester,
Warwickshire B49 6ES
Tel: 01789 400357
Fax: 01789 400359
E-mail: enquires@avtsystems.co.uk
Web site: www.avtsystems.co.uk

BRADTECH LTD
Unit 3, Ladford Covert, Seighford,
Stafford ST18 9QL
Tel: 01785 282800
Fax: 01785 282558
E-mail: sales@bradtech.ltd.uk
Web site: www.bradtech.ltd.uk

CARLYLE BUS & COACH LTD
Carlyle Business Park, Great Bridge Street,
Swan Village, West Bromwich B70 0X4
Tel: 0121 524 1200
Fax: 0121 524 1201
E-mail: admin@carlyleplc.co.uk
Web site: www.carlyleplc.co.uk

CRESCENT FACILITIES LTD
72 Willow Crescent, Chapeltown,
Sheffield S35 1QS
Tel/Fax: 0114 245 1050
E-mail: cfl.chris@btinternet.com
Web site: www.cflparts.com

DIRECT PARTS LTD
Unit 1, Churnet Court, Churnetside Business
Park, Harrison Way, Cheddleton ST13 7EF
Tel: 01538 361777
Fax: 01538 369100
E-mail: sales@direct-group.co.uk
Web site: www.direct-group.co.uk

EXPRESS COACH REPAIRS LTD
Outgang Lane, Pickering YO18 7JA
Tel: 01751 475215
Fax: 01751 475215
E-mail: info@expresscoachrepairs.co.uk
Web site: www.expresscoachrepairs.co.uk

INTELLITEC LTD
VIP Trading Estate, Anchor & Hope Lane
Charlton, London SE7 7RY
Tel/Fax: 020 8858 3781

E-mail: sales@intellitec.co.uk
Web site: www.intellitec.co.uk

INVERTEC LTD
Whelford Road, Fairford GL7 4DT
Tel: 01285 713550
Fax: 01285 713548
Mobile: 07802 793828
E-mail: ian@invertec.co.uk
Web site: www.invertec.co.uk

KCP CAR & COMMERCIAL LTD
Unit 15, Hillside Business Park,
Kempson Way, Bury St Edmunds,
Suffolk IP32 7EA
Tel: 01284 750777
Fax: 01284 750773
E-mail: info@kcpcarandcommercial.co.uk
Web site: www.kcpcarandcommercial.co.uk

KARIVE LIMITED
PO Box 205, Southam,
Warwickshire CV47 0ZL
Tel: 01926 813938
Fax: 01926 814898
E-mail: karive.ltd@btinternet.com
Web site: www.karive.co.uk

NEALINE WINDSCREEN WIPER PRODUCTS
Unit 1, The Sidings Industrial Estate,
Birdingbury Road, Marton CV23 9RX
Tel: 01926 633256
Fax: 01926 632600

OPTARE PARTS DIVISION (Rotherham)
Denby Way, Hellaby, Rotherham S66 8HR
Tel: 01709 792000
Fax: 01709 792009
E-mail: parts@optare.com

PACET MANUFACTURING LTD
Wyebridge House, Cores End Road,
Bourne End SL8 5HH
Tel: 01628 526754
Fax: 01628 810080
E-mail: sales@pacet.co.uk
Web site: www.pacet.co.uk

PARTLINE LTD
Dockfield Road, Shipley BD17 7AZ
Tel: 01274 531531
Fax: 01274 531088
E-mail: sales@partline.co.uk
Web site: www.partline.co.uk

PLAXTON PARTS
Ryton Road, Anston, Sheffield S25 4DL
Tel: 0844 822 6224
Fax: 01909 550050
E-mail: parts@plaxtonlimited.co.uk
Web site: www.plaxtonaftercare.co.uk

PLAXTON SERVICE
Ryton Road, Anston, Sheffield S25 4DL
Tel: 01909 551155
Fax: 01909 550050
E-mail: service@plaxtonlimited.co.uk
Web site: www.plaxtonaftercare.co.uk

PNEUMAX LTD
Unit 8, Venture Industrial Park,
Fareham Road, Gosport PO13 0BA
Tel: 01329 823999
Fax: 01329 822345
E-mail: sales@pneumax.co.uk
Web site: www.pneumax.co.uk

PRESTOLITE ELECTRIC
Unit 48, The Metropolitan Park,
12-16 Bristol Road,
Greenford UB6 8UP
Tel: 020 8231 1000
Fax: 020 8575 9575
E-mail: eu_info@prestolite.com
Web site: www.prestolite.com

Electronic Control

ACTIA UK LTD
Unit 81, Mochdre Industrial Estate,
Newtown SY16 4LE
Tel: 01686 611150
Fax: 01686 621068
E-mail: mail@actia.co.uk
Web site: www.actia.co.uk

ARRIVA BUS AND COACH
Lodge Garage, Whitehall Road West,
Gomersal, Cleckheaton, West Yorkshire
BD19 4BJ
Tel: 01274 681144
Fax: 01274 651198
E-mail: whiter@arriva.co.uk
Web site: www.arrivabusandcoach.co.uk

CRESCENT FACILITIES LTD
72 Willow Crescent, Chapeltown,
Sheffield S35 1QS
Tel/Fax: 0114 245 1050
E-mail: cfl.chris@btinternet.com
Web site: www.cflparts.com

INTELLITEC LTD
14a Church Street, Rothersthorpe,
Northampton NN7 3JD
Tel/Fax: 01604 830 690
E-mail: sales@intellitec.co.uk
Web site: www.intellitec.co.uk

KCP CAR & COMMERCIAL LTD
Unit 15, Hillside Business Park,
Kempson Way, Bury St Edmunds,
Suffolk IP32 7EA
Tel: 01284 750777

Fax: 01284 750773
E-mail: info@kcpcarandcommercial.co.uk
Web site: www.kcpcarandcommercial.co.uk

KNORR-BREMSE SYSTEMS FOR COMMERCIAL VEHICLES LTD
Douglas Road, Kingswood, Bristol BS15 8NL
Tel: 0117 984 6100
Fax: 0117 984 6101
Web site: www.knorr-bremse.com

OPTARE PARTS DIVISION (Rotherham)
Denby Way, Hellaby, Rotherham S66 8HR
Tel: 01709 792000
Fax: 01709 792009
E-mail: parts@optare.com

PLAXTON PARTS
Ryton Road, Anston, Sheffield S25 4DL
Tel: 0844 822 6224
Fax: 01909 550050
E-mail: parts@plaxtonlimited.co.uk
Web site: www.plaxtonaftercare.co.uk

PLAXTON SERVICE
Ryton Road, Anston, Sheffield S25 4DL
Tel: 01909 551155
Fax: 01909 550050
E-mail: service@plaxtonlimited.co.uk
Web site: www.plaxtonaftercare.co.uk

VDO KIENZLE UK LTD
36 Gravelly Industrial Park, Birmingham B24 8TA
Tel: 0121 326 1234.
Fax: 0121 326 1299

WABCO AUTOMOTIVE UK
Texas Street, Morley LS27 0HQ.
Tel: 0113 251 2510
Fax: 0113 251 2844
Web site: www.wabco-auto.com

Emission Control Devices

ARRIVA BUS AND COACH
Lodge Garage, Whitehall Road West, Gomersal, Cleckheaton, West Yorkshire BD19 4BJ
Tel: 01274 681144
Fax: 01274 651198
E-mail: whiter@arriva.co.uk
Web site: www.arrivabusandcoach.co.uk

CUMMINS UK
Rutherford Drive, Park Farm South, Wellingborough NN8 6AN
Tel: 01933 334200
Fax: 01933 334198
E-mail: cduksales@cummins.com
Web site: www.cummins-uk.com

DINEX EXHAUSTS LTD
14 Chesford Grange, Woolston, Warrington WA1 3BT
Tel: 01925 849849
Fax: 01925 849850
E-mail: dinex@dinex.co.uk

EMISSION CONTROL LIMITED
Global Works, 1/6 Crescent Mews (off Crescent Road), London N22 7GG
Tel: 020 8888 4982
Fax: 020 8826 4736
E-mail: info@emissioncontroluk.com
Web site: www.emissioncontroluk.com

KCP CAR & COMMERCIAL LTD
Unit 15, Hillside Business Park, Kempson Way, Bury St Edmunds, Suffolk IP32 7EA
Tel: 01284 750777
Fax: 01284 750773
E-mail: info@kcpcarandcommercial.co.uk
Web site: www.kcpcarandcommercial.co.uk

OPTARE PARTS DIVISION (Rotherham)
Denby Way, Hellaby, Rotherham S66 8HR
Tel: 01709 792000
Fax: 01709 792009
E-mail: parts@optare.com

PLAXTON SERVICE
Ryton Road, Anston, Sheffield S25 4DL
Tel: 01909 551155
Fax: 01909 550050
E-mail: service@plaxtonlimited.co.uk
Web site: www.plaxtonaftercare.co.uk

Engineering

ARRIVA BUS AND COACH
Lodge Garage, Whitehall Road West, Gomersal, Cleckheaton, West Yorkshire BD19 4BJ
Tel: 01274 681144
Fax: 01274 651198
E-mail: whiter@arriva.co.uk
Web site: www.arrivabusandcoach.co.uk

BRITCOM INTERNATIONAL LTD
York Road, Market Weighton, East Yorkshire YO43 3QX
Tel: 01430 871010
Fax: 01430 872492
E-mail: sales@britcom.co.uk
Web site: www.britcom.co.uk

BULWARK BUS & COACH ENGINEERING LTD
Unit 5, Bulwark Business Park, Bulwark, Chepstow NP16 6QZ
Tel: 01291 622326
Fax: 01291 622726
E-mail: bulwarkbusandcoach@tiscali.co.uk
Web site: www.bulwarkbusandcoach.co.uk

BUSS BIZZ
Goughs Transport Depot, Morestead, Winchester SO21 1JD
Tel: 01962 715555/66
Fax: 01962 714868

COACH-AID
Unit 2, Brindley Close, Tollgate Industrial Estate, Stafford ST16 3sU
Tel: 01785 222666
E-mail: workshop@coach-aid.com
Web site: www.coach-aid.com

CUMMINS UK
Rutherford Drive, Park Farm South, Wellingborough NN8 6AN
Tel: 01933 334200
Fax: 01933 334198
E-mail: cduksales@cummins.com
Web site: www.cummins-uk.com

DIRECT PARTS LTD
Unit 1, Churnet Court, Churnetside Business Park, Harrison Way, Cheddleton ST13 7EF
Tel: 01538 361777
Fax: 01538 369100
E-mail: sales@direct-group.co.uk
Web site: www.direct-group.co.uk

FTA VEHICLE INSPECTION SERVICE
Hermes House, St John's Road, Tunbridge Wells TN4 9UZ
Tel: 01892 526171
Fax: 01892 534989
E-mail: enquiries@fta.co.uk
Web site: www.fta.co.uk

THOMAS HARDIE COMMERCIALS LTD
Newstet Road, Knowsley Industrial Park, Liverpool L33 7TJ
Tel: 0151 549 3000
E-mail: info@thardie.co.uk

HART BROTHERS (ENGINEERING) LTD
Soho Works, Soho Street, Oldham OL4 2AD
Tel: 0161 737 6791

HILTech DEVELOPMENTS LTD
22 Larbre Crescent, Whickham, Newcastle upon Tyne NE16 5YG
Tel: 0191 488 6258
Fax: 0191 488 9158
E-mail: executive@hiltechdevelopments.com
Web site: www.hiltechdevelopments.com

IMPERIAL ENGINEERING
Delamare Road, Cheshunt, Hertfordshire EN8 9UD
Tel: 01992 634255
Fax: 01992 630506
E-mail: orders@imperialengineering.co.uk
Web site: www.imperialengineering.co.uk

JBF SERVICES LTD
Southedge Works, Hipperholme, Halifax HX3 8EF
Tel: 01422 202840
Fax: 01422 206070
E-mail: jbfservices@aol.com

KCP CAR & COMMERCIAL LTD
Unit 15, Hillside Business Park, Kempson Way, Bury St Edmunds, Suffolk IP32 7EA
Tel: 01284 750777
Fax: 01284 750773
E-mail: info@kcpcarandcommercial.co.uk
Web site: www.kcpcarandcommercial.co.uk

LEYLAND PRODUCT DEVELOPMENTS LTD
Croston Road, Leyland, Preston PR26 6LZ
Tel: 01772 621400
Web site: www.leylandtrucksltd.co.uk

LH GROUP SERVICES LTD
Graycar Business Park, Barton under Needwood, Burton-on-Trent DE13 8EN
Tel: 01283 722600
Fax: 01283 722622
E-mail: lh@lh-group.com
Web site: www.lh-group.com

MARSHALLS COACHES LLP
Firbank Way, Leighton Buzzard LU7 3BD
Tel: 01525 376077
Fax: 01525 850967
E-mail: info@marshalls-coaches.co.uk
Web site: www.marshalls-coaches.co.uk

MASS SPECIAL ENGINEERING LTD
Houghton Road, North Anston, Sheffield S25 4JJ
Tel: 01909 550480
Fax: 01909 550486

OPTARE PARTS DIVISION (Rotherham)
Denby Way, Hellaby, Rotherham S66 8HR
Tel: 01709 792000
Fax: 01709 792009
E-mail: parts@optare.com

OPTARE PRODUCT SUPPORT LONDON
Unit 9, Eurocourt, Olivers Close, West Thurrock RM20 3EE
Tel: 08444 123222
Fax: 01708 869920
E-mail: london.service@optare.com

OPTARE PRODUCT SUPPORT ROTHERHAM
Denby Way, Hellaby, Rotherham S66 8HR
Tel: 01709 535101
Fax: 01709 535103
E-mail: rotherham.service@optare.com

Trade Directory

OPTARE PRODUCT SUPPORT SCOTLAND
Unit 7, Cumbernauld Business Park,
Ward Park Road,
Cumbernauld G67 3JZ
Tel: 01236 726738
Fax: 01236 795651
E-mail: scotland.service@optare.com

PLAXTON SERVICE
Ryton Road, North Anston,
Sheffield S25 4DL
Tel: 01909 551155
Fax: 01909 550050
E-mail: service@plaxtonlimited.co.uk
Web site: www.plaxtonaftercare.co.uk

PNEUMAX LTD
Unit 8, Venture Industrial Park,
Fareham Road, Gosport PO13 0BA
Tel: 01329 823999
Fax: 01329 822345
E-mail: sales@pneumax.co.uk
Web site: www.pneumax.co.uk

QUEENSBRIDGE (PSV) LTD
Milner Way, Longlands Industrial Estate,
Ossett WF5 9JE
Tel: 01924 281871
Fax: 01924 281807
E-mail: enquiries@queensbridgeltd.co.uk
Web site: www.queensbridgeltd.co.uk

TRANSPORT DESIGN INTERNATIONAL
12 Waterloo Road Estate,
Bidford on Avon B50 4JH
Tel: 01789 490370
Fax: 01789 490592
E-mail: enquiries@tdi.uk.com
Web site: www.tdi.uk.com

TTS UK
Total Tool Solutions Ltd,
Newhaven Business Park,
Lowergate, Milnsbridge,
Huddersfield HD3 4HS
Tel: 01484 642211
Fax: 01484 461002
E-mail: sales@ttsuk.com
Web site: www.ttsuk.com

Engines

ARRIVA BUS AND COACH
Lodge Garage, Whitehall Road West,
Gomersal, Cleckheaton,
West Yorkshire BD19 4BJ
Tel: 01274 681144
Fax: 01274 651198
E-mail: whiter@arriva.co.uk
Web site: www.arrivabusandcoach.co.uk

BUSS BIZZ
Goughs Transport Depot, Morestead,
Winchester SO21 1JD
Tel: 01962 715555/66.
Fax: 01962 714868.

CREWE ENGINES
Warmingham Road, Crewe CW1 4PQ
Tel: 01270 526333
Fax: 01270 526433
E-mail: sales@creweengines.co.uk
Web site: www.creweengines.co.uk

CUMMINS UK
Rutherford Drive, Park Farm South,
Wellingborough NN8 6AN
Tel: 01933 334200
Fax: 01933 334198
E-mail: cduksales@cummins.com
Web site: www.cummins-uk.com

DAF COMPONENTS LTD
Eastern Bypass, Thame OX9 3FB
Tel: 01844 261111
Fax: 01844 217111
Web site: www.daftrucks.com.

DIESEL POWER ENGINEERING
Goughs Transport Depot, Morestead,
Winchester SO21 1JD
Tel/Fax: 01962 711314

FUEL THEFT SOLUTIONS LTD
20 Yew Tree Court, Alsager, Stoke-on-Trent
ST7 2WR
Tel: 0845 077 3921
Fax: 0845 077 3922
E-mail: sales@dieseldye.com
Web site: www.dieseldye.com

IMEXPART LTD
Links 31, Willowbridge Way, Whitwood,
Castleford WF10 5NP
Tel: 0845 605 0404
Fax: 01977 513412
E-mail: sales@imexpart.com
Web site: www.imexpart.com

IVECO
Iveco Ford Truck Ltd, Iveco Ford House,
Station Road, Watford WD1 1SR
Tel: 01923 246400
Fax: 01923 240574

KCP CAR & COMMERCIAL LTD
Unit 15, Hillside Business Park, Kempson
Way, Bury St Edmunds, Suffolk IP32 7EA
Tel: 01284 750777
Fax: 01284 750773
E-mail: info@kcpcarandcommercial.co.uk
Web site: www.kcpcarandcommercial.co.uk

LH GROUP SERVICES LTD
Graycar Business Park, Barton under
Needwood, Burton-on-Trent DE13 8EN
Tel: 01283 722600
Fax: 01283 722622
E-mail: lh@lh-group.com
Web site: www.lh-group.com

MAN TRUCK & BUS UK LTD
Frankland Road, Blagrove,
Swindon SN5 8YU
Tel: 01793 448000
Fax: 01793 448262
Web site: www.manbusandcoach.co.uk

NEXT BUS LTD
The Coach Yard, Vincients Road,
Bumpers Farm Industrial Estate,
Chippenham SN14 6QA
Tel: 01249 462462
Fax: 01249 448844
E-mail: sales@next-bus.co.uk
Web site: www.next-bus.co.uk

OPTARE PARTS DIVISION
(Rotherham)
Denby Way, Hellaby, Rotherham S66 8HR
Tel: 01709 792000
Fax: 01709 792009
E-mail: parts@optare.com

OPTARE PRODUCT SUPPORT LONDON
Unit 9, Eurocourt, Olivers Close, West
Thurrock RM20 3EE
Tel: 08444 123222
Fax: 01708 869920
E-mail: london.service@optare.com

OPTARE PRODUCT SUPPORT ROTHERHAM
Denby Way, Hellaby, Rotherham S66 8HR
Tel: 01709 535101
Fax: 01709 535103
E-mail: rotherham.service@optare.com

OPTARE PRODUCT SUPPORT SCOTLAND
Unit 7, Cumbernauld Business Park,
Ward Park Road, Cumbernauld G67 3JZ
Tel: 01236 726738
Fax: 01236 795651
E-mail: scotland.service@optare.com

PERKINS GROUP LTD
Peterborough PE1 5NA
Tel: 01733 567474.
Fax: 01733 582240.
Web site: www.perkins.com

QUEENSBRIDGE (PSV) LTD
Longlands Industrial Estate, Milner Way,
Ossett WF5 9JE
Tel: 01924 281871
Fax: 01924 281807
E-mail: craig@queensbridgeltd.co.uk
Web site: www.queensbridgeltd.co.uk

SHAWSON SUPPLY LTD
12 Station Road, Saintfield,
County Down, Northern Ireland BT24 7DU
Tel: 028 9751 0994
Fax: 028 9751 0816
E-mail: info@shawsonsupply.com
Web site: www.shawsonsupply.com

CRAIG TILSLEY & SON LTD
Moorfield Industrial Estate, Cotes Heath,
Stoke on Trent ST21 6QY
Tel: 01782 781524
Fax: 01782 791316

TTS UK
Total Tool Solutions Ltd,
Newhaven Business Park,
Lowergate, Milnsbridge,

Trade Directory

Huddersfield HD3 4HS
Tel: 01484 642211
Fax: 01484 461002
E-mail: sales@ttsuk.com
Web site: www.ttsuk.com

WALSH'S ENGINEERING LTD
Barton Moss Road, Eccles, Manchester M30 7RL
Tel: 0161 787 7017
Fax: 0161 787 7038
E-mail: walshs@gardnerdiesel.co.uk
Web site: www.gardnerdiesel.co.uk

WEALDSTONE ENGINEERING
Sanders Lodge Industrial Estate, Rushden NN10 6AZ
Tel: 01933 354600
Fax: 01933 354601
Web site: www.wealdstone.co.uk

Engine Oil Drain Valves

ARRIVA BUS AND COACH
Lodge Garage, Whitehall Road West, Gomersal, Cleckheaton, West Yorkshire BD19 4BJ
Tel: 01274 681144
Fax: 01274 651198
E-mail: whiter@arriva.co.uk
Web site: www.arrivabusandcoach.co.uk

FUMOTO ENGINEERING OF EUROPE LTD
Normandy House, 35 Glategny Esplanade, St Peter Port, Guernsey GY1 2BP
Tel: 01481 716987
Fax: 01481 700374
E-mail: sales@fumoto-valve.com

PARTLINE LTD
Dockfield Road, Shipley BD17 7AZ
Tel: 01274 531531
Fax: 01274 531088
E-mail: sales@partline.co.uk
Web site: www.partline.co.uk

WALLMINSTER LTD
Unit 22, Chelsea Wharf, 15 Lots Road, London SW10 0QJ
Tel: 020 7352 2727 **Fax:** 020 7352 3990
E-mail: info@tankcontainers.co.uk

Exhaust Systems

ARRIVA BUS AND COACH
Lodge Garage, Whitehall Road West, Gomersal, Cleckheaton, West Yorkshire BD19 4BJ
Tel: 01274 681144
Fax: 01274 651198
E-mail: whiter@arriva.co.uk
Web site: www.arrivabusandcoach.co.uk

ARVIN MERITOR
Unit 21, Suttons Park Avenue, Reading RG6 1LA
Tel: 0118 935 9126
Fax: 0118 935 9138
E-mail: james.randall@arvinmeritor.com
Web site: www.arvinmeritor.com

BUSS BIZZ
Goughs Transport Depot, Morestead, Winchester SO21 1JD
Tel: 01962 715555/66.
Fax: 01962 714868.

CARLYLE BUS & COACH LTD
Carlyle Business Park, Great Bridge Street, Swan Village, West Bromwich B70 0X4
Tel: 0121 524 1200
Fax: 0121 524 1201
E-mail: admin@carlyleplc.co.uk
Web site: www.carlyleplc.co.uk

CRESCENT FACILITIES LTD
72 Willow Crescent, Chapeltown, Sheffield S35 1QS
Tel/Fax: 0114 245 1050
E-mail: cfl.chris@btinternet.com
Web site: www.cflparts.com

DINEX EXHAUSTS LTD
14 Chesford Grange, Woolston, Warrington WA1 3BT
Tel: 01925 849849
Fax: 01925 849850
E-mail: dinex@dinex.co.uk

EMINOX LTD
North Warren Road, Gainsborough DN21 2TU
Tel: 01427 810088
Fax: 01427 810061
E-mail: enquiry@eminox.com
Web site: www.eminox.com

Eminox design and manufacture exhaust and emission control systems for commercial vehicles. Our emissions systems are approved for retrofitting to buses and coaches for the London LEZ and E-Zones across Europe.

LEZ freephone: 0808 156 2012
T: 01427 810088
F: 01427 810061
E: enquiry@eminox.com
www.eminox.com

North Warren Road, Gainsborough, Lincolnshire DN21 2TU

IMEXPART LTD
Links 31, Willowbridge Way, Whitwood, Castleford WF10 5NP
Tel: 0845 605 0404
Fax: 01977 513412
E-mail: sales@imexpart.com
Web site: www.imexpart.com

KCP CAR & COMMERCIAL LTD
Unit 15, Hillside Business Park, Kempson Way, Bury St Edmunds, Suffolk IP32 7EA
Tel: 01284 750777
Fax: 01284 750773
E-mail: info@kcpcarandcommercial.co.uk
Web site: www.kcpcarandcommercial.co.uk

OPTARE PARTS DIVISION (Rotherham)
Denby Way, Hellaby, Rotherham S66 8HR
Tel: 01709 792000
Fax: 01709 792009
E-mail: parts@optare.com

OPTARE PRODUCT SUPPORT LONDON
Unit 9, Eurocourt, Olivers Close, West Thurrock RM20 3EE
Tel: 08444 123222
Fax: 01708 869920
E-mail: london.service@optare.com

OPTARE PRODUCT SUPPORT ROTHERHAM
Denby Way, Hellaby, Rotherham S66 8HR
Tel: 01709 535101
Fax: 01709 535103
E-mail: rotherham.service@optare.com

OPTARE PRODUCT SUPPORT SCOTLAND
Unit 7, Cumbernauld Business Park, Ward Park Road, Cumbernauld G67 3JZ
Tel: 01236 726738
Fax: 01236 795651
E-mail: scotland.service@optare.com

PARTLINE LTD
Dockfield Road, Shipley BD17 7AZ
Tel: 01274 531531
Fax: 01274 531088
E-mail: sales@partline.co.uk
Web site: www.partline.co.uk

TTS UK
Total Tool Solutions Ltd, Newhaven Business Park, Lowergate, Milnsbridge, Huddersfield HD3 4HS
Tel: 01484 642211
Fax: 01484 461002
E-mail: sales@ttsuk.com
Web site: www.ttsuk.com

Fans & Drive Belts

ARRIVA BUS AND COACH
Lodge Garage, Whitehall Road West, Gomersal, Cleckheaton, West Yorkshire BD19 4BJ
Tel: 01274 681144
Fax: 01274 651198
E-mail: whiter@arriva.co.uk
Web site: www.arrivabusandcoach.co.uk

BRT BEARINGS LTD
21-24 Regal Road, Wisbech, Cambridgeshire PE13 2RQ
Tel: 01945 464 097
Fax: 01945 464 523
E-mail: info@brt-group.com

The Little Red Book 2011 - in association with tbf Transport Benevolent Fund

Trade Directory

CARLYLE BUS & COACH LTD
Carlyle Business Park, Great Bridge Street, Swan Village, West Bromwich B70 0X4
Tel: 0121 524 1200
Fax: 0121 524 1201
E-mail: admin@carlyleplc.co.uk
Web site: www.carlyleplc.co.uk

CLAYTON HEATERS LTD
Hunter Terrace, Fletchworth Gate, Burnsall Road, Coventry CV5 6SP
Tel: 02476 691 916
Fax: 02476 691 969
E-mail: admin@claytoncc.co.uk
Web site: www.claytoncc.co.uk

CUMMINS UK
Rutherford Drive, Park Farm South, Wellingborough NN8 6AN
Tel: 01933 334200
Fax: 01933 334198
E-mail: cduksales@cummins.com
Web site: www.cummins-uk.com

DIRECT PARTS LTD
Unit 1, Churnet Court, Churnetside Business Park, Harrison Way, Cheddleton ST13 7EF
Tel: 01538 361777
Fax: 01538 369100
E-mail: sales@direct-group.co.uk
Web site: www.direct-group.co.uk

KCP CAR & COMMERCIAL LTD
Unit 15, Hillside Business Park, Kempson Way, Bury St Edmunds, Suffolk IP32 7EA
Tel: 01284 750777
Fax: 01284 750773
E-mail: info@kcpcarandcommercial.co.uk
Web site: www.kcpcarandcommercial.co.uk

OPTARE PARTS DIVISION (Rotherham)
Denby Way, Hellaby, Rotherham S66 8HR
Tel: 01709 792000
Fax: 01709 792009
E-mail: parts@optare.com

PACET MANUFACTURING LTD
Wyebridge House, Cores End Road, Bourne End SL8 5HH
Tel: 01628 526754 **Fax:** 01628 810080
E-mail: sales@pacet.co.uk
Web site: www.pacet.co.uk

PARTLINE LTD
Dockfield Road, Shipley BD17 7AZ
Tel: 01274 531531
Fax: 01274 531088
E-mail: sales@partline.co.uk
Web site: www.partline.co.uk

QUEENSBRIDGE (PSV) LTD
Longlands Industrial Estate, Milner Way, Ossett WF5 9JE
Tel: 01924 281871
Fax: 01924 281807
E-mail: craig@queensbridgeltd.co.uk
Web site: www.queensbridgeltd.co.uk

Fare Boxes

CUBIC TRANSPORTATION SYSTEMS LTD
AFC House, Honeycrock Lane, Salfords, Redhill RH1 5LA
Tel: 01737 782200
Fax: 01737 789759
Web site: www.cubic.com

ETMSS LTD
c/o Ground Floor, Austin House, 43 Poole Road, Westbourne, Bournemouth BH4 9DN
Tel: 0844 800 9299

E-mail: info@etmss.com
Web Site: www.etmss.com

JOHN GROVES TICKET SYSTEMS
Unit 10, North Circular Business Centre, 400 NCR, London NW10 0JG
Tel: 020 8830 1222
Fax: 020 8830 1223
E-mail: sales@jgts.co.uk
Web site: www.jgts.co.uk

MARK TERRILL TICKET MACHINERY
5 De Grey Close, Lewes BN7 2JR
Tel: 01273 474816
Fax: 01273 474816
E-mail: mark.terrill@ukonline.co.uk

TICKETER
Riverside Centre, 82 Station Road, Barnes, London SW13 0LS
Tel: 0844 800 9299
E-mail: sales@ticketer.co.uk
Web site: www.ticketer.co.uk

Fire Extinguishers

ARRIVA BUS AND COACH
Lodge Garage, Whitehall Road West, Gomersal, Cleckheaton, West Yorkshire BD19 4BJ
Tel: 01274 681144
Fax: 01274 651198
E-mail: whiter@arriva.co.uk
Web site: www.arrivabusandcoach.co.uk

CARLYLE BUS & COACH LTD
Carlyle Business Park, Great Bridge Street, Swan Village, West Bromwich B70 0X4
Tel: 0121 524 1200
Fax: 0121 524 1201
E-mail: admin@carlyleplc.co.uk
Web site: www.carlyleplc.co.uk

EXPRESS COACH REPAIRS LTD
Outgang Lane, Pickering YO18 7JA
Tel: 01751 475215
Fax: 01751 475215
E-mail: info@expresscoachrepairs.co.uk
Web site: www.expresscoachrepairs.co.uk

FIREMASTER EXTINGUISHER LTD
Firex House, 174-176 Hither Green Lane, London SE13 6QB
Tel: 020 8852 8585
Fax: 020 8297 8020
E-mail: info@firemaster.co.uk
Web site: www.firemaster.co.uk

HAPPICH V & I COMPONENTS LTD
Unit 30/31, Fort Industrial Park, Fort Parkway, Castle Bromwich B35 7AR
Tel: 0121 747 4400
Fax: 0121 747 4977
E-mail: sales@happich.co.uk
Web site: www.happich.co.uk

KCP CAR & COMMERCIAL LTD
Unit 15, Hillside Business Park, Kempson Way, Bury St Edmunds, Suffolk IP32 7EA
Tel: 01284 750777
Fax: 01284 750773
E-mail: info@kcpcarandcommercial.co.uk
Web site: www.kcpcarandcommercial.co.uk

KELLETT (UK) LTD
8 Stevenson Way, Sheffield S9 3WZ.
Tel: 0114 261 1122
Fax: 0114 261 1199
E-mail: sales@kellett.co.uk

LAWTON SERVICES LTD
Knutsford Road, Church Lawton, Stoke-on-Trent ST7 3DN
Tel: 01270 882056
Fax: 01270 883014

E-mail: andrea@lawtonservices.co.uk
Web site: www.lawtonservices.co.uk

PARTLINE LTD
Dockfield Road, Shipley BD17 7AZ
Tel: 01274 531531
Fax: 01274 531088
E-mail: sales@partline.co.uk
Web site: www.partline.co.uk

PLAXTON PARTS
Ryton Road, Anston, Sheffield S25 4DL
Tel: 0844 822 6224
Fax: 01909 550050
E-mail: parts@plaxtonlimited.co.uk
Web site: www.plaxtonaftercare.co.uk

PSV PRODUCTS
The Red House, Underbridge Lane, Higher Walton, Warrington WA4 5QR
Tel: 01925 210220
Fax: 01925 601534
E-mail: info@psvproducts.com
Web site: www.psvproducts.com

First Aid Equipment

ARRIVA BUS AND COACH
Lodge Garage, Whitehall Road West, Gomersal, Cleckheaton, West Yorkshire BD19 4BJ
Tel: 01274 681144
Fax: 01274 651198
E-mail: whiter@arriva.co.uk
Web site: www.arrivabusandcoach.co.uk

BRADTECH LTD
Unit 3, Ladford Covert, Seighford, Stafford ST18 9QL
Tel: 01785 282800
Fax: 01785 282755
E-mail: sales@bradtech.ltd.uk
Web site: www.bradtech.ltd.uk

CARLYLE BUS & COACH LTD
Carlyle Business Park, Great Bridge Street, Swan Village, West Bromwich B70 0X4
Tel: 0121 524 1200
Fax: 0121 524 1201
E-mail: admin@carlyleplc.co.uk
Web site: www.carlyleplc.co.uk

EXPRESS COACH REPAIRS LTD
Outgang Lane, Pickering YO18 7JA
Tel: 01751 475215
Fax: 01751 475215
E-mail: info@expresscoachrepairs.co.uk
Web site: www.expresscoachrepairs.co.uk

FIREMASTER EXTINGUISHER LTD
Firex House, 174-176 Hither Green Lane, London SE13 6QB
Tel: 020 8852 8585
Fax: 020 8297 8020
E-mail: info@firemaster.co.uk
Web site: www.firemaster.co.uk

HAPPICH V & I COMPONENTS LTD
Unit 30/31, Fort Industrial Park, Fort Parkway, Castle Bromwich B35 7AR
Tel: 0121 747 4400
Fax: 0121 747 4977
E-mail: sales@happich.co.uk
Web site: www.happich.co.uk

KCP CAR & COMMERCIAL LTD
Unit 15, Hillside Business Park, Kempson Way, Bury St Edmunds, Suffolk IP32 7EA
Tel: 01284 750777
Fax: 01284 750773
E-mail: info@kcpcarandcommercial.co.uk
Web site: www.kcpcarandcommercial.co.uk

Trade Directory

LAWTON SERVICES LTD
Knutsford Road, Church Lawton,
Stoke-on-Trent ST7 3DN
Tel: 01270 882056
Fax: 01270 883014
E-mail: andrea@lawtonservices.co.uk
Web site: www.lawtonservices.co.uk

PLAXTON PARTS
Ryton Road, Anston, Sheffield S25 4DL
Tel: 0844 822 6224
Fax: 01909 550050
E-mail: parts@plaxtonlimited.co.uk
Web site: www.plaxtonaftercare.co.uk

PSV PRODUCTS
The Red House, Underbridge Lane,
Higher Walton, Warrington WA4 5QR
Tel: 01925 210220
Fax: 01925 601534
E-mail: info@psvproducts.com
Web site: www.psvproducts.com

Floor Coverings

ALTRO TRANSFLOR
Works Road, Letchworth Garden City
SG6 1NW
Tel: 01462 707600
Fax: 01462 480010
E-mail: info@altro.com
Web site: www.altrotransflor.com

ARRIVA BUS AND COACH
Lodge Garage, Whitehall Road West,
Gomersal, Cleckheaton, West Yorkshire
BD19 4BJ
Tel: 01274 681144
Fax: 01274 651198
E-mail: whiter@arriva.co.uk
Web site: www.arrivabusandcoach.co.uk

AUTOMATE WHEEL COVERS LTD
California Mills, Oxford Road, Gomersal,
Cleckheaton BD19 4HQ
Tel: 01274 862700
Fax: 01274 851989
E-mail: sales@wheelcovers.co.uk
Web site: www.wheelcovers.co.uk

AUTOMOTIVE TEXTILE INDUSTRIES
Unit 15 & 16, Priest Court, Springfield
Business Park, Grantham NG31 7BG
Tel: 01476 593050
Fax: 01476 593607
E-mail: sales@autotex.com
Web site: www.autotex.com

CARLYLE BUS & COACH LTD
Carlyle Business Park, Great Bridge Street,
Swan Village, West Bromwich B70 0X4
Tel: 0121 524 1200
Fax: 0121 524 1201
E-mail: admin@carlyleplc.co.uk
Web site: www.carlyleplc.co.uk

COACH CARPETS
Unit 12, Hamilton Street, Blackburn BB2 4AJ
Tel: 01254 53549
Fax: 01254 261873

CONCEPT COACHCRAFT LTD
Far Cromwell Road, Stockport,
Cheshire SK6 2SE
Tel: 0161 406 9322
Fax: 0161 406 9588
E-mail: sales@conceptcoachcraft.co.uk
Web site: www.conceptcoachcraft.com

EXPRESS COACH REPAIRS LTD
Outgang Lane, Pickering YO18 7JA
Tel: 01751 475215
Fax: 01751 475215
E-mail: info@expresscoachrepairs.co.uk
Web site: www.expresscoachrepairs.co.uk

LAWTON SERVICES LTD
Knutsford Road, Church Lawton, Stoke-on-
Trent ST7 3DN
Tel: 01270 882056
Fax: 01270 883014
E-mail: andrea@lawtonservices.co.uk
Web site: www.lawtonservices.co.uk

MARTYN INDUSTRIALS LTD
5 Brunel Way, Durranhill, Harraby,
Carlisle CA1 3NQ
Tel: 01228 544000
Fax: 01228 544001
E-mail: enquiries@martyn-industrials.co.uk
Web site: www.martyn-industrials.com

PLAXTON PARTS
Ryton Road, Anston, Sheffield S25 4DL
Tel: 0844 822 6224
Fax: 01909 550050
E-mail: parts@plaxtonlimited.co.uk
Web site: www.plaxtonaftercare.co.uk

TIFLEX LTD
Tiflex House, Liskeard PL14 4NB
Tel: 01579 320808
Fax: 01579 320802
E-mail: marketing@tiflex.co.uk
Web site: www.tiflex.co.uk

TRIMPLEX SAFETY TREAD LTD
Trident Works, Mulberry Way, Belvedere
DA17 6AN
Tel: 020 8311 2101
Fax: 020 8312 1400
E-mail: safetytread@btconnect.com
Web site: www.safetytread.co.uk

Fuel, Fuel Management & Lubricants

ARRIVA BUS AND COACH
Lodge Garage, Whitehall Road West,
Gomersal, Cleckheaton, West Yorkshire
BD19 4BJ
Tel: 01274 681144
Fax: 01274 651198
E-mail: whiter@arriva.co.uk
Web site: www.arrivabusandcoach.co.uk

CUMMINS UK
Rutherford Drive, Park Farm South,
Wellingborough NN8 6AN
Tel: 01933 334200
Fax: 01933 334198
E-mail: cduksales@cummins.com
Web site: www.cummins-uk.com

FUEL THEFT SOLUTIONS LTD
20 Yew Tree Court, Alsager,
Stoke on Trent ST7 2WR
Tel: 0845 077 3921
Fax: 0845 077 3922
E-mail: sales@dieseldye.com
Web site: www.dieseldye.com

INTERLUBE SYSTEMS LTD
St Modwen Road,
Plymouth PL6 8LH
Tel: 01752 676000
Fax: 01752 676001
E-mail: info@interlubesystems.com
Web site: www.interlubesystems.com

J MURDOCH WIGHT LTD
Systems House, Pentland Industrial Estate,
Loanhead, Midlothian EH20 9QH
Tel: 0131 440 3633
Fax: 0131 440 3637
Web site: www.jmw-group.co.uk

TRISCAN SYSTEMS LTD
Phoenix Park, Blakewater Road,
Blackburn, Lancashire BB1 5SJ
Tel: 0845 225 3100
Fax: 0845 225 3101
E-mail: info@triscansystems.com
Web site: www.triscansystems.com

Garage Equipment

ARRIVA BUS AND COACH
Lodge Garage, Whitehall Road West,
Gomersal, Cleckheaton,
West Yorkshire BD19 4BJ
Tel: 01274 681144
Fax: 01274 651198
E-mail: whiter@arriva.co.uk
Web site: www.arrivabusandcoach.co.uk

AUTOMOTIVE SUPPLIES DIRECT LTD
Unit 1, Meadowcroft Way,
Leigh Business Park, Leigh WN7 3XZ
Tel: 01942 609200
Fax: 01942 609770
E-mail: sales@automotive-supplies.co.uk
Web site: www.automotive-supplies.co.uk

BUTTS OF BAWTRY GARAGE EQUIPMENT
Station Yard, Station Road, Bawtry,
Doncaster DN10 6QD
Tel: 01302 710868
Fax: 01302 719481
E-mail: info@buttsequipment.com
Web site: www.jhmbuttco.com

TERENCE BARKER TANKS
Phoenix Road, Haverhill,
Suffolk CB9 7EA
Tel: 01376 330661
Fax: 01440 715460
E-mail: sales.tbtanks.co.uk
Web site: www.terencebarkertanks.co.uk

DIRECT PARTS LTD
Unit 1, Churnet Court,
Churnetside Business Park,
Harrison Way, Cheddleton ST13 7EF
Tel: 01538 361777
Fax: 01538 369100
E-mail: sales@direct-group.co.uk
Web site: www.direct-group.co.uk

FUEL THEFT SOLUTIONS LTD
20 Yew Tree Court, Alsager,
Stoke on Trent ST7 2WR
Tel: 0845 077 3921
Fax: 0845 077 3922
E-mail: sales@dieseldye.com
Web site: www.dieseldye.com

GEMCO EQUIPMENT LTD
153-156 Bridge Street,
Northampton NN1 1QG
Tel: 01604 828500
Fax: 01604 633159
E-mail: sales@gemco.co.uk
Web site: www.gemco.co.uk

KCP CAR & COMMERCIAL LTD
Unit 15, Hillside Business Park,
Kempson Way, Bury St Edmunds,
Suffolk IP32 7EA
Tel: 01284 750777
Fax: 01284 750773
E-mail: info@kcpcarandcommercial.co.uk
Web site: www.kcpcarandcommercial.co.uk

KISMET GARAGE EQUIPMENT LTD
PO Box 273, Wirral CH32 9AE
Tel: 0844 879 3298
Fax: 0560 344 6213
E-mail: kismet2@btconnect.com
Web site: www.vehicle-lifts.co.uk

MAJORLIFT HYDRAULIC EQUIPMENT LTD
Arnold's Field Industrial Estate,

Trade Directory

TTS UK
Total Tool Solutions Limited
Newhaven Business Park
Lowergate
Milnsbridge
Huddersfield
HD3 4HS
T: 01484 642211
F: 01484 461002
E: sales@ttsuk.com
W: www.ttsuk.com

Wickwar, Wotton-under-Edge,
Gloucestershire GL12 8JD
Tel: 01454 299299
Fax: 01454 294003
E-mail: sales@majorlift.com
Web site: www.majorlift.com

SOMERS TOTALKARE LTD
15 Forge Trading Estate,
Mucklow Hill, Halesowen
B62 8TR
Tel: 0121 585 2700
Fax: 0121 585 2725
E-mail: sales@somerstotalkare.co.uk
Web site: www.somerstotalkare.co.uk

STERTIL UK LTD
Unit A, Brackmills Business Park,
Caswell Road, Northampton
NN4 7PW
Tel: 0870 770 6607
Fax: 01604 662014
E-mail: info@stertiluk.com
Web site: www.stertiluk.com

TTS UK
Total Tool Solutions Ltd, Newhaven
Business Park, Lowergate, Milnsbridge,
Huddersfield HD3 4HS
Tel: 01484 642211
Fax: 01484 461002
E-mail: sales@ttsuk.com
Web site: www.ttsuk.com

VARLEY & GULLIVER LTD
57 Alfred Street, Sparkbrook,
Birmingham B12 8JR
Tel: 0121 773 2441.
Fax: 0121 766 6875.
Web site: www.v-and-g.co.uk

V L TEST SYSTEMS LTD
3-4 Middle Slade, Buckingham Industrial
Park, Buckingham MK18 1WA
Tel: 01280 822488
Fax: 01280 822489
E-mail: sales@vltestuk.com
Web site: www.vltest.com

Gearboxes

ALLISON TRANSMISSION
Millbrook Proving Ground, Millbrook,
Bedford MK45 2JQ
Tel: 01525 408600
Fax: 01525 408610
Web site: www.allisontransmission.com

ARRIVA BUS AND COACH
Lodge Garage, Whitehall Road West,
Gomersal, Cleckheaton, West Yorkshire
BD19 4BJ

Tel: 01274 681144
Fax: 01274 651198
E-mail: whiter@arriva.co.uk
Web site: www.arrivabusandcoach.co.uk

DAVID BROWN VEHICLE TRANSMISSIONS LTD
Park Gear Works, Lockwood,
Huddersfield HD4 5DD
Tel: 01484 465500
Fax: 01484 465518

BUSS BIZZ
Goughs Transport Depot, Morestead,
Winchester SO21 1JD
Tel: 01962 715555/66.
Fax: 01962 714868.

GARDNER PARTS LTD
Centurion Court, Centurion Way,
Leyland, Lancashire PR25 3UQ
Tel: 01772 642460
Fax: 01772 621333
E-mail: sales@gardnerparts.co.uk
Web site: www.gardnerparts.co.uk

HL SMITH TRANSMISSIONS LTD
Enterprise Business Park, Cross Road,
Albrighton, Wolverhampton WV7 3BJ
Tel: 01902 373011
Fax: 01902 373608
Web site: www.hlsmith.co.uk

KCP CAR & COMMERCIAL LTD
Unit 15, Hillside Business Park,
Kempson Way, Bury St Edmunds,
Suffolk IP32 7EA
Tel: 01284 750777
Fax: 01284 750773
E-mail: info@kcpcarandcommercial.co.uk
Web site: www.kcpcarandcommercial.co.uk

LH GROUP SERVICES LTD
Graycar Business Park,
Barton under Needwood,
Burton-on-Trent DE13 8EN
Tel: 01283 722600
Fax: 01283 722622
E-mail: lh@lh-group.com
Web site: www.lh-group.com

OPTARE PARTS DIVISION
(Rotherham)
Denby Way, Hellaby, Rotherham S66 8HR
Tel: 01709 792000
Fax: 01709 792009
E-mail: parts@optare.com

OPTARE PRODUCT SUPPORT LONDON
Unit 9, Eurocourt, Olivers Close, West
Thurrock RM20 3EE
Tel: 08444 123222

Fax: 01708 869920
E-mail: london.service@optare.com

OPTARE PRODUCT SUPPORT ROTHERHAM
Denby Way, Hellaby,
otherham S66 8HR
Tel: 01709 535101
Fax: 01709 535103
E-mail: rotherham.service@optare.com

OPTARE PRODUCT SUPPORT SCOTLAND
Unit 7, Cumbernauld Business Park,
Ward Park Road, Cumbernauld G67 3JZ
Tel: 01236 726738
Fax: 01236 795651
E-mail: scotland.service@optare.com

QUEENSBRIDGE (PSV) LTD
Longlands Industrial Estate, Milner Way,
Ossett WF5 9JE
Tel: 01924 281871
Fax: 01924 281807
E-mail: craig@queensbridgeltd.co.uk
Web site: www.queensbridgeltd.co.uk

SHAWSON SUPPLY LTD
12 Station Road, Saintfield, County Down,
North Ireland BT24 7DU
Tel: 028 9751 0994
Fax: 028 9751 0816
E-mail: info@shawsonsupply.com
Web site: www.shawsonsupply.com

VOITH TURBO LTD
6 Beddington Farm Road,
Croydon CR0 4XB
Tel: 020 8667 0333
Fax: 020 8667 0403
E-mail: david.holdsworth@voith.com
Web site: www.voithturbo.com

VOITH
Engineered reliability.

Voith Turbo Ltd.
6 Beddington Farm Road,
Croydon, Surrey, CR0 4XB
Phone 0208 667 0333
Fax 0208 667 0403
david.holdsworth@voith.com

TREVOR WIGLEY & SONS BUS LTD
Passenger Vehicle Dismantling/Spares
Works: Boulder Bridge Lane, off Shaw
Lane, Barnsley S71 3HJ
Correspondence: 148 Royston Road,
Cudworth, Barnsley S72 8BN
Tel: 01226 713636
Fax: 01226 700199
E-mail: wigleys@btintenet.com
Web site: www.twigley.com

ZF POWERTRAIN
Stringes Close, Willenhall WV13 1LE
Tel: 01902 366000
Fax: 01902 366504
E-mail: sales@powertrain.org.uk
Web site: www.powertrain.org.uk

Hand Driers (in coaches)

BRADTECH LTD
Unit 3, Ladford Covert, Seighford,
Stafford ST18 9QL
Tel: 01785 282800
Fax: 01785 282558
E-mail: sales@bradtech.ltd.uk
Web site: www.bradtech.ltd.uk

CARLYLE BUS & COACH LTD
Carlyle Business Park, Great Bridge Street,
Swan Village, West Bromwich B70 0X4
Tel: 0121 524 1200
Fax: 0121 524 1201
E-mail: admin@carlyleplc.co.uk
Web site: www.carlyleplc.co.uk

CROWN COACHBUILDERS LTD
32 Flemington Industrial Park, Flemington,
Motherwell ML1 1SN
Tel: 01698 276087
Fax: 01698 262676
E-mail: davidgreer@hotmail.com
Web site: www.crowncoachbuilders.co.uk

DEANS POWERED DOORS
PO Box 8, Borwick Drive, Grovehill,
Beverley HU17 0HQ
Tel: 01482 868111
Fax: 01482 881890
E-mail: info@deans-doors.com

HAPPICH V & I COMPONENTS LTD
Unit 30/31, Fort Industrial Park, Fort
Parkway, Castle Bromwich B35 7AR
Tel: 0121 747 4400
Fax: 0121 747 4977
E-mail: sales@happich.co.uk
Web site: www.happich.co.uk

JBF SERVICES LTD
Southedge Works, Hipperholme,
Halifax HX3 8EF
Tel: 01422 202840
Fax: 01422 206070
E-mail: jbfservices@aol.com

PLAXTON PARTS
Ryton Road, Anston, Sheffield S25 4DL
Tel: 0833 822 6224
Fax: 01909 550050
E-mail: parts@plaxtonlimited.co.uk
Web site: www.plaxtonaftercare.co.uk

PLAXTON SERVICE
Ryton Road, Anston, Sheffield S25 4DL
Tel: 01909 551155
Fax: 01909 550050
E-mail: service@plaxtonlimited.co.uk
Web site: www.plaxtonaftercare.co.uk

SHADES TECHNICS LTD
Units E3 & E4, Rd Park, Stephenson Close,
Hoddesdon, Hertfordshire EN11 0BW
Tel: 01992 501683
Fax: 01992 501669
E-mail: sales@shades-technics.com
Web site: www.shades-technics.com

UNWIN SAFETY SYSTEMS
Unwin House, The Horseshoe,
Coat Road, Martock TA12 6EY
Tel: 01935 827740
Fax: 01935 827760
E-mail: sales@unwin-safety.co.uk
Web site: wwwunwin-safety.com

Handrails

ABACUS TRANSPORT PRODUCTS LTD
Abacus House, Highlode Industrial Estate,
Stockingfen Road,
Ramsey PE26 2RB
Tel: 01487 710700
Fax: 01487 710626
E-mail: f.riola@abacus-tp.com
Web site: www.abacus-tp.com

ARRIVA BUS AND COACH
Lodge Garage, Whitehall Road West,
Gomersal, Cleckheaton, West Yorkshire
BD19 4BJ
Tel: 01274 681144
Fax: 01274 651198
E-mail: whiter@arriva.co.uk
Web site: www.arrivabusandcoach.co.uk

EXPRESS COACH REPAIRS LTD
Outgang Lane,
Pickering YO18 7JA
Tel: 01751 475215
Fax: 01751 475215
E-mail: info@expresscoachrepairs.co.uk
Web site: www.expresscoachrepairs.co.uk

GABRIEL & CO LTD
Abro Works, 10 Hay Hall Road,
Tyseley, Birmingham B11 2AU
Tel: 0121 248 3331 **Fax:** 0121 248 3330
E-mail: john.gabriel@gabrielco.com
Web site: www.gabrielco.com

LAWTON SERVICES LTD
Knutsford Road, Church Lawton,
Stoke-on-Trent ST7 3DN
Tel: 01270 882056
Fax: 01270 883014
E-mail: andrea@lawtonservices.co.uk
Web site: www.lawtonservices.co.uk

PLAXTON PARTS
Ryton Road, Anston, Sheffield S25 4DL
Tel: 0833 822 6224
Fax: 01909 550050
E-mail: parts@plaxtonlimited.co.uk
Web site: www.plaxtonaftercare.co.uk

PLAXTON SERVICE
Ryton Road, Anston, Sheffield S25 4DL
Tel: 01909 551155
Fax: 01909 550050
E-mail: service@plaxtonlimited.co.uk
Web site: www.plaxtonaftercare.co.uk

TRAMONTANA
Chapelknowe Road, Carfin,
Motherwell ML1 5LE
Tel: 01698 861790
Fax: 01698 860778
E-mail: wdt90@tiscali.co.uk
Web site: www.tramontanacoach.co.uk

Headrest Covers & Curtains

ARRIVA BUS AND COACH
Lodge Garage, Whitehall Road West,
Gomersal, Cleckheaton, West Yorkshire
BD19 4BJ
Tel: 01274 681144
Fax: 01274 651198
E-mail: whiter@arriva.co.uk
Web site: www.arrivabusandcoach.co.uk

DUOFLEX LTD
Trimmingham House, 2 Shires Road,
Buckingham Road Industrial Estate,
Brackley NN13 7EZ
Tel: 01280 701366
Fax: 01280 704799
E-mail: sales@duoflex.co.uk
Web site: www.duoflex.co.uk

EXPRESS COACH REPAIRS LTD
Outgang Lane, Pickering YO18 7JA
Tel: 01751 475215
Fax: 01751 475215
E-mail: info@expresscoachrepairs.co.uk
Web site: www.expresscoachrepairs.co.uk

**LEISUREWEAR DIRECT LTD,
inc. AHEAD OF THE REST**
4A South Street North, New Whittington,
Chesterfield S43 2AB
Tel: 01246 454447
Fax: 0870 755 9842
Web site: www.leisureweardirect.com

ORVEC INTERNATIONAL LTD
Malmo Road, Hull HU7 0YF
Tel: 01482 625333
Fax: 01482 625335.
E-mail: service@orvec.com
Web site: www.orvec.co.uk

PLAXTON PARTS
Ryton Road, Anston, Sheffield S25 4DL
Tel: 0833 822 6224
Fax: 01909 550050
E-mail: parts@plaxtonlimited.co.uk
Web site: www.plaxtonaftercare.co.uk

Heating & Ventilation Systems

AIRCONCO LTD
Unit 10, Middleton Trade Park,
Oldham Road, Middleton M24 1QZ
Tel: 0845 402 4014
Fax: 0845 402 4041
E-mail: mail@airconco.carriersutrak.co.uk
Web site: www.airconco.ltd.uk

ARRIVA BUS AND COACH
Lodge Garage, Whitehall Road West,
Gomersal, Cleckheaton, West Yorkshire
BD19 4BJ
Tel: 01274 681144 **Fax:** 01274 651198
E-mail: whiter@arriva.co.uk
Web site: www.arrivabusandcoach.co.uk

CARLYLE BUS & COACH LTD
Carlyle Business Park, Great Bridge Street,
Swan Village, West Bromwich B70 0X4
Tel: 0121 524 1200
Fax: 0121 524 1201
E-mail: admin@carlyleplc.co.uk
Web site: carlyleplc.co.uk

CLAYTON HEATERS LTD
Hunter Terrace, Fletchworth Gate,
Burnsall Road, Coventry CV5 6SP
Tel: 02476 691 916
Fax: 02476 691 969
E-mail: admin@claytoncc.co.uk
Web site: www.claytoncc.co.uk

CONSERVE (UK) LTD
Suite 7, Logistics House, Kingsthorpe Road,
Northampton NN2 6LJ
Tel: 01604 710055
Fax: 01604 710065
E-mail: information@conserveuk.co.uk
Web site: www.conserveuk.co.uk

EBERSPACHER (UK) LTD
Headlands Business Park, Salisbury Road,
Ringwood BH24 3PB
Tel: 01425 480151
Fax: 01425 480152
E-mail: enquiries@eberspacher.com
Web site: www.eberspacher.com

HAPPICH V & I COMPONENTS LTD
Unit 30/31, Fort Industrial Park,
Fort Parkway, Castle Bromwich
B35 7AR
Tel: 0121 747 4400
Fax: 0121 747 4977
E-mail: sales@happich.co.uk
Web site: www.happich.co.uk

KARIVE LIMITED
PO Box 205, Southam,
Warwickshire CV47 0ZL
Tel: 01926 813938

Fax: 01926 814898
E-mail: karive.ltd@btinternet.com
Web site: www.karive.co.uk

KELLETT (UK) LTD
8 Stevenson Way,
Sheffield S9 3WZ
Tel: 0114 261 1122
Fax: 0114 261 1199
E-mail: sales@kellett.co.uk

NEALINE WINDSCREEN WIPER PRODUCTS
Unit 1, The Sidings Industrial Estate,
Birdingbury Road, Marton CV23 9RX
Tel: 01926 633256
Fax: 01926 632600

OPTARE PARTS DIVISION
(Rotherham)
Denby Way, Hellaby,
Rotherham S66 8HR
Tel: 01709 792000
Fax: 01709 792009
E-mail: parts@optare.com

PIONEER WESTON
206 Cavendish Place,
Birchwood Park,
Warrington WA3 6WU
Tel: 01925 853000
Fax: 01925 853030
E-mail: info@pwi-ltd.com
Web site: www.pwi-ltd.com

PLAXTON PARTS
Ryton Road, Anston,
Sheffield S25 4DL
Tel: 0833 822 6224
Fax: 01909 550050
E-mail: parts@plaxtonlimited.co.uk
Web site: www.plaxtonaftercare.co.uk

PLAXTON SERVICE
Ryton Road, Anston,
Sheffield S25 4DL
Tel: 01909 551155
Fax: 01909 550050
E-mail: service@plaxtonlimited.co.uk
Web site: www.plaxtonaftercare.co.uk

SHADES TECHNICS LTD
Units E3 & E4, Rd Park, Stephenson Close,
Hoddesdon, Hertfordshire EN11 0BW
Tel: 01992 501683
Fax: 01992 501669
E-mail: sales@shades-technics.com
Web site: www.shades-technics.com

WEBASTO PRODUCT UK LTD
Webasto House, White Rose Way,
Doncaster Carr, South Yorkshire DN4 5JH
Tel: 01302 322232
Fax: 01302 322231
E-mail: info@webastouk.com
Web site: www.webasto.co.uk

Hub Odometers

ARRIVA BUS AND COACH
Lodge Garage, Whitehall Road West,
Gomersal, Cleckheaton, West Yorkshire
BD19 4BJ
Tel: 01274 681144
Fax: 01274 651198
E-mail: whiter@arriva.co.uk
Web site: www.arrivabusandcoach.co.uk

FUMOTO ENGINEERING OF EUROPE LTD
Normandy House, 35 Glategny Esplanade,
St Peter Port, Guernsey GY1 2BP
Tel: 01481 716987
Fax: 01481 700374
E-mail: sales@fumoto-valve.com

KCP CAR & COMMERCIAL LTD
Unit 15, Hillside Business Park, Kempson
Way, Bury St Edmunds, Suffolk IP32 7EA
Tel: 01284 750777
Fax: 01284 750773
E-mail: info@kcpcarandcommercial.co.uk
Web site: www.kcpcarandcommercial.co.uk

ROADLINK INTERNATIONAL LTD
Strawberry Lane, Willenhall WV13 3RL
Tel: 01902 636206
Fax: 01902 631515
E-mail: sales@roadlink-international.co.uk
Web site: www.roadlink-international.co.uk

In-coach Catering Equipment

AVT SYSTEMS LTD
Unit 3, Tything Road, Arden Forest Trading
Estate, Alcester, Warwickshire B49 6ES
Tel: 01789 400357
Fax: 01789 400359
E-mail: enquiries@avtsystems.co.uk
Web site: www.avtsystems.co.uk

BRADTECH LTD
Unit 3, Ladford Covert, Seighford, Stafford
ST18 9QL
Tel: 01785 282800
Fax: 01785 282558
E-mail: sales@bradtech.ltd.uk
Web site: www.bradtech.ltd.uk

EXPRESS COACH REPAIRS LTD
Outgang Lane, Pickering YO18 7JA
Tel: 01751 475215
Fax: 01751 475215
E-mail: info@expresscoachrepairs.co.uk
Web site: www.expresscoachrepairs.co.uk

PLAXTON PARTS
Ryton Road, Anston, Sheffield S25 4DL
Tel: 0833 822 6224
Fax: 01909 550050
E-mail: parts@plaxtonlimited.co.uk
Web site: www.plaxtonaftercare.co.uk

PLAXTON SERVICE
Ryton Road, Anston, Sheffield S25 4DL
Tel: 01909 551155
Fax: 01909 550050
E-mail: service@plaxtonlimited.co.uk
Web site: www.plaxtonaftercare.co.uk

PSV PRODUCTS
The Red House, Underbridge Lane, Higher
Walton, Warrington WA4 5QR
Tel: 01925 210220
Fax: 01925 601534
E-mail: info@psvproducts.com
Web site: www.psvproducts.com

SHADES TECHNICS LTD
Units E3 & E4, Rd Park,
Stephenson Close, Hoddesdon,
Hertfordshire EN11 0BW
Tel: 01992 501683
Fax: 01992 501669
E-mail: sales@shades-technics.com
Web site: www.shades-technics.com

Labels, Nameplates & Decals

ARRIVA BUS AND COACH
Lodge Garage, Whitehall Road West,
Gomersal, Cleckheaton, West Yorkshire
BD19 4BJ
Tel: 01274 681144
Fax: 01274 651198
E-mail: whiter@arriva.co.uk
Web site: www.arrivabusandcoach.co.uk

FUEL THEFT SOLUTIONS LTD
20 Yew Tree Court, Alsager,
Stoke on Trent ST7 2WR

Tel: 0845 077 3921
Fax: 0845 077 3922
E-mail: sales@dieseldye.com
Web site: www.dieseldye.com

McKENNA BROTHERS LTD
McKenna House, Jubilee Road,
Middleton, Manchester M24 2LX
Tel: 0161 655 3244
Fax: 0161 655 3059
E-mail: info@mckennabrothers.co.uk
Web site: www.mckennabrothers.co.uk

PLAXTON PARTS
Ryton Road, Anston,
Sheffield S25 4DL
Tel: 0833 822 6224
Fax: 01909 550050
E-mail: parts@plaxtonlimited.co.uk
Web site: www.plaxtonaftercare.co.uk

Lifting Equipment

AUTOLIFT LTD
Unit 440/41, Alma Works,
Sticker Lane, Bradford BD1 8RL
Tel: 01274 680744
Fax: 01274 680042
E-mail: sales@autoliftuk.co.uk
Web site: www.autoliftuk.co.uk

Lifts/Ramps (Passenger)

ARRIVA BUS AND COACH
Lodge Garage, Whitehall Road West,
Gomersal, Cleckheaton, West Yorkshire
BD19 4BJ
Tel: 01274 681144
Fax: 01274 651198
E-mail: whiter@arriva.co.uk
Web site: www.arrivabusandcoach.co.uk

AVS STEPS LTD
Unit 1, Mereside Industrial Park,
Fenns Bank, Whitchurch,
Shropshire SY13 3PA
Tel: 01948 781000
Fax: 01978 780098
E-mail: sales@avssteps.co.uk
Web site: www.avssteps.co.uk

COMPAK RAMPS LTD
VIP Trading Estate, Anchor & Hope Lane,
London SE7 7RY
Tel: 020 8858 3781
Fax: 020 8858 3781
E-mail: tony.rodwell@dsl.pipex.com

CROWN COACHBUILDERS LTD
32 Flemington Industrial Park, Flemington,
Motherwell ML1 1SN
Tel: 01698 276087
Fax: 01698 262676
E-mail: davidgreer@hotmail.com
Web site: www.crowncoachbuilders.co.uk

DIRECT PARTS LTD
Unit 1, Churnet Court,
Churnetside Business Park,
Harrison Way, Cheddleton ST13 7EF
Tel: 01538 361777
Fax: 01538 369100
E-mail: sales@direct-group.co.uk
Web site: www.direct-group.co.uk

EXPRESS COACH REPAIRS LTD
Outgang Lane, Pickering YO18 7JA
Tel: 01751 475215
Fax: 01751 475215
E-mail: info@expresscoachrepairs.co.uk
Web site: www.expresscoachrepairs.co.uk

LAWTON SERVICES LTD
Knutsford Road, Church Lawton,
Stoke-on-Trent ST7 3DN

Tel: 01270 882056
Fax: 01270 883014
E-mail: andrea@lawtonservices.co.uk
Web site: www.lawtonservices.co.uk

PASSENGER LIFT SERVICES
Unit 1C, Pearsall Drive, Oldbury, West Midlands B69 2RA
Tel: 0121 552 0660
Fax: 0121 552 0200
E-mail: enquiries@pls-access.co.uk
Web site: www.passengerliftservices.co.uk

PLAXTON PARTS
Ryton Road, Anston, Sheffield S25 4DL
Tel: 0833 822 6224
Fax: 01909 550050
E-mail: parts@plaxtonlimited.co.uk
Web site: www.plaxtonaftercare.co.uk

PLAXTON SERVICE
Ryton Road, Anston, Sheffield S25 4DL
Tel: 01909 551155
Fax: 01909 550050
E-mail: service@plaxtonlimited.co.uk
Web site: www.plaxtonaftercare.co.uk

PNEUMAX LTD
Unit 8, Venture Industrial Park, Fareham Road, Gosport PO13 0BA
Tel: 01329 823999
Fax: 01329 822345
E-mail: sales@pneumax.co.uk
Web site: www.pneumax.co.uk

RATCLIFF PALFINGER
Bessemer Road, Welwyn Garden City AL7 1ET
Tel: 01707 325571
Fax: 01707 327752
E-mail: info@ratcliffpalfinger.co.uk
Web site: www.ratcliffpalfinger.co.uk

RICON UK LIMITED
Littlemoss Business Park, Littlemoss Road, Droylsden, Manchester M43 7EF
Tel: 0800 435677 **Fax:** 0161 301 6050
E-mail: info@riconuk.com
Web site: www.riconuk.com

TRUCKALIGN CO LTD
VIP Trading Estate, Anchor & Hope Lane, London SE7 7RY
Tel: 020 8858 3781
Fax: 020 8858 3781
E-mail: tony.rodwell@dsl.pipex.com

Lighting & Lighting Design

ARRIVA BUS AND COACH
Lodge Garage, Whitehall Road West, Gomersal, Cleckheaton, West Yorkshire BD19 4BJ
Tel: 01274 681144
Fax: 01274 651198
E-mail: whiter@arriva.co.uk
Web site: www.arrivabusandcoach.co.uk

BRITAX PMG LTD
Bressingby Industrial Estate, Bridlington, East Yorkshire YO16 4SJ
Tel: 01262 670161
Fax: 01262 605666
E-mail: info@britax-pmg.com
Web site: www.britax-pmg.com

CARLYLE BUS & COACH LTD
Carlyle Business Park, Great Bridge Street, Swan Village, West Bromwich B70 0XA
Tel: 0121 524 1200
Fax: 0121 524 1201
E-mail: admin@carlyleplc.co.uk
Web site: www.carlyleplc.co.uk

CSM LIGHTING
Suite 1b, Cobb House, Oyster Lane, Byfleet KT14 7DU
Tel: 01932 349661
Fax: 01932 349991
Web site: www.csmauto.com

EXPRESS COACH REPAIRS LTD
Outgang Lane, Pickering YO18 7JA
Tel: 01751 475215
Fax: 01751 475215
E-mail: info@expresscoachrepairs.co.uk
Web site: www.expresscoachrepairs.co.uk

HAPPICH V & I COMPONENTS LTD
Unit 30/31, Fort Industrial Park, Fort Parkway, Castle Bromwich B35 7AR
Tel: 0121 747 4400
Fax: 0121 747 4977
E-mail: sales@happich.co.uk
Web site: www.happich.co.uk

INVERTEC LTD
Whelford Road, Fairford GL7 4DT
Tel: 01285 713550
Fax: 01285 713548
Mobile: 07802 793828
E-mail: ian@invertec.co.uk
Web site: www.invertec.co.uk

KCP CAR & COMMERCIAL LTD
Unit 15, Hillside Business Park, Kempson Way, Bury St Edmunds, Suffolk IP32 7EA
Tel: 01284 750777
Fax: 01284 750773
E-mail: info@kcpcarandcommercial.co.uk
Web site: www.kcpcarandcommercial.co.uk

KELLETT (UK) LTD
8 Stevenson Way, Sheffield S9 3WZ.
Tel: 0114 261 1122.
Fax: 0114 261 1199.
E-mail: sales@kellett.co.uk

OPTARE PARTS DIVISION (Rotherham)
Denby Way, Hellaby, Rotherham S66 8HR
Tel: 01709 792000
Fax: 01709 792009
E-mail: parts@optare.com

PARTLINE LTD
Dockfield Road, Shipley BD17 7AZ
Tel: 01274 531531
Fax: 01274 531608
E-mail: sales@partline.co.uk
Web site: www.partline.co.uk

PLAXTON PARTS
Ryton Road, Anston, Sheffield S25 4DL
Tel: 0833 822 6224
Fax: 01909 550050
E-mail: parts@plaxtonlimited.co.uk
Web site: www.plaxtonaftercare.co.uk

PLAXTON SERVICE
Ryton Road, Anston, Sheffield S25 4DL
Tel: 01909 551155
Fax: 01909 550050
E-mail: service@plaxtonlimited.co.uk
Web site: www.plaxtonaftercare.co.uk

RESCROFT LTD
20 Oxleasow Road, East Moons Moat, Redditch B98 0RE
Tel: 01527 521300
Fax: 01527 521301
E-mail: info@rescroft.com
Web site: www.rescroft.com

Mirrors/Mirror Arms

ASHTREE GLASS LTD
Brownroyd Street, Bradford BD8 9AF
Tel: 01274 546732

Fax: 01274 548525
E-mail: sales@ashtreeglass.co.uk
Web site: www.ashtreeglass.co.uk

EXPRESS COACH REPAIRS LTD
Outgang Lane, Pickering YO18 7JA
Tel: 01751 475215
Fax: 01751 475215
E-mail: info@expresscoachrepairs.co.uk
Web site: www.expresscoachrepairs.co.uk

LAWTON SERVICES LTD
Knutsford Road, Church Lawton, Stoke-on-Trent ST7 3DN
Tel: 01270 882056
Fax: 01270 883014
E-mail: andrea@lawtonservices.co.uk
Web site: www.lawtonservices.co.uk

PLAXTON PARTS
Ryton Road, Anston, Sheffield S25 4DL
Tel: 0833 822 6224
Fax: 01909 550050
E-mail: parts@plaxtonlimited.co.uk
Web site: www.plaxtonaftercare.co.uk

Oil Management Systems

ARRIVA BUS AND COACH
Lodge Garage, Whitehall Road West, Gomersal, Cleckheaton, West Yorkshire BD19 4BJ
Tel: 01274 681144
Fax: 01274 651198
E-mail: whiter@arriva.co.uk
Web site: www.arrivabusandcoach.co.uk

FUEL THEFT SOLUTIONS LTD
20 Yew Tree Court, Alsager, Stoke on Trent ST7 2WR
Tel: 0845 077 3921
Fax: 0845 077 3922
E-mail: sales@dieseldye.com
Web site: www.dieseldye.com

GROENEVELD UK LTD
The Greentec Centre, Gelders Hall Road, Shepshed, Leicestershire LE12 9NH
Tel: 01509 600033
Fax: 01509 602000
E-mail: info@groeneveld.co.uk
Web site: www.groeneveld.co.uk

INTERLUBE SYSTEMS LTD
St Modwen Road, Plymouth PL6 8LH
Tel: 01752 676000
Fax: 01752 676001
E-mail: info@interlubesystems.co.uk
Web site: www.interlubesystems.co.uk

MARTYN INDUSTRIALS LTD
5 Brunel Way, Durranhill, Harraby, Carlisle CA1 3NQ
Tel: 01228 544000
Fax: 01228 544001
E-mail: enquiries@martyn-industrials.co.uk
Web site: www.martyn-industrials.com

STERTIL UK LTD
Unit A, Brackmills Business Park, Caswell Road, Northampton NN4 7PW
Tel: 0870 7706607
Fax: 01604 668014
E-mail: info@stertiluk.com
Web site: www.stertiluk.com

Painting & Signwriting

ARRIVA BUS AND COACH
Lodge Garage, Whitehall Road West, Gomersal, Cleckheaton, West Yorkshire BD19 4BJ
Tel: 01274 681144
Fax: 01274 651198

Trade Directory

E-mail: whiter@arriva.co.uk
Web site: www.arrivabusandcoach.co.uk

BLACKPOOL COACH SERVICES
Burton Road, Blackpool
FY4 4NN.
Tel/Fax: 01253 698686

BULWARK BUS & COACH ENGINEERING LTD
Gate 3, Bulwark Industrial Estate,
Chepstow NP16 5QZ
Tel: 01291 622326
Fax: 01291 622726

CHANNEL COMMERCIALS PLC
Unit 6, Cobbs Wood Industrial Estate,
Brunswick Road,
Ashford TN23 1EH
Tel: 01233 629272
Fax: 01233 636322
E-mail: info@ccplc.co.uk
Web site: www.channelcommercials.co.uk

EXPRESS COACH REPAIRS LTD
Outgang Lane,
Pickering YO18 7JA
Tel: 01751 475215
Fax: 01751 475215
E-mail: info@expresscoachrepairs.co.uk
Web site: www.expresscoachrepairs.co.uk

HANTS & DORSET TRIM LTD
Canada Road,
West Wellow SO51 6DE.
Tel: 02380 644200
Fax: 02380 647802
E-mail: dclack@hdtrim.co.uk
Web site: www.hantsanddorsettrim.co.uk

LANCES MOBILE PAINTING
20 Hillham Crescent, Boost Town,
Worsley, Manchester M28 1FY
Tel: 07974 862022

LAWTON SERVICES LTD
Knutsford Road, Church Lawton,
Stoke-on-Trent ST7 3DN
Tel: 01270 882056
Fax: 01270 883014
E-mail: andrea@lawtonservices.co.uk
Web site: www.lawtonservices.co.uk

NORBURY BLINDS LTD
41-45 Hanley Street, Newtown,
Birmingham B19 3SP
Tel: 0121 359 4311
Fax: 0121 359 6388
E-mail: info@norbury-blinds.com
Web site: www.norbury-blinds.com

OPTARE PRODUCT SUPPORT LONDON
Unit 9, Eurocourt, Olivers Close,
West Thurrock RM20 3EE
Tel: 08444 123222
Fax: 01708 869920
E-mail: london.service@optare.com

OPTARE PRODUCT SUPPORT ROTHERHAM
Denby Way, Hellaby,
Rotherham S66 8HR
Tel: 01709 535101
Fax: 01709 535103
E-mail: rotherham.service@optare.com

OPTARE PRODUCT SUPPORT SCOTLAND
Unit 7, Cumbernauld Business Park,
Ward Park Road,
Cumbernauld G67 3JZ
Tel: 01236 726738
Fax: 01236 795651
E-mail: scotland.service@optare.com

RH BODYWORKS
A140 Ipswich Road, Brome,
Eye IP23 8AW
Tel: 01379 870666
Fax: 01379 872106
E-mail: mike.ball@rhbodyworks.co.uk
Web site: www.rhbodyworks.co.uk

VOLVO BUS AND COACH CENTRE
Parts Sales & Body Repair/
Refurbishment Specialists
Byron Street Extension,
Loughborough LE11 5HE
Tel: 01509 217700
Fax: 01509 238770
E-mail (Body Support):
dporter@volvocoachsales.co.uk
Web site: www.volvo.com

Parts Suppliers

AIR DOOR SERVICES
Unit D, The Pavillions,
Holly Lane Industrial Estate,
Atherstone CV9 2QZ.
Tel: 01827 711660
Fax: 01827 713577
Web site: www.airdoorservices.co.uk

ARRIVA BUS AND COACH
Lodge Garage, Whitehall Road West,
Gomersal, Cleckheaton,
West Yorkshire BD19 4BJ
Tel: 01274 681144
Fax: 01274 651198
E-mail: whiter@arriva.co.uk
Web site: www.arrivabusandcoach.co.uk

ASHTREE GLASS LTD
Brownroyd Street,
Bradford BO8 9AF
Tel: 01274 546 732
Fax: 01274 548 525
E-mail: sales@ashtreeglass.co.uk
Web site: www.ashtreeglass.co.uk

M BARNWELL SERVICES LTD
Reginald Road,
Smethwick B67 5AS
Tel: 0121 429 8011
Fax: 0121 434 3016
E-mail: sales@barnwell.co.uk
Web site: www.barnwell.co.uk

BRT BEARINGS LTD
21-24 Regal Road, Wisbech,
Cambridgeshire PE13 2RQ
Tel: 01945 464 097
Fax: 01945 464 523
E-mail: info@brt-group.com

BUSS BIZZ
Goughs Transport Depot, Morestead,
Winchester SO21 1JD
Tel: 01962 715555/66
Fax: 01962 714868

CARLYLE BUS & COACH LTD
Carlyle Business Park, Great Bridge Street,
Swan Village, West Bromwich B70 0X4
Tel: 0121 524 1200
Fax: 0121 524 1201
E-mail: admin@carlyleplc.co.uk
Web site: www.carlyleplc.co.uk

CLAYTON HEATERS LTD
Hunter Terrace, Fletchworth Gate,
Burnsall Road, Coventry CV5 6SP
Tel: 02476 691 916
Fax: 02476 691 969
E-mail: admin@claytoncc.co.uk
Web site: www.claytoncc.co.uk

COACH-AID
Unit 2, Brindley Close, Tollgate Industrial Estate, Stafford ST16 3SU
Tel: 01785 222666
E-mail: workshop@coach-aid.com
Web site: www.coach-aid.com

CONSERVE (UK) LTD
Suite 7, Logistics House,
1 Horsley Road, Kingsthorpe Road,
Northampton NN2 6LJ
Tel: 01604 710055
Fax: 01604 710065
E-mail: information@conserveuk.co.uk
Web site: www.conserveuk.co.uk

CRESCENT FACILITIES LTD
72 Willow Crescent, Chapeltown,
Sheffield S35 1QS
Tel/Fax: 0114 245 1050
E-mail: cfl.chris@btinternet.com
Web site: www.cflparts.com

CREST COACH CONVERSIONS
Unit 5, Holmeroyd Road,
Bentley Moor Lane, Carcroft,
Doncaster DN6 7BH
Tel: 01302 723723
Fax: 01302 724724

CREWE ENGINES
Warmingham Road, Crewe CW1 4PQ
Tel: 01270 526333
Fax: 01270 526433
E-mail: sales@creweengines.co.uk
Web site: www.creweengines.co.uk

CUMMINS UK
Rutherford Drive, Park Farm South,
Wellingborough NN8 6AN
Tel: 01933 334200
Fax: 01933 334198
E-mail: cduksales@cummins.com
Web site: www.cummins-uk.com

DINEX EXHAUSTS LTD
14 Chesford Grange, Woolston,
Warrington WA1 3BT
Tel: 01925 849849
Fax: 01925 849850
E-mail: dinex@dinex.co.uk

DIRECT PARTS LTD
Unit 1, Churnet Court, Churnetside Business Park, Harrison Way, Cheddleton ST13 7EF
Tel: 01538 361777
Fax: 01538 369100
E-mail: sales@direct-group.co.uk
Web site: www.direct-group.co.uk

ERENTEK LTD
Malt Kiln Lane, Waddington,
Lincoln LN5 9RT
Tel: 01522 720065
Fax: 01522 729155
E-mail: sales@erentek.co.uk
Web site: www.erentek.co.uk

EXPRESS COACH REPAIRS LTD
Outgang Lane, Pickering YO18 7JA
Tel: 01751 475215
Fax: 01751 475215
E-mail: info@expresscoachrepairs.co.uk
Web site: www.expresscoachrepairs.co.uk

GARDNER PARTS LTD
Centurion Court, Centurion Way,
Leyland, Lancashire PR25 3UQ
Tel: 01772 642460
Fax: 01772 621333
E-mail: sales@gardnerparts.co.uk
Web site: www.gardnerparts.co.uk

HAPPICH V & I COMPONENTS LTD
Unit 30/31, Fort Industrial Park, Fort Parkway, Castle Bromwich B35 7AR
Tel: 0121 747 4400

Fax: 0121 747 4977
E-mail: sales@happich.co.uk
Web site: www.happich.co.uk

HART BROTHERS (ENGINEERING) LTD
Soho Works, Soho Street,
Oldham OL4 2AD
Tel: 0161 737 6791

THOMAS HARDIE COMMERCIALS LTD
Newstet Road, Knowsley Industrial Park,
Liverpool L33 7TJ
Tel: 0151 549 3000
E-mail: info@thardie.co.uk

IMEXPART LTD
Links 31, Willowbridge Way,
Whitwood, Castleford WF10 5NP
Tel: 0845 605 0404
Fax: 01977 513412
E-mail: sales@imexpart.com
Web site: www.imexpart.com

IMPERIAL ENGINEERING
Delamare Road, Cheshunt,
Hertfordshire EN8 9UD
Tel: 01992 634255
Fax: 01992 630506
E-mail: orders@imperialengineering.co.uk
Web site: www.imperialengineering.co.uk

KCP CAR & COMMERCIAL LTD
Unit 15, Hillside Business Park,
Kempson Way, Bury St Edmunds,
Suffolk IP32 7EA
Tel: 01284 750777
Fax: 01284 750773
E-mail: info@kcpcarandcommercial.co.uk
Web site: www.kcpcarandcommercial.co.uk

KARIVE LIMITED
PO Box 205, Southam CV47 0ZL
Tel: 01926 813938
Fax: 01926 814898
E-mail: karive.ltd@btinternet.com
Web site: www.karive.co.uk

KELLETT (UK) LTD
8 Stevenson Way,
Sheffield S9 3WZ
Tel: 0114 261 1122
Fax: 0114 261 1199
E-mail: sales@kellett.co.uk

KNORR-BREMSE SYSTEMS FOR COMMERCIAL VEHICLES LTD
Douglas Road, Kingswood,
Bristol BS15 8NL
Tel: 0117 984 6100
Fax: 0117 984 6101
Web site: www.knorr-bremse.com

LAWTON SERVICES LTD
Knutsford Road, Church Lawton,
Stoke-on-Trent ST7 3DN
Tel: 01270 882056
Fax: 01270 883014
E-mail: andrea@lawtonservices.co.uk
Web site: www.lawtonservices.co.uk

LH GROUP SERVICES LTD
Graycar Business Park,
Barton under Needwood,
Burton-on-Trent DE13 8EN
Tel: 01283 722600
Fax: 01283 722622
E-mail: lh@lh-group.com
Web site: www.lh-group.com

MOCAP LIMITED
Hortonwood 35,
Telford TF1 7YW
Tel: 01952 670247
Fax: 01952 670241

E-mail: sales@mocap.co.uk
Web site: www.mocap.co.uk

MOSELEY (PCV) LTD
Elmsall Way, Dale Lane,
South Elmsall, Pontefract WF9 2XS
Tel: 01977 609000
Fax: 01977 609900
E-mail: sales@moseleycoachsales.co.uk
Web site: www.moseleycoachsales.co.uk

NEXT BUS LTD
The Coach Yard, Vincients Road, Bumpers Farm Industrial Estate, Chippenham SN14 6QA
Tel: 01249 462462
Fax: 01249 448 844
E-mail: sales@next-bus.co.uk
Web site: www.next-bus.co.uk

OPTARE PARTS DIVISION
(Rotherham)
Denby Way, Hellaby, Rotherham S66 8HR
Tel: 01709 792000
Fax: 01709 792009
E-mail: parts@optare.com

PARTLINE LTD
Dockfield Road, Shipley BD17 7AZ
Tel: 01274 531531
Fax: 01274 531088
E-mail: sales@partline.co.uk
Web site: www.partline.co.uk

PLAXTON PARTS
Ryton Road, Anston, Sheffield S25 4DL
Tel: 0833 822 6224
Fax: 01909 550050
E-mail: parts@plaxtonlimited.co.uk
Web site: www.plaxtonaftercare.co.uk

PNEUMAX LTD
Unit 8, Venture Industrial Park, Fareham Road, Gosport PO13 0BA
Tel: 01329 823999
Fax: 01329 822345
E-mail: sales@pneumax.co.uk
Web site: www.pneumax.co.uk

PSV GLASS
Hillbottom Road, High Wycombe HP12 4HJ
Tel: 01494 533131
Fax: 01494 462675
E-mail: sales@psvglass.co.uk
Web site: www.psvglass.com

Q'STRAINT
73-76 John Wilson Business Park,
Whitstable, Kent CT5 3QU
Tel: 01227 773035
Fax: 01227 770035

E-mail: info@qstraint.co.uk
Web site: www.qstraint.com

QUEENSBRIDGE (PSV) LTD
Longlands Industrial Estate, Milner Way,
Ossett WF5 9JE
Tel: 01924 281871
Fax: 01924 281807
E-mail: craig@queensbridgeltd.co.uk
Web site: www.queensbridgeltd.co.uk

ROADLINK INTERNATIONAL LTD
Strawberry Lane, Willenhall, West Midlands WV13 3RL
Tel: 01902 636206
Fax: 01902 631515
E-mail: sales@roadlink-international.co.uk
Web site: www.roadlink-international.co.uk

ROUTEMASTER BUSES LTD
PO Box 407, Crewe CW1 9AF
Tel: 0870 720 2920
E-mail: routemasterbuses@hotmail.com
Web site: www.routemasterbuses.co.uk

SHADES TECHNICS LTD
Units E3 & E4, Rd Park, Stephenson Close, Hoddesdon, Hertfordshire EN11 0BW
Tel: 01992 501683
Fax: 01992 501669
E-mail: sales@shades-technics.com
Web site: www.shades-technics.com

SHAWSON SUPPLY LTD
12 Station Road, Saintfield, County Down, Northern Ireland BT24 7DU
Tel: 028 9751 0994
Fax: 028 9751 0816
E-mail: info@shawsonsupply.com
Web site: www.shawsonsupply.com

CRAIG TILSLEY & SON LTD
Moorfield Industrial Estate, Cotes Heath, Stoke on Trent ST21 6QY
Tel: 01782 781524
Fax: 01782 791316

TTS UK
Total Tool Solutions Ltd, Newhaven Business Park, Lowergate, Milnsbridge, Huddersfield HD3 4HS
Tel: 01484 642211
Fax: 01484 461002
E-mail: sales@ttsuk.com
Web site: www.ttsuk.com

VOLVO BUS AND COACH CENTRE
Parts Sales & Body Repair/Refurbishment Specialists
Byron Street Extension,
Loughborough LE11 5HE

TTS UK
Total Tool Solutions Limited
Newhaven Business Park
Lowergate
Milnsbridge
Huddersfield
HD3 4HS
T: 01484 642211
F: 01484 461002
E: sales@ttsuk.com
W: www.ttsuk.com

The Little Red Book 2011 - in association with tbf Transport Benevolent Fund

Tel: 01509 217700
Fax: 01509 238770
E-mail (Parts):
csparts@volvocoachsales.co.uk
Web site: www.volvo.com

WABCO AUTOMOTIVE UK LTD
Texas Street, Morley LS27 0HQ
Tel: 0113 251 2510.
Fax: 0113 251 2844.
Web site: www.wabco-auto.com

WACTON COACH SALES & SERVICES
Linton Trading Estate,
Bromyard HR7 4QL
Tel: 01885 482782.
Fax: 01885 482127

WALSH'S ENGINEERING
Barton Moss Road, Eccles,
Manchester M30 7RL
Tel: 0161 787 7017
Fax: 0161 787 7038
E-mail: walshs@gardnerdiesel.co.uk
Web site: www.gardnerdiesel.co.uk

TREVOR WIGLEY & SON BUS LTD
Passenger Vehicle Dismantling/Spares
Works: Boulder Bridge Lane,
off Shaw Lane, Barnsley S71 3HJ
Correspondence: 148 Royston Road,
Cudworth, Barnsley S72 8BN
Tel: 01226 713636
Fax: 01226 700199
E-mail: wigleys@btintenet.com
Web site: www.twigley.com

ZF POWERTRAIN
Stringes Close,
Willenhall WV13 1LE
Tel: 01902 366000
Fax: 01902 366504
E-mail: sales@powertrain.org.uk
Web site: www.powertrain.org.uk

Passenger Information Systems

ARRIVA BUS AND COACH
Lodge Garage, Whitehall Road West,
Gomersal, Cleckheaton, West Yorkshire
BD19 4BJ
Tel: 01274 681144
Fax: 01274 651198
E-mail: whiter@arriva.co.uk
Web site: www.arrivabusandcoach.co.uk

AVT SYSTEMS LTD
Units 3 & 4, Tything Road, Arden Forest
Industrial Estate, Alcester,
Warwickshire B49 6ES
Tel: 01789 400357
Fax: 01789 400359
E-mail: enquiries@avtsystems.co.uk.co.uk
Web site: www.avtsystems.co.uk

M BISSELL DISPLAY LTD
Unit 15, Beechwood Business Park,
Burdock Close, Cannock,
Staffordshire WS11 7GB
Tel: 01543 502115
Fax: 01543 502118
E-mail: sales@bisselldisplay.com
Web site: www.bisselldisplay.com

HANOVER DISPLAYS LTD
Unit 24, Cliffe Industrial Estate,
Lewes BN8 6JL
Tel: 01273 477528
Fax: 01273 407766
E-mail: hanover@hanoverdisplays.com
Web site: www.hanoverdisplays.com

INIT GMBH – INNOVATION IN TRANSPORT
32A Stoney Street, The Lace Market,
Nottingham NG1 1LL
Tel: 0870 890 4648
Fax: 0115 988 6917
E-mail: sales@init.co.uk
Web site: www.init.co.uk

J MURDOCH WIGHT LTD
Systems House, Pentland Industrial Estate,
Loanhead, Midlothian EH20 9QH
Tel: 0131 440 3633
Fax: 0131 440 3637
Web site: www.jmw-group.co.uk

JOURNEY PLAN LTD
Dickson Street, Dunfermline
KY12 7SL
Tel: 01383 731048
Fax: 01383 731788
Web site: www.journeyplan.co.uk

McKENNA BROTHERS LTD
McKenna House, Jubilee Road,
Middleton, Manchester M24 2LX
Tel: 0161 655 3244
Fax: 0161 655 3059
E-mail: info@mckennabrothers.co.uk
Web site: www.mckennabrothers.co.uk

MOTIONAL MEDIA LTD
Hillington Park Innovation Centre,
1 Ainslie Road, Hillington Industrial Estate,
Glasgow G52 4RU
Tel: 0141 585 6438
Fax: 0141 585 6301
Web site: www.momedia.tv

SSL SIMULATION SYSTEMS LTD
Unit 12, Market Industrial Estate,
Yatton BS49 4RF
Tel: 01934 838803
Fax: 01934 876202
E-mail: ssl@simulation-systems.co.uk
Web site: www.simulation-systems.co.uk

TRAPEZE GROUP (UK) LTD
The Mill, Staverton, Nr Trowbridge,
Bath BA14 6PH
Tel: 01225 784200
Fax: 01225 784222
E-Mail: info@trapezegroup.co.uk
Web site: www.trapezegroup.co.uk

VULTRON INTERNATIONAL LTD
Unit 2, Stadium Way, Elland Road,
Leeds LS11 0EW
Tel: 0113 387 7310
Fax: 0113 387 7317
E-mail: jmoorhouse@vultron.co.uk

Pneumatic Valves/Cylinders

OPTARE PARTS DIVISION (Rotherham)
Denby Way, Hellaby,
Rotherham S66 8HR
Tel: 01709 792000
Fax: 01709 792009
E-mail: parts@optare.com

PNEUMAX LTD
Unit 8, Venture Industrial Park,
Fareham Road, Gosport PO13 0BA
Tel: 01329 823999
Fax: 01329 822345
E-mail: sales@pneumax.co.uk
Web site: www.pneumax.co.uk

Rapid Transit/Priority Equipment

ALSTOM TRANSPORT SA
48 rue Albert Dhalenne,
F-93482 Saint-Ouen Cedex, France
Tel: 00 33 1 41 66 90 00
Fax: 00 33 1 41 66 96 66
Web site: www.transport.alstom.com

BALFOUR BEATTY RAIL PLANT LTD
PO Box 5065, Raynesway,
Derby DE21 7QZ
Tel: 07967 669551
Fax: 01332 288222
E-mail: info.bbrpl@bbrail.com
Web site: www.bbrail.com

BRECKNELL WILLIS & CO LTD
PO Box 10, Chard TA20 2DE
Tel: 01460 64941
Fax: 01460 66122
Web site: www.brecknell-willis.co.uk

BRISTOL ELECTRIC RAILBUS LTD
Heron House, Chiswick Mall,
London W4 2PR
Tel: 020 8995 3000
Fax: 020 8994 6060
E-mail: james@skinner.demon.co.uk

PARRY PEOPLE MOVERS LTD
Overend Road, Cradley Heath,
Dudley B64 7DD
Tel: 01384 569553
Fax: 01384 637753
E-mail: jpmparry@aol.com
Web site: www.parrypeoplemovers.com

SIEMENS TRAFFIC CONTROLS LTD
Sopers Lane, Poole BH17 7ER
Tel: 01202 782000
Web site: www.siemenstraffic.com

SUSTRACO LTD
Heron House, Chiswick Mall,
London W4 2PR
Tel: 020 8995 3000
Fax: 020 8994 6060
Web site: www.ultralightrail.com

Repairs/Refurbishment - see Body Repairs, above

Retarders & Speed Control Systems

ARRIVA BUS AND COACH
Lodge Garage, Whitehall Road West,
Gomersal, Cleckheaton, West Yorkshire
BD19 4BJ
Tel: 01274 681144
Fax: 01274 651198
E-mail: whiter@arriva.co.uk
Web site: www.arrivabusandcoach.co.uk

BUSS BIZZ
Goughs Transport Depot, Morestead,
Winchester SO21 1JD
Tel: 01962 715555/66.
Fax: 01962 714868.

CHASSIS DEVELOPMENTS LTD
Grovebury Road,
Leighton Buzzard LU7 8SL
Tel: 01525 374151
Fax: 01525 370127
Web site: www.chassisdevelopments.co.uk

GROENEVELD UK LTD
The Greentec Centre,
Gelders Hall Road, Shepshed,
Leicestershire LE12 9NH
Tel: 01509 600033
Fax: 01509 602000
E-mail: info@groeneveld.co.uk
Web site: www.groeneveld.co.uk

NUTEXA FRICTIONS LTD
PO Box 11, New Hall Lane,
Hoylake,
Wirral CH47 4DH
Tel: 0151 632 5903
Fax: 0151 632 5908
E-mail: sales@nutexafrictions.co.uk
Web Site: www.sergeant.co.uk

Trade Directory

TELMA RETARDER LTD
25 Clarke Road, Mount Farm,
Milton Keynes MK1 1LG
Tel: 01908 642822
Fax: 01908 641348
E-mail: telma@telma.co.uk
Web site: www.telma.co.uk

VOITH TURBO LTD
6 Beddington Farm Road,
Croydon CR0 4XB
Tel: 020 8667 0333
Fax: 020 8667 0403
E-mail: david.holdsworth@voith.com
Web site: www.voithturbo.com

WABCO AUTOMOTIVE UK LTD
Texas Street, Morley LS27 0HQ.
Tel: 0113 251 2510.
Fax: 0113 251 2844
Web site: www.wabco-auto.com

Reversing Safety Systems

ARRIVA BUS AND COACH
Lodge Garage, Whitehall Road West,
Gomersal, Cleckheaton,
West Yorkshire BD19 4BJ
Tel: 01274 681144
Fax: 01274 651198
E-mail: whiter@arriva.co.uk
Web site: www.arrivabusandcoach.co.uk

AUTOSOUND LTD
4 Lister Street, Dudley Hill,
Bradford BD4 9PQ
Tel: 01274 688990
Fax: 01274 651318
Web site: www.autosound.co.uk
E-mail: sales@autosound.co.uk

ASHTREE GLASS LTD
Brownroyd Street, Bradford BO8 9AF
Tel: 01274 546 732
Fax: 01274 548 525
E-mail: sales@ashtreeglass.co.uk
Web site: www.ashtreeglass.co.uk

AVT SYSTEMS LTD
Unit 3 & 4, Tything Road,
Arden Forest Trading Estate,
Alcester,
Warwickshire B49 6ES
Tel: 01789 400357
Fax: 01789 400359
E-mail: enquiries@avtsystems.co.uk
Web site: www.avtsystems.co.uk

BRIGADE ELECTRONICS PLC
Brigade House, The Mills, Station Road,
South Darenth DA4 9BD
Tel: 01322 420 300
Fax: 01322 420 343
E-mail: info@brigade-electronics.co.uk
Web site: www.brigade-electronics.com

CARLYLE BUS & COACH LTD
Carlyle Business Park,
Great Bridge Street, Swan Village,
West Bromwich B70 0XA
Tel: 0121 524 1200
Fax: 0121 524 1201
E-mail: admin@carlyleplc.co.uk
Web site: carlyleplc.co.uk

CLAN TOOLS & PLANT LTD
3 Greenhill Avenue, Giffnock,
Glasgow G46 6QX
Tel: 0141 638 8040 **Fax:** 0141 638 8881
E-mail: clantools@btconnect.com
Web site: www.clantools.com

EXPRESS COACH REPAIRS LTD
Outgang Lane, Pickering YO18 7JA
Tel: 01751 475215
Fax: 01751 475215
E-mail: info@expresscoachrepairs.co.uk
Web site: www.expresscoachrepairs.co.uk

GROENEVELD UK LTD
The Greentec Centre, Gelders Hall Road,
Shepshed, Leicestershire LE12 9NH
Tel: 01509 600033
Fax: 01509 602000
E-mail: info@groeneveld.co.uk
Web site: www.groeneveld.co.uk

KCP CAR & COMMERCIAL LTD
Unit 15, Hillside Business Park,
Kempson Way, Bury St Edmunds,
Suffolk IP32 7EA
Tel: 01284 750777
Fax: 01284 750773
E-mail: info@kcpcarandcommercial.co.uk
Web site: www.kcpcarandcommercial.co.uk

KELLETT (UK) LTD
8 Stevenson Way, Sheffield S9 3WZ
Tel: 0114 261 1122
Fax: 0114 261 1199
E-mail: sales@kellett.co.uk

PLAXTON PARTS
Ryton Road, Anston, Sheffield S25 4DL
Tel: 0833 822 6224
Fax: 01909 550050
E-mail: parts@plaxtonlimited.co.uk
Web site: www.plaxtonaftercare.co.uk

PLAXTON SERVICE
Ryton Road, Anston, Sheffield S25 4DL
Tel: 01909 551155
Fax: 01909 550050
E-mail: service@plaxtonlimited.co.uk
Web site: www.plaxtonaftercare.co.uk

Roller Blinds - Passenger & Driver

ARRIVA BUS AND COACH
Lodge Garage, Whitehall Road West,
Gomersal, Cleckheaton, West Yorkshire
BD19 4BJ
Tel: 01274 681144
Fax: 01274 651198
E-mail: whiter@arriva.co.uk
Web site: www.arrivabusandcoach.co.uk

CARLYLE BUS & COACH LTD
Carlyle Business Park, Great Bridge Street,
Swan Village, West Bromwich B70 0XA
Tel: 0121 524 1200
Fax: 0121 524 1201
E-mail: admin@carlyleplc.co.uk
Web site: carlyleplc.co.uk

HAPPICH V & I COMPONENTS LTD
Unit 30/31, Fort Industrial Park, Fort
Parkway, Castle Bromwich B35 7AR
Tel: 0121 747 4400
Fax: 0121 747 4977
E-mail: sales@happich.co.uk
Web site: www.happich.co.uk

PLAXTON PARTS
Ryton Road, Anston, Sheffield S25 4DL
Tel: 0833 822 6224
Fax: 01909 550050
E-mail: parts@plaxtonlimited.co.uk
Web site: www.plaxtonaftercare.co.uk

PLAXTON SERVICE
Ryton Road, Anston, Sheffield S25 4DL
Tel: 01909 551155
Fax: 01909 550050
E-mail: service@plaxtonlimited.co.uk
Web site: www.plaxtonaftercare.co.uk

TEMPLE MANUFACTURING CO LTD
Unit 2, First Avenue, West Denbigh,
Bletchley, Milton Keynes MK1 1 DX
Tel: 01908 642233
Fax: 01908 373396
E-mail: iantemple@btconnect.com

WIDNEY UK LTD
Plume Street, Aston, Birmingham B6 7SA
Tel: 0121 327 5500
Fax: 0121 328 2466
E-mail: richard@widney.co.uk
Web site: www.widney.co.uk

Roof-Lining Fabrics

ARDEE COACH TRIM LTD
Artnalivery, Ardee, Co Louth,
Republic of Ireland
Tel: 00 353 41 685 3599
Fax: 00 353 41 685 7016
E-mail: ardeecoachtrim@eircom.net

ARRIVA BUS AND COACH
Lodge Garage, Whitehall Road West,
Gomersal, Cleckheaton, West Yorkshire
BD19 4BJ
Tel: 01274 681144
Fax: 01274 651198
E-mail: whiter@arriva.co.uk
Web site: www.arrivabusandcoach.co.uk

AUTOMATE WHEEL COVERS LTD
California Mills, Oxford Road,
Gomersal BD19 4HQ
Tel: 01274 862700
Fax: 01274 851989
E-mail: sales@wheelcovers.co.uk
Web site: www.euroliners.com

AUTOMOTIVE TEXTILE INDUSTRIES
Unit 15 & 16, Priest Court, Springfield
Business Park, Grantham NG31 7BG
Tel: 01476 593050
Fax: 01476 593607
E-mail: sales@autotex.com
Web site: www.autotex.com

EXPRESS COACH REPAIRS LTD
Outgang Lane, Pickering YO18 7JA
Tel: 01751 475215
Fax: 01751 475215
E-mail: info@expresscoachrepairs.co.uk
Web site: www.expresscoachrepairs.co.uk

HAPPICH V & I COMPONENTS LTD
Unit 30/31, Fort Industrial Park, Fort
Parkway, Castle Bromwich B35 7AR
Tel: 0121 747 4400
Fax: 0121 747 4977
E-mail: sales@happich.co.uk
Web site: www.happich.co.uk

MARTYN INDUSTRIALS LTD
5 Brunel Way, Durranhill, Harraby,
Carlisle CA1 3NQ
Tel: 01228 544000
Fax: 01228 544001
E-mail: enquiries@martyn-industrials.co.uk
Web site: www.martyn-industrials.com

Seat Belts/Restraint Systems

ABACUS TRANSPORT PRODUCTS LTD
Abacus House, Highlode Industrial Estate,
Stockingfen Road,
Ramsey PE26 2RB
Tel: 01487 710700
Fax: 01487 710626
E-mail: f.riola@abacus-tp.com
Web site: www.abacus-tp.com

ARDEE COACH TRIM LTD
Artnalivery, Ardee, Co Louth,
Republic of Ireland
Tel: 00 353 41 685 3599
Fax: 00 353 41 685 7016
E-mail: ardeecoachtrim@eircom.net

Trade Directory

ARRIVA BUS AND COACH
Lodge Garage, Whitehall Road West,
Gomersal, Cleckheaton,
West Yorkshire BD19 4BJ
Tel: 01274 681144
Fax: 01274 651198
E-mail: whiter@arriva.co.uk
Web site: www.arrivabusandcoach.co.uk

CARLYLE BUS & COACH LTD
Carlyle Business Park,
Great Bridge Street, Swan Village,
West Bromwich B70 0XA
Tel: 0121 524 1200
Fax: 0121 524 1201
E-mail: admin@carlyleplc.co.uk
Web site: www.carlyleplc.co.uk

ELITE SERVICES LTD
Unit 3/6, Adswood Industrial Estate,
Adswood Road, Stockport SK3 8LF
Tel: 0161 480 0617
Fax: 0161 480 3099

EXPRESS COACH REPAIRS LTD
Outgang Lane, Pickering
YO18 7JA
Tel: 01751 475215
Fax: 01751 475215
E-mail: info@expresscoachrepairs.co.uk
Web site: www.expresscoachrepairs.co.uk

KCP CAR & COMMERCIAL LTD
Unit 15, Hillside Business Park,
Kempson Way, Bury St Edmunds,
Suffolk IP32 7EA
Tel: 01284 750777
Fax: 01284 750773
E-mail: info@kcpcarandcommercial.co.uk
Web site: www.kcpcarandcommercial.co.uk

LAWTON SERVICES LTD
Knutsford Road, Church Lawton,
Stoke-on-Trent ST7 3DN
Tel: 01270 882056
Fax: 01270 883014
E-mail: andrea@lawtonservices.co.uk
Web site: www.lawtonservices.co.uk

PARTLINE LTD
Dockfield Road,
Shipley BD17 7AZ
Tel: 01274 531531
Fax: 01274 531088
E-mail: sales@partline.co.uk
Web site: www.partline.co.uk

PLAXTON PARTS
Ryton Road, Anston, Sheffield S25 4DL
Tel: 0833 822 6224
Fax: 01909 550050
E-mail: parts@plaxtonlimited.co.uk
Web site: www.plaxtonaftercare.co.uk

PLAXTON SERVICE
Ryton Road, Anston, Sheffield S25 4DL
Tel: 01909 551155
Fax: 01909 550050
E-mail: service@plaxtonlimited.co.uk
Web site: www.plaxtonaftercare.co.uk

Q'STRAINT
Units 72-76 John Wilson Business Park,
Whitstable, Kent CT5 3QT
Tel: 01227 773 035
Fax: 01227 770 035
E-mail: tina@qstraint.co.uk
Web site: www.qstraint.com

RESCROFT LTD
20 Oxleasow Road, East Moons Moat,
Redditch B98 0RE
Tel: 01527 521300
Fax: 01527 521301
E-mail: info@rescroft.com
Web site: www.rescroft.com

SAFETEX LTD
Unit 16/17, Bookham Industrial Park,
Church Road, Bookham KT23 3EV
Tel: 01372 451272
Fax: 01372 451282
E-mail: sales@safetex.com
Web site: www.safetex.com

SECURON (AMERSHAM) LTD
The Hill, Winchmore Hill,
Amersham HP7 0NZ
Tel: 01494 434455
Fax: 01494 726499
E-mail: uksp@securon.co.uk
Web site: www.securon.co.uk

TRAMONTANA
Chapelknowe Road, Carfin,
Motherwell ML1 5LE
Tel: 01698 861790
Fax: 01698 860778
E-mail: wdt90@tiscali.co.uk
Web site: www.tramontanacoach.co.uk

UNWIN SAFETY SYSTEMS
Unwin House, The Horseshoe,
Coat Road, Martock TA12 6EY
Tel: 01935 827740
Fax: 01935 827760
E-mail: sales@unwin-safety.co.uk
Web site: wwwunwin-safety.com

Seats/Seat Cushions & Seat Frames

ABACUS TRANSPORT PRODUCTS LTD
Abacus House, Highlode Industrial Estate,
Stockingfen Road,
Ramsey PE26 2RB
Tel: 01487 710700
Fax: 01487 710626
E-mail: f.riola@abacus-tp.com
Web site: www.abacus-tp.com

holdsworth
...moving forward to a greener future

second nature
sustainability is Second Nature

Environmental plush moquette seating fabrics with a complementary range of high performance flat-wovens & coordinating trim fabrics.

Holdsworth Fabrics **T:** 01924 481144   **F:** 01924 495605   www.holdsworthfabrics.com

The Little Red Book 2011 - in association with Transport Benevolent Fund

Trade Directory

ARDEE COACH TRIM LTD
Artnalivery, Ardee, Co Louth,
Republic of Ireland
Tel: 00 353 41 685 3599
Fax: 00 353 41 685 7016
E-mail: ardeecoachtrim@eircom.net

ARRIVA BUS AND COACH
Lodge Garage, Whitehall Road West,
Gomersal, Cleckheaton, West Yorkshire
BD19 4BJ
Tel: 01274 681144
Fax: 01274 651198
E-mail: whiter@arriva.co.uk
Web site: www.arrivabusandcoach.co.uk

BERNSTEIN ENGINEERING LTD
Unit 4, East 41 Garside Way, Stocklake,
Aylesbury HP20 1BH
Tel: 01296 395889
Fax: 01296 394939
E-mail: contact@bernsteinengineering.co.uk
Web site: www.bernsteinengineering.co.uk

CARLYLE BUS & COACH LTD
Carlyle Business Park, Great Bridge Street,
Swan Village, West Bromwich B70 0XA
Tel: 0121 524 1200
Fax: 0121 524 1201
E-mail: admin@carlyleplc.co.uk
Web site: www.carlyleplc.co.uk

CHAPMAN DRIVER SEATING
68 Burners Lane, Kiln Farm,
Milton Keynes MK11 3HD
Tel: 0845 838 2305
Fax: 0845 838 2909
E-mail: sales@chapmandriverseating.com
Web site: www.chapmandriverseating.com

COGENT PASSENGER SEATING LTD
Prydwen Road, Swansea West Industrial
Estate, Swansea SA5 4HN
Tel: 01792 585444
Fax: 01792 588191
E-mail: enquiries@cogentseating.co.uk
Web site: www.cogentseating.co.uk

DUOFLEX LTD
Trimmingham House, 2 Shires Road,
Buckingham Road Industrial Estate,
Brackley NN13 7EZ
Tel: 01280 701366
Fax: 01280 704799
E-mail: sales@duoflex.co.uk
Web site: www.duoflex.co.uk

EXPRESS COACH REPAIRS LTD
Outgang Lane, Pickering YO18 7JA
Tel: 01751 475215
Fax: 01751 475215
E-mail: info@expresscoachrepairs.co.uk
Web site: www.expresscoachrepairs.co.uk

HAPPICH V & I COMPONENTS LTD
Unit 30/31, Fort Industrial Park, Fort
Parkway, Castle Bromwich B35 7AR
Tel: 0121 747 4400
Fax: 0121 747 4977
E-mail: sales@happich.co.uk
Web site: www.happich.co.uk

HOLDSWORTH FABRICS LTD
Hopton Mills, Mirfield WF1 8HE
Tel: 01924 481144
Fax: 01924 495605
E-mail: info@camirafabrics.co.uk
Web site: www.holdsworthfabrics.com

JBF SERVICES LTD
Southedge Works, Hipperholme,
Halifax HX3 8EF
Tel: 01422 202840 **Fax:** 01422 206070
E-mail: jbfservices@aol.com

KAB SEATING LTD
Round Spinney, Northampton NN3 8RS
Tel: 01604 790500
Fax: 01604 790155
E-mail: infouk@cvgrp.com
Web site: www.kabseating.com

LAWTON SERVICES LTD
Knutsford Road, Church Lawton,
Stoke-on-Trent ST7 3DN
Tel: 01270 882056
Fax: 01270 883014
E-mail: andrea@lawtonservices.co.uk
Web site: www.lawtonservices.co.uk

PHOENIX SEATING LTD
Unit 47, Bay 3, Second Avenue,
Pensnett Estate,
Kingswinford DY6 7UZ
Tel: 01384 296622
Fax: 01384 287831
E-mail: sales@phoenixseating.co.uk
Web site: www.phoenixseating.com

P.L. TRIM LTD
Burton Road, Blackpool FY4 4NW
Tel: 01253 696033
Fax: 01253 696033
E-mail: enquiries@pltrim.co.uk
Web site: www.pltrim.co.uk

PLAXTON PARTS
Ryton Road, Anston,
Sheffield S25 4DL
Tel: 0833 822 6224
Fax: 01909 550050
E-mail: parts@plaxtonlimited.co.uk
Web site: www.plaxtonaftercare.co.uk

PLAXTON SERVICE
Ryton Road, Anston,
Sheffield S25 4DL
Tel: 01909 551155
Fax: 01909 550050
E-mail: service@plaxtonlimited.co.uk
Web site: www.plaxtonaftercare.co.uk

RESCROFT LTD
20 Oxleasow Road, East Moons Moat,
Redditch B98 0RE
Tel: 01527 521300
Fax: 01527 521301
E-mail: info@rescroft.com
Web site: www.rescroft.com

SCANDUS UK
Unit 21, Gainsborough Trading Estate,
Rufford Road,
Stourbridge DY9 7ND
Tel: 01384 443409
Fax: 01384 443 932
Web site: www.scandusuk.co.uk

TUBE PRODUCTS LTD
PO Box 13, Hope Lane, Oldbury,
Warley B69 4PF
Tel: 0121 552 1511
Fax: 0121 544 6026

WOODBRIDGE FOAM UK LTD
Stakehill Industrial Estate,
Manchester M24 2SJ
Tel: 0161 654 2500
Fax: 0161 653 4433

Shelters/Street Furniture

M BISSELL DISPLAY LTD
Unit 15, Beechwood Business Park,
Burdock Close, Cannock, Staffordshire
WS11 7GB
Tel: 01543 502115
Fax: 01543 502118
E-mail: sales@bisselldisplay.com
Web site: www.bisselldisplay.com

BUS SHELTERS LTD
Dyffryn Business Park,
Llantwit Major Road, Llandow,
Cardiff CF71 7PY
Tel: 01446 795444
Fax: 01446 793344
E-mail: bus@shelters.co.uk
Web site: www.shelters.co.uk

CARMANAH TECHNOLOGIES GROUP
UK Retailer: Green Solar Solutions Ltd,
Brighton
Tel: 01273 549345
E-mail: sales@greensolarsolutions.co.uk
Web site: www.greensolarsolutions.co.uk

GABRIEL & COMPANY LTD
Abro Works, 10 Hay Hall Road,
Tyseley, Birmingham B11 2AU
Tel: 0121 248 3333
Fax: 0121 248 3330
E-mail: john.gabriel@gabrielco.com
Web site: www.gabrielco.com

MACEMAIN + AMSTAD
Boyle Road, Willowbrook Industrial Estate,
Corby NN17 5XU
Tel: 01536 401331
Fax: 01536 401298
E-mail: enquiries@macemainamstad.com
Web site: www.macemainamstad.com

QUEENSBURY SHELTERS
Queensbury House, Fitzherbert Road,
Farlington, Portsmouth PO6 1SE
Tel: 023 9221 0052
Fax: 023 9221 0059
Web site: www.queensbury.org

TRUEFORM ENGINEERING LTD
Unit 4, Pasadena Trading Estate,
Pasadena Close, Hayes UB3 3NQ
Tel: 020 8561 4959
Fax: 020 8848 1397
E-mail: sales@trueform.co.uk
Web site: www..trueform.co.uk

WHITELEY ELECTRONICS
Victoria Street,
Mansfield NG18 5RW
Tel: 01623 415600
Fax: 01623 420484
E-mail: sales@whiteleyelectronics.com
Web site: www.whiteleyelectronics.com

Shock Absorbers/Suspension

ARRIVA BUS AND COACH
Lodge Garage, Whitehall Road West,
Gomersal, Cleckheaton, West Yorkshire
BD19 4BJ
Tel: 01274 681144
Fax: 01274 651198
E-mail: whiter@arriva.co.uk
Web site: www.arrivabusandcoach.co.uk

CRESCENT FACILITIES LTD
72 Willow Crescent, Chapeltown, Sheffield
S35 1QS
Tel/Fax: 0114 245 1050
E-mail: cfl.chris@btinternet.com
Web site: www.cflparts.com

DIRECT PARTS LTD
Unit 1, Churnet Court, Churnetside Business
Park, Harrison Way,
Cheddleton ST13 7EF
Tel: 01538 361777
Fax: 01538 369100
E-mail: sales@direct-group.co.uk
Web site: www.direct-group.co.uk

ERENTEK LTD
Malt Kiln Lane, Waddington,
Lincoln LN5 9RT

Trade Directory

Tel: 01522 720065
Fax: 01522 729155
E-mail: sale@erentek.co.uk
Web site: www.erentek.co.uk

GLIDE RITE
Mill Lane, Passfield, Liphook GU30 7RP
Tel: 01428 751711 **Fax:** 01428 751677
Web site: www.glide-rite.net

IMEXPART LTD
Links 31, Willowbridge Way,
Whitwood, Castleford WF10 5NP
Tel: 0845 605 0404
Fax: 01977 513412
E-mail: sales@imexpart.com
Web site: www.imexpart.com

KCP CAR & COMMERCIAL LTD
Unit 15, Hillside Business Park,
Kempson Way, Bury St Edmunds,
Suffolk IP32 7EA
Tel: 01284 750777
Fax: 01284 750773
E-mail: info@kcpcarandcommercial.co.uk
Web site: www.kcpcarandcommercial.co.uk

KELLETT (UK) LTD
8 Stevenson Way, Sheffield S9 3WZ.
Tel: 0114 261 1122
Fax: 0114 261 1199
E-mail: sales@kellett.co.uk

OPTARE PARTS DIVISION
(Rotherham)
Denby Way, Hellaby, Rotherham S66 8HR
Tel: 01709 792000
Fax: 01709 792009
E-mail: parts@optare.com

PARTLINE LTD
Dockfield Road, Shipley BD17 7AZ
Tel: 01274 531511
Fax: 01274 531088
E-mail: sales@partline.co.uk
Web site: www.partline.co.uk

POLYBUSH
Clywedog Road South, Wrexham Industrial
Estate, Wrexham LL13 9XS
Tel: 01978 664316
Fax: 01978 661190
E-mail: sales@polybush.co.uk
Web site: www.polybush.co.uk

ROADLINK INTERNATIONAL LTD
Strawberry Lane, Willenhall, West Midlands
WV13 3RL
Tel: 01902 636206
Fax: 01902 631515
E-mail: sales@roadlink-international.co.uk
Web site: www.roadlink-international.co.uk

SHAWSON SUPPLY LTD
12 Station Road, Saintfield, County Down,
Northern Ireland BT24 7DU
Tel: 028 9751 0994
Fax: 028 9751 0816
E-mail: info@shawsonsupply.com
Web site: www.shawsonsupply.com

Steering

ARRIVA BUS AND COACH
Lodge Garage, Whitehall Road West,
Gomersal, Cleckheaton, West Yorkshire
BD19 4BJ
Tel: 01274 681144
Fax: 01274 651198
E-mail: whiter@arriva.co.uk
Web site: www.arrivabusandcoach.co.uk

CRESCENT FACILITIES LTD
72 Willow Crescent, Chapeltown, Sheffield
S35 1QS

Tel/Fax: 0114 245 1050
E-mail: cfl.chris@btinternet.com
Web site: www.cflparts.com

DIRECT PARTS LTD
Unit 1, Churnet Court, Churnetside Business
Park, Harrison Way, Cheddleton ST13 7EF
Tel: 01538 361777
Fax: 01538 369100
E-mail: sales@direct-group.co.uk
Web site: www.direct-group.co.uk

HL SMITH TRANSMISSIONS LTD
Enterprise Business Park, Cross Road,
Albrighton, Wolverhampton WV7 3BJ
Tel: 01902 373011
Fax: 01902 373608
Web site: www.hlsmith.co.uk

IMEXPART LTD
Links 31, Willowbridge Way, Whitwood,
Castleford WF10 5NP
Tel: 0845 605 0404
Fax: 01977 513412
E-mail: sales@imexpart.com
Web site: www.imexpart.com

IMPERIAL ENGINEERING
Delamare Road, Cheshunt, Hertfordshire
EN8 9UD
Tel: 01992 634255
Fax: 01992 630506
E-mail: orders@imperialengineering.co.uk
Web site: www.imperialengineering.co.uk

KCP CAR & COMMERCIAL LTD
Unit 15, Hillside Business Park, Kempson
Way, Bury St Edmunds, Suffolk IP32 7EA
Tel: 01284 750777
Fax: 01284 750773
E-mail: info@kcpcarandcommercial.co.uk
Web site: www.kcpcarandcommercial.co.uk

OPTARE PARTS DIVISION (Rotherham)
Denby Way, Hellaby, Rotherham S66 8HR
Tel: 01709 792000
Fax: 01709 792009
E-mail: parts@optare.com

OPTARE PRODUCT SUPPORT LONDON
Unit 9, Eurocourt, Olivers Close, West
Thurrock RM20 3EE
Tel: 08444 123222
Fax: 01708 869920
E-mail: london.service@optare.com

OPTARE PRODUCT SUPPORT ROTHERHAM
Denby Way, Hellaby, Rotherham S66 8HR
Tel: 01709 535101
Fax: 01709 535103
E-mail: rotherham.service@optare.com

OPTARE PRODUCT SUPPORT SCOTLAND
Unit 7, Cumbernauld Business Park,
Ward Park Road, Cumbernauld G67 3JZ
Tel: 01236 726738
Fax: 01236 795651
E-mail: scotland.service@optare.com

PARTLINE LTD
Dockfield Road, Shipley BD17 7AZ
Tel: 01274 531511
Fax: 01274 531088
E-mail: sales@partline.co.uk
Web site: www.partline.co.uk

PSS - STEERING & HYDRAULICS DIVISION
Folgate Road, North Walsham NR28 0AJ
Tel: 01692 406017
Fax: 01692 406957
E-mail: sales@pss.co.uk
Web site: www.pss.co.uk

ROADLINK INTERNATIONAL LTD
Strawberry Lane, Willenhall,
West Midlands WV13 3RL
Tel: 01902 636206
Fax: 01902 631515
E-mail: sales@roadlink-international.co.uk
Web site: www.roadlink-international.co.uk

SHAWSON SUPPLY LTD
12 Station Road, Saintfield, County Down,
Northern Ireland BT24 7DU
Tel: 028 9751 0994
Fax: 028 9751 0816
E-mail: info@shawsonsupply.com
Web site: www.shawsonsupply.com

ZF POWERTRAIN
Stringes Close, Willenhall WV13 1LE
Tel: 01902 366000
Fax: 01902 366504
E-mail: sales@powertrain.org.uk
Web site: www.powertrain.org.uk

Surveillance Systems

AUTOSOUND LTD
4 Lister Street, Dudley Hill,
Bradford BD4 9PQ
Tel: 01274 688990
Fax: 01274 651318
E-mail: sales@autosound.co.uk
Web site: www.autosound.co.uk

AVT SYSTEMS LTD
Unit 3 & 4, Tything Road, Arden Forest
Trading Estate, Alcester,
Warwickshire B49 6ES
Tel: 01789 400 357
Fax: 01789 400 359
E-mail: enquiries@avtsystems.co.uk
Web site: www.avtsystems.co.uk

BRIGADE ELECTRONICS PLC
Brigade House, The Mills, Station Road,
South Darenth DA4 9BD
Tel: 01322 420 300
Fax: 01322 420 343
E-mail: info@brigade-electronics.co.uk
Web site: www.brigade-electronics.com

CLAN TOOLS & PLANT LTD
3 Greenhill Avenue, Giffnock,
Glasgow G46 6QX
Tel: 0141 638 8040
Fax: 0141 638 8881
E-mail: clantools@btconnect.com
Web site: www.clantools.com

CYBERLYNE COMMUNICATIONS LTD
Unit 5, Hatfield Way,
South Church Enterprise Park,
Bishop Auckland,
Durham DL14 6XF
Tel: 01388 773761
Fax: 01388 773778
E-mail: sales@cyberlyne.co.uk
Web site: www.cyberlyne.co.uk

DIRECT PARTS LTD
Unit 1, Churnet Court,
Churnetside Business Park,
Harrison Way,
Cheddleton ST13 7EF
Tel: 01538 361777
Fax: 01538 369100
E-mail: sales@direct-group.co.uk
Web site: www.direct-group.co.uk

FUEL THEFT SOLUTIONS LTD
20 Yew Tree Court, Alsager,
Stoke on Trent ST7 2WR
Tel: 0845 077 3921
Fax: 0845 077 3922
E-mail: sales@dieseldye.com
Web site: www.dieseldye.com

Trade Directory

GROENEVELD UK LTD
The Greentec Centre, Gelders Hall Road, Shepshed, Leicestershire LE12 9NH
Tel: 01509 600033
Fax: 01509 602000
E-mail: info@groeneveld.co.uk
Web site: www.groeneveld.co.uk

KELLETT (UK) LTD
8 Stevenson Way, Sheffield S9 3WZ.
Tel: 0114 261 1122
Fax: 0114 261 1199
E-mail: sales@kellett.co.uk

KNORR-BREMSE SYSTEMS FOR COMMERCIAL VEHICLES LTD
Douglas Road, Kingswood, Bristol BS15 8NL
Tel: 0117 984 6100
Fax: 0117 984 6101
Web site: www.knorr-bremse.com

LOOK CCTV LTD
Unit 4, Wyrefields, Poulton-le-Fylde FY6 8JX
Tel: 01253 891222
Fax: 01253 891221
E-mail: enquiries@lookcctv.com
Web site: www.lookcctv.com

PSV PRODUCTS
The Red House, Underbridge Lane, Higher Walton, Warrington WA4 5QR
Tel: 01925 210220
Fax: 01925 601534
E-mail: info@psvproducts.com
Web site: www.psvproducts.com

WABCO AUTOMOTIVE UK LTD
Texas Street, Morley LS27 0HQ.
Tel: 0113 251 2510
Fax: 0113 251 2844
Web site: www.wabco-auto.com

Suspension

ARRIVA BUS AND COACH
Lodge Garage, Whitehall Road West, Gomersal, Cleckheaton, West Yorkshire BD19 4BJ
Tel: 01274 681144
Fax: 01274 651198
E-mail: whiter@arriva.co.uk
Web site: www.arrivabusandcoach.co.uk

CRESCENT FACILITIES LTD
72 Willow Crescent, Chapeltown, Sheffield S35 1QS
Tel/Fax: 0114 245 1050
E-mail: cfl.chris@btinternet.com
Web site: www.cflparts.com

ERENTEK LTD
Malt Kiln Lane, Waddington, Lincoln LN5 9RT
Tel: 01522 720065
Fax: 01522 729155
E-mail: sales@erentek.co.uk
Web site: www.erentek.co.uk

IMEXPART LTD
Links 31, Willowbridge Way, Whitwood, Castleford WF10 5NP
Tel: 0845 605 0404
Fax: 01977 513412
E-mail: sales@imexpart.com
Web site: www.imexpart.com

PARTLINE LTD
Dockfield Road, Shipley BD17 7AZ
Tel: 01274 531531
Fax: 01274 531088
E-mail: sales@partline.co.uk
Web site: www.partline.co.uk

PLAXTON SERVICE
Ryton Road, Anston, Sheffield S25 4DL
Tel: 01909 551155
Fax: 01909 550050
E-mail: service@plaxtonlimited.co.uk
Web site: www.plaxtonaftercare.co.uk

ROADLINK INTERNATIONAL LTD
Strawberry Lane, Willenhall, West Midlands WV13 3RL
Tel: 01902 636206
Fax: 01902 631515
E-mail: sales@roadlink-international.co.uk
Web site: www.roadlink-international.co.uk

Tachographs

ARRIVA BUS AND COACH
Lodge Garage, Whitehall Road West, Gomersal, Cleckheaton, West Yorkshire BD19 4BJ
Tel: 01274 681144
Fax: 01274 651198
E-mail: whiter@arriva.co.uk
Web site: www.arrivabusandcoach.co.uk

CHASSIS DEVELOPMENTS LTD
Grovebury Road, Leighton Buzzard LU7 8SL.
Tel: 01525 374151
Fax: 01525 370127
E-mail: Sales@chassisdevelopments.com
Web site: www.chassisdevelopment.co.uk

THOMAS HARDIE COMMERCIALS LTD
Newstet Road, Knowsley Industrial Park, Liverpool L33 7TJ
Tel: 0151 549 3000
E-mail: info@thardie.co.uk

KCP CAR & COMMERCIAL LTD
Unit 15, Hillside Business Park, Kempson Way, Bury St Edmunds, Suffolk IP32 7EA
Tel: 01284 750777
Fax: 01284 750773
E-mail: info@kcpcarandcommercial.co.uk
Web site: www.kcpcarandcommercial.co.uk

MARSHALLS COACHES LLP
Firbank Way, Leighton Buzzard LU7 3BD
Tel: 01525 376077
Fax: 01525 850967
E-mail: info@marshalls-coaches.co.uk
Web site: www.marshalls-coaches.co.uk

OPTARE PRODUCT SUPPORT LONDON
Unit 9, Eurocourt, Olivers Close, West Thurrock RM20 3EE
Tel: 08444 123222
Fax: 01708 869920
E-mail: london.service@optare.com

OPTARE PRODUCT SUPPORT ROTHERHAM
Denby Way, Hellaby, Rotherham S66 8HR
Tel: 01709 535101
Fax: 01709 535103
E-mail: rotherham.service@optare.com

OPTARE PRODUCT SUPPORT SCOTLAND
Unit 7, Cumbernauld Business Park, Ward Park Road, Cumbernauld G67 3JZ
Tel: 01236 726738
Fax: 01236 795651
E-mail: scotland.service@optare.com

PLAXTON SERVICE
Ryton Road, Anston, Sheffield S25 4DL
Tel: 01909 551155
Fax: 01909 550050
E-mail: service@plaxtonlimited.co.uk
Web site: www.plaxtonaftercare.co.uk

SIEMENS VDO TRADING LTD
36 Gravelly Industrial Park, Birmingham B24 8TA
Tel: 0121 326 1234
Fax: 0121 326 1299
Web site: www.siemens-datatrack.com

WARD INTERNATIONAL CONSULTING LTD
Funtley Court, 19 Funtley Hill, Fareham PO16 7UY
Tel: 01329 280280
Fax: 01329 221010
E-mail: info@wardint.co.uk
Web site: www.wardint.com

Tachograph Calibrators

ARRIVA BUS AND COACH
Lodge Garage, Whitehall Road West, Gomersal, Cleckheaton, West Yorkshire BD19 4BJ
Tel: 01274 681144
Fax: 01274 651198
E-mail: whiter@arriva.co.uk
Web site: www.arrivabusandcoach.co.uk

MARSHALLS COACHES LLP
Firbank Way, Leighton Buzzard LU7 3BD
Tel: 01525 376077
Fax: 01525 850967
E-mail: info@marshalls-coaches.co.uk
Web site: www.marshalls-coaches.co.uk

OPTARE PRODUCT SUPPORT LONDON
Unit 9, Eurocourt, Olivers Close, West Thurrock RM20 3EE
Tel: 08444 123222
Fax: 01708 869920
E-mail: london.service@optare.com

OPTARE PRODUCT SUPPORT ROTHERHAM
Denby Way, Hellaby, Rotherham S66 8HR
Tel: 01709 535101
Fax: 01709 535103
E-mail: rotherham.service@optare.com

OPTARE PRODUCT SUPPORT SCOTLAND
Unit 7, Cumbernauld Business Park, Ward Park Road, Cumbernauld G67 3JZ
Tel: 01236 726738
Fax: 01236 795651
E-mail: scotland.service@optare.com

PLAXTON SERVICE
Ryton Road, Anston, Sheffield S25 4DL
Tel: 01909 551155
Fax: 01909 550050
E-mail: service@plaxtonlimited.co.uk
Web site: www.plaxtonaftercare.co.uk

SIEMENS VDO TRADING LTD
36 Gravelly Industrial Park, Birmingham B24 8TA
Tel: 0121 326 1234
Fax: 0121 326 1299
Web site: www.siemens-datatrack.com

Tachograph Chart Analysis Service

CHASSIS DEVELOPMENTS LTD
Grovebury Road, Leighton Buzzard LU7 8SL.
Tel: 01525 374151
Fax: 01525 370127
E-mail: sales@chassisdevelopments.com
Web site: www.chassissdevelopments.co.uk

IBPTS
43 Cage Lane, Felixstowe,

BUSES magazine

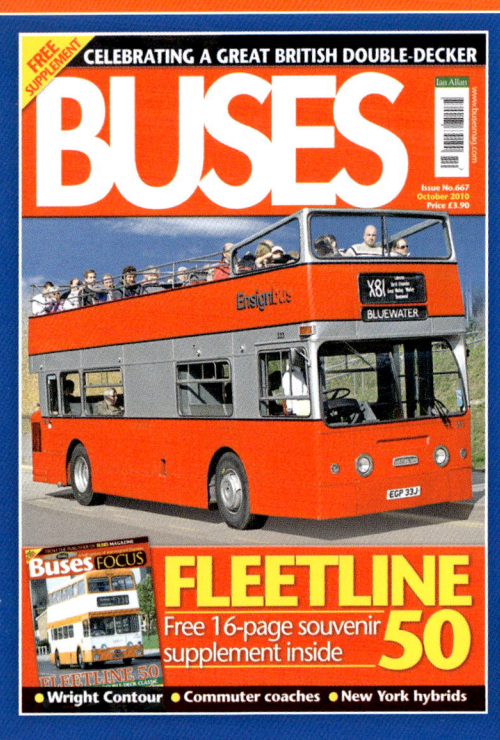

Buses offers unrivalled content and superb coverage of the bus and coach industry

- Get the latest news on the bus and coach industries
- The most comprehensive photographic coverage of new developments
- Receive each issue 'hot off the press' before the shops
- Convenient home delivery so that you never miss an issue
- **FREE** membership to the Ian Allan Publishing Subs Club
- **FREE** personalised Subscription Loyalty Card
- **EXCLUSIVE** access to new online site with great subscriber benefits, offers and competitions.

Visit www.ianallanmagazines.com/subsclub for more details

CONTACT OUR SUBSCRIPTIONS DEPARTMENT TO FIND OUT ABOUT OUR LATEST OFFERS!

CALL +44 (0)1932 266622

QUOTE CODE LRB11 - SUBSCRIBE TODAY!

Suffolk OP11 9BJ
Tel: 01394 672 344
Fax: 01394 672 344
E-mail: info@ibpts.co.uk
Web site: www.ibpts.co.uk

SIEMENS VDO TRADING LTD
36 Gravelly Industrial Park,
Birmingham B24 8TA
Tel: 0121 326 1234
Fax: 0121 326 1299
Web site: www.siemens-datatrack.com

TRANSPORT & TRAINING SERVICES LTD
Warrington Business Park, Long Lane,
Warrington WA2 8TX
Tel: 01925 243 500
Fax: 01925 243 000
E-mail: tachographsuk@aol.com
Web site: www.transporttrainingservices.com

Tickets, Ticket Machines and Ticket Systems

ACT - APPLIED CARD TECHNOLOGIES
Langley Gate, Kington Langley,
Chippenham SN15 5SE
Tel: 01249 751200
Fax: 01249 751201
E-mail: info@card.co.uk
Web site: www.card.co.uk

ALMEX UK
Metric House,
Westmead Industrial Estate Westlea,
Swindon SN5 7AD
Tel: 01793 647934
Fax: 01793 647932
E-mail: info@almex.co.uk
Web site: www.almex.co.uk

ATOS ORIGIN
4 Triton Square, Regents Place,
London NW1 3HG
Tel: 020 7830 4444
Fax: 020 7830 4445
Web site: www.atosorigin.co.uk

BEMROSEBOOTH LTD
Stockholm Road, Sutton Fields Industrial Estate, Hull HU7 0XY
Tel: 01482 826343
Fax: 01482 371386
E-mail: lprecious@bemrosebooth.com
Web site: www.bemrosebooth.com

CANN PRINT
Commercial Centre, Main Road,
Kilmarnock KA3 6LX
Tel: 01563 572440
Fax: 01563 544933
E-mail: info@cannprint.com
Web site: www.cannprint.com

CUBIC TRANSPORTATION SYSTEMS LTD
AFC House, Honeycrock Lane,
Salfords, Redhill RH1 5LA
Tel: 01737 782200
Fax: 01737 789759
Web site: www.cubic.com

DE LA RUE
De La Rue House, Jays Close,
Viables, Basingstoke RG22 4BS
Tel: 01256 605000
Fax: 01256 605004
Web site: www.delarue.com

KEITH EDMONDSON TICKET ROLLS
Garden House, Tittensor Road,
Tittensor Stoke-on-Trent
ST12 9HQ
Tel: 01782 372305
Fax: 01782 351136
E-mail: keith@ticketrolls.co.uk
Web site: www.ticketrolls.co.uk

ETMSS LTD
c/o Ground Floor, Austin House,
43 Poole Road, Westbourne,
Bournemouth BH4 9DN
Tel: 0844 800 9299
E-mail: info@etmss.com
Web Site: www.etmss.com

JOHN GROVES TICKET SYSTEMS
Unit 10, North Circular Business Centre,
400 NCR, London NW10 0JG
Tel: 020 8830 1222
Fax: 020 8830 1223
E-Mail: sales@jgts.co.uk
Web site: www.jgts.co.uk

INIT GmbH – INNOVATION IN TRANSPORT
32a Stoney Street, The Lace Market,
Nottingham NG1 1LL
Tel: 0870 890 4648
Fax: 0115 988 6917
E-mail: sales@init.co.uk
Web site: www.init-ka.de

MARK TERRILL TICKET MACHINERY
5 De Grey Close, Lewes BN7 2JR
Tel: 01273 474816
Fax: 01273 474816
E-mail: mark.terrill@ukonline.co.uk

PAYPOINT PLC
1 The Boulevard, Shire Park, Welwyn Garden City AL7 1EL
Tel: 01707 60300
E-mail: grahambloye@paypoint.co.uk
Web site: www.paypoint.co.uk

SCAN COIN LTD
110 Broadway, Salford Quays
M50 2UW
Tel: 0161 873 0505
Fax: 0161 873 0501
E-mail: sales@scancoin.co.uk
Web site: www.scancoin.co.uk

SCHADES LTD
Brittain Drive, Codnor Gate Business Park,
Ripley DE5 3RZ
Tel: 01773 748721
Fax: 01773 745601
Web site: www.schades.com
E-mail: sales@schades.co.uk

STUART MANUFACTURING CO LTD
Craft House, 135 Hayes Lane,
Kenley CR8 5JR
Tel: 020 8668 8107
Fax: 020 8668 8277
E-mail: sales@smco.co.uk
Web site: www.smco.co.uk

THOMAS AUTOMATION LTD
5 Weldon Road, Loughborough
LE11 5RN
Tel: 01509 265692
Fax: 0700 600 7749
E-mail: sales@thomasa.co.uk
Web site: www.thomasa.co.uk

TICKETER
Riverside Centre, 82 Station Road,
Barnes, London SW13 0LS
Tel: 0844 800 9299
E-mail: sales@ticketer.co.uk
Web site: www.ticketer.co.uk

TRANSPORT TICKET SERVICES LTD
Yew Tree Cottage, Newcastle,
Monmouth NP25 5NT
Tel/Fax: 01600 750650
E-mail: ttservices@tiscali.co.uk
Web site: www.ticket-machines.co.uk

WAYFARER (PARKEON TRANSIT) LTD
10 Willis Way, Fleets Industrial Estate,
Poole, Dorset BH15 3SS
Tel: 01202 339339
Fax: 01202 339369
E-mail: sales_uk@parkeon.com
Web site: www.parkeon.com

Timetable Display Frames

M BISSELL DISPLAY LTD
Unit 15, Beechwood Business Park,
Burdock Close, Cannock,
Staffordshire WS11 7GB
Tel: 01543 502115
Fax: 01543 502118
E-mail: sales@bisselldisplay.com
Web site: www.bisselldisplay.com

BROADWATER MOULDINGS LTD
Benacre House, Ellough, Beccles,
Suffolk NR34 7XD
Tel: 01502 719310
Fax: 01502 471942
E-mail: info@broadwater.co.uk
Web site: www.broadwater.co.uk

Toilet Equipment

ARRIVA BUS AND COACH
Lodge Garage, Whitehall Road West,
Gomersal, Cleckheaton,
West Yorkshire BD19 4BJ
Tel: 01274 681144
Fax: 01274 651198
E-mail: whiter@arriva.co.uk
Web site: www.arrivabusandcoach.co.uk

BRADTECH LTD
Unit 3, Ladford Covert, Seighford,
Stafford ST18 9QL
Tel: 01785 282800
Fax: 01785 282558
E-mail: sales@bradtech.ltd.uk
Web site: www.bradtech.ltd.uk

CARLYLE BUS & COACH LTD
Carlyle Business Park,
Great Bridge Street, Swan Village,
West Bromwich B70 0XA
Tel: 0121 524 1200
Fax: 0121 524 1201
E-mail: admin@carlyleplc.co.uk
Web site: www.carlyleplc.co.uk

ELSAN LTD
Bellbrook Park, Uckfield, East Sussex
TN22 1QF
Tel: 01825 748200
Fax: 01825 761212
E-mail: sales@elsan.co.uk
Web site: www.elsan.co.uk

EXPRESS COACH REPAIRS LTD
Outgang Lane, Pickering YO18 7JA
Tel: 01751 475215
Fax: 01924 475215
E-mail: info@expresscoachrepairs.co.uk
Web site: www.expresscoachrepairs.co.uk

LAWTON SERVICES LTD
Knutsford Road, Church Lawton,
Stoke-on-Trent ST7 3DN
Tel: 01270 882056
Fax: 01270 883014
E-mail: andrea@lawtonservices.co.uk
Web site: www.lawtonservices.co.uk

PLAXTON SERVICE
Ryton Road, Anston, Sheffield S25 4DL

Trade Directory

The Little Red Book 2011 - in association with *tbf* Transport Benevolent Fund

Trade Directory

Tel: 01909 551155
Fax: 01909 550050
E-mail: service@plaxtonlimited.co.uk
Web site: www.plaxtonaftercare.co.uk

PSV PRODUCTS
The Red House, Underbridge Lane, Higher Walton, Warrington WA4 5QR
Tel: 01925 210220
Fax: 01925 601534
E-mail: info@psvproducts.com
Web site: www.psvproducts.com

SHADES TECHNICS LTD
Units E3 & E4, Rd Park, Stephenson Close, Hoddesdon, Hertfordshire EN11 0BW
Tel: 01992 501683
Fax: 01992 501669
E-mail: sales@shades-technics.com
Web site: www.shades-technics.com

Transmission Overhaul

ARRIVA BUS AND COACH
Lodge Garage, Whitehall Road West, Gomersal, Cleckheaton, West Yorkshire BD19 4BJ
Tel: 01274 681144
Fax: 01274 651198
E-mail: whiter@arriva.co.uk
Web site: www.arrivabusandcoach.co.uk

BUSS BIZZ
Goughs Transport Depot, Morestead, Winchester SO21 1JD
Tel: 01962 715555/66
Fax: 01962 714868.

GARDNER PARTS LTD
Centurion Court, Centurion Way, Leyland, Lancashire PR25 3UQ
Tel: 01772 642460
Fax: 01772 621333
E-mail: sales@gardnerpars.co.uk
Web site: www.gardnerparts.com

HL SMITH TRANSMISSIONS LTD
Enterprise Business Park, Cross Road, Albrighton, Wolverhampton WV7 3BJ
Tel: 01902 373011
Fax: 01902 373608
Web site: www.hlsmith.co.uk

LH GROUP SERVICES LTD
Graycar Business Park, Barton under Needwood, Burton-on-Trent DE13 8EN
Tel: 01283 722600
Fax: 01283 722622
E-mail: lh@lh-group.com
Web site: www.lh-group.com

OPTARE PARTS DIVISION (Rotherham)
Denby Way, Hellaby, Rotherham S66 8HR
Tel: 01709 792000
Fax: 01709 792009
E-mail: parts@optare.com

OPTARE PRODUCT SUPPORT LONDON
Unit 9, Eurocourt, Olivers Close, West Thurrock RM20 3EE
Tel: 08444 123222
Fax: 01708 869920
E-mail: london.service@optare.com

OPTARE PRODUCT SUPPORT ROTHERHAM
Denby Way, Hellaby, Rotherham S66 8HR
Tel: 01709 535101
Fax: 01709 535103
E-mail: rotherham.service@optare.com

OPTARE PRODUCT SUPPORT SCOTLAND
Unit 7, Cumbernauld Business Park, Ward Park Road, Cumbernauld G67 3JZ
Tel: 01236 726738
Fax: 01236 795651
E-mail: scotland.service@optare.com

SHAWSON SUPPLY LTD
12 Station Road, Saintfield, County Down, Northern Ireland BT24 7DU
Tel: 028 9751 0994
Fax: 028 9751 0816
E-mail: info@shawsonsupply.com
Web site: www.shawsonsupply.com

TTS UK
Total Tool Solutions Ltd, Newhaven Business Park, Lowergate, Milnsbridge, Huddersfield HD3 4HS
Tel: 01484 642211
Fax: 01484 461002
E-mail: sales@ttsuk.com
Web site: www.ttsuk.com

VOITH TURBO LTD
6 Beddington Farm Road, Croydon CR0 4XB
Tel: 020 8667 0333
Fax: 020 8667 0403
E-mail: david.holdsworth@voith.com
Web site: www.voithturbo.co.uk

VOR TRANSMISSIONS LTD
Little London House, St Anne's Road, Willenhall WV13 1DT
Tel: 01902 604141
Fax: 01902 603868
E-mail: sueh@vor.co.uk

ZF POWERTRAIN
Stringes Close, Willenhall WV13 1LE
Tel: 01902 366000
Fax: 01902 366504
E-mail: sales@powertrain.org.uk
Web site: www.powertrain.org.uk

Tree Guards

ARRIVA BUS AND COACH
Lodge Garage, Whitehall Road West, Gomersal, Cleckheaton, West Yorkshire BD19 4BJ
Tel: 01274 681144
Fax: 01274 651198
E-mail: whiter@arriva.co.uk
Web site: www.arrivabusandcoach.co.uk

GABRIEL & COMPANY LTD
Abro Works, 10 Ham Hall Road, Birmingham B11 2AU
Tel: 0121 248 3333
Fax: 0121 248 3330
E-mail: john.gabriel@gabrielco.com
Web site: www.gabrielco.com

PLAXTON SERVICE
Ryton Road, Anston, Sheffield S25 4DL
Tel: 01909 551155
Fax: 01909 550050
E-mail: service@plaxtonlimited.co.uk
Web site: www.plaxtonaftercare.co.uk

Tyres

DUNLOP TYRES LTD
Tyre Fort, 88-98 Wingfoot Way, Birmingham B24 9HY
Tel: 0121 306 6000
Fax: 0121 306 6437
Web site: www.dunloptyres.co.uk

OPTARE PRODUCT SUPPORT LONDON
Unit 9, Eurocourt, Olivers Close, West Thurrock RM20 3EE
Tel: 08444 123222
Fax: 01708 869920
E-mail: london.service@optare.com

OPTARE PRODUCT SUPPORT ROTHERHAM
Denby Way, Hellaby, Rotherham S66 8HR
Tel: 01709 535101
Fax: 01709 535103
E-mail: rotherham.service@optare.com

OPTARE PRODUCT SUPPORT SCOTLAND
Unit 7, Cumbernauld Business Park, Ward Park Road, Cumbernauld G67 3JZ
Tel: 01236 726738
Fax: 01236 795651
E-mail: scotland.service@optare.com

SNOWCHAINS EUROPRODUCTS
Borough Green TN15 8DG
Tel: 01732 884408
Fax: 01732 884564
Web site: www.snowchains.co.uk

Uniforms

ALLEN & DOUGLAS CORPORATE CLOTHING LTD
Unit 8, Lombard Way, Banbury OX16 3EZ
Tel: 01295 228452
Fax: 01295 257937
E-mail: sales@aandd.co.uk
Web site: www.aandd.co.uk

HANDLEY BUS & COACH UNIFORMS
Unit 3, 18 Croydon Street, Leeds LS11 9RT
Tel: 0113 245 7008
Fax: 0113 245 9643
E-mail: tor@tordesigns.com
Web-Site: www.tordesigns.com

IMAGE 1ST CLOTHING LTD
Unit 3, Eagle Industrial Estate, Torre Road, Leeds LS10 1BX
Tel: 0113 200 9147
Fax: 0113 249 8172
E-Mail: reception@image-first.co.uk
Web site: www.image-first.co.uk

LEISUREWEAR DIRECT LTD, inc. AHEAD OF THE REST
4A South Street North, New Whittington, Chesterfield S43 2AB
Tel: 01246 454447
Fax: 0870 755 9842
Web site: www.leisureweardirect.com

RAINBOW CORPORATEWEAR
Gosforth Road, Derby DE24 8HU
Tel: 01332 342616
Fax: 01332 362328
Web site: www.rainbow-corporatewear.co.uk

Upholstery

ABACUS TRANSPORT PRODUCTS LTD
Abacus House, Highlode Industrial Estate, Stockingfen Road, Ramsey PE26 2RB
Tel: 01487 710700
Fax: 01487 710626
E-mail: f.riola@abacus-tp.com
Web site: www.abacus-tp.com

ARDEE COACH TRIM LTD
Artnalivery, Ardee, Co Louth, Republic of Ireland
Tel: 00 353 41 685 3599
Fax: 00 353 41 685 7016
E-mail: ardeecoachtrim@eircom.net

AUTOMOTIVE TEXTILE INDUSTRIES
Unit 15 & 16, Priest Court, Springfield Business Park, Grantham NG31 7BG
Tel: 01476 593050
Fax: 01476 593607
E-mail: sales@autotex.com
Web site: www.autotex.com

Trade Directory

BLACKPOOL TRIM SHOPS LTD
Brun Grove,
Blackpool FY1 6PG
Tel: 01253 766762
Fax: 01253 798443
E-mail: sales@blackpooltrimshops.co.uk
Web site: www.blackpooltrimshops.co.uk

BRIDGE OF WEIR LEATHER CO LTD
Baltic Works, Bridge of Weir,
Paisley PA11 33RH
Tel: 01505 612132
Fax: 01505 614964
E-mail: mail@bowleather.co.uk
Web site: www.bowleather.co.uk

DUOFLEX LTD
Trimmingham House,
2 Shires Road,
Buckingham Road Industrial Estate,
Brackley NN13 7EZ
Tel: 01280 701366
Fax: 01280 704799
E-mail: sales@duoflex.co.uk
Web site: www.duoflex.co.uk

EXPRESS COACH REPAIRS LTD
Outgang Lane,
Pickering YO18 7JA
Tel: 01751 475215
Fax: 01924 475215
E-mail: info@expresscoachrepairs.co.uk
Web site: www.expresscoachrepairs.co.uk

HOLDSWORTH FABRICS LTD
Hopton Mills,
Mirfield WF1 8HE
Tel: 01924 481144
Fax: 01924 495605
E-mail: info@camirafabrics.co.uk
Web site: www.camirafabrics.com

MARTYN INDUSTRIALS LTD
5 Brunel Way, Durranhill,
Harraby, Carlisle CA1 3NQ
Tel: 01228 544000
Fax: 01228 544001
E-mail: enquiries@martyn-industrials.co.uk
Web site: www.martyn-industrials.com

P.L. TRIM LTD
Burton Road, Blackpool
FY4 4NW
Tel: 01253 696033
Fax: 01253 696033
E-mail: enquiries@pltrim.co.uk
Web site: www.pltrim.co.uk

TTS UK
Total Tool Solutions Ltd, Newhaven
Business Park, Lowergate, Milnsbridge,
Huddersfield HD3 4HS
Tel: 01484 642211
Fax: 01484 461002
E-mail: sales@ttsuk.com
Web site: www.ttsuk.com

WIDNEY UK LTD
Plume Street, Aston, Birmingham B6 7SA
Tel: 0121 327 5500
Fax: 0121 328 2466
E-mail: richard@widney.co.uk

Vacuum Systems

RESCROFT LTD
20 Oxleasow Road, East Moons Moat,
Redditch B98 0RE
Tel: 01527 521300
Fax: 01527 521301
E-mail: info@rescroft.com
Web site: www.rescroft.com

SMART CENTRAL COACH SYSTEMS
5 Kings Acre House, 329 Kings Acre Road,
Hereford HR4 0SL
Tel: 01432 276380
E-mail: info@smartcoachsystems.co.uk
Web site: www.smartcoachsystems.co.uk

TTS UK
Total Tool Solutions Ltd, Newhaven
Business Park, Lowergate, Milnsbridge,
Huddersfield HD3 4HS
Tel: 01484 642211
Fax: 01484 461002
E-mail: sales@ttsuk.com
Web site: www.tts.co.uk

Vehicle Washing & Washers

ARRIVA BUS AND COACH
Lodge Garage, Whitehall Road West,
Gomersal, Cleckheaton, West Yorkshire
BD19 4BJ
Tel: 01274 681144
Fax: 01274 651198
E-mail: whiter@arriva.co.uk
Web site: www.arrivabusandcoach.co.uk

ATLANTIS INTERNATIONAL LTD
18 Weldon Road, Loughborough LE11 5RA
Tel: 01509 233770
Fax: 01509 210542
E-mail: sales@atlantisint.co.uk
Web site: www.atlantisinternational.co.uk

EXPRESS COACH REPAIRS LTD
Outgang Lane, Pickering YO18 7JA
Tel: 01751 475215
Fax: 01924 475215
E-mail: info@expresscoachrepairs.co.uk
Web site: www.expresscoachrepairs.co.uk

KISMET GARAGE EQUIPMENT LTD
PO Box 273, Wirral CH32 9AE
Tel: 0844 879 3298
Fax: 0560 344 6213
E-mail: kismet2@btconnect.com
Web site: www.vehicle-lifts.co.uk

MARSHALLS COACHES LLP
Firbank Way, Leighton Buzzard LU7 3BD
Tel: 01525 376077
Fax: 01525 850967
E-mail: info@marshalls-coaches.co.uk
Web site: www.marshalls-coaches.co.uk

MONOWASH
(BRUSH REPLACEMENT SERVICE)
8 Contessa Close, Farnborough BR6 7ER
Tel: 01689 860061
Fax: 01689 861469

NATIONWIDE CLEANING & SUPPORT SERVICES LTD
Airport House, Purley Way,
Croydon CR0 0XZ
Tel: 020 8288 3580
Fax: 020 8288 3581
Web site: www.nationwidefm.com

SMITH BROS & WEBB LTD
Britannia House, Arden Forest Industrial
Estate, Alcester, Warwickshire B49 6EX
Tel: 01789 400096
Fax: 01789 400231
E-mail: sales@vehicle-washing-systems.co.uk
Web site: www.vehicle-washing-systems.co.uk

SOMERS TOTALKARE LTD
15 Forge Trading Estate, Mucklow Hill,
Halesowen B62 8TR
Tel: 0121 585 2700
Fax: 0121 585 2725
E-mail: sales@somerstotalkare.co.uk
Web site: www.somerstotalkare.co.uk

Wheels, Wheeltrims & Covers

ABACUS TRANSPORT PRODUCTS LTD
Abacus House, Highlode Industrial Estate,
Stockingfen Road, Ramsey PE26 2RB
Tel: 01487 710700
Fax: 01487 710626
E-mail: f.riola@abacus-tp.com
Web site: www.abacus-tp.com

ALCOA WHEEL PRODUCTS EUROPE
Industrieweg 135, 3583 PAAL, Belgium
Tel: 00 32 11 458464
Fax: 00 21 11 455630
E-mail: info.wheels@alcoa.com
Web site: www.alcoawheels.com

ARRIVA BUS AND COACH
Lodge Garage, Whitehall Road West,
Gomersal, Cleckheaton, West Yorkshire
BD19 4BJ
Tel: 01274 681144
Fax: 01274 651198
E-mail: whiter@arriva.co.uk
Web site: www.arrivabusandcoach.co.uk

AUTOMATE WHEEL COVERS LTD
California Mills, Oxford Road, Gomersal
BD19 4HQ
Tel: 01274 862700
Fax: 01274 851989
E-mail: sales@wheelcovers.co.uk
Web site: www.euroliners.com

TTS UK
Total Tool Solutions Limited
Newhaven Business Park
Lowergate
Milnsbridge
Huddersfield
HD3 4HS
T: 01484 642211
F: 01484 461002
E: sales@ttsuk.com
W: www.ttsuk.com

The Little Red Book 2011 - in association with **tbf** Transport Benevolent Fund

Trade Directory

EXPRESS COACH REPAIRS LTD
Outgang Lane, Pickering YO18 7JA
Tel: 01751 475215
Fax: 01924 475215
E-mail: info@expresscoachrepairs.co.uk
Web site: www.expresscoachrepairs.co.uk

HATCHER COMPONENTS LTD
Broadwater Road, Framlingham IP13 9LL
Tel: 01728 723675
Fax: 01728 724475
E-mail: info@hatchercomp.co.uk

J. HIPWELL & SON
427 Warwick Road, Greet, Birmingham B20 1JE.
Tel: 0121 706 5471
Fax: 0121 706 0502

OPTARE PARTS DIVISION (Rotherham)
Denby Way, Hellaby, Rotherham S66 8HR
Tel: 01709 792000
Fax: 01709 792009
E-mail: parts@optare.com

PLAXTON PARTS
Ryton Road, Anston, Sheffield S25 4DL
Tel: 0844 822 6224
Fax: 01909 550050
E-mail: parts@plaxtonlimited.co.uk
Web site: www.plaxtonaftercare.co.uk

Windows and Windscreens

ARRIVA BUS AND COACH
Lodge Garage, Whitehall Road West, Gomersal, Cleckheaton, West Yorkshire BD19 4BJ
Tel: 01274 681144
Fax: 01274 651198
E-mail: whiter@arriva.co.uk
Web site: www.arrivabusandcoach.co.uk

AUTOGLASS COACH & BUS SERVICES
PO Box 343, Goldington Road, Bedford MK40 3BX
Tel: 01234 279572 **Fax:** 01234 279460
Tel: 01234 279559

BRITAX PMG LTD
Bressingby Industrial Estate, Bridlington YO16 4SJ
Tel: 01262 670161
Fax: 01262 605666
E-mail: info@britax-pmg.com
Web site: www.britax-pmg.com

BUS & COACH GLAZING
Ryton Road, Anston, Sheffield S25 4DL
Tel: 0800 220077
Fax: 01909 550050
E-mail: glazing@plaxtonlimited.co.uk
Web site: www.plaxtonaftercare.co.uk

CARLYLE BUS & COACH LTD
Carlyle Business Park, Great Bridge Street, Swan Village, West Bromwich B70 0XA
Tel: 0121 524 1200
Fax: 0121 524 1201
E-mail: admin@carlyleplc.co.uk
Web site: www.carlyleplc.co.uk

EXPRESS COACH REPAIRS LTD
Outgang Lane, Pickering YO18 7JA
Tel: 01751 475215
Fax: 01924 475215
E-mail: info@expresscoachrepairs.co.uk
Web site: www.expresscoachrepairs.co.uk

B HEPWORTH & CO LTD
4 Merse Road, Redditch B98 9HL
Tel: 01527 61243
Fax: 01527 66836
Web site: www.b-hepworth.com
E-mail: bhepworth@b-hepworth.com

INDUSTRIAL & COMMERCIAL WINDOW CO LTD
Unit 2, Caldervale Industrial Estate, Horbury Junction, Wakefield WF4 5ER
Tel: 01924 260106
Fax: 01924 260152

J W GLASS LTD
Units 6 & 7, Scropton Road, Hatton DE65 5DT
Tel: 01283 520202
Fax: 01283 520022
E-mail: info@jwglass.co.uk
Web site: www.jwglass.co.uk

LAWTON SERVICES LTD
Knutsford Road, Church Lawton, Stoke-on-Trent ST7 3DN
Tel: 01270 882056
Fax: 01270 883014
E-mail: andrea@lawtonservices.co.uk
Web site: www.lawtonservices.co.uk

NEALINE WINDSCREEN WIPER PRODUCTS
Unit 1, The Sidings Industrial Estate, Birdingbury Road, Marton CV23 9RX
Tel: 01926 633256
Fax: 01926 632600

NUTEXA FRICTIONS LTD
PO Box 11, New Hall Lane, Hoylake, Wirral CH47 4DH
Tel: 0151 632 5903
Fax: 0151 632 5908
E-mail: sales@nutexafrictions.co.uk
Web Site: www.sergeant.co.uk

OPTARE PARTS DIVISION (Rotherham)
Denby Way, Hellaby, Rotherham S66 8HR
Tel: 01709 792000
Fax: 01709 792009
E-mail: parts@optare.com

OPTARE PRODUCT SUPPORT LONDON
Unit 9, Eurocourt, Olivers Close, West Thurrock RM20 3EE
Tel: 08444 123222
Fax: 01708 869920
E-mail: london.service@optare.com

OPTARE PRODUCT SUPPORT ROTHERHAM
Denby Way, Hellaby, Rotherham S66 8HR
Tel: 01709 535101
Fax: 01709 535103
E-mail: rotherham.service@optare.com

OPTARE PRODUCT SUPPORT SCOTLAND
Unit 7, Cumbernauld Business Park, Ward Park Road, Cumbernauld G67 3JZ
Tel: 01236 726738
Fax: 01236 795651
E-mail: scotland.service@optare.com

PERCY LANE PRODUCTS LTD
Lichfield Road, Tamworth B79 7TL
Tel: 01827 63821
Fax: 01827 310159
E-mail: sales@percy-lane.co.uk
Web site: www.percy-lane.co.uk

PLAXTON PARTS
Ryton Road, Anston, Sheffield S25 4DL
Tel: 01909 550044
Fax: 01909 550050
E-mail: parts@plaxtonlimited.co.uk
Web site: www.plaxtonaftercare.co.uk

PSV GLASS
Hillbottom Road, High Wycombe HP12 4HJ
Tel: 01494 533131
Fax: 01494 462675

E-mail: sales@psvglass.co.uk
Web site: www.psvglass.com

TRAMONTANA
Chapelknowe Road, Carfin, Motherwell ML1 5LE
Tel: 01698 861790
Fax: 01698 860778
E-mail: wdt90@tiscali.co.uk
Web site: www.tramontanacoach.co.uk

TTS UK
Total Tool Solutions Ltd, Newhaven Business Park, Lowergate, Milnsbridge, Huddersfield HD3 4HS
Tel: 01484 642211
Fax: 01484 461002
E-mail: sales@ttsuk.com
Web site: www.ttsuk.com

VOLVO BUS AND COACH CENTRE
Parts Sales & Body Repair/Refurbishment Specialists
Byron Street Extension, Loughborough LE11 5HE
Tel: 01509 217700
Fax: 01509 238770
E-mail (Body Support): dporter@volvocoachsales.co.uk
E-mail (Parts): csparts@volvocoachsales.co.uk
Web site: www.volvo.com

WIDNEY UK LTD
Plume Street, Aston, Birmingham B6 7SA
Tel: 0121 327 5500
Fax: 0121 328 2466
E-mail: richard@widney.co.uk

INDUSTRY SERVICE PROVIDERS

Accident Investigation

KERNOW ASSOCIATES
18 Tresawla Court, Tolvaddon, Camborne TR14 0HF
Tel/Fax: 01209 711870
E-mail: 106472.3264@compuserve.com

Accountancy & Audit

BARRONS CHARTERED ACCOUNTANTS
Monometer House, Rectory Grove, Leigh on Sea SS9 2HN
Tel: 01702 481910
Fax: 01702 481911
E-mail: garyr@barrons-bds.com
Web site: www.barrons-bds.com

PRE METRO OPERATIONS LTD
21 Woodglade Croft, Kings Norton, Birmingham B38 8TD
Tel: 0121 243 9906
Fax: 0121 243 9906
E-mail: info@premetro.co.uk
Web site: www.premetro.co.uk

Advisory Services

AD COACH SALES
Newbridge Coach Depot, Witheridge, Devon EX16 8PY
Tel: 01884 860787
Fax: 01884 860711
E-mail: enquiries@adcoachsales.co.uk
Web site: www.adcoachsales.co.uk

ADG TRANSPORT TRAINING
Oak Cottage, Royal Oak, Machen, Caerphilly CF83 8SN
Tel: 01633 441491
Fax: 01633 440591
E-mail: a.dgettins@btinternet.com

Trade Directory

TTS UK
Total Tool Solutions Limited
Newhaven Business Park
Lowergate
Milnsbridge
Huddersfield
HD3 4HS
T: 01484 642211
F: 01484 461002
E: sales@ttsuk.com
W: www.ttsuk.com

ANDY IZATT
10 Briton Court, St Thomas's Road,
Spalding PE11 2TS
Tel: 01775 712542
E-mail: andy.izatt@btinternet.com
Web site: andy.izatt.btinternet.co.uk

AUSTIN ANALYTICS
Crown House, 183 High Street,
Bottisham,
Cambridge CB25 9BB
Tel: 07730 943415
Fax: 07005 946854
E-mail: john@analytics.co.uk
Web site: www.analytics.co.uk

COLIN BUCHANAN
10 Eastbourne Terrace,
London W2 6LG
Tel: 020 7053 1300
Fax: 020 7053 1301
E-mail: london@cbuchanan.co.uk
Web site: www.colinbuchanan.com

CAPOCO DESIGN
Stone Cross House, Chickgrove,
Salisbury SP3 6NA
Tel: 01722 716722
Fax: 01722 716226
E-mail: design@capoco.co.uk

CHADWELL ASSOCIATES LTD
3 Caledonian Close,
Ilford, IG3 9QF
Tel: 0208 590 5697
E-mail: ib@chadwellassociates.co.uk

ETMSS LTD
c/o Ground Floor, Austin House,
43 Poole Road, Westbourne,
Bournemouth BH4 9DN
Tel: 0844 800 9199
E-mail: info@etmss.com
Web Site: www.etmss.com

GOSKILLS LTD
Concorde House, Trinity Park,
Solihull B37 7UQ
Tel: 01216 355520
Fax: 01216 355521
E-mail: info@goskills.org
Web site: www.goskills.org

IBPTS
43 Cage Lane, Felixstowe,
Suffolk OP11 9BJ
Tel: 01394 672344
Fax: 01394 672344
E-mail: info@ibpts.co.uk
Web site: www.ibpts.co.uk

LEONARD GREEN ASSOCIATES
4 Crawshaw Drive, Reedsholme,
Rawtenstall, Rossendale BB4 8PT
Tel: 01706 218539
E-mail: lgreen22@ntlworld.com

LEYLAND PRODUCT DEVELOPMENTS LTD
Aston Way, Leyland, Preston PR26 7TZ
Tel: 01772 435834
E-mail: sales@lpdl.co.uk
Web site: www.lpdl.co.uk

MINIMISE YOUR RISK
11 Chatsworth Park, Telscombe Cliffs,
East Sussex BN10 7DZ
Tel: 01273 580189
Fax: 01273 580189
E-mail: alec@minimiseyourrisk.co.uk
Web site: www.minimiseyourrisk.co.uk

STEPHEN C MORRIS
PO Box 119,
Shepperton TW17 8UX
Tel: 01932 232574
E-ail: buswriter@btinternet.com

MVA
Duke Street, Woking GU21 5DH
Tel: 01483 728051
Fax: 01483 755207
Web site: www.mvaconsultancy.com

PEAK LEGAL SERVICES LTD
41 Longmoor Road, Simmondley,
Glossop, Derbyshire SK13 6NH
Tel/Fax: 01457 855141
Mobile: 07989 092835
E-mail: ford414@btinternet.com

PRE METRO OPERATIONS LTD
21 Woodglade Croft, Kings Norton,
Birmingham B38 8TD
Tel: 0121 243 9906
Fax: 0121 243 9906
E-mail: info@premetro.co.uk
Web site: www.premetro.co.uk

PROFESSIONAL TRANSPORT SERVICES LTD
12 Silverdale, Stanford-le-Hope
SS17 8BG
Tel: 01375 675262
Web site: www.proftranserv.co.uk
E-mail: enquiries@proftranserv.com

SALTIRE COMMUNICATIONS
39 Lilyhill Terrace, Edinburgh EH8 7DR
Tel: 0131 652 0205
E-mail: gavin.booth@btconnect.com

TRANSPORT & TRAVEL RESEARCH LTD
Minster House, Minster Pool Walk,
Lichfield, Staffordshire WS13 6QT
Tel: 01543 416416
Fax: 01543 416681
E-mail: enquiries@ttr-ltd.com
Web site: www.ttr-ltd.com

TTS UK
Total Tool Solutions Ltd, Newhaven
Business Park, Lowergate, Milnsbridge,
Huddersfield HD3 4HS
Tel: 01484 642211
Fax: 01484 461002
E-mail: sales@ttsuk.com
Web site: www.ttsuk.com

WARD INTERNATIONAL CONSULTING LTD
Funtley Court, 19 Funtley Hill, Fareham
PO16 7UY
Tel: 01329 280280
Fax: 01329 221010
E-mail: info@wardint.co.uk
Web site: www.wardint.com

Artwork

BEST IMPRESSIONS
15 Starfield Road,
London W12 9SN
Tel: 020 8740 6443
Fax: 020 8740 9134
E-mail: talk2us@best-impressions.co.uk
Web site: www.best-impressions.co.uk

EXPRESS COACH REPAIRS LTD
Outgang Lane, Pickering YO18 7JA
Tel: 01751 475215
Fax: 01751 475215
E-mail: info@expresscoachrepairs.co.uk
Web site: www.expresscoachrepairs.co.uk

FWT
Aztec House, 397-405 Archway Road,
London N6 4EY
Tel: 020 7347 3700
Fax: 020 7347 3701
E-mail: sales@fwt.co.uk
Web site: www.fwt.co.uk

GRAPHIC EVOLUTION LTD
Ad House, East Parade,
Harrogate HG1 5LT
Tel: 01423 706680
Fax: 01423 502522
E-mail: info@graphic-evolution.co.uk
Web site: www.graphic-evolution.co.uk

TONY GREAVES GRAPHICS
19 Perth Mount, Horsforth, Leeds LS18 5SH
Tel/Fax: 0113 258 4795
E-mail: tony@greavesgraphics.fsnet.co.uk

HATTS GARAGE SERVICES
Foxham, Chippenham SN15 4NB
Tel: 01249 740444
Fax: 01249 740447
E-mail: mike@hattstravel.co.uk
Web site: www.hattsgarageservices.co.uk

MCV BUS & COACH LTD
Sterling Place, Elean Business Park,
Sutton CB6 2QE
Tel: 01353 773000
Fax: 01353 773001
E-mail: vernon.edwards@mcv-uk.com

NEERMAN & PARTNERS
c/o 22 Larbre Crescent, Whickham,
Newcastle-upon-Tyne NE16 5YG
Tel: 0191 488 6258
Fax: 0191 488 9158
E-mail: info@neerman.net
Web site: www.neerman.net

The Little Red Book 2011 - in association with *tbf* Transport Benevolent Fund

Trade Directory

PLUM DIGITAL PRINT
Suite 1, Cornerstone House, Stafford Park 13, Telford, Shropshire TF3 3AZ
Tel: 01952 204920
E-mail: nigel.greenaway@busandcoach.com
Web site: www.plumdigitalprint.co.uk

TIME TRAVEL UK
247 Bradford Road, Stanningley, Pudsey, Leeds LS28 6QB
Tel: 0113 255 1188
E-mail: nick.baldwin@tinyworld.co.uk

VETRO DESIGN
247 Bradford Road, Pudsey, Leeds LS28 6QB
Tel: 0113 255 1188
E-mail: nick@vetrodesign.co.uk

Breakdown & Recovery Services

NB - Operator lists also indicate bus and coach operators able to provide breakdown and recovery services.

AD COACH SALES
Newbridge Coach Depot, Witheridge, Devon EX16 8PY
Tel: 01884 860767
Fax: 01884 860711
E-mail: enquiries@adcoachsales.co.uk
Web site: www.adcoachsales.co.uk

BUZZLINES LTD
Unit G1, Lympne Industrial Park, Hythe CT21 4LR
Tel: 01303 261870
Fax: 01303 230093
E-mail: sales@buzzlines.co.uk
Web site: www.buzzlines.co.uk

CHANNEL COMMERCIALS PLC
Unit 6, Cobbs Wood Industrial Estate, Brunswick Road, Ashford TN23 1EH
Tel: 01233 629272
Fax: 01233 636322
E-mail: info@ccplc.co.uk
Web site: www.channelcommercials.co.uk

COACH-AID
Unit 2, Brindley Close, Tollgate Industrial Estate, Stafford ST16 3SU
Tel: 01785 222666
E-mail: workshop@coach-aid.com
Web site: www.coach-aid.com

HATTS GARAGE SERVICES
Foxham, Chippenham SN15 4NB
Tel: 01249 740444
Fax: 01249 740447
E-mail: mike@hattstravel.co.uk
Web site: www.hattsgarageservices.co.uk

J & K RECOVERY LTD
3 Grovebury Road, Leighton Buzzard, Bedfordshire LU7 4SQ
Tel: 01525 851011 **Fax:** 01525 850361
UK Call Centre: 0800 434 6106

LANTERN RECOVERY SPECIALISTS PLC
Lantern House, 39/41 High Street, Potters Bar EN6 5AJ
Tel: 0870 6090333
Fax: 01707 640450
Web site: www.lanternrecovery.org

LAWTON SERVICES LTD
Knutsford Road, Church Lawton, Stoke-on-Trent ST7 3DN
Tel: 01270 882056
Fax: 01270 883014
E-mail: andrea@lawtonservices.co.uk
Web site: www.lawtonservices.co.uk

MARSHALLS COACHES LLP
Firbank Way, Leighton Buzzard, Bedfordshire LU7 3BD
Tel: 01525 376077
Fax: 01525 850967
E-mail: info@marshalls-coaches.co.uk
Web site: www.marshalls-coaches.co.uk

MASS SPECIAL ENGINEERING LTD
Houghton Road, North Anston S25 4JJ.
Tel: 01909 550480
Fax: 01909 550486

OPTARE PRODUCT SUPPORT LONDON
Unit 9, Eurocourt, Olivers Close, West Thurrock RM20 3EE
Tel: 08444 123222
Fax: 01708 869920
E-mail: london.service@optare.com

OPTARE PRODUCT SUPPORT ROTHERHAM
Denby Way, Hellaby, Rotherham S66 8HR
Tel: 01709 535101
Fax: 01709 535103
E-mail: rotherham.service@optare.com

OPTARE PRODUCT SUPPORT SCOTLAND
Unit 7, Cumbernauld Business Park, Ward Park Road, Cumbernauld G67 3JZ
Tel: 01236 726738
Fax: 01236 795651
E-mail: scotland.service@optare.com

PLAXTON SERVICE
Ryton Road, Anston, Sheffield S25 4DL
Tel: 01909 551155
Fax: 01909 550050
E-mail: service@plaxtonlimited.co.uk
Web site: www.plaxtonaftercare.co.uk

TOURMASTER RECOVERY
Alderlands, James Road, Crowland, Peterborough PE6 0AA
Tel: 01733 211639
Fax: 01733 211378
E-mail: Tourmaster@btconnect.com
Contact: David Dinsey

TRUCKALIGN CO LTD
VIP Trading Estate, Anchor & Hope Lane, London SE7 7RY
Tel: 020 8858 3781
Fax: 020 8858 3781

Cleaning services

EXPRESS COACH REPAIRS LTD
Outgang Lane, Pickering YO18 7JA
Tel: 01751 475215
Fax: 01751 475215
E-mail: info@expresscoachrepairs.co.uk
Web site: www.expresscoachrepairs.co.uk

SMART CENTRAL COACH SYSTEMS
5 Kings Acre House, 329 Kings Acre Road, Hereford HR4 0SL
Tel: 01432 276380
E-mail: info@smartcoachsystems.co.uk
Web site: www.smartcoachsystems.co.uk

TARA SUPPORT SERVICES LTD
32 Derby Road, Enfield EN3 4AW
Tel: 0845 450 0607
Fax: 0845 450 0608
E-mail: info@tarasupport.co.uk
Web site: www.tarasupport.co.uk

Coach Driver Agencies

ANTAL INTERNATIONAL NETWORK
Kestrel House, 111 Heath Road, Twickenham TW1 1AF
Tel: 0870 770 1604
E-mail: bcoyne@antal.com
Web site: www.antal.com

COUNTY RECRUITMENT & TRAINING LTD
5 White Cliffs Business Centre, Honeywood Road, Whitfield, Dover, Kent CT16 3EH
Tel: 01304 826220
Fax: 01304 822551
E-mail: admin@crtweb.co.uk
Web site: www.crtweb.co.uk

DRIVER HIRE CANTERBURY
East Suite, Parsonage Office, Nackington, Canterbury CT4 7AD
Tel: 01227 479529
Fax: 01227 479531
E-mail: canterbury@driver-hire.co.uk
Web site: www.driverhire.co.uk

Coach Hire Brokers/Vehicle Rental

COACH DIRECT LTD
22 South Street, Rochford, Essex SS4 1BQ
Tel: 0843 084 3001
Fax: 0843 084 3002
E-mail: info@coachdirect.co.uk
Web site: www.coachdirect.co.uk

Trade Directory

COACHFINDER LTD
Woodbank House, 24 Matley Close,
Newton, Hyde SK14 4UE
Tel: 0161 368 7877
E-mail: enquiries@coachfinder.uk.com
Web site: www.coachfinder.uk.com

DAWSONRENTALS BUS AND COACH LTD
Delaware Drive, Tongwell, Milton Keynes MK15 8JH
Tel: 01908 218111
Fax: 01908 610156
E-mail: info@dawsongroup.co.uk
Web site: www.dawsongroup.co.uk

HAYWARD TRAVEL (CARDIFF)
2 Murch Crescent, Dinas Powys,
Cardiff CF64 4RF
Tel: 029 2051 5551
Fax: 029 2051 5113
E-mail: haytvl@aol.com
Web site: haywardtravel.co.uk

NEXT BUS LTD
The Coach Yard, Vincients Road,
Bumpers Farm Industrial Estate,
Chippenham SN14 6QA
Tel: 01249 462462
Fax: 01249 448844
E-mail: sales@next-bus.co.uk
Web site: www.next-bus.co.uk

SANTANDER ASSET FINANCE
Taylor Road, Trafford Park,
Manchester M41 7JQ
Tel: 0161 747 5698
Fax: 0161 275 4501
E-mail: steve.moult@hansar.co.uk
Web site: www.buses247.co.uk

YORKSHIRE BUS & COACH SALES
254A West Ella Road, West Ella,
Hull HU10 7SF
Tel: 01482 653302
Fax: 01482 653302
E-mail: craig.porteous@virgin.net

Coach Interchange & Parking Facilities

SAMMYS GARAGE
Victoria Coach Station, Arrivals Hall,
3 Eccleston Place, London SW1W 9NF
Tel: 020 7793 7533/7730/8867

TRAVELGREEN COACHES
Canda Lodge, Hampole Bank Lane,
Skellow, Doncaster DN6 8LF
Tel: 01302 722227
Fax: 01302 727999
(also B&B accommodation)

VICTORIA COACH STATION LTD
164 Buckingham Palace Road, London SW1W 9TP
Tel: 020 7027 2520
Fax: 020 7027 2511
Web site: www.tfl.gov.uk

Computer Systems/Software

ACIS
ACIS House, Knaves Beech Business Centre, Loudwater, Buckinghamshire HP10 9QR
Tel: 01628 524900
Fax: 01628 523222
E-mail: enquiries@acis.uk.com
Web site: www.acis.uk.com

ALMEX UK
Metric House, Westmead Industrial Estate
Westlea, Swindon SN5 7AD
Tel: 01793 647934
Fax: 01793 647932

E-mail: info@almex.co.uk
Web site: www.almex.co.uk

AUTOPRO SOFTWARE
1 Kingsmeadow, Norton Cross, Runcorn WA7 6PB
Tel: 01928 715962
Fax: 01928 714538
E-mail: sales@autoprouk.com
Web site: www.autoprosoftware.co.uk

DISTINCTIVE SYSTEMS LTD
Amy Johnson Way, York YO30 4XT
Tel: 01904 692269
Fax: 01904 690810
E-mail: sales@distinctive-systems.com
Web site: www.distinctive-systems.com

ETMSS LTD
c/o Ground Floor, Austin House, 43 Poole Road, Westbourne, Bournemouth BH4 9DN
Tel: 0844 800 9299
E-mail: info@etmss.com
Web Site: www.etmss.com

INIT GmbH – INNOVATION IN TRANSPORT
32A Stoney Street, The Lace Market,
Nottingham NG1 1LL
Tel: 0870 890 4648
Fax: 0115 988 6917
E-mail: sales@init.co.uk
Web site: www.init.co.uk

OMNIBUS
Hollinwood Business Centre, Albert Street,
Hollinwood, Oldham, Lancashire OL8 3QL
Tel: 0161 683 3100
Fax: 0161 683 3102
Web site: www.omnibus.uk.com

PROFESSIONAL TRANSPORT SERVICES
12 Silverdale, Stanford-le-Hope SS17 8BG
Tel: 01375 675262
Web site: www.proftranserv.co.uk
E-mail: enquiries@proftranserv.com

ROEVILLE COMPUTER SYSTEMS
Station House, East Lane, Stainforth,
Doncaster DN7 5HF
Tel: 01302 841333
Fax: 01302 843966
E-mail: sales@roeville.com
Web site: www.roeville.com

TAGTRONICS LTD
Suite 408, Daisyfield Business Centre,
Appleby Street, Blackburn BB1 3BL
Tel: 01254 297730
Fax: 01254 698484
E-mail: info@tagtronics.co.uk
Web site: www.tagtronics.co.uk

TICKETER
Riverside Centre, 82 Station Road,
Barnes, London SW13 0LS
Tel: 0844 800 9299
E-mail: sales@ticketer.co.uk
Web site: www.ticketer.co.uk

TRANMAN SOLUTIONS
Thornbury Office Park, Midland Way,
Thornbury, Gloucestershire BS35 2BS
Tel: 01454 874000
Fax: 01454 874001
E-mail: tranman@civica.co.uk

TRAPEZE GROUP (UK) LTD
The Mill, Staverton, Trowbridge,
Bath BA14 6PH
Tel: 01225 784200
Fax: 01225 784222
E-mail: info@trapezegroup.co.uk
Web site: www.trapezegroup.co.uk

TRAVEL INFORMATION SYSTEMS
Grand Union House,
20 Kentish Town Road,
London NW1 9NX
Tel: 020 7428 1288
Fax: 020 7267 2745
E-mail: enquiries@travelinfosystems.com
Web site: www.tranman@civica.co.uk

Consultants

ADG TRANSPORT TRAINING
Oak Cottage, Royal Oak, Machen,
Caerphilly CF83 8SN
Tel: 01633 441491
Fax: 01633 440591
E-mail: a.dgettins@btinternet.com

AUSTIN ANALYTICS
Crown House, 183 High Street,
Bottisham, Cambridge CB25 9BB
Tel: 07730 943415
Fax: 07005 946854
E-mail: john@analytics.co.uk
Web site: www.analytics.co.uk

AUTOPRO SOFTWARE
1 Kingsmeadow, Norton Cross,
Runcorn WA7 6PB
Tel: 01928 715962
Fax: 01928 714538
E-mail: sales@autoprouk.com
Web site: www.autoprosoftware.co.uk

BESTCHART LTD
6A Mays Yard, Down Road,
Horndean, Waterlooville,
Hampshire PO8 0YP
Tel: 023 9259 7707
Fax: 023 9259 1700
E-mail: info@bestchart.co.uk
Web site: www.bestchart.co.uk

COLIN BUCHANAN
10 Eastbourne Terrace,
London W2 6LG
Tel: 020 7053 1300
Fax: 020 7053 1301
E-mail: london@cbuchanan.co.uk
Web site: www.colinbuchanan.com

CAREYBROOK LTD
PO Box 205, Southam,
Warwickshire CV47 0ZL
Tel: 01926 813619
Fax: 01926 814898
E-mail: cb.ltd@btinternet.com
Web site: www.careybrook.com

CHADWELL ASSOCIATES LTD
3 Caledonian Close, Ilford IG3 9QF
Tel: 0208 590 5697
E-mail: ib@chadwellassociates.co.uk

CRONER (WOLTERS KLUWER UK LTD)
145 London Road,
Kingston upon Thames KT2 6SR
Tel: 020 8547 3333
Fax: 020 8547 2637
E-mail: info@croner.co.uk
Web site: www.croner.co.uk

DCA DESIGN INTERNATIONAL
19 Church Street, Warwick CV34 4AB
Tel: 01926 499461
Fax: 01926 401134
Web site: www.dca-design.com/transport

ELLIS TRANSPORT SERVICES
61 Bodycoats Road,
Chandlers Ford SO53 2HA
Tel: 023 8027 0447
Fax: 023 8027 6736
E-mail: info@ellistransportservices.com
Web site: www.ellistransportservices.co.uk

Trade Directory

ETMSS LTD
c/o Ground Floor, Austin House,
43 Poole Road, Westbourne,
Bournemouth BH4 9DN
Tel: 0844 800 9299
E-mail: info@etmss.com
Web Site: www.etmss.com

4 FARTHINGS INTERNATIONAL RECRUITMENT
128 Percy Road, Hampton,
Middlesex TW12 2JW
Tel: 0870 770 1604, 020 8941 3147
E-mail: info@4farthings.co.uk
Web site: www.4farthings.co.uk

HILTech DEVELOPMENTS LTD
22 Larbre Crescent, Whickham,
Newcastle upon Tyne NE16 5YG
Tel: 0191 488 6258
Fax: 0191 488 9158
E-mail: executive@hiltechdevelopments.com
Web site: www.hiltechdevelopments.com

IBPTS
43 Cage Lane, Felixstowe,
Suffolk OP11 9BJ
Tel: 01394 672 344
Fax: 01394 672 344
E-mail: info@ibpts.co.uk
Web site: www.ibpts.co.uk

JACOBS BABTIE GROUP LTD
School Green, Shinfield,
Reading RG2 9HL
Tel: 0118 988 1555.
Fax: 0118 988 1653.

KERNOW ASSOCIATES
18 Tresawla Court, Tolvaddon,
Camborne TR14 0HF
Tel/Fax: 01209 711870
E-mail: 106472.3264@compuserve.com

LEONARD GREEN ASSOCIATES
4 Crawshaw Drive, Reedsholme,
Rawtenstall, Rossendale BB4 8PR
Tel: 01706 218539
E-mail: lgreen22@ntlworld.com

LEYLAND PRODUCT DEVELOPMENTS LTD
Aston Way, Leyland,
Preston PR26 7TZ
Tel: 01772 435834
E-mail: sales@lpdl.co.uk

MASS SPECIAL ENGINEERING LTD
Houghton Road North Anston,
Sheffield S25 4SJ
Tel: 01909 550480.
Fax: 01909 550486.

MINIMISE YOUR RISK
11 Chatsworth Park, Telscombe Cliffs,
East Sussex BN10 7DZ
Tel: 01273 580189
Fax: 01273 580189
E-mail: alec@minimiseyourrisk.co.uk
Web site: www.minimiseyourrisk.co.uk

MOTT MACDONALD
St Anne House, Wellesley House,
Croydon CR9 2UL
Tel: 020 8774 2000
Fax: 020 8681 5706
E-mail: marketing@mottmac.com
Web site: www.mottmac.com

NEERMAN & PARTNERS
c/o 22 Larbre Crescent, Whickham,
Newcastle-upon-Tyne NE16 5YG
Tel: 0191 488 6258
Fax: 0191 488 9158

E-mail: info@neerman.net
Web site: www.neerman.net

PARRY PEOPLE MOVERS LTD
Overend Road, Cradley Heath,
Dudley B64 7DD
Tel: 01384 569553
Fax: 01384 637753
E-mail: jpmparry@aol.com
Web site: www.parrypeoplemovers.com

PJA LTD
Locks House, Locks Lane, Wantage,
Oxon OX12 9EH
Tel: 01235 771 791
E-mail: info@pj-associates.co.uk
Web site: www.pj-associates.co.uk

PRE METRO OPERATIONS LTD
21 Woodglade Croft, Kings Norton,
Birmingham B38 8TD
Tel: 0121 243 9906
Fax: 0121 243 9906
E-mail: info@premetro.co.uk
Web site: www.premetro co.uk

PROFESSIONAL TRANSPORT SERVICES
12 Silverdale,
Stanford-le-Hope SS17 8BG
Tel: 01375 675262
E-mail: enquiries@proftranserv.com
Web site: www.proftranserv.co.uk

ROBERTSON TRANSPORT CONSULTING LTD
Field House, Braceby, Sleaford,
Lincolnshire NG34 0SZ
Tel: 01529 497354
E-mail: robertson@rtclincs.co.uk

SALTIRE COMMUNICATIONS
39 Lilyhill Terrace, Edinburgh EH8 7DR
Tel: 0131 652 0205
E-mail: gavin.booth@btconnect.com

SPECIALIST TRAINING & CONSULTANCY SERVICES LTD
6 Venture Court, Metcalfe Drive,
Altham Industrial Estate,
Accrington BB5 5TU
Tel: 01282 687090
Fax: 01282 687091
E-mail: enquiries@specialisttraining.co.uk
Web site: www.specialisttraining.co.uk

TAS PARTNERSHIP LTD
Guildhall House, Guildhall Street,
Preston PR1 3NU
Tel: 01772 204988
Fax: 01722 562070
Web site: www.tas.uk.net

THOMAS KNOWLES - TRANSPORT CONSULTANT
41 Redhills, Eccleshall,
Staffordshire ST21 6JW
Tel: 01785 859414
Fax: 01785 859414
E-mail: thmsknw@aol.com

TRANSPORT CONSULTANCY – R W FAULKS
Penthouse J, Ross Court,
Putney Hill, London SW15 3NY
Tel: 020 8785 1585
E-mail: rexfaulks@aol.com

TRANSPORT DESIGN INTERNATIONAL
12 Waterloo Road Estate,
Bidford on Avon B50 4JH
Tel: 01789 490370
Fax: 01789 490592
E-mail: enquiries@tdi.uk.com
Web site: www.tdi.uk.com

TRANSPORT & TRAVEL RESEARCH LTD
Minster House, Minster Pool Walk,
Lichfield, Staffordshire WS13 6QT
Tel: 01543 416416
Fax: 01543 416681
E-mail: enquiries@ttr-ltd.com
Web site: www.ttr-ltd.com

TTS UK
Total Tool Solutions Ltd,
Newhaven Business Park,
Lowergate, Milnsbridge,
Huddersfield HD3 4HS
Tel: 01484 642211
Fax: 01484 461002
E-mail: sales@ttsuk.com
Web site: www.ttsuk.com

VCA
No1, The Eastgate Office Centre,
Eastgate Road,
Bristol BS5 6XX
Tel: 0117 951 5151
Fax: 0117 952 4103
E-mail: paul.cooke@vca.gov.uk
Web site: www.vca.gov.uk

WARD INTERNATIONAL CONSULTING LTD
Funtley Court, 19 Funtley Hill,
Fareham PO16 7UY
Tel: 01329 280280
Fax: 01329 221010
E-mail: info@wardint.co.uk
Web site: www.wardint.com

WEST END TRAVEL & RUTLAND TRAVEL
The Lakeside Bus & Coach Centre,
Dixon Drive, Off Leicester Road,
Melton Mowbray,
Leicestershire LE13 0DA
Tel: 01664 563498
Fax: 01664 568568

Driver Supply

WEBB'S
St Peters Farm, Middle Drove,
Peterborough PE14 8JJ
Tel: 01945 430123
E-mail: webb-s-cant@fsbdial.co.uk

Driver Training

ADG TRANSPORT CONSULTANCY
Oak Cottage, Royal Oak,
Machen, Caerphilly CF83 8SN
Tel: 01633 441491
Fax: 01633 440591
E-mail: a.dgettins@btinternet.com

BUZZLINES LTD
Unit G1, Lympne Industrial Park,
Hythe CT21 4LR
Tel: 01303 261870
Fax: 01303 230093
Web site: www.buzzlines.co.uk

DATS (DAVE'S ACCIDENT & TRAINING SERVICES)
13 Kingfisher Close, The Willows,
Torquay TQ2 7TF
Tel: 07747 686789
E-Mail: davepboulter@btinternet.com
Web site: www.datservices.org

GOSKILLS LTD
Concorde House, Trinity Park,
Solihull B37 7UQ
Tel: 01216 355520
Fax: 01216 355521
E-mail: info@goskills.org
Web site: www.goskills.org

Trade Directory

HATTS GARAGE SERVICES
Foxham, Chippenham SN15 4NB
Tel: 01249 740444
Fax: 01249 740447
E-mail: mike@hattstravel.co.uk
Web site: www.hattsgarageservices.co.uk

IBPTS
43 Cage Lane, Felixstowe,
Suffolk OP11 9BJ
Tel: 01394 672 344
Fax: 01394 672 344
E-mail: info@ibpts.co.uk
Web site: www.ibpts.co.uk

MIDLAND RED COACHES/WHEELS HERITAGE
Postal Office, 23 Broad Street, Brinklow,
Warwickshire CV23 0LS
Tel: 02476 633624, 07733 884914
Fax: 02476 354900
E-mail: ashley@wheels.co.uk
Web site: www.wheels.co.uk

MINIMISE YOUR RISK
11 Chatsworth Park, Telscombe Cliffs,
East Sussex BN10 7DZ
Tel: 01273 580189
Fax: 01273 580189
E-mail: alec@minimiseyourrisk.co.uk
Web site: www.minimiseyourrisk.co.uk

OMNIBUS TRAINING LTD
2 Purley Way, Croydon CR0 3JT
Tel: 020 8006 7259
Fax: 020 8009 7001
E-mail: enquiries@omnibusltd.com

SPECIALIST TRAINING & CONSULTANCY SERVICES LTD
6 Venture Court, Metcalfe Drive, Altham Industrial Estate, Accrington BB5 5TU
Tel: 01282 687090
Fax: 01282 687091
E-mail: enquiries@specialisttraining.co.uk
Web site: www.specialisttraining.co.uk

VOSA
Vehicle & Operator Services Agency,
Commercial Projects Unit, Berkeley House,
Croydon Street, Bristol BS5 0DA
Tel: 0117 954 3359
Fax: 0117 954 3212
E-mail: commercial.training@vosa.gov.uk

Exhibition/Event Organisers

EXPO MANAGEMENT LTD
Olympus Avenue,
Leamington Spa CV34 6BF
Tel: 01926 888123
Fax: 01926 888004
E-mail: info@expom.co.uk
Web site: www.expom.co.uk

MCI EXHIBITIONS LTD
1Rye Hill Office Park, Birmingham Road,
Allesley, Coventry CV5 9AB
Tel: 02476 408020
Fax: 02476 408019
E-mail: gina@motorcycleshow.co.uk
Web site: www.motorcycleshow.co.uk

THE LONDON BUS EXPORT CO
PO Box 12, Chepstow NP16 5UZ
Tel: 01291 689 741
Fax: 01291 689 361
E-mail: lonbusco@globalnet.co.uk
Web site: www.london-bus.co.uk

UK COACH RALLY
21 The Poynings, Richings Park,
Iver, Buckinghamshire SL0 9DS
Tel: 01753 631170
Fax: 01753 655980

E-mail: info@coachdisplays.co.uk
Web site: www.coachdisplays.co.uk
Contact: Ann Cousins

Ferry Operators

BRITTANY FERRIES GROUP TRAVEL
The Brittany Centre, Wharf Road,
Portsmouth PO2 8RU
Tel: 0870 901 2100
Fax: 0870 901 3100
E-mail: grouptravel@brittany-ferries.co.uk
Web site: www.brittany-ferries.co.uk/grouptravel

CALEDONIAN MACBRAYNE LTD
Head Office, The Ferry Terminal,
Gourock PA19 1QP
Tel: 01475 650100
Web site: www.calmac.co.uk

CONDOR FERRIES LTD
Condor House, New Harbour Road South,
Hamworthy, Poole BH15 4AJ
Tel: 01202 207207
Fax: 01202 685184
E-mail: reservations@condorferries.co.uk
Web site: www.condorferries.co.uk

DFDS SEAWAYS
Scandinavia House, Refinery Road,
Parkeston CO12 4QG
Tel: 08771 882 0881
Web site: www.dfdsseaways.co.uk

EUROTUNNEL
PO Box 2000,
Folkestone CT18 8XY
Tel: 08702 430401
Fax: 01303 288909
Web site: www.eurotunnel.com

IRISH FERRIES LTD
Groups Department, Salt Island,
Holyhead LL65 1DR
Tel: 08705 329129
Fax: 01407 760340
Web site: www.irishferries.com

ISLE OF MAN STEAM PACKET COMPANY
Imperial Buildings, Douglas IM1 2BY
Tel: 01624 661661
Fax: 01624 645618
E-mail: resesteam-packet.com
Web site: www.steam-packet.com

NORFOLKLINE
Norfolk House, Eastern Dock,
Dover CT16 1JA
Tel: 0870 870 1020
Web site: www.norfolkline.com

NORTHLINK FERRIES LTD
Stromness Ferry Terminal, Ferry Road,
Stromness, Orkney KW16 3BH
Tel: 01856 885500
Fax: 01856 851795
E-mail: info@northlinkferries.co.uk
Web site: www.northlinkferries.co.uk

P&O FERRIES
Channel House, Channel View Road,
Dover CT17 9TJ
Tel: 08716 641641
Fax: 08707 625325
E-mail: groups@poferries.com
Web site: www.poferries.com

PENTLAND FERRIES
Pier Road, St Margaret's Hope,
Orkney KW17 2SW
Tel: 01856 831226
Fax: 01856 831697
Web site: www.pentlandferries.co.uk

RED FUNNEL
Red Funnel Travel Centre,
12 Bugle Street, Southampton SO14 2JY
Tel: 0844 844 9988
Fax: 0844 844 2698
E-mail: post@redfunnel.co.uk
Web site: www.redfunnel.co.uk

SEAFRANCE
Whitfield Court, Honeywood Close,
Whitfield, Dover CT16 3PX
Tel: 0871 222 2800
Fax: 0871 282 8549
E-mail: groups@seafrance.fr
Web site: www.seafrance.com

STENA LINE
Station Approach, Holyhead LL65 1DQ
Tel: 08705 20 44 02
E-mail: groups@stenaline.com
Web site: www.stenaline.co.uk/groups

TRANSMANCHE FERRIES
Newhaven Ferry Port, Railway Approach,
Newhaven BN9 0DF
Tel: 0800 917 1201
Web site: www.transmancheferries.co.uk,
www.ldlines.com

TRAVELPATH 3000
PO Box 32, Grantham NG31 7JA
Tel: 01476 570187
Fax: 01476 572718
E-mail: info@travelpath3000.com
Web site: www.travelpath3000.com

WIGHTLINK ISLE OF WIGHT FERRIES
70 Broad Street, Portsmouth PO1 2LB
Tel: 0870 582 7744
Fax: 023 9285 5257
E-mail: sales@wightlink.co.uk
Web site: www.wightlink.co.uk

Finance and Leasing

AD COACH SALES
Newbridge Coach Depot, Witheridge,
Devon EX16 8PY
Tel: 01884 860767
Fax: 01884 860711
E-mail: enquiries@adcoachsales.co.uk
Web site: www.adcoachsales.co.uk

DAWSONRENTALS BUS AND COACH LTD
Delaware Drive, Tongwell, Milton Keynes
MK15 8JH
Tel: 01908 218111
Fax: 01908 218 444
E-mail: contactus@dawsongroup.co.uk
Web site: www.dawsongroup.co.uk

LANDMARK FINANCE LTD
Suite 4, Old Grove House, 13 Vine Street,
Hazel Grove, Stockport,
Cheshire SK7 4JS
Tel: 0161 456 4242
Fax: 0161 483 3733
E-mail: landmarkfinance@btconnect.com
Web site: www.landmarkltd.co.uk

LHE FINANCE LTD
21 Headlands Business Park, Salisbury
Road, Ringwood, Hampshire BH24 3PB
Tel: 01425 474070
Fax: 01425 474090
E-mail: mfox@lhefinance.co.uk
Web site: www.dawsongroup.co.uk

MCV BUS & COACH LTD
Sterling Place, Elean Business Park,
Sutton CB6 2QE
Tel: 01353 773000
Fax: 01353 773001
E-mail: vernon.edwards@mcv-uk.com

Trade Directory

MISTRAL BUS & COACH PLC
Booths Hall, Chelford Road,
Knutsford WA16 8QZ
Tel: 01565 621881
Fax: 01565 621882
E-mail: sales@mistral-group.com
Web site: www.mistral-group.com

NORTON FOLGATE FG PLC
50A St Andrew Street,
Hertford SG14 1JA
Tel: 01992 537735
Fax: 01992 537733
E-mail: help@nortonfolgate.co.uk
Web site: www.nortonfolgate.co.uk

ROADLEASE
Crossroads, Anston, Sheffield S25 7ES
Tel: 01909 551177
Fax: 01909 567994
E-mail: roadlease@kirkbycoachandbus.com
Web site: www.roadlease.com

SANTANDER ASSET FINANCE
Taylor Road, Trafford Park,
Manchester M41 7JQ
Tel: 0161 747 5698
Fax: 0161 275 4501
E-mail: steve.moult@hansar.co.uk
Web site: www.buses247.co.uk

VOLVO FINANCIAL SERVICES
Wedgnock Lane, Warwick CV34 5YA
Tel: 01926 498888
Fax: 01926 410278
Web site: www.volvo.com

Graphic Design

BEST IMPRESSIONS
15 Starfield Road, London W12 9SN
Tel: 020 8740 6443
Fax: 020 8740 9134
E-mail: talk2us@best-impressions.co.uk
Web site: www.best-impressions.co.uk

EXPRESS COACH REPAIRS LTD
Outgang Lane,
Pickering YO18 7JA
Tel: 01751 475215
Fax: 01751 475215
E-mail: info@expresscoachrepairs.co.uk
Web site: www.expresscoachrepairs.co.uk

FWT
Aztec House 397-405 Archway Road,
London N6 4EY
Tel: 020 7347 3700
Fax: 020 7347 3701
E-mail: sales@fwt.co.uk
Web site: www.fwt.co.uk

GRAPHIC EVOLUTION LTD
Ad House, East Parade,
Harrogate HG1 5LT
Tel: 01423 706680
Fax: 01423 502522
E-mail: info@graphic-evolution.co.uk
Web site: www.graphic-evolution.co.uk

HATTS GARAGE SERVICES
Foxham, Chippenham
SN15 4NB
Tel: 01249 740444
Fax: 01249 740447
E-mail: mike@hattstravel.co.uk
Web site: www.hattsgarageservices.co.uk

LAWTON SERVICES LTD
Knutsford Road, Church Lawton, Stoke-on-Trent ST7 3DN
Tel: 01270 882056
Fax: 01270 883014
E-mail: andrea@lawtonservices.co.uk
Web site: www.lawtonservices.co.uk

NEERMAN & PARTNERS
c/o 22 Larbre Crescent, Whickham,
Newcastle-upon-Tyne NE16 5YG
Tel: 0191 488 6258
Fax: 0191 488 9158
E-mail: info@neerman.net
Web site: www.neerman.net

PLUM DIGITAL PRINT
Suite 1, Cornerstone House, Stafford Park
13, Telford, Shropshire TF3 3AZ
Tel: 01952 204 920
E-mail:
nigel.greenaway@busandcoach.com
Web site: www.plumdigitalprint.co.uk

RH BODYWORKS
A140 Ipswich Road, Brome,
Eye IP23 8AW
Tel: 01379 870666
Fax: 01379 872138
E-mail: mike.ball@rhbodyworks.co.uk
Web site: www.rhbodyworks.co.uk

TIME TRAVEL UK
247 Bradford Road, Stanningley,
Pudsey, Leeds LS28 6QB
Tel: 0113 255 1188
E-mail: nick.baldwin@tinyworld.co.uk

VETRO DESIGN
247 Bradford Road, Pudsey,
Leeds LS28 6QB
Tel: 01132 551188
E-mail: nick@vetrodesign.co.uk

Health & Safety

GAUNTLET RISK MANAGEMENT (COVENTRY)
11 Little Church Street,
Rugby CV21 3AW
Tel: 07944 092681
Web site: www.gauntletgroup.com/coventry
Contact: Laura Jennings

Hotel Agents

TRAVELPATH 3000
PO Box 32, Grantham NG31 7JA
Tel: 01476 570187
Fax: 01476 572718
E-mail: info@travelpath3000.com
Web site: www.travelpath3000.com

Insurance

BELMONT INTERNATIONAL LTD
Becket House, Vestry Road, Otford,
Sevenoaks TN14 5EL
Tel: 01732 744700
Fax: 01732 740276
E-mail: phil.white@belmontint.com
Web site: www.belmontint.com

R. L. DAVISON & CO LTD
Bury House, 31 Bury Street,
London EC3A 5AH.
Tel: 020 7816 9876
Fax: 020 7816 9880
Web site: www.rlddavison.co.uk

GAUNTLET RISK MANAGEMENT (COVENTRY)
11 Little Church Street,
Rugby CV21 3AW
Tel: 07944 092681
Web site: www.gauntletgroup.com/coventry
Contact: Laura Jennings

P J HAYMAN & CO LTD
Stansted House, Rowlands Castle,
Hampshire PO9 6BR
Tel: 08452 393 526
Web site: www.pjhayman.com

OMNI WHITTINGTONS
Arthur Castle House, 33 Creechurch Lane,
London EC3A 5EB
Tel: 020 7709 9991
Fax: 020 7456 1225.
Web site: whittingtoninsurance.com

PEAK LEGAL SERVICES LTD
41 Longmoor Road, Simmondley,
Glossop, Derbyshire SK13 6NH
Tel/Fax: 01457 855141
Mobile: 07989 092835
E-mail: ford414@btinternet.com

RIGTON INSURANCE SERVICES LTD
Chevin House, Otley Road, Guiseley,
Leeds LS20 8BH
Tel: 01943 879539
Fax: 01943 875529
E-mail: enquiries@rigtoninsurance.co.uk
Web site: www.rigtoninsurance.co.uk

TOWERGATE CHAPMAN STEVENS
Towergate House, 22 Wintersells Road,
Byfleet, Surrey KT14 7LF
Tel: 01932 334140
Fax: 01932 351238
E-mail: tcs@towergate.co.uk
Web site:
www.towergatechapmanstevens.co.uk

VOLVO INSURANCE SERVICES
Wedgnock Lane, Warwick CV34 5YA
Tel: 01926 401777
Fax: 01926 407407
Web site: www.volvo.com

WILLIS LTD
10 Trinity Square, London EC3P 3AX
Tel: 020 7488 8111
Fax: 020 7975 2884
E-mail: warren.dann@willis.com
Web site: www.willis.com

WRIGHTSURE GROUP
799 London Road,
West Thurrock RM20 3LH
Tel: 01708 865553
Fax: 01708 865100
E-mail: info@wrightsure.com
Web site: www.wrightsure.com

Legal & Operations Advisers

BORLAND NINDER DIXON LLP
3 Axe View, Axe Road, Drimpton,
Beaminster, Dorset DT8 3RJ
Tel: 01460 72 769
Fax: 01460 271680
E-mail: chris.borland@tiscali.co.uk

ELLIS INTERNATIONAL TRANSPORT CONSULTING LTD
61 Bodycoats Road, Chandlers Ford,
Hampshire SO53 2HA
Tel: 023 8027 0447
Fax: 023 8027 6736
E-mail: info@ellistransportservices.co.uk
Web site: www.ellistransportservices.co.uk

FREIGHT TRANSPORT ASSOCIATION
Hermes House, St John's Road,
Tunbridge Wells TN4 9UZ
Tel: 01892 526171
Fax: 01892 534989
E-mail: enquiries@fta.co.uk
Web site: www.fta.co.uk

IBPTS
43 Cage Lane, Felixstowe,
Suffolk OP11 9BJ
Tel: 01394 672 344
Fax: 01394 672 344
E-mail: info@ibpts.co.uk
Web site: www.ibpts.co.uk

Trade Directory

KERNOW ASSOCIATES
18 Tresawla Court, Tolvaddon, Camborne TR14 0HF
Tel/Fax: 01209 711870.
E-mail: 106472.3264@compuserve.com

PEAK LEGAL SERVICES LTD
41 Longmoor Road, Simmondley, Glossop, Derbyshire SK13 6NH
Tel/Fax: 01457 855141
Mobile: 07989 092835
E-mail: ford414@btinternet.com

PELLYS LLP SOLICITORS
The Old Monastery, Windmill, Bishops, Stortford, Hertfordshire CM23 2ND
Tel: 01279 758 080
Fax: 01279 467 565
E-mail: office@pellys.co.uk
Web site: www.pellys.co.uk

PRE METRO OPERATIONS LTD
21 Woodglade Croft, Kings Norton, Birmingham B38 8TD
Tel: 0121 243 9906
Fax: 0121 243 9906
E-mail: info@premetro.co.uk
Web site: www.premetro.co.uk

PROFESSIONAL TRANSPORT SERVICES
12 Silverdale, Stanford-le-Hope SS17 8BG
Tel: 01375 675262
E-mail: enquiries@proftranserv.com
Web site: www.proftranserv.co.uk

WARD INTERNATIONAL CONSULTING LTD
Funtley Court, 19 Funtley Hill, Fareham PO16 7UY
Tel: 01329 280280
Fax: 01329 221010
E-mail: info@wardint.co.uk
Web site: www.wardint.com

WEDLAKE SAINT
91-93 Farringdon Road, London EC1M 3LN.
Tel: 020 7400 4100.
Fax: 020 7242 3100.
Web site: www.wedlakesaint.co.uk

Livery Design

BEST IMPRESSIONS
15 Starfield Road, London W12 9SN
Tel: 020 8740 6443
Fax: 020 8740 9134
E-mail: talk2us@best-impressions.co.uk
Web site: www.best-impressions.co.uk

CHANNEL COMMERCIALS PLC
Unit 6, Cobbs Wood Industrial Estate, Brunswick Road, Ashford TN23 1EH
Tel: 01233 629272
Fax: 01233 636322
E-mail: info@ccplc.co.uk
Web site: www.channelcommercials.co.uk

EXPRESS COACH REPAIRS LTD
Outgang Lane, Pickering YO18 7JA
Tel: 01751 475215
Fax: 01751 475215
E-mail: info@expresscoachrepairs.co.uk
Web site: www.expresscoachrepairs.co.uk

GRAPHIC EVOLUTION LTD
Ad House, East Parade, Harrogate HG1 5LT
Tel: 01423 706680
Fax: 01423 502522
E-mail: info@graphic-evolution.co.uk
Web site: www.graphic-evolution.co.uk

TONY GREAVES GRAPHICS
19 Perth Mount, Horsforth, Leeds LS18 5SH
Tel/Fax: 0113 258 4795
E-mail: tony@greavesgraphics.fsnet.co.uk

HATTS GARAGE SERVICES
Foxham, Chippenham SN15 4NB
Tel: 01249 740444
Fax: 01249 740447
E-mail: mike@hattstravel.co.uk
Web site: www.hattsgarageservices.co.uk

LAWTON SERVICES LTD
Knutsford Road, Church Lawton, Stoke-on-Trent ST7 3DN
Tel: 01270 882056
Fax: 01270 883014
E-mail: andrea@lawtonservices.co.uk
Web site: www.lawtonservices.co.uk

THE LONDON BUS EXPORT CO
PO Box 12, Chepstow NP16 5UZ
Tel: 01291 689741
Fax: 01291 689361
E-mail: lonbusco@globalnet.co.uk

McKENNA BROTHERS
McKenna House, Jubilee Road, Middleton, Manchester M24 2LX
Tel: 0161 655 3244
Fax: 0161 655 3059
E-mail: info@mckennabrothers.co.uk
Web site: www.mckennabrothers.co.uk

NEERMAN & PARTNERS
c/o 22 Larbre Crescent, Whickham, Newcastle-upon-Tyne NE16 5YG
Tel: 0191 488 6258
Fax: 0191 488 9158
E-mail: info@neerman.net
Web site: www.neerman.net

PLUM DIGITAL PRINT
Suite 1, Cornerstone House, Stafford Park 13, Telford, Shropshire TF3 3AZ
Tel: 01952 204 920
E-mail: nigel.greenaway@busandcoach.com
Web site: www.plumdigitalprint.co.uk

TIME TRAVEL UK
247 Bradford Road, Stanningley, Pudsey, Leeds LS28 6QB
Tel: 0113 255 1188
E-mail: nick.baldwin@tinyworld.co.uk

VETRO DESIGN
247 Bradford Road, Pudsey, Leeds LS28 6QB
Tel: 01132 551188
E-mail: nick@vetrodesign.co.uk

Maps for the Bus Industry

BEST IMPRESSIONS
15 Starfield Road, London W12 9SN
Tel: 020 8740 6443
Fax: 020 8740 9134
E-mail: talk2us@best-impressions.co.uk
Web site: www.best-impressions.co.uk

FWT
Aztec House, 397-405 Archway Road, London N6 4EY
Tel: 020 7347 3700
Fax: 020 7347 3701
E-mail: sales@fwt.co.uk
Web site: www.fwt.co.uk

TONY GREAVES GRAPHICS
19 Perth Mount, Horsforth, Leeds LS18 5SH
Tel/Fax: 0113 258 4795
E-mail: tony@greavesgraphics.fsnet.co.uk

PINDAR PLC
31 Edison Road, Aylesbury HP19 8TE
Tel: 01296 390100
Fax: 01296 381233
Web site: www.pindar.com

TIME TRAVEL UK
247 Bradford Road, Stanningley, Pudsey, Leeds LS28 6QB
Tel: 0113 255 1188
E-mail: nick.baldwin@tinyworld.co.uk

VETRO DESIGN
247 Bradford Road, Pudsey, Leeds LS28 6QB
Tel: 01132 551188
E-mail: nick@vetrodesign.co.uk

Marketing Services

ADG TRANSPORT CONSULTANCY
Oak Cottage, Royal Oak, Machen, Caerphilly CF83 8SN
Tel: 01633 441491
Fax: 01633 440591
E-mail: a.dgettins@btinternet.com

KERNOW ASSOCIATES
18 Tresawla Court, Tolvaddon, Camborne TR14 0HF
Tel/Fax: 01209 711870.
E-mail: 106472.3264@compuserve.com

Mechanical Investigation

KERNOW ASSOCIATES
18 Tresawla Court, Tolvaddon, Camborne TR14 0HF
Tel/Fax: 01209 711870.
E-mail: 106472.3264@compuserve.com

OPTARE PRODUCT SUPPORT LONDON
Unit 9, Eurocourt, Olivers Close, West Thurrock RM20 3EE
Tel: 08444 123222
Fax: 01708 869920
E-mail: london.service@optare.com

OPTARE PRODUCT SUPPORT ROTHERHAM
Denby Way, Hellaby, Rotherham S66 8HR
Tel: 01709 535101
Fax: 01709 535103
E-mail: rotherham.service@optare.com

OPTARE PRODUCT SUPPORT SCOTLAND
Unit 7, Cumbernauld Business Park, Ward Park Road, Cumbernauld G67 3JZ
Tel: 01236 726738
Fax: 01236 795651
E-mail: scotland.service@optare.com

PLAXTON SERVICE
Ryton Road, Anston, Sheffield S25 4DL
Tel: 01909 551155
Fax: 01909 550050
E-mail: service@plaxtonlimited.co.uk
Web site: www.plaxtonaftercare.co.uk

On-Bus Advertising

BEST IMPRESSIONS
15 Starfield Road, London W12 9SN
Tel: 020 8740 6443
Fax: 020 8740 9134
E-mail: talk2us@best-impressions.co.uk
Web site: www.best-impressions.co.uk

M BISSELL DISPLAY LTD
Unit 15, Beechwood Business Park, Burdock Close, Cannock, Staffordshire WS11 7GB
Tel: 01543 502115

Trade Directory

Fax: 01543 502118
E-mail: sales@bisselldisplay.com
Web site: www.bisselldisplay.com

CYBERLYNE COMMUNICATIONS LTD
Unit 5, Hatfield Way, South Church
Enterprise Park, Bishop Auckland,
Durham DL14 6XF
Tel: 01388 773761
Fax: 01388 773778
E-mail: sales@cyberlyne.co.uk
Web site: www.cyberlyne.co.uk

DECKER MEDIA LTD
Adbus Ltd, Decker House,
Lowater Street, Carlton,
Nottingham NG4 1JJ
Tel: 0115 940 2406
Fax: 0115 940 2407
E-mail: sales@deckermedia.co.uk
Web site: www.deckermedia.co.uk

TIME TRAVEL UK
247 Bradford Road, Stanningley,
Pudsey, Leeds LS28 6QB
Tel: 0113 255 1188
E-mail: nick.baldwin@tinyworld.com

TITAN BUS UK LTD
St Johns House, John Street,
Harrogate HG1 1NH
Tel: 01423 727636
Fax: 01423 564453
E-mail: enquiries@titanbus.co.uk
Web site: www.titanbus.co.uk

Printing and Publishing

BEMROSEBOOTH LTD
Stockholm Road, Sutton Fields Industrial
Estate, Hull HU7 0XY
Tel: 01482 826343
Fax: 01482 371386
E-mail: lprecious@bemrosebooth.com
Web site: www.bemrosebooth.com

BEST IMPRESSIONS
15 Starfield Road, London W12 9SN
Tel: 020 8740 6443
Fax: 020 8740 9134
E-mail: talk2us@best-impressions.co.uk
Web site: www.best-impressions.co.ukl

M BISSELL DISPLAY LTD
Unit 15, Beechwood Business Park,
Burdock Close, Cannock, Staffordshire
WS11 7GB
Tel: 01543 502115
Fax: 01543 502118
E-mail: sales@bisselldisplay.com
Web site: www.bisselldisplay.com

THE HENRY BOOTH GROUP
Stockholm Road, Sutton Fields Industrial
Estate, Hull HU7 0XY
Tel: 01482 826343
Fax: 01482 839767
E-mail: mshanley@henrybooth.co.uk
Web site: www.henrybooth.co.uk

FWT
Aztec House, 397-405 Archway Road,
London N6 4EY
Tel: 020 7347 3700
Fax: 020 7347 3701
E-mail: sales@fwt.co.uk
Web site: www.fwt.co.uk

GRAPHIC EVOLUTION LTD
Ad House, East Parade,
Harrogate HG1 5LT
Tel: 01423 706680
Fax: 01423 502522
E-mail: info@graphic-evolution.co.uk
Web site: www.graphic-evolution.co.uk

TONY GREAVES GRAPHICS
19 Perth Mount, Horsforth,
Leeds LS18 5SH
Tel/Fax: 0113 258 4795
E-mail: tony@greavesgraphics.fsnet.co.uk

HB PUBLICATIONS LTD
3 Ingham Grove, Hartlepool TS25 2LH
Tel: 01429 293611
E-mail: sales@hbpub.co.uk
Web site: www.hbpub.co.uk

IAN ALLAN PRINTING LTD
Riverdene Business Park, Molesey Road,
Hersham, Surrey KT12 4RG
Tel: 01932 266600
Fax: 01932 266601
E-mail:
jonathan.bingham@ianallanprinting.co.uk
Web site: www.ianallanprinting.co.uk

IMAGE & PRINT GROUP
Unit 9, Oakbank Industrial Estate,
Garscube Road, Glasgow G20 7LU
Tel: 0141 353 1900
Fax: 0141 353 8611
E-mail: alan@imageandprint.co.uk
Web site: www.imageandprint.co.uk

MIDLAND COUNTIES PUBLICATIONS
4 Watling Drive, Hinckley LE10 3EY
E-mail: midlandbooks@compuserve.com

PINDAR PLC
31 Edison Road, Aylesbury HP19 8TE
Tel: 01296 390100
Fax: 01296 381233
Web site: www.pindar.com

PLUM DIGITAL PRINT
Suite 1, Cornerstone House,
Stafford Park 13, Telford, Shropshire TF3 3AZ
Tel: 01952 204 920
E-mail: nigel.greenaway@buscoach.com
Web site: www.plumdigitalprint.co.uk

TIME TRAVEL UK
247 Bradford Road, Stanningley,
Pudsey LS28 6QB
Tel: 0113 255 1188
E-mail: nick.baldwin@tinyworld.co.uk

TRANSPORT STATIONERY SERVICES
61 Bodycoats Road, Chandlers Ford,
Hampshire SO53 2HA
Tel: 07041 471008
Fax: 07041 471009
E-mail:
info@transportstationeryservices.co.uk

VETRO DESIGN
247 Bradford Road, Pudsey,
Leeds LS28 6QB
Tel: 0113 255 1188
E-mail: nick@vetrodesign.co.uk

Promotional Material

BEST IMPRESSIONS
15 Starfield Road,
London W12 9SN
Tel: 020 8740 6443
Fax: 020 8740 9134
E-mail: talk2us@best-impressions.co.uk
Web site: www.best-impressions.co.uk

M BISSELL DISPLAY LTD
Unit 15, Beechwood Business Park,
Burdock Close, Cannock, Staffordshire
WS11 7GB
Tel: 01543 502115
Fax: 01543 502118
E-mail: sales@bisselldisplay.com
Web site: www.bisselldisplay.com

FWT
Aztec House, 397-405 Archway Road,
London N6 4EY
Tel: 020 7347 3700
Fax: 020 7347 3701
E-mail: sales@fwt.co.uk
Web site: www.fwt.co.uk

GRAPHIC EVOLUTION LTD
Ad House, East Parade,
Harrogate HG1 5LT
Tel: 01423 706680
Fax: 01423 502522
E-mail: info@graphic-evolution.co.uk
Web site: www.graphic-evolution.co.uk

IBPTS
43 Cage Lane, Felixstowe,
Suffolk OP11 9BJ
Tel: 01394 672 344
Fax: 01394 672 344
E-mail: info@ibpts.co.uk
Web site: www.ibpts.co.uk

MARKET ENGINEERING
43-44 North Bar, Banbury OX16 0TH
Tel: 01295 277050
Fax: 01295 277030
E-mail: contact@m-eng.co.uk
Web site: www.marketengineering.co.uk

PINDAR PLC
31 Edison Road, Aylesbury HP19 8TE
Tel: 01296 390100
Fax: 01296 381233
Web site: www.pindar.com

PLUM DIGITAL PRINT
Suite 1, Cornerstone House,
Stafford Park 13, Telford,
Shropshire TF3 3AZ
Tel: 01952 204 920
E-mail:
nigel.greenaway@busandcoach.com
Web site: www.plumdigitalprint.co.uk

STEPHEN C MORRIS
PO Box 119, Shepperton TW17 8UX
Tel: 01932 232574
E-mail: buswriter@btinternet.com

TIME TRAVEL UK
247 Bradford Road, Stanningley,
Pudsey, Leeds LS28 6QB
Tel: 0113 255 1188
E-mail: nick.baldwin@tinyworld.co.uk

TONY GREAVES GRAPHICS
19 Perth Mount, Horsforth,
Leeds LS18 5SH
Tel/Fax: 0113 258 4795
E-mail: tony@greavesgraphics.fsnet.co.uk

VETRO DESIGN
247 Bradford Road, Pudsey,
Leeds LS28 6QB
Tel: 01132 551188
E-mail: nick@vetrodesign.co.uk

Publications – Magazines & Books

BRITISH BUS PUBLISHING LTD
16 St Margaret's Drive,
Telford TF1 3PH
Tel: 01952 255 669
E-mail: bill@britishbuspublishing.co.uk
Web site: www.britishbuspublishing.co.uk

BUS & COACH BUYER
The Publishing Centre, 1 Woolram Wygate,
Spalding PE11 1NU
Tel: 01775 711777
Fax: 01775 711737
E-mail: bcbsales@busandcoachbuyer.com
Web site: www.busandcoachbuyer.com

Trade Directory

BUS & COACH PROFESSIONAL
Suite 1, Cornerstone House, Stafford Park 13, Telford TF3 3AZ
Tel: 01952 204 920
E-mail: jo.taylor@busnadcoach.com
Web site: www.busandcoach.com

BUS USER
Bus Users UK, PO Box 2950, Stoke on Trent ST4 9EW
Tel: 01782 442885
Fax: 01782 442886
E-mail: enquiries@bususers.org
Web site: www.bususers.org

BUSES
Ian Allan Publishing Ltd, Riverdene Business Park, Molesey Road, Hersham, Surrey KT12 4RG
Tel: 01932 266600
Fax: 01932 266601
Web site: www.busesmag.com

BUSES WORLDWIDE
37 Oyster Lane, Byfleet, Surrey KT14 7HS
Tel: 01932 352351
E-mail: membership@busesworldwide.org
Web site: www.busesworldwide.org

COACH & BUS WEEK
3 The Office Village, Cygnet Park, Hampton, Peterborough PE7 8FD
Tel: 01733 293240
Fax: 0845 2802927
E-mail: jacqui.grobler@rouncymedia.co.uk
Web site: www.cbwnet.co.uk

CRONER (WOLTERS KLUWER UK LTD)
145 London Road, Kingston upon Thames KT2 6SR
Tel: 020 8547 3333
Fax: 020 8547 2637
E-mail: info@croner.co.uk
Web site: www.croner.co.uk

HB PUBLICATIONS LTD
3 Ingham Grove, Hartlepool TS25 2LH
Tel: 01429 293611
E-mail: sales@hbpub.co.uk
Web site: www.hbpub.co.uk

JANES URBAN TRANSPORT SYSTEMS
163 Brighton Road, Coulsdon CR5 2YH
Tel: 020 8700 3700
Web site: www.janes.com/www.juts.janes.com

PLUM DIGITAL PRINT
Suite 1, Cornerstone House, Stafford Park 13, Telford, Shropshire TF3 3AZ
Tel: 01952 204920
E-mail: nigel.greenaway@busandcoach.com
Web site: www.plumdigitalprint.co.uk

ROUTE ONE
Expo Publishing, Suite 4, Century House, Towermead Business Park, Fletton, Peterborough PE2 9DY
Tel: 0870 241 8745
Fax: 0870 241 8891
E-mail: mike.morgan@route-one.net
Web site: www.route.one.net

SALTIRE COMMUNICATIONS
39 Lilyhill Terrace, Edinburgh EH8 7DR
Tel: 0131 652 0205
E-mail: gavin.booth@btconnect.com

SOE
22 Greencoat Place, London SW1 1PR
Tel: 02076 301 111
Fax: 02076 306 667
E-mail: soe@soe.org.uk
Web site: www.soe.org.uk

STEPHEN C MORRIS
PO Box 119, Shepperton TW17 8UX
Tel: 01932 232574
E-mail: buswriter@btinternet.com

TIME TRAVEL UK
247 Bradford Road, Stanningley, Pudsey, Leeds LS28 6QB
Tel: 0113 255 1188
E-mail: nick.baldwin@tinyworld.co.uk

TRAMWAYS & URBAN TRANSIT
c/o LRTA, PO Box 26, Sawtry PE28 5WY
E-mail: editor@lrta.org
Web site: www.lrta.org

TRANSIT MAGAZINE
Quadrant House, 250 Kennington Lane, London SE11 5RD
Tel: 0845 270 7954
Fax: 0845 270 7961
E-mail: ed.transit@landor.co.uk
Web site: www.transitmagazine.co.uk

VETRO DESIGN
247 Bradford Road, Pudsey, Leeds LS28 6QB
Tel: 0113 255 1188
E-mail: nick@vetrodesign.co.uk

Quality Management Systems

FTA VEHICLE INSPECTION SERVICE
Hermes House, St John's Road, Tunbridge Wells TN4 9UZ
Tel: 01892 526171
Fax: 01892 534989
E-mail: enquiries@fta.co.uk
Web site: www.fta.co.uk

IBPTS
43 Cage Lane, Felixstowe, Suffolk OP11 9BJ
Tel: 01394 672344
Fax: 01394 672344
E-mail: info@ibpts.co.uk
Web site: www.ibpts.co.uk

INIT GmbH – INNOVATION IN TRANSPORT
32A Stoney Street, The Lace Market, Nottingham NG1 1LL
Tel: 0870 890 4648
Fax: 0115 988 6917
E-mail: sales@init.co.uk
Web site: www.init.co.uk

MYSTERY TRAVELLERS
6A Mays Yard, Down Road, Horndean, Waterlooville, Hampshire PO8 0YP
Tel: 023 9259 7707
Fax: 023 9259 1700
E-mail: info@bestchart.co.uk
Web site: www.bestchart.co.uk

PROFESSIONAL TRANSPORT SERVICES
12 Silverdale, Stanford-le-Hope SS17 8BG
Tel: 01375 675262
E-mail: enquiries@proftranserv.com
Web site: www.proftranserv.co.uk

TRANSPORT STATIONERY SERVICES
61 Bodycoats Road, Chandlers Ford, Hampshire SO53 2HA
Tel: 07041 471 008
Fax: 07041 471 009
E-mail: info@transportstationeryservices.co.uk

TTS UK
Total Tool Solutions Ltd, Newhaven Business Park, Lowergate, Milnsbridge, Huddersfield HD3 4HS
Tel: 01484 642211
Fax: 01484 461002
E-mail: sales@ttsuk.com
Web site: www.ttsuk.com

VCA
No1, The Estate Office Centre, Eastgate Road, Bristol BS5 6XX
Tel: 0117 952 4126
Fax: 0117 952 4104
E-mail: paul.cooke@vca.gov.uk
Web site: www.vca.gov.uk

VOSA COMMERCIAL PROJECTS UNIT
Berkeley House, Croydon Street, Bristol BS5 0DA
Tel: 0117 954 3359
Fax: 0117 954 3496
E-mail: commercial.training@vosa.gov.uk

Recruitment

COUNTY RECRUITMENT & TRAINING LTD
5 White Cliffs Business Centre, Honeywood Road, Whitfield, Dover, Kent CT16 3EH
Tel: 01304 826220
Fax: 01304 822551
E-mail: admin@crtweb.org
Web site: www.crtweb.org

4 FARTHINGS INTERNATIONAL RECRUITMENT
128 Percy Road, Hampton, Middlesex TW12 2JW
Tel: 0870 770 1604, 020 8941 3147
E-mail: info@4farthings.co.uk
Web site: www.4farthings.co.uk

Reference Books

BRITISH BUS PUBLISHING LTD
16 St Margaret's Drive, Telford TF1 3PH
Tel: 01952 255669
E-mail: bill@britishbuspublishing.co.uk
Web site: www.britishbuspublishing.co.uk

HB PUBLICATIONS LTD
3 Ingham Grove, Hartlepool TS25 2LH
Tel: 01429 293611
E-mail: sales@hbpub.co.uk
Web site: www.hbpub.co.uk

Timetable Production

BEMROSEBOOTH LTD
Stockholm Road, Sutton Fields Industrial Estate, Hull HU7 0XY
Tel: 01482 826343
Fax: 01482 371386
E-mail: lprecious@bemrosebooth.com
Web site: www.bemrosebooth.com

BEST IMPRESSIONS
15 Starfield Road, London W12 9SN
Tel: 020 8740 6443
Fax: 020 8740 9134
E-mail: talk2us@best-impressions.co.uk
Web site: www.best-impressions.co.uk

M BISSELL DISPLAY LTD
Unit 15, Beechwood Business Park, Burdock Close, Cannock, Staffordshire WS11 7GB
Tel: 01543 502115
Fax: 01543 502118
E-mail: sales@bisselldisplay.com
Web site: www.bisselldisplay.com

The Little Red Book 2011 - in association with *tbf* Transport Benevolent Fund

Trade Directory

FWT
Aztec House, 397-405 Archway Road,
London N6 4EY
Tel: 020 7347 3700 **Fax:** 020 7347 3701
E-mail: sales@fwt.co.uk
Web site: www.fwt.co.uk

TONY GREAVES GRAPHICS
19 Perth Mount, Horsforth,
Leeds LS18 5SH
Tel/Fax: 0113 258 4795
E-mail: tony@greavesgraphics.fsnet.co.uk

IBPTS
43 Cage Lane, Felixstowe,
Suffolk OP11 9BJ
Tel: 01394 672344 **Fax:** 01394 672344
E-mail: info@ibpts.co.uk
Web site: www.ibpts.co.uk

PINDAR PLC
31 Edison Road, Aylesbury HP19 8TE
Tel: 01296 390100
Fax: 01296 381233
Web site: www.pindar.com

PLUM DIGITAL PRINT
Suite 1, Cornerstone House, Stafford Park
13, Telford, Shropshire TF3 3AZ
Tel: 01952 204920
E-mail: nigel.greenaway@busandcoach.com
Web site: www.plumdigitalprint.co.uk

PROFESSIONAL TRANSPORT SERVICES
12 Silverdale, Stanford-le-Hope SS17 8BG
Tel: 01375 675262
E-mail: enquiries@proftranserv.com
Web site: www.proftranserv.co.uk

TIME TRAVEL UK
247 Bradford Road, Stanningley, Pudsey,
Leeds LS28 6QB
Tel: 0113 255 1188
E-mail: nick.baldwin@tinyworld.co.uk

TRAVEL INFORMATION SYSTEMS
Grand Union House, 20 Kentish Town Road,
London NW1 9NX
Tel: 020 7428 1288
Fax: 020 7267 2745
E-mail: enquiries@travelinfosystems.com
Web site: www.travelinfosystems.com

VETRO DESIGN
247 Bradford Road, Pudsey,
Leeds LS28 6QB
Tel: 0113 255 1188
E-mail: nick@vetrodesign.co.uk

Tour Wholesalers

ACTION TOURS
5 Aston Street, Shifnal,
Shropshire TR11 8DW
Tel: 01952 462462 **Fax:** 01952 462555
E-mail: info@actiontours.co.uk
Web site: www.actionotours.co.uk

ALBATROSS TRAVEL GROUP LTD
Albatross House, 14 New Hythe Lane,
Larkfield, Kent ME20 6AB
Tel: 01732 879191
Fax: 01732 522968
E-mail: sales@albatross-tours.com
Web site: www.albatross-tours.com

CIE TOURS INTERNATIONAL
35 Lower Abbey Street, Dublin 1,
Republic of Ireland
Tel: 00 353 1 703 1888
Fax: 00 353 1 874 5564
E-mail: info@cietours.ie
Web site: www.cietours.com

GREATDAYS TRAVEL GROUP
2 Stamford Park Road,
Altrincham WA15 9EN
Tel: 0161 928 9966
Fax: 0161 928 1332
E-mail: sales@greatdays.co.uk
Web site: www.greatdays.co.uk

GREATDAYS TRAVEL GROUP
10A Thurloe Place, London SW7 2RZ
Tel: 020 7584 0748
Fax: 020 7591 0375
E-mail: travel@london.greatday.co.uk
Web site: www.greatdays.co.uk

INDEPENDENT COACH TRAVEL (WHOLESALING) LTD
South Quay Travel and Leisure Ltd,
Studios 20/21, Colman's Wharf,
45 Morris Road, London E14 6PA
Tel: 020 7538 4627
Fax: 020 7538 8239
E-mail: aheaton@ictsqt.co.uk
Web site: www.ictsqt.co.uk

TRAVELPATH 3000
PO Box 32 Grantham NG31 7JA
Tel: 01476 570187
Fax: 01476 572718
E-mail: info@travelpath3000.com
Web site: www.travelpath3000.com

Training Services

ADG TRANSPORT CONSULTANCY
Oak Cottage, Royal Oak, Machen,
Caerphilly CF83 8SN
Tel: 01633 441491
Fax: 01633 440591
E-mail: a.dgettins@btinternet.com

BUZZLINES LTD
Unit G1, Lympne Industrial Park,
Hythe, Kent CT21 4LR
Tel: 01303 261870
Fax: 01303 230093
Web site: www.buzzlines.co.uk

COUNTY RECRUITMENT & TRAINING LTD
5 White Cliffs Business Centre, Honeywood
Road, Whitfield, Dover, Kent CT16 3EH
Tel: 01304 826220
Fax: 01304 822551
E-mail: admin@crtweb.co.uk
Web site: www.crtweb.co.uk

DATS (DAVE'S ACCIDENT & TRAINING SERVICES)
13 Kingfisher Close, The Willows,
Torquay TQ2 7TF
Tel: 07747 686789
E-Mail: davepboulter@btinternet.com
Web site: www.datservices.org

GOSKILLS
Concorde House, Trinity Park,
Solihull B37 7UQ
Tel: 0121 635 5520
Fax: 0121 635 5521
E-mail: info@goskills.org
Web site: www.goskills.org

IBPTS
43 Cage Lane, Felixstowe,
Suffolk OP11 9BJ
Tel: 01394 672344
Fax: 01394 672344
E-mail: info@ibpts.co.uk
Web site: www.ibpts.co.uk

MARKET ENGINEERING
43-44 North Bar, Banbury OX16 0TH
Tel: 01295 277050
Fax: 01295 277030

E-mail: contact@m-eng.com
Web site: www.marketengineering.com

MIDLAND RED COACHES/WHEELS HERITAGE
Postal Office, 23 Broad Street,
Brinklow, Warwickshire CV23 0LS
Tel: 02476 633624, 07733 884914
Fax: 02476 354900
E-mail: ashley@wheels.co.uk
Web site: www.wheels.co.uk

OMNIBUS TRAINING LTD
Unit 3, Lombard House, 2 Purley Way,
Croydon CR0 3JP
Tel: 020 8006 7259
Fax: 020 8684 7835
E-mail: enquiries@omnibusltd.com
Web site: www.omnibusltd.com

PROFESSIONAL TRANSPORT SERVICES
12 Silverdale, Stanford-le-Hope SS17 8BG
Tel: 01375 675262
E-mail: enquiries@proftranserv.com
Web site: www.proftranserv.co.uk

SOE
22 Greencoat Place, London SW1 1PR
Tel: 02076 301 111 **Fax:** 02076 306 667
E-mail: soe@soe.org.uk
Web site: www.soe.org.uk

SPECIALIST TRAINING & CONSULTANCY SERVICES LTD
6 Venture Court, Metcalfe Drive,
Altham Industrial Estate,
Accrington BB5 5TU
Tel: 01282 687090
Fax: 01282 687091
E-mail: enquiries@specialisttraining.co.uk
Web site: www.specialisttraining.co.uk

TRANSPORT & TRAINING SERVICES LTD
Warrington Business Park, Long Lane,
Warrington WA2 8TX
Tel: 01925 243500
Fax: 01925 243000
E-mail: tachographsuk@aol.com
Web site: www.transporttrainingservices.com

TTS UK
Total Tool Solutions Ltd,
Newhaven Business Park, Lowergate,
Milnsbridge, Huddersfield HD3 4HS
Tel: 01484 642211
Fax: 01484 461002
E-mail: sales@ttsuk.com
Web site: www.ttsuk.com

WEST END TRAVEL & RUTLAND TRAVEL
The Lakeside Bus & Coach Centre,
Dixon Drive, Off Leicester Road, Melton
Mowbray, Leicestershire LE13 0DA
Tel: 01664 563498
Fax: 01664 568568

Vehicle Certification

PLAXTON SERVICE
Ryton Road, Anston, Sheffield S25 4DL
Tel: 01909 551155 **Fax:** 01909 550050
E-mail: service@plaxtonlimited.co.uk
Web site: www.plaxtonaftercare.co.uk

VCA
No1, The Estate Office Centre, Eastgate
Road, Bristol BS5 6XX
Tel: 0117 952 4126
Fax: 0117 952 4104
E-mail: paul.cooke@vca.gov.uk
Web site: www.vca.gov.uk

Section 2

Tendering & Regulatory Authorities

- Tendering & Regulatory Authorities etc
- PTAs
- PTEs
- Integrated Transport Regional Authorities
- Transport Coordinating Offiicers
- Traffic Commissioners
- Office of Fair Trading
- Department for transport

Tendering & Regulatory Authorities

INTEGRATED TRANSPORT AUTHORITIES

Greater Manchester ITA
PO Box 532, Town Hall,
Manchester M60 2LA
Tel: 0161 234 3335
Fax: 0161 236 6459
Web site: www.gmita.gov.uk
Chairman: Cllr I Macdonald
Vice-Chairman: Cllr K Whitmore
Clerk: Sir Howard Bernstein.

Merseyside ITA
24 Hatton Garden, Liverpool L3 2AN
Tel: 0151 227 5181
Fax: 0151 236 2457
Web site: www.merseytravel.gov.uk
Chair: Cllr Mark Dowd
Clerk: Steve Maddox
Gen Man Mersey Tunnels: John Gillard
Operates with Merseyside PTE (qv) as Merseytravel

South Yorkshire ITA
PO Box 37, Regent Street,
Barnsley S70 2PQ
Tel: 01226 772848
Tel: 01226 772899
Web site: www.southyorks.org.uk
Chairman: Cllr M Jameson
Vice-Chairman: Cllr Ms J Wilson
Clerk/Treasurer: W J Wilkinson.

Tyne & Wear ITA
Civic Centre, Newcastle upon Tyne
NE99 2BN
Tel: 0191 203 3209
Fax: 0191 203 3180
Web site: www.twpta.org.uk
Chairman: Cllr David Wood
Vice-Chair: Cllr John Scott
Clerk: K G Lavery
Deputy Clerk & Treasurer: D Johnson
Engineer: J Millar
Legal advisor: V A Dodds

West Midlands ITA
Room 120, Centro House,
16 Summer Lane, Birmingham B19 3SD
Tel: 0121 214 7507
Fax: 0121 233 1841
Web site: www.wmpta.org.uk
E-mail for Councillors:
tateam@centro.org.uk
E-mail for Committee Team:
ptateam@centro.org.uk
Chair: Cllr A Adams
Vice-Chair: Cllr J Hunt
Clerk: Ms S Manzie
Deputy Clerk/Solicitor: C Hinde
Treasurer: Ms A Ridgewell
Head of Communications: Conrad Jones

West Yorkshire ITA
Wellington House, 40-50 Wellington Street,
Leeds LS1 2DE
Tel: 0113 251 7272
Fax: 0113 251 7373
Web site: www.wypta.gov.uk
Chairman: Cllr C Greaves
Vice-Chairman: Cllr R Downes
Clerk to the Authority: K T Preston, OBE.

PASSENGER TRANSPORT EXECUTIVES

Centro (West Midlands PTE)
Centro House, 16 Summer Lane,
Birmingham B19 3SD
Tel: 0121 200 2787
Fax: 0121 214 7010
Web site: www.centro.org.uk

The Executive is responsible to the West Midlands Integrated Transport Authority
Director General: Geoff Inskip
Passenger Services Director: Stephen Rhodes
Strategy & Commissioning Director: Tom Magrath
Corporate Services Director: Steve Chatwin
Finance & Planning Director: James Aspinall
Rail & Rapid Transit Director: Nigel Pennington
Non Executive Directors: Richard Hyde, Keith Kerr, Denise Plumpton
Member of Executive/Treasurer to ITA: Angie Rigwell
ITA Committee: Dan Essex, Marion Cheatham

GMPTE
2 Piccadilly Place,
Manchester M1 3BG
Tel: 0161 244 1000
Web site: www.gmpte.com
GMPTE is responsible to the Greater Manchester Integrated Transport Authority. The PTE is responsible for contracting socially necessary bus services and supporting the local rail service. It also owns the Metrolink light rail system on behalf of the Authority and is responsible for planning for the future of the Metrolink network.
 GMPTE and the Authority are also committed to developing accessible transport, funding Ring and Ride, a fully accessible door to door transport service for people with mobility difficulties.
 The PTE administers the concessionary fares scheme, which allows participants (pensioners, children and people with disabilities) either free or reduced rate travel. GMPTE owns and is responsible for the upkeep of bus stations and on-street infrastructure. It also provides information about public transport through telephone information lines, timetables, general publicity and Travelshops.
Chief Executive: David Leather
Finance & Corporate Services Director: Steve Warrener
Organisational Development Director: Urvashi Bramwell
Director of Bus & Rail: Michael Renshaw
Interim Projects Director: Paul Griffiths

Merseyside Integrated Transport Authority and Executive (Merseytravel)
24 Hatton Garden, Liverpool L3 2AN
Tel: 0151 227 5181
Fax: 0151 236 2457
Web site: www.merseytravel.gov.uk
Merseytravel ensures the availability of public transport in Merseyside, including financial support for the Merseyrail rail network and those bus services not provided for by the private sector.
 It also promotes public transport by providing bus stations and infrastructure, comprehensive travel tickets and free travel with minimum restrictions for the elderly and those with mobility difficulties.
 Merseytravel also owns and operates the Mersey ferries and Mersey tunnels.
Chair to ITA: Cllr M Dowd
Chief Executive ITA & Director General PTE: Neil Scales OBE
Clerk to ITA: Steve Maddox
Director of Resources: John Wilkinson
Director of Resources: Jim Barclay
Director of Operations: Alan Stilwell
Head of Media & Communications: Ian Kenyon

Nexus (Tyne & Wear PTE)
Nexus House, St James Boulevard,
Newcastle upon Tyne NE1 4AX
Tel: 0191 203 3333
Fax: 0191 203 3180
Director General: Bernard Garner
Director, Metro: Mick Carbro
Web site: www.nexus.org.uk
Metro: www.tyneandwearmetro.co.uk
Nexus operates within the policies of the Tyne & Wear Integrated Transport Authority. Nexus owns both the Tyne & Wear Metro system and the Shields Ferry (between North Shields and South Shields). Nexus ensures that bus services not operated commercially are provided where there is evidence of social need; operates a demand-responsive transport system, U-call; and organises the provision of special transport for those who can only use ordinary public transport with difficulty if at all. Nexus administers the Concessionary Travel scheme and provides comprehensive travel information and sales outlets for countywide season tickets, as well as related administrative support for the scheme.
Rolling Stock: 90 light rail cars
Ferries: MFs 'Pride of the Tyne' and 'Shieldsman'

South Yorkshire Passenger Transport Executive
PO Box 801, Exchange Street,
Sheffield S2 5YT
Tel: 0114 276 7575
Fax: 0114 275 9908
Web site: www.sypte.co.uk
The Executive is responsible to the South Yorkshire Integrated Transport Authority.
Director General: David Brown
Director, Strategy: Ben Still
Director, Customer Experience: David Young

West Yorkshire Passenger Transport Executive (Metro)
Wellington House, 40-50 Wellington Street,
Leeds LS1 2DE
Tel: 0113 251 7272
Fax: 0113 251 7333
Web site: www.wymetro.com
WYPTE activities are conducted under the corporate name Metro. Metro is financed and supported by the West Yorkshire Integrated Transport Authority.
Director General: Kieran Preston, OBE
Director of Passenger Services: John Henkel
Director of Development: David Hoggarth

PASSENGER TRANSPORT REGIONAL AUTHORITIES

Strathclyde Partnership for Transport (SPT)
Consort House, 12 West George Street,
Glasgow G2 1HN
Tel: 0141 332 6811
Fax: 0141 332 3076
Web site: www.spt.co.uk
Chair: Cllr Jonathan Findlay
Vice Chair: Cllr D Fagan
Chief Executive: Gordon MacLennan
Dep Chief Executive: Valerie Davidson
Asst Chief Executive: Eric Stewart
Director, Finance: Neil Wylie

Transport for London
Windsor House, 42-50 Victoria Street,
London SW1H 0TL
Tel: 020 7941 4500
Web Site: www.tfl.gov.uk
Chairman: Boris Johnson

Deputy Chairman: Daniel Moylan
Board Members: Peter Anderson, Claudia Arney, Charles Belcher, Christopher Garnett, Baroness Tanni Grey-Thompson, Sir Mike Hodgkinson, Judith Hunt, Eva Lindholm, Steven Norris, Bob Oddy, Patrick O'Keeffe, Kulveer Ranger, Tony West, Keith Williams, Steve Wright

Transport for London (TfL) took over most of the functions of London Transport from July 2000. It is under the control of the Mayor of London and Greater London Authority. TfL assumed control of London Underground Ltd in 2003.
Commissioner for Transport: Peter Hendy, CBE
Managing Director, Finance: Steve Allen
Managing Director, Surface Transport: David Brown
Managing Director, London Rail: Ian Brown
Managing Director, London Underground: Mike Brown
Managing Director, Planning: Michele Dix
Managing Director, Marketing & Communications: Vernon Everitt
General Counsel: Howard Carter
Chief Executive, Crossrail: Rob Holden

TfL subsidiary companies:
London Buses
Palestra, 197 Blackfriars Road,
London SE1 8NJ
Tel: 020 7222 5600
Director of Performance: Clare Kavanagh
Director of Operations: Mike Weston
Head of Contracts: Mark O'Donovan
Head of Network Development: John Barry
Victoria Coach Station Ltd
164 Buckingham Palace Road, London SW1W 9TP.
Tel: 020 7027 2520
Fax: 020 7027 2511
London River Services Ltd
Palestra, 197 Blackfriars Road,
London SE1 8NJ
Tel: 020 7222 5600
General Manager: Andy Griffiths
London Underground Ltd
55 Broadway, London SW1H 0BD
Tel: 020 7222 5600
Managing Director: Mike Brown

TRANSPORT CO-ORDINATING OFFICERS

Under the Transport Act 1978 the non-Metropolitan Counties were given power to co-ordinate public transport facilities in their areas. From 1 April 1996 Welsh Counties and Scottish Regions were replaced by new single-tier authorities. At the same time and subsequently, certain English Counties have been replaced by new single-tier authorities. The major role is now to secure socially necessary services which are not provided commercially. Where provided, the names of most of the responsible officers are set out below.

ENGLAND

Bath & North East Somerset Council
Guildhall, High Street, Bath BA1 5AW
Group Manager (Transport & Planning Policy): Peter Dawson
Transportation Planning Manager: Adrian Clarke
Public Transport Team Leader: Andy Strong
Tel: 01225 477000
Fax: 01225 394335
E-mail: transportation@bathnes.gov.uk
Web site: www.bathnes.gov.uk
A Unitary Authority in South West England, and part of the West of England Partnership.

Bedford Borough Council, Central Bedfordshire Council
Chris Pettifer, Integrated Passenger Transport Manager, Integrated Passenger Transport Unit, County Hall, Cauldwell Street, Bedford MK42 9AP
Tel: 01234 228881
Fax: 01234 228720
Web site: Bedford Borough: www.bedford.gov.uk
Web site: Central Bedfordshire: www.centralbedfordshire.gov.uk

Blackburn with Darwen Borough Council
Transport Policy Group, Old Town Hall, Blackburn BB1 7DY
Tel: 01245 585585
E-mail: transportpolicy@blackburn.gov.uk
Web site: www.blackburn.gov.uk

Blackpool Council
Transportation Division, Layton Depot, Plymouth Road, Blackpool FY3 7HW
Tel: 01253 476172
Fax: 01253 476198
E-mail: transport.policy@blackpool.gov.uk
Web site: www.blackpool.gov.uk

Bournemouth Borough Council
Mike Holmes, Director of Planning and Transport Services, Town Hall Annex, St Stephen's Road, Bournemouth BH2 6EA
Tel: 01202 451199
Fax: 01202 451000
E-mail: highways@bournemouth.gov.uk
Web site: www.bournemouth.gov.uk

Bracknell Forest Borough Council
Transport Group, Time Square, Market Street, Bracknell RG12 1JD
Tel: 01344 424642
E-mail: customer.services@bracknell-forest.gov.uk
Web site: www.bracknell-forest.gov.uk

Brighton & Hove City Council
Public Transport Team, King's House, Grand Avenue, Hove BN3 2LS
Tel: 01273 292480
Web site: www.brighton-hove.gov.uk

Bristol City Council
Public Transport Section, Brunel House, St George's Road, Bristol BS1 5UY
Tel: 0117 922 4454
Fax: 0117 922 3539
E-mail: public.transport@bristol.gov.uk
Web site: www.bristol.gov.uk

Buckinghamshire County Council
Andy Clarke, Passenger Transport Contract Manager, Transport for Buckinghamshire, 10th Floor, County Hall, Walton Street, Aylesbury HP20 1UY
Tel: 0845 2302882
E-mail: passtrans@buckscc.gov.uk
Web site: www.buckscc.gov.uk

Cambridgeshire County Council
B. E. Jackson, Head of Passenger Transport, Department of Environment & Transport, Mailbox ET1015, Shire Hall, Castle Hill, Cambridge CB3 0AP.
Tel: 01223 717744
Fax: 01223 717789
Web site: www.cambridgeshire.gov.uk

Cheshire East Council, Cheshire West & Chester Council
Integrated Transport Service, Rivacre Business Centre, Mill Lane, Ellesmere Port CH66 3TL
Tel: 01244 972387
Fax: 01244 603200
Web site: Cheshire East: www.cheshireeast.gov.uk
Web site: Cheshire West & Chester: www.cheshirewestandchester.gov.uk

Cornwall Council
Passenger Transport Unit, County Hall, Truro TR1 3AY
Tel: 01872 322003
Fax: 01872 323844
E-mail: snicholson@cornwall.gov.uk
Web site: www.cornwall.gov.uk

Cumbria County Council
Lonsdale Building, The Courts, Carlisle CA3 8NA
Tel: 01228 606720
Fax: 01228 606755
E-mail: graham.whiteley@cumbriacc.gov.uk
Web site: www.cumbriacc.gov.uk

Darlington Borough Council
Local Motion Team, Units 8-11, The Beehive, Lingfield Point, Darlington DL1 1YN
Tel: 0800 4589810
E-mail: dothelocalmotion@darlington.gov.uk
Web site: www.darlington.gov.uk

Derby City Council
Integrated Passenger Transport Unit, Room C338, Roman House, Friar Gate, Derby DE1 1XB
Tel: 01332 641744
Fax: 01332 641740
Web site: www.derby.gov.uk

Derbyshire County Council
T. M. Hardy, Public Transport Manager, County Hall, Matlock DE4 3AG
Tel: 01629 580000
Fax: 01629 585740
E-mail: publictransport@derbyshire.gov.uk
Web site: www.derbyshire.gov.uk

Devon County Council
Bruce Thompson, Transport Co-ordination Service Manager, County Hall, Exeter EX2 4QW
Tel: 01392 383244
Fax: 01392 382904
E-mail: bruce.thompson@devon.gov.uk
Web site: www.devon.gov.uk

Dorset County Council
David Dawkins, Integrated Transport Unit Manager, County Hall, Dorchester DT1 1XJ
Tel: 01305 224660
Fax: 01305 225166
E-mail: d.dawkins@dorsetcc.gov.uk
Web site: www.dorsetcc.gov.uk

Durham County Council
County Hall, Durham DH1 5UQ
Tel: 0191 383 3435
Fax: 0191 383 4096
Web site: www.durham.gov.uk

East Riding of Yorkshire Council
David R Boden, Passenger Services Manager, 1st Floor, The Offices, Beverley Depot, Annie Reed Road, Beverley HU17 0LF
Tel: 01482 887700
Fax: 01482 395090
E-mail: passenger.services@eastriding.gov.uk

Web site: www.eastriding.gov.uk
The Passenger Services Unit is responsible for all passenger transport (public transport and schools and SEN transport) in the East Riding.

East Sussex County Council
N Smith, Group Manager (Passenger Transport), Transport & Environment, County Hall, St Anne's Crescent, Lewes BN7 1UE.
Tel: 01273 482326
Fax: 01273 474361
E-mail: nick.smith@eastsussexcc.gov.uk
Web site: www.eastsussex.gov.uk

Essex County Council
John Pope, Head of Passenger Transport, County Hall, Chelmsford CM1 1QH
Tel: 01245 437506
Fax: 01245 496764
E-mail: john.pope@essex.gov.uk
Web site: www.essex.gov.uk

Gloucestershire County Council
Integrated Transport Unit, Environment Directorate, Shire Hall, Gloucester GL1 2TH
Tel: 01452 425543
Fax: 01452 425995
E-mail: timetables@gloucestershire.gov.uk
Web site: www.gloucestershire.gov.uk

Halton Borough Council
Transport Co-ordination, Grosvenor House, Halton Lea, Runcorn WA7 2GW
Tel: 0151 471 7600
Fax: 0151 471 7521
Web site: www.halton.gov.uk

Hampshire County Council
K Wilcox, Head of Passenger Transport, Hampshire County Council, Environment Department, The Castle, Winchester SO23 8UD
Tel: 01962 846997
Fax: 01962 845855
E-mail: keith.wilcox@hants.gov.uk
Web site: www.hampshire.gov.uk

Hartlepool Borough Council
Ian Jopling, Transport Team Leader, Department of Neighbourhood Services, Bryan Hanson House, Hanson Square, Hartlepool TS24 7BT
Tel: 01429 284140
Fax: 01429 860830
E-mail: ian.jopling@hartlepool.gov.uk
Web site: www.hartlepool.gov.uk

Herefordshire Council
James Davies, Public Transport Manager, Sustainable Communities Directorate, PO Box 236, Plough Lane, Hereford HR4 0WZ
Tel: 01432 260948
Fax: 01432 383031
E-mail: public.transport@herefordshire.gov.uk
Web site: www.herefordshire.info

Hertfordshire County Council
Passenger Transport Unit, PO Box 99, Hertford SG13 8TJ
Tel: 01992 556725
E-mail: feedback.ptu@hertscc.gov.uk
Web site: www.intalink.org.uk

Hull City Council
Passenger Transport Services, Kingston House, Bond Street, Hull HU1 3ER
Tel: 01482 300300
E-mail: passengertransport@hullcc.gov.uk
Web site: www.hullcc.gov.uk

Isle of Wight Council
Martyn Mullins, Public Transport Officer, Highways & Transport, Enterprise House, St Cross Business Park, Monks Brook, Newport PO30 5WB
Tel: 01983 823780
Fax: 01983 823707
E-mail: transport.info@iow.gov.uk
Web site: www.iwight.com

Kent County Council
Commercial Services, Gibson Drive, Kings Hill, West Malling ME19 4QG
Transport Integration Manager: Kenneth Cobb
School Transport Manager: Tim Edwards
Local Bus & Information Team Manager: Steve Pay
Tel: 01622 605481
Fax: 01622 605084
E-mail: transport.integration@kent.gov.uk
Web site: www.kent.gov.uk
Transport Integration plans, procures and manages Kent County Council's public, school and client transport. It also works for neighbouring councils and other organisations in related transport fields of data management, consultancy and CRB checks.

Lancashire County Council
Stuart Wrigley, Head of Transport Policy, PO Box 9, Guild House, Cross Street, Preston PR1 8RD
Tel: 01772 534660
Fax: 01772 533833
Web site: www.lancashire.gov.uk

Leicester City Council
Transport Development Section, New Walk Centre, Welford Place, Leicester LE1 6ZG
Tel: 0116 223 2121
E-mail: transportdevelopment@leicester.gov.uk
Web site: www.leicester.gov.uk

Leicestershire County Council
Tony Kirk, Group Manager (Public Transport), Department of Highways, Transportation & Waste Management, County Hall, Glenfield, Leicester LE3 8RJ
Tel: 0116 265 6270
Fax: 0116 265 7181
E-mail: tkirk@leics.gov.uk
Web site: www.leics.gov.uk

Lincolnshire County Council
A R Cross, Head of Transport Services, 4th Floor, City Hall, Beaumont Fee, Lincoln LN1 1DN
Tel: 01522 553132
Fax: 01522 568735
Web site: www.lincolnshire.gov.uk

Luton Borough Council
Passenger Transport Unit, Central Depot, Kingsway, Luton LU4 8AU
Tel: 01582 547219
Fax: 01582 547254
E-mail: ptu@luton.gov.uk
Web site: www.luton.gov.uk

Medway Council
Integrated Transport Team, Gun Wharf, Dock Road, Chatham ME4 4TR
Tel: 01634 331398
Fax: 01634 331625
E-mail: customer.first@medway.gov.uk
Web site: www.medway.gov.uk

Milton Keynes Council
Passenger Transport Group, Environment Directorate, Civic Offices, 1 Saxon Gate East, Milton Keynes MK9 3EJ
Tel: 01908 691691
E-mail: passenger.transport@milton-keynes.gov.uk
Web site: www.milton-keynes.gov.uk

Norfolk County Council
Tracey Jessop, Head of Passenger Transport, Department of Planning & Transportation, County Hall, Martineau Lane, Norwich NR1 2SG
Tel: 01603 224368
Fax: 01603 222144
Web site: www.norfolk.gov.uk

Northamptonshire County Council
Sustainable Transport Manager, Riverside House, Riverside Way, Bedford Road, Northampton NN1 5NX
Tel: 01604 236711
Web site: www.northamptonshire.gov.uk

Northumberland County Council
Integrated Transport Unit, County Hall, Morpeth NE61 2EF
Tel: 0845 600 6400
Fax: 01670 533409
E-mail: ask@northumberland.gov.uk
Web site: www.northumberland.gov.uk

North Lincolnshire Council
Public Transport Team, PO Box 42, Church Square House, Scunthorpe DN15 6XQ
Tel: 01724 297460
Fax: 01724 297066
E-mail: public.transport@northlincs.gov.uk
Web site: www.northlincs.gov.uk

North East Lincolnshire Council
Public Transport Section, Municipal Offices, Town Hall Square, Grimsby DN31 1HU
Tel: 01472 313131
E-mail: transport@nelincs.gov.uk
Web site: www.nelincs.gov.uk

North Somerset Council
Sustainable Travel Team, Somerset House, Oxford Street, Weston-super-Mare BS23 1TG
Tel: 01934 426426
E-mail: sustainable.travel@n-somerset.gov.uk
Web site: www.n-somerset.gov.uk

North Yorkshire County Council
R Owens, Passenger Transport Officer, County Hall, Northallerton DL7 8AH
Tel: 01609 780780, Ext 2870
Fax: 01609 779838
Web site: www.northyorks.gov.uk

Nottingham City Council
Public Transport Team, Exchange Buildings North, Smithy Row, Nottingham NG1 2BS
Tel: 0115 915 5492
E-mail: public.transport@nottinghamcity.gov.uk
Web site: www.nottinghamcity.gov.uk

Nottinghamshire County Council
County Hall, West Bridgford, Nottingham NG2 7QP
Tel: 0115 982 3823
E-mail: enquiries@nottscc.gov.uk
Web site: www.nottinghamshire.gov.uk

Oxfordshire County Council
R Helling, Public Transport Officer, Environmental Services, Speedwell House, Speedwell Street, Oxford OX1 1NE
Tel: 01865 815859

Fax: 01865 815085
E-mail: dick.helling@oxfordshire.gov.uk
Web site: www.oxfordsshire.gov.uk

Peterborough City Council
Accessibility & Travel Group,
Midgate House, Midgate,
Peterborough PE1 1TN
Tel: 01733 747474 **Fax:** 01733 317499
E-mail: buses@peterborough.gov.uk
Web site: www.peterborough.gov.uk

Plymouth City Council
Sustainable Transport Team, Plymouth
Transport & Highways, Department of
Development, Civic Centre, Armada Way,
Plymouth PL1 2AA
Tel: 01752 307790
Fax: 01752 305593
E-mail: publictransport@plymouth.gov.uk
Web site: www.plymouth.gov.uk

Borough of Poole
Transportation Services, St John's House,
1 Serpentine Road, Poole BH15 2DX
Tel: 01202 262000
E-mail: transportation@poole.gov.uk
Web site: www.boroughofpoole.com

Portsmouth City Council
Passenger Transport Group, Transport &
Street Management, Guildhall Square,
Portsmouth PO1 2BG
Tel: 023 9282 2251
Web site: www.portsmouth.gov.uk

Reading Borough Council
Mrs P Baxter, Civic Centre,
Reading RG1 7TD
Tel: 0118 939 0813
Web site: www.reading.gov.uk

Redcar & Cleveland Council
Joint Public Transport Group,
Belmont House, Rectory Lane,
Guisborough TS14 7FD
Tel: 0845 6126126
E-mail: public_transport@redcar-cleveland.gov.uk
Web site: www.redcar-cleveland.gov.uk

Rutland County Council
Integrated Transport Team, Catmose,
Oakham LE15 6HP
Tel: 01572 722577
E-mail: enquiries@rutland.gov.uk
Web site: www.rutland.gov.uk

Shropshire County Council
Development Services, Shirehall,
Abbey Foregate, Shrewsbury SY2 6ND
Tel: 0345 678 9006
E-mail: transport@shropshire.gov.uk
Web site: www.shropshire.gov.uk

Slough Borough Council
R Fraser, PO Box 570, Slough SL1 1FA
Tel: 01753 475111
E-mail: enquiries@slough.gov.uk
Web site: www.slough.gov.uk

Somerset County Council
Mark Pedlar, Group Manager, Passenger
Transport Unit, County Hall, The Crescent,
Taunton TA1 4DY
Tel: 01823 358176
Fax: 01823 351356
E-mail: transport@somerset.gov.uk
Web site: www.somerset.gov.uk

Southampton City Council
Passenger Transport Team, Planning &
Sustainability, Floor 1, Castle Way,
Southampton SO14 2PD

Tel: 0800 519 1919
E-mail: public.transport@southampton.gov.uk
Web site: www.southampton.gov.uk

Southend-on-Sea Borough Council
Civic Centre, Victoria Avenue,
Southend-on-Sea SS2 6ER
Tel: 01702 215000
E-mail: council@southend.gov.uk
Web site: www.southend.gov.uk

South Gloucestershire Council
Integrated Transport Unit,
PO Box 2081, Council Offices,
Castle Street, Thornbury BS35 9BP
Tel: 01454 868004
Fax: 01454 864473
E-mail: itu@southglos.gov.uk
Web site: www.southglos.gov.uk

Staffordshire County Council
Charles Soutar, Head of Passenger
Transport, Development Services
Department, Riverway, Stafford ST16 3TJ
Tel: 01785 276735
Fax: 01785 276621
Web site: www.staffordshire.gov.uk

City of Stoke-on-Trent
Passenger Transport Team, Transport
Planning Group, PO Box 630,
Civic Centre, Stoke-on-Trent ST4 1RF
Tel: 01782 234500
Fax: 01782 233243
E-mail: transportation@stoke.gov.uk
Web site: www.stoke.gov.uk

Suffolk County Council
Mitchell Bradshaw, Public Transport
Manager, Environment & Transport
Department, Endeavour House,
8 Russell Road, Ipswich IP1 2BX
Tel: 01473 265050
Fax: 01473 216884
E-mail: mitchell.bradshaw@et.suffolkcc.gov.uk
Web site: www.suffolk.gov.uk

Surrey County Council
A Teer, Group Manager Passenger
Transport, Room 306, County Hall,
Penrhyn Road, Kingston-on-Thames
KT1 2DY
Tel: 020 8541 9371
Fax: 020 8541 9389
E-mail: alan.teer@surreycc.gov.uk
Web site: www.surreycc.gov.uk/passenger_transport

Swindon Borough Council
Passenger Transport Team, Premier House,
Station Road, Swindon SN1 1TZ
Tel: 01793 466214
E-mail: passengertransport@swindon.gov.uk
Web site: www.swindon.gov.uk

Telford & Wrekin Council
Planning & Transport Department,
Darby House, Lawn Central,
Telford TF3 4JA
Tel: 01952 202172
Web site: www.telford.gov.uk

Thurrock Council
Passenger Transport Section, Strategic
Planning & Transportation, Civic Offices,
New Road, Grays, Essex RM17 6SL
Tel: 01375 413882
Fax: 01375 413891
E-mail: passengertransport@thurrock.gov.uk
Web site: www.thurrock.gov.uk

Torbay Council
Strategic Transportation Team, Roebuck
House, Abbey Road, Torquay TQ2 5TF
Tel: 01803 208823
Fax: 01803 208882
E-mail: transportation@torbay.gov.uk
Web site: www.torbay.gov.uk

Warrington Borough Council
Passenger Transport Unit, Palmyra House,
Palmyra Square North, Warrington
WA1 1JN
Tel: 01925 442620
Web site: www.warrington.gov.uk

Warwickshire County Council
K McGovern, Passenger Transport
Operations Manager, Environment &
Economy Directorate, PO Box 43,
Shire Hall, Warwick CV34 4SX
Tel: 01926 412930
Fax: 01926 418041
E-mail: passengertransport@warwickshire.gov.uk
Web site: www.warwickshire.gov.uk

West Berkshire Council
Transport Services Team, Highways &
Engineering, Faraday Road,
Newbury RG14 2AF
Tel: 01635 503248
Fax: 01635 519979
E-mail: transport@westberks.gov.uk
Web site: www.westberks.gov.uk

West Sussex County Council
Mark Miller, Group Manager,
Transport Co-ordination, Highways and
Transport, The Grange, Tower Street,
Chichester PO19 1RH
Tel: 01243 777811
E-mail: highwaysandtransporthq@westsussex.gov.uk
Web site: www.westsussex.gov.uk

Wiltshire Council
I White, Head of Service - Passenger
Transport, Passenger Transport Unit,
County Hall, Bythesea Road,
Trowbridge BA14 8JN
Tel: 01225 713322
Fax: 01225 713317
E-mail: ian.white@wiltshire.gov.uk
Web site: www.wiltshire.gov.uk

Royal Borough of Windsor & Maidenhead
Passenger Transport Team, Highways &
Engineering, Community Services, Town
Hall, St Ives Road, Maidenhead SL6 1RF
Tel: 01628 796666
Fax: 01628 796774
E-mail: customerservice@rbwm.gov.uk
Web site: www.rbwm.gov.uk

Wokingham Borough Council
Places & Neighbourhoods, PO Box 153,
Wokingham RG40 1WL
Tel: 0118 974 6000
E-mail: transportplanning@wokingham.gov.uk
Web site: www.wokingham.gov.uk

Worcestershire County Council
Passenger Transport Group, PO Box 82,
Pershore Lane, Worcester WR4 0AA
Tel: 01905 768411
Fax: 01905 768438
Web site: www.worcestershire.gov.uk

City of York Council
Transport Planning Unit,
9 St Leonard's Place, York YO1 7ET

Tel: 01904 551550
Fax: 01904 551340
E-mail: transportplanning@york.gov.uk
Web site: www.york.gov.uk

WALES

Isle of Anglesey County Council
Highways & Transportation Service,
Council Offices, Llangefni,
Anglesey LL77 7TW
Tel: 01248 752457
Fax: 01248 757332
E-mail: dwrpl@anglesey.gov.uk
Web site: www.anglesey.gov.uk

Blaenau Gwent County Borough Council
Joint Passenger Transport Unit,
Civic Centre, Ebbw Vale NP3 6XB
Tel: 01495 355440
Fax: 01495 301255
Web site: www.blaenau-gwent.gov.uk

Bridgend County Borough Council
Transport Co-ordinating Manager,
Communities Directorate,
Waterton Lane, Waterton,
Bridgend CF31 3YP
Tel: 01656 642559
Fax: 01656 642859
E-mail: transportation@bridgend.gov.uk
Web site: www.bridgend.gov.uk

Caerphilly County Borough Council
Huw Morgan, Principal Passenger Transport Officer, Council Offices, Pontllanfraith,
Blackwood NP12 2YW
Tel: 01495 235089
Fax: 01495 235045
E-mail: morgash@caerphilly.gov.uk
Web site: www.caerphilly.gov.uk

Cardiff County Council
Traffic & Transportation Service,
County Hall, Atlantic Wharf,
Cardiff CF10 4UW
Tel: 029 2087 2087
E-mail: c2c@cardiff.gov.uk
Web site: www.cardiff.gov.uk

Carmarthenshire County Council
Public Transport Section, Director of Technical Services, Llansteffan Road,
Carmarthen SA31 3LZ
Tel: 0845 634 0661
E-mail: publictransport@carmarthenshire.gov.uk
Web site: www.carmarthenshire.gov.uk

Ceredigion County Council
Mrs S A Witts, Acting Manager, Corporate Passenger Transport Unit (CPTU), Canolfan Rheidol, Rhodfa Padarn, Llanbadarn Fawr, Aberystwyth SY23 3UE
Tel: 01970 633555
Fax: 01970 633559
E-mail: cptu@ceredigion.gov.uk
Web site: www.ceredigion.gov.uk

Conwy County Borough Council
Bus Conwy, The Heath, Penmaenmawr Road, Llanfairfechan LL33 0PF
Tel: 01492 575414
E-mail: bwsconwy@conwy.gov.uk
Web site: www.conwy.gov.uk

Denbighshire County Council
Passenger Transport Group, Transport & Infrastructure Department, Caledfryn,
Smithfield Road, Denbigh LL16 3RJ
Tel: 01824 706968
Fax: 01824 706970
Web site: www.denbighshire.gov.uk

Flintshire County Council
Transportation Unit, Directorate of Environment & Regeneration,
County Hall, Mold CH7 6NF
Tel: 01352 704530
Fax: 01352 704540
Web site: www.flintshire.gov.uk

Gwynedd Council
Public Transport Officer, Council Offices,
Shirehall, Caernarfon LL55 1SH.
Tel: 01286 679541
Fax: 01286 673324
E-mail: bwsgwynedd@gwynnedd.gov.uk
Web site: www.gwynedd.gov.uk

Merthyr Tydfil County Borough Council
Martin Haworth, Senior Transport Officer,
Civic Centre, Castle Street,
Merthyr Tydfil CF47 8AN
Tel: 01685 726288
Fax: 01685 387982
E-mail: martin.howarth@merthyr.gov.uk
Web site: www.merthyr.gov.uk

Monmouthshire County Council
Monmouthshire Passenger Transport Unit,
County Hall, Cwmbran NP44 2XH
Tel: 01633 644644
Fax: 01633 644777
E-mail: transport@monmouthshire.gov.uk
Web site: www.monmouthshire.gov.uk

Neath Port Talbot County Borough Council
S Colinese, Passenger Transport Manager,
The Quays, Brunel Way,
Baglan Energy Park, Neath SA11 2GG
Tel: 01639 686658
Fax: 01639 686107
E-mail: s.colinese@npt.gov.uk
Web site: www.neath-porttalbot.gov.uk

Newport City Council
Director of Development/Transport,
Civic Centre, Newport NP9 4UR
Tel: 01633 244491
Fax: 01633 244721
Web site: www.newport.gov.uk

Pembrokeshire County Council
M Hubert, Transport and Fleet Manager,
County Hall, Haverfordwest SA61 1TP
Tel: 01437 764551
Fax: 01437 775008
E-mail: hubert.mathias@pembrokeshire.gov.uk
Web site: www.pembrokeshire.gov.uk

Powys County Council
J Forsey, Passenger Transport Manager,
Passenger Transport Unit, County Hall,
Llandrindod Wells LD1 5LG
Tel: 0845 607 6060
Web site: www.powys.gov.uk

Rhondda Cynon Taf County Borough Council
Integrated Transport Unit,
Sardis House, Sardis Road,
Pontypridd CF37 1DU
Head of Service – Transportation:
Roger Waters
Integrated Transport Unit Manager:
Charlie Nelson
Principal Transport Officers:
Gwyneth Elliott, Caroline Harries,
Adrian Morgan
Tel: 01443 494700
Fax: 01443 494875
E-mail: transportation@rhondda-cynon-taff.gov.uk
Web site: www.rhondda-cynon-taff.gov.uk

City & County of Swansea
Environment Dept – Transportation,
Civic Centre, Oystermouth Road,
Swansea SA1 3SN
Tel: 01792 637250
Fax: 01792 635270
E-mail: transportation.engineering@swansea.gov.uk
Web site: www.swansea.gov.uk

Torfaen County Borough Council
Torfaen County Borough Council,
Civic Centre, Pontypool NP4 6YB
Joint Passenger Transport Unit
(with Blaenau Gwent), Civic Centre,
Ebbw Vale NP3 6XB
Tel: 01495 762200
Fax: 01495 755513
Web site: www.torfaen.gov.uk

Vale of Glamorgan Council
C Edwards, Senior Transportation Officer,
Passenger Transport Unit, The Dock Offices,
Barry Docks, Barry CF63 4RT
Tel: 01446 700111
Fax: 01446 704891
E-mail: cedwards@valeofglamorgan.gov.uk
Web site: www.valeofglamorgan.gov.uk

Wrexham County Borough Council
Transport Co-ordination, Crown Buildings,
Chester Street, Wrexham LL13 8BG
Tel: 01978 292000
Fax: 01978 292106
Web site: www.wrexham.gov.uk

SCOTLAND

Councils whose names are marked with an asterisk (*) are the 12 member councils of Strathclyde Partnership for Transport (SPT) (see above), which is responsible for co-ordinating public transport services and infrastructure.

Aberdeen City Council
Ian Mason, Public Transport Unit,
St Nicholas House, Broad Street,
Aberdeen AB10 1WL
Tel: 01224 523073
Fax: 01224 523764.
E-mail: imason@aberdeencity.gov.uk.
Web site: www.aberdeencity.gov.uk

Aberdeenshire Council
Richard McKenzie, Public Transport Manager, Public Transport Unit,
Transportation & Infrastructure,
Woodhill House, Westburn Road,
Aberdeen AB16 5GB
Tel: 01224 664585
Fax: 01224 662005
E-mail: richard.mckenzie@aberdeenshire.gov.uk
Web site: www.aberdeenshire.gov.uk

Angus Council
Planning & Transport Infrastructure Services,
County Buildings, Market Street,
Forfar DD8 3LG
Tel: 01307 461774
Fax: 01307 475037
E-mail: plntransport@angus.gov.uk
Web site: www.angus.gov.uk

Argyll and Bute Council*
Facility Services, Integrated Transport,
Kilmory, Lochgilphead PA31 8RT
Integrated Transport Manager:
Janne Leckie
Public Transport Officer:
Douglas Blades
Tel: 01546 604193

Fax: 01546 604291
E-mail: public.transport@argyll-bute.gov.uk
Web site: www.argyll-bute.gov.uk

Clackmannanshire Council
Public Transport Officer, Roads,
Traffic & Transportation, Kilncraigs,
Greenside Street, Alloa FK10 1EB
Tel: 01259 450000
E-mail: roads@clacks.gov.uk
Web site: www.clacksweb.org.uk

Dundee City Council
Mark Devine, Transport Officer,
Planning & Transportation Department,
Floor 16, Tayside House, Crichton Street,
Dundee DD1 3RB.
Tel: 01382 433831
Fax: 01382 433313
E-mail: mark.devine@dundeecity.gov.uk.
Web site: www.dundeecity.gov.uk

Dumfries & Galloway Council
Douglas Kirkpatrick, Team Leader
(Sustainable Travel), Council Offices,
English Street, Dumfries DG1 2DD
Tel: 03033 333000
Fax: 01387 260583
E-mail: pe.travel.info@dumgal.gov.uk
Web site: www.dumgal.gov.uk

East Ayrshire Council*
Council Headquarters,
London Road, Kilmarnock
KA3 7BU
Tel: 01563 576000
Web site: www.east-ayrshire.gov.uk

East Dunbartonshire Council*
Civic Way, Kirkintilloch G66 4TJ
Tel: 0845 045 4510
E-mail:
contact.centre@eastdunbarton.gov.uk
Web site: www.eastdunbarton.gov.uk

East Lothian Council
Transport Planning Manager,
John Muir House, Haddington
EH41 3HA
Tel: 01620 827661
E-mail: policy&projects@eastlothian.gov.uk
Web site: www.eastlothian.gov.uk

East Renfrewshire Council*
Council Headquarters,
Eastwood Park, Giffnock G46 6UG
Tel: 0141 577 3425
Web site: www.eastrenfrewshire.gov.uk

City of Edinburgh Council
Max Thomson, Public Transport Manager,
City Development, 1 Cockburn Street,
Edinburgh EH1 1BJ
Tel: 0131 469 3631 **Fax:** 0131 469 3635.
E-mail: max.thomson@edinburgh.gov.uk
Web site: www.edinburgh.gov.uk

Falkirk Council
Stephen Bloomfield, Public Transport
Co-ordinator, Development Services,
Abbotsfold House, David's Loan,
Falkirk FK2 7YZ
Tel: 01324 504723
Fax: 01324 504914
Web site: www.falkirk.gov.uk

Fife Council
Trond Haugen, Transportation Manager -
Transportation Services, Fife House,
North Street, Glenrothes KY7 5LT
Tel: 01592 413106
Fax: 01592 413061
E-mail: trond.haugen@fife.gov.uk
Web site: www.fifedirect.org.uk

Glasgow City Council*
Land & Environmental Services,
Richmond Exchange,
20 Cadogan Street, Glasgow G2 7AD
Tel: 0141 287 9000
Fax: 0141 287 9059
E-mail: land@glasgow.gov.uk
Web site: www.glasgow.gov.uk

The Highland Council
David Summers, Transport Development
Officer, Public Transport Dept,
Glenurquhart Road, Inverness
IV3 5NX
Tel: 01463 702457
Fax: 01463 702606
E-mail: public.transport@highland.gov.uk
Web site: www.highland.gov.uk

Inverclyde Council*
Municipal Buildings, Greenock
PA15 1LY
Tel: 01475 717171
Fax: 01475 712181
Web site: www.inverclyde.gov.uk

Midlothian Council
Travel Team - Room 9, Dundas Buildings,
62A Polton Street, Bonnyrigg,
Midlothian EH19 3YD
Tel: 0131 561 5443
Fax: 0131 654 2797
E-mail: karl.vanters@midlothian.gov.uk
Web site: www.midlothian.gov.uk

Moray Council
Peter Findlay, Public Transport Manager,
Council Office, Academy Street,
Elgin IV30 1LL
Tel: 01343 562569
Fax: 01343 545628.
E-mail: transport@moray.gov.uk
Web site: www.moray.gov.uk

North Ayrshire Council*
Cunningham House, Irvine KA12 8EE
Tel: 0845 603 0590
Fax: 01294 324144
Web site: www.north-ayrshire.gov.uk

North Lanarkshire Council*
Civic Centre, Windmillhill Street,
Motherwell ML1 1AB
Tel: 01698 403200
Web site: www.northlanarkshire.gov.uk

Orkney Islands Council
Council Offices, School Place,
Kirkwall KW15 1NY
Tel: 01856 873535
E-mail: transport@orkney.gov.uk
Web site: www.orkney.gov.uk

Perth & Kinross Council
Andrew J Warrington, Public Transport
Manager, The Environment Service,
Pullar House, 35 Kinnoull Street,
Perth PH1 5GD
Tel: 01738 476530
Fax: 01738 476510
E-mail: publictransport@pkc.gov.uk
Web site: www.pkc.gov.uk

Renfrewshire Council*
North Building, Renfrewshire House,
Cotton Street, Paisley PA1 1WB
Tel: 0141 842 5000
Web site: www.renfrewshire.gov.uk

Scottish Borders Council
B Young, Transport Policy Manager,
Council Headquarters, Newtown St
Boswells, Melrose TD6 0SA
Tel: 01835 824000

Fax: 01835 823008
Web site: www.scotborders.gov.uk

Shetland Islands Council
Ian Bruce, Service Manager - Transport
Operations, Infrastructure Service Dept.,
Grantfield, Lerwick ZE1 0NT
Tel: 01595 744872
Fax: 01595 744869
E-mail: ian.bruce@sic.shetland.gov.uk
Web site: www.shetland.gov.uk

South Ayrshire Council*
County Buildings, Wellington Square,
Ayr KA7 1DR
Tel: 0845 601 2020
Web site: www.south-ayrshire.gov.uk

South Lanarkshire Council*
Council Offices, Almada Street,
Hamilton ML3 0AA
Tel: 01698 454444
Web site: www.southlanarkshire.gov.uk

Stirling Council
Council Headquarters, Viewforth,
2 Pitt Place, Stirling FK8 2ET
Tel: 0845 277 7000
Web site: www.stirling.gov.uk

West Dunbartonshire Council*
Council Offices, Garshake Road,
Dunbarton, G82 3PU
Tel: 01389 737633
Web site: www.west-dunbarton.gov.uk

Western Isles Council
Western Isles Council (Comhairle nan
Eilean Siar), Sandwick Road, Stornoway,
Isle of Lewis HS1 2BW
Tel: 01851 703773
E-mail: enquiries@cne-siar.gov.uk
Web site: www.cne-siar.gov.uk

West Lothian Council
Ian Forbes, Public Transport Manager,
County Buildings, Linlithgow
EH49 7EZ
Tel: 01506 775282
Fax: 01506 775265
E-mail: ian.forbes@westlothian.gov.uk
Web site: www.westlothian.gov.uk

TRAFFIC COMMISSIONERS

Web site: www.vosa.gov.uk
Senior Traffic Commissioner: Philip Brown

EASTERN TRAFFIC AREA
City House, 126-130 Hills Road, Cambridge
CB2 1NP
Tel: 0300 123 9000
Fax: 01223 309684
Traffic Commissioner: Richard Turfitt
Deputy Traffic Commissioners: Marcia
Davis, Gillian Ekins, Fiona Harrington,
Mary Kane, Roger Seymour.
Area covered: Buckinghamshire,
Cambridgeshire, Essex, Hertfordshire,
Leicestershire, Lincolnshire, Norfolk,
Northamptonshire, Suffolk, Bedford, Central
Bedfordshire, Leicester, Luton, Milton
Keynes, Peterborough, Rutland, Southend-
on-Sea, Thurrock.

NORTH EASTERN TRAFFIC AREA
Hillcrest House, 386 Harehills Lane, Leeds
LS9 6NF
Tel: 0300 123 9000
Fax: 0113 249 8142
Traffic Commissioner: Tom Macartney
Deputy Traffic Commissioners: Mark
Hinchcliffe, Patrick Mulvenna, Liz Perrett.

Area covered: Durham, Northumberland, Nottinghamshire, North Yorkshire, South Yorkshire, Tyne & Wear, West Yorkshire, Darlington, East Riding, Hartlepool, Kingston upon Hull, Middlesbrough, North Lincolnshire, North East Lincolnshire, Nottingham, Redcar & Cleveland, Stockton-on-Tees, York.

NORTH WESTERN TRAFFIC AREA
Suite 4, Stone Cross place,
Stone Cross Lane, Golborne,
Warrington WA3 2SH
Tel: 0300 123 9000
Fax: 01942 728297
Traffic Commissioner: Beverley Bell.
Deputy Traffic Commissioners:
Mark Hinchcliffe, Patrick Mulvenna, Liz Perrett.
Area covered: Cumbria, Derbyshire, Greater Manchester, Lancashire, Merseyside, Blackburn with Darwen, Blackpool, Cheshire East, Cheshire West & Chester, City of Derby, Halton, Warrington.

SCOTTISH TRAFFIC AREA
Level 6, The Stamp Office,
10 Waterloo Place, Edinburgh
EH1 3EG
Tel: 0300 123 9000
Fax: 0131 229 0682
Traffic Commissioner: Miss Joan Aitken
Deputy Traffic Commissioner:
Richard McFarlane
Area covered: Scotland

SOUTH EASTERN & METROPOLITAN TRAFFIC AREA
Ivy House, 3 Ivy Terrace,
Eastbourne BN21 4QT
Tel: 0300 123 9000
Fax: 01323 726679
Traffic Commissioner: Philip Brown
Deputy Traffic Commissioners:
Chris Heaps, Mary Kane, Jonathan Black.
Area covered: East Sussex, Greater London, Kent, Surrey, West Sussex, Brighton & Hove, Medway.

WELSH TRAFFIC AREA
38 George Road, Edgbaston,
Birmingham B15 1PL
Tel: 0300 123 9000
Fax: 0121 609 4250
Traffic Commissioner: Nick Jones
Deputy Traffic Commissioners:
J Astle, M Dorrington, T Seculer, C R Seymour.
Area covered: Wales.

WEST MIDLAND TRAFFIC AREA
38 George Road, Edgbaston,
Birmingham B15 1PL
Tel: 0121 123 9000
Fax: 0121 609 4250
Traffic Commissioner: Nick Jones
Deputy Traffic Commissioners:
J Astle, M Dorrington, T Seculer, C R Seymour.
Area covered: Herefordshire, Shropshire, Staffordshire, Warwickshire, West Midlands, Worcestershire, Stoke-on-Trent, Telford & Wrekin.

WESTERN TRAFFIC AREA
2 Rivergate, Temple Quay,
Bristol BS1 6EH
Tel: 0300 123 9000
Fax: 0117 929 8352
Traffic Commissioner: Sarah Bell
Deputy Traffic Commissioners:
Jonathan Black, Fiona Harrington, Tim Hayden, Lester Maddrell.
Administrative Director: Tim Hughes.

Area covered: Cornwall, Devon, Gloucestershire, Hampshire, Oxfordshire, Somerset, Wiltshire, Bath & North East Somerset, Bournemouth, Bracknell Forest, Bristol, Isle of Wight, North Somerset, Plymouth, Poole, Portsmouth, Reading, Slough, Southampton, South Gloucestershire, Swindon, Torbay, West Berkshire, Windsor & Maidenhead, Wokingham.

OFFICE OF FAIR TRADING

The Office of Fair Trading (OFT) plays a leading role in promoting and protecting consumer interests throughout the UK, while ensuring that businesses are fair and competitive. The tools to carry out this work are the powers granted to the OFT under consumer and competition legislation.
Address: Fleetbank House,
2-6 Salisbury Square,
London EC4Y 8JX
Tel: 020 7211 8000
Fax: 020 7211 8800
Web site: www.oft.gov.uk
E-mail: enquiries@oft.gsi.gov.uk
Enquiries: 08457 22 44 99

DEPARTMENT FOR TRANSPORT

4/24 Great Minster House,
76 Marsham Street, London SW1P 4DR
Tel: 020 7944 3000
Web site: www.dft.gov.uk

Permanent Secretary: Robert Devereux
Director General, Railways & National Works: Dr Mike Mitchell

Executive Agencies: (include)
Driving Standards Agency (DSA)
Driver and Vehicle Licensing Agency (DVLA)

Highways Agency (HA)
Chief Executive: Archie Robertson
Tel: 08457 50 40 30
Web Site: www.highways.gov.uk

Vehicle Certification
VCA
No1, The Estate Office Centre,
Eastgate Road, Bristol BS5 6XX
Tel: 0117 952 4126
Fax: 0117 952 4104
E-mail: paul.cooke@vca.gov.uk
Web site: www.vca.gov.uk

Vehicle and Operator Services Agency (VOSA)
(see also Driver Training,
A-Z Manufacturers section)
Berkeley House, Croydon Street,
Bristol BS5 0DA
Tel: 0300 123 9000
Fax: 0117 954 3212
E-mail: enquiries@vosa.gov.uk
Web site: www.vosa.gov.uk
Chief Executive: Alistair Peoples

Advisory Non-Departmental Bodies: (include)

Commission for Integrated Transport
Chairman: Peter Hendy
Tel: 020 7944 8300
E-mail: cfit@dft.gsi.gov.uk

Disabled Persons Transport Advisory Committee
E-mail: dptac@dft.gsi.gov.uk

Executive Non-departmental Bodies: (include)
Health and Safety Commission
Health and Safety Executive
Tribunals
Traffic Areas

Public Corporations
Civil Aviation Authority
Transport for London

The Disabled Persons Transport Advisory Committee
Great Minster House,
76 Marsham Street, London
SW1P 4DR
Tel: 020 7944 8011
Minicom: 020 7944 3277
Fax: 020 7944 6998
E-mail: dptac@dft.gov.uk
Web site: www.dptac.gov.uk
Chair: Neil Betteridge
The Disabled Persons Transport Advisory Committee (DPTAC) is a statutory body established under Section 125 of the Transport Act 1985 to advise the Secretary of State for Transport on matters affecting the transport needs of disabled people. Membership is limited to a Chairman plus twenty members, at least half of whom must be disabled.

Mobility and Inclusion Unit
(address as above)
Tel: 020 7944 8021
Minicom: 020 7944 3277
Fax: 020 7944 6102
E-mail: miu@dft.gsi.gov.uk
Web site: www.dptac.gov.uk
Disability Rights Commission
Web site: www.drc-gb.org.uk

Rail Accident Investigation Branch
The Wharf, Stores Road, Derby
DE21 4BA
Chief Inspector: Carolyn Griffiths
Tel: 01332 253300
Fax: 01332 253301
E-mail: enquiries@raib.gov.uk
Web site: www.raib.gov.uk
RAIB is the independent railway accident investigation organisation for the UK and is listed in LRB because its remit covers street tramways.

Notes

Section 3

Organisations and Societies

- British Operators Organisations
- Institutions
- International Associations
- Other Organisations
- First Aid and Sports Associations
- Trade Organisations
- Societies
- Passenger Transport Museums

British Operators' Organisations

ALBUM – ASSOCIATION OF LOCAL BUS COMPANY MANAGERS
The Association represents the professional views of the Executive Directors and Senior Managers of those bus companies owned by district councils and major independent operators on matters specifically affecting locally-owned bus company management and operations.
Chairperson: M Howarth, Western Greyhound Ltd, Western House, St Austell Street, Summercourt, Newquay, Cornwall TR8 5DR
Tel: 01637 871871
Secretary: Thomas W W Knowles, 41 Redhills, Eccleshall, Stafford ST21 6JW
Tel & Fax: 01785 859414
Web site: www.album-bus.co.uk

THE COACH TOURISM COUNCIL
10 Bermondsey Exchange, 179-181 Bermondsey St, London SE1 3UW
Tel: 0870 850 2839
Fax: 020 7407 6880
E-mail: admin@coachtourismcouncil.co.uk
Web site: www.coachtourismcouncil.co.uk, www.findacoachholiday.com
Chairman: Sean Taggart
Chief Executive: Chris Wales
Administration: Paul Ovington
The CTC's mission is to promote tourism and travel by coach.

COMMUNITY TRANSPORT ASSOCIATION
Highbank, Halton Street, Hyde SK14 2NY
Tel: 0161 351 1475
Fax: 0161 351 7221
Advice Service Tel: 0845 130 6195
E-mail: infi@ctauk.org
Web site: www.ctauk.org
The community transport sector is vast. There are over 100,000 minibuses serving over 10 million passengers every year being operated for use by voluntary and community groups, schools, colleges and Local Authorities, or to provide door-to-door transport for people who are unable to use other public transport. This door-to-door transport is not limited to minibuses though; there are very many voluntary car schemes throughout the UK where volunteers will use their own cars to provide transport for individuals. Overcoming social exclusion is at the heart of what community transport has always been about. The CTA is committed to helping its members achieve this objective in their area both in terms of the direct support it can offer such as training, developmental support etc. but also by lobbying on behalf of the movement with government and other important agencies.

CONFEDERATION OF PASSENGER TRANSPORT UK
Drury House, 34-43 Russell Street, London WC2B 5HA
Tel: 020 7240 3131
Fax: 020 7240 6565
E-mail: cpt@cpt-uk.org
Web site: www.cpt-uk.org
The Confederation of Passenger Transport UK (CPT) is the trade association representing the UK's bus and coach operators and the light rail sector. CPT has wide responsibilities ranging from representation on government working parties (national, local, EU); establishing operating codes of practice; advising on legal, technical and mechanical standards; management of the Bonded Coach Holiday Scheme, a government recognised consumer travel protection scheme and Coach Marque, an industry quality standard; 24-hour Crisis Control service for members; organisation of industry events and the first point of contact for the media on transport and other related issues.

OFFICERS AND COUNCIL
President: Steve Whiteway
Chairman: Giles Fearnley
Chief Executive: Simon Posner
Manager, Chief Executive's Office: Miss Ling Tang
Finance Director: Bill Wright
Communications Director: John Major
Operations Director: Stephen Smith
Media Relations Manager: Hassaid Stackpoole
Director of Membership: Peter Gomersall
Director of Policy Development: Steven Salmon
Director of Coaching: Steven Barber
Technical Executive: Colin Copelin
Deputy Director, Operations: John Burch
Fixed Track Executive: David Walmsley

Director of Government Relations, Scotland: George Mair
29 Drumsheugh Gardens, Edinburgh EH3 7RN
Tel: 0131 272 2150
Fax: 0131 272 2152

Director of Government Relations, Wales: John Pockett
70 Hillside View, Craigwen, Pontypridd CF37 2LG
Tel: 01443 485814
Fax: 01443 485816

Director of Government Relations, EU: David Watson
Drury House, 34-43 Russell Street, London WC2B 5HA
Tel: 020 7240 3131
Fax: 020 7240 6565

Regional Managers
East Midlands & Yorkshire: Keith McNally
Tel: 0121 633 7770
E-mail: keithm@cpt-uk.org
London & Home Counties: Karen Tiley
Drury House, 34-43 Russell Street, London WC2B 5HA
Tel: 020 7240 3131
E-mail: karent@cpt-uk.org
Northern: David Holding
Foxwood House, 6 The Dene, Chester Moor, Chester-le-Street DH2 3TB
Tel: 0191 388 7694
E-mail: davidh@cpt-uk.org
North Western: Phillipa Sudlow
210 Crow Lane East, Newton le Willows, Merseyside WA12 9UA
Tel: 01925 229497
E-mail: phillipas@cpt-uk.org
Scotland: Jeremy Tinsley
29 Drumsheugh Gardens, Edinburgh EH3 7RN
Tel: 0131 272 2150
E-mail: jeremyt@cpt-uk.org
Wales: Colin Thomas
Tel: 01633 270800
E-mail: colint@cpt-uk.org
West Midlands: Phil Bateman
3A Broadlane North, Wednesfield, Wolverhampton WV12 5UH
Tel: 07768 145445
E-mail: philb@cpt-uk.org
South West: John Burch
"Avercombe", 28 Belmont Road, Ilfracombe, Devon EX34 8DR
Tel: 07940 929881
E-mail: johnb@cpt-uk.org

PASSENGER TRANSPORT EXECUTIVE GROUP
Wellington House, 40-50 Wellington Street, Leeds LS1 2DE
Tel: 0113 251 7204
Fax: 0113 251 7333
Web site: www.pteg.net
Chair: Neil Scales
Director, PTEG Support Unit: Jonathan Bray
PTEG brings together and promotes the interests of the six Passenger Transport Executives (PTEs) in England. Leicester City Council, Nottingham City Council, Strathclyde Partnership for Transport and Transport for London are associate members.

Institutions

THE CHARTERED INSTITUTE OF LOGISTICS & TRANSPORT
Logistics & Transport Centre, Earlstrees Court, Earlstrees Road, Corby NN17 4AX
Tel: 01536 740100
Fax: 01536 740101
E-mail: enquiry@ciltuk.org.uk.
Web site: www.ciltuk.org.uk
President: Sir Moir Lockhead
The Chartered Institute of Logistics and Transport (UK) is the professional body for individuals and organisations involved in all disciplines, modes and aspects of logistics and transport.
The Institute's 22,000 members have privileged access to a range of benefits and services, which support them, professionally and personally, throughout their careers and help connect them with world-wide expertise.
For further information and to join please contact Membership Services,
Tel: 01536 740104 or visit the CILT(UK) web site above

THE INSTITUTE OF THE MOTOR INDUSTRY
Fanshaws, Brickendon, Hertford SG13 8PQ
Tel: 01992 511521
Fax: 01992 511548
E-mail: imi@motor.org.uk
Web site: www.motor.org.uk
The Institute of the Motor Industry (IMI) is the professional association for individuals working in the retail motor industry and is the leading awarding body of vocational qualifications in the automotive sector. With some 25,000 members and 45,000 registered students at 350 assessment centres, the IMI is focused on improving professional standards through the recognition, qualification and development of individuals.
Qualifications offered by the Institute include NVQs/SVQs, technical certificates, vehicle sales awards, Quality Assured Awards and Certificate/Diploma in automotive retail management (ARMS).
The IMI governs the industry's Automotive Technician Accreditation (ATA) initiative, which has more than 4500 nationally-accredited technicians since launching in 2005.

OFFICERS AND VICE PRESIDENTS
Patron: HRH Prince Michael of Kent KCVO FIMI.
President: Garel Rhys CBE FIMI
Honorary Treasurer: Edward Clark FIMI.
Chairman of the Council: Steve Nash FIMI
Chief Executive: Sarah Sillars FIMI
Company Secretary: Alan Tyrer FIMI

THE INSTITUTE OF TRANSPORT ADMINISTRATION
The Old Studio, 25 Greenfield Road,
Westoning MK45 5JD
Tel: 01525 634940
Fax: 01525 750016
E-mail: director@iota.org.uk
Web site: www.iota.org.uk
Registered Friendly Society: No 53 SA

OFFICERS
President: Wing Cdr Peter Green FInstTA
Deputy President: Alan Whittington FInstTA, FRSA, FIBC
Trustees: Brian Bigwood FInstTA, Christopher Sullivan MInstTA, Dirk Duwel MInstTA
National Treasurer and Chairman, Finance & General Purposes Committee: Clive Aisbitt FInstTA
Chairman Education, Membership & Training Committee: Eric Davies FInstTA
Chairman External Affairs Committee: Mike Walker FInstTA
Director of the Institute: David J S Dalglish MInstTA, FRSA

THE INSTITUTION OF MECHANICAL ENGINEERS
1 Birdcage Walk,
London SW1H 9JJ
Tel: 020 7222 7899
Fax: 020 7222 4557
Web site: www.imeche.org.uk
Chief Executive: William Edgar
President: William M Banks
Engineering Director: Dr Colin Brown C Eng FIMechE
The Institute was founded in 1847, and incorporates as the Automobile Division the former Institution of Automobile Engineers and as the Railway Division the former Institution of Locomotive Engineers.

SOE
22 Greencoat Place,
London SW1P 1PR
Tel: 020 7630 1111
Fax: 020 7630 6677
E-mail: soe@soe.org.uk
Web site: www.soe.org.uk
The SOE is the umbrella professional body for those working in road transport and plant engineering. The IRTE is a professional sector within the SOE.

TRL LTD (TRANSPORT RESEARCH LABORATORY)
Crowthorne House, Nine Mile Ride,
Wokingham RG40 3GA
Tel: 01344 773131
Fax: 01344 770356
E-mail: enquiries@trl.co.uk
Web site: www.trl.co.uk

International Associations

INTERNATIONAL ROAD TRANSPORT UNION (IRU)
Founded in 1948 in Geneva, the IRU is an international association of national road transport federations which has consultative status in the United Nations. One of its two Transport Councils is concerned with road passenger transport.
General Secretariat:
IRU, Centre International,
3 Rue de Varembe, B.P.44,
1211 Geneva 20, Switzerland
Tel: 00 41 22 918 2700
Fax: 00 41 22 918 2741
E-mail: info@iru.org
Web site: www.iru.org

UITP, THE INTERNATIONAL ASSOCIATION OF PUBLIC TRANSPORT
President: Roberto Cavalieri (Italy)
Secretary General: Hans Rat
Offices: Rue Sainte Marie 6,
B-1080, Bruxelles, Belgium
Tel: 00 32 2 673 6100
Fax: 00 32 2 660 1072
E-mail: info@uitp.org
Web site: www.uitp.org

WORLD ROAD ASSOCIATION (PIARC)
Hon Sec/Hon Treasurer:
John Smart IHT
6 Endsleigh Street,
London WC1H 0DZ
Tel: 0207 391 9927
E-mail: john.smart@iht.org
Web site: www.piarc.org
The Association is an international body with headquarters in Paris, administered by an elected President and other office bearers. Members are recruited from governments, local authorities, technical and industrial groups and private individuals whose interests are centred on roads and road traffic. The association is maintained by subscriptions from its members. International congresses are held every four years.

OFFICE BEARERS
President: O Michaud (Switzerland)
International Vice-Presidents: P Anguitas Salas (Chile), C Jordan (Australia),
K Ghellab (Morocco)
Secretary General: J F Corte, PIARC,
La Grande Arche, Paroi Nord, Niveau 8,
92055 La Defense Cedex, France
Tel: 00 33 1 47 96 81 21
Fax: 00 33 1 49 00 02 02
The British National Committee's role is to ensure adequate representation of British methods and experience on PIARC's international committees and Congresses, to disseminate the findings of those committees and generally look after British interests. The present officers of this committee are:
Patron: Minister for Transport.
UK President: Steve Lee
UK Chairman: W J McCoubrey
Vice-Chairman: S Clarke
Hon Treasurer: C B Goodwillie
Hon Secretary/Hon Treasurer: J Smart

Other Organisations

ASSOCIATION OF TRANSPORT CO-ORDINATING OFFICERS (ATCO)
c/o Ian White, Passenger Transport Unit, Wiltshire Council, County Hall, Trowbridge BA14 8JN
Tel: 01225 713322
Fax: 01225 713317
E-mail: ian.white@wiltshire.gov.uk
Chairman: Tony Moreton, Lancashire County Council
Tel: 01772 530714
E-mail: tony.moreton@lancashire.gov.uk
Chairman (from November 2010): Bruce Thompson, Devon County Council
Tel: 01392 383244
E-mail: bruce.thompson@devon.gov.uk
Chairman, Bus Executive: Mark Pedlar, Somerset County Council
Tel: 01823 356968
E-mail: mcpedlar@somerset.gov.uk
Web site: www.atco.org.uk
The Association of Transport Co-ordinating Officers was formed in 1974 to bring together local authority officers whose work involved what were then new county council responsibilities for passenger transport.
ATCO members include senior staff directly concerned with strategic policy development and implementation for securing of passenger transport services for a wide range of public authorities. These include shire counties and unitary councils in England, Wales and Scotland, Passenger Transport Executives, TfL, the Isle of Man, the States of Jersey and Northern Ireland.
Through exchanging information and views the Association helps formulate policies and standards and promotes transport initiatives aimed at achieving better passenger transport services for all.
Members give advice to the Local Government Association and the Convention of Scottish Local Authorities. ATCO co-operates with the Community Transport Association and Passenger Transport Executive Group.

BUS USERS UK
PO Box 2950, Stoke-on-Trent ST4 9EW
Tel: 01782 442855
Fax: 01782 442856
E-mail: enquiries@bususers.org
Web site: www.bususers.org
Bus Users UK was formed in 1985 to bring together national and local organisations with an interest in bus services and concerned individual bus users to seek to give an effective voice to the consumer. It is actively involved in developing constructive dialogue between the users and providers of bus services. It publishes a quarterly newsletter – Bus User.
Life President: Dr Caroline Cahm MBE
Chairman: Gavin Booth
Vice Chairman: Jeff Anderson
Treasurer: Stephen Le Bras

Senior Officer for Wales:
Mrs Margaret Everson
Officer for Wales: Barclay Davies
Welsh Office: PO Box 1045,
Cardiff CF11 1JE
Tel: 029 2022 1370
E-mail: wales@bususers.org

Bus User Editor: Stephen Morris
PO Box 119, Shepperton TW17 8UX
Tel: 01932 232574
Fax: 01932 246394
E-mail: editor@bususers.org

BUSK
18 Windsor Road, Newport NP19 8NS
Tel: 01633 274944
E-mail: buskuk@aol.com
Formerly known for its Belt Up School Kids campaign, BUSK is now known through the European Union as an authority on vehicular safety for children and young people.

COACH DRIVERS CLUB
Unit 4, Minerva Business Park,
Lynch Wood, Peterborough PE2 6FT
Tel: 01733 405738
Fax: 01733 405745
E-mail: lauren.kirt@coachdriversclub.com
Web site: www.coachdriversclub.com
The Coach Drivers Club is a membership club for coach drivers, coaching and tourism. It offers accident cover, magazine, yearbook, members' website, legal advice.

GOSKILLS
Concorde House, Trinity Park,
Solihull B37 7UQ
Tel: 0121 635 5520
Fax: 0121 635 5521
Web site: goskills.org
Director of Operations: Ruth Exelby
GoSkills is the Sector Skills Council for passenger transport.

British Operators' Organisations

LIGHT RAIL TRANSIT ASSOCIATION
c/o 8 Berwick Place, Welwyn Garden City AL7 4TU
E-mail: office@lrta.org
Web site: www.lrta.org
Founded in 1937 to advocate and encourage interest in light rail and modern tramways. Monthly magazine is Tramways & Urban Transit. Membership enquiries to:
Membership Secretary: Roger Morris
E-mail: membership@lrta.org
President: Geoffrey Claydon
Chairman: Geoff Lusher
Deputy Chairman: Andrew Braddock
Editor in Chief, Tramways & Urban Transit: Howard Johnston

LOCAL GOVERNMENT ASSOCIATION
Local Government House, Smith Square, London SW1P 3HZ
Tel: 020 7664 3131
Fax: 020 7664 3030
Web Site: www.lga.gov.uk
The Local Government Association was formed by the merger of the Association of County Councils, the Association of District Councils and the Association of Metropolitan Authorities in 1997. The LGA has just under 500 members, including all shire district councils; metropolitan district councils; county councils; new unitary authorities; London authorities; and Welsh authorities. In addition, the LGA represents police authorities, fire authorities and passenger transport authorities. The LGA provides the national voice for local communities in England and Wales; its members represent over 50 million people, employ more than 2 million staff and spend over £65 billion on local services.

Amongst the LGA's policy priorities is integrated transport; local authorities lead the way in encouraging the use of public transport and thereby reducing congestion, ill-health and environmental damage through a programme of partnerships between local authorities and other agencies.
President: Lord Richard Best
Chairman: Margaret Eaton OBE (Conservative, Bradford)
Vice-Chairs: Sir Jeremy Beecham (Labour, Newcastle), David Shakespeare OBE (Conservative, Buckinghamshire)
Deputy Chairs:
Ian Swithenbank CBE (Labour, Northumberland), Richard Kemp (Liberal Democrat, Liverpool), Keith Ross OBE (Independent, West Somerset), David Parsons (Conservative, Leicestershire)
Chief Executive: John Ransford

LONDON TRAVELWATCH
6 Middle Street, London EC1A 7JA
Tel: 020 7505 9000
Fax: 020 7505 9003
E-mail: info@londontravelwatch.org.uk
Web site: www.londontravelwatch.org.uk
Formerly the London Transport Users Committee, London TravelWatch is the independent statutory body set up to represent the interests of the users of all transport for which the Greater London Authority and Transport for London is responsible for operating, providing, procuring and licensing. London TravelWatch is also the Rail Passengers Committee for London.
Interim Chair: David Leibling
Chief Executive: Janet Cooke

PASSENGER FOCUS
5th Floor, Wellington House, 39-41 Piccadilly, Manchester M1 1LQ
Tel: 0300 123 2140
Fax: 0161 244 5981
E-mail: info@passengerfocus.org.uk
Web site: www.passengerfocus.org.uk
Passenger Focus is the independent passenger watchdog, set up by the Government to protect the interests of rail passengers and bus passengers in England (outside London).
Chairman: Colin Foxall CBE
Board Members: David Burton, Christine Knights, Dr Derek Langslow CBE, David Leibling, Deryk Mead CBE, Bill Samuel, Barbara Saunders OBE, Stella Mair Thomas, Nigel Walmsley
Chief Executive: Anthony Smith
Rail Passenger Director: Ashwin Kumar
Bus Passenger Director: David Sidebottom

ROAD OPERATORS' SAFETY COUNCIL (ROSCO)
Osborn House, 20 High Street South, Olney, Buckinghamshire MK46 5JF
Tel: 01234 714420
E-mail: admin@rosco-uk.org
Web site: www.rosco-uk.org
'ROSCO' operates the industry's leading safe driver award scheme. Over 100 operators and 50,000 drivers annually register for the scheme which provides diplomas, badges and insignia for drivers who complete a year's safe driving.
Chairman: P J S Shipp
Vice Chairman: J E H Miller
Executive Officer: A M Edmondson

THE ROYAL SOCIETY FOR THE PREVENTION OF ACCIDENTS
Edgbaston Park, 353 Bristol Road, Birmingham B5 7ST
Tel: 0121 248 2000
Fax: 0121 248 2001
RoSPA promotes safety at work and in the home, at leisure and in schools, on (or near water) and on the roads, through providing information, publicity, training and consultancy.

The Society works with central and local government, the caring services, the police and public and private sector organisations large and small. Some work is funded by grant and sponsorship, but most relies on the support of the Society's membership.

The Society also produces and supplies a comprehensive selection of publications ranging from reference books to low-cost booklets for mass distribution.
Training Offered: Training courses cover practical skills and management training through to professional qualifications in Health and Safety.
Chief Executive: Tom Mullarkey

STATUS
c/o Michael Hughes, Manchester Metropolitan University, Chester Street, Manchester M1 5GD
Tel: 0161 247 6240
Fax: 0161 247 6779
Web site: www.status.org.uk
E-mail: m.p.hughes@mmu.ac.uk
STATUS others members, from all areas of the specialist road transport industry, with engineering development and test services, technical legislative consultancy and a range of general technical information.

It is involved on behalf of its members in contributing to consultation documents, influencing transport related legislation and lobbying government departments and agencies.

The organisation can call on a diverse range of personnel to help deal with more difficult problems. A primary benefit is the availability of telephone consultancy on technical or legislative matters.

STATUS plays a prominent role in representing its members' interests on legislative matters and lobbies government agencies on behalf of members.

A monthly newsletter is published, featuring industry related stories.

TRANSPORT 2000
1st Floor, The Impact Centre, 12-18 Hoxton Street, London N1 6NG
Tel: 020 7613 0743
Fax: 020 7613 5280.
Web site: www.bettertransport.org.uk
E-mail: info@bettertransport.org.uk
Transport 2000 is a campaign and research group that seeks greener, cleaner transport patterns through greater use of public transport, walking and cycling.
President: Michael Palin
Executive Director: Stephen Joseph

TRANSPORT BENEVOLENT FUND
22-25 Finsbury Square, London EC2A 1DX
Tel: 08450 100 500 **Fax:** 0870 831 2882
Web site: www.tbf.org.uk
E-mail: help@tbf.org.uk
TBF is a Registered Charity (No 1058032) and was founded in 1923. Membership is open to most staff engaged in the public transport industry. Members pay £1 a week and in return are granted, at the discretion of the Trustees, cash help, convalescence, recuperation, a wide range of complementary medical treatments, legal advice, and medical equipment in times of need. Membership covers the employee and their partner and dependent children. Subject to age and length of membership, free membership may be awarded on leaving the industry. There are payroll deduction facilities in many companies.
Director: Chris Godbold
Senior Trustee: Ray Jordan (President)
Patrons: Sir Wilfrid Newton, CBE (Past Chairman, London Transport), Brian Souter (Stagecoach Group), Lew Adams OBE (BT Police Authority), Sir Moir Lockhead OBE (FirstGroup), Peter Hendy CBE (Transport for London), Robert Crow (RMT), Graham Stevenson (UNITE), Gerry Doherty (TSSA), Keith Norman (ASLEF), David Martin (Arriva), Keith Ludeman (Go-Ahead Group), Roger Bowker CBE (East London Bus Group), Bob Rixham (UNITE), Nigel Stevens (Transdev), John O'Brien (Veolia Transport UK), Ian Coucher (Network Rail) Simon Posner (CPT).

Sports Associations

NATIONAL PASSENGER TRANSPORT SPORTS ASSOCIATION
President: Ian Davies
Vice President: Geoff Lusher
Chairman: Murray McDonald
Treasurer: Jack McLean
Secretary: Paul Bishop, National Express West Midlands, Unit 35, Second Avenue, Pensnett Trading Estate, Kingswinford, West Midlands DY6 7UH
Tel: 01384 555507
Fax: 01384 555510
E-mail: paul.bishop@nationalexpress.com
Web site: www.tran-sport.co.uk
The association organises inter-company sporting activities for the bus, coach, light rail and heavy rail industries. Currently 16 different sports are covered, each with competitions through the year, with trophies

provided often by bus sponsors. A regular magazine is published. Corporate membership is provided to large transport undertakings. Further information is available from the Secretary, address above.

Trade Organisations and Associations

BEAMA LTD
The British Electrotechnical & Allied Manufacturers' Association Founded 1902, Incorporated 1905.
Offices: Westminster Tower, 3 Albert Embankment, London SE1 7SL
Tel: 020 7793 3000
Fax: 020 7793 3003
E-mail: info@beama.org.uk
Objectives: By co-operative action to promote the interests of the industrial, electrical and electronic manufacturing industries of Great Britain.
Director-General: A. A. Bullen

FEDERATION OF ENGINE REMANUFACTURERS
49 Mewstone Avenue, Wembury, Plymouth PL9 0JT
Director: Brian Ludford
Tel: 01752 863681
Web Site: www.fer.co.uk.

FREIGHT TRANSPORT ASSOCIATION VEHICLE INSPECTION SERVICE
Hermes House, St John's Road, Tunbridge Wells TN4 9UZ
Tel: 01892 526171
Web Site: www.fta.co.uk.
The Freight Transport Association represents the interests of over 11,000 companies throughout the UK. FTA carries out over 100,000 vehicle inspections each year including many PSVs. The FTA Vehicle Inspection Service supports operators in maintaining their vehicles in a roadworthy condition - both mechanically and legally.
Further details are available from Alan Osborne, Head of Vehicle Inspection Services, FTA, Tunbridge Wells (01892 526171).
Publications: Freight (monthly journal), FTA Yearbook.
Chief Executive: Richard Turner.

LOW CARBON VEHICLE PARTNERSHIP
83 Victoria Street,
London SW1H 0HW
Tel: 020 3178 7859
E-mail: secretariat@lowcvp.org.uk
Web site: www.lowcvp.org.uk
The LowCVP is an action and advisory group providing a forum through which partners can work together towards shared goals and take the lead in the transition to a low-carbon future for road transport in the UK.
Bus Working Group Chairman: Bob Bryson (Alexander Dennis)

MIRA LTD
Registered Office: MIRA Ltd, Watling Street, Nuneaton CV10 0TU
Tel: 024 7635 5000.
Fax: 024 7635 5355.
MIRA is an independent product engineering and technology centre and offers skills in innovation, problem-solving and consultancy.
Chairman: M Beasley
Executive Directors:
Managing Director: J. R. Wood
Director of Finance & Company Secretary: C J N Phillipson
Director of Engineering: G. Townsend

SOCIETY OF MOTOR MANUFACTURERS & TRADERS (SMMT)
Forbes House, Halkin Street, London SW1X 7DS
Tel: 020 7235 7000
E-mail: buscoachweb@smmt.co.uk
Web site: www.smmt.co.uk

THE VEHICLE BUILDERS & REPAIRERS ASSOCIATION
Belmont House, Gildersome, Leeds LS27 7TW
Tel: 0113 253 8333
Fax: 0113 238 0496
E-mail: vbra@vbra.co.uk
Web site: www.vbra.co.uk
The VBRA is the representative organisation for vehicle manufacturers and vehicle/car body repairers.
An OFT approved Code of Practice has been drawn up to govern the conduct of members.
Director General: Malcolm Tagg

Societies

THE ASSOCIATION OF FRIENDS OF THE BRITISH COMMERCIAL VEHICLE MUSEUM TRUST
The Association was formed when The British Commercial Vehicle Museum was opened in 1983. Its aims are to support the full-time staff in matters of publicity, fund raising, maintenance and documentation of exhibits, work in the archives, organising rallies, etc. Facilities for members include a newsletter, free admission to the museum to undertake museum work and socialise with colleagues. New members are always welcome and special rates exist for families, students and senior citizens.
Hon Chairman: H Hatcher
Hon Secretary: A Pritchard
Hon Treasurer: A Pritchard
Members of the Committee:
E Simister, D Lewis, J Gardner
Museum Manager: A Buchan
Address:
The British Commercial Vehicle Museum, King Street, Leyland,
Preston PR25 2LE
Tel: 01772 451011

ASTON MANOR ROAD TRANSPORT MUSEUM
The Old Tram Depot, 208-216 Witton Lane, Aston, Birmingham B6 6QE
Tel: 0121 322 2298
Web site: www.amrtm.org.uk
Company limited by guarantee. Registered as a charity.
The museum is uniquely housed in a former depot of Birmingham's first-generation tramways. The display of commercial and passenger vehicles reflects the history of construction and operation in the West Midlands, and there are numerous displays of transport artefacts, tickets, notices and photographs. Joining as a Friend of the Museum gives entitlement to free entry and a quarterly newsletter. The museum is open on Saturdays, Sundays and Bank Holidays throughout the year, with a range of special events featuring a free heritage bus service to and from the city centre. The Museum is situated on Travel West Midland's bus services 7 and 11 and close to Aston railway station.
Further information from:
Chairman: Geoff Lusher, 86 Heritage Court, Warstone Lane, Jewellery Quarter, Birmingham B18 6HU

BRITISH BUS PRESERVATION GROUP
25 Oldfield Road, Bexleyheath DA7 4DX
Membership enquiries: 51 Market Close, Shirebrook, Mansfield NG20 8AE
Tel: 07940 771439
E-mail: info@bbpg.co.uk
Web site: www.bbpg.co.uk
The BBPG was formed in 1990 and has been responsible for securing the future of more than 250 historic buses and coaches, many of which were saved at extremely short notice from being broken up. The society has more than 600 members, both individuals and preservation groups. The BBPG caters for all bus enthusiasts, whether or not they own a bus.
Chairman: Glyn Matthews.
General Secretary: Mike Lloyd.
Membership Secretary: Steve Mortimore.

BRITISH TROLLEYBUS SOCIETY
Formed as the Reading Transport Society in 1961, the present title was adopted in 1971, having acquired a number of trolleybuses for preservation from all over Britain. In 1969 it founded the Trolleybus Museum at Sandtoft, near Doncaster, where its vehicles are housed and regularly operate on mains power from the overhead wiring. West Yorkshire Transport Circle merged into the Society in January 1991. Currently membership stands at about 320. Members receive the monthly journal Trolleybus containing news and articles from home and abroad. Additionally members can subscribe to Bus Fare and Wheels, monthly magazines for motorbus operation in the Thames Valley and West Yorkshire areas respectively. Monthly meetings are also held in Reading, London and Bradford.
Secretary: A. J. Barton, 2 Josephine Court, Southcote Road, Reading RG30 2DG
Tel: 0118 958 3974

BUSES WORLDWIDE
37, Oyster Lane, Byfleet, Surrey KT14 7HS
Tel: 01932 352351
E-mail: membership@busesworldwide.org
Web site: www.busesworldwide.org
Buses Worldwide is an international society for those interested in buses and coaches throughout the world. Regular publications include Buses Worldwide, Maltese Transport News and British Buses Abroad.
Chairman/Managing Editor: Richard Stedall
Vic-Chairman/Membership Secretary: Steve Guess
News Editor: Norman Bartlett
Features Editor: David Corke
Secretary: Simon Brown

CLASSIC BUS HERITAGE TRUST (INCORPORATING THE ROUTEMASTER HERITAGE TRUST)
The Classic Bus Heritage Trust aims to advance preservation of buses and coaches by fostering the interests of the general public. It is a Registered Charity.
Treasurer & Hon Sec: W. Ackroyd, 8 Twining Road, Ventnor, Isle of Wight PO38 1TX

ESSEX BUS ENTHUSIASTS' GROUP
272 Shoebury Road, Southend-on-Sea, Essex SS1 3TT
E-mail: admin@signal-training.com
Web site: www.essexbus.org.uk
EBEG was formed in 1962, under its previous title, Eastern National Enthusiasts' Group. The present title was adopted in 1987 to reflect more fully the activities of the group. EBEG publishes a monthly illustrated magazine "Essex Bus News", holds regular

British Operators' Organisations

meetings in South and North Essex, and offers publications, photo sales, and coach tours. Annual subscription of £20 includes 12 issues of Essex Bus News.
Chairman: Chris Stewart
Secretary: Alan Osborne
Treasurer: Richard Delahoy
Editor: David Harman

GB BUS GROUP
Membership Enquiries:
192 Alvechurch Road, West Heath, Birmingham B31 3PW
Tel: 0121 624 8641
Chairman: G Nichols
Secretary: M Brown
Treasurer: F Gold
The GB Bus Group was formed in 2006 to help attract new enthusiasts to the hobby. It provides a monthly magazine as well as a full range of bus and coach fleet books covering UK and Ireland. The GB Bus Group is a member of the UK Transport Group.

HISTORIC COMMERCIAL VEHICLE SOCIETY
The Society was founded in 1958 and four years later absorbed the Vintage Passenger Vehicle Society and the London Vintage Taxi Club. Its membership of over 4,000 owns more than 6,000 preserved vehicles. Activities include the organisation of rallies, among them the well known London to Brighton and Trans-Pennine runs. The club caters for all commercial vehicles over 20 years old.

OFFICERS
President: Lord Montagu of Beaulieu
Senior Exec Officer and Vice-President: M. Banfield, Iden Grange, Cranbrook Road, Staplehurst TN12 0ET
Tel: 01580 892929
Fax: 01580 893227
E-mail: hcvs@btinternet.com
Web site: www.hcvs.co.uk

LEYLAND NATIONAL GROUP
E-mail: secretary@leylandnationalgroup.org
Web site: www.leylandnationalgroup.org
The Leyland National Group was formed in 1997 and has members throughout Great Britain and abroad. Although the group does not own any vehicles itself, some of its members are bus owners. There are more than 100 Leyland Nationals from a variety of operators preserved by group members. However, one does not need to own a bus to join the group, as membership is open to anyone with an interest in Leyland Nationals. The group also caters for those interested in the derivatives of the Leyland National; the Leyland-DAB, Leyland B21 and Leyland National bodied rail vehicles. Members receive a colour illustrated quarterly magazine, exclusive access to the members' only area on the group's website as well as other benefits. Please contact the Membership Secretary for more information about the group, the benefits of membership and to receive a membership application form.
Chairman: Mick Berg
Secretary:
D Lefevre, 2 Forest Cottages, Whatlington, Battle, East Sussex TN33 0NT
E-mail: secretary@leylandnationalgroup.org
Treasurer: Mike Bellinger
Magazine Editor: Claire Barrett
Membership Secretary: Tim Wild, 27 Dukeshill Road, Bracknell, RG42 2DU
Tel: 01344 640095
E-mail: membership@leylandnationalgroup.org

LINCOLNSHIRE VINTAGE VEHICLE SOCIETY
Road Transport Museum, Whisby Road, North Hykeham LN6 5TR
Tel: 01522 500566/689497
The LVVS was founded in 1959 by local businessmen with the aim of forming a road transport museum. Charitable status was obtained some time ago, and with a capital grant from its local district council, it has now completed the first stage of its new museum project. Over 60 vehicles dating from the 1920s to the 1980s can be seen in the new exhibition hall with many more in the workshop.
Opening times: November–April Sundays 13.00-16.00. May–October Mon-Fri 12.00-16.00, Sun 10.00-16.00.
Chairman: S Milner
Hon Treasurer: J Child
Secretary: Mrs J Jefford
Web site: www.lvvs.org.uk

LONDON OMNIBUS TRACTION SOCIETY (LOTS)
Unit N305, Westminster Business Square, 1-45 Durham Street, Vauxhall, London SE11 5JH
Web site: www.lots.org.uk
Formed in 1964, LOTS has nearly 2,500 members and is the largest bus enthusiast society in the United Kingdom.

A colour Illustrated monthly newsletter is sent to all members. This covers all the current operators in the former London Transport central and country areas, and includes General and Industry News, Route Developments, Vehicle News, Publicity News, as well as subsequent disposal information for vehicles and Service Vehicle information. Monthly meetings as normally held in central London featuring guest speakers, slide and film presentations during the year as well as the annual free bus rides from central London using vehicles of London interest.

Regular LOTS publications include fleet allocations, route working and service vehicle publications, an annual review of the routes, vehicles and operations of London Buses, as well as the popular annual London Bus and Tram Fleet book. A quarterly 64-page glossy magazine, the London Bus Magazine (LBM) has been produced for over 35 years.

Regular sales lists are produced and sent out to all members through the year. An information service is also available to all members to help with those historical queries.

The Autumn Transport Spectacular (ATS) is held in London every autumn and is one of London's biggest transport sales.

All enquiries should be directed to the above address.

THE M & D AND EAST KENT BUS CLUB
42 St Albans Hill, Hemel Hempstead HP3 9NG
E-mail: n.king112@btinternet.com
Web site: www.mdekbusclub.org.uk
This club was formed in 1952 with the object of bringing together all those interested in road passenger transport in an area covering Kent and East Sussex. Facilities for members include a monthly news booklet (illustrated), information service, tours, meetings, vehicle photograph sales and vehicle preservation. A series of publications is also produced, including illustrated fleet histories.
Hon Chairman: J. V. Spillett
Hon Sec: P J Evans
Hon Editor: N D King
Hon Treasurer: N D King
Membership Officer: J. A. Fairley
Photographic Officer: B.Weeden
Sales Officer: to be appointed
Tours Officer: D. R. Cobb
Management Committee: N. D. King, R. A. Lewis, J. V. Spillett, P. J. Evans, D M Jones. There are Area Organisers in Ashford, Dover, Folkestone, Hastings, North-East Kent, Maidstone and the Medway Towns.

THE NATIONAL TRAMWAY MUSEUM
Crich, Matlock DE4 5DP
Tel: 01773 854321
Fax: 01773 854320
The Society was founded in 1955 to establish and operate a working tramway museum. The Museum is at Crich Tramway Village, Crich, near Matlock, in Derbyshire, and owns over 70 English, Irish, Scottish, Welsh and overseas tramcars. Members receive a copy of the Society's quarterly journal and can participate in the running of the museum.
Patron: HRH The Duke of Gloucester GCVO
Vice-Presidents: G. S. Hearse, W. G. S. Hyde, G. B. Claydon, D. J. H. Senior, A W Bond
Chairman: C. Heaton
Vice-Chairman: R T Pennyfather
Hon Secretary: I. M. Dougill
Hon Treasurer: P R Moore
Operations Superintendent: K. B. Hulme

NATIONAL TROLLEYBUS ASSOCIATION
2 St John's Close, Claines, Worcester WR3 7PT
Tel: 01449 740876
Web site: www.trolleybus.co.uk/nta
Formed in 1963, and incorporated in 1968 as The Trolleybus Museum Co Ltd. The vehicles and ancillary equipment collected by the NTA since its inception are now owned by the company, which is limited by guarantee and is a registered charity. Members receive Trolleybus Magazine, a printed and illustrated bi-monthly journal documenting all aspects of trolleybus operation past and present throughout the world.
Chairman: R. D. Helliar-Symons
Secretary: J. H. Ward
Treasurer: I Martin
Membership Secretary: I Martin
Enquiries: tmbmembsec@hotmail.com

THE OMNIBUS SOCIETY LTD
The Omnibus Society was founded in 1929. Today it is a nationwide organisation with a network of provincial branches, offering a comprehensive range of facilities for those interested in the bus and coach industry. The Society has accumulated a wealth of information on public road transport. Members have the opportunity to receive and exchange data on every aspect of the industry including route developments, operational/traffic matters and fleet changes. Each branch has a full programme of activities and publishes its own Branch Bulletin to give local news of route changes, etc. A scheme exists whereby members subscribe to receive bulletins from branches other than that of which they are a member. A programme of indoor meetings is customary during winter, including film shows, invited speakers and discussions. In the summer months visits to manufacturers and tours to operators are featured. The Society maintains a comprehensive library and archive which may be visited by members and non-members undertaking

research, together with separate photographic and ticket collections.
Address: 100 Sandwell Street, Walsall WS1 3EB
Tel: 01922 629358
E-mail: oslibrary@btconnect.com
Web site: www.omnibussoc.org.

OFFICERS
President (2010): Mark Howarth
Vice-Presidents: F P Groves, A W Mills, G Wedlake, T F McLachlan, K W Swallow, Professor John Hibbs.
Chairman: B. Le Jeune.
Secretary: A. J. Francis, 185 Southlands Road, Bromley BR2 9QZ.
Treasurer: H. L. Barker, 31 High Street, Tarporley CW6 0DP.
Librarian/Archivist: Alan Mills
Editor, Society's Publications: Cyril McIntyre
Members of the Council: I D Barlex, G Booth, D M Persson, D Roy, J Howie, S Morris and nominations from each branch
Branch Officers:
Midland Branch: C R Warn, 11 The Meadows, Shawbury, Shrewsbury SY4 4HS
South Wales and West Branch: A J Armstrong, 16 Stanley Grove, Weston-super-Mare BS23 3EB
Northern Branch: Dave Sturrock, 8 Whiteley Grove, Newton Aycliffe DL5 4NH
North Western & Yorkshire Branch: P. Wilkinson, 10 Bradley Close, Timperley, Altrincham WA15 6SH
Scottish Branch: I. Allan, 10 Miller Avenue, Crossford, Dunfermline KY12 8PY
Essex & South Suffolk Group: J. L. Rugg, 86 Worthing Road, Laindon SS15 6JU
East Midland Group: A. Oxley, 4 Gordon Close, Attenborough, Nottingham NN4 9UF
Herts & Beds Group: R. C. Barton, 5 Viscount Court, Knights Field, Luton LU2 7LD
London Historical Research Group: D A Ruddom, 57 Bluebridge Road, Brookmans Park, Hatfield AL9 7UW
Provincial Historical Research Group: A E Jones, 8 Poplar Drive, Church Stretton S76 7BW

THE PSV CIRCLE
Unit 1R, Leroy House, 436 Essex Road, London N1 3QP
E-mail: enquiries@psv-circle.org.uk
Web site: www.psv-circle.org.uk
The aim of the PSV Circle is to be the definitive source of all knowledge on Public Service Vehicles and Operators throughout the United Kingdom. We produce a wide range of Publications including operator fleet histories, chassis lists, body lists, as well as current fleet lists covering Great Britain and Ireland.
HONORARY OFFICERS
Chairman: Mike Still
Secretary: John Skilling
Treasurer: Mike Bissex
Membership Secretary: Steve Fitzgerald
Rally Sales Team & Website Manager: Paul Young
News Sheet Despatch Manager: Adrian Clarke

RIBBLE ENTHUSIASTS' CLUB
23 Richmond Road, Hindley Green, Wigan WN2 4ND
Tel: 01942 253497
E-mail: mjyat@msn.com
Web site: http://homepage.manx.net/JHL/REC/index.htm

Founded in 1954 by the late T. B. Collinge for the study of road transport past and present and in particular Ribble Motor Services and associated companies. Meetings are held and a monthly news sheet produced.
Life President: A E Chapman
Life Vice President: M. Shires
Vice President: C Bowles
Committee Chairman: D Bailey MBE
Secretary/Tours: M J Yates, 23 Richmond Road, Hindley Green, Wigan WN2 4ND
Treasurer: R A Harpum, 107 New Road, West Parley, Ferndown, Dorset BH22 8EA
Records: S Blake, 23 Fairfield Road, North Shore, Blackpool FY1 2RA
Sales Dept: Mrs T Ashcroft, 11 Regent Road, Walton le Dale, Preston PR5 4QA
Sales Dept: Assistant: Mrs J Yates, 23 Richmond Road, Hindley Green, Wigan WN2 4ND
Archive: B Ashcroft, 11 Regent Road, Walton Le Dale, Preston PR5 4QA
Editor: R Kenyon, 18 Hatfield Road, Accrington BB5 6DF
Membership Sec: B Downham, 203 Brindle Road, Bamber Bridge, Preston PR5 6YL

ROADS AND ROAD TRANSPORT HISTORY ASSOCIATION
Web site: www.rrtha.org.uk
Founded in 1992, the association promotes, encourages and co-ordinates the study of the history of roads and road transport, both passenger and freight. It aims to encourage those interested in a particular aspect of transport to understand their chosen subject in the context of developments in other areas and at other periods. It publishes a newsletter four times a year and holds an annual conference each autumn. Membership is open to professional bodies/transport societies, museums and individuals.
President: Professor John Hibbs, OBE
Chairman: Garry Turvey, CBE
Hon. Secretary: Christopher Hogan, 124 Shenstone Avenue, Stourbridge DY8 3EJ
E-mail: roadsandRTHA@aol.com

ROUTEMASTER ASSOCIATION
Easton House, Easton Lane, Bozeat, Northamptonshire NN29 7NN
Web site: www.routemaster.org.uk
The Routemaster Association was set up in 1988 to provide assistance, advice and news for operators, owners and enthusiasts of these vehicles. From the specification of a screw to a complete bus, the Association provides authoritative technical and parts information. Bus rallies and events are occasionally organised and other selected events are supported from time to time.
Members receive a quarterly magazine and the regular Suppliers' Handbook, as well as discounts on various parts, spares and accessories including maintenance manuals, owners' handbook, summaries of technical bulletins, badges, vinyls, window rubbers, indicator ears rubbers, B-frame sandwich rubbers, rear engine mountings, bulkhead windows, Treadmaster flooring and nosings, bodywork fixings and many other unique products for the vehicle.
In 2001/02, large batches of Routemaster spares were acquired from the London Buses RM refurbishment programme, including original specification mechanical units, electrical items and bodywork spares. In 2009/10, several more batches of second-hand spares have been acquired for the benefit of our members.
All enquiries should be directed to the above address, or via the *contact page* on the website.
President: Colin Curtis OBE
Vice President: George Watson
Chairman & Vice President: Andrew Morgan
E-mail: andrewmorgan1368@tiscali.co.uk
Sales Officer: Rob Duker
Press & Publicity Officer: Dave Paskell

THE SAMUEL LEDGARD SOCIETY
58 Kirklees Drive, Farsley, Pudsey, West Yorkshire LS28 5TE
Tel: 0113 236 3695
Fax: 0113 259 1125
E-mail: rennison@cc-email.co.uk
Web Site: wwwsamuelledgardsociety.org.uk
The Samuel Ledgard Society was formed in 1998 at the Rose & Crown Inn, Otley, during the second annual reunion of the devotees of this well-known bus company. Reunions are held twice yearly at Armley during April and Otley on or about October 14. A Christmas dinner is also part of the established calendar of events. The quarterly journal of the Society, The Chat, is published in March, June, September and December each year. Founding officers were Barry Rennison, Tony Greaves and Don Bate, all of whom have a wealth of knowledge about the Samuel Ledgard company. Membership is open to all with a subscription of £5 - contact any member of the Committee for details.
Hon President: Mrs Jenny Barton
COMMITTEE
Chairman: Barry Rennison
Vice-Chairman: Tony Edwards
Treasurer: Bryan Whitham
Secretary: Margaret Rennison

SCOTTISH TRAMWAY & TRANSPORT SOCIETY
PO Box 7342, Glasgow G51 4YQ
Tel: 0141 445 3883
Fax: 0141 440 2955
E-mail: stt.glasgow@virgin.net
Web site: www.scottishtransport.org
Founded in 1951 as the Scottish Tramway Museum Society, the Society claims to be 'Scotland's foremost tramway enthusiast organisation', publishing books and videos on tramways and other transport subjects and supporting the National Tramway Museum. Monthly meetings are held and a newsletter is produced.
Hon Chairman: Alastair Murray
Gen Secretary: Hugh McAulay
Hon Treasurer: Allan Ramsay
Members of Committee: A Murray, N Bates, A Muir, B Quinn, F W B Mitchell, I Stewart

SOUTH YORKSHIRE TRANSPORT MUSEUM
Waddington Way, Aldwarke, Rotherham S65 3SH
Tel: 0114 255 3010
The Sheffield Bus Museum Trust was formed in 1987 with the purpose of co-ordinating the bus preservation movement in Sheffield and to establish a permanent museum. This was initially achieved at the former Sheffield Tramways Company's Tinsley Tram Depot but in 2007 the Trust moved its collection to new premises at Aldwarke, Rotherham. At the same time the museum was re-branded to the name above. The majority of the Trust's collection is local and extremely varied, ranging from a 1926 Sheffield tramcar to a 1985 Dennis

British Operators' Organisations

Domino. In recent years the Museum Trust has benefitted from Heritage Fund Lottery grants. The museum is an educational charity and promotes an ever-expanding schools visits programme. The museum is open to the public on a monthly basis from March to December.
Chairman: M W Greenwood
Membership Secretary:
Dr. John Willis, 2 Pwll-Y-Waen,
Ty'n-Y-Groes, Conwy LL32 8TQ

SOUTHDOWN ENTHUSIASTS' CLUB
Web site:
www.southdownenthusiastsclub.org.uk
This club was founded in 1954 to bring together people interested in the vehicles, routes and history of Southdown Motor Services Ltd and now includes Stagecoach South (Eastbourne Buses, Hastings & District, South Coast Buses, Southdown, Hampshire Bus, Hants & Surrey, East Kent), Brighton & Hove, and First Hampshire and Dorset. There is a monthly news publication and winter meetings. Membership is open to persons aged 14 years and over and details may be had from the Hon Secretary.
Hon Chairman: J Allpress,
9 Phoenix Way, Southwick,
Brighton BN42 4HQ
Hon Secretary: N Simes,
11 High Cross Fields,
Crowborough TN6 2SN
Hon Treasurer: D E Still,
12 Westway Close, Mile Oak,
Portslade BN42 2RT
Hon Sales Officer: D Chalkley,
6 Valebridge Drive, Burgess Hill RH15 0RW
Hon News Sheet Editor: P Gainsbury,
Park Cottage, Guestling TN35 4LT
Hon Publications Officer: J Smith,
1 Sackville Way, Worthing BN14 8BJ
Committee Member: J Barley,
84 Kipling Avenue, Brighton BN2 6UE.
Hon Photographic Officer: C Churchill,
53 Monks Close, Lancing BN15 9DB

SWINDON VINTAGE OMNIBUS SOCIETY
10 Fraser Close, Nythe,
Swindon SN3 3RP
Tel: 01793 526001
E-mail: davenicol@talktalk.net
The group owns a preserved Daimler Weymann double deck, ex Swindon Corporation Society vehicle, also a Bristol RESL ECW ex-Thamesdown Transport.
Chairman: M Naughton
Secretary: D Nicol
Treasurer: D Mundy

THE TRANSPORT MUSEUM SOCIETY OF IRELAND LTD
National Transport Museum, Heritage Depot, Howth Castle Demesne, Howth, Dublin 13
Tel: 00 353 1 832 0427
E-mail: info@nationaltransportmuseum.org
Web site:
www.nationaltransportmuseum.org
A commercial vehicle collection of trams, buses, fire appliances, military vehicles, lorries and horse-drawn vehicles. Open daily (June to August), Sat/Sun/Bank Holidays (Sept-May): Mondays to Fridays 1000-1700, Sat/Sun/Bank Holidays 1400-1700.
Hon President: Michael Corcoran
Hon Chairman: John Kelleher
Hon Secretary: John Molloy

THE TRANSPORT MUSEUM, WYTHALL
Birmingham & Midland Motor Omnibus Trust, The Transport Museum, Chapel Lane, Wythall, Worcestershire B47 6JX
Tel: 01564 826471
E-mail: enquiries@wythall.org.uk
Web site: www.wythall.org.uk
The Trust dates back to 1973, taking its present title in 1977, when it became a registered educational charity to establish and develop a regional transport museum.
The museum comprises an exhibition hall, plus two other halls, housing 100 buses, coaches and battery-electric vehicles, mostly operated and/or built in the Midlands. The Museum is also licensed as a bus operator and some exhibits can be hired for appropriate work.
Trustees: David Taylor (Chairman), Paul Gray, Phil Ireland, Malcolm Keeley.

TRAMWAY & LIGHT RAILWAY SOCIETY
Web site: www.tramwayinfo.co.uk
Founded in 1938, the Tramway & Light Railway Society caters for those interested in all aspects of tramways. Members receive Tramfare, a bi-monthly illustrated magazine. There are regular meetings throughout the country. The Society promotes tramway modelling, drawings, castings, and technical details are available to modellers. There are also comprehensive library facilities. For fuller details of the Society and of membership please write to the Membership Secretary.
HONORARY OFFICERS
President: P J Davis.
Vice-Presidents: E R Oakley,
G B Claydon, C.B
Chairman: J R Prentice,
216 Brentwood Road, Romford RM1 2RP.
Secretary: G R Tribe,
47 Soulbury Road, Linslade, Leighton Buzzard LU7 7RW.
Membership Secretary: H J Leach,
6 The Woodlands,
Brightlingsea CO7 0RY.

THE TRANSPORT TICKET SOCIETY (TTS)
The TTS is for anyone interested in transport tickets, past and present. Facilities include a monthly illustrated journal, regular meetings, ticket exchange pools, monthly ticket distributions, and postal auctions of scarce tickets.
Membership Secretary:
Steve Skeavington, 6 Breckbank,
Forest Town, Mansfield NG19 0PZ
Web site: www.transport-ticket.org.uk

THE TRANSPORT TRUST
202 Lambeth Road, London SE1 7JW
Tel: 020 7928 6464
Fax: 020 7928 6565
E-mail: hq@thetransporttrust.org.uk
Web Site: www.thetransporttrust.org.uk
The Trust is the national charity for the preservation and restoration of Britain's transport heritage.

Passenger Transport Museums

This list is in addition to those shown in the main Society section above.

ABBEY PUMPING STATION
Contact address: Corporation Road,
Leicester LE4 5PX
Tel: 0116 299 5111
Fax: 0116 299 5125
Web site: www.leicester.gov.uk/museums, www.leicestermuseums.ac.uk

AMBERLEY WORKING MUSEUM
Amberley, Arundel BN18 9LT
Tel: 01798 831370
Fax: 01798 831831
E-mail: office@amberleymuseum.co.uk
Web site: www.amberleymuseum.co.uk

ASTON MANOR ROAD TRANSPORT MUSEUM
See Societies section

BLACK COUNTRY LIVING MUSEUM TRANSPORT GROUP
Tipton Road, Dudley DY1 4SQ
Tel: 0121 557 9643
Web site: wwww.bclm.co.uk

BRISTOL ROAD TRANSPORT COLLECTION
E-mail: william.staniforth@virgin.net
Web site: www.bristolbusevents.co.uk

BRITISH COMMERCIAL VEHICLE MUSEUM
King Street, Leyland PR25 2LE
Tel: 01772 451011 **Fax:** 01772 451015
E-mail: enquiries@bcvm.co.uk
Web site: www.bcvm.co.uk

CASTLE POINT TRANSPORT MUSEUM
105 Point Road, Canvey
Island SS8 7TP
Tel: 01268 684272

CAVAN AND LEITRIM RAILWAY
Narrow Gauge Station, Station Road,
Dromod, Co Leitrim, Ireland
Tel/Fax: 00353 71 9638599
E-mail: info@irish-railway.com
Web site: www.irish-railway.com

COBHAM BUS MUSEUM - THE LONDON BUS PRESERVATION TRUST LTD
Redhill Road, Cobham, Surrey, KT11 1EF
Tel/Fax: 01932 868665
E-mail: cobhambusmuseum@aol.com
Web site: www.lbpt.org

COVENTRY TRANSPORT MUSEUM
Millennium Place, Hales Street,
Coventry CV1 1PN
Tel: 024 7623 4270 **Fax:** 024 7623 4284
E-mail: enquiries@transport-museum.com

DOVER TRANSPORT MUSEUM
Willingdon Road, Port Zone White Cliffs Business Park, Whitfield,
Dover CT16 2HJ
Tel: 01304 822409

EAST ANGLIA TRANSPORT MUSEUM
Chapel Road, Carlton Colville,
Lowestoft NR33 8BL
Tel: 01502 518459
Fax: 01502 584658
E-mail: enquiries@eatm.org.uk
Web site: www.eatm.org.uk

GRAMPIAN TRANSPORT MUSEUM
Alford, Aberdeenshire AB33 8AE
Tel: 01975 562292
Fax: 01975 562180
E-mail: info@g-t-m.freeserve.co.uk
Web site: www.gtm.org.uk

IPSWICH TRANSPORT MUSEUM
Old Trolleybus Depot, Cobham Road,
Ipswich IP3 9JD
Tel: 01473 715666
E-mail: enquiries@ipswichtransportmuseum.co.uk
Web site:
www.ipswichtransportmuseum.co.uk
Chairman: Tony King
Vice Chairman: Mark Smith
Secretary: Mike Abbott
Finance: Bernard Simpson
An independent museum, run by volunteers,

devoted to telling the story of transport and engineering in the Ipswich area. Exhibits range from horse drawn carriages to an electric tram, trolleybuses and motor buses.

ISLE OF WIGHT BUS MUSEUM
Contact address:
28 Westmill Road, Newport PO30 5RG
Tel: 01983 526422
E-mail: nharris.westmill@tiscali.co.uk

KEIGHLEY BUS MUSEUM TRUST
Contact address: 47 Brantfell Drive, Burnley BB12 8AW
Tel: 01282 413179
E-Mail: shmdboard@aol.com
Web site: www.kbmt.org.uk
Chairman: R G Mitchell
Secretary: G A Jones
Treasurer: M J Jessop
A registered charity, the Trust holds a varied collection of some 60 buses, coaches, trolleybuses and ancillary vehicles, mainly from the West Yorkshire area, covering the period from 1924 up to the 1990s.

LONDON TRANSPORT MUSEUM
39 Wellington Street,
London WC2E 7BB.
Tel: 020 7379 6344; recorded information 020 7565 7299
E-mail: resourcedesk@ltmuseum.co.uk
Web site: www.ltmuseum.co.uk

MIDLAND ROAD TRANSPORT GROUP - BUTTERLEY
Contact address: 21 Ash Grove, Mastin Moor, Chesterfield S43 3AW
Tel: Midland Road Transport Group - 01246 473619
Tel: Midland Railway 01773 747674, Visitor Information Line (01773) 570140.

MUSEUM OF TRANSPORT
Kelvin Hall, 1 Bunhouse Road,
Glasgow G3 8DP
Tel: 0141 287 2720 (school bookings on 0141 565 4112/3)
Fax: 0141 287 2692

MUSEUM OF TRANSPORT, GREATER MANCHESTER
Boyle Street, Cheetham,
Manchester M8 8UW

Tel: 0161 205 2122
Fax: 0161 202 1110
E-mail: email@gmts.co.uk
Web site: www.gmts.co.uk
Chairman, Greater Manchester Transport Society:
Dennis Talbot
The museum charts the development of public transport in Greater Manchester, with exhibits ranging from a Victorian horse-drawn bus to a full size prototype Metrolink tram.

NATIONAL MUSEUM OF SCIENCE AND INDUSTRY
Exhibition Road, London SW7 2DD
Tel: 0207 942 4105 or 01793 814466
E-mail: s.evans@nmsi.ac.uk

THE NORTH OF ENGLAND OPEN AIR MUSEUM
Beamish, Durham DH9 0RG
Tel: 0191 370 4000
Fax: 0191 370 4001
E-mail: museum@beamish.org.uk
Web site: www.beamish.org.uk

THE NATIONAL TRAMWAY MUSEUM
See Societies Section

NORTH WEST MUSEUM OF ROAD TRANSPORT
The Old Bus Depot, 51 Hall Street,
St Helens WA10 1DU
E-mail: general@hallstreetdepot.info
Web site: www.hallstreetdepot.info

NOTTINGHAM TRANSPORT HERITAGE CENTRE
Contact address: Mere Way, Ruddington, Nottingham NG11 6NX
Tel: 0115 940 5705
E-mail: geoffrey.clark3@ntworld.com
Web site: http://www.nthc.co.uk

OXFORD BUS MUSEUM
Station Yard, Long Hanborough,
Witney OX29 8LA
Tel: 01993 883617
Web site: www.oxfordbusmuseum.org.uk
The museum collection was started by the Oxford Bus Preservation Syndicate, who acquired a 1949 semi-coach in 1967. In 1984 the vehicles were moved to the museum's present location in Long Hanborough. It traces the story of public transport in the Oxford area from the 19th century to the present day. Vehicles of local operators are strongly represented, from the 1920s to the minibus era of the 1980s, with several in running order. A total of some 40 vehicles are on display, and there is a conservation workshop with public viewing gallery.

SCOTTISH VINTAGE BUS MUSEUM
M90 Commerce Park, Lathalmond,
Dunfermline, Fife KY12 OSJ
Tel: 01383 623380
Web site: www.busweb.co.uk/svbm

THE TRANSPORT MUSEUM, WYTHALL
Birmingham & Midland Motor Omnibus Trust
See Societies section

TRANSPORT MUSEUM SOCIETY OF IRELAND
Howth Castle Demesne, Howth,
Dublin 13, Ireland
Tel/Fax: 00 353 1 848 0831
E-mail: info@nationaltransportmuseum.org
Web site:
www.nationaltransportmuseum.org

THE TROLLEYBUS MUSEUM AT SANDTOFT
Belton Road, Sandtoft,
North Lincolnshire DN8 5SX
Tel: 01724 711391
Fax: 01724 711846
E-mail: trolleybusmuseum@sandtoft.org
Web site: www.sandtoft.org
The museum is home to the world's largest collection of historic trolleybuses, and is open selected weekends from Easter to October.

ULSTER FOLK & TRANSPORT MUSEUM
Contact address: Cultra, Holywood,
Belfast BT18 0EU
Tel: 028 9042 8428

WIRRAL TRANSPORT MUSEUM
Pacific Road, Birkenhead L41 5HN
Tel: 0151 666 2756

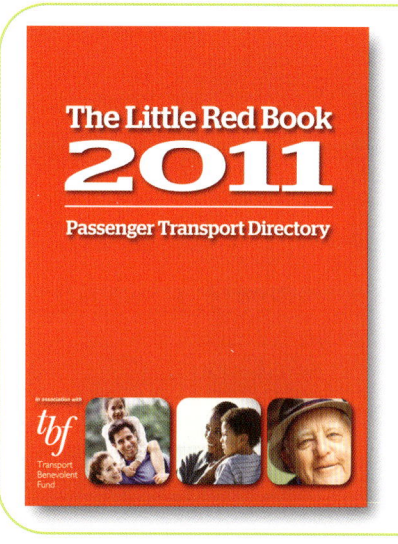

British Operators' Organisations

Advertising in the Little Red Book

For information regarding advertising contact:
Graham Middleton

Tel: 01780 484632
Fax: 01780 763388
E-mail:
graham.middleton@ianallanpublishing.co.uk

The Little Red Book 2011 - in association with *tbf* Transport Benevolent Fund

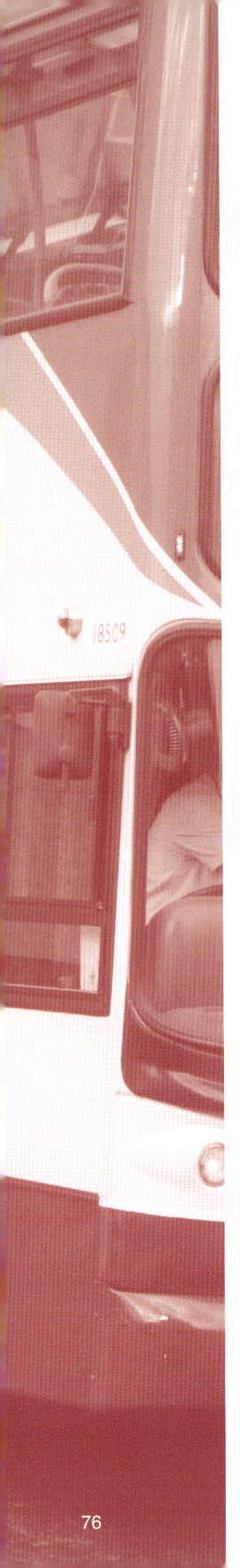

Section 4

British Isles Operators

Major Groups 78

English Operators

Bedford, Central Bedfordshire, Luton 83
Berkshire (including Bracknell Forest,
Reading, Slough, West Berkshire,
Windsor & Maidenhead, Wokingham) 84
Bristol, South Gloucestershire 85
Buckinghamshire, Milton Keynes 87
Cambridgeshire, City of Peterborough 88
Cheshire East, Cheshire West & Chester, Halton,
Warrington 92
Cornwall 94
Cumbria 95
Derbyshire, Derby 97
Devon, Plymouth, Torbay 101
Dorset, Bournemouth, Poole 104
Durham, Hartlepool, Stockton-on-Tees 107
East Riding of Yorkshire,
City of Kingston upon Hull 110
East Sussex, Brighton & Hove 111
Essex, Southend on Sea, Thurrock 112
Gloucestershire 117
Greater Manchester 118
Hampshire, Portsmouth, Southampton 122
Herefordshire 125
Hertfordshire 126
Isle of Wight 128
Kent, Medway 129
Lancashire, Blackburn & Darwen, Blackpool 132
Leicestershire, City of Leicester,
Rutland 135
Lincolnshire 137
London & Middlesex 139
Merseyside 145
Norfolk 147
North and North East Lincolnshire 150
North Yorkshire, Darlington, Middlesbrough,
Redcar & Cleveland, York 151
Northamptonshire 154
Northumberland 155
Nottinghamshire, Nottingham 156
Oxfordshire 159
Shropshire, Telford & Wrekin 160
Somerset, Bath & NE Somerset,
North Somerset 162
South Yorkshire 165
Staffordshire, City of Stoke on Trent 168
Suffolk 170
Surrey 172
Tyne & Wear 174
Warwickshire 176
West Midlands 176
West Sussex 179
West Yorkshire 181
Wiltshire, Swindon 184
Worcestershire 185

Channel Islands Operators

Alderney 187
Guernsey 187
Jersey 187

Isle of Man Operators

Isle of Man 187

Isles of Scilly Operators

Isles of Scilly 187

Scottish Operators

Aberdeen, City of 188
Aberdeenshire 188
Angus 189
Argyll & Bute 189
Borders 190
Clackmannanshire 190
Dumfries & Galloway 191
Dundee, City of 191
East Ayrshire 192
East Lothian 192
East Renfrewshire 192
Edinburgh, City of 192
Falkirk 193
Fife 193
Glasgow, City of 194
Highland 194
Inverclyde 195
Midlothian 195
Moray 196
North Ayrshire 196
North Lanarkshire 196
Orkney 197
Perth & Kinross 197
Renfrewshire 198
Shetland 198
South Ayrshire 199
South Lanarkshire 199
Stirling 200
West Dunbartonshire 200
West Lothian 200
Western Isles 201

Welsh Operators

Anglesey 202
Blaenau Gwent 202
Bridgend 202
Caerphilly 203
Cardiff 203
Carmarthenshire 203
Ceredigion 204
Conwy 205
Denbighshire 205
Flintshire 206
Gwynedd 206
Merthyr Tydfil 207
Monmouthshire 207
Neath & Port Talbot 207
Newport 208
Pembrokeshire 208
Powys 208
Rhondda Cynon Taf 210
Swansea, City & County of 210
Torfaen 210
Vale of Glamorgan 211
Wrexham 211

Northern Ireland Operators

Northern Ireland 212

Republic of Ireland Operators

Republic of Ireland 213

76 The Little Red Book 2011 - in association with Transport Benevolent Fund

Providing help and advice to public transport employees in need for over 85 years - and meeting the needs of today.

For just £1 a week all these benefits are available to those working in the public transport industry in Great Britain...

Cash Grants
Medical Consultations
Scans and Tests
Physiotherapy
Osteopathy
Acupuncture
Chiropractic Treatment
Homeopathy
Reflexology
Convalescence
Legal Advice
Medical Equipment
Debt Counselling
Prescription Seasons

Our Patrons include leading figures in all transport groups and the trades unions. The Trustees all work in the industry and decide on all benefits.

new address

tbf

Transport Benevolent Fund

22-25 Finsbury Square
London EC2A 1DX

☎ 08450 100 500
email help@tbf.org.uk
www.tbf.org.uk

The Transport Benevolent Fund (known as TBF) is a registered charity in England and Wales (1058032) and in Scotland (SC040013)

MAJOR GROUPS

ARRIVA

ARRIVA PLC

1 Admiral Way, Doxford International Business Park, Sunderland SR3 3XP
Tel: 0191 520 4000
Fax: 0191 520 4001
E-mail: enquiries@arriva.co.uk
Web site: www.arriva.co.uk

Chairman:
Sir Richard Broadbent KCB
Chief Executive: David Martin
Group Finance Director:
Steve Lonsdale
Non-Executive Directors:
Angie Risley, Simon Batey,
Nick Buckles, Steve Williams

Managing Director – Mainland Europe:
David Evans
Managing Director – UK Trains:
Bob Holland

Arriva Passenger Services
487 Dunstable Road, Luton, LU4 8DS
Tel: 01582 587000

Managing Director – UK Bus:
Mike Cooper
Operations and Commercial Director – UK Bus: Mark Yexley
Engineering Director – UK Bus:
Ian Tarran
Finance & Business Development Director – UK Bus: Peter Telford
People & Change Director – UK Bus:
Jo Humphreys
Regional Director, North East & Scotland:
Jonathan May
Regional Director, North West & Wales:
Phil Stone
Regional Director, Shires & Southern Counties: Heath Williams

Operating Regions, Group Companies, Principal Depots (UK Bus):

• **Arriva Scotland West**
(see Renfrewshire)
Depots at Inchinnan, Johnstone

• **Arriva Yorkshire**
(see North Yorkshire, West Yorkshire)
Depots at Castleford, Dewsbury, Heckmondwike, Selby, Wakefield

• **Arriva North East**
(see Tyne & Wear)
Depots at Ashington, Belmont, Blyth, Darlington, Durham, Newcastle, Redcar, Stockton, Whitby

• **Arriva North West**
(see Greater Manchester Merseyside)
Depots at Birkenhead, Bolton, Bootle, Liverpool, Manchester, Runcorn, St Helens, Skelmersdale, Southport, Winsford, Wythenshawe

• **Arriva Buses Wales**
(see Conwy)
Depots at Aberystwyth, Bangor, Chester, Llandudno, Rhyl, Wrexham

• **Arriva Midlands**
(see Derbyshire, Leicestershire, Shropshire, Staffordshire)
Depots at Bridgnorth, Burton on Trent, Cannock, Coalville, Derby, Oswestry, Shrewsbury, Stafford, Tamworth, Telford, Thurmaston, Wigston

• **Arriva Shires**
(see Bedfordshire, Buckinghamshire, Hertfordshire)
Depots at Aylesbury, Hemel Hempstead, High Wycombe, Luton, Milton Keynes (MK Metro), Stevenage, Ware, Watford

• **Arriva London**
(see London & Middlesex)
Depots at Barking, Battersea, Brixton, Clapton, Croydon, Edmonton, Enfield, Hackney, Norwood, Palmers Green, Stamford Hill, Thornton Heath, Tottenham, Wood Green

• **Arriva Southern Counties**
(see Essex, Kent, Surrey)
Depots at Cranleigh, Dartford, Gillingham, Grays, Guildford, Maidstone, Northfleet, Southend, Tonbridge (New Enterprise), Tunbridge Wells

• **The Original Tour**
(see London)

• **T G M Group Ltd**
(see Durham, Essex, London & Middlesex, Surrey)
Includes Classic Coaches, Excel Passenger Logistics, Flight Delay Services, Linkline Coaches, Network Colchester, OFJ Connections, Tellings Golden Miller Coaches
Depots include Colchester, Gatwick, Harlesden, Harlow, Heathrow, Stansted

• **Other Operations**
Huddersfield Bus Company, K-Line Travel (jointly owned with Centrebus)
Depots at Huddersfield, Elland

Overseas Interests:
Arriva has extensive overseas interests in the Czech Republic (bus), Denmark (bus and rail), Germany (bus and rail), Hungary (bus), Italy (bus), Netherlands (bus and rail), Poland (rail), Portugal (bus), Slovakia (bus), Spain (bus), Sweden (bus and rail)

UK Rail Franchises:
Arriva Trains Wales, Cross Country

Other Interests:
Arriva Bus & Coach
(see Trade Directory)

Note: At the time of going to press, Arriva is in the process of acquisition by DB UK Holding Ltd, which is a subsidiary of Deutsche Bahn AG of Germany

First

transforming travel

FIRSTGROUP PLC

395 King Street, Aberdeen AB24 5RP
Tel: 01224 650100
Fax: 01224 650140
Web Site: www.firstgroup.com

Chairman:
Martin Gilbert
Deputy Chairman and Chief Executive:
Sir Moir Lockhead
**Chief Operating Officer
& Deputy Chief Executive:**
Tim O'Toole
Group Finance Director:
Jeff Carr
Commercial Director & Company Secretary:
Sidney Barrie
Non-Executive Directors:
Audrey Baxter, David Begg, Colin Hood, John Sievwright, Martyn Williams

UK Bus
Managing Director Bus & Rail:
Mary Grant
Business Efficiency & Engineering Director:
David Liston
Customer Service & Communications Director:
Leon Daniels
Finance Director:
Graeme Jenkins
Safety Director:
Janet Ault
Regional Managing Director, North:
Dave Alexander
Regional Managing Director, Scotland:
Mark Savelli
Regional Managing Director, South East & Midlands:
Nigel Barrett
Regional Managing Director, London:
Adrian Jones
Regional Managing Director, South West & Wales:
Justin Davies

Operating Regions, Group Companies, Principal Depots (UK Bus):

- **First Aberdeen, First Aberdeen Coaching Unit**
(Includes Grampian Coaches, Kirkpatrick of Deeside, Mairs Coaches)
(see City of Aberdeen)

- **First Scotland East**
(see Stirling)
Depots at Balfron, Bannockburn, Dalkeith, Galashiels, Larbert, Linlithgow, Livingston, Musselburgh, North Berwick

- **First Glasgow**
(see City of Glasgow)
Depots at Blantyre, Cumbernauld, Dumbarton, Glasgow, Overtown

- **First West Yorkshire**
(Includes First in York)
(see North Yorkshire, West Yorkshire)
Depots at Bradford, Halifax, Huddersfield, Leeds, York

- **First South Yorkshire**
(see South Yorkshire)
Depots at Doncaster, Rotherham, Sheffield

- **First Manchester**
(Includes First Cheshire, First Pioneer Bus)
(see Cheshire, Greater Manchester, Merseyside)
Depots at Bolton, Bury, Chester, Ince, Manchester, Oldham, Tameside, Wigan, Wirral, Wrexham

- **First Midlands**
(Includes First Leicester, First Northampton, First North Staffordshire, First Wyvern)
(see Leicestershire, Northamptonshire, Staffordshire, Worcestershire)
Depots at Hereford, Kidderminster, Leicester, Newcastle under Lyme, Northampton, Redditch, Stoke, Worcester

- **First East of England**
(Includes First Eastern Counties, First Essex)
(see Essex, Norfolk)
Depots at Basildon, Braintree, Chelmsford, Clacton, Colchester, Great Yarmouth, Hadleigh, Harwich, Ipswich, Kings Lynn, Lowestoft, Norwich

- **First London**
(see London & Middlesex)
Depots at Alperton, Dagenham, Greenford, Hayes, Leyton, Northumberland Park, Uxbridge, Westbourne Park, Willesden Junction

- **First in Berkshire**
(see Berkshire)
Depots at Bracknell, Slough

- **First Cymru**
(see City & County of Swansea)
Depots at Bridgend, Carmarthen, Haverfordwest, Llanelli, Pontardawe, Port Talbot, Swansea

- **First Bristol**
(see Bristol)

- **First in Hampshire & Dorset**
(see Hampshire)
Depots at Bridport, Fareham, Portsmouth, Southampton, Weymouth

- **First Somerset & Avon**
(see Somerset)
Depots at Bath, Bridgwater, Bristol, Taunton, Weston super Mare, Yeovil

- **First Devon & Cornwall**
(see Cornwall, Devon)
Depots at Barnstaple, Camborne, Plymouth, Truro

- **Greyhound UK Ltd**
(see London)

Overseas Interests:
First has a bus operation in the Republic of Ireland - Aircoach (See Republic of Ireland) and in Germany and the USA

UK Rail Operations:
First Capital Connect,
First Great Western, First Trans Pennine Express, First ScotRail,
First GB Railfreight,
First Hull Trains

Go-Ahead

GO-AHEAD GROUP PLC

6th Floor, 1 Warwick Row,
London SW1E 5ER
Tel: 020 7821 3939 **Fax:** 0191 221 0315
E-mail: admin@go-ahead.com
Web Site: www.go-ahead.com

Non-Executive Chairman:
Sir Patrick Brown
Group Chief Executive: Keith Ludeman
Group Finance Director: Nicholas Swift
Group Company Secretary:
Carolyn Sephton
Non-Executive Directors:
Andrew Allner, Katherine Innes Ker,
Rupert Pennant-Rea

UK Bus
Managing Director, Bus Development:
Martin Dean

Operating Regions - Group Companies
Principal Depots - (UK Bus):
• Go North East
(see Tyne & Wear)
Depots at Chester le Street, Gateshead,
Hexham, Newcastle, Peterlee, Stanley,
Sunderland, Washington, Winlaton

• Oxford Bus Company *(see Oxfordshire)*
Depot at Oxford

• Konectbus Ltd *(see Norfolk)*
Depot at Dereham

• Go-Ahead London
(includes Blue Triangle, Docklands Buses,
East Thames Buses, London Central,
London General)
(see Essex, London & Middlesex)
Depots at Belvedere, Bexleyheath,
Camberwell, Merton, New Cross, Peckham,
Putney, Rainham, Silvertown, Southwark,
Stockwell, Sutton, Waterloo, Wimbledon

• Metrobus
(see West Sussex)
Depots at Crawley, Croydon, Orpington

• Brighton & Hove Bus & Coach
Company
(see East Sussex)
Depots at Brighton, Hove

• Go South Coast
(includes Bells Coaches, Bluestar, Damory
Coaches, Kingston Coaches, Levers
Coaches, Marchwood Motorways, Southern
Vectis, Tourist Coaches, Wilts & Dorset)
*(see Dorset, Hampshire, Isle of Wight,
Wiltshire)*
Depots at Blandford, Eastleigh, Figheldean,
Lymington, Newport IOW, Poole, Ringwood,
Salisbury, Swanage, Totton

• Plymouth Citybus *(see Devon)*
Depot at Plymouth

Other interests:
Meteor Parking

UK Rail Franchises:
London Midland, South Eastern, Southern

national express

NATIONAL EXPRESS GROUP PLC

7 Triton Square,
London NW1 3HG
Tel: 0845 130130
E-mail: info@nationalexpress.com
Web Site:
www.nationalexpressgroup.com

Executive Chairman:
John Devaney
Group Finance Director:
Jez Maiden
Group Chief Executive:
Dean Finch
Deputy Chairman:
Jorge Cosmen
Non-Executive Directors:
Miranda Curtis, Roger Devlin,
Sir Andrew Foster, Tim Score
Company Secretary:
Tony McDonald
Acting UK Chief Executive:
David Franks
Chief Executive, ALSA Group:
Javier Carbajo
Interim Chief Executive Officer,
North America:
John Elliott

UK Bus
Chief Executive, UK Bus:
Neil Barker
Operations Director,
UK Bus & Coach:
Alex Perry

Operating Regions
Group Companies
Principal Depots
(UK Bus):

• Kings Ferry Travel Group
 (see Kent)

• National Express Coach
 (See West Midlands)

• National Express Dundee
 (see Dundee City)

• Midland Metro
 (see West Midlands)

• National Express
  West Midlands
 (See West Midlands)
Depots at Birmingham, Coventry,
Dudley, Walsall, West Bromwich,
Wolverhampton

Overseas interests:
National Express has extensive interests in
Spain (ALSA, Continental Auto),
Canada (Stock Transportation) and the
USA (Durham School Services)

UK Rail Franchises:
c2c, National Express East Anglia

TRANSDEV
Developing mobility

TRANSDEV PLC

3rd Floor, 401 King Street,
Hammersmith,
London W6 9NJ
Tel: 020 8600 5650
Fax: 020 8600 5651
E-mail: information@transdevplc.co.uk
Web Site:
www.transdevplc.co.uk

Group Managing Director:
Francois Xavier Perin
Chief Operating Officer, Transdev
International:
Charlie Beaumont
UK Divisional Director and CEO,
Transdev PLC:
Nigel Stevens
Finance Director:
Peter Brogden
Light Rail & Corporate
Services Director:
Julia Thomas

Operating Regions
Group Companies
Principal Depots
(UK Bus):

• Blazefield Lancashire
(includes Burnley & Pendle, Lancashire
United)
(see Lancashire)
Depots at Blackburn, Burnley

• Blazefield Yorkshire
(includes Harrogate & District, Keighley &
District, Transdev York, Yorkshire Coastliner)
(see North Yorkshire, West Yorkshire)
Depots at: Harrogate, Keighley, Malton, York

• London United Busways
(see London & Middlesex)
Depots at Fulwell, Hounslow, Hounslow
Heath, Park Royal, Shepherd's Bush,
Stamford Brook, Tolworth, Twickenham

• London Sovereign
(see London & Middlesex)
Depots at Edgware, Harrow

• Nottingham City Transport
(part owned)
(see Nottinghamshire)

• Nottingham Express Transit
(part of operating group)

• Transdev Yellow Buses (Bournemouth
Transport)
(see Dorset)

Overseas interests:
Transdev has bus and rail interests in
Australia, Canada, France, Germany, Italy,
the Netherlands and Portugal

Parent Group:
Transdev's Parent Group is Transdev SA,
part of the French Group Caisse des Depots

Major Groups

Stagecoach

STAGECOACH GROUP PLC
10 Dunkeld Road, Perth PH1 5TW
Tel: 01738 442111
Fax: 01738 643648
Web Site: www.stagecoachgroup.com

Non-Executive Chairman:
Sir George Mathewson
(from 1 January 2011)
Chief Executive:
Brian Souter
Finance Director:
Martin Griffiths
Non-Executive Directors:
Ewan Brown CBE, Ann Gloag OBE,
Helen Mahy, Garry Watts, Phil White
Managing Director UK Bus:
Les Warneford
Regional Directors:
Robert Andrew, Sam Greer,
Bob Montgomery

Operating Regions
Group Companies
Principal Depots
(UK Bus):

• Stagecoach East Scotland
(Includes Bluebird Buses, JW Coaches, Rennies of Dunfermline, Fife Scottish Omnibuses, Stagecoach Highland, Stagecoach in Orkney, Stagecoach in Perth, Strathtay Scottish Omnibuses)
(see City of Aberdeen, Aberdeenshire, City of Dundee, Fife, Highland, Orkney, Perth & Kinross)
Depots at Aberdeen, Arbroath, Banchory, Blairgowrie, Cowdenbeath, Dundee, Dunfermline, Elgin, Forfar, Fort William, Glenrothes, Inverness, Kirkwall, Methil, Montrose, Perth, Peterhead, St Andrews, Tain, Thurso, Wick

• Stagecoach West Scotland
(Includes Stagecoach Glasgow, Western Buses)
(see South Ayrshire)

Depots at Ardrossan, Arran, Ayr, Cumnock, Dumfries, Glasgow, Kilmarnock, Stranraer

• Scottish Citylink Coaches (part owned)
(see City of Glasgow)

• Stagecoach North East
(Includes Stagecoach Hartlepool, Newcastle, South Shields, Sunderland, Teesside, Transit)
(see Durham, Tyne & Wear)
Depots at Hartlepool, Newcastle, South Shields, Stockton, Sunderland

• Stagecoach North West
(Includes Stagecoach in Cumbria, Lancashire, Lancaster, Preston Bus)
(see Cumbria, Lancashire)
Depots at Barrow, Carlisle, Chorley, Kendal, Lancaster, Preston, Whitehaven

• Stagecoach Merseyside
(see Merseyside)
Depot at Liverpool

• Stagecoach Manchester
(see Greater Manchester)
Depots at Manchester, Stockport, Tameside

• Manchester Metrolink
(see Greater Manchester)

• Stagecoach Yorkshire
(Includes Stagecoach Sheffield, Stagecoach Supertram, Stagecoach Yorkshire)
(see South Yorkshire)
Depots at Barnsley, Doncaster, Rawmarsh, Shafton, Sheffield

• Stagecoach East Midlands
(Includes Stagecoach East Midlands, Hull, Lincolnshire)
(see Derbyshire, East Riding, Lincolnshire)
Depots at Chesterfield, Gainsborough, Grimsby, Hull, Lincoln, Mansfield, Newark, Scunthorpe, Skegness, Worksop

• Stagecoach East
(Includes Stagecoach in Bedfordshire, Cambridgeshire, Peterborough, The Fens)
(see Bedfordshire, Cambridgeshire)
Depots at Bedford, Cambridge, Ely, Fenstanton, Peterborough

• Stagecoach Oxfordshire
(see Oxfordshire)
Depots at Banbury, Oxford, Witney

• Stagecoach Midlands
(see Northamptonshire, Warwickshire)
Depots at Corby, Kettering, Leamington Spa, Northampton, Nuneaton, Rugby, Stratford upon Avon

• Stagecoach West
(Includes Stagecoach Cheltenham, Cotswolds, Gloucester, Swindon, Wye & Dean)
(see Gloucestershire)
Depots at Cheltenham, Coleford, Gloucester, Stroud, Swindon

• Stagecoach South East
(Includes Stagecoach in East Kent & East Sussex, Hampshire, Hants & Surrey, Stagecoach South)
(see East Sussex, Hampshire, Kent, West Sussex)
Depots at Aldershot, Andover, Ashford, Basingstoke, Chichester, Dover, Eastbourne, Folkestone, Hastings, Herne Bay, Portsmouth, Thanet, Winchester, Worthing

• Stagecoach South West
(Includes Stagecoach Devon, Stagecoach Somerset)
(see Devon, Somerset)
Depots at Barnstaple, Chard, Exeter, Exmouth, Honiton, Paignton, Torquay, Wellington

• Stagecoach in South Wales
(see Torfaen)
Depots at Aberdare, Blackwood, Brynmawr, Caerphilly, Cwmbran, Merthyr, Porth

Overseas Interests:
The group has significant bus and coach operations in North America

UK Rail Franchises:
East Midlands Trains, Island Line, South West Trains, Virgin West Coast (joint venture)

ABELLIO

2nd Floor, 1 Ely Place, London EC1N 6RY
Tel: 020 7430 8270
Fax: 020 7430 2239
E-mail: info@abellio.com
Web site: www.abellio.com
Chief Executive: Anton Valk
Chief Operating Officer: Dominic Booth
Chief Financial Officer: Richard Emmerink
Finance Director, UK: Lesley Batty
Non-Executive Director: David Quarmby

Group Companies (UK Bus)
Abellio London
(see London & Middlesex)
Depots at Beddington, Battersea, Walworth
Abellio Surrey
(see Surrey)

Depots at Byfleet, Fulwell, Hayes
Overseas Interests
Abellio has bus and rail interests in Germany and a bus operation (Probo Bus) in the Czech Republic
UK Rail Franchises
Merseyrail, Northern Rail
Parent Company
Abellio is part of the NedRail Group

CENTREBUS GROUP

37 Wenlock Way,
Leicester LE4 9HU
Tel: 0116 246 0030
Fax: 0116 246 7221
E-mail: centrebusltd@btconnect.com
Web site: www.centrebus.co.uk
Directors: Peter Harvey,

Julian Peddle, Keith Hayward,
David Shelley
Group Operations:
• Bowers Coaches
(see Derbyshire)
Depot at Chapel-en-le-Frith
• Centrebus in Essex, Hertfordshire and Bedfordshire
(see Bedfordshire, Essex, Hertfordshire)
Depots at Dunstable, Harlow, Stevenage
• Centrebus in Leicestershire
(see Leicestershire)
Depots at Hinckley, Leicester
• Centrebus in Lincolnshire
(see Lincolnshire)
Depot at Grantham
• Centrebus in West Yorkshire
(see West Yorkshire)
Includes Huddersfield Bus Company (Jointly owned with Arriva)

Depots at Elland, Huddersfield
K-Line Travel (Jointly owned with Arriva)
Depot at Huddersfield
White Rose Bus Company
Depot at Leeds
• Galleon Travel
 (see Essex)
Depot at Harlow

COMFORT DELGRO

Hygeia House, 66-68 College Road,
Harrow, HA1 1BE
Tel: 020 8218 8888
Fax: 020 8218 8899
Web Site: www.comfortdelgro.com.sg
Chief Executive, UK & Ireland:
Jaspal Singh

Group Companies (UK Bus):

• Metroline Travel
(see London & Middlesex)
Depots at Brentford, Cricklewood,
Edgware, Harrow Weald, Holloway,
Kings Cross, Perivale, Potters Bar,
West Perivale, Willesden
• Scottish Citylink Coaches (part owned)
(see City of Glasgow)
• Westbus Coach Services
(see London & Middlesex)

Other Interests:

Citylink (Ireland)
(see Republic of Ireland)
Also Computer Cab and other taxi interests

Overseas Interests:
The group has extensive interests in
Australia, China, Malaysia, Singapore and
Vietnam

Parent Company:
Comfort DelGro Corporation

Overseas Interests:
The group has major bus and taxi
operations in Australia, China,
Malaysia, Singapore and Vietnam

EAST LONDON BUS GROUP

Stephenson Street, Canning Town,
London E16 4SA
Tel: 020 8553 3420
Fax: 020 8477 7200
E-mail: pr.london@elbg.com
Web Site: www.elbg.com
Chief Executive: Jon Gatfield
Chief Financial Officer: Paul Cox
Engineering Director: Peter Sumner
Human Resources Director: Sarah Rennie
Health & Safety Director: John Carmichael

Group Trading Names:
• East London
Depots at Barking, Bow, Leyton,
Romford, Upton Park, West Ham
• Selkent
Depots at Bromley, Catford,
Plumstead
• Thameside

Depot at Rainham
(see London & Middlesex)

EYMS GROUP LTD

252 Anlaby Road, Hull HU3 2RS
Tel: 01482 327142
Fax: 01482 212040
Web Site: www.eymsgroup.co.uk
Chairman: Peter Shipp
Finance Director: Peter Harrison

Group Companies:

• East Yorkshire Motor Services
(including Scarborough &
District Motor Services)
(see East Riding, North Yorkshire)
Depots at Beverley, Bridlington, Driffield,
Elloughton, Hornsea, Hull, Pocklington,
Scarborough, Withernsea
• Finglands Coachways
(see Greater Manchester)
• Whittle Coach & Bus
(see Shropshire)

ROTALA PLC

Beacon House, Long Acre,
Birmingham B7 5JJ
Tel: 0121 322 2222
Fax: 0121 322 2718
E-Mail: info@rotalaplc.co.uk
Web Site: www.rotalaplc.co.uk
Chairman: John Gunn
Chief Executive: Simon Dunn
Finance Director: Kim Taylor
Non-Executive Directors:
Robert Dunn, Geoffrey Flight

Group Companies:

• Central Connect
(see West Midlands)
Depot at Birmingham
• Diamond Bus
(See West Midlands, Worcestershire)
Depots at Droitwich, Oldbury, Redditch
• Flights Hallmark
(See London & Middlesex, West Midlands,
West Sussex)
Depots at Birmingham, Crawley,
Heathrow, Isleworth
• Wessex Connect, Bath Connect
(see Bristol, Somerset)
Depots at Bristol, Keynsham

VEOLIA TRANSPORT (UK) LTD

King's Place, 90 York Way,
London N1 9RG
Tel: 020 7843 8500
Fax: 020 7843 8560
Web Site: www.veolia-transport.co.uk
Chairman: John O'Brien
Chief Executive Officer: Vincent Bech
Chief Financial Officer: Gary Smith
Managing Director, Veolia Transport Cymru: Vacant
Managing Director, Veolia Transport England: Steve Campbell
Human Resources Director: Tracie Paul

Legal Adviser & Company Secretary:
Jenny Eades

Group Companies (UK Bus):
• Astons Coaches Ltd
(see Worcestershire)
• Veolia Transport Cymru PLC
(Formerly Bebb Travel PLC, Long's
Coaches, Pullman Coaches, Thomas of
Barry)
(see Rhondda Cynon Taf, City & County of
Swansea)
Depots at Abercrave, Cowbridge, Cross
Gates, Nantgarw, Newport, Penclawdd,
Talgarth
• Veolia Transport England PLC
(Formerly Dunn Line Holdings, Paul James
Coaches)
(See Leicestershire, Nottinghamshire,
South Yorkshire, Tyne & Wear)
Depots at Birmingham, Coalville, Heanor,
Melton Mowbray, Nottingham, Rotherham,
Houghton le Spring

Other Subsidiaries:
Connex Transport (Jersey) Ltd
(See Jersey)
LUAS (Operating Concession)
(See Republic of Ireland)

Overseas interests:
Veolia has substantial worldwide transport
interests
Parent Company:
Veolia Environnement

WELLGLADE LTD

Mansfield Road, Heanor,
Derbyshire DE75 7BG
Tel: 01773 536309
Fax: 01773 536310
Chairman: B R King
Deputy Chairman: R I Morgan
Group Finance Director: G Sutton

Group Companies:

• Derby Community Transport
(see Derbyshire)
• Kinchbus
(see Leicestershire)
• Notts & Derby
(see Derbyshire)
• TM Travel
(see South Yorkshire)
• Trent Barton
(see Derbyshire)

Advertising in LRB
For information regarding advertising contact:
Graham Middleton
Tel: 01780 484632
Fax: 01780 763388
E-mail:
graham.middleton@ianallanpublishing.co.uk

♿	Vehicle suitable for disabled	🛇	Seat belt-fitted Vehicle
T	Toilet-drop facilities available	🍴	Coach(es) with galley facilities
R	Recovery service available	❄	Air-conditioned vehicle(s)
🚌	Open top vehicle(s)	🚻	Coaches with toilet facilities
R24	24 hour recovery service	🔧	Replacement vehicle available
🚍	Vintage Coach(es) available		

BEDFORD, CENTRAL BEDFORDSHIRE, LUTON

AtoB TRAVEL (LUTON) LTD
♿🛇
UNIT 54, BILTON WAY, LUTON LU1 1UU
Tel: 01582 733333
Fax: 01582 733331
Web site: www.atobexec.com
Fleet: 50 – single-deck coach, minicoach, midicoach
Chassis incl: Ford, Mercedes.
Bodies incl: Ford, Mercedes.
Ops incl: school contracts, private hire
Livery: Silver

ARRIVA THE SHIRES LTD
♿🚻❄R🛇T
487 DUNSTABLE ROAD, LUTON LU4 8DS
Tel: 01582 587000/08701 201088
Web site: www.arrivabus.co.uk
Fleet Name: Arriva the Shires & Essex.
Regional Man Dir: Heath Williams
Area Man Dir: Paul Adcock
Comm Dir: Kevin Hawkins
Eng Dir: Brian Barraclough
Fin Dir: Beverley Lawson
Fleet: 622 – 124 double-deck bus, 169 single-deck bus, 58 single-deck coach, 187 midibus, 84 minibus.
Chassis: Alexander Dennis, DAF, Dennis, Leyland, Mercedes, Optare, Scania, Van Hool, VDL, Volvo.
Ops incl: local bus services, school contracts, excursions & tours, private hire, express.
Liveries: Arriva UK Bus, Green Line.
Ticket System: Wayfarer 3, Prestige.

BARFORDIAN COACHES LTD
❄🍴🛇🔧
500 GOLDINGTON ROAD, BEDFORD MK41 0DX
Tel: 01234 355440
Fax: 01234 355310
E-mail: info@barfordiancoaches.co.uk
Web site: www.barfordiancoaches.co.uk
Man: J Bullard
Fleet: 19 - 3 double-deck bus, 1 single-deck bus, 9 single-deck coach, 2 double-deck coach, 3 midicoach, 1 minibus.
Chassis: 1 Bedford, 9 Bova, 3 Leyland, 3 Mercedes, 2 Neoplan, 1 Toyota.
Ops incl: local bus services, school contracts, excursions & tours, private hire, continental tours.
Livery: Orange/Yellow/White
Ticket System: Almex
A subsidiary of Souls Coaches Ltd (see Buckinghamshire)

CEDAR COACHES
🍴🛇❄
ARKWRIGHT ROAD, BEDFORD MK42 0LE.
Tel: 01234 354054
Fax: 01234 219210
E-mail: nikki@cedarcoaches.co.uk
Web site: www.cedarcoaches.co.uk
Man Dir: Eric Reid **Co Sec:** Nichola Graham **Dirs:** Donna Reid, Kevin Reid

Fleet: 30 - 17 double-deck bus, 4 single-deck bus, 6 single-deck coach, 1 double-deck coach, 2 minicoach.
Chassis: Ayats, Bova, Irisbus, Iveco, Leyland, Scania, Volvo.
Bodies: Ayats, Beulas, Bova
Ops incl: local bus services, school contracts, excursions & tours, private hire.
Livery: Red/Yellow

CENTREBUS LTD
♿
UNIT 34, HUMPHRYS ROAD, WOODSIDE INDUSTRIAL ESTATE, DUNSTABLE, LU5 4TP
Tel: 0844 357 6520
E-mail: info@centrebus.com
Web site: www.centrebus.co.uk
Man Dir: Peter Harvey
Ops Dir: Neil Harris
Fleet (Bedfordshire):
46 – 2 single-deck bus, 44 midibus.
Chassis: 30 Dennis, 1 MAN, 9 Optare, 2 Scania, 2 VDL.
Bodies: 2 Alexander, 4 Caetano, 1 East Lancs, 5 Northern Counties, 9 Optare, 25 Plaxton.
Ops incl: local bus services
Livery: Blue/Orange/White
Ticket system: Wayfarer 3
Part of the Centrebus Group

CHILTERN TRAVEL
🛇🍴❄🔧
THE COACH HOUSE, BARFORD ROAD, BLUNHAM MK44 3NA
Tel: 01767 641400
Fax: 01767 641358
E-mail: chilterntravel@hotmail.com
Web Site: www.chilterntravel.com
Proprietor: Trevor Boorman
Fleet: 18 single-deck coach.
Chassis: 2 Bova, 1 Mercedes, 5 Setra, 10 Volvo.
Bodies: 2 Bova, 10 Jonckheere, 1 Mercedes, 5 Setra.
Ops incl: private hire, continental tours, school contracts.
Livery: White/Blue

EXPRESSLINES LTD
♿🛇❄
FENLAKE ROAD INDUSTRIAL ESTATE, BEDFORD MK42 0HB
Tel: 01234 268704
Fax: 01234 272212
E-mail: info@expresslinesltd.co.uk
Web site: www.expresslinesltd.co.uk
Dirs: Chris Spriggs, Richard Harris
Fleet: 15 - 4 midibus, 3 midicoach, 8 minicoach.
Chassis: 6 Ford Transit, 5 Mercedes, 4 Optare.
Bodies: 8 Optare, 7 other.
Ops incl: local bus services, school contracts, private hire.
Livery: Red/White/Silver
Ticket System: Wayfarer & Almex

FLIGHTS HALLMARK
See West Midlands

GRANT PALMER PASSENGER SERVICES
♿🛇
UNIT 2, LAWRENCE WAY, DUNSTABLE LU6 1BD
Tel/Fax: 01582 600844
E-mail: info@grantpalmer.com
Web site: www.grantpalmer.com
Dirs: Grant Palmer, Peter Morgan, Jeff Wilson.
Fleet: 26 - 6 double deck bus, 2 single deck bus, 18 midibus.
Chassis: Dennis, Leyland, MAN, Mercedes, Plaxton, Volvo
Bodies: Alexander Dennis, ECW, East Lancs, Northern Counties, Plaxton, Roe
Ops incl: local bus services, school contracts, private hire.
Livery: Red/White
Ticket System: Wayfarer 3

HERBERTS TRAVEL
🛇❄🔧
UNIT 5, OLD ROWNEY FARM, SHEFFORD SG17 5QH
Tel: 01234 382000
Fax: 01234 381117
E-mail: booking@herberts-travel.co.uk
Web site: www.herberts-travel.co.uk
Man Dir: D M Dougall **Ops Dir:** D S Dougall **Fleet Eng:** S Myers
Fleet: 21 - 6 double-deck bus, 5 midibus, 4 midicoach, 1 minibus, 5 minicoach.
Chassis: 5 Ford Transit, 5 Leyland, 3 MCW, 4 Mercedes, 2 Optare, 1 Toyota, 1 Volvo.
Bodies: 4 Alexander, 1 Caetano, 2 ECW, 1 Leyland, 1 MCW, 4 Optare, 1 Plaxton, 6 other.
Ops incl: private hire, school contracts, local bus services.
Livery: White.
Ticket system: Wayfarer

MARSHALLS COACHES LLP
♿🍴🍴❄T
FIRBANK WAY, LEIGHTON BUZZARD LU7 4YP
Tel: 01525 376077
Fax: 01525 850967
E-mail: info@marshalls-coaches.co.uk
Web site: www.marshalls-coaches.co.uk
Prop: G Marshall **Ops Man:** I White
Workshop Man: B Barnard
Fleet: 28 - 3 double-deck bus, 22 single-deck coach, 2 double-deck coach, 1 minicoach.
Chassis: 2 Alexander Dennis, 3 Ayats, 1 Bristol, 4 Dennis, 1 Iveco, 1 Mercedes, 15 Volvo.
Bodies: 3 Ayats, 1 Beulas, 2 East Lancs, 5 Jonckheere, 1 Mercedes, 15 Plaxton.
Ops incl: local bus services, private hire, school contracts, continental tours.
Livery: Blue/Multicoloured.

PREMIER CONNECTIONS TRAVEL LTD
THE COACH YARD, EATON GREEN PARK, EATON GREEN ROAD, LUTON AIRPORT, LU2 9HD

Tel: 01582 424140
Fax: 01582 727093
E-mail: sales@premier.gb.com
Web site: www.premiercoachhire.co.uk
Ops incl: school contracts, private hire
Livery: Silver/White (coaches), Yellow (school buses)

RED KITE COMMERCIAL SERVICES
UNIT 2, LEYS YARD, DUNSTABLE ROAD, TILSWORTH, LEIGHTON BUZZARD LU7 9PU
Tel: 01525 211441
Props: D. Hoar, R. H. Savage
Fleet: 18 - 13 double-deck bus, 3 single-deck coach, 2 midibus.
Chassis: Bedford, Leyland, Optare, Volvo
Ops incl: local bus services, school contracts, excursions and tours, private hire, school contracts.
Livery: Red/Blue

SAFFORD COACHES LTD
See Cambridgeshire

SHOREYS TRAVEL
119 CLOPHILL ROAD, MAULDEN MK45 2AE
Tel: 01525 860694
Fax: 01525 861850
E-mail: shoreystravel@talk21.com
Prop: E C J Shorey **Partners:** D Shorey, G Shorey **Ch Eng:** D Bunker
Ops incl: school contracts, private hire.
Livery: White/Green
Ticket System: Wayfarer.

STAGECOACH EAST
BEDFORD BUS STATION, ALL HALLOWS, BEDFORD MK40 1LT
Tel: 01604 676060
Fax: 01604 662286
E-mail: east.enquiries@stagecoachbus.com
Web site: www.stagecoachbus.com/bedford
Fleet Name: Stagecoach in Bedfordshire
Regional Man Dir: Robert Andrew
Man Dir: Andy Campbell
Comm Dir: Philip Norwell
Eng Dir: Bob Dennison
Ops incl: local bus services, school contracts, private hire, express.
Livery: Stagecoach UK Bus
Ticket System: ERG

TATES COACHES
44 HIGH STREET, MARKYATE AL3 8PA
Tel: 01582 840297
Fax: 01582 840014
E-mail: info@tatescoaches.co.uk
Web site: www.tatescoaches.co.uk
Dirs: A M Tate, A J Tate, S W Tate
Fleet: 9 single-deck coach
Chassis: 1 Bova, 1 DAF, 1 Dennis, 1 MAN, 1 Mercedes, 1 Neoplan, 3 Scania.
Bodies: 1 Bova, 1 Caetano, 1 Hispano, 2 Irizar, 1 Neoplan, 2 Van Hool, 1 Wadham Stringer.
Ops incl: school contracts, excursions & tours, private hire, continental tours.
Livery: Cream/Blue/Orange

THREE STAR COACHES.COM
UNIT 1, GUARDIAN BUSINESS PARK, DALLOW ROAD, LUTON LU1 1NA
Tel: 01582 722626
Fax: 01582 484034
E-mail: sales@threestarcoaches.com
Web Site: www.threestarcoaches.com
Man Dir: Colin Dudley,
Ops Man: Kevin Green
Ch Eng: Michael Nallaby
Co Sec: Isabelle Dudley
Fleet: 13 – 1 single-deck bus, 7 single-deck coach, 2 double-deck coach, 3 midicoach.
Chassis: 3 Alexander Dennis, 1 Ayats, 5 Mercedes, 1 Optare, 1 Scania, 1 Volvo
Bodies incl: 2 Ayats, 2 Beulas.
Ops incl: school contracts, excursions & tours, private hire.
Livery: Blue

THE VILLAGER MINIBUS (SHARNBROOK) LTD
SHARNBROOK UPPER SCHOOL, ODELL ROAD, SHARNBROOK MK44 1JL
Tel: 01234 781920
E-mail: villager.sharn@btconnect.com
Man: Stan Jones
Fleet: 1 minibus
Chassis: 1 Mercedes
Body: 1 Mellor
Ops incl: local bus services, private hire

BERKSHIRE (WEST BERKSHIRE, BRACKNELL FOREST, READING, SLOUGH, WINDSOR & MAIDENHEAD, WOKINGHAM)

ALDERMASTON COACHES
ALDERMASTON, READING RG7 5PP
Tel: 0118 971 3257
Fax: 0118 971 2722
E-mail: anne@aldermastoncoaches.co.uk
Prop: Philip M Arlott
Fleet: 9 – single-deck coach, minicoach
Chassis: 1 LDV, 3 Mercedes, 6 Volvo
Bodies: 1 Jonckheere, 3 Mercedes, 5 Plaxton, 1 Sunsundegui
Ops incl: private hire, school contracts.
Livery: White

BURGHFIELD MINI COACHES LTD
BURGHFIELD FARM, MILL ROAD, BURGHFIELD, READING RG30 3SS
Tel/Fax: 0118 959 0719
E-mail: burghfield.coaches@virgin.net
Dir: Susan McCouid
Fleet: 38 - 30 minibus, 8 minicoach.
Chassis: Citroen, Dennis, Leyland, Mercedes, Optare, Renault.
Ops incl: local bus services, school contracts, private hire.

COURTNEY COACHES LTD
UNIT 1, BERKSHIRE BUSINESS CENTRE, DOWNMILL ROAD, BRACKNELL RG12 1QS
Tel: 01344 412302
Fax: 01344 868980
E-mail: sales@courtneycoaches.com
Web site: www.courtneycoaches.com
Man Dir: William Courtney-Smith
Dirs: Miss Hayley Smith, Miss Belinda Smith **Tran Man:** Trevor Springett
Fleet: 38 - 7 double-deck bus, 30 double-deck bus, 1 midibus.
Chassis: 7 Alexander Dennis, 2 DAF, 25 Optare, 1 Renault, 3 Volvo.
Bodies: 5 Alexander Dennis, 5 East Lancs, 25 Optare, 3 Volvo
Ops incl: local bus services, school contracts.
Livery: Orange/White.
Ticket System: Ticketer

FERNHILL TRAVEL LTD
LONGSHOT LANE, BRACKNELL RG12 1RL
Tel: 01344 621413
Fax: 01344 488669
E-mail: office@fernhill.co.uk
Web site: www.fernhill.co.uk
Ops incl: school contracts, private hire
Livery: Red/White

FIRST BEELINE BUSES LTD
COLDBOROUGH HOUSE, MARKET STREET, BRACKNELL RG12 1JA
Tel: 01344 782200
Fax: 01344 868332
E-mail: contact.berkshire@firstgroup.com
Web site: www.firstgroup.com
Regional Man Dir: Adrian Jones
Chief Operating Officer: Chris Dexter.
Fleet: 109 - 16 double-deck bus, 51 single-deck bus, 14 single-deck coach, 28 midibus.
Chassis: 8 Bluebird, 2 BMC, 35 Dennis, 28 Mercedes, 6 Optare, 21 Scania, 9 Volvo.
Bodies: 13 Alexander, 8 Bluebird, 2 BMC, 8 Irizar, 6 Marshall, 28 Mercedes, 5 Northern Counties, 6 Optare, 9 Plaxton, 8 Transbus, 16 Wright.
Ops incl: local bus services, express.
Livery: FirstGroup UK Bus/Green Line/Specials
Ticket System: Wayfarer 3 & TGX.

HAYWARDS COACHES
169 NEW GREENHAM PARK, THATCHAM RG19 6HN
Tel: 0118 947 4561
Fax: 01635 821128
E-mail: info@haywardscoaches.co.uk
Web site: www.haywardscoaches.co.uk
Dir: Simon Weaver
Fleet: 23 – 13 single-deck coach, 9 double-deck coach, 1 minicoach
Chassis: 4 Irisbus, 10 MAN, 1 Mercedes, 8 Volvo.
Ops incl: private hire.
Livery: Electric Blue
A subsidiary of Weavaway Travel

HODGE'S COACHES (SANDHURST) LTD
100 YORKTOWN ROAD, SANDHURST GU47 9BH.
Tel: 01252 873131
Fax: 01252 874884.
E-mail: enquiries@hodges-coaches.co.uk
Web site: www.hodges-coaches.co.uk
Man Dir: P Hodge **Dirs:** M Hodge, M Hodge
Fleet: 21 - 18 single-deck coach, 1 midicoach, 2 minicoach.
Chassis: 4 Bedford, 2 DAF, 1 MAN, 2 Toyota, 12 Volvo.
Bodies: 10 Berkhof, 7 Caetano, 1 Duple, 3 Plaxton.

Ops incl: excursions & tours, private hire, continental tours, school contracts.
Livery: Blue/Gold

HORSEMAN COACHES LTD
2 ACRE ROAD, READING RG2 0SU
Tel: 0118 975 3811
Fax: 0118 975 3515
Recovery: 0118 975 3811
E-mail: privatehire@horsemancoaches.co.uk
Web site: www.horsemancoaches.co.uk
Man Dir: Keith Horseman
Ops Dir: James Horseman
Ch Eng: Derrick Holton
Personnel: Ann Fletcher
Sales Man: Trevor Underwood
Fleet: 59 - 50 coach, 9 midicoach.
Chassis: 1 Dennis, 4 Iveco, 9 Toyota, 45 Volvo.
Bodies: 3 Berkhof, 4 Beulas, 9 Caetano, 42 Plaxton, 1 UVG.
Ops incl: local bus services, school contracts, private hire, continental tours.
Livery: multi-coloured

KINGFISHER MINI COACHES
357 BASINGSTOKE ROAD, READING RG2 0JA
Tel: 0118 931 3454
Fax: 0118 931 1322
Prop: Kevin Pope
E-mail: info@kingfisherminicoaches.co.uk
Web site: www.minicoachhirereading.co.uk
Fleet: 13 - 10 minibus, 3 minicoach
Chassis: 2 Ford Transit, 6 LDV, 5 Mercedes.
Ops incl: private hire, school contracts
Livery: White/Orange

MEMORY LANE VINTAGE OMNIBUS SERVICES
78 LILLIBROOKE CRESCENT, MAIDENHEAD SL6 3XQ
Tel: 01628 825050
Fax: 01628 825851
E-mail: admin@memorylane.co.uk
Web site: www.memorylane.co.uk
Prop: M J Clarke
Fleet: 6 - 3 double-deck bus, 3 single-deck bus
Chassis: 6 AEC.
Bodies: 2 ECW, 3 Park Royal, 1 Willowbrook.
Ops incl: private hire
Livery: Original operators

NEWBURY & DISTRICT
169 NEW GREENHAM PARK, THATCHAM RG19 6HN
Tel: 01635 33855

Fax: 01635 821128
Dir: Simon Weaver
Fleet: 8 single-deck bus
Chassis: 3 Alexander Dennis, 5 MAN
Bodies: 3 Alexander Dennis, 2 MCV, 3 Optare.
Ops incl: local bus services
Livery: Silver/Black
Ticket System: Wayfarer 3
A subsidiary of Weavaway Travel

READING & WOKINGHAM COACHES
33 MURRAY ROAD, WOKINGHAM RG41 2TA
Tel: 0118 979 3983 **Fax:** 0118 979 4330
Web site: www.readingandwokinghamcoaches.co.uk
Props: Mark Way, Sharon Way.
Fleet: 10 - 8 single-deck coach, 2 minibus
Chassis: 1 Dennis, 1 Iveco, 1 Mercedes, 1 Setra, 1 Toyota, 5 Volvo.
Bodies: 2 Berkhof, 1 Beulas, 1 Caetano, 1 Ikarus, 1 Jonckheere, 1 Mercedes, 1 Setra, 2 Van Hool.
Ops incl: excursions & tours, private hire, school contracts, continental tours.
Livery: White

READING HERITAGE TRAVEL
PO BOX 147, READING RG1 6BD
Tel: 07850 220151
Prop & Tran Man: M J Russell
Fleet: 1 double-deck bus.
Chassis: 1 AEC
Bodies: 1 Park Royal
Ops incl: private hire
Livery: Red/Cream

READING TRANSPORT LTD
GREAT KNOLLYS STREET, READING RG1 7HH
Tel: 0118 959 4000
Fax: 0118 957 5379
Recovery: 0118 958 7625
E-mail: info@reading-buses.co.uk.
Web site: www.reading-buses.co.uk
Fleet Name: Reading Buses, Newbury Buses
Chairman: Stuart Singleton-White
Ch Exec Off: James Freeman
Fin Dir: Greg Chambers **Perf Dir:** Jaqui Gavaghan **HR Dir:** Caroline Anscombe
Ch Eng: Keith Ward **Comm Man & Co Sec:** Norman Fryer-Saxby
Fleet: 156 - 89 double-deck bus, 57 single-deck bus, 10 midibus.
Chassis: 4 Alexander Dennis, 3 MAN, 23 Optare, 125 Scania, 1 Transbus.
Bodies: 4 Alexander Dennis, 41 East Lancs, 10 Optare, 61 Scania, 1 Transbus, 39 Wright.
Ops incl: local bus services.
Livery: various brand liveries
Ticket System: Wayfarer TGX150

STEWARTS OF MORTIMER (PRIVATE HIRE) LTD
JAMES LANE, GRAZELEY GREEN, READING, RG7 1NE
Tel: 0118 983 1231
Fax: 0118 983 1232
E-mail: quotes@somph.co.uk
Web site: www.somph.co.uk
Fleet incl: single-deck coach, midicoach, minibus, minicoach.
Ops incl: private hire
Livery: Silver

TOP TRAVEL COACHES
See Hampshire

WEAVAWAY TRAVEL
169 NEW GREENHAM PARK, THATCHAM RG19 6HN
Tel: 01635 820028
Fax: 01635 821128
Web site: www.weavaway.co.uk
Dir: Simon Weaver
Fleet: 23 - 13 single-deck coach, 9 double-deck coach, 1 minicoach.
Chassis: 4 Irisbus, 10 MAN, 1 Mercedes, 8 Volvo.
Ops incl: private hire.
Liveries: Black, Black & Blue

WHITE BUS SERVICES
NORTH STREET GARAGE, WINKFIELD, WINDSOR SL4 4TP
Tel: 01344 882612
Fax: 01344 886403
E-mail: office@whitebus.co.uk
Web site: www.whitebus.co.uk
Man Dir: Doug Jeatt
Fleet: 15 – 5 single-deck bus, 10 single-deck coach.
Chassis: 2 Alexander Dennis, 3 DAF, 6 Dennis, 2 Optare, 2 Volvo.
Ops incl: local bus services, school contracts, private hire.
Livery: White/grey
Ticket System: Wayfarer 3 & Saver

WINDSORIAN COACHES
373 HATTON ROAD, BEDFONT, FELTHAM TW14 9QS
Tel: 01753 860131
Fax: 020 8751 5054
Web site: www.windsoriancoaches.co.uk
Man Dir: Martin Cornell
Gen Man: Gilbert Parsons
Fleet: 10 - 8 single-deck coach, 2 midicoach.
Chassis: 7 Dennis, 2 Mercedes, 1 Volvo.
Bodies: 2 Mellor, 8 Plaxton.
Ops incl: school contracts, excursions & tours, private hire, continental tours.
Livery: White/Blue

BERKSHIRE (WEST BERKSHIRE, BRACKNELL FOREST, READING, SLOUGH, WINDSOR & MAIDENHEAD, WOKINGHAM)

BRISTOL, SOUTH GLOUCESTERSHIRE

ABUS LTD
104 WINCHESTER ROAD, BRISLINGTON BS4 3NL
Tel: 0117 977 6126
E-mail: alan@abus.co.uk
Web site: www.abus.co.uk
Man Dir: Alan Peters
Fleet: 25 - 21 double-deck bus, 4 midibus,
Chassis: 1 Bristol, 13 DAF, 3 Leyland, 4 Optare, 2 Scania, 2 Volvo.
Bodies: 2 Alexander Dennis, 1 ECW, 3 East Lancs, 2 Northern Counties, 17 Optare.
Ops incl: local bus services
Livery: Cream/White/Maroon
Ticket System: Wayfarer 3

AZTEC COACH TRAVEL
6/8 EMERY ROAD, BRISLINGTON BS4 5PF
Tel: 0117 329 7959
Fax: 0117 977 4431
E-mail: myrtletree@holding4337.freeserve.co.uk
Web site: www.azteccoaches.co.uk
Man Dir: Iain Fortune
Fleet Eng: D Harvey
Ops Man: P Rixon.
Fleet: 15 - 13 midicoach, 2 minibus.
Chassis: 1 Freight Rover, 14 Mercedes.
Bodies: 4 Autobus Classique, 2 Optare, 7 Reeve Burgess.
Ops incl: excursions & tours, private hire,

The Little Red Book 2011 - in association with *tbf* Transport Benevolent Fund

continental tours, school contracts.
Livery: White with diagonal red/orange stripes.

BERKELEY COACH & TRAVEL
HAM LANE, PAULTON BS39 7PL
Tel: 01761 413196
Fax: 01761 416469
Web Site: www.berkeleycoachandtravel.co.uk
Proprietor: Mr T. Pow
Fleet: 8 - 8 single-deck coach
Chassis: 8 Volvo
Ops incl: school contracts, private hire.

BLAGDON LIONESS COACHES LTD
See Somerset

BLUE IRIS COACHES
25 CLEVEDON ROAD, NAILSEA BS48 1EH
Tel: 01275 851121
Fax: 01275 856522
E-mail: enquiry@blueiris.co.uk
Web site: www.blueiris.co.uk
Dirs: Philip Hatherall, Tony Spiller
Fleet: 17 - 2 single-deck bus, 9 single-deck coach, 6 midicoach.
Chassis: 2 Optare, 9 Scania, 6 Toyota.
Bodies: 1 Berkhof, 6 Caetano, 6 Irizar, 2 Optare, 2 Van Hool.
Ops incl: local bus services, school contracts, private hire, continental tours.
Livery: 2-tone Blue/White.
Ticket System: Wayfarer

PETER CAROL PRESTIGE COACHING
BAMFIELD HOUSE, WHITCHURCH BS14 0XD
Tel: 01275 839839
Fax: 01275 835604
E-mail: charter@petercarol.co.uk
Web site: www.luxurycoach.co.uk
Gen Man: Peter Collis
Fleet: 9 - 9 single-deck coach.
Chassis: 1 BMC, 2 Bova, 1 MAN, 5 Mercedes.
Bodies: 1 BMC, 2 Bova, 5 Mercedes, 1 other body.
Ops incl: excursions & tours, private hire.

CITISTAR LTD
2 CARTER ROAD, PAULTON, BRISTOL BS39 7LL
E-mail: bus@citistar.co.uk
Web site: www.citistar.co.uk
Dir: Andrew Fear
Ops incl: local bus services

EAGLE COACHES
FIRECLAY HOUSE, NETHAM ROAD, ST GEORGE BS5 8HU
Tel: 0117 955 4541
Fax: 0117 941 1107
E-mail: james@eagle-coaches.co.uk
Web site: www.eagle-coaches.co.uk
Partners: A J Ball, J A Ball
Fleet: 21 – 18 single-deck coach, 2 midicoach, 1 minibus.
Chassis: 17 DAF, 2 Mercedes, 1 Volvo.
Bodies: 2 Ikarus, 1 Jonckheere, 2 Reeve Burgess, 15 Van Hool.
Ops incl: excursions & tours, continental tours.
Livery: Yellow

EASTVILLE COACHES LTD
15 ASHGROVE ROAD, REDLAND BS6 6NA
Tel: 0117 971 0657
Fax: 0117 971 5824
Man Dir: T. Reece.
Fleet: 9 - 4 double-deck bus, 1 double-deck coach, 4 single-deck coach.
Chassis: 1 Bova, 3 Leyland, 5 Volvo.
Bodies: 2 Alexander, 1 Bova, 1 ECW, 1 Northern Counties, 4 Van Hool.
Ops incl: local bus services, school contracts, private hire, continental tours.
Livery: Myosotis Blue/White.

EUROTAXIS LTD
JORROCKS ESTATE, WESTERLEIGH ROAD, WESTERLEIGH BS30 5LT
Tel: 0871 250 5555
Fax: 0871 250 4444
Recovery: 0871 250 3333
E-mail: juan@eurotaxis.com
Web site: www.eurotaxis.com
Man Dir: Anne Sanzo
Co Sec: Juan Sanzo
Gen Man: Keith Sanzo
HR Manager: William Sanzo
Joint Ops Mans: Fred Taylor, Tony Lavoie
Fleet: 165 – incl 11 double-deck bus, 2 single-deck bus, 25 single-deck coach, 12 midibus, 14 midicoach, 15 minibus, 16 minicoach.
Chassis incl: 30 Citroen, 2 Dennis, 32 Fiat, 45 Mercedes, 2 Peugeot, 6 Setra, 2 Toyota, 2 Volkswagen, 12 Volvo, 11 Other.
Ops incl: local bus services, school contracts, private hire, excursions & tours, continental tours.
Livery: All White
Ticket system: Wayfarer 2

FIRST BRISTOL
ENTERPRISE HOUSE, EASTON ROAD, BRISTOL BS5 0DZ
Tel: 0117 955 8211
Fax: 0117 955 1248
Web site: www.firstgroup.com
Man Dir: Tony McNiff **Eng Dir:** Richard Noble **Fin Dir:** Mike Gahan
Ops Dir: Jenny McLeod
Fleet: 266 - 155 double-deck bus, 37 single-deck bus, 3 articulated bus, 61 midibus, 10 coach.
Chassis: 22 Alexander Dennis, 67 Dennis, 3 Mercedes, 4 Scania, 170 Volvo.
Bodies: 22 Alexander Dennis, 25 Alexander, 8 East Lancs, 4 Irizar, 3 Mercedes, 2 Northern Counties, 57 Plaxton, 5 Transbus, 140 Wright.
Ops incl: local bus services, school contracts.
Livery: FirstGroup UK Bus
Ticket System: Wayfarer

GLENVIC OF BRISTOL LTD
THE OLD COLLIERY, STANTON WICK, PENSFORD BS39 4BZ
Tel: 01761 490116
Fax: 0117 907 7032
Dirs: Paul Holvey, Philip Holvey
Ops Man/Co Sec: Paul Holvey
Eng: Nick Reed
Fleet: 13 - 4 double-deck bus, 5 single-deck coach, 4 minicoach.
Chassis: 2 LDV, 7 Leyland, 2 Mercedes, 2 Volvo.

GRAHAM'S COACHES OF BRISTOL
7 WYCK BECK ROAD, BRENTRY BS10 7JD
Tel/Fax: 0117 950 9398
E-mail: wyckbeck@yahoo.co.uk
Props: Graham P Smith, Yvonne M E Smith
Fleet: 6 - 3 double-deck bus, 3 single deck coach.
Chassis: 1 DAF, 3 Leyland, 2 Volvo.
Bodies incl: 1 Jonckheere, 2 Van Hool.
Ops incl: private hire, school contracts.
Livery: White/Red/Maroon

ARNOLD LIDDELL COACHES
89 JERSEY AVENUE, BRISLINGTON BS4 4QX.
Tel: 0117 977 2011
Web site: www.arnoldliddellcoaches.com
Prop: Michael Liddell
Gen Man: Arnold. Liddell **Fleet Eng:** Robert Liddell
Fleet: 2 - 1 single-deck coach, 1 midicoach.
Chassis: 1 Leyland, 1 Mercedes.
Ops incl: excursions & tours, school contracts.
Livery: Blue/White.

MARTINS SELF DRIVE MINICOACH HIRE
GRINDELL ROAD GARAGE, 1 GRINDELL ROAD, REDFIELD BS5 9PG
Tel: 0117 955 1042
Fax: 0117 939 3383
Fleet: 12 - 12 minibus.
Chassis: 12 Ford Transit.
Ops incl: Self Drive Minicoach Hire.

NORTH SOMERSET COACHES
UNIT 3A, COATES ESTATE, SOUTHFIELD ROAD, NAILSEA BS48 1JN
Tel/Fax: 01275 859123
E-mail: talktous@northsomersetcoaches.co.uk
Web site: www.northsomersetcoaches.co.uk
Prop: David Fricker
Fleet: 10 – 1 double-deck bus, 4 single-deck bus, 4 single–deck coach, 1 minibus.
Chassis: 2 Bristol, 1 DAF,, 1 Optare, 6 Volvo.
Bodies: 2 Alexander Dennis, 1 Berkhof, 2 ECW, 2 Optare, 3 Plaxton.
Ops incl: local bus services, school contracts, excursions & tours, private hire.
Livery: white/cream/black
Ticket System: Wayfarer Saver

PREMIER TRAVEL LTD
ALBERT CRESCENT, ST PHILIPS, BRISTOL BS2 0SU
Tel: 0117 9300 5550
Fax: 0117 9300 5551
Man Dir: Glenn Bond
Fleet: 5 - 1 double-deck bus, 2 single-deck coach, 1 double-deck coach, 1 minicoach.
Chassis: 1 Bova, 1 DAF, 1 Freight Rover, 1 Leyland, 1 Volvo.
Bodies: 1 Bova, 1 ECW, 2 Van Hool.
Ops incl: school contracts, continental

tours, private hire.
Livery: White/Red with blue lettering.

SOUTH GLOUCESTERSHIRE BUS & COACH COMPANY
THE COACH DEPOT, PEGASUS PARK, GYPSY PATCH LANE, PATCHWAY BS34 6QD
Tel: 0117 931 4340
Fax: 0117 979 9400
E-mail: sgbc@btconnect.com
Web site: www.southgloucestershirebus.co.uk
Man Dir: Roger Durbin
Gen Man: Mike Owen
Workshop Man: Mark Wood
Route Man: Martyn Edney
Fleet: 54 – 9 double-deck bus, 4 single-deck bus, 37 single-deck coach, 4 minibus.
Chassis: 6 DAF, 8 Leyland, 4 Mercedes, 8 Scania, 28 Volvo.

Bodies: 5 Alexander, 6 Caetano, 1 ECW, 3 East Lancs, 1 Frank Guy, 1 Keillor, 1 Leyland, 1 Mellor, 16 Plaxton, 18 Van Hool, 1 Wadham Stringer.
Ops incl: local bus service, school contracts, excursions & tours, private hire, continental tours, express.
Livery: Blue/White.
Ticket system: Wayfarer 2

SOMERBUS LTD
See Somerset

TURNERS COACHWAYS (BRISTOL) LTD
59 DAYS ROAD, ST PHILIPS BS2 0QS
Tel: 0117 955 9086
Fax: 0117 955 6948
E-mail: admin@turnerscoachways.co.uk
Web site: www.turners-coachways.co.uk

Man Dir: Tony Turner
Private Hire Man: Liz Venn
Traf Man: Tony Harvey
Fleet: 31 - 30 single-deck coach, 1 minicoach.
Chassis: 7 Scania, 2 Setra, 1 Toyota, 20 Volvo.
Bodies: 2 Berkhof, 7 Irizar, 14 Jonckheere, 1 Optare, 2 Plaxton, 2 Setra, 2 Van Hool.
Ops incl: school contracts, private hire
Livery: Silver/Blue

WESSEX CONNECT
PEGASUS PARK, GYPSY PATCH LANE, PATCHWAY BS34 6QD
Tel: 0117 969 8661
Fax: 0117 969 8662
E-mail: info@connectbuses.com
Web site: www.wessexconnect.net
Ops incl: local bus services.
Part of Flights Hallmark, a subsidiary of Rotala

BUCKINGHAMSHIRE, MILTON KEYNES

BRAZIERS MINI COACHES
17 VICARAGE ROAD, WINSLOW, BUCKINGHAM MK18 3BE
Tel: 01296 712201
E-mail: pbrazier@btconnect.com
Web site: www.brazierscoaches.co.uk
Prop: Peter Brazier
Fleet: 3 minicoach.
Chassis/Bodies: 3 LDV
Ops incl: private hire, school contracts

CAROUSEL BUSES
THE BUS GARAGE, LANSDALES ROAD, HIGH WYCOMBE HP11 2PB
Tel: 01494 533436
E-mail: enquiries@carouselbuses.com
Web site: www.carouselbuses.com
Man Dir: Steve Burns
Fin Dir: John Robinson
Ops Man: Noel Clark
Eng Man: Mick Cook
Fleet: 56 - 27 double-deck bus, 28 single-deck bus, 1 open-top bus.
Chassis: 2 AEC, 4 Alexander Dennis, 2 DAF, 3 Irisbus, 7 Leyland, 5 MAN, 11 MCW, 3 Mercedes, 1 VDL, 10 Volvo, 4 Other.
Bodies: 5 East Lancs, 10 Marshall/MCV, 11 MCW, 3 Mercedes, 4 Northern Counties, 4 Plaxton, 19 Other.
Ops incl: local bus services, school contracts.
Livery: Red
Ticket system: Wayfarer 3

CLIFF'S COACHES
UNIT 6, BINDERS INDUSTRIAL ESTATE, CRYERS HILL, HIGH WYCOMBE HP15 6LJ
Tel: 01494 714878
Fax: 01494 713491
E-mail: info@cliffscoaches.co.uk
Web site: www.cliffscoaches.co.uk
Fleet incl: single-deck coach, midicoach, minibus
Ops incl: excursions & tours, private hire
Livery: Blue/White

DRP TRAVEL
1 THE MEADWAY, LOUGHTON, MILTON KEYNES MK5 8AN
Tel: 01908 394141
E-mail: drptravel@talktalk.net

Web site: www.drptravel.co.uk
Man: D R Pinnock
Fleet: 2 minibus
Chassis: 1 Mercedes, 1 Renault.
Ops incl: school contracts, private hire.
Livery: Blue/White

HOWLETTS COACHES
UNIT 2, STATION ROAD INDUSTRIAL ESTATE, WINSLOW MK18 3DZ
Tel: 01296 713201   **Fax:** 01296 715879
Prop: R. S. Durham
Fleet: 8 - 2 double-deck bus, 6 single-deck coach.
Chassis: 1 Bedford, 4 DAF, 2 MCW, 1 Setra.
Ops incl: private hire, continental tours, school contracts.
Livery: Brown/White.

J & L TRAVEL LTD
MOUNT PLEASANT, TAYLORS LANE, ST LEONARDS, TRING HP23 6LU
Tel: 01296 696046
E-mail: info@jlcoaches.com
Web site: www.jlcoaches.com
Ops incl: excursions & tours, private hire, school contracts
Livery: White with Red lettering

LANGSTON & TASKER
23 QUEEN CATHERINE ROAD, STEEPLE CLAYDON MK18 2PZ
Tel/Fax: 01296 730347
Partners: Mrs J Langston, Mrs M A Fenner **Man:** J Langston
Ops Man: A P Price
Fleet: 19 - 13 single-deck coach, 6 minibus.
Chassis: 1 Bedford, 4 Dennis, 1 Iveco, 2 Leyland, 4 Mercedes, 1 Toyota, 6 Volvo.
Bodies: 1 Autobus, 2 Caetano, 3 Duple, 2 Jonckheere, 3 Mercedes, 6 Plaxton, 1 Transbus, 1 Wadham Stringer.
Ops incl: local bus services, school contracts, private hire.
Livery: White/Red
Ticket system: Wayfarer

MAGPIE TRAVEL LTD
BINDERS INDUSTRIAL ESTATE, CRYERS HILL, HIGH WYCOMBE HP15 6LJ

Tel: 01494 715381
Dir: David Harris **Co Sec:** Amanda Ash
Fleet: 14 – 1 double-deck bus, 2 single-deck bus, 7 single-deck coach, 4 midibus.
Chassis: 1 Dennis, 1 Leyland, 1 MCW, 6 Mercedes, 5 Volvo.
Bodies: 1 Alexander Dennis, 1 Jonckheere, 1 Leyland, 1 MCV, 1 Mellor, 1 Optare, 2 Plaxton, 2 Reeve Burgess, 2 Van Hool, 2 Other.
Ops incl: local bus services, school contracts, private hire.
Livery: White/Black
Ticket System: Almex

MASONS COACHES
3 THE GREEN, CHEDDINGTON LU7 0RJ
Tel: 01296 661604 **Fax:** 01296 660341
E-mail: info@masonsminicoachhire.co.uk
Web site: www.masonsminicoachhire.co.uk
Fleet: 6 single-deck coach, midicoach.
Ops incl: excursions & tours, private hire, school contracts

MK METRO LTD
52 COLTS HOLM ROAD, OLD WOLVERTON, MILTON KEYNES MK12 5RN
Tel: 01908 225100
Fax: 01908 313553
Web site: www.mkmetro.co.uk
Man Dir: Paul Adcock
Comm Dir: Kevin Hawkins
Eng Dir: Brian Barraclough
Fin Dir: Beverley Lawson
Fleet: 120 - double-deck bus, single-deck bus, single-deck coach, midibus.
Chassis: DAF, Dennis, Mercedes, Optare, Scania, Volvo.
Bodies: Alexander, Caetano, Optare, Plaxton, Wright.
Ops incl: local bus services, school contracts, express.
Livery: Arriva UK Bus, National Express Coach
Ticket System: Wayfarer 3
Part of Arriva The Shires (see Bedfordshire)

MOTTS COACHES (AYLESBURY) LTD
GARSIDE WAY, AYLESBURY HP20 1BH
Tel: 01296 398300

The Little Red Book 2011 - in association with tbf Transport Benevolent Fund   87

Buckinghamshire, Milton Keynes

Fax: 01296 398386
E-mail: info@mottstravel.com
Web site: www.mottstravel.com
Fleet Name: Motts Travel
Man Dir: M R Mott
Ops Dir: C J Mott **Eng Dir:** I Scutt
Tours Dir: C Joel
Traf Man: S Lane
Fleet: 53 - 6 double-deck bus,
4 single-deck bus, 32 single-deck coach,
2 double-deck coach, 2 midibus,
7 midicoach
Chassis: 4 Leyland, 9 Mercedes,
4 Neoplan, 4 Scania, 32 Volvo.
Bodies: 10 Alexander Dennis, 3 Irizar,
12 Jonckheere, 4 Neoplan, 12 Plaxton,
3 Sitcar, 1 Sunsundegui, 2 Unvi, 6 Other.
Ops incl: local bus services, school
contracts, excursions & tours, private hire,
continental tours.
Livery: White/Yellow/Green.
Ticket System: Wayfarer.

REDLINE BUSES
8 GATEHOUSE WAY, AYLESBURY
HP19 8DB
Tel/Fax: 01296 426786
E-mail: kwk@redlinebuses.com
Web site: www.redlinebuses.com
Prop: Khan Wali
Fleet: 24-7 double-deck bus,
6 single-deck bus, 4 single-deck coach,
7 minibus.
Chassis: 1 Alexander Dennis, 2 Dennis,
1 Enterprise, 1 Ford, 3 Leyland,
3 Mercedes, 3 Optare, 10 Volvo.
Bodies: 5 Alexander Dennis,
2 Jonckheere, 3 Northern Counties,
3 Optare, 6 Plaxton, 1 Van Hool, 3 Wright,
1 Other.
Ops incl: local bus services, school
contracts, private hire.
Livery: Red
Ticket System: Wayfarer TGX.

RED ROSE TRAVEL
OXFORD ROAD, DINTON, AYLESBURY
HP17 8TT
Tel: 01296 747926
Fax: 01296 612196
E-mail: admin@redrosetravel.com
Web site: www.redrosetravel.com
Dirs: Christopher Day, Taj Khan
Fleet: 27 – 2 double-deck bus,
25 single-deck bus.
Chassis: Alexander Dennis, Dennis,
Mercedes, Volvo.
Bodies: Alexander Dennis, Caetano,
East Lancs, Optare, Plaxton, Transbus

Ops incl: local bus services, private hire.
Livery: Red/Yellow
Ticket System: Wayfarer 3.

SOULS COACHES LTD
2 STILEBROOK ROAD, OLNEY
MK46 5EA
Tel: 01234 711242 **Fax:** 01234 240130
Recovery: 07739 097775
E-mail: sales@souls-coaches.co.uk
Web site: www.souls-coaches.co.uk
Man Dir: David Soul
Sales Man: Wendy Cheshire
Traf Man: Neil McCormick
Ops Man: Steve Neale **Workshop Man:**
Drew Blunt
Fleet: 41 - 4 double-deck bus,
2 single-deck bus, 31 coach, 1 double-
deck coach, 3 minicoach.
Chassis: 5 Dennis, 2 Leyland, 1 MAN,
2 Mercedes, 5 Setra, 3 Toyota, 14 Volvo.
Bodies: 5 Jonckheere, 2 Leyland,
2 Mercedes, 1 Neoplan, 3 Optare,
15 Plaxton, 5 Setra.
Ops incl: local bus services, school
contracts, excursions & tours, private hire,
continental tours.
Livery: Red/Gold
Ticket System: Wayfarer.

STAR TRAVEL
19 KINGS ROAD, AYLESBURY HP21
7RR
Tel: 01296 422225
Fleet incl: midibus, minibus
Ops incl: local bus services

THREE STAR COACHES.COM
UNIT 1, GUARDIAN BUSINESS PARK,
DALLOW ROAD, LUTON LU1 1NA
Tel: 01582 722626
Fax: 01582 484034
E-mail: sales@threestarcoaches.com
Web Site: www.threestarcoaches.com
Man Dir: Colin Dudley
Ops Man: Kevin Green
Ch Eng: Michael Nallaby
Co Sec: Isabelle Dudley
Fleet: 13 – 1 single-deck bus, 7 single-
deck coach, 2 double-deck coach,
3 midicoach.
Chassis: 3 Alexander Dennis, 1 Ayats,
5 Mercedes, 1 Optare, 1 Scania, 1 Volvo
Bodies incl: 2 Ayats, 2 Beulas.
Ops incl: school contracts, excursions &
tours, private hire.
Livery: Blue

VALE TRAVEL
61 FLEET STREET, AYLESBURY
HP20 2PA
Tel: 01296 484348
Fax: 01296 435309
E-mail: vale_travel@yahoo.co.uk
Web site: www.valetravel.co.uk
Prop: Wazir Zaman
Fleet: 16 – 6 single-deck bus, 2 midibus,
2 midicoach, 6 minibus.
Chassis incl: Alexander Dennis, DAF,
Dennis, Ford Transit, Mercedes, Optare,
Renault, Volvo.
Bodies incl: Alexander Dennis,
Leyland, Optare, Plaxton, Van Hool,
Wright.
Ops Inc: local bus services, school
contracts, private hire.
Livery: Multi
Ticket System: Wayfarer

WOOTTENS
THE COACH YARD, LYCROME ROAD,
LYE GREEN, CHESHAM HP5 3LG
Tel: 01494 774411
Fax: 01494 784597
E-mail: info@woottens.co.uk
Web site: www.woottens.co.uk
Dirs: N H Wootten, M J Wootten
Ops Man: P Williams
Chief Eng: R A Gomm
Fleet Names: Woottens (coaches),
Tiger Line (buses)
Fleet: 25 - 2 double-deck bus,
6 single-deck bus, 17 single-deck coach.
Chassis: Leyland, Volvo.
Bodies: Alexander, Berkhof, ECW,
East Lancs, Jonckheere, Leyland,
Plaxton.
Ops incl: local bus services, excursions
and tours, continental tours, private hire,
school contracts.
Livery: White with coloured swirls.
Ticket System: Wayfarer.

Z & S INTERNATIONAL
AYLESBURY BUSINESS CENTRE,
CHAMBERLAIN ROAD,
AYLESBURY HP19 8DY
Tel/Fax: 01296 415468
E-mail: info@zands.co.uk
Web site: www.zands.co.uk
Fleet incl: double-deck bus,
double-deck coach, single-deck coach,
midibus, midicoach.
Ops incl: local bus services, school
contracts, excursions & tours,
private hire.

CAMBRIDGESHIRE, CITY OF PETERBOROUGH

AARDVARK & FIRST CHOICE COACHES
GOODMANS BUSINESS PARK,
THIRD DROVE, FENGATE,
PETERBOROUGH PE1 5QR
Tel: 01733 561222 **Fax:** 01733 349268
E-mail: aardvarkcoaches@aol.com
Web site:
www.aardvarkcoaches.webeden.co.uk
Ops incl: school contracts, private hire,
excursions & tours.
Livery: White.

ANDREWS COACHES
20 CAMBRIDGE ROAD, FOXTON
CB22 6SH
Tel: 0844 3570602

Fax: 0844 3576992
E-mail: andrewscoaches@aol.com
Web site: www.andrewscoaches.co.uk
Man Dir: F Miller **Dir:** J Miller
Ops Sup: A Miller
E-mail: andrewscoaches@aol.co.uk
Web site: www.andrewscoaches.co.uk
Fleet: 7 single-deck coach
Chassis: 4 Dennis, 1 Scania, 2 Volvo.
Bodies: 1 Berkhof, 3 Duple, 1
Jonckheere, 1 Plaxton, 1 Van Hool.
Ops incl: school contracts, excursions &
tours, private hire, continental tours.
Livery: White

BURTONS COACHES
DUDDERY HILL, HAVERHILL CB9 8DR
Tel: 01440 702257
Fax: 01440 713287

Recovery: 01440 760391
E-mail: hire@burtons-bus.co.uk
Web site: www.burtonscoaches.com
Man Dir: Paul J Cooper
Dir: Tracy Atkinson-Cooper
Traffic Man: Paul Steed
Workshop Man: Steve Freemantle
Fleet: 32 - 9 double-deck bus,
4 single-deck bus, 15 single-deck coach,
1 midicoach, 2 minibus, 1 minicoach.
Chassis: Alexander Dennis, DAF,
Leyland, Mercedes, Scania, Volvo.
Bodies: Alexander Dennis, Bova,
Caetano, East Lancs, Irizar, Northern
Counties, Plaxton, Van Hool.
Ops incl: local bus services, school
contracts, excursions & tours, private hire,
continental tours.
Livery: Blue/White/Yellow
Ticket system: Almex A90

C & G COACHES
HONEYSOME LODGE, HONEYSOME ROAD, CHATTERIS PE16 6SB
Tel: 01354 692200
Fax: 01354 694433
Recovery: 07771 962 105
E-mail: info@candgcoaches.co.uk
Web site: www.candgcoaches.co.uk
Partners: Mrs C Day, G Ellwood, R Day
Ops Man: C Smith
Fleet: 24 - 1 double-deck bus, 23 single-deck coach.
Chassis: 3 Bedford, 1 Bova, 2 Leyland, 1 MCW, 1 Neoplan, 11 Scania, 5 Volvo.
Bodies: 2 Berkhof, 1 Bova, 2 Duple, 1 ECW, 8 Irizar, 1 MCW, 1 Neoplan, 8 Plaxton, 1 Van Hool.
Ops incl: school contracts, excursions & tours, private hire, continental tours.
Livery: White/Red/Yellow

COLLINS COACHES
UNIT 4, CAMBRIDGE ROAD INDUSTRIAL ESTATE, CAMBRIDGE CB4 6AZ
Tel: 01223 420462
Fax: 01223 424739
E-mail: collinscoaches@sagehost.co.uk office@collinscoaches.net
Partners: C. R. Collins, R. T. Collins
Off Man: Jacky Liptrot
Garage Man: R D Curtis
Fleet: 19 - 3 single-deck coach, 3 midicoach, 13 minibus.
Chassis: 1 Bedford, 2 Dennis, 5 Ford Transit, 2 Freight Rover, 4 Iveco, 2 LDV.
Ops incl: excursions & tours, school contracts, private hire.
Livery: White/Orange

DECKER BUS
70-72 AARON ROAD INDUSTRIAL ESTATE, WHITTLESEY PE7 2EX
Tel: 01733 351694
Fax: 01733 359438
Recovery: 07521 194734
E-mail: anthea@deckerbus.co.uk
Web site: www.deckerbus.co.uk
Prop: Anthea Head
Fleet: 11 – incl 3 double-deck bus, 5 single-deck coach, 1 open top bus, 1 minicoach.
Chassis incl: 1 Bova, 2 Leyland, 3 MAN, 3 Scania.
Bodies incl: 1 Bova
Ops incl: school contracts, excursions & tours, private hire, express.
Livery: Various Colours

RON W DEW & SONS LTD
CHATTERIS ROAD, SOMERSHAM PE17 3DN
Tel: 01487 740241
Fax: 01487 740341
E-mail: sales@dews-coaches.com
Web site: www.dews-coaches.com
Man Dir: Simon Dew
Ops Dir: Jim Darr
Maintenance Man: Tom Williams

Fleet incl: double-deck bus, single-deck bus, single-deck coach, midibus.
Chassis: Bedford, Iveco, Leyland, Mercedes, Optare, Scania, Setra, Volvo.
Bodies: Alexander, Beulas, Duple, East Lancs, Irizar, Jonckheere, Marshall, Mercedes, Optare, Plaxton, Van Hool.
Ops incl: local bus services, excursions & tours, private hire, continental tours, school contracts.
Livery: Green/Grey.

EMBLINGS COACHES
BRIDGE GARAGE, GUYHIRN, WISBECH PE13 4ED
Tel: 01945 450253
Fax: 01945 450770
Man Dir: John Embling
Ops incl: local bus services, school contracts, private hire.

FENN HOLIDAYS
WHITTLESEY ROAD, MARCH PE15 0AG
Tel: 01354 653329
Fax: 01354 650647
E-mail: info@fennholidays.co.uk
Web site: www.fennholidays.co.uk
Man Dir: Peter Fenn
Dir: Margaret Fenn
Fleet: 3 single-deck coach, 1 minibus.
Chassis: 1 Bova, 1 Mercedes, 2 Van Hool integral.
Bodies: 1 Bova, 2 Van Hool.
Ops incl: excursions & tours, private hire, continental tours
Livery: Multicoloured
Ticket System: Setright.

FREEDOM TRAVEL COACHES
98 BROAD STREET, ELY CB7 4BE
Tel: 01353614451
E-mail: info@freedomtravelcoaches.co.uk
Web site: www.freedomtravelcoaches.co.uk
Ops incl: local bus services, school contracts, private hire.
Livery: White.

GRETTON'S COACHES
ARNWOOD CENTRE, NEWARK ROAD, PETERBOROUGH PE1 5YH
Tel: 01733 311008
Fax: 01733 319859
Prop: Roger Gretton
Fleet: 15 - 12 single-deck coach, 3 midicoach.
Chassis: 1 Bedford, 2 Mercedes, 12 Scania.
Bodies: 10 Plaxton, 5 Van Hool.
Ops incl: school contracts, excursions & tours, private hire.
Livery: Silver/Red/Maroon

GREYS OF ELY
41 COMMON ROAD, WITCHFORD, ELY CB6 2HY
Tel: 01353 662300
Fax: 01353 662412
E-mail: sales@greysofely.co.uk

Web site: www.greysofely.co.uk
Man Dir: R Grey
Ops Man: C Covill
Fleet: 23 – 5 double deck bus, 3 single-deck bus, 13 single-deck coach, 2 midicoach.
Chassis: 3 Alexander Dennis, 1 DAF, 8 Dennis, 3 Leyland, 2 Mercedes, 1 Transbus, 5 Volvo.
Bodies: 1 Alexander, 1 Caetano, 3 Duple, 1 ECW, 3 Jonckheere, 2 Optare, 9 Plaxton, 1 Sunsundegui, 2 Transbus.
Ops incl: school contracts, private hire
Livery: Cream/Green

JANS COACHES
23 TOWNSEND, SOHAM CB7 5DD
Tel: 01353 721344
Fax: 01353 721341
E-mail: janscoaches@aol.com
Dirs: Roland Edwards, Janet Edwards, Stuart Edwards
Fleet: 8 - 3 double-deck bus, 3 single-deck coach, 1 double-deck coach, 1 minicoach.
Chassis: 1 Dennis, 1 Iveco, 1 Leyland, 2 MAN, 2 MCW, 1 Neoplan.
Bodies: 1 Berkhof, 1 Indcar, 2 MCW, 3 Neoplan, 1 Northern Counties.
Ops incl: excursions & tours, private hire, continental tours, school contracts.
Livery: White.

KIDDLES COACHES
HEATH ROAD, WARBOYS, HUNTINGDON PE28 2UU
Tel: 01487 824003
Fax: 01487 824044
E-mail: kiddlescoaches@btconnect.com
Web site: www.kiddlescoaches.com
Dirs: R Willmore, J Willmore.
Ops incl: school contracts, private hire, continental tours.
Livery: White.

MIL-KEN TRAVEL LTD
11 LYNN ROAD, LITTLEPORT, ELY CB6 1QG
Tel: 01353 860705
Fax: 01353 863222
E-mail: milken@btconnect.com
Web-site: www.milkentravel.com
Man Dir: Jason Miller
Fleet Eng: Ian Martin
Fleet: 32 - 29 single-deck coach, 2 minibus, 1 minicoach.
Chassis: 1 Dennis, 2 LDV, 1 Mercedes, 2 VDL, 26 Volvo.
Bodies: 2 LDV, 25 Plaxton, 1 Sitcar, 4 Van Hool.
Ops incl: school contracts, private hire.
Livery: White with Red, Blue, Yellow.

C G MYALL & SON
CHERRY TREE HOUSE, THE CAUSEWAY, BASSINGBOURN, ROYSTON SG8 5JA
Tel: 01763 243225
Ops incl: local bus services, school contracts, private hire.
Livery: White

♿	Vehicle suitable for disabled	🔒	Seat belt-fitted Vehicle	R24	24 hour recovery service
T	Toilet-drop facilities available	🍽	Coach(es) with galley facilities		Replacement vehicle available
R	Recovery service available	❄	Air-conditioned vehicle(s)		Vintage Coach(es) available
	Open top vehicle(s)	🚻	Coaches with toilet facilities		

Cambridgeshire, City of Peterborough

The Little Red Book 2011 - in association with *tbf* Transport Benevolent Fund

NEAL'S TRAVEL LTD
102 BECK ROAD, ISLEHAM, ELY
CB7 5QP
Tel: 01638 780066
Fax: 01638 780011
E-mail: sales@nealstravel.com
Web site: www.nealstravel.com
Dirs: Bridget Paterson, Graham Neal, Lionel Neal, Nancy Neal
Fleet: 16 – 9 single-deck coach, 1 midibus, 4 midicoach, 2 minibus.
Chassis: 9 Mercedes, 7 Volvo.
Bodies: 2 Autobus, 5 Jonckheere, 2 Mercedes, 1 Plaxton, 2 Sunsundegui, 4 Other.
Ops incl: local bus services, school contracts, private hire.
Livery: White/Blue, Silver/Blue
Ticket system: Wayfarer

D A PAYNE COACH HIRE
MANOR FARM, PAPWORTH ROAD, GRAVELEY, ST NEOTS
PE19 6PL
Tel: 01480 831303
Fax: 01480 831664
E-mail: david@dapaynecoachhire.co.uk
Web site: www.dapaynecoachire.co.uk
Prop: D A Payne
Sec: Mrs Carole Allen
Ops Man: R Wood
Fleet: 10 - 3 single-deck coach, 1 midibus, 1 midicoach, 2 minibus, 3 minicoach.
Ops incl: school contracts, excursions & tours, private hire.

PETERBOROUGH TRAVEL CONSULTANTS
12 BUCKLAND CLOSE, NETHERTON, PETERBOROUGH PE3 9UQ
Tel: 01733 267025
Fax: 01733 267025
E-mail: petertravelcon@aol.com
Web site: www.peterboroughtravelconsultants.co.uk
Prop: Mrs P C Greeves
Fleet: 3 - 2 single-deck coach, 1 minibus.
Chassis: 1 LDV, 2 Setra.
Ops incl: excursions & tours, school contracts, private hire, continental tours.
Livery: Blue/White/Red

RICHMOND'S COACHES
THE GARAGE, HIGH STREET, BARLEY, ROYSTON SG8 8JA
Tel: 01763 848226
Fax: 01763 848105
E-mail: postbox@richmonds-coaches.co.uk
Web site: www.richmonds-coaches.co.uk
Dirs: David Richmond, Michael Richmond, Andrew Richmond
Sales & Marketing Man: Rick Ellis
Asst Ops Man: Craig Ellis
Ch Eng: Patrick Granville
Exc & Tours Man: Natalie Richmond
Fleet: 25 – 18 single-deck coach, 1 double-deck coach, 5 midibus, 1 midicoach.
Chassis: 9 Bova, 5 DAF, 4 Mercedes, 2 Optare, 5 Volvo.
Bodies: 9 Bova, 2 Optare, 3 Plaxton, 1 Sitcar, 10 Van Hool.
Ops incl: local bus services, school contracts, excursions & tours, private hire, continental tours.
Livery: Cream/Brown
Ticket System: Wayfarer 3

ROBINSON KIMBOLTON
19 THRAPSTON ROAD, KIMBOLTON PE28 0HW
Tel: 01480 860581
E-mail: robinsoncharles@btconnect.com
Web site: www.robinsonkimbolton.co.uk
Man Dir: Charles Robinson
Fleet: 9 - 8 single-deck coach, 1 minibus
Chassis: 7 Dennis, 1 Scania, 1 Toyota.
Bodies: 3 Berkhof, 1 Caetano, 1 Duple, 3 Plaxton, 1 Van Hool.
Ops incl: private hire, school contracts.
Livery: Cream/Brown/Red

SAFFORD COACHES LTD
THE DRIFT, LITTLE GRANSDEN, SANDY SG19 3DP
Tel: 01767 677395
Fax: 01767 677742
E-mail: saffordscoaches@btconnect.com
Web site: www.saffordscoaches.co.uk
Dirs: Miss Tracey Gillett, Mrs Shirley Gillett, Mr Chris Chapman.
Fleet: 13 - 1 single-deck bus, 9 single-deck coach, 1 midicoach, 1 minibus, 1 minicoach.
Chassis: 1 Bova, 1 Ford Transit, 3 Mercedes, 8 Volvo.
Bodies: 1 Berkhof, 1 Bova,

2 Jonckheere, 3 Mercedes, 5 Plaxton.
Ops incl: local bus services, school contracts, excursions & tours, private hire, continental tours.
Livery: White with Blue/Yellow

SHAWS OF MAXEY
49 HIGH STREET, MAXEY
PE6 9EF
Tel: 01778 342224
Fax: 01778 380378
E-mail: enquiries@shawscoaches.co.uk
Web site: www.shawscoaches.co.uk
Partners: Jane Duffelen, Richard Shaw, Christopher Shaw
Fleet: 20 - 1 single-deck bus, 16 single-deck coach, 3 midicoach.
Chassis: 2 Bova, 1 DAF, 1 Dennis, 1 Iveco, 2 Mercedes, 1 Optare, 1 Toyota, 11 Volvo.
Bodies: 1 Autobus, 1 Berkhof, 1 Beulas, 2 Bova, 3 Jonckheere, 1 Optare, 10 Plaxton, 1 Reeve Burgess.
Ops incl: local bus services, school contracts, excursions & tours, private hire, continental tours.
Livery: Blue/White

STAGECOACH CAMBRIDGESHIRE
100 COWLEY ROAD,
CAMBRIDGE CB4 0DN
Tel: 01223 420544
Fax: 01223 433275
E-mail: cambridge.enquiries@stagecoachbus.com
Web site: www.stagecoachbus.com
Fleet Names: Stagecoach in Cambridge, Stagecoach in the Fens, Stagecoach in Peterborough
Man Dir: Andy Campbell
Comm Dir: Philip Norwell
Eng Dir: Bob Dennison
Fleet: 292 - 154 double-deck bus, 59 single-deck bus, 6 single-deck coach, 60 midibus, 7 minibus, 6 open-top bus.
Ops incl: local bus services.
Livery: Stagecoach UK Bus
Ticket system: Wayfarer 3
Part of Stagecoach East (with Stagecoach in Bedford)

SUN FUN INTERNATIONAL
SUN FUN HOUSE, MEADOW DROVE,
EARITH PE28 3SA
Tel: 01487 843333 **Fax:** 01487 843285
E-mail: sales@sunfunholidays.co.uk
Web site: www.sunfunholidays.co.uk
Ops incl: excursions & tours, private hire, continental tours.

TOWLERS COACHES LTD
CHURCH ROAD, EMNETH,
WISBECH PE14 8AA
Tel: 01945 583645
Fax: 01945 583645
E-mail: towlerscoaches@btconnect.com
Web site: www.towlerscoaches.co.uk
Dirs: Mark Towler, Wendy Shepherd, Anton Towler, Joanne Walton
Fleet: 9 - 4 double-deck bus, 5 single-deck coach.
Chassis: 1 Iveco, 4 Leyland, 2 Scania, 2 Volvo.
Bodies incl: 1 Beulas, 2 Berkhof, 4 Northern Counties, 1 Van Hool.
Ops incl: school contracts, excursions & tours, private hire.
Livery: White

UPWELL & DISTRICT COACHES
THE COACH DEPOT, SCHOOL ROAD,
UPWELL PE14 9EW
Tel: 01945 773461
Partners: Caroline Parsons, William Hircock.
Fleet: 3 single-deck coach.
Chassis: 1 Alexander Dennis, 1 MAN, 1 Scania.
Bodies: 1 Irizar, 1 Jonckheere, 1 Plaxton
Ops incl: excursions & tours, private hire, school contracts.
Livery: Red/White/Blue.

VEAZEY COACHES LTD
WINWICK GARAGE, HAMERTON
ROAD, HUNTINGDON PE28 5PX
Tel: 01832 293263
Fax: 01832 293142

VICEROY OF ESSEX LTD
See Essex

WEBB'S
ST PETER'S FARM,
MIDDLE DROVE PE14 8JJ
Tel: 01945 430123
E-mail: webb-s-cant@fsbdial.co.uk
Prop: Barry Webb
Fleet: 3 - 1 midicoach, 1 minicoach, 1 minibus.
Ops incl: local bus services

WHIPPET COACHES LTD
UNIT 1 & 2, ROWLES WAY,
BUCKINGWAY BUSINESS PARK,
SWAVESEY CB24 4UG
Tel: 01480 463792
Fax: 01480 495264
Web site: www.go-whippet.co.uk
Dirs: J. T. Lee, P. H. Lee, M. H. Lee.
Fleet: double-deck bus, single-deck bus, single-deck coach, midibus, minibus.
Chassis: Dennis, Leyland, Scania, Volvo.
Bodies: Alexander, Duple, East Lancs, Leyland, Northern Counties, Plaxton, Van Hool.
Ops incl: local bus service, school contracts, excursions & tours, private hire, express.
Livery: Blue/Cream with logo.
Ticket System: Almex Eurofare.

W & M TRAVEL
211 MAIN ROAD, CHURCH END,
PARSON DROVE, WISBECH
PE13 4LF
Tel: 01945 700492
Fax: 01945 700964
E-mail: bill@norman.wanadoo.co.uk
Dir: W Norman
Fleet: 6 single-deck coach.
Chassis: 5 Dennis, 1 Scania.
Ops incl: local bus services, school contracts, excursions & tours, private hire.

Advertising in the

The Little Red Book 2011

Passenger Transport Directory for the British Isles

For information regarding advertising contact:

Graham Middleton
Tel: 01780 484632
Fax: 01780 763388
E-mail:
graham.middleton@ianallanpublishing.co.uk

Ian Allan
PUBLISHING

Riverdene Business Park,
Molesey Road, Hersham,
Surrey KT12 4RG
Tel: 01932 266600
Fax: 01932 266601

Cambridgeshire, City of Peterborough

CHESHIRE EAST, CHESHIRE WEST & CHESTER, HALTON, WARRINGTON

ANGEL TRAVEL
108 GORSEY LANE,
WARRINGTON WA2 7RY
Tel: 07090 741550
Fax: 01925 445591
E-mail: angeltravelwarrington@yahoo.co.uk
Dir: Richard Keane
Fleet: 3 minibus.
Chassis: LDV, Mercedes.
Ops incl: school contracts, private hire, excursions & tours.
Livery: Blue/White

ANTHONYS TRAVEL
8 CORMORANT DRIVE,
RUNCORN WA7 4UD
Tel: 01928 561460
Fax: 01928 561460
Emergency: 07920 154240
E-mail: enquiries@anthonystravel.co.uk
Web site: www.anthonys-travel.co.uk
Partners: Richard Bamber, Anthony Bamber, Anne Bamber
Ops Man: Jodie Waring
Ch Eng: Stephen Knight
Fleet: 16 – 2 single-deck bus, 10 single-deck coach, 4 minicoach.
Chassis: 2 LDV, 3 MAN, 9 Mercedes, 2 Scania.
Bodies: 1 Berkhof, 1 Irizar, 2 LDV, 4 Mercedes, 5 Neoplan, 2 Optare, 1 Setra.
Ops incl: local bus services, school contracts, private hire, excursion & tours.
Livery: multi coloured
Ticket system: Wayfarer

ARRIVA NORTH WEST & WALES
Runcorn, Winsford operations – see Arriva Manchester (Greater Manchester)
Chester operations – see Arriva Buses Wales (Conwy)

ARROWEBROOK COACHES LTD
THE OLD COACH YARD,
WERVIN ROAD, CROUGHTON
CH2 4DA
Tel: 01244 382444
Fax: 01244 379777
Dirs: A. G. Parsons, P. A. Parsons
Ops Incl: local bus services
Livery: White/Green.

BARRATT'S COACHES LTD
UNIT 15, MILLBANK WAY, SPRINGVALE INDUSTRIAL ESTATE, ELWORTH
CW11 3GQ
Tel: 08450 625096
Fax: 08450 627728
E-mail: barrattscoaches@aol.com
Man Dir: Gillian Barratt
Fleet: 12 – 10 single-deck coaches, 1 double-deck coach, 1 midicoach.
Chassis: 1 Dennis, 1 Mercedes, 1 Neoplan, 9 Volvo.
Bodies: 1 Alexander Dennis, 1 Jonckheere, 1 Mercedes, 1 Neoplan, 4 Plaxton, 4 Van Hool.
Ops incl: local bus services, school contracts, excursions & tours, private hire.
Livery: White.

BENNETT'S TRAVEL
ATHLONE ROAD, LONGFORD,
WARRINGTON WA2 8JJ
Tel/Fax: 01925 415299
Fleetname: Warrington Coachways
Props: B. A. Bennett, D. B. Bennett.
Ops incl: local bus services
Livery: White/Blue.

BOSTOCK'S COACHES
SPRAGG STREET GARAGE,
CONGLETON CW12 1QH
Tel: 01260 273108
Fax: 01260 276338
E-mail: sales@holmeswood.uk.com
Web site: www.holmeswood.uk.com
Dirs: J F Aspinall, M Aspinall, C H Aspinall, D E Aspinall, M F Aspinall, M J Forshaw
Ops Man: M E Bostock
Tours Man: J Bostock-Gibson
Ch Eng: M Boniface
Fleet: 40 - 3 double-deck bus, 33 single-deck coach, 1 double-deck coach, 2 midicoach, 1 minicoach.
Chassis: 1 Ayats, 1 Bova, 7 DAF, 6 Dennis, 2 Iveco, 4 Leyland, 4 MAN, 9 Scania, 6 Volvo.
Bodies: 1 Ayats, 1 Beulas, 2 Berkhof, 1 Bova, 3 Caetano, 2 ECW, 1 East Lancs, 4 Ikarus, 1 Indcar,1 Irizar, 6 Marcopolo, 8 Plaxton, 9 Van Hool.
Ops incl: local bus services, excursions & tours, private hire, continental tours, school contracts.
Livery: Green
(Subsidiary of Holmeswood Coaches, Lancashire)

DOBSON'S BUSES LTD
OFF CHAPEL STREET, WINCHAM,
NORTHWICH CW9 6DA
Tel/Fax: 01606 350200
Man Dir: Ian Dobson
Ch Eng: Paul Dobson
Office Man: Richard Dobson
Fleet: 12 - 5 double-deck bus, 1 single-deck bus, 2 single-deck coach, 1 midibus, 3 midicoach.
Chassis: 3 Dennis, 1 Iveco, 3 Leyland, 1 MCW, 3 Mercedes, 1 Volvo.
Ops incl: school contracts
Livery: Red/Cream

FIRST IN CHESTER & THE WIRRAL
669 NEW CHESTER ROAD,
ROCK FERRY CH42 1PZ
Tel: 0151 645 8661
See First Manchester. Includes former Chester City Transport

JOHN FLANAGAN COACH TRAVEL
2 REDDISH HALL COTTAGES,
BROAD LANE, GRAPPENHALL,
WARRINGTON WA4 3HS
Tel: 01925 266115
Fax: 01925 261100
Recovery: 01925 266115
E-mail: admin@flanagancoaches.co.uk
Web site: www.flanagancoaches.co.uk
Fleet: 7 - 3 single-deck coach, 1 midicoach, 3 minicoach.
Chassis: 1 Dennis, 1 Ford, 3 Mercedes, 2 Volvo.
Bodies: 1 Berkhof, 1 Esker, 2 Mercedes, 1 UVG, 1 Van Hool, 1 other.
Ops incl: private hire, school contracts, excursions and tours.
Livery: Red/Black/White
(Subsidiary of Holmeswood Coaches, Lancashire)

GOLDEN GREEN TRAVEL
COWBROOK LANE, GAWSWORTH,
MACCLESFIELD SK11 0JH
Tel: 01260 223453
E-mail: goldengreentravel@hotmail.com
Web site: www.goldengreentravel.co.uk
Partners: John Worth, Gill Worth, Derek J Lownds
Fleet: 11 single-deck coaches
Chassis and Bodies: Mercedes
Ops incl: local bus services, school contracts, excursions & tours, private hire

HALTON BOROUGH TRANSPORT LTD
MOOR LANE, WIDNES WA8 7AF
Tel: 0151 423 3333
Fax: 0151 424 2362
E-mail: enquiries@haltontransport.co.uk
Web site: www.haltontransport.co.uk
Fleet Name: Halton Transport
Man Dir: Chris Adams
Eng Man: Phil Matthews
Traf Man: David Steadman
Fin Man: Adele Cookson
Fleet: 65 single-deck bus.
Chassis: 59 Alexander Dennis, 6 Leyland.
Bodies: 21 East Lancs, 6 Leyland, 38 Marshall/MCV.
Ops incl: local bus services.
Livery: Red/Cream.
Ticket System: Wayfarer III

HULME HALL COACHES LTD
1 STANLEY ROAD,
CHEADLE HULME SK8 6PL
Tel: 0161 486 1187
Fax: 0161 482 8125
E-mail: hulmehallcoaches@talk21.com
Gen Man: Philip Keogh
Traf Man: Ian Johnson
Fleet Eng: Philip Henshall
Fleet: 14 - 4 double-deck bus,

	Vehicle suitable for disabled	Seat belt-fitted Vehicle	24 hour recovery service
	Toilet-drop facilities available	Coach(es) with galley facilities	Replacement vehicle available
	Recovery service available	Air-conditioned vehicle(s)	Vintage Coach(es) available
	Open top vehicle(s)	Coaches with toilet facilities	

The Little Red Book 2011 - in association with *tbf* Transport Benevolent Fund

7 single-deck bus, 3 single-deck coach.
Chassis: 4 Leyland, 10 Volvo.
Bodies: 4 Alexander Dennis, 3 ECW, 2 Northern Counties, 5 Plaxton.
Ops incl: school contracts, private hire.
Livery: Red/Cream
Ticket System: Wayfarer 2

LAMBS COACHES
2A BUXTON STREET, HAZEL GROVE, STOCKPORT SK7 4BB
Tel: 0161 456 1515
Fax: 0161 483 5011
E-mail: lambs139@aol.com
Web site: www.lambscoaches.net
Man Dir: Geoff Lamb
Dir: Graham Lamb
Comp Sec: Christine Lamb
Fleet: 7 - 7 single-deck coach
Chassis: 2 DAF, 2 Scania, 1 Setra, 2 Volvo.
Bodies: 1 Setra, 6 Van Hool.
Ops incl: private hire, school contracts.
Livery: White/Blue

LE-RAD COACHES & LIMOUSINES
328 HYDE ROAD, WOODLEY SK6 1PF
Tel: 0161 430 2032
Prop: Derek & Jean Mycock
E-mail: le.radtravel@yahoo.co.uk
Fleet: 3 - 2 single-deck coach, 1 minicoach.
Chassis: 1 DAF, 1 Ford, 1 LDV.
Bodies: 1 Caetano, 1 LDV, 1 Plaxton.
Ops incl: excursions & tours, private hire.

ROY McCARTHY COACHES
THE COACH DEPOT, SNAPE ROAD, MACCLESFIELD SK10 2NZ
Tel: 01625 425060
Fax: 01625 619853
E-mail: sales@roymccarthycoaches.co.uk
Web site: www.roymccarthycoaches.co.uk
Senior Partner: Andy McCarthy
Fleet: 10 single-deck coach.
Chassis: 1 Bedford, 2 Dennis, 7 Volvo.
Bodies: 10 Plaxton.
Ops incl: school contracts, excursions & tours, private hire, continental tours.
Livery: Blue/Cream

MARPLE MINI COACHES
5 GROSVENOR ROAD, MARPLE SK6 6PR.
Tel: 0161 881 9111
Owner: G. W. Cross
Fleet: 2 minicoach
Chassis: Ford Transit, LDV.
Ops incl: school contracts, private hire.
Livery: White/Gold.

MAYNE COACHES LTD
MARSH HOUSE LANE, WARRINGTON WA1 7ET
Tel: 0161 223 2035
Fax: 0161 223 1835
E-mail: coaches@mayne.co.uk
Web site: www.mayne.co.uk
Dirs: S B Mayne (**Chairman & Man Dir**), D Mayne (**Co Sec**), C S Mayne, S L Mayne **Gen Man:** R W Vernon
Sales Mans: A J Dykes, D Williams
Eng Dir: C F Pannel
Eng Man: E Sutcliffe
Traffic Man: J Drake

Fleet: 38 - 2 double-deck bus, 36 single-deck coach.
Chassis: 4 Alexander Dennis, 3 Bova, 31 Scania.
Bodies: 3 Bova, 2 East Lancs, 24 Irizar, 7 Plaxton, 2 UVG.
Ops incl: local bus services, school contracts, excursions & tours, private hire.
Livery: Cream/Red

MEREDITHS COACHES LTD
LYDGATE, WELL STREET, MALPAS SK14 8DE
Tel: 01948 860405
Fax: 01948 860162
E-mail: info@meredithscoaches.co.uk
Web site: www.meredithscoaches.co.uk
Dirs: J K Meredith, Mrs M E Meredith, D J Meredith **Co Sec:** Mrs Kirin Meredith
Ch Eng: C Bellis
Fleet: 18 single-deck coach
Chassis: Leyland, Scania, Volvo.
Bodies: Irizar, Jonckheere, Plaxton.
Ops incl: local bus services, school contracts, private hire.
Livery: Cream with Red/Yellow

MILLMANS COACHES
STATION YARD, GREEN LANE, PADGATE, WARRINGTON WA1 4JR
Tel: 01925 822298
Fax: 01925 813181
Prop: Eric Millman
Fleet: 7 single-deck coach
Chassis: 1 DAF, 6 Leyland.
Ops incl: local bus services, school contracts, excursions & tours, private hire.
Livery: Blue/White

MOORE'S COACHES LTD
53 REES CRESCENT, HOLMES CHAPEL CW4 7NL
Tel/Fax: 01477 537004
Dirs: D. M. Moore, J. C. Moore.
Fleet: 4 single-deck coach.
Chassis: 1 Dennis, 1 Scania, 1 Volvo, 1 Van Hool.
Bodies: 1 Jonckheere, 1 Plaxton, 2 Van Hool.
Ops incl: excursions & tours, private hire, express, continental tours, school contracts.
Livery: Moore's Coaches/Nat. Express.

SELWYNS TRAVEL SERVICES
CAVENDISH FARM ROAD, WESTON, RUNCORN WA7 4LU
Tel: 01928 564515
Fax: 01928 591872
Recovery: 01928 572108
E-mail: sales@selwyns.co.uk
Web site: www.selwyns.co.uk
Man Dir: Selwyn A Jones
Gen Man: Alan P Williamson
Co Sec/Acct: Richard E Williams
Fleet Eng: Cledwyn Owen
Fleet: 44 - 9 single-deck bus, 33 single-deck coach, 1 midibus, 1 minicoach.
Chassis: 31 DAF, 1 Caetano, 1 Dennis, 2 Mercedes, 1 Optare, 6 Tecnobus, 2 Volvo.
Bodies: 1 Caetano, 3 Ikarus, 2 Mercedes, 1 Optare, 6 Pantheon, 2 Plaxton, 27 Van Hool.
Ops incl: local bus services, school contracts, excursions & tours, private hire, express, continental tours.
Livery: White/Blue/Orange/Green
Ticket System: Wayfarer
See also Greater Manchester

SHEARINGS HOLIDAYS
BARLEYCASTLE LANE, APPLETON, WARRINGTON WA4 4FR
Tel: 01925 214600
Fax: 01925 262606
See Shearings Holidays, Greater Manchester.

SMITHS OF MARPLE
72 CROSS LANE, MARPLE SK6 7PZ
Tel: 0161 427 2825
Fax: 0161 449 7731
Dirs: Anthony Vernon, Angie Vernon
Fleet: 12 - 5 double-deck bus, 2 single-deck bus, 3 single-deck coach, 2 midicoach
Ops incl: local bus services, school contracts, excursions & tours, private hire.
Livery: White/Orange-Rose.
Ticket System: Wayfarer

JIM STONES COACHES
THE JAYS, LIGHT OAKS ROAD, GLAZEBURY, WARRINGTON WA3 5LH
Tel/Fax: 01925 766465
E-mail: jimstones@ic24.net
Web site: www.jimstonescoaching.com
Partners: J B Stones, Mrs J P Stones
Gen Man: R Dyson
Fleet Eng: S Mayo
Fleet: 16 - single-deck bus.
Chassis: 11 Alexander Dennis, 1 Dennis, 3 Leyland, 1 Volvo.
Bodies: 1 Alexander, 11 Alexander Dennis, 1 DAB, 1 East Lancs, 1 Plaxton, 1 Wright
Ops incl: local bus services, school contracts
Livery: Blue/White
Ticket System: Almex, Wayfarer 3, Setright

WARRINGTON BOROUGH TRANSPORT LTD
WILDERSPOOL CAUSEWAY, WARRINGTON WA4 6PT
Tel: 01925 634296
Fax: 01925 418382
Web site: www.warringtonboroughtransport.co.uk
Fleet Name: Network Warrington
Man Dir: David Squire
Comm Man: Phil Pearson
Eng Man: Damian Graham
Fleet: 126 - 24 double-deck bus, 93 midibus, 9 minibus.
Chassis: 6 DAF, 33 Dennis, 13 Leyland, 9 Optare, 23 Volvo, 42 VDL.
Bodies: 17 Alexander Dennis, 1 East Lancs, 29 Marshall, 4 MCV, 6 Northern Counties, 9 Optare, 60 Wright.
Ops incl: local bus services, school contracts, private hire.
Livery: Red/Cream
Ticket System: Wayfarer 3

WHITEGATE TRAVEL LTD
15 BEAUTY BANK, WHITEGATE, NORTHWICH CW8 2BP
Tel: 01606 882760
Fax: 01606 883356
Owner: K. Prince
Fleet: 12 minibus
Chassis: 1 Ford Transit, 2 Freight Rover, 2 Iveco, 5 LDV, 2 Mercedes.
Ops incl: local bus services, school contracts, private hire.
Livery: Yellow/White

CORNWALL

BAKER'S COACHES
THE GARAGE, DULOE, LISKEARD
PL14 4PL
Tel: 01503 262359
Fax: 01503 262422
E-mail: KBaker5678@aol.com
Fleet Name: KTM Coaches
Fleet incl: single-deck coach, midicoach, minibus
Ops incl: school contracts, private hire.

CARADON RIVIERA TOURS
THE GARAGE, UPTON CROSS,
LISKEARD PL14 5AX
Tel: 01579 362226
Fax: 01579 362220
Prop: John K. Deeble.
Fleet: 31 – 12 single-deck bus,
10 single-deck coach, 2 midibus,
4 midicoach, 3 minicoach.
Chassis: 8 Alexander Dennis, 3 LDV,
12 Leyland, 8 MCW.
Bodies: 3 Duple, 1 Leicester, 1 Mellor,
8 Optare, 12 Plaxton, 1 Reeve Burgess,
2 UVG, 3 Wadham Stringer.
Ops incl: school contracts, private hire.
Livery: Cream/Blue.

DAC COACHES LTD
RYLANDS GARAGE, ST ANN'S
CHAPEL, GUNNISLAKE PL18 9HW
Tel: 01822 834571
Fax: 01822 833881
Recovery: 01822 834571
E-mail: dac.coaches@btconnect.com
Web site: www.daccoaches.co.uk
Dirs: Bernard Harding, Nick Smith
Fleet: 16 – 8 single-deck bus,
6 single-deck coach, 2 midicoach.
Chassis: 3 Iveco, 8 Mercedes, 5 Volvo.
Bodies: 3 Beulas, 1 Caetano,
1 Jonckheere, 2 Mercedes, 8 Plaxton,
1 Van Hool.
Ops incl: local bus services, school contracts, excursions & tours, private hire, continental tours.
Livery: White
Ticket System: Almex A90.

DARLEY FORD TRAVEL
DARLEY FORD, LISKEARD PL14 5AS
Tel: 01579 362272
Fax: 01579 363425
Owner: Albert J Deeble
Fleet: 8 – 8 single-deck coaches
Chassis: 2 Scania, 6 Volvo.
Ops incl: private hire, excursions & tours, continental tours.
Livery: White

FIRST DEVON & CORNWALL LTD
See Devon

GROUP TRAVEL
DUNMERE ROAD GARAGE, DUNMERE
ROAD, BODMIN PL31 2QN
Tel: 01208 77989
Fax: 01208 77989
E-mail: benneymoon@btinternet.com
Web site: www.grouptravelcoachhire.com
Dirs: Dawn Moon, David Benny
Fleet: 21 - 7 single-deck coach,
2 midicoach, 11 minibus, 1 minicoach.
Chassis: 2 Autosan, 1 Bova, 2 Dennis,

1 MAN, 1 Marshall, 10 Mercedes,
1 Optare, 1 Setra, 2 Volvo.
Bodies: 1 Bova, 1 Caetano,
1 Jonckheere, 1 Marshall, 5 Mellor,
1 Optare, 5 Plaxton, 1 Setra, 1 Van Hool,
4 other.
Ops incl: local bus services, school contracts, excursions & tours, private hire
Livery: Avalon Signs
Ticket system: Almex A90

HILLS SERVICES LTD
See Devon

HOOKWAYS JENNINGS
LANSDOWNE ROAD, BUDE EX23 8BN
Tel: 01288 352359
Fax: 01288 352140
Recovery: 07850 038707
E-mail: barry@hookways.com
Web site: www.hookways.com
Man Dir: Alistair Gray **Dirs:** Kym Hookway **(Holidays)**, Susan Hookway, Jason Hookway **(Traffic)**, Martin Hookway **(Eng)**, Julie Hookway **(Sec)**
Fleet: See Devon
Ops incl: local bus services, school contracts, excursions & tours, private hire, express, continental tours.
Livery: Yellow
Part of Hookways Pleasureways (Devon)

HOPLEYS COACHES LTD
GOVER FARM, GOVER HILL,
MOUNT HAWKE, TRURO TR4 8BH
Tel: 01872 553786
E-mail: hopleyscoaches@tiscali.co.uk
Web site: www.hopleyscoaches.com
Partners: B. Hopley, D. R. Hopley,
N. A. Hopley.
Fleet: 16 - 1 double-deck bus, 4 single-deck bus, 11 single-deck coach.
Ops incl: local bus services, school contracts, excursions & tours, private hire.
Livery: Red/White/Grey.
Ticket System: Wayfarer 3.

MOUNTS BAY COACHES
4 ALEXANDRA ROAD, PENZANCE
TR18 4LY
Tel: 01736 363320
Fax: 01736 366985
E-mail: mountsbaycoaches@btconnect.com
Web site: www.mountsbaycoaches.co.uk
Dir: Jeff Oxenham
Fleet: 8 - 6 single-deck coach,
2 midicoach.
Chassis: 2 Toyota, 6 Volvo.
Bodies: 2 Caetano, 6 Van Hool.
Ops incl: school contracts, excursions & tours, private hire.
Livery: Blue/White

OTS MINIBUS & COACH HIRE
48 FORE STREET, CONSTANTINE,
FALMOUTH TR11 5AB
Tel: 01326 340703
Fax: 01326 340404
E-mail: salots@hotmail.com
Web site: www.otsfalmouth.co.uk
Co Sec: Stephen Moore
Ops Man: Benjamin Moore
Fleet: 5 - 1 single-deck coach,
1 midicoach, 2 minibus, 1 minicoach.
Chassis: 4 Mercedes, 1 Volvo.

Bodies: 3 Mercedes, 1 Sitcar,
1 Van Hool.
Ops incl: local bus services, school contracts, excursions & tours, private hire.
Livery: White with Blue & Brown
Ticket system: Microfare

PENMERE MINIBUS SERVICES
28 BOSMOOR ROAD, FALMOUTH
TR11 4PU
Tel/Fax: 01326 314165
E-mail: enquiries@penmereminibus.co.uk
Web site: www.penmereminibus.co.uk
Man: Ben Moore
Fleet: 2 - 1 minibus, 1 minicoach.
Chassis: 2 Mercedes.
Ops incl: local bus services,
school contracts, private hire.
Livery: Blue/Brown stripes.
Ticket system: Manual

ROSELYN COACHES LTD
MIDDLEWAY GARAGE, ST BLAZEY
ROAD, PAR PL24 2JA
Tel: 01726 813737 **Fax:** 01726 813737
Recovery: 01726 813737
E-mail: jonathan.ede@roselyncoaches.co.uk
Web site: www.roselyncoaches.co.uk
Man Dir: Jonathan Ede **Dir:** Karen Paramor **Ch Eng:** Graham Paramor
Ops Man: John Stoneman
Fleet: 44 - 10 double-deck bus, 34 single-deck coach.
Chassis: 3 DAF, 10 Leyland, 3 Scania,
28 Volvo.
Bodies: 3 Alexander Dennis, 2 Bova,
1 Caetano, 1 Jonckheere, 10 Northern Counties, 14 Plaxton, 14 Van Hool.
Ops incl: school contracts, private hire, continental tours.
Livery: Green/Gold

SUMMERCOURT TRAVEL LTD
THE OLD COACH GARAGE,
ST AUSTELL STREET,
SUMMERCOURT TR8 5DR
Tel: 01726 861108
Fax: 01726 860093
E-mail: rob@summercourttravel.com
Web site: www.summercourttravel.com
Dirs: R D Ryder, S M Ryder **(Ops)**
Fleet: 20 – 2 double-deck bus,
1 single-deck bus, 15 midibus, 2 minibus.
Chassis: 2 Dennis, 2 LDV, 1 Leyland,
15 Mercedes.
Ops incl: local bus services, school contracts, excursions & tours, private hire.
Livery: White

TAVISTOCK COMMUNITY TRANSPORT
GREENLANDS, ST ANN'S CHAPEL,
GUNNISLAKE PL18 9HW
Tel: 01822 833574
E-mail: keithp44@btinternet.com
Fleet Name: Tavistock Country Bus
Chmn: K W Potter **Sec:** A Everitt
Fleet: 1 minibus
Chassis: Iveco
Body: G M Coachwork.
Ops incl: local bus services, private hire.
Livery: Red/White
Ticket System: Wayfarer

TILLEY'S COACHES
THE COACH STATION, WAINHOUSE CORNER, BUDE EX23 0AZ
Tel: 01840 230244
Fax: 01840 230752
Man Dir: Paul Tilley
Fleet: 12 single-deck coaches
Ops incl: school contracts, private hire, excursions & tours
Livery: White/Cream/Maroon.

TRELEY COACH HIRE
ST BURYAN GARAGE, ST BURYAN, PENZANCE TR19 6DZ
Tel: 01736 810322
Fax: 01736 810708
Man Dir: J Ley **Dir:** A J Ley
Co Sec: A D Ley
Fleet: 4 - 3 single-deck coach, 1 minicoach
Chassis: 3 Alexander Dennis, 1 Mercedes.
Bodies incl: 1 Berkhof, 1 Duple.

WESTERN GREYHOUND LTD
WESTERN HOUSE, ST AUSTELL STREET, SUMMERCOURT, NEWQUAY TR8 5DR
Tel: 01637 871871
Recovery: 01872 510511 Ext 25
E-mail: enquiries@westerngreyhound.com
Web site: www.westerngreyhound.com
Man Dir: Mark Howarth **Co Sec:** Mari Howarth **Dir:** Robin Orbell **Ops Man:** Brian James
Fleet: 122 - 21 double-deck bus, 30 single-deck bus, 60 midibus, 4 minibus, 1 open-top bus, 6 heritage.
Chassis: 5 AEC, 2 Alexander Dennis, 2 Bristol, 6 Dennis, 71 Mercedes, 23 Optare, 13 Volvo.
Bodies: 2 Alexander Dennis, 2 ECW, 15 East Lancs, 7 Mercedes, 1 Metro-Cammell, 23 Optare, 4 Park Royal, 64 Plaxton, 4 UVG.
Ops incl: local bus services, school contracts, excursions & tours, private hire.
Livery: Green/White
Ticket System: ERG

WHEAL BRITON TRAVEL
MOOR COTTAGE, BLACKWATER, TRURO TR4 8ET
Tel: 01872 560281
Fax: 01872 560691
Web site: www.whealbritontravel.com
Prop: Stephen J Palmer
Fleet: 22- 20 single-deck coach, 1 midicoach,1 minibus.
Chassis: 1 LDV, 1 Toyota, 20 Volvo.
Bodies: 1 Caetano, 5 Jonckheere, 14 Plaxton, 2 Van Hool.
Ops incl: school contracts, excursions & tours, private hire, continental tours.
Livery: Cream

WILLIAMS TRAVEL
DOLCOATH INDUSTRIAL PARK, DOLCOATH ROAD, CAMBORNE TR14 8RA
Tel: 01209 717152
Fax: 01209 612511
E-mail: enquiries@williams-travel.co.uk
Web site: www.williams-travel.co.uk
Prop: Fred Williams **Operations:** Garry Williams **Workshop:** John Williams
Fleet: 51 – 7 double-deck bus, 4 single-deck bus, 15 single-deck coach, 3 midicoach, 20 minibus, 2 minicoach.
Chassis: 2 Alexander Dennis, 2 Bova, 3 DAF, 4 Ford Transit, 12 Iveco, 2 LDV, 2 Leyland Tiger, 5 Mercedes, 19 Volvo.
Bodies: 2 Bova, 5 ECW, 1 East Lancs, 1 Esker, 1 Jonckheere, 2 Mellor, 1 Northern Counties, 2 Plaxton, 4 Reeve Burgess, 17 Van Hool, 1 Wadham Stringer, 14 Other.
Ops incl: local bus services, school contracts, excursions & tours, private hire, continental tours.
Livery: White Base with Black & Gold.

CUMBRIA

FRANK ALLISON LTD
MAIN STREET, BROUGH, KIRKBY STEPHEN CA17 4AY
Tel: 01768 341328
Fax: 01768 341517
Web site: www.grand-prix-services.com
E-mail: frank@grandprixservices.co.uk
Fleet Name: Grand Prix Services
Dir: Frank Allison
Fleet: 14 – 1 single-deck bus, 5 single-deck coach, 2 midicoach, 6 minibus.
Chassis: 1 Ford, 1 LDV, 2 Mercedes, 1 VDL, 6 Volvo, 3 Other.
Bodies: 1 Caetano, 1 Duple, 1 LDV, 1 Mercedes, 3 Plaxton, 1 Van Hool, 1 Wright, 5 Other.
Ops incl: local bus services, school contracts, excursions & tours, private hire.
Livery: White
Ticket System: Wayfarer TGX150

APOLLO 8 TRAVEL
KNOTT HALL FARM, LOWGILL, KENDAL LA8 9DG
Tel: 01539 824086
Fax: 01539 824239
E-mail: info@apollo8travel.co.uk
Web site: www.apollo8travel.co.uk
Ops incl: local bus services, private hire
Livery: White

ROBERT BENSON COACHES LTD
7 MAIN ROAD, SEATON, WORKINGTON CA14 1ES
Tel: 01900 511245
Web site: www.robertbensonworkington.co.uk
Fleet incl: single-deck coach, midicoach, minibus, minicoach
Chassis: Mercedes, Volkswagen, Volvo
Ops incl: private hire, school contracts

D K & N BOWMAN
BURTHWAITE HILL, BURTHWAITE, WREAY, CARLISLE CA4 0RT
Tel: 01697 473262
Fax: 01697 473262
E-mail: enquiries@bowmans-coaches.co.uk
Web site: www.bowmans-coaches.co.uk
Partners: David K Bowman, Nora Bowman **Manager:** Andrew Bowman
Fleet: 8 – 7 single-deck coach, 1 vintage coach.
Chassis: 3 AEC, 4 Scania, 1 Volvo.
Bodies: 1 Irizar, 1 Jonckheere, 2 Plaxton, 3 Van Hool, 1 Other.
Ops incl: school contracts, excursions and tours, private hire.
Livery: Royal Ivory/Red

S H BROWNRIGG
ENNERDALE MILL, EGREMONT CA22 2PN
Tel: 01946 822926
Fax: 01946 821919
E-mail: enquiries@shbrownrigg.co.uk
Web site: www.shbrownrigg.co.uk
Dir: R J Cook **Ops Man:** B Marshall
Senior Officers: Mrs D Marshall, Mrs L Holliday
Fleet: 22 - 12 single-deck coach, 6 midibus, 4 minibus.
Chassis: 2 Ford Transit, 6 Mercedes, 1 Scania, 12 Volvo.
Bodies: Plaxton, Van Hool.
Ops incl: school contracts, private hire.
Livery: Purple/White

CALDEW COACHES LTD
6 CALDEW DRIVE, DALSTON, CARLISLE CA5 7NS

Tel/Fax: 01228 711690
E-mail: caldewcoachesltd@aol.com
Web site: www.caldewcoaches.co.uk
Dirs: Hugh McKerrell, Ann McKerrell, Bill Rogers **Co Sec:** Mandy Rogers
Fleet: 14 - 2 single-deck coach, 8 midicoach, 4 minicoach.
Chassis: 1 Bova, 12 Mercedes, 1 Other.
Bodies: 1 Bova, 12 Mercedes, 1 Other.
Ops incl: school contracts, excursions & tours, private hire.
Livery: Red/White

CARR'S COACHES
CONTROL TOWER, THE AIRFIELD, SILLOTH CA7 4NS
Tel: 01697 331276
Fax: 01697 333826
Web site: www.carrs-coaches.co.uk
Prop: A J Markley **Ch Eng:** Fred Gill
Fleet: 9 - 4 single-deck coach, 2 midibus, 1 midicoach, 2 minibus.
Chassis: 1 Dennis, 3 Ford Transit, 1 Leyland, 2 Mercedes, 2 Scania.
Bodies: 2 Duple, 1 Optare, 2 Van Hool.
Ops incl: local bus services, school contracts, private hire.
Livery: Blue/White.

CLARKSON COACHWAYS LTD
UNIT 2B, ASHBURNER WAY, WALNEY ROAD INDUSTRIAL ESTATE, BARROW IN FURNESS LA14 5UZ
Tel: 01229 828022
Fax: 01229 828022
E-mail: info@clarksoncoachways.co.uk
Web site: www.clarksoncoachways.co.uk
Dirs: Susan Clarkson, Neil Clarkson
Fleet: 13 - 8 single-deck coach, 1 open-top bus, 3 midicoach, 1 minicoach.
Chassis: 5 Dennis, 1 Ford, 1 Leyland, 3 MAN, 1 Mercedes.
Bodies: 1 Alexander, 4 Berkhof, 3 Caetano, 1 Crest, 1 Marcopolo, 1 Optare.
Ops incl: school contracts, excursions & tours, private hire.
Livery: two-tone Green

COAST TO COAST PACKHORSE LTD
CHESTNUT HOUSE, CROSBY GARRETT, KIRKBY STEPHEN CA17 4PR
Tel: 01768 371777
Fax: 01768 371777
E-mail: packhorse@cumbria.com
Web site: www.cumbria.com/packhorse
Operator: J. Bowman.
Fleet: 2 minibus.
Chassis: 2 Ford Transit.
Ops incl: local bus services, school contracts, private hire.

CUMBRIA COACHES LTD
ALGA HOUSE, BRUNEL WAY, DURRANHILL INDUSTRIAL ESTATE, CARLISLE CA1 3NQ
Tel: 01228 404300
Fax: 01228 404309
Dirs: Dennis Smith, H. Humble
Ops Man: S. Hall.
Fleet: 12 - 8 single-deck coach, 4 double-deck coach.
Chassis: 2 Neoplan, 2 Setra, 8 Volvo.
Bodies: 4 Duple, 2 Jonckheere, 2 Neoplan, 2 Plaxton, 2 Setra.
Ops incl: excursions & tours, private hire,

express, continental tours, school contracts.

JOHN HOBAN TRAVEL LTD
22 KING STREET, WORKINGTON CA14 4DJ
Tel: 01900 603579 **Fax:** 01900 605528
E-mail: johnahoban@aol.com
Partners: John Hoban, Allison Hoban
Fleet: 10 - 6 minicoach, 4 midicoach.
Chassis/Bodies: 10 Mercedes
Ops incl: local bus services, private hire

IRVINGS COACH HIRE LTD
JESMOND STREET, CARLISLE CA1 2DE
Tel: 01228 521666
Fax: 01228 515792
Recovery: 07803 833845
E-mail: office@irvings-coaches.co.uk
Web site: www.irvings-coaches.co.uk
Man Dir: R Irving **Dir:** Miss A Irving
Tran Man: J K Cartner
Fleet: 10 - 10 single-deck coach.
Chassis: 2 DAF, 8 Volvo.
Bodies: 2 Bova, 1 Caetano, 1 Duple, 1 Jonckheere, 1 Plaxton, 1 Sunsundegui, 3 Van Hool.
Ops incl: excursions & tours, private hire, school contracts.
Livery: Orange/Black/White.

K & B TRAVEL LTD
33 KING STREET, PENRITH CA11 7AY
Tel: 01768 868600 **Fax:** 01768 862715
E-mail: mail@kbtravel.co.uk
Web site: www.kbtravel.co.uk
Man Dir: G Lund **Dirs:** B Bainbridge (**Co Sec**), T Lund
Fleet: 15 - 10 single-deck coach, 1 minibus, 4 midibus.
Chassis: 5 MAN, 5 Mercedes, 4 Volvo.
Bodies: 1 Berkhof, 4 Mercedes, 5 Neoplan, 1 Optare, 4 Van Hool.
Ops incl: local bus services, excursions & tours, private hire, school contracts, continental tours.
Livery: Blue with Green lettering

LAKES SUPERTOURS
1 HIGH STREET, WINDERMERE LA23 1AF
Tel: 01539 442751
Fax: 01539 446026
Dirs: R. Minford, A. Dobson
Fleet: 3 minibus.
Chassis: 2 Renault, 1 Vauxhall.
Ops incl: excursions & tours.
Livery: White/Purple/Gold.

LECKS TRAVEL
HAVERTHWAITE, ULVERSTON LA12 8AB
Tel: 01539 587128
Fax: 01539 531225
Web site: www.leckstravelinternationalla12.co.uk
Ops incl: local bus services, private hire

MESSENGERS COACHES LTD
MEALSGATE STATION, WIGTON CA7 1JP
Tel: 01697 371111
Fax: 01697 371112
Web site: www.messengerscoaches.co.uk
Man Dir: Liam Walker **Dir:** Mrs Angie Walker
Fleet: 10 - 9 single-deck coach, 1 midicoach.

Chassis: 1 Mercedes, 9 Volvo.
Bodies: 2 Jonckheere, 2 Plaxton, 6 Van Hool.
Ops incl: school contracts, excursions & tours, private hire, continental tours.

MOUNTAIN GOAT LTD
VICTORIA STREET, WINDERMERE LA23 1AD
Tel: 015394 45161
Fax: 015394 45164
E-mail: enquiries@mountain-goat.com
Web site: www.mountain-goat.com
Dirs: Peter Nattrass, Stephen Broughton, Norman Stoller **Fleet Man:** Steve Loveland **Office Man:** Sue Todd
Fleet: 15 - 14 minicoach, 1 car.
Chassis: 6 Mercedes, 8 Renault.
Ops incl: local bus services, excursions & tours, private hire, continental tours.
Livery: Green/Red on White
Ticket system: Wayfarer

NBM HIRE LTD
CROMWELL ROAD, PENRITH CA11 7JW
Tel: 01768 892727
Fax: 01768 899680
E-mail: sales@nbmtravel.co.uk
Web site: www.nbmtravel.co.uk
Ops incl: excursions & tours, private hire, school contracts

REAYS COACHES LTD
STRAWBERRY FIELDS, SYKE PARK, WIGTON CA7 9NE
Tel: 016973 49999 **Fax:** 016973 49900
E-mail: info@reays.co.uk
Web site: www.reays.co.uk
Man Dir: Chris Reay **Dir:** Nicola Reay
Ops Man: Chris Bowness
Fleet: 40 - 2 single-deck bus, 18 single-deck coach, 1 midicoach, 8 minibus, 11 minicoach.
Chassis: 2 Alexander Dennis, 10 Bova, 4 Iveco, 13 Mercedes, 9 Volvo.
Bodies incl: 10 Bova, 1 Mercedes, 15 Plaxton.
Ops incl: local bus services, school contracts, excursions & tours, private hire, continental tours.
Livery: Reays Blue & White Triangles.
Ticket System: Wayfarer

ROBINSONS COACHES
STATION ROAD GARAGE, APPLEBY CA16 6TX
Tel: 01768 351424
Fax: 01768 352199
Prop: S E Graham
Fleet: 9 - 5 single-deck coach, 4 minibus.
Chassis: 2 Dennis, 1 Iveco, 2 LDV, 1 Mercedes, 1 Scania, 2 Volvo.
Bodies: include: 1 Alexander Dennis, 1 Jonckheere, 2 LDV, 1 Plaxton, 1 Van Hool, 1 Wadham Stringer.
Ops incl: local bus services, school contracts, private hire.
Livery: Green/White

KEN ROUTLEDGE TRAVEL
ALLERDALE HOUSE WORKSHOPS, LOW ROAD, BRIGHAM, COCKERMOUTH CA13)XH
Tel: 01900 822795
Fax: 01900 822593
Fleet incl: single-deck coach, midicoach. Minicoach
Chassis: Mercedes
Ops incl: local bus services, private hire.

SIMS TRAVEL
HUNHOLME GARAGE, BOOT, HOLMROOK CA19 1TF
Tel: 019467 23227
Fax: 019467 23158
E-mail: info@simstravel.co.uk
Web site: www.simstravel.co.uk
Partners: Andrew Sim, Peter Sim
Fleet: 10 - 6 coach, 2 midicoach, 2 minibus.
Chassis incl: 2 Bova, 1 Neoplan, 3 Volvo.
Bodies incl: 1 Berkhof, 2 Bova, 1 Neoplan, 2 Van Hool.
Ops incl: excursions & tours, private hire, school contracts.
Livery: White/Red/Maroon

STACEY'S COACHES LTD
UNIT 3, MILLRACE ROAD, WILLOWHOLME INDUSTRIAL ESTATE, CARLISLE CA2 3RS
Tel: 01228 511127
Web site: www.staceys-coaches.co.uk
Fleet: 40 – single-deck coach, midicoach, minibus
Ops incl: local bus services, excursions & tours, school contracts, private hire

STAGECOACH NORTH WEST LTD
BROADACRE HOUSE, 16-20 LOWTHER STREET, CARLISLE CA3 8DA
Tel: 01228 597222
Fax: 01228 597888
E-mail: enquiries.northwest@stagecoachbus.com
Web site: www.stagecoachbus.com
Fleet Name: Stagecoach in Cumbria/Lancashire
Man Dir: Christopher J Bowles
Eng Dir: Paul W Lee
Ops Dir: Philip C Smith
Comm Man: James P Mellor
Fleet: 490 - 180 double-deck bus, 115 single-deck bus, 13 single-deck coach, 8 open-top bus, 78 midibus, 96 minibus.
Chassis: 140 Alexander Dennis, 25 Leyland, 45 MAN, 12 Mercedes, 97 Optare, 31 Scania, 140 Volvo.
Bodies: 335 Alexander Dennis, 9 East Lancs, 6 Jonckheere, 12 Marshall/MCV,

1 Northern Counties, 97 Optare, 24 Plaxton, 6 Transbus.
Ops incl: local bus services, school contracts, excursions & tours, private hire, express.
Livery: Stagecoach UK Bus
Ticket System: Wayfarer TGX

F W STAINTON & SON LTD
39 BURTON ROAD, KENDAL LA9 7LJ
Tel: 01539 720156
Fax: 01539 740287
Web site: www.staintons coaches.co.uk
Fleet Name: Staintons Olympic Holidays.
Man Dir: R. S. Stainton
Ops Man: C. J. Stainton
Ch Eng: I. M Stainton.
Fleet: 24 - 21 single-deck coach, 2 midicoach, 1 minicoach.
Chassis: 2 Bova, 8 DAF, 4 Mercedes, 5 Setra, 5 Volvo.
Ops incl: excursions & tours, private hire, continental tours.
Livery: Blue/Green/Silver.

TITTERINGTON COACHES LTD
THE GARAGE, BLENCOW, PENRITH CA11 0DG
Tel: 01768 483228
Fax: 01768 483680
E-mail: enquiries@titteringtoncoaches.co.uk
Web site: www.titteringtonholidays.co.uk
Dirs: Ian Titterington, Paul Titterington, Colin Titterington
Fleet: 12 single-deck coach.
Chassis: 3 Mercedes, 9 Volvo.
Bodies: 5 Jonckheere, 1 Mercedes, 3 Plaxton, 2 Setra, 1 Van Hool.
Ops incl: excursions & tours, private hire, continental tours, school contracts
Livery: Mustard/White/Brown

TOWER COACHES
THE GARAGE, BURNFOOT, WIGTON CA7 9HL
Tel: 01697 349600
Props: M D Sellars, Mrs T Sellars
Fleet: 5 - 2 single-deck coach, 2 midibus, 1 minibus.
Chassis: 1 DAF, 1 Leyland, 2 Mercedes, 1 Renault.
Bodies: 1 Alexander, 1 Holdsworth,

2 Plaxton, 1 Reeve Burgess.
Ops incl: local bus services, school contracts, private hire.
Livery: Dark Blue/Grey
Ticket System: Almex A

THE TRAVELLERS CHOICE
See Lancashire

TUERS MOTORS LTD
BRIDGE HOUSE, MORLAND, PENRITH CA10 3AY
Tel: 01931 714224
Fax: 01931 714236
Fleet: 7 - 4 single-deck coach, 1 midicoach, 2 minicoach
Chassis: 1 AEC, 1 DAF, 1 Ford Transit, 1 Mercedes, 1 Toyota, 2 Volvo.
Bodies: 1 Caetano, 3 Plaxton, 2 Reeve Burgess, 1 Van Hool.
Ops incl: excursions & tours, private hire, school contracts, continental tours.
Livery: Cream/Red

WOOFS OF SEDBERGH
UNIT 2, BUSK LANE, SEDBERGH LA10 5HF
Tel: 01539 620414
Ops incl: local bus services, school contracts, private hire.

WRIGHT BROS (COACHES) LTD
CENTRAL GARAGE, NENTHEAD, ALSTON CA9 3NP
Tel: 01434 381200
Fax: 01434 382089
E-mail: wrightbros@btinternet.com
Web site: www.wrightscoaches.co.uk
Chmn/Man Dir: J. G. Wright
Dir: C. I. Wright.
Fleet: 12 - 10 single-deck coach, 2 double-deck coach.
Chassis: 5 Bedford, 2 Scania, 5 Volvo.
Bodies: 1 Ikarus, 2 Jonckheere, 7 Plaxton, 2 Van Hool.
Ops incl: local bus services, school contracts, private hire, continental tours.
Livery: Cream/Black/Gold.
Ticket System: Almex.

DERBYSHIRE, DERBY

ANDREW'S OF TIDESWELL LTD
ANCHOR GARAGE, TIDESWELL SK17 8RB
Tel: 01298 871222
Fax: 01298 872412
E-mail: info@andrews-of-tideswell.co.uk
Web site: www.andrews-of-tideswell.co.uk
Dirs: R. B. Andrew, P. D. Andrew
Fleet: 18 - 2 double-deck bus, 11 single-deck coach, 2 double-deck coach, 2 midicoach, 1 minicoach.
Chassis: 2 Ford, 2 Leyland, 3 Mercedes, 1 Scania, 2 Setra, 8 Volvo.
Bodies: 2 Alexander, 3 Mercedes, 5 Plaxton, 2 Setra, 6 Van Hool.
Ops incl: excursions & tours, private hire, continental tours, school contracts
Livery: Cream/Ivory/Red flash.

ARRIVA MIDLANDS LTD
852 MELTON ROAD, LEICESTER LE4 8BT
Tel: 0116 264 0400
Fax: 0116 260 5605
Web site: www.arriva.co.uk
Fleet Name: Arriva serving Derby
Man Dir: R A Hind **Fin Dir:** J Barlow
Ops Dir: A Lloyd **Eng Dir:** M Evans
Area Business Man (Derbyshire): R Godfrey
Fleet: 658 - 134 double-deck bus, 176 single-deck bus, 3 articulated bus, 232 midibus, 113 minibus.
Chassis: 116 DAF, 222 Dennis, 9 Leyland, 3 Mercedes, 66 Optare, 69 Scania, 54 VDL, 125 Volvo
Bodies: 55 Alexander, 1 Caetano, 73 East Lancs, 3 Mercedes, 5 Marshall, 21 Northern Counties, 66 Optare,

176 Plaxton, 44 Scania, 8 UVG, 206 Wright.
Ops incl: local bus services.
Livery: Arriva
Ticket System: Wayfarer

BAGNALLS COACHES
THE COACH STOP, GEORGE HOLMES WAY, SWADLINCOTE DE11 9DF
Tel: 01283 551964
Fax: 01283 552287
E-mail: info@bagnallscoaches.com
Web site: www.bagnallscoaches.com
Dir/Ops Man: John Bagnall
Dir/Clerk: Pat Bagnall
Dir/Ch Eng: Karl Bagnall
Dir/Clerk: Gavin Bagnall
Fleet: 15 - 1 single-deck bus, 13 single-deck coach, 1 midicoach
Chassis: Volvo, Mercedes

Derbyshire, Derby

Bodies: 1 East Lancs, 2 Jonckheere, 2 Plaxton, 9 Van Hool.
Ops incl: local bus services, excursions & tours, private hire, school contracts.
Livery: various

BAKEWELL COACHES
24 MOORHALL ESTATE,
BAKEWELL DE45 1FP
Tel: 01629 813995

BOWERS COACHES
ASPINCROFT GARAGE,
CHAPEL-EN-LE-FRITH SK23 0NU
Tel: 01298 812204
Fax: 01298 816103
E-mail: enquiries@bowerscoaches.co.uk
Web site: www.bowersbuses.com
Fleet: 29 - 2 single-deck bus,
3 single-deck coach, 24 midibus.
Chassis: 4 DAF, 7 Mercedes, 14 Optare, 4 Scania.
Bodies: 4 Alexander, 14 Optare, 5 Plaxton, 3 Van Hool, 3 Wright.
Ops incl: local bus services, school contracts, excursions & tours, private hire, continental tours.
Livery: Red/Yellow/White.
Part of the Centrebus Group

CLOWES COACHES
BARROWMOOR,
LONGNOR NEAR BUXTON
SK17 0QP
Tel: 01298 83292
Fax: 01298 83838
E-mail: clowescoach@btconnect.com
Prop: George Clowes
Fleet: 14 – 9 single-deck coach, 4 midibus, 1 minicoach
Bodies: 4 Alexander Dennis, 6 Duple, 2 Irizar, 2 Van Hool.
Ops incl: local bus services, school contracts, excursions & tours, private hire.
Livery: Cream
Ticket system: Card

COX'S OF BELPER
GOODS ROAD, BELPER DE56 1UU
Tel: 01773 822395 **Fax:** 01773 821157
E-mail: bernardbembridge@btinternet.com
Prop: Bernard Bembridge
Fleet: 6 - 4 single-deck coach, 1 midicoach, 1 minibus.
Chassis: 1 Dennis, 1 LDV, 2 Mercedes, 2 Volvo.
Bodies: 1 Esker, 1 Jonckheere, 1 LDV, 1 Optare, 1 Plaxton, 1 Van Hool.
Ops incl: excursions & tours, private hire, school contracts.
Livery: White/Blue

CRESSWELL'S COACHES (GRESLEY) LTD
3 SHORTHEATH ROAD, MOIRA,
SWADLINCOTE DE12 6AL
Tel: 01283 217215
Fax: 01283 550043
E-mail: sales@cresswellscoaches.com
Web site: www.cresswellscoaches.com
Man Dir: David Cresswell
Ch Eng: Steve Lloyd
Fleet: 15 - 11 single-deck coach, 1 midibus, 1 midicoach, 2 minibus
Chassis: 4 Iveco, 3 Mercedes, 1 Optare, 7 Volvo.
Bodies: 4 Beulas, 1 Jonckheere, 2 Mercedes, 1 Optare, 6 Plaxton, 1 Van Hool.
Ops incl: local bus services, school contracts, excursions & tours, private hire, continental tours.
Livery: White/Orange
Ticket System: Wayfarer

CRISTAL HIRE COACHES OF SWANWICK
19 CROMWELL DRIVE,
SWANWICK DE55 1DB
Tel: 01773 604932

Prop: A. Hunt
Co Sec: Mrs Christine Hunt.
Fleet: 2 single-deck coach.
Chassis: 1 Bova, 1 Leyland.
Ops incl: excursions & tours, private hire, school contract.

DAWSON'S MINICOACHES
10 HOLLAND CLOSE,
MORTON DE55 6HE
Tel: 01773 873149
Prop: S. R. Dawson
Fleet: 4 - 2 minibus, 2 minicoach.
Chassis: 2 Ford Transit, 2 Freight Rover.
Ops incl: private hire, school contracts.
Livery: Grey/White/Blue stripe.

DERBY COMMUNITY TRANSPORT
MEADOW ROAD GARAGE,
MEADOW ROAD,
DERBY DE1 2BH
Tel: 01332 380738
E-mail: derbyct@btinternet.com
Fleet: 18 minibus
Chassis: Fiat, Mercedes.
Ops incl: local bus services, school contracts
Part of the Wellglade Group

K & H DOYLE LTD
LYDFORD ROAD, ALFRETON
DE55 7RQ
Tel: 01773 546546
Fax: 01773 546547
E-mail: info@doylescoaches.co.uk
Web site: www.doylescoaches.co.uk
Prop: K Doyle
Fleet: 28 – single-deck coach, single-deck bus, midibus, midicoach, minibus.
Ops incl: local bus services, school contracts, private hire.
Livery: Green.

TIM DRAPER'S GOLDEN HOLIDAYS
SEVERN SQUARE,
ALFRETON   DE55 7BQ
Tel: 01773 590808 **Fax:** 01773 590034
E-mail: tim.draper@btconnect.com
Web site: www.timdrapers.co.uk
Dirs: Tim Draper, Pam Draper, Claire Draper
Fleet: 10 - 1 double-deck bus, 6 single-deck coach, 1 midibus, 2 minibus.
Chassis: 1 DAF, 1 Iveco, 1 LDV, 1 MAN, 1 MCW, 2 Mercedes, 3 Volvo.
Bodies: 1 Beulas, 1 MCW, 2 Mercedes, 1 Noge, 2 Plaxton, 2 Van Hool.
Ops incl: excursions & tours, school contracts, private hire
Livery: White/Red/Yellow
Ticket System: Almex, Wayfarer 3, Setright

DUNN MOTOR TRACTION
DELVES ROAD, HEANOR GATE INDUSTRIAL ESTATE,
HEANOR DE75 7SJ
Tel: 0844 800 0196
Fax: 0844 800 0197
Web site: www.brightsites.org.uk/yourbus
Fleet Name: Your Bus
Man Dir: Scott Dunn
Fleet: 31 – 8 double-deck bus, 8 single-deck bus, 15 midibus.
Chassis: 24 Dennis, 7 Volvo.
Bodies: 5 Alexander, 2 Northern Counties, 19 Plaxton, 5 Wright.
Operations incl: local bus services.
Livery: Magenta.

'E' COACHES OF ALFRETON
1 MANOR COURT, RIDDINGS
DE55 4DG
Tel/Fax: 01773 541222
E-mail: bacon-k@sky.com
Web site: www.ecoachesofalfreton.co.uk
Owner: Kieron Bacon
Fleet: 6 – 1 single-deck coach, 5 midicoach.
Chassis: 1 Iveco, 5 Mercedes.
Bodies: 1 Beulas, 4 Plaxton, 1 Other.
Ops incl: local bus services, school contracts, excursions & tours, private hire.
Livery: White/Blue.

FELIX BUS SERVICES LTD
157 STATION ROAD, STANLEY,
ILKESTON DE7 6FJ
Tel: 0115 932 5332   **Fax:** 0115 932 6096
E-mail: office@felixbusandcoach.co.uk
Web site: www.felixbuxandcoach.co.uk
Dirs: G Middup, I Middup, C Middup
Fleet: 11 - 6 single-deck bus, 3 single-deck coach, 2 midibus.
Chassis: 2 Iveco, 2 Optare, 3 Scania, 2 VDL, 2 Volvo.
Bodies: 2 Alexander Dennis, 2 Optare, 4 Plaxton, 3 Wright.
Ops incl: local bus services, school contracts, excursions & tours, private hire, continental tours.
Livery: Red/White
Ticket system: Wayfarer TGX150

FLIGHTS HALLMARK
See West Midlands

GLOVERS COACHES LTD
MOOR FARM ROAD EAST,
ASHBOURNE DE6 1HD
Tel/Fax: 01335 300043
E-mail: gloverscoaches@btconnect.com
Web site: www.gloverscoaches.co.uk
Dirs: Stephen Mason, Heather Mason
Fleet: 16 – 2 single-deck bus, 14 single-deck coach.
Chassis: 2 Dennis, 14 Volvo.
Bodies: 1 Alexander Dennis, 1 Northern Counties, 14 Plaxton.
Ops incl: local bus services, school contracts, excursions & tours, private hire, continental tours.
Livery: Blue/Cream.
Ticket System: Wayfarer

GOLDEN GREEN LUXURY TRAVEL
See Cheshire

HARPUR'S COACHES
WINCANTON CLOSE,
DERBY DE24 8NB
Tel: 01332 757677   **Fax:** 01332 757259
E-mail: harpurscoaches@tiscali.co.uk
Web site: www.harpurscoaches.co.uk
Man Dir: Nick Harpur
Fleet: 27 - 10 double-deck bus, 4 single-deck bus, 13 single-deck coach.
Chassis: 1 AEC, 2 Leyland, 9 MCW, 11 Volvo.
Bodies: 7 MCW, 1 Park Royal, 15 Plaxton.
Ops incl: school contracts, excursions & tours, private hire.
Livery: Cream/Brown

HAWKES TOURS
EAGLE CENTRE MARKET,
DERBY DE1 2AZ
Tel: 01332 205400 **Fax:** 01332 202024
E-mail: david@hawkescoaches.freeserve.co.uk
Web site: www.hawkestours.co.uk
Fleet: 11 - double-deck bus, single-deck coach.
Ops incl: school contracts, excursions & tours, private hire.
Livery: Blue

HENSHAWS COACHES LTD
57 PYE HILL ROAD,
JACKSDALE NG16 5LR
Tel: 01773 607909
Prop: Paul Henshaw
E-mail: paul@henshawscoaches.co.uk
Web site: www.henshawscoaches.co.uk
Fleet: 5 - 4 single-deck coach, 1 midicoach
Chassis: 1 BMC, 1 Bova, 1 DAF, 2 Mercedes
Bodies: 1 BMC, 1Bova, 2 Mercedes, 1 Van Hool.
Ops incl: excursions & tours, private hire, school contracts, continental tours.
Livery: White/Orange

G & J HOLMES (COACHES) LTD
124A MARKET STREET,
CLAY CROSS S45 9LY
Tel/Fax: 01246 863232
E-mail: gj.holmes@tiscali.co.uk
Web site: www.gandjholmescoachesltd.co.uk
Fleet Name: Hallmark
Fleet: 11 – 2 single-deck coach, 3 midicoach, 6 midibus.
Chassis: 4 Mercedes, 5 Optare, 2 Volvo.
Bodies: 5 Plaxton, 6 Optare.
Ops incl: local bus services, school contracts, private hire.
Livery: White, or Silver/Blue

HULLEYS OF BASLOW
DERWENT GARAGE, BASLOW,
BAKEWELL DE45 1RP
Tel: 01246 582246 **Fax:** 01246 583161
E-mail: info@hulleys-of-baslow.co.uk
Web site: office2008@hulleys-of-baslow.co.uk
Dirs: Peter Eades, Richard Eades
Fleet: 19 - 13 single-deck bus, 3 single-deck coach, 3 midibus.
Chassis: 4 Alexander Dennis, 1 DAF, 6 Dennis, 4 MAN, 3 Optare, 1 Volvo.
Bodies: 5 MCV, 8 Optare, 5 Plaxton, 1 Wright.
Ops incl: local bus services, school contracts, private hire.
Livery: Buses: Cream/Blue; Coaches: White/Blue
Ticket System: Wayfarer 3

JOHNSON BROS TOURS LTD
GREEN ACRES, GREEN LANE,
HODTHORPE, WORKSOP S80 4XR
Tel: 01909 720337 / 721847
Fax: 01909 722886
Recovery: 07774 005863
E-mail: lee@johnsonstours.co.uk
Web site: www.johnsonstours.co.uk
Dirs: Tony Johnson, Lee Johnson, Antony Johnson, Scott Johnson, Sheila Johnson **(Co Sec)**
Fleet: 116 - 70 double-deck bus, 2 single-deck bus, 35 single-deck coach, 3 double-deck coach, 3 midibus, 2 midicoach, 1 minicoach.
Chassis: 1 Ayats, 2 Bova, 50 Bristol, 1 DAF, 1 Ford Transit, 10 Iveco, 10 MCW, 7 Neoplan, 2 Optare, 10 Scania, 6 Transbus, 4 VDL, 10 Volvo.
Bodies: Ayats, Beulas, Berkhof, Bova, Irizar, Jonckheere, Neoplan, Northern Counties, Optare, Plaxton, Scania, Setra, Sunsundegui, Transbus, Van Hool, Volvo.
Ops incl: local bus services, school contracts, excursions & tours, private hire, express, continental tours.
Livery: Blue with Stars
Ticket System: Almex
See also Redfern Travel Ltd

LEANDER TRAVEL
7 WORDSWORTH AVENUE,
SWADLINCOTE DE11 0DZ
Tel/Fax: 01283 213780
E-mail: pat@leandercoaches.co.uk
Web site: www.leandercoaches.co.uk
Fleet Name: Leander Coaches
Prop: M. W. Bugden
Fleet: 4 single-deck coach, 1 minicoach.
Chassis: 3 DAF, 1 LDV, 1 Volvo.
Ops incl: excursions & tours, private hire, school contracts, continental tours.

LITTLE TRANSPORT LTD
HALLAM FIELDS ROAD, ILKESTON
DE7 4AZ
Tel/Fax: 0115 932 8581
Recovery: 0115 932 8581
E-mail: enqiries@littlestravel.co.uk
Web site: www.littlestravel.co.uk
Fleet Name: Little's Travel
Dirs: Steve Wells, Paul Wright
Fleet: 25 - double-deck bus, single-deck bus, single-deck coach.
Chassis: 3 DAF, 2 Iveco, 4 Leyland, 1 MCW, 1 Mercedes, 3 Optare, 5 Scania, 1 VDL, 5 Volvo.
Bodies: 2 Beulas, 4 ECW, 3 East Lancs,

Derbyshire, Derby

5 Irizar, 2 Marcopolo, 1 MCW, 3 Optare, 5 Plaxton.
Ops incl: local bys services, school contracts, excursions & tours, private hire, continental tours.
Livery: White
Ticket system: Almex

MACPHERSON COACHES LTD
THE GARAGE, HILL STREET, DONISTHORPE DE12 7PL
Tel: 01530 270226 **Fax:** 01530 273669
E-mail: travel@macphersoncoaches.co.uk
Web site: www.macphersoncoaches.co.uk
Man Dir: D MacPherson
Sales Man: P. Krawse
Fleet Eng: C.Underwood
Fleet: 16 - 1 single-deck bus, 10 single-deck coach, 3 midibus, 2 midicoach.
Chassis: 1 Dennis, 5 Mercedes, 1 Optare, 8 Setra, 1 Volvo.
Bodies: 3 Mercedes, 1 Optare, 3 Plaxton, 8 Setra, 1 other.
Ops incl: local bus services, school contracts, excursions & tours, private hire, continental tours.
Livery: Cream/Red
Ticket System: Wayfarer.

NOTTS & DERBY TRACTION CO LTD
MANSFIELD ROAD, HEANOR DE75 7BG
Fleet: 65 - 15 double-deck bus, 38 single-deck bus, 7 midibus, 5 minibus.
Chassis: 6 Dennis, 1 Mercedes, 14 Optare, 1 Transbus, 43 Volvo.
Bodies: 15 Alexander, 28 Northern Counties, 14 Optare, 8 Plaxton.
Livery: Blue/Green
Ticket System: Almex
Part of the Wellglade Group

PROTOURS LTD
UNIT 2, RYDER CLOSE, SWADLINCOTE DE11 9EU
Tel: 01283 217012 **Fax:** 01283 550685
E-mail: kramsdall@protours.co.uk
Web Site: www.protours.co.uk
Dept Man: Kevin Ramsdall
Fleet: 18 - 17 single-deck coach, 1 midicoach.
Chassis: 1 BMC, 1 Scania, 16 Volvo.
Bodies: 10 Berkhof, 1 BMC, 1 Irizar, 1 Plaxton, 5 Van Hool.
Ops incl: excursions & tours, private hire, express, continental tours, school contracts
Livery: Blue & White

REDFERN TRAVEL LTD
THE SIDINGS, DEBDALE LANE, MANSFIELD WOODHOUSE, MANSFIELD NG19 7FE
Tel: 01623 627653 **Fax:** 01909 625787
Recovery: 07774 005863
E-mail: lee@johnsonstours.co.uk
Web site: www.johnsonstours.co.uk
Dirs: Tony Johnson, Sheila Johnson **(Co Sec)**, Anthony Johnson, Lee Johnson, Scott Johnson

Fleet: 67 – 40 double-deck bus, 1 single-deck bus, 20 single-deck coach, 2 double-deck coach, 1 midibus, 1 midicoach, 1 minibus, 1 minicoach.
Chassis: 1 Ayats, 2 Bova, 20 Bristol, 2 DAF, 3 Irisbus, 1 Iveco, 1 Mercedes, 4 Neoplan, 5 Scania, 2 Setra, 2 Toyota, 10 Transbus, 4 Volvo.
Bodies incl: Ayats, Beulas, Berkhof, Bova, ECW, Irizar, Jonckheere, MCW, Neoplan, Northern Counties, Optare, Sitcar, Scania, Setra, Sunsundegui, Volvo.
Ops incl: local bus services, excursions & tours, private hire, express, continental tours, school contracts.
Livery: Green/Stars
(Subsidiary of Johnson Bros Tours Ltd)

SLACKS TRAVEL (K V & G L SLACK LTD)
THE TRAVEL CENTRE, LUMSDALE, MATLOCK DE4 5LB
Tel: 01629 582826 **Fax:** 01629 580519
E-mail: enquiries@slackscoaches.co.uk
Web site: www.slackscoaches.co.uk
Man Dir: G L Slack **Ch Eng:** R M Slack
Co Sec: D R Slack **Tran Man:** J Gough
Fleet: 19 - 15 single-deck coach, 2 midicoach, 2 minibus.
Chassis: 5 DAF, 3 Dennis, 2 Ford, 2 Ford Transit, 3 Iveco, 2 Mercedes, 1 Neoplan, 1 Scania, 1 Volvo.
Bodies: 1 Autobus, 3 Beulas, 1 Jonckheere, 1 Mercedes, 1 Neoplan, 5 Plaxton, 5 Van Hool.
Ops incl: excursions & tours, private hire, continental tours, school contracts

STAGECOACH EAST MIDLANDS
PO BOX 15, DEACON ROAD, LINCOLN LN2 4JB
Tel: 01522 522255 **Fax:** 01522 538229
Fleet Names incl: Stagecoach in Chesterfield
Web site: www.stagecoachbus.com
Man Dir: Gary Nolan **Eng Dir:** John Taylor
Comm Dir: Dave Skepper
Ops Dir: Richard Kay
Fleet: 501 – 236 double-deck bus, 85 single-deck bus, 15 single-deck coach, 147 midibus, 18 minibus.
Chassis: 269 Alexander Dennis, 4 DAF, 1 Leyland, 49 MAN, 4 MCW, 27 Optare, 9 Scania, 138 Volvo.
Bodies: 315 Alexander Dennis, 1 Caetano, 60 East Lancs, 4 Jonckheere, 4 MCW, 14 Northern Counties, 27 Optare, 62 Plaxton, 14 Wright.
Ops incl: local bus services.
Livery: Stagecoach UK Bus
Ticket System: ERG TP5000.

TM TRAVEL LTD
See South Yorkshire

TRENT BARTON
MANSFIELD ROAD, HEANOR DE75 7BG
Tel: 01773 712265 **Fax:** 01773 536333
E-mail: customer.services@trentbarton.co.uk

Web site: www.trentbarton.co.uk
Chairman: B R King
Deputy Chairman: R I Morgan
Man Dir: J Counsell
Group Fin Dir: G Sutton
Comm Dir: A Hornby
Head of Development: K L Shayshutt
Fleet: 291 - 204 single-deck bus, 15 single-deck coach, 72 midibus.
Chassis: 8 Dennis, 7 Mercedes, 121 Optare, 92 Scania, 63 Volvo.
Bodies: 8 Irizar, 6 Mercedes, 121 Optare, 16 Plaxton, 135 Wright.
Ops incl: local bus services.
Livery: Red
Ticket System: Init
Part of the Wellglade Group

WARRINGTON COACHES LTD
ILAM MOOR LANE, ILAM, ASHBOURNE DE6 2AZ
Tel: 01335 350204
Fax: 01335 350204
E-mail: info@warringtoncoaches.co.uk
Web site: www.warringtoncoaches.co.uk
Dirs: Lynton Boydon, Maureen Boydon, Keith Warrington
Fleet: 9 - 4 single-deck coaches, 2 midicoach, 2 minibus, 1 minicoach
Chassis: 1 BMC, 3 Dennis, 1 Ford Transit, 2 LDV, 1 Mercedes.
Bodies: 1 BMC, 1 Marcopolo, 2 Optare, 3 Plaxton, 2 other.
Ops incl: local bus services, school contracts, excursions & tours, private hire
Livery: White/Silver with Red/Gold/Black

P J WILDE & D A WARD
t/a ALBERT WILDE COACHES, 121 PARKSIDE, HEAGE, BELPER DE56 2AG
Tel/Fax: 01773 856655
Dirs: Philip J Wilde, David Ward
Fleet: 5 single-deck coach.
Chassis: 4 DAF, 1 Leyland.
Ops incl: excursions & tours, school contracts.

WOODWARD'S COACHES LTD
100 HIGH STREET EAST, GLOSSOP SK13 8QF
See Courtesy Coaches, Greater Manchester

YESTERYEAR MOTOR SERVICES
10 LADY GATE, DISEWORTH, DERBY DE74 2QF
Tel/Fax: 01332 810774
E-mail: yesteryear10@hotmail.com
Prop: D. J. Moores
Fleet: 2 - 1 single-deck bus, 1 single-deck coach.
Chassis: Bedford, Leyland.
Bodies: Duple, ECW.
Ops incl: private hire.
Livery: Green/Cream.
Ticket System: Bell Punch.

	Vehicle suitable for disabled	R24	24 hour recovery service
T	Toilet-drop facilities available		Replacement vehicle available
R	Recovery service available		Vintage Coach(es) available
	Open top vehicle(s)		Seat belt-fitted Vehicle
	Coach(es) with galley facilities		Air-conditioned vehicle(s)
	Coaches with toilet facilities		

Derbyshire, Derby

DEVON, PLYMOUTH, TORBAY

A B COACHES LTD
WILLS ROAD, TOTNES INDUSTRIAL ESTATE, TOTNES TQ9 5XN
Tel: 01803 864161
Fax: 01803 864008
E-mail: abcoaches@btconnect.com
Web site: www.abcoaches.co.uk
Dirs: B T Smith, Mrs L Smith, M Chalk, Mrs R Chalk
Fleet: 14 single-deck coach.
Bodies: 2 Berkhof, 5 Duple, 3 Plaxton, 4 Van Hool.
Ops incl: school contracts, excursions & tours, private hire.
Livery: Cream/Red

AST TEIGNBRIDGE COMMUNITY TRANSPORT
THE MANOR HOUSE, OLD TOWN STREET, DAWLISH EX7 9AP
Tel: 01626 888890
Fax: 01626 889253
E-mail: etcta@lineone.net
Man: Jenny Connor
Coordinator: Jan Green
Fleet: 3 minibus, 3 car.
Chassis: 1 Fiat, 1 Ford, 1 Ford Transit, 1 LDV, 1 Renault, 1 Volkswagen
Ops incl: school contracts, excursions and tours, private hire.

AXE VALLEY MINI TRAVEL
BUS DEPOT, 26 HARBOUR ROAD, SEATON EX12 2NA
Tel/Fax: 01297 625959
Fleet Name: AVMT
Prop: Mrs F. M. Searle
Traf Man: J. R. Paddon.
Fleet: 9 - 5 double-deck bus, 4 midibus.
Chassis: 1 Dodge, 2 Iveco, 1 Leyland, 4 MCW, 1 Optare.
Bodies: 1 Leyland, 1 Reeve Burgess, 4 MCW, 2 Dormobile, 1 Optare.
Ops incl: local bus services.
Livery: Maroon/White.
Ticket System: Wayfarer.

AYREVILLE COACHES
202 NORTH PROSPECT ROAD, PLYMOUTH PL2 2PR
Tel: 01752 605450
Fax: 01752 219366
E-mail: ayrevillecoaches@tinyonline.co.uk
Owner: M. J. Buley.
Fleet: 6 - 3 midicoach, 3 minibus.
Chassis: 1 Ford, 1 Iveco, 4 Mercedes.
Bodies: 2 Carlyle, 1 Devon Conversion, 2 Pilcher Green, 1 Reeve Burgess.
Ops incl: private hire, school contracts.
Livery: White.

BEACON BUS
DOLTON BEACON GARAGE, DOLTON, WINKLEIGH EX19 8PS
Tel: 01805 804240
Fleet incl: single-deck bus, single-deck coach, midibus, minibus.
Ops incl: local bus services, school contracts, private hire.

BLAKES COACHES LTD
EAST ANSTEY, TIVERTON EX16 9JJ
Tel: 01398 341160
Fax: 01398 341594
E-mail: info@blakescoaches.co.uk
Web site: www.blakescoaches.co.uk
Dirs: David Blake, Janet Blake
Fleet: 8 - 7 single-deck coach, 1 midicoach
Chassis: 1 MAN, 5 Scania, 1 Toyota, 1 Volvo.
Bodies: 1 Beulas, 1 Caetano, 2 Irizar, 4 Van Hool.
Ops incl: excursions & tours, private hire, continental tours
Livery: Silver/Green/Blue

CARMEL COACHES
STATION ROAD, NORTHLEW, OKEHAMPTON EX20 3BN
Tel: 01409 221237
Fax: 01409 221226
E-mail: info@carmelcoaches.co.uk
Web site: www.carmelcoaches.co.uk
Prop: Tony Hazell
Fleet: 32 - 8 single-deck bus, 21 single-deck coach, 2 midicoach, 1 minicoach.
Chassis: 8 Bova, 2 DAF, 5 Dennis, 1 King Long, 1 LDV, 9 Mercedes, 1 Optare, 2 Scania, 3 Volvo.
Bodies: 1 Alexander Dennis, 1 Berkhof, 8 Bova, 2 Irizar, 1 Jonckheere, 1 King Long, 1 Marcopolo, 1 Marshall/MCV, 1 Optare, 9 Plaxton, 1 Sitcar, 1 Sunsundegui, 1 UVG, 1 Van Hool.
Ops incl: local bus services, school contracts, excursions & tours, private hire
Livery: White
Ticket System: Almex

COUNTRY BUS
KING CHARLES BUSINESS PARK, OLD NEWTON ROAD, HEATHFIELD, NEWTON ABBOT TQ12 6UT
Tel: 01626 833664
Fax: 01626 835648
E-mail: info@countrybusdevon.co.uk
Web site: www.countrybusdevon.co.uk
Man Dir: Ms A Ellison
Ops incl: local bus services, school contracts, private hire.
Livery: White with Blue.
Ticket System: Setright.

CRUDGE COACHES LTD
TURBURY FARM, DUNKESWELL, HONITON EX14 4QN
Tel: 01404 841657
Fax: 01404 841668
E-mail: kscrudge@btinternet.com
Dirs: K W Crudge, Mrs S Crudge
Fleet: 10 – 7 single deck coach, 2 midibus, 1 minibus.
Chassis: 2 Dennis, 3 Iveco, 2 Mercedes, 1 Neoplan, 2 Volvo
Bodies: 2 Beulas, 2 Berkhof, 1 Indcar, 1 Mercedes, 1 Neoplan, 2 Plaxton, 1 Van Hool.
Ops incl: school contracts, excursions & tours, private hire.

DAISH'S TRAVEL
PARKHILL ROAD, TORQUAY TQ1 2DY
Tel: 0870 902 1412
Web site: www.daishs.com
Fleet: 9 single-deck coach
Ops incl: excursions & tours, private hire, continental tours

DARTLINE COACHES
LANGDONS BUSINESS PARK, CLYST ST MARY, EXETER EX5 1AF
Tel: 01392 872900
Fax: 01392 872909
E-mail: info@dartline-coaches.co.uk
Web site: www.dartline-coaches.co.uk
Dirs: David Dart, Dave Hounslow
Ops Dir: Kevin Busby
Fleet: 34 - 6 single-deck bus, 19 single-deck coach, 3 midicoach, 6 minibus
Chassis: 3 Bova, 5 Dennis, 6 Optare, 1 Scania, 10 Volvo.
Bodies: 1 Berkhof, 3 Bova, 1 Caetano, 1 Irizar, 14 Plaxton, 1 Sunsundegui, 1 Van Hool
Ops incl: local bus services, school contracts, excursions & tours, private hire.
Livery: White/Green
Ticket System: Almex.

DOWN MOTORS & OTTER COACHES
1 MILL STREET, OTTERY ST MARY EX11 1AB
Tel: 01404 812002
Fax: 01404 811128
Partners: W M Down, A G Down, C P Down
Fleet: 10 - 9 single-deck coach, 1 midicoach.
Chassis: 2 Bedford, 1 Bova, 4 Dennis, 1 Iveco, 1 MAN, 1 Toyota.
Bodies: 1 Beulas, 1 Bova, 4 Caetano, 2 Duple, 2 Plaxton.
Ops incl: school contracts, excursions & tours, private hire.
Livery: Ivory/red

C.J. DOWN
THE GARAGE, MARY TAVY, TAVISTOCK PL19 9PA
Tel: 01822 664925
Fax: 01822 810242
E-mail: downscoaches@aol.com
Web site: www.cjdowncoachhiretavistock.co.uk
Proprietors: Mr & Mrs. C J Down
Ops Man: W J Wakem
Chief Eng: W J Lashbrook
Fleet: 15 - 15 single-deck coach
Chassis: 15 Volvo.
Bodies: 1 Duple, 8 Jonckheere, 6 Plaxton.
Ops incl: school contracts, excursions & tours, private hire.
Livery: Cream

EASTWARD COACHES
1 BARLANDS WAY, DOLTON, WINKLEIGH EX19 8QB
Tel: 01805 804659
Fax: 01805 804659
E-mail: eastwardcoaches@btopenworld.com
Props: Karen Wonnacott, Nick Woolacott
Tran Man: Mike Yedermann
Fleet: 6 - 5 single-deck coach, 1 minibus.
Chassis: 1 AEC, 2 Bedford, 1 DAF, 1 Ford, 1 Freight Rover.
Bodies: 1 Carlyle, 4 Plaxton, 1 Van Hool.
Ops incl: school contracts, excursions & tours, private hire.
Livery: White with Green/Red stripes

The Little Red Book 2011 - in association with *tbf* Transport Benevolent Fund

Devon, Plymouth, Torbay

101

FILERS TRAVEL LTD
SLADE LODGE, SLADE ROAD,
ILFRACOMBE EX34 8LB
Tel: 01271 863819
Fax: 01271 867281
E-mail: info@filers.co.uk
Web site: www.filers.co.uk
Man Dir: Roy Filer **Office & Tours Man:** Christina King **Ch Eng:** George Rogers
Fleet: 20 - 11 single-deck coach, 7 midibus, 1 midicoach, 1 minibus.
Chassis: 4 Bova, 1 Iveco, 2 MAN, 5 Mercedes, 1 Scania, 1 Volkswagen, 3 Volvo.
Bodies inc: 4 Bova, 1 Caetano, 1 Irizar, 3 Plaxton, 2 Van Hool.
Ops incl: local bus services, excursions & tours, private hire, school contracts, continental tours.
Livery: White/Royal Blue/Gold
Ticket system: Almex

FIRST DEVON & CORNWALL LTD
THE RIDE, CHELSON MEADOW, PLYMOUTH PL9 7JT
Tel: 01752 495250
Fax: 01752 495225
E-mail: firstdevonandcornwall@firstgroup.com
Web site: www.firstgroup.com
Man Dir: Marc Reddy
Eng Dir: Simon Marsh **Comm Dir:** Simon Newport **Ops Dir:** Steve Grigg
Fleet: 331 – 95 double-deck bus, 195 single-deck bus, 32 single-deck coach, 6 open-top bus, 3 articulated bus.
Chassis: 159 Alexander Dennis, 2 Autosan, 1 Enterprise, 2 Ford, 10 Leyland, 9 Mercedes, 25 Optare, 123 Volvo.
Bodies: 66 Alexander Dennis, 2 Caetano, 26 East Lancs, 1 Marshall/MCV, 3 Mercedes, 30 Northern Counties, 25 Optare, 113 Plaxton, 3 Van Hool, 58 Wright, 4 Other.
Ops incl: local bus services, school contracts, excursions & tours, private hire, express, continental tours.
Livery: FirstGroup UK Bus
Ticket System: Almex

GREY CARS OF TORBAY
6/7 DANEHEATH BUSINESS PARK, HEATHFIELD,
NEWTON ABBOT TQ12 6TL
Tel: 01626 833038
Fax: 01626 835920
E-mail: office@greycars.com
Web site: www.greycars.com
Man Dir: Duncan Millman
Dir: Bruce Millman
Ops Manager: Colin Holt
Fleet: 16 - 14 single-deck coach, 1 midicoach, 1 minicoach.
Chassis: 2 Mercedes, 14 Volvo.
Bodies: 3 Berkhof, 1 Caetano, 1 Jonckheere, 7 Plaxton, 4 Van Hool.
Ops incl: school contracts, excursions & tours, private hire, continental tours.
Livery: Grey with Yellow/Red stickers

GUSCOTT'S COACHES LTD
THE GARAGE, CROFT GATE, HALWILL, BEAWORTHY EX21 5TL
Tel: 01409 221661
Fax: 01409 221435
Dirs: C D Guscott, T Guscott.
Fleet: 5 single-deck coach.

Chassis: 5 Volvo.
Bodies: 1 Caetano, 1 Jonckheere, 3 Plaxton.
Ops incl: local bus services, school contracts, private hire.
Livery: Cream/Blue/Red

HARVEY'S BUS LTD
UNIT 5, STATION ROAD, MORETONHAMPSTEAD TQ13 8SA
Tel: 01647 441221
Web site: www.harveysbus.com
Dirs: P Denton, M Murray
Fleet incl: midicoach, minibus, minicoach
Ops incl: school contracts, private hire
Livery: White with Blue

HEARDS COACHES
FORE STREET, HARTLAND, BIDEFORD EX39 6BD
Tel: 01237 441233
Fax: 01237 441789
E-mail: info@heardscoaches.co.uk
Web Site: www.heardscoaches.co.uk
Fleet Name: Heards Coaches
Dirs: G Heard, B Heard.
Fleet: 14 single-deck coach.
Chassis: 2 Dennis, 1 MAN, 2 Scania, 9 Volvo.
Bodies: 2 Berkhof, 1 Caetano, 2 Irizar, 1 Noge, 2 Plaxton, 6 Van Hool.
Ops incl: school contracts, private hire.

HEMMINGS COACHES LTD
POWLERS PIECE GARAGE, EAST PUTFORD, HOLSWORTHY EX22 7XW
Tel: 01237 451282
Fax: 01237 451920
E-mail: hemmingscoaches@aol.com
Web site: www.hemmingscoaches.co.uk
Dirs: Ken & Linda Hemmings.
Fleet: 6 - 5 single-deck coach, 1 minicoach.
Chassis: 1 MAN, 4 Mercedes, 1 Volvo.
Bodies: 1 Berkhof, 2 Mercedes, 2 Setra, 1 Volvo.
Ops incl: excursions & tours, private hire, continental tours, school contracts
Livery: Gold

HILLS SERVICES LTD
THE GARAGE, STIBB CROSS, LANGTREE, TORRINGTON EX38 8LH
Tel: 01805 601102, 601203
Fax: 01805 601131
E-mail: hills.servicesltd@btinternet.com
Web site: www.hillsholidays.co.uk
Dirs: David J Hearn, Mrs D Hearn, Mrs M E Hearn
Fleet: 30 - 13 single-deck coach, 5 midicoach, 12 minibus.
Chassis: 3 Bova, 2 DAF, 1 Ford Transit, 10 LDV, 6 Mercedes, 8 Volvo.
Bodies: 3 Bova, 10 LDV, 6 Neoplan, 2 Plaxton, 6 Van Hool, 3 Other.
Ops incl: excursions & tours, private hire, school contracts.

HOOKWAYS
PEEK HOUSE, PINHOE TRADING ESTATE, VENNY BRIDGE, EXETER EX4 8JN
Tel: 01392 469210
Fax: 01392 466036
Recovery: 07850 038707
E-mail: alistair@hookways.com
Web site: www.hookways.com
Fleet Name: Hookways Greenslades

Man Dir: Alistair Gray **Dirs:** Kym Hookway (**Holidays**), Susan Hookway, Jason Hookway (**Traffic**), Martin Hookway (**Eng**), Julie Hookway (**Sec**)
Fleet: 56 – 2 double-deck bus, 45 single-deck coach, 1 midibus, 2 minicoach, 6 MPV.
Chassis: 3 Mercedes, 6 Volkswagen, 47 Volvo.
Bodies: 2 Alexander Dennis, 2 Berkhof, 2 Crest, 16 Jonckheere, 19 Plaxton, 2 Sunsundegui, 7 Van Hool, 6 Other.
Ops incl: local bus services, school contracts, excursions & tours, private hire, express, continental tours.
Livery: Yellow
Ticket System: Wayfarer
Incorporating Hookways Classic Tours, Hookways Jennings (Cornwall), Hookways Pleasureways Coaches

IVYBRIDGE & DISTRICT COMMUNITY TRANSPORT
DOURO COURT, BROOK ROAD, IVYBRIDGE PL21 0LS
Tel: 01752 690444
Fleet Name: Ivybridge Ring & Ride.
Co-ordinator: Mrs S Jenkins
Chairman: I Martin.
Fleet: 1 minibus.
Chassis/Body: LDV.
Ops incl: local bus services, private hire.

KINGDOM'S TOURS LTD
WESTFIELD GARAGE, EXETER ROAD, TIVERTON EX16 5NZ
Tel/Fax: 01884 252646
E-mail: kingdomstours@btconnect.com
Web site: www.kingdoms-tours.co.uk
Dirs: Steven J Kingdom, Russell S Kingdom, Ronald V Kingdom
Fleet: 24 – 10 single-deck coach, 6 midicoach, 6 minicoach, 2 Tram.
Chassis: 1 Bova, 1 DAF, 4 Iveco, 12 Mercedes, 2 Scania, 4 Volvo.
Bodies: 2 Beulas, 2 Berkhof, 1 Bova, 1 Irizar, 7 Mercedes, 5 Optare, 4 Van Hool, 2 Other.
Ops incl: local bus services, school contracts, excursions & tours, private hire, continental tours.
Livery: White/Red/Orange

MID DEVON COACHES
STATION ROAD, BOW, CREDITON EX17 6JD
Tel/Fax: 01363 82200
E-mail: enquiries@middevoncoaches.co.uk
Web site: www.middevoncoaches.co.uk
Prop: Mrs L A Hamilton
Fleet: 22 - 18 single-deck coach, 2 minicoach, 2 minibus.
Chassis: 2 DAF, 3 Ford, 3 Ford Transit, 5 Leyland, 4 Scania, 2 Toyota, 2 Volvo.
Bodies: 2 Bova, 2 Caetano, 1 Irizar, 2 Jonckheere, 10 Plaxton.
Ops incl: school contracts, excursions & tours, private hire, continental tours.
Livery: Green/Cream.

PARAMOUNT COACHES LTD
6 VENN CRESCENT, HARTLEY, PLYMOUTH PL5 5PJ
Tel: 01752 767255 **Fax:** 01752 767255
Prop: B M Couch
Touring Man: Brian Madge
Fleet: 5 - 1 midicoach, 2 minibus, 2 minicoach.

♿	Vehicle suitable for disabled	🎗	Seat belt-fitted Vehicle	R24	24 hour recovery service
T	Toilet-drop facilities available	🍴	Coach(es) with galley facilities	🔧	Replacement vehicle available
R	Recovery service available	❄	Air-conditioned vehicle(s)	🚌	Vintage Coache(s) available
🚌	Open top vehicle(s)	🚻	Coaches with toilet facilities		

Chassis: 2 Ford Transit, 1 Leyland, 2 Mercedes.
Ops incl: excursions & tours, private hire, school contracts.
Associated company: Eastward Coaches (see above)

PLYMOUTH CITYBUS LTD
♿ 🚌 🎗 ❄ 🚌 🔧 R24 R T
MILEHOUSE, PLYMOUTH
PL3 4AA
Tel: 01752 662271
Fax: 01752 567209
Recovery: 01752 264215
E-mail: customer.services@plymouthbus.co.uk
Web site: www.plymouthcitybus.co.uk
Man Dir: Andrew Wickham
Ops Dir: Tom Piggott
Eng Dir: Karl Duncan
Fin Cont: Iain Perring
Fleet: 184 - 35 double-deck bus, 137 single-deck bus, 11 single-deck coach, 1 open-top bus.
Ops incl: local bus services, excursions & tours, private hire, continental tours, school contracts.
Chassis: Alexander Dennis, Dennis, Leyland, Mercedes, Optare, Transbus, Volvo.
Bodies: Alexander Dennis, East Lancs, MCW, Mercedes, Optare, Plaxton.
Livery: Red/White
Ticket system: Wayfarer TGX
A subsidiary of the Go-Ahead Group

POWELLS COACHES
🎗 🚻 ❄
2 BARRIS, LAPFORD,
CREDITON EX17 6PT
Tel/Fax: 01363 83468
Props: James P Powell, Mrs D.M.Powell, W R Powell
Fleet: 5 single-deck coach
Chassis: 1 DAF, 1 Leyland, 1 Mercedes, 2 Volvo.
Bodies: 1 Jonckheere, 1 Mercedes, 1 Plaxton, 2 Van Hool.
Ops incl: school contracts, excursions & tours, private hire.

RADMORES TRAVEL
♿
4 WOODFORD CRESCENT,
PLYMPTON PL7 4QY
Tel/Fax: 01752 335391
Owner: John Williams
Man: Sarah Hale
Fleet Name: Radmores Coaches
Fleet: 5 - 1 double-deck bus, 2 midibus, 2 midicoach.
Chassis: 1 DAF, 1 Ford Transit, 1 Iveco, 1 Toyota.
Bodies: 1 Caetano, 1 Mellor, 1 Reeve Burgess.
Ops incl: local bus services, school contracts, excursions & tours, private hire.
Livery: Red/Gold

RAYS COACHES
88 KINGS TAMERTON ROAD,
ST BUDEAUX PL5 2BW
Tel: 01752 369000

REDWOODS TRAVEL
♿ 🎗 🍴 ❄ 🔧
INDUSTRIAL PARK, HEMYOCK,
CULLOMPTON EX15 3SE
Tel: 01823 680288
Fax: 01823 681096
Recovery: 01823 680288
E-mail: info@redwoodstravel.com
Web site: www.redwoodstravel.com
Dirs: Paul Redwood, Jacquie Redwood
Ch Eng: Garry Morrissey
Fleet: 28 – 20 single-deck coach, 8 minibus.
Chassis: 1 BMC, 1 Ford Transit, 5 LDV, 3 MAN, 3 Mercedes, 6 Scania, 10 Volvo.
Bodies: 1 BMC, 1 Duple, 6 Irizar, 4 Jonckheere, 5 LDV, 3 Noge, 3 Plaxton, 2 Van Hool.
Ops incl: school contracts, excursions & tours, private hire, continental tours
Livery: White/Red/Green with Palm Trees

RIVER LINK
♿ 🚌
5 LOWER STREET,
DARTMOUTH TQ6 9AJ
Tel: 01803 834488 **Fax:** 01803 835248
E-mail: sales@riverlink.co.uk
Web site: www.riverlink.co.uk
Chairman: Sir William McAlpine
Dirs: David Allan, John Butt, Norman Christy **Co Sec:** Philip Smallwood
Group Gen Man: Andrew Pooley
Tran Man: Michael Palmer
Fleet: 7 - 2 double-deck bus, 1 single-deck bus, 2 open-top bus, 2 midibus.
Chassis: 3 Bristol, 1 Dennis, 1 Leyland, 2 Mercedes.
Ops incl: local bus services, private hire.
Livery: Dark Blue/Ivory
Ticket System: Almex.

SEWARDS COACHES
🎗 ❄ 🔧
GLENDALE, DALWOOD, AXMINSTER
EX13 7EJ
Tel/Fax: 01404 881343
Partners: Richard M Seward, Ivy A Seward, Catherine E Seward
Fleet: 19 - 11 single-deck coach, 1 midibus, 5 midicoach, 2 minicoach.
Chassis: 2 Bova, 1 DAF, 5 Dennis, 1 Iveco, 1 Leyland, 2 MAN, 4 Mercedes, 1 Renault, 1 Temsa, 1 Toyota.
Bodies: 1 Berkhof, 2 Bova, 3 Caetano, 1 Hispano, 1 Marcopolo, 4 Plaxton, 1 Sitcar, 1 UVG, 5 Other
Ops incl: local bus services, school contracts, private hire.
Livery: Cream with Orange/Green

SHEARINGS HOLIDAYS
BARTON HILL WAY, TORQUAY TQ2 8JG
Tel: 01803 326016
Fax: 01803 316059
Depot Man: David Braund
See Shearings Holidays, Greater Manchester

STAGECOACH SOUTH WEST
♿ ❄
BELGRAVE ROAD, EXETER EX1 2LB
Tel: 01392 439539
Fax: 01392 889727
Web site: www.stagecoachbus.com
Man Dir: Ms Michelle Hargreaves
Ops Dir: Richard Stevens
Ops Man: Richard McAllister
Eng Man: Adrian Noel
Fleet: 362 - 135 double-deck bus, 9 single-deck bus, 112 midibus, 04 minibus, 2 other.
Chassis: 15 Alexander Dennis, 207 Dennis, 2 LDV, 3 Leyland, 32 Mercedes, 65 Optare, 12 Scania, 1 Volkswagen, 50 Volvo.
Bodies: 216 Alexander, 1 Autobus, 1 Caetano, 3 Marshall, 3 Northern Counties, 65 Optare, 48 Plaxton, 1 UVG, 25 Other.
Ops incl: local bus services, school contracts
Livery: Stagecoach UK Bus
Ticket System: ERG EP5000

STREETS COACHWAYS LTD
🎗 🚻 ❄ 🔧
THE OLD AERODROME, CHIVENOR,
BARNSTAPLE EX31 4AY
Tel: 01271 815069
Fax: 01271 817333
E-mail: lyn@streetscoachways.co.uk
Dirs: M Street, S M Street
Fleet: 15 - 6 single-deck coach, 2 midicoach, 7 minibus.
Chassis: 1 Bova, 1 DAF, 2 Dennis, 1 Ford Transit, 6 LDV, 1 MAN, 3 Mercedes.
Bodies: 1 Berkhof, 1 Bova, 1 Jonckheere, 7 LDV, 1 Marshall, 1 Mercedes, 1 Neoplan, 1 Sitcar, 1 Van Hool.
Ops incl: private hire, school contracts.

TALLY HO! COACHES LTD
♿ 🚻 🎗 ❄ R24
STATION YARD INDUSTRIAL ESTATE,
KINGSBRIDGE TQ7 1ES
Tel: 01548 853081
Fax: 01548 853602
E-mail: info@tallyhocoaches.com
Web site: www.tallyhocoaches.com
Dir: Don McIntosh
Head of Transport: Steve Pengelly
Head of Engineering: Adam Wilson
Fleet: 49 – 2 double-deck bus, 16 single-deck bus, 25 single-deck coach, 6 minibus.
Ops incl: local bus services, school contracts, excursions & tours, private hire.
Livery: Blue/White
Ticket system: Almex

TARGET TRAVEL
EAGLE ROAD, LANGAGE BUSINESS PARK, PLYMOUTH PL7 5JY
Tel: 01752 242000
Fax: 01752 345700
E-mail: admin@targettravel.info
Web site: www.targettravel.co.uk
Ops incl: local bus services, private hire
Livery: Green/White

TAVISTOCK COMMUNITY TRANSPORT
See Cornwall

Devon, Plymouth, Torbay

TAW & TORRIDGE COACHES LTD
♿♿♿R24♿T
GRANGE LANE, MERTON,
OKEHAMPTON EX20 3ED
Tel: 01805 603400
Fax: 01805 603559
Recovery: 01805 603400
E-mail: enquiries@tawandtorridge.co.uk
Web site: www.tawandtorridge.co.uk
Man Dir: Tony Hunt
Dir/Ops Man: Mark Hunt
Dir/Co Sec: Linda Hunt
Dir: Tracey Laughton
Fleet Eng/Dir: Chris Laughton
Fleet: 37 – 1 single-deck bus,
28 single-deck coach, 7 minibus,
1 midicoach
Chassis: 1 DAF, 9 Dennis, 2 Ford Transit, 1 LDV, 5 Mercedes, 19 Volvo.
Bodies: 1 Berkhof, 8 Jonckheere, 1 Mercedes, 7 Plaxton, 2 Van Hool, 8 Wadham Stringer, 8 Other.
Ops incl: school contracts, excursions & tours, private hire, continental tours.
Livery: Miami Blue/Silver

TRATHENS TRAVEL SERVICES
♿♿♿♿
BURRINGTON WAY,
PLYMOUTH PL5 3LS
Tel: 01752 794545/790585
Fax: 01752 777931
Chairman: D I Park
Dir: John Bettinson
Fleet: 50 - 49/70/83-seat single and double-deck coach, sleeper coach.
Ops incl: express, continental tours.
Livery: White with Red and Yellow lining;

National Express: White.
A subsidiary of Parks of Hamilton (see South Lanarkshire)

TURNERS TOURS
♿♿♿♿♿♿T
BACK LANE INDUSTRIAL ESTATE,
CHULMLEIGH EX18 7AA
Tel: 01769 580242
Fax: 01769 581281
E-mail: coaches@turnerstours.co.uk
Web site: www.turnerstours.co.uk
Dirs: S.L. Gilson, P.C.Gilson
Fleet: 28 - 16 single-deck coach,
7 single-deck bus, 2 midibus,
2 midicoach, 1 minibus.
Chassis: Alexander Dennis, LDV, Mercedes, Volvo.
Bodies: Alexander Dennis, Caetano, Jonckheere, Marshall/MCV, Mercedes, Plaxton, Reeve Burgess, Other
Ops incl: local bus services, school contracts, excursions & tours, private hire, express, continental tours.
Livery: Cream.
Ticket System: Almex

T. W. COACHES LTD
♿♿♿
HACCHE LANE, SOUTH MOLTON
EX36 3EH
Tel: 01769 572139
Fax: 01769 574182
E-mail: twcoaches@ukf.net
Dirs: C Tearall, N Williams
Fleet: 18 – single-deck bus, single-deck coach, midibus, midicoach, minibus, minicoach.
Chassis: 3 Dennis, 11 Mercedes, 4 Optare.

Bodies: 1 Berkhof, 2 Jonckheere,
11 Mercedes, 4 Optare.
Ops incl: local bus services, school contracts, excursions & tours, private hire, continental tours.
Livery: Blue
Ticket system: Almex

WESTERN GREYHOUND LTD
See Cornwall

WILLS MINI COACHES
2 LOWER UNION ROAD,
KINGSBRIDGE TQ7 1EF
Tel/Fax: 01548 852140
Man Dir: E. G. Wills
Dir/Co Sec: Mrs G. M. Wills.
Fleet: 5 minibus.
Chassis: 4 LDV, 1 Mercedes.
Ops incl: school contracts, private hire.

WOOD BROTHERS TRAVEL LTD
HAREWOOD GARAGE,
BOSSELL ROAD,
BUCKFASTLEIGH TQ11 0AL
Tel: 01364 642666
Fax: 01364 643870
E-mail: woodbrotherstravel@hotmail.co.uk
Man Dir: R C Wood
Comp Sec: S Wood
Dirs: R D Wood, R Wood, A S Carter
Fleet: 14 - 9 single-deck coach,
1 midicoach, 3 minibus, 1 minicoach.
Chassis: 4 Dennis, 2 Leyland,
4 Mercedes, 1 Volkswagen, 3 Volvo.
Ops incl: local bus service, school contracts, private hire.
Livery: Yellow/White.

DORSET, BOURNEMOUTH, POOLE

BARRY'S COACHES LTD
♿♿♿♿♿
9 CAMBRIDGE ROAD,
GRANBY INDUSTRIAL ESTATE,
WEYMOUTH DT4 9TJ
Tel: 01305 784850
Fax: 01305 782252
E-mail: barryscoaches@hotmail.co.uk
Web site: www.barryscoachesdorset.com
Fleet: 25 – 21 single-deck coach,
1 double-deck coach, 3 midicoach.
Man Dir: Mrs M Newsam
Chassis: MAN, Mercedes, Scania, Volvo.
Ops incl: school contracts, excursions & tours, private hire, continental tours.
Livery: White/Blue/Yellow

BLUEBIRD COACHES (WEYMOUTH) LTD
♿♿♿♿R24♿T
450 CHICKERELL ROAD,
WEYMOUTH DT3 4DH
Tel: 01305 786262
Fax: 01305 766223
Recovery: 01305 786262/07771 561060
E-mail: martyn@bluebirdcoaches.com
Web site: www.bluebirdcoaches.com
Dirs: Martyn Hoare, Stephen Hoare
Fleet: 22 - 20 single-deck coach,
1 midicoach, 1 minibus.
Chassis: 7 DAF, 1 Mercedes, 2 Neoplan, 1 Volkswagen, 11 Volvo.
Bodies: 7 Bova, 1 Caetano,

3 Jonckheere, 2 Neoplan, 4 Plaxton,
5 Van Hool.
Ops incl: school contracts, excursions & tours, private hire, continental tours.
Livery: White/Blue/Orange

CAVENDISH LINER LTD
BANBURY ROAD, NUFFIELD
INDUSTRIAL ESTATE,
POOLE BH17 0GA
Tel: 01202 660620
Fax: 01202 660220
E-mail: sales@cavendishliner.com
Web site: www.cavendishliner.com
Fleet incl: single-deck coach, double-deck coach, midicoach, minicoach.
Ops incl: schools contracts, private hire
Livery: Grey/Black

COACH HOUSE TRAVEL
♿♿♿
UNIT 16, POUNDBURY WEST
INDUSTRIAL ESTATE,
DORCHESTER DT1 2PG
Tel: 01305 267614
Fax: 01305 260608
E-mail: admin@coachhousetravel.fsnet.co.uk
Web site: www.coachhousetravel.co.uk
Prop: Les Watts **Ch Eng:** Phillip Watts
Fleet: 14 - 3 single-deck bus, 6 single-deck coach, 1 midicoach, 3 minibus,
1 minicoach.

Chassis: 1 Bova, 1 DAF, 1 Dennis,
2 Ford Transit, 1 Iveco, 5 Mercedes,
5 Volvo.
Bodies: Bova, Mellor, Mercedes, Plaxton.
Ops incl: local bus services, school contracts, excursions & tours, private hire, continental tours.
Livery: White/Red/Blue

DAMORY COACHES
♿♿♿♿♿♿
UNIT 1, CLUMP FARM, SHAFTESBURY
LANE, BLANDFORD FORUM
DT11 7TD
Tel: 01258 452545
Fax: 01258 451930
E-mail: igray@damorycoach.co.uk
Web site: www.damorycoach.co.uk
Local Man: Ian Gray
Man Dir: Alex Carter
Eng Dir: Steve Hamilton
Fin Dir: Matt Dolphin
Fleet: 48 - 18 double-deck bus,
7 single-deck bus, 9 single-deck coach,
1 double-deck coach, 6 midibus,
1 midicoach, 6 minibus.
Chassis: 1 Bristol, 2 DAF, 1 Ford Transit, 2 Iveco, 5 LDV, 11 Leyland,
1 MAN, 6 Optare, 1 Scania, 8 Volvo.
Bodies: 2 Beulas, 1 Caetano, 1 ECW,
1 East Lancs, 1 Ford Transit, 4 Ikarus,
5 LDV, 11 Leyland, 2 Northern Counties,
10 Optare, 6 Plaxton, 4 Van Hool.
Ops incl: local bus services, school

contracts, excursions & tours, private hire, continental tours.
Livery: Two tone Blue/Black
Ticket system: Wayfarer
Part of the Go-Ahead Group

DOLPHIN COACHES LTD
UNIT 6, STONE LANE INDUSTRIAL ESTATE, WIMBORNE MINSTER BH21 1HB
Tel: 01202 883134
Fax: 01202 883132
E-mail: markself@dolphincoaches.co.uk
Web site: www.dolphincoaches.co.uk
Man Dir: T J Hann
Fin Dir: Mrs S Hann
Ops Man: M R Self
Fleet: 10 – 9 single-deck coach, 1 midicoach.
Chassis: 3 Bova, 1 Dennis, 1 MAN, 1 Optare, 4 Scania
Bodies: 3 Bova, 1 Caetano, 1 Noge, 1 Optare, 4 Van Hool
Ops incl: local bus services, school contracts, excursions & tours, private hire, express, continental tours.
Livery: Cream & Blue
Ticket System: Wayfarer

DORSET COUNTY COUNCIL – DORSET PASSENGER TRANSPORT
DPT GARAGE, GROVE TRADING ESTATE, DORCHESTER DT1 1ST
Tel: 01305 224540 **Fax:** 01305 225166
E-mail: K.R.Clark@dorsetcc.gov.uk
Ops Man: David Besant
Fleet Sup: Kevin Clark
Fleet: 103 – 4 single-deck coach, 6 single-deck bus, 22 midibus, 68 minibus, 3 wheelchair accessible cars
Chassis: 2 Dennis, 30 Fiat, 7 Iveco, 1 Leyland, 23 Mercedes, 21 Optare, 3 Peugeot, 9 Renault, 6 Scania, 1 Volvo.
Bodies: 3 Expert, 30 Fiat, 7 Irisbus, 6 Irizar, 23 Mercedes, 21 Optare, 4 Plaxton, 9 Renault.
Ops incl: school contracts, welfare contracts, adult day centre transport, school excursions, park & ride.
Livery: Silver/Green (large vehicles: Yellow)

EXCELSIOR COACHES LTD
CENTRAL BUSINESS PARK, BOURNEMOUTH BH1 3SJ
Tel: 01202 652220
Fax: 01202 652223
E-mail: krobins@excelsior-coaches.com
Web site: www.excelsior-coaches.com
Man Dir: Kathy Tilbury
Fin Dir: Ken Robins
Fleet: 31 - 27 coach, 4 minibus.
Chassis: 6 Mercedes, 25 Volvo.
Bodies: 5 Caetano, 4 Crest, 2 Esker, 2 Jonckheere, 13 Plaxton, 5 Sunsundegui.
Ops incl: excursions & tours, private hire, express, continental tours.
Livery: Cream, also National Express

MIKE HALFORD COACHES
KISEM, NORTH MILLS, BRIDPORT DT6 3AH
Tel/Fax: 01308 421106
Prop: M G Halford
Fleet: 7 - 3 midicoach, 4 minibus
Chassis: 7 Mercedes
Ops incl: local bus services, private hire, school contracts

HERRINGTON COACHES LTD
MANOR FARM, SANDLEHEATH ROAD, ALDERHOLT, FORDINGBRIDGE SP6 3EG
Tel: 01425 652842
E-mail: herringtoncoaches@live.co.uk
Web site: www.herringtoncoaches.com
Props: Alan Herrington, Mrs Janet Herrington
Fleet: 6 - 3 single-deck coach, 3 minibus.
Chassis: 3 Mercedes, 1 Scania, 2 Volvo.
Bodies: 2 Jonckheere, 3 Mercedes, 1 Van Hool
Ops incl: local bus services, school contracts, private hire.
Livery: Red/Grey
Ticket System: Setright

HOMEWARD BOUND TRAVEL
137 LYNWOOD DRIVE, WIMBORNE BH21 1UU
Tel: 01202 884491
Fax: 01202 885664
E-mail: enquiries@homewardboundtravel.co.uk
Web site: www.homewardboundtravel.co.uk
Prop: Louisa Fairhead
Fleet: 4 minicoach
Chassis: 4 Renault
Ops incl: excursions & tours, private hire, continental tours.
Livery: Silver /Purple/Green

HOOKWAYS
See Devon

LAGUNA HOLIDAYS
LAGUNA HOTEL, 6 SUFFOLK ROAD SOUTH, BOURNEMOUTH BH2 6AZ
Tel: 01202 767022
Web site: www.lagunaholidays.com
Fleet incl: double-deck coach, single-deck coach
Ops incl: excursions & tours, private hire
Livery: White with Red Lettering

LINKRIDER COACHES LTD
FLOWER MEADOW, HAYCRAFTS LANE, HARMANS CROSS, SWANAGE BH19 3EB
Tel: 01929 477344
Fax: 01929 477345
E-mail: linkridercoaches@btconnect.com
Web site: www.linkridercoaches.co.uk
Fleet Names: Linkrider Coaches, South Dorset Coaches
Dirs: Nick & Anne Hubbard
Ops Man: Ben Banks
Ch Eng: Barry Goodwin
Fleet incl: single-deck coach, midicoach
Chassis: Alexander Dennis, Bova, Mercedes, Setra, Toyota.
Bodies: Alexander Dennis, Bova, Mercedes, Setra.
Ops incl: local bus services, school contracts, excursions & tours, private hire, continental tours.

POWELLS COACHES
THORNFORD GARAGE, THORNFORD DT9 6QN
Tel: 01935 872390
Fleet: 3 single-deck coach.
Ops incl: local bus services, excursions & tours, private hire.
Livery: Red/White.

RAMON TRAVEL
7 HARCOURT ROAD, BOSCOMBE BH5 2JG
Tel: 01202 432690
Fax: 01202 432690
Owner/Ops: C. Rochester.
Fleet: 6 - 1 single-deck coach, 1 midicoach, 4 minibus.
Chassis: 1 Bedford, 4 Freight Rover.
Ops incl: excursions & tours, private hire, school contracts.

SEA VIEW COACHES (POOLE) LTD
10-12 FANCY ROAD, POOLE BH12 4QZ
Tel: 01202 741439
Fax: 01202 740241
E-mail: info@seaviewcoaches.com
Web site: www.seaviewcoaches.com
Man Dir: David Tarr
Fleet: 22 - 18 single-deck coach, 3 minibus, 1 midicoach.
Chassis incl: 2 DAF, 16 MAN.
Bodies incl: 7 Beulas, 4 Neoplan, 7 Noge.
Ops incl: school contracts, excursions & tours, private hire.
Livery: Silver with Blue/Red

SHAFTESBURY & DISTRICT MOTOR SERVICES LTD
UNIT 2, MELBURY WORKSHOPS, CANN COMMON, SHAFTESBURY SP7 0EB
Tel/Fax: 01747 854359
E-mail: info@sdbuses.co.uk
Web site: www.sdbuses.co.uk
Dir: Roger Brown **Co Sec:** Liam Stacey
Fleet: 15 - 5 double-deck bus, 1 single-deck bus, 5 single-deck coach, 3 midibus, 1 minicoach.
Chassis: 5 AEC, 4 Leyland, 3 Mercedes, 1 Toyota, 2 Volvo.
Bodies: 1 Caetano, 1 Duple, 1 Jonckheere, 1 MCW, 1 Optare, 4 Plaxton, 1 Wadham Stringer, 5 Other.
Ops incl: local bus services, school contracts, private hire.
Livery: Red/Cream/Maroon
Ticket System: Wayfarer TGX

SHAMROCK BUSES LTD
UNIT 50A, HOLTON HEATH TRADING PARK, POOLE BH16 6LT
Tel: 01202 621581
Fax: 01202 623657
E-mail: office@shamrockbuses.co.uk
Web site: www.shamrockandrambler.co.uk
Man Dir Ops: Keith Baynton
Man Dir Finance: Martin Judge
Eng Dir: Steve Bracher
Fleet: 44 – 40 double-deck bus, 4 single-deck bus, 1 2 heritage vehicles.
Chassis: Dennis, Leyland, Volvo.
Ops Inc: local bus services, school contracts, private hire
Livery: Orange/Cream
Ticket System: Wayfarer TGX

SHORELINE BUS & COACH TRAVEL
13 CHESHIRE DRIVE, BOURNEMOUTH BH8 0JU
Tel/Fax/Recovery: 01202 391285
E-mail: shoreline@shorelinetravel.co.uk

Web site: www.shorelinetravel.co.uk
Prop: Trevor Shore
Tran Man: Shirley Shore
Fleet: 4 – 2 double-deck bus, 2 single-deck coach.
Chassis: 1 DAF, 2 Leyland, 1 Scania.
Bodies: 2 Van Hool.
Ops incl: local bus services, school contracts, excursions & tours, private hire.
Livery: Red.

SOUTH WEST COACHES LTD/SOUTH WEST TOURS LTD
UNIT 17, TRADECROFT INDUSTRIAL ESTATE, PORTLAND DT5 2LN
Tel: 01305 823039
See Somerset

SOVEREIGN COACHES
PINE LODGE, SIDMOUTH ROAD, ROUSDON, LYME REGIS DT7 3RD
Tel: 01297 23000
Fax: 01297 22466
E-mail: sov_coaches@btinternet.com
Web site: www.sovereigncoaches.co.uk
Partners: Ronald A Keech, Mrs Cynthia M Keech, Richard C Keech
Fleet: 8 - 5 midicoach, 3 minicoach.
Chassis: 1 Iveco, 1 LDV, 5 Mercedes, 1 Toyota.
Bodies: 1 Crest, 1 Esker, 1 Onyx, 1 Plaxton, 1 Sitcar, 3 Other.
Ops incl: school contracts, excursions & tours, private hire.
Livery: White

DAVID THOMPSON TOURS LTD
NEWLYN, 11 LINCOLN AVENUE, CHRISTCHURCH BH23 2SG
Tel: 01202 490333
Fax: 01202 480026
Web site: www.thompsonstours.co.uk
Dir: David Thompson
Ops incl: local bus services, excursions & tours, private hire, continental tours.
Livery: White with Blue Lettering

TRAVEL GUEST
63 PINEVALE CRESCENT, REDHILL, BOURNEMOUTH BH10 6BG
Tel: 01202 383643

Web site: www.dorsetsprinter.com
Fleet Name: Dorset Sprinter
Ops incl: local bus services, private hire

WILTS & DORSET BUS COMPANY LTD
TOWNGATE HOUSE, 2-8 PARKSTONE ROAD, POOLE BH15 2PR
Tel: 01202 680888/673555
Fax: 01202 670244
E-mail: enquiries-poole@wdbus.co.uk
Web site: www.wdbus.co.uk
Man Dir: A Carter
Divisional Dir: E Wills
Eng Dir: G Parsons
Fleet: 344 - 132 double-deck bus (incl. convertible open-top), 64 single-deck bus, 7 single-deck coach, 141 minibus.
Chassis: 25 Bristol, 96 DAF, 16 Leyland, 30 Mercedes, 156 Optare, 51 Volvo.
Bodies: 2 Duple, 35 ECW, 13 East Lancs, 30 Mercedes, 7 Northern Counties, 237 Optare, 11 Plaxton, 2 Roe, 3 Van Hool, 34 Wright.
Ops incl: local bus services, school contracts, private hire, express.
Livery: Red/White/Black, Red/Blue
Ticket System: Wayfarer TGX
Part of the Go-Ahead Group

YELLOW BUSES
YEOMANS WAY, BOURNEMOUTH BH8 0BQ
Tel: 01202 636000
Fax: 01202 636001
E-mail: mail@yellowbuses.co.uk
Web site: www.bybus.co.uk
Man Dir: D A Lott
Eng Dir: G C Corrie
Fin Dir & Co Sec: A Smith
Head of Marketing: Mrs J Wilkinson
Fleet: 140 - 45 double-deck bus, 79 single-deck bus, 16 single-deck coach.
Chassis: 12 Alexander Dennis, 1 DAF, 43 Dennis, 29 Optare, 2 Scania, 53 Volvo.
Bodies: 5 Alexander Dennis, 10 Caetano, 58 East Lancs, 1 Jonckheere, 29 Optare, 15 Plaxton, 18 Wright, 4 Other.
Ops incl: local bus services, school contracts, express.
Livery: Yellow

Ticket System: Wayfarer TGX200
A subsidiary of the Transdev Group

2 & 4th LIMITED
5 HEATHFIELD WAY, WEST MOORS, FERNDOWN BH22 0DA
Tel/Fax: 01202 870724
E-mail: nwiain@aol.com
Web site: www.2and4th.com
Man Dir: Lian Newman
Dir: Gillian Newman
Fleet: 3 - 1 single deck coach, 1 midicoach, 1 minicoach
Chassis: 1 LDV, 1 Mercedes, 1 Scania
Bodies: 1 Plaxton, 2 Other
Ops incl: school contracts, excursion & tour, private hire, express
Livery: White

Advertising in the The Little Red Book 2011
Passenger Transport Directory for the British Isles

For information regarding advertising contact:

Graham Middleton
Tel: 01780 484632
Fax: 01780 763388
E-mail: graham.middleton@ianallanpublishing.co.uk

Notes

DURHAM, HARTLEPOOL, STOCKTON ON TEES

ALFA COACHES LTD
17 RAMSGATE, STOCKTON-ON-TEES
TS18 1BS
Tel: 01642 678066
Fax: 01642 673462
Fleet Name: Gladwin Tours
Man Dir: P. Sawbridge
Man: M. Gladwin
Co Sec: P. Sawbridge
Ops Man: D. Squire
Ops incl: excursions & tours, private hire, continental tours
Livery: Beige with Blue lettering
See also Alfa Travel, Lancashire

ARRIVA NORTH EAST
See Tyne & Wear

BROWNS OF DURHAM
1 LEESFIELD DRIVE, MEADOWFIELD, DURHAM DH7 8NG
Tel: 0191 3780398
Recovery: 0191 378 0393
E-mail: info@brownscoachesltd.com
Dir: Ralph Brown
Fleet: 6 single-deck coach
Chassis: 1 Bova, 5 DAF.
Bodies: include LAG. EOS
Ops incl: excursions & tours, private hire, continental tours.

CLASSIC COACHES LTD
CLASSIC HOUSE, MORRISON ROAD, ANNFIELD PLAIN, STANLEY DH9 7RX
Tel: 01207 282288
Fax: 01207 281333
E-mail: ian.shipley@tgmgroup.co.uk
Web site: www.classic-coaches.co.uk
Man Dir: Ian Shipley
Tran Man: John Shipley
Ch Eng: Eric Bowerbank
Fleet: 41 - 3 double-deck bus, 10 single-deck bus, 25 single-deck coach, 3 double-deck coach.
Chassis incl: 1 Ayats, 1 Leyland, 1 MAN, 4 Mercedes, 11 Scania, 10 VDL, 5 Volvo.
Bodies incl: 4 Irizar, 4 Mercedes, 10 Optare, 2 Van Hool.
Ops incl: local bus services, school contracts, excursions & tours, private hire, express, continental tours
Livery: Red
Part of the TGM Group, a subsidiary of Arriva

COCHRANE'S
4 FARADAY ROAD, NORTH EAST INDUSTRIAL ESTATE, PETERLEE SR8 5AP
Tel: 0191 586 2136
Fax: 0191 586 5566
Fleet Name: Cochrane's Kelvin Travel
Owner: I. P. Cochrane
Fleet: 7 - 5 single-deck bus, 2 minicoach.
Chassis: 4 Bedford, 1 DAF, 1 Ford, 1 Freight Rover.
Bodies: 5 Plaxton, 2 others.
Ops incl: school contracts.
Livery: Orange/Black.
Ticket System: Setright.

COMPASS ROYSTON TRAVEL LTD
BOWESFIELD LANE INDUSTRIAL ESTATE, STOCKTON-ON-TEES
TS18 3EG
Tel: 01642 606644
Fax: 01642 608617
Man Dir: G Walton
Trans Man: M. Metcalfe
Fleet: 55 - double-deck bus, single-deck coach, midicoach.
Chassis: Ayats, Ford, Mercedes, Neoplan, Optare, Setra, Volvo.
Bodies: Berkhof, Jonckheere, Mercedes, Optare, Neoplan, Plaxton, Van Hool.
Ops incl: excursions & tours, private hire, express, continental tours, school contracts.
Livery: White with Red/Maroon stripe.
Associated with Procters Coaches, North Yorkshire

DURHAM CITY COACHES LTD
BRANDON LANE, BRANDON, DURHAM DH7 8PG
Tel: 0191 378 0540
Fax: 0191 378 1985
E-mail: sales@durhamcitycoaches.co.uk
Web site: www.durhamcitycoaches.co.uk
Man Dir: Michael Lightfoot
Fleet: 16 - 12 single-deck coach, 4 midicoach.
Chassis: 3 Bova, 5 Mercedes, 8 Volvo.
Ops incl: excursions & tours, private hire, continental tours, school contracts.
Livery: Black/Red/Gold

ENTERPRISE TRAVEL
19 PINE GROVE, DARLINGTON
DL3 8JF
Tel/Fax: 01325 286924
E-mail: coachhire@aol.com
Web site: www.enterprisecoachhire.co.uk
Dirs: B R Brown, Mrs B M Brown
Fleet: 6 - 5 single-deck coach, 1 minicoach.
Chassis: 1 Bova, 1 Dennis, 1 Toyota, 2 Setra.
Bodies: 1 Berkhof, 1 Bova, 1 Caetano, 2 Setra, 1 Van Hool.
Ops incl: private hire, school contracts, excursions & tours.
Livery: White with red/green reliefs.

GARDINERS TRAVEL
COULSON STREET, SPENNYMOOR
DL16 7RS
Tel: 01388 818235
Fax: 01388 811466
E-mail: info@gardinerstravel.co.uk
Web site: www.nmctours.co.uk
Man Dir: John Gardiner
Tran Man: Harry Revel
Fleet incl: single-deck coach.
Ops incl: excursions & tours, private hire, continental tours.
Livery: Cream/Maroon
Ticket system: AES

GARNETT'S COACHES
UNIT E1, ROMAN WAY INDUSTRIAL ESTATE, TINDALE CRESCENT, BISHOP AUCKLAND DL14 9AW
Tel: 01388 604419
Fax: 01388 609549
E-mail: bookings@garnettscoaches.com
Web site: www.garnettscoaches.com
Fleet Ops Man: Paul Garnett

Fleet incl: double-deck bus, single-deck coach.
Ops incl: school contracts, excursions & tours, private hire, continental tours.
Livery: Yellow/Red/Black.

GO NORTH EAST
See Tyne & Wear

GRIERSONS COACHES
SEDGEFIELD ROAD GARAGE, FISHBURN, STOCKTON-ON-TEES
TS21 4DD
Tel: 01740 620209
Fax: 01740 621243
Props: C & D Grierson.
Fleet: 20 - 5 double-deck bus, 6 single-deck bus, 4 single-deck coach, 1 midicoach, 4 minibus.
Chassis: 1 DAF, 1 Ford, 1 Ford Transit, 2 Freight Rover, 2 Mercedes, 1 Scania, 13 Volvo.
Bodies: 1 Carlyle, 3 Jonckheere, 2 Mercedes, 13 Plaxton, 1 Reeve Burgess, 1 Van Hool.
Ops incl: excursions & tours, private hire, express, continental tours.
Livery: Blue/Red.

HODGSONS COACHES
16 GALGATE, BARNARD CASTLE
DL12 8BG
Tel: 01833 630730
Fax: 01833 630830
E-mail: hodgsons@rapidial.co.uk
Web site: www.hodgsonscoachtravel.co.uk
Props: J K Hodgson, G A Hodgson.
Fleet: 6 - 2 single-deck coach, 1 midicoach, 3 minicoach.
Chassis: 1 Bedford, 1 Bova, 1 Leyland, 1 Mercedes.
Bodies: 1 Bova, 1 Plaxton, 1 Elme, 3 Concept Coach Craft.
Ops incl: local bus services, school contracts, excursions & tours, private hire, continental tours.
Livery: White/Blue

HUMBLES COACHES
UP YONDER, ROBSON STREET, SHILDON DL4 1EB
Tel: 01388 772772
Fax: 01388 772211
E-mail: Malcolm.humble@sky.com
Dirs: Malcolm Humble, Mrs Pamela West
Fleet: 6 - 1 single-deck coach, 2 midicoach, 2 minicoach, 1 wheelchair minibus
Chassis: 3 LDV, 2 Mercedes, 1 Volvo.
Ops incl: school contracts, excursions & tours, private hire.
Livery: White

HUNTER BROS LTD
THE GARAGE, TANTOBIE, STANLEY DH9 9TG
Tel: 01207 232392
Fax: 01207 290575
Ops incl: local bus services.
Livery: Black/White.

J & C COACHES
COACH DEPOT, GROAT DRIVE, AYCLIFFE INDUSTRIAL PARK, NEWTON AYCLIFFE DL5 6HY

The Little Red Book 2011 - in association with *tbf* Transport Benevolent Fund

107

Tel: 01325 312728
Fax: 01325 320385
Snr Partner: J. N. Jones
Partners: A. Jones, N. Jones, D. Jones.
Fleet: 10 - 6 single-deck coach, 1 midicoach, 3 minicoach.
Chassis: 4 DAF, 1 Dennis, 1 Ford Transit, 1 Freight Rover, 2 Mercedes, 1 Setra.
Bodies: 4 Bova, 1 Duple, 1 Leyland, 2 Mercedes, 1 Setra.
Ops incl: school contracts, excursions & tours, private hire, continental tours.
Livery: various

JSB TRAVEL
13 HILLSIDE ROAD, COUNDON
DL14 8LS
Tel: 07900 426206
Web site: www.jsbtravel.co.uk
Ops incl: local bus services, private hire.
Fleet: midibus, minibus.
Chassis: Mercedes, Optare.
Livery: Maroon/White

JAYLINE BAND SERVICES LTD
UNIT 8A, KILBURN DRIVE,
SEAVIEW INDUSTRIAL ESTATE,
HORDEN SR8 4TQ
Tel: 0191 586 5787

Fax: 0191 586 5836
E-mail: jaylinetravel@hotmail.com
Web site: jaylinetravel.com
Prop: Jason Rogers
Dir: Neil Tait
Fleet: 6 - 2 single-deck band coach, 4 double-deck band coach.
Chassis: 2 Scania, 2 Setra, 2 Volvo.
Bodies: Berkhof, Jonckheere, Setra, Van Hool
Ops incl: private hire (band buses, film crews)
Livery: Blue

KINGSLEY COACHES LTD
See Tyne & Wear

LEE'S COACHES LTD
MILL ROAD GARAGE,
LITTLEBURN INDUSTRIAL ESTATE,
LANGLEY MOOR DH7 8HE
Tel: 0191 378 0653 **Fax:** 0191 378 9086
E-mail: info@leescoaches.co.uk
Web site: www.leescoaches.co.uk
Man Dir: Malcolm Lee
Dir: Colin Lee
Co Sec: Mrs Jean Lee
Fleet: 15 - 14 singe-deck coach, 1 minibus
Chassis: 1 Bova, 1 MAN, 1 Mercedes, 12 Volvo.

Bodies: 3 Berkhof, 1 Bova, 3 Caetano, 2 Jonckheere, 1 Mercedes, 1 Neoplan, 1 Plaxton, 3 Van Hool.
Ops incl: school contracts, excursions & tours, private hire, continental tours
Livery: Blue/Silver

MAUDES COACHES
REDWELL GARAGE,
HARMIRE ROAD, BARNARD CASTLE
DL12 8QJ
Tel: 01833 637341
Fax: 01833 631888
Prop: Stephen Maude
Fleet: 6 - 4 single-deck coach, 1 midicoach, 1 minicoach.
Chassis: 2 Mercedes, 4 Volvo.
Bodies: 1 Jonckheere, 2 Mercedes, 1 Plaxton, 2 Van Hool.
Ops incl: local bus services, school contracts, excursions & tours, private hire.
Livery: Red/White.

METRO COACHES
THE CONIFERS, DARLINGTON ROAD,
STOCKTON-ON-TEES TS21 1PE
Tel: 01642 219555
E-mail: info@coachiremiddlesbrough.co.uk
Web site: www.coachhirestockton.co.uk

	Vehicle suitable for disabled	R24	24 hour recovery service
	Toilet-drop facilities available		Replacement vehicle available
R	Recovery service available		Vintage Coache(s) available
	Open top vehicle(s)		Seat belt-fitted Vehicle
	Coach(es) with galley facilities		
	Air-conditioned vehicle(s)		
	Coaches with toilet facilities		

NORTON MINI TRAVEL
5 PLUMER DRIVE, NORTON
TS20 1HF
Tel: 01642 555832
Owner: R. Spears.
Fleet: 2 minicoach.
Chassis: 1 Iveco, 1 Freight Rover.
Ops incl: private hire, school contracts.
Livery: White/Purple.

RICHARDSON COACHES
3 OXFORD ROAD, HARTLEPOOL
TS25 5SS
Tel/Fax: 01429 272235
Man Dir/Ch Eng: T. Richardson
Dir/Co Sec/Traf Man: D. Richardson.
Fleet: 9 - 3 single-deck coach,
2 midicoach, 4 minibus.
Chassis: 4 Ford, 2 Leyland,
2 Mercedes, 1 Scania.
Bodies: 4 Ford, 5 Plaxton.
Ops incl: excursions & tours, private hire.
Livery: Green/Red/White.

ROBERTS TOURS
36 NORTH ROAD WEST,
WINGATE TS28 5AP
Tel: 01429 838268
Fax: 01429 838228
E-mail: robertstours@aol.com
Web site: www.robertstours.com
Dirs: T. G. Roberts, D Roberts,
C. A. Harper.
Fleet: 14 single-deck coach, 1 midibus.
Chassis: 5 Bova, 5 DAF, 2 Leyland,
2 Volvo.
Bodies: 5 Bova, 8 Plaxton, 1 Wadham Stringer.
Ops incl: excursions & tours, private hire, express, school contracts.
Livery: Cream/Green.

SCARLET BAND
WELFARE GARAGE, STATION ROAD,
WEST CORNFORTH,
FERRYHILL DL17 9LA
Tel: 01740 654247
Fax: 01740 656068
E-mail: s.band@btconnect.com
Dirs: Graeme Torrance
Traffic Man: Andrew Dolan
Fleet: 26 - 1 double-deck bus, 3 single-deck bus, 6 single-deck coach, 7 midibus,
9 minibus.
Chassis: 8 Leyland, 9 Mercedes,
8 Optare, 1 Volvo.
Bodies: 7 Optare, 5 Plaxton, 1 Van Hool,
13 Other.
Ops incl: local bus services, school contracts, private hire.
Livery: Red and Cream with Scarlet Band
Ticket System: Wayfarer 3

SHERBURN VILLAGE COACHES
FRONT STREET, SHERBURN VILLAGE
DH6 1QY
Tel: 0191 372 1531
Fax: 0191 372 1531
E-mail: sherburncoaches@btconnect.com
Prop: John Cousins.
Fleet: 7 - 2 single-deck coach, 3 midibus,
2 midicoach.
Chassis: 1 MAN, 4 Mercedes, 2 Volvo.
Bodies: 1 Autobus, 1 Berkhof,
1 Caetano, 3 Plaxton, 1 Wadham Stringer.

Ops incl: local bus services, excursions & tours, private hire.
Livery: Red/White
Ticket System: AES.

SIESTA INTERNATIONAL HOLIDAYS LTD
NEWPORT SOUTH BUSINESS PARK,
LAMPORT STREET,
MIDDLESBROUGH TS1 5QL
Tel: 01642 257920
Fax: 01642 219153
Recovery: 07739 679957
E-mail: sales@siestaholidays.co.uk
Web site: www.siestaholidays.co.uk
Chairman: Paul R Herbert
Dirs: C Herbert, J Herbert, J Cofton
Ops Mans: K Keelan, J Potter
Fleet: 9 - 2 single-deck coach,
6 double-deck coach, 1 minibus.
Chassis: 1 Ford Transit, 8 Scania.
Bodies: 8 Berkhof, 1 Ford.
Ops incl: excursions & tours, private hire, continental tours.
Livery: Metallic Blue.

SNOWDON COACHES
SEASIDE LANE, EASINGTON
SR8 3TW
Tel: 0191 527 0535
Fax: 0191 527 3280
E-mail: snowdoncoaches@gmail.com
Web site: www.snowdoncoaches.co.uk
Props: Alan Snowdon, Andrew Snowdon
Fleet: 9 single-deck coach.
Chassis: 1 DAF, 8 Volvo.
Bodies: 7 Plaxton, 2 Van Hool.
Ops incl: private hire, school contracts.
Livery: White

STAGECOACH TRANSIT
CHURCH ROAD, STOCKTON ON TEES
TS18 2HW
Tel: 01642 602112
Web site: www.stagecoachbus.com
Man Dir: John Conroy
Fleet: See Stagecoach North East
(Tyne & Wear)
Ops incl: local bus services
Livery: Stagecoach UK Bus

STANLEY TRAVEL
THE BUS STATION,
STANLEY DH9 OTD
Tel: 01207 237424
Fax: 01207 233233
Web site: www.minicoachhire.co.uk
Dir: Robert Scott
Fleet: 36 - 2 single-deck bus, 10 minibus,
14 minicoach, 7 taxi-bus
Ops incl: local bus services, private hire
Livery: White/Orange

TEES VALLEY LUXURY COACHES LTD
EAGLESCLIFFE LOGISTICS CENTRE,
DURHAM LANE, EAGLESCLIFFE,
STOCKTON-ON-TEES TS16 0RW
Tel: 01642 781150
Fax: 01642 780666
E-mail: info@teesvalleycoachtravel.co.uk
Web site:
www.teesvalleycoachtravel.co.uk
Fleet Name: Tees Valley Coach Travel
Fleet incl: double-deck bus, single-deck bus, single-deck coach, midibus.
Ops incl: local bus services, school contracts, private hire
Livery: Blue/White

TOWN & COUNTRY MOTOR SERVICES LTD
UNIT 2, HENSON ROAD, YARM ROAD
BUSINESS PARK,
DARLINGTON DL1 4QD
Tel: 01325 489966.
E-mail: sales@townandcountrycoaches.co.uk
Web site: www.townandcountrycoaches.co.uk
Fleet Name: Town & Country
Man Dir: Philip Notman
Fleet: 3 - 1 single-deck bus, 1 midibus,
1 midicoach.
Chassis: 1 Leyland, 2 Mercedes.
Bodies: 1 Duple, 1 Marshall, 1 Plaxton.
Ops incl: local bus services, school contracts, private hire.
Livery: White/Blue.
Ticket System: Almex.

PAUL WATSON TRAVEL
BRIDGE HOUSE, MOOR ROAD,
STAINDROP,
DARLINGTON DL2 3LF
Tel/Fax: 01833 660471
E-mail: paul.watson9@btconnect.com
Web site: www.paulwatsontravel.co.uk
Dir: Paul Watson
Co Sec: Joanne Watson
Fleet: 4 - 2 single-deck coach,
1 midicoach, 1 minibus.
Chassis: 1 DAF, 1 Ford Transit, 2 Volvo.
Ops incl: school contracts, excursions & tours, private hire, continental tours.
Livery: White

WEARDALE MOTOR SERVICES LTD
39 EAST END, STANHOPE
DL13 2YQ
Tel: 01388 528235
Fax: 01388 526080
E-mail:
enquiries@weardalemotorservices.co.uk
Web site: www.weardale-travel.co.uk
Dirs: Messrs Gibson
Ops Man: C Adams
Fleet: 30 - 11 double-deck bus,
4 single-deck bus, 10 single-deck coach,
3 minibus, 1 midicoach, 1 midibus.
Chassis: DAF, Irisbus, Leyland, MAN, Mercedes, Neoplan, Optare, Scania, Volvo.
Bodies: Alexander, Berkhof, Beulas, Ikarus, Mercedes, Neoplan, Optare, Plaxton, Van Hool, Wright.
Ops incl: local bus services, excursions & tours, school contracts, private hire, express, continental tours.
Livery: Red/White
Ticket System: Wayfarer

Advertising in LRB
For information regarding advertising contact:
Graham Middleton
Tel: 01780 484632
Fax: 01780 763388
E-mail:
graham.middleton@ianallanpublishing.co.uk

EAST RIDING OF YORKSHIRE, CITY OF KINGSTON UPON HULL

ABBEY COACHWAYS LTD
See North Yorkshire

ACKLAMS COACHES LTD
BARMSTON CLOSE,
BEVERLEY HU17 0LA
Tel: 01482 887666
Fax: 01482 874949
Web site: www.acklams-coaches-beverley.co.uk
Prop: Paul Acklam
Fleet: 20 – 4 double-deck bus,
6 single-deck coach, 3 midibus,
1 midicoach, 6 minibus.
Chassis: 1 Dennis, 1 Ford, 4 LDV,
1 Mazda, 1 Mercedes, 3 Optare,
1 Transbus, 8 Volvo.
Bodies: Alexander, Ford, Optare,
Plaxton.
Ops incl: local bus services, school
contracts, private hire.
Livery: Red/Grey

R DRURY COACHES
6 BLENHEIM DRIVE,
GOOLE DN14 6LP
Tel/Fax: 01405 763440
E-mail: rdrurycoaches@aol.com
Dirs: Roland Drury, Richard Drury
Fleet: 6 - 4 single-deck coach,
1 midibus, 1 midicoach
Chassis: 2 Mercedes, 4 Volvo.
Bodies: 6 Plaxton.
Ops incl: school contracts, private hire.
Livery: Green/White

EAST YORKSHIRE MOTOR SERVICES LTD
252 ANLABY ROAD,
HULL HU3 2RS
Tel: 01482 327142
Fax: 01482 212040
E-mail: enquiries@eyms.co.uk
Web site: www.eyms.co.uk
Chairman: Peter Shipp
Fin Dir: Peter Harrison
Comm Man: Bob Rackley
Ch Eng: David Heptinstall
Co Sec: Paul Leeman
Ops Man: Ray Hill
Fleet: 320 - 153 double-deck bus,
90 single-deck bus, 27 single-deck coach,
8 open-top bus, 42 midibus, 42 minibus.
Chassis: Alexander Dennis, AEC,
Bedford, Bristol, Dennis, Enterprise,
Leyland, MAN, Mercedes, Optare,
Transbus, Volvo.
Bodies: Alexander Dennis, Berkhof,
Caetano, Duple, ECW, East Lancs,
Mercedes, Northern Counties, Optare,
Park Royal, Plaxton, Transbus,
Willowbrook, Wright
Ops incl: local bus services, school
contracts, excursion & tours, private hire,
express, continental tours.
Livery: buses - Burgundy/Cream.
Ticket System: Wayfarer TGX150

ELLIE ROSE TRAVEL LTD
BANKSIDE INDUSTRIAL ESTATE,
VALLETTA STREET, HEDON ROAD,
HULL HU9 5NP
Tel: 01482 890616
Fax: 01482 899359
E-mail: jim@ellierosetravel.karoo.co.uk
Dirs: James Houghton, Mrs Sheila Houghton
Fleet: 65 - 27 double-deck bus,
6 single-deck bus, 20 single-deck coach,
1 open top bus, 2 midicoach, 3 minibus,
6 service vehicles.
Chassis: DAF, Dennis, LDV, Leyland,
MCW, Optare, Scania, Setra, Volvo.
Bodies: ECW, LDV, MCW, Optare,
Plaxton, Scania, Setra, Volvo.
Ops incl: local bus services, school
contract, excursions & tours, private hire.
Livery: White
Ticket system: Wayfarer.

NATIONAL HOLIDAYS
THE TRAVEL CENTRE, SPRINGFIELD
WAY, ANLABY, HULL HU10 6RJ
Tel: 01482 572572
Fax: 01482 569004
E-mail: s.hart@nationalholidays.com
Web site: www.nationalholidays.com
Man Dir: G Rogers
Ops Man: A Hutchinson
Traffic Man: P Joyce
Fleet: 90 single-deck coach
Chassis: 30 Setra, 60 Volvo.
Ops incl: excursions & tours.
Livery: White & Blue

Subsidiary company of Shearings
Holidays, see Greater Manchester

PEARSON COACHES LTD
9 HEADLANDS ROAD,
ALDBROUGH, HU11 4RR
Tel: 01964 527260
Fax: 01964 527774
E-mail: enquiries@pearsonscoaches.co.uk
Web site: www.pearsonscoaches.co.uk
Dirs: Mrs V Pearson, S Colley
Fleet: 10 - 5 single-deck coach,
5 minicoach.
Chassis: 5 Mercedes, 5 Volvo.
Bodies: 4 Mercedes, 1 UVG, 5 Van Hool.
Ops incl: local bus services, school
contracts, excursions & tours, private hire.
Livery: Grey with Red & Burgundy stripes.
Ticket system: Wayfarer 2

SHAW'S OF WHITLEY
See North Yorkshire

STAGECOACH EAST MIDLANDS
PO BOX 15, DEACON ROAD,
LINCOLN LN2 4JB
Tel: 01522 522255
Fax: 01522 538229
Fleet Name: Stagecoach in Hull
Web site: www.stagecoachbus.com
Man Dir: Gary Nolan
Eng Dir: John Taylor
Comm Dir: Dave Skepper
Ops Dir: Richard Kay
Fleet: 501 - 236 double-deck bus,
85 single-deck bus, 15 single-deck coach,
147 midibus, 18minibus.
Chassis: 269 Alexander Dennis, 4 DAF,
1 Leyland, 49 MAN, 4 MCW, 27 Optare,
9 Scania, 138 Volvo.
Bodies: 315 Alexander Dennis,
1 Caetano, 60 East Lancs, 4 Jonckheere,
4 MCW, 14 Northern Counties, 27 Optare,
62 Plaxton, 14 Wright.
Ops incl: local bus services.
Livery: Stagecoach UK Bus
Ticket System: ERG TP5000.

SWEYNE COACHES
LONGSHORE, REEDNESS ROAD,
SWINEFLEET DN14 8ER
Tel: 01405 704263
E-mail: mail@sweyne.co.uk
Web site: www.sweyne.co.uk
Fleet: 13 – 4 double-deck bus,
3 single-deck bus, 6 single-deck coach.
Chassis: 7 DAF, 2 Dennis, 4 Leyland.
Bodies: 4 Alexander, 5 Ikarus,
2 Plaxton, 2 Van Hool.
Ops incl: local bus services, school
contracts, private hire.
Livery: Blue/White/Gold

EAST SUSSEX, BRIGHTON & HOVE

BARCROFT TOURS & EVENTS
247 LONDON ROAD,
ST LEONARDS ON SEA TN37 6LU
Tel: 01424 200201
Fax: 01424 200206
Recovery: 07977 004371
E-mail: info@barcrofttours.co.uk
Web site: www.barcrofttours.co.uk
Fleet: 2 single-deck coach.
Chassis: 1 Scania, 1 Volvo
Bodies: 1 Caetano, 1 Irizar.
Ops incl: excursions & tours, private hire, continental tours.
Livery: White

BRIGHTON & HOVE BUS & COACH COMPANY
43 CONWAY STREET, HOVE BN3 3LT
Tel: 01273 886210
Fax: 01273 822073
E-mail: info@buses.co.uk
Web site: www.buses.co.uk
Fleet Name: Brighton & Hove
Chairman: Keith Ludeman
Dir: Nick Swift **Man Dir:** Roger French
Fin Dir: Philip Woodgate
Ops Dir: Mike Best
Eng Dir: Adrian Mitchell
Fleet Eng: Alan Wabey
Coaching Man: Ian Miller
Fleet: 288 - 233 double-deck bus, 44 single-deck bus, 7 single-deck coach, 4 articulated bus.
Chassis: 1 AEC, 1 Bristol, 108 Dennis, 4 Mercedes, 1 Optare, 160 Scania, 13 Volvo.
Bodies: 7 Alexander, 1 ECW, 157 East Lancs, 5 Irizar, 4 Mercedes, 1 Optare, 1 Park Royal, 63 Plaxton, 38 Scania, 11 Wright.
Ops incl: local bus services, school contracts, excursions & tours, private hire, continental tours.
Livery: Red/Cream/Black
Ticket System: Wayfarer TGX
A subsidiary of the Go-Ahead Group

BRIGHTONIAN COACHES
3 THE AVENUE, BRIGHTON
BN2 4GF
Tel: 01273 696195
Props: Laurence R Walker, Susan M Walker
Fleet: 2 coach
Chassis: 2 Volvo.
Bodies: 1 Duple ,1 Plaxton.
Ops incl: school contracts, private hire.
Livery: White

C & S COACH TRAVEL LTD
STATION ROAD, HEATHFIELD
TN21 8DF
Tel: 01435 866600
Fax: 01435 868264
E-mail: info@candscoaches.co.uk
Partners: Chris Hicks, Geoff Shaw, Bob Hodgetts, Roger Belcher
Ch Eng: Paul Matthews
Fleet: 37 - incl 1 double-deck coach, 1 midicoach.
Chassis: 20 DAF, 2 Leyland, 6 Scania, 9 Volvo.
Bodies: 2 Jonckheere, 6 Plaxton, 1 Reeve Burgess, 28 Van Hool.

Ops incl: school contracts, private hire.
Livery: White with red/black/grey graphics
A Countryliner Group Company – see Surrey

COASTAL COACHES
18 WEST POINT,
NEWICK BN8 4NK
Tel: 01825 723024
E-mail: enquires@coastalcoaches.com
Web site: www.coastalcoaches.com
Prop: Peter Jenkins
Fleet: 10 - 10 single-deck bus.
Chassis: 10 Alexander Dennis.
Bodies: 10 Alexander Dennis.
Ops incl: local bus services
Livery: Green/white/blue
Ticket System: Wayfarer 3

COUNTRYLINER (SUSSEX) LTD
A Countryliner Group company
– see Surrey

CUCKMERE COMMUNITY BUS LTD
THE OLD RECTORY, LITLINGTON,
POLEGATE BN26 5RB
Tel: 01323 870032
Web site: www.cuckmerebus.freeuk.com
Chairman: Mrs Beryl Smith
Organiser: Philip Ayers
Deputy Organiser: John Bunce
Co Sec: Mrs Susan de Angeli
Treasurer: Andrew Cottingham
Fleet: 8 - 8 minibus
Chassis: 8 Mercedes.
Bodies: 1 Alexander, 2 Constable, 3 Mellor, 2 Mercedes.
Ops incl: local bus services, private hire.
Livery: Green/Cream
Ticket system: Wayfarer TGX

L J EDWARDS COACH HIRE
BELLBANKS CORNER, MILL ROAD,
HAILSHAM BN27 2HR
Tel: 01323 440622
Fax: 01323 442555
E-mail: info@ljedwards.co.uk
Web site: www.ljedwards.co.uk
Prop: John Edwards
Gen Man: Antony Burkill
Co Acct: David Maynard
Fleet: 14 - 9 single-deck coach, 2 midicoach, 3 minibus.
Chassis: 6 Bova, 1 Irisbus, 2 Mercedes, 2 Toyota, 3 Volkswagen.
Bodies: 1 Beulas, 6 Bova, 2 Caetano, 2 Mercedes, 3 Volkswagen
Ops incl: school contracts, excursions & tours, private hire, continental tours.
Livery: White with Red detail

EMPRESS COACHES LTD
10/11 ST MARGARETS ROAD,
ST LEONARDS-ON-SEA TN37 6EH
Tel/Fax: 01424 430621
E-mail: info@empresscoaches.com
Web site: www.empresscoaches.com
Dir: Stephen Dine
Ch Eng: Bill Sweetman
Fleet: 10 - 2 midicoach, 6 minibus, 2 minicoach.

Chassis: 3 Ford Transit, 6 Mercedes, 1 Other.
Bodies: 2 Autobus, 1 Mellor, 2 Optare, 5 Other.
Ops incl: school contracts, private hire.
Livery: Claret/Cream

HAMS TRAVEL
THE WHITE HOUSE, LONDON ROAD,
FLIMWELL TN5 7PL
Tel: 01580 879537
Fax: 01580 879629
E-mail: info@hamstravel.co.uk
Web site: www.hamstravel.co.uk
Fleet incl: double-deck bus, double-deck coach, single-deck coach, midicoach, minibus.
Ops incl: excursions & tours, school contracts, private hire.
Livery: Red/Orange/Brown.

OCEAN COACHES
19 STONERY CLOSE,
PORTSLADE BN41 2TD
Tel/Fax: 01273 278385
Recovery: 07887 815798
Web site: www.oceancoaches.net
E-mail: info@oceancoaches.net
Prop: Peter Woodcock.
Fleet: 1 single-deck coach.
Chassis: Volvo.
Body: Ikarus.
Ops incl: private hire, school contracts, excursions & tours.
Livery: Blue/White

PAVILION COACHES
144 NEVILL AVENUE,
HOVE BN3 7NH
Tel: 01273 732405
E-mail: nicky2168@hotmail.com
Web-site: www.pavilioncoaches.co.uk
Joint owners: Peter Hammer, Nicky Hammer
Fleet: 2 – 1 double-deck bus, 1 single-deck coach
Chassis: 1 Leyland, 1 Volvo.
Bodies: 1 Park Royal, 1 Plaxton
Ops incl: excursions & tours, private hire, continental tours

RAMBLER COACHES
WESTRIDGE MANOR, WHITWORTH
ROAD, HASTINGS TN37 7PZ
Tel: 01424 752505
Fax: 01424 751815
Partners: Colin Rowland, J. Goodwin.
Fleet: 38 - 5 single-deck bus, 26 coach, 1 midibus, 3 midicoach. 1 minicoach.
Chassis: 8 Bedford, 4 Dennis, 2 Leyland National, 5 Mercedes, 1 Scania, 18 Volvo.
Bodies: 5 Berkhof, 1 Duple, 1 Hispano, 2 Leyland National, 2 Optare, 17 Plaxton, 1 Reeve Burgess, 7 Van Hool, 1 Wadham Stringer, 1 Wright..
Ops incl: local bus services, school contracts, excursions & tours, private hire, continental tours.
Livery: White, Green/Black.
Ticket System: Wayfarer.

RENOWN COACHES LTD
1A BEECHING ROAD, BEXHILL-ON-SEA
TN39 3LG
Tel: 01424 210744
Fax: 01424 212651

E-mail: renowncoaches@yahoo.co.uk
Web Site: www.renowncoaches.co.uk
Man Dir: Christian Harmer
Ops incl: local bus services, school contracts, excursions & tours, private hire, continental tours.

STAGECOACH IN EAST KENT & EAST SUSSEX

BUS STATION, ST GEORGE'S LANE, CANTERBURY CT1 2SY
Tel: 01227 828103
Fax: 01227 828150
E-mail: dawn.cannon@stagecoachbus.com
Web site: www.stagecoachbus.com
Fleet Names: Stagecoach in Eastbourne, Stagecoach in Hastings
Man Dir: Phil Medlicott
Ops Dir: Neil Instrall
Eng Dir: Jason Bush
Comm Dir: Jeremy Cooper

Fleet: 420 - 154 double-deck bus, 69 single-deck bus, 28 single-deck coach, 104 midibus, 65 minibus.
Chassis: Alexander Dennis, DAF, Dennis, Leyland, MAN, Mercedes, Optare, Scania, Transbus, Volvo.
Bodies: Alexander, Alexander Dennis, Caetano, East Lancs, Ikarus, Marshall, MCV, Northern Counties, Optare, Plaxton, Transbus, Wright.
Ops incl: local bus services, express.
Livery: Stagecoach UK Bus; National Express (White).
Ticket System: ERG/Wayfarer.

SUSSEX COUNTRY COACH HIRE

TERMINAL BUILDING, SHOREHAM AIRPORT BN43 5FF
Tel: 01273 465500
Fax: 01273 453040
E-mail: sxcountry@tiscali.co.uk
Web site: www.sussex-country.co.uk

Partners: A Wright, Mrs M Keates
Fleet: 4 - 2 single-deck coach, 1 midicoach, 1 minibus
Chassis: 1 LDV, 1 Mercedes, 2 Volvo.
Bodies: 1 Plaxton, 1 Van Hool, 2 Other.
Ops incl: school contracts, excursions & tours, private tours, continental tours
Livery: Blue/Yellow/Green on White

WISE COACHES LTD

74 HIGH STREET, HAILSHAM BN27 1AU
Tel: 01323 844321
E-mail: info@wisecoaches.co.uk
Web site: www.wisecoaches.co.uk
Fleet: 4 single-deck coach.
Chassis: 4 DAF.
Bodies: 1 Ikarus, 1 Ovi, 2 Van Hool.
Ops incl: excursions & tours, private hire, school contracts.
Livery: Red/Silver

ESSEX, SOUTHEND ON SEA, THURROCK

ANITA'S COACHES

ROOMS 4-5, AIRWAYS HOUSE, FIRST AVENUE, STANSTED AIRPORT CM24 1RY
Tel: 01279 661551
Fax: 01279 661771
E-mail: anitas.coaches@btconnect.com
Web site: www.anitascoaches.com
Dirs: E A S Wheeler, Mrs V A Wyatt
Fleet: 7 - 5 single-deck coach, 1 midicoach, 1 minicoach.
Chassis: 2 DAF, 1 MAN, 1 Mercedes, 3 Volvo.
Bodies: 2 Bova, 4 Caetano, 1 Plaxton
Ops incl: local bus services, school contracts, private hire, continental tours.

APT COACHES LTD

UNIT 27, RAWRETH INDUSTRIAL ESTATE, RAWRETH LANE, RAYLEIGH SS6 9RL
Tel: 01268 783878
Fax: 01268 782656
E-mail: admin@aptcoaches.co.uk
Web site: www.aptcoaches.co.uk
Fleet Name: APT Travel
Dir: Peter Thorn
Fleet: 13 - 12 single-deck coach, 1 minibus.
Chassis: 1 Bova, 1 Dennis, 1 Leyland, 2 Mercedes, 6 Scania, 2 Volvo.
Bodies: 1 Bova, 1 Caetano, 1 Crest, 1 East Lancs, 5 Irizar, 1 Neoplan, 2 Van Hool, 1 Wadham Stringer.
Ops incl: school contracts, private hire, continental tours
Livery: White/Pink

ARRIVA SOUTHEND LTD

20 SHORT STREET, SOUTHEND ON SEA, SS2 5BY
Tel: 01622 697000   Fax: 01702 697001
Web site: www.arrivabus.co.uk
Regional Man Dir: Heath Williams
Comm Dir: Kevin Hawkins
Eng Dir: Brian Barraclough
Fin Dir: Beverley Lawson
A division of Arriva Southern Counties - See Kent

B J S TRAVEL

61A HIGH STREET, GREAT WAKERING SS3 0EF

Tel: 01702 219403
Prop: Brian Snow
Fleet: 1 single-deck coach.
Chassis: 1 Scania.
Bodies: 1 Irizar.
Ops incl: school contracts, private hire.
Livery: White, Red & Gold.

BLUE DIAMOND COACHES

37 HOLMES MEADOW, HARLOW CM19 5SG
Tel: 01279 427524   Fax: 01279 427525
E-mail: beau.aukett@ntlworld.com
Prop: J. Robilliard
Sec: A. Aukett
Fleet: 4 - 1 single-deck bus, 2 midibus, 1 midicoach.
Chassis: 1 Alexander Dennis, 3 Mercedes.
Bodies: 4 Plaxton.
Ops incl: school contracts, private hire.
Livery: Blue/White.

BLUE TRIANGLE LTD

18 MERTON HIGH STREET, LONDON SW19 1DN
Tel: 020 8545 6100
Fax: 020 8545 6101
E-mail: enquiries@go-ahead-london.com
Web site: www.go-ahead-london.com
Fleet: 67 – 23 double-deck bus, 44 single-deck bus.
Chassis: 27 Alexander Dennis, 17 Transbus, 23 Volvo.
Bodies: 19 Alexander Dennis, 8 MCV, 6 Northern Counties, 1 Plaxton, 17 Transbus, 16 Wright.
Ops incl: local bus services, school contracts, private hire.
Livery: Red
Part of the Go-Ahead Group

BORDACOACH

25B, EASTWOOD ROAD, RAYLEIGH SS6 7JD
Tel: 07729 009303
Prop: David J Stubbington
Fleet: 1 single-deck coach.
Chassis: 1 Volvo.
Body: 1 Van Hool.
Ops incl: school contracts, excursions & tours, private hire.
Livery: White

BRENTWOOD COACHES

79 WASH ROAD, HUTTON, BRENTWOOD CM13 1DL
Tel: 01277 233144
Fax: 01277 201386
E-mail: brentwoodcoach@tiscali.co.uk
Web site: www.brentwoodcoach.co.uk
Prop: A. J. Brenson
Ch Eng: K. Wright
Sec: Mrs P. Alexander Traf Man: B. Pierce.
Fleet: 11 single-deck coach.
Chassis: MAN, Volvo.
Bodies: Caetano, Jonckheere, Plaxton, Van Hool.
Ops incl: excursions & tours, private hire, school contracts, continental tours.
Livery: White/Brown/Orange/Yellow.
Ticket System: Almex.

C I CLUB CLASS TRAVEL

POOLS LANE, HIGHWOOD, CHELMSFORD CM1 3QL
Tel: 01245 24866
E-mail: cicoachlines@btopenworld.com
Props: S Lodge, I Lodge,
Fleet: 8 - 6 single-deck coach, 1 midicoach, 1 minibus
Chassis: 4 Iveco, 1 Optare, 1 Temsa
Bodies incl: 4 Beulas
Ops incl: local bus service, private hire, school contracts, continental tours
Livery: Silver

C N ENTERPRISES LTD

9 BARTHOLOMEW DRIVE, HAROLD WOOD RM3 0WB
Tel/Fax: 01708 379700
E-mail: cnenterprise1@aol.com
Man Dir: Colin Nossek
Dir: Vena Nossek
Fleet: 1 single-deck coach.
Chassis: 1 Volvo.
Bodies: 1 Jonckheere.
Ops incl: excursions & tours, private hire.

CEDRIC COACHES

THE ARDLEIGH TRUCK STOP, A120 NORTH, ARDLEIGH, COLCHESTER CO7 7SL
Tel: 01206 231212
Fax: 01206 231029
E-mail: info@cedriccoaches.com

112   The Little Red Book 2011 - in association with *tbf* Transport Benevolent Fund

Web site: www.cedriccoaches.com
Fleet: 20 - 10 double-deck bus, 7 single-deck coach, 1 double-deck coach, 1 midicoach, 1 minibus.
Chassis: 2 Bova, 5 DAF, 6 Leyland, 2 Scania, 1 Toyota, 4 Volvo.
Bodies: 2 Berkhof, 2 Bova, 1 Caetano, 6 ECW, 2 Irizar, 2 Jonckheere, 4 Optare, 1 Van Hool.
Ops incl: local bus services, school contracts, private hire.
Livery: Orange/Red/Yellow/White
Ticket system: Wayfarer

CENTREBUS LTD
TOPRAK HOUSE, RIVERWAY, HARLOW CM20 2DR
Tel: 01279 428702
Fax: 01279 417809
E-mail: info@centrebus.com
Web site: www.centrebus.co.uk
Man Dir: Peter Harvey
Ops Dir: Neil Harris
Fleet (Essex): 21 – 9 single-deck bus, 12 midibus.
Chassis: 5 Alexander Dennis, 7 Dennis, 1 MAN, 1 Optare, 4 Scania, 3 Transbus.
Bodies: 1 Alexander Dennis, 4 MCV, 3 Marshall, 2 Optare, 2 Plaxton, 3 Transbus, 6 Wright.
Ops incl: local bus services
Livery: Blue/Orange/White
Ticket system: Wayfarer 3
Part of the Centrebus Group

CHADWELL HEATH COACHES
30 REYNOLDS AVENUE, CHADWELL HEATH RM6 4NT
Tel: 020 8590 7505
Fax: 020 8597 8883
Props: John Thompson, Lynn Thompson.
Fleet: 5 single-deck coach.
Chassis: 2 Leyland, 3 Volvo.
Bodies: 3 Berkhof, 1 Duple, 1 Plaxton.
Ops incl: excursions & tours, private hire, school contracts.
Livery: Country cream

CHARIOTS OF ESSEX LTD
1 ONE TREE HILL, STANFORD-LE-HOPE SS17 9NH
Tel: 01268 581444
Fax: 01268 581555
E-mail: chariots@btconnect.com
Web site: www.chariots-coaches.co.uk
Man Dir: K T Flavin
Dir: W J Collier
Fleet: 18 - 3 double-deck bus, 2 single-deck bus, 4 single-deck coach, 1 midicoach, 7 minibus, 1 minicoach.
Chassis: Bova, DAF, Freight Rover, Iveco, Mercedes, Toyota.
Bodies: Bova, Caetano, Marshall/MCV, MCW.
Ops incl: school contracts, private hire, express.
Livery: Orange/Yellow
Ticket system: Wayfarer

CLINTONA MINICOACHES
LITTLE WARLEY HALL LANE, BRENTWOOD CM13 3HA
Tel: 01277 215526
Fax: 01277 200038
E-mail: enquiries@clintona.co.uk
Web site: www.clintona.co.uk
Fleet Name: Clintona
Partners: Robin Staines, Barbara Staines.

Fleet: 20 - 4 midibus, 9 midicoach, 7 minicoach.
Chassis: 2 Alexander Dennis, 1 Ford Transit, 3 LDV, 14 Mercedes.
Ops incl: local bus services, school contracts, private hire.
Livery: White/Blue
Ticket System: Wayfarer 2

COOKS COACHES
607 LONDON ROAD, WESTCLIFF-ON-SEA SS0 9PE
Tel: 01702 344702
Fax: 01702 436887
E-mail: info@cookscoaches.co.uk
Web site: www.cookscoaches.co.uk
Prop: W E Cook
Fleet: 12 single-deck coach
Chassis: 12 Bova.
Bodies: 12 Bova
Ops incl: excursions & tours, private hire, continental tours.
Livery: Red & White

COUNTY COACHES
2 CRESCENT ROAD, BRENTWOOD CM14 5JR
Tel: 01277 201505
Fax: 01277 225918
E-mail: enquiries@countycoaches.com
Web site: www.countycoaches.com
Off Man: C A Jee
Tran Man: R J Pratt
Fleet: 12 – 1 single-deck bus, 8 single-deck coach, 3 midibus.
Chassis: 2 MAN, 3 Mercedes, 7 Volvo.
Ops incl: school contracts, excursions & tours, private hire.
Livery: Green/White

STAINES CRUSADER COACHES
CRUSADER BUSINESS PARK, STEPHENSON ROAD WEST, CLACTON-ON-SEA CO15 4HP
Tel: 01255 425453
Fax: 01255 222683
Recovery: 01255 431777
E-mail: info@crusader-holidays.co.uk
Web site: www.crusader-holidays.co.uk
CEO: Martyn Burke
Fleet: 26 - 26 single-deck coach
Chassis/Bodies: 26 Setra
Ops incl: excursions & tours, continental tours, private hire
Livery: White/Blue/Red

CUNNINGHAM CARRIAGE COMPANY
THE CARRIAGE HOUSE, FOBBING ROAD, CORRINGHAM SS17 9BG
Tel: 01375 676578
Fax: 01375 679719
Prop: Pat Cunningham
Junior Partner: Sarah Cunningham
Fleet: 1 single-deck coach.
Chassis: 1 Scania.
Bodies: 1 Irizar.
Ops incl: private hire, express.
Livery: White
Ticket System: Setright.

DOCKLANDS BUSES LTD
See London

DONS COACHES DUNMOW LTD
PARSONAGE DOWNS, GREAT DUNMOW CM6 2AT
Tel: 01371 872644
Fax: 01371 876055
E-mail: jamie@donscoaches.fsnet.co.uk
Web: www.donscoaches.fsnet.co.uk
Dir: S D Harvey
Fleet: 16 - 3 double-deck bus, 10 single-deck coach, 2 midicoach, 1 minicoach.
Chassis: 1 Ayats, 1 Caetano, 1 Dennis, 1 Jonckheere, 1 Mercedes, 3 Neoplan, 2 Plaxton.
Bodies: 2 Alexander, 1 Ayats, 2 Caetano, 2 Duple, 1 Marcopolo, 3 Neoplan, 3 Plaxton.
Ops incl: private hire, school contracts.
Livery: Red/Yellow/Blue

EAST LONDON BUS GROUP
See London

EDS MINIBUS & COACH HIRE
257 PRINCESS MARGARET ROAD, EAST TILBURY RM18 8SB
Tel/Fax: 01375 858049
Props: E Sammons, Mrs S Sammons
Fleet: 2 - 1 single-deck coach, 1 minibus.
Chassis/Body: MAN/Caetano Algarve.
Ops incl: Private hire, excursions & tours

ENSIGN BUS COMPANY LTD
JULIETTE CLOSE, PURFLEET INDUSTRIAL PARK, PURFLEET RM15 4YF
Tel: 01708 865656
Fax: 01708 864340
E-mail: sales@ensignbus.com
Web site: www.ensignbus.com
Chairman: Peter Newman
Comm Dir: Ross Newman
City Sightseeing Dir: Steve Newman
Eng Dir: Brian Longley
Fin Man: Tony Astle
Comm Man: John Lupton
Eng Man: Roger Jackson
Fleet (Purfleet): 80 - 51 double-deck bus, 23 single-deck bus, 1 single-deck coach, 5 open-top bus.
Chassis: 14 AEC, 1 Bristol, 30 Dennis, 7 Leyland, 2 MCW, 26 Volvo.
Bodies: 21 Alexander Dennis, 1 Duple, 1 ECW, 3 East Lancs, 19 Marshall, 2 MCW, 10 Optare, 2 Plaxton, 1 UVG, 20 Other.
Ops incl: local bus services, private hire.
Livery: Blue/Silver
Ticket System: Wayfarer TGX150

EXCALIBUR COACH TRAVEL
44 MOUNTVIEW CRESCENT, ST LAWRENCE BAY, SOUTHMINSTER CM0 7NR
Tel: 01621 779980
Fax: 01621 778928
E-mail: info@excaliburcoach.co.uk
Web site: www.excaliburcoach.co.uk
Prop: Trevor Wynn
Fleet: 3 minibus.
Chassis: 1 Ford Transit, 1 LDV.
Ops incl: private hire, school contracts.

FARGO COACHLINES
ALLVIEWS, SCHOOL ROAD, RAYNE, BRAINTREE CM7 6SS
Tel: 01376 321817
Fax: 01376 551236
E-mail: enquiries@fargocoachlines.co.uk

Symbol	Meaning	Symbol	Meaning	Symbol	Meaning
♿	Vehicle suitable for disabled	🔒	Seat belt-fitted Vehicle	R24	24 hour recovery service
T	Toilet-drop facilities available	🍴	Coach(es) with galley facilities		Replacement vehicle available
R	Recovery service available	❄	Air-conditioned vehicle(s)		Vintage Coach(es) available
	Open top vehicle(s)	🚻	Coaches with toilet facilities		

Web site: www.fargocoachlines.co.uk
Prop: L J Smith
Fleet: 8 minibus
Ops incl: private hire
Livery: White

FERRERS COACHES LTD
♿ 🔒
117B HULLBRIDGE ROAD,
SOUTH WOODHAM FERRERS CM3 5LL
Tel: 01245 320456
Dir: A. Read, G. Read.
Fleet: 4 – 2 single-deck coach, 2 minibus.
Chassis: 2 Dennis, 1 Ford Transit,
1 Freight Rover.
Ops incl: excursions & tours, private hire, school contracts.

FIRST EAST OF ENGLAND
(formerly FIRST ESSEX BUSES)
♿
WESTWAY, CHELMSFORD CM1 3AR
Tel: 01245 293400
Web site: www.firstgroup.com
Man Dir: Alan Pilbeam
Eng Dir: Phil Pannell
Fin Dir: Jacky Cato
Comm & Customer Services Dir:
Steve Wickers
Fleet: 699 - 174 double-deck bus,
222 single-deck bus, 19 single-deck coach, 244 midibus, 40 minibus.
Chassis: AEC, BMC, Dennis, Leyland, Mercedes, Optare, Scania, Volvo.
Ops incl: local bus services, school contracts.
Livery: FirstGroup UK Bus
Ticket System: Wayfarer

FLORIDA COACHES
♿ 🔒 🍴 ❄ 🚻 T
LITTLE STUBLEYS FARM,
SUDBURY ROAD, HALSTEAD CO9 2BB
Tel: 01787 477701
Fax: 01787 475209
E-mail: info@coachcompany.co.uk
Web site: www.coachcompany.co.uk
Man Dir: Patrick Keeble
Ops Man: Murray Dean
Eng: Paul Twyman
Office Man: Lisa Whellem
Fleet: 14 – 3 double-deck bus,
2 single-deck bus, 7 single-deck coach,
1 midicoach, 1 minicoach.
Chassis: 2 Dennis, 2 Leyland, 3 MAN,
1 Neoplan, 1 Renault, 2 Setra, 1 Toyota,
2 Volvo
Bodies: 2 Alexander Dennis, 2 Caetano,
2 East Lancs, 1 Jonckheere, 1 Neoplan,
2 Noge, 1 Northern Counties, 2 Setra,
1 Other.
Ops incl: local bus services, school contracts, excursions & tours, private hire, continental tours.
Livery: Various
Ticket System: Almex

FORDS COACHES
🍴 ❄
THE GARAGE, FAMBRIDGE ROAD,
ALTHORNE CM3 6BZ
Tel: 01621 740326
Fax: 01621 742781
Web site: www.fordscoaches.co.uk

Prop: A A W Ford Ch Eng: A W Ford
Fleet: 22 - 8 double-deck bus,
1 single-deck bus, 8 single-deck coach,
3 double-deck coach, 2 midicoach
Chassis: 6 Alexander Dennis, 1 AEC,
1 Bedford, 8 Leyland, 3 Scania.
Bodies: 2 Alexander, 1 Ayats, 1 Beulas,
2 Berkhof, 1 Caetano, 6 ECW, 1 Indcar,
1 Mellor, 1 Optare, 2 Plaxton, 4 Van Hool.
Ops incl: local bus services, school contracts, excursions & tours, private hire.
Livery: White/Multi-colour stripe
Ticket system: Wayfarer

GALLEON TRAVEL LTD
♿ 🍴 ❄ R
TOPRAK HOUSE, RIVERWAY,
HARLOW CM20 2DR
Tel: 0800 294 9534
E-mail: sales@galleontravel.co.uk
Web site: www.galleontravel.co.uk
Man Dir: Peter Harvey
Fleet: 4 - 2 single-deck coach,
1 double-deck coach, 1 midicoach
Chassis: 1 Ayats, 1 Mercedes, 2 Scania.
Bodies: 1 Ayats, 2 Irizar, 1 Plaxton.
Ops incl: private hire.
Liveries: Maroon, White
Part of the Centrebus Group

GATWICK FLYER LTD
DANES ROAD, ROMFORD RM7 0HL
Tel: 01708 730555
Fax: 01708 751231
Web site: www.gatwickflyer.co.uk
Fleet Names: Gatwick Flyer, Avon Coaches
Fleet: 15 - 6 single-deck coach,
9 minicoach.
Ops incl: private hire, express.

GENIAL TRAVEL
♿
43 PEACE ROAD, STANWAY,
COLCHESTER CO3 0HL
Tel/Fax: 01206 571513
Prop: Trevor Brookes
Fleet: 1 single-deck coach.
Chassis: 1 DAF
Body: 1 Van Hool
Ops incl: excursions & tours, private hire.
Livery: White/Blue/Yellow.

PETER GODWARD COACHES
🍴 🚻 ♿ ❄
UNITS 3&4, MILLS COURT,
SWINBOURNE ROAD,
BURNT MILLS INDUSTRIAL ESTATE,
BASILDON SS13 1EH
Tel: 01268 591834 Fax: 01268 591835
E-mail: peter.godward@virgin.net
Props: P R Godward (Ops), J Godward
(Ops), Mrs A M Godward (Co Sec)
Fleet: 13 – 3 double-deck bus,
10 single-deck coach.
Chassis incl: 4 Iveco, 6 Scania.
Bodies incl: 4 Beulas, 6 Irizar.
Ops incl: school contracts, excursions & tours, private hire, express, continental tours.
Livery: White

GOLDEN BOY COACHES
See Hertfordshire

GOODWIN'S COACHES
ALWYNN, LONDON ROAD,
BLACK NOTLEY, BRAINTREE CM7 8QQ
Tel: 01376 321096
Prop: A. M. Goodwin
Sec: I. B. Goodwin.
Fleet: 6 - 5 single-deck coach, 1 minibus.
Chassis: 3 Bedford, 2 Volvo.
Bodies: 1 Berkhof, 1 Crystal, 4 Plaxton.
Ops incl: excursions & tours, private hire.
Livery: White/Blue/Grey stripes.

GRAHAM'S COACHES LTD
STATION ROAD, KELVEDON
CO5 9NP
Tel: 01376 570150.
Fax: 01376 570657
E-mail: info@grahamscoaches.ltd.uk
Web site: www.grahamscoaches.com
Prop: G. Ellis.
Livery: White/Blue.

HAILSTONE TRAVEL LTD
♿ ❄
82 BRACKLEY CRESCENT,
BASILDON SS13 1RA
Tel: 0845 388 3848
Fax: 0845 388 3856
E-mail: info@hailstonetravel.co.uk
Web site: www.hailstonetravel.co.uk
Dirs: Mrs Tina Hailstone, Lawrence Hailstone
Fleet: 7 minicoach.
Chassis/Bodies: 7 Mercedes.
Ops incl: school contracts, excursions & tours, private hire
Livery: White

HARDY MILES COACHES LTD
259 HAMSTEL ROAD,
SOUTHEND ON SEA SS2 4LB
Tel: 01701 612222
Fax: 01702 546461
E-mail: info@hardymilestravel.co.uk
Web site: www.hardymilestravel.co.uk
Prop: Richard Jordan, Michael Chapman
Fleet: 3 - 2 double-deck bus,
1 single-deck coach.
Chassis: 2 MCW, 1 Scania
Bodies: 1 Irizar, 2 MCW
Ops incl: excursions & tours, private hire.

HEDINGHAM & DISTRICT OMNIBUSES LTD
♿
WETHERSFIELD ROAD,
SIBLE HEDINGHAM CO9 3LB
Tel: 01787 460621
Fax: 01787 462852
E-mail: services@hedingham.co.uk
Web site: www.hedingham.co.uk
Man Dir: R J MacGregor
Fleet: 103 - 42 double-deck bus,
43 single-deck bus, 18 single-deck coach.
Chassis: 29 ADL/Dennis/Transbus,
2 Bristol, 22 Leyland, 50 Volvo.
Bodies: 27 Alexander Dennis, 13 ECW,
1 East Lancs, 3 Leyland, 17 Northern Counties, 23 Plaxton, 1 Willowbrook,
3 Wright.
Ops incl: local bus services, school contracts, excursions & tours, private hire.
Livery: Red/Cream.
Ticket System: Wayfarer TGX

IMPERIAL BUS CO LTD
COMPOUND 6, MILL FARM ESTATE,
WHALEBONE LANE NORTH,
ROMFORD, RM6 5QT
Tel: 0208 597 7368
Web site: www.imperialbus.co.uk
Man Dir: M Biddell
Fleet: 31 - 17 double-deck bus,
2 single-deck bus, 12 midibus.
Chassis: 6 AEC, 12 Dennis, 8 Leyland,
3 MCW, 2 Mercedes.
Bodies: 1 Alexander Dennis, 2 ECW,
1 Leyland, 3 MCW, 4 Marshall, 5 Northern
Counties, 7 Park Royal, 7 Plaxton, 1 Roe.
Ops incl: local bus services, school
contracts, private hire
Livery: Green.

KINGS COACHES
364 LONDON ROAD, STANWAY,
COLCHESTER CO3 8LT
Tel: 01206 210332
Fax: 01206 213861
E-mail: andrew@kings-coaches.co.uk
Web site: www.kings-coaches.co.uk
Prop: Andrew B Cousins
Fleet: 7 single-deck coach.
Chassis: 7 Bova.
Bodies: 7 Bova.
Ops incl: excursions & tours, private hire.
Livery: Green/Cream

KIRBYS COACHES (RAYLEIGH) LTD
2 PRINCESS ROAD,
RAYLEIGH SS6 8HR
Tel: 01268 777777
Fax: 01702 202555
E-mail: kirbyscoaches@hotmail.co.uk
Web site: www.kirbyscoaches.co.uk
Dir: Edward Kirby
Co Sec: Elizabeth Kirby
Fleet: 9 single-deck coach.
Chassis/Bodies: 9 Setra.
Ops incl: excursions & tours, private hire,
continental tours.
Livery: Lilac/Turquoise

LINKFAST LTD t/a S&M COACHES
93 ROSEBERRY AVENUE,
BENFLEET SS7 4JF
Tel/Fax: 01268 795763
Props: B. W. Smith (**Ch Eng**),
W. N. May (**Sec**).
Fleet: 10 - 9 double-deck bus,
1 single-deck coach.
Chassis: Daimler, Leyland.
Bodies: ECW, Northern Counties,
Park Royal, Plaxton.
Ops incl: school contracts, private hire.
Livery: Mixed.

J W LODGE & SONS LTD
THE GARAGE, HIGH EASTER,
CHELMSFORD CM1 4QT
Tel: 01245 231262 **Fax:** 01245 231825
E-mail:
administrator@lodgecoaches.co.uk
Web site: www.lodgecoaches.co.uk
Fleet Name: Lodge Coaches
Dirs: R C Lodge (**Co Sec**), A D Lodge,
C J Lodge **Ch Eng:** P Hartley
Fleet: 25 - 6 double-deck bus,
2 single-deck bus 12 single-deck coach,
2 minicoach, 3 vintage coach.
Chassis: 3 Bedford, 3 Dennis, 1 Iveco,
6 Leyland, 1 MAN, 4 Mercedes, 1 Optare,
2 Scania, 4 Setra.
Bodies: 1 Alexander Dennis, 3 Duple.
5 Leyland, 2 Mellor, 3 Mercedes,
2 Optare, 3 Plaxton, 4 Setra, 2 Van Hool
Ops incl: local bus services, school
contracts, excursions & tours, private hire,
continental tours.
Livery: Blue/Cream
Ticket System: Wayfarer

MIKES COACHES
THE GRANARY, PIPPS HILL ROAD
NORTH, CRAYS HILL,
BASILDON CM11 2UJ
Tel: 01268 525900
Fax: 01268 453654
Partners: M. Orphan, D. Orphan,
P. Brown.
Fleet: 6 - 5 single-deck coach,
1 midicoach.
Chassis: 2 Bedford, 1 DAF, 3 Volvo.
Bodies: 5 Plaxton, 1 Van Hool.
Ops incl: local bus services, school
contracts, private hire.

W. H. NELSON (COACHES) LTD
THE COACH STATION, BRUCE GROVE,
WICKFORD SS11 8BZ
Tel: 01268 767870
Fax: 01268 735307
E-mail: info@nibsbus.com
Web site: www.nibsbus.com
Fleet Name: Nelsons Independent Bus
Services
Fleet: double-deck bus, midibus.
Ops incl: local bus services, school
contracts
Livery: Yellow.

NETWORK COLCHESTER LTD
UNIT 4 HEATH BUSINESS PARK,
GRANGE WAY,
COLCHESTER CO2 8GH
Tel: 01206 877620
Fax: 01206 766345
Web site: www.networkcolchester.co.uk
Fleet Name: Network Colchester
Fleet: 44 - 16 double-deck bus, 7 single-
deck bus, 21 midibus.
Chassis: 2 DAF, 18 Dennis, 5 Optare,
7 Scania, 12 Volvo.
Bodies: 7 Alexander, 6 Caetano,
10 East Lancs, 4 Northern Counties,
5 Optare, 2 Plaxton, 10 Transbus.
Ops incl: local bus services, excursions
& tours, school contracts, private hire,
continental tours.
Livery: Blue/Yellow on White base
A subsidiary of TGM Group Ltd, part of
Arriva

NEW HORIZON TRAVEL LTD
GREAT BENTLEY ROAD, FRATING,
CO7 7HN
Tel: 01206 255255
Fax: 01206 255033
E-mail: nhtltd@aol.com
Web Site: www.newhorizontravel.co.uk
Man Dir: R Connor
Ops incl: school contracts, excursions &
tours, private hire
Livery: White, with Blue, Red, Yellow

OLYMPIAN COACHES LTD
TEMPLE BANK, RIVERWAY,
HARLOW CM20 2DY
Tel: 01279 868868
Fax: 01279 868867
E-mail: mel@olympiancoaches.com
Web site: www.olympiancoaches.com
Dirs: C. Marino
Co Sec: Mrs D. K. Higgins
Ops Dir: B. Gunton
Fleet: 40 – single-deck bus, single-deck
coach, minibus.
Ops incl: local bus services, school
contracts, excursions & tours, private hire,
express continental tours.

P & M COACHES
74 CHURCHEND LANE,
WICKFORD SS11 7JG
Tel: 01268 763616

PHILLIPS COACHES
117B HULLBRIDGE ROAD, SOUTH
WOODHAM FERRERS CM3 5LL
Tel/Fax: 01245 323039
Prop: L. Phillips.
Fleet: 3 - 2 single-deck coach, 1 minibus.
Chassis: 1 Freight Rover, 2 Volvo.
Bodies: Plaxton, Van Hool.
Ops incl: excursions & tours, private hire,
school contracts.
Livery: Cream/Maroon.

RAYLEIGH ROADWAYS LTD
SHOT FARM, SHOTGATE, WICKFORD
SS11 8RZ
Tel: 01268 765240
Fax: 01268 570221
E-mail: info@rayleighroadways.co.uk
Web site: www.rayleighroadways.co.uk
Fleet: singe-deck coaches
Ops incl: school contracts, private hire,
excursions & tours, continental tours.

REGAL BUSWAYS LTD
LANDVIEW, COOKSMILL GREEN,
CHELMSFORD CM1 3SR
Tel: 01702 291001
E-mail: info@regalbusways.com
Web site: www.regalbusways.com
Man Dir: Adrian McGarry
Ops Dir: Lee Whitehead
Dir: Mandy McGarry
Fleet Names: Essex Pullman,
Regal Busways
Fleet: 35 - 4 double-deck bus,
9 single-deck bus, 22 midibus.
Chassis: 1 Alexander Dennis, 19 Dennis.
5 Leyland, 2 MAN, 8 Optare.
Bodies: 3 Alexander Dennis, 4 ECW,
1 Leyland, 1 MCV, 8 Optare, 16 Plaxton,
2 Wright.
Ops incl: local bus services, private hire,
school contracts.
Livery: Maroon/Cream
Ticket system: ERG

RELIANCE LUXURY COACHES
54 BROOK ROAD,
BENFLEET SS7 5JF
Tel/Fax: 01268 758426
Web site: www.reliancecoaches.co.uk
Prop: Martyn J Titchen
Fleet: 4 - 1 double-deck coach,
3 single-deck coach
Chassis: 1 MAN, 3 Scania.
Bodies: 1 Jonckheere Monaco,
3 Irizar Century Club.
Ops incl: private hire.
Livery: Yellow/White/Orange/Red.

RICHMOND'S COACHES
THE GARAGE, HIGH STREET,
BARLEY, ROYSTON SG8 8JA

Tel: 01763 848226
Fax: 01763 848105
E-mail: postbox@richmonds-coaches.co.uk
Web site: www.richmonds-coaches.co.uk
Dirs: David Richmond, Michael Richmond, Andrew Richmond
Sales & Marketing Man: Rick Ellis
Asst Ops Man: Craig Ellis
Ch Eng: Patrick Granville
Exc & Tours Man: Natalie Richmond
Fleet: 25 – 18 single-deck coach, 1 double-deck coach, 5 midibus, 1 midicoach.
Chassis: 9 Bova, 5 DAF, 4 Mercedes, 2 Optare, 5 Volvo.
Bodies: 9 Bova, 2 Optare, 3 Plaxton, 1 Sitcar, 10 Van Hool.
Ops incl: local bus services, school contracts, excursions & tours, private hire, continental tours.
Livery: Cream/Brown
Ticket System: Wayfarer 3

STALLION COACHES
STACEYS FARM BUNGALOW, BROOMFIELD, CHELMSFORD CM1 7HF
Tel/Fax: 01245 443500
Partners: D. A. Brewster, Miss J. C. Pinkerton.
Fleet: 2 midicoach.
Chassis: 1 Mercedes, 1 Toyota.
Bodies: 1 Caetano, 1 Reeve Burgess.
Ops incl: school contracts, private hire.

STAN'S COACHES
THE COACH-HOUSE, BECKINGHAM ROAD, GREAT TOTHAM, MALDON CM9 8DY
Tel: 01621 891959
Fax: 01621 891365
Web site: www.stans-coaches.co.uk
Prop: S. J. Porter.
Fleet: 6 - 5 single-deck coach, 1 minibus.
Chassis: 1 Bedford, 3 Bova, 1 Mercedes, 1 Volvo.
Bodies: 3 Bova, 1 Duple, 1 Mercedes, 1 Plaxton.
Ops incl: excursions & tours, school contracts, private hire, continental tours.
Livery: White with Blue/Grey stripes.

STEPHENSONS OF ESSEX LTD
RIVERSIDE INDUSTRIAL ESTATE, SOUTH STREET, ROCHFORD SS4 1BS
Tel: 01702 541511
Fax: 01702 549461
E-mail: sales@stephensonsofessex.com
Web site: www.stephensonsofessex.com
Man Dir: Bill Hiron
Fin Dir: Lyn Watson
Fleet: 60 - 41 double-deck bus, 17 single-deck bus, 2 single-deck coach.
Chassis: 4 Alexander Dennis, 6 Dennis, 28 Leyland, 6 Optare, 3 Scania, 10 Volvo.
Bodies: 18 Alexander Dennis, 1 East Lancs, 25 Northern Counties, 9 Optare, 7 Plaxton.
Ops incl: local bus services, school contracts, private hire.
Livery: White/Green
Ticket System: Wayfarer 3

SUPREME COACHES
REAR OF SOUTHERN COUNTIES, SOUTHEND ROAD, RETTENDON COMMON, CHELMSFORD CM3 8DZ
Tel: 01702 401541
Fax: 01702 616590
E-mail: admin@supremecoaches.co.uk
Web site: www.supremecoaches.co.uk
Man Dir: John Bridge
Fleet Eng: Toby Lyster-Bridge
Fleet: 12 - 6 double-deck bus, 6 single-deck coach.
Chassis: 6 MCW, 4 Scania, 1 Setra, 1 Volvo.
Ops incl: school contracts, excursions & tours, private hire, continental tours.
Livery: Red/White/Blue

SWALLOW COACH CO LTD
1 BARLOW WAY SOUTH, FAIRVIEW INDUSTRIAL ESTATE, MARSH WAY, RAINHAM RM13 8BT
Tel: 01708 630555
Fax: 01708 555135
E-mail: info@swallowcoach.co.uk
Web site: www.swallowcoach.com
Chairman: D. R. Webb
Man Dir: K. I. Webb
Sec: Mrs. S. D. Webb.
Fleet: 26 - 17 single-deck coach, 5 midicoach, 4 minicoach.
Chassis: 1 DAF, 1 Dennis, 1 Ford, 1 Ford Transit, 3 Freight Rover, 3 Leyland, 1 MAN, 2 Mercedes, 1 Setra, 1 Toyota, 11 Volvo.
Bodies: 5 Caetano, 1 Carlyle, 4 Jonckheere, 2 Mercedes, 6 Plaxton, 1 Setra, 2 Van Hool.
Ops incl: Private hire.
Livery: Various.

TALISMAN COACH LINES
THE COACH STATION, HARWICH ROAD, GREAT BROMLEY, COLCHESTER CO7 7UL
Tel: 01206 252472
Fax: 01206 251742
E-mail: sales@talismancoachlines.co.uk
Web site: www.talismancoachlines.com
Man Dir: Terry Smith
Fleet incl: 18 – 4 double-deck bus, 12 single-deck coach, 2 open-top bus.
Chassis: 1 Bristol, 3 Leyland, 1 MCW, 1 Optare, 1 Scania, 11 Setra.
Bodies: 4 ECW, 1 Irizar, 1 MCW, 1 Optare, 11 Setra.
Ops incl: excursions & tours, private hire, continental tours.
Livery: White

TGM GROUP LTD
FOURTH AVENUE, HARLOW CM20 1DU
Tel: 01279 681800
Fax: 01279 682268
Recovery: 07770 873614
E-mail: mail@excelpl.co.uk
Web site: www.excelcoaches.co.uk
Ops incl: local bus services, school contracts
Incorporates Excel Passenger Logistics.
A subsidiary of Arriva

VICEROY OF ESSEX LTD
12 BRIDGE STREET, SAFFRON WALDEN CB10 1BU
Tel: 01799 508010
Fax: 01799 506106
E-mail: enquiries@viceroycoaches.co.uk
Web site: www.viceroycoaches.co.uk
Man Dir: A R Moore
Man Dir/Eng: S A Moore
Ops Man: A L Moore
Fleet: 7 - 1 dingle-deck bus, 4 single-deck coach, 1 midibus, 1 minicoach.
Chassis: 1 BMC, 1 DAF, 4 Mercedes, 1 Scania.
Bodies: 1 BMC, 1 Bova, 2 Hispano, 1 Mercedes, 1 Plaxton.
Ops incl: local bus services, school contracts, excursions & tours, private hire, continental tours.
Livery: White
Ticket System: Wayfarer 3

WALDEN TRAVEL LTD
126 THAXTED ROAD, SAFFRON WALDEN CB11 3BJ
Tel/Fax: 01799 516878
Man Dir: Peter Blanchard
Non-Exec Dirs: John Wilson, David Grimmett.
Fleet: 8 - 4 single-deck coach, 3 midibus, 1 minibus.
Chassis: 2 Dennis, 1 Ford Transit, 3 Mercedes, 2 Volvo
Bodies: 1 Jonckheere, 6 Plaxton, 1 other.
Ops incl: local bus services, school contracts, excursions & tours, private hire.
Livery: White
Ticket System: ERG

WEST'S COACHES LTD
See London

GLOUCESTERSHIRE

ALEXCARS LTD
11 LOVE LANE, CIRENCESTER GL7 1YG
Tel: 01285 653985
Fax: 01285 652964
E-mail: info@alexcars.co.uk
Web site: www.alexcars.co.uk
Man Dir: Rod Hibberd
Tran Man: Will Jarvis
Co Sec: Jenny Jarvis
Ch Mech: Steve Hall
Fleet: 22 - 16 single-deck coach, 3 midicoach, 3 minicoach.
Chassis: 2 Alexander Dennis, 1 Bedford, 1 Iveco, 1 MAN, 4 Mercedes, 10 Scania, 3 Toyota.
Bodies: 3 Caetano, 1 Duple, 1 Indcar, 11 Irizar, 4 Mercedes, 1 Plaxton, 1 Wadham Stringer, 1 Other.
Ops incl: school contracts, excursions & tours, private hire, continental tours.
Livery: Dual Blue

BAKERS COACHES
COTSWOLD BUSINESS VILLAGE, MORETON-IN-THE-MARSH GL56 0JQ
Tel: 0845 688 7707
Fax: 0845 688 7660
E-mail: enquiries@bakerscoaches.co.uk
Web site: www.bakerscoaches.co.uk
Dir: Mike Baker **Ops Man:** Dave Goodall
Fleet: 17 - 14 single-deck coach, 2 midicoach, 1 minibus.
Chassis: 2 Dennis, 2 Iveco, 3 Mercedes, 1 Scania, 2 Transbus, 7 Volvo.
Bodies: Alexander, Irizar, Plaxton.
Ops incl: local bus services, excursions & tours, school contracts, private hire, continental tours.
Livery: White/Red

B. E. W. BEAVIS/BEAVIS HOLIDAYS
BUSSAGE GARAGE, BUSSAGE, STROUD GL6 8BA
Tel: 01453 882297
Fax: 01453 731019
E-mail: admin@beavisholidays.co.uk
Web site: www.beavisholidays.co.uk
Props/Partners: Brian Beavis, Anita Baxter **Ch Eng:** Chris Beavis
Fleet: 8 - 5 single-deck coach, 1 midicoach, 1 minibus, 1 minicoach.
Chassis: 1 DAF, 4 Neoplan, 1 Scania, 1 Toyota, 1 Volkswagen.
Bodies: 1 Caetano, 1 EOS, 1 Irizar, 4 Neoplan, 1 Volkswagen.
Ops incl: excursions & tours, private hire, school contracts, continental tours.
Livery: Gold/Orange/Red/Yellow.

BENNETT'S COACHES
EASTERN AVENUE, GLOUCESTER GL4 4LP
Tel: 01452 527809
Fax: 01452 384448
E-mail: info@bennettscoaches.co.uk
Web site: www.bennettscoaches.co.uk
Senior Partner: Peter Bennett
Ops Man: Gavin Bennett
Sales Man: Paul O'Connor
Fleet: 24 - 5 double-deck bus, 5 single-deck bus, 14 single-deck coach.
Chassis: 4 DAF, 1 MAN, 11 Mercedes, 3 Neoplan, 5 Volvo

Bodies incl: 1 Ikarus, 11 Mercedes, 3 Neoplan, 4 Van Hool.
Ops incl: local bus services, school contracts, private hire.
Livery: Blue/Orange or Silver.

JAMES BEVAN (LYDNEY) LTD
THE BUS STATION, HAMS ROAD, LYDNEY GL15 5PE
Tel/Fax: 01594 842859
E-mail: jamesbevancoaches@tiscali.co.uk
Web site: www.jamesbevancoaches.com
Man Dir: James Bevan
Ops Dir: J Zimmerman
Eng Dir: M Zimmerman
Fleet: 12 – 2 single-deck bus, 5 single-deck coach, 5 midibus.
Chassis: 5 Dennis, 2 Mercedes, 1 Optare, 4 Volvo.
Bodies: 1 Alexander, 1 Optare, 3 Plaxton, 2 Sunsundegui, 3 UVG, 2 Wadham Stringer.
Ops incl: local bus services, school contracts, private hire.
Livery: Silver
Ticket System: Wayfarer

CASTLEWAYS LTD
CASTLE HOUSE, GREET ROAD, WINCHCOMBE GL54 5PU
Tel: 01242 603715
Fax: 01242 604454
Web site: www.castleways.co.uk
Man Dir: John Fogarty **Dir:** Mrs Rowena McCubbin **Ch Eng:** Trevor Wood
Fleet: 13 - 4 single-deck bus, 8 single-deck coach, 1 midicoach
Chassis: 1 Bova, 1 Dennis, 2 Mercedes, 1 Optare, 4 Setra, 1 Temsa, 1 Toyota, 2 Volvo.
Bodies: 1 Bova, 1 Caetano, 2 Mercedes, 1 Optare, 2 Plaxton, 4 Setra, 1 Sunsundegui, 1 Temsa.
Ops incl: local bus services, school contracts, private hire.
Livery: Dark Blue/Silver/Gold
Ticket System: Wayfarer

CATHEDRAL COACHES LTD
18 QUAY STREET, GLOUCESTER GL1 2JS
Tel: 01452 524591
Fax: 01452 524595
E-mail: paul@cathedralcoaches.fsnet.co.uk
Web site: www.cathedralcoaches.co.uk
Dirs: Irene Chandler, Paul Chandler
Fleet: 9 - 5 single-deck coach, 2 midicoach, 2 minicoach.
Chassis: 1 DAF, 3 Dennis, 3 Mercedes, 1 Toyota, 1 Volvo.
Bodies: 2 Caetano, 1 Optare, 5 Plaxton, 1 Reeve Burgess.
Ops incl: school contracts, private hire.
Livery: Blue/Grey/Red/White

COLEFORDIAN (WILLETTS) LTD
CROWN PARK ESTATE, EDENWALL ROAD, COALWAY, COLEFORD GL16 7HW
Tel: 01594 810080
Fax: 01594 834480
E-mail: colefordian@tiscali.co.uk

Web site: www.colefordian.co.uk
Fleet: 6 single-deck coach
Chassis: 6 Volvo
Bodies: 2 Jonckheere, 2 Plaxton, 2 Van Hool
Ops incl: excursions & tours, private hire, continental tours.

COTSWOLD GREEN LTD
UNIT 27A, NAILSWORTH MILLS ESTATE, AVENING ROAD, NAILSWORTH GL6 0DS
Tel: 01453 835153
Fleet: 20 - single-deck bus, midibus, minibus.
Chassis: Dennis, MAN, Mercedes, Optare, Scania, Volvo.
Ops incl: local bus services, school contracts.
Livery: Green/White.

EAGLE LINE TRAVEL
ANDOVERSFORD TRADING ESTATE, ANDOVERSFORD GL54 4LB
Tel/Fax: 01242 820535
E-mail: brian@eaglelinetravel.co.uk
Web site: www.eaglelinetravel.co.uk
Man Dirs: Brian Davis, Martin Davis, Wayne Hodge
Ch Eng: Tony Mezzone
Fleet: 22 - 10 single-deck coach, 2 double-deck coach, 2 midibus, 4 midicoach, 2 minicoach, 2 minibus.
Chassis: 2 DAF, 2 Dennis, 4 Ford Transit, 6 Mercedes, 1 Neoplan, 1 Scania, 1 Toyota, 5 Volvo.
Bodies: 2 Autobus, 2 Berkhof, 1 Caetano, 2 Mercedes, 4 Ford Transit, 1 Neoplan, 2 Plaxton, 6 Van Hool, 2 Volkswagen.
Ops incl: school contracts, excursions & tours, private hire, continental tours.
Livery: Dark Blue/Silver/Silver Blue

EBLEY COACHES LTD
UNIT 27, NAILSWORTH MILLS ESTATE, AVENING ROAD, NAILSWORTH GL6 0BS
Tel/Fax: 01453 839333
Dirs: C C Levitt, G A Jones.
Fleet: single-deck bus, single-deck coach.
Ops incl: school contracts, excursions & tours, private hire.
Livery: White.

DAVID FIELD
WHEATSTONE HOUSE, WATERY LANE, NEWENT GL18 1PY
Tel: 01531 820979
Web site: www.davidfieldtravel.co.uk
Prop: David Field MSOE, MIRTE
Fleet: 8 - 6 single-deck coach, 1 midicoach, 1 minicoach.
Chassis: 1 DAF, 1 Dennis, 1 Iveco, 1 Leyland, 2 Mercedes, 1 Setra, 1 Toyota.
Ops incl: school contracts, private hire.
Livery: Black/White
Ticket System: Setright

GRINDLES COACHES LTD
4 DOCKHAM ROAD, CINDERFORD GL14 2DD.
Tel: 01594 822110
Fax: 01594 823189

The Little Red Book 2011 - in association with Transport Benevolent Fund

Man Dir: P R Grindle
Co Sec: W H R Grindle.
Fleet: 7 single-deck coach.
Chassis: 3 Bedford, 1 Bova, 3 DAF.
Bodies: 1 Bova, 5 Plaxton, 1 Van Hool.
Ops incl: local bus services, private hire.

MARCHANTS COACHES
61 CLARENCE STREET,
CHELTENHAM GL50 3LB
Tel: 01242 257714
Fax: 01242 251360
E-mail: sales@marchants-coaches.com
Web site: www.marchants-coaches.com
Man Dir: Roger Marchant
Dir/Ops/Tran Man: Richard Marchant
Ch Eng: Russell Marchant
Co Sec: Mrs Jean Ellis
Fleet: 26 - 6 double-deck bus,
3 single-deck bus, 11 single-deck coach,
2 double-deck coach, 3 midibus,
1 midicoach.
Chassis: 2 Bristol, 4 Leyland,
1 Mercedes, 2 Neoplan, 1 Optare,
16 Volvo.
Bodies: 2 Alexander, 3 ECW,
1 East Lancs, 4 Jonckheere, 2 Neoplan,
1 Optare, 9 Plaxton, 4 Wright.
Ops incl: local bus services, school
contracts, excursions & tours, private hire,
continental tours.
Livery: Red/Gold
Ticket System: Wayfarer

PULHAM & SONS (COACHES) LTD
STATION ROAD GARAGE,
BOURTON ON THE WATER, GL54 2EN
Tel: 01451 820369
E-mail: info@pulhamscoaches.com
Web site: www.pulhamscoaches.com
Fleet: 27 – 20 single-deck coach,
3 midibus, 4 midicoach
Chassis: Dennis, Leyland, Mercedes,
Optare, Toyota, Volvo
Bodies: Caetano, Optare, Plaxton,
Van Hool
Ops incl: local bus services, school
contracts, excursions & tours, private hire.
Livery: Red

ROVER EUROPEAN LTD
THE COACH HOUSE, THE STREET,
HORSLEY, STROUD GL6 0PU
Tel: 01453 832121
Fax: 01453 832722
E-mail: info@rovereuropean.co.uk
Web site: www.rovereuropean.co.uk
Man Dir: David Hand **Dir:** Carole Hand
Fleet: 9 - 8 single-deck coach,
1 minicoach
Chassis: 6 Bova, 2 Dennis, 1 Mercedes.
Bodies: 6 Bova, 2 Plaxton.
Ops incl: school contracts, excursions &
tours, private hire, continental tours.
Livery: Cream base with Light Blue/Dark
Blue/Orange.

STAGECOACH WEST
3RD FLOOR, 65 LONDON ROAD,
GLOUCESTER GL1 3HF
Tel: 01452 418630
Fax: 01452 304857
E-Mail: west@stagecoachbus.com
Web site: www.stagecoachbus.com
Man Dir: Ian Manning
Eng Dir: Peter Sheldon
Ops Dir: Sholto Thomas
Comm Man: Craig Lockley.
Fleet: 233 - 94 double-deck bus,
24 single-deck bus, 6 single-deck coach,
90 midibus, 19 minibus.
Chassis: 151 Dennis, 13 MAN,
2 Mercedes, 18 Optare, 19 Scania,
30 Volvo.
Bodies: 186 Alexander Dennis,
6 Caetano, 3 Northern Counties,
18 Optare, 20 Plaxton.
Ops incl: local bus services, school
contracts, private hire, express.
Livery: Stagecoach UK Bus
Ticket System: Wayfarer

SWANBROOK TRANSPORT LTD
GOLDEN VALLEY, STAVERTON,
CHELTENHAM GL51 0TE
Tel: 01452 712386 **Fax:** 01452 859217
E-mail: enquiries@swanbrook.co.uk
Web site: www.swanbrook.co.uk

Fleet Name: Swanbrook
Chairman: D J Thomas **Man Dir:** K J
Thomas **Eng Dir:** J A Thomas **Ops Dir:**
Mrs K J West **Ops Man:** M Dowle
Workshop Man: R Barnes
Fleet: 25 - 9 double-deck bus,
4 single-deck bus, 5 single-deck coach,
7 midibus.
Chassis: 5 Leyland, 3 MCW,
7 Mercedes, 3 Optare, 7 Volvo.
Bodies: 7 Alexander Dennis,
1 East Lancs, 3 MCW, 3 Optare, 8
Plaxton, 2 Van Hool, 1 Other.
Ops incl: local bus services, school
contracts, private hire.
Livery: White/Green/Purple
Ticket System: Wayfarer II

F R WILLETTS & CO (YORKLEY) LTD
DEAN RISE, MAIN ROAD,
PILLOWELL GL15 4QY
Tel: 01594 562511
Fax: 01594 564373
Man Dir: Geoff Willetts
Sec: Sue Willetts
Fleet: 6 - 4 single-deck coach,
1 minicoach, 1 minibus.
Chassis: 1 Dennis, 1 Leyland,
2 Mercedes, 1 Setra, 1 Volvo.
Bodies: 1 Mercedes, 4 Plaxton, 1 Setra.
Ops incl: local bus services, school
contracts, excursions & tours, private hire.
Livery: Red
Ticket System: Setright

MAL WITTS EXECUTIVE TRAVEL
1 YEW TREE COTTAGE, BRISTOL
ROAD, HARDWICKE, GLOUCESTER
GL2 4QZ
Tel/Fax: 01452 724072
E-mail: mal@malwittstravel.co.uk
Web site: www.malwittstravel.co.uk
Owners: Mal Witts, Lynn Witts
Fleet: 4 - 2 minicoach, 2 people carrier.
Bodies: 2 Mercedes, 2 Volkswagen.
Ops incl: private hire, continental tours,
excursions & tours, school contracts.

GREATER MANCHESTER (BOLTON, BURY, OLDHAM, ROCHDALE, SALFORD, TAMESIDE, WIGAN)

ADLINGTON TAXIS AND MINICOACHES
LODGE FARM, SANDY LANE,
HORWICH BL6 6RS
Tel: 01204 697577
E-mail: frank@fjohnson7.wanado.co.uk
Fleet: 5 - 2 single-deck bus,
1 single-deck coach, 2 midicoach.
Chassis: 1 Bedford, 2 Freight Rover,
2 Iveco.
Ops incl: local bus services, private hire.
Ticket System: Wayfarer

ARRIVA NORTH WEST
73 ORMSKIRK ROAD, AINTREE,
LIVERPOOL L9 5AE
Tel: 0151 522 2800
Fax: 0151 525 9556
Web site: www.arrivabus.co.uk
Fleet Name: Arriva Manchester
Regional Man Dir: Phil Stone
Area Man Dir: John Rimmer
Eng Dir: Philip Cummins
Fin Dir: Simon Mills
Head of Eng: Peter Gent

Fleet (Manchester): 309 - 53 double-
deck bus, 215 single-deck bus,
41 midibus.
Chassis: 10 Alexander Dennis, 33 DAF,
88 Dennis, 4 MAN, 15 Optare, 7 Scania,
122 VDL, 30 Volvo
Ops incl: local bus services, school
contracts, private hire
Livery: Arriva UK Bus
Ticket System: Wayfarer

BATTERSBY'S COACHES
73 BRIDGEWATER ROAD,
WALKDEN M28 3AF
Tel/Fax: 0161 790 2842
Dirs: R W Griffiths, S. J. Griffiths
Fleet: 3 single-deck coach.
Chassis: 1 Leyland, 2 Setra.
Ops incl: private hire, school contracts.

BLUEBIRD BUS & COACH
ALEXANDER HOUSE, GREENGATE,
MIDDLETON M24 1RU
Tel: 0161 653 1900
Fax: 0161 653 6602

Web site: www.bluebirdbus.co.uk
Gen Man: Michael T G Dunstan
Fleet: 50 single-deck bus.
Chassis: 44 Alexander Dennis, 2 DAF,
1 MAN, 3 Optare.
Bodies: 33 Alexander, 3 Caetano,
2 East Lancs, 9 MCV, 3 Plaxton.
Ops incl: local bus services.
Livery: two tone Blue
Ticket system: ERG

R BULLOCK & CO (TRANSPORT) LTD
COMMERCIAL GARAGE, STOCKPORT
ROAD, CHEADLE SK8 2AG
Tel: 0161 428 5265
Fax: 0161 428 9074
Web site: www.bullockscoaches.co.uk
Fleet: 43 – 15 double-deck bus,
6 single-deck bus, 19 single-deck coach,
3 midicoach.
Chassis: Irisbus, Leyland, Mercedes,
Scania, Toyota, Volvo.
Bodies: Alexander, Caetano, East Lancs,
Irizar, Northern Counties, Plaxton, Scania,
Vehixel.

118 The Little Red Book 2011 - in association with Transport Benevolent Fund

Ops incl: local bus services, school contracts, excursions & tours, private hire
Livery: Red/White.

BU-VAL BUSES LTD
UNIT 5, PARAGON INDUSTRIAL ESTATE, SMITHYBRIDGE, LITTLEBOROUGH OL15 8QF
Tel: 01706 372787
Fax: 01706 372121
E-mail: sales@bu-val.co.uk
Web site: www.bu-val.co.uk
Man Dir: Daniel Booth
Gen Man: David Beames
Fleet: 18 single-deck bus.
Chassis: 16 Alexander Dennis, 1 Mercedes, 1 Optare.
Bodies: 14 Alexander Dennis, 2 Caetano, 1 Optare, 1 UVG.
Ops incl: local bus services
Livery: White/Red
Ticket System: Wayfarer

LES BYWATER & SONS LTD
SPARTH BOTTOMS ROAD, ROCHDALE OL11 4HT
Tel: 01706 648573
Man Dir: M. T. Bywater
Dir: N. L. Bywater.
Fleet: 3 - 1 single-deck coach, 1 midicoach, 1 minibus.
Chassis: 1 Dennis, 2 Iveco.
Bodies: 1 Duple, 2 Robin Hood.
Ops incl: private hire, school contracts.
Livery: White/Blue/Black.

CARSVILLE COACHES
51A HIGHER ROAD, URMSTON M41 9AP
Tel: 0161 748 2698
Fax: 0161 747 2694
Recovery: 07812 964367
E-mail: janetcarsville@hotmail.com
Man Dir: D Nickson
Man: Mrs J Nickson
Fleet: 10 – 8 single-deck coach, 1 double-deck coach, 1 minibus.
Chassis: 1 Ford, 1 Ford Transit, 1 Iveco, 1 MAN, 5 Scania, 1 Volvo.
Bodies: 1 Ayats, 5 Irizar, 4 Plaxton.
Ops incl: private hire, excursions & tours, school contracts, continental tours.
Livery: White/Purple.

COACH OPTIONS LTD
768 MANCHESTER ROAD, CASTLETON, ROCHDALE OL11 3AW
Tel: 01706 713966
Fax: 01706 759996
Recovery: 01706 655808
E-mail: coach.options@freeuk.com
Web site: www.optionstours.co.uk
Dir: Paul Stone Man: Adrian Duffy
Fleet: 10 - 6 single-deck coach, 2 midicoach, 2 minibus.
Chassis incl: 2 Bova, 3 Scania, 1 Volvo.
Bodies incl: 2 Bova, 3 Irizar, 1 Van Hool.
Ops incl: school contracts, excursions & tours, private hire, continental tours.
Livery: Blue

COURTESY COACHES LTD
P.O. BOX 632, OLDHAM OL1 9HN
Tel: 0845 045 0344
Fax: 0161 287 3344
E-mail: sales@courtesycoaches.co.uk
Web site: www.courtesycoaches.co.uk
Fleet Names: Hartshead Travel, Hebble Travel, Yelloway.

Ops incl: private hire, excursions & tours, continental tours.
Livery: White with multicolour logos.

CROPPER COACHES
316 BURY ROAD, TOTTINGTON BL8 3DT
Tel: 01204 885322
Prop: L. Donnell.
Fleet: 7 minibus.
Chassis: Ford Transit, Freight Rover.
Ops incl: private hire, school contracts.

DAM EXPRESS
GROVE HOUSE, 27 MANOR STREET, ARDWICK GREEN M12 6HE
Tel: 0161 273 1234
Fax: 0161 274 4141
Fleet Name: Don Travel
Prop/Ops Man: D. Francis
Sales Man: W. Lee
Co Sec: Miss T. Wilding.
Fleet: 3 - 1 single-deck coach, 2 double-deck coach.
Ops incl: excursions & tours, private hire, express, continental tours.

ELLEN SMITH (TOURS) LTD
MANDALE PARK, CORPORATION ROAD, ROCHDALE OL11 4HJ
Tel: 01706 345000
Fax: 01706 345970
E-mail: p.targett@ellensmith.co.uk
Web site: www.ellensmith.co.uk
Man Dir: Paul Targett
Fleet: 6 - 4 single-deck coach, 2 minibus
Chassis: 2 Bova, 1 Iveco, 1 Mercedes, 2 VW.
Bodies: 1 Beulas, 2 Bova, 1 Mercedes.

ELITE SERVICES LTD
UNITS 3/6, ADSWOOD ROAD INDUSTRIAL ESTATE, ADSWOOD ROAD, STOCKPORT SK3 8LF
Tel: 0161 480 0617
Fax: 0161 480 3099
Dirs: Dave Nickson
Fleet: 21 - 2 double-deck bus, 17 single-deck coach, 2 double-deck coach.
Chassis: 1 Ayats, 1 Ford, 15 Scania, 2 Volvo.
Ops incl: excursions & tours, private hire, continental tours, school contracts.
Livery: White/Purple/Pink

FINGLANDS COACHWAYS LTD
261 WILMSLOW ROAD, RUSHOLME, MANCHESTER M14 5LJ
Tel: 0161 224 3341
Fax: 0161 257 3154
E-mail: enquiry@finglands.co.uk
Web site: www.finglands.co.uk
Fleet Name: Finglands
Chairman: Peter Shipp
Dirs: David Shurden, Peter Harrison
Fleet Eng: Tim Jenkins
Traf Man: Fred Walton
Fleet: 57 - 42 double-deck bus, 5 single-deck bus, 10 single-deck coach
Chassis: 5 Alexander Dennis, 4 Dennis, 49 Volvo.
Bodies: 23 Alexander, 15 Northern Counties, 15 Plaxton, 4 Wright, 1 Other
Ops incl: local bus services, school contracts, private hire.
Livery: White/Orange/Brown

Ticket System: Wayfarer TGX150
Subsidiary of East Yorkshire Motor Services Ltd – see East Riding

FIRST IN MANCHESTER
WALLSHAW STREET, OLDHAM OL1 3TR
Tel: 0161 627 2929
Fax: 0161 627 5845
Fleet Name: First
Man Dir: Richard Soper
Fin Dir: Martin Wilson
Service Delivery Dir: Robert Mason
Network Dir: Simon Bennett
Fleet: 776 - 236 double-deck bus, 363 single-deck bus, 149 midibus, 19 articulated bus, 9 minibus.
Chassis: BMC, Dennis, Irisbus, Leyland, Mercedes, Optare, Scania, Volvo.
Ops incl: local bus services, school contracts, private hire.
Livery: FirstGroup UK Bus
Ticket System: ERG TP4004

FREEBIRD
REVERS STREET GARAGE, WOODHILL, BURY BL8 1AQ
Tel: 0161 797 6633
Fax: 08712 773124
E-mail: info@freebirdcoaches.co.uk
Web site: www.freebirdcoaches.co.uk
Proprietor: Paul Dart
Fleet: 12 – 10 single-deck coach, 1 midicoach 1 minibus.
Chassis: 1 DAF, 3 Dennis, 5 Irisbus, 1 Iveco, 1 LDV, 1 Mercedes.
Bodies: 1 Beulas, 1 Berkhof, 1 Caetano, 1 Crest, 1 Marcopolo, 1 Mercedes, 1 Van Hool, 5 Vehixel.
Ops incl: private hire, school contracts.
Livery: White

GO-GOODWINS COACHES
LYNTOWN TRADING ESTATE, 186 OLD WELLINGTON ROAD, ECCLES, MANCHESTER M30 9QG
Tel: 0161 789 4545
Fax: 0161 789 0939
E-mail: gogoodwins@btinternet.com
Web site: www.gogoodwins.co.uk
Fleet: 22 – single-deck bus, single-deck coach, midibus
Chassis: Bova, DAF, Dennis, Irisbus, Mercedes, Optare, Van Hool, Volvo.
Prop: Geoff Goodwin
Co Sec: Suzanne Goodwin
Ops incl: local bus services, school contracts, private hire.

GPD TRAVEL
27 HARTFORD AVENUE, HEYWOOD OL10 4XM
Tel: 01706 622297
Fax: 01706 361494
E-mail: janinedawson@hotmail.com
Web site: www.gpdtravel.co.uk
Proprietor: Gary Dawson
Fleet: 5 - 4 single-deck coach, 1 midicoach.
Chassis: 1 Mercedes-Benz, 4 Volvo.
Ops incl: school contracts, excursions & tours, private hire, continental tours.
Livery: White with red lettering

GRAYWAY COACHES
237 MANCHESTER ROAD, INCE, WIGAN WN2 2AE
Tel: 01942 243165
Fax: 01942 824807
E-mail: enquiries@grayway.co.uk
Web site: www.grayway.co.uk

Greater Manchester

Greater Manchester

Proprietors: Janet Gray, Michael Gray
Fleet: 33 - 24 single-deck coach, 6 minicoach.
Chassis: 2 DAF, 6 Mercedes, 25 Volvo.
Bodies: 20 Jonckheere, 2 Plaxton, 7 Van Hool, 4 Other
Ops incl: school contracts, excursions & tours, private hire, continental tours.
Livery: Cream/Orange/Red

HAYTON'S EXECUTIVE TRAVEL LTD
VELOS HOUSE, UNIT 3, FROXMER STREET, GORTON, MANCHESTER M19 2HS
Tel: 0161 223 3103
Fax: 0161 223 9528
Web site: www.haytonstravel.co.uk
Prop: Barry Hayton
Dir/Sec: Barry A Hayton
Fleet: 47 - 4 single-deck bus, 28 single-deck coach, 1 double-deck coach, 12 midibus, 1 minibus, 1 midicoach.
Chassis: Alexander Dennis, DAF, Dennis, MAN, Mercedes, Optare, Scania, Volvo.
Bodies: Alexander Dennis, Ikarus, Berkhof, Caetano, Jonckheere, Marcopolo, Noge, Optare, Plaxton, Van Hool.
Ops incl: local bus services, school contracts, excursions & tours, private hire, express, continental tours.
Livery: White

HEALINGS INTERNATIONAL COACHES
251 HIGGINSHAW LANE, ROYTON, OLDHAM OL2 6HW
Tel: 0161 624 8975
Fax: 0161 652 0203
Partners: Philip Healing, Richard Healing
Fleet: 7 – 5 single-deck coach, 1 midicoach, 1 minicoach.
Chassis: 1 DAF, 1 Mercedes, 1 Scania, 1 Toyota, 1 Volvo, 2 Duple 425
Ops incl: school contracts, excursions & tours, private hire, continental tours.
Livery: White with coloured decals

JONES EXECUTIVE COACHES LTD
THE COACH STATION, SHARP STREET, WALKDEN, MANCHESTER M28 3LX
Tel: 0161 790 9495
Fax: 0161 790 9400
Web site: www.jonesexecutive.co.uk
E-mail: simon@jonesexecutive.co.uk
Man Dir: Simon Jones
Fleet: 7 single-deck coach.
Chassis: 2 DAF, 2 Irisbus, 2 Scania, 1 Volvo.
Bodies: 2 Beulas, 5 Van Hool.
Ops incl: school contracts, private hire.
Livery: White

JP EXECUTIVE TRAVEL
THE COACH HOUSE, JOSHUA LANE, MIDDLETON, MANCHESTER M24 2AZ
Tel: 0161 643 4182
Fax: 0161 653 3404
E-mail: info@jptbuses.co.uk
Web site: www.jptbuses.co.uk
Fleet Name: JPT
Fleet: 39 – 4 double-deck bus, 8 single-deck bus, 27 midibus.
Chassis: Alexander Dennis, Dennis, MAN, Mercedes, Optare, Scania
Bodies: Alexander Dennis, ast Lancs, Optare, Plaxton, Wright
Ops incl: local bus services
Livery: Blue/Yellow

LAINTON COACHES LTD t/a ASHALL'S COACHES
UNIT 11, FROXMER STREET, GORTON, MANCHESTER M18 8EF
Tel: 0161 231 7777
Fax: 0161 231 7787
E-mail: info@ashallscoaches.co.uk
Web site: www.ashallscoaches.co.uk
Dirs: James A Ashall, Aaron Ashworth
Fleet: 13 – 3 single-deck bus, 9 single-deck coach, 1 minicoach.
Chassis: 1 DAF, 1 Dennis, 1 MAN, 1 Mercedes, 2 Scania, 7 Volvo.
Bodies: 1 Alexander, 3 Caetano, 1 Ikarus, 1 Irizar, 1 Jonckheere, 1 Onyx, 1 Optare, 3 Plaxton, 1 Van Hool.
Ops incl: school contracts, private hire (UK only).
Livery: White
Ticket System: Wayfarer 2

LAMBS
BUXTON STREET, HAZEL GROVE, STOCKPORT SK7 4BB
Tel: 0161 456 1515
Fax: 0161 483 5011
E-mail: lambs139@aol.com
Web site: www.lambscoaches.net
Man Dir: Geoffrey Lamb
Dir: Graham Lamb
Fleet: 7 single-deck coach
Chassis: 3 DAF, 1 Mercedes, 2 Scania, 1 Volvo.
Bodies: 1 Setra, 6 Van Hool.
Ops incl: private hire, school contracts.
Livery: White/Blue

MARPLE MINI COACHES
5 GROSVENOR ROAD, MARPLE SK6 6PR
Tel: 0161 881 9111
Owner: G. W. Cross.

120   The Little Red Book 2011 - in association with *tbf* Transport Benevolent Fund

Fleet: 2 minicoach.
Chassis: Ford Transit, LDV.
Ops incl: school contracts, private hire.
Livery: White/Gold.

MAYNE COACHES LTD
MARSH HOUSE LANE,
WARRINGTON WA1 7ET
Tel: 0161 223 2035
Fax: 0161 223 1835
E-mail: coaches@mayne.co.uk
Web site: www.mayne.co.uk
Dirs: S B Mayne (**Chairman & Man Dir**),
D Mayne (**Co Sec**), C S Mayne, S L
Mayne **Gen Man:** R W Vernon
Sales Mans: A J Dykes, D Williams
Eng Dir: C F Pannel
Eng Man: E Sutcliffe
Traffic Man: J Drake
Fleet: 38 - 2 double-deck bus,
36 single-deck coach.
Chassis: 4 Alexander Dennis, 3 Bova,
31 Scania.
Bodies: 3 Bova, 2 East Lancs, 24 Irizar,
7 Plaxton, 2 UVG.
Ops incl: local bus services, school
contracts, excursions & tours, private hire.
Livery: Cream/Red

MAYTREE TRAVEL LTD
CUTHBERT STREET, BOLTON BL3 3SD
Tel: 01204 651800
E-mail: info@maytreetravel.co.uk
Web site: www.maytreetravel.co.uk
Dir: G Hawthorne
Fleet: 25 midibus
Chassis: 8 Alexander Dennis,
17 Optare
Bodies: 8 Alexander Dennis,
17 Optare
Ops incl: local bus services
Livery: White

METROLINK
METROLINK HOUSE, QUEENS ROAD,
MANCHESTER M8 0RY
Tel: 0161 205 8685
Fax: 0161 205 8699
Web site: www.metrolink.co.uk
Man Dir: Phil Smith
Fleet: 28 tram
Chassis: GEC Alsthom
Bodies: Firema
Ops incl: tram service

DAVID PLATT COACHES & MINITRAVEL OF LEES
8 THE WOODS, GROTTON,
SADDLEWORTH, OLDHAM OL4 4LP
Tel/Fax: 0161 633 4845
Prop: David Platt
Fleet: 2 - 1 single-deck coach,
1 minicoach.
Chassis: 1 Bedford, 1 Toyota.
Bodies: 1 Caetano, 1 Plaxton.
Ops incl: private hire.
Livery: Aqua/White

SELWYNS TRAVEL SERVICES
BUILDING 77, TERMINAL 2,
MANCHESTER AIRPORT M90 1QX
Tel: 0161 489 5720
Fax: 0161 499 9157
Recovery: 01928 572108
E-mail: sales@selwyns.co.uk
Web site: www.selwyns.co.uk
Man Dir: Selwyn A Jones
Co Sec/Acct: Richard E Williams
Gen Man: Geoff Prince

Fleet Eng: Paul Trill
Ops Man: Alan Spilman
Fleet: 12 - 4 single-deck coach,
5 minicoach, 3 minicoach.
Chassis: 4 DAF, 8 Mercedes.
Bodies: 8 Mercedes, 4 Van Hool.
Ops incl: local bus services, school
contracts, private hire.
Livery: White/Blue/Orange/Green
Ticket System: Wayfarer
See also Selwyns Travel Services,
Runcorn (Cheshire)

SHEARINGS HOLIDAYS
MIRY LANE, WIGAN WN3 4AG
Tel: 01942 244246
Fax: 01942 242518
Web site: www.washearings.com
Fleet Names: Shearings Holidays,
Euro Tourer, Grand Tourer, National
Holidays (see East Riding)
Chairman: Bernard Norman
Ch Exec: Dennis Wormwell
Fin Dir: David Newbold
Tran Dir: Chris Brown
Eng Dir: Mick Forbes
Group HR Dir: Jane Burke
Fleet: 206 - 201 single-deck coach,
5 minibus.
Chassis: 5 Ford Transit, 60 Setra,
141 Volvo.
Bodies: 5 Ford, 26 Jonckheere,
46 Plaxton, 60 Setra, 69 Van Hool.
Ops incl: excursions & tours, private hire,
continental tours.
Livery: Blue or Gold

SOUTH LANCS TRAVEL
UNIT 22/23, CHANTERS INDUSTRIAL
ESTATE, ATHERTON M46 9BF
Tel: 01942 888893
Fax: 01942 894010
E-mail: southlancs@btconnect.com
Web site: www.southlancs.com
Man Dir: Martin Bott
Eng Dir: D A Stewart
Tran Man: W Peach
Fleet: 50 – 4 double-deck bus,
42 single-deck bus, 4 midibus.
Chassis: 13 Dennis, 4 MAN,
4 Mercedes, 15 Optare, 11 Scania,
3 Volvo.
Bodies: 1 Alexander, 3 Caetano,
3 East Lancs, 1 Marshall, 16 Optare,
11 Plaxton, 2 Scania, 1 UVG, 12 Wright.
Ops incl: local bus services, school
contracts.
Livery: Yellow/Blue
Ticket System: Wayfarer TGX

SPEEDWELLBUS LTD
RAGLAN STREET, HYDE SK14 2DX
Tel: 0161 367 8588
Fax: 0161 367 8589
E-mail: enquiries@speedwellbus.com
Web site: www.speedwellbus.com
Fleet: 35 - 4 double-deck bus,
5 single-deck bus, 26 midibus
Chassis: Alexander Dennis, Dennis,
Leyland, Mercedes, Optare
Bodies: Alexander, Marshall, Northern
Counties, Optare, Plaxton
Ops incl: local bus services, school
contracts

STAGECOACH MANCHESTER
HEAD OFFICE, HYDE ROAD,
MANCHESTER M12 6JS
Tel: 0161 273 3577

Fax: 0161 276 2594
E-mail: manchester.enquiries@stagecoachbus.com
Web site: www.stagecoachbus.com/manchester
Man Dir: M Threapleton
Ops Dir: E Tasker
Comm Dir: R A Cossins
Eng Dir: D Roe **Ser Performance Man:**
C Icely **Network Man:** J K Young
Marketing Man: K Coventry
Personnel Man: J E Crenigan
Fleet: 730 - 510 double-deck bus,
165 single-deck bus, 3 single-deck coach,
32 midibus, 20 minibus.
Chassis: Alexander Dennis, DAF,
Dennis, MAN, Mercedes, Optare, Scania,
Volvo.
Ops incl: local bus services.
Livery: Stagecoach UK Bus
Ticket System: ERG

STOTT'S TOURS (OLDHAM) LTD
144 LEES ROAD, OLDHAM OL4 1HT
Tel: 0161 624 4200
Fax: 0161 628 2969
Props: A. Stott, G Stott, S Stott.
Fleet: 27 - 14 double-deck bus,
1 single-deck bus, 2 single-deck coach,
10 midibus
Ops incl: local bus services, school
contracts.
Livery: Cream/Red/Black.

SWANS TRAVEL
STANLEY HOUSE, BROADGATE,
CHADDERTON, OLDHAM OL9 9XA
Tel: 0161 681 0999
Fax: 0161 681 0777
E-mail: enquiries@swanstravel.com
Web site: www.swanstravel.co.uk
Man Dir: Kieran Swindells
Ops incl: local bus services, private hire.
Livery: White.

VIKING COACHES
DOCTOR FOLD FARM,
DOCTOR FOLD LANE, BIRCH,
HEYWOOD OL10 2QE
Tel: 01706 368999
Fax: 01706 620011
E-mail: viking@coaches76.freeserve
Web site: www.coach-day-trips
Owners: A. Warburton, Ms A. Warburton.
Fleet: 4 single-deck coach.
Chassis: Iveco, Volvo.
Bodies: Beulas, Plaxton, Van Hool.
Ops incl: excursions & tours, private hire,
continental tours, school contracts.
Livery: Viking Ship.

WRIGLEY'S COACHES LTD
4 FIDDLERS LANE, IRLAM M44 6QE
Tel: 0161 775 2414
Fax: 0161 775 1558
E-mail: sales@wrigleyscoaches.com
Web site: www.wrigleyscoaches.com
Man Dir: Colin Wrigley
Co Sec/Dir: Lesley Wrigley
Ops Man: Alan Grice
Fleet: 8 - 1 double-deck bus, 4 single-
deck coach, 2 double-deck coach,
1 minicoach.
Chassis: 1 Leyland, 2 MAN, 1 Neoplan,
1 Setra, 1 Toyota, 2 Volvo.
Bodies: 1 Alexander, 1 Caetano,
3 Neoplan, 1 Plaxton, 1 Setra,
1 Van Hool.
Ops incl: private hire, school contracts.
Livery: Blue/White

Greater Manchester

The Little Red Book 2011 - in association with *tbf* Transport Benevolent Fund

HAMPSHIRE, PORTSMOUTH, SOUTHAMPTON

AIRLYNX TRAVEL
THE SYCAMORES, OAKLEY ROAD,
SOUTHAMPTON SO16 4LJ
Tel: 023 8039 9078 **Fax:** 023 8077 7724
E-mail: us@airlynx.co.uk
Web site: www.airlynx.co.uk
Dir: Gary Gregory **Co Sec:** Sharon Lucas
Fleet: 9 - 1 single-deck bus, 1 midicoach,
8 minibus, 8 minicoach
Chassis: 3 Ford Transit, 4 Mercedes,
1 Volkswagen.
Ops incl: private hire, school contracts,
local bus services.
Livery: Blue/Yellow

ALTONIAN COACHES LTD
1A WESTBROOK WALK, MARKET
SQUARE, ALTON GU34 1HZ
Tel: 01420 84845 **Fax:** 01420 541429
E-mail: sales@altoniancoaches.co.uk
Web site: www.altoniancoaches.co.uk
Man Dir: Derek Wheeler
Depot Man: David Butcher
Tours Man: Ian McKee
Fleet: 20 - 13 single-deck coach,
2 midicoach, 3 minibus, 2 minicoach.
Chassis: 1 Ayats, 1 Bova, 1 BMC,
1 Daimler, 1 Irisbus, 1 Iveco, 1 King Long,
3 LDV, 2 MAN, 3 Mercedes, 2 Renault,
1 Scania, 2 Volvo.
Ops incl: school contracts, excursions &
tours, private hire, continental tours.
Livery: Blue & Orange
Associated with Wheelers Travel Ltd,
Southampton

AMK CHAUFFEUR DRIVE LTD
MILL LANE, PASSFIELD,
LIPHOOK GU30 7RP
Tel: 01428 751675 **Fax:** 01428 751677
E-mail: info@amkxl.com
Web site: www.amkxl.com
Man Dir: G Fraser **Fin Dir:** M Dummer
Fleet: 78 - 65 minibus, 3 midibus,
10 minicoach.
Ops incl: local bus services, school
contracts, excursions & tours, private hire.

AMPORT & DISTRICT COACHES LTD
EASTFIELD HOUSE,
AMESBURY ROAD, THRUXTON,
ANDOVER SP11 8ED
Tel: 01264 772307 **Fax:** 01264 773020
E-mail: tedd@onetel.net
Dirs: P J Tedd, A M Tedd, N B Tedd
Fleet: 9 - 7 single-deck coach,
2 midicoach.
Chassis: 2 Mercedes, 3 Scania,
1 Setra, 3 Volvo.
Bodies: 1 Autobus, 3 Berkhof, 1 Esker,
2 Plaxton, 1 Setra, 1 Van Hool.
Ops incl: private hire, continental tours,
school contracts.
Livery: White/Silver

ANGELA COACHES LTD
OAKTREE HOUSE, LOWFORD,
BURSLEDON, SOUTHAMPTON
SO31 8ES
Tel: 023 8040 3170 **Fax:** 023 8040 6487
E-mail: robert@angelacoaches.com
Web site: www.angelacoaches.com
Man Dir: M J Pressley
Co Sec: Mrs H M Pressley

Ops Dir: R J Pressley
Ch Eng: D Evans **Ops Man:** J Davies
Fleet: 11 - 5 single-deck coach,
1 midicoach, 5 minicoach.
Chassis: 3 Iveco, 5 MAN, 1 Mercedes,
2 Toyota.
Bodies: 2 Beulas, 2 Caetano, 2 Indcar,
4 Neoplan, 1 other.
Ops incl: private hire, school contracts,
excursions & tours, continental tours
Livery: Maroon/White

AVENSIS COACH TRAVEL LTD
29 PREMIER WAY, ABBEY PARK
INDUSTRIAL ESTATE,
ROMSEY SO51 9DQ
Tel: 01794 515260 **Fax:** 01794 512260
E-mail: info@avensiscoaches.co.uk
Web site: www.avensiscoaches.co.uk
Dirs: Graham Humby, Simon Humby
Fleet: 8 single-deck coach.
Chassis: 8 Scania.
Bodies: 8 Irizar.
Ops incl: excursions & tours, private hire,
continental tours.
Livery: Yellow/Purple

BLACK & WHITE MOTORWAYS LTD
31 STONEY LANE, WINCHESTER
SO22 6DP
Tel: 01962 883398
Fax: 01962 620169
Recovery: 07810 772074
E-mail: peter.bailey50@ntlworld.com
Web site: www.bwmotorways.co.uk
Dirs: Peter Bailey, Eve Bailey
Ch Eng: Michael Elliott
Fleet: 5 double-deck bus, 5 single-deck bus
Chassis: 1 Bristol, 1 Daimler, 8 Dennis
Bodies: 1 Alexander Dennis, 1 ECW,
3 East Lancs, 2 Plaxton, 3 UVG.
Ops incl: local bus services, school
contracts, excursions & tours, private hire.
Livery: Black & White
Ticket System: Setright

BLACK VELVET TRAVEL LTD
SUITE A, BINNING HOUSE, 4A HIGH
STREET EASTLEIGH S050 5LA
Tel: 023 8061 2288
Fax: 023 8064 4881
E-mail: info@blackvelvettravel.co.uk
Web site: www.velvetbus.info
Chairman: Terry Stockley
Comp Sec: Rosalind Stockley
Man Dir: Phil Stockley
Ops Man: Taz Keeley **Dir:** David Huber
Fleet: 10 - 6 double-deck bus. 4 single-deck bus
Chassis: 4 DAF, 3 Leyland, 3 Volvo.
Bodies: 3 Alexander Dennis, 4 East
Lancs, 3 Northern Counties.
Ops incl: local bus services, private hire.
Livery: Purple
Ticket System: Wayfarer 3

A. S. BONE & SONS LTD
LONDON ROAD, HOOK RG27 9EQ
Tel: 01256 761388, 762106
Fleet Name: Newnham Coaches
Man Dir: J. E. Bone
Co Sec: Mrs M. Bone.
Fleet: 5 - 3 double-deck bus,
2 single-deck bus.
Chassis: 1 Bristol, 2 Daimler,
2 Leyland National.

Ops incl: private hire.
Livery: Cream/Blue.

BRIJAN TOURS LTD
THE COACH STATION, UNITS 4/5,
BOTTINGS INDUSTRIAL ESTATE,
CURDRIDGE SO30 2DY
Tel: 01489 788138 **Fax:** 01489 789395
Recovery: 07711 435189
E-mail: sales@brijantours.com
Web site: www.brijantours.com
Man Dir: Brian Botley **Co Sec:** Janet Botley
Ops Man: Brian Bedford
Fleet Eng: Ben Cresswell
Asst Man: David Thompson
Fleet: 28 - 12 double-deck bus,
8 single-deck bus, 8 single-deck coach.
Chassis: 2 Alexander Dennis, 7 Dennis, 1
Iveco, 9 Leyland, 3 MCW, 3 Mercedes, 2
Scania, 1 Volvo.
Bodies: 1 Alexander Dennis, 1 Duple,
7 ECW, 1 Irizar, 1 Jonckheere, 3 MCW,
1 Northern Counties, 12 Plaxton,
1 Van Hool.
Ops incl: local bus services, school
contracts, excursions & tours, private hire,
continental tours.
Livery: Cream/Burgundy.
Ticket system: Wayfarer

CLEGG & BROOKING LTD
WHITE HORSE SERVICE STATION,
MIDDLE WALLOP, STOCKBRIDGE
SO20 8DZ
Tel: 01264 781283 **Fax:** 01264 781679
E-mail:
cleggandbrooking@btconnect.com
Dirs: Kevin Brooking, Jeanette Cook,
John Cook, Sarah Glasspool
Fleet: 11 - 7 single-deck coach,
1 midicoach, 3 minicoach.
Chassis: 2 Dennis, 2 Mercedes,
4 Scania, 2 Toyota, 2 Volvo.
Bodies: 1 Berkhof, 4 Caetano, 2 Irizar,
2 Plaxton, 1 Sitcar, 1 Sunsundegui.
Ops incl: local bus services, private hire,
school contracts.
Livery: Blue/Grey

COLISEUM COACHES LTD
BOTLEY ROAD GARAGE, WEST END,
SOUTHAMPTON SO30 3JA
Tel: 023 8047 2377 **Fax:** 023 8047 6537
E-mail: info@coliseumcoaches.co.uk
Web site: www.coliseumcoaches.co.uk
Dirs: David Pitter, Kerry Pitter
Fleet: 12 coach
Chassis: 12 MAN
Bodies: 3 Beulas, 9 Neoplan.
Ops incl: excursions & tours, private hire.
Livery: Silver

COOPERS COACHES
31-35 LAKE ROAD, WOOLSTON
SO19 9EB
Tel: 023 8039 3393
Fax: 023 8044 4929
E-mail: cooperscoaches@yahoo.co.uk
Props: Stephen & Ellen Cooper
Fleet: 6 - 4 single-deck coach, 2 minibus.
Chassis: 1 DAF, 1 Dennis, 1 Ford
Transit, 2 Scania, 1 Volvo.
Bodies: 1 Berkhof, 1 Caetano, 1 Ikarus,
1 Plaxton, 1 Scania.
Ops incl: local bus services, school
contracts, private hire.

COUNTRYLINER GROUP
See Surrey

COUNTYWIDE TRAVEL
169 NEW GREENHAM PARK, THATCHAM RG19 6HN
Tel: 01256 780079
Fax: 01635 821128
Web site: www.countywidetoptravel.co.uk
Dir: Simon Weaver
Fleet: 23 – 13 single-deck coach, 9 double-deck coach, 1 minicoach.
Chassis: 4 Irisbus, 10 MAN, 1 Mercedes, 8 Volvo.
Ops incl: private hire
Liveries: Black, Black & Blue
A subsidiary of Weavaway Travel, Berkshire

COUNTYWIDE TRAVEL (FLEET) LTD
BOWENHURST FARM, CRONDALL FARNHAM, GU10 5RP
Tel: 01252 851009
Fax: 01252 852009
E-mail: info@countywidetravel.co.uk
Web site: www.countywide.co.uk
Fleet Name: Fleet Buzz
Man Dir: John C Chadwick
Fleet: 22 - 6 single-deck bus, 14 midibus, 2 minibus.
Chassis: 2 Dennis, 1 Iveco, 1 LDV, 9 Mercedes, 8 Optare.
Bodies: 2 Caetano, 2 LDV, 1 Mellor, 8 Optare, 9 Plaxton.
Ops incl: local bus services, school contracts.
Livery: Black & Yellow
Ticket system: Wayfarer II

EASSONS COACHES LTD
44 WODEHOUSE ROAD, ITCHEN, SOUTHAMPTON SO19 2EQ
Tel: 023 8044 8153
Fax: 023 8044 1635
Dirs: D.H.Easson, R.A.Easson.
Fleet: 7 - 5 single-deck coach, 2 midicoach.
Chassis: 2 Mercedes, 1 Neoplan, 3 Setra, 1 Volvo.
Bodies: 1 Neoplan, 1 Plaxton, 3 Setra, 2 Sitcar.
Ops incl: excursions & tours, private hire.
Livery: Cream & Khaki Brown

EMSWORTH & DISTRICT MOTOR SERVICES LTD
THE BUS GARAGE, CLOVELLY ROAD, SOUTHBOURNE PO10 8PE
Tel: 01243 378337
Fax: 01243 389424
E-mail: caren@emsworthanddistrict.co.uk
Web site: www.emsworthanddistrict.co.uk
Man Dir: Paul Lea
Fleet: 33 - 4 double-deck bus, 20 single-deck bus, 7 single-deck coach, 2 midicoach
Chassis: 21 Alexander Dennis, 1 AEC, 4 Bedford, 1 Bova, 4 DAF, 2 Mercedes.
Ops incl: local bus services, school contracts, excursions & tours, private hire, continental tours
Livery: Green/Silver.
Ticket system: Wayfarer

FIRST HAMPSHIRE & DORSET LTD
226 PORTSWOOD ROAD, SOUTHAMPTON SO17 2BE
Tel: 023 8058 4321
Fax: 023 8067 1448
Web site: www.firstgroup.com
E-mail: hampshire-dorset.csc@firstgroup.com
Man Dir: Marc Reddy **Eng Dir:** David Toy
Fin Dir: Ian Stone **Ops Dir:** Mike Smith
Ops Man: Chris Bainbridge **Ops Eng:** Mike Britten **Comm Man:** Kenneth Cobb
Fleet: 375 - 74 double-deck bus, 97 single-deck bus, 8 coach, 1 open-top bus, 148 midibus, 47 minibus.
Chassis: 4 Alexander Dennis, 16 BMC, 1 Bristol, 136 Dennis, 9 Leyland, 47 Mercedes, 9 Optare, 26 Scania, 135 Volvo.
Bodies: 4 Alexander Dennis, 26 Alexander, 16 BMC, 1 Caetano, 2 ECW, 6 East Lancs, 16 Marshall, 41 Northern Counties, 9 Optare, 151 Plaxton, 1 Roe, 20 Scania, 6 UVG, 76 Wright, 80 Other.
Ops incl: local bus services, school contracts, private hire.
Livery: FirstGroup UK Bus

GEMINI TRAVEL SOUTHAMPTON LTD
NORTH ROAD, MARCHWOOD INDUSTRIAL PARK, MARCHWOOD, SOUTHAMPTON SO40 4BL
Tel: 023 8066 0066
Fax: 023 8087 1308
E-mail: kenhatch@btconnect.com
Dirs: Ken Hatch, Mark Bennett
Gen Man: Nigel Smith
Fleet: 10 - 2 double-deck coach, 5 midicoach, 3 minicoach.
Chassis: 2 Ford, 1 LDV, 5 Mercedes, 2 Volvo.
Bodies: 1 LDV, 3 Optare, 2 Plaxton, 4 other.
Ops incl: private hire, school contracts.
Livery: White/Blue

HERRINGTON COACHES LTD
See Dorset

HYTHE & WATERSIDE COACHES LTD
1A HIGH STREET, HYTHE SO45 6AG
Tel: 023 8084 4788
Fax: 023 8020 7284
E-mail: enquiries@watersidetours.co.uk
Web site: www.watersidetours.co.uk
Fleet Name: Waterside Tours
Man Dir: Roy Barker
Dirs: Pam Barker, Jackie Withey
Fleet: 7 – 4 single-deck coach, 2 midicoach, 1 minibus.
Chassis: 3 Mercedes, 1 Scania, 3 Volvo.
Bodies: 3 Berkhof, 2 Esker, 1 Mercedes, 1 Scania.
Ops incl: excursions & tours, private hire, continental tours, school contracts.
Livery: White/Burgundy/Gold.

KING ALFRED MOTOR SERVICES LTD
UNIT 6, THE GRAINSTORE, PENTON MEWSEY, ANDOVER SP11 0RG
Tel: 01264 771616
Fax: 01264 772074
Recovery: 07825 224723
E-mail: kingalfredmotorservices@ntlworld.com
Web site: www.kingalfredmotorservices.co.uk
Dirs: Peter Bailey, Eve Bailey
Eng: Graham True
Fleet: 16 – 5 double-deck bus, 4 single-deck bus, 3 single-deck coach, 2 double-deck coach, 2 open-top bus.
Chassis: 4 AEC, 2 Bristol, 1 DAF, 2 Daimler, 4 Dennis, 2 Leyland, 1 Neoplan.
Bodies: 2 ECW, 1 East Lancs, 1 MCW, 1 Neoplan, 1 Northern Counties, 3 Park Royal, 4 Plaxton, 1 UVG, 2 Wadham Stringer.
Ops incl: local bus services, school contracts, excursions & tours, private hire.
Livery: Apple Green/Pale Yellow
Ticket System: Setright

LUCKETTS TRAVEL
BROADCUT, WALLINGTON, FAREHAM PO16 8TB
Tel: 01329 823755
Fax: 01329 823855
E-mail: info@lucketts.co.uk
Web site: www.lucketts.co.uk
Chairman: David Luckett
Joint Man Dirs: Steven Luckett, Ian Luckett
Eng Dir: Mark Jordan
Ops Man: Tony Harper
Fleet: 61 – 1 single-deck bus, 47 single-deck coach, 1 double-deck coach, 4 midicoach, 8 minibus.
Chassis: 2 Bova, 5 Dennis, 12 Mercedes, 1 Neoplan, 1 Optare, 35 Scania, 3 Toyota, 2 Volvo.
Bodies: 5 Berkhof, 2 Bova, 17 Caetano, 2 Hispano, 18 Irizar, 9 Mercedes, 1 Neoplan, 1 Optare, 4 Plaxton, 2 Scania.
Ops incl: school contracts, excursions & tours, private hire, express, continental tours.
Livery: Grey/White/Orange

MARCHWOOD MOTORWAYS
200 SALISBURY ROAD, TOTTON SO40 3PE
Tel: 023 8066 3700
Fax: 023 8066 7762
E-mail: ian.harley@marchwoodmotorways.co.uk
Web site: www.southerncoachhire.com
Ops Man: Ian Harley
Asst Man: Paul Dawson
Fleet: 19 – 3 double-deck bus, 16 single-deck coach
Chassis: 12 DAF, 4 Scania, 3 Volvo.
Bodies: 3 East Lancs, 4 Ikarus, 4 Irizar, 3 Plaxton, 5 Van Hool.
Ops incl: school contracts, excursions & tours, private hire, continental tours.
Livery: Light Blue/Dark Blue/White
A subsidiary of Solent Blue Line, part of the Go-Ahead Group

MERVYN'S COACHES
THE NEW COACH HOUSE, INNERSDOWN, MICHELDEVER SO21 3BW
Tel/Fax: 01962 774574
E-mail: mervynscoaches@btconnect.com
Web site: www.mervynscoaches.com
Partners: Mervyn Annetts, Carol Annetts, Linda Porter, James Annetts.
Fleet: 6 - 5 single-deck coach, 1 midicoach

Chassis: 4 Bedford, 2 Volvo.
Chassis: 1 Duple, 4 Plaxton, 1 other
Ops incl: local bus services, school contracts, excursions & tours, private hire.
Livery: Brown/Cream
Ticket System: Setright

PIKE'S COACHES LTD

77 SCOTT CLOSE, WALWORTH INDUSTRIAL ESTATE, ANDOVER SP10 5NU
Tel: 01264 334328
Fax: 01264 334329
Web site: www.pikecoaches-andover.co.uk
Props: J S Pike, Jenny Pike, C Pike, R Pike.
Fleet: 15 - 4 double-deck bus, 5 single-deck coach, 2 midicoach, 4 minibus.
Chassis: Bristol, Ford Transit, Iveco, Mercedes, Volvo.
Bodies: Mercedes, Plaxton, ECW.
Ops incl: local bus services, school contracts, excursions & tours, private hire, continental tours.
Livery: White.
Ticket System: Setright.

PRINCESS COACHES LTD

PRINCESS COACHES GARAGE, BOTLEY ROAD, WEST END, SOUTHAMPTON SO30 3HA
Tel: 023 8047 2150
Fax: 023 8039 9944
E-mail: enquiries@princesscoaches.com
Web site: www.princesscoaches.co.uk
Dirs: Y B Barfoot, D K Brown, P A Brown
Fleet: 16 - 12 single-deck coach, 2 double-deck coach, 1 minibus, 1 minicoach.
Chassis: 1 Ford, 14 Scania, 1 Toyota.
Bodies: 2 Berkhof, 1 Caetano, 8 Irizar, 4 Jonckheere, 1 other.
Ops incl: private hire, school contracts, continental tours.
Livery: White with multi-coloured flashes

SOLENT BLUE LINE

UNIT 4, BARTON PARK INDUSTRIAL ESTATE, CHICKENHALL LANE, EASTLEIGH SO50 6RR
Tel: 023 8061 4459
Fax: 023 8062 9613
E-mail: enquiries@bluestarbus.co.uk
Web site: www.bluestarbus.com
Fleet Names: Bluestar, Unilink
Man Dir: Alex Carter
Divisional Dir: Ed Wills
Eng Dir: Steve Hamilton
Eng Man: Steve Prewett
Fleet: 94 – incl. double-deck bus, single-deck bus, open-top bus, midibus.
Chassis: 6 Alexander Dennis, 20 DAF, 1 Iveco, 3 Leyland, 10 Mercedes, 11 Optare, 25 Scania, 8 Transbus, 10 Volvo.

Bodies: 6 Alexander Dennis, 16 East Lancs, 9 Ikarus, 3 Leyland, 10 Mercedes, 2 Northern Counties, 11 Optare, 12 Wright, 25 Other.
Ops incl: local bus services, school contracts.
Livery: Royal Blue
Ticket System: Wayfarer 3
(Part of the Go-Ahead Group)

SOLENT COACHES LTD

BROOKSIDE GARAGE, CROW LANE, RINGWOOD BH24 3EA
Tel: 01425 473188
Fax: 01425 473669
Recovery: 0784 326 6720/1
E-mail: enquiries@solentcoaches.co.uk
Web site: www.solentcoaches.co.uk
Man Dir/Co Sec: John Skew
Dir/Ch Eng: Paul Skew.
Fleet: 9 - 7 single-deck coach, 1 minibus, 1 midicoach.
Chassis: 1 Mercedes, 6 Scania, 1 Setra, 1 Toyota.
Bodies: 1 Caetano, 2 Irizar, 1 Mercedes, 1 Setra, 4 Van Hool.
Ops incl: excursions & tours, private hire, continental tours, school contracts.
Livery: White/Blue

STAGECOACH IN HAMPSHIRE

THE BUS STATION, FESTIVAL PLACE, CHURCHILL WAY, BASINGSTOKE RG21 7BE
Tel: 0845 121 0180
Web site: www.stagecoachbus/com/hampshire
Man Dir: Andrew Dyer
Eng Dir: Richard Alexander
Fin Dir: Martin Stoggell
Div Man: Matthew Callow.
Fleet: 172 - 46 double-deck bus, 24 single-deck bus, 3 single-deck coach, 87 midibus, 12 minibus.
Chassis: Alexander Dennis, Dennis, Leyland, Mercedes, Optare, Volvo.
Bodies: Alexander, Alexander Dennis, Jonckheere, Optare, Plaxton.
Ops incl: local bus services, school contracts.
Livery: Stagecoach UK Bus
Ticket System: Wayfarer.

STAGECOACH IN HANTS & SURREY

HALIMOTE ROAD, ALDERSHOT GU11 1NJ
Tel: 01256 464501
Man Dir: Andrew Dyer
Eng Dir: Richard Alexander
Fin Dir: Martin Stoggell.
Fleet: 93 - 17 double-deck bus, 20 single-deck bus, 38 midibus, 18 minibus.
Chassis: Alexander Dennis, Dennis, MAN, Mercedes, Optare, Volvo.
Bodies: Alexander, Alexander Dennis, Northern Counties, Optare, Plaxton.
Ops incl: local bus services, school contracts.

Livery: Stagecoach UK Bus
Ticket System: Wayfarer

TEST VALLEY TRAVEL LTD

BANNISTER BARN, NEWTON LANE, WHITEPARISH SP5 2QQ
Tel/Fax: 01794 884555
Man Dir: John M Norman
Co Sec: Mrs Angeline N Norman
E-mail: falconlomax@hotmail.co.uk
Fleet: 3 minibus.
Chassis/Bodies: 3 LDV.
Ops incl: private hire, school contracts.
Livery: Green, Gold on White

TRUEMANS COACHES (FLEET) LTD

TRUEMANS END, LYNCHFORD ROAD, ASH VALE, GU12 5PQ
Tel: 01252 373303
Fax: 01252 373393
Dir: Richard Trueman
Fleet: 15 single deck coach.
Chassis: 5 Iveco, 10 MAN.
Bodies: 5 Beulas, 6 Neoplan, 4 Plaxton.
Ops incl: school contracts, private hire, excursions & tours, continental tours.
Livery: Electric Blue

VISION TRAVEL

3A SPUR ROAD, COSHAM, PORTSMOUTH PO6 3DY
Tel: 02392 359168
Fax: 02392 361253
E-mail: visiontravels@aol.com
Web site: www.visiontravel.co.uk
Dir: Peter Sharpe
Fleet: 37 - 29 single-deck coach, 2 double-deck coach, 4 midicoach, 2 minibus.
Ops incl: school contracts, excursions & tours, private hire, continental tours.
Livery: Yellow/Red/White

WHEELERS TRAVEL LTD

UNIT 9, GROVE FARM, UPPER NORTHAM DRIVE, HEDGE END, SOUTHAMPTON SO30 4BG
Tel: 02380 471800
Fax: 02380 470414
E-mail: sales@wheelerstravel.co.uk
Web site: www.wheelerstravel.co.uk
Man Dir: Derek Wheeler
Gen Man: Paul Barker
Traffic Man: Keith Trenchard
Assistant Traffic Man: Nigel Taylor
Fleet: 22
Chassis: 1 Ayats, 1 Bova, 2 Iveco, 1 King Long, 5 LDV, 5 Mercedes, 2 Renault, 2 Scania, 3 Volvo.
Bodies incl: 1 Ayats, 2 Beulas, 1 Esker, 2 Indcar, 2 Marcopolo, 1 Noge, 2 Plaxton, 1 Van Hool.
Ops incl: private hire, excursions & tours, school contracts, continental tours.
Livery: Blue Body, Orange Mirrors

♿	Vehicle suitable for disabled		Seat belt-fitted Vehicle	R24	24 hour recovery service
T	Toilet-drop facilities available		Coach(es) with galley facilities		Replacement vehicle available
R	Recovery service available		Air-conditioned vehicle(s)		Vintage Coach(es) available
	Open top vehicle(s)		Coaches with toilet facilities		

HEREFORDSHIRE

BOWYER'S COACHES
QUARRY GARAGE, PETERCHURCH
HR2 0TF
Tel: 01981 550206
Prop: Fernley C. Anning,
Anthony H. Anning.
Fleet: 9 - 5 single-deck coach, 4 minibus.
Chassis: Bedford, LDV.
Ops incl: private hire, school contracts.
Livery: White/Red.

BROMYARD OMNIBUS COMPANY
STREAMHALL GARAGE, LINTON
TRADING ESTATE, BROMYARD HR7 4QL
Tel: 01885 482782
Fax: 01885 482127
Prop: Martin Perry
Fleet Eng: Michael Simcock
Fleet: 11 - 6 single-deck bus,
3 single-deck coach, 1 midibus,
1 minicoach.
Chassis: 1 Bedford, 2 Leyland,
2 Mercedes, 4 Optare, 1 Volvo, 1 Trojan.
Bodies: 2 Autobus, 1 Caetano, 1 Duple,
4 Optare, 2 Plaxton, 1 Trojan.
Ops incl: local bus services, school contracts, private hire.
Livery: Red/Cream
Ticket System: Wayfarer Saver

COACH COMPANIONS LTD
MAGNOLIA HOUSE 12 ST BOTOLPH'S
GREEN, LEOMINSTER HR6 8ER
Tel: 01568 620279
Fax: 01568 616906
E-mail:
enquiries@coachcompanions.co.uk
Web site: www.coachcompanions.co.uk
Dir: Richard Asghar-Sandys
Fleet: 1 midicoach.
Chassis: 1 Mercedes.
Bodies: 1 other.
Ops incl: private hire.
Livery: White

D R M BUS AND CONTRACT SERVICES
THE COACH GARAGE, BROMYARD
HR7 4NT
Tel: 01885 483219
Prop: David R. Morris
Fleet: 9 single-deck bus
Chassis: 3 Scania, 6 Volvo.
Bodies: 2 Alexander, 3 East Lancs,
1 Leyland National, 3 Scania.
Ops incl: local bus services, school contracts.
Livery: Blue/Silver-White
Ticket System: Wayfarer 3

GOLDEN PIONEER TRAVEL
BRANDON, REDHILL, HEREFORD
HR2 8BH
Tel: 01432 274307
Fax: 01432 275809
E-mail: crockbrey@aol.com
Web site: www.goldenpioneertravel.com
Prop: Bryan Crockett **Dir:** J Crockett.
Fleet: 3 single-deck coach.
Chassis incl: King Long.
Bodies incl: Van Hool.
Ops incl: excursions & tours, private hire, continental tours.
Livery: Black/Gold/Red/Green/Yellow

GOLD STAR TRAVEL
See Worcestershire

P. W. JONES COACHES
HILBREY GARAGE, BURLEY GATE,
HEREFORD HR1 3QL
Tel: 01432 820214
Fax: 01432 820521
Recovery: 01432 820214
E-mail: coaches@p.w.jones.com
Owner: Philip W Jones
Fleet: 19 - 17 single-deck coach,
1 midicoach, 1 minicoach.
Chassis: 1 Bedford, 1 Bova, 8 Dennis,
1 Leyland, 1 MAN, 2 Mercedes,
1 Neoplan, 1 Toyota, 3 Volvo.
Bodies: 1 Bova, 1 Caetano, 1 Duple,
1 Neoplan, 15 Plaxton.
Ops incl: excursions & tours, private hire, continental tours, school contracts.
Livery: Multi Colours

LUGG VALLEY PRIMROSE TRAVEL LTD
SOUTHERN AVENUE,
LEOMINSTER HR6 0QF
Tel: 01432 344341
Fax: 01432 356206
E-mail: sales@luggvalleytravel.co.uk
Man Dir: N D Yeomans
Ops Man: I Davies
Chief Eng: D W Jones
Fleet: 25 – 4 single-deck bus,
7 single-deck coach, 13 midibus,
1 midicoach.
Chassis: 4 Dennis, 1 Mercedes,
13 Optare, 2 Scania, 5 Volvo.
Bodies: 1 Berkhof, 1 Carlyle, 1 Duple,
1 Esker, 2 Irizar, 1 Jonckheere,
13 Optare, 5 Plaxton.
Ops incl: local bus services, school contracts, excursions & tours, private hire
Livery: Green/Cream/Orange
Ticket System: ERG

M & S COACHES OF HEREFORDSHIRE LTD
UNIT 3, BRIERLEY WAY,
SOUTHERN AVENUE,
LEOMINSTER HR6 0QF
Tel: 01568 612803
E-mail: les@mscoaches.co.uk
Web site: www.mscoaches.co.uk
Dirs: Maurice Peruffo, Mrs Susan Peruffo, Les Allen
Fleet: 9 – midicoach, minicoach.
Chassis: 7 Mercedes, 2 Toyota.
Bodies: 2 Caetano, 2 Esker, 3 Optare,
2 Sitcar.
Ops incl: school contracts, excursions & tours, private hire, continental tours.

NEWBURY COACHES
LOWER ROAD TRADING ESTATE,
LEDBURY HR8 2DJ
Tel: 01531 633483
Fax: 01531633650
Livery: Blue/White.

NICK MADDY COACHES
171 WIDEMARSH STREET,
HEREFORD HR4 9HE
Tel: 01432 266211
Fax: 01432 356645
Prop: Nick Maddy

Fleet: 5 – 1 single-deck bus, 4 minibus.
Chassis: 2 Iveco, 2 LDV, 1 Optare.
Ops incl: local bus services, school contracts, private hire.

SARGEANTS BROS LTD
MILL STREET, KINGTON
HR5 3AL
Tel: 01544 230481
Fax: 01544 231892
E-mail: mike@sargeantsbros.com
Web site: www.sargeantsbros.com
Prop: Michael Sargeant
Fleet: 22 - 1 double-deck bus,
4 single-deck bus, 5 single-deck coach,
7 midibus, 5 minibus.
Chassis: 1 Blue Bird, 1 DAF, 1 Dennis,
2 Ford Transit, 1 LDV, 9 Mercedes,
2 Plaxton, 2 Van Hool, 5 Other.
Bodies: 1 Autobus, 2 Jonckheere,
1 LDV, 9 Optare, 2 Plaxton, 2 Van Hool,
6 Other.
Ops incl: local bus services, school contracts, private hire.
Livery: Red
Ticket System: ERG

SMITHS MOTORS (LEDBURY) LTD
COACH GARAGE, HOMEND,
LEDBURY HR8 1BA
Tel: 01531 632953
Dirs: F. W. B. Sterry, M. Sterry.
Ops incl: private hire, continental tours.
Livery: White with Green/Blue/Red stripe.
Ticket System: Setright.

STAGECOACH IN SOUTH WALES
See Torfaen

YEOMANS CANYON TRAVEL LTD
THE TRAVEL CENTRE,
OLD SCHOOL LANE, HEREFORD
HR1 1EX
Tel: 01432 356201
Fax: 01432 356206
E-mail: sales@yeomanstravel.co.uk
Web site:
www.yeomanscoachholidays.com
Man Dir: N D Yeomans
Ops Man: I Davies
Ch Eng: C Taylor
Fleet: 36 – 4 single-deck bus,
23 single-deck coach, 8 midibus,
1 midicoach.
Chassis: 2 BMC, 8 Dennis, 1 Neoplan,
8 Optare, 9 Scania, 8 Volvo.
Bodies: 1 Berkhof, 2 BMC, 5 Caetano,
1 Duple, 2 Irizar, 2 Marcopolo,
1 Marshall/MCV, 1 Neoplan, 1 Northern Counties, 8 Optare, 10 Plaxton,
2 Van Hool.
Ops incl: local bus services, school contracts, excursions & tours, private hire, express, continental tours.
Livery: Green/Cream/Orange
Ticket System: ERG

HERTFORDSHIRE

A R TRAVEL LTD
40 PERRY GREEN, HEMEL HEMPSTEAD HP2 7ND
Tel: 01442 408093
Fax: 01442 389899
E-mail: artravelltd@hotmail.com
Web site: www.artravelltd.co.uk
Dir: Terry Hill
Fleet: 4 minicoach.
Chassis: 3 Mercedes, 1 Volkswagen.
Ops incl: excursions & tours, private hire, school contracts, continental tours.
Livery: Silver

ARRIVA THE SHIRES LTD
See Bedfordshire

CENTREBUS LTD
ALBANY HOUSE, PIN GREEN, WEDGEWOOD WAY, STEVENAGE SG1 4PX
Tel: 0844 357 6520
E-mail: info@centrebus.com
Web site: www.centrebus.com
Fleet (Hertfordshire): 23 – 1 single-deck bus, 22 midibus.
Chassis: 2 Dennis, 16 Optare, 1 Scania, 4 VDL.
Bodies: 1 Alexander, 1 East Lancs, 16 Optare, 5 Plaxton.
Ops incl: local bus services.
Livery: Blue/Orange/White.
Ticket System: Wayfarer 3.
Part of the Centrebus Group

CHAMBERS COACHES (STEVENAGE) LTD
38 TRENT CLOSE, STVENAGE SG1 3RT
Tel: 01438 352920
Fax: 01462 486616
E-mail: chamberscoaches@btconnect.com
Web site: www.chamberscoaches.com
Man Dir: M R Chambers
Dir & Comp Sec: D C Tidey
Fleet: 26 - 22 single-deck coach, 3 midicoach, 1 minicoach.
Chassis: 1 BMC, 12 Dennis, 3 Iveco, 1 LDV, 2 Mercedes, 2 Toyota, 1 VDL.
Bodies: 1 BMC, 2 Marcopolo, 2 Mercedes, 15 Plaxton, 2 UGV, 1 Wadham Stringer.
Ops incl: school contracts, private hire.
Livery: Red/White/Blue

COZY TRAVEL LTD
661 SAUNDERS CLOSE, GREEN LANE, LETCHWORTH SG6 1PF
Tel: 01462 481707
Fax: 01462 673875
E-mail: info@cozys.co.uk
Web site: www.cozys.co.uk
Fleet Name: Cozy's.
Dirs: N Powell, G Powell, B Powell
Fleet: 17 – 2 double-deck bus, 2 single-deck bus, 8 single-deck coach, 1 double-deck coach, 2 midibus, 2 minicoach.
Chassis: 2 Dennis, 2 Iveco, 1 MAN, 1 Mercedes, 1 Neoplan, 2 Optare, 2 Scania, 1 Toyota, 5 Volvo.
Bodies: 2 Alexander Dennis, 2 East Lancs, 2 Irizar, 1 Jonckheere, 1 Mercedes, 1 Neoplan, 1 Noge, 2 Optare, 2 Plaxton, 3 Other.

Ops incl: local bus services, private hire, school contracts, excursions & tours, continental tours.
Livery: White/Multicoloured.

GOLDEN BOY COACHES (JETSIE LTD)
JOHN TERENCE HOUSE, GEDDINGS ROAD, HODDESDON EN11 0NT
Tel: 01992 465747
Fax: 01992 450957
E-mail: sales@goldenboy.co.uk
Web site: www.goldenboy.co.uk
Joint Man Dirs: G A McIntyre, T P McIntyre
Tran Man: G Jaikens
Ch Eng: P Murdoch
Fleet: 36 - 3 single-deck bus, 18 single-deck coach, 12 midicoach, 3 minicoach.
Chassis: 3 Dennis, 2 MAN, 16 Mercedes, 15 Volvo.
Bodies: 3 Alexander Dennis, 1 Euro, 1 Mercedes, 3 Optare, 9 Plaxton, 1 Sitcar, 18 Van Hool.
Ops incl: local bus services, private hire, school contracts, excursions & tours, continental tours.
Livery: Black/Red/Gold.
Ticket System: Wayfarer

GRAVES COACHES & MINIBUSES
134 WINFORD DRIVE, BROXBOURNE EN10 6PN
Tel/Fax: 01992 445556
E-mail: m.graves@btinternet.com
Prop: Michael Graves
Fleet: 2 -1 minicoach, 1 minibus
Chassis: 1 Mercedes, 1 Toyota.
Bodies: 1 Caetano, 1 Mercedes.
Ops incl: private hire, school contracts.

GROVE COACHES
101 MANDEVILLE ROAD, HERTFORD SG13 8JL
Tel: 01992 583417
Fleet Name: Pride of Hertford
Driver/operator: R A Bowers
Fleet: 1 single-deck coach.
Chassis: Volvo.
Body: Plaxton.
Ops incl: private hire, school contracts.
Livery: Brown/Orange

KENZIES COACHES LTD
6 ANGLE LANE, SHEPRETH SG8 6QH
Tel: 01763 260288
Fax: 01763 262012
Fleet: 20 single-deck coach.
Chassis: 2 Bedford, 18 Volvo.
Bodies: 6 Plaxton, 14 Van Hool.
Ops incl: private hire, school contracts.
Livery: Blue with logos.

LITTLE JIM'S BUSES
5 WILLIAM FISKE HOUSE, CASTLE STREET, BERKHAMSTED HP4 2HF
Tel: 01442 870029
E-mail: littlejimbuses@aol.com
Prop: James H Petty
Fleet: 3 - 1 single-deck bus, 1 midibus, 1 midicoach.

Chassis: 2 Mercedes, 1 Optare.
Bodies: 1 Optare, 2 Plaxton.
Ops incl: local bus services, school contracts, excursions & tours, private hire, continental tours.
Livery: Red & White.
Ticket System: Almex

LWB LTD
9 ELTON WAY, WATFORD WD25 8HH
Tel: 01923 247444
Fax: 01923 817066
Fleet Name: Cantabrica Coaches
Web site: www.cantabricacoaches.co.uk
Gen Man: Colin Brown
Ops Man: Paul Cram
Fleet: 14 - 12 single-deck coach, 2 minicoach.
Chassis: 1 LDV, 1 Peugeot, 12 Volvo.
Bodies: 12 Berkhof, 2 Other.
Ops incl: excursions & tours, private hire, continental tours.
Livery: Blue with Red relief

MARSHALLS COACHES
FIRBANK WAY, LEIGHTON BUZZARD LU7 4YP
Tel: 01525 376077 **Fax:** 01525 850967
E-mail: info@marshalls-coaches.co.uk
Web site: www.marshalls-coaches.co.uk
Prop: G Marshall
Ops Man: I White
Workshop Man: B Barnard
Fleet: 28 - 3 double-deck bus, 22 single-deck coach, 2 double-deck coach, 1 minicoach.
Chassis: 2 Alexander Dennis, 3 Ayats, 1 Bristol, 4 Dennis, 1 Iveco, 1 Mercedes, 15 Volvo.
Bodies: 3 Ayats, 1 Beulas, 2 East Lancs, 5 Jonckheere, 1 Mercedes, 15 Plaxton.
Ops incl: local bus services, private hire, school contracts, continental tours.
Livery: Blue/Multicoloured.

MASTER TRAVEL COACHES
9-12 PEARTREE FARM, WELWYN GARDEN CITY AL7 3UW
Tel: 01707 334040
Fax: 01707 334366
E-mail: mastertravel@btclick.com
Partners: R J Goulden, S Goulden
Fleet: 16 - 1 single-deck bus, 13 single-deck coach, 2 minibus.
Chassis: 1 BMC, 4 Dennis, 2 Ford Transit, 3 Mercedes, 1 Neoplan, 2 Scania, 1 Optare, 1 Autosan, 1 Volvo.
Bodies: 1 Berkhof, 1 BMC, 1 Caetano, 2 Irizar, 2 Marcopolo, 1 Neoplan, 1 Northern Counties, 1 Optare, 1 UGV, 4 other.
Ops incl: school contracts, private hire.
Livery: White/Blue, White

MERIDIAN LINE TRAVEL
UNIT 2, WIRELESS STATION PARK, CHESTNUT LANE, BASSINGBOURN, ROYSTON SG8 5JH
Tel: 01763 241999
Fax: 01763 245697
E-mail: meridianline@dial.pipex.com
Web site: www.mltravel.co.uk
Prop: Norman Dawes
Ops incl: local bus services, school contracts, private hire, excursions & tours.
Livery: White/Multicolour.

MINIBUS SERVICES LTD
773 ST ALBANS ROAD, WATFORD
WD25 9LA
Tel: 01923 663432
Fax: 01923 337347
E-mail: minibusservices@btconnect.com
Props: Russell Crowson, Gillian Crowson.
Fleet: 4 - 1 single-deck coach, 1minibus, 2 midicoach.
Chassis: 1 Ford Transit, 1 Mercedes, 1 Toyota, 1 Volvo.
Bodies: include Caetano, Plaxton.
Ops incl: school contracts, private hire

MULLANY'S COACHES
BROOKDELL TRANSPORT YARD,
ST ALBANS ROAD, WATFORD
WD25 0GB
Tel: 01923 279991
Fax: 01923 682212
E-mail: coachbookings@mullanyscoaches.com
Web site: www.mullanyscoaches.com
Fleet Name: Mullany's Starline
Dir: Kevin Crawford
Fleet: double-deck bus, single-deck bus, single-deck coach, midibus.
Ops incl: local bus services, school contracts, private hire.
Livery: White with Blue.

PARKSIDE TRAVEL LTD
PARADISE WILDLIFE PARK,
WHITE STUBBS LANE,
BROXBOURNE EN10 7QA
Tel: 01992 444477
Fax: 01992 465441
Fleet Name: Parkside Travel
Dirs: P C Sampson, G F Sampson
Fleet: 7 minibus.
Chassis: 7 Ford Transit.
Ops incl: school contracts, private hire.
Livery: Light Blue

PROVENCE PRIVATE HIRE (P.P.H. COACHES)
HEATH FARM LANE, ST ALBANS
AL3 5AE
Tel: 01727 864988
Fax: 01727 855275
E-mail: office@pphcoaches.com
Web site: www.pphcoaches.com
Dirs: Andrew Hayes, Ronald Hayes
Ch Eng: Derek Higgins
Fleet: 30 - 4 double-deck bus, 19 single-deck coach, 1 double-deck coach, 4 midicoach, 2 minibus, 1 Bova.
Chassis: 2 DAF, 4 Dennis, 2 LDV, 3 Leyland, 1 MCW, 3 Mercedes, 9 Scania, 1 Toyota, 4 Volvo.
Bodies: 1 Bova, 2 Caetano, 3 East Lancs, 1 Hispano, 8 Irizar, 2 LDV, 1 MCW, 1 Mercedes, 4 Optare, 6 Plaxton, 1 Van Hool.
Ops incl: school contracts, excursions & tours, private hire, continental tours.
Livery: Yellow.

REG'S COACHES LTD
113 - 115 CODICOTE ROAD,
WELWYN AL6 9TY
Tel: 01483 822000
Fax: 01483 822003
E-mail: regscoaches@btconnect.com
Web site: www.regscoaches.co.uk
Man Dir: Terry Hunt
Dir: Mrs Beverly Hunt
Acting Man: D Witt

Chief Eng: Dicken Baxter
Fleet: 18 - 2 single-deck bus, 14 single-deck coach, 2 midicoach.
Chassis: 7 Alexander Dennis, 3 Mercedes, 8 Volvo.
Bodies: 1 Berkhof, 1 Mercedes, 1 Optare, 11 Plaxton, 2 Van Hool, 1 Wright, 1 Other.
Ops incl: local bus services, school contracts, excursions & tours, private hire.
Livery: Black/Green/Orange
Ticket System: Wayfarer 2/Almex

REYNOLDS DIPLOMAT COACHES
285 LOWER HIGH STREET, WATFORD
WD17 2HY
Tel: 01923 296877
Fax: 01923 210020
E-mail: enquiries@reynoldscoaches.com
Web site: www.reynoldscoaches.com
Partners: Richard Reynolds, Mrs Susan Reynolds
Fleet: 17 - 12 single-deck coach, 2 double-deck coach, 1 midicoach, 2 minicoach.
Chassis incl: 3 Scania, 6 Setra, 1 Toyota, 3 Volvo.
Bodies incl: 1 Caetano, 3 Jonckheere, 6 Setra, 3 Van Hool.
Ops incl: excursions & tours, private hire, continental tours, school contracts.
Livery: Gold

RICHMOND'S COACHES
THE GARAGE, HIGH STREET,
BARLEY, ROYSTON SG8 8JA
Tel: 01763 848226
Fax: 01763 848105
E-mail: postbox@richmonds-coaches.co.uk
Web site: www.richmonds-coaches.co.uk
Dirs: David Richmond, Michael Richmond, Andrew Richmond
Sales & Marketing Man: Rick Ellis
Asst Ops Man: Craig Ellis
Ch Eng: Patrick Granville
Exc & Tours Man: Natalie Richmond
Fleet: 25 – 18 single-deck coach, 1 double-deck coach, 5 midibus, 1 midicoach.
Chassis: 9 Bova, 5 DAF, 4 Mercedes, 2 Optare, 5 Volvo.
Bodies: 9 Bova, 2 Optare, 3 Plaxton, 1 Sitcar, 10 Van Hool.
Ops incl: local bus services, school contracts, excursions & tours, private hire, continental tours.
Livery: Cream/Brown
Ticket System: Wayfarer 3

SMITH BUNTINGFORD
CLAREMONT, BALDOCK ROAD,
BUNTINGFORD SG9 9DJ
Tel/Fax: 01763 271516
Prop: Graham H Smith
Fleet Eng: Stewart C Smith
Fleet: 6 minicoach.
Chassis: 1 Ford Transit, 3 Mercedes, 1 Renault, 1 Vauxhall
Bodies: 1 Autobus, 1 Courtside, 1 Ford, 1 Mellor, 1 Stanford.
Ops incl: private hire, school contracts
Livery: White/Orange

SMITHS OF TRING
THE GARAGE, WIGGINTON HP23 6EJ
Tel: 01442 322555
Fax: 08707 627292

Dirs: G. A. Smith
(Man Dir), Mrs S. N. Smith, J. Smith.
Fleet: 8 - 6 single-deck coach, 1 midicoach, 1 minicoach.
Chassis: 2 Mercedes, 6 Volvo.
Bodies: 2 Mercedes, 1 Plaxton, 1 Reeve Burgess.
Ops incl: local bus services, excursions & tours, private hire, continental tours.
Livery: Red/Cream.

SOUTH MIMMS TRAVEL LTD
WARRENGATE ROAD,
NORTH MYMMS AL9 7TU
Tel: 01707 322555
Fax: 08707 627292
E-mail: info@southmimmstravel.com
Web site: www.southmimmstravel.co.uk
Man Dir: S. J. Griffiths.
Fleet: 10 single-deck coach.
Chassis incl: Dennis, MCW, Neoplan, Volvo.
Bodies incl: Berkhof, Bova, MCW, Neoplan, Plaxton.
Ops incl: school contracts, excursions & tours, private hire, continental tours.
Livery: Red/Black/Gold

SULLIVAN BUSES LTD
FIRST FLOOR, DEARDS HOUSE
ST ALBANS ROAD, POTTERS BAR
EN6 3NE
Tel: 01707 646803
Fax: 01707 646804
E-mail: admin@sullivanbuses.com
Web site: www.sullivanbuses.com
Man Dir: Dean Sullivan
Fleet Eng: Neal Hogg
Fleet: 53 - 35 double-deck bus, 9 single-deck bus, 9 midibus.
Chassis: 1 Alexander Dennis, 5 AEC, 14 Dennis, 6 Leyland, 2 MCW, 9 Transbus, 16 Volvo.
Bodies: 1 Alexander Dennis, 7 Caetano, 1 Duple, 9 East Lancs, 2 MCW, 9 Northern Counties, 11 Park Royal, 10 Plaxton, 2 Transbus, 1 Wright.
Ops incl: local bus services, private hire, rail replacement
Livery: Red
Ticket system: Wayfarer TGX

TATES COACHES
44 HIGH STREET, MARKYATE
AL3 8PA
Tel: 01582 840297
Fax: 01582 840014
E-mail: info@tatescoaches.co.uk
Web site: www.tatescoaches.co.uk
Dirs: A M Tate, A J Tate, S W Tate
Fleet: 9 single-deck coach
Chassis: 1 Bova, 1 DAF, 1 Dennis, 1 MAN, 1 Mercedes, 1 Neoplan, 3 Scania.
Bodies: 1 Bova, 1 Caetano, 1 Hispano, 2 Irizar, 1 Neoplan, 2 Van Hool, 1 Wadham Stringer.
Ops incl: school contracts, excursions & tours, private hire, continental tours.
Livery: Cream/Blue/Orange

TERRY'S COACHES
3 NORTHRIDGE WAY, HEMEL
HEMPSTEAD HP1 2AE
Tel: 01442 265850
Dirs: Terry Bunyan, Shirley Bunyan.
Fleet: 5 - 1 midibus, 2 midicoach, 2 minicoach.
Chassis: 1 Iveco, 1 LDV, 2 Mercedes.

Bodies: 1 Leicester, 2 Optare, 2 other.
Ops incl: school contracts, private hire.
Livery: Blue/White

THREE STAR COACHES.COM
UNIT 1, GUARDIAN BUSINESS PARK,
DALLOW ROAD, LUTON LU1 1NA
Tel: 01582 722626
Fax: 01582 484034
E-mail: sales@threestarcoaches.com
Web Site: www.threestarcoaches.com
Man Dir: Colin Dudley,
Ops Man: Kevin Green **Ch Eng:** Michael Nallaby **Co Sec:** Isabelle Dudley
Fleet: 13 – 1 single-deck bus, 7 single-deck coach, 2 double-deck coach, 3 midicoach.
Chassis: 3 Alexander Dennis, 1 Ayats, 5 Mercedes, 1 Optare, 1 Scania, 1 Volvo

Bodies incl: 2 Ayats, 2 Beulas.
Ops incl: school contracts, excursions & tours, private hire.
Livery: Blue

TIMEBUS TRAVEL
See London

UNICORN COACHES
PO BOX 45, HATFIELD AL9 5LD
Tel: 0845 658 5000
E-mail: unicorncoaches@aol.com
Web site: www.unicorncoaches.com
Man Dir: Mrs J E Pleshette
Gen Man: S T Saltmarsh
Fleet: 4 – 2 single-deck coach, 2 minibus.
Chassis: 2 Setra, 2 Volkswagen.
Ops incl: private hire, continental tours.
Livery: White

UNO LTD
GYPSY MOTH AVENUE, HATFIELD BUSINESS PARK, HATFIELD AL10 9BS
Tel: 01707 255764
Web site: www.unobus.info
Man Dir: Jim Thorpe
Fleet: 89 - 11 double deck bus, 72 single deck bus, 6 midibus.
Chassis: 4 Alexander Dennis, 7 DAF, 22 Dennis, 23 Mercedes, 5 Optare, 9 Scania, 18 Transbus, 1 Volvo.
Bodies: 1 Alexander Dennis, 4 Caetano, 6 East Lancs, 22 Mercedes, 6 Optare, 15 Plaxton, 4 Scania, 18 Transbus, 12 Wright.
Ops incl: local bus services, school contracts.
Livery: Pink/Purple.
Ticket System: Wayfarer 3 Inform

ISLE OF WIGHT

GANGES COACHES
77 PLACE ROAD,
COWES PO31 7AE
Tel: 01983 296666
Fax: 01983 296666
Prop: John Gange
Fleet: 9 - 4 single-deck coach, 3 midicoach, 1 minibus, 1 minicoach.
Chassis: 1 AEC, 1 Bedford, 1 Ford, 1 Leyland, 3 Mercedes, 1 Peugeot/Talbot, 1 Renault.
Bodies: 2 Duple, 1 Mercedes, 3 Plaxton, 3 other.
Ops incl: private hire
Livery: Red/Cream and Blue/Cream

ISLE OF WIGHT COUNTY TRANSPORT DEPARTMENT
21 WHITCOMBE ROAD,
CARISBROOKE, NEWPORT
PO30 1YS
Tel: 01983 823782
Fax: 01983 825818
E-mail: transport.info@iow.gov.uk
Fleet Name: Wightbus.
Tran Man: A A Morris
Ops Man: J Lamb.
Fleet: 34 - single-deck bus, single-deck coach, midibus, minibus.
Chassis: Dennis, Iveco, Mercedes, Optare.

Bodies: Alexander, Caetano, Plaxton, UVG, Wadham Stringer.
Ops incl: local bus services, school contracts, excursions & tours, private hire.
Livery: White with Orange and Blue stripes.
Ticket System: Setright.

KARDAN TRAVEL LTD
1ST FLOOR, 35A ST JAMES STREET,
NEWPORT PO30 1LG
Tel: 01983 520995
Fax: 01983 821288
E-mail: info@kardan.co.uk
Web site: www.kardan.co.uk
Dirs: R Hodgson, L Hodgson
Fleet: 5 single-deck coach
Chassis: 3 Setra, 2 Volvo.
Bodies: 2 Plaxton, 3 Setra.
Ops incl: excursions & tours, private hire, continental tours
Livery: Yellow/White

A & M A ROBINSON SEAVIEW SERVICES LTD
COLLEGE FARM INDUSTRIAL ESTATE,
FAULKNER LANE,
SANDOWN PO36 9AZ
Tel: 01983 407070
Fax: 01983 407045
Recovery: 07739 237361
E-mail: mail@seaview-services.com
Web site: www.seaview-services.com
Chairman: Philip Robinson
Ops Man: Lorraine Bunce
Ch Engs: Peter Brand, Jim Wood
Ch Body Eng: Dennis Bunce
Fleet: 8 - 7 single-deck coach, 1 midicoach.
Chassis: 1 Mercedes, 1 Setra, 6 Volvo.
Bodies: 2 Caetano, 3 Plaxton, 1 Setra, 2 Van Hool.
Ops incl: school contracts, excursions & tours, private hire, continental tours, express.
Livery: Silver/Green/Red

THE SOUTHERN VECTIS OMNIBUS CO LTD
NELSON ROAD, NEWPORT
PO30 1RD
Tel: 01983 827000
Fax: 01983 524961
Recovery: 01983 821135
E-mail: talk2us@islandbuses.info
Web site: www.islandbuses.info

Fleet Names: Southern Vectis, Island Breezers, Fountain Coaches, Moss Motor Tours, West Wight Bus & Coach Company
Man Dir: Alex Carter
Div Dir: Marc Morgan-Huws
Fleet: 99 - 51 double-deck bus, 2 single-deck bus, 20 single-deck coach, 9 open-top bus, 12 midibus, 1 midicoach, 4 minicoach.
Chassis: 10 Alexander Dennis, 1 Bristol, 1 Bova, 8 DAF, 1 Dennis, 5 Leyland, 3 Mercedes, 33 Scania, 2 Transbus, 3 Toyota, 32 Volvo.
Bodies: 1 Autobus, 1 Bova, 3 Caetano, 1 ECW, 9 East Lancs, 1 Ikarus, 2 Mercedes, 15 Northern Counties, 32 Plaxton, 28 Scania, 2 Transbus, 4 Van Hool.
Ops incl: local bus services, school contracts, private hire.
Livery: Green
Ticket system: Wayfarer 3
Part of the Go-Ahead Group

WIGHTROLLERS
UNIT C7, SPITHEAD BUSINESS CENTRE, NEWPORT ROAD,
SANDOWN PO36 9PH
Tel: 01983 404028
Fax: 01983 404772
Recovery: 07774 186449
E-mail: wightrollers@supanet.com
Web site: www.wightrollers.co.uk
Dirs: Patricia Steele, Tracey Steele
Ch Eng: Colin Steele
Fleet: 14 - 12 single-deck coach, 1 minibus, 1 minicoach
Chassis incl: 5 Dennis, 1 Optare, 1 Renault, 6 Volvo.
Bodies incl: 1 Caetano, 3 Plaxton.
Ops incl: excursions & tours, private hire.
Livery: White

JOHN WOODHAMS VINTAGE TOURS
WOODSTOCK, GROVE ROAD, RYDE
PO33 3LH
Tel: 01983 812147
E-mail: vintagetours@btconnect.com
Web site: www.vintagetours.co.uk
Prop: John Woodhams
Fleet: 3 midicoach.
Chassis: 3 Bedford.
Bodies: 3 Duple.
Ops incl: excursions & tours, private hire
Livery: Two tone Green

KENT, MEDWAY

ARRIVA SOUTHERN COUNTIES
INVICTA HOUSE, ARMSTRONG ROAD, MAIDSTONE ME15 6TX
Tel: 01622 697000
Fax: 01622 697001
Web site: www.arriva.co.uk
Fleet Names: Arriva Kent & Sussex, Arriva Kent Thameside, Arriva Medway Towns, Arriva Southend, New Enterprise Coaches
Regional Man Dir: Heath Williams
Comm Dir: Kevin Hawkins
Eng Dir: Brian Barraclough
Fin Dir: Beverley Lawson
Fleet: 654 – 146 double-deck bus, 63 single-deck bus, 17 single-deck coach, 416 midibus, 12 minibus.
Chassis: Alexander Dennis, DAF, Dennis, Leyland, Mercedes, Optare, Scania, VDL, Volvo.
Ops incl: local bus services, school contracts, excursions & tours, express, continental tours, private hire.
Livery: Arriva UK Bus.
Ticket System: Wayfarer 3 & TGX150

ASM COACHES
8 THE OAZE, WHITSTABLE CT5 4TQ
Tel: 01227 280254
E-mail: info@asmcoaches.co.uk
Web site: www.asmcoaches.co.uk
Prop/Tran Man: Steve Morrish
Fleet: 3 – 1 midicoach, 1 minibus, 1 minicoach
Chassis: 1 Fiat, 1 Iveco, 1 Mercedes.
Ops incl: school contracts, excursions & tours, private hire, continental tours.
Livery: Purple/Silver & White

AUTOCAR BUS & COACH SERVICES LTD
64 WHETSTED ROAD, FIVE OAK GREEN, TONBRIDGE TN12 6RT
Tel: 01892 833830
Fax: 01892 836977
Dir: Julian Brown
Ops Dir: Eric Baldock
Fleet: 12 – 2 double-deck bus, 5 single-deck bus, 2 single-deck coach, 2 midibus, 1 minibus
Chassis: 1 DAF, 4 Dennis, 2 Leyland, 2 Mercedes, 2 Optare, 1 Scania.
Bodies: 2 Duple, 2 East Lancs, 1 Leyland, 2 Optare, 2 Plaxton, 2 Reeve Burgess, 1 Wadham Stringer.
Ops incl: local bus services, private hire.
Livery: White/Purple/Pink
Ticket System: Wayfarer 2

BRITANNIA COACHES
HOLLOW WOOD ROAD, DOVER CT17 0UB
Tel: 01304 228111
Fax: 01304 215350
E-mail: enq@britannia-coaches.co.uk
Web site: www.britannia-coaches.co.uk
Partners: Barry Watson, Danny Lawson.
Fleet: 30 minicoach.
Chassis/Bodies: 20 Mercedes, 10 Renault.
Ops incl: private hire, school contracts, excursions & tours.

BROWNS COACHES
OAKTREE COTTAGE, MANOR POUND LANE, BRABOURNE, ASHFORD TN25 5LG
Tel: 01303 813555
Fax: 01303 812070
Prop: Patrick Browne
Fleet: 4 - 3 single-deck coach, 1 minibus.
Chassis: 1 LDV, 3 Volvo.
Ops incl: school contracts, private hire

BUZZLINES TRAVEL LTD
LYMPNE INDUSTRIAL PARK, LYMPNE CT21 4LR
Tel: 01303 261870
Fax: 01303 230093
Recovery: 07767 475625
Web site: www.buzzlinestravel.co.uk
Man Dir: Nigel Busbridge
Co Sec: Mrs Kathryn Busbridge
Fleet: 36 – single-deck coach, double-deck coach, midicoach, minibus, minicoach.
Chassis incl: 7 Ford Transit, 5 Mercedes, 3 Toyota.
Bodies incl: 1 Alexander Dennis, 5 Irizar, 1 Neoplan, 2 Scania, 7 Setra.
Ops incl: excursions & tours, private hire, continental tours.
Livery: White.

BZEE BUS & TRAVEL LTD
UNIT 2F, DEACON TRADING ESTATE, FORSTAL ROAD, AYLESFORD ME20 7SP
Tel: 01622 882288
Fax: 01622 718070
Dirs: D Quick, N Kemp
Fleet: 7

CENTAUR COACHES & MINICOACHES
188 HALFWAY STREET, SIDCUP DA15 8DJ
Tel: 020 8300 3001
Fax: 020 8302 5959
Man Dir: M. Sims
Dirs: P Sims, S Durrant
E-mail: matt@minicoaches.com
Web site: www.minicoaches.com
Fleet: 107 – incl 7 single-deck bus, 12 midibus, 22 midicoach, 41 minibus, 20 minicoach.
Chassis incl: 25 Ford Transit, 17 LDV, 12 Mercedes.
Bodies incl: Alexander Dennis, Mercedes, Reeve Burgess.
Ops incl: private hire, school contracts, excursions & tours.

CENTRAL MINI COACHES
177 LOWER ROAD, DOVER CT17 0RE
Tel/Fax: 01304 823030
Prop: P. Hull.
Fleet: 6 - 5 minibus, 1 minicoach.
Chassis: 3 Bedford, 1 Mercedes, 1 Renault.
Ops incl: private hire, school contracts.

CHALKWELL COACH HIRE & TOURS
195 CHALKWELL ROAD, SITTINGBOURNE ME10 1BJ
Tel: 01795 423982
Fax: 01795 431855
E-mail: coachhire@chalkwell.co.uk
Web site: www.chalkwell.co.uk
Fleet Name: Chalkwell
Man Dir: Clive Eglinton
Ops Man: Roland Eglinton
Finance & Admin Man: Louise Eglinton
Fleet: 45 - 5 double-deck bus, 21 single-deck coach, 16 midibus, 2 midicoach, 1 minibus.
Chassis: 1 DAF, 11 Dennis, 8 Mercedes, 6 Optare, 6 Scania, 13 Volvo.
Bodies: 8 Alexander Dennis, 6 Irizar, 4 Jonckheere, 6 Optare, 14 Plaxton, 3 UVG, 3 Wadham Stringer, 1 Other.
Ops incl: local bus services, school contracts, excursions & tours, private hire, express, continental tours.
Livery: White/Red/Black
Ticket System: Almex

COUNTRYLINER GROUP
See Surrey

COUNTRYWIDE TRAVEL SERVICES LTD t/a DAWNEY HOLIDAYS
ABBEY WORKS, WHITEWAY ROAD, QUEENBOROUGH ME11 5PP
Tel: 01795 662688
Fax: 01795 662730
E-mail: stephen.smith@cwts.co.uk
Web sites: www.dawneyholidays.com
Man Dir: Stephen Smith
Dir: Steve Mason
Fleet: 8 - incl: double-deck bus, single-deck coach, midibus, midicoach.
Chassis: 1 BMC, 4 Irisbus, 1 Mercedes, 2 Volvo.
Bodies incl: 2 Alexander Dennis, 4 Beulas, 1 BMC, 1 Mercedes.
Ops incl: excursions & tours, private hire, continental tours.
Livery: White/Green lettering

CROSSKEYS COACHES LTD
CROSSKEYS BUSINESS PARK, CAESARS WAY, FOLKESTONE CT19 4AL
Tel: 01303 272625
Fax: 01303 274085
E-mail: coachhire@crosskeys.uk.com
Web site: www.crosskeys.uk.com
Dir: Alan Johnson
Fleet: 18 - 2 single-deck bus, 15 single-deck coach, 1 minicoach.
Chassis incl: 3 Alexander Dennis, 8 Bova, 2 Leyland National, 2 Setra, 2 Volvo.
Bodies incl: 8 Bova, 1 Jonckheere, 4 Plaxton, 2 Setra.
Ops incl: school contracts, excursions & tours, private hire, continental tours.
Livery: Orange

EASTONWAYS LTD
MANSTON ROAD, RAMSGATE CT12 6HJ
Tel: 01843 588944
Fax: 01843 582300
E-mail: info@eastonways.co.uk
Web site: www.eastonways.co.uk
Man Dir: D. Austin
Co Sec: Mrs Y. M. Easton
Gen Man: S. Bishop.
Fleet: 29 - 6 double-deck bus,

15 single-deck bus, 1 single-deck coach,
4 midibus, 3 minicoach.
Chassis incl: 15 Alexander Dennis.
Ops incl: local bus services, school
contracts, private hire, continental tours.
Livery: Coaches: Blue/Silver. Buses:
Red.
Ticket System: Wayfarer.

EUROLINK FOKESTONE
GREATWORTH, CANTERBURY ROAD,
ETCHINGHILL, FOLKESTONE
CT18 8BS
Tel: 01303 862767
Fax: 01303 862484
E-mail: eurolinkcoaches@btconnect.com
Partners: Andy Williams, Lyn Williams
Fleet: 5 - 3 midicoach, 2 minicoach.
Chassis: 1 Ford, 1 MAN, 3 Mercedes.
Bodies: 1 Caetano, 1 Esker, 1 Mercedes,
2 other.
Ops incl: school contracts, private hire.
Livery: White/Grey/Orange

FARLEIGH COACHES
ST PETERS WORKS, HALL ROAD,
WOULDHAM, ROCHESTER
ME1 3XL
Tel: 01634 201065
Fax: 01634 660350
Prop: D R Smith
Livery: White/Yellow/Red/Black.

FERRYMAN TRAVEL
RECTORY LANE NORTH,
LEYBOURNE ME19 5HD
Tel/Fax: 01732 843396
Fleet: 4 minibus.
Chassis: 3 DAF, 1 Ford Transit.
Ops incl: school contracts, excursions &
tours, private hire, continental tours.

G & S TRAVEL
14 PYSONS ROAD, RAMSGATE
CT12 6TS
Tel: 01843 591105
Fax: 01843 596274
E-mail: shirleygstravel@fismail.net
Dirs: Shirley Rimmer, George Rimmer
Ops Man: Malcolm Wood
Ch Eng: Darren Doyle
Fleet: 12 - 8 single-deck coach,
2 minibus, 2 midicoach.
Chassis: 2 LDV, 2 Toyota, 8 Volvo.
Bodies: 5 Caetano, 5 Plaxton,
1 Van Hool, 2 other.
Ops incl: school contracts, excursions &
tours, private hire, continental tours.
Livery: White.

GRIFFIN BUS
SALTS FARM, FAWKHAM ROAD,
LONGFIELD DA3 7BJ
Tel: 01474 709415
Fax: 01474 703872
Recovery: 01474 709402
E-mail: griffinbus@aol.com
Web site: www.griffinbuses.com
Man Dir: David Booker
Ops Man: Steve Ellis
Eng Man: Richard Caplin
24 Hr Recovery: Paul Hands
Fleet: 12 – 8 double-deck bus,
1 single-deck bus, 2 single-deck coach,
1 minibus.
Chassis: 1 Bova, 3 Leyland, 6 MCW,
2 Volvo.
Bodies: 1 Bova, 3 East Lancs, 6 MCW,
2 Volvo.

Ops incl: local bus services, school
contracts, excursions & tours, private hire.
Livery: Red/White
Ticket System: Wayfarer

KENT COACH TOURS LTD
THE COACH STATION, MALCOLM
SARGENT ROAD, ASHFORD
TN23 6JW
Tel/Recovery: 01233 627330
Fax: 01233 612977
Web site: www.kentcoachtours.co.uk
Dirs: David Farmer, Ann Farmer,
Andrew Farmer **(Co Sec)**, Brian Farmer
(Ch Eng)
Fleet: 13 - 1 single-deck bus,
7 single-deck coach, 5 minibus.
Chassis: 1 MAN, 5 Mercedes, 1 Optare,
7 Volvo.
Bodies: 1 Optare, 12 Plaxton.
Ops incl: local bus services, school
contracts, excursions & tours, private hire.
Livery: Blue
Ticket System: Wayfarer

KENT COUNTY COUNCIL
PASSENGER SERVICES,
FORSTAL ROAD, AYLESFORD
ME20 7HB
Tel: 01622 605935
Fax: 01622 790338
Fleet Name: Kent Top Travel
Tran Man: Kenneth Cobb
Ops Controller: Roger Faunch
Asst Ops Controller: Mick Curd.
Fleet: 48 - 2 double-deck bus,
12 single-deck bus, 4 single-deck coach,
2 midibus, 1 midicoach, 27 minibus.
Chassis: 5 Dennis, 27 Iveco, 4 Leyland,
3 Mercedes, 4 Optare, 1 Volvo.
Bodies: 1 Alexander, 1 Caetano,
27 Euromotive, 7 Leicester, 2 Leyland,
4 Optare, 6 Plaxton.
Ops incl: local bus services, school
contracts, private hire.
Livery: Red on White.
Ticket System: Almex.

THE KINGS FERRY LTD
THE TRAVEL CENTRE,
GILLINGHAM ME8 6HW
Tel: 01634 377577
Fax: 01634 370656
E-mail: sales@thekingsferry.co.uk
Web site: www.thekingsferry.co.uk
Dir: Ian Fraser **Comm Dir:** Danny Elford
Ops Man: Graham Birch
Eng Man: Mick Keohane
Fleet: 66 - single-deck bus, single-deck
coach, double-deck coach, midicoach,
minibus, minicoach.
Chassis: 1 Alexander Dennis, 1 Bova,
2 DAF, 2 Dennis, 2 Iveco, 10 MAN,
15 Mercedes, 2 Optare, 22 Scania,
2 Setra, 9 Volvo.
Bodies: 1 Alexander Dennis, 13 Berkhof,
1 Bova, 2 Caetano, 1 Castrosua, 2 Indcar,
9 Irizar, 3 Mercedes, 10 Noge, 5 Optare,
2 Setra, 5 Sunsundegui, 5 Van Hool.
Ops incl: local bus services, school
contracts, excursions & tours, private hire,
express, continental tours.
Livery: Yellow with green stripe
Part of the National Express Group

KINGSMAN INTERNATIONAL TRAVEL
57 BRAMLEY AVENUE, FAVERSHAM
ME13 8LP

Tel: 01795 501746
Fax: 01795 536798
E-mail: jonathanamancini@tiscali.co.uk
Web site:
www.kingsmaninternationalme13.co.uk
Props: J A Mancini, J Mancini
Fleet: 8 - single-deck bus, single-deck
coach, midicoach.
Chassis: Mercedes, Neoplan.
Bodies: Mercedes, Neoplan, Plaxton.
Ops incl: local bus services, excursions
& tours, private hire, continental tours.

LOGANS TOURS LTD
1 AND 2 THE COTTAGES,
NORTHFLEET GREEN DA13 9PT
Tel: 01474 833876
E-mail: dave@loganstours.co.uk
Web site: www.loganstours.co.uk
Dir: David Logan
Fleet: 2 single-deck coach.
Chassis: 1 Dennis, 1 Raba.
Bodies: 1 Caetano, 1 Ikarus.
Ops incl: excursions & tours, private hire,
continental tours
Livery: Pink/White

NEW ENTERPRISE COACHES
CANNON LANE, TONBRIDGE
TN9 1PP
Tel: 01732 355256
Fax: 01732 357716
Prop: Arriva Southern Counties
Man Dir: Heath Williams
Gen Man: Chris Lawrence
Eng Man: Andy Weber
Fleet: 24 - 5 double-deck bus,
2 single-deck bus, 17 single-deck coach.
Ops incl: local bus services, school
contracts, excursions & tours, private hire,
continental tours.
Livery: White/Red/Blue.
Ticket System: Wayfarer II.

NU-VENTURE COACHES LTD
UNIT 2F, DEACON TRADING ESTATE,
FORSTAL ROAD, AYLESFORD
ME20 7SP
Tel: 01622 882288
Fax: 01622 718070
E-mail:
nuventurecoachesltd@yahoo.co.uk
Web site: www.nu-venture.co.uk
Dir: D Quick
Co Sec: N Kemp
Fleet: 28 - 11 double-deck bus,
14 single-deck bus, 3 single-deck coach.
Chassis: 10 Dennis, 13 Leyland, 1 MAN,
1 Mercedes, 2 Optare, 1 Scania.
Bodies: 5 Alexander, 1 Caetano,
12 Leyland, 1 Marcopolo, 2 Marshall,
2 Optare, 1 Plaxton, 1 Reeve Burgess,
2 UVG, 1 Van Hool.
Ops incl: local bus services, school
contracts, private hire, excursions & tours.
Livery: White/Blue
Ticket System: Wayfarer 3

POYNTERS COACHES LTD
WYE COACH DEPOT,
WYE TN25 5BX
Tel: 01233 812002
Fax: 01233 813210
Recovery: 07770 874631
E-mail: poyntercoaches@aol.com
Man Dir: B Poynter
Ch Eng: B Poynter
Fleet: 15 - 1 double-deck bus,
8 single-deck bus, 5 single-deck coach,

1 double-deck coach.
Chassis: 2 DAF, 3 Dennis, 2 Leyland, 1 MAN, 7 Volvo.
Bodies: 4 Alexander, 1 Berkhof, 1 Bova, 1 Jonckheere, 2 Leyland, 2 Neoplan, 1 Optare, 2 Reeve Burgess, 1 Van Hool
Ops incl: local bus services, school contracts, excursions & tours, private hire, continental tours.
Livery: White
Ticket System: Wayfarer

R. K. F. TRAVEL
R24
19 COBB CLOSE, STROOD
ME2 3TY
Tel/Fax: 01634 715897
Dir: Ray Fraser.
Fleet: 2 minibus.
Chassis: 1 LDV, 1 Volkswagen.
Ops incl: private hire.

THE RAINHAM COACH COMPANY
1A SPRINGFIELD ROAD,
GILLINGHAM ME7 1YJ
Tel & Recovery: 01634 852020
Fax: 01634 582020
E-mail: info@rainhamcoach.co.uk
Web site: www.rainhamcoach.co.uk
Senior Partner: David Graham
Gen Man: Richard Graham
Traffic Man: Louise Salisbury
Ch Eng: Geoff Birdock
Fleet: 20 - 4 midicoach, 16 minicoach.
Chassis/Bodies: 1 Ford Transit, 19 Mercedes.
Ops incl: school contracts, excursions & tours, private hire.
Livery: White/Magenta/Grey

RED ROUTE BUSES LTD
GRANBY COACHWORKS, GROVE ROAD, NORTHFLEET DA11 9AX
Tel: 01474 353896 **Fax:** 01424 358475
E-mail: redroutebuses@btconnect.com
Web site: www.redroutebuses.com
Ops Dir: Jason Mee
Eng Dir: Terry Mee
Ops Man: Chris Carman
Fleet: 15 - 8 double-deck bus, 2 single-deck bus, 3 single-deck coach, 1 midicoach, 1 open top bus.
Chassis incl: 4 AEC Routemaster, 2 DAF, 1 Daimler
Bodies incl: 2 LDV, 1 MCW, 1 Mercedes, 4 Park Royal, 3 Volvo, 1 Other.
Ops incl: local bus services, school contracts, private hire
Livery: Red/White
Ticket System: Wayfarer Saver

REGENT COACHES
UNIT 16, ST AUGUSTINE'S BUSINESS PARK, SWALECLIFFE CT5 2QJ
Tel: 01227 794345
Fax: 01227 795127
E-mail: info@regentcoaches.com
Web site: www.regentcoaches.co.uk
Partners: Paul Regent, Kerry Regent
Tran Man: Colin MacDonald

Workshop Man: Robert Wildish
Office Man: Sam Regent
Asst Tran Man: Nigel Andrews
Fleet: 22 – 2 single-deck bus, 10 minibus, 10 midicoach.
Chassis: 2 Alexander Dennis, 6 Iveco, 1 MAN, 9 Mercedes, 4 Renault.
Bodies: 2 Alexander Dennis, 1 Ayats, 1 Beulas, 2 Esker, 4 Indcar, 10 Other.
Ops incl: local bus services, school contracts, excursions & tours, private hire, continental tours.
Livery: Ivory with Red/Orange lettering.
Ticket system: Ticketer

SCOTLAND & BATES
HEATH ROAD, APPLEDORE
TN26 2AJ
Tel: 01233 758325
Fax: 01233 758611
E-mail: info@scotlandandbates.co.uk
Web site: www.scotlandandbates.co.uk
Partners: Richard Bates, Mrs Georgina Bates.
Fleet: 18 single-deck coach.
Chassis: 18 Volvo.
Bodies: 2 Plaxton, 16 Van Hool.
Ops incl: local bus services, private hire
Livery: Cream/Brown/Orange

SEATH COACHES
THE FIELDINGS, STONEHEAP ROAD, EAST STUDDAL, DOVER CT15 5BU
Tel: 01304 620825
Fax: 01304 620825
Prop: Philip J Seath
Fleet: 4 - single-deck coach, midicoach, minibus.
Chassis: Ford Transit, MAN, Volvo.
Ops incl: school contracts, private hire.
Livery: White/Blue

SPOT HIRE TRAVEL
STATION APPROACH, BEARSTED STATION, WARE STREET, MAIDSTONE ME14 4PH
Tel: 01622 736660
Fax: 01622 630406
E-mail: sales@spothire.co.uk
Web site: www.spothire.co.uk
Prop: Ross Young
Tours & Excursions Man:
Ms Jodie Follett
Fleet: 9 - 3 single-deck coach, 3 midicoach, 3 minicoach.
Chassis: 1 Ford, 5 Mercedes, 3 Volvo
Bodies: 3 Esker, 1 Jonckheere, 2 Van Hool, 3 Other.
Ops incl: excursions & tours.
Livery: Cream with three stripes

STAGECOACH IN EAST KENT & EAST SUSSEX
BUS STATION, ST GEORGE'S LANE, CANTERBURY CT1 2SY
Tel: 01227 828103
Fax: 01227 828150
E-mail: dawn.cannon@stagecoachbus.com
Web site: www.stagecoachbus.com

Fleet Name: Stagecoach in East Kent
Man Dir: Phil Medlicott
Ops Dir: Neil Instrall
Eng Dir: Jason Bush
Comm Dir: Jeremy Cooper
Fleet: 420 - 154 double-deck bus, 69 single-deck bus, 28 single-deck coach, 104 midibus, 65 minibus.
Chassis: Alexander Dennis, DAF, Dennis, Leyland, MAN, Mercedes, Optare, Scania, Transbus, Volvo.
Bodies: Alexander, Alexander Dennis, Caetano, East Lancs, Ikarus, Marshall, MCV, Northern Counties, Optare, Plaxton, Transbus, Wright.
Ops incl: local bus services, express.
Livery: Stagecoach UK Bus; National Express (White).
Ticket System: ERG/Wayfarer.

STREAMLINE (KENT) LTD
WEST STATION APPROACH, MAIDSTONE ME16 8RJ
Tel: 01622 750000
Fax: 01622 752978
E-mail: coaches@streamline.travel
Web site: www.streamline.travel
Man Dir: Ron Parker
Co Sec: Angela Parker
Fleet: 8 - 3 midicoach, 5 minicoach.
Chassis/Bodies: 1 Iveco, 7 Mercedes.
Ops incl: school contracts, excursions & tours, private hire, continental tours.
Livery: Silver/Blue.

THOMSETT'S COACHES
50 GOLF ROAD, DEAL CT14 6QB
Tel/Fax: 01304 374731
E-mail: thomsettscoaches@fsmail.net
Web site: www.thomsettscoaches.com
Prop: S. J. Thomsett
Fleet: 4 - 3 single-deck coach, 1 midicoach.
Chassis: 1 MAN, 3 Scania.
Bodies: 1 Caetano, 3 Van Hool.
Ops incl: school contracts, private hire.
Livery: White/Red

TRACKS VEHICLE SERVICES LTD
THE FLOTS, BROOKLAND, ROMNEY MARSH TN29 9TG
Tel: 01797 344164
Fax: 01797 344135
E-mail: info@tracks-travel.com
Web site: tracks-travel.com
Man Dir: Andrew Toms.
Ops incl: private hire, continental tours.

TRAVELMASTERS
R24
DORSET ROAD INDUSTRIAL ESTATE, DORSET ROAD, SHEERNESS ME12 1LT
Tel: 01795 660066
Fax: 01795 660088
Recovery: 07850 848008
E-mail: sales.travel@btconnect.com
Dirs: T Lambkin, C Smith
Fleet: 23 - 4 double-deck bus, 2 single-deck bus, 10 single-deck coach,

---

	Vehicle suitable for disabled		Seat belt-fitted Vehicle	R24	24 hour recovery service
T	Toilet-drop facilities available		Coach(es) with galley facilities		Replacement vehicle available
R	Recovery service available		Air-conditioned vehicle(s)		Vintage Coach(es) available
	Open top vehicle(s)		Coaches with toilet facilities		

The Little Red Book 2011 - in association with *tbf* Transport Benevolent Fund

2 double-deck coach, 2 midibus,
1 midicoach, 3 minibus.
Chassis: 1 Dennis, 2 Leyland,
5 Mercedes, 4 Scania, 11 Volvo.
Bodies: 2 Alexander, 2 ECW,
3 Mercedes, 2 Northern Counties,
5 Plaxton, 9 Van Hool.
Ops incl: school contracts, excursions &
tours, private hire, continental tours.

VIKING MINICOACHES

UNIT 1, LYSANDER CLOSE,
PYSONS ROAD INDUSTRIAL ESTATE,
BROADSTAIRS CT10 2YJ
Tel: 01843 860876
Fax: 01843 866975
Prop: Paul Troke
Fleet: 7 - 2 midicoach, 5 minibus.
Chassis/Bodies: 2 Iveco, 1 LDV,
2 Mercedes, 1 Renault, 1 Toyota,
1 Caetano
Ops incl: school contracts, private hire.

WESTERHAM COACHES

15 BARROW GREEN ROAD,
OXTED RH8 0NJ
Tel: 01883 713663
Fax: 01883 730279
E-mail: info@skinners.travel
Web site: www.skinners.travel
Partners: Stephen Skinner,
Deborah Skinner
Fleet: 13 – 10 single-deck coach,
2 midicoach, 1 minicoach.
Chassis: 4 Alexander Dennis, 1 MAN,
2 Mercedes, 6 Setra.

Bodies: 1 Duple, 1 Mercedes, 4 Neoplan,
1 Optare, 6 Setra.
Ops incl: school contracts, excursions &
tours, private hire, continental tours.
A subsidiary of Skinners of Oxted – see
Surrey

WEST KENT BUSES

THE COACH STATION,
LONDON ROAD, WEST KINGSDOWN
TN15 6AR

Tel: 01474 855444
Fax: 01474 855454
E-Mail: info@westkentbuses.co.uk
Proprietor: Stuart Gilkes
Ch Eng: Paul Jones
Fleet: 7 - 5 double-deck bus,
2 single-deck bus.
Chassis: 4 Leyland, 3 Volvo.
Bodies: 1 Alexander, 3 Leyland,
1 Northern Counties, 1 Plaxton,
1 Van Hool.
Ops incl: school contracts, private hire.
Livery: Maroon/Cream

LANCASHIRE, BLACKBURN & DARWEN, BLACKPOOL

ADLINGTON TAXIS & MINICOACHES
See Greater Manchester

ALFA TRAVEL

EUXTON LANE, EUXTON,
CHORLEY PR7 6AF
Tel: 0845 130 5777
Fax: 0845 130 3777
E-mail: req@alfatravel.co.uk
Web site: www.alfatravel.co.uk
Man Dir: Paul Sawbridge
Fin Dir: Peter Sawbridge
Head of Ops: Neil McMurdy
Ops Man: Tom Smith
Fleet: 39 single-deck coach.
Chassis: 15 Alexander Dennis, 24 Volvo.
Bodies: 39 Plaxton.
Ops incl: excursions & tours, private hire,
continental tours.
Livery: Cream

J & F ASPDEN (BLACKBURN) LTD

LANCASTER STREET,
BLACKBURN BB2 1UA.
Tel: 01254 52020
Fax: 01254 57474
Fleet Name: Aspdens Coaches.
Ops incl: school contracts, excursions &
tours, private hire, continental tours.
Livery: Yellow/Black.
A subsidiary of Holmeswood Coaches

BATTERSBY SILVER GREY COACHES

THE COACH STATION, MIDDLEGATE,
WHITE LUND BUSINESS PARK,
MORECAMBE LA3 3PE
Tel: 01524 380000
Fax: 01524 380800
Recovery: 01524 380000
E-mail: tony@battersbys.co.uk
Web site: www.battersbys.co.uk
Chairman: J A Harrison
Co Sec: M F Harrison
Fleet: 29 - 24 single-deck coach,
5 midicoach.
Chassis: 4 Dennis, 5 Mercedes,
20 Volvo.
Bodies: 2 Jonckheere, 1 Mercedes,
21 Plaxton, 1 Van Hool, 4 Wadham
Stringer
Ops incl: local bus services, excursions
& tours, private hire, continental tours,
school contracts.
Livery: Silver Grey
Ticket system: Wayfarer

BLACKPOOL TRANSPORT SERVICES LTD

RIGBY ROAD, BLACKPOOL FY1 5DD
Tel: 01253 473001
Fax: 01253 473101
E-mail:
debbie.vallance@blackpooltransport.com
Web site: www.blackpooltransport.com
Fleet Name: Metro Coastlines
Man Dir: Trevor Roberts
Eng Dir: Dave Hislop
Fin Dir: Sue Kennerley
Ops Man: Guy Thornton
Fleet: 249 - 70 double-deck bus,
44 single-deck bus, 7 open top bus,
57 midibus, 12 minibus, 62 tram.
Chassis: 37 Alexander Dennis, 24 DAF,

34 Leyland, 86 Optare, 6 Volvo, 62 Tram.
Bodies: 24 ECW, 44 East Lancs,
6 Northern Counties, 110 Optare, 3 Roe.
Ops incl: local bus services, tram
services.
Livery: Yellow plus route branded route
colours.
Ticket System: Wayfarer/Almex A90

BRADSHAWS TRAVEL

46 WESTBOURNE ROAD,
KNOTT END ON SEA,
POULTON-LE-FYLDE FY6 0BS
Tel/Fax: 01253 810058
Proprietor: Mrs Jill Swift
Fleet: 10 - 9 single-deck coach,
1 minibus.
Chassis: 1 DAF, 2 Dennis, 3 Leyland,
1 Mercedes, 3 Volvo.
Bodies: 1 Mercedes, 7 Plaxton,
2 Van Hool.
Ops incl: private hire, school contracts.
Livery: White/Yellow
Ticket System: Almex

COACH OPTIONS
See Greater Manchester

COASTAL COACHES

65 CHURCH STREET, WARTON,
PRESTON PR4 1BD
Tel: 01772 635820
Web site: www.coastalcoaches.co.uk
Props: W Holder, Mrs H Holder
Fleet: 12 – single-deck coach, midibus,
midicoach, minicoach
Chassis: Mercedes, Optare, Setra
Ops incl: local bus services, private hire
Livery: Blue & White

132 | The Little Red Book 2011 - in association with *tbf* Transport Benevolent Fund

COLRAY COACHES
14 PRESTBURY AVENUE, BLACKPOOL FY4 1PT
Tel: 01253 349481
Dirs: Geoffrey Shaw, V Shaw
Fleet: 4 – single-deck coach, midibus, midicoach.
Chassis: 1 Mercedes, 1 Setra, 2 Toyota, 1 Volvo.
Bodies: 1 Caetano, 1 Mercedes, 1 Plaxton, 1 Setra
Ops incl: excursions & tours, school contracts, private hire, continental tours.
Livery: White/Blue

COSGROVE'S TOURS
133 WOODPLUMPTON ROAD, PRESTON PR2 3LF
Tel: 01772 460748
Web site: www.cosgroveafton.co.uk
Fleet: 7 – 6 single-deck coach, 1 midicoach
Chassis: 6 DAF/VDL, 1 Mercedes
Bodies: 1 Mercedes, 6 Van Hool
Ops incl: excursions & tours, private hire
Livery: White with logos

EAVESWAY TRAVEL LTD
BRYN SIDE, BRYN ROAD, ASHTON-IN-MAKERFIELD WN4 8BT
Tel: 01942 727985
Fax: 01942 271234
E-mail: sales@eaveswaytravel.com
Web site: www.eaveswaytravel.com
Man Dir: Mike Eaves
Dir: Phil Rogers
Ops Man: Tim Presley
Service Man: Mick Mullen
Fleet: 30 – 16 double-deck coach, 14 single-deck coach.
Chassis: 28 DAF, 2 MAN.
Bodies: 30 Van Hool.
Ops incl: express, private hire.
Livery: Silver/Blue/Green.

JOHN FISHWICK & SONS
GOLDEN HILL LANE, LEYLAND PR25 3LE
Tel: 01772 421207
Fax: 01772 622407
E-mail: enquiries@fishwicks.co.uk
Web site: www.fishwicks.co.uk
Dirs: John C Brindle, James F Hustler
Fleet: 38 - 8 double-deck bus, 26 single-deck bus, 4 single-deck coach.
Chassis: 29 DAF/VDL, 1 Leyland, 1 Leyland National, 7 Volvo.
Bodies: 7 Alexander Dennis, 1 East Lancs, 4 Plaxton, 4 Van Hool, 21 Wright.
Ops incl: local bus services, school contracts, excursions & tours, private hire, continental tours.
Livery: Green.
Ticket System: Wayfarer.

FLIGHTS HALLMARK
See West Midlands

FREEBIRD
See Greater Manchester

GPD TRAVEL
27 HARTFORD AVENUE, HEYWOOD OL10 4XH
Tel: 01706 622297 **Fax:** 01706 361494
Web site: www.gpdtravel.freeserve.co.uk
E-mail: gary@gpdtravel.freeserve.co.uk
Props: Gary Dawson, Janine Dawson
Fleet: 7 - 3 single-deck coach,

2 minicoach, 2 midibus.
Chassis: 2 DAF, 4 Mercedes, 1 Volvo.
Bodies: 1 Autobus, 1 Caetano, 2 Plaxton.
Ops incl: school contracts, excursions & tours, private hire, continental tours.
Livery: Red/Gold stripes.

G-LINE HOLIDAYS LTD
54 ST DAVIDS ROAD SOUTH, ST ANNES FY8 1TS
Tel: 01253 725999 **Fax:** 01253 781843
Web site: www.g-linecoaches.co.uk
E-mail: info@g-linecoaches.co.uk
Prop: Mr E Bradshaw
Tours Man: Mr A Nayler
Coach Man: Mr R Smith
Office Man: Mrs P Jenkinson
Fleet: 9 single-deck coach
Chassis: 5 VDL, 4 Volvo.
Bodies: 1 Berkhof, 3 Plaxton, 5 Van Hool.
Ops incl: excursions & tours, private hire, continental tours.
Livery: White and Maroon

JEFF GRIFFITHS COACHES
22 MYERSCOUGH AVENUE, ST ANNES-ON-SEA FY8 2HY
Tel: 01253 714230
Fax: 01253 640560
E-mail: jeff-griffiths@comserve.com
Dir: Jeff Griffiths
Fleet: 1 single-deck coach
Chassis: Volvo.
Bodies: Plaxton
Ops incl: excursions & tours, private hire.
Livery: White

HEALINGS INTERNATIONAL COACHES
See Greater Manchester

HODDER MOTOR SERVICES LTD
3 ALDERFORD CLOSE, CLITHEROE BB7 2QP
Tel: 01200 422473
Fax: 01200 422590
E-mail: hoddercoaches@hotmail.co.uk
Dir: Paul Hodgson
Co Sec: Janice Hodgson.
Fleet: 2 single-deck coach
Chassis: 1 Neoplan, 1 Volvo.
Body: 1 Neoplan, 1 Van Hool.
Ops incl: school contracts, private hire,

excursions & tours.
Livery: Silver/Grey

HOLMESWOOD COACHES LTD
SANDY WAY, HOLMESWOOD, ORMSKIRK L40 1UB
Tel: 01704 821245
Fax: 01704 822090
E-mail: sales@holmeswood.uk.com
Web site: www.holmeswood.uk.com
Dirs: J F Aspinall, M Aspinall, D G Aspinall, C H Aspinall, M F Aspinall, M J Aspinall
Fleet Names: Bostock's Coaches, Congleton; Walkers Coaches, Northwich; Aspden's Coaches, Blackburn; John Flanagan Coaches, Warrington.
Fleet: 125 - 14 double-deck bus, 82 single-deck coach, 2 double-deck coach, 3 midibus, 14 midicoach, 10 minicoach.
Chassis: DAF, Dennis, Irisbus, Iveco, Leyland, MAN, Mercedes, Neoplan, Scania, VDL, Volvo.
Bodies: Alexander Dennis, Beulas, Caetano, ECW, East Lancs, Esker, Ikarus, Irizar, Jonckheere, Marcopolo, Neoplan, Northern Counties, Plaxton, Van Hool.
Ops incl: local bus services, school contracts, excursions & tours, private hire, continental tours.
Livery: Green
Ticket system: Wayfarer

JACKSONS COACHES
JACKSON HOUSE, BURTON ROAD, BLACKPOOL FY4 4NW
Tel: 01253 792222
Fax: 01253 692070
Partner: Jon Paul Jackson
Fleet: 6 single-deck coach.
Chassis: 1 Iveco, 3 Scania, 2 Volvo.
Bodies: 2 Irizar, 3 Plaxton, 1 Van Hool.
Ops incl: school contracts, private hire, excursions & tours, continental tours.
Livery: White/Blue.
Ticket System: Setright

KIRKBY LONSDALE COACH HIRE LTD
OLD STATION YARD, WARTON ROAD, CARNFORTH LA5 9EU
Tel: 01524 733831
Fax: 01524 733821

Lancashire, Blackburn & Darwen, Blackpool

Recovery: 07814 371079
E-mail: sutton@klch.bbfree.co.uk
Web site:
www.kirkbylonsdalecoachhire.co.uk
Dirs: Mrs Jane Sutton, Stephen Sutton
Ops Man: Matthew Sutton
Fleet: 22 – 1 single-deck bus,
5 single-deck coach, 12 midibus,
3 minicoach, 1 minicoach.
Chassis: 3 DAF, 1 Dennis, 16 Mercedes,
1 Setra, 1 Volvo.
Bodies: 1 Bova, 1 Marshall, 1 Mellor,
5 Optare, 11 Plaxton, 1 Setra, 1 Van Hool,
1 Wadham Stringer.
Ops incl: local bus services, school
contracts, excursions & tours, private hire.
Livery: White/Maroon
Ticket System: Wayfarer TGX, Almex

LAKELAND COACHES
SMITHY ROW, HURST GREEN,
CLITHEROE BB7 9QA
Tel: 01254 826007
Fleet: 9 – 7 single-deck coach,
2 midicoach
Chassis: Mercedes, Scania, Volvo
Ops incl: excursions & tours, private hire

NORTH WEST COACHES & LIMOS
HILLHOUSE INTERNATIONAL
BUSINESS PARK, WEST ROAD,
THORNTON CLEVELEYS FY5 4DQ
Tel: 01253 855000
Fax: 01253 522845
Recovery: 07850 500015
E-mail: stewart.farrel@tiscali.co.uk
Web site: www.northwestcoaches.co.uk
Owner/Operator: Stuart J Farrell
Ops Man: Paul Portisman
Head Fitter: John Keen
Fleet: 18 - 1 double-deck coach,
3 single-deck coach, 2 minibus,
5 midicoach, 7 minibus.
Chassis: 1 DAF, 1 Iveco, 5 Mercedes,
1 Neoplan, 8 Renault, 2 Volvo.
Ops incl: local bus services, excursions
& tours, school contracts, private hire

OLYMPIA TRAVEL UK LTD
44 ARGYLE STREET, HINDLEY,
WIGAN WN2 3PH
Tel: 01942 522322
Fax: 01942 255845
Recovery: 07736 329133
E-mail: olympia@coach-hire.net
Web site: www.coach-hire.net
Props: Joseph Lewis, Shaun Lewis.
Fleet: 19 – double-deck bus, single-deck
coach, midicoach, minibus, minicoach.
Chassis: 4 Mercedes, 15 Volvo.
Bodies: 1 East Lancs, 4 Jonckheere,
2 Mercedes, 6 Plaxton, 6 Van Hool,
1 Other.
Ops incl: local bus services, school
contracts, excursions & tours, private hire,
continental tours.
Livery: White with blue stripes
Ticket System: Wayfarer

PRESTON BUS LTD
221 DEEPDALE ROAD,
PRESTON PR1 6NY
Tel: 01772 253671
Fax: 01772 555840
Recovery: 01772 253671
E-mail: enquiries@prestonbus.co.uk
Web site: www.prestonbus.co.uk
Ops incl: local bus services, school
contracts.

Livery: Blue/Cream, Stagecoach UK Bus
Ticket System: Wayfarer TGX150
Part of Stagecoach North West

REDLINE TRAVEL
25 GOWER GROVE, WALMER BRIDGE,
PRESTON PR4 5QJ
Tel: 01772 611612
Fax: 01772 611613
E-mail: info@lancashirecoachhire.co.uk
Web site:
www.lancashirecoachhire.co.uk
Props: R. G. H. & S. R. Nuttall.

REEVES COACH SERVICE
34 MONKS DRIVE, WITHNELL,
CHORLEY PR6 8SG
Tel/Fax: 01254 830545
E-mail: info@reevescoachholidays.com
Web site: www.reevescoachholidays.com
Prop: John Reeves
Fleet: 1 single-deck coach
Chassis/Body: Setra.
Ops incl: excursions & tours, private hire,
continental tours.
Livery: Blue/Silver

RIGBY'S EXECUTIVE COACHES LTD
MOORFIELD INDUSTRIAL ESTATE,
MOORFIELD DRIVE, ALTHAM,
ACCRINGTON BB5 5WG
Tel: 01254 388866
Fax: 01254 232505
Web site: www.rigbyscoachcentre.co.uk
Man Dir: Derek Moorhouse
Eng Dir: Mel Mellor
Dir/Tran Man: Andrew Knowles
Fleet: 23 - 20 single-deck coach,
2 minibus, 1 minicoach.
Chassis: 1 Ford Transit, 2 Mercedes,
1 Scania, 19 Volvo.
Bodies: 2 Berkhof, 1 Irizar, 2 Jonckheere,
1 Reeve Burgess, 16 Van Hool. 1 Wright.
Ops incl: school contracts, excursions &
tours, private hire.
Livery: Orange
Ticket System: Almex

ROBINSONS HOLIDAYS
PARK GARAGE, GREAT HARWOOD
BB6 7SP
Tel: 01254 889900
Fax: 01254 884708
E-mail: info@robinsons-holidays.co.uk
Web site: www.robinsons-holidays.co.uk
Dirs: D D Lord, J E Bannister (**Sec**),
J McMillan **Ops Man:** C Skeen
Engineer: P Godwin
Off Man: B Cooke
Sales Man: G Holdsworth
Fleet: 19 single-deck coach
Chassis: 3 MAN, 6 Neoplan, 10 Volvo.
Bodies: 3 Jonckheere, 6 Neoplan,
3 Noge, 5 Plaxton, 2 Sunsundegui.
Ops incl: excursions & tours, private hire,
continental tours, school contracts.
Livery: Blue

ROSSENDALE TRANSPORT LTD
KNOWSLEY PARK WAY,
HASLINGDEN BB4 4RS
Tel: 01706 390520
Fax: 01706 390530
Web site: www.rossendalebus.co.uk
E-mail: info@rossendalebus.co.uk
Man Dir: Edgar Oldham
Comm Dir: Barry Drelincourt

Fleet: 110 - 16 double-deck bus,
48 single-deck bus, 3 single-deck coach,
43 midibus.
Chassis: 1 Bova, 48 Dennis, 3 MAN,
23 Optare, 35 Volvo.
Bodies: 4 Alexander, 1 Bova, 5 Caetano,
20 East Lancs, 3 MCV, 2 Marshall,
13 Northern Counties, 23 Optare,
22 Plaxton, 17 Wright.
Ops incl: local bus services, school
contracts, private hire, express,
continental tours.
Livery: White/Red/Cream.
Ticket System: Wayfarer TGX

SANDGROUNDER COACHES
28 WARWICK STREET, SOUTHPORT
PR8 5ES
Tel: 01704 541194
E-mail: gerry@dohe.wanadoo.co.uk
Web site: sgccoaches.co.uk
Dir: Gerry Doherty
Ops incl: excursions & tours, private hire,
continental tours.

STAGECOACH NORTH WEST
BROADACRE HOUSE,
16-20 LOWTHER STREET,
CARLISLE CA3 8DA
Tel: 01228 597222   **Fax:** 01228 597888
E-mail:
enquiries.northwest@stagecoachbus.com
Web site: www.stagecoachbus.com
Fleet Name: Stagecoach in
Cumbria/Lancashire
Man Dir: Christopher J Bowles
Eng Dir: Paul W Lee
Ops Dir: Philip C Smith
Comm Man: James P Mellor
Fleet: 490 - 180 double-deck bus,
115 single-deck bus, 13 single-deck
coach, 8 open-top bus, 78 midibus,
96 minibus.
Chassis: 140 Alexander Dennis,
25 Leyland, 45 MAN, 12 Mercedes,
97 Optare, 31 Scania, 140 Volvo.
Bodies: 335 Alexander Dennis,
9 East Lancs, 6 Jonckheere,
12 Marshall/MCV, 1 Northern Counties,
97 Optare, 24 Plaxton, 6 Transbus.
Ops incl: local bus services, school
contracts, excursions & tours, private hire,
express.
Livery: Stagecoach UK Bus
Ticket System: Wayfarer TGX

TRANSDEV BURNLEY & PENDLE
QUEENSGATE BUS DEPOT,
COLNE ROAD, BURNLEY BB10 1HH
Tel: 0845 604 0110
E-mail: enquire@burnleyandpendle.co.uk
Web site: www.lancashirebus.co.uk
Fleet Names: Mainline, Starship,
The Witch Way
Prop: Blazefield Holdings Ltd.
Man Dir: Russell Revill
Comm Dir: David Wilson
Fleet: 96 – 32 double-deck bus,
39 single-deck bus, 2 single-deck coach,
23 midibus.
Chassis: Dennis, Leyland, Optare,
Scania, Volvo.
Bodies: Alexander, ECW, Leyland,
Northern Counties, Optare, Plaxton,
Wright.
Livery: Red/Cream.
Ticket System: ERG.
(Part of the Blazefield group which is
owned by Transdev)

TRANSDEV LANCASHIRE UNITED
INTACK GARAGE, WHITEBIRK ROAD, INTACK, BLACKBURN BB1 3JD
Tel: 0845 272 7272
Fax: 01234 693964
E-mail: enquire@lancashireunited.co.uk
Web site: www.lancashirebus.co.uk
Fleet Names: Spot On, The Lancashire Way
Prop: Blazefield Holdings Ltd
Man Dir: Russell Revill
Business Dir: John Threlfall
Fleet: 120 - 38 double-deck bus, 62 single-deck bus, 20 midibus.
Chassis: Dennis, Leyland, Optare, Volvo.
Bodies: Alexander, ECW, Leyland, Northern Counties, Optare, Plaxton, Wright.
Livery: Blue/Cream.
Ticket System: ERG.
(Part of the Blazefield group which is owned by Transdev)

THE TRAVELLERS CHOICE
THE COACH & TRAVEL CENTRE, SCOTLAND ROAD, CARNFORTH LA5 9RQ
Tel: 01524 720033
Fax: 01524 720044
E-mail: info@travellerschoice.co.uk
Web site: www.travellerschoice.co.uk
Chairman: R Shaw
Man Dirs: J Shaw, D Shaw
Co Sec: P Shaw
Dir: M Shaw
Fleet: 74 – single-deck coach, midicoach, minicoach.
Chassis: 13 Mercedes, 6 Scania, 55 Volvo.
Bodies: 4 Berkhof, 6 Caetano, 2 Esker, 1 Irizar, 30 Jonckheere, 8 Mercedes, 1 Optare, 9 Plaxton, 13 Sunsundegui.
Ops incl: local bus services, school contracts, excursions & tours, private hire, continental tours, express.
Livery: White with blue/yellow/red stripe

R S TYRER LTD
168 CHORLEY ROAD, ADLINGTON PR6 9LQ
Tel: 01257 480929
Web site: www.tyrerscoaches.co.uk
Fleet: 16 – 5 double-deck bus, 7 single-deck coach, 2 double-deck coach, 2 midicoach
Chassis: DAF, Scania, Volvo
Bodies: Alexander, East Lancs, Northern Counties, Optare, Plaxton, Van Hool
Ops incl: school contracts, excursions & tours, private hire
Livery: Blue & White

TYRER TOURS LTD
16 KIRBY ROAD, LOMESHAYE INDUSTRIAL ESTATE, NELSON BB9 6RS
Tel: 0845 130 1716
Fax: 01282 615541
E-mail: ask@tyrerbus.myzen.co.uk
Web site: www.tyrertours.com
Fleet Name: Tyrer Bus
Dir: R Tyrer
Fleet: 29 midibus.
Chassis: Dennis, Mercedes, Optare.
Ops incl: Local bus services.
Livery: White with Blue/Gold

LEICESTERSHIRE, CITY OF LEICESTER, RUTLAND

ABBEY TRAVEL
RMC YARD, THURMASTON FOOTPATH, HUMBERSTONE LANE, LEICESTER LE4 9JU
Tel: 0116 246 1755
Fax: 0116 246 1755
Recovery: 07900 438428
Partners: Bryan A Garratt, Pauline Garratt (**Co Sec**), Paul Garratt
Fleet: 21 – 4 double-deck bus, 16 single-deck coach, 1 minibus.
Chassis incl: Alexander Dennis, Bova, Dennis, Freight Rover, MAN, Neoplan, Scania, Volvo.
Bodies: Berkhof, Bova, Caetano, Hispano, Jonckheere, Mercedes, Neoplan, Plaxton, Scania, Volvo.
Ops incl: local bus services, school contracts, excursions & tours, private hire, continental tours.
Livery: White/Green/Red

ARRIVA MIDLANDS LTD
852 MELTON ROAD, LEICESTER LE4 8BT
Tel: 0116 264 0400 **Fax:** 0116 260 5605
Web site: www.arriva.co.uk
Man Dir: R A Hind **Fin Dir:** J Barlow
Ops Dir: A Lloyd **Eng Dir:** M Evans
Area Business Man (Leicestershire): S Smith
Fleet: 658 - 134 double-deck bus, 176 single-deck bus, 3 articulated bus, 232 midibus, 113 minibus.
Chassis: 116 DAF, 222 Dennis, 9 Leyland, 3 Mercedes, 66 Optare, 69 Scania, 54 VDL, 125 Volvo
Bodies: 55 Alexander, 1 Caetano, 73 East Lancs, 3 Mercedes, 5 Marshall, 21 Northern Counties, 66 Optare, 176 Plaxton, 44 Scania, 8 UVG, 206 Wright.
Ops incl: local bus services.
Livery: Arriva
Ticket System: Wayfarer

ASMAL COACHES
70 KEDLESTONE ROAD, LEICESTER LE5 5HW
Tel/Fax: 0116 249 0443
Man Dir: Mehboob M. Asmal.

AUSDEN CLARK GROUP
DYSART WAY, LEICESTER LE1 2JY
Tel: 0116 262 9492
Fax: 0116 251 5551
Recovery: 0116 262 9492
E-mail: afrost@ausdenclark.co.uk
Web Site: www.ausdenclark.co.uk
Man Dir: Paul Ausden-Clark
Dir: Danny Smith
Gen Man: Susan Ward
Ops Man: Adam Frost
Tran Man: Les Gent-Watts
Fleet: 72 – 8 double-deck bus, 11 double-deck coach, 43 single-deck coach, 8 midicoach, 2 minicoach.
Chassis: 1 MAN, 9 Mercedes, 62 Scania.
Bodies: 6 Autobus, 14 Berkhof, 6 East Lancs, 1 Esker, 6 Irizar, 2 Mercedes, 2 Northern Counties, 1 Plaxton, 34 Van Hool.
Ops incl: local bus services, school contracts, excursions & tours, private hire, express, continental tours.
Livery: Pink/Black/Purple on Metallic Silver.

CENTREBUS LIMITED
37 WENLOCK WAY, LEICESTER LE4 9HU
Tel: 0116 246 0030 **Fax:** 0116 276 7221
E-mail: centrebusltd@btconnect.com
Web Site: www.centrebus.co.uk
Dirs: Peter Harvey, Mark O Mahony
Fin Controller: Chris Holmes
Fleet (Leicestershire)**:** 91 – 21 double-deck bus, 10 single-deck bus, 60 midibus.
Chassis: 17 Dennis, 3 Leyland, 7 MCW, 30 Mercedes, 8 Optare, 23 Scania, 3 VDL, 2 Volvo.
Bodies: 29 Alexander, 8 East Lancs, 2 Leyland, 7 MCW, 1 Northern Counties, 8 Optare, 27 Plaxton, 1 Reeve Burgess, 2 Scania, 1 UVG, 5 Wright.
Ops Inc: local bus services
Livery: Blue/Orange/White
Part of the Centrebus Group

CONFIDENCE
30 SPALDING STREET, LEICESTER LE5 4PH
Tel/Fax: 0116 276 2171
E-mail: confidencebus@btclick.com
Web site: www.confidencebus.co.uk
Man Dir: K M Williams
Dirs: A P Williams, Mrs C A Dalby, Mrs S J Williams **Ops Man:** A Harris
Ch Eng: R Allen **Sec:** Mrs M Daines
Fleet: 27 - 18 double-deck bus, 9 single-deck coach.
Chassis: 1 AEC, 1 Alexander Dennis, 20 Leyland, 5 Volvo.
Bodies: 1 Alexander Dennis, 1 Duple, 11 ECW, 2 Optare, 1 Park Royal, 7 Plaxton, 3 Roe, 1 Van Hool.
Ops incl: school contracts, private hire.
Livery: Buses: Black/Grey; Coaches: Black/Red.
Ticket System: Setright

COUNTY MINI COACHES
31 EDENHURST AVENUE, LEICESTER LE3 2PH
Tel/Fax: 0116 289 7205
Owner: F. Bradshaw.
Fleet: 3 - 2 midicoach, 1 minibus.
Chassis: 1 DAF, 1 Freight Rover, 1 Iveco.
Ops incl: school contracts, private hire.

COUNTRY HOPPER
213 MELBOURNE ROAD, IBSTOCK LE67 6NQ
Tel: 01530 260888

FIRST MIDLANDS
PO BOX 8324, LEICESTER LE41 9BF
Tel: 0116 251 6691
Fax: 0116 268 9198
Fleet Name: First Leicester
Man Dir: Ken Poole **Eng Dir:** C. Stafford
Fin Dir: J. Hollis
Gen Man Ops: C. Lara.
Fleet: 102 – 66 double-deck bus, 36 single-deck bus.
Chassis: 102 Volvo.
Bodies: 47 Alexander, 55 Wright.
Ops incl: local bus services, school contracts, excursions & tours, private hire, express, continental tours.
Livery: FirstGroup UK Bus.
Ticket System: Wayfarer 3

The Little Red Book 2011 - in association with *tbf* Transport Benevolent Fund

PAUL JAMES COACHES
UNIT 5, GRANGE FARM BUSINESS PARK, GRANGE ROAD, HUGGLESCOTE LE67 2BT
Tel: 01530 832399 **Fax:** 01530 836128
E-mail: info@pauljamescoaches.co.uk
Web site: www.pauljamescoaches.co.uk
Gen Man: Wayne Smith
Fleet: 35 - single-deck bus, single-deck coach, midibus.
Chassis: 3 Bedford, 2 Bova, 1 Dennis, 2 Leyland, 6 Mercedes, 6 Optare, 1 Setra, 6 Volvo.
Bodies: 5 Alexander, 1 Autobus, 2 Bova, 6 Optare, 10 Plaxton, 2 Van Hool.
Ops incl: excursions & tours, private hire, local bus services, school contracts, continental tours.
Livery: Red/White
Ticket System: Wayfarer 3
Part of Veolia Transport UK

KINCHBUS LTD
SULLIVAN WAY, SWINGBRIDGE ROAD, LOUGHBOROUGH LE11 5QS
Tel: 01509 815637
E-mail: customer.services@kinchbus.co.uk
Web site: www.kinchbus.co.uk
Ops Man: James Cheatle
Fleet: 31 - 3 double-deck bus, 18 single-deck bus, 3 midibus, 7 minibus.
Chassis: 3 Leyland, 14 Optare, 8 Scania, 6 Volvo.
Bodies: 3 ECW, 14 Optare, 6 Plaxton, 8 Wright.
Ops incl: local bus services, school contracts.
Livery: Blue/Yellow
Ticket System: Wayfarer
Part of the Wellglade Group

MACPHERSON COACHES LTD
See Derbyshire

NESBIT BROS LTD
BURROUGH ROAD, SOMERBY, MELTON MOWBRAY LE14 2PP
Tel: 01664 454284 **Fax:** 01664 454106
Dirs: I Foster, J Townsend
Fleet: 13 single-deck coach.
Chassis: 13 Volvo.
Bodies: 7 Plaxton, 6 Van Hool.
Ops incl: school contracts, private hire

NIGEL JACKSON TRAVEL
THURMASTON FOOTPATH, HUMBERSTONE LANE, LEICESTER LE4 7JU
Tel: 0116 276 9456
Fax: 0116 276 1969
E-mail: nigeljackson@tiscali.co.uk
Prop: N Jackson
Fleet: 7 - 4 double-deck bus, 2 single-deck coach, 1 midicoach.
Chassis: 2 Bova, 4 MCW, 1 Toyota.
Bodies: 2 Bova, 1 Caetano, 4 MCW.
Ops incl: local bus services, school contracts, excursions & tours, private hire.
Livery: Coaches - White; Buses - Blue/Red

NOTTINGHAM CITY COACHES
BUILDING 3, ASHBY ROAD CENTRAL, SHEPSHED, LOUGHBOROUGH LE12 9BS
Tel: 01509 506188 **Fax:** 01509 506388
E-mail: coachhire@moseleygroup.co.uk
Web site: www.nottinghamcitycoaches.co.uk
Prop: A H Moseley **Chairman:** K Lower
Chief Exec: P J Harper
Co Sec: R Graham
Ops Man: N Carver-Smith
Fleet: 10 single-deck coach
Chassis: 4 Iveco, 5 Volvo.
Bodies: 5 Beulas, 5 Plaxton.
Ops incl: school contracts, excursions & tours, private hire, continental tours.
Livery: Gold/Green.

REDFERN TRAVEL LTD
See Nottinghamshire

ROBERTS COACHES LTD
THE LIMES, MIDLAND ROAD, HUGGLESCOTE LE67 2FX
Tel: 01530 817444
Fax: 01530 817666
Recovery: 07785 572526
E-mail: info@robertscoaches.co.uk
Web site: www.robertscoaches.co.uk
Man Dir: Jonathan Hunt **Ops Man:** Andrew Lomas **Chief Eng:** Mick Crawford
Fleet: 42 - 20 double-deck bus, 12 single-deck coach, 2 double-deck coach, 1 open-top bus, 3 midibus, 2 midicoach, 2 minibus.
Chassis: 1 LDV, 20 MCW, 1 Mercedes, 4 Optare, 14 Volvo, 2 Other.
Bodies: 2 East Lancs, 10 Jonckheere, 20 MCW, 4 Optare, 4 Van Hool, 2 Other.
Ops incl: local bus services, school contracts, excursions & tours, private hire, continental tours
Livery: White with Vinyls.
Ticket System: Wayfarer 3

TRAVEL-WRIGHT
64 ROCKHILL DRIVE, MOUNTSORREL LE12 7DT
Tel: 0116 230 2887
Fax: 0116 230 2223
E-mail: trwright@demon.co.uk
Dir: C. Wright.
Fleet: 5 minibus.
Chassis: 1 DAF, 2 Mercedes, 2 Volkswagen.
Bodies: 1 Advanced, 2 Crystals, 2 Volkswagen.
Ops incl: private hire, school contracts.

WEST END TRAVEL/RUTLAND TRAVEL
LAKESIDE BUS & COACH CENTRE, DIXON DRIVE, LEICESTER ROAD, MELTON MOWBRAY LE13 0DA
Tel: 01664 563498
Fax: 01664 568568
Fleet: 24 - 7 single-deck bus, 11 single-deck coach, 2 midibus, 2 midicoach, 2 minibus.

Chassis incl: 2 Leyland, 6 Mercedes, 1 Scania, 5 Setra, 4 Volvo.
Bodies: 3 Alexander Dennis, 1 Jonckheere, 1 Mercedes, 12 Plaxton, 5 Setra, 2 Other.
Ops incl: local bus services, school contracts, excursions & tours, private hire.
Livery: White with Maroon Flashes.
Ticket System: Wayfarer 3

WIDE HORIZON
48 COVENTRY ROAD, BURBAGE, HINCKLEY LE10 2HP
Tel: 01455 615915
Fax: 01455 230767
Partners: Reg Clarke, Jon Clarke.
Fleet: 16 - 9 double-deck bus, 7 single-deck coach.
Chassis: 1 Bova, 3 DAF, 1 Dennis, 1 Leyland, 1 MAN, 1 Mercedes, Neoplan, 1 Scania, 1 Volvo.
Bodies: 2 Berkhof, 1 Bova, 2 Plaxton, 2 Setra.
Ops incl: local bus services, excursions & tours, school contracts, private hire, continental tours.
Livery: White

PAUL S WINSON COACHES LTD
ROYAL WAY, BELTON PARK, LOUGHBOROUGH LE11 5XR
Tel: 01509 232354
Fax: 01509 265110
Recovery: 01509 237999
Web site: www.winsoncoaches.co.uk
E-mail: sales@winsoncoaches.co.uk
Man Dir: Paul S Winson
Ch Eng: Paul B Winson **Ops Man/Co Sec:** Anthony J Winson
Fleet: 30 - double-deck bus, single-deck bus, single-deck coach, midibus, midicoach, minibus, minicoach.
Chassis: 3 Alexander Dennis, 6 Bova, 2 DAF, 1 Dennis, 1 Leyland, 4 Mercedes, 1 Scania, 6 Volvo.
Ops incl: local bus services, school contracts, excursions & tours, private hire, continental tours.
Livery: Red/White/Blue.
Ticket system: Wayfarer

WOODS COACHES LTD
211 GLOUCESTER CRESCENT, WIGSTON LE18 4YH
Tel: 0116 278 6374 **Fax:** 0116 247 7819
E-mail: sales@woods-coaches.co.uk
Web site: www.woodscoaches.com
Chairman: Mark Wood **Man Dir:** Kevin Brown **Co Sec:** Jacqui Bates **Eng Dir:** Ian Trigg **Traffic Manager:** Bill Tanser
Fleet: 16- 15 single-deck coach, 1 midicoach.
Chassis: 1 Mercedes, 4 Neoplan, 11 Volvo.
Bodies: 1 Mercedes, 4 Neoplan, 11 Plaxton.
Ops incl: school contracts, excursions & tours, private hire, express, continental tours.
Livery: Blue base – Orange/Yellow/White relief

Symbol	Meaning	Symbol	Meaning	Symbol	Meaning
♿	Vehicle suitable for disabled	🔒	Seat belt-fitted Vehicle	R24	24 hour recovery service
T	Toilet-drop facilities available	🍴	Coach(es) with galley facilities	🔑	Replacement vehicle available
R	Recovery service available	❄	Air-conditioned vehicle(s)	🚌	Vintage Coach(es) available
	Open top vehicle(s)	🚻	Coaches with toilet facilities		

LINCOLNSHIRE

APPLEBYS COACH TRAVEL
CONISHOLME, LOUTH LN11 7LT
Tel: 01507 357900
Fax: 01507 357910
Recovery: 07764 278466
E-mail: coach@applebyscoaches.co.uk
Web site: www.applebyscoaches.co.uk
Fleet Name: L F Bowen
Tran Man: Neil Warne
Man Dir: Rob Lyng
Group Ops Man: Nick Tetley
Fleet Eng: David Hoy
Fleet: 17 – 13 single-deck coach, 4 minibus
Chassis: 1 Dennis, 12 Scania, 4 Volkswagen
Bodies: 8 Irizar, 4 Volkswagen, 5 Other
Ops incl: excursions & tours, private hire, continental tours.
(Subsidiary of L F Bowen Ltd, Staffordshire)

BARNARD COACHES
STATION ROAD, KIRTON LINDSEY, GAINSBOROUGH DN21 4BD
Tel: 01652 648381
Fax: 01652 640377
Fleet: 13 single-deck coach.

MARK BLAND TRAVEL LTD
ESSENDINE ROAD, RYHALL, STAMFORD PE9 4JN
Tel: 01780 751671
Fleet incl: double-deck bus, single-deck bus, single-deck coach.
Ops incl: local bus services, school contracts.
Livery: Red/Cream

BRYLAINE TRAVEL LTD
291 LONDON ROAD, BOSTON PE21 7DD
Tel: 01205 364087
Fax: 01205 359504
Man Dir: Brian W Gregg, Elaine R Gregg
Co Sec: Susan E Bradshaw
Eng Dir: Brian P Gregg
Ops Dir: Malcolm P Wheatley
Fleet: 45 - 16 double-deck bus, 29 single-deck bus.
Chassis: 3 BMC, 7 DAF, 5 Dennis, 4 Leyland, 2 MCW, 14 Optare, 2 VDL, 8 Volvo.
Ops incl: local bus services, school contracts
Livery: Various
Ticket system: Wayfarer

J W CARNELL LTD
72 BRIDGE ROAD, SUTTON BRIDGE PE12 9UA.
Tel: 01406 350482
Fax: 01406 350600
E-mail: enquiries@carnellscoaches.co.uk
Web site: www.carnellscoaches.co.uk
Dirs: John Grindwood, Mervyn Emmet
Fleet: 22 - 3 double-deck bus, 16 single-deck coach, 2 midicoach, 1 minicoach.
Chassis: 2 Bedford, 1 Bova, 2 DAF, 5 Leyland, 1 MAN, 3 MCW, 2 Toyota, 6 Volvo.
Bodies: 1 Bova, 3 Caetano, 8 Duple, 3 MCW, 6 Plaxton, 1 Van Hool.
Ops incl: local bus services, school contracts, excursions and tours.
Livery: Silver/Red/Orange.
Ticket system: Setright.

CENTREBUS LTD
TOLLEMARCHE ROAD SOUTH, SPITALGATE LEVEL, GRANTHAM NG31 7UH
Tel: 0844 351 1120
E-mail: grantham@centrebus.com
Web site: www.centrebus.com
Fleet (Lincolnshire): 25 - 13 double-deck bus, 5 single-deck bus, 7 midibus.
Chassis: Alexander Dennis, DAF, Dennis, Leyland, MCW, Mercedes, Optare, Volvo.
Bodies: Alexander Dennis, Alexander, East Lancs, Ikarus, MCW, Marshall, Northern Counties, Optare, Plaxton, UVG.
Ops incl: local bus services, school contracts.
Livery: Blue/Orange/White
Part of the Centrebus Group

CROPLEY COACHES
MAIN ROAD, FOSDYKE, BOSTON PE20 2BH
Tel: 01205 260226
Fax: 01205 260246
Web site: www.cropleycoach.co.uk
E-mail: enquiries@cropleycoach.co.uk
Man Dir: John Cropley
Co Sec: Mrs Sandra Cropley
Ch Eng: Chris Cropley
Fleet: 12 single-deck coach.
Chassis: 12 Volvo.
Bodies: 1 Plaxton, 11 Sunsundegui
Ops incl: local bus services, school contracts, excursions & tours, private hire, continental tours.
Livery: Turquoise & White

DELAINE BUSES LTD
8 SPALDING ROAD, BOURNE PE10 9LE
Tel: 01778 422866
Fax: 01778 425593
Web site: www.delainebuses.com
Chairman: I Delaine-Smith **Man Dir:** A Delaine-Smith **Dirs:** M Delaine-Smith, K Delaine-Smith **Sec:** Mrs B P Tilley
Fleet: 20 - 16 double-deck bus, 4 single-deck bus.
Chassis: 20 Volvo.
Bodies: 16 East Lancs, 4 Wright.
Ops incl: local bus services
Livery: Light/Dark Blue & Cream.
Ticket System: Almex A90

DICKINSON'S COACHES
BROADGATE, WRANGLE, BOSTON, PE22 9DY
Tel/Fax: 01205 870333
E-mail: enquiries@dickinsons-coaches.co.uk
Web site: www.dickinsons-coaches.co.uk
Fleet: 11 – single-deck coach, minibus.
Ops incl: school contracts, private hire, excursions & tours.
Livery: White with Orange/Green.

EAGRE COACHES LTD
CROOKED BILLET STREET, MORTON, GAINSBOROUGH DN21 3AG
Tel: 01427 612098
Fax: 01427 811340
E-mail: sales@eagre.co.uk
Web site: www.eagre.co.uk
Man Dir: Mrs S M Scholey
Dirs: P G Haxby, N G Haxby
Ch Eng: P Whitaker

Tours Man: M Barron
Fleet: 8 single-deck coach.
Chassis: 2 Iveco, 1 MAN, 5 Scania.
Bodies: 3 Beulas, 5 Irizar.
Ops incl: excursions & tours, private hire, continental tours
Livery: Red & White
A subsidiary of Wilfreda Beehive - see South Yorkshire

FOWLERS TRAVEL
155 DOG DROVE SOUTH, HOLBEACH DROVE, SPALDING PE12 0SD
Tel: 01406 330232
Fax: 01406 330923
E-mail: andrew@fowlerstravel.com
Web site: www.fowlerstravel.com
Dir: Andrew Fowler
Fleet: 20 - 9 double-deck bus, 2 single-deck bus, 8 single-deck coach, 1 minibus.
Chassis: 2 DAF, 2 Leyland, 1 Mercedes, 15 Volvo
Bodies: 9 Alexander Dennis, 1 Duple, 2 Jonckheere, 3 Northern Counties, 4 Plaxton, 1 Van Hool.
Ops incl: local bus services, school contracts, excursions & tours, private hire.
Livery: Cream/Red/Orange
Ticket System: Wayfarer

GRAYSCROFT BUS & COACH SERVICES LTD
15A VICTORIA ROAD, MABLETHORPE LN12 2AF
Tel: 01507 473236
Fax: 01507 477073
E-mail: Grayscroft.ltd@btconnect.com
Web site: www.grayscroft.co.uk
Dirs: C W Barker, N Barker, N W Barker, D Birt.
Fleet: 16 - 5 double-deck bus, 2 single-deck bus, 9 single-deck coach.
Chassis: 2 Mercedes, 2 Neoplan, 1 Optare, 9 Volvo.
Bodies: 1 Caetano, 1 Hispano, 4 Jonckheere, 2 Noge, 2 Northern Counties, 1 Optare, 2 Plaxton, 3 Van Hool.
Ops incl: local bus services, school contracts, excursions & tours, private hire.
Livery: Cream, Blue & Orange
Ticket system: Wayfarer

PHIL HAINES COACHES
RALPHS LANE, FRAMPTON WEST, BOSTON PE20 1QU
Tel/Fax: 01205 722359
Props: N. A. & F. E. Haines.

HODSON COACHES LTD
SAXILBY ENTERPRISE PARK, SKELLINGTHORPE ROAD, SAXILBY, LINCOLN LN1 2LR
Tel: 01522 706030
Fax: 01522 706031
E-mail: sales@hodsoncoaches.co.uk
Web Site: www.hodsoncoaches.co.uk
Man Dir: Alistair Gooseman
Ops Dir: Tim Gooseman
Dir: Sue Gooseman
Fleet: 14 - 8 single-deck coach, 4 minibus, 2 minicoach.
Chassis: 2 Mercedes, 12 Setra.
Ops incl: school contracts, excursions & tours, private hire, continental tours.
Livery: Lemon/Purple
Ticket system: Almex

Lincolnshire

HORNSBY TRAVEL SERVICES LTD
See North Lincolnshire

F HUNT COACH HIRE LTD
2/3 WEST STREET, ALFORD LN13 9DG
Tel/Fax: 01507 463000
E-mail: travel.office@hunts-coaches.co.uk
Web site: www.hunts-coaches.co.uk
Fleet Name: Hunts Travel
Dirs: Michael Hunt, Charles Hunt, Dave Eales
Fleet: 19 - 1 double-deck bus, 5 single-deck bus, 10 single-deck coach, 3 midibus.
Chassis: 3 Dennis, 1 Leyland, 3 Mercedes, 1 Optare, 11 Volvo.
Bodies: 2 Alexander, 3 Mercedes, 1 Optare, 10 Van Hool, 3 Wright.
Ops incl: local bus services, school contracts, excursions & tours, private hire, express, continental tours.
Livery: White/Red/Grey
Ticket System: Almex

R KIME & CO LTD
3 SLEAFORD ROAD, FOLKINGHAM, SLEAFORD NG34 0SB
Tel: 01529 497251
Fax: 01529 497554
E-mail: enquiries@kimesbuses.co.uk
Web site: www.kimesbuses.co.uk
Man Dir: Paul Brown
Dirs: Geoff Blanchard, Angela Cliff
Fleet: 26 - 13 double-deck bus, 13 single-deck bus.
Chassis: DAF, Leyland, Mercedes, Volvo, Optare, Scania.
Bodies: Alexander, Leyland, Northern Counties, Optare, Plaxton, Ikarus, Wright.
Ops incl: local bus services, school contracts, excursions & tours, private hire.
Livery: Cream/Green
Ticket System: Almex

LAWTON'S EXECUTIVE COACHES
LAST MOORINGS, EAST FEN LANE, STICKNEY, BOSTON PE22 8DE
Tel: 01205480462
Fax: 01205 480709
Recovery: 07879 444085
E-mail: info@lawtonscoaches.co.uk
Web site: www.lawtonscoaches.co.uk
Props: Geoff & Liz Lawton
Fleet: 8 – 2 double-deck bus, 2 single-deck bus, 4 single-deck coach
Chassis: 2 DAF, 3 Leyland, 1 MAN, 2 Volvo
Bodies: 1 Alexander Dennis, 2 Bova, 1 Jonckheere, 2 Northern Counties, 1 Plaxton, 1 Setra
Ops incl: school contracts, excursions & tours, private hire
Livery: White

MEMORY LANE COACHES
ELM HOUSE, OLD BOLINGBROKE, SPILSBY PE23 4HF
Tel: 01790 763394
Prop: John B Dorey
Fleet: 5 - 3 single-deck coach, 2 midicoach.
Chassis: 2 Bedford, 1 Iveco, 1 Leyland, 1 Mercedes.
Bodies: 1 Carlyle, 3 Duple, 1 Plaxton.
Ops incl: school contracts, private hire.
Livery: White/Green/Red.

PC COACHES OF LINCOLN LTD
17 CROFTON ROAD, LINCOLN LN3 4NL
Tel: 01522 533605
Fax: 01522 560402
Man Dir: Peter Smith
Ops Dir: Miss Sarah Smith
Dir International Ops: Chris Bristow
Ops incl: local bus services, school contracts, private hire, continental tours.
Livery: White/Maroon/Red

PULFREYS COACHES
271 HARLAXTON ROAD, GRANTHAM NG31 7SL
Tel: 01476 564144
Dir: Andrew Pulfrey.
Fleet: 3 - 2 single-deck coach, 1 midicoach.
Chassis: 1 Dennis, 1 Iveco, 1 Mercedes.
Bodies: 1 Beulas, 2 Plaxton.
Ops incl: school contracts, excursions & tours, private hire, continental tours.
Livery: Blue/White
Ticket System: Wayfarer

RADLEY COACH TRAVEL
THE TRAVEL OFFICE, 11 CHAPEL STREET, BRIGG DN20 8JZ
Tel: 01652 653583
Fax: 01652 656020
Fleet Name: Radley Holidays
E-mail: radleytravel@aol.com
Web site: www.radleytravel.co.uk
Owner: Kevin Radley.
Fleet: 4 single-deck coach
Chassis: 4 Scania.
Bodies: 1 Berkhof, 1 Irizar, 2 Scania Omni Express
Ops incl: excursions & tours, private hire, continental tours.
Livery: Maroon/Gold

ROY PHILLIPS
69 STATION ROAD, RUSKINGTON NG34 9DF
Tel: 01526 832279
Prop: R Phillips.
Fleet: 6 single-deck coach.
Chassis: 1 Leyland, 5 Volvo.
Bodies: 1 Jonckheere, 2 Plaxton, 3 Van Hool.
Ops incl: private hire, school contracts.

REDFERN TRAVEL LTD
See Nottinghamshire

SLEAFORDIAN COACHES
PRIDE PARKWAY, EAST ROAD, SLEAFORD NG34 8GL
Tel: 01529 303333
Fax: 01529 303324
E-mail: office@sleafordian.co.uk
Web site: www.sleafordian.co.uk
Dirs: Mark Broughton (**Man Dir**), Mrs Lisa Broughton, Don Broughton (**Co Sec**), Mrs Jean Broughton
Chief Eng: Phil Kerr
Fleet: 25 - 9 double-deck bus, 11 single-deck coach, 1 double-deck coach, 3 midibus, 1 midicoach.
Chassis: 2 Dennis, 2 Leyland, 1 Mercedes, 11 Volvo, 9 Other.
Bodies: 4 East Lancs, 1 Neoplan, 4 Northern Counties, 2 Optare, 7 Plaxton, 5 Van Hool, 2 Other.
Ops incl: local bus services, school contracts, excursions & tours, private hire, continental tours.
Livery: White/Orange/Blue
Ticket System: Wayfarer TGX, Setright

SMITHS COACHES, CORBY GLEN
THE GREEN, CORBY GLEN NG33 4NR
Tel: 01476 550285
Fax: 01476 550032
Partners: H. J. and Mary J. Smith.
Fleet: 7 - 5 single-deck coach, 1 double-deck coach, 1 minibus.
Chassis: 1 Bedford, 1 Bova, 1 Ford, 1 Freight Rover, 2 MAN, 1 Mercedes.
Bodies: 1 Bova, 1 Carlyle, 1 Duple, 2 MAN, 1 Neoplan, 1 Plaxton.
Ops incl: excursions & tours, private hire, continental tours, school contracts.
Livery: Blue/White.

STAGECOACH EAST MIDLANDS
PO BOX 15, DEACON ROAD, LINCOLN LN2 4JB
Tel: 01522 522255
Fax: 01522 538229
Fleet Names incl: Stagecoach in Lincolnshire
Web site: www.stagecoachbus.com
Man Dir: Gary Nolan
Eng Dir: John Taylor
Comm Dir: Dave Skepper
Ops Dir: Richard Kay
Fleet: 501 - 236 double-deck bus, 85 single-deck bus, 15 single-deck coach, 147 midibus, 18 minibus.
Chassis: 269 Alexander Dennis, 4 DAF, 1 Leyland, 49 MAN, 4 MCW, 27 Optare, 9 Scania, 138 Volvo.
Bodies: 315 Alexander Dennis, 1 Caetano, 60 East Lancs, 4 Jonckheere, 4 MCW, 14 Northern Counties, 27 Optare, 62 Plaxton, 14 Wright.
Ops incl: local bus services.
Livery: Stagecoach UK Bus
Ticket System: ERG TP5000.

TOURMASTER COACHES
ALDERLANDS, JAMES ROAD, CROWLAND, PETERBOROUGH PE6 0AA
Tel: 01733 211710
Fax: 01733 2113369
Recovery: 01733 211639
E-mail: tourmaster@btconnect.com
Prop: David Dinsey
Fleet: 12 - 1 double-deck bus, 11 single-deck coach.
Chassis: 3 DAF, 1 Dennis, 3 Leyland, 5 Volvo.
Bodies: 1 Berkhof, 3 Bova, 1 Jonckheere, 3 Van Hool, 1 Volvo, 3 Other.
Ops incl: school contracts, private hire.
Livery: Blue/Red/Turquoise.

TRANSLINC
JARVIS HOUSE, 157 SADLER ROAD, LINCOLN LN6 3RS
Tel: 01522 503400
Fax: 01522 503406
E-mail: logistics@translinc.co.uk
Web site: www.translinc.co.uk
Man Dir: Paul Roberts
Fleet: 193 - 18 single-deck coach, 19 midibus, 136 minibus, 20 minicoach (8 seats & under)
Chassis: 16 Citroen, 2 DAF, 10 Dennis, 8 Fiat, 104 Iveco, 7 LDV, 20 Mercedes, 2 Optare, 13 Renault, 2 Scania, 4 Toyota,

1 Volkswagen, 4 Volvo.
Ops incl: local bus services, school contracts, excursions & tours, private hire, express.

A C WILLIAMS LTD
ERMINE STREET, ANCASTER, GRANTHAM NG32 3QN
Tel: 01400 230833
Fax: 01400 230296
Recovery: 01400 230491
E-mail: coaches@acwilliams.co.uk
Web site: www.acwcoaches.co.uk
Man Dir: A D C Williams
Dirs: Mrs M Williams, Mrs A Parker
Coach Man: Ian Mansell
Fleet: 22- 4 double-deck bus, 16 single-deck coach, 1 double-deck coach, 1 minicoach.
Chassis: 2 Alexander Dennis, 1 DAF, 2 Leyland, 1 MAN, 5 Scania, 2 Setra, 1 Toyota, 8 Volvo.
Bodies: 2 Alexander Dennis, 5 Irizar, 1 Neoplan, 2 Northern Counties, 2 Setra, 8 Van Hool, 2 Other.
Ops incl: school contracts, excursions & tours, private hire, continental tours.
Livery: White

LONDON & MIDDLESEX

This section includes those operators in the London and Middlesex postal areas, as well as operators who have asked to appear under this heading. Other operators within Greater London with a non-London postal address, eg Kingston, Surrey; Bromley, Kent; etc, may be found under their respective postal counties.

AA, KNIGHTS OF THE ROAD
WREN ROAD, SIDCUP DA14 4NA
Tel: 020 8309 7741
Prop: J. V. H. Knight
Ch Eng: D. Knight
Fleet: 10 - 6 single-deck coach, 2 double-deck coach, 2 minicoach.
Chassis: 6 DAF, 2 Mercedes, 2 Volvo.
Bodies: 6 Bova, 2 Jonckheere, 2 Mercedes.
Ops incl: excursions & tours, private hire, continental tours, school contracts.
Livery: Cream/Beige.

ABELLIO LONDON LTD
301 CAMBERWELL NEW ROAD, LONDON SE5 0TF
Tel: 020 7788 8550
Fax: 020 7805 3510
E-mail: customer.care@abellio.co.uk
Web site: www.abellio.co.uk
Man Dir: Paul McGowan
Ops Dir: Bill Weatherley
Eng Dir: Steve Hamilton
Fin Dir: Ross Hanley
Fleet: 589 - 325 double-deck bus, 136 single-deck bus, 128 midibus
Chassis: 188 Alexander Dennis, 237 Dennis, 8 Optare, 78 Transbus, 73 Volvo, 5 Wright.
Bodies: 208 Alexander Dennis, 141 Alexander, 41 Caetano, 4 East Lancs, 8 Optare, 52 Plaxton, 57 Transbus, 78 Wright.
Ops incl: local bus services
Liveries: Red (London), Red/White (Surrey CC)
Ticket system: Wayfarer, Almex

ABELLIO LONDON WEST LTD
See Surrey

ANDERSON TRAVEL GROUP
178A TOWER BRIDGE ROAD, LONDON SE1 3LS
Tel: 020 7403 8118 **Fax:** 020 7403 8421
E-mail: kp@andersontravel.co.uk
Web site: www.andersontravel.co.uk
Man Dir: Mark Anderson
Comm Man: Keith Payne
Ops Man: Peter Gilbert
Fleet: 28 - 22 single-deck coach, 4 midicoach, 2 minibus.
Chassis incl: 8 Bova, 8 Mercedes, 1 Volkswagen, 8 Volvo.
Bodies incl: 8 Bova, 4 Mercedes, 7 Plaxton.
Ops incl: school contracts, excursions & tours, private hire, express, continental tours.
Livery: White with Green lettering

ARRIVA LONDON
16 WATSONS ROAD LONDON N22 7TZ
Tel: 020 8271 0101 **Fax:** 020 8271 0120
Web site: arrivabus.co.uk
Man Dir: Bob Scowen
Eng Dir: Tony Ward
Fleet: 1460 - incl: double-deck bus, single-deck bus, articulated bus.
Chassis incl: AEC, DAF, Dennis, Mercedes, Volvo.
Bodies incl: Alexander, Mercedes, Park Royal, Plaxton, Wright
Ops incl: local bus services, excursions & tours, private hire.
Livery: Red

ASHFORD LUXURY COACHES
373 HATTON ROAD, FELTHAM TW14 9QS
Tel: 020 8890 6394
Fax: 020 8751 5054
Web site: www.ashfordluxurycoaches.co.uk
Man Dir: Martin Cornell
Fleet: 10 - 1 single-deck bus, 6 single-deck coach, 2 midicoach, 1 minicoach.
Chassis: 7 Dennis, 3 Mercedes.
Bodies: 3 Mellor, 7 Plaxton.
Ops incl: local bus services, private hire, school contracts.

ATBUS LTD
41 MANOR ROAD, ASHFORD TW15 2SL
Tel: 07949 140437
Fax: 01784 241094
E-mail: info@atbus.co.uk
Web site: www.atbus.org.uk
Man Dir: Andrew Tanner
Co Sec: Clifford Tanner
Ops incl: school contracts, rail replacement.
Livery: Red with Grey Stripe
Ticket System: Wayfarer

BACK ROADS TOURING CO LTD
LEVEL 2, 107 POWER ROAD, CHISWICK, LONDON W4 5PY
Tel: 020 8987 0990
E-mail: info@backroadstouring.co.uk
Web site: www.backroadstouring.co.uk
Man Dir: Bruce Cherry **Fin Dir:** Erika Harcz **Ops Dir:** Alex Newmann
Fleet: 22 minibus.
Chassis/Bodies: 16 Mercedes, 6 Renault

Ops incl: excursions & tours, private hire, continental tours.
Livery: White

BEECHES TRAVEL
23 POWDER MILL LANE, WHITTON, TWICKENHAM TW2 6EE
Tel/Fax: 020 8898 7048
E-mail: info@beeches-travel.co.uk
Web site: www.beeches-travel.co.uk
Prop: C. Miller.
Fleet: 4 minicoach.
Chassis: Ford Transit, Freight Rover.
Ops incl: school contracts, excursions & tours, private hire.
Livery: White/Yellow.

BESSWAY TRAVEL LTD
THE IMPACT BUSINESS PARK, 7-9 WADSWORTH ROAD, PERIVALE, GREENFORD UB6 7JD
Tel: 020 8997 1297
Fax: 020 8998 6853
E-mail: info@besswaytravel.co.uk
Web site: www.besswaytravel.co.uk
Prop: Michael Heffernan.
Fleet: 11 - 3 single-deck coach, 2 midicoach, 2 minicoach, 4 minibus.
Chassis: 2 Iveco, 2 LDV, 4 Mercedes, 2 Scania, 1 Volvo.
Bodies: 3 Crest, 1 Excel, 3 Ferqui, 2 Plaxton, 2 Scania.
Ops incl: private hire, school contracts.
Livery: White with Blue/Red

BIG BUS COMPANY
GROSVENOR GARDENS HOUSE, 35-37 GROSVENOR GARDENS, LONDON SW1W 0BS
Tel: 020 7233 8722
Fax: 020 7233 8766
E-mail: info@bigbustours.com
Web site: www.bigbustours.com
Fleet: 75 open-top bus.
Chassis: 27 Dennis, 20 Leyland, 8 MCW, 20 Volvo.
Bodies: 10 Alexander, 12 East Lancs, 8 MCW, 20 Optare, 25 Other.
Ops incl: excursions & tours, private hire.
Livery: Burgundy/Cream
Ticket system: Almex

BLUEWAYS GUIDELINE COACHES LTD
49 WINDERS ROAD, LONDON SW11 3HE
Tel: 020 7228 3515
Fax: 020 7228 0290
E-mail: blueways@clara.co.uk
Web site: www.bluewaysguideline.co.uk

Dirs: Philip Bruton, Janet Bruton, Thomas McKechnie.
Fleet: 6 - 4 single-deck coach. 2 minicoach.
Chassis: 1 Mercedes, 3 Scania, 2 Toyota
Bodies: 2 Caetano, 3 Irizar, 1 Mercedes.
Ops incl: excursions & tours, private hire, continental tours, school contracts.
Livery: 2 White/two-tone Blue, 2 White, 2 England sponsors.

BM COACHES
SHACKLES DOCK, SILVERDALE ROAD, HAYES UB3 3BN
Tel: 0845 555 7711
Fax: 0845 555 7722
E-mail: info@bmcoaches.co.uk
Web site: www.bmcoaches.co.uk
Fleet: 38 – double-deck coach, single-deck coach, midicoach, minibus, minicoach
Chassis: Mercedes, Scania, Temsa, Van Hool, VDL, Volvo
Ops incl: excursions & tours, private hire

BRENTONS OF BLACKHEATH
27 FORDMILL ROAD, CATFORD, LONDON SE6 3JL
Tel: 020 8698 6834   **Fax:** 020 8461 0110
E-mail: davee@brentonsofblackheath.co.uk
Web site: www.brentonsselfdrivehire.co.uk
Prop: C Clark
Coach Man: D Eaton
Ch Eng: I Powell
Fleet: 14 - 11 single-deck coach, 1 midicoach, 2 minicoach.
Chassis: 2 Dennis, 5 Leyland, 3 Mercedes, 5 Volvo.
Bodies: 1 Berkhof, 2 Duple, 3 Mercedes, 7 Plaxton, 1 Van Hool.
Ops incl: private hire, school contracts, excursions and tours.
Livery: Red/Cream/Grey

BRYANS OF ENFIELD
19 WETHERLEY ROAD, ENFIELD EN2 0NS
Tel: 020 8366 0062
Owner: B. Nash.
Fleet: 6 - 3 double-deck bus, 1 single-deck bus, 1 single-deck coach, 1 double-deck coach.
Chassis: 1 AEC, 1 DAF, 2 Daimler, 1 Leyland, 1 MCW.
Bodies: 1 ECW, 2 MCW, 2 Park Royal, 1 Van Hool.
Ops incl: school contracts, private hire.
Livery: Red.

CABIN COACHES
1 PARSONAGE CLOSE, HAYES UB3 2LZ
Tel: 020 8573 1100
Fax: 020 8573 8604
E-mail: info@cabincoaches.com
Web site: www.cabincoaches.com
Prop: P Martin
Fleet: 4 - 3 single-deck coach, 1 midicoach.
Chassis: 1 BMC, 3 Scania.
Bodies: 1 BMC, 2 Irizar, 1 Van Hool.
Ops incl: excursions & tours, school contracts, private hire.
Livery: White with Purple/Light Blue

CARAVELLE COACHES
9 CHESTNUT AVENUE, EDGWARE HA8 7RA
Tel/Fax: 020 8952 4025
Dir: H Lawrence.
Fleet: 2 - 1 midibus, 1 minibus.
Chassis: 1 Iveco, 1 Mercedes.
Ops incl: school contracts, private hire.

CAVALIER TRAVEL SERVICES
ASH COURT, LAND "C", PHOENIX DISTRIBUTION PARK, PHOENIX WAY, HESTON TW5 9NB
Tel: 0845 125 9379
Fax: 0845 833 2295
E-mail: bookings@cavaliercoaches.com
Web site: www.cavaliercoaches.com
Dirs: Andrew W Pagan, Denise H Pagan
Fleet: 8 - 4 single-deck coach, 2 midicoach, 2 minicoach.
Chassis: 2 Iveco, 2 Mercedes, 2 Optare, 2 Transbus.
Bodies: 2 Beulas, 2 Caetano, 4 Mercedes+.
Ops incl: private hire
Livery: White, White/Blue

CENTAUR COACHES & MINICOACHES
188 HALFWAY STREET, SIDCUP DA15 8DJ
Tel: 020 8300 3001
Fax: 020 8302 5959
Man Dir: M. Sims
Dirs: P Sims, S Durrant
E-mail: matt@minicoaches.com
Web site: www.minicoaches.com
Fleet: 107 – incl 7 single-deck bus, 12 midibus, 22 midicoach, 41 minibus, 20 minicoach.
Chassis incl: 25 Ford Transit, 17 LDV, 12 Mercedes.
Bodies incl: Alexander Dennis, Mercedes, Reeve Burgess.
Ops incl: private hire, school contracts, excursions & tours.

CHALFONT COACHES OF HARROW LTD
200 FEATHERSTONE ROAD, SOUTHALL UB2 5AQ
Tel: 020 8843 2323
Fax: 020 8574 0939
E-mail: chalfontcoaches@btopenworld.com
Web site: www.chalfontcoaches.co.uk
Man Dir: C J Shears
Dirs: I Shears, M Shears
Ops Man: P Williams
Ch Eng: R Arents
Co Sec: G Shears
Fleet: 18 - 16 single-deck coach, 2 minibus.
Chassis: 1 Bova, 1 LDV, 1 Mercedes, 15 Volvo.
Bodies: 1 Bova, 15 Van Hool, 2 Other.
Ops incl: school contracts, excursions & tours, private hire, express, continental tours.
Livery: Mauve/White

CHALFONT LINE LTD
4 PROVIDENCE ROAD, WEST DRAYTON UB7 8HJ
Tel: 01895 459540
Fax: 01895 459549
E-mail: info@chalfont-line.co.uk
Web site: www.chalfont-line.co.uk
Chairman: T J Reynolds
Man Dir: R Chadija
Dir: M Kerr

Tran Man: Lynn Young
Fleet: 84 minibus.
Chassis: 64 DAF, 6 Ford Transit, 8 Mercedes, 6 Renault.
Ops incl: school contracts, excursions & tours, private hire, continental tours.
Livery: White/Green

CITY CIRCLE (UK) LTD
WEST LONDON COACH CENTRE, NORTH HYDE GARDENS, HAYES UB4 3QT
Tel: 020 8561 2112
Fax: 020 8561 2010
E-mail: go@citycircleuk.com
Web site: www.citycircleuk.com
Man Dir: Neil Pegg
Fin Dir: Johnson Mitchell
Fleet: 34 single-deck coach, midicoach
Chassis: Mercedes, Neoplan, Setra, Van Hool, VDL, Volvo
Bodies: Jonckheere, Mercedes, Neoplan, Setra, Van Hool
Ops incl: excursions & tours, private hire
Livery: White with Red/Grey

CLARKES OF LONDON
KANGLEY BRIDGE ROAD, LOWER SYDENHAM, LONDON SE26 5AT
Tel: 020 8778 6697
Fax: 020 8778 0389
E-mail: info@clarkescoaches.co.uk
Web site: www.clarkescoaches.co.uk
Man Dir: Mrs D Newman
Comm Dir: J Devacmaker
Fin Dir: S Reeve
Fleet: 55 - 51 single-deck coach, 4 midicoach.
Chassis: 11 Mercedes, 9 Setra, 31 Scania, 4 Toyota.
Bodies: 7 Berkhof, 4 Caetano, 24 Irizar, 11 Mercedes, 9 Setra.
Ops incl: excursions & tours, private hire, express, continental tours.
Livery: Green/Silver.

COACHES EXCETERA
120 BEDDINGTON LANE, CROYDON CR9 4ND
Tel: 020 8665 5561
Fax: 020 8664 8694
E-mail: info@coachesetc.com
Web site: www.coachesetc.com
Man Dir: Alex Mazza
Gen Man: Richard Hill.
Fleet: single-deck coach, midicoach, minibus, minicoach.
Chassis: Mercedes, Scania, Setra, Volvo.
Livery: White with logo.

COLLINS COACHES LTD
UNIT 6, WATERSIDE TRADING CENTRE, TRUMPERS WAY, LONDON W7 2QD
Tel: 020 8843 2145
Fax: 020 8843 2357
E-mail: collinscoaches@aol.com
Web site: www.collins-coaches.co.uk
Man Dir: Eric Collins
Sec: Pauline Collins
Dir: Alfred Collins
Fleet: 11 single-deck coach.
Chassis: 2 Scania, 9 Volvo.
Bodies: 3 Jonckheere, 4 Plaxton, 2 Van Hool, 2 Other.
Ops incl: private hire, school contracts, excursions & tours, continental tours.
Livery: Red/White.

CONISTON COACHES LTD
88 CONISTON ROAD, BROMLEY
BR1 4JB
Tel/Fax: 020 8460 3432
E-mail: ricksmock@oal.com
Web site: www.conistoncoaches.co.uk
Dir: Richard Smock
Fleet: 5 - 5 single-deck coach
Chassis: 5 Volvo
Bodies: 1 Caetano, 4 Plaxton.
Ops incl: private hire, school contracts.
Livery: White/Red.

COUNTY COACHES
See Essex

DAVID CORBEL OF LONDON LTD
6 CAMROSE AVENUE, EDGWARE
HA8 6EG
Tel: 020 8952 1300
Fax: 020 8952 8641
E-mail: corbeloflondon@aol.com
Web site: www.corbel-coaches.com
Dir: Robert Whelan
Fleet: 10 single-deck coach
Chassis: 3 Scania, 7 Volvo.
Bodies: 3 Irizar, 7 Plaxton.
Ops incl: school contracts, private hire.
Livery: Pink/Blue.

CROWN COACHES
68 CANON ROAD, BICKLEY BR1 2SP
Tel: 020 8313 3020
Fleet: 9 – 4 double-deck bus,
2 single-deck coach, 1 open-top bus,
2 minibus
Chassis incl: 2 Ford Transit,
1 Mercedes, 2 Setra
Ops incl: school contracts, excursions & tours, private hire, continental tours.

CRYSTALS COACHES LTD
1 ELKSTONE ROAD, LONDON
W10 5NT
Tel: 020 8960 8800
Ops Man: G. Betts.
Fleet: 30 - 15 minibus, 15 minicoach.
Chassis: Ford Transit, Freight Rover, Mercedes.
Ops incl: local bus services, school contracts, private hire.

CT PLUS LTD
ASH GROVE DEPOT, MARE STREET,
LONDON, E8 4RH
Tel: 020 7275 2400 **Fax:** 020 7275 2450
E-mail: info@hctgroup.org
Web site: www.hctgroup.org
Ch Exec: Dai Powell
CFO: Douglas Downie
Fleet: 68 - 26 double deck bus,
12 single-deck bus, 17 midibus,
13 minibus.
Chassis: 9 Alexander Dennis, 12 Dennis, 13 Optare, 10 Scania, 24 Transbus
Bodies: 2 Alexander Dennis, 21 Caetano, 20 East Lancs, 13 Optare, 10 Scania, 2 Transbus
Ops incl: Local bus services
Livery: Red/Yellow

CUMFI-LUX COACHES
69 CORWELL LANE, HILLINGDON
UB8 3DE
Tel: 020 8561 6948

Fax: 020 8569 3809
Prop: N. R. Farrow (**Traf Man**)
Sec: Mrs T. K. Lovell.
Fleet: 3 - 1 single-deck coach, 1 minibus, 1 minicoach.
Chassis: 2 Mercedes, 1 Scania.
Ops incl: excursions & tours, private hire.
Livery: Orange/White (coach); White (minibuses).

DANS LUXURY TRAVEL LTD
ROYAL FOREST COACH HOUSE,
109 MAYBANK ROAD, LONDON
E18 1EZ
Tel: 020 8505 8833
Fax: 020 8519 1937
Man Dir: D. J. Brown
Dir: S. A. Brown.
Fleet: 43, including single-deck coach, midicoach, minicoach.
Chassis: 19 Ford Transit, 24 Mercedes
Bodies incl: 24 Mercedes, 7 Optare, 5 Reeve Burgess, 1 Ford
Ops incl: school contracts, excursions & tours, private hire, continental tours.

DAVIAN COACHES LTD
1-3 BECKET ROAD, EDMONTON,
LONDON N18 3PN
Tel: 020 8807 1515
Fax: 020 8807 2323
E-mail: daviancoaches@btconnect.com
Web site: www.daviancoaches.co.uk
Man Dir: Darren Wardle
Dir & Co Sec: Judy Wardle
Comm Man: David Bee
Transport Man: Richard Window
Fleet: 24 - 11 single-deck coach,
13 minibus.
Chassis: 2 Autosan, 1 BMC, 1 Iveco,
2 King Long, 10 LDV, 3 Mercedes,
4 Scania, 1 Volvo.
Bodies: 1 Beulas, 5 BMC, 4 Irizar,
10 LDV, 3 Mercedes, 1 Plaxton.
Ops incl: excursions & tours, school contracts, private hire, continental tours.
Livery: Orange and Blue on White

DOCKLANDS BUSES LTD
18 MERTON HIGH STREET, LONDON
SW19 1DN
Tel: 020 8545 6100
Fax: 020 8545 6101
E-mail: enquiries@go-ahead-london.com
Web site: www.go-ahead-london.com
Ch Exec: John Trayner
Eng Dir: Phil Margrave
Fin Dir: Paul Reeves
Ops Dir: David Cutts
Fleet: 54 – 16 double-deck bus,
30 single-deck bus, 8 midibus.
Chassis: 30 Alexander Dennis,
9 Dennis, 14 Scania, 1 Volvo.
Bodies: 10 Alexander Dennis, 5 East Lancs, 20 MCV, 10 Plaxton, 9 Scania.
Ops incl: local bus services, school contracts, private hire.
A subsidiary of the Go Ahead Group

EAST LONDON BUS GROUP
STEPHENSON STREET, CANNING
TOWN, LONDON E16 4SA
Tel: 020 8553 3420
Fax: 020 8477 7200
E-mail: pr.london@elbg.com
Web site: www.elbg.com
Fleet Names: East London, Selkent, Thameside
Acting CEO: Jon Gatfield

Ch Fin Off: Paul Cox **HR Dir:** Sarah Rennie **H&S Director:** John Carmichael
Eng Dir: Peter Sumner
Asst Eng Dir: Richard Smith
Fleet: 1378 - 1038 double-deck bus, 203 single-deck bus, 86 midibus, 51 articulated bus.
Chassis: 1123 Alexander Dennis/Transbus, 11 AEC, 51 Mercedes, 19 Optare, 174 Scania.
Bodies: 1106 Alexander Dennis/Transbus, 51 Mercedes, 19 Optare, 11 Park Royal, 18 Plaxton, 174 Scania.
Ops incl: local bus services
Livery: Red
Ticket System: Wayfarer
(Includes East London Bus & Coach Co Ltd, East London Bus Ltd, South East London & Kent Bus Co Ltd)

EASYBUS LTD
HAMILTON HOUSE, NORTH CIRCULAR
ROAD, LONDON NW10 7PX
Web site: www.easybus.co.uk
Man Dir: Jonathan Crick
Fleet: 30 minibus
Chassis: 30 Mercedes
Bodies: 30 Ferqui
Operations: Express
Livery: Orange
Buses are also provided by Arriva The Shires & Essex

P & J ELLIS LTD
UNIT 3, RADFORD ESTATE, OLD OAK
LANE, LONDON NW10 6UA
Tel: 020 8961 1141 **Fax:** 020 8965 5995
E-mail: enquiries@pjellis.co.uk
Web site: www.pjellis.co.uk
Dirs: Matthew Ellis, J Ellis
Fleet: 16 - 15 single-deck coach,
1 midicoach.
Chassis: 1 Mercedes, 15 Volvo.
Bodies: 13 Jonckheere, 1 Plaxton,
2 Sunsundegui.
Ops incl: excursions & tours, private hire, continental tours.

ELTHAM EXECUTIVE CHARTER LTD
21-23 CROWN WOODS WAY, LONDON
SE9 2NL
Tel: 020 8850 2011
Fax: 020 8850 5210
E-mail: enquiries@eec-minicoaches.co.uk
Web site: www.eec-minicoaches.co.uk
Dirs: Ray Lawrence, Jill Lawrence, Fiona Lawrence
Fleet: 6 - 3 midicoach, 1 minibus,
2 minicoach
Chassis: 1 Ford, 5 Iveco.
Bodies: 3 Indcar, 1 Optare, 2 other
Ops incl: private hire.
Livery: White with blue and gold graphics

EXCALIBUR COACHES
NYES WHARF, FRENSHAM STREET,
LONDON SE15 6TH
Tel: 020 7358 1441
Fax: 020 7358 1661
E-mail: excaliburcoaches@btconnect.com
Web site: www.excaliburcoaches.com
Man Dir: Mark Jewell
Fleet: 25 single-deck coach.
Chassis: 20 Scania, 5 Volvo.
Bodies: 2 Caetano, 19 Irizar, 1 Plaxton, 1 Van Hool, 2 Volvo.

Ops incl: school contracts, excursions & tours, private hire, express, continental tours.
Livery: Blue

FALCON TRAVEL
123 NUTTY LANE, SHEPPERTON TW17 0RQ
Tel: 01932 787752
Fax: 01932 785521
Prop: A Risby
Fleet: 5 - 4 single-deck coach, 1 minicoach.
Chassis: 1 Mercedes, 4 Volvo.
Bodies: 4 Van Hool, 1 other.
Ops incl: private hire, school contracts, excursions & tours.
Livery: White/Black/Crimson

FIRST LONDON
3RD FLOOR, MACMILLAN HOUSE, PADDINGTON STATION, LONDON W2 1TY
Tel: 020 7298 7300
Fax: 020 7706 8789
Web site: www.firstgroup.co.uk
Man Dir: Adrian Jones.
Fleet: 1169 - 684 double-deck bus, 281 single-deck bus, 7 single-deck coach, 120 midibus, 71 articulated bus.
Chassis: 12 AEC, 258 Alexander Dennis, 417 Dennis, 81 Mercedes, 6 Optare, 4 Scania, 121 Transbus, 271 Volvo, 9 Wrightbus.
Bodies: 1 Alexander, 258 Alexander Dennis, 4 Berkhof, 53 Caetano, 191 Marshall, 81 Mercedes, 3 Northern Counties, 6 Optare, 12 Park Royal, 176 Plaxton, 192 Transbus, 202 Wright.
Ops incl: local bus services, school contracts, private hire.
Livery: Red with Yellow.
Ticket System: Prestige (TfL).

FLIGHTS HALLMARK
See West Midlands, West Sussex

FORESTDALE COACHES LTD
68 VINEY BANK, COURTWOOD LANE, FORESTDALE, ADDINGTON CR0 9JT
Tel/Fax: 020 8651 1359
Chairman/Man Dir: V J Holub
Co Sec: Mrs P R Holub
Fleet: 1 single-deck coach.
Chassis/Body: Bova.
Ops incl: excursions & tours, private hire, continental tours.
Livery: Red with Gold sign writing

GOLDENSTAND (SOUTHERN) LTD
13 WAXLOW ROAD, LONDON NW10 7NY
Tel: 020 8961 9974/5
Fax: 020 8961 9949
Web site: www.goldenstand.co.uk
Chairman: J Chivrall **Sec:** J Kemp
Fleet: 8 - 5 single-deck coach, 3 minibus.
Chassis: 3 LDV, 5 Scania.
Bodies: 5 Jonckheere, 3 Leyland
Ops incl: school contracts, private hire, excursions & tours
Livery: Red/White

THE GOLD STANDARD
94A HORSENDEN LANE NORTH, GREENFORD UB6 7QH
Tel: 020 8795 0075

Fax: 020 8900 9630
E-mail: paul@luxurymincoaches.co.uk
Web site: www.luxuryminicoach.co.uk
Prop: Paul Grant
Fleet: 1 minicoach.
Chassis: Optare.
Ops incl: excursions & tours, private hire.

A GREEN COACHES LTD
357A HOE STREET, WALTHAMSTOW, LONDON E17 9AP
Tel: 020 8520 1138
Fax: 020 8520 1139
E-mail: agreencoaches357@aol.com
Web site: www.agreencoaches.co.uk
Dirs: Keith Richards, Janis Grover
Fleet: 6 single-deck coach
Chassis: 1 Scania, 5 Volvo
Ops incl: school contracts, private hire.
Livery: White.

GREYHOUND UK LTD
50 EASTBOURNE TERRACE, PADDINGTON, LONDON W2 6LX
Tel: 0900 096 0000
E-mail: support@greyhounduk.com
Web site: www.greyhounduk.com
Man Dir: Alex Warner
Fleet: 11 single-deck coach
Chassis: 11 Scania
Bodies: 11 Irizar
A subsidiary of FirstGroup

HAMILTON OF UXBRIDGE
589-591 UXBRIDGE ROAD, HAYES END UB4 8HP
Tel: 01895 232266 **Fax:** 01895 810454.
Web site: www.hamiltoncoaches.com
Prop: D. L. Bennett.
Fleet: 9 - 8 single-deck coach, 1 midicoach.
Chassis: 1 Toyota, 8 Volvo.
Bodies: 1 Berkhof, 6 Caetano, 1 Jonckheere, 1 Sunsundegui.
Ops incl: private hire, express, continental tours.

HEARNS COACHES
801 KENTON LANE, HARROW WEALD HA3 6AH
Tel: 020 8954 0444
Fax: 020 8954 5959
E-mail: info@hearns-coaches.co.uk
Web site: www.hearns-coaches.co.uk
Prop: R J Hearn
Ops Man: Ged Newham
Ch Eng: Dave Berry
Fleet: 33 - 29 single-deck coach, 2 midicoach, 2 minicoach.
Chassis: 2 MAN, 9 Mercedes, 2 Neoplan, 9 Scania, 11 Setra.
Ops incl: private hire, school contracts, excursions & tours, continental tours.
Livery: Blue

JOHN HOUGHTON LUXURY MINI COACHES
2 ELGAR AVENUE, EALING, LONDON W5 3JU
Tel: 020 8567 0056
Fax: 020 8567 5781
E-mail: john@luxuryminicoaches.co.uk
Web site: www.luxuryminicoaches.co.uk
Man Dir: John Houghton
Co Sec: M Houghton
Fleet: 3 minicoach.
Chassis/Bodies: 3 Mercedes.
Ops incl: private hire
Livery: White

HOUNSLOW COMMUNITY TRANSPORT
9 MONTAGUE ROAD, HOUNSLOW TW3 1JY
Tel: 020 8572 8204
Fax: 020 8572 0997
E-mail: haightim@aol.com
Ch Officer: Tim Haigh
Fleet Co-ordinator: Steve Cann
Fleet: 9 minibus

HOUNSLOW MINI COACHES
2 VINEYARD ROAD, HIGH STREET, FELTHAM TW13 4HQ
Tel: 020 8890 8429
Fax: 020 8893 1736
E-mail: hounslowminicoaches@btconnect.com
Web site: www.hounslowminicoaches.co.uk
Fleet: 19 - 3 midicoach, 4 minibus, 4 minicoach, 8 people carrier.
Chassis: 2 Ford Transit, 1 Iveco, 5 LDV, 7 Mercedes, 1 Toyota.
Bodies: 1 Caetano, 3 Mellor, 4 Mercedes, 5 Optare, 3 other.
Ops incl: school contracts, private hire.

HOUSTON'S OF LONDON
83 GLADESMORE ROAD, LONDON N15 6TL
Tel/Fax: 020 8800 4576
Prop: H. Jones.
Fleet: 2 single-deck coach.
Chassis: Leyland.
Ops incl: school contracts, excursions & tours, private hire.

VIC HUGHES & SON LTD
61 FERN GROVE, FELTHAM TW14 9AY
Tel: 020 8831 0770
Fax: 020 8831 0660
Man Dir: V B Hughes
Co Sec: Mrs V. Hughes **Dir:** K. Hughes.
Fleet: 21 - 4 midicoach, 5 minibus, 12 ambulance.
Chassis: Ford, Mercedes.
Ops incl: school contracts, excursions & tours, private hire.
Livery: White/Black.

IMPACT OF LONDON
7-9 WADSWORTH ROAD, GREENFORD UB6 7JZ
Tel: 020 8579 9922
Fax: 020 8840 4880
E-mail: info@impactgroup.co.uk
Web site: www.impactgroup.co.uk
Dir: A Hill **Gen Man:** A Palmer
Engs: H Louis, L Singh.
Fleet: 85 – 1 double-deck bus, 14 single-deck coach, 2 midibus, 25 midicoach, 43 minibus.
Chassis: Alexander Dennis, DAF, Dennis, Iveco, LDV, Leyland, Mercedes, Scania, Volvo.
Ops incl: excursions & tours, private hire, express, continental tours, school contracts.
Livery: White.

IMPERIAL COACHES LTD
80 SCOTTS ROAD, SOUTHALL UB2 5DE
Tel: 020 8574 0028
Fax: 020 8574 0061
E-mail: imperialcoaches1@hotmail.com

Web site: www.imperialcoaches.co.uk
Fleet: 8 – double-deck coach, single-deck coach
Chassis: Volvo
Bodies: Optare, Van Hool
Ops incl: school contracts, excursions & tours, private hire
Livery: White

INTERNATIONAL COACH LINES LTD
19 NURSERY ROAD, THORNTON HEATH CR7 8RE
Tel: 020 8684 8308, 2995
Fax: 020 8689 3483
Web site: www.internationalcoaches.co.uk
Dir: Mrs S. Bailey.
Fleet: 18 - 3 double-deck bus, 1 single-deck bus, 10 single-deck coach, 4 minicoach.
Ops incl: excursions & tours, private hire, express, continental tours.
Livery: Blue/White.

J & D EUROTRAVEL
58 WEALD LANE, HARROW WEALD HA3 5EX
Tel: 020 8861 1829
Fax: 020 8424 2585
E-mail: jdetravel1@aol.com
Man Dir: J T Thomas
Fleet: 10 - 3 single-deck coach, 3 midicoach, 2 minibus, 2 minicoach.
Ops incl: school contracts, excursions & tours, private hire, express, continental tours.

THE KINGS FERRY
See Kent

LEOLINE TRAVEL
UPPER SUNBURY ROAD, HAMPTON TW12 2DW
Tel: 020 8941 3370
Fax: 020 8941 3372
E-mail: leolinecoaches@aol.com
Web site: www.leolinetravel.co.uk
Prop: David Baker
Ops Man: Judy Dale
Fleet: 6 - 5 single-deck coach, 1 midicoach.
Chassis: 3 Iveco, 1 Toyota, 2 Volvo.
Bodies: 3 Beulas, 1 Caetano, 2 Van Hool.
Ops incl: excursions & tours, private hire, school contracts.
Livery: Blue/Orange

LEWIS TRAVEL
UNIT 2, BUILDING 3, ASHLEIGH COMMERCIAL ESTATE, 86 WESTMOOR STREET, CHARLTON SE7 8NQ
Tel: 020 8858 0031
Fax: 020 8858 7631
E-mail: sales@lewistravel.co.uk
Web site: www.lewistravel.co.uk
Fleet: 14 - 9 single-deck coach, 3 minibus, 2 minicoach.
Chassis: DAF, Mercedes, Volvo.
Ops incl: school contracts, excursions & tours, private hire, continental tours.
Livery: incl. Red

LINK LINE COACHES LTD
1 WROTTESLEY ROAD, LONDON NW10 5XA
Tel: 020 8965 2221
Fax: 020 8961 3680
E-mail: info@linkline-coaches.co.uk
Web site: wwwlinkline-coaches.co.uk
Dir: T. J. Russell.
Fleet: 10 - 9 midibus, 2 minibus.
Chassis: 2 Alexander Dennis, 6 Dennis, 1 Mercedes, 1 Optare.
Bodies: 1 Alexander Dennis, 7 Caetano, 1 Optare, 1 Other.
Ops incl: contracts, private hire.
Livery: White.
A subsidiary of TGM Group Ltd, part of Arriva

THE LITTLE BUS COMPANY
HOME FARM, ALDENHAM ROAD, ELSTREE WD6 3AZ
Tel: 020 8953 0202
Fax: 020 8953 9553
E-mail: enquiry@littlebus.co.uk
Web site: www.littlebus.co.uk
Prop: Jeremy Reese
Fleet: 7 minibus.
Chassis: 5 LDV, 2 Ford Transit.
Ops incl: school contracts, private hire.

LONDON CENTRAL BUS CO LTD
18 MERTON HIGH STREET, LONDON SW19 1DN
Tel: 020 8545 6100
Fax: 020 8545 6101
E-mail: enquiries@go-ahead-london.com
Web site: www.go-ahead-london.com
Fleet Name: London Central
Ch Exec: John Trayner
Eng Dir: Phil Margrave
Fin Dir: Paul Reeves
Ops Dir: David Cutts
Fleet: 614 - 430 double-deck bus, 120 single-deck bus, 64 articulated bus.
Chassis: 45 Alexander Dennis, 4 AEC, 113 Dennis, 64 Mercedes, 1 VDL, 380 Volvo.
Bodies: 91 Alexander Dennis, 64 Mercedes, 7 Northern Counties, 4 Park Royal, 377 Plaxton, 71 Wright.
Ops incl: local bus services, school contracts, excursions & tours, private hire.
Livery: Red
A subsidiary of the Go Ahead Group

LONDON GENERAL TRANSPORT SERVICES LTD
18 MERTON HIGH STREET, LONDON SW19 1DN
Tel: 020 8545 6100
Fax: 020 8545 6101
E-mail: enquiries@go-ahead-london.com
Web site: www.go-ahead-london.com
Fleet Name: London General
Ch Exec: John Trayner
Eng Dir: Phil Margrave
Fin Dir: Paul Reeves
Ops Dir: David Cutts
Fleet: 779 - 557 double-deck bus, 166 single-deck bus, 56 articulated bus.
Chassis: 181 Alexander Dennis, 4 AEC, 118 Dennis, 56 Mercedes, 420 Volvo.
Bodies: 99 Alexander, 24 East Lancs, 56 Mercedes, 38 Northern Counties, 85 Optare, 4 Park Royal, 263 Plaxton, 210 Wright.
Ops incl: local bus services, school contracts, excursions & tours, private hire.
Livery: Red
A subsidiary of the Go Ahead Group

LONDON SOVEREIGN
BUSWAYS HOUSE, WELLINGTON ROAD, TWICKENHAM TW2 5NX
Tel: 020 8400 6600
Web site: www.sovereignlondonbuses.co.uk
Man Dir: Paul Matthews
Deputy Man Dir: Richard Casling
Fleet: See London United.
Ops Incl: local bus services, private hire
Livery: Red
Ticket System: TfL Prestige.
A subsidiary of the Transdev Group

LONDON TRAMLINK
COOMBER WAY, CROYDON CR0 4TQ
Tel: 020 8665 9695
Web site: www.tfl.gov.uk/trams
Ops Dir: John Ryman
Head of Safety: C Tomlinson
Fleet: 24 trams
Chassis/Bodies: Bombardier
Ops incl: local tram services
Livery: Red/White

LONDON UNITED BUSWAYS LTD
BUSWAYS HOUSE, WELLINGTON ROAD, TWICKENHAM TW2 5NX
Tel: 020 8400 6605
Fax: 020 8943 2688
E-mail: customer@lonutd.co.uk
Web site: www.lonutd.co.uk
Man Dir: Paul Matthews
Deputy Man Dir: Richard Casling
Human Res Dir: Karen Fuller
Eng Dir: Les Birchley
Comm Man: Steffan Evans
Fleet: 916 - 547 double-deck bus, 344 single-deck bus, 25 midibus.
Chassis: 1 AEC, 137 Alexander Dennis, 186 Dennis, 38 Optare, 254 Scania, 168 Transbus, 170 Volvo.
Bodies: 114 Alexander, 137 Alexander Dennis, 119 East Lancs, 38 Optare, 1 Park Royal, 197 Plaxton, 190 Scania, 153 Transbus, 3 Wright.
Ops Incl: local bus services, private hire
Livery: Red
Ticket system: TfL Prestige.
A subsidiary of the Transdev Group

M C H MINIBUSES LTD
47 WALLINGFORD ROAD, UXBRIDGE UB8 2XS
Tel: 01895 230643
Fax: 01895 234891
E-mail: info@mchbuses.demon.co.uk
Web site: www.mch-coaches.co.uk
Fleet: 40 - double-deck coach, single-deck coach, midicoach, midicoach, minibus.
Chassis incl: Irisbus, King Long, Mercedes, Neoplan, Setra.
Ops incl: excursions & tours, private hire, continental tours.
Livery: White with Blue

MEMORY LANE VINTAGE OMNIBUS SERVICES
78 LILLIBROOKE CRESCENT, MAIDENHEAD SL6 3XQ
Tel: 01628 825050
Fax: 01628 825851
E-mail: admin@memorylane.co.uk
Web site: www.memorylane.co.uk
Prop: M J Clarke
Fleet: 6 - 3 double-deck bus, 3 single-deck bus

London & Middlesex

Chassis: 6 AEC.
Bodies: 2 ECW, 3 Park Royal,
1 Willowbrook.
Ops incl: private hire
Livery: Original operators

METROBUS LTD
See West Sussex

METROLINE TRAVEL LTD
66 COLLEGE ROAD, HARROW
HA1 1BE
Tel: 020 8218 8888
Fax: 020 8218 8899
E-mail: info@metroline.co.uk
Web site: www.metroline.co.uk
Chief Exec Off: Jaspal Singh
Ch Op Officer: Sean O'Shea
Fin Dir: Damian Rowbotham
Fleet: 1195 - 781 double-deck bus,
381 single-deck bus, 33 midibus.
Chassis: 3 AEC, 309 Alexander Dennis,
317 Dennis, 38 MAN, 5 Optare,
33 Scania, 263 Transbus, 327 Volvo.
Bodies: 84 Alexander, 308 Alexander Dennis, 33 East Lancs, 48 MCV,
5 Optare, 3 Park Royal, 325 Plaxton,
459 Transbus, 22 Wright.
Ops incl: local bus services, school contracts, private hire.
Livery: Red/Blue.
Ticket System: Wayfarer (London Buses spec)
A subsidiary of the Comfort Delgro Group

M T P CHARTER COACHES
39 GROSVENOR ROAD,
LONDON E11 2EW
Tel/Fax: 020 8989 0211
Prop: M Powis
Fleet: 2 - 1 single-deck coach,
1 minicoach.
Chassis/Bodies: 1 Setra, 1 Caetano.
Ops incl: private hire, excursions & tours, continental tours.
Livery: White

NEW BHARAT COACHES LTD
1A PRIORY WAY, SOUTHALL UB2 5EB
Tel: 020 8574 6817
Fax: 020 8813 9555
E-mail: bharatcoaches@aol.com
Web site: www.newbharat.co.uk
Dir: Surjit Singh Dhaliwal
Ch Eng: Alan Littlemore
Fleet: 10 – 2 double-deck coach,
6 single-deck coach, 2 midicoach
Chassis: 2 Mercedes, 8 Volvo
Ops incl: school contracts, excursions & tours, private hire, express, continental tours.
Livery: Red/Yellow/Blue on white base.

NEWBOURNE COACHES
FIRBANK WAY, LEIGHTON BUZZARD
LU7 4YP
Tel: 020 7837 6663
Fax: 01525 850967
E-mail: info@marshalls-coaches.co.uk
Web site: www.marshalls-coaches.co.uk
Prop: G R Marshall
Ops Man: Ian White
Ch Eng: Bob Barnard
Fleet: See Marshalls Coaches
Ops incl: private hire, school contracts, local bus services.
Livery: Blue/Multicoloured.
(part of Marshalls Coaches - see Bedfordshire)

OFJ CONNECTIONS LTD
BUILDING 16300 MT2, ELECTRA AVENUE, HEATHROW AIRPORT, HOUNSLOW, MIDDLESEX, TW6 2DN
Tel: 020 8754 7375
Fax: 020 8759 6589
E-mail: enquiries@ofjbus.com
Web site: www.ofjbus.com
Ops Inc: school contracts, private hire, Airport transfers
Livery: White
A subsidiary of TGM Group Ltd, part of Arriva

THE ORIGINAL LONDON TOUR
JEWS ROW, LONDON SW18 1TB
Tel: 020 8877 1722
Fax: 020 8877 1968
E-mail: info@theoriginaltour.com
Web site: www.theoriginaltour.com
Man Dir: Colin Atkins
Head of Comm Devt: Ms N Crump
Fleet: 107 - 14 double-deck bus,
93 open-top bus.
Chassis: 14 DAF, 38 Leyland,
21 MCW, 34 Volvo.
Bodies: 38 Alexander, 10 Ayats,
10 East Lancs, 21 MCW, 14 Plaxton,
4 Transbus.
Ops incl: local bus services, London sightseeing tours.
Liveries: Red (buses) Red/Cream (sightseeing buses)
Ticket systems: Almex/Wayfarer
Subsidiary of Arriva

REDWING COACHES
10 DYLAN ROAD, LONDON SE24 0HL
Tel: 020 7733 1124 **Fax:** 020 7733 5194
E-mail: redwing@redwing-coaches.co.uk.
Web site: www.redwing-coaches.co.uk.
Ops Man: Barry Nunn
Gen Man: Paul Hockley
Ch Eng: Robbie Hodgekiss
Reservations: Jeff Johnson
Fleet: 61 - 56 single-deck coach,
1 midicoach, 4 minicoach.
Chassis: 26 Mercedes, 7 Neoplan,
28 Setra.
Bodies: 4 Ferqui, 22 Mercedes,
7 Neoplan, 28 Setra
Ops incl: excursions & tours, private hire, continental tours.
Livery: Red/Cream
A subsidiary of Addison Lee PLC

ROUNDABOUT BUSES
25 OLDFIELD ROAD, BEXLEYHEATH
DA7 4DX
Tel: 020 8302 7551
E-mail: info@roundaboutbuses.co.uk
Web site: www.roundaboutbuses.co.uk
Man Dir: Glyn Matthews.
Fleet: 6 – 4 double-deck bus,
1 single-deck bus, 1 minibus.
Chassis: 1 AEC, 2 Iveco, 3 Leyland.
Bodies: 2 ECW, 1 Marshall,
1 Park Royal, 1 Roe, 1 Robin Hood.
Ops incl: local bus services, school contracts.
Livery: Green/Cream.
Ticket System: Wayfarer.

ROYALE EUROPEAN COACHES
47 WALLINGFORD ROAD, UXBRIDGE
UB8 2XS
Tel: 01895 233748
Fax: 01895 258119
E-mail: royaleuropean@aol.com
Web site: www.royaleuropean.co.uk
Fleet: 8 – double-deck coach, single-deck coach, midicoach
Chassis: Mercedes, Neoplan, Volvo
Ops incl: private hire
Livery: Red/Grey/White

SILVERDALE LONDON LTD
1 LYMINSTER CLOSE, HAYES UB4 9YB
Tel: 020 8961 1812
Fax: 020 8961 5677
E-mail: info@silverdalelondon.com
Web site: www.silverdalelondon.co.uk
Dirs: John Doherty, Shaun Doherty, Robert Green
Tran Man: Richard Cassell
Ops incl: school contracts, excursions & tours, private hire, express, continental tours.
Livery: White/Red
A subsidiary of Silverdale Tours - see Nottinghamshire

SOUTHGATE & FINCHLEY COACHES LTD
231A COLNEY HATCH LANE,
LONDON N11 3DG
Tel: 020 8368 0040
Fax: 020 8361 1934
Web site: www.coaches.org.uk
Man Dir: M. P. Rice
Dirs: Mrs V. M. Rice (**Co Sec**),
P. M. Rice, Mrs E. B. Scrivens.
Fleet: 24 - 23 single-deck coach,
1 minibus.
Chassis: 1 Iveco, 23 Volvo.
Bodies: 5 Jonckheere, 18 Plaxton,
1 Other.
Ops incl: school contracts, excursions and tours, private hire
Livery: Yellow/Blue/Orange

SUNBURY COACHES
204A CHARLTON ROAD,
SHEPPERTON TW17 0SJ
Tel: 01932 785153
Fax: 01932 789937
E-mail: sunburycoaches@tiscali.co.uk
Dirs: P Jones, D Jones.
Fleet: 6 - 4 single-deck coach,
1 midicoach, 1 minicoach.
Chassis: 2 DAF, 3 Iveco, 1 Toyota.
Bodies: 3 Beulas, 1 Caetano, 1 Plaxton,
1 Van Hool.
Ops incl: school contracts, excursions & tours, private hire.
Livery: White/Turquoise/Navy Blue.

TGM GROUP LTD
BUILDING 16300 MT2, ELECTRA AVENUE, HEATHROW AIRPORT, HOUNSLOW TW6 2DN
Tel: 020 8757 4700
Fax: 020 8757 4719
E-mail: info@tellings.co.uk
Web site: www.tellingsgoldenmiller.co.uk
Fleet Name: Tellings Golden Miller
Group Man Dir: Stephen Telling
Regional Man Dir (South): Paul Churchman **Group Ops Dir:** Richard Telling **Fin Dir/Co Sec:** Basil Taylor
Ops Dir: Paul Cowell
Eng Man: Ian Foster
Fleet: 75 - 58 single-deck coach,
14 minicoach, 3 minicoach.
Chassis: 2 Iveco, 15 Mercedes, 3 Setra,
2 Toyota, 53 Volvo.

Bodies: 2 Beulas, 6 Caetano, 3 Mercedes, 59 Plaxton, 3 Setra, 2 Van Hool.
Ops incl: school contracts, excursions & tours, private hire, express, continental tours.
Livery: White/Blue/Yellow
A subsidiary of Arriva

TIMEBUS TRAVEL
7 BOLEYN DRIVE, St LBANS AL1 2BP
Tel: 01727 866248
Web site: www.timebus.co.uk
Fleet Name: Timebus
Prop: David Pring
Fleet: 15 - 12 double-deck bus, 1 single-deck bus, 2 open-top bus.
Chassis: 15 AEC.
Bodies: 1 Metro-Cammell, 13 Park Royal, 1 Weymann.
Ops incl: private hire
Livery: Red with grey lining

TOMORROWS TRANSPORT
GIBBS STORAGE, GIBBS ROAD, LONDON N18 3PU
Tel: 020 8807 4555
Fax: 020 8807 4603
Prop: V A Daniels
Fleet: 3 - 2 single-deck coach, 1 midicoach
Chassis: 1 DAF, 1 Leyland, 1 Toyota.
Bodies: 1 Caetano, 1 Duple, 1 Van Hool.
Ops incl: private hire

VENTURE TRANSPORT (HENDON) (1965) LTD
307 PINNER ROAD, HARROW HA1 4HG
Tel: 020 8427 0101
Fax: 020 8427 1707
Ops incl: private hire

A subsidiary of Hearns Coaches, Harrow Weald

WESTBUS COACH SERVICES LTD
27A SPRING GROVE ROAD, HOUNSLOW TW3 4BE
Tel: 020 8572 6348
Fax: 020 8570 2234
Recovery: 020 8572 6348
E-mail: reservations@westbus.co.uk
Web site: www.westbus.co.uk
Gen Man: Tim Miles
Ops Man: Chris Shaw
Ch Eng: Graham Bessant
Fleet: 37 – 3 double-deck bus, 29 single-deck coach, 2 double-deck coach, 3 midicoach.
Chassis: DAF, Mercedes, Scania, Setra, Van Hool, VDL, Volvo.
Bodies: Alexander, Berkhof, Irizar, Setra, Sitcar, Van Hool.
Ops incl: private hire, continental tours, excursions & tours, school contracts.
Livery: Red/Beige
Part of the Comfort Delgro Corporation

WEST'S COACHES LTD
198/200 HIGH ROAD, WOODFORD GREEN, IG8 9EF
Tel: 020 8504 9747
Fax: 020 8559 1085
E-mail: info@westscoaches.myzen.co.uk
Web site: www.westscoaches.co.uk
Dirs: R L West, E J M West
Fleet: 15 single-deck coach.
Chassis: 8 Alexander Dennis, 1 Irisbus, 6 Volvo.
Bodies: 2 Marcopolo, 11 Plaxton, 2 UVG.
Ops incl: excursions & tours, private hire, school contracts, continental tours.
Livery: White/Red/Blue

WESTWAY COACH SERVICES LTD
7A RAINBOW INDUSTRIAL ESTATE, STATION APPROACH, RAYNES PARK, LONDON SW20 0JY
Tel: 020 8944 1277
Fax: 020 8947 5339
E-mail: info@westway-coaches.co.uk
Web site: www.westwaycoachservices.com
Prop: David West
Gen Man: Arthur Richardson
Ops Man: Kevin Pates
Fleet: 22 - 12 single-deck coach, 7 double-deck coach, 1 midicoach, 2 minicoach.
Chassis: 2 Mercedes, 1 Scania, 19 Volvo
Bodies: 7 Jonckheere, 2 Plaxton, 13 Van Hool.
Ops incl: school contracts, excursions & tours, private hire, continental tours.
Livery: Blue/Orange

WINGS LUXURY TRAVEL LTD
47 WALLINGFORD ROAD, UXBRIDGE UB8 2XS
Tel: 020 8573 8388
Fax: 020 8573 7773
E-mail: info@wingstravel.co.uk
Web site: www.wingstravel.co.uk
Chairman: F L Gritt
Gen Man: W Gritt
Ops Man: S Hughes
Fleet: 14 - 7 midicoach, 4 minicoach, 3 minibus
Chassis: 14 Mercedes
Ops Incl: school contracts, excursions and tours, private hire
Livery: White

MERSEYSIDE (ST HELENS, KNOWSLEY, LIVERPOOL, SEFTON, WIRRAL)

A1A LTD
373 CLEVELAND STREET, BIRKENHEAD CH41 4JW
Tel: 0151 650 1616
Fax: 0151 650 0007
Web site: www.a1atravel.co.uk
Prop: Barbara Ashworth
Fleet: 26 - 7 single-deck bus, 8 midibus, 11 minibus.
Chassis: 7 Dennis, 8 LDV, 1 Mazda, 5 Mercedes, 1 Volkswagen.
Ops incl: local bus services, school contracts, private hire.
Livery: White/Blue

A.2.B TRAVEL UK LTD
PRENTON WAY, NORTH CHESHIRE TRADING ESTATE, PRENTON CH43 3DU
Tel: 0151 609 0600
Fax: 0151 609 0601
E-mail: info@a2b-travel.com
Web site: www.a2b-travel.com
Dirs: G Evans, D Evans
Fleet: 26 - 2 single-deck coach, 2 midibus, 12 midicoach, 10 minibus
Chassis: 1 Dennis, 4 Ford, 6 Ford Transit, 10 Freight Rover, 2 Iveco, 1 MAN, 4 Mercedes, 1 Renault.
Bodies: 1 Beulas, 1 Caetano, 2 Mercedes, 1 Plaxton.
Ops incl: school contracts, private hire, excursions & tours.
Livery: White/Blue

AINTREE COACHLINE
11 CLARE ROAD, BOOTLE L20 9LY
Tel: 0151 922 8630
Fax: 0151 933 6994
Ops incl: local bus services, school contracts, private hire.
Livery: Red/Cream.
Also owns Helms of Eastham.

ALS COACHES LTD
400 CELEVELAND STREET, BIRKENHEAD CH41 8EQ
Tel: 0151 6530222
Fax: 0151 6700509
E-mail: dan@happyals.com
Web site: www.happyals.com
Fleet Name: Happy Al's
Man Dir: T.A Cullinan
Gen Man: M Cullinan
Tran Man: C Cullinan
Fleet: 48 - 25 double-deck bus, 8 single-deck bus, 15 single-deck coach.
Chassis: 13 DAF, 2 MAN, 8 Volvo.
Bodies: 1 Bova, 10 East Lancs, 11 Ikarus, 15 Leyland, 1 Plaxton, 2 Van Hool.
Ops incl: school contracts, private hire, excursions & tours.
Ticket System: Wayfarer

ARRIVA NORTH WEST & WALES
73 ORMSKIRK ROAD, AINTREE, LIVERPOOL L9 5AE
Tel: 0151 522 2800
Fax: 0151 525 9556
Web site: www.arriva.co.uk
Regional Man Dir: Phil Stone
Area Man Dir: Howard Farrall
Eng Dir: Phil Cummins
Ops Dir: John Rimmer
Fin Dir: Simon Mills
Head of Ops: Rick Halsall
Fleet: 1236 - 196 double-deck bus, 927 single-deck bus, 108 midibus, 15 open-top bus..
Chassis: 49 Alexander Dennis, 487 DAF/VDL, 378 Dennis, 7 Leyland, 5 MAN, 3 MCW, 54 Optare, 83 Scania, 170 Volvo
Bodies: 137 Alexander Dennis, 69 East Lancs, 10 Ikarus, 64 Marshall/MCV, 3 MCW, 117 Northern Counties, 54 Optare, 276 Plaxton, 3 Scania, 505 Wright.
Ops incl: local bus services, school contracts, private hire.
Livery: Arriva UK Bus
Ticket System: Wayfarer TGX

G. ASHTON COACHES
WATERY LANE, ST HELENS WA9 3JA
Tel: 01744 733275
Fax: 01744 454122
E-mail: enquiries@gashtoncoaches.f2s.com

Merseyside (St Helens, Knowsley, Liverpool, Sefton, Wirral)

Web site: www.gashtoncoachholidays.co.uk
Prop: Simon Ashton
Fleet: 6- 5 single-deck coach, 1 midicoach
Chassis: 2 DAF, 2 Scania, 1 Toyota.
Bodies: 1 Berkhof, 1 Caetano, 3 Irizar, 1 Van Hool.
Ops incl: excursions & tours, private hire, continental tours.
Livery: Multicoloured

AVON COACH AND BUS COMPANY

10 BROOKWAY, NORTH CHESHIRE TRADING ESTATE, PRENTON CH43 3DT
Tel: 0151 608 8000
Fax: 0151 608 9955
Props: Larry Smith, George Lewis
Ops Man: George Lewis
Fleet: 1 single-deck bus, 36 midibus.
Chassis: 14 Alexander Dennis, 18 Dennis, 1 Enterprise, 4 Volvo.
Bodies: 2 Alexander, 3 Alexander Dennis, 1 Berkhof, 6 East Lancs, 11 MCV, 4 Marshall, 6 Plaxton, 2 Wright
Ops incl: local bus services, school contracts, excursions & tours, private hire.
Livery: Cream with Blue and Gold stripe.
Ticket System: Wayfarer.

BLUELINE TRAVEL

54 STATION ROAD, MAGHULL L31 3DB
Tel/Fax: 0151 526 8888
Prop: C. P. Carr
Fleet: 12 - 3 single-deck coach, 4 midicoach, 5 minicoach.
Ops incl: private hire, school contracts.

CUMFYBUS LTD

178 CAMBRIDGE ROAD, SOUTHPORT PR9 7LW
Tel: 01704 227321
Fax: 01704 505781

E-mail: info@cumfybus.co.uk
Web site: www.cumfybus.co.uk
Man Dir: M. R. Vickers
Admin: Mrs P. Lyon.
Fleet: 109 – 2 double-deck bus, 12 single-deck bus, 68 midibus, 27 minibus.
Chassis: 8 DAF, 4 Dennis, 4 Fiat, 2 Leyland, 88 Optare, 3 Renault.
Bodies: 4 Caetano, 8 East Lancs, 2 Leyland, 88 Optare, 7 Other.
Ops incl: local bus services, school contracts.
Livery: Yellow

FIRST MANCHESTER

THE PEBBLES, LIVERPOOL ROAD, CHESTER CH2 1AE
Tel: 08708 500 868
Fax: 01782 592541
Web site: www.firstgroup.com
Fleet Name: First in Chester and the Wirral
See Greater Manchester

FIVE STAR TRAVEL

SNAPE GATE, FOX'S BANK LANE, WHISTON, PRESCOTT L35 3SS
Tel: 0151 481 0000
Fax: 0151 493 9999
E-mail: phil@fivestar.freeserve.co.uk
Web site: www.fivestartravel.co.uk
Prop: Phil Riley
Fleet: 2 single-deck coach.
Chassis: 2 DAF
Bodies: 2 Bova.
Ops incl: excursions & tours, private hire, continental tours.
Livery: White

FORMBY COACHWAYS LTD

38 STEPHENSON WAY, FORMBY L37 8EG
Tel: 01704 834448
Fax: 01704 878820
Fleet Name: Freshfield Coaches.

Man Dir: K W Bradley
Sec: D A Bradley
Fleet: 1 minicoach.
Chassis/Body: Mercedes.
Ops incl: school contracts, private hire.
Livery: Green/Silver

HARDINGS TOURS LTD

CAVENDISH FARM ROAD, WESTON VILLAGE, RUNCORN WA7 4LU
Tel: 0151 647 7831
Fax: 0151 650 1033
Web site: www.hardingstours.co.uk
Man Dir: Selwyn A Jones
Ops Man: Ken Pickavance
Fleet Eng: Cledwyn Owen
Fleet: 13 - 11 single-deck coach, 1 minibus, 1 minicoach
Chassis: 1 Caetano, 2 Mercedes, 8 Scania, 2 Volvo.
Bodies: 1 Berkhof, 1 Caetano, 7 Irizar, 2 Mercedes, 2 Van Hool.
Ops incl: school contracts, excursions & tours, private hire, continental tours.
Livery: White/Red/Orange/Yellow.
A subsidiary of Selwyn's Travel – see Cheshire

HATTON'S TRAVEL

WALKERS LANE, ST HELENS WA9 4AF
Tel: 01744 822818
E-mail: enquiries@hattonstravel.co.uk
Web site: www.hattonstravel.co.uk
Ops incl: local bus services, school contracts, private hire, excursions & tours, continental touring
Livery: White with Blue/Red

HUYTON TRAVEL LTD

37 WILSON ROAD, LIVERPOOL L36 6AN
Tel: 0151 449 3868
Fleet Name: HTL Buses
Fleet: 81 – 9 single-deck bus, 27 midibus, 45 minibus.
Chassis incl: Alexander Dennis, Dennis,

Fiat, Ford, Iveco, LDV, MAN, Mercedes, Optare, Renault, Transbus.
Bodies incl: Alexander Dennis, Alexander, East Lancs, Koch, Marshall, Optare, Plaxton, Transbus, UVG.
Ops incl: local bus services, school contracts.

MAYPOLE COACHES
SPENCERS LANE,
MELLING L31 1HB
Tel: 0151 547 2713
Fax: 0151 548 2849
Prop: Andrew Donnelly
Fleet: 10 - 2 double-deck bus, 2 single-deck bus, 4 single-deck coach, 2 midicoach.
Chassis: 2 Bluebird, 1 DAF, 1 Ford Transit, 2 Leyland National, 4 Volvo.
Ops incl: school contracts, excursions & tours, private hire, Livery: White.
Livery: Blue/Green

GAVIN MURRAY & ELLISONS TRAVEL SERVICES
QUEENS GARAGE,
61 BOUNDARY ROAD,
ST HELENS WA10 2LX
Tel: 01744 22882
Fax: 01744 24402
Web site: www.ellisonstravel.com
Dirs: A. Magowan, M. Magowan.
Fleet: 21 – 18 single-deck coach, 3 midicoach.
Chassis: 8 VDL Bova, 6 Mercedes, 3 Van Hool, 4 Volvo.
Bodies: 8 VDL Bova, 4 Jonckheere, 3 Mercedes, 3 Neoplan, 3 Van Hool.
Ops incl: private hire.
Livery: White/Red/Yellow.

DAVID OGDEN COACHES
BAXTERS LANE, SUTTON,
ST HELENS WA9 3DH
Tel: 01744 606176
Fax: 01744 822146
E-mail: ogdenssutton@btconnect.com
Web site: www.davidogdenholidays.co.uk

Prop: John David Ogden
Co Sec: Carol Ogden.
Fleet: 17 - 1 single-deck bus, 11 single-deck coach, 1 midicoach, 4 minibus.
Chassis: 1 Bova, 7 DAF, 3 EOS, 3 Ford Transit, 1 Mercedes.
Bodies: 1 Berkhof, 1 Bova, 1 Ikarus, 1 Mercedes, 1 Plaxton, 8 Van Hool.
Ops incl: school contracts, excursions & tours, private hire, continental tours.
Livery: Red/White/Blue.

PEOPLES BUS LTD
CUSTOMER SERVICE CENTRE,
PO BOX 57, LIVERPOOL
L9 8YZ
Tel: 0151 523 4010
E-mail: queries@peoplesbus.com
Web site: www.peoplesnus.com
Dir: Andrew Cawley
Ops incl: local bus services, school contracts, private hire.

SANDGROUNDER COACHES
28 WARWICK STREET,
SOUTHPORT PR8 5ES
Tel: 01704 541194
E-mail: gerry@dohe.wanadoo.co.uk
Web site: sgccoaches.co.uk
Dir: Gerry Doherty
Ops incl: excursions & tours, private hire, continental tours.

STAGECOACH MERSEYSIDE
EAST LANCASHIRE ROAD,
LIVERPOOL L11 0BB
Tel: 0151 330 6204
E-mail: enquiries.merseyside@stagecoachbus.com
Web site: www.stagecoachbus.com
Man Dir: Stephen Riggans
Ops Dir: Les Burton
Eng Dir: Paul Lee
Fleet: 172 - 5 double-deck bus, 155 single-deck bus, 12 midibus.
Chassis: 44 Alexander Dennis,

26 Dennis, 46 MAN, 6 Optare, 7 Transbus, 43 Volvo.
Bodies: 13 Alexander, 90 Alexander Dennis, 6 East Lancs, 6 Northern Counties, 6 Optare, 7 Plaxton, 7 Transbus, 37 Wright.
Ops incl: local bus services, express.
Livery: Stagecoach UK Bus
Ticket System: ERG

STRAWBERRY
ROLLING SOLUTIONS LTD,
UNIT 18, LINKWAY DISTRIBUTION PARK, ELTON HEAD ROAD,
ST HELENS WA9 5BW
Tel: 01744 850016
Web site: www.strawberrybus.co.uk
Dirs: O S Howarth, L Howarth, D Reeves
Fleet: 11 single-deck bus
Chassis: 5 Alexander Dennis, 4 DAF, 2 Scania
Bodies: 5 Alexander Dennis, 6 Wright
Ops incl: local bus services, school contracts
Livery: Lime Green and Red
Ticket System: Wayfarer

SUPERTRAVEL OMNIBUS LTD
STC HOUSE, SPEKE HALL ROAD,
SPEKE, LIVERPOOL
L24 9HD
Tel: 0151 486 3994
Fax: 0151 448 1216
E-mail: 96.supertravel@btconnect.com
Web site: www.supertravelltd.com
Man Dir: Graham Bolderson.
Fleet: 28 - 4 single-deck bus, 23 midibus, 1 minibus.
Chassis: 12 Dennis, 2 MAN, 13 Optare, 1 Renault.
Bodies: 5 Alexander, 13 Optare, 9 Plaxton, 1 Other.
Ops incl: local bus services, school contracts, private hire.

NORFOLK

AMBASSADOR TRAVEL (ANGLIA) LTD
JAMES WATT CLOSE,
GAPTON HALL INDUSTRIAL ESTATE,
GREAT YARMOUTH
NR31 0NX
Tel/Recovery: 01493 440350
Fax: 01493 440367
E-mail: ambassador-travel@hotmail.co.uk
Man Dir: M C Green
Ops Man: B Picton
Dep Ops Man: M Pleasants
Fleet: 46 - 1 double-deck bus, 3 single-deck bus, 38 single-deck coach, 4 midibus.
Chassis: 6 Scania, 40 Volvo.
Bodies: 5 Caetano, 2 Irizar, 4 Jonckheere, 5 Optare, 26 Plaxton, 4 Sunsundegui.
Ops incl: local bus services, school contracts, private hire, express, excursions & tours.
Livery: White.
Ticket System: Setright/Almex/Wayfarer

ANGLIAN COACHES LTD
See Suffolk

CHENERY TRAVEL
THE GARAGE, DICKLEBURGH,
DISS IP21 4NJ
Tel: 01379 741221 **Fax:** 01379 740728
Recovery: 01379 741656
E-mail: julia@chenerytravel.co.uk
Web site: www.chenerytravel.co.uk
Dir: Mrs P Garnham
Gen Man: Mrs J M McGraffin
Fleet: 21 single-deck coach.
Chassis: 1 Bedford, 17 Setra, 3 Volvo.
Bodies: 1 Duple, 3 Jonckheere, 17 Setra.
Ops incl: school contracts, excursions & tours, private hire, express, continental tours.
Livery: Silver/Blue.

COACH SERVICES LTD
1A HOWLETT WAY, THETFORD
IP24 1HZ

Tel: 01842 821509 **Fax:** 01842 766581
E-mail: info@coachservicesltd.co.uk
Web site: www.coachservicesltd.co.uk
Prop: A Crawford **Tran Man:** R Crawford
Fleet: 37 - 1 double-deck bus, 4 single-deck bus, 21 single-deck coach, 7 midibus, 4 minibus.
Chassis: 1 AEC Routemaster, 1 Alexander Dennis, 2 DAF, 2 Dennis, 3 Ford Transit, 1 Iveco, 1 MAN, 7 Mercedes, 10 Scania, 9 Volvo.
Bodies: 3 Alexander Dennis, 1 Beulas, 1 Bova, 6 Irizar, 4 Jonckheere, 1 Mercedes, 1 Neoplan, 3 Optare, 1 Park Royal, 6 Plaxton, 2 Scania, 3 Van Hool, 2 Wright.
Ops incl: local bus services, school contracts, excursions & tours, private hire.
Livery: White
Ticket System: Almex

CRUSADER HOLIDAYS
See Essex

D-WAY TRAVEL
See Suffolk

♿	Vehicle suitable for disabled	🔒	Seat belt-fitted Vehicle	R24	24 hour recovery service
T	Toilet-drop facilities available	🍽	Coach(es) with galley facilities	✹	Replacement vehicle available
R	Recovery service available	❄	Air-conditioned vehicle(s)	🚍	Vintage Coach(es) available
🚌	Open top vehicle(s)	🚻	Coaches with toilet facilities		

A. W. EASTONS COACHES LTD
T ♿ 🍽 ❄
THE OLD COACH HOUSE, STRATTON STRAWLESS, NORWICH NR10 5LR
Tel/Fax: 01603 754253
E-mail: admin@eastonsholidays.co.uk
Web site: www.eastonsholidays.co.uk
Dirs: Robert Easton, Derek Easton
Fleet: 10 - 1 single-deck bus, 9 single-deck coach.
Chassis: 2 Bova, 1 Dennis, 1 Setra, 7 Val Hool.
Bodies: 2 Bova, 1 Optare, 1 Setra, 7 Van Hool.
Ops incl: local bus services, excursions & tours, school contracts, private hire, continental tours.
Livery: Purple
Ticket System: Almex

EUROSUN COACHES
🚻 🍽 ♿ ❄ 🔒 T
25 REGENT ROAD, LOWESTOFT NR32 1PA
Tel: 01520 501015
Fax: 01502 589382
E-mail: eurosuncoaches@hotmail.com
Web site: www.eurosuncoaches.co.uk
Dirs: Phil Overy, Jack Overy
Ch Eng: Adam Goffin
Sales & Marketing Man: Tony Porter
Fleet: 19 - 16 single-deck coach, 3 double-deck coach.
Chassis: 7 DAF, 4 Leyland, 3 MAN, 2 Mercedes, 5 Neoplan.
Bodies: 3 Bova, 2 Leyland, 5 Neoplan, 6 Plaxton, 2 Van Hool, 1 other.
Ops incl: school contracts, excursions & tours, private hire, continental tours.
Livery: Red and Gold

FARELINE COACH SERVICES
See Suffolk

FIRST EAST OF ENGLAND (formerly FIRST EASTERN COUNTIES)
♿ 🔒 🚍 ❄
ROUEN HOUSE, ROUEN ROAD, NORWICH NR1 1RB
Tel: 08456 020 121
Fax: 01603 615439
Web site: www.firstgroup.com
Man Dir: Alan Pilbeam
Fin Dir: Jacky Cato
Eng Dir: Phil Pannell **Comm & Customer Services Dir:** Steve Wickers
Fleet: 699 - 174 double-deck bus, 222 single-deck bus, 19 single-deck coach, 244 midibus, 40 minibus.
Chassis: AEC, BMC, Dennis, Leyland, Mercedes, Optare, Scania, Volvo.
Ops incl: local bus services, school contract, private hire.
Livery: FirstGroup UK Bus.
Ticket System: Wayfarer 3

FREESTONES COACHES LTD
♿ 🔒 🍽 ❄ 🔒
GREEN LANE, BEETLEY, DEREHAM NR20 4DL
Tel: 01362 860236 **Fax:** 01362 860276
Dir: Mrs Gloria Feeke
Ops Man: Robert Tibbles
Co Sec: Gary Feeke
Web site: www.freestonescoaches.co.uk
E-mail: freestonescoachesltd@tiscali.co.uk
Fleet: 11 - 1 single-deck bus, 9 single-deck coach, 1 minibus.
Chassis: 1 BMC, 2 Iveco, 1 Mercedes, 2 Scania 1 Volkswagen, 4 Volvo.
Bodies: 2 Beulas, 1 BMC, 1 Hispano, 1 Irizar, 1 Plaxton, 4 Van Hool.
Ops incl: local bus services, excursions & tours, school contracts, private hire, continental tours.

D&H HARROD (COACHES) LTD
🔒 🍽 ❄ 🔒 T
BEXWELL AERODROME, DOWNHAM MARKET PE38 9LU
Tel: 01366 381111
Fax: 01366 382010
E-mail: paulharrod@btconnect.com
Web site: www.harrodcoaches.co.uk
Prop: Derek Harrod
Ops Man: Paul Harrod.
Fleet: 12 – single-deck coach, midicoach.
Chassis: 1 Dennis, 1 Iveco, 1 Mercedes, 9 Volvo.

Bodies: Jonckheere, Mercedes, Plaxton, UVG, Van Hool.
Ops incl: local bus services, school contracts, excursions & tours, private hire, continental tours.
Livery: Gold/Cream & Blue

KONECTBUS LTD
♿
JOHN GOSHAWK ROAD, DEREHAM NR19 1SY
Tel: 01362 851210
Fax: 01362 851215
E-mail: feedback@konectbus.co.uk
Web site: www.konectbus.co.uk
Man Dir: Steve Challis
Ops & Comm Dir: Julian Patterson
Eng Dir: Andy Warnes
Fleet: 44 - 12 double-deck bus, 32 single-deck bus.
Chassis: 5 Alexander Dennis, 2 Leyland, 1 Leyland National, 31 Optare, 5 VDL.
Bodies: 7 Alexander Dennis, 1 Leyland National, 31 Optare, 5 Wright.
Ops incl: local bus services
Livery: Blue/Yellow/Grey
Ticket System: Wayfarer TGX
A subsidiary of the Go-Ahead Group

MATTHEWS COACHES
♿
50 WESTGATE STREET, SHOULDHAM, KING'S LYNN PE33 0BN
Tel: 01366 347220
Fax: 01366 347293
E-mail: john@matthewscoaches.co.uk
Man Dir: John Lloyd
Fleet: 5 - 4 single-deck coach, 1 minibus
Chassis: 1 DAF, 3 Dennis, 1 LDV.
Bodies: 1 Berkhof, 1 LDV, 2 Plaxton, 1 Van Hool.
Ops incl: school contracts, private hire.
Livery: White/Blue

NEAVES COACHES
♿ 🔒 🍽 🍽 ❄ R
THE STREET, CATFIELD, GREAT YARMOUTH NR29 5AA
Tel: 01692 580383
Fax: 01692 582977
E-mail: info@neavescoaches.com
Web site: www.neavescoaches.com
Man Dir: Mrs Daphne Holburn
Gen Man: Richard Hipkiss
Fleet: 9 – 2 single-deck bus, 5 single-deck coach, 1 midicoach, 1 minibus.
Chassis: 1 DAF, 1 Dennis, 1 Marshall, 2 Mercedes, 2 Optare, 1 Scania, 1 Volvo.
Bodies: 1 Jonckheere, 2 Mercedes, 2 Optare, 2 Plaxton, 1 Van Hool, 1 Wright.
Ops incl: local bus services, school contracts, excursions & tours, private hire.
Livery: White, Red & Grey
Ticket System: Wayfarer

NORFOLK GREEN
♿
HAMLIN WAY, KINGS LYNN PE31 6HA
Tel: 01553 776980
Fax: 01553 770891
E-mail: enquiries@norfolkgreen.co.uk
Web site: www.norfolkgreen.co.uk

Man Dir: Ben Colson
Dir: Keith Shayshutt
Fleet Eng: Nigel Firth
Ops Man: Richard Pengelly
Accountant: Simon Carr
Fleet: 66 – 3 double-deck bus, 15 single-deck bus, 44 midibus, 4 minibus.
Chassis: 3 DAF, 1 Dennis, 3 Irisbus, 4 Mercedes, 51 Optare, 4 Renault.
Bodies: 1 Alexander, 3 Irisbus, 54 Optare, 4 Plaxton, 4 Other.
Ops incl: local bus services
Livery: two-tone Green
Ticket System: Wayfarer TGX

PEELINGS COACHES
THE GARAGE, CLAY HILL, TITTLESHALL, KING'S LYNN PE32 2RQ
Tel/Fax: 01328 701531
Web site: www.peelings-coaches.co.uk
E-mail: jonathon.joplin@btinternet.com
Prop: Jonathan Joplin
Comp Sec: Ruth Joplin
Ch Eng: Jonathan Sayer
Fleet: 6 - single-deck coach.
Chassis: 1 Dennis, 1 Iveco, 4 Volvo.
Bodies: 1 Beulas, 1 Jonckheere, 4 Plaxton.
Ops incl: local bus services, school contracts, excursions & tours, private hire, express.
Livery: White/Blue/Silver
Ticket System: Setright

REYNOLDS COACHES LTD
THE GARAGE, ORMESBY ROAD, CAISTER-ON-SEA, GREAT YARMOUTH NR30 5QJ
Tel: 01493 720312
Fax: 01493 721512
E-mail: reynolds.coaches@gtyarmouth.co.uk
Web site: www.reynolds-coaches.co.uk
Man Dir: Charles Reynolds
Tours Dir: Mrs Julie Reynolds
Co Sec: Mrs Grace Reynolds
Ch Eng: Jeffrey Buckle
Fleet: 17 - single-deck coach, midicoach, minicoach.
Chassis: 7 Alexander Dennis, 1 Bova, 1 EOS, 1 Iveco, 3 Toyota, 3 Volvo, 1 Other.
Bodies: 2 Beulas, 1 Bova, 3 Caetano, 1 Duple, 7 Plaxton, 2 Van Hool, 1 Other.

Ops incl: school contracts, excursions & tours, private hire, continental tours.
Livery: Silver.

SANDERS COACHES LTD
HEATH DRIVE, HEMPSTEAD ROAD INDUSTRIAL ESTATE, HOLT NR25 6ER
Tel: 01263 712800
Fax: 01263 710920
E-mail: sales@sanderscoaches.com
Web site: www.sanderscoaches.com
Man Dir: Charles Sanders
Ops Dir: Paul Sanders
Head of Tours & Finance: Carole Willimott
Fleet Eng: Andrew Sanders
Fleet: 78 - 7 double-deck bus, 40 single-deck bus, 18 single-deck coach, 3 midibus, 5 midicoach, 5 minibus.
Chassis: 5 Alexander Dennis, 2 Bedford, 2 Bova, 43 DAF, 12 Mercedes, 2 Optare, 3 Scania, 2 Setra, 4 VDL, 3 Volvo.
Bodies: 2 Bova, 8 East Lancs, 20 Ikarus, 8 Optare, 14 Plaxton, 5 Reeve Burgess, 2 Setra, 16 Van Hool, 3 Wright.
Ops incl: local bus services, school contracts, excursions & tours, private hire, continental tours.
Livery: Orange/Yellow/Blue
Ticket System: Wayfarer

H SEMMENCE & CO LTD
34 NORWICH ROAD, WYMONDHAM NR18 0NS
Tel: 01953 602135
Fax: 01953 605867
E-mail: sales@semmence.co.uk
Web site: www.semmence.co.uk
Man Dir: Sean Green
Ops incl: local bus services, school contracts, excursions & tours, express, private hire
Livery: White
Ticket System: Wayfarer
(Associated with Ambassador Travel)

SIMONDS OF BOTESDALE LTD
ROSWALD HOUSE, OAK DRIVE, DISS IP22 4GX
Tel/Recovery: 01379 647300
Fax: 01379 647350
E-mail: info@simonds.co.uk

Web site: www.simonds.co.uk
Fleet Name: Simonds Coach & Travel
Man Dir: Martyn Simonds
Dirs: Robin Simonds, Adrian Tant
Fleet: 43 - single-deck bus, single-deck coach, midibus, minicoach.
Chassis: 7 MAN, 5 Mercedes, 27 Volvo, 4 Other.
Bodies: 1 Alexander Dennis, 1 Jonckheere, 7 MCV, 1 Mercedes, 1 Optare, 10 Plaxton, 22 Van Hool.
Ops incl: local bus services, school contracts, excursions & tours, private hire, continental tours.
Livery: White with Red/Gold leaves
Ticket system: Wayfarer/Paycell

SPRATTS COACHES (EAST ANGLIAN & CONTINENTAL) LTD
THE GARAGE, WRENINGHAM, NORWICH NR16 1AZ
Tel: 01508 489262
Fax: 01508 489404
E-mail: sprattscoaches@btconnect.com
Web site: www.sprattscoaches.co.uk
Dirs: Richard Spratt, Christine Bilham
Fleet: 9 - 6 single-deck coach, 3 midicoach.
Chassis: 1 Bova, 2 MAN, 1 Mercedes, 4 Scania, 1 Volvo.
Bodies: 1 Berkhof, 1 Bova, 1 Caetano, 1 Optare, 5 Van Hool.
Ops incl: school contracts, excursions & tours, private hire, continental tours.
Livery: White

SUNBEAM COACHES LTD
WESTGATE STREET, HEVINGHAM, NORWICH NR10 5NH
Tel/Fax: 01603 754211
E-mail: sunbeamcoaches@aol.com
Man Dir: G M Coldham
Fleet: 6 – 1 single-deck bus, 4 single-deck coach, 1 minicoach.
Chassis: 1 Dennis, 2 MAN, 1 Mercedes, 1 Toyota, 1 Volvo.
Bodies: 1 Caetano, 2 Neoplan, 2 Plaxton, 1 Van Hool.
Ops incl: local bus service, school contracts, private hire, excursions & tours.
Livery: White with Orange/Blue/Yellow

Norfolk

The Little Red Book 2011
Passenger Transport Directory for the British Isles

For information regarding advertising contact:

Graham Middleton
Tel: 01780 484632
Fax: 01780 763388
E-mail: graham.middleton@ianallanpublishing.co.uk

NORTH AND NORTH EAST LINCOLNSHIRE

APPLEBYS COACH TRAVEL
CONISHOLME, LOUTH LN11 7LT
Tel: 01507 357900
Fax: 01507 357910
Recovery: 07764 278466
E-mail: coach@applebyscoaches.co.uk
Web site: www.applebyscoaches.co.uk
Fleet Name: L F Bowen
Tran Man: Neil Warne
Man Dir: Rob Lyng **Group Ops Man:** Nick Tetley **Fleet Eng:** David Hoy
Fleet: 17 – 13 single-deck coach, 4 minibus
Chassis: 1 Dennis, 12 Scania, 4 Volkswagen
Bodies: 8 Irizar, 4 Volkswagen, 5 Other
Ops incl: excursions & tours, private hire, continental tours.
(Subsidiary of L F Bowen Ltd, Staffordshire)

BEN GEORGE TRAVEL LTD
39 ESTATE AVENUE, BROUGHTON, BRIGG DN20 0JZ
Tel: 01652 654681
Fax: 01652 650224
E-mail: s.p.easton@btinternet.com
Dirs: Stephen & John Easton
Fleet: 4 - 3 single-deck coach, 1 minicoach.
Chassis: 1 Alexander Dennis, 1 Toyota, 2 Volvo.
Bodies: 1Caetano, 2 Plaxton, 1 Van Hool.
Ops incl: school contracts, private hire.
Livery: Red/White/Blue

EMMERSON COACHES LTD
BLUESTONE LANE, IMMINGHAM DN40 2EL
Tel: 01469 578166
Fax: 01469 575278
E-mail: emmersoncoaches@tiscali.co.uk
Web site: www.emmersoncoaches.com
Dir: Alan Brumby
Fleet: 7 single-deck coach.
Chassis: 1 Leyland, 2 MAN, 3 Mercedes, 1 Volvo.
Bodies: 1 Ikarus, 2 Mercedes, 1 Neoplan, 1 Noge, 1 Plaxton, 1 Van Hool.
Ops incl: school contracts, private hire.
Livery: White, Orange & Brown.

EXPERT COACH SERVICES LTD
2 PASTURE STREET, GRIMSBY DN31 1QD
Tel: 01472 350650
Fax: 01472 351926
E-mail: sales@expertcoaches.co.uk
Web site: www.expertcoaches.co.uk
Man Dir: L A Harniess
Dir: C J Cator
Fleet: 2 single-deck coach
Chassis: 2 Scania.
Bodies: 1 Berkhof, 1 Plaxton.
Ops incl: excursions & tours, private hire, continental tours.
Livery: Blue/White.

HOLLOWAY COACHES LTD
COTTAGE BECK ROAD, SCUNTHORPE DN16 1TP
Tel: 01724 282277, 281177
Fax: 01724 289945
Man Dir: F. S. Holloway
Dir: P. A. Holloway
Fleet: 14 - 7 double-deck bus, 6 single-deck coach, 1 minicoach.
Chassis: 1 Bedford, 2 Dennis, 11 Leyland.
Bodies: 7 Alexander, 6 Plaxton, 1 other.
Ops incl: local bus services, school contracts, excursions & tours, express.
Livery: Red/White/Blue.

HORNSBY TRAVEL SERVICES LTD
51 ASHBY HIGH STREET, SCUNTHORPE DN16 2NB
Tel: 01724 282255
E-mail: office@hornsbytravel.co.uk
Web site: www.hornsbytravel.co.uk
Man Dir: R Hornsby
Gen Man: N Hornsby
Fleet: 30 - 4 double-deck bus, 17 single-deck bus, 9 single-deck coach, 1 minibus
Chassis: 1 BMC, 4 DAF, 13 Dennis, 2 Leyland, 2 MCW, 2 Plaxton, 1 Vauxhall, 2 Volvo.
Bodies: 3 Alexander, 1 BMC, 2 MCW, 19 Plaxton, 1 Transbus, 4 Wright, 1 other.
Ops incl: local bus services, excursions & tours, private hire, school contracts
Livery: Silver/Blue.
Ticket System: Almex

MILLMAN COACHES
17 WILTON ROAD, HUMBERSTON, GRIMSBY DN36 4AW
Tel: 01472 210297
Fax: 01472 595915
E-mail: enquiries@millmancoaches.co.uk
Web site: www.millmancoaches.co.uk
Partners: Marjorie Millman, David Millman, Amanda J Millman
Fleet: 9 - 6 single-deck coach, 2 midicoach, 1 minibus.
Chassis: 2 Cummins, 1 Dennis, 2 Leyland, 1 Mercedes, 3 Volvo.
Bodies: 2 Duple, 2 Jonckheere, 1 Mercedes, 4 Plaxton.
Ops incl: private hire, school contracts.
Livery: White/Blue/Yellow

RADLEY COACH TRAVEL
THE TRAVEL OFFICE, 11 CHAPEL STREET, BRIGG DN20 8JZ
Tel: 01652 653583
Fax: 01652 656020
Fleet Name: Radley Holidays
E-mail: radleytravel@aol.com
Web site: www.radleytravel.co.uk
Owner: Kevin Radley.
Fleet: 4 single-deck coach
Chassis: 4 Scania.
Bodies: 1 Berkhof, 1 Irizar, 2 Scania Omni Express
Ops incl: excursions & tours, private hire, continental tours.
Livery: Maroon/Gold

SHERWOOD TRAVEL
19 QUEENS ROAD, IMMINGHAM DN40 1QR
Tel: 01469 571140
Fax: 01469 574937
E-mail: enquiries@sherwoodtravel.co.uk
Web site: www.sherwoodtravel.co.uk
Dirs: Stuart Oakland, Jane Oakland, Lucy Oakland
Fleet: 10 - 4 single-deck coach, 3 midicoach, 1 minibus, 2 minicoach.
Chassis incl: 3 Mercedes, 1 Van Hool, 4 Volvo.
Ops incl: school contracts, excursions & tours, private hire.

SOLID ENTERTAINMENTS
46 WELLOWGATE, GRIMSBY DN32 0RA
Tel: 01472 349222
Fax: 01472 362275
Web site: www.solidentertainments.com
Prop: S. J. Stanley.
Fleet: 2 - 1 single-deck coach, 1 minibus.
Chassis incl: 1 Scania.
Bodies incl: 1 Irizar.
Ops incl: excursions & tours, private hire, continental tours.
Livery: Black.

STAGECOACH EAST MIDLANDS
PO BOX 15, DEACON ROAD, LINCOLN LN2 4JB
Tel: 01522 522255
Fax: 01522 538229
Fleet Names incl: Stagecoach in Grimsby
Web site: www.stagecoachbus.com
Man Dir: Gary Nolan
Eng Dir: John Taylor
Comm Dir: Dave Skepper
Ops Dir: Richard Kay
Fleet: 501 - 236 double-deck bus, 85 single-deck bus, 15 single-deck coach, 147 midibus, 18 minibus.
Chassis: 269 Alexander Dennis, 4 DAF, 1 Leyland, 49 MAN, 4 MCW, 27 Optare, 9 Scania, 138 Volvo.
Bodies: 315 Alexander Dennis, 1 Caetano, 60 East Lancs, 4 Jonckheere, 4 MCW, 14 Northern Counties, 27 Optare, 62 Plaxton, 14 Wright.
Ops incl: local bus services.
Livery: Stagecoach UK Bus
Ticket System: ERG TP5000.

Notes

NORTH YORKSHIRE, DARLINGTON, MIDDLESBOROUGH, REDCAR & CLEVELAND, YORK

ABBEY COACHWAYS LTD
MEADOWCROFT GARAGE, LOW STREET, CARLTON, GOOLE DN14 9PH
Tel: 01405 860337
Fax: 01405 869433
Dirs: Mrs L E Baker, J Stockdale.
Fleet: 5 single-deck coaches.
Chassis: 1 Scania, 4 Volvo.
Bodies: 1 Jonckheere, 4 Plaxton.
Ops incl: school contracts, private hire
Livery: White/Blue

G. ABBOTT & SONS
AUMANS HOUSE, LEEMING, NORTHALLERTON DL7 9RZ
Tel: 01677 422858/422571
Fax: 01677 424971
Fleet Name: Abbotts of Leeming
Partners: David C Abbott, Clifford G Abbot.
Fleet: 89 - 59 single-deck coach, 1 double-deck coach, 12 midibus, 4 midicoach, 13 minibus.
Chassis: 1 Bedford, 8 DAF, 1 Fiat, 4 Ford Transit, 6 LDV, 15 Leyland, 14 Mercedes, 4 Optare, 16 Scania, 4 Van Hool, 16 Volvo.
Bodies: 2 Caetano, 14 Duple, 1 Euro, 1 Ford, 2 Ikarus, 9 Irizar, 6 LDV, 3 Mercedes, 4 Optare, 20 Plaxton, 3 Reeve Burgess, 6 Sunsundegui, 1 Transbus, 10 Van Hool, 7 Other.
Ops incl: local bus services, school contracts, excursions & tours, private hire, express, continental tours.
Livery: Orange/Cream/Red.

ARRIVA YORKSHIRE LTD
24 BARNSLEY ROAD, WAKEFIELD WF1 5JX
Tel: 01924 231300
Fax: 01924 200106
Man Dir: Nigel Featham
Fin Dir: David Cocker
Fleet: 335 - 137 double-deck bus, 117 single-deck bus, 81 midibus.
Chassis: 31 Alexander Dennis, 104 DAF, 64 Dennis, 13 Optare, 35 VDL, 79 Volvo, 8 Wrightbus.
Bodies: 136 Alexander Dennis, 14 East Lancs, 7 Ikarus, 8 Northern Counties, 71 Optare, 50 Plaxton, 49 Wright.
Ops incl: local bus services.
Livery: Arriva UK Bus.

H ATKINSON & SONS (INGLEBY) LTD
NORWOOD GARAGE, INGLEBY ARNCLIFFE, NORTHALLERTON DL6 3LN
Tel: 01609 882222
Fax: 01609 882476
E-mail: office@atkinsoncoaches.co.uk
Web site: www.atkinsoncoaches.co.uk
Dirs: M T Atkinson, D Atkinson, R Atkinson
Fleet: 11 - 10 single-deck coach, 1 midicoach
Chassis: 2 Bova, 2 Irisbus, 2 MAN, 1 Scania, 2 Setra, 2 Volvo.
Bodies: 2 Beulas, 2 Bova, 1 Indcar, 1 Irizar, 1 Jonckheere, 1 Plaxton, 2 Setra, 1 Van Hool.
Ops Incl: schools contracts, excursions & tours, private hire, continental tours.
Livery: Yellow with Maroon/Gold

BALDRY'S COACHES
LEYLANDII, SELBY ROAD, HOLME-ON-SPALDING-MOOR YO43 4HB
Tel/Fax: 01430 860992
E-mail: baldryscoaches@live.co.uk
Prop: A. Baldry.
Fleet: 5 single-deck coach.
Chassis: Bedford, Ford.
Bodies: Duple, Plaxton.
Ops incl: school contracts, excursions & tours, private hire.
Livery: Two-tone Green.

BARNARD CASTLE COACHES (BURRELLS)
SOUTH VIEW GARAGE, NEWSHAM, RICHMOND DL11 7RA
Tel: 01833 621302 **Fax:** 01833 621431
E-mail: qlburrell@hotmail.com
Dirs: Alan Burrell, Mrs Sandra Burrell
Fleet: 6 - 5 single-deck coach, 1 minibus
Chassis: 1 Leyland, 1 Mercedes, 4 Volvo.
Bodies: 1 Duple, 1 Mercedes, 4 Van Hool.
Ops incl: school contracts, excursions & tours, private hire, express, continental tours.
Livery: Yellow/White

BEECROFT COACHES
POST OFFICE, FEWSTON HG3 1SG
Tel/Fax: 01943 880206
Prop: D. Beecroft.
Fleet: 6 - 3 single-deck coach, 1 midicoach, 2 minibus.
Chassis: 1 DAF, 1 Dodge, 2 Freight Rover, 1 Scania, 1 Volvo.
Bodies: 1 Alexander, 1 Bova, 3 Carlyle, 1 Duple, 1 Plaxton, 1 Van Hool.
Ops incl: local bus services, school contracts, excursions & tours, private hire, continental tours.
Livery: Green/Orange/White.

BIBBY'S OF INGLETON LTD
INGLETON INDUSTRIAL ESTATE, INGLETON LA6 3NU
Tel: 01524 241330 **Fax:** 01524 242216
E-mail: bibbys_travel@talk21.com
Man Dir: P Bibby **Co Sec:** Mrs S Holcroft
Ch Eng: M Stephenson.
Fleet: 24 - 19 single-deck coach, 3 midicoach, 1 minicoach, 1 minibus.
Chassis: 13 DAF, 5 Mercedes, 3 Temsa, 3 VDL.
Bodies: 1 Crest, 2 Esker, 7 Ikarus, 1 Onyx, 3 Temsa, 9 Van Hool.
Ops incl: school contracts, excursions & tours, private hire, continental tours.
Livery: Blue/Grey/Red with white stripes.

BOTTERILLS MINIBUSES
HIGH STREET GARAGE, THORNTON LE DALE, PICKERING YO18 7QW
Tel: 01751 474210
E-mail: botterills@hotmail.com
Web site: www.botterills.org.uk
Fleet: 4 minibus
Chassis/Bodies: 4 Mercedes
Ops incl: local bus services, school contracts, private hire.
Livery: White

EDDIE BROWN TOURS LTD
UNIT 370, THORP ARCH TRADING ESTATE, WETHERBY, YORK LS23 7EG
Tel: 01423 321248
Fax: 01423 326213
Recovery: 07736 692702
E-mail: enquiries@eddiebrowntours.com
Web site: www.eddiebrowntours.com
Dir: Philip Brown **Dir/Co Sec:** Mrs Deirdre Brown **Ch Eng:** John Firth
Ops Man: John Bywater
Fleet: 43 – 3 double-deck bus, 31 single-deck coach, 9 midicoach.
Chassis: 4 Dennis, 2 MAN, 10 Mercedes, 2 Scania, 25 Volvo.
Bodies: 3 East Lancs, 36 Plaxton, 4 Van Hool.
Ops incl: school contracts, excursions & tours, private hire, continental tours.
Livery: White Base with Red/Orange/Maroon

CHARTER COACH LTD
THE CONTROL TOWER OFFICES, THE AIRFIELD, TOCKWITH YO26 7QF
Tel: 01423 359655
Fax: 01423 359459
E-mail: expert.coaches@btinternet.com
Dir: Antoni La Pilusa.

COASTAL AND COUNTRY COACHES
THE GARAGE, FAIRFIELD WAY, WHITBY BUSINESS PARK, WHITBY YO22 4PU
Tel: 01947 602922
Fax: 01947 600830
E-mail: enquiries@coastalandcountry.co.uk
Web site: www.coastalandcountry.co.uk
Chairman: J Vasey **Man Dir:** C Vasey
Ch Eng: A Caley
Fleet: 20 - 13 single-deck coach, 2 open-top bus, 2 midicoach, 1 minibus, 2 midibus, 1 vintage.
Chassis incl: 1 Bedford, 1 Bristol, 1 Dennis, 5 Mercedes, 13 Volvo.
Bodies: 1 Duple, 2 ECW, 1 Jonckheere, 2 Mercedes, 14 Plaxton, 1 Van Hool.
Ops incl: local bus services, school contracts, excursions & tours, private hire.
Livery: White/Blue.
Ticket system: Wayfarer

COLLINS COACHES
CLIFFE SERVICE STATION, YORK ROAD, CLIFFE, SELBY YO8 6NN
Tel: 01757 638591
Fax: 01757 630196
E-mail: collins.coaches@hotmail.co.uk
Web site: www.collinscoaches.co.uk
Prop: Alan Collins.
Fleet: 5 - 4 single-deck coach, 1 midicoach
Chassis: 1 Mercedes, 4 Volvo.
Bodies: 1 Plaxton, 4 Van Hool.
Ops incl: school contracts, private hire.
Livery: White

JOHN DODSWORTH (COACHES) LTD
WETHERBY ROAD, BOROUGHBRIDGE YO5 9HS
Tel: 01423 322236 **Fax:** 01423 324682
Dir: John Dodsworth.

The Little Red Book 2011 - in association with *tbf* Transport Benevolent Fund

Fleet: 13 - 10 single-deck coach, 1 midibus, midicoach, 1 minibus.
Chassis: 4 Mercedes, 4 Setra, 1 Volkswagen, 4 Volvo.
Bodies: 1 Autobus, 1 Concept, 1 Jonckheere, 1 Mercedes, 4 Plaxton, 4 Setra, 1 Volkswagen.
Ops incl: excursions & tours, private hire, continental tours, school contracts.
Livery: Cream/Orange.

FIRST YORK
45 TANNER ROW, YORK YO1 6JP
Tel: 01904 883000
Fax: 01904 883057
Web site: www.firstgroup.com
Dirs: see First West Yorkshire
Fleet: 100 - double-deck bus, single-deck bus, midibus, articulated bus.
Chassis: Volvo, Optare.
Bodies: Alexander, Optare, Wright.
Ops incl: local bus services, school contracts.
Livery: FirstGroup UK Bus.
Ticket System: Wayfarer.

HANDLEY'S COACHES
NORTH ROAD, MIDDLEHAM, LEYBURN DL8 4PJ
Tel: 01969 623216
Fax: 01969 624546
Dirs: Mr M Anderson, Mrs J Anderson, Mrs L Cooke
Fleet: 12 - 5 single-deck coach, 1 midibus, 4 midicoach, 2 minicoach.
Chassis: 1 LDV, 2 Leyland, 6 Mercedes, 1 Scania, 2 Volvo.
Bodies: 1 Autobus, 1 LDV, 2 Mercedes, 1 Optare, 6 Plaxton, 1 Reeve Burgess, 1 Van Hool.
Ops incl: private hire, school contracts.
Livery: White

HARGREAVES COACHES
BRIDGE HOUSE, HEBDEN, SKIPTON BD23 5DE
Tel: 01756 752567
Fax: 01756 753768
E-mail: info@hargreaves.coaches.co.uk
Web site: www.hargreavescoaches.co.uk
Prop: Andrew C Howick
Fleet: 7 - 3 single-deck coach, 1 double-deck coach, 2 midicoach, 1 minibus.
Chassis: 1 DAF, 3 MAN, 2 Mercedes, 1 Neoplan.
Bodies incl: 1 Ayats, 1 LDV, 1 Neoplan, 1 Noge, 2 Plaxton, 1 Van Hool.
Ops incl: local bus services, school contracts, excursions & tours, private hire, continental tours.
Livery: Pink/Cream

HARROGATE COACH TRAVEL LTD
6 ST THOMAS'S WAY, GREEN HAMMERTON, YORK YO26 8BE
Tel: 01423 339600
Fax: 01423 339785
Web site: www.harrogatecoachtravel.com
E-mail: harrogatecoach@aol.com
Man Dir: Craig Temple
Fin Dir: Julie Temple
Fleet: 16 - 4 double-deck bus, 9 single-deck bus, 1 single-deck coach, 2 midibus.
Chassis: 2 Leyland, 1 Mercedes, 1 Optare, 11 Scania, 1 Volvo.
Bodies incl: 2 Northern Counties,

1 Optare, 2 Plaxton, 2 Scania.
Ops incl: local bus services, school contracts, private hire.
Livery: Green/White
Ticket System: Wayfarer

P & D A HOPWOOD
22 MAIN STREET, ASKHAM BRYAN, YORK YO23 3QU
Tel: 01904 707394
Dirs: P Hopwood, D A Hopwood, R C Baker, A J Baker.
Fleet: 2 single-deck coach.
Chassis: 2 Dennis
Bodies: 1 Duple, 1 Plaxton
Ops incl: school contracts, private hire.

INGLEBY'S LUXURY COACHES LTD
24 HOSPITAL FIELDS ROAD, FULFORD ROAD, YORK YO10 4DZ
Tel: 01904 637620
Fax: 01904 612944
Dir: C Ingleby
Fleet Eng: R Atkinson
Ops: A Evans
Fleet: 12 - 8 single-deck coach, 2 midicoach, 2 minibus.
Chassis: 1 Bova, 1 Dennis, 4 Mercedes, 6 Volvo.
Bodies: 1 Bova, 2 Mercedes, 2 Plaxton, 1 Sitcar, 6 Van Hool.
Ops incl: private hire.
Livery: Blue/Cream

J. R. TRAVEL
36 CALF CLOSE, HAXBY, YORK YO3 3NS
Tel: 01904 766233
Partners: R. Flatt, J. Smith.
Fleet: 10 - 3 double-deck bus, 3 single-deck coach, 4 double-deck coach.
Chassis: 3 Daimler, 3 Mercedes, 4 Neoplan.
Bodies: 1 East Lancs, 2 Neoplan, 2 Northern Counties, 2 Plaxton, 3 Taz.
Ops incl: local bus services, school contracts, excursions & tours, private hire, continental tours.
Livery: White with green/red stripes.

KINGS LUXURY COACHES
FERRY ROAD, MIDDLESBROUGH TS2 1PL
Tel: 01642 243687
Fax: 01642 213109
E-mail: enquiries@kingscoaches.co.uk
Web site: www.kingscoaches.co.uk
Prop: Ken King
Fleet: 5 - 2 double-deck bus, 3 single-deck coach.
Chassis: 2 Scania, 3 Setra.
Bodies: 1 Jonckheere, 3 Setra, 1 Van Hool.
Ops incl: private hire, continental tours.
Livery: Cream with Orange/Black.

LEVEN VALLEY COACHES
TILBURY ROAD, SOUTH BANK, MIDDLESBROUGH TS6 6AW
Tel: 01642 722068
Prop: P Thompson
Fleet: 10 midibus
Chassis: 7 Alexander Dennis, 3 Optare
Bodies: 7 Alexander Dennis, 3 Optare
Ops incl: local bus services
Livery: Red/Yellow

PENNINE MOTOR SERVICES
BROUGHTON ROAD, SKIPTON BD23 1TE
Tel: 01756 795515
E-mail: penninemotors@btconnect.com
Web site: www.pennine-bus.co.uk
Fleet: midibus
Chassis: Dennis
Bodies: Plaxton, Wright
Ops incl: local bus services
Livery: Orange/Black

PERRY'S COACHES
RICCAL DRIVE, YORK ROAD INDUSTRIAL PARK, MALTON YO17 6YE
Tel: 01653 690500
Fax: 01653 690800
Web site: www.perrystravel.com
E-mail: info@perrystravel.com
Partners: D J Perry (**Gen Man/Ch Eng**), Mrs A Holtby (**Co Sec**)
Fleet: 19 - 11 single-deck coach, 6 midicoach, 2 minicoach.
Chassis: 1 Dennis, 7 Mercedes, 1 Toyota, 9 Volvo.
Bodies: 1 Caetano, 2 Crest, 1 Jonckheere, 9 Plaxton, 2 Sitcar, 3 Van Hool.
Ops incl: local bus services, school contracts, excursions & tours, private hire, continental tours.
Livery: Red/White.

PROCTERS COACHES (NORTH YORKSHIRE) LTD
TUTIN ROAD, LEEMING BAR INDUSTRIAL ESTATE, LEEMING BAR, NORTHALLERTON DL7 9UJ
Tel: 01677 425203
Fax: 01677 426550
E-mail: enquiries@procterscoaches.co.uk
Web site: www.procterscoaches.co.uk
Man Dir: Kevin J Procter
Fleet Eng: Philip Kenyon
Tran Man: Andrew Fryatt
Fleet: 55 - 18 single-deck coach, 1 double-deck coach, 22 midibus, 1 midicoach, 10 minibus, 3 minicoach.
Chassis incl: DAF, Dennis, Ford Transit, 1 Leyland, 13 Mercedes, 9 Optare, 1 Setra, 1 Van Hool, 23 Volvo.
Bodies incl: Alexander, Autobus, Berkhof, Jonckheere, Mercedes, Optare, Plaxton, Setra, Transbus, Van Hool, Wright.
Ops incl: local bus services, school contracts, excursions & tours, private hire, continental tours.
Livery: White
Ticket System: Wayfarer 3

RELIANCE MOTOR SERVICES
RELIANCE GARAGE, YORK ROAD, SUTTON-ON-FOREST, YORK YO61 1ES
Tel/Fax: 01904 768262
E-mail: reliance.motors@btconnnect.com
Web site: www.reliancemotorservices.co.uk
Props: John H Duff, Margaret Duff
Fleet: 10 - 4 double-deck bus, 6 single-deck bus.
Chassis: 10 Volvo.
Bodies: 1 Alexander Dennis, 2 East Lancs, 7 Wright.
Ops incl: local bus services, school contracts.
Livery: Cream/Green
Ticket System: Wayfarer TGX 150

SCARBOROUGH & DISTRICT
BARRY'S LANE, SCARBOROUGH YO12 4HA
Tel: 01723 500064
Fax: 01723 370064
E-mail: sd@eyms.co.uk
Web site: www.eyms.co.uk
Chairman: P J S Shipp
Fin Dir: P Harrison
Comm Man: R Rackley
Eng & Ops Man: R Graham
Ops incl: local bus services, school contracts, excursions & tours, private hire, express, continental tours.
Livery: Burgundy/Cream
Ticket system: Wayfarer TGX150
A division of East Yorkshire Motor Services Ltd

SHAW'S OF WHITLEY
WHITLEY FARM, SILVER STREET, WHITLEY, GOOLE DN14 0JG
Tel: 01977 661214
Fax: 01977 662036
Recovery: 07802 249878
E-mail: info@shawsofwhitley.co.uk
Web site: www.shawsofwhitley.co.uk
Prop: Mrs Marjorie Shaw
Ops Man: Philip Shaw
Secs: Ann Johnson, Julie Gordge
Fleet: 6 – 1 double-deck bus, 4 single-deck coach, 1 minibus.
Chassis: 1 MAN, 1 Mercedes, 1 Optare, 2 Setra, 1 Volvo.
Bodies incl: 1 Optare, 2 Setra, 1 Van Hool.
Ops incl: school contracts, excursions & tours, private hire, continental tours.
Livery: White with name & logo.

SIESTA INTERNATIONAL HOLIDAYS LTD
NEWPORT SOUTH BUSINESS PARK, LAMPORT STREET, MIDDLESBROUGH TS1 5QL
Tel: 01642 257920
Fax: 01642 219153
Recovery: 07739 679957
E-mail: sales@siestaholidays.co.uk
Web site: www.siestaholidays.co.uk
Chairman: Paul R Herbert
Dirs: C Herbert, J Herbert, J Cofton
Ops Mans: K Keelan, J Potter
Fleet: 9 - 2 single-deck coach, 6 double-deck coach, 1 minibus.
Chassis: 1 Ford Transit, 8 Scania.
Bodies: 8 Berkhof, 1 Ford.
Ops incl: excursions & tours, private hire, continental tours.
Livery: Metallic Blue.

JOHN SMITH & SONS LTD
THE AIRFIELD, DALTON, THIRSK YO7 3HE
Tel/Recovery: 01845 577250
Fax: 01845 577752
E-mail: admin@johnsmithandsons.net
Web site: www.johnsmithandsons.net
Man Dir: Neville Smith
Ops Man: John Smith
Ch Eng: Ivan Smith
Co Sec: Sarah Smith
Fleet: 22 - 1 single-deck bus, 13 single-deck coach, 3 midibus, 3 midicoach, 1 minicoach, 1 vintage coach.
Chassis: 10 DAF, 2 Dennis, 1 Leyland, 1 MAN, 6 Mercedes, 2 Neoplan.
Bodies: 1 Berkhof, 1 Duple, 6 Mercedes, 5 Neoplan, 5 Plaxton, 3 Van Hool.
Ops incl: local bus services, school contracts, excursions & tours, private hire, continental tours.
Livery: Green/Cream/Gold
Ticket system: Wayfarer

STEPHENSONS OF EASINGWOLD LTD
MOOR LANE INDUSTRIAL ESTATE, THOLTHORPE, YORK YO61 1SR
Tel: 01347 838990
Fax: 01347 830189
E-mail: sales@stephensonsofeasingwold.co.uk
Web site: www.stephensonsofeasingwold.co.uk
Chairman: Harry J Stephenson
Man Dir/Co Sec: David A Stephenson
Fleet: 59 - 10 double-deck bus, 9 single-deck bus, 35 single-deck coach, 5 midibus.
Chassis: 4 Alexander Dennis, 1 DAF, 7 Leyland, 5 Mercedes, 10 Scania, 32 Volvo.
Bodies: 1 Jonckheere, 27 Plaxton, 3 Van Hool, 4 Wright, 14 Other.
Ops incl: local bus services, school contracts, private hire.
Livery: Red/Orange/Cream/Gold
Ticket system: Wayfarer

STEVE STOCKDALE COACHES (Validford Ltd t/a)
76 GREEN LANE, SELBY YO8 9AW
Tel: 01757 703549
Fax: 01757 210956
Dirs: S. Stockdale, J. Stockdale, Julie O'Neill **(Co Sec)**
Fleet: 6 - 2 double-deck bus, 4 single-deck coach
Chassis: 2 Bedford, 2 Bristol, 2 Leyland.
Bodies: 2 Alexander, 2 Duple, 2 Plaxton.
Ops incl: local bus services, school contracts, private hire.
Livery: Red/White.
Ticket System: Almex.

TEES VALLEY STAGE CARRIAGE
6 WHITSTABLE GARDENS, REDCAR TS10 4GE
Tel: 01642 498622
E-mail: wayne@stagecarriage.co.uk
Web site: www.eastcleveland.co.uk
Props: W Brown, I Peacock
Fleet: 3 double-deck bus, 4 single-deck coach.
Chassis: 2 Bova, 1 Leyland, 4 Volvo.
Bodies: 2 Bova, 2 East Lancs, 1 Northern Counties, 1 Plaxton, 1 Van Hool
Ops incl: local bus services, school contracts, excursions & tours, private hire.

THORNES INDEPENDENT LTD
THE COACH STATION, HULL ROAD, HEMINGBOROUGH, SELBY YO8 6QG
Tel: 01757 630777
Fax: 01757 630666
Web site: www.thornes.info
E-mail: coaches@thornes.info
Man Dir: P Thornes
Ch Eng: S Cotton
Co Sec: Mrs C Thornes
Ops Man: Ms L J Thornes
Fleet: 17 - 2 double-deck bus, 1 single-deck bus, 8 single-deck coach, 2 midicoach, 4 vintage coaches.
Chassis: 1 Alexander Dennis, 1 Beadle, 1 Bedford, 1 Bristol, 1 DAF, 2 Dennis, 1 Leyland, 2 Mercedes, 1 Seddon, 6 Volvo.
Bodies: 1 Beadle, 1 Duple, 3 East Lancs, 1 Harrington, 1 Optare, 9 Plaxton, 1 Van Hool.
Ops incl: local bus services, school contracts, excursions & tours, private hire, continental tours
Livery: Blue/Grey
Ticket System: Wayfarer Saver

TRANSDEV HARROGATE & DISTRICT
PROSPECT PARK, BROUGHTON WAY, STARBECK, HARROGATE HG2 7NY
Tel: 01423 566061 **Fax:** 01423 885670
E-mail: enquire@harrogateanddistrict.co.uk
Web site: www.harrogatebus.co.uk
Fleet Name: Harrogate & District.
Ch Exec: Martin Gilbert
Fin Dir: Jim Wallace
Fleet: 72 - 17 double-deck bus, 30 single-deck bus, 11 single-deck coach, 14 midibus.
Chassis: 11 Dennis, 61 Volvo.
Bodies: 2 Alexander, 14 Plaxton, 56 Wright.
Ops incl: local bus services, school contracts.
Livery: Red/Cream.
Ticket System: Wayfarer 3
(Part of the Blazefield Group which is owned by Transdev)

TRANSDEV YORK
23 HOSPITAL FIELDS ROAD, FULFORD INDUSTRIAL ESTATE, YORK YO10 4EW
Tel: 01904 655585 **Fax:** 01904 655587
E-mail: info@transdevyork.co.uk
Web sites: www.yorkbus.co.uk
Fleet Names: Transdev York, York City Sightseeing
Chief Exec: Martin Gilbert
Fin Dir: Jim Wallace
Fleet: 25 - 3 double-deck bus, 8 single-deck bus, 7 open-top bus, 7 midibus.
Chassis: 3 Dennis, 4 Leyland, 3 MCW, 13 Optare, 2 Volvo.
Bodies: 3 Alexander, 4 East Lancs, 3 MCW, 13 Optare, 2 Wright.
Ops incl: local bus services, city sightseeing tours, school contracts.
Livery: Red
Ticket System: Almex A90/Wayfarer TGX150
(Part of the Blazefield Group which is owned by Transdev)

TRANSDEV YORKSHIRE COASTLINER
BUS STATION, RAILWAY STREET, MALTON YO17 7NR
Tel: 01653 692556
Fax: 01653 695341
E-mail: enquire@coastliner.co.uk
Web site: www.yorkbus.co.uk
Ops Man: Brian Kneeshaw.
Fleet: 20 double-deck bus.
Chassis: 20 Volvo.
Bodies: 20 Wright.
Ops incl: local bus services.
Livery: Cream/Blue.
Ticket System: Wayfarer 3
(Part of the Blazefield group which is owned by Transdev)

North Yorkshire, Darlington, Middlesborough, Redcar & Cleveland, York

The Little Red Book 2011 - in association with *tbf* Transport Benevolent Fund

WINN BROS
8 MILL HILL CLOSE, BROMPTON,
NORTHALLERTON DL6 2QP
Tel: 01609 773520
Fax: 01609 775234

WISTONIAN COACHES
PLANTATION GARAGE, CAWOOD
ROAD, WISTOW, SELBY YO8 0XB
Tel/Fax: 01757 269303
Partners: John Firth, Gordon Firth.
Fleet: 6 - 4 single-deck coach,
2 midicoach.
Chassis: 1 Bedford, 1 Mercedes,
4 Volvo.
Bodies: 6 Plaxton.

Ops incl: private hire.
Livery: Cream with Red/Orange/Yellow stripes.

YORK PULLMAN
WETHERBY ROAD, RUFFORTH,
YORK YO23 3QA
Tel: 01904 622992 **Fax:** 01904 622993
Recovery: 07753 670742
E-mail: sales@yorkpullmanbus.co.uk
Web site: www.yorkpullmanbus.co.uk
Man Dir: Tom James
Accts Man: Maxine James
Ops Man: Kevin Walker
Chief Eng: Paul Hirst
Bus Service Man: Stuart Fillingham

Fleet: 50 - 10 double-deck bus,
7 single-deck bus, 20 single-deck coach,
7 open-top bus, 4 midicoach, 1 minibus,
1 minicoach.
Chassis: 2 AEC, 2 Bedford, 1 Bristol,
2 DAF, 4 Dennis, 1 Ford, 2 Irisbus,
6 Leyland, 1 Leyland National, 2 MCW,
6 Scania, 1 Toyota, 17 Volvo.
Bodies: 1 Berkhof, 1 Caetano, 3 Duple,
1 ECW, 3 East Lancs, 1 Ikarus, 1 Irizar,
1 Jonckheere, 2 Leyland, 1 Leyland
National, 3 Marshall/MCV, 2 MCW,
1 Northern Counties, 2 Park Royal,
17 Plaxton, 6 Van Hool, 1 Wright.
Ops incl: local bus services, school contracts, private hire, continental tours.
Livery: Cream/Yellow/Maroon
Ticket system: Wayfarer 3

NORTHAMPTONSHIRE

GEOFF AMOS COACHES LTD
THE COACH STATION, WOODFORD
ROAD, EYDON, DAVENTRY NN11 3PL
Tel: 01327 260522
Fax: 01327 262883
Recovery: 01327 260522
E-mail: sales@geoffamos.co.uk
Web site: www.geoffamos.co.uk
Dir: Shirley Smith (**Fin**), Brian Amos
(**Trans Man**) **Ops Man:** Brian Ellard
Ch Eng: Kevin Wilson
Fleet: 26 - 10 double-deck bus,
8 single-deck bus, 7 single-deck coach,
1 midicoach
Chassis: 1 Dennis, 10 Leyland, 4 MAN,
1 Mercedes, 1 Optare, 7 Volvo.
Bodies: 1 Caetano, 4 ECW,
2 Jonckheere, 5 MCV, 6 Northern
Counties, 1 Optare, 1 Plaxton,
4 Sunsundegui.
Ops incl: local bus services, school contracts, excursions & tours, private hire, continental tours.
Livery: Buses: Yellow; Coaches: Metallic
Ticket system: Almex

L F BOWEN LTD t/a JEFFS COACHES LTD
STATION ROAD, HELMDON,
BRACKLEY NN13 5QT
Tel: 01295 768292
Fax: 01295 760365
E-mail: admin@jeffscoaches.com
Web site: www.jeffscoaches.com
Chairman & Ch Exec: Kevin Lower
Man Dir (Coaching): R Lyng
Group Ops Man: N G Tetley
Group Eng Man: D Hoy
Fin Dir: R Graham
Man Dir (Retail): N Stones
Property Dir: N Ellis
Dirs: A H Moseley, C J Padbury, K G York
Fleet: 58 - 8 double-deck bus,
1 single-deck bus, 47 single-deck coach,
2 midicoach.
Chassis: 4 Dennis, 6 Iveco, 8 Leyland,
2 Toyota, 38 Volvo.
Bodies: 6 Beulas, 23 Caetano,
8 Jonckheere, 8 Leyland, 9 Plaxton,
2 Van Hool, 2 other.
Ops incl: school contracts, excursions & tours.
Livery: White /Red/Green/Silver

L F BOWEN LTD t/a YORKS COACHES
SHORT LANE, COGENHOE,
NORTHAMPTON NN7 1LE
Tel: 01604 890210
Fax: 01604 891153
E-mail: yorksco@yorks-travel.co.uk
Web site: www.yorkscoaches.com
Chairman & Ch Exec: Kevin Lower
Man Dir (Coaching): R Lyng
Group Ops Man: N G Tetley
Group Eng Man: D Hoy
Fin Dir: R Graham **Man Dir (Retail):**
N Stones **Property Dir:** N Ellis
Dirs: A H Moseley, C J Padbury, K G York
Fleet: 28 – 3 double-deck bus,
23 single-deck coach, 2 midicoach.
Chassis incl: 2 Dennis, 2 Iveco, 5 MAN,
2 Scania, 2 Setra, 2 Toyota, 10 Volvo.
Bodies incl: 2 Beulas, 2 Caetano,
2 Irizar, 2 Marcopolo, 5 Noge, 9 Plaxton,
2 Setra, 1 Van Hool.
Ops incl: local bus services, excursions & tours, school contracts, private hire, express, continental tours.
Livery: Silver
Ticket System: Almex

COUNTRY LION (NORTHAMPTON) LTD
87 ST JAMES MILL ROAD,
ST JAMES BUSINESS PARK,
NORTHAMPTON NN5 5JP
Tel: 01604 754566
Fax: 01604 759770
Web site: www.countrylion.co.uk
Dirs: J S F Bull, A J Bull
Fleet: 38 – 9 double-deck bus,
2 single-deck bus, 23 single-deck coach,
3 midicoach, 1 minibus.
Chassis: Bristol, Dennis, Ford, Iveco,
Leyland, Mercedes, Scania, Toyota,
Volvo.
Bodies: Alexander, Beulas, Caetano,
Duple, East Lancs, Irizar, Marshall,
Optare, Plaxton, Wadham Stringer
Ops incl: local bus services, school contracts, excursions & tours, continental tours, private hire.

FIRST MIDLANDS
ST JAMES' ROAD, NORTHAMPTON
NN5 5JD
Tel: 01604 751431
Fax: 01604 590522
Fleet Name: First Northampton
Man Dir: Ken Poole
Fin Dir: A Bhimani
Fleet: 52 - 11 double-deck bus,
31 single-deck bus, 1 single-deck coach,
1 articulated bus, 8 midibus.
Chassis: 4 BMC, 8 Optare, 1 Scania,
39 Volvo.
Bodies: 8 Alexander, 4 BMC,
1 East Lancs, 1 Irizar, 8 Optare,
30 Wright.
Ops incl: local bus services, school contracts, private hire.
Livery: FirstGroup UK Bus
Ticket System: Wayfarer 3

GOODE COACHES
47 BURFORD AVENUE,
BOOTHVILLE, NORTHAMPTON
NN3 6AF
Tel: 01604 862700
Prop: David Goode
Tran Man: Andrew Wall
Fleet: 5 – 4 single-deck coach,
1 midicoach.
Ops incl: local bus services, school contracts, private hire.
Livery: Cream/Maroon.

HAMILTON'S COACHES
3 FOX STREET, ROTHWELL,
KETTERING NN14 6AN
Tel: 01536 710344
Fax: 01536 712244
Recovery: 07887 945564
E-mail: hamiltonscoaches@googlemail.com
Prop: Minesh Uka.
Fleet: 22 - 11 double-deck bus,
9 single-deck coach, 1 double-deck coach, 1 midicoach.
Chassis: 8 MCW, 1 Mercedes, 13 Volvo.
Bodies: 1 Alexander Dennis,
1 Jonckheere, 8 MCW, 2 Northern
Counties, 10 Plaxton.
Ops incl: local bus services, school contracts, excursions & tours, private hire, continental tours.
Livery: White with Yellow, Orange & Red stripes

J.C.S COACHES
2 THE JAMB, CORBY
NN17 1AY
Tel: 01536 202660
Fax: 01536 406299
E-mail: info@jambtravel.co.uk
Web site: www.jambtravel.co.uk
Props: Jackie Burton, Michael Burton
Fleet: 6 - 5 single-deck coach,
1 midicoach.
Chassis: 2 Bova, 3 DAF, 1 Mercedes.
Bodies: 2 Bova, 1 Caetano, 1 Ikarus,
1 Marshall, 1 Van Hool.
Ops incl: school contracts, excursions & tours, private hire.
Livery: Silver

JUDGE'S MINI COACHES
24 STALBRIDGE WALK,
CORBY NN18 0DT
Tel: 01536 200317
Fax: 01536 394387
Prop: J. D. Judge
Fleet: single-deck coach, midibus, minibus.
Ops incl: local bus services, school contracts, excursions & tours, private hire
Business sold to the Centrebus Group as this edition of LRB goes to press

R S LAWMAN COACHES LTD
7 ROBINSON WAY, KETTERING
NN16 8PT
Tel: 01536 517664
Fax: 01536 513474
Web site: www.lawmanscoaches.co.uk
Fleet incl: single-deck coach, minibus
Chassis incl: Bova, LDV, Mercedes, Volvo
Livery: White with Green/Orange

MERIDIAN BUS
23 MILLBROOK CLOSE, ST JAMES,
NORTHAMPTON NN5 5JF
Tel: 01604 590480
Web site: www.meridianbus.co.uk
Fleet incl: midibus, minibus
Ops incl: local bus services
Livery: Red/Blue/White

R B TRAVEL
ISHAM ROAD, PYTCHLEY NN4 1EW
Prop: Roger Bull
Tel/Fax: 01536 791066
Fleet: 10 single-deck coach
Chassis: 6 DAF, 4 MAN.
Bodies: 2 Plaxton, 8 Van Hool.

RODGER'S COACHES LTD
102 KETTERING ROAD,
WELDON NN17 3JG
Tel: 01536 200500 **Fax:** 01536 407407
Recovery: 01536 200500
E-mail: rodgerscoaches@hotmail.com
Props: James Rodger, Linda Rodger
Fleet: 20 - 10 double-deck bus, 8 single-deck coach, 2 double-deck coach.
Ops incl: school contracts.
Livery: White/Red

SOUL BROTHERS
See Buckinghamshire

STAGECOACH MIDLANDS
ROTHERSTHORPE AVENUE,
NORTHAMPTON NN4 8UT
Tel/Fax: 01604 662260
E-mail: eastenquiries@stagecoachbus.com
Web site: www.stagecoachbus.com
Regional Man Dir: Bob Montgomery
Man Dir: Steve Burd **Ops Dir:** Liz Esnouf
Eng Dir: Keith Dyball
Ops incl: local bus services, school contracts, private hire, express.
Livery: Stagecoach UK Bus
Ticket System: ERG

NORTHUMBERLAND

ADAMSON'S COACHES
8 PORLOCK COURT, NORTHBURN
CHASE, CRAMLINGTON NE23 3TT
Tel/Fax: 01670 734050
Recovery: 07721 633351
E-mail: adamsonscoaches@btconnect.com
Web site: www.adamsonscoaches.co.uk
Prop: Allen Mullen
Ch Eng: Paul Mullen
Co Sec: Mrs Wendy Mullen
Fleet: 3 single-deck coach
Chassis: 3 DAF
Bodies: 3 Van Hool
Ops incl: excursions & tours, private hire
Livery: White/Rosewood

ARRIVA NORTH EAST
See Tyne & Wear

HENRY COOPER
See Tyne & Wear

COOPER'S TOURMASTER LTD
RIVERSIDE, KITTYBREWSTER
BRIDGE, BEDLINGTON
NE22 7BS
Tel: 01670 824900
Fax: 01670 824800
E-mail: helen@cooperstourmaster.co.uk
Web site: www.cooperstourmaster.co.uk
Fleet incl: double-deck bus, single-deck bus, single-deck coach, minibus
Ops incl: school contracts, private hire, excursions & tours
Livery: Blue & Orange

CRAIGGS TRAVEL EUROPEAN
1 CENTRAL AVENUE, AMBLE,
MORPETH NE65 0NQ
Tel/Fax: 01665 710614
E-mail: classicalholiday@tiscali.co.uk
Web site: www.coachhireandholidays.co.uk
Props: Ian Craiggs, Joan Craiggs, Lawrence Craiggs
Fleet: 4 single-deck coach, 1 minibus.
Chassis: 1 DAF, 1 LDV, 2 Setra, 1 Volvo.
Bodies: 1 LDV, 1 Plaxton, 2 Setra, 1 Van Hool.

Ops incl: excursions & tours, private hire, continental tours.
Livery: Red

DREADNOUGHT COACHES
198 ALLERBURN LEA,
ALNWICK NE66 2QR
Tel: 01665 603022
Web site: www.dreadnoughtcoaches.co.uk
Fleet: 9 – 7 double-deck bus, 2 single-deck bus
Props: P Gilroy, Mrs C Gilroy
Ops incl: local bus services, park & ride, private hire
Livery: Red & Cream

GLEN VALLEY TOURS LTD
STATION ROAD, WOOLER
NE71 6SP
Tel: 01668 281578
Fax: 01668 281169
E-mail: enquiries@glenvalley.co.uk
Web site: www.glenvalley.co.uk
Ops incl: local bus services, school contracts, private hire, excursions & tours
Livery: Green & White

GO NORTH EAST
See Tyne & Wear.

HILLARYS COACHES
20 CASTLE VIEW, PRUDHOE
NE42 6NG
Tel/Fax: 01661 832560
Props: Lawrence Hillary
Fleet: 5 - 3 single-deck bus, 1 midicoach, 1 minibus.
Chassis: 1 Ford, 1 MAN, 1 Mercedes, 1 Toyota, 1 Volkswagen.
Ops incl: school contracts, excursions & tours, private hire.

LONGSTAFF'S COACHES
UNIT 107, COQUET ENTERPRISE
PARK, AMBLE, MORPETH
NE65 0PE
Tel: 01665 713300
Fax: 01665 710987
E-mail: fred@longstaffcoaches.co.uk
Web site: www.longstaffcoaches.co.uk

Dirs: Frederick Longstaff, Edward Longstaff
Fleet: 7 single-deck coach.
Chassis: Neoplan, Volvo.
Bodies: Jonckheere, Mercedes, Neoplan, Plaxton, Van Hool.
Ops incl: school contracts, excursions & tours, private hire, continental tours.
Livery: White.

PERRYMAN'S BUSES
NORTH ROAD INDUSTRIAL ESTATE,
BERWICK UPON TWEED TD15 1TX
Tel: 01289 308719
Fax: 01289 309970
Web site: www.perrymansbuses.com
Dirs: R J Perryman L M Perryman
Fleet: 35 - 20 single deck bus, 5 single-deck coach, 6 midicoach, 4 minibus.
Chassis: MAN, Mercedes, Optare, Renault, Volvo.
Bodies: Alexander Dennis, MCV, Optare, Plaxton.
Ops Inc: Local bus services, school contracts, private hire
Ticket System: Wayfarer.
Livery: White with Red/Blue.

ROTHBURY MOTORS
HAWTHORN CLOSE, LIONHEART
ENTERPRISE PARK,
ALNWICK NE66 2HT
Tel: 01665 606616
E-mail: rothburymotors@btconnect.com
Web site: www.rothburymotors.co.uk
Ops incl: local bus services, school contracts, private hire, excursions & tours
Livery: White with Blue Lettering

ROWELL COACHES
3B DUKES WAY, PRUDHOE
NE42 6PQ
Tel: 01661 832316
Fax: 01661 834485
E-mail: sales@rowellcoaches.co.uk
Web site: www.rowellcoaches.co.uk
Dirs: Mr S Gardiner, Mrs B Gardiner
Fleet: 7 single-deck coach
Chassis: 6 Bova, 1 Leyland.
Ops incl: school contracts, excursions & tours, private hire.
Livery: White

Symbol	Meaning	Symbol	Meaning	Symbol	Meaning
♿	Vehicle suitable for disabled	🔒	Seat belt-fitted Vehicle	R24	24 hour recovery service
T	Toilet-drop facilities available	🍴	Coach(es) with galley facilities		Replacement vehicle available
R	Recovery service available	❄	Air-conditioned vehicle(s)		Vintage Coach(es) available
	Open top vehicle(s)	🚻	Coaches with toilet facilities		

SERENE TRAVEL
♿🍴🔒▭R T
86A FRONT STREET EAST,
BEDLINGTON NE22 5AB
Tel: 01670 829636
Fax: 01670 827961
Web site: www.yell.co.uk/sites/serenetravel
Man Dir: Mrs C. E. Fielding
Fleet Eng: G. J. Balsdon
Co Sec: D. A. Fielding
Fleet: 17 - 7 single-deck bus, 6 single-deck coach, 2 midicoach, 2 minibus
Chassis: 1 AEC, 2 Bedford, 1 Ford Transit, 1 Iveco, 3 Leyland, 6 Leyland National, 2 MCW, 1 Volvo.
Bodies: 2 Carlyle, 2 Duple, 6 Leyland National, 2 Optare, 4 Plaxton, 1 Burlingham.
Ops incl: local bus services, school contracts, excursions & tours, private hire, express.
Livery: Blue/Cream.
Ticket System: Wayfarer II.

HOWARD SNAITH COACHES
THE COACH HOUSE, BRIERLEY GARDENS, OTTERBURN NE19 1HB
Tel: 01830 520609
E-mail: howardsnaith@btconnect.com
Web site: www.howardsnaith.co.uk
Ops incl: local bus services, school contracts, private hire, excursions & tours, continental tours
Livery: White with Blue/Red

STAGECOACH NORTH EAST
See Tyne & Wear

TRAVELSURE
♿🔒❄🚻
STATION ROAD, BELFORD NE70 7DT
Tel: 01668 219291
Fax: 01668 213947
E-mail: travelsure@travelsure.co.uk
Web site: www.travelsure.co.uk
Props: Barrie Patterson, Karen Patterson
Fleet: 24 - 6 single-deck bus, 12 single-deck coach, 3 midicoach, 1 minibus, 2 minicoach.
Chassis: 2 Alexander Dennis, 1 Bova, 2 DAF, 3 Dennis, 2 Irisbus, 2 Iveco, 1 LDV, 3 Mercedes, 1 Optare, 1 Renault, 1 Scania, 3 Setra, 2 Transbus.
Bodies: 2 Alexander Dennis, 4 Beulas, 1 Bova, 1 Caetano, 1 Irizar, 1 Mellor, 2 Optare, 2 Plaxton, 1 Reeve Burgess, 1 Sitcar, 3 Setra, 2 Transbus, 1 Van Hool, 2 Other.
Ops incl: local bus services, school contracts, excursions & tours, private hire.
Livery: Blue.
Ticket System: Wayfarer

TYNEDALE GROUP TRAVEL
♿🍴🔒❄🚻
TOWNFOOT GARAGE, HALTWHISTLE NE49 0EJ
Tel: 01434 322944 **Fax:** 01434 322955
E-mail: admin@tynedalegrouptravel.co.uk
Web site: www.tynedalegrouptravel.co.uk
Partner: Andy Sinclair.
Fleet: 4 - 3 single-deck coach, 1 minicoach.
Chassis: 1 Mercedes, 3 Neoplan.
Bodies: 3 Neoplan, 1 Other.
Ops incl: local bus services, school contracts, excursions & tours, private hire, continental tours.

TYNE VALLEY COACHES LTD
🔒❄
ACOMB, HEXHAM NE46 4QT
Tel: 01434 602217
Fax: 01434 604150
Dir: Mrs K M Weir
Fleet: 20 - 2 single-deck bus, 18 single-deck coach.
Chassis: 2 DAF, 13 Leyland, 5 Volvo.
Bodies: 3 Duple, 1 East Lancs, 1 Optare, 14 Plaxton, 1 Van Hool.
Ops incl: local bus services, school contracts, private hire
Livery: Blue/Silver
Ticket System: AES

NOTTINGHAMSHIRE, NOTTINGHAM

BAILEY'S COACHES LTD
♿🔒T
EEL HOLE FARM, LONG LANE, WATNALL NG16 1HY
Tel: 0115 968 0141
Fax: 0115 968 1101.
Dirs: T. Bailey **(Gen Man & Traf Man),** Mrs J. Bailey **(Sec) Ch Eng:** G. Payne.
Fleet: 10 - 2 double-deck bus, 6 single-deck coach 2 double-deck coach.
Chassis: Bristol, DAF, Volvo.
Ops incl: local bus services, school contracts, excursions & tours, private hire, continental tours.
Livery: White with Yellow/Brown/Orange stripes.

BELLAMY COACHES LTD
ARTIC HOUSE, GLAISDALE DRIVE WEST, BILBOROUGH, NOTTINGHAM NG8 4GY
Tel: 0115 928 8833
Fax: 0115 928 4500
E-mail: bellamycoaches@btconnect.com
Web site: www.bellamy-holidays.co.uk
Ops incl: school contracts, excursions & tours, private hire, express.
Livery: Yellow.

BUTLER BROTHERS COACHES
♿🔒❄🚻
60 VERNON ROAD, KIRKBY IN ASHFIELD NG17 8ED
Tel: 01623 753260 **Fax:** 01623 754581
E-mail: butlerscoaches@btconnect.com
Dirs: Robert Butler, Anita Butler, James Butler.

Fleet: 9 - 1 double-deck bus, 7 single-deck coach, 1 midicoach.
Chassis: 2 DAF, 3 Dennis, 1 Leyland, 2 MAN, 1 Volvo.
Bodies: 1 Berkhof, 2 Caetano, 1 East Lancs, 2 Plaxton, 3 Van Hool.
Ops incl: school contracts, excursions & tours, private hire, continental tours.
Livery: Dual Blue
Ticket System: Wayfarer

DUNN MOTOR TRACTION (YOUR BUS)
See Derbyshire

GILL'S TRAVEL
106 ILKESTON ROAD, TROWELL, NOTTINGHAM NG9 3PX
Tel: 0115 944 1400
Fleet incl: single-deck bus
Ops incl: local bus services, school contracts
Livery: Yellow

GOSPEL'S COACHES
🔒❄🚻
27 ASCOT DRIVE, HUCKNALL NG15 6JA
Tel: 0115 963 3894
Dirs: T Gospel, G Gospel, G T Gospel
Fleet: 4 - 2 double-deck bus, 2 single-deck coach.
Chassis: 2 Leyland, 2 Volvo.
Bodies: 1 Alexander, 1 Northern Counties, 2 Plaxton.
Ops incl: excursions & tours, private hire, school contracts.
Livery: White/Blue.

HENSHAWS COACHES
♿🔒❄
57 PYE HILL ROAD, JACKSDALE NG16 5LR
Tel: 01773 607909
Prop: Paul Henshaw
Fleet: 5 - 4 single-deck coach, 1 midicoach
Chassis: 1 BMC, 1 Bova, 1 DAF, 2 Mercedes
Bodies: 1 BMC, 1 Bova, 2 Mercedes, 1 Van Hool.
Ops incl: excursions & tours, private hire, school contracts, continental tours.
Livery: White/Orange

JOHNSON BROS TOURS LTD
♿🔒♿🍴▭❄R R24🚻T
GREEN ACRES, GREEN LANE, HODTHORPE, WORKSOP S80 4XR
Tel: 01909 720337 / 721847
Fax: 01909 722886
Recovery: 07774 005863
E-mail: lee@johnsonstours.co.uk
Web site: www.johnsonstours.co.uk
Dirs: Tony Johnson, Lee Johnson, Antony Johnson, Scott Johnson, Sheila Johnson **(Co Sec)**
Fleet: 116 - 70 double-deck bus, 2 single-deck bus, 35 single-deck coach, 3 double-deck coach, 3 midibus, 2 midicoach, 1 minicoach.
Chassis: 1 Ayats, 2 Bova, 50 Bristol, 1 DAF, 1 Ford Transit, 10 Iveco, 10 MCW, 7 Neoplan, 2 Optare, 10 Scania, 6 Transbus, 4 VDL, 10 Volvo.
Bodies: Ayats, Beulas, Berkhof, Bova, Irizar, Jonckheere, Neoplan, Northern

Counties, Optare, Plaxton, Scania, Setra, Sunsundegui, Transbus, Van Hool, Volvo.
Ops incl: local bus services, school contracts, excursions & tours, private hire, express, continental tours.
Livery: Blue with Stars
Ticket System: Almex
See also Redfern Travel Ltd

K & S COACHES

21 CLIFTON GROVE, MANSFIELD NG18 4HY
Tel/Fax: 01623 656768
Prop: K. & Sue Burnside.
Fleet: 4 - 1 midicoach, 3 minicoach.
Chassis/Bodies: Ford Transit, Mercedes, Renault, Talbot.
Ops incl: school contracts, excursions & tours, private hire.
Livery: White/Red/Grey.

KETTLEWELL (RETFORD) LTD

GROVE STREET, RETFORD DN22 6LA
Tel: 01777 860360
Fax: 01777 710351
E-mail: paulkettlewell@btconnect.com
Web site: www.kettlewellretfordltd.co.uk
Man Dir: P C Kettlewell
Dirs: A S Kettlewell, C C Kettlewell
Senior Officer: M Burton
Ops Man: T Bradley
Fleet: 17 - 1 double-deck coach, 12 single-deck coach, 3 double-deck coach, 1 minicoach.
Chassis: 1 Leyland, 1 MAN, 1 Mercedes, 3 Neoplan, 10 Scania, 1 Volvo.
Bodies: 1 East Lancs, 10 Irizar, 1 Jonckheere, 1 Mercedes, 3 Neoplan, 1 Plaxton.
Ops incl: local bus services, school contracts, excursions & tours, private hire, continental tours.
Livery: White
Ticket System: Wayfarer

McEWENS TRAVEL

MILLENNIUM BUSINESS PARK, CHESTERFIELD ROAD, MANSFIELD NG19 7JX
Tel: 01623 646733
Fax: 01623 621366
E-mail: mcewentravel@hotmail.com
Web site: www.mcewentravel.co.uk
Dirs: J McEwen, Mrs T McEwen
Ops Man: A Poyser **Comm Man:** C Elkin
Fleet: 20 – 8 double-deck bus, 10 single-deck coach, 1 midicoach, 1 minibus.
Chassis incl: 1 Bedford, 1 Irisbus, 1 LDV, 8 Leyland, 1 MAN.
Bodies: 1 Beulas, 1 Berkhof, 1 East Lancs, 1 Irizar, 2 Jonckheere, 1 LDV, 1 Marcopolo, 7 Northern Counties, 5 Plaxton.
Ops incl: school contracts, excursions & tours, private hire, continental tours.
Livery: Red & White

MARSHALLS OF SUTTON-ON-TRENT LTD

11 MAIN STREET, SUTTON-ON-TRENT NG23 6PF
Tel: 01636 821138
Fax: 01636 822227
E-mail: office@marshallscoaches.co.uk
Web site: www.marshallscoaches.co.uk
Man Dir: John Marshall
Eng Dir: Paul Marshall
Financial Dir: Sally Sloan

Ops Man: Kenneth Tagg
Fleet: 27 - 9 double-deck bus, 8 single-deck bus, 6 single-deck coach, 3 midicoach.
Chassis: 2 Dennis, 1 Iveco, 3 Leyland, 1 MAN, 1 Mercedes, 1 Neoplan, 7 Optare, 11 Volvo.
Bodies: 6 Alexander Dennis, 1 Berkhof, 2 East Lancs, 1 Indcar, 1 Mercedes, 1 Neoplan, 7 Optare, 6 Plaxton, 1 Transbus, 1 Wright.
Ops incl: local bus services, school contracts, excursions & tours, private hire, continental tours.
Livery: Blue/Cream.
Ticket System: Wayfarer

C. W. MOXON LTD

MALTBY ROAD, OLDCOTES, WORKSOP S81 8JN
Tel: 01909 730345
Fax: 01909 733670
Web site: www.moxons-tours.co.uk
Fleet Name: Moxons Coaches.
Dirs: Mrs L. Marlow, Mrs M. Moxon
Co Sec: Mrs J. Holder
Ch Eng: M. Marlow.
Fleet: 15 - 3 double-deck bus, 12 single-deck coach.
Chassis: 2 Bedford, 3 Bristol, 7 DAF, 2 Leyland, 1 Iveco.
Bodies: 2 Bova, 1 Duple, 1 EOS, 3 MCW, 5 Plaxton, 3 Van Hool.
Ops incl: excursions & tours, private hire, continental tours, school contracts.
Livery: Cream/Red.

NOTTINGHAM CITY TRANSPORT

LOWER PARLIAMENT STREET, NOTTINGHAM NG1 1GG
Tel: 0115 950 5745
Fax: 0115 950 4425
E-mail: shiela.swift@nctx.co.uk, info@nctx.co.uk
Web site: www.nctx.co.uk
Chairman: Brian Parbutt
Man Dir: Mark Fowles
Eng Dir: Barry Baxter
Fin Dir/Co Sec: Rob Hicklin
Marketing & Communications Dir: Nicola Tidy **Comm Man:** Barrie Burch
Fleet Eng: Farrell Smith

Fleet: 335 - 161 double-deck bus, 74 single-deck bus, 5 articulated bus, 95 midibus.
Chassis: 54 Dennis, 108 Optare, 149 Scania, 23 Volvo.
Bodies: 114 East Lancs, 51 Scania, 54 Transbus, 5 Wright.
Ops incl: local bus services
Livery: Multi-Branded
Ticket system: Almex

NOTTINGHAM EXPRESS TRANSIT

LAWRENCE HOUSE, TALBOT STREET, NOTTINGHAM NG1 5NT
Tel: 0115 915 6600
Web site: www.thetram.net, www.nottinghamcity.gov.uk, www.nottinghamexpresstransitco.uk, www.netphasetwo.com
Concession Co: Arrow Light Rail (Bombardier, Carillion, Transdev, Nottingham City Transport, Innisfree, CDC Projects)
Commercial Manager: Colin Lea
Fleet: 15 tram
Chassis/bodies: Bombardier
Ops incl: tram service
Livery: Green/White

PREMIERE TRAVEL LTD

TRENT WHARF, MEADOW LANE, NOTTINGHAM NG2 3HR
Tel: 0115 985 1111
Fax: 0115 986 3366
E-mail: sales@premiere-travel.co.uk
Web sites: www.premiere-travel.co.uk, www.local-bus.co.uk
Ops incl: local bus services, private hire, school contracts.
Livery: Red/Silver

REDFERN TRAVEL LTD

THE SIDINGS, DEBDALE LANE, MANSFIELD WOODHOUSE, MANSFIELD NG19 7FE
Tel: 01623 627653
Fax: 01909 625787
Recovery: 07774 005863
E-mail: lee@johnsonstours.co.uk
Web site: www.johnsonstours.co.uk
Dirs: Tony Johnson, Sheila Johnson (Co

Sec), Anthony Johnson, Lee Johnson, Scott Johnson
Fleet: 67 – 40 double-deck bus, 1 single-deck bus, 20 single-deck coach, 2 double-deck coach, 1 midibus, 1 midicoach, 1 minibus, 1 minicoach.
Chassis: 1 Ayats, 2 Bova, 20 Bristol, 2 DAF, 3 Irisbus, 1 Iveco, 1 Mercedes, 4 Neoplan, 5 Scania, 2 Setra, 2 Toyota, 10 Transbus, 4 Volvo.
Bodies incl: Ayats, Beulas, Berkhof, Bova, ECW, Irizar, Jonckheere, MCW, Neoplan, Northern Counties, Optare, Sitcar, Scania, Setra, Sunsundegui, Volvo.
Ops incl: local bus services, excursions & tours, private hire, express, continental tours, school contracts.
Livery: Green/Stars
(Subsidiary of Johnson Bros Tours Ltd)

SHARPE & SONS (NOTTINGHAM) LTD
UNIT 10, CANALSIDE INDUSTRIAL PARK, CROPWELL BISHOP, NOTTINGHAM NG12 3BE
Tel: 0115 989 4466
Fax: 0115 989 4666
E-mail: enquiries@sharpesofnottingham.com
Web site: www.sharpesofnottingham.com
Man Dir: Trevor Sharpe
Ops Dir: James Sharpe
Dirs: Russell Sharpe, Neil Sharpe
Fin Dir: Simon Sharpe
Fleet: 34 - 12 double-deck bus, 4 single-deck bus, 15 single-deck coach, 1 double-deck coach, 2 minibus.
Chassis: 1 DAF, 2 Ford Transit, 4 Leyland, 1 MAN, 7 MCW, 19 Volvo.
Bodies incl: 4 Alexander Dennis, 3 Berkhof, 1 Bova, 12 Van Hool
Ops incl: school contracts, private hire, continental tours, excursions & tours.
Livery: Silver/Two Tone Blue
Ticket System: Wayfarer

SILVERDALE TOURS LTD
LITTLE TENNIS STREET SOUTH, NOTTINGHAM NG2 4EU
Tel: 0115 912 1000
Fax: 0115 912 1558
E-mail: info@silverdaletours.co.uk
Web site: www.silverdaletours.co.uk
Dirs: Shaun Doherty, John Doherty
Fleet: 39 - 6 double-deck bus, 3 single-deck bus, 26 single-deck coach, 2 double-deck coach, 2 midicoach
Chassis: 2 Ayats, 2 DAF, 3 Leyland National, 2 Mercedes, 30 Volvo.
Bodies: 5 Beulas, 19 Caetano, 3 Jonckheere, 3 Leyland National, 8 Plaxton, 1 Van Hool.
Ops incl: local bus services, private hire, express, school contracts, continental tours.
Livery: Yellow/Red/Black

SKILLS MOTOR COACHES LTD
BELGRAVE ROAD, BULWELL, NOTTINGHAM NG6 8LY
Tel: 0115 977 0080
Fax: 0115 977 7439
E-mail: pete.hallam@skillsholidays.co.uk
Web site: www.skillsholidays.co.uk
Man Dir: Nigel Skill
Fin Dir: Simon Skill
Ops Dir: Pete Hallam
Fleet: 48 - 14 double-deck bus,

30 single-deck coach, 4 midicoach.
Chassis: 1 Bova, 2 MAN, 4 Mercedes, 1 Optare, 16 Setra, 25 Volvo.
Bodies: 9 Alexander, 1 Bova, 5 East Lancs, 7 Jonckheere, 1 Optare, 3 Plaxton, 16 Setra, 6 Van Hool.
Ops incl: school contracts, excursions & tours, private hire, continental tours.
Livery: Green

STAGECOACH EAST MIDLANDS
PO BOX 15, DEACON ROAD, LINCOLN LN2 4JB
Tel: 01522 522255
Fax: 01522 538229
Fleet Names incl: Stagecoach in Bassetlaw
Web site: www.stagecoachbus.com
Man Dir: Gary Nolan
Eng Dir: John Taylor
Comm Dir: Dave Skepper
Ops Dir: Richard Kay
Fleet: 501 - 236 double-deck bus, 85 single-deck bus, 15 single-deck coach, 147 midibus, 18 minibus.
Chassis: 269 Alexander Dennis, 4 DAF, 1 Leyland, 49 MAN, 4 MCW, 27 Optare, 9 Scania, 138 Volvo.
Bodies: 315 Alexander Dennis, 1 Caetano, 60 East Lancs, 4 Jonckheere, 4 MCW, 14 Northern Counties, 27 Optare, 62 Plaxton, 14 Wright.
Ops incl: local bus services.
Livery: Stagecoach UK Bus
Ticket System: ERG TP5000.

TIGER EUROPEAN
UNIT E PRIVATE ROAD, NO.4 COLWICK INDUSTRIAL ESTATE, NOTTINGHAM NG2 2JT
Tel: 01159 404040
Fax: 01159 404030
E-mail: info@tiger-european.com
Web site: www.tiger-european.co.uk.
Dirs: Mr G Golaz, Mrs B Golaz.
Fleet: 15 - 2 double-deck bus, 3 single-deck bus, 3 single-deck coach, 1 double-deck coach, 1 midicoach, 5 minibus
Chassis: 4 Ford, 1 LDV, 3 Leyland, 1 MAN, 1 MCW, 2 Mercedes, 3 Volvo.
Bodies: 1 Caetano, 2 Jonckheere, 2 Leyland, 1 Marshall/MCV, 1 Plaxton, 8 Other.
Ops incl: School contracts, private hire

TRANSIT EXPRESS TRAVEL
UNIT 7, EVANS BUSINESS PARK, RADMARSH ROAD, LENTON, NOTTINGHAM NG7 2GN
Tel: 0115 970 2900
Fax: 0115 970 5515
E-mail: garycrosby@hotmail.com
Prop: Gary M Crosby
Fleet: 8 - 4 single-deck coach, 2 midicoach, 2 minicoach.
Chassis: 1 Bedford, 2 Ford, 2 Ford Transit, 2 Leyland, 1 MAN.
Bodies: 1 Caetano, 1 Duple, 2 Plaxton, 1 Reeve Burgess, 3 other.
Ops incl: private hire.
Livery: Blue/White

TRAVEL WRIGHT LTD
BRUNEL BUSINESS PARK, JESSOP CLOSE, NEWARK NG24 2AG
Tel: 01636 703813
Fax: 01636 674641
E-mail: info@travelwright.fsnet.co.uk

Web site: www.travelwright.co.uk
Dirs: T D Wright, D C Wright, C A Wright, M Wright
Co Sec: P J Allen
Fleet: 30 – 1 double-deck bus, 8 single-deck bus, 19 single-deck coach, 2 midicoach.
Chassis: 1 Alexander Dennis, 8 Dennis, 6 MAN, 6 Mercedes, 2 Neoplan, 2 Optare, 1 Scania, 1 Setra, 3 Volvo.
Bodies: 1 Alexander Dennis, 2 Berkhof, 6 Caetano, 4 Mercedes, 3 Neoplan, 2 Noge, 3 Optare, 4 Plaxton, 1 Setra, 3 Van Hool, 1 Wadham Stringer.
Ops incl: local bus services, school contracts, excursions & tours, private hire, continental tours.
Livery: Cream/Red/Black.
Ticket System: Wayfarer

UNITY COACHES
BECK GARAGE, CLAYWORTH DN22 9AG
Tel: 07777 817556.
Partners: F. Marriott, Mrs J. Marriott.
Livery: Blue/Grey/Cream.

VEOLIA TRANSPORT ENGLAND PLC
BEECHDALE ROAD, BEECHDALE, NOTTINGHAM NG8 3EU
Tel: 0115 916 9000
Fax: 0115 942 0578
Web site: www.veolia-transport.co.uk
Fleet: 230 - double-deck bus, single-deck bus, single-deck coach, double-deck coach, open-top bus, midibus, minibus.
Chassis: Alexander Dennis, Bova, DAF, Dennis, MAN, Mercedes, Optare, Scania, Transbus, Volvo.
Bodies: Alexander, Bova, Caetano, East Lancs, Irizar, MCV/Marshall, Mellor, Mercedes, Northern Counties, Optare, Plaxton, Sunsundegui, Transbus, Van Hool.
Ops incl: local bus services, school contracts, private hire, express, continental tours.
Livery: Red/White

WALLIS COACHWAYS
100 GRILLINGTON ROAD, BILSTHORPE NG22 8SP
Tel: 01623 870655
Fax: 01623 870655
Prop: Stephen Wallis
Fleet: 2 - 1 midibus, 1 midicoach.
Chassis/Bodies: 1 Mercedes, 1 Toyota
Ops incl: school contracts, private hire
Livery: White
Ticket system: Almex

The Little Red Book 2011
Passenger Transport Directory for the British Isles

For information regarding advertising contact:

Graham Middleton
Tel: 01780 484632
Fax: 01780 763388
E-mail: graham.middleton@ianallanpublishing.co.uk

OXFORDSHIRE

ABINGDON COACHES
169, NEW GREENHAM PARK,
THATCHAM RG19 6HN
Tel: 01235 420520
Fax: 01635 821128
E-mail: info@abingdoncoaches.co.uk
Web site: www.abingdoncoaches.co.uk
Dir: Simon Weaver
Fleet: 23 - 13 single-deck coach,
9 double-deck coach, 1 minicoach.
Chassis: 4 Irisbus, 10 MAN, 1 Mercedes,
8 Volvo.
Ops incl: private hire
Livery: Blue
A subsidiary of Weavaway Travel,
Berkshire

BAKERS COMMERCIAL SERVICES
COTSWOLD BUSINESS VILLAGE,
MORETON-IN-THE-MARSH
GL56 0JQ
Tel: 0845 688 7707
Fax: 0845 688 7660
E-mail: enquiries@bakerscoaches.co.uk
Web site: www.bakerscoaches.co.uk
Dir: Mike Baker
Ops Man: Dave Goodall
Fleet: 17 - 14 single-deck coach,
2 midicoach, 1 minibus.
Chassis: 2 Dennis, 2 Iveco, 3 Mercedes,
1 Scania, 2 Transbus, 7 Volvo.
Bodies: Alexander, Irizar, Plaxton.
Ops incl: local bus services, excursions
& tours, school contracts, private hire,
continental tours.
Livery: White/Red

BANBURYSHIRE ETA LTD
UNIT 17, BEAUMONT BUSINESS
CENTRE, BEAUMONT CLOSE,
BANBURY OX16 7TN
Tel: 01295 263777
Fax: 01295 273186
E-mail: bcta@msn.com
Fleet Name: Cherwell District Dial-A-Ride
Fleet: 3 minibus
Chassis/Bodies: 2 Mercedes, 1 Peugeot
Ops incl: local bus services, private hire

BLUNSDON'S COACH TRAVEL
13 HAMBLESIDE, BICESTER
OX26 2GA
Tel: 01993 811320
Fax: 01993 811416
E-mail: blunsdonsct@talktalk.net
Prop: Michael Blunsdon
Fleet: 7 single-deck coach
Chassis: 5 Dennis, 2 Mercedes.
Bodies: 2 Hispano, 1 Neoplan. 4 Plaxton
Ops incl: private hire, school contracts
Livery: White

CHARLTON-ON-OTMOOR SERVICES
THE GARAGE,
CHARLTON-ON-OTMOOR
OX5 2UQ
Tel: 01865 331249
Fax: 01865 316189
Ops incl: local bus services, school
contracts, private hire.
Livery: Blue

CHENEY COACHES LTD
THORPE MEAD, BANBURY
OX16 4RZ
Tel: 01295 254254
Fax: 01295 271990
E-mail: travel@cheneycoaches.co.uk
Web site: www.cheneycoaches.co.uk
Chairman: G W Peace
Man Dir: M R Peace
Co Sec: S A Peace
Dir: A G Peace
Fleet Eng: Tony Piotrowski
Fleet: 45 - 1 double-deck bus,
34 single-deck coach, 1 midicoach,
9 minibus.
Chassis: 2 DAF, 1 Dennis, 7 Ford
Transit, 1 LDV, 2 Mercedes, 1 Neoplan,
4 Scania, 23 Volvo, 3 other.
Bodies: 1 Berkhof, 4 Caetano,
11 Jonckheere, 2 Mercedes, 1 Neoplan,
7 Plaxton, 10 Van Hool.
Ops incl: school contracts, private hire

HARTWOOL LTD t/a GRAYLINE COACHES
STATION APPROACH,
BICESTER OX26 6HU
Tel: 01869 246461
Fax: 01869 240087
Recovery: 07980 796028
E-mail: paul@grayline.co.uk
Web site: www.grayline.co.uk
Man Dir: Brian Gray
Co Sec: Alan Gray
Ops Man: Paul Gray
Traffic Man: Stuart Gray
Fleet Eng: Geoff Willoughby
Fleet: 18 – 7 single-deck bus,
11 single-deck coach.
Chassis: 1 Bedford, 2 Dennis, 5 Iveco,
1 MAN, 5 Mercedes, 3 Volvo.
Bodies: 5 Beulas, 1 Mercedes, 3 Optare,
9 Plaxton.
Ops incl: local bus services, school
contracts, excursions & tours, private hire,
continental tours.
Livery: White/Red with Blue bands
Ticket System: Wayfarer 3

HEYFORDIAN TRAVEL LTD
MURDOCK ROAD,
BICESTER OX26 4PP
Tel: 01869 241500
Fax: 01869 360011
E-mail: info@heyfordian.co.uk
Web site: www.heyfordian.co.uk
Dir: Graham Smith
Fleet: 85 - double-deck bus, single-deck
coach, double-deck coach, midibus,
minibus, minicoach.
Chassis: Alexander Dennis, Bova, DAF,
Dennis, Leyland, MAN, Optare, Scania,
Volvo.
Bodies: Alexander, Alexander Dennis,
Bova, Caetano, Jonckheere, Neoplan,
Optare, Plaxton, Van Hool.
Ops incl: local bus services, school
contracts, excursions & tours, private hire,
continental tours.
Livery: White/Red/Orange/Black.
Ticket System: Wayfarer.

McLEANS COACHES
GATEWAY HOUSE, WINDRUSH PARK
ROAD, WITNEY OX29 7EY
Tel: 01993 771445
Fax: 01993 779556
E-mail: info@mcleanscoaches.co.uk
Web site: www.mcleanscoaches.co.uk
Dirs: Roger Alder, Mark Hepden
Man: Paul Skidmore
Ch Eng: Paul Rose
Fleet: 27 - 26 single-deck coach,
1 minibus.
Chassis: 3 Ford, 1 Ford Transit,
5 Mercedes, 17 Volvo.
Bodies: 2 Beulas, 4 Caetano, 1 Ikarus,
1 Neoplan, 9 Plaxton, 2 Setra,
4 Sunsundegui, 1 Van Hool.
Ops incl: school contracts, excursions &
tours, private hire, continental tours.
Livery: White/Red.

OXFORD BUS COMPANY
COWLEY HOUSE, WATLINGTON
ROAD, OXFORD OX4 6GA
Tel: 01865 785400
Fax: 01865 774611
E-mail: info@oxfordbus.co.uk
Web site: www.oxfordbus.co.uk
Fleet Names: Brookes Bus, City, Oxford
Express, The Airline.
Man Dir: Philip Kirk
Ops Dir: Louisa Weeks
Eng Dir: Ray Woodhouse
Fin & Comm Dir: Helen Le Fevre
Fleet: 163 – 56 double-deck bus,
70 single-deck bus, 37 single-deck coach.
Chassis: 1 Alexander Dennis, 1 DAF,
24 Dennis, 48 Mercedes, 43 Scania,
46 Volvo.
Bodies: 20 Alexander, 32 Alexander
Dennis, 12 Irizar, 6 Jonckheere,
48 Mercedes, 24 Plaxton, 21 Wright.
Ops incl: local bus services, express.
Liveries: Red (City bus) Green (Oxford
Express/park & ride) Blue (Brookes Bus,
The Airline)
Ticket System: Wayfarer TGX150
A subsidiary of the Go-Ahead Group

PEARCES PRIVATE HIRE
TOWER ROAD INDUSTRIAL ESTATE,
BERINSFIELD,
WALLINGFORD OX10 7LN
Tel: 01865 340560
Fax: 01865 341582
Web site: www.coachhireoxford.com
Props: Clive Pearce, Martin Pearce.
Fleet: 12 - 8 single-deck coach,
2 midicoach, 2 minicoach.
Chassis: 1 Bova, 6 Dennis, 2 Mercedes,
1 Scania, 2 Toyota.
Bodies: 1 Bova, 2 Caetano, 2 Neoplan,
6 Plaxton, 1 Van Hool.
Ops incl: school contracts, excursions
and tours, private hire.
Livery: Yellow/White

PLASTOWS COACHES
134 LONDON ROAD,
WHEATLEY OX33 1JH
Tel: 01865 872270
Fax: 01865 875066
E-mail:
plastowscoaches@btconnect.com
Web site: www.plastows.co.uk
Fleet: 9 single-deck coach.
Chassis: 9 Volvo.
Ops incl: private hire, school contracts.

RH TRANSPORT SERVICES
NORTH BUNGALOW, DOWNS ROAD,

WITNEY OX29 0SY
Tel: 01993 869100
E-mail: rhbuses@googlemail.com
Web sites: www.rhbuses.com, www.rhcoaches.com
Fleet incl: double-deck bus, single-deck bus, double-deck coach, single-deck coach, midibus, minibus.
Ops incl: local bus services, school contracts, private hire
Livery: Blue & Cream

STAGECOACH IN OXFORDSHIRE
HORSPATH ROAD, COWLEY OX4 2RY
Tel: 01865 772250
Fax: 01865 405500
E-mail: oxford.enquiries@stagecoachbus.com
Web site: www.stagecoachbus.com/warwickshire
Man Dir: Martin Sutton
Service Delivery Dir: Paul O'Callaghan
Fleet Man: Simon Weaver
Fleet: 194 - 66 double-deck bus, 50 single-deck bus, 7 single-deck coach, 26 double-deck coach, 26 midibus, 19 minibus.
Chassis: Alexander Dennis, Dennis, MAN, Optare, Scania, Van Hool, Volvo.
Bodies: Alexander, Alexander Dennis, Caetano, Optare, Plaxton, Van Hool.
Ops incl: local bus services, express, school contracts.
Livery: Stagecoach UK Bus
Ticket system: Wayfarer 3

TAPPINS COACHES
COLLETT ROAD, SOUTHMEAD PARK, DIDCOT OX11 7ET
Tel: 01235 819393
Fax: 01235 816464
E-mail: coaches@tappins.co.uk
Web site: www.tappins.co.uk
Man Dir: Graham Smith
Comp Sec: Jeremy Smith

Dirs: Andrew Smith, Roland Smith
Fleet: 45 - 1 double-deck bus, 2 single-deck bus, 39 single-deck coach, 1 double-deck coach, 2 minicoach.
Chassis incl: Neoplan, Volvo.
Bodies incl: Caetano, Plaxton, Van Hool.
Ops incl: local bus services, school contracts, excursions & tours, private hire, express.
Livery: Orange/Black
Ticket System: Wayfarer.
A subsidiary of Heyfordian Travel

TOM TAPPIN LTD
No 1 SHOP, OXFORD RAILWAY STATION, PARK END STREET, OXFORD OX1 1HS
Tel: 01865 790522
Fax: 01865 202154
E-mail: info@citysightseeingoxford.com
Web site: www.citysightseeingoxford.com
Fleet Names: Guide Friday, City Sightseeing Oxford
Chairman: Bill Allen
Gen Man: Jane Marshall
Ops Man: Jonathan Harwood
Consultant: Thomas Knowles
Fleet: 11 open top bus
Chassis: 4 Dennis, 5 Leyland, 2 Volvo
Bodies: 5 Alexander Dennis, 6 East Lancs
Ops incl: open top city sightseeing tours, private hire.
Livery: City Sightseeing Red with pictorial vinyls.
Ticket System: Sion Workabout

THAMES TRAVEL
WYNDHAM HOUSE, LESTER WAY, WALLINGFORD OX10 9TD
Tel: 01491 837988
Fax: 01491 838562
E-mail: office@thames-travel.co.uk
Web site: www.thames-travel.co.uk
Man Dir: John Wright
Dir: Barbara Wood

Fleet Eng: Paul Jupp
Fleet: 46 - 4 double-deck bus, 21 single-deck bus, 21 midibus.
Chassis: 13 Alexander Dennis, 1 Dennis, 14 MAN, 9 Optare, 8 Scania, 1 Volvo.
Bodies: 1 Alexander, 8 Alexander Dennis, 16 MCV, 9 Optare, 4 Plaxton, 8 Scania.
Ops incl: local bus services, school contracts
Livery: Green/Blue
Ticket system: Wayfarer

WHITES COACHES
90 COLWELL ROAD, BERINSFIELD, WALLINGFORD OX10 7NU
Tel: 01865 340516
E-mail: sue@whitescoaches.com
Web site: www.whitescoaches.com
Fleet incl: single-deck coach, midibus, midicoach
Ops incl: local bus services, school contracts, excursions & tours, private hire.
Liveries: Buses – Yellow; Coaches: White with Red/Blue.

WORTHS MOTOR SERVICES LTD
ENSTONE, CHIPPING NORTON OX7 4LQ
Tel: 01608 677322
Fax: 01608 677298
E-mail: worths.coaches@ukonline.co.uk
Web site: www.worthscoaches@ukonline.co.uk
Dirs: Richard Worth, Paul Worth
Fleet: 16 - 2 single-deck bus, 12 single-deck coach, 1 midibus, 1 midicoach.
Chassis: 1 Dennis, 2 Mercedes, 13 Volvo.
Bodies: 1 Caetano, 1 Jonckheere, 1 Mercedes, 1 Optare, 12 Plaxton.
Ops incl: school contracts, continental tours, private hire.
Livery: Silver/Blue
Ticket System: Wayfarer

SHROPSHIRE, TELFORD & WREKIN

ARRIVA MIDLANDS LTD
852 MELTON ROAD, LEICESTER LE4 8BT
Tel: 0116 264 0400
Fax: 0116 260 5605
Web site: www.arriva.co.uk
Man Dir: R A Hind **Fin Dir:** J Barlow
Ops Dir: A Lloyd **Eng Dir:** M Evans
Area Business Man (Shropshire): G Frost
Fleet: 658 - 134 double-deck bus, 176 single-deck bus, 3 articulated bus, 232 midibus, 113 minibus.
Chassis: 116 DAF, 222 Dennis, 9 Leyland, 3 Mercedes, 66 Optare, 69 Scania, 54 VDL, 125 Volvo.
Bodies: 55 Alexander, 1 Caetano, 73 East Lancs, 3 Mercedes, 5 Marshall, 21 Northern Counties, 66 Optare, 176 Plaxton, 44 Scania, 8 UVG, 206 Wright.
Ops incl: local bus services.
Livery: Arriva
Ticket System: Wayfarer

BOULTONS OF SHROPSHIRE LTD
SUNNYSIDE, CARDINGTON, CHURCH STRETTON SY6 7JZ

Tel: 01694 771226
Fax: 01694 771296
Dir: Mick Boulton,
E-mail: info@boultonsofshropshire.co.uk
Web site: www.boultonsofshropshire.co.uk
Fleet: 22 - 7 single-deck bus, 9 single-deck coach, 4 midicoach, 1 minibus.
Chassis incl: 4 Alexander Dennis, 2 Autosan, 6 Bova, Mercedes, Optare, Scania.
Bodies: Alexander Dennis, BMC, Bova, Marcopolo, Mercedes, Scania.
Ops incl: local bus services, school contracts, excursions & tours, private hire, continental tours.
Livery: Cream/Orange/Brown
Ticket System: Microfare

A T BROWN (COACHES) LTD
FREEMAIN HOUSE, HORTON ENTERPRISE PARK, HORTON WOOD, TELFORD TF1 7GZ
Tel: 01952 605531
Fax: 01952 608011
E-mail: atbrowncoaches@aol.com
Web site: www.atbrowncoaches.co.uk
Dirs: Nina Macleod, Ewen Macleod

Fleet: 12 - 10 single-deck coach, 2 midicoach
Chassis: 9 DAF, 1 Dennis, 2 Mercedes.
Bodies: 1 Autobus, 3 Caetano, 1 Ikarus, 5 Plaxton, 2 Van Hool.
Ops incl: school contracts, private hire, excursions & tours.
Livery: Sky Blue/Navy

CARADOC COACHES LTD
2 NURSERY FIELDS, RUSHBURY ROAD, RUSHBURY, CHURCH STRETTON SY6 7DY
Tel/Fax/Recovery: 01694 724522
Prop: G Gough
Fleet: 9 - 2 single-deck coach, 2 midicoach, 4 minibus, 1 minicoach
Chassis: 1 Iveco, 4 LDV, 1 Leyland, 1 Mercedes, 1 Toyota, 1 Volvo.
Bodies: 1 Caetano, 1 Mercedes, 3 Plaxton, 4 other.
Ops incl: local bus services, school contracts, excursions & tours, private hire.

COURTESY TRAVEL
2 WOODFIELD AVENUE, SHREWSBURY SY3 8HT
Tel/Fax: 01743 358209
E-mail: courtesy@talktalkbusiness.net

Prop: John Amies.
Fleet: 2 - 1 minicoach, 1 midicoach.
Chassis: 1 LDV, 1 Mercedes.
Ops incl: excursions & tours, private hire.
Livery: Blue/White

ELCOCK REISEN
THE MADDOCKS, MADELEY,
TELFORD TF7 5HA
Tel: 01952 585712
Fax: 01952 582577
Man Dir: J C Elcock
Dirs: J H Prince, J D Ashley
Ops Man: Mark Perkins
E-mail: enquiries@elcockreisen.co.uk
Web site: www.elcockreisen.co.uk
Fleet: 35 - 27 single-deck coach,
5 midicoach, 3 minicoach.
Chassis: 8 Mercedes, 27 Volvo.
Bodies: 2 Autobus, 3 Esker, 20 Plaxton,
10 Van Hool.
Ops incl: local bus services, school
contracts, excursions & tours, private hire,
express, continental tours.
Livery: Silver/Red/Gold

HAPPY DAYS COACHES
See Staffordshire

HOLMES GROUP TRAVEL
CHAPEL HOUSE, 6 STAFFORD ROAD,
NEWPORT TF10 7LY
Tel: 01952 820477
Fax: 01952 270607
Fax: 07831 258084
Dir: C Holmes
Fleet: 3 single-deck coach
Chassis incl: Mercedes, Volvo.
Bodies incl: Mercedes, Plaxton.
Ops incl: excursions & tours, private hire.
Livery: White with flag emblem

HORROCKS BUS LTD
IVY HOUSE, BROCKTON, LYDBURY
NORTH SY7 8BA
Tel: 01588 680364
Prop: A P Horrocks
Fleet: 9 - 2 double-deck bus,
2 single-deck bus, 5 midibus.
Chassis: 1 Bedford, 1 Bristol, 1 Daimler,
1 Dodge, 1 LDV, 4 Mercedes, 1 Volvo.
Ops incl: school contracts, private hire
Livery: White/Blue

LAKESIDE COACHES LTD
THE COACH CENTRE,
ELLESMERE BUSINESS PARK,
ELLESMERE SY12 0EW
Tel: 01691 622761
Fax: 01691 623694
E-mail: mailbox@lakesidecoaches.co.uk
Web site: www.lakesidecoaches.co.uk
Man Dir: John Davies
Dirs: Dorothy Davies, Gareth Davies
Gen Man: Neal Hall
Fleet: 22 - 16 single-deck coach,
5 midicoach, 1 minicoach
Chassis: 1 DAF, 2 Dennis, 3 Mercedes,
4 Toyota, 12 Volvo.
Bodies: 6 Caetano, 1 Excel, 3 Mercedes,
1 Optare, 12 Plaxton, 1 Sitcar,
1 Van Hool.

Ops incl: local bus service, excursions &
tours, private hire, school contracts.
Livery: Green/White

LONGMYND TRAVEL LTD
THE COACH DEPOT, LEA CROSS,
SHREWSBURY SY5 8HX
Tel: 01743 861999 **Fax:** 01743 861901
E-mail: info@longmyndtravel.co.uk
Web Site: www.longmyndtravel.co.uk
Dirs: T G Evans, F J Evans,
V M Sheppard-Evans, D M Sheppard.
Fleet: 22 - 19 single-deck coach,
2 midicoach, 1 minibus
Chassis: 3 Bova, 1 Toyota, 18 Volvo.
Bodies: 1 Berkhof, 3 Bova,
1 Caetano, 1 Jonckheere, 15 Plaxton,
1 Sunsundegui.
Ops incl: school contracts, private hire.
Livery: Red/White

M & J TRAVEL
COACH GARAGE, NEWCASTLE,
CRAVEN ARMS SY7 8QL
Tel: 01588 640273
Prop: W. M. Price.
Fleet: 13 - 7 coach, 1 midicoach,
5 minibus.
Chassis: 4 Bedford, 2 Dennis, 1 Toyota,
1 Talbot.
Bodies: 1 Caetano, 2 Duple, 4 Plaxton.
Ops incl: school contracts, excursions &
tours, private hire, continental tours.
Livery: White/Black/Gold.
Ticket System: Setright.

M P MINICOACHES LTD
14 REDBURN CLOSE, KETLEY
GRANGE, TELFORD TF2 0EE
Tel: 01952 415607
Fax: 01952 619188
Recovery: 07767 250246
E-mail: mpminicoaches@hotmail.com
Fleet Name: MPM of Telford
Dirs: M Perkins, A Perkins, N Perkins
Fleet: 3 – 1 midicoach, 2 minicoach.
Chassis: 2 Iveco, 1 Mercedes.
Bodies: 2 Crest, 1 Plaxton
Ops incl: local bus services, school
contracts, private hire.
Livery: Two-tone Blue

MINSTERLEY MOTORS
STIPERSTONES, MINSTERLEY,
SHREWSBURY SY5 0LZ
Tel: 01743 791208
Fax: 01743 790101
E-mail: john@minsterleymotors.co.uk
Web site: www.minsterleymotors.co.uk
Dirs: John B Jones, Carl Evans
Fleet: 23 - 8 single-deck bus,
12 single-deck coach, 3 midicoach.
Chassis: 3 Mercedes, 6 Scania,
14 Volvo.
Bodies: 5 Berkhof, 2 Jonckheere,
15 Plaxton, 1 Wright.
Ops incl: local bus services, school
contracts, excursions & tours, private hire,
continental tours.
Livery: 2 Tone Blue/White
Ticket system: ERG

N.C.B. MOTORS LTD
EDSTASTON GARAGE, WEM,
SHREWSBURY SY4 5RF
Tel: 01939 232379
Fax: 01939 234892
E-mail: paul@ncb-motors.co.uk
Web site: www.ncb-motors.co.uk
Dirs: Paul R Brown, Derek N Brown
Fleet: 14 single-deck coach
Chassis: 14 Volvo.
Bodies: 7 Jonckheere, 7 Plaxton
Ops incl: private hire, school contracts.
Livery: Brown/Cream

OWENS COACHES LTD
36 BEATRICE STREET,
OSWESTRY SY11 1QG
Tel: 01691 652126
Fax: 01691 670047
E-mail: mike@owenstravel.co.uk
Web site: www.owenstravel.co.uk
Dir: Michael Owen
Ops Man: Peter Worthy
Fleet: 22 - 3 single-deck bus,
16 single-deck coach, 3 midicoach.
Chassis: 3 BMC, 2 Dennis, 1 Irisbus,
1 Iveco, 4 MAN, 5 Mercedes,
1 Scania, 5 Volvo.
Bodies: 2 Ayats, 1 Beulas, 2 Berkhof,
3 BMC, 2 Mercedes, 1 Noge,
8 Plaxton, 1 UVG, 2 Van Hool.
Ops incl: local bus services, excursions
& tours, private hire, continental tours,
school contracts.
Livery: White with Blue/Red stripes.
Ticket System: Wayfarer

R & B TRAVEL
PLEASANT VIEW, KNOWLE,
CLEE HILL, LUDLOW SY8 3NE
Tel/Fax: 01584 890770
E-mail: radnorradnor@supanet.com
Prop: A T Radnor, Mrs L Radnor.
Fleet: 15 – 6 single-deck coach,
5 midibus, 2 midicoach, 2 minibus
Chassis: 2 Bedford, 1 Dennis, 1 LDV,
2 MAN, 1 Mercedes, 5 Optare, 1 Renault,
1 Scania, 1 Toyota.
Bodies: 1 Beulas, 1 Caetano, 1 Carlyle,
1 LDV, 1 Marcopolo, 5 Optare,
2 Plaxton, 1 Wright, 1 Other.
Ops incl: Local bus services, school
contracts, private hire, excursions & tours.
Livery: Grey, Orange and Red over Grey
or White
Ticket System: Wayfarer

RIVERSIDE COACHWAYS LTD
HEATH HILL, DAWLEY
TF4 2JU
Tel: 01952 505490
Fax: 01952 505590
Prop: K H Pollen
Fleet: 13 - double-deck bus, single-deck
coach, double-deck coach.
Chassis: Bristol, Ford, Volvo.
Ops Incl: private hire, school contracts
Livery: Blue/Silver and Blue/White

	Vehicle suitable for disabled	Seat belt-fitted Vehicle	R24 24 hour recovery service
T	Toilet-drop facilities available	Coach(es) with galley facilities	Replacement vehicle available
R	Recovery service available	Air-conditioned vehicle(s)	Vintage Coach(es) available
	Open top vehicle(s)	Coaches with toilet facilities	

The Little Red Book 2011 - in association with *tbf* Transport Benevolent Fund

SHROPSHIRE COUNTY COUNCIL
INTEGRATED TRANSPORT UNIT,
107 LONGDEN ROAD,
SHREWSBURY SY3 9DS
Tel: 01743 245300
Fax: 01743 253279
E-mail: peter.ralphs@shropshire-cc.gov.uk
Web site: www.shropshireonline.gov.uk
Fleet Name: Fleet Operations
Ch Exec: Carolyn Downs
Gen Man Transport: Adrian Millard
Fleet Ops Off: Peter Ralphs.
Fleet: 55 - 1 single-deck bus, 51 minibus, 2 midicoach, 1 midibus.
Chassis: 1 Ford Transit, 30 Iveco, 13 LDV, 8 Mercedes, 1 Optare, 2 Renault.
Ops incl: local bus services, school contracts.
Livery: White
Ticket system: Almex

WORTHEN MOTORS/TRAVEL
BENTHALL STONE FARM BUILDINGS, ALDERBURY ROAD, FORD,
SHREWSBURY SY5 9NA
Tel: 01743 861360
Fax: 01743 851356
E-mail: jackie@worthentravel.freeserve.co.uk
Prop: D A Pye
Sec: J Davies
Fleet: 4 - 4 single-deck coach.
Chassis incl: 3 DAF.
Bodies incl: 1 Plaxton.
Ops incl: school contracts, excursions & tours, private hire.
Livery: White/Blue

SOMERSET, BATH & N E SOMERSET, N SOMERSET

A1 TRAVEL
80 HIGHFIELD ROAD, YEOVIL BA21 4RJ
Tel/Fax: 01935 477722
Web site: www.a1travelservices.com
Dir: Ian Watson
Fleet: 5 - 2 midibus, 3 minibus.
Chassis: 1 Ford. 2 Freight Rover, 2 LDV, 1 Mercedes, 1 Setra.
Bodies: include 1 Plaxton, 1 Setra.
Ops incl: school contracts, private hire.

ARLEEN COACH HIRE & SERVICES LTD
14 BATH ROAD, PEASEDOWN ST JOHN, BATH BA2 8DH
Tel: 01761 434625 **Fax:** 01761 436578
E-mail: arleen.coach-hire@virgin.net
Web site: www.arleen.co.uk
Chairman: Alan Spiller
Co Sec: Mrs Mary Spiller
Dir/Office Man: Ms Carol Spiller
Dir/Ops Man: Justin Spiller
Ch Eng: Kristian Spiller
Fleet: 18 - 13 single-deck coach, 2 midibus, 3 midicoach.
Chassis: 2 Alexander Dennis, 6 DAF, 2 Leyland, 3 Mercedes, 2 Neoplan, 3 Volvo.
Bodies: 1 Alexander Dennis, 1 Berkhof, 3 Duple, 4 Mercedes, 2 Neoplan, 1 Optare, 4 Plaxton, 1 Van Hool, 1 Wadham Stringer.
Ops incl: school contracts, excursions & tours, private hire, continental tours.
Livery: Red/White/Blue

AXE VALE COACHES
BIDDISHAM, AXBRIDGE BS26 2RD
Tel: 01934 750321 **Fax:** 01934 750334
E-mail: enquiries@axevale.com
Web site: www.axevale.com
Partners: C P Bailey, J I Bailey, J Bailey
Fleet: 13 - 12 single-deck coach, 1 midibus.
Chassis: 1 Autosan, 8 Bova, 1 DAF, 1 Dennis, 1 Mercedes, 1 Volvo.
Bodies: 8 Bova, 3 Plaxton, 1 UVG, 1 Other.
Ops incl: local bus services, school contracts, excursions & tours, private hire, continental tours.
Livery: White
Ticket system: Setright

BAKERS COACHES YEOVIL
8 BUCKLAND ROAD, YEOVIL BA21 5EA
Tel: 01935 428401 **Fax:** 01935 410423
Recovery: 01935 428401
E-mail: bakers@bakerscoaches.1global.org.uk
Dir: S Baker
Fleet: 13 - 10 single-deck coach, 2 midicoach, 1 minicoach.
Chassis: DAF, Ford Transit, Iveco, Volvo
Bodies: Beulas, Jonckheere, Mercedes, Van Hool.
Ops incl: school contracts, excursions & tours, private hire, continental tours.
Livery: White

BAKERS DOLPHIN COACH TRAVEL
48 LOCKING ROAD,
WESTON-SUPER-MARE BS23 3DN
Tel: 01934 635635
Fax: 01934 641162
E-mail: coach.hire@bakersdolphin.com
Web site: www.bakersdolphin.com
Chairman: John Baker
Man Dir: Max Fletcher
Ch Eng: Mark Vearncombe
Marketing Dir: Amanda Harrington
Fin Dir: Steve Hunt
Ops Man: Chris Rubery
Fleet: 75 - 68 single-deck coach, 3 double-deck coach, 1 midicoach, 2 minibus, 1 minicoach
Chassis: 4 Bedford, 1 Bova, 1 Dennis, 5 Iveco, 2 LDV, 15 Leyland, 2 Mercedes, 45 Volvo.
Bodies: 5 Beulas, 1 Bova, 3 Jonckheere, 2 LDV, 1 Mercedes, 1 Optare, 34 Plaxton, 28 Van Hool.
Ops incl: local bus services, excursions & tours, private hire, express, continental tours, school contracts.
Livery: Blue/White/Green/Yellow.
Ticket System: Setright

BATH BUS COMPANY
6 NORTH PARADE, BATH BA1 1LF
Tel: 01225 330444 **Fax:** 01225 330727
E-mail: hq@bathbuscompany.com
Web site: www.bathbuscompany.com
Chairman: Peter Newman
Man Dir: Martin Curtis **Dir:** Dr. Mike Walker
Eng Dir: Collin Brougham-Field
Co Sec/Dir: Rob Bromley
Com Dir: Keith Tazewell.
Fleet: 11 double-deck bus, 7 single-deck bus, 3 minibus.
Chassis: 1 AEC, 6 Bristol, 6 Dennis, 3 Leyland-DAB, 3 Leyland, 3 MCW, 4 Mercedes.
Bodies: 1 Alexander, 6 ECW, 1 Leyland, 3 MCW, 1 Park Royal, 3 Plaxton, 6 Wright.
Ops incl: local bus services, excursions & tours, private hire.
Livery: Red/Primrose.
Ticket System: Wayfarer/BBC punch system.
A subsidiary of Ensignbus (see Essex)

BATH CONNECT
A subsidiary of Wessex Connect – see Bristol

BERRY'S COACHES (TAUNTON) LTD
CORNISHWAY WEST, NEW WELLINGTON ROAD,
TAUNTON TA1 5NB
Tel: 01823 331356
Fax: 01823 322347
E-mail: info@berryscoaches.co.uk
Web site: www.berryscoaches.co.uk
Dir: S A Berry
Fleet: 30 - 26 single-deck coach, 4 double-deck coach.
Chassis: 30 Volvo.
Bodies: 5 Jonckheere, 2 Plaxton, 22 Van Hool, 1 Other.
Ops incl: local bus services, school contracts, excursions & tours, private hire, express, continental tours.
Livery: White/Red/Orange
Ticket system: Setright

BLAGDON LIONESS COACHES LTD
MENDIP GARAGE, BLAGDON BS40 7TL
Tel: 01761 462250
Fax: 01761 463237
Recovery: 01761 462250
Dir: T M Lyons
Gen Man: M A Lyons
Fleet: 3 - 2 single-deck coach, 1 minibus
Chassis: 1 Bova, 1 Leyland, 1 Mercedes
Bodies: 1 Bova, 2 Plaxton.
Ops incl: local bus services, excursions & tours, private hire, school contracts.
Livery: White
Ticket System: Wayfarer

BLUE IRIS COACHES
25 CLEVEDON ROAD,
NAILSEA BS48 1EH
Tel: 01275 851121
Fax: 01275 856522
E-mail: enquiry@blueiris.co.uk
Web site: www.blueiris.co.uk
Dirs: Philip Hatherall, Tony Spiller
Fleet: 17 - 2 single-deck bus, 9 single-deck coach, 6 midicoach.
Chassis: 2 Optare, 9 Scania, 6 Toyota.
Bodies: 1 Berkhof, 6 Caetano, 6 Irizar, 2 Optare, 2 Van Hool.
Ops incl: local bus services, private hire, continental tours.
Livery: 2-tone Blue/White.
Ticket System: Wayfarer

BUGLERS COACHES LTD
29 VICTORIA BUILDINGS, LOWER BRISTOL ROAD, BATH BA2 3EH
Tel: 01225 444422
Fax: 01225 466665
E-mail: info@buglercoaches.co.uk
Web site: www.buglercoaches.co.uk
Prop: Computer Village Group
Ops Incl: local bus services, private hire, school contracts
Livery: Red/White/Yellow

CENTURION TRAVEL LTD
WEST ROAD GARAGE, WELTON, MIDSOMER NORTON, RADSTOCK BA3 2TP
Tel: 01761 417392
Fax: 01761 417369
E-mail: coach-hire@centuriontravel.co.uk
Web site: www.centuriontravel.co.uk
Man Dir: Martin Spiller
Fleet: 22 - 18 single-deck coach, 1 midibus, 3 midicoach.
Chassis: 2 Bedford, 2 Bova, 4 DAF, 4 Dennis, 2 Leyland, 5 Mercedes, 1 Scania, 1 Temsa, 2 Volvo.
Bodies: 1 Autobus, 1 Berkhof, 2 Bova, 1 Caetano, 3 Duple, 1 Esker, 1 Irizar, 3 Jonckheere, 1 Marcopolo, 2 Optare, 3 Plaxton, 2 Van Hool
Ops incl: school contracts, private hire, continental tours.
Livery: Red/Cream/Burgundy

CLAPTON COACHES
1 HAYDON ESTATE, RADSTOCK BA3 3RD
Tel: 01761 431936 **Fax:** 01761 431935
E-mail: claptonholidays@btconnect.com

Dirs: S C Lippet, M C Lippet.
Fleet: 11 - 6 single-deck coach, 5 minicoach.
Ops incl: excursions & tours, private hire, continental tours.
Livery: Lilac

COOMBS TRAVEL
COOMBS HOUSE, SEARLE CRESCENT, WESTON-SUPER-MARE BS23 3YX
Tel: 01934 428555
Fax: 01934 428559
E-mail: coombscoaches@aol.com
Dirs: Brian F Coombs, Ruth A Coombs
Ops Man: Mrs June Carroll
Admin: Mrs M Lillie
Fleet: 30 - 1 double-deck bus, 18 single-deck coach, 6 midicoach, 5 minibus.
Chassis incl: 3 Dennis, 3 Ford Transit, 5 Mercedes, 8 Scania.
Bodies incl: 8 Plaxton, 2 Scania, 3 Van Hool
Ops incl: local bus services, school contracts, excursions & tours, private hire.
Livery: Yellow/White
Ticket system: Wayfarer

FIRST SOMERSET & AVON LTD
OLDMIXON CRESCENT, WESTON SUPER MARE BS24 9AY
Tel: 01934 620122
Fax: 01934 415859
Recovery: 0117 955 4442
Web site: www.firstgroup.com
Man Dir: Tony McNiff
Fin Dir: Mike Gahan
Fleet: 396 - 53 double-deck bus, 12 articulated single-deck bus, 133 single-deck bus, 15 single-deck coach, 139 midibus, 44 minibus.
Chassis: Alexander Dennis, Dennis, Leyland, Mercedes, Optare, Scania, Volvo.
Ops incl: local bus services, school contracts, excursions & tours, express, private hire.
Livery: FirstGroup UK Bus
Ticket System: Wayfarer

FROME MINIBUSES LTD
GEORGES GROUND, FROME BA11 4RP
Tel: 01373 471474
Fax: 01373 455294
Man Dir: Andrew Young
Ops incl: local bus services.
Livery: White.

HATCH GREEN COACHES
HATCH GREEN GARAGE, HATCH BEAUCHAMP, TAUNTON TA3 6TN
Tel: 01823 480338
Fax: 01823 480500
E-mail: info@hatchgreencoaches.com
Web site: www.hatchgreencoaches.co.uk
Fleet incl: midibus, midicoach, minicoach.
Ops incl: local bus services, school contracts, private hire.
Livery: White/Grey/Black

HUTTON COACH HIRE
95 MOORLAND ROAD, WESTON-SUPER-MARE BS23 4HS
Tel: 01934 618292

Somerset, Bath & N E Somerset, N Somerset

Fax: 01934 641362
E-mail: jnjlawrence@onetel.com
Owner: John Lawrence
Man: Wendy Dover
Fleet: 5 - 3 single-deck coach, 2 midibus.
Chassis: 1 Alexander Dennis, 1 DAF, 1 MAN, 1 Mercedes, 1 Volvo.
Bodies: 1 Autobus, 1 Caetano, 1 UVG, 2 Van Hool.
Ops incl: school contracts, excursions & tours, private hire.
Livery: White with orange/green logo

NORTH SOMERSET COACHES
See Bristol

QUANTOCK MOTOR SERVICES LTD
UNIT 13A, TAUNTON TRADING ESTATE, TAUNTON TA2 6RX
Tel: 01823 251140
Fax: 01823 251833
E-mail: sales@quantockmotorservices.co.uk
Web site: www.quantockmotorservices.co.uk
Man Dir: Steve Morris
Dir: Liz Ranson
Gen Man: Peter McNaughton
Fleet Eng: Paul Smith
Supervisor: William Ricketts
Fleet: 55 - 14 double-deck bus, 8 single-deck bus, 22 single-deck coach, 8 open-top bus, 3 minibus.
Chassis incl: 4 AEC, 12 Bristol, 8 Dennis, 1 Scania, 4 Volvo.
Bodies incl: 7 Bova, ECW, Esker, 22 Northern Counties, Plaxton, Scania, 22 Van Hool.
Ops incl: local bus services, private hire, school contracts, excursions & tours, express.
Livery: Red
Ticket system: Wayfarer 2/3

RIDLERS LTD
JURY ROAD GARAGE, DULVERTON TA22 9EJ
Tel: 01398 323398
Fax: 01398 324398
E-mail: info@ridlers.co.uk
Web site: www.ridlers.co.uk
Dirs: G Ridler, S Ridler
Ops Man: M E Jamieson
Fleet: 18 - 15 single-deck coach, 3 midicoach.
Chassis: 6 Dennis, 1 Iveco, 2 Leyland, 1 Mercedes, 6 Scania, 2 Toyota.
Bodies: 1 Berkhof, 2 Caetano, 5 Duple, 2 Irizar, 5 Plaxton, 3 Van Hool.
Ops incl: local bus services, school contracts, excursions & tours, continental tours, private hire
Livery: White/Red/Silver.
Ticket system: Almex

D. W. SKELTON
90 BROADWAY, CHILTON POLDEN TA7 9EQ
Tel: 01278 722066
Fax: 01278 722608
Fleet Name: Skelton Tours.
Prop: D. W. Skelton.
Fleet: 3 single-deck coach.
Chassis: 1 Ford, 2 MAN.
Bodies: 1 MAN, 1 Neoplan, 1 Plaxton.
Ops incl: excursions & tours, private hire, continental tours.
Livery: Black/Green/Gold.

SMITH'S COACHES (B.E. & G.W. SMITH)
BYFIELDS, PYLLE BA4 6TA
Tel: 01749 830126
Fax: 01749 830888
Prop: Graham Smith
Fleet: 14 single-deck coach.
Chassis: 3 Bedford, 3 Leyland, 8 Volvo.
Bodies: 14 Plaxton.
Ops incl: school contracts, private hire.
Livery: Maroon/Cream

SOMERBUS LIMITED
64 BROOKSIDE, PAULTON, BRISTOL BS39 7YR
Tel/Fax: 01761 415456
Web site: www.somerbus.co.uk
E-mail: somerbus@tinyworld.co.uk
Dir: Tim Jennings
Fleet: 5 - 5 single-deck bus.
Chassis: 5 Optare.
Bodies: 5 Optare.
Ops incl: local bus services, school contracts
Livery: Orange/White
Ticket system: Wayfarer

SOUTH WEST COACHES LTD /SOUTH WEST TOURS LTD
SOUTHGATE ROAD, WINCANTON BA9 9EB
Tel: 01963 33124 **Fax:** 01963 31599
E-mail: info@southwestcoaches.co.uk
Web site: www.southwestcoaches.co.uk
Man Dir: A M Graham
Co Sec: Mrs S Graham
Comm Dir: S P Caine
Ops Dir: P Fairey
Eng Man: K Jeffrey
Services Man: L Trahar
Fleet: 95 - 29 single-deck bus, 50 single-deck coach, 2 midicoach, 14 minibus.
Chassis: 1 BMC, 2 DAF, 12 Dennis, 3 Ford, 3 LDV, 8 Leyland, 4 MAN, 19 Mercedes, 5 Optare, 3 Scania, 8 Setra, 1 Volkswagen, 26 Volvo.
Bodies: 6 Alexander Dennis, 5 Berkhof, 1 BMC, 5 Caetano, 1 Duple, 2 Irizar, 5 Jonckheere, 3 LDV, 5 MCV, 3 Mercedes, 5 Optare, 19 Plaxton, 1 Reeve Burgess, 8 Setra, 1 UVG, 3 Van Hool, 4 Wright, 18 Other.
Ops incl: local bus services, school contracts, excursions & tours, private hire, continental tours.
Livery: White with Red/Blue stripes
Ticket Systems: Wayfarer, Almex

STAGECOACH SOUTH WEST (formerly COOKS COACHES)
BELGRAVE ROAD, EXETER EX1 2LB
Tel: 01392 439439
Fax: 01392 889727
Web site: www.stagecoachbus.com
Officers: See Stagecoach South West (Devon)
Fleet: See Stagecoach South West (Devon)
Ops incl: local bus services, school contracts.
Livery: Stagecoach UK Bus

STONES OF BATH
LOWER BRISTOL ROAD, BATH BA2 3DR
Tel: 01225 422267

Fax: 01225 442209
E-mail: stonescoaches@btconnect.com
Web site: www.stonescoaches.co.uk
Senior Partner: D G Stone
Ops Man: C G Stone
Ch Eng: S M Stone
Sec/Fin: Mrs N R Russell
Fleet: 13 - 10 single-deck coach, 3 midicoach
Chassis: DAF, Neoplan, Scania, Toyota.
Bodies: Bova, Irizar, Neoplan, Van Hool.
Ops incl: excursions & tours, school contracts, private hire, continental tours.
Livery: Cream/Red

TAYLORS COACH TRAVEL LTD
PLOT 10, BYMPTON WAY, LYNX WEST TRADING ESTATE, YEOVIL BA20 2HP
Tel: 01935 427556
Fax: 01935 423177
E-Mail: taylorscoachtravel@tintinhull.fsworld.co.uk
Web site: www.taylorscoachtravel.co.uk
Man Dir: D D J Elliott
Co Sec: Mrs T R Elliott
Eng Dir: D Porter
Ops Dir: M D Kirkland
Fleet: 46 - 34 single-deck coach, 7 midicoach, 5 minibus.
Chassis: 2 Autosan, 2 Bova, 4 BMC, 3 DAF, 3 Dennis, 4 Irisbus, 4 Iveco, 2 LDV, 6 Leyland, 1 Mercedes, 15 Volvo.
Bodies: 2 Autosan, 3 Alexander, 4 BMC, 2 Bova, 2 Duple, 3 Indcar, 2 Leyland, 1 Mercedes, 10 Plaxton, 1 Reeve Burgess, 12 Van Hool, 3 Vehixel, 1 Wadham Stringer.
Ops incl: local bus services, private hire, school contracts, excursions & tours, continental tours
Livery: Burgundy/White/Yellow/Gold
Ticket system: Wayfarer

TRAVELINE
SUMMERLAND CAR PARK, MINEHEAD TA24 5BN
Tel: 01643 704774, 821883
Fax: 01643 821883
Dirs: D. C. & P. A. Grimmett.
Fleet: 1 single-deck coach.
Chassis/Body: Bova.
Ops incl: excursions & tours, private hire, continental tours.

WEBBER BUS
UNIT 8C, BEECH BUSINESS PARK, BRISTOL ROAD, BRIDGWATER TA6 4FF
Tel: 0800 096 3039
Fax: 01278 455250
E-mail: sales@webberbus.com
Web site: www.webberbus.com
Man Dir: Tim Gardner
Eng & Ops Dir: David Webber
Fleet: 38 - 25 single-deck coach, 3 midicoach, 7 minibus, 3 midibus.
Chassis incl: 2 Bova, 1 DAF, 5 Ford Transit, 5 Irisbus, 2 LDV, 4 Optare.
Bodies incl: 2 Bova, 4 Optare, 11 Plaxton, 4 Van Hool.
Ops incl: local bus services, school contracts, excursions & tours, private hire
Ticket system: Wayfarer

SOUTH YORKSHIRE

ANDERSON COACHES LTD
36 BONET LANE, BRINSWORTH, ROTHERHAM S60 5NE
Tel: 0114 239 9231
Fax: 01709 364750
Fleet: 5 - 3 single-deck coach, 2 minibus.
Chassis: 2 Dennis, 1 Ford Transit, 1 LDV, 1 MAN.
Ops incl: excursions & tours, private hire

ASHLEY TRAVEL LTD t/a GRANT & McALLIN
RENISHAW SERVICE STATION, RENISHAW S21 3WF
Tel: 0114 251 1234
Fax: 0114 251 1900
Dirs: R. Atack (**Gen Man/Traf Man**) T. F. Atack (**Ch Eng/Sec**)
Fleet: 7 single-deck coach.
Chassis: 7 Volvo.
Bodies: 1 Berkhof, 1 Jonckheere, 2 Plaxton, 3 Van Hool.
Ops incl: excursions & tours, private hire.
Livery: Turquoise/Blue/White.

BUCKLEYS TOURS LTD
THORNE ROAD, BLAXTON, DONCASTER DN9 3AX
Tel: 01302 770379
E-mail: info@buckleysholidays.co.uk
Web site: www.buckleysholidays.co.uk
Man Dir: Richard Buckley.
Fleet: 6 single-deck coach.
Chassis: 3 DAF, 1 Mercedes, 2 Neoplan.
Ops incl: private hire, excursions & tours.
Livery: Orange

BURDETTS COACHES LTD
8 STATION ROAD, MOSBOROUGH, SHEFFIELD S20 5AD
Tel: 0114 321 4597
Fax: 0114 247 5733
Web site: www.burdettscoachessheffield.co.uk
Fleet: 4 single-deck coach.
Chassis: 4 Volvo.
Bodies: 4 Van Hool.
Ops incl: school contracts, excursions & tours, private hire

BYRAN TOURS LTD
31 SUSSEX STREET, SHEFFIELD S4 7YY
Tel/Fax: 0114 270 0060
Dir/Owner: Julie Scott
Dir: Dennis Heaton
Fleet: 6 - 3 minibus, 3 minicoach.
Chassis incl: 1 Ford, 4 Mercedes.
Bodies incl: 1 Setra.
Ops incl: school contracts, excursions & tours, private hire.
Livery: White/Jade/Black.

CENTRAL TRAVEL
313 COLEFORD ROAD, DARNALL, SHEFFIELD S9 5NF
Tel: 0114 276 7000
Fax: 0114 275 9060
Recovery: 0114 276 9869
E-mail: paulharrison4@btconnect.com
Props: Paul Harrison, Joy Harrison
Fleet: 34 – 4 single-deck bus, 8 single-deck coach, 2 midibus, 2 midicoach, 10 minibus, 8 minicoach

Chassis incl: 1 Bova, 2 Dennis, 5 Ford Transit, 3 Mercedes, 1 Neoplan, 1 Optare, 1 Peugeot, 1 Renault, 3 Setra, 1 Volvo.
Ops incl: school contracts, excursions & tours, private hire, continental tours

CLARKSONS HOLIDAYS
See West Yorkshire

COOPERS TOURS LTD
ALDRED CLOSE, NORWOOD INDUSTRIAL ESTATE, KILLAMARSH S21 2JH
Tel: 0114 248 2859
Fax: 0114 248 3867
E-mail: sales@cooperstours.co.uk
Web site: www.cooperstours.co.uk
Dirs: Alan Cooper, Graham Cooper.
Fleet: 8 single-deck coach.
Chassis: 1 AEC, 2 Leyland, 1 MAN, 3 Volvo.
Bodies: 2 Berkhof, 4 Plaxton, 2 Van Hool.
Ops incl: excursions & tours, private hire, continental tours.
Livery: Yellow/White.

ELLENDERS COACHES
71 HURLFIELD AVENUE, SHEFFIELD S12 2TL
Tel: 0114 321 9364
Web site: www.ellenderscoachessheffield.co.uk
Partners: P. J. D. Ellender, C. S. Ellender
Fleet: 2 coach.
Chassis: Volvo.
Bodies: Jonckheere.
Ops incl: excursions & tours, private hire, continental tours, school contracts.

EXPRESSWAY COACHES
DERWENT WAY, WATH WEST INDUSTRIAL ESTATE, WATH ON DEARNE, ROTHERHAM S63 6EX
Tel: 01709 875358
Fax: 01709 879919
E-mail: expresswaycoaches@btconnect.com
Dirs: Peter Regan
Fleet: 16 - 1 single-deck bus 4 single-deck coach, 5 midicoach, 6 minicoach.
Chassis: 1 Alexander Dennis, 1 MAN, 11 Mercedes, 1 Volkswagen, 2 Volvo.
Bodies: 1 Alexander Dennis, 8 Mercedes, 1 Neoplan, 5 Plaxton, 1 Other.
Ops incl: local bus service, private hire, continental tours, school contracts, excursions & tours.
Livery: Orange/Yellow/White
Ticket system: Wayfarer II

FIRST SOUTH YORKSHIRE
MIDLAND ROAD, ROTHERHAM S61 1TF
Tel: 01709 566000
Fax: 01709 566063
E-mail: enquiries@firstgroup.com
Web site: www.firstgroup.com
Man Dir: Bob Hamilton
Deputy Man Dir: Brandon Jones
Eng Dir: Brian Wilkinson
Ops Dir: Phil Robinson
Fleet: 544 - 209 double-deck bus, 287 single-deck bus, 48 midibus.

Chassis: 39 Dennis, 13 Optare, 6 Scania, 485 Volvo.
Bodies: 77 Alexander, 47 Northern Counties, 13 Optare, 35 Plaxton, 15 Transbus, 357 Wright.
Ops incl: local bus services
Livery: FirstGroup UK Bus
Ticket System: Wayfarer 3

L. FURNESS & SONS
48 THOMPSON HILL, HIGH GREEN, SHEFFIELD S30 4JU
Tel: 0114 284 8365
Partners: G. Furness, A. Furness
Ch Eng: P. Hayes.
Fleet: 8 - 7 single-deck coach, 1 minicoach.
Chassis: 3 DAF, 3 Ford, 1 Leyland, 1 Mercedes.
Bodies: 1 Duple, 7 Plaxton.
Ops incl: excursions & tours, private hire.
Livery: Red/Cream.

GEE-VEE TRAVEL
173 DONCASTER ROAD, BARNSLEY S70 1UF
Tel: 01226 287403
Fax: 01226 284783
Web site: www.geeveetravel.co.uk
Owner: Gordon Clark
Fleet: 13 single-deck coach.
Chassis: 13 Bova.
Bodies: 13 Bova.
Ops incl: excursions & tours, private hire, continental tours

W GORDON & SONS
CHESTERTON ROAD, EASTWOOD TRADING ESTATE, ROTHERHAM S65 1SU
Tel: 01709 363913
Fax: 01709 830570
Dir: D Gordon
Fleet: 10 – 8 single-deck coach, 2 midicoach.
Chassis: 1 EOS, 1 Irisbus, 2 MAN, 1 Mercedes, 5 Volvo.
Bodies: 1 Esker, 5 Plaxton, 1 Sunsundegui, 3 Van Hool
Ops incl: school contracts, excursions & tours, private hire.
Livery: Red/Ivory

GRAYS LUXURY TRAVEL
30-32 SHEFFIELD ROAD, HOYLAND COMMON S74 0DQ
Tel: 01226 743109
Fax: 01226 749430
E-mail: stephen@grays-travel.co.uk
Web site: www.grays-travel.co.uk
Man Dir: S. Gray **Ch Eng:** P. Winter.
Fleet: 10 - 7 single-deck coach, 1 midicoach, 1 minibus, 1 minicoach.
Chassis: 1 Bova, 6 DAF, 2 Dennis, 1 Toyota.
Bodies: 1 Berkhof, 1 Caetano, 2 Duple, 6 Plaxton.
Ops incl: excursions & tours, private hire, school contracts.
Livery: White/Blue/Yellow.

HEATON'S OF SHEFFIELD LTD
31 SUSSEX STREET, SHEFFIELD S3 7YY
Tel/Fax: 0114 230 9184
E-mail: info@heatonscoachhire.com

Web site: www.heatonscoachhire.com
Fleet: 10 - 4 single-deck coach,
2 midicoach, 4 minicoach.
Chassis: 1 Ford, 4 Mercedes, 5 Setra.
Bodies: 4 Mercedes, 1 Plaxton, 5 Setra.
Ops incl: school contracts, excursions & tours.
Livery: White.

ISLE COACHES
97 HIGH STREET, OWSTON FERRY DN9 1RL
Tel: 01427 728227
Props: J. & C. Bannister.
Ch Eng: E. Scotford Sec: Jill Bannister.
Fleet: 12 - 2 double-deck bus,
3 single-deck bus, 6 single-deck coach,
1 minibus.
Ops incl: local bus services, excursions & tours, private hire.
Livery: Blue/Cream.
Ticket System: Almex.

JEMS TRAVEL
27 BOYNTON ROAD, SHIRECLIFFE, SHEFFIELD S5 7HJ
Tel: 0114 242 0885
Fax: 0114 242 0885
E-mail: info@jemstravel.co.uk
Web Site: www.jemstravel.co.uk
Prop: Malcolm S Mallender
Fleet: 1 minibus.
Chassis: 1 LDV
Bodies: 1 Mellor
Ops incl: school contracts, excursions & tours, private hire.

JOHN POWELL TRAVEL LTD
UNIT 2, 6 HELLABY LANE, HELLABY, ROTHERHAM S66 8HA
Tel: 01709 700900
Fax: 01709 701521
E-mail: jane@johnpowelltravel.co.uk
Dir: Ian Powell Co Sec: Jane Powell
Chief Eng: Ian Slater
Office Man: Lynn Oliver
Supervisor: Jerry Smith
Fleet: 40 – 8 double-deck bus,
7 single-deck bus, 10 single-deck coach,
15 midibus
Chassis: Alexander Dennis, BMC, Dennis, Iveco, Leyland, MCW, Optare, Scania, Volvo.
Ops incl: local bus services, school contracts, excursions & tours, private hire.
Livery: Blue/Yellow/Orange
Ticket system: Wayfarer III

JOHNSON BROS TOURS LTD
GREEN ACRES, GREEN LANE, HODTHORPE, WORKSOP S80 4XR
Tel: 01909 720337 / 721847
Fax: 01909 722886
Recovery: 07774 005863
E-mail: lee@johnsonstours.co.uk
Web site: www.johnsonstours.co.uk
Dirs: Tony Johnson, Lee Johnson, Antony Johnson, Scott Johnson, Sheila Johnson (Co Sec)
Fleet: 116 - 70 double-deck bus,
2 single-deck bus, 35 single-deck coach,
3 double-deck coach, 3 midibus,
2 midicoach, 1 minicoach.
Chassis: 1 Ayats, 2 Bova, 50 Bristol,
1 DAF, 1 Ford Transit, 10 Iveco, 10 MCW,
7 Neoplan, 2 Optare, 10 Scania,
6 Transbus, 4 VDL, 10 Volvo.
Bodies: Ayats, Beulas, Berkhof, Bova, Irizar, Jonckheere, Neoplan, Northern Counties, Optare, Plaxton, Scania, Setra, Sunsundegui, Transbus, Van Hool, Volvo.
Ops incl: local bus services, school contracts, excursions & tours, private hire, express, continental tours.
Livery: Blue with Stars
Ticket System: Almex
See also Redfern Travel Ltd (Nottinghamshire)

JOURNEYS-DESTINATION
42-45 WILSON STREET, NEEPSEND, SHEFFIELD S3 8DD
Tel: 0800 298 1938
Fax: 0114 242 0885
E-mail: info@journeys-destination.com
Web site: www.journeys-destination.com
Prop: Mrs Patricia R Russell
Fleet: 3 minibus
Chassis: 2 Iveco, 1 LDV
Ops incl: school contracts, excursions & tours, private hire.

K. M. MOTORS LTD
WILSON GROVE, LUNDWOOD, BARNSLEY S71 5JS
Tel: 01226 245564
Fax: 01226 213004
Man Dir: Keith Meynell
Fleet: 11 - 8 single-deck coach,
3 minibus.
Chassis: 5 Bova, 1 Ford Transit,
2 Mercedes, 3 Scania.
Bodies: 5 Bova, 1 Constable, 1 Ford,
1 Mercedes, 3 Van Hool.
Ops incl: excursions & tours, continental tours, private hire.
Livery: Gold/Maroon/White.

LADYLINE
47 BERNARD STREET, RAWMARSH S62 5NR
Tel: 01709 522422
Fax: 01709 525558
Owner: C. B. Goodridge
Fleet: 6 single-deck coach
Chassis: 2 AEC, 3 Bova, 1 DAF.
Bodies: 3 Bova, 1 Caetano, 2 Plaxton.
Ops incl: local bus services, school contracts, excursions & tours, private hire, continental tours.
Livery: Blue/White.

LINBURG BUS & COACH
UNIT 7, 35 CATLEY ROAD, DARNALL, SHEFFIELD S9 5JF
Tel: 0114 261 9172
Fax: 0114 256 1159
E-mail: info@linburg.co.uk
Web site: www.linburg.co.uk
Dirs: John Hadaway, Gill Dawson
Fleet: 15 – 7 double-deck bus,
8 single-deck coach
Chassis: 6 DAF, 8 Leyland, 1 Volvo
Ops incl: school contracts, private hire, express.
Livery: White/Multi
Ticket System: Wayfarer 2

MALCYS
27 BOYNTON ROAD, SHIRECLIFFE, SHEFFIELD S5 7HJ
Tel: 0114 242 0885
Fax: 0114 242 0885
E-mail: info@jemstravel.co.uk
Web site: www.malcystravel.co.uk
Prop: Malcolm S Mallender
Fleet: 1 minicoach
Chassis: 1 LDV.
Ops incl: school contracts, excursions & tours, private hire.

WALTER MARTIN COACHES
57 OLD PARK AVENUE, GREENHILL, SHEFFIELD S8 7DQ
Tel: 0114 274 5004
Prop: John Martin, June Martin.
Fleet: 3 coach.
Chassis: 3 Volvo.
Ops incl: excursions & tours, private hire.

MASS BRIGHT BUS
HOUGHTON ROAD, ANSTON, SHEFFIELD S25 4JJ
Tel: 01909 550480   Fax: 01909 550486
Recovery: 01909 550480
Web site: www.brightbus.co.uk
Fleet Name: Brightbus
Man Dir: Mick Strafford
Co Sec: Carol Morton
Eng Man: Richard Harrison
Fleet: 57 - 55 double-deck bus,
2 single-deck bus.
Chassis: 15 DAF, 12 Dennis, 16 Leyland, 12 Scania.
Bodies: 16 Alexander, 12 Duple,
12 Northern Counties, 15 Optare,
2 Plaxton.
Ops incl: local bus services, school contracts.

J A MAXFIELD & SONS LTD
172 AUGHTON ROAD, AUGHTON, SHEFFIELD S26 3XE
Tel: 0114 287 2622
Fax: 0114 287 5003
E-mail: info@maxfieldstravel.co.uk
Web site: www.maxfieldstravel.co.uk

MOSLEYS TOURS
LEES HALL ROAD, THORNHILL LEES, DEWSBURY WF12 9EQ.
Tel: 01226 382243 Fax: 01924 458665
Dirs: A. Gath-Bragg, J. R. Bragg
Gen Man: P. R. Emerton
Fleet: 3 - 2 single-deck coach,
1 midicoach.
Chassis: 1 Dennis, 1 Leyland, 1Volvo.
Ops incl: school contracts, private hire, continental tours, excursions and tours, express
Livery: Grey/Cream

NIELSEN TRAVEL SERVICE
23 WINN GROVE, MIDDLEWOOD, SHEFFIELD S6 1UW
Tel/Fax: 0114 234 2961
E-mail: niel@nielsenstravel.co.uk
Web site: www.nielsenstravel.co.uk
Fleet: 2 minibus
Chassis: 2 Mercedes.
Ops incl: school contracts, private hire, excursions & tours

ROYLES TRAVEL
114 TUNWELL AVENUE, SHEFFIELD S5 9FG
Tel: 0114 245 4519
Fax: 0114 257 8585
E-mail: info@roylestravel.co.uk
Web site: www.roylestravel.co.uk
Partners: Ricky Eales, Roy Eales.
Fleet: 2 single-deck coach.
Chassis: 1 Bova, 1 Iveco.
Bodies: 1 Beulas, 1 Bova.
Ops incl: excursions & tours, private hire.

SLEIGHTS COACHES
COACH HOUSE, MAIN STREET,
MEXBOROUGH S64 9DU
Tel: 01709 584561   **Fax:** 01709 582016
Owner: J. Sleight
Fleet: 3 single-deck coach
Chassis: DAF
Bodies: Jonckheere
Ops incl: excursions & tours, private hire, continental tours, school contracts.
Livery: Orange/Cream

STAGECOACH YORKSHIRE
UNIT 4 ELDON ARCADE,
BARNSLEY S70 4PP
Tel: 01226 202555   **Fax:** 01226 282313
E-mail: yorkshire@stagecoach.com
Web site: www.stagecoachbus.com
Man Dir: Paul Lynch
Eng Dir: Joe Gilchrist
Ops Dir: Sue Hayes
Comm Dir: Rupert Cox
Fleet: 439 – 43 double-deck bus, 150 single-deck bus, 31 single-deck coach, 173 midibus, 42 minibus.
Chassis: DAF, Dennis, Leyland, MAN, Optare, Scania, Volvo.
Bodies: Alexander, East Lancs, Hispano, Jonckheere, Marshall/MCV, Northern Counties, Optare, Plaxton, Transbus, Wright.
Ops incl: local bus services, school contracts, excursions & tours, private hire, express, continental tours.
Livery: Stagecoach UK Bus
Ticket system: Wayfarer

STAGECOACH SHEFFIELD
GREEN LANE, ECCLESFIELD,
SHEFFIELD S35 9WY
Tel: 014 247 0777
E-mail: sheffield@stagecoachbus.com
Web site: www.stagecoachbus.com
Man Dir: Paul Lynch
Eng Dir: Joe Gilchrist
Ops Dir: Sue Hayes
Comm Dir: Rupert Cox
Fleet: See Stagecoach Yorkshire
Livery: Stagecoach UK Bus
Ticket machines: Wayfarer

STAGECOACH SUPERTRAM
NUNNERY DEPOT, WOODBURN ROAD,
SHEFFIELD S9 3LS
Tel: 0114 275 9888
Fax: 0114 279 8120
E-mail: enquiries@supertram.com
Web site: www.supertram.com
Man Dir: A Morris
Fleet: 25 tramcars
Chassis/Bodies: Siemens
Ops incl: tram services.
Livery: White/Orange/Red

SWIFTS HAPPY DAYS TRAVEL
THORNE ROAD, BLAXTON,
DONCASTER DN9 3AX
Tel/Fax: 01302 770999
A subsidiary of Buckley's Tours

TATE'S TRAVEL GROUP
WHALEY ROAD, BARNSLEY
S75 1HT
Tel: 01226 205800
Fax: 01226 390048
E-mail: info@tates-travel.com
Web site: www.tates-travel.com
Props: Graham Mallinson, Scott Woolley
Fleet: 42 – 2 double-deck bus, 13 single-deck bus, 9 single-deck coach, 14 midibus, 2 minicoach.
Chassis: DAF, Dennis, Leyland, Mercedes, Optare, Volvo
Bodies: Alexander, Duple, Ikarus, Jonckheere, Optare, Plaxton, Van Hool, Wright
Ops incl: local bus services, private hire, excursions & tours.
Livery: Blue/White.

TM TRAVEL
HALFWAY BUS GARAGE, STATION
ROAD, HALFWAY S20 3GZ
Tel: 0114 263 3890
Fax: 0114 263 3899
Web site: www.tmtravel.co.uk
E-mail: info@tmtravel.co.uk
Gen Man: Paul Hopkinson
Eng Man: Mark Clare
Fleet: 102 - 31 double-deck bus, 25 single-deck bus, 7 single-deck coach, 37 midibus, 2 midicoach.
Chassis: 2Alexander Dennis, 12 DAF, 7 Dennis, 1 Enterprise, 19 Leyland, 3 MAN, 7 Mercedes, 37 Optare, 3 Scania, 11 Volvo.
Bodies: 20 Alexander Dennis, 2 ECW, 7 East Lancs, 1 Ikarus, 5 Northern Counties, 37 Optare, 29 Plaxton, 1 Van Hool.
Ops incl: local bus services, school contracts, excursions & tours, private hire, express, continental tours.
Livery: Red/Cream/Maroon
Ticket system: Wayfarer TGX 150.
Part of the Wellglade Group

TRAVELGREEN COACHES
CANDA LODGE, HAMPOLE BALK
LANE, SKELLOW,
DONCASTER DN6 8LF
Tel/Recovery: 01302 722227
Web site: www.travelgreen.co.uk
E-mail: travelgreen@btconnect.com
Dir: David Green
Fleet: 7 – 1 double-deck bus, 2 midicoach, 4 minicoach.
Chassis: 1 AEC, 6 Mercedes.
Bodies: 1 Mercedes, 2 Optare, 1 Park Royal, 2 Plaxton.
Ops incl: excursions & tours, private hire, continental tours.
Livery: Maroon/White

VEOLIA TRANSPORT ENGLAND PLC
ALDWARKE ROAD, PARKGATE,
ROTHERHAM S62 6BZ
See Nottinghamshire

WILFREDA BEEHIVE COACHES LTD
APEX HOUSE, CHURCH LANE,
ADWICK-LE-STREET, DONCASTER
DN6 7AY
Tel: 01302 330330
Fax: 01302 330204
E-mail: sales@wilfreda.co.uk
Web site: www.wilfreda.co.uk
Man Dir: Mrs S M Scholey
Dirs: P G Haxby, N G Haxby
Ops Man: I Kaye
Ch Eng: P Whitaker
Fleet: 45 - 4 double-deck bus, 1 single-deck bus, 21 single-deck coach, 12 midibus, 2 minibus, 5 minicoach.
Chassis: 4 BMC, 1 Dennis, 2 Iveco, 1 Leyland, 4 MAN, 10 Mercedes, 10 Optare, 13 Scania.
Bodies: 5 Beulas, 4 BMC, 2 East Lancs, 11 Irizar, 7 Mercedes, 10 Optare, 3 Plaxton, 1 Van Hool.
Ops incl: local bus services, school

South Yorkshire

	Vehicle suitable for disabled		Seat belt-fitted Vehicle	R24	24 hour recovery service
T	Toilet-drop facilities available		Coach(es) with galley facilities		Replacement vehicle available
R	Recovery service available		Air-conditioned vehicle(s)		Vintage Coach(es) available
	Open top vehicle(s)		Coaches with toilet facilities		

The Little Red Book 2011 - in association with *tbf* Transport Benevolent Fund

contracts, excursions & tours, private hire, continental tours.
Livery: Blue & Silver
Ticket System: Wayfarer TGX150

WILKINSONS TRAVEL
2 REDSCOPE CRESCENT, KIMBERWORTH PARK, ROTHERHAM S61 3LX
Tel: 01709 553403 **Fax:** 01709 550550
Owner: M. D. Wilkinson.
Fleet: 9 - 2 single-deck coach, 3 minibus, 4 minicoach.
Chassis: AEC, Volvo.
Bodies: Berkhof, Duple, Ikarus, Jonckheere.
Ops incl: excursions & tours, private hire, continental tours, school contracts.

WILLIAMSONS OF ROTHERHAM
19 VICTORIA STREET, CATCLIFFE S60 5SJ
Tel: 01709 366856
Fax: 01709 828241
Prop: P. Williamson.
Fleet: 3 single-deck coach.

Chassis: 1 Bedford, 1 DAF, 1 Leyland.
Bodies: 1 Duple, 1 Leyland, 1 Van Hool.
Ops incl: school contracts, excursions & tours, private hire, continental tours.
Livery: White.

WILSON'S COACHES
PLOT 5, BANKWOOD LANE INDUSTRIAL ESTATE, ROSSINGTON, DONCASTER DN11 0PS
Tel: 01302 866193
E-mail: info@wilson-tours.co.uk
Web site: www.wilson-tours.co.uk
Prop: E Wilson
Fleet: 3 single-deck coach.
Chassis: 1 EOS, 2 Volvo.
Bodies: 1 Berkhof, 2 Van Hool.
Ops incl: excursions & tours, private hire, continental tours.

WOMBWELL COACH TOURS LTD
1 CEMETARY ROAD, WOMBWELL, BARNSLEY S73 8HZ
Tel: 01226 753903
Fleet: single-deck coach, midicoach, minibus

Ops incl: school contracts, excursions & tours, private hire
Livery: White with Blue

WOODS COACHES
NEW LODGE, WAKEFIELD ROAD, BARNSLEY S71 1PA
Tel: 01226 286830
E-mail: contact@woodscoachesbarnsley.co.uk
Web site: www.woodscoaches.co.uk
Fleet: 4 single-deck coach
Chassis: 4 VDL
Bodies: 4 Van Hool
Ops incl: excursions & tours, private hire
Livery: White with Blue/Yellow

YORKSHIRE ROSE COACHES
28 BRANKSOME AVENUE, BARNSLEY S70 6XH
Tel: 0808 166 2924
Web site: www.yorkshireroseholidays.co.uk
Fleet: 5 – 4 single-deck coaches, 1 midicoach
Chassis: 1 DAF, 1 Mercedes, 3 Volvo
Bodies: 1 Unvi, 3 Van Hool, 1 Volvo
Ops incl: private hire, excursions & tours
Livery: White with Blue/Red

STAFFORDSHIRE, CITY OF STOKE ON TRENT

ACE TRAVEL
10 BIDDULPH PARK, IRONSTONE ROAD, BURNTWOOD WS7 1LG
Tel: 01543 279068
Prop: G. E. Elson.
Fleet: 1 midicoach.
Chassis: Toyota.
Ops incl: excursions & tours, private hire, continental tours, school contracts.

ARRIVA MIDLANDS LTD
852 MELTON ROAD, LEICESTER LE4 8BT
Tel: 0116 264 0400 **Fax:** 0116 260 5605
Web site: www.arriva.co.uk
Fleet Name: Arriva serving the North Midlands
Man Dir: R A Hind **Fin Dir:** J Barlow
Ops Dir: A Lloyd **Eng Dir:** M Evans
Area Business Man (Staffordshire): K Walker
Fleet: 658 - 134 double-deck bus, 176 single-deck bus, 3 articulated bus, 232 midibus, 113 minibus.
Chassis: 116 DAF, 222 Dennis, 9 Leyland, 3 Mercedes, 66 Optare, 69 Scania, 54 VDL, 125 Volvo
Bodies: 55 Alexander, 1 Caetano, 73 East Lancs, 3 Mercedes, 5 Marshall, 21 Northern Counties, 66 Optare, 176 Plaxton, 44 Scania, 8 UVG, 206 Wright.
Ops incl: local bus services.
Livery: Arriva
Ticket System: Wayfarer

BAKERS COACHES
THE COACH TRAVEL CENTRE, PROSPECT WAY, VICTORIA BUSINESS PARK, BIDDULPH ST8 7PL
Tel: 01782 522101
Fax: 01782 522363
E-mail: sales@bakerscoaches.com
Web site: www.bakerscoaches.com
Man Dir: Philip Baker **Ops Man:** Dave Machin **Co Sec:** Susan Baker
Fleet: 56 - 15 single-deck bus, 15 single-

deck coach, 24 midibus, 2 midicoach.
Chassis: 11 Alexander Dennis, 11 Mercedes, 4 Optare, 9 Scania, 3 VDL, 18 Volvo.
Bodies: 10 Alexander Dennis, 3 Berkhof, 2 Caetano, 2 Irizar, 2 Jonckheere, 4 Optare, 21 Plaxton, 1 Sitcar, 3 Scania, 2 Van Hool, 6 Wright.
Ops incl: local bus services, school contracts, excursions & tours, private hire, continental tours.
Livery: Coach – Green/White; Bus – Yellow/Blue
Ticket System: Wayfarer TGX150

BENNETTS TRAVEL (CRANBERRY) LTD
CRANBERRY, COTES HEATH ST21 6SQ
Tel: 01782 791468
Prop/Gen Man: J. P. McDonnell.
Fleet: 27 – single-deck bus, single-deck coach, midibus, minibus.
Chassis: Bedford, Ford Transit, Leyland, Mercedes.
Bodies: Mercedes, Plaxton.
Ops incl: local bus services, excursions & tours, private hire.
Livery: Blue/White

L F BOWEN LTD
104 MARINER, LICHFIELD ROAD INDUSTRIAL ESTATE, TAMWORTH B79 7UL
Tel: 01827 300000 **Fax:** 01827 300009
E-mail: coachhire@bowenstravel.com
Web site: www.bowenstravel.com
Chairman & Ch Exec: Kevin Lower
Man Dir (Coaching): R Lyng
Group Ops Man: N G Tetley
Group Eng Man: D Hoy
Fin Dir: R Graham **Man Dir (Retail):** N Stones **Property Dir:** N Ellis
Dirs: A H Moseley, C J Padbury, K G York
Fleet: 39 - 27 single-deck coach, 2 midicoach, 10 minibus
Chassis: 10 MAN, 15 Scania, 2 Toyota, 10 Volkswagen, 2 Volvo
Bodies: 15 Irizar, 2 Marcopolo. 8 Noge, 2 Plaxton.

Ops incl: school contracts, private hire, express, continental tours, excursions & tours.
Livery: Silver/sun emblem

TERRY BUSHELL TRAVEL
14 DERBY STREET, BURTON-ON-TRENT DE14 2LA
Tel/Fax: 01283 538242
E-mail: info@terrybushelltravel.co.uk
Web site: www.terrybushelltravel.co.uk
Prop: Terry Bushell
Fleet: 3 - 2 single-deck coach, 1 minicoach.
Chassis: 2 Mercedes, 1 Volvo.
Bodies: 1 Mercedes, 1 Neoplan, 1 Van Hool.
Ops incl: excursions & tours, private hire, continental tours.
Livery: Red/Poppy/Gold

CLOWES COACHES
See Derbyshire

COPELAND TOURS (STOKE-ON-TRENT) LTD
1009 UTTOXETER ROAD, MEIR, STOKE ON TRENT, ST3 6HE
Tel: 01782 324466
Fax: 01782 319401
Recovery: 01782 324466
E-mail: mb@copelandtours.co.uk
Web site: www.copelandtours.co.uk
Chairman/Man Dir: J E M Burn
Dir: Mrs P Burn **Ch Eng:** J C Burn
Co Sec: J E M Burn
Fleet: 26 - 1 single-deck bus, 22 single-deck coach, 2 midibus, 1 midicoach.
Chassis: 1 AEC, 14 DAF, 1 Dennis, 7 Leyland, 1 MAN, 2 Mercedes.
Bodies: 1 Duple, 1 Jonckheere, 1 Marshall, 17 Plaxton, 4 Van Hool, 2 Wadham Stringer.
Ops incl: local bus services, school contracts, excursions & tours, private hire, express, continental tours.
Livery: Blue-Blue/Orange.
Ticket System: Wayfarer.

CRUSADE TRAVEL LTD
THE COACHYARD, COPPICE FARM, TEDDESLEY, HUNTINGDON, PENKRIDGE ST19 5RP
Tel: 01785 714124 **Fax:** 01543 579678
E-mail: crusade-tvl@tiscali.co.uk
Web site: www.crusade-travel.com
Ops Man: Gavin Pardoe
Fleet incl: single-deck coach, midicoach, minibus, minicoach.
Chassis: 1 Dennis, 3 Mercedes, 2 Volvo.
Ops incl: school contracts, excursions & tours, private hire.

D & G COACH AND BUS LTD
MOSSFIELD ROAD, ADDERLEY GREEN ST3 5BW
Tel: 01782 332337 **Fax:** 01782 337864
E-mail: dreeves@dgbus.co.uk
Web site: www.dgbus.co.uk
Man Dir: D Reeves
Fleet Eng: M Johnson
Depot Eng: K Mitchell
Fleet: 49 - 14 single-deck coach, 35 midibus.
Chassis: 10 Dennis, 1 Ford, 33 Mercedes, 5 Optare.
Bodies: 7 Alexander, 2 Carlyle, 3 East Lancs, 1 Marshall, 6 Optare, 12 Plaxton, 2 Reeve Burgess, 1 Wadham Stringer, 4 Wright, 11 Other.
Ops incl: local bus services, school contracts.
Livery: Cream/Blue
Ticket system: Wayfarer

D H CARS OF DENSTONE LTD
9 HAWTHORN CLOSE, DENSTONE, UTTOXETER ST14 5HB
Tel: 01889 590819 **Fax:** 01889 591888
Dir: Donald Handley
Sec: Alison Williams
Fleet: 2 - 1 single-deck coach, 1 minicoach.
Chassis: 1 Mercedes, 1 Scania.
Bodies: 1 Crest, 1 Irizar
Ops incl: private hire
Livery: White with Gold/Blue lining.

FIRST MIDLANDS
ADDERLEY GREEN GARAGE, DIVIDY ROAD, STOKE ON TRENT ST3 0AJ
Tel: 01782 592500 **Fax:** 01782 592541
Man Dir: Ken Poole
Ops incl: local bus services, school contracts
Livery: FirstGroup UK Bus

GOLDEN GREEN TRAVEL
COWBROOK LANE, GAWSWORTH, MACCLESFIELD SK11 0JH
Tel: 01260 223453
E-mail: goldengreentravel@hotmail.com
Web site: www.goldengreentravel.co.uk
Partners: John Worth, Gill Worth, Derek J Lownds
Fleet: 11 single-deck coaches
Chassis and Bodies: Mercedes
Ops incl: local bus services, school contracts, excursions & tours, private hire

HAPPY DAYS COACHES
GREYFRIARS COACH STATION, GREYFRIARS WAY, STAFFORD ST16 2SH
Tel/Recovery: 01785 229797
Fax: 01785 229790
E-mail: info@happydayscoaches.co.uk
Web site: www.happydayscoaches.co.uk
Joint Man Dirs: Richard Austin, Neil Austin **Dir:** Brian Austin.
Fleet: 29 - 25 single-deck coach, 3 minicoach, 1 minibus.
Chassis: 3 DAF, 4 Mercedes, 5 Scania, 17 Volvo.
Bodies: 2 Bova, 2 Irizar, 1 Jonckheere, 12 Plaxton, 2 Scania, 10 Van Hool.
Ops incl: local bus services, excursions & tours, private hire, express, school contracts, continental tours
Livery: Rising Sun
Ticket System: Setright

HOLLINSHEAD COACHES LTD
BEMERSLEY ROAD, KNYPERSLEY ST8 7PZ
Tel: 01782 512209
Fleet: 10 single-deck coach
Chassis: 1 DAF, 2 Leyland, 7 Volvo.
Ops incl: school contracts, excursions & tours, private hire

JOSEPHS MINI COACHES
171 CRACKLEY BANK, CHESTERTON, NEWCASTLE-UNDER-LYME ST5 7AB
Tel: 01782 564944
Prop: Joseph Windsor
Fleet: 1 minicoach.
Chassis/Body: 1 Mercedes.
Ops incl: private hire
Livery: White

LEONS COACH TRAVEL (STAFFORD) LTD
DOUGLAS HOUSE, TOLLGATE, BEACONSIDE, STAFFORD ST16 3EE
Tel: 01785 244575
Fax: 01785 258444
E-mail: andy@leons.co.uk
Web site: www.leons.co.uk
Dirs: Andrew Douglas, Robert Douglas, Leon Douglas **Co Sec:** Sylvia Douglas
Fleet: 30 - 23 single-deck coach, 7 midicoach.
Chassis: 3 Bova, 1 DAF, 2 Ford, 2 MAN, 11 Scania, 4 Volvo.
Bodies: 2 Berkhof, 3 Bova, 2 Duple, 5 Irizar, 1 Plaxton, 4 Reeve Burgess, 6 Van Hool.
Ops incl: excursions & tours, school contracts, private hire, continental tours.
Livery: Red/Yellow/Orange/Purple

MIDLAND CLASSIC LTD
UNIT 5, 290 STANTON ROAD, BURTON-ON-TRENT DE15 9SQ
Tel/Fax: 01283 500228
E-mail: info@midlandclassic.com
Web site: www.midlandclassic.com
Dirs: James Boddice, Julian H Peddle, David B Reeves, John Mitcheson
Fleet: 9 – 1 double-deck bus, 7 single-deck bus, 1 midibus.
Chassis: 1 AEC, 4 Alexander Dennis, 1 Optare, 3 Volvo.
Bodies: 1 Optare, 4 Plaxton, 3 Wright, 1 Other.
Ops incl: local bus services, private hire.
Livery: LT Red/Stevensons Yellow
Ticket System: Wayfarer 3.

PARAGON TRAVEL LTD
THE GARAGE, SPATH ST14 5AE
Tel: 01889 569899
Fax: 01889 563518
Recovery: 01889 569899
E-mail: phil@paragontravel.co.uk
Web site: www.paragontravel.co.uk
Dir: P L Smith
Fleet: 14 single-deck coach
Chassis: 1 Leyland, 1 Mercedes, 2 Scania, 10 Volvo
Bodies: 1 Alexander, 3 Jonckheere, 4 Plaxton, 6 Van Hool.
Ops incl: local bus services, school contracts, excursions & tours, continental tours, private hire.
Livery: White with Blue/Red lettering.
Ticket system: Setright

PARRYS INTERNATIONAL TOURS LTD
LANDYWOOD GREEN, CHESLYN HAY WS6 7QX
Tel: 01922 414576 **Fax:** 01922 413416
E-mail: info@parrys-international.co.uk
Web site: www.parrys-international.co.uk
Man Dir: David Parry
Fleet: 16 - 13 single-deck coach, 3 minicoach.
Chassis: 3 Mercedes, 13 Van Hool.
Bodies: 3 Mercedes, 13 Van Hool.
Ops incl: excursions & tours
Livery: Red/Gold

PLANTS LUXURY TRAVEL LTD
167 TEAN ROAD, CHEADLE ST10 1LS
Tel: 01538 753561
Fax: 01538 757025
E-mail: julie.plant@plantsluxurytravel.co.uk
Web site: www.plantsluxurytravel.co.uk
Partners: T J Plant, M P Plant
Fleet: 4 - 1 midicoach, 3 minicoach.
Chassis: 3 Mercedes, 1 Toyota.
Bodies incl: 1 Optare.
Ops incl: private hire, school contracts.
Livery: Silver with Burgundy/Gold/Mustard stripes

F PROCTER & SON LTD
DEWSBURY ROAD, FENTON ST4 2TE
Tel: 01782 846031 **Fax:** 01782 744732
Dirs: R Walker, J Walker.
Fleet: 16
Chassis: 2 Bova, 5 DAF, 1 Iveco, 6 Leyland, 2 Scania.
Ops incl: local bus services, school contracts, excursions & tours, private hire.
Livery: Blue/White
Ticket System: Wayfarer

ROBIN HOOD TRAVEL LTD
HIGHWAY GARAGE, MACCLESFIELD ROAD, LEEK ST13 8PS
Tel: 01538 306618
Fax: 01538 306079
Web site: www.robinhoodtravel.co.uk
Fleet: 12 - 3 single-deck bus, 7 single-deck coach, 1 midicoach, 1 minicoach.
Chassis incl: 6 Bova
Ops incl: school contracts, excursions & tours, private hire, continental tours
Livery: Green/Gold stars

SHIRE TRAVEL INTERNATIONAL LTD
UNIT 4:02 CANNOCK ENTERPRISE CENTRE, WALKERS RISE, HEDNESFORD WS12 0QU
Tel/Fax: 01543 871605
E-mail: hire@shiretravel.co.uk
Web site: www.shiretravel.co.uk

Dir: Robert Garrington **Comp Sec:** Michelle Wassell
Fleet: 9 - 3 single-deck coach, 1 midibus, 5 minibus.
Chassis incl: 1 Scania, 2 Setra, 5 Mercedes.
Bodies: 1 Irizar, 6 Mercedes, 2 Setra.
Ops incl: private hire, school contracts, excursions & tours, continental tours.
Livery: White/Red + end three lions flag

SOLUS COACH TRAVEL LTD
LICHFIELD ROAD INDUSTRIAL ESTATE, TAMWORTH B79 7TA
Tel: 01827 51736
Fax: 0871 900 4124
Recovery: 01785 222666
E-mail: info@soluscoaches.co.uk
Web site: www.soluscoaches.co.uk
Man Dir: Andy Garratt
Co Sec: Lucy Garratt
Ch Eng: Graham Hopkins
Ops Man: Dave Wakelin
Fin Dir: David Baldwin
Fleet: 24 – single-deck bus, single-deck coach, midibus, minibus, midicoach, minicoach.
Chassis incl: 2 Bova, 4 DAF, 8 Ford Transit, 1 Mercedes, 3 Scania, 1 Setra, 4 Temsa.
Bodies incl: 2 Bova, 3 Irizar, 1 Mercedes, 1 Plaxton, 1 Scania, 1 Setra, 4 Van Hool, 4 Volvo, 1 Other.
Ops incl: local bus services, school contracts, excursions & tours, private hire, continental tours.
Livery: Red/Black/Grey
Ticket System: Wayfarer

STANWAYS COACHES
ODLUMS GARAGE, KNUTSFORD ROAD, RODE HEATH, STOKE-ON-TRENT ST7 3QT
Tel: 01270 884242
Fax: 01270 884262
E-mail: stanwayscoaches@yahoo.co.uk

Partners: David Elliot, Paul Richman,
Fleet: 11 - 1 single-deck bus, 8 single-deck coach, 2 midibus.
Chassis: 1 DAF, 3 Dennis, 4 Leyland, 1 Optare, 1 Scania, 4 Volvo.
Bodies: 1 Alexander Dennis, 1 Berkhof, 1 Caetano, 1 Duple, 3 Plaxton, 4 Other.
Ops incl: local bus services, school contracts, private hire.
Livery: various
Ticket System: Wayfarer

STODDARDS LTD
GREENHILL GARAGE, LEEK ROAD, CHEADLE ST10 1JF
Tel: 01538 752253 **Fax:** 01538 750375
E-mail: info@stoddards.co.uk
Web site: www.stoddards.co.uk
Man Dir: Judith Stoddard
Fin Dir: Peter Stoddard
Workshop/Vehicles: Paul Stoddard
Co Sec: Brian Stoddard
Fleet: 5 - 5 single-deck coach.
Chassis: 5 DAF
Bodies: 5 Bova.
Ops incl: excursions & tours, private hire, school contracts.
Livery: Silver/Blue

SWIFTSURE TRAVEL (BURTON-UPON-TRENT) LTD
UNIT 6, 290 STANTON ROAD, BURTON-UPON-TRENT DE15 9SQ
Tel: 01283 512974
Fax: 01283 516728
E-mail: info@swiftsure-travel.co.uk
Web site: www.swiftsure-travel.co.uk
Man Dir: Richard Hackett
Dirs: Julian Peddle, Brian Kershaw
Co Sec: Kathleen Hackett
Fleet: 7 - 4 single-deck coach, 2 midicoach, 1 minicoach.
Chassis: 1 Bova, 1 DAF, 1 LDV, 2 Mercedes, 1 Scania, 1 Toyota.
Bodies: 1 Bova, 1 Caetano, 2 Optare, 1 Scania, 1 Van Hool, 1 Other.

Ops incl: school contracts, excursions & tours, express, private hire.
Livery: White/Blue/Green

TAMWORTH COACH CO
66 FAZELEY ROAD, TAMWORTH B78 3JN
Tel: 01827 51736
Fax: 0871 900 4124
Prop: Thomas Garratt
Fleet: 3 single-deck coach.
Chassis/Bodies: 3 Setra.
Ops incl: private hire.
Livery: White.

WARDLE TRANSPORT
DOUGLAS HOUSE, RAFFERTY BUSINESS PARK, SNEYD TRADING ESTATE, BURSLEM ST6 2BY
Tel: 01782 827282 **Fax:** 01782 833679
Web site: www.wardletransport.co.uk
Fleet: double-deck bus, single-deck coach, midibus, minibus
Ops incl: local bus services, school contracts, private hire.
Livery: Red & White

WARRINGTON COACHES
See Derbyshire

WINTS COACHES
MONTANA, WETTON ROAD, BUTTERTON ST13 7ST
Tel/Fax: 01538 713938
Web site: www.wintscoachesleek.co.uk
Props: Andrew Wint, Maxine Wint.
Fleet: 10 - 8 single-deck coach, 2 minicoach.
Chassis: 1 DAF, 1 Dennis, 6 Mercedes, 1 Optare, 1 Volvo.
Bodies: 1 Bova, 6 Mercedes, 1 Neoplan, 1 Optare, 1 Plaxton.
Ops incl: school contracts, excursions & tours, private hire, continental tours.

SUFFOLK

ANGLIAN BUS & COACH LTD
BECCLES BUSINESS PARK, BECCLES NR34 7TH
Tel: 01502 711109
Fax: 01502 711161
E-mail: office@angliancoaches.co.uk
Web site: www.anglianbus.co.uk
Fleet: 62 - 6 double-deck bus, 24 single-deck bus, 1 single-deck coach, 23 midibus, 8 minibus.
Chassis: 1 Alexander Dennis, 2 Dennis, 7 Mercedes, 28 Optare, 22 Scania, 2 Volvo.
Bodies: 2 Alexander, 1 Alexander Dennis, 1 Mercedes, 28 Optare, 7 Plaxton, 17 Scania, 1 Wadham Stringer, 5 Wright.
Ops incl: local bus services, school contracts.
Livery: Yellow with blue stripes
Ticket System: Wayfarer 3

AWAYDAYS LTD, t/a GEMINI TRAVEL
UNIT 20, STERLING COMPLEX, FARTHING ROAD, IPSWICH IP1 5AP
Tel: 01473 462721
Fax: 01473 462731
E-mail: info@geminiofipswich.co.uk

Web site: www.geminiofipswich.co.uk
Dir: Ed Nicholls
Fleet: 7 – 2 midicoach, 1 minibus, 4 minicoach.
Chassis: 6 Mercedes, 1 Renault.
Bodies: 1 Mellor, 5 Optare, 1 Reeve Burgess.
Ops incl: excursions & tours, private hire, school contracts, continental tours
Livery: Red/White

BEESTONS (HADLEIGH) LTD
THE COACH DEPOT, IPSWICH ROAD, HADLEIGH IP7 6BG
Tel: 01473 823243
Fax: 01473 823608
Recovery: 07748 988555
E-mail: info@beestons.co.uk
Web site: www.beestons.co.uk
Man Dir: P R Munson
Co Sec: S J Munson
Ops Man: T Munson
Fleet: 10 - 1 double-deck bus, 6 single-deck coach, 2 double-deck coach, 1 minicoach.
Chassis: 1 Mercedes, 2 Scania, 6 Volvo, 1 Other.
Bodies: 1 Optare, 1 Plaxton, 8 Van Hool.
Ops incl: school contracts, excursions & tours, private hire.
Livery: Gold/Black

BURTONS COACHES
DUDDERY HILL, HAVERHILL CB9 8DR
Tel: 01440 702257
Fax: 01440 713287
Recovery: 01440 760391
E-mail: hire@burtons-bus.co.uk
Web site: www.burtonscoaches.com
Man Dir: Paul J Cooper
Dir: Tracy Atkinson-Cooper
Traffic Man: Paul Steed
Workshop Man: Steve Freemantle
Fleet: 32 - 9 double-deck bus, 4 single-deck bus, 15 single-deck coach, 1 midicoach, 2 minibus, 1 minicoach.
Chassis: Alexander Dennis, DAF, Leyland, Mercedes, Scania, Volvo.
Bodies: Alexander Dennis, Bova, Caetano, East Lancs, Irizar, Northern Counties, Plaxton, Van Hool.
Ops incl: local bus services, school contracts, excursions & tours, private hire, continental tours.
Livery: Blue/White/Yellow
Ticket system: Almex A90

CARTERS COACH SERVICES
LONDON ROAD, CAPEL ST MARY, IPSWICH IP9 2JT

Tel: 01473 378018
E-mail: enquiries@cartersbusdepot.demon.co.uk
Web site: www.carterscoachservices.co.uk
Fleet: 18 - 4 double-deck bus, 4 single-deck bus, 5 midibus, 1 minibus, 4 vintage
Chassis: 3 Alexander Dennis, 1 DAF, 4 Dennis, 1 Enterprise, 1 Mercedes, 1 Optare, 3 Volvo.
Bodies: 2 Alexander, 3 Alexander Dennis, 1 Koch, 1 MCV, 1 Northern Counties, 1 Optare, 5 Plaxton.
Ops incl: local bus services, school contracts, private hire.
Livery: Red/Yellow/Black

H C CHAMBERS & SON LTD
HIGH STREET, BURES CO8 5AB
Tel: 01787 227233
Fax: 01787 227042
Recovery: 07770 886834
E-mail: info@chamberscoaches.co.uk
Web site: www.chamberscoaches.co.uk
Ops Dir: Alec Chambers
Eng Dir: Robert Chambers
Fleet: 30 - 19 double-deck bus, 6 single-deck bus, 4 single-deck coach, 1 minibus
Chassis: 5 Dennis, 3 Mercedes, 22 Volvo.
Bodies: 15 Alexander, 4 East Lancs, 2 Mercedes, 6 Northern Counties, 1 Plaxton, 1 Van Hool, 1 Wright.
Ops incl: local bus services, excursions & tours, private hire.
Livery: Red
Ticket System: Wayfarer

CONSTABLE COACHES LTD
THE COACH DEPOT, IPSWICH ROAD, HADLEIGH IP7 6BG
Tel: 01473 828555
Web site: www.constablecoachesltd.co.uk
Man Dir: P R Munson
Co Sec: S J Munson
Ops Man: T Munson
Fleet: 21 – 10 double-deck bus, 7 single-deck bus, 4 minibus.
Chassis: 4 Mercedes, 11 Scania, 6 Volvo.
Bodies: 1 Alexander, 6 East Lancs, 1 Northern Counties, 1 Optare, 4 Plaxton, 2 Scania, 6 Wright.
Ops incl: local bus services, school contracts.
Livery: All over Dark Blue
Ticket System: Wayfarer 3
Associated with Beestons (Hadleigh) Ltd

CUTTINGS COACHES
HAWKS FARM, BROCKLEY, BURY ST EDMUNDS IP29 4AQ
Tel/Fax: 01284 830368
Prop: Roger D Stittle
Fleet: 5 – 4 single-deck coach, 1 minibus.
Chassis incl: 2 DAF, 1 Setra, 1 Volvo.
Bodies incl: 1 Plaxton, 1 Setra, 2 Van Hool.
Ops incl: school contracts, excursions & tours.
Livery: Red/White/Blue

D-WAY TRAVEL
GREENWAYS, THE STREET, EARSHAM, BUNGAY NR35 2TZ
Tel: 01986 895375

Fax: 05600 751425
E-mail: david@dwaytravel.com
Web site: www.dwaytravel.com
Prop: David Thompson
Fleet: 12 - 7 single-deck coach, 1 minibus, 2 minicoach, 2 midicoach.
Chassis incl: 1 Ford, 1 Ford Transit, 7 MAN, 2 Mercedes.
Ops incl: school contracts, excursions & tours, private hire, continental tours.

FAR EAST TRAVEL
UNIT 20, STERLING COMPLEX, FARTHING ROAD, IPSWICH IP1 5AP
Tel: 01473 462721
Fax: 01473 462731
E-mail: info@geminiofipswich.co.uk
Web site: www.geminiofipswich.co.uk
Man Dir: Ed Nicholls
Fleet: 8 – 8 single-deck bus
Chassis: 2 Alexander Dennis, 1 Marshall, 4 Mercedes, 1 Optare.
Bodies: 2 Alexander Dennis, 1 Marshall/MCV, 1 Optare, 4 Plaxton.
Ops incl: local bus services, school contracts.
Livery: Red/White
Ticket System: Wayfarer
Associated with Awaydays Ltd, t/a Gemini Travel

FARELINE BUS & COACH SERVICES
OLD ROSES, SYLEHAM ROAD, WINGFIELD, EYE IP21 5RF
Tel: 01379 668151
Prop: Jeff Morss
Fleet: 1 single-deck coach
Chassis: 1 Bedford.
Body: 1 Plaxton
Ops incl: local bus services, school contracts, excursions & tours, private hire.
Livery: Blue/Cream
Ticket System: Setright Mk 3

FELIX OF LONG MELFORD
8 WINDMILL HILL, LONG MELFORD, SUDBURY CO10 9AD
Tel: 01787 310574, 372125
Fax: 01787 310584
Web site: www.felixcoaches.co.uk
Ops incl: local bus services, school contracts, excursions & tours, private hire
Livery: White with Red/Black

FIRST EAST OF ENGLAND (formerly FIRST EASTERN COUNTIES)
ROUEN HOUSE, ROUEN ROAD, NORWICH NR1 1RB
Tel: 08456 020 121
Fax: 01603 615439
Web site: www.firstgroup.com
Man Dir: Alan Pilbeam
Fin Dir: Jacky Cato
Eng Dir: Phil Pannell
Comm & Customer Services Dir: Steve Wickers
Fleet: 699 - 174 double-deck bus, 222 single-deck bus, 19 single-deck coach, 244 midibus, 40 minibus.
Chassis: AEC, BMC, Dennis, Leyland, Mercedes, Optare, Scania, Volvo.
Ops incl: local bus services, school contract, private hire.
Livery: FirstGroup UK Bus.
Ticket System: Wayfarer 3

FORGET-ME-NOT (TRAVEL) LTD
CHAPEL ROAD, OTLEY, IPSWICH IP6 9NT
Tel: 01473 890268 **Fax:** 01473 890748
E-mail: sales@forgetmenot-travel.co.uk
Web site: www.forgetmenottravel.co.uk
Fleet Name: Soames
Dirs: A F Soames, Mrs M A Soames (**Co Sec**), A M Soames (**Ch Eng**)
Fleet: 16 - 16 single-deck coach, 1 midicoach.
Chassis: 1 Mercedes, 16 Volvo.
Bodies: 1 Esker, 1 Jonckheere, 13 Plaxton, 1 Van Hool.
Ops incl: private hire, school contracts.
Livery: Three tone Blue

GALLOWAY EUROPEAN COACHLINES LTD
DENTERS HILL, MENDLESHAM, STOWMARKET IP14 5RR
Tel: 01449 766323
Fax: 01449 766241
E-mail: david@gallowayeuropean.co.uk
Web: www.gallowayeuropean.com
Man Dir: David Cattermole
Comm Dir: John Miles **Fin Dir:** Roger Stedman **Fleet Man:** Andy Kemp
Ops Man: Richard Smith
Comm Man: Liz Palfrey
Training Man: Ian Brain
Fleet: 44 - 2 double-deck bus, 14 single-deck bus, 25 single-deck coach, 3 midicoach.
Chassis: 28 DAF/VDL, 1 Iveco, 10 Mercedes, 1 Scania, 2 Setra, 2 Temsa.
Bodies: 1 Beulas, 4 Ikarus, 3 Optare, 14 Plaxton, 3 Setra, 1 UVG, 14 Van Hool, 4 Wright.
Ops incl: local bus services, school contracts, excursions & tours, private hire, express.
Livery: Multi Globe & Star based.
Ticket System: Wayfarer 3.

HARLEQUIN TRAVEL
77 LANERCOST WAY, IPSWICH IP2 9DP
Tel: 01473 407408
E-mail: paul.lewis80@ntlworld.com
Web site: www.harlequin-travel.co.uk
Dirs: P D Lewis, Mrs L M Lewis
Fleet: 3 - 2 midicoach, 1 minibus.
Chassis: 2 Mercedes, 1 Peugeot
Bodies incl: 1 Autobus, 1 Plaxton.
Ops incl: school contracts, private hire
Livery: Maroon/White

IPSWICH BUSES LTD
7 CONSTANTINE ROAD, IPSWICH IP1 2DL
Tel: 01473 232600 **Fax:** 01473 232062
Recovery: 01473 344817
E-mail: info@ipswichbuses.co.uk
Web site: www.ipswichbuses.co.uk
Man Dir: Malcolm Robson
Chair: Paul West
Fleet: 71 - 28 double-deck bus, 1 open-top bus, 33 single-deck bus, 9 midibus.
Chassis: 1 Bristol, 11 DAF, 24 Dennis, 10 Leyland, 13 Optare, 9 Scania, 3 Volvo.
Bodies: 2 Alexander, 8 ECW, 35 East Lancs, 18 Optare, 1 Roe, 6 Scania Omnicity
Ops incl: local bus services, school contracts.
Livery: Green/White
Ticket System: Wayfarer TGX150

Suffolk

The Little Red Book 2011 - in association with *tbf* Transport Benevolent Fund

LAMBERT'S COACHES (BECCLES) LTD
UNIT 4A, MOOR BUSINESS PARK, BENACRE ROAD, BECCLES NR34 7TQ
Tel: 01502 717579
Fax: 01502 711209
E-mail: lorraine@lambertscoaches.co.uk
Web site: www.lambertscoaches.co.uk
Chairman: D M Reade
Dir: Miss L K Reade
Fleet: 7 single-deck coach.
Chassis: 5 DAF, 2 Volvo.
Bodies: 7 Van Hool.
Ops incl: private hire, school contracts.
Livery: White with Blue Signwriting

MIL-KEN TRAVEL LTD
GRASSMERE, BURY ROAD, KENTFORD, NEWMARKET CB8 7PZ
Tel: 01353 860705
Fax: 01353 863222
E-mail: milken@btconnect.com
Web site: www.milkentravel.com
Man Dir: Jason Miller
Fleet Man: Ian Martin
Fleet: 32 - 29 single-deck coach, 2 minibus, 1 minicoach.
Chassis: 1 Dennis, 2 LDV, 1 Mercedes, 2 VDL, 26 Volvo.
Bodies: 2 LDV, 25 Plaxton, 1 Sitcar, 4 Van Hool.
Ops incl: school contracts, private hire.
Livery: White with Red, Blue, Yellow.
See also Mil-Ken Travel Ltd, Cambridgeshire

MINIBUS & COACH HIRE
LINGS FARM, BLACKSMITHS LANE, FORWARD GREEN, EARL STONHAM IP14 5ET.
Tel: 01449 711117
Fax: 01449 711977
Owner: Mrs L. J. Eustace.
Fleet: 11 - 3 single-deck coach, 8 minibus.

Chassis: 3 Bedford, 1 Iveco, 6 LDV, 1 Nissan.
Ops incl: local bus services, school contracts, excursions & tours, private hire.

MULLEYS MOTORWAYS LTD
STOW ROAD, IXWORTH, BURY ST EDMUNDS IP31 2JB.
Tel: 01359 230234
Fax: 01359 232451
E-mail: enquiries@mulleys.co.uk
Web site: www.mulleys.co.uk
Dir/Co Sec: Jayne D Munson
Man Dir: David J Munson
Ops Man: Daniel Munson
Fleet: 43 - 9 double-deck bus, 6 single-deck bus, 17 single-deck coach, 1 double-deck coach, 2 midicoach, 7 midibus, 1 minibus.
Chassis: 3 BMC, 1 Ford Transit, 1 Irisbus, 2 Iveco, 10 Leyland, 8 Mercedes, 6 Scania, 2 Setra, 10 Volvo.
Bodies: 3 Alexander, 3 BMC, 2 Beulas, 3 ECW, 3 East Lancs, 1 Euro, 1 Ford, 1 Indcar, 1 Irizar, 7 Jonckheere, 1 Northern Counties, 6 Plaxton, 2 Setra, 2 Transbus, 5 Van Hool.
Ops incl: local bus services, school contracts, excursions & tours, private hire, continental tours.
Livery: Orange/Silver.
Ticket System: Wayfarer.

ROUTESPEK COACH HIRE LTD
3 ELMS CLOSE, EARSHAM, NR BUNGAY NR35 2TD
Tel/Fax: 01968 893035
Dirs: Mr K Reeve, Mrs R Reeve
Fleet: 4 - 1 double-deck bus, 3 single-deck coach.
Chassis: 1 Bristol, 2 Leyland, 1 Volvo.
Bodies: 1 ECW, 3 Van Hool.
Ops incl: local bus service, school contracts, private hire.
Livery: Fawn
Ticket System: hand m/c

B R SHREEVE & SONS LTD
HADENHAM ROAD, LOWESTOFT NR33 7NF
Tel: 01502 532000 **Fax:** 01502 532009
E-mail: info@bellecoaches.co.uk
Web site: www.bellecoaches.co.uk
Fleet Name: Belle Coaches.
Man Dirs: Ken Shreeve, Robert Shreeve
Co Sec: Susan Speed
Fleet: 45 - 38 single-deck coach, 3 midicoach, 4 minibus
Chassis: 1 DAF, 2 Ford Transit, 3 MAN, 21 Mercedes, 7 Scania, 1 Toyota, 2 Volkswagen, 8 Volvo.
Bodies: 1 Caetano, 1 Duple, 7 Plaxton, 19 Setra, 9 Van Hool, 8 other.
Ops incl: school contracts, excursions & tours, private hire, continental tours.
Livery: Blue

SQUIRRELL'S COACHES
THE COACH HOUSE, THE CAUSEWAY, HITCHAM, IPSWICH IP7 7NF
Tel/Fax: 01449 740582
E-mail: info@squirrellscoaches.co.uk
Web site: www.coachhire4less.co.uk
Fleet: 7 - 5 single-deck coach, 2 midicoach.
Chassis: 1 Leyland, 2 Mercedes, 4 Volvo.
Bodies: 1 Autobus, 1 Reeve Burgess, 5 Van Hool.
Ops incl: school contracts, private hire.
Livery: Silver/Black/Orange

WHINCOP'S COACHES
THE GARAGE, PEASENHALL, SAXMUNDHAM IP17 2HJ
Tel: 01728 660233 **Fax:** 01728 660156
Owner: Paul S Whincop
Fleet: 10 single-deck coach.
Chassis: 10 Volvo.
Bodies: 2 Jonckheere, 6 Plaxton, 2 Van Hool.
Ops incl: school contracts, excursions & tours, private hire.

SURREY

ABELLIO WEST LONDON LTD
301 CAMBERWELL ROAD, LONDON SE5 0TF
Tel: 020 7788 8550
Fax: 020 7805 3502
E-mail: customer.care@abellio.co.uk
Web site: www.abellio.co.uk
Fleet Name: Abellio Surrey
Man Dir: Paul McGowan
Fleet: see Abellio London Ltd (London)
Ops incl: local bus services.
Livery: Red/White
A division of the Abellio Group

ARRIVA SOUTHERN COUNTIES
FRIARY BUS STATION, GUILDFORD GU1 4YP
Tel: 01483 505693
Fleet Name: Arriva serving Guildford & West Surrey.
Man Dir: Heath Williams
Comm Dir: Kevin Hawkins
Eng Dir: Brian Barraclough
Fin Dir: Beverley Lawson.
Fleet: see Arriva Southern Counties (Kent)
Ops incl: local bus services.
Livery: Arriva UK Bus.
Ticket System: Wayfarer 3

BANSTEAD COACHES LTD
1 SHRUBLAND ROAD, BANSTEAD SM7 2ES
Tel: 01737 354322 **Fax:** 01737 371090
E-mail: sales@bansteadcoaches.co.uk
Web site: www.bansteadcoaches.co.uk
Dirs: D C Haynes, C J Haynes, M C Haynes.
Fleet: 17 - 16 single-deck coach, 1 midicoach.
Chassis: 1 Bedford, 8 Dennis, 4 Mercedes, 1 Toyota, 2 Volvo.
Bodies: 4 Berkhof, 4 Caetano, 1 Mercedes, 1 Neoplan, 7 Plaxton.
Ops incl: school contracts, private hire.
Livery: Pink/White.

BUSES4U
EAST SURREY RURAL TRANSPORT PARTNERSHIP, TANDRIDGE DISTRICT COUNCIL, STATION ROAD EAST, OXTED RH8 0BT
Tel: 01730 815518
Web site: www.buses4u.org.uk

CALL-A-COACH
CAPRI HOUSE, WALTON-ON-THAMES KT12 2LY
Tel: 01932 223838

Fax: 01932 269109
Owner: Arthur Freakes
Fleet: 8 – 3 single-deck coach, 2 midicoach, 3 minicoach
Chassis: 2 DAF, 3 LDV, 2 Mercedes.
Bodies: 2 Bova, 3 LDV, 2 Mercedes, 1 Van Hool.
Ops incl: school contracts, excursions & tours, private hire.

CHEAM COACHES
11 FREDERICK CLOSE, CHEAM SM1 2HY
Tel: 01372 742527
Fax: 01372 742528
E-mail: cheamco@aol.com
Web site: www.cheamcoaches.co.uk
Props: Michael Mower, Lise Cyr-Mower
Fleet: 6 - 2 single-deck coach, 4 minibus.
Chassis: 4 Mercedes, 1 Setra, 1 Volvo.
Bodies: 1 Jonckheere, 4 Mercedes, 1 Setra.
Ops incl: private hire, school contracts.

CHIVERS COACHES LTD
13A ROSS PARADE, WALLINGTON SM6 8QG
Tel: 020 8647 6648 **Fax:** 020 8647 6649
E-mail: chivlyn@aol.com

Dirs: Lynne Lucas, Melanie Chivers
Fleet: 4 - 2 single-deck coach, 1 midicoach, 1 minibus.
Chassis: 1 LDV, 1 Mercedes, 2 Volvo.
Bodies incl: 2 Van Hool.
Ops Incl: private hire, school contracts.
Livery: White with blue graphics

COUNTRYLINER GROUP
GB HOUSE, MERROW LANE, GUILDFORD GU4 7BQ
Tel: 01483 506919
Fax: 01483 506913
E-mail: info@countryliner-coaches.com
Web site: www.countryliner-coaches.co.uk
Dirs: R Hodgetts, R Belcher
Gen Man: N Hatcher
Ops Man: M Bishop **Eng Man:** G Mills
Fleet: 186 - double-deck bus, double-deck coach, single-deck bus, single-deck coach, midibus, midicoach.
Chassis: 80 Alexander Dennis, 25 DAF, 4 Leyland, 9 MAN, 1 Marshall, 10 MCW, 5 Mercedes, 2 Neoplan, 15 Optare, 15 Scania, 20 Volvo.
Bodies incl: 1 Berkhof, 4 Caetano, 5 ECW, 1 East Lancs, 1 Hispano, 11 Marshall/MCV, 4 Mercedes, 2 Neoplan, 3 Northern Counties, 83 Plaxton, 20 Van Hool.
Ops incl: local bus services, school contracts, private hire.
Livery: Green/White.
Ticket System: Wayfarer

CRUISERS LIMITED
UNIT M, KINGSFIELD BUSINESS CENTRE, REDHILL RH1 4DP
Tel: 01737 770036 **Fax:** 01737 770046
E-mail: info@cruisersltd.co.uk
Web site: www.cruisersltd.co.uk
Dir: M J Walter
Fleet: 35 - 3 single-deck bus, 9 single-deck coach, 20 minibus, 3 minicoach.
Chassis incl: Dennis, LDV, Mercedes, Volvo.
Bodies incl: Plaxton.
Ops incl: local bus services, school contracts, private hire.
Livery: Various Metallic
Ticket System: Almex

EPSOM COACHES GROUP
BLENHEIM ROAD, LONGMEAD BUSINESS PARK, EPSOM KT19 9AF
Tel: 01372 731700 **Fax:** 01372 731740
E-mail: sales@epsomcoaches.com
Web site: www.epsomcoaches.com
Fleet Names: Epsom Coaches, Quality Line
Chairman: R B Richmond MBE
Man Dir: A J Richmond
Comm Dir: S R Whiteway
Coach Hire Man: J Fowler
Bus Services Man: J Ball
Ch Eng: I Norman
Fin Controller: N Mandria
Fleet: 81 - 10 double-deck bus, 51 single-deck bus, 14 single-deck coach, 2 midicoach, 4 minibus.
Chassis: 31 Alexander Dennis, 7 Mercedes, 29 Optare, 14 Setra.
Bodies: 15 Alexander Dennis, 16 East Lancs, 5 Mercedes, 29 Optare, 2 Plaxton, 14 Setra.
Ops incl: local bus services, school contracts, excursions & tours, private hire, express, continental tours.
Livery: Red/Cream
Ticket system: Wayfarer

FARNHAM COACHES
See Safeguard Coaches

HARDINGS COACHES
WELLWOOD, WELLHOUSE LANE, BETCHWORTH RH3 7HH
Tel: 01737 842103 **Fax:** 01737 842831
E-mail: sales@hardings-coaches.co.uk
Fleet: 13 - 6 single-deck coach, 3 midicoach, 4 minicoach.
Chassis: 1 MAN, 5 Mercedes, 2 Scania, 4 Volvo.
Bodies: 2 Berkhof, 2 Autobus, 1 Caetano, 2 Esker, 2 Irizar, 3 Plaxton.
Ops incl: private hire

HARWOOD COACHES
51 ELLESMERE ROAD, WEYBRIDGE KT13 0HW
Tel: 01932 842073, 227272
Prop: G. A. Harwood.
Fleet: 5 single-deck coach.
Chassis: 2 Bedford, 3 Volvo.
Bodies: 2 Duple, 3 Van Hool.
Ops incl: private hire.
Livery: Beige/Red/Brown.

HILLS OF HERSHAM
129 BURWOOD ROAD HERSHAM KT12 4AN
Tel: 01932 254795
Fax: 01932 222671
Dir: D Hill
Fleet: 6 - single-deck coach, midicoach, minicoach, minibus.
Chassis: 1 Iveco, 1 LDV, 1 Mercedes, 1 Renault, 2 Volvo.
Bodies: 1 Beulas, 1 Jonckheere, 1 Mercedes, 1 Van Hool.
Ops incl: school contracts, private hire
Livery: White/Red

MAYDAY TRAVEL
UNIT 7, MILL LANE TRADING ESTATE, MILL LANE, CROYDON CR0 4AA
Tel: 020 8680 5111
Fax: 020 8680 8624
E-mail: info@coachhirelondon.co.uk
Web site: www.coachhirelondon.co.uk
Fleet: single-deck coach, midibus, minibus.
Ops incl: private hire, excursions & tours.
Livery: Silver/White/Blue

M&E COACHES
11 VAUX CRESCENT, HERSHAM KT12 4HE
Tel: 01932 244664
Prop/Gen Man: M. W. Oram
Sec: Mrs A. E. Oram.
Fleet: 3 single-deck coach.
Chassis: 1 MAN, 2 Mercedes.
Ops incl: school contracts, excursions & tours, private hire.
Livery: Blue/White.

MEMORY LANE VINTAGE OMNIBUS SERVICES
78 LILLIBROOKE CRESCENT, MAIDENHEAD SL6 3XQ
Tel: 01628 825050
Fax: 01628 825851
E-mail: admin@memorylane.co.uk
Web site: www.memorylane.co.uk
Prop: M J Clarke
Fleet: 6 - 3 double-deck bus, 3 single-deck bus
Chassis: 6 AEC.
Bodies: 2 ECW, 3 Park Royal, 1 Willowbrook.
Ops incl: private hire
Livery: Original operators

MERTON COMMUNITY TRANSPORT
JUSTIN PLAZA 3, SUITE 3, LONDON ROAD, MITCHAM CR4 4BE
Tel: 020 8648 7727
E-mail: mertonct@ukonline.co.uk

PICKERING COACHES
12 HAYSBRIDGE COTTAGES, WHITE WOOD LANE, SOUTH GODSTONE RHG 8JN
Tel/Fax: 01342 843731
Props: R. Pickering, Ms D. Pickering.
Fleet: 5 single-deck coach.
Chassis: Volvo.
Bodies: 2 Duple, 1 Jonckheere, 2 Plaxton.
Ops incl: private hire, school contracts.

SAFEGUARD COACHES LTD
GUILDFORD PARK ROAD, GUILDFORD GU2 7TH
Tel: 01483 561103
Fax: 01483 455865
E-mail: sales@safeguardcoaches.co.uk
Web site: www.safeguardcoaches.co.uk
Man Dir: Andrew Halliday
Ops Man: Chris West
Fleet: 35 - 7 single-deck bus, 25 single-deck coach, 3 midicoach.
Chassis: 1 AEC, 4 Dennis, 4 Mercedes, 6 Optare, 2 Setra, 19 Volvo.
Bodies: 1 Carlyle, 1 Hispano, 1 Mercedes, 7 Optare, 16 Plaxton, 2 Setra, 7 Van Hool, 1 Other.
Ops incl: local bus services, school contracts, private hire.
Livery: Red/Cream.
Ticket System: Wayfarer TGX 150 (Incorporating Farnham Coaches)

SKINNERS OF OXTED
15 BARROW GREEN ROAD, OXTED RH8 0NJ
Tel: 01883 713633
Fax: 01883 730079

Symbol	Meaning	Symbol	Meaning	Symbol	Meaning
♿	Vehicle suitable for disabled		Seat belt-fitted Vehicle	R24	24 hour recovery service
T	Toilet-drop facilities available		Coach(es) with galley facilities		Replacement vehicle available
R	Recovery service available		Air-conditioned vehicle(s)		Vintage Coach(es) available
	Open top vehicle(s)		Coaches with toilet facilities		

E-mail: enquiries@skinners.travel
Web site: www.skinners.travel
Partners: Stephen Skinner, Deborah Skinner.
Fleet: 13 - 10 single-deck coach, 2 midicoach, 1 minicoach.
Chassis: 4 Alexander Dennis, 1 MAN, 2 Mercedes, 6 Setra.
Bodies: 1 Duple, 1 Mercedes, 4 Neoplan, 1 Optare, 6 Setra.
Ops incl: excursions & tours, private hire, school contracts, continental tours.
Livery: Brown & Cream
(Incorporating Westerham Coaches)

STAGECOACH IN HANTS & SURREY
See Hampshire

SUNRAY TRAVEL LTD
79 ASHLEY ROAD, EPSOM KT18 5BN
Tel: 01372 740400 **Fax:** 01372 800778
E-mail: enquiries@gosunray.com
Web site: www.sunraytravel.co.uk
Fleet Name: Go Sunray.com
Dir: Noel Millier
Fleet: 7 - 4 single-deck bus, 3 single-deck coach
Chassis: 3 Dennis, 1 Leyland, 3 Volvo.
Bodies: Alexander, Carlyle, Plaxton.
Ops incl: local bus services, school contracts, excursions & tours, private hire, continental tours.
Livery: Blue with yellow/orange/red sun rays

SURELINE COACHES
UNIT 8, MARTLANDS INDUSTRIAL ESTATE, SMARTS HEATH LANE, MAYFORD, WOKING GU22 0RQ
Tel: 01483 234649
Fax: 01483 236464

E-mail: sureline@btclick.com
Prop: John McCracken
Fleet: 10 - 8 single-deck coach, 2 midicoach.
Chassis: 4. Bova, 2 MAN, 1 Mercedes, 2 Setra, 1 Toyota.
Bodies: 4 Bova, 2 Caetano, 1 Neoplan, 2 Setra, 1 other.
Ops incl: excursions & tours, private hire, school contracts, continental tours.
Livery: White with red signage

SURREY CONNECT
GATWICK COACH CENTRE, OLD BRIGHTON ROAD, LOWFIELD HEATH, CRAWLEY RH4 0PR
Tel: 01293 596831
See Flights Hallmark, West Sussex

SUTTON COMMUNITY TRANSPORT
UNIT 3, BROOKMEAD, JESSOPS WAY, CROYDON CR0 4TS
Tel: 020 8683 3944
Web site: www.suttonct.co.uk
Ch Exec: Mike Skinner
Ops Man: Christian Evans
Dirs: Philip Hewitt (**Chair**), Oumouly Ba, Peter Morley, Bob Harris, Brian Wilson, Pam Wilson, Andrew Theobald, Peter Talboys, Tony Pattison.
Fleet: 29 minibus.
Chassis/Bodies: Ford Transit, Iveco, LDV, Mercedes, Optare, Volkswagen.
Ops incl: school contracts, excursions & tours, private hire.
Livery: White with purple logo

TELLINGS GOLDEN MILLER COACHES LTD
See Middlesex

EDWARD THOMAS & SON
442 CHESSINGTON ROAD, EPSOM, SURREY KT19 9EJ
Tel: 020 8397 4276
Fax: 020 8397 5276
E-mail: edwardthomasandson@btconnect.com
Web site: www.edwardthomasandson.com
Owner: Ivan Thomas
Ch Eng: Manny Seager
Ops Man: Neil Seager
Fleet: 33 - 1 double-deck bus, 4 single-deck bus, 28 single-deck coach
Ops incl: local bus services, school contracts, private hire.
Livery: Green/Cream

W H MOTORS
See West Sussex

WESTERHAM COACHES
See Skinners of Oxted

WOKING COMMUNITY TRANSPORT
MOORCROFT, OLD SCHOOL PLACE, WESTFIELD, WOKING GU22 9LY
Tel: 01483 744800
Fax: 01483 757115
E-mail: enquiries@wokingbustler.co.uk
Web site: www.wokingbustler.org.uk
Fleet Name: Woking Bustler
Chairman: Jacquie Chamberlain
Ch Exec: Vic Clare
Sec: Sheila Rapley
Dir of Fin: Ron Bell
Fleet: 28 minibus
Ops incl: local bus services, private hire
Livery: Yellow

TYNE & WEAR

A & J COACHES OF WASHINGTON
6 SKIRLAW CLOSE, GLEBE VILLAGE, WASHINGTON NE38 7RE
Tel: 0191 417 2564 **Fax:** 0191 415 4672
Recovery: 07702 068063
E-mail: info@ajcoaches.co.uk
Dir: Ian Ashman **Co Sec:** Jean Ashman
Fleet: 1 single-deck coach
Chassis: 1 Volvo
Bodies: 1 Plaxton
Ops incl: school contracts, private hire.
Livery: Blue/White

A LINE COACHES
UNIT 1, PELAW INDUSTRIAL ESTATE, GATESHEAD NE10 0UW
Tel/Fax: 0191 495 2424
Recovery: 07984 501243
E-mail: david@a-linecoaches.co.uk
Web site: www.a-linecoaches.co.uk
Partners: David C Annis, Leslie B Annis
Fleet: 7 - 2 single-deck bus, 2 single-deck coach, 3 midibus.
Chassis: 1 Alexander Dennis, 1 DAF, 3 Dennis, 1 Mercedes, 1 Optare.
Bodies: 1 Berkhof, 1 Duple, 1 Optare, 2 Plaxton, 1 Van Hool, 1 Other.
Ops incl: local bus services, school contracts, excursions & tours, private hire, continental tours.
Livery: Red/White
Ticket System: AES 2000 Datafare

ALTONA COACH SERVICES LTD
BRS DEPOT, EARLSWAY, TEAM VALLEY TRADING ESTATE, GATESHEAD NE11 8UG
Tel: 0191 469 2193
Fax: 0191 469 3025
Fleet Name: Altona Travel
Prop: A. C. Hunter
Ops Man: A. I. Hunter
Office Man: R. Dudding.
Fleet: 9 - 5 single-deck coach, 2 midicoach, 2 minicoach.
Chassis: 1 DAF, 1 Dennis, 2 Mercedes, 1 Toyota, 3 Volvo.
Bodies: 2 Caetano, 2 Duple, 1 LAG, 2 Plaxton, 1 Robin Hood, 1 Bus Craft Impala.
Ops incl: excursions & tours, private hire, continental tours.
Livery: Two tone Blue and Orange.

ARRIVA NORTH EAST
ADMIRAL WAY, DOXFORD INTERNATIONAL BUSINESS PARK, SUNDERLAND SR3 3XP
Tel: 0191 520 4200
Fax: 0191 520 4222
Web site: www.arriva.co.uk
Regional Man Dir: Jonathan May
Man Dir: Iain McInroy
Eng Dir: J Greaves
Fin Dir: Sue Richardson
Fleet: 650 - 117 double-deck bus, 326 single-deck bus, 8 single-deck coach, 199 minibus.
Chassis: DAF, Dennis, Iveco, Leyland, MAN, MCW, Mercedes, Optare, Scania, Transbus, Volvo.
Bodies: Alexander, ECW, East Lancs, Ikarus, Leyland, MCW, Mercedes, Northern Counties, Optare, Plaxton, Transbus, Van Hool, Wright.
Ops incl: local bus services, school contracts, private hire, express.
Livery: Arriva UK Bus.
Ticket System: Wayfarer 3

COACHLINERS OF TYNESIDE
16 BRANDLING COURT, SOUTH SHIELDS NE34 8PA
Tel/Fax: 0191 427 1515
E-mail: coachliners@yahoo.co.uk
Prop: John Dorothy
Fleet: 2 midicoach
Chassis: 2 Mercedes.
Bodies: 2 Plaxton.
Ops incl: school contracts, excursions & tours, private hire.
Livery: White with red stripes

HENRY COOPER
LANE END GARAGE, ANNITSFORD NE23 7BD
Tel: 0191 250 0260 **Fax:** 0191 250 1820
E-mail: graham@henrycoopercoaches.com

Web site: www.henrycoopercoaches.com
Partners: Graham, Lily, Pamela Greaves
Fleet: 8 – 1 double-deck bus,
1 single-deck bus, 6 single-deck coach.
Chassis: 1 AEC, 1 Leyland National,
6 Volvo.
Bodies: 1 Park Royal, 1 Leyland
National, 6 Plaxton.
Ops incl: school contracts, private hire.
Livery: Orange/Cream.

ERB SERVICES LTD
HANNINGTON PLACE, BYKER,
NEWCASTLE UPON TYNE NE6 1JU
Tel: 0191 224 0002
Fax: 0191 224 0030
E-mail: sales@erb.entadsl.com
Web site: www.erbservices.co.uk
Man Dir: David Brown **Dir:** Edmund
Brown **Business Man:** Frank Billender
Fleet: 20 – 6 single-deck coach,
2 midibus, 3 midicoach, 9 minibus.
Chassis incl: 2 Dennis, 1 Neoplan,
1 Scania, 1 Setra, 3 Volvo.
Bodies incl: 1 Irizar, 7 Mercedes,
1 Neoplan, 1 Setra, 2 Van Hool.
Ops incl: school contracts, excursions &
tours, private hire
Livery: White

GO NORTH EAST
117 QUEEN STREET, GATESHEAD
NE8 2UA
Tel: 0191 420 5050
Fax: 0191 420 0225
E-mail: customerservices@
gonortheast.co.uk
Web site: www.simplygo.co.uk
Man Dir: P G Huntley
Ops Dir: K Carr **Fin Dir:** G C McPherson
Comm Dir: M P Harris
Fleet: 668 - 131 double-deck bus,
376 single-deck bus, 20 single-deck
coach, 141 minibus.
Chassis: 1 Blue Bird, 60 DAF,
216 Dennis, 21 Leyland, 35 Mercedes,
16 Optare, 137 Scania, 26 Transbus,
6 VDL, 150 Volvo.
Bodies: 18 Alexander, 22 Caetano,
30 East Lancs, 3 Leyland,
24 Marshall/MCV, 35 Mercedes,
92 Northern Counties, 23 Optare,
123 Plaxton, 70 Transbus, 187 Wright,
41 Other.
Ops incl: local bus services, school
contracts, express.

Livery: Various route brands
Ticket System: Wayfarer 3

JIM HUGHES COACHES LTD
WEAR STREET, LOW SOUTHWICK,
SUNDERLAND SR5 2BH
Tel: 0191 548 9600
Fax: 0191 549 3728
E-mail: jhcoaches@hotmail.co.uk
Man Dir: James Hughes
Dir: Valerie Hughes **Sec:** Jean Fisher
Ch Eng: Stephen McGuinness
Fleet: 7 single-deck coach
Chassis: 1 MAN, 1 Mercedes, 5 Volvo.
Bodies: 3 Plaxton, 2 Setra, 2 Van Hool.
Ops incl: excursions & tours, private hire,
continental tours.

KINGSLEY COACHES LTD
UNIT 20, PENSHAW WAY,
PORTOBELLO INDUSTRIAL ESTATE,
BIRTLEY DH3 2SA
Tel: 0191 492 1299
Fax: 0191 410 9281
E-mail:
accounts@kingsleycoaches.co.uk
Dir: David Kingsley (senior)
Ch Eng: David Kingsley (junior)
Co Sec: Mrs Eileen Kingsley
Fleet: 23 - 9 double-deck bus,
4 single-deck bus, 2 double-deck coach,
6 single-deck coach, 1 midicoach,
1 minibus.
Chassis incl: 1 LDV, 2 MAN, 10 MCW,
1 Mercedes, 1 Scania, 3 Volvo.
Bodies incl: 1 Berkhof, 1 Duple,
2 Marshall/MCV, 10 MCW, 2 Optare,
1 Plaxton, 1 Van Hool.
Ops incl: school contracts, excursions &
tours, private hire
Livery: Blue/White.
Ticket System: Wayfarer 3

PRIORY COACH & BUS LTD
59 CHURCH WAY, NORTH SHIELDS
NE29 0AD
Tel/Fax: 0191 257 0283
E-mail: info@priorycoaches.com
Web site: www.priorycoaches.com
Dirs: S Kirkpatrick, P Harris, I Fenwick,
L Stewart.
Fleet: 10 - 9 single-deck coach,
1 minibus.
Chassis: 1 LDV, 1 Leyland, 8 Volvo.
Bodies: 1 Berkhof, 1 Caetano,

2 Plaxton, 4 Van Hool, 1 Other.
Ops incl: excursions & tours, private hire,
school contracts.
Livery: White/Blue vinyls

ROWLANDS GILL COACHES & TAXIS
1 THORNEY VIEW, ROWLANDS GILL,
TYNE & WEAR NE39 1QL
Tel: 01207 543118
E-mail: ashleycoaches@aol.com
Prop: David Murphy
Fleet: 8 – 2 midibus, 2 minicoach,
2 minibus, 2 minicoach.
Chassis: 2 Mercedes, 2 Peugeot,
4 Renault.
Ops incl: school contracts, private hire.
Livery: Blue

STAGECOACH NORTH EAST
WHEATSHEAF, NORTH BRIDGE
STREET, SUNDERLAND SR5 1AQ
Tel: 0191 567 5251
Fax: 0191 566 0202
E-mail:
info.northeast@stagecoachbus.com
Web site: www.stagecoachgroup.com
Man Dir: John Conroy
Ops Dir: Nigel Winter
Eng Dir: David Kirsopp
Comm Dir: Robin Knight
Fleet: 505 - 97 double-deck bus,
236 single-deck bus, 4 single-deck coach,
5 open top bus, 163 midibus.
Chassis: 182 Alexander Dennis,
5 Leyland, 225 MAN, 83 Volvo, 10 other.
Bodies: 462 Alexander Dennis,
25 Northern Counties, 8 Plaxton, 10 other
Ops incl: local bus services, school
contracts.
Livery: Stagecoach UK Bus
Ticket System: ERG TP5000

THIRLWELL'S COACHES
MILLERS BRIDGE, WHICKHAM BANK,
SWALWELL, NEWCASTLE NE16 3BP
Tel/Fax: 0191 488 4948
E-mail: enquiries@thrilwellcoaches.co.uk
Web site: www.thirlwellcoaches.co.uk
Fleet: 7 – 6 single-deck coach,
1 midicoach
Chassis: 1 Mercedes, 6 Volvo
Bodies: 4 Plaxton, 2 Van Hool, 1 Other
Ops incl: excursions & tours, private hire
Livery: Red & Grey

VEOLIA TRANSPORT ENGLAND PLC
COLLIERY LANE, HETTON-LE-HOLE,
HOUGHTON LE SPRING DH5 0BG
Tel: 0191 517 0122
See Nottinghamshire

Tyne & Wear

WARWICKSHIRE

A-LINE COACHES
BRANDON ROAD, BINLEY, COVENTRY CV3 2JD
Tel: 024 7645 0808 **Fax:** 024 7645 6434
E-mail: office@a-linecoaches.com
Web site: www.a-linecoaches.com
Dirs: B Haywood, K Prosser
Fleet: 23 - 1 single-deck bus, 13 single-deck coach, 6 midibus, 2 minibus, 1 minicoach
Chassis: 5 Bova, 1 DAF, 3 Mercedes, 2 Optare, 2 Scania, 10 Volvo
Bodies: 5 Alexander, 2 Berkhof, 5 Bova, 1 Jonckheere, 3 Optare, 5 Plaxton, 2 Other
Ops incl: local bus services, private hire, school contracts
Livery: White

CATTERALLS COACHES
74 COVENTRY STREET, SOUTHAM CV47 0EA
Tel: 01926 813192 **Fax:** 01926 813915
Recovery: 01926 813192
E-mail: info@travelcatteralls.co.uk
Web site: www.travelcatteralls.co.uk
Dir: Paul Catterall
Fleet: 35 – 2 double-deck bus, 30 single-deck coach, 2 double-deck coach, 1 midicoach.
Ops incl: local bus services, school contracts, excursions & tours, private hire, continental tours.
Livery: Blue, Yellow and White

CHAPEL END COACHES
WILSON HOUSE, 3 OASTON ROAD, NUNEATON CV11 6JX
Tel: 024 7635 4588 **Fax:** 024 7635 6406
Web site: www.chapelendcoaches.co.uk
E-mail: cecoaches@ukonline.co.uk
Man Dir/Trans Man: Ian Wilson
Dir/Sec: Mrs Tracey Wilson
Fleet: 11 single-deck coaches.
Ops incl: local bus services, excursions & tours, private hire, continental tours, school contracts.
Livery: White/Red/Black

MIKE DE COURCEY TRAVEL LTD
See West Midlands.

MARTIN'S OF TYSOE
20 OXHILL ROAD, MIDDLE TYSOE CV35 0SX
Tel: 01295 680642
Prop: Martin Thomas.

MIDLAND RED COACHES/WHEELS HERITAGE
POSTAL OFFICE, 23 BROAD STREET, BRINKLOW, WARWICKSHIRE CV23 0LS
Tel: 02476 633624, 07733 884914
Fax: 02476 354900
E-mail: buses@wheels.co.uk
Web site: www.wheels.co.uk
Props: Ashley Wakelin, Rob Paramour
Fleet: vintage vehicles
Ops incl: private hire, excursions & tours, bus driver experiences
Livery: Midland Red

SKYLINERS LTD
19 BOND STREET, NUNEATON CV11 4NX
Tel: 024 7632 5682
Fax: 024 7635 4626
E-mail: haydn@skyliners.co.uk
Dir: Haydon J. Dawkins
Fleet: 1 double-deck coach.
Body: Neoplan.
Ops incl: excursions & tours, private hire, continental tours.

STAGECOACH IN WARWICKSHIRE
RAILWAY TERRACE, RUGBY CV21 3HS
Tel: 01788 562036
Fax: 01788 566094
E-mail: warksenquiries@stagecoachbus.com
Web site: www.stagecoachbus.com/warwickshire
Man Dir: Steve Burd
Ops Dir: Liz Esnouf
Eng Dir: Keith Dyball
Comm Mgr: Clive Jones
Marketing Man: Adam Rideout
Fleet: 206 - 34 double-deck bus, 7 single-deck bus, 16 single-deck coach, 7 open top bus, 99 midibus, 33 minibus.
Chassis: 1 AEC, 59 Dennis, 5 Leyland, 14 MAN, 38 Optare, 5 Scania, 84 Volvo.
Bodies: 115 Alexander, 6 Jonckheere, 1 Northern Counties, 38 Optare, 1 Park Royal, 20 Plaxton, 5 Scania, 10 Transbus, 1 Other.
Ops incl: local bus services, school contracts, private hire, express
Livery: Stagecoach UK Bus
Ticket System: ERG

WEST MIDLANDS

ADAMS TOURS
75 SANDBANK, BLOXWICH, WALSALL WS3 2HL
Tel/Fax: 01922 406469
Prop: David Adams
Fleet: 7 - 4 single-deck coach, 3 midicoach.
Chassis: 4 DAF, 3 Mercedes.
Bodies: 2 Autobus, 1 Plaxton, 4 Van Hool.
Ops incl: private hire, school contracts, excursions & tours.
Livery: Cream.

AIRPARKS SERVICES LTD
WILLOW HOUSE, PINEWOOD BUSINESS PARK, COLESHILL ROAD, MARSTON GREEN, BIRMINGHAM B37 7HJ
Tel: 0121 717 5300
Fax: 0121 788 0778
E-mail: david.rowe@airparks.co.ik
Web site: www.airparks.co.uk
Ops Dir: Paul Humphrey
Group Fleet Man: David Rowe
Trans Man: Matt Lawton
Co Sec: Elisabeth Hirlemann
Fleet: 32 - 27 single-deck bus, 5 minibus.
Chassis: 11 Alexandra Dennis, 4 Ford Transit, 16 MAN, 1 Volkswagen.
Bodies: 11 Alexander Dennis, 16 MCV
Ops incl: local bus services, private hire, - car park to airport shuttle.

AM-PM TRAVEL
BIRMINGHAM TRUCK STOP, WHARFDALE ROAD, TYSELEY, BIRMINGHAM B11 2DA
Tel: 0121 707 5511
Fax: 0121 707 5522
E-mail: info@ampm-travel.co.uk
Web site: www.ampm-travel.co.uk
Man Dir: Mel Kang
Ops incl: local bus services.
Livery: Blue/White/Green.

B B COACHES LTD
22 VICTORIA AVENUE, HALESOWEN B62 9BL
Tel: 0121 422 4501 **Fax:** 0121 602 2040
Dirs: Mick Bird, Barbara Blewitt
Fleet: 1 single-deck coach.
Chassis: Volvo
Bodies: Plaxton
Ops incl: excursions & tours, private hire
Livery: Cream

BEACON COACHES
24 CHICHESTER GROVE, CHELMSLEY WOOD B37 5RZ
Tel: 0121 783 2221
Fax: 0121 680 2582
E-mail: enquiries@beaconcoaches.co.uk
Web site: www.beaconcoaches.co.uk
Fleet: 6 - 2 double-deck coach, 1 midicoach, 1 minicoach, 2 minibus.
Chassis: 1 MAN, 2 Scania, 1 Toyota, LDV.
Bodies incl: 3 Jonckheere.
Ops incl: excursions & tours, private hire, school contracts, continental tours.
Livery: White /Red/Grey.

BIRMINGHAM INTERNATIONAL COACHES LTD
10 FORTNUM CLOSE, TILE CROSS, BIRMINGHAM B33 0JT
Tel: 0121 783 4004
Fax: 0121 785 0967
E-mail: Birmingham.intl@btconnect.com
Web site: www.birminghaminternationalcoaches.co.uk
Dirs: M Watkiss, A Watkiss, N Watkiss
Fleet: 11 – 1 double-deck bus, 10 single-deck coach.
Chassis: 11 DAF.
Bodies: 10 Bova, 1 Optare.
Ops incl: school contracts, excursions & tours, private hire, continental tours.
Livery: Grey/Red

L F BOWEN LTD
See Staffordshire

CENTRAL BUSES LTD
177 NEW TOWN ROW, NEWTOWN BIRMINGHAM B6 4QZ
Tel: 0121 333 4533 **Fax:** 0870 199 2923
E-mail: email@centralbuses.com

Web site: www.centralbuses.com
Man Dir: Geoff Cross
Fleet: 12 single-deck bus.
Chassis: 4 Alexander Dennis, 9 Dennis.
Bodies: 3 Marshall, 10 Plaxton.
Ops incl: local bus services, school contracts.
Livery: Red/Grey
Ticket System: Wayfarer TGX200

CENTRAL CONNECT
BEACON HOUSE, LONG ACRE,
BIRMINGHAM B7 5JJ
Tel: 0121 322 2222 **Fax:** 0121 322 2718
Recovery: 07973 939103
E-mail: buses@connectbuses.com
Web site: www.connectbuses.net
Fleet: single-deck bus, single-deck coach, minibus.
Chassis: Dennis, Enterprise, LDV, MAN, Neoplan, Setra, Volvo.
Bodies: Caetano, Duple, Neoplan, Plaxton, Setra, Van Hool.
Ops incl: local bus services, school contracts, excursions & tours, private hire, express, continental tours
Livery: White with Blue, Red
Ticket System: Wayfarer TGX
Part of Rotala PLC - Incorporating Birmingham Motor Traction, North Birmingham Busways & Zak's Bus & Coach Services.

DEN CANEY COACHES LTD
THE COACH STATION, STONE HOUSE LANE, BARTLEY GREEN, BIRMINGHAM B32 3AH
Tel: 0121 427 2078
Fax: 0121 427 8905
E-mail: enquiry@dencaneycoaches.co.uk
Web site: www.dencaneycoaches.co.uk
Man Dir: D Stevens **Dir:** M Stevens
Ch Eng: A Doggett **Ops Man:** J Clarke
Administrator: Mrs D Johnston
Fleet: 9 single-deck coach
Chassis: Dennis, Leyland, Toyota, Volvo
Ops incl: private hire, school contracts

CHAUFFEURS OF BIRMINGHAM
CREST HOUSE, 7 HIGHFIELD ROAD, EDGBASTON, BIRMINGHAM B15 3ED.
Tel: 0121 456 3355
E-mail: enquiries@c-o-b.co.uk
Web site: www.chauffeursbirmingham.co.uk
Fleet incl: single-deck coach, midicoach, minicoach.

CHOICE TRAVEL SERVICES
PLANETARY ROAD, WEDNESFIELD, WOLVERHAMPTON WV13 3SW
Tel: 01902 305181
Fax: 01902 307454
E-mail: info@midlandbus.net
Web site: www.midlandbus.net
Fleet Name: Midland
Man Dir: David Reeves
Ops Dir: Shaz Ali
Ops incl: local bus services
Livery: Blue/White
Associated with D&G Coach & Bus Ltd – see Staffordshire

CLARIBEL COACHES LTD
10 FORTNUM CLOSE, TILE CROSS, BIRMINGHAM B33 0JT
Tel: 0121 789 7878
Fax: 0121 785 0967

E-mail: Birmingham.intl@btconnect.com
Web site: www.claribelcoaches.co.uk
Dirs: M J Watkiss, M Watkiss, A Watkiss, N Watkiss
Fleet: 24 - 2 double-deck bus, 22 single-deck bus.
Chassis: DAF, VDL
Bodies: 1 East Lancs, 1 Optare, 22 Wright.
Ops incl: local bus services, school contracts, private hire.
Livery: Blue/White.
Ticket System: Wayfarer TGX

COURTESY TRAVELS
See Shropshire

N N CRESSWELL
See Worcestershire

DAIMLER
99 SAREHOLE ROAD,
BIRMINGHAM B28 8ED
Tel: 0121 778 2837 **Fax:** 0121 702 2843
E-mail: roy@daimlertours.wanadoo.co.uk
Prop: Roy Picken
Fleet: 1 single-deck coach
Chassis/Body: 1 Neoplan
Ops incl: excursions & tours
Livery: White/Burgundy

DIAMOND BUS LTD
CROSS QUAYS BUSINESS PARK,
HALLBRIDGE WAY, TIVDALE,
OLDBURY, WEST MIDLANDS B69 3HW
Tel: 0121 557 7337
Fax: 0121 520 4999
Web site: www.diamondbuses.com
Fleet Names: Black Diamond, Red Diamond
Fleet incl: single-deck bus, midibus.
Man Dir: Scott Dunn
Ops incl: local bus services
Livery: Red/Black
Part of Rotala PLC

MIKE DE COURCEY TRAVEL LTD
ROWLEY DRIVE, COVENTRY CV3 4FG
Tel: 024 7630 2656
Fax: 024 7663 9276
E-mail: bob@traveldecourcey.com
Web site: www.traveldecourcey.com
Fleet Name: Travel De Courcey
Man Dir: Mike de Courcey
Co Sec: Adrian de Courcey
Gen Man: Bob Wildman
Fleet Eng: Neville Collins
Fleet: 80 - 28 double-deck bus, 36 single-deck bus, 16 single-deck coach.
Chassis: 2 Alexander Dennis, 1 Daimler, 16 Leyland, 37 MAN, 6 Mercedes, 5 Scania, 3 Volvo.
Bodies: 2 Alexander Dennis, 6 Marcopolo, 3 Marshall/MCV, 14 MCW, 7 Mercedes, 4 Northern Counties, 4 Optare, 6 Plaxton, 2 Van Hool.
Ops incl: local bus services, school contracts, excursions & tours, private hire, continental tours.
Livery: White/Blue/Orange.
Ticket System: Wayfarer TGX

DIRECT COACH TOURS
68 BERKELEY ROAD EAST, HAYMILLS,
BIRMINGHAM B25 8NP
Tel: 0121 772 0664
Fax: 0121 773 8649
Tours Man: Brian Bourne
Fleet: 7 - 6 single-deck coach,

1 midicoach.
Chassis: 1 Toyota, 6 Volvo.
Bodies: 1 Caetano, 6 Plaxton.
Ops incl: excursions & tours, private hire.

ENDEAVOUR COACHES LTD
30 PLUME STREET, ASTON,
BIRMINGHAM B6 7RT
Tel: 0121 326 4994 **Fax:** 0121 326 4999
E-mail: enquiries@endeavourcoaches.co.uk
Web site: www.endeavourcoaches.co.uk
Dirs: J Mitchell, G Mitchell, D Mitchell
Fleet: 14 – 10 single-deck coach, 4 minibus.
Chassis: 2 Ford Transit, 2 Freight Rover, 1 MAN, 2 VDL, 7 Volvo.
Bodies incl: 2 Bova, 1 Marcopolo, 7 Van Hool.
Ops incl: school contracts, excursions & tours, private hire, continental tours.
Livery: Silver

EUROLINERS
See Worcestershire

FLIGHTS HALLMARK LTD
BEACON HOUSE, LONG ACRE,
BIRMINGHAM B7 5JJ
Tel: 0121 322 2222
Fax: 0121 322 2224
Recovery: 0121 322 2710
E-mail: sales@flightshallmark.com
Web site: www.flightshallmark.com
Chairman: John Gunn
Ch Exec: Kim Taylor
Man Dir: Simon Dunn **Dir:** Geoff Flight
Eng Man: Dave Russell
Bus Dev Man: Anthony Goozee
Comm Man: Ian Pollard
Ops Mans: Paul Williams (coach), Steve Elms (bus)
Fleet: double-deck bus, single-deck bus, single-deck coach, midicoach.
Chassis: DAF, Dennis, LDV, MAN, Mercedes, Optare, Toyota, Volvo.
Bodies: Alexander, Caetano, Jonckheere, MCW, Mercedes, Neoplan, Optare, Plaxton, Sunsundegui, Van Hool, Wright.
Ops incl: local bus services, school contracts, excursions & tours, private hire, express, continental tours.
Ticket system: Wayfarer, ERG
Part of Rotala PLC

HARDINGS INTERNATIONAL
See Worcestershire

J. R. HOLYHEAD INTERNATIONAL
32 CROSS STREET,
WILLENHALL WV13 1PG
Tel: 01902 607364
Fax: 01902 609772
Owner: J. R. Holyhead.
Fleet: 5 single-deck coach.
Chassis: 2 Bova, 3 Volvo.
Bodies: 2 Bova, 3 Plaxton.
Ops incl: excursions & tours, private hire, express, continental tours.
Livery: White.

JOHNSONS COACH & BUS TRAVEL
LIVERIDGE HOUSE, LIVERIDGE HILL,
HENLEY-IN-ARDEN,
SOLIHULL B95 5QS
Tel: 01564 797000 **Fax:** 01564 797050

E-mail: info@johnsonscoaches.co.uk
Web site: www.johnsonscoaches.co.uk
Dirs: Peter Johnson, John Johnson
Fleet: 84 – 3 double-deck bus, 26 single-deck bus, 40 single-deck coach, 1 midicoach, 11 minibus, 3 minicoach.
Chassis: 38 Bova, 3 DAF, 4 Dennis, 11 Ford, 22 Optare, 6 Scania.
Bodies: 38 Bova, 2 East Lancs, 1 Ikarus, 3 Irizar, 22 Optare, 4 Transbus, 14 Other.
Ops incl: local bus services, school contracts, excursions & tours, private hire, express, continental tours.
Livery: Yellow/Blue/White
Ticket system: Wayfarer TGX150

JOSEPHS MINI COACHES
See Staffordshire

KEN MILLER TRAVEL
10 CHURCHILL ROAD, SHENSTONE WS14 0LP
Tel: 01827 60494   **Fax:** 01827 60494
Recovery: 07976 303951
E-mail: ken.m.traveluk@amserve.net
Fleetname: Ken Miller Recovery
Prop: Ken Miller
Fleet: 2 single-deck bus, 2 minibus.
Chassis: LDV, Volvo.
Ops incl: school contracts, private hire, express, continental tours.
Livery: Blue/Silver
Ticket system: Wayfarer.

KINGSNORTON COACHES
40 BISHOPS GATE, NORTHFIELD, BIRMINGHAM B31 4AJ
Tel: 0121 550 8519
Fax: 0121 501 6554
E-mail: info@kingsnortoncoaches.co.uk
Web site: www.kingsnortoncoaches.co.uk
Prop: Richard Egan
Fleet: 23 – 1 midibus, 1 midicoach, 20 minibus, 1 minicoach.
Chassis: 1 Iveco, 20 LDV, 1 MAN, 1 Mercedes.
Ops incl: school contracts, excursions & tours, private hire.
Livery: Red/White

KINGSWINFORD COACHWAYS
HIGH STREET, PENSNETT, BRIERLEY HILL DY6 8XB
Tel: 01384 401626
Fax: 01384 401580
Recovery: 07831 148626
Dir: David William Edmunds
Ch Eng: Robert Lamesdale
Sec: Robert Morgan
Advisor: David Moor
Fleet: 7 - 6 single-deck coach, 1 midibus.
Chassis: 6 Volvo.
Body: 2 Plaxton, 1 Reeve Burgess, 4 Van Hool
Ops incl: school contracts, private hire.
Livery: White/Yellow/Red.

LAKESIDE COACHES LTD
See Shropshire

MEADWAY PRIVATE HIRE LTD
28-32 BERKELEY ROAD, HAY MILLS, BIRMINGHAM B25 8NG
Tel: 0121 773 8389, 8380
Fax: 0121 693 7171
E-mail: meadwaycoaches@btconnect.com
Fleet Name: Meadway Coaches
Fleet: 10 single-deck coach.
Chassis: Alexander Dennis, DAF, Volvo.
Ops incl: private hire, school contracts.

MIDLAND METRO
METRO CENTRE, POTTERS LANE, WEDNESBURY WS10 0AR
Tel: 0121 502 2006
Fax: 0121 556 6299
Web site: www.travelmetro.co.uk
Fleet: 16 articulated tramcars
General Manager: Fred Roberts
Chassis/Bodies: Ansaldo
Ops incl: tram service
Part of National Express West Midlands

NASH COACHES LTD
83 RAGLAN ROAD, SMETHWICK B66 3TT
Tel: 0121 558 0024
Fax: 0121 558 0907
E-mail: info@nashcoaches.co.uk
Web site: www.nashcoaches.co.uk
Dirs: Ian Powell, Linda Powell
Fleet: 8 - single-deck coach, midicoach, minicoach.
Chassis: 6 Mercedes, 1 Toyota, 1 Volvo.
Bodies: 1 Berkhof, 1 Caetano, 2 Neoplan, 1 Plaxton, 3 Setra.
Ops incl: excursions & tours, private hire, express, continental tours, school contracts.
Livery: Multi stars/Firework

NATIONAL EXPRESS LTD
1 HAGLEY ROAD, EDGBASTON, BIRMINGHAM B16 8TG
Tel: 0121 625 1122
Fax: 0121 456 1397
E-mail: reception@nationalexpress.com
Web site: www.nationalexpress.com
Man Dir: Paul Bunting
Ops Dir: Alex Perry
Ops incl: express.
Livery: Red/White/Blue.
Ticket System: Pre-sale, Wayfarer.

NATIONAL EXPRESS WEST MIDLANDS
51 BORDESLEY GREEN, BIRMINGHAM B9 4BZ
Tel: 0121 254 7200
Fax: 0121 254 7277
Web site: www.travelwm.co.uk
Man Dir: Neil Barker
Fin Dir: Peter Coates
Eng Dir: Jack Henry
Marketing & Dev Dir: Martin Hancock
Fleet: 1700 - 929 double-deck bus, 31 articulated bus, 689 single-deck bus, 51 minibus.
Chassis: DAF, Dennis, Mercedes, Optare, Scania, Volvo.
Bodies: Alexander, Mercedes, Optare, Plaxton, Scania, Wright.
Ops incl: local bus services, school contracts, private hire.
Livery: Red/White/Blue

NEWBURY TRAVEL
NEWBURY LANE, OLDBURY B69 1HF
Tel: 0121 552 3262
Fax: 0121 552 0230
E-mail: newburytravel@aol.com
Web site: www.newburytravel.co.uk
Man Dir: David Greenhouse
Ch Eng: Chris Phillips
Fleet: 11 - 5 single-deck coach, 3 midicoach, 3 minicoach.
Chassis: 1 Ford Transit, 2 LDV, 3 Mercedes, 5 Volvo.
Bodies: 1 Berkhof, 3 Mercedes, 4 Van Hool.
Ops incl: school contracts, private hire.
Livery: White

PROSPECT COACHES (WEST) LTD
81 HIGH STREET, LYE, STOURBRIDGE DY9 8NG
Tel: 01384 895436
Fax: 01384 898654
E-mail: enquiries@prospectcoaches.co.uk
Web site: www.prospectcoaches.co.uk
Man Dirs: Geoffrey Watts, Roslynd A D Hadley
Tran Man: Nathan Hadley
Ops Man: David Price
Garage Man: Martin Hadley
Fleet: 34 single-deck coach.
Chassis: 30 Alexander Dennis, 1 Neoplan, 3 Volvo.
Bodies: 1 Marcopolo, 1 Neoplan, 32 Plaxton.
Ops incl: school contracts, private hire.
Livery: Silver with Red/Blue/White stripes.

HARRY SHAW
MILL HOUSE, MILL LANE, BINLEY, COVENTRY CV3 2DU
Tel: 024 7665 0650
Fax: 024 7663 5684
E-mail: john@harryshaw.co.uk
Web site: www.harryshaw.co.uk
Fleet: 21 - 19 single-deck coach, 1 midicoach, 1 minibus.
Chassis: 1 Bova, 1 DAF, 2 Dennis, 2 Mercedes, 4 Scania, 2 Setra, 9 Volvo.
Bodies: 5 Berkhof, 1 Bova, 1 Excel, 1 Ikarus, 3 Irizar, 1 Jonckheere, 1 Mercedes, 2 Setra, 3 Van Hool, 2 Wadham Stringer.
Ops incl: local bus services, excursions & tours, school contracts, private hire, continental tours.
Livery: Orange

SHEARINGS HOLIDAYS
BAYTON ROAD, EXHALL CV7 9EJ
Tel: 024 7664 4633
Fax: 024 7636 0304
Gen Man: Carol Carpenter.
See also Shearings Holidays, Greater Manchester.

SILVERLINE LANDFLIGHT LTD
ARGENT HOUSE, VULCAN ROAD, SOLIHULL B91 2JY
Tel: 0121 705 5555   **Fax:** 0121 709 0556
E-mail: silverline@landflight.co.uk
Web site: www.landflight.co.uk
Man Dir: M E Breakwell
Ops Dir: R G Knott
Bus Dev Dir: W J Matthews
Eng Man: R J Nowlan
Fleet: 16 - 6 single-deck bus, 7 single-deck coach, 3 midicoach.
Chassis: 1 DAF, 1 Dennis, 2 MAN, 7 Mercedes, 2 Scania, 3 Toyota.
Bodies: 3 Caetano, 2 Esker, 2 Irizar, 2 Neoplan, 5 Optare, 2 Scania.
Ops incl: local bus services, private hire, continental tours.
Livery: Silver/Blue
Ticket System: Parkeon/ITSO

SOLUS COACH TRAVEL LTD
See Staffordshire

STAGECOACH IN WARWICKSHIRE
See Warwickshire

T. N. C. COACHES
257 CHESTER ROAD, CASTLE BROMWICH B36 0ET
Tel: 0121 747 5722
Fax: 0121 747 5722
Dirs: N T Cunningham, K M Cunningham.
Fleet: 5 - 2 single-deck coach, 3 minibus.
Chassis: 1 DAF, 1 Leyland, 3 LDV.
Bodies: Duple. Van Hool
Ops incl: school contracts, excursions & tours, private hire.

TERRYS COACH HIRE
21 PANDORA ROAD, COVENTRY CV2 2FU
Tel/Fax: 024 7636 2975
E-mail: enquiries@terrys-coaches.co.uk
Web site: www.terrys-coaches.co.uk
Prop: T Hall **Ops Man:** L Hall
Chief Engs: J Hall, D Harrison
Co Sec: S Hall
Fleet: 11 – 2 single-deck bus, 8 single-deck coach, 1 double-deck coach.
Chassis: 1 Ayats, 6 MAN, 1 Neoplan, 3 Volvo.
Bodies: 1 Ayats, 1 Jonckheere, 2 Neoplan, 4 Noge, 3 Plaxton.
Ops incl: excursions & tours, private hire, continental tours, school contracts.
Livery: Gold/Green leaf

THE TRANSPORT MUSEUM, WYTHALL
See Worcestershire

TRAVEL EXPRESS LTD
30 COTON ROAD, PENN, WOLVERHAMPTON WV41 5AT
Tel/Fax: 01902 330653
E-mail: kishan.chumber@sky.com
Props: Kishan Chumber, Nirmal Chumber
Fleet: 10 - 10 single-deck bus
Chassis incl: 9 Alexander Dennis
Bodies: 6 Carlyle, 3 Duple, 1 Reeve Burgess
Ops incl: local bus service.
Livery: mixed
Ticket System: Wayfarer

WEST MIDLANDS SPECIAL NEEDS TRANSPORT
218-220 WINDSOR STREET, NECHELLS, BIRMINGHAM B7 4NE
Tel: 0121 333 3107 **Fax:** 0121 333 3345
E-mail: enquiries@wmsnt.org
Web site: www.wmsnt.org
Ch Exec: E B Connor
Ops Man: D Rogers **Co Sec:** J Frater
Fleet: 260 minibus.
Chassis: 260 Volkswagen.
Bodies: 260 Concept.
Ops incl: local bus services, school contracts.
Livery: Red/White/Blue, Blue/Yellow
Ticket system: manual/receipts

WHITTLE COACH & BUS LTD
See Worcestershire

WICKSONS TRAVEL
COPPICE ROAD, BROWNHILLS WS8 7DG
Tel: 01543 372247 **Fax:** 01543 374271
Web site: www.wicksons.co.uk
Fleet: 11 - 8 coach, 1 midibus, 2 midicoach
Chassis: 5 DAF, 1 MAN, 1 Mercedes, 4 Volvo
Bodies: 1 Autobus, 1 Noge, 9 Van Hool.

Ops incl: school contracts, excursions & tours, private hire, continental tours.
Livery: White/Blue/Orange

WINDSOR-GRAY TRAVEL
186 GRIFFITHS DRIVE, WEDNESFIELD, WOLVERHAMPTON WV11 2JR
Tel: 01902 722392
Fax: 01902 722339
E-Mail: grahamwgt@hotmail.co.uk
Owner: Graham Williams
Fleet: 1 midicoach.
Chassis: 1 Dennis.
Bodies: 1 Duple.
Ops incl: private hire, excursions & tours.
Livery: Cream/Brown/Orange.

YARDLEY TRAVEL LTD
68 BERKELEY ROAD EAST, HAY MILLS, BIRMINGHAM B25 8NP
Tel: 0121 772 3700
Fax: 0121 773 8649
E-mail: info@yardleytravel.co.uk
Web site: www.yardleytravel.co.uk
Dirs: Mr Mohammed Saleem, Mrs Tasneem Saleem
Fleet: 11 - 8 coach, 3 midicoach
Chassis: Volvo.
Bodies: Plaxton.
Ops incl: school contracts, excursions & tours, excursions & tours, private hire.
Livery: White/Yellow/Black.

YOUNGS OF ROMSLEY
MALVERN VIEW, DAYHOUSE BANK, ROMSLEY, HALESOWEN B62 0EU
Tel/Fax: 01562 710717
Prop: R J Young
Fleet: 3 - 1 single-deck coach, 1 midicoach, 1 minibus
Chassis: 2 Mercedes, 1 Volkswagen.
Ops incl: excursions & tours, private hire, continental tours.
Livery: Gold

WEST SUSSEX

ARUN COACHES/FAWLTY TOURS
1 NORFOLK TERRACE, HORSHAM RH12 1DA
Tel: 01403 272999 **Fax:** 01403 272777
Prop/Ch Eng: H. Miller.
Fleet: 4 single-deck coach.
Chassis: 1 AEC, 1 Bristol, 2 Hestair/Duple.
Bodies: 2 Duple, 1 ECW, 1 Plaxton.
Ops incl: private hire.
Livery: Red/Gold.

C. L. COACHES
UNIT 13, CHARTWELL ROAD, LANCING BN15 8TU
Tel: 01903 752555 **Fax:** 01903 752777
Man Dir: D Brown **Dir:** G Brown, D Brown **Man:** H Ticehurst.
Fleet: 15 - 1 double-deck bus, 14 single-deck coach
Chassis: 15 Volvo
Bodies: 1 Alexander, 14 Plaxton
Ops incl: private hire, school contracts.
Livery: Cream/Green/Grey

COMPASS TRAVEL
FARADAY CLOSE, WORTHING BN13 3RB
Tel: 01903 690025 **Fax:** 01903 690015

E-mail: office@compass-travel.co.uk
Web site: www.compass-travel.co.uk
Man Dir: Chris Chatfield
Eng Dir: Malcolm Gallichan
Co Sec: Roger Cotterell
Fleet: 50 - 25 single-deck bus, 11 single-deck coach, 8 midibus, 4 midicoach, 2 minibus.
Chassis: 25 Alexander Dennis, 4 DAF, 1 Dennis, 1 Ford Transit, 1 Irisbus, 4 Mercedes, 7 Optare, 4 Scania, 3 Volvo.
Bodies: 25 Alexander Dennis, 1 Autobus, 1 Ikarus, 1 Indcar, 2 Irizar, 2 Optare, 3 Plaxton, 7 Van Hool, 8 Other.
Ops incl: local bus services, school contracts, private hire.
Livery: White/Burgundy.
Ticket System: Wayfarer

COUNTRYLINER GROUP
See Surrey

CRAWLEY LUXURY
STEPHENSON WAY, THREE BRIDGES RH10 1TN
Tel: 01293 521002
Fax: 01293 522450
E-mail: crawleylux@aol.com
Fleet Name: Crawley Luxury Coaches.

Dirs: David Brown, Darren Brown, Gavin Brown **Ops Man:** Stephen Burse
Fleet: 56 - 2 double-deck bus, 51 single-deck coach, 1 minicoach, 2 minibus.
Chassis: 1 Bedford, 1 Ford, 1 LDV, 1 Mercedes, 52 Volvo.
Bodies: 2 Alexander, 1 Devon, 1 Duple, 1 Ford, 1 LDV, 51 Plaxton.
Ops incl: private hire, school contracts.
Livery: Cream/Green/Grey.

FLIGHTS HALLMARK LTD
GATWICK COACH CENTRE, OLD BRIGHTON ROAD, LOWFIELD HEATH, CRAWLEY RH1 0PR
Tel: 01293 596831
Fax: 01293 596837
E-mail: gatwick@flightshallmark.com
Web site: www.connectbuses.org
Chairman: S Dunn
Gen Man: D Dow
Fleet: 11 – 3 double-deck bus, 6 single-deck bus, 2 midibus.
Chassis: Dennis, Mercedes, Volvo.
Bodies incl: Mercedes.
Ops incl: local bus services, school contracts, excursions & tours, private hire, express.
Part of Rotala PLC

West Sussex

METROBUS LTD
WHEATSTONE CLOSE, CRAWLEY
RH10 9UA
Tel: 01293 449192
Fax: 01293 404281
E-mail: info@metrobus.co.uk
Web site: www.metrobus.co.uk
Man Dir: Alan Eatwell
Fin Dir: Kevin Lavender
Ops Dir: Kevin Carey
Ch Eng: Les Bishop
Fleet: 443 - 170 double-deck bus, 69 single-deck bus, 202 midibus, 2 minibus.
Chassis: 6 Alexander Dennis, 140 Dennis, 23 MAN, 2 Optare, 269 Scania, 3 Volvo.
Bodies: 18 Alexander Dennis, 18 Caetano, 163 East Lancs, 33 Marshall/MCV, 32 Optare, 38 Plaxton, 105 Scania, 36 Transbus.
Ops incl: local bus services.
Livery: Two Tone Blue (Home Counties), Red (London).
Ticket System: Parkeon
Part of the Go-Ahead Group

PAVILION COACHES
See East Sussex

RICHARDSON TRAVEL LTD
RUSSELL HOUSE, BEPTON ROAD, MIDHURST GU29 9NB
Tel: 01730 813304
Fax: 01730 815985
E-mail: sales@richardson-travel.co.uk
Web site: www.richardson-travel.co.uk
Man Dir: R W Richardson
Fleet: 18 - 6 double-deck bus, 3 single-deck bus, 7 single-deck coach, 2 midicoach.
Chassis: 2 Mercedes, 16 Volvo
Bodies: 5 Alexander Dennis, 2 East Lancs, 10 Plaxton, 1 Wright.
Ops incl: local bus services, school contracts, excursions & tours, private hire, continental tours.
Livery: Blue
Ticket System: Paper

ROADMARK TRAVEL LTD
UNIT 15, GERSTON BUSINESS PARK, GREYFRIARS LANE, STORRINGTON, PULBOROUGH RH20 4HE
Tel: 01903 741233 **Fax:** 01903 741232
E-mail: coaches@roadmarktravel.co.uk
Web site: www.roadmarktravel.co.uk
Man Dir: David Coster
Fleet: 3 - 2 single-deck coach, 1 open-top bus
Chassis: 1 Leyland, 2 Mercedes
Bodies: 2 Mercedes
Ops incl: excursions & tours, private hire, continental tours.
Livery: White/Blue

RUTHERFORDS TRAVEL
BRAMFIELD HOUSE, CHURCH LANE, EASTERGATE, CHICHESTER
PO20 3UZ
Tel: 01243 543673
E-mail: rutherfordstravel@hotmail.co.uk
Owner: George Bell
Fleet: 9 single-deck coach.
Chassis: 2 Dennis, 5 Leyland, 1 MAN, 1 Scania.
Bodies: 2 Alexander Dennis, 2 Duple, 1 Noge, 4 Plaxton
Ops incl: private hire, school contracts.
Livery: White

SOUTHDOWN PSV LTD
SILVERWOOD, SNOW HILL, COPTHORNE RH10 3EN
Tel: 01342 715222
Fax: 01342 719617
E-mail: info@southdownpsv.co.uk
Web site: www.southdownpsv.co.uk
Man Dir: Steve Swain
Eng Dir: Simon Stanford
Fin Dir: Peter Larking
Ops Dir: Gary Wood
Fleet: 21 - 3 double-deck bus, 18 single-deck bus.
Chassis: 5 Alexander Dennis, 2 DAF, 11 Dennis, 1 MAN, 1 VDL, 1 Volvo.
Bodies: 5 Alexander Dennis, 1 East Lancs, 1 Ikarus, 13 Plaxton, 1 Wright.
Ops incl: local bus services, school contracts
Livery: Green/White/Blue
Ticket System: Wayfarer TGX

STAGECOACH SOUTH
BUS STATION, SOUTHGATE, CHICHESTER PO19 8DG
Tel: 01243 536161
Fax: 01243 528743
E-mail: enquiries.south@stagecoachbus.com
Web site: www.stagecoachbus.com/south
Fleet Names: Stagecoach in the South Downs, Stagecoach in Portsmouth
Man Dir: Andrew Dyer **Ops Dir:** Tom Bridge
Eng Dir: Richard Alexander
Comm Dir: Mark Turner
Fleet: 188 – 38 double-deck bus, 32 single-deck bus, 2 single-deck coach, 104 midibus, 12 minibus.
Chassis: Alexander Dennis, Dennis, Leyland, Mercedes, Optare, Scania, Transbus, Volvo.
Bodies: Alexander, Alexander Dennis, Optare, Plaxton, Transbus.
Ops incl: local bus services, school contracts, private hire.
Livery: Stagecoach UK Bus
Ticket system: Wayfarer

SUSSEX COUNTRY COACH HIRE
TERMINAL BUILDING, SHOREHAM AIRPORT BN43 5FF
Tel: 01273 465500
Fax: 01273 453040
E-mail: sxcountry@tiscali.co.uk
Web site: www.sussex-country.co.uk
Ops incl: private hire, school contracts, excursions & tours.
Livery: Blue/Yellow/Green on White
A subsidiary of Compass Travel

W+H MOTORS
KELVIN WAY, CRAWLEY
RH10 9SF
Tel: 01293 510220
Fax: 01293 513263
Recovery: 01293 548111
E-mail: sales@wandhgroup.co.uk
Web site: www.wandhgroup.co.uk
Man Dir: George M Heron
Fleet: 17 – 11 single-deck coach, 2 double-deck coach, 4 midicoach.
Chassis: 2 Ayats, 1 Iveco, 3 MAN, 3 Toyota, 6 Volvo, 2 Other.
Bodies: 2 Ayats, 3 Caetano, 2 Jonckheere, 3 Noge, 6 Sunsundegui, 1 Other.
Ops incl: excursions and tours, private hire, school contracts, express, continental tours
Livery: White

WESTRINGS COACHES LTD
53 STOCKS LANE, EAST WITTERING, CHICHESTER PO20 8NH
Tel: 01243 672411
E-mail: westringscoaches@btconnect.com
Web site: www.westringscoaches.co.uk
Dir: W J Buckland
Co Sec: T S West
Fleet: 6 - 1 single-deck bus, 4 single-deck coach, 1 minibus.
Ops incl: school contracts, excursions & tours, private hire.

WOODS TRAVEL LTD
PARK ROAD, BOGNOR REGIS
PO21 2PX
Tel: 01243 868080
Fax: 01243 871669
E-mail: info@woodstravel.co.uk
Web site: www.woodstravel.co.uk
Man Dir: R Elsmere
Transport Man: R Barnes
Excursions: L Glue
Tours: K Elsmere
Fleet: 13 - 12 single-deck coach, 1 midicoach.
Chassis: 12 Bova, 1 Mercedes.
Bodies: 12 Bova, 1 Mercedes.
Ops incl: excursions & tours, private hire, continental tours, school contracts.
Livery: Red/White/Blue.

WORTHING COACHES
117 GEORGE V AVENUE, WORTHING BN11 5SA.
Tel: 01903 505805
Prop: Lucketts of Fareham
Fleet: 15 – 14 single-deck coach, 1 double-deck coach.
Chassis: 15 Scania.
Bodies: 1 East Lancs, 14 Irizar.
Ops incl: excursions & tours, private hire, continental tours.
Livery: Red/White/Yellow
A subsidiary of Lucketts Travel - see Hampshire

Symbol	Meaning	Symbol	Meaning	Symbol	Meaning
	Vehicle suitable for disabled		Seat belt-fitted Vehicle	R24	24 hour recovery service
T	Toilet-drop facilities available		Coach(es) with galley facilities		Replacement vehicle available
R	Recovery service available		Air-conditioned vehicle(s)		Vintage Coach(es) available
	Open top vehicle(s)		Coaches with toilet facilities		

WEST YORKSHIRE

ANDERSON'S COACHES
HOLMFIELD HOUSE, STRANGLANDS LANE, FERRYBRIDGE WF11 8SD
Tel: 01977 552980
Fax: 01977 557823
E-mail: paulanthonyanderson@btinternet.com
Props: Paul Anderson, Gillian Anderson
Fleet: 1 single-deck coach
Chassis: 1 Setra.
Bodies: 1 Setra.
Ops incl: excursions & tours, private hire, continental tours

ARRIVA YORKSHIRE LTD
24 BARNSLEY ROAD, WAKEFIELD WF1 5JX
Tel: 01924 231300
Fax: 01924 200106
Man Dir: Nigel Featham
Fin Dir: David Cocker
Fleet: 335 - 137 double-deck bus, 117 single-deck bus, 81 midibus.
Chassis: 31 Alexander Dennis, 104 DAF, 64 Dennis, 13 Optare, 35 VDL, 79 Volvo, 8 Wrightbus.
Bodies: 136 Alexander Dennis, 14 East Lancs, 7 Ikarus, 8 Northern Counties, 71 Optare, 50 Plaxton, 49 Wright.
Ops incl: local bus services.
Livery: Arriva UK Bus.

B & J TRAVEL
3 SANDY LANE, MIDDLESTOWN, WAKEFIELD WF4 4PW
Tel: 01924 263334
Prop: J. S. Bendle.
Fleet: 2 single-deck coach.
Chassis: DAF, Volvo.
Bodies: Jonckheere, Plaxton.
Ops incl: school contracts, excursions & tours, private hire.
Livery: Red/White/Blue.

B L TRAVEL
10 GRANGE VIEW, HEMSWORTH, NR PONTEFRACT WF9 4ER
Tel: 01977 610313
Fax: 01977 613999
E-mail: bltravelcoaches@aol.com
Proprietors: Brian Lockwood, Paul Lockwood
Fleet: 18 - 8 single-deck bus, 2 single-deck coach, 8 minibus.
Chassis: - 2 Ford, 4 Mercedes, 4 Optare, 1 VDL, 7 Volvo.
Bodies incl: - 2 Ford, 4 Optare, 2 Plaxton, 1 Van Hool, 6 Wright.
Ops incl: local bus services, school contracts, excursions & tours, private hire, express.
Livery: Blue/Yellow.

BAILDON MOTORS LTD
VICTORIA ROAD, GUISELEY, LEEDS LS20 8DG
Tel: 01943 873420
Fax: 01943 878227
E-mail: dalesmancoaches@btconnect.com
Web site: www.dalesmancoaches.co.uk
Fleet Name: Dalesman
Dirs: K Hartshorne, Mrs P J Hartshorne
Fleet: 6 – 2 single-deck coach, 2 midicoach, 2 minicoach
Chassis: 4 Mercedes, 2 VDL

Ops incl: school contracts, excursions & tours, private hire, continental tours.
Livery: White & Blue
See also Dalesman

BRITANNIA TRAVEL
BRITANNIA HOUSE, 113 WESTON LANE, OTLEY LS21 2DX
Tel/Fax: 01943 465591
Props: Antony Broome, Mrs Susan Eastwood.
Fleet: 1 single-deck coach.
Chassis: Setra.
Body: Setra.
Ops incl: private hire.
Livery: Silver/Red.

BROWNS COACHES (SK) LTD
WHITE APRON STREET, SOUTH KIRKBY, PONTEFRACT WF9 3HQ
Tel: 01977 644777
Fax: 01977 643210
E-mail: sales@brownscoaches.com
Web site: www.brownscoaches.com
Fleet Name: Browns
Man Dir: Mrs J M Brown
Co Sec: A Stoppard
Gen Man: A Griffith **Eng Man:** D Brown
Fleet: 12 - 5 single-deck coach, 4 midicoach, 3 minibus.
Chassis: 1 Ford, 3 Iveco, 4 Mercedes, 2 Scania, 2 Temsa.
Bodies: 1 Beulas, 3 Crest, 2 Esker, 1 Irizar, 1 Plaxton, 4 other.
Ops incl: private hire, school contracts, continental tours.
Livery: White

CENTRAL GARAGE
STANSFIELD ROAD, TODMORDEN OL14 5DL
Tel/Fax: 01706 813909
E-mail: tonygled@hotmail.co.uk
Man Dir: David Paul Guest
Man: A J Gledhill.
Fleet: 3 - 2 midibus, 1 minicoach.
Chassis/bodies: 3 Mercedes.
Ops incl: school contracts, private hire.

CITY TRAVEL YORKSHIRE LTD
10A MANYWELLS INDUSTRIAL ESTATE, CULLINGWORTH, BRADFORD BD13 5DX
Tel: 01535 275522
Fax: 01533 274400
E-mail: enquires@citytravel.com
Web site: www.citytravel.co.uk
Fleet: 10 - 6 single-deck bus, 3 single-deck coach, 1 minibus.
Chassis: 6 BMC, 1 DAF, 1 Ford Transit, 1 Iveco, 1 MAN.
Bodies: 1 Berkhof, 6 BMC, 1 Noge, 1 Van Hool.
Ops incl: school contracts, private hire.

CLARKSONS HOLIDAYS
52 DONCASTER ROAD, SOUTH ELMSALL, PONTEFRACT WF9 2JN
Tel: 01977 642385
Fax: 01977 640158
E-mail: info@clarksonscoaches.co.uk
Web site: www.clarksoncoaches.co.uk
Chairman: Ken Clarkson
Dir/Co Sec: John Hancock
Dir: Paul Clarkson
Fleet: 9 - 7 single-deck coach, 1 minicoach, 1 midicoach.

Chassis: 4 Mercedes, 5 Neoplan.
Bodies: 5 Mercedes, 4 Neoplan.
Ops incl: excursions & tours, continental tours.
Livery: Blue

DALESMAN
VICTORIA ROAD, GUISELEY, LEEDS LS20 8DG
Tel: 01943 870228 **Fax:** 01943 878227
E-mail: dalesmancoaches@btconnect.com
Web site: www.dalesmancoaches.co.uk
Dirs: K Hartshorne, Mrs P J Hartshorne
Fleet: 8 - 4 single-deck coach, 2 midicoach, 2 minicoach.
Chassis: 1 DAF, 4 Mercedes, 3 VDL
Bodies: 4 Van Hool, 4 Other
Ops incl: excursions & tours, private hire, excursions & tours.
Livery: Blue/White

DEWHIRST COACHES LTD
TRAVEL TECH HOUSE, THORNCLIFFE ROAD, BRADFORD BD8 7DD
Tel/Fax: 01274 481208
E-mail: dewhirstcoaches@hotmail.com
Web site: www.dewhirstcoaches.co.uk
Dir: S Dewhirst
Co Sec: Mrs L Dewhirst
Fleet: 7 - 4 double-deck bus, 3 single-deck coach.
Chassis: 1 EOS, 1 Scania, 3 VDL, 2 Volvo.
Bodies: 1 Alexander Dennis, 3 East Lancs, 3 Van Hool.
Ops incl: school contracts, excursions & tours, private hire, continental tours.
Livery: Blue/White

FIRST WEST YORKSHIRE
HUNSLET PARK, DONISTHORPE STREET, LEEDS LS10 1PL
Tel: 0113 381 5000
Fax: 0113 242 9721
E-mail: contact.us@firstgroup.com
Web site: www.firstgroup.com
Man Dir: Ian Humphreys
Ops Dir: Ben Gilligan
Fin Dir: Janet Burgess
Eng Dir: Colin Stafford
Comm Dir: Richard Harris
Fleet: 1077 – 501 double-deck bus, 428 single-deck bus, 63 midibus, 43 articulated bus, 42 minibus.
Chassis incl: BMC, Dennis, Mercedes, Optare, Scania, Volvo.
Bodies incl: Alexander, BMC, Marshall, Mercedes, Northern Counties, Optare, Plaxton, Wright.
Ops incl: local bus services, school contracts
Livery: FirstGroup UK Bus
Ticket System: Wayfarer 3.

FOURWAY COACHES
FOURWAY'S GARAGE, LOW MILLS, GHYLL ROYD, GUISELEY, LEEDS LS20 9LT
Tel: 0113 250 5800
E-mail: fourway@freezone.co.uk
Web site: www.fourwaycoaches.co.uk
Fleet: 34 – single-deck coach, midicoach, minibus.
Chassis incl: DAF, Irisbus, Iveco, LDV, Mercedes, Volvo.

Ops incl: private hire, excursions & tours.
Livery: White/Multicoloured.

GAIN TRAVEL EXPERIENCE
6 FAIR ROAD, WIBSEY, BRADFORD BD6 1QN
Tel: 01274 603224 **Fax:** 01274 678274
E-mail: gail@gaintravel.co.uk
Web site: www.gaintravel.co.uk
Man Dir: Gail Bottomley
Dirs: Ian Bottomley, Darren Bottomley
Man: Beryl LeaRoyd
Fleet: 5 - 4 single-deck coach, 1 minibus.
Chassis incl: 3 DAF, 1 MAN.
Bodies incl: 4 Van Hool.
Ops incl: excursions & tours, private hire

STANLEY GATH (COACHES) LTD
WHALEY ROAD, BARNSLEY S75 1HT
Tel: 01226 205800 **Fax:** 01226 390048
E-mail: info@stanley-gath.co.uk
Web site: www.stanley-gath.co.uk
Ops incl: excursions & tours, private hire, school contracts
Livery: Grey/Cream
Subsidiary of Tate's Travel – see South Yorkshire

GELDARD'S COACHES LTD
1 CHAPEL LANE, ARMLEY, LEEDS LS12 2DJ
Tel: 0113 263 9491 **Fax:** 0113 231 1447
E-mail: info@geldardscoaches.co.uk
Web site: www.geldardscoaches.co.uk
Fleet: 48 - 38 double-deck bus, 2 single-deck bus, 8 single-deck coach.
Ops incl: local bus services, school contracts, private hire.

J D GODSON
65 STATION ROAD, CROSSGATES LS15 8DT
Tel: 0113 264 6166 **Fax:** 0113 390 9669
E-mail: godsonscoaches@hotmail.com
Web site: www.godsonluxurycoachesleeds.co.uk
Man Dir: David Godson
Fleet: 8
Chassis: 2 Bova, 3 DAF, 3 Volvo.
Bodies: 2 Bova, 1 Caetano, 5 Plaxton.
Ops incl: local bus services, private hire.
Livery: Pink/White/Brown

G. W. GOULDING
64 THE RIDGEWAY, KNOTTINGLEY WF11 0JS
Tel: 01977 672265, 672059
Fax: 01977 670276
Fleet Name: B. Goulding.
Prop: G. W. Goulding.
Fleet: 5 - 3 single-deck coach, 1 midicoach, 1 minicoach.
Chassis: 1 Bristol, 1 Leyland, 1 Toyota, 2 Volvo.
Bodies: 1 Caetano, 4 Plaxton.
Ops incl: excursions & tours, private hire, continental tours.
Livery: White with Red/Yellow/Blue stripes.

HALIFAX BUS COMPANY
18 STONECROFT MOUNT, SOWERBY BRIDGE HX6 2SB
Tel: 01422 363600
Fleet: midibus, minibus
Ops incl: local bus services
Livery: Red

HALIFAX JOINT COMMITTEE
1 VICAR PARK ROAD, NORTON TOWER, HALIFAX HX2 0NL
Tel: 01422 353330
Fleet: double-deck bus, single-deck bus, midibus
Ops incl: local bus services, school contracts, private hire
Livery: Green/Orange

HUDDERSFIELD BUS COMPANY
PENISTONE ROAD, WATERLOO, HUDDERSFIELD HD5 5QU
Tel: 0843 289 5135
Web site: www.centrebus.com
Fleet Name: Centrebus
Fleet: 55 –7 double-deck bus, 34 single-deck bus, 14 minibus.
Chassis: 6 DAF, 7 Dennis, 3 Leyland, 18 Optare, 4 Scania, 7 VDL, 10 Volvo.
Bodies: 18 East Lancs, 2 Marshall, 4 Northern Counties, 18 Optare, 11 Plaxton, 2 Wright.
Ops incl: local bus services.
Liveries: Blue/Orange, Green.
Jointly owned by Centrebus and Arriva

HUNTER COACHES LTD
30 TYNWALD ROAD, LEEDS LS17 5ED
Tel: 0113 239 0034
Fax: 0113 239 0101
E-mail: sales@huntercoaches.co.uk
Web site: www.huntercoaches.co.uk
Ops incl: school contracts, private hire, excursions & tours.
Livery: White/Blue.

INDEPENDENT COACHWAYS LTD
LOW FOLD GARAGE, NEW ROAD SIDE, HORSFORTH, LEEDS LS18 4DR
Tel: 0113 258 6491
Fax: 0113 259 1125
E-mail: sales@independentcoachways.com
Dirs: P & C Thornes
Fleet: 7 - 1 single-deck bus, 6 single-deck coach.
Chassis: 1 Optare 6 Volvo.
Bodies: 1 Optare, 5 Plaxton, 1 Van Hool.
Ops incl: private hire.
Livery: Blue/Grey
A subsidiary of Thornes Independent – see East Riding

K-LINE TRAVEL
STATION YARD, STATION ROAD, HONLEY, HUDDERSFIELD HD9 6BF
Tel: 0843 289 5135
Fleet: 32 – 19 single-deck bus, 13 minibus.
Chassis incl: BMC, DAF, Optare.
Bodies incl: BMC, Ikarus, Northern Counties, Optare, Plaxton, Wright.
Ops incl: local bus services, school contracts.
Livery: Blue/White.
Jointly owned by Centrebus and Arriva

J J LONGSTAFF & SONS LTD
EASTFIELD GARAGE, STONEY LANE, MIRFIELD WF14 0DX
Tel: 01924 463122
Web site: www.longstaffofmirfield.com

E-mail: jjlongstaff@btconnect.com
Fleet Name: Longstaff of Mirfield
Dirs: G Kaye, S Kaye
Fleet: 2 - 2 single-deck bus.
Chassis: 2 Volvo.
Bodies: 2 Wright.
Ops incl: local bus service, school contracts.
Livery: Blue/Blue Grey
Ticket System: Wayfarer

A. LYLES & SON
156 COMMONSIDE, BATLEY WF17 6LA
Tel: 01924 464771
Fax: 01924 469267
E-mail: alyles&son@aol.com
Senior Partner: Terence Lyles
Partner: Howard Lyles.
Fleet: 6 - 1 single-deck bus, 5 single-deck coach
Chassis: 2 DAF, 4 MAN.
Bodies: 1 Berkhof, 1 Duple, 1 Indcar, 1 Optare, 2 Van Hool
Ops incl: local bus services, school contracts, excursions & tours, private hire, continental tours.
Livery: Beige/Brown/Red

DAVID PALMER COACHES LTD
THE TRAVEL OFFICE, WAKEFIELD ROAD, NORMANTON WF6 2BT
Tel: 01924 895849 **Fax:** 01924 897750
E-mail: info@davidpalmercoaches.co.uk
Web site: www.davidpalmercoaches.co.uk
Dirs: Andrew Palmer, Lisa Palmer.
Fleet: 9 – 1 double-deck bus, 4 single-deck coach, 1 open top bus, 1 minibus, 2 minicoach.
Chassis incl: 4 DAF, 2 Mercedes.
Bodies incl: 4 Van Hool.
Ops incl: school contracts, excursions & tours, private hire, continental tours.
Livery: Silver

PULLMAN DINER
THE HAWTHORNS, GREAT NORTH ROAD, KNOTTINGLEY WF11 0BS
Tel: 07860 302018 **Fax:** 07860 677554
Web site: www.pullmandiner.co.uk
Prop: Michael Hartley
Fleet: 1 single-deck coach
Chassis: 1 MAN
Bodies: 1 Van Hool.
Ops incl: excursions & tours, private hire, continental tours

RED ARROW COACHES LTD
ASPLEY HOUSE, LINCOLN STREET, HUDDERSFIELD HD1 6RX
Tel: 01484 420993
Fax: 01484 540409
E-mail: info@redarrowcoaches.co.uk
Web site: www.redarrowcoaches.co.uk
Dirs: Steven R. Moore, Suichwant Singh.
Fleet: 10 - 9 single-deck coach, 1 midicoach.
Chassis: 1 Ayats, 2 Bova, 2 DAF, 1 Dennis, 2 MAN, 2 Scania.
Bodies: 1 Ayats, 2 Bova, 1 Caetano, 2 Plaxton, 4 Van Hool.
Ops incl: excursions & tours, private hire, continental tours, school contracts.

JOHN RIGBY TRAVEL
231 BRADFORD ROAD, BATLEY WF17 6JL
Tel: 01924 485151 **Fax:** 01924 485161

E-mail: rigbytransport@hotmail.co.uk
Web site: www.johnrigby.co.uk
Props: John Rigby, Nick Barker
Fleet: 7 - 5 single-deck coach,
1 midicoach, 1 minicoach.
Chassis: 1 Dennis, 2 EOS, 2 MAN,
1 Mercedes, 2 Volvo.
Bodies: 2 Caetano, 1 Marcopolo,
2 Van Hool, 3 Other.
Ops incl: private hire, school contracts.
Livery: White

ROLLINSON SAFEWAY LTD

RSL HOUSE, 65 HALL LANE,
LEEDS LS12 1PQ
Tel: 0113 231 1355
Fax: 0113 231 1344
Web site: www.rollinson.co.uk
Fleet Name: Air-Line Connections
Man Dir: Paul Rollinson
Dir: Peter Rollinson
Contracts Man: M. J. Joyce.
Fleet: 72 minibus
Chassis: 1 Fiat, 3 Ford Transit, 3 Iveco,
20 Mercedes, 45 Renault.
Ops incl: private hire, school contracts.
Liveries: Brown/Gold, White with
Blue/Red.

ROSS TRAVEL

THE GARAGE, ALLISON STREET,
FEATHERSTONE WF7 5BL
Tel: 01977 791738
Fax: 01977 690109
E-mail: info@rosstravelgroup.co.uk
Web Site: www.rosstravelgroup.co.uk
Props: Peter Ross, Mary Ross,
Andrew Stirling, Stephen Ross.
Fleet: 18 - 10 single-deck bus,
5 single-deck coach, 3 midicoach.
Chassis: 2 DAF, 7 Mercedes, 5 Optare,
2 Scania, 2 Volvo.
Bodies: 1 Alexander Dennis, 2 Bova,
5 Optare, 5 Plaxton, 2 Sitcar,
2 Van Hool, 1 Volvo.
Ops incl: local bus services, school
contracts, private hire, continental tours.
Livery: Red/White
Ticket System: Wayfarer

SHEARINGS HOLIDAYS

MILL LANE, NORMANTON WF6 1RF
Tel: 01977 603088 **Fax:** 01977 603114
Ops Man: Martin Guy
See also Shearings Holidays,
Greater Manchester

STEELS LUXURY COACHES LTD

61 MAIN STREET, ADDINGHAM
LS29 0PD
Tel: 01943 830206 **Fax:** 01943 831499
E-mail: info@steelscoaches.co.uk
Web site: www.steelscoaches.co.uk
Dir: T Steel
Co Sec: Mrs J Steel
Fleet: 6 - 2 single-deck coach,
3 midicoach, 1 minicoach.
Chassis: 1 Iveco, 4 Mercedes, 1 Volvo.
Bodies: 4 Plaxton, 2 Other.
Ops incl: excursions & tours, private hire,
school contracts, continental tours.
Livery: White/Red/Black

STEVENSONS TRAVEL

THE WILLOWS, LIDGATE CRESCENT,
SOUTH KIRKBY,
PONTEFRACT WF9 3NR
Tel: 01977 645060.

E-mail: stevensonstravel@hotmail.co.uk
Partners: Ricky Stevenson, Michelle Mills.
Fleet: 7 minibus.
Chassis: 3 Ford Transit, 3 Iveco, 1 LDV.
Ops incl: school contracts, excursions &
tours, private hire.

E STOTT & SONS LTD

COLNE VALE GARAGE, OFF SAVILE
STREET, MILNSBRIDGE,
HUDDERSFIELD HD3 4PG
Tel: 01484 460463 **Fax:** 01484 461463
E-mail: info@stottscoaches.co.uk
Web site: www.stottscoaches.co.uk
Dirs: Mark Stott, Carl Stott
Fleet: 30 - 5 single-deck bus,
12 single-deck coach, 2 midibus,
11 minibus.
Chassis: 5 Dennis, 5 Mercedes,
8 Optare, 12 Volvo.
Bodies: 8 Optare, 18 Plaxton,
4 Sunsundegui.
Ops incl: local bus services, school
contracts, excursions & tours, private hire.
Livery: White with Red/Black/Silver
Ticket System: Wayfarer 3

STRINGERS PONTEFRACT MOTORWAYS

102 SOUTHGATE, PONTEFRACT
WF8 1PN
Tel: 01977 600205 **Fax:** 01977 704178
E-mail:
enquires@stringerscoaches.co.uk
Web: www.stringerscoaches.co.uk
Prop: Mark G Stringer
Ops Man: Mark E Stringer
Sec: Sonia A Stringer
Ch Eng: Chris Palmer
Fleet: 10 - 3 single-deck coach,
6 midibus, 1 midicoach.
Chassis: 5 Alexander Dennis,
1 Mercedes, 1 Optare, 3 Volvo.
Bodies: 2 Jonckheere, 1 Optare,
3 Plaxton, 3 Transbus, 1 Van Hool.
Ops incl: local bus services, school
contracts, excursions & tours, private hire.
Livery: Black/White/Red
Ticket system: Wayfarer

TETLEYS MOTOR SERVICES LTD

76 GOODMAN STREET,
LEEDS LS10 1NY
Tel: 0113 276 2276 **Fax:** 0113 276 2277
E-mail: sales@tetleyscoaches.com
Web site: www.tetleyscoaches.com
Dir: Ian Tetley **Co Sec:** Angela Tetley
Ch Eng: David Leach
Ops Man: Stephen Cunniff
Fleet: 17 – 2 double-deck bus,
11 single-deck coach, 2 midicoach,
2 minicoach
Chassis: 1 Alexander Dennis, 1 Iveco,
2 Mercedes, 2 Renault, 11 Volvo.
Bodies: 2 East Lancs, 13 Plaxton,
2 Other.
Ops incl: school contracts, private hire,
express.
Livery: Blue lettering on White

TLC TRAVEL LTD

7 LINTON STREET, BRADFORD BD4 7EZ
Tel: 01274 727811 **Fax:** 01274 723640
E-mail: enquiries@tlctravelltd.co.uk
Web site: www.tlctravelltd.co.uk
Fleet: 24 midibus, minibus
Chassis: Mercedes, Optare
Ops incl: local bus services

TRANSDEV KEIGHLEY & DISTRICT

CAVENDISH HOUSE, 91-93
CAVENDISH STREET,
KEIGHLEY BD21 3DG
Tel: 01535 603284 **Fax:** 01535 610065
E-mail:
enquire@keighleyanddistrict.co.uk
Web site: www.keighleybus.co.uk
Fleet Name: The Zone
Chief Exec: Martin Gilchrist
Fleet: 104 - 21 double-deck bus,
67 single-deck bus, 16 midibus.
Chassis: 15 Dennis, 11 Leyland,
78 Volvo.
Bodies: 1 Alexander, 3 ECW,
16 Northern Counties, 17 Plaxton,
7 Wright.
Ops incl: local bus services, school
contracts
Livery: Blue/White, Blue/Red
Part of the Blazefield group which is
owned by Transdev

TWIN VALLEY COACHES

INDUSTRIAL ROAD, SOWERBY
BRIDGE HX6 2RA
Tel/Fax: 01422 833358.
Dirs: D Pilling, E Pilling.
Fleet: 5 - 2 single-deck coach,
2 midicoach, 1 minicoach.
Chassis: 2 Dennis, 1 LDV, 1 MAN,
2 Mercedes.
Bodies: 1 Caetano, 2 Optare, 1 Plaxton.
Ops incl: private hire, school contracts.
Livery: Green/White.

WELSH'S COACHES LTD

FIELD LANE, UPTON, PONTEFRACT
WF9 1BH
Tel: 01977 643873 **Fax:** 01977 648143
E-mail: info@welshscoaches.com
Web site: www.welshscoaches.com
Dirs: John Welsh, Judy Welsh
Fleet: 8 - 5 single-deck coach,
3 minicoach.
Chassis: 3 Mercedes, 5 Setra.
Bodies: 3 Mercedes, 5 Setra.
Ops incl: excursions & tours, private hire,
continental tours.
Livery: Green/White/Red

WHITE ROSE BUS COMPANY LTD

5 SUMMERBANK CLOSE,
DRIGHLINGTON,
BRADFORD BD11 1LQ
Tel: 0843 289 5135
Fleet: 10 single-deck bus
Chassis: 2 MAN, 8 Scania
Ops incl: local bus services
Jointly owned by Centrebus and Arriva

Notes

West Yorkshire

WILTSHIRE, SWINDON

AD-RAINS OF BRINKWORTH
THE COACH YARD, THE COMMON, BRINKWORTH SN15 5DX
Tel: 01666 510874
Recovery: 07831 303295
Prop: Adrain Griffiths
Ops Man: Colin Minchin
Fleet: 8 - 3 single-deck bus, 4 single-deck coach, 1 minibus.
Chassis: 1 LDV, 2 Leyland, 3 Mercedes, 2 Volvo.
Bodies: 7 Plaxton, 1 Reeve Burgess.
Ops incl: local bus services, school contracts, private hire.
Livery: White/Blue/Yellow
Ticket system: Wayfarer

ANDREW JAMES QUALITY TRAVEL (ANDYBUS AND COACH LTD)
UNIT 6, WHITEWALLS, EASTON GREY, MALMESBURY SN16 0RD
Tel: 01666 825655
Fax: 01666 825651
Recovery: 07740 88710
E-mail: ajcoaches@andrew-james.co.uk
Web site: www.andrew-james.co.uk
Dir: Andrew James
Fleet: 16 - 3 single-deck coach, 6 single-deck bus, 6 midibus, 1 midicoach.
Chassis: 3 Bova, 2 DAF, 4 Dennis, 1 Leyland, 2 MAN, 1 Marshall, 5 Mercedes, 1 Optare, 1 Toyota.
Bodies: 3 Bova, 1 Caetano, 1 East Lancs, 1 Ikarus, 1 Marshall/MCV, 2 Optare, 8 Plaxton
Ops incl: local bus services, school contracts, private hire.
Livery: Bus - Cream/Orange; Coach - Yellow/Black
Ticket System: Wayfarer

APL TRAVEL LTD
PEAR TREE COTTAGE, CRUDWELL SN16 9ES
Tel: 01666 577774
Fax: 01249 721402
E-mail: apltravel@btconncet.com
Web site: www.apltravel.co.uk
Dirs: Alan Legg, Shane Legg
Fleet: 15 - 6 single-deck bus, 6 single-deck coach, 2 midicoach, 1 minicoach.
Chassis: 3 Alexander Dennis, 1 Bedford, 1 DAF, 2 Dennis, 1 Iveco, 1 Leyland, 3 MAN, 3 Mercedes.
Bodies: 2 Berkhof, 1 Bova, 2 Ikarus, 2 Mercedes, 1 Noge, 3 Optare, 2 Plaxton.
Ops incl: local bus services, school contracts, excursions & tours, private hire.
Livery: White
Ticket System: Wayfarer

BARNES COACHES
UNIT E, WOODSIDE ROAD, SOUTH MARSTON BUSINESS PARK, SWINDON SN3 4AQ
Tel: 01793 821303
Fax: 01793 828486
E-mail: travel@barnescoaches.co.uk
Web site: www.barnescoaches.co.uk
Dirs: Lionel Barnes, Terry Barnes, Luke Barnes, Matt Barnes
Fleet: 25 - 25 single-deck coaches
Chassis: 10 Bova, 15 Volvo.

Bodies: 10 Bova, 15 Van Hool.
Ops incl: local bus services, excursions & tours, school contracts, private hire, continental tours
Livery: Green

BEELINE (R & R) COACHES LTD
BISHOPSTROW ROAD, WARMINSTER BA12 9HQ
Tel: 01985 213503
Fax: 01985 213922
E-mail: markhayball@beelinecoaches.co.uk
Web site: www.beelinecoaches.co.uk
Dirs: Mark Hayball, Andrew Hayball
Gen Man: Noel Ennis
Fleet: 32 - 20 single-deck coach, 8 midicoach, 4 minibus.
Chassis: 4 LDV, 14 Mercedes, 14 Volvo.
Bodies: 4 Jonckheere, 4 LDV, 19 Plaxton, 5 Van Hool.
Ops incl: local bus services, school contracts, private hire
Livery: White/Beige
Ticket system: Setright

BETTER MOTORING SERVICES
104a SWINDON ROAD, STRATTON ST MARGARET, SWINDON SN3 4PT
Tel: 01793 823747
Fax: 01793 831898
E-mail: bmscoaches@btconnect.com
Fleet Name: BMS Coaches.
Prop: D G Miles
Fleet Eng: M J Hopkins
Sec: Mrs M Mulhern
Fleet: 11 - 9 midicoach, 2 minicoach.
Chassis: 2 Ford, 9 Mercedes.
Bodies: 2 Autobus, 2 Esker, 2 Mellor, 3 Optare, 2 Other.
Ops incl: school contracts, excursions & tours, private hire, continental tours.
Livery: Coffee/Cream

BODMAN COACHES
88 HIGH STREET, WORTON, DEVIZES SN10 5RU
Tel: 01380 722393
Fax: 01380 721969
E-Mail: bodmancoaches@btinternet.com
Tran Man: Nigel Denny
Ops Man: Graham Carter
Fleet: 39 - 20 single-deck bus, 19 single-deck coach.
Chassis: 7 Alexander Dennis, 18 Dennis, 1 Leyland, 2 MAN, 4 Mercedes, 7 Volvo.
Bodies: 7 Alexander Dennis, 2 Berkhof, 2 Marshall/MCV, 1 MCW, 26 Plaxton, 1 Van Hool.
Ops incl: local bus services, school contracts, excursions & tours, private hire.
Livery: White/Green
Ticket System: Wayfarer

CHANDLERS COACH TRAVEL
158 CHEMICAL ROAD, WEST WILTS TRADING ESTATE, WESTBURY BA13 4JN
Tel: 01373 824500
Fax: 01373 824300
E-mail: info@chandlerscoach.co.uk
Web site: www.chandlerscoach.co.uk

Prop: Margaret l'Anson
Fleet Eng: Christopher l'Anson
Fleet: 10 - 9 single-deck coach, 1 minibus.
Chassis: 1 Renault, 9 Volvo.
Bodies: 4 Plaxton, 1 Renault, 5 Van Hool.
Ops incl: school contracts, excursions & tours, private hire, continental tours.
Livery: White/Burgundy/Gold

COACHSTYLE LTD
HORSDOWN GARAGE, NETTLETON, CHIPPENHAM SN14 7LN
Tel/Fax: 01249 782224
E-mail: mail@coachstyle.ltd.uk
Web site: www.coachstyle.ltd.uk
Owners: Andrew Jones, Mrs A L Jones
Fleet: 15 - 2 single-deck bus, 13 single-deck coach.
Chassis: 4 DAF, 3 Leyland, 1 Scania, 6 Volvo.
Bodies: 3 Berkhof, 1 Caetano, 2 Duple, 3 Jonckheere, 2 Mercedes, 3 Van Hool.
Ops incl: local bus services, school contracts, excursions & tours, private hire, continental tours.
Livery: White with Purple

ELLISON'S COACHES
THE GARAGE, HIGH ROAD, ASHTON KEYNES, SWINDON SN6 6NX
Tel: 01285 861224
Fax: 01285 862115
E-mail: sales@ellisonscoaches.co.uk
Web site: www.ellisonscoaches.co.uk
Prop: Alan Ellison
Fleet: 20 single-deck coach.
Chassis: 1 Autosan, 1 BMC, 4 Dennis, 1 Mercedes, 11 Neoplan.
Ops incl: school contracts, excursions & tours, private hire, continental tours.
Livery: White/Green/Red

FARESAVER BUSES
THE COACH YARD, VINCIENTS ROAD, BUMPERS FARM INDUSTRIAL ESTATE, CHIPPENHAM SN14 6QA
Tel: 01249 444444
Fax: 01249 448844
E-mail: sales@faresaver.co.uk
Web site: www.faresaver.co.uk
Prop: J V Pickford
Ch Eng: D Watts
Ops Man: D J Pickford
Ops Man: D Beard
Fleet: 55 - 15 single-deck bus, 30 midibus, 10 midicoach.
Chassis: Dennis, Mercedes.
Bodies: Alexander Dennis, Caetano, Mercedes, Plaxton
Ops incl: local bus services, school contracts, private hire.
Liveries: White/Mauve, Silver & Purple.
Ticket System: Wayfarer 3

G-LINE MINICOACHES
UNIT 1, TRANSFER BRIDGE INDUSTRIAL ESTATE, COUNTY ROAD, SWINDON SN1 2EL
Tel/Fax: 01793 422832
E-mail: gline@btinternet.com
Chairman: P McGarry
Man Dir: N McGarry
Service Dir: J McGarry

Tpt Man: N McGarry.
Fleet: 30 - 4 minicoach, 26 midicoach
Chassis incl: 4 Ford Transit, 2 Iveco, 10 LDV, 5 Mercedes.
Ops incl: private hire, school contracts.

HATTS TRAVEL
HAM VILLA, FOXHAM, CHIPPENHAM SN15 4NB
Tel/Recovery: 01249 740444
Fax: 01249 740447
E-mail: info@hattstravel.co.uk
Web site: www.hattstravel.co.uk
Man Partner: Adrian Hillier
Ops Man: Andy Bridgeman
Traffic Man: Phil Turner
Workshop Man: Mike Henderson
Bodyshop Man: Ashley Davis
Accts Man: Lynne Pegler
Holidays: Pat Huston
Group Sales Man: Marilyn Nelson
Fleet: 69 – 4 single-deck bus, 33 single-deck coach, 2 double-deck coach, 10 midibus, 10 midicoach, 7 minibus, 3 minicoach.
Chassis: 10 Alexander Dennis, 4 Ayats, 4 Bova, 5 DAF, 7 Ford Transit, 2 Iveco, 14 MAN, 27 Mercedes, 3 Neoplan, 4 Optare, 2 Toyota, 8 Volvo.
Bodies: 4 Alexander Dennis, 6 Autobus, 4 Ayats, 2 Berkhof, 2 Beulas, 4 Bova, 1 Caetano, 1 Esker, 2 Ikarus, 4 Marcopolo, 4 Mellor, 16 Mercedes, 3 Neoplan, 1 Noge, 5 Optare, 11 Plaxton, 3 Van Hool.
Ops incl: local bus services, school contracts, excursions & tours, private hire, continental tours.
Livery: Purple/White
Ticket System: Wayfarer

MANSFIELD'S COACHES
27 FINCHDALE, COVINGHAM, SWINDON SN3 5AL
Tel/Fax: 01793 525375
Prop: R E Mansfield
Man: A. Mansfield
Tran Man: P Mansfield
Sec: Mrs M S Mansfield.
Fleet: 6 – 5 single-deck coach, 1 midicoach.
Chassis: 3 MAN, 2 Mercedes, 1 Toyota.
Ops incl: excursions & tours, private hire, express, school contracts.
Livery: Yellow/Green/Red.
Ticket System: Setright.

PEWSEY VALE COACHES
HOLLYBUSH LANE, PEWSEY SN9 5BB
Tel/Fax: 01672 562238
E-mail: pewseyvalecoaches@aol.com
Web site: www.pewseyvalecoaches.co.uk
Dirs: Andrew Thorne, Dawn Thorne, Anne Thorne
Fleet: single-deck coach, minicoach.
Chassis incl: Bova, Leyland, Mercedes, Volvo.
Bodies incl: Bova, Plaxton, Van Hool.
Ops incl: local bus services, school contracts, excursions & tours, private hire, continental tours
Livery: White/Blue/Red
Ticket system: Almex

SEAGER'S COACHES LTD
EASTON LANE, CHIPPENHAM SN14 0RW
Tel: 01249 654949 **Fax:** 01249 652581
E-mail: seagerscoaches@hotmail.com
Web site: www.seagerscoaches.co.uk
Dirs: Ms J Seager, T Woods, A Watts, Ms A Truscott
Fleet: 19 - 1 single-deck coach, 14 minibus, 2 midicoach.
Chassis: 1 DAF, 9 Ford Transit, 4 Iveco, 3 LDV, 2 Mercedes.
Ops incl: private hire, school contracts.
Livery: White

STAGECOACH WEST
See Gloucestershire

TEST VALLEY TRAVEL LTD
BANNISTER BARN, NEWTON LANE, WHITEPARISH SP5 2QQ
Tel/Fax: 01794 884555
Man Dir: John M Norman
Co Sec: Mrs Angeline N Norman
E-mail: falconlomax@hotmail.co.uk
Fleet: 3 minibus.
Chassis/Bodies: 3 LDV.
Ops incl: private hire, school contracts.
Livery: Green, Gold on White

THAMESDOWN TRANSPORT
BARNFIELD ROAD, SWINDON SN2 2DJ
Tel: 01793 428400

Fax: 01793 428405
Recovery: 01793 428432
E-mail: customerservices@thamesdown-transport.co.uk
Web site: www.thamesdown-transport.co.uk
Man Dir: Paul Jenkins
Eng Dir: Nigel Mason
Fin Controller/Co Sec: Cliff Connor
Ops Dir: David Burch
Fleet: 101 - 25 double-deck bus, 76 single-deck bus.
Chassis incl: 1 Daimler, 26 Dennis, 9 Leyland, 28 Scania, 22 Transbus, 15 Volvo
Bodies: 23 Alexander, 1 ECW, 1 Northern Counties, 30 Plaxton, 18 Transbus, 28 Wright.
Ops incl: local bus services, school contracts.
Livery: Blue/Green
Ticket System: Wayfarer TGX

TOURIST COACHES LTD
(Incorporating Bells Coaches Ltd, Kingston Coaches, Levers Coaches Ltd)
162 CASTLE STREET, SALISBURY SP1 3UA
Tel: 01722 338359
Fax: 01722 412681
Web site: www.touristcoaches.co.uk
Man Dir: A Carter
Divisional Dir: M Morgan-Huws
Fleet: 32 - 21 single-deck coach, 4 midibus, 3 midicoach, 2 minicoach, 2 minibus
Chassis: 9 DAF, 5 Dennis, 2 LDV, 5 Mercedes, 3 Optare, 1 Toyota, 7 Volvo.
Bodies: 1 Autobus, 1 Caetano, 2 Ferqui, 1 Mercedes, 3 Optare, 11 Plaxton, 1 Reeve Burgess, 8 Van Hool, 5 other.
Ops incl: local bus services, school contracts, excursions & tours, private hire, continental tours
Livery: Orange/Cream.
(Subsidiary of Wilts & Dorset Bus Company – see Dorset)

WILTS & DORSET BUS COMPANY LTD
See Dorset

WORCESTERSHIRE

ASTONS COACHES
BROOMHALL, CLERKENLEAP, WORCESTER WR5 3HR
Tel: 01905 820201 **Fax:** 01905 829249
Recovery: 07860 693712
E-mail: info@astons-coaches.co.uk
Web site: www.astons-coaches.co.uk
Gen Man: Richard Conway
Tran Man: Matthew Wells
Ops Man: Jon Elsdon
New Bus Dev Man: Becki Muir
Sales & Mktg Man: Anna Woodward
Fleet: 36 - 4 double-deck bus, 9 single-deck bus, 18 single-deck coach, 3 midibus, 2 minibus.
Chassis: 1 Alexander Dennis, 1 MAN, 6 Mercedes, 7 Optare, 12 Scania, 8 Volvo.
Bodies: 1 Berkhof, 1 Duple, 4 East Lancs, 3 Irizar, 1 Jonckheere, 7 Optare, 3 Sunsundegui, 6 Van Hool, 8 Other.

Ops incl: local bus services, school contracts, private hire, express, continental tours.
Ticket system: ERG
A subsidiary of Veolia Transport UK

N N CRESSWELL COACH HIRE
WORCESTER ROAD, EVESHAM WR11 4RA
Tel: 01386 48655
Fax: 01386 48656
E-mail: nncresswell@btinternet.com
Props: Mrs Mary Shephard, Mrs Sue Everatt
Fleet: 21 - 14 single-deck coach, 5 minibus, 2 midicoach.
Chassis: 2 Bedford, 12 Dennis, 7 Mercedes.
Bodies: 21 Plaxton
Ops incl: local bus services, school contracts, excursions & tours, private hire.
Livery: Blue/White
Ticket System: Wayfarer.

DIAMOND BUS LTD
See West Midlands

DUDLEY'S COACHES
POPLAR GARAGE, ALCESTER ROAD, RADFORD, WORCESTER WR7 4LS
Tel: 01386 792206 **Fax:** 01386 793373
E-mail: info@dudleys-coaches.co.uk
Web site: www.dudleys-coaches.co.uk
Fleet: 17 - 16 single-deck coach, 1 minibus.
Chassis: 1 Leyland, 1 Toyota, 15 Volvo.
Bodies: 1 Caetano, 1 Jonckheere, 10 Plaxton, 5 Van Hool.
Ops incl: local bus services, school contracts, excursions & tours, private hire
Livery: Green/Cream.

The Little Red Book 2011
Passenger Transport Directory for the British Isles

For information regarding advertising contact:

Graham Middleton
Tel: 01780 484632
Fax: 01780 763388
E-mail: graham.middleton@ianallanpublishing.co.uk

Worcestershire

EUROLINERS
1631 BRISTOL ROAD SOUTH, REDNAL, BIRMINGHAM BH45 9UA
Tel: 0121 453 5151
Fax: 0121 453 5504
E-mail: info@euroliners.co.uk
Web site: www.euroliners.co.uk
Prop: Anthony Armstrong
Fleet: 15 - 2 single-deck coach, 5 midicoach, 8 minicoach.
Chassis: 5 LDV, 10 Mercedes.
Bodies: 6 Mercedes, 4 Optare, 5 Plaxton.
Ops incl: local bus services, school contracts, private hire.

FIRST MIDLANDS
HERON LODGE, LONDON ROAD, WORCESTER WR5 2EU
Tel: 01905 359393
Fax: 01905 351104
Man Dir: Ken Poole
Fleet Name: First Wyvern
Fleet: 170 – 10 double-deck bus, 113 single-deck bus, 7 single-deck coach, 45 minibus.
Chassis: 46 Alexander Dennis, 1 BMC, 84 Dennis, 1 Leyland, 15 Optare, 5 Transbus, 19 Volvo.
Bodies: 46 Alexander Dennis, 1 BMC, 5 Caetano, 2 Northern Counties, 15 Optare, 83 Plaxton, 5 Transbus, 13 Wright.
Ops incl: local bus services, school contracts.
Livery: FirstGroup UK Bus
Ticket System: Wayfarer

HARDINGS INTERNATIONAL
OXLEASOW ROAD, REDDITCH B98 0RE
Tel: 01527 525200
Fax: 01527 523800
E-mail: john@hardingscoaches.com
Web site: www.hardingscoaches.co.uk
Man Dir: Malcolm Chance
Dir: Malcolm Playford
Fleet: 43 - 5 single-deck bus, 35 single-deck coach, 4 minibus.
Chassis: 3 DAF, 5 Leyland, 4 MAN, 9 Mercedes, 20 Scania, 3 Volvo.
Bodies: 2 Berkhof, 1 East Lancs, 1 Ikarus, 13 Irizar, 5 Leyland, 9 Mercedes, 13 Van Hool.

Ops incl: local bus services, school contracts, excursions & tours, private hire, continental tours.
Livery: Silver/Red/Blue

HARRIS EXECUTIVE TRAVEL
58 MEADOW ROAD, CATSHILL, BROMSGROVE B61 0JL
Tel: 01527 872857
Fax: 01527 872708
E-mail: accountsharristravel@msn.com
Joint Man Dirs: J G Harris, S W Harris
Fleet: 7 - 6 single-deck coach, 1 minicoach.
Chassis: 7 Mercedes.
Bodies: 1 Cacciamali, 6 Neoplan.
Ops incl: excursions & tours, private hire, continental tours.
Livery: White/Red/Yellow/Orange.

KESTREL COACHES
UNITS 1&2, BARRACKS ROAD, SANDY LANE, STOURPORT-ON-SEVERN DY13 9QB
Tel/Fax: 01299 829689
Prop: M Wood.
Fleet: 10 - 4 single-deck coach, 3 midicoach, 3 minibus.
Chassis: 1 Bedford, 2 Bova, 1 Citroën, 1 DAF, 1 LDV, 2 Mercedes, 2 Toyota.
Bodies: 2 Bova, 3 Caetano, 1 Leyland, 2 Mercedes, 1 Relay, 1 Van Hool.
Ops incl: local bus services, school contracts, private hire.
Livery: White
Ticket System: Almex

WHITTLE COACH & BUS LTD
FOLEY BUSINESS PARK, STOURPORT ROAD, KIDDERMINSTER DY11 7QL
Tel: 01562 820002
Fax: 01562 820027
E-mail: webenquiries@whittlecoach.co.uk
Web site: www.whittlecoach.co.uk
Chairman: Peter Shipp
Man Dir: David Shurden
Dir: Peter Harrison
Fleet: 26 – 6 single-deck bus, 14 single-deck coach, 6 midibus.
Chassis: 18 Dennis, 8 Volvo.
Bodies: 26 Plaxton.

Ops incl: local bus services, school contracts, excursions & tours, private hire, continental tours.
Livery: White/Blue/Yellow.
Ticket system: Wayfarer III
Part of the EYMS Group

WOODSTONES COACHES LTD
ARTHUR DRIVE, HOO FARM INDUSTRIAL ESTATE, WORCESTER ROAD, KIDDERMINSTER DY11 7RA
Tel: 01562 823073
Fax: 01562 827277
E-mail: enquiries@woodstones.org.uk
Web site: www.woodstones.org.uk
Man Dir: Ivan Meredith
Dir: Richard Meredith
Fleet: 6 single-deck coach
Chassis: 6 Volvo.
Bodies: 6 Plaxton.
Ops incl: school contracts, excursions & tours, private hire
Livery: White/Orange/Yellow/Red

YARRANTON BROS LTD
EARDISTON GARAGE, TENBURY WELLS WR15 8JL
Tel: 01584 881229
E-mail: info@yarrantons.co.uk
Web site: www.yarrantons.co.uk
Dirs: A. L. Yarranton (**Gen Man**), M. L. Yarranton, D. A. Yarranton.
Fleet: 12 – 1 single-deck bus, 9 single-deck coach, 1 minibus, 1 minicoach.
Chassis: 3 Bedford, 3 Dennis, 3 Mercedes, 1 Toyota, 2 Volvo.
Bodies: 2 Berkhof, 2 Caetano, 1 Duple, 1 Jonckheere, 2 Mercedes, 4 Plaxton.
Ops incl: local bus services, school contracts, excursions & tours, private hire, continental tours.
Livery: Green/White/Orange

	Vehicle suitable for disabled		Seat belt-fitted Vehicle
T	Toilet-drop facilities available		Coach(es) with galley facilities
R	Recovery service available		Air-conditioned vehicle(s)
	Open top vehicle(s)v		Coaches with toilet facilities
R24	24 hour recovery service		Replacement vehicle available
			Vintage Coach(es) available

Ian Allan PUBLISHING

186   The Little Red Book 2011 - in association with   *tbf*   Transport Benevolent Fund

CHANNEL ISLANDS

ALDERNEY

RIDUNA BUSES
ALLEE ES FEES, ALDERNEY
GY9 3XD
Tel: 01481 823760
Fax: 01481 823030
Prop: A. J. Curtis.
Fleet: 5 - 2 single-deck bus,
2 single-deck coach, 1 minibus.
Chassis: 3 Bedford, 1 Freight Rover.
Bodies: 2 Duple, 1 Heaver, 1 Pennine.
Ops incl: local bus services, excursions & tours, private hire.

GUERNSEY

ISLAND COACHWAYS LTD
THE TRAMSHEDS, LES BANQUES,
ST PETER PORT GY1 2HZ
Tel: 01481 720210
Fax: 01481 710109
E-mail: admin@icw.gg
Web site: www.icw.gg
Man Dir: Hannah Beacom
Dir: Ben Boucher
Ops Man: Tom Whyte
Strategic Planning Man: Rob Branigan
Fleet Man: Tom Wilson
Sales Man: Isabel de Menezes
Fleet: 56 - 41 single-deck bus,
6 single-deck coach, 6 midicoach,
1 minibus, 2 minicoach.
Chassis: 41 Alexander Dennis, 1 Ford Transit, 3 Iveco, 6 Mercedes, 4 Renault, 1 Other.
Bodies: 8 Caetano, 33 East Lancs, 1 Leicester, 6 Plaxton, 8 Other.
Ops incl: local bus services, school contracts, excursions & tours, private hire
Livery: Green/Cream, Green/Yellow
Ticket System: Wayfarer TGX150

JERSEY

CONNEX TRANSPORT (JERSEY) LTD
1A COLLETTE STREET,
ST HELIER JE2 3NX
Tel: 01534 877772 **Fax:** 01534 723999
Gen Man: Phillipe Juhles
Fleet Name: Connex
Fleet: 46 single-deck buses
Chassis: 46 Dennis
Bodies: 46 Caetano
Subsidiary of Veolia Transport

TANTIVY BLUE COACH TOURS
70/72 LA COLOMBERIE,
ST HELIER JE2 4QA
Tel: 01534 706706 **Fax:** 01534 706705
E-mail: info@jerseycoaches.com
Web site: www.tantivybluecoach.com
Man Dir: Mike Cotilard
Ops Dir: Paul Young
Fleet: 80 - 60 single-deck coach,
20 minibus.
Ops incl: school contracts, excursions & tours, private hire.
Livery: Blue.

WAVERLEY COACHES LTD
UNIT 3, LA COLLETTE, ST HELIER JE2 3NX
Tel: 01534 758360 **Fax:** 01534 732627
Web site: www.norfolkhoteljersey.co.uk/waverley
Dir/Gen Man: S. E. Pedersen
Ch Eng: Peter Evans.
Fleet: 18 - 12 single-deck coach,
2 midicoach, 4 minibus.
Chassis: 7 Bedford, 5 Leyland,
2 Mercedes, 1 Renault, 3 Volkswagen.
Bodies: 7 Duple, 5 Wadham Stringer, 4 Other.
Ops incl: excursions & tours, private hire.
Livery: Yellow/White

ISLE OF MAN

DOUGLAS CORPORATION TRAMWAY
STRATHALLAN CRESCENT,
DOUGLAS IM2 4NR
Tel: 01624 696420
Fleet: 22 tramcars
Ops incl: tram services, private hire.

ISLE OF MAN TRANSPORT
TRANSPORT HEADQUARTERS,
BANKS CIRCUS, DOUGLAS IM1 5PT
Tel: 01624 663366 **Fax:** 01624 663637
E-mail: info@busandrail.dtl.gov.im
Director of Public Transport: Ian Longworth
Fleet Name: Bus Vannin
Fleet: 109 - 73 double-deck bus,
12 single-deck bus, 24 tram.
Chassis: 9 Alexander Dennis, 32 DAF, 22 Dennis, 2 Leyland, 6 Transbus, 3 VDL, 11 Volvo.
Bodies: 58 East Lancs, 11 Marshall, 2 Northern Counties, 3 Optare, 11 Wright.
Ops incl: local bus/tram services, private hire
Livery: Red/Cream.
Ticket System: Wayfarer.

PROTOURS ISLE OF MAN LTD
AIRPORT GARAGE, BALLASALLA
IM9 2AN
Tel: 01624 822611 **Fax:** 01624 822389
E-mail: info@protours.co.im
Chairman & Man Dir: W R Lightfoot
Dirs: J F Cairns, F G Kinnear **Ops Man:** D Bennett **Ch Eng:** A Lancaster
Fleet: 28 - 3 single-deck bus, 13 single-deck coach, 2 midibus, 5 midicoach, 3 minibus, 2 vintage coach.
Chassis: 2 Bedford, 2 BMC, 1 Bova, 3 DAF, 4 Iveco, 1 LAG, 4 Leyland, 1 MAN, 2 Mercedes, 1 Optare, 5 Scania, 1 Toyota, 2 Volvo, 1 Other.
Bodies: 3 Berkhof, 2 BMC, 1 Bova, 4 Duple, 4 Irizar, 3 Leicester, 1 Optare, 3 Plaxton, 2 Van Hool, 1 Wadham Stringer, 4 Other.
Ops incl: school contracts, excursions & tours, private hire, express, continental tours.
Livery: White/Blue/Green/Yellow

ISLES OF SCILLY

HERITAGE TOUR
SANTAMANA, 9 RAMS VALLEY,
ST MARY'S TR21 0JX
Tel: 01720 422387
Props: G. Twynham, Mrs P. Twynham.
Fleet: 1 single-deck bus (1948 vehicle).
Chassis: Austin K2.
Body: Barnard.
Ops incl: excursions & tours, private hire.
Livery: Blue/Cream.

ISLAND ROVER
THE NOOK, CHURCH STREET, ST MARYS TR21 OJT
Tel/Fax: 01720 422131
E-mail: admin@islandrover.co.uk
Web site: www.islandrover.co.uk
Prop: Glynne Lucas
Fleet: 2 single-deck coach, 1 open top bus.
Chassis: 1 Austin, 1 Bedford, 1 Leyland.
Bodies: 1 East Lancs, 1 Plaxton, 1 Other.

LRB 2012

Work on the preparation of LRB 2012 will start in Spring 2011 when we update our address lists and prepare to send out questionnaires to trade suppliers, authorities, organisations and operators. We are planning to update the design of the questionnaires next year to reflect fleet developments and other changes.

However, you do not have to wait until you hear from us. If your entry becomes outdated, why not contact us in advance and we will publish a revision in our monthly update column in Buses Magazine, as well as making note of the change
for the next edition of LRB.

Please write to The Editor, Little Red Book,
Ian Allan Publishing Ltd, Foundry Road,
Stamford, Lincolnshire PE9 2PP

ABERDEEN, CITY OF

BLUEBIRD BUSES LTD
UNION SQUARE BUS STATION,
GUILD STREET, ABERDEEN AB11 6NA
Tel: 01224 597590 **Fax:** 01224 584202
Recovery: 01224 591381
E-mail: bluebird.enquiries@stagecoachbus.com
Web site: www.stagecoachbus.com
Fleet Name: Stagecoach Bluebird
Man Dir: Andrew Jarvis
Ops Dir: Robert Hall
Eng Dir: John MacPherson
Ops Man: George Devine **Depot Eng:** Dave Cabine **Comm Man:** Jim Gardner
Fleet: 369 - 65 double-deck bus, 141 single-deck bus, 17 single-deck coach, 61 midibus, 85 minibus.
Chassis: Dennis, Leyland, MAN, Mercedes, Optare, Scania, Volvo.
Bodies: Alexander, Jonckheere, Leyland, Neoplan, Optare, Plaxton, Wright.
Ops incl: local bus services, school contracts, excursions & tours, private hire, express.
Livery: Stagecoach UK Bus/Megabus/Citylink
Ticket System: ERG

FIRST IN ABERDEEN
395 KING STREET, ABERDEEN AB24 5RP
Tel: 01224 650000
Fax: 01224 650099
Web site: www.firstgroup.com
Man Dir: David Stewart
Ops Dir: Duncan Cameron
Eng Dir: Iain Ferguson
Fleet: 167 - 34 double-deck bus, 107 single-deck bus, 20 articulated bus, 4 open top bus, 2 vintage.
Ops incl: local bus services, school contracts, private hire.
Livery: FirstGroup UK Bus.

FIRST ABERDEEN LTD, COACHING UNIT
FIRST ABERDEEN LTD, 395 KING STREET, ABERDEEN AB24 5RP
Tel: 01224 650000 **Fax:** 01224 650123
Recovery: 01224 650151
E-mail: coachhire.aberdeen@firstgroup.com
Web site: www.firstgroup.com
Man Dir: David Stewart
Ops Dir: Duncan Cameron
Eng Dir: Iain Ferguson
Coaching Ops Man: Tom Gordon
Fleet: 24 - 19 single-deck coach, 4 midicoach, 1 minibus.
Chassis: 2 BMC, 4 Mercedes, 1 Optare, 5 Scania, 12 Volvo.
Bodies: 2 BMC, 5 Irizar, 2 Jonckheere, 1 Optare, 14 Plaxton.
Ops incl: school contracts, excursions & tours, private hire, continental tours.
Livery: First Group Magenta/Blue/Grey
A subsidiary of First Group

FOUNTAIN EXECUTIVE
HILL OF GOVAL, DYCE, ABERDEEN AB21 7NX
Tel: 01224 729090 **Fax:** 01224 729898
E-mail: fountainexe@hotmail.com
Web site: www.fountainexecutive.co.uk
Prop: Michael Ewen
Fleet: 12 - 5 single-deck coach, 4 midicoach, 3 minicoach.

Chassis: 7 Mercedes, 5 Scania.
Bodies: 4 Esker, 5 Irizar, 3 Mercedes.
Ops incl: private hire, continental tours.
Livery: Gold

WHYTES COACHES LTD
SCOTSTOWN ROAD, NEWMACHAR, ABERDEEN AB21 7PP
Tel: 01651 862211
Fax: 01651 862918
E-mail: sales@whytes.co.uk
Web site: www.whytes.co.uk
Man Dir: Steven W Whyte
Fleet: 27 - 10 single-deck coach, 17 midicoach.
Chassis: 10 DAF, 2 Ford, 14 Mercedes, 1 Volkswagen.
Bodies: 10 Bova, 3 Esker, 7 Plaxton, 7 Other.
Ops incl: school contracts, excursions & tours, private hire, express, continental tours.
Livery: Light Green

ABERDEENSHIRE

ALLAN & BLACK
DRUMDUAN DEPOT, DESS, ABOYNE AB34 5BN
Tel: 01339 886326
Fax: 01339 886008
Recovery: 07801 294322
E-mail: info-enq@allanandblackcoaches.co.uk
Web site: www.allanandblackcoaches.co.uk
Props: Andrew C Brown, Murray W Brown, Jane W Brown, Cameron W Brown
Fleet: 10 - 1 double-deck bus, 7 single-deck coach, 2 minibus.
Chassis: 1 Iveco, 4 Mercedes, 4 Scania, 1 Volvo.
Bodies: 1 Alexander Dennis, 2 Berkhof, 1 Neoplan, 2 Setra, 2 Van Hool, 2 Other.
Ops incl: local bus services, school contracts, excursions & tours, private hire.
Ticket System: Almex.

AMBER TRAVEL
CROSSFIELDS FARMHOUSE, TURRIFF AB53 7QY
Tel: 01888 563474
Fax: 01888 563474
Props: D. Cheyne, S. Cheyne.
Fleet: 5 - 4 single-deck coach, 1 midibus.
Chassis: 1 Bedford, 1 Mercedes, 3 Volvo.
Ops incl: school contracts, private hire.
Livery: White/Red/Amber

J & M BURNS
DINNESWOOD, TARVES, ELLON AB41 7LR
Tel: 01651 851279
Fax: 01651 851844
E-mail: info@burnscoaches.co.uk
Web site: www.burnscoaches.co.uk
Fleet incl: single-deck coach, midicoach, minicoach.
Ops incl: school contracts, private hire, excursions & tours.
Livery: Purple.

CHEYNES COACHES
ALLANDALE, DAVIOT, INVERURIE AB51 0EJ
Tel: 01467 671400 **Fax:** 01467 671479
E-mail: lesley@cheynescoaches.co.uk

Web site: www.cheynescoaches.co.uk
Partners: W A Cheyne, R Cheyne, L A Cheyne, M F Cheyne.
Fleet: 10 - 3 single-deck bus, 3 single-deck coach, 1 minibus, 3 minicoach.
Chassis: 1 DAF, 1 Ford Transit, 3 Leyland, 2 Volvo.
Bodies: 1 Bova, 2 Optare, 4 Plaxton, 2 Van Hool.
Ops incl: school contracts, excursions & tours, private hire.
Livery: Silver/Pink/Purple

DEVERON COACHES
6 UNION ROAD, MACDUFF AB44 1UJ
Tel: 01261 498000
Ops incl: local bus services, school contracts, private hire, excursions & tours.
Livery: Red/White

J W COACHES LTD
DYKEHEAD GARAGE, BLACKHALL, BANCHORY AB31 6PS
Tel/Fax: 01330 823300
Ops incl: local bus services, school contracts, excursions & tours, private hire.
Livery: White.
Ticket System: Setright.
A subsidiary of Bluebird Buses, part of Stagecoach

KINEIL COACHES LTD
ANDERSON PLACE, WEST SHORE INDUSTRIAL ESTATE, FRASERBURGH AB43 9LG
Tel: 01346 510200
Fax: 01346 514774
Man Dir: Ian Neilson
Fleet: 27 - 19 single-deck coach, 1 midibus, 3 midicoach, 4 minibus.
Chassis: 1 DAF, 8 Mercedes, 1 Scania, 17 Van Hool.
Bodies: 1 Jonckheere, 5 Mercedes, 1 Scania, 17 Volvo.
Ops incl: local bus services, school contracts, excursions & tours, private hire, continental tours.
Livery: Blue/White/Red

ALEX MILNE COACHES
THE GARAGE, 4 MAIN STREET, NEW BYTH AB53 5XD
Tel: 01888 544340 **Fax:** 01888 544154
E-mail: info@alexmilnecoaches.co.uk
Web site: www.alexmilnecoaches.co.uk
Partners: Alex Milne Brian Milne
Fleet: 14 - 1 single-deck bus, 4 single-deck coach, 3 minicoach, 6 minibus.
Ops incl: local bus services, school contracts, private hire, excursions & tours
Livery: Blue/White
Ticket system: Wayfarer

MAYNES COACHES LTD
4 MARCH ROAD WEST, BUCKIE AB56 4BU
Tel: 01542 831219
Fax: 01542 833572
E-mail: info@maynes.co.uk
Web site: www.maynes.co.uk
Dirs: Gordon Mayne, Sandra Mayne, David Mayne, Kevin Mayne
Fleet: 30 - 1 single-deck bus, 22 single-deck coach, 2 midibus, 5 midicoach.
Chassis: 12 MAN, 5 Mercedes, 1 Optare, 2 Renault, 10 Volvo.
Bodies: 2 Berkhof, 4 Marcopolo, 7 Neoplan, 1 Optare, 1 Onyx, 5 Plaxton, 8 Van Hool, 2 Other.

Ops incl: local bus services, school contracts, excursions & tours, private hire, continental tours.
Livery: Blue/Silver.
Ticket System: Setright.

M W NICOLL'S COACH HIRE
THE BUSINESS PARK, ABERDEEN ROAD, LAURENCEKIRK AB30 1EY
Tel: 01561 377262
Fax: 01561 378822
E-mail: malcolm.nicoll@lineone.net
Web site: www.nicoll-coaches.co.uk
Man Dir: M. W. Nicoll **Dir:** I. J. Nicoll
Service Man: A. Gordon
Office Man: M Forrest
Fleet: 24 - 2 single-deck bus, 6 single-deck coach, 3 midibus, 6 midicoach, 2 minibus, 5 minicoach.
Chassis: 1 Bova, 4 Ford Transit, Leyland, 9 Mercedes, 1 Optare, 2 Toyota, 6 Volvo.
Bodies: 1 Bova, 2 Caetano, 1 Duple, 10 Mercedes, 1 Solo, 6 Van Hool, 3 Others.
Ops incl: local bus services, private hire.
Livery: White.
Ticket System: Almex.

J D PEACE CO ABDN LTD
FARE PARK, ECHT, WESTHILL AB32 7AL
Tel: 01330 860542
Fax: 01330 860543
E-mail: info@peacescoaches.co.uk
Web: www.peacescoaches.co.uk
Dirs: David J Collie, Kathleen Collie.
Fleet: 13 - 5 single-deck coach, 1 midicoach, 7 minibus.
Chassis incl: 5 Bova, 1Volvo.
Bodies incl: 5 Bova, 1 Van Hool.
Ops incl: school contracts, private hire.

RS TAXIS & MINICOACH HIRE
BLACKSTONE, SAUCHEN, INVERURIE AB51 7RD
Tel: 01330 833314
Ops incl: local bus services, private hire.

REIDS OF RHYNIE
22 MAIN STREET, RHYNIE, BY HUNTLY AB54 4HB
Tel/Fax: 01464 861212
Recovery: 07831 173681
Owner: Colin Reid.
Fleet: 14 - 4 single-deck coach, 2 midibus, 1 midicoach, 7 minibus.
Chassis: 4 Ford Transit, 4 LDV, 3 Mercedes, 4 Volvo.
Bodies incl: 3 Caetano, 2 Mercedes, 1 Van Hool.
Ops incl: local bus services, school contracts, private hire.
Livery: White/Blue/Water Green
Ticket system: Wayfarer 3

SHEARER OF HUNTLY LTD
OLD TOLL ROAD, HUNTLY AB54 6JA
Tel: 01466 792410
Fax: 01466 793926
Dirs: James W Shearer, Irene E Shearer.
Fleet: 10 - 1 single-deck coach, 1 midicoach, 6 minibus, 2 minicoach.
Chassis: 1 Dennis, 6 Ford Transit, 2 LDV, 1 Mercedes.
Bodies incl: 1 UVG, 1 Wadham Stringer.
Ops incl: school contracts, private hire.

SIMPSON'S COACHES
21 UNION STREET, ROSEHEARTY, FRASERBURGH AB43 7JQ
Tel: 01346 571610
Fax: 01346 571070
E-mail: info@simpsonscoaches.co.uk
Web site: www.simpsonscoaches.co.uk
Prop: Ron Simpson, Pat Simpson.
Fleet: 6 single-deck coach.
Chassis: 1 Iveco, 5 Volvo.
Bodies: 1 Beulas, 2 Berkhof, 3 Caetano.
Ops incl: excursions & tours, private hire, continental tours.
Livery: Silver/Blue.

VICTORIA COACHES
LONGSIDE ROAD, PETERHEAD AB42 3LA
Tel: 01779 480480
E-mail: info@victoriacoaches.co.uk
Web site: www.victoriacoaches.co.uk
Props: Mr & Mrs Ewan Mowat & son.
Fleet: 22 – 6 single-deck coach, 8 minicoach, 8 minibus.
Ops incl: school contracts, excursions & tours, private hire.
Livery: White with logos.

WATERMILL COACHES
88 COLLEGE BOUNDS, FRASERBURGH AB43 9QS
Tel/Fax: 01346 513050
E-mail: info@watermillcoaches.co.uk
Web site: www.watermillcoachesltd.co.uk
Ops incl: school contracts, private hire, excursions & tours.

ANGUS

GLENESK TRAVEL CO LTD
5 MANSE ROAD, EDZELL DD9 7TJ
Tel: 01356 648666
Ops incl: local bus services, private hire.
Livery: White with Blue

JP MINICOACHES
UNIT 3, ORCHARDBANK INDUSTRIAL ESTATE, FORFAR DD8 1TD
Tel: 01307 461431
Fax: 01307 467028
E-mail: jpminicoaches@btconnect.com
Ops incl: local bus services, private hire.

RIDDLER'S COACHES LIMITED
CAIRNIE LOAN, ARBROATH DD11 4DS
Tel: 01241 873464
Fax: 01241 873504
E-mail: charles_riddler@btconnect.com
Web site: www.riddlerscoaches.co.uk
Dirs: C W Riddler, Mrs G M Riddler
Fleet: 6 single-deck coach.
Chassis: 6 Volvo.
Ops incl: excursions & tours, private hire
Livery: Blue/White

SIDLAW EXECUTIVE TRAVEL (SCOTLAND) LTD
UNIT 5, ARDYLE INDUSTRIAL ESTATE, PERRY STREET, DUNDEE DD2 2RD
Tel: 01382 610410 **Fax:** 01382 624733
E-mail: travel@sidlaw.co.uk
Web site: www.sidlaw.co.uk
Dir: Bob Costello
Fleet Eng: Jamie Costello
Fleet: 14 - 2 single-deck coach, 4 minicoach, 4 midicoach, 4 minicoach.

Chassis: 1 MAN, 13 Mercedes.
Ops incl: school contracts, excursions & tours, private hire.
Livery: White/Silver.

TEEJAY TRAVEL LTD
27 BRUCE DRIVE, CARNOUSTIE DD7 7DE
Tel: 01241 854717
E-mail: tomjordan@teejaytravel.co.uk
Web site: www.teejaytravel.co.uk
Ops incl: local bus services, private hire
Livery: White with Blue lettering

ARGYLL & BUTE

BOWMAN'S COACHES (MULL) LTD
SCALLCASTLE, CRAIGNURE, ISLE OF MULL PA65 6BA
Tel: 01680 812313
E-mail: info@bowmanstours.co.uk
Web site: www.bowmanstours.co.uk
Props: A. Bowman, S. Bowman, I. Bowman, I. Bowman
Gen Man: A. Bowman.
Fleet: 12 single-deck bus and coach.
Chassis: Bedford, DAF, Dennis, Ford, Leyland.
Bodies: Duple, Jonckheere, Plaxton, Wright.
Ops incl: local bus services, excursions & tours, private hire.
Livery: Cream/Red.
Ticket System: Setright, Almex.

CRAIG OF CAMPBELTOWN LTD
BENMHOR, CAMPBELTOWN PA28 6DN
Tel: 01586 552319 **Fax:** 01586 552344
E-mail: enquiries@westcoastmotors.co.uk
Web site: www.westcoastmotors.co.uk
Fleet Name: West Coast Motors
Chairman/Man Dir: W G Craig
Dir: C R Craig **Co Sec:** J M Craig
Tran Man: D M Halliday
Fleet Eng: D Martin
Fleet: 71 - 6 double-deck bus, 28 single-deck bus, 30 single-deck coach, 2 midibus, 3 midicoach, 1 minibus.
Chassis: 1 Bedford, 26 DAF/VDL, 17 Dennis, 1Freight Rover, 5 Leyland, 1 MAN, 5 Mercedes, 5 Optare, 9 Volvo.
Bodies: 15 Alexander, 1 Ikarus, 1 Jonckheere, 1 Mellor, 1 Onyx, 5 Optare, 4 Park Royal, 13 Plaxton, 27 Van Hool, 2 Wright.
Ops incl: local bus services, school contracts, excursions & tours, private hire, express.
Livery: Red/Cream.
Ticket System: Wayfarer.
See also Oban & District Buses, Glasgow Citybus, Glasgow Sightseeing.

GARELOCHHEAD COACHES
WOODLEA GARAGE, MAIN ROAD, GARELOCHHEAD PA65 6BA
Tel: 01436 810200
Fax: 01436 810050
Web site: www.garelochheadcoaches.co.uk
Prop: Stuart McQueen
Ops incl: local bus services.

HIGHLAND HERITAGE COACH TOURS
CENTRAL ADMINISTRATION OFFICE, DALMALLY PA33 1AY
Tel: 01838 200453

Scottish Operators

E-mail: info@highlandheritage.co.uk
Web site: www.highlandheritage.co.uk
Man Dir: Ian Cleaver
Gen Man: Sheena Thompson
Fleet: 18 single-deck coach.
Chassis: 18 Volvo.
Bodies: 18 Van Hool.
Ops incl: excursions & tours
Livery: Gold

HIGHLAND ROVER COACHES

AWE SERVICE STATION,
TAYNUILT PA35 1HT
Tel/Fax: 01866 822612
E-mail: angus@crunachy.plus.com
Prop: Angus Douglas
Fleet: 3 - 1 single-deck coach, 1 minibus, 1 minicoach.
Chassis: 3 Mercedes.
Bodies: 1 Beulas, 1 Mercedes, 1 Onyx.
Ops incl: local bus services, school contracts, excursions & tours, private hire
Livery: Brown/Orange/White
Ticket system: Almex.

ISLAY COACHES

BARDARAVINE, TARBERT PA29 6YF
Tel: 01496 840273
Prop: B Mundell Ltd
Ops incl: local bus services
Fleet incl: single-deck coach, midibus.
Livery: Green/White.

McCOLLS OF ARGYLL LTD

Mc COLLS HOTEL, WEST BAY,
DUNOON PA23 7HN
Tel: 01369 702764
Fax: 01369 702764
Web site: www.mccollshotel.co.uk
Dir: David Wilkinson
Fleet: 8 single-deck coach
Chassis: 8 Iveco
Bodies: 8 Beulas
Ops incl: excursions & tours
Livery: Red/yellow

OBAN & DISTRICT BUSES LTD

GLENGALLAN ROAD, OBAN PA34 4HH
Tel: 01631 570500
Fax: 01631 567252
E-mail: enquiries@westcoastmotors.co.uk
Web site: www.westcoastmotors.co.uk
Fleet Name: Oban & District.
Man Dir: Colin Craig
Dir: W. G. Craig
Depot Controllers: David Hannah, Donnie McDougal
Workshop Supervisor: Iain McDonald
Fleet: 23 - 16 single-deck bus, 2 single-deck coach, 2 midicoach, 2 minibus, 1 midibus.
Chassis: 4 DAF, 3 Dennis, 2 LDV, 10 Leyland, 2 Mercedes, 1 Optare, 1 Volvo.
Bodies: 10 Alexander, 2 KL Conversions, 1 Onyx, 1 Optare, 5 Plaxton, 4 Wright.
Ops incl: local bus services, school contracts, private hire, express.
Livery: Red/Blue/Honeysuckle
Ticket System: Wayfarer 3
A subsidiary of West Coast Motors

WILSON'S OF RHU

RHU GARAGE, MANSE BRAE,
RHU G84 8RE
Tel: 01436 820300
Fax: 01436 820337
E-mail: info@wilsonsofrhu.co.uk
Web site: www.wilsonsofrhu.co.uk
Ops incl: local bus services, private hire.
Livery: Grey/White/Red.

BORDERS

AUSTIN TRAVEL

STATION ROAD, EARLSTON TD4 6BZ
Tel: 01896 849360
Fax: 01896 849623
E-mail: austin@travel.gbtbroadband.co.uk
Web site: www.scotlinetours.co.uk
Partners: Douglas Austin, Barry Austin.
Fleet: 7 - 4 single-deck coach, 2 midicoach, 1 minicoach.
Chassis: 2 Bova, 3 Mercedes, 2 Setra.
Bodies: 2 Bova, 2 Esker, 2 Setra, 1 Other.
Ops incl: school contracts, excursions & tours, private hire, continental tours.
Livery: Pearlescent white

FIRST SCOTLAND EAST LTD
See Stirling

JAMES FRENCH & SON

THE GARAGE, COLDINGHAM,
EYEMOUTH TD14 5NS
Tel/Fax: 01890 771283
Man Dir: Peter Redden
E-mail: frenchs.garage@virgin.net
Web site: www.jamesfrenchandson.com
Fleet inc: single-deck coach.
Ops incl: excursions & tours, private hire.

MUNRO'S OF JEDBURGH LTD

OAKVALE GARAGE, BONGATE,
JEDBURGH TD8 6DU
Tel: 01835 862253 Fax: 01835 864297
E-mail: ewan@munrosofjedburgh.co.uk
Web site: www.munrosofjedburgh.co.uk
Dir/Co Sec: Ewan Farish
Eng Dir: Bruce Campbell
Fleet: 34 - 20 single-deck bus, 9 single-deck coach, 4 midicoach, 1 minicoach.
Chassis: 6 Alexander Dennis, 3 DAF, 1 Dennis, 2 Enterprise, 6 EOS, 1 Iveco, 7 MAN, 4 Mercedes, 4 Optare.
Bodies: 3 Alexander Dennis, 1 Crest, 2 Ikarus, 7 MCV, 4 Optare, 8 Plaxton, 7 Van Hool, 1 Wadham Stringer, 1 Other.
Ops incl: local bus services, school contracts, private hire.
Livery: White with Red stripes
Ticket System: Wayfarer TGX150

PERRYMAN'S BUSES

NORTH ROAD INDUSTRIAL ESTATE,
BERWICK UPON TWEED TD15 1UN
Tel: 01289 308719 Fax: 01289 309970
Web site: www.perrymansbuses.com
Dirs: R J Perryman, L M Perryman.
Fleet: 35 - 20 single-deck bus, 5 single-deck coach, 6 midicoach, 4 minibus
Chassis: MAN, Mercedes, Optare, Renault, Volvo.
Bodies: Alexander Dennis, MCV, Optare, Plaxton.
Ops incl: local bus services, school contract, private hire
Ticket System: Wayfarer.
Livery: White with Red/Blue.

TELFORD'S COACHES LTD

1 GEORGE STREET, NEWCASTLETON TD9 0RA
Tel/Fax: 01387 375677
Recovery: 07711 280475
E-mail: alistair@telfordscoaches.com
Web site: www.telfordscoaches.com
Man Dir: Alistair S Telford
Co Sec: Doreen S Telford
Ch Eng: Rod Swan
Ops Man: Sarah Little
Fleet: 17 - 9 single-deck coach, 2 midicoach, 4 minibus, 2 minicoach.
Chassis: 1 DAF, 1 Ford, 1 Ford Transit, 6 Mercedes, 8 Volvo.
Bodies: 1 Bova, 2 Jonckheere, 4 Mercedes, 10 Plaxton.
Ops incl: local bus services, school contracts, excursions & tours, private hire, express, continental tours.
Livery: White with Blue vinyls
Ticket System: Almex

A WAIT & SON

WEST END GARAGE, CHIRNSIDE,
DUNS TD11 3UJ
Tel/Fax: 01890 818216
Ops incl: local bus services, school contracts, private hire.

CLACKMANNANSHIRE

FIRST SCOTLAND EAST LTD
See Stirling

HUNTERS EXECUTIVE COACHES

GREYGORAN HOUSE, GREYGORAN, SAUCHIE, ALLOA FK10 3EH
Tel: 01259 215560
Fax: 01259 723638
E-mail: hunterscoaches@btconnect.com
Web site: www.huntersexecutivecoaches.co.uk
Ops incl: school contracts, private hire, excursions & tours.

M LINE

THE COACH HOUSE, KELLIEBANK, ALLOA FK10 1NT
Tel: 01259 212802
E-mail: info@m-line.co.uk.
Web Site: www.m-line.co.uk.
Ops Man: Tom Matchett, Andy McLellan
Eng: Dave Craig
Fleet: 16 - 7 double-deck bus, 1 single-deck bus, 5 single-deck coach, 1 midicoach, 2 minibus..
Chassis: 1 Alexander Dennis, 1 Ford, 2 Scania, 12 Volvo.
Ops incl: local bus services, school contracts, excursions & tours, private hire, continental tours.
Livery: Cream/Beige.

MACKIE'S COACHES

32 GLASSHOUSE LOAN, ALLOA FK10 1PE
Tel: 01259 216180
Fax: 01259 217508
E-mail: enquiries@mackiescoaches.com
Web site: www.mackiescoaches.com
Fleet incl: single-deck bus, single-deck coach
Chassis incl: Bova, Volvo.
Bodies incl: Bova, Jonckheere, Van Hool, Wright.
Ops incl: local bus services, school contracts, excursions & tours, private hire.
Livery: White/Brown/Beige.
Ticket System: Wayfarer.

WOODS COACHES
2 GOLF VIEW, TILLICOULTRY
FK13 6DH
Tel: 01259 751753
Fax: 01259 751824
E-mail: jwcoaches@btinternet.com
Web site: www.woodscoaches.net
Owner: James Woods
Ops Man: John Woods
Fleet: 10 – single-deck coach, midicoach, minicoach
Chassis: 2 Bova, 8 Mercedes.
Bodies: 2 Bova, 2 Esker, 6 Mercedes.
Ops incl: school contracts, excursions & tours, private hire
Livery: Silver

DUMFRIES & GALLOWAY

ANDERSON'S COACHES
UNIT 1, WHITSHIELS INDUSTRIAL ESTATE, LANGHOLM DG13 0HX
Tel: 01387 380553
Fax: 01387 380553
Partners: I. R. Anderson, K. Irving
Ch Eng: C. Anderson
Fleet: 6 - 2 single-deck bus, 2 minibus, 2 minicoach.
Chassis: 1 AEC, 3 Ford Transit, 1 Freight Rover, 1 Leyland.
Bodies: 2 Plaxton, 1 PMT, 1 Robin Hood, 1 Other.
Ops incl: local bus services, school contracts, private hire.
Livery: Red/Orange/Yellow stripe.
Ticket System: Almex.

WILLIAM BROWNRIGG
THE GARAGE, THORNHILL DG3 5LZ
Tel/Fax: 01848 330203
Dir: William Brownrigg
Fleet: 9 - 5 single-deck coach, 1 midicoach, 3 minibus.
Chassis: Bova, Mercedes, Volvo.
Bodies: Alexander Dennis, Bova, Reeve Burgess, Van Hool.
Ops incl: local bus services, school contracts, excursions & tours, private hire.
Livery: Orange/White
Ticket System: Almex.

DGC BUSES
DUMFRIES & GALLOWAY COUNCIL, COUNCIL OFFICES, ENGLISH STREET, DUMFRIES DG1 2HR
Tel: 01387 260136
Prop: Dumfries & Galloway Council
Fleet: 49 – 18 single-deck bus, 19 midibus, 12 minibus.
Chassis: 3 Alexander Dennis, 3 BMC, 3 DAF, 9 Dennis, 6 LDV, 1 Leyland, 21 Mercedes, 2 Optare, 1 Renault.
Bodies: 8 Alexander Dennis, 3 BMC, 1 Ikarus, 2 Marshall/MCV, 2 Mercedes, 4 Optare, 12 Plaxton, 5 Wright, 12 Other.
Ops incl: local bus services, school contracts.
Livery: Red/Yellow
Ticket System: Almex.

HOUSTON'S MINICOACHES
13 STEVENSON AVENUE, LOCKERBIE DG11 2PG
Tel: 01576 203874
Fleet incl: single-deck coach, single-deck bus, midibus, midicoach, minibus.
Ops incl: local bus services, school contracts, private hire, excursions & tours.
Livery: Blue/White.

A & F IRVINE & SON
99 MAIN STREET, GLENLUCE DG8 0PT
Tel: 01581 300345
Fleet: 5 – midibus, midicoach.
Ops incl: local bus services, private hire, excursions & tours.
Livery: White with Red lettering.

JAMES KING COACHES
36 MAIN STREET, KIRKCOWAN, NEWTON STEWART DG8 0HG
Tel: 01671 830284
Fax: 01671 830499
E-mail: enquiries@kingscoachhire.com
Web site: www.kingscoachhire.com
Fleet: 25 - 8 single-deck bus, 12 single-deck coach, 5 midicoach.
Chassis: 5 Optare, 12 Volvo.
Bodies: 1 Caetano, 2 Jonckheere, 5 Optare, 5 Plaxton, 12 Van Hool.
Ops incl: local bus services, school contracts, excursions & tours, private hire.
Livery: White:
Ticket System: Wayfarer

KIWI LUXURY TRAVEL
80 QUEEN STREET, NEWTON STEWART DG8 6JL
Tel: 01671 404294
Fax: 01671 403310
E-mail: kiwitravel@btconnect.com
Web site: www.kiwitravelltd.co.uk
Dirs: Ian Allison, Janet Allison
Fleet: 4 - 3 single-deck coach, 1 minicoach
Chassis incl: 3 Volvo
Bodies incl: 1 Caetano.
Ops incl: local bus services, school contracts, excursions & tours, private hire.

MacEWAN'S COACH SERVICES
JOHNFIELD, AMISFIELD, DUMFRIES DG1 3LS
Tel: 01387 256533 **Fax:** 01387 711123
Prop: John Mac Ewan
Ch Eng: Peter Maxwell
Fleet: 65 - 5 double-deck, 22 single-deck bus, 9 single-deck coach, 1 double-deck coach, 12 midibus, 4 midicoach, 12 minibus
Chassis: 1 AEC, 2 Bedford, 1 Bristol, 1 DAF, 3 Dennis, 3 Ford Transit, 1 Iveco, 4 LDV, 2 Leyland, 5 MAN, 5 MCW, 18 Mercedes, 3 Optare, 5 Scania, 2 Transbus, 9 Volvo.
Bodies: 10 Alexander, 2 Autobus, 3 Crystal, 1 DAB, 2 Drinkwater, 2 Duple, 1 ECW, 1 East Lancs, 1 Irizar, 1 Jonckheere, 4 LDV, 4 Marshall/MCV, 5 MCW, 2 Montano, 3 Optare, 17 Plaxton, 2 Transbus, 1 Van Hool, 3 Wright.
Ops incl: local bus services, school contracts
Livery: White/Red/Blue
Ticket system: ERG Transit 400

Mc CULLOCH AND SON
MAIN ROAD, STONEYKIRK, STRANRAER DG9 9DH
Tel/Fax: 01776 830236
E-mail: mcculloch.coaches@virgin.net
Fleet Name: McCulloch Coaches
Partners: D F McCulloch, E A McCulloch
Fleet: 8 - 1 single-deck bus, 3 single-deck coach, 1 midibus, 1 midicoach, 1 minicoach.
Chassis: 1 Bedford, 4 Mercedes, 2 Optare, 3 Volvo.
Bodies: 1 Caetano, 1 Duple, 2 Optare, 4 Plaxton.
Ops incl: local bus services, excursions & tours, school contracts, private hire
Livery: White/Blue lettering
Ticket System: Ticket books

OOR COACHES LTD
SWORDWELL COTTAGE, ANNAN DG12 6QZ
Tel: 01461 202159
E-mail: info@oorcoaches.co.uk
Web site: www.oorcoaches.co.uk
Ops incl: local bus services, private hire.

STAGECOACH WEST SCOTLAND
See South Ayrshire

DUNDEE CITY

FISHERS TOURS
R24
16 WEST PORT, DUNDEE DD1 5EP
Tel/Fax: 01382 461999
Recovery: 07974 180771
E-mail: fisherstours@btconnect.com
Web site: www.fisherstours.co.uk
Props: James Cosgrove, Catherine Cosgrove
Fleet: 26 – 23 single-deck coach, 3 midibus.
Chassis: 2 DAF, 5 Dennis, 3 Iveco, 5 Leyland, 2 Mercedes, 9 Volvo.
Bodies: 1 Beulas, 1 Duple, 1 Hispano, 1 Leicester, 1 Marcopolo, 1 Marshall, 8 Plaxton, 9 Van Hool, 3 Wadham Stringer.
Ops incl: local bus services, school contracts, excursions & tours, private hire, express, continental tours.
Livery: White.
Ticket System: Almex.

NATIONAL EXPRESS DUNDEE
44-48 EAST DOCK STREET, DUNDEE DD1 3JS
Tel: 01382 201121
Fax: 01382 201997
E-mail: mailbox@traveldundee.co.uk
Web site: www.traveldundee.co.uk
Fleet Names: Travel Dundee, Travel Greyhound (coaches), Travel Wishart
Dir: Lawrence Davie
Traffic Man: William Murphy
Ch Eng: Frank Sheach
Business Man: Elsie Turbyne
Fleet: 135 - 23 double-deck bus, 66 single-deck bus, 8 single-deck coach, 13 midibus, 4 midicoach, 20 minibus, 1 minicoach
Chassis: Dennis, Mercedes, Optare, Scania, Volvo.
Bodies: Alexander, Berkhof, Northern Counties, Optare, Plaxton, Scania, Wright
Ops incl: local bus services, school contracts, excursions & tours, private hire. Part of the National Express Group

SIDLAW EXECUTIVE TRAVEL (SCOTLAND) LTD
UNIT 5 ARDYLE IND ESTATE, PERRIE STREET, DUNDEE DD2 2RD
Tel: 01382 610410
Fax: 01382 624333
E-mail: travel@sidlaw.co.uk
Web site: www.sidlaw.co.uk
Dir: Bob Costello
Fleet Eng: Jamie Costello

Fleet: 14 - 2 single-deck coach, 4 minicoach, 4 midicoach, 4 minicoach.
Chassis: 1 MAN, 13 Mercedes.
Ops incl: school contracts, excursions & tours, private hire.
Livery: White/Silver

STRATHTAY SCOTTISH OMNIBUSES LTD
OFFICES 47-51, EVANS BUSINESS CENTRE, JOHN SMITH BUSINESS PARK, KIRKCALDY KY2 6HD
Tel: 01382 614550
Fax: 01382 614552
Recovery: 01382 228345
E-mail: eastscotland@stagecoachbus.com
Web site: www.stagecoachbus.com
Fleet Name: Stagecoach Strathtay
Man Dir: Doug Fleming
Eng Dir: Jim Penrose
Ops Man: Martin Hall
Depot Eng: Alan Hughes
Fleet: 132 - 43 double-deck bus, 51 single-deck bus, 11 single deck coach, 12 midibus, 15 minibus.
Chassis: 16 Alexander Dennis, 5 Dennis, 17 MAN, 13 Mercedes, 11 Optare, 69 Volvo.
Bodies: 30 Alexander Dennis, 16 Alexander, 27 East Lancs, 4 Jonckheere, 7 Northern Counties, 11 Optare, 24 Plaxton, 1 Transbus, 10 Wright, 2 Other.
Ops incl: local bus services, school contracts, excursions & tours, private hire, express.
Livery: Stagecoach UK Bus/Citylink/Megabus
Ticket System: ERG
Part of the Stagecoach Group

EAST AYRSHIRE

LIDDELL'S COACHES
1 MAUCHLINE ROAD, AUCHINLECK KA18 2BJ
Tel: 01290 424300/420717
Fax: 01290 425637
Prop: J. Liddell **Ch Eng:** J. Quinn
Co Sec: Ms J. Samson
Ops Man: Ms M. Milroy
Fleet: 24 - 8 double-deck bus, 10 single-deck coach, 4 midicoach, 2 minibus.
Chassis: 1 Bova, 3 DAF, 2 Dodge, 2 Freight Rover, 10 Leyland, 6 Volvo.
Bodies: 8 Alexander, 1 Bova, 1 Caetano, 3 Duple, 1 ECW, 1 East Lancs, 2 Jonckheere, 4 Plaxton, 2 Reeve Burgess, 1 Wright.
Ops incl: local bus services, school contracts, excursions & tours, private hire, express.
Livery: White with Brown/Orange/Lemon stripes.
Ticket System: Setright.

MILLIGAN'S COACH TRAVEL LTD
LOAN GARAGE, 20 THE LOAN, MAUCHLINE, KA5 6AN
Tel/Recovery: 01290 550365
Fax: 01290 553291
E-mail: enquiries@milliganscoachtravel.co.uk
Web site: www.milliganscoachtravel.co.uk
Dir: William J Milligan
Fleet: 20 - 18 single -deck coach, 1 midicoach, 1 minibus.

Chassis: 5 Bova, 1 DAF, 1 Ford Transit, 2 Leyland, 2 MAN, 3 Scania, 6 Volvo.
Ops incl: school contracts, excursions & tours, private hire.
Livery: Black and Silver.

ROWE & TUDHOPE
UNIT 2, PALMERMOUNT INDUSTRIAL PARK, KILMARNOCK ROAD, DUNDONALD KA2 9BL
Tel: 0845 217 9853
E-mail: rowesales@fsmail.net
Web site: www.roweandtudhope.com
Prop: George Rowe
Fleet: 17 - 8 single-deck coach, 3 midicoach, 10 minicoach.
Chassis: 2 Bova, 2 Ford Transit, 1 Iveco, 6 Mercedes, 1 Scania, 5 Volvo.
Bodies: 2 Berkhof, 2 Bova, 1 Esker, 1 Irizar, 1 Jonckheere, 4 Mercedes, 1 Plaxton, 1 Sitcar, 2 Van Hool, 2 Other.
Ops incl: school contracts, excursions & tours, private hire.
Livery: White with Blue vinyls.

STAGECOACH WEST SCOTLAND
See South Ayrshire

EAST LOTHIAN

EVE CARS & COACHES
SPOTT ROAD, DUNBAR EH42 1RR
Tel: 01368 865500 **Fax:** 01368 865400
E-mail: admin@eveinfo.co.uk
Web site: www.eveinfo.co.uk
Partners: Gary Scougall, Vona Scougall.
Ops incl: local bus services, school contracts, private hire.

FIRST SCOTLAND EAST LTD
See Stirling

PRENTICE COACHES LTD
STATION GARAGE, HOSPITAL ROAD, HADDINGTON EH41 3BH
Tel: 01620 822620
Fax: 01620 823544
E-mail: mail@prentice.info
Web site: www.prenticeofhaddington.info
Fleet: 18 – 6 single-deck coach, 2 midibus, 10 midicoach.
Chassis: 1 Alexander Dennis, 1 Bedford, 1 Dennis, 1 Irisbus, 12 Mercedes, 1 Scania, 2 Volvo.
Bodies: 15 Plaxton, 3 Other.
Ops incl: local bus services, school contracts, excursions & tours, private hire.
Livery: Silver/Blue
Ticket System: Wayfarer

EAST RENFREWSHIRE

ARRIVA SCOTLAND WEST
See Renfrewshire

HENRY CRAWFORD COACHES LTD
SHILFORD MILL, NEILSTON G78 3BA
Tel: 01505 850456
Fax: 01505 850479
E-mail: henrycrawford@talk21.com
Web site: www.henrycrawfordcoaches.co.uk
Dirs: James Crawford (Ops), John Crawford (Eng), Isobel Crawford(Co Sec).
Fleet: 26 - 21 single-deck coach, 5 minicoach.

Chassis: 1 Bova, 2 Leyland, 5 Mercedes, 18 Volvo.
Bodies: 1 Bova, 2 Duple, 1 Indcar, 1 Optare, 3 Plaxton, 16 Van Hool, 2 Other.
Ops incl: private hire, school contracts.
Livery: White/Red

RIVERSIDE TRANSPORT LTD
15 CARLIBAR ROAD, BARRHEAD G78 1AA
Tel: 0141 881 1104 **Fax:** 0141 881 1130
Web site: www.riversidetransport.co.uk
Ops incl: local bus services.

SOUTHERN COACHES (NM) LTD
LOCHIBO ROAD, BARRHEAD G78 1LF
Tel: 0141 881 1147
Fax: 0141 881 1148
E-mail: reservations@southerncoaches.co.uk.
Web site: www.southerncoaches.co.uk
Dirs: R. Wallace, D. Wallace, Mary Wallace.
Fleet: 19 - 17 single-deck coach, 2 minicoach.
Chassis: 2 DAF, 2 Toyota, 15 Volvo.
Bodies: 2 Caetano, 1 Jonckheere, 8 Plaxton, 8 Van Hool.
Ops incl: school contracts, excursions & tours, private hire, express.
Livery: Cream/Blue/Orange.

EDINBURGH, CITY OF

AAA COACHES
UNIT 7, RAW CAMPS INDUSTRIAL ESTATE, KIRKNEWTON EH27 8DF
Tel: 01506 883000
Fax: 01506 884000
E-mail: info@aaacoaches.co.uk
Web site: www.aaacoaches.co.uk
Man Dir: Mr J T Renton
Fleet: 17 - 13 single-deck coach, 3 midibus, 1 minibus.
Chassis: 1 Bova, 1 Dennis, 1 LDV, 4 MAN, 3 Mercedes, 7 Volvo.
Bodies: 4 Jonckheere, 2 Leyland, 4 Marcopolo, 2 Plaxton, 2 Sunsundegui.

ALLAN'S COACHES EDINBURGH
THE COACH YARD, NEWTONLOAN TOLL, GOREBRIDGE EH23 4LZ
Tel/Recovery: 01875 820377
Fax: 01875 822468
E-mail: coaches@allanscoaches.co.uk
Web Site: www.allanscoaches.co.uk
Prop & Ops Man: David W Allan
Ch Eng: Neil Mitchell
Office Man: Mrs Dawn Allan
Fleet: 10 - 8 single-deck coach, 1 midicoach, 1 minibus.
Chassis: 2 DAF, 4 Iveco, 3 Mercedes.
Bodies: 2 Bova, 2 Mercedes, 5 Plaxton.
Ops incl: school contracts, excursions & tours, private hire, express.
Livery: Allan's Blue.

CITY CIRCLE UK LTD
BUTLERFIELD INDUSTRIAL ESTATE, BONNYRIGG EH19 3JQ
Tel: 0131 220 1066 **Fax:** 01875 822762
E-mail: edi@citycircleuk.com
Web site: www.citycircleuk.com
Man Dir: Neil Pegg **Fin Dir:** Johnson Mitchell **Ops Man:** John Blair

Asst Ops Man: Jennifer Gibson
Eng: James Mellon
Fleet: 15 single-deck coach.
Ops incl: excursions & tours, private hire, continental tours.
Livery: White with Grey, Red
A subsidiary of City Circle, London

EDINBURGH TOURS LTD
ANNANDALE STREET, EDINBURGH EH7 4AZ
Tel: 0131 554 4494 **Fax:** 0131 554 3942
E-mail: info@edinburghtour.com
Web site: www.edinburghtour.com
Man Dir: W Ian G Craig
Fin Dir: Norman J Strachan
Ops Dir: William W Campbell
Eng Dir: William Devlin
Marketing & Comms Dir: Iain G Coupar
Fleet: 61 – 2 double-deck bus, 59 open-top bus.
Chassis: 13 AEC, 32 Dennis, 14 Leyland, 2 Volvo.
Bodies: 21 Alexander Dennis, 27 Plaxton, 13 Park Royal.
Livery: Various
Ticket system: Casio
A subsidiary of Lothian Buses

EDINBURGH COACH LINES LTD
81 SALAMANDER STREET, LEITH, EDINBURGH EH6 7JZ
Tel: 0131 554 5413 **Fax:** 0131 553 3721
E-mail: enquiries@edinburghcoachlines.com.
Web site: www.edinburghcoachlines.com.
Dir: Patrick Kavanagh
Gen Man: Peter Fyvie
Traffic Man: Gary Forbes-Burns
Fleet: 24 – 3 single-deck bus, 17 single-deck coach, 3 midicoach, 1 minicoach.
Chassis: 1 Dennis, 3 MAN, 3 Mercedes, 17 Scania.
Bodies: 7 Irizar, 3 Plaxton, 10 Van Hool, 3 Other.
Ops incl: local bus services, school contracts, excursions & tours, private hire, continental tours.
Livery: Pink/Purple/White.
Ticket System: Wayfarer TGX.
A subsidiary of Bernard Kavanagh & Sons – see Republic of Ireland

FAIRWAY TRAVEL
6 BRIARBANK TERRACE, EDINBURGH EH11 1ST
Tel: 0131 467 6717
Fax: 0131 467 6717
E-mail: davy@fairwaytravel.freeserve
Web site: www.fairwaytravel.co.uk
Prop: D. Innes.
Fleet: 4 - 1 single-deck coach, 2 midicoach, 1 minibus.
Chassis: 1 DAF, 1 Setra, 2 Toyota.
Bodies: 2 Caetano, 1 Leyland, 1 Setra.
Ops incl: school contracts, excursions & tours, private hire, continental tours.
Livery: Blue and Red on White.

FIRST SCOTLAND EAST LTD
See Stirling

LIBERTON TRAVEL
17-29 ENGINE ROAD, LOANHEAD EH20 9RF
Tel: 0131 440 4400 **Fax:** 0131 448 0008
E-mail: sales@libertontravel.co.uk

Dirs: Iain Smith, Alan Boyd
Fleet: 10 - 7 single-deck coach, 2 minibus, 1 minicoach.
Chassis: 1 Dennis, 1 Ford Transit, 1 Freight Rover, 1 Mercedes, 6 Volvo.
Bodies incl: 1 Caetano, 1 Marcopolo, 4 Plaxton.
Ops incl: school contracts, excursions & tours, private hire.
Livery: White

LOTHIAN BUSES PLC
ANNANDALE STREET, EDINBURGH EH7 4AZ
Tel: 0131 554 4494 **Fax:** 0131 554 3942
E-mail: mail@lothianbuses.com
Web site: www.lothianbuses.com
Man Dir: W Ian G Craig **Fin Dir:** Norman J Strachan **Ops Dir:** William W Campbell
Eng Dir: William Devlin
Marketing & Comms Dir: Iain G Coupar
Chairman: David Mackay
Non Exec Dirs: I Kitson, A Ross, R Hewitt, A Faulds, D Macleod, M Rodger, J Gray
Fleet: 624 - 486 double-deck bus, 70 single-deck bus, 68 midibus.
Chassis: 226 Dennis, 6 Optare, 15 Scania, 377 Volvo.
Bodies: 6 Optare, 233 Plaxton, 15 Scania, 370 Wright.
Ops incl: local bus services.
Livery: Maroon/Red/White/Gold
Ticket system: Wayfarer TGX200

FALKIRK

FIRST SCOTLAND EAST LTD
CARMUIRS HOUSE, 300 STIRLING ROAD, LARBERT FK5 3NJ
Tel: 01324 602200 **Fax:** 01324 611287
Customer Service Centre: 08708 727271
E-mail: contact.scotlandeast@firstgroup.com
Web site: www.firstgroup.com/scotlandeast
Fleet Names: First Scotland East, Midland Bluebird
Man Dir: Paul Thomas
Fleet: 419 – 155 double-deck bus, 196 single-deck bus, 10 single-deck coach, 57 midibus, 1 minicoach.
Chassis: 50 Alexander Dennis, 4 Dennis, 8 Leyland, 6 Mercedes, 167 Scania, 5 Transbus, 179 Volvo.
Bodies: 93 Alexander Dennis, 24 East Lancs, 6 Marshall/MCV, 14 Northern Counties, 5 Optare, 59 Plaxton, 4 Transbus, 214 Wright.
Ops incl: local bus services, school contracts, private hire.
Livery: FirstGroup UK Bus.
Ticket System: Almex

KELVIN VALLEY
RICHARD BRUCE HOUSE, HEAD OF MUIR, FALKIRK FK6 5NA
Tel/Fax: 01236 734883
E-mail: kvc@blueyonder.co.uk
Props: Robert B Mackenzie
Fleet: 4 midibus.
Chassis: 1 Alexander Dennis, 3 Mercedes.
Bodies: 1 Leicester, 1 Marshall/MCV, 1 Plaxton, 1 Wadham Stringer.
Ops incl: local bus services, school contracts, private hire.
Livery: Mint and Green.
Ticket System: Wayfarer TGX150.

P. WOODS MINICOACHES
20 CALDER PLACE, HALLGLEN FK1 2QQ.
Tel: 01324 613085.
Fax: 01324 717976.

FIFE

FIFE SCOTTISH OMNIBUSES LTD
OFFICES 47-51, EVANS BUSINESS CENTRE, JOHN SMITH BUSINESS PARK, KIRKCALDY KY2 6HD
Tel: 01592 642394
Fax: 01592 645677
Recovery: 01383 511911
E-mail: eastscotland@stagecoachbus.com
Web site: www.stagecoachbus.com
Fleet Name: Stagecoach in Fife
Man Dir: Doug Fleming
Chief Eng: Mike Williams
Fleet: 330 - 132 double-deck bus, 114 single-deck bus, 6 single-deck coach, 44 midibus, 34 minibus.
Chassis: 45 Dennis, 14 Leyland, 37 MAN, 19 Mercedes, 15 Optare, 10 Scania, 190 Volvo.
Bodies: 177 Alexander Dennis, 2 Jonckheere, 88 Northern Counties, 15 Optare, 48 Plaxton.
Ops incl: local bus services, school contracts, excursions & tours, private hire, express.
Livery: Stagecoach UK Bus/Citylink
Ticket System: ERG

KINGDOM COACHES
DEN WALK, METHIL KY8 3JH
Tel: 01333 26109
Fleet: 3 single-deck coach.
Chassis: 2 DAF, 1 Ford.
Bodies: 2 Plaxton, 1 Van Hool.
Ops incl: private hire.
Livery: Yellow/White.

MOFFAT & WILLIAMSON LTD
OLD RAILWAY YARD, ST FORT, NEWPORT-ON-TAY DD6 8RG
Tel: 01382 541159
Fax: 01382 541169
E-mail: enquiries@moffat-williamson.co.uk
Web site: www.moffat-williamson.co.uk
Dirs: John Williamson, Iain Williamson
Accounts Asst: Sharon Smith
Fleet: 63 - 26 single-deck bus, 22 single-deck coach, 10 midibus, 3 midicoach, 2 minicoach.
Chassis: DAF, Dennis, LDV, MAN, Mercedes, Optare, Volvo.
Bodies: Alexander Dennis, Ikarus, Marshall/MCV, Mercedes, Optare, Plaxton, UVG, Wadham Stringer.
Ops incl: local bus services, school contracts, excursions & tours, private hire, express.
Livery: Brown/Cream/Orange

RENNIES OF DUNFERMLINE LTD
WELLWOOD, DUNFERMLINE KY12 0PY
Tel: 01383 620600
Fax: 01383 620624
E-mail: gordon@rennies.co.uk
Web site: www.rennies.co.uk
Gen Man: Gordon Menzies **Tran Man:** Iain Robertson **Ch Eng:** George Clark
Fleet: 60 - 23 double-deck bus, 15 single-

deck bus, 14 single-deck coach,
4 midibus, 4 minicoach.
Chassis: 4 Autosan, 2 BMC, 13 Dennis,
4 Mercedes, 37 Volvo.
Bodies: 4 Autosan, 3 Alexander, 2 BMC,
5 Caetano, 5 Jonckheere, 20 Northern
Counties, 9 Plaxton, 1 Sunsundegui,
1 Van Hool, 6 Wadham Stringer, 4 Other.
Ops incl: local bus services, school
contracts, excursions & tours, private hire,
continental tours.
Livery: Blue/White.
Ticket system: Almex
A subsidiary of the Stagecoach Group

ST ANDREWS EXECUTIVE TRAVEL
BROWNHILLS GARAGE,
ST ANDREWS KY16 8PL
Tel: 01334 470080
Fax: 01334 470081
E-mail: orders@saxtravel.co.uk
Web Site: www.saxtravel.co.uk
Dir: Gordon Donaldson
Fleet: 10 - 2 minicoach, 8 midicoach.
Chassis: 10 Mercedes

Ops incl: excursions & tours, private hire.
Livery: White and Green

GLASGOW, CITY OF

ALLANDER COACHES LTD
19 CLOBERFIELD, MILNGAVIE,
GLASGOW G62 7LN
Tel: 0141 956 1234
Fax: 0141 956 6669
E-mail: enquiries@allandercoaches.co.uk
Web site: www.allandertravel.co.uk
Man Dir: J F Wilson **Dir:** Mrs E E Wilson
Ch Eng: G S Wilson
Co Sec: Miss M Brown
Ops Man: G F Wilson
Fleet: 26 - 3 double-deck bus,
7 single-deck bus, 12 single-deck coach,
1 midibus, 1 midicoach.
Chassis: 16 DAF, 7 Dennis, 3 Mercedes.
Bodies: 4 Alexander Dennis, 19 Bova,
2 Esker, 1 Wadham Stringer.
Ops incl: local bus services, school
contracts, excursions & tours, private hire,
continental tours.
Livery: Black/Orange/Gold.

ARRIVA SCOTLAND WEST
See Renfrewshire

CITY SIGHTSEEING GLASGOW
ST GEORGE'S BUILDING, 153 QUEEN
STREET, GLASGOW G1 3BJ
Tel: 0141 204 0444
Fax: 0141 248 6582
Web site: www.citysightseeingglasgow.co.uk
E-mail: info@citysightseeingglasgow.co.uk
Man Dir: Colin Craig
Ops Man: Donald Booth
Fleet: 10 open top bus.

Chassis: 4 Scania, 6 Volvo.
Bodies: 2 Alexander Dennis, 2 East
Lancs, 2 Optare.
Ops incl: excursions & tours, private hire.
Livery: City Sightseeing Red
Ticket system: Wayfarer 3
A subsidiary of West Coast Motors – see
Argyll & Bute

DOIGS OF GLASGOW LTD
TRANSPORT HOUSE, SUMMER
STREET, GLASGOW G40 3TB
Tel: 0141 554 5555
Fax: 0141 551 9000
E-mail: andy@doigs.com
Web site: www.doigs.com
Chairman/Man Dir: Andrew Forsyth
Co Sec: Iain Forsyth
Fleet: 15 - 1 double-deck bus, 1 single-deck bus, 1 articulated bus, 8 single-deck coach, 1 midicoach, 3 minicoach.
Chassis incl: DAF, Dennis, LDV,
Mercedes, Scania, 3 Volvo.
Bodies: 1 Caetano, 1 East Lancs,
7 Irizar, 1 Marcopolo, 2 Mercedes,
1 Optare, 3 Sunsundegui, 1 Wright.
Ops incl: school contracts, excursions &
tours, private hire, continental tours.
Livery: Silver/Red lettering

FIRST GLASGOW
197 VICTORIA ROAD,
GLASGOW G42 7AD
Tel: 0141 423 6600 **Fax:** 0141 636 3228
Web Site: www.firstgroup.com.
Man Dir: Ronnie Park
Fleet: 953 - incl: double-deck bus,
single-deck bus, minibus.
Chassis: Dennis, Leyland, MCW,
Mercedes, Optare, Plaxton, Wright.
Ops incl: local bus services.
Livery: FirstGroup UK Bus.

GLASGOW CITYBUS LTD
729 SOUTH STREET,
GLASGOW G14 0BX
Tel: 0141 954 2255
Email: mail@glasgowcitybus.co.uk
Web site: www.glasgowcitybus.co.uk
Man Dir: Colin Craig
Fleet: 27 – 1 double-deck bus,
8 single-deck bus, 18 midibus.
Chassis: 7 Alexander Dennis, 6 DAF,
8 Dennis, 2 Optare, 1 Scania, 3 VDL
Bodies: 7 Alexander Dennis,
1 Alexander, 1 East Lancs, 2 Optare,
9 Plaxton, 1 UVG, 6 Wright
Ops incl: local bus services
Livery: Red/White/Blue/Yellow
A subsidiary of West Coast Motors – see
Argyll & Bute

JOHN MORROW COACHES
18 ALBION INDUSTRIAL ESTATE,
HALLEY STREET, YOKER,
GLASGOW G13 4DJ
Tel: 0141 951 8888
Fax: 0141 952 6445
E-mail: info@clantours.com
Web site: www.clantours.com
Prop: John Morrow.
Fleet: 19 - 16 single-deck bus, 1 single-

deck coach, 1 midicoach, 1 minicoach.
Chassis: 2 Alexander Dennis, 1 Leyland,
7 Mercedes, 5 Optare, 1 Toyota, 3 Volvo.
Ops incl: local bus services, school
contracts, excursions & tours, private hire.
Livery: Brown/Cream
Ticket system: Almex

SCOTTISH CITYLINK COACHES LTD
BUCHANAN BUS STATION,
KILLERMONT STREET,
GLASGOW G2 3NP
Tel: 0141 352 4454
E-mail: info@citylink.co.uk.
Web site: www.citylink.co.uk.
Ops incl: private hire, express.
Livery: Blue/yellow
Ticket system: Wayfarer

SELVEY'S COACHES
HILLCREST HOUSE, 33 HOWIESHILL
ROAD, CAMBUSLANG G72 8PW
Tel: 0141 641 1080
Fax: 0141 641 2065
Owner: A. G. Selvey.
Fleet: 8 - 5 single-deck coach,
2 midicoach, 1 minicoach.
Chassis: 3 Bedford, 2 Leyland,
1 Mercedes, 2 Volvo.
Bodies: 1 Duple,1 Jonckheere,
1 Mercedes, 3 Plaxton.
Ops incl: excursions & tours, private hire,
school contracts.
Livery: Maroon/Red/Yellow

STAGECOACH GLASGOW
See Stagecoach West Scotland
– South Ayrshire

HIGHLAND

D&E COACHES LTD
39 HENDERSON DRIVE,
INVERNESS IV1 1TR
Tel: 01463 222444 **Fax:** 01463 226700
Recovery: 07770 222612
E-mail: decoaches@aol.com
Web site: www.decoaches.co.uk
Man Dir: Donald Mathieson
Dir: Elizabeth Mathieson
Co Sec: Gayle Kennedy **Ops Man:** Willie Bell **Ch Eng:** Bryan Fiddy
Fleet: 24 – 2 double-deck bus, 2 single-deck bus, 9 single-deck coach, 4 midibus,
3 midicoach, 2 minibus, 2 minicoach.
Chassis: 7 Bova, 1 DAF, 2 Dennis,
9 Mercedes, 2 Volkswagen, 3 Volvo.
Bodies: 2 Alexander, 2 Berkhof, 7 Bova,
1 Duple, 3 Esker, 4 Plaxton, 2 Reeve Burgess, 2 Van Hool, 2 Volkswagen.
Ops incl: local bus services, school
contracts, private hire.
Livery: White
Ticket system: Almex

TIM DEARMAN COACHES
INCHNAVIE LOWER, NEWBRIDGE,
ARDROSS, ROSS-SHIRE IV17 0XL
Tel: 01348 883585
Fax: 01348 884193

♿	Vehicle suitable for disabled	R24	24 hour recovery service
T	Toilet-drop facilities available		Replacement vehicle available
R	Recovery service available		Air-conditioned vehicle(s)
	Open top vehicle(s)		Vintage Coach(es) available
	Seat belt-fitted Vehicle		
	Coach(es) with galley facilities		
	Coaches with toilet facilities		

E-mail:
tim.dearman@timdearmancoaches.co.uk.
Web site:
www.timdearmancoaches.co.uk
Owner: Tim Dearman.
Fleet: 6 - 3 single-deck bus,
2 single-deck coach, 1 midibus.
Chassis: 1 Cannon, 1 Iveco, 3 Mercedes,
1 Optare.
Bodies: 1 Beulas, 1 Esker, 1 Leicester,
1 Optare, 2 Plaxton.
Ops incl: local bus services, school
contracts, private hire.
Livery: Maroon/Red
Ticket system: Almex

SCOTBUS LTD
5 DARNAWAY AVENUE, INVERNESS
IV2 3HY
Tel: 01463 214410
E-mail: info@scotbus.co.uk
Web site: www.scotbus.co.uk
Fleet incl: double-deck bus, single-deck
bus, single-deck coach, minibus
Ops incl: local bus services, school
contracts, private hire

SHIEL BUSES
BLAIN GARAGE, ACHARACLE
PH36 4JY
Tel/Fax: 01967 431272
E-mail: shiel.buses@virgin.net
Dir: Donnie MacGillivray.
Fleet: 10 - 4 single-deck coach,
6 midibus.
Chassis: 1 Ford Transit, 4 Mercedes,
4 Volvo.
Bodies: 2 Mercedes, 2 Onyx, 2 Plaxton,
2 Van Hool.
Ops incl: local bus services, school
contracts, private hire.
Livery: Red/White
Ticket system: Amex
Incorporates White Heather Travel

SPA COACHES
KINETTAS, STRATHPEFFER IV14 9BH
Tel: 01997 421311 **Fax:** 01997 421983
Web site: www.spacoaches.com
Prop: N. MacArthur.
Fleet: 28 - 6 double-deck bus, 13 single-
deck coach, 5 midibus, 2 minibus.
Chassis: 1 DAF, 2 Ford Transit,
5 Mercedes, 14 Volvo.
Bodies: 1 Duple, 7 Alexander, 2 Caetano,
3 Jonckheere, 5 Plaxton, 6 Van Hool,
4 other.
Ops incl: local bus services, school
contracts, excursions & tours, private hire,
continental tours.
Livery: Orange/White.
Ticket System: Punch Tickets.

STAGECOACH HIGHLAND
6 BURNETT ROAD, LONGMAN
INDUSTRIAL ESTATE,
INVERNESS IV1 1TF
Tel: 01463 239292 **Fax:** 01463 251360
Recovery: 01463 239292
E-mail:
highland.enquiries@stagecoachbus.com
Web site: www.stagecoachbus.com
Fleet Name: Stagecoach in the
Highlands
Man Dir: Steve Walker **Ops Dir:** Bob Hall
Eng Dir: Russell Henderson
Traffic Man: Scott Pearson
Eng Man: Callum MacGregor
Comm Man: William Mainus
Ops Man: Ali Mac Donald

Fleet: 211 - 29 double-deck bus,
118 single-deck bus, 36 single-deck
coach, 23 midibus, 4 minibus,
1 minicoach (excludes Orkney
– see separate entry).
Chassis: 39 Alexander Dennis,
34 Dennis, 1 MAN, 12 Mercedes,
10 Optare, 1 Toyota, 16 Transbus,
98 Volvo.
Bodies: 39 Alexander Dennis,
35 Alexander, 4 East Lancs,
3 Jonckheere, 1 Marshall, 4 Northern
Counties, 10 Optare, 88 Plaxton,
17 Transbus, 1 Van Hool, 5 Wright,
4 Other.
Ops incl: local bus services, school
contracts, excursions & tours, private hire,
express.
Livery: Stagecoach UK
Bus/Citylink/Megabus
Ticket System: Wayfarer/ERG

GRAHAM URQUHART TRAVEL LTD
28 MIDMILLS ROAD,
INVERNESS IV2 3NY
Tel: 01463 222292 **Fax:** 01463 238880
E-mail:
graham@urquharttravel.fsnet.co.uk
Web site:
www.grahamurquharttravel.co.uk
Dir: John G Urquhart **Sec:** John G Prant
Fleet: 8 - 4 single-deck coach,
2 midicoach, 2 minicoach.
Chassis: 4 Mercedes, 4 Scania.
Bodies: 4 Irizar, 4 Esker.
Ops incl: excursions & tours, private hire.

INVERCLYDE

ARRIVA SCOTLAND WEST
See Renfrewshire

GILLEN'S COACHES LTD
11 DELLINGBURN STREET,
GREENOCK PA15 4RN
Tel/Fax: 01475 744618
Recovery: 07785 873299
Dir: Samuel McPherson
Fleet: 14 - single-deck bus, midicoach,
minibus, minicoach
Ops incl: local bus services, excursions
& tours, private hire.
Livery: White
Ticket system: Wayfarer

HARTE BUSES
OCEAN TERMINAL, PATRICK STREET,
GREENOCK PA16 8UU
Tel/Fax: 01475 787781
E-mail: info@hartebuses.co.uk
Web site: www.hartebuses.co.uk
Dir: Peter Harte MBE
Fleet: 3 single-deck bus, 1 single-deck
coach
Chassis/Bodies: 1 Bova, 1 FAST,
2 Mercedes
Operations: local bus services.
Livery: Orange/Gold.

McGILLS BUS SERVICE LTD
99, EARNHILL ROAD, LARKFIELD
INDUSTRIAL ESTATE, GREENOCK
PA16 0EQ
Tel: 01475 711122 **Fax:** 01475 711133
Web Site: www.mcgillsbuses.co.uk
Chairman: J Easdale
Man Dir: R Roberts **Fin Dir:** G Davidson
Gen Man: B Hendry
Ops incl: local bus services
Livery: Blue/White

PRIDE OF THE CLYDE COACHES LTD
11 DELLINGBURN STREET,
GREENOCK PA15 4RN
Tel: 01475 888000
Fax: 01475 888333
E-mail: info@prideoftheclyde.net
Web site: www.prideoftheclyde.net
Fleet incl: single-deck coach, midicoach,
minicoach, minibus
Ops incl: private hire
Livery: White with Blue

MIDLOTHIAN

ALLAN'S COACHES EDINBURGH
THE COACH YARD, NEWTONLOAN
TOLL, GOREBRIDGE EH23 4LZ
Tel/Recovery: 01875 820377
Fax: 01875 822468
E-mail: coaches@allanscoaches.co.uk
Web Site: www.allanscoaches.co.uk
Prop & Ops Man: David W Allan
Ch Eng: Neil Mitchell
Office Man: Mrs Dawn Allan
Fleet: 10 - 8 single-deck coach,
1 midicoach, 1 minibus.
Chassis: 2 DAF, 4 Iveco, 3 Mercedes.
Bodies: 2 Bova, 2 Mercedes, 5 Plaxton.
Ops incl: school contracts, excursions &
tours, private hire, express.
Livery: Allan's Blue.

CITY CIRCLE UK LTD
BUTTERFIELD INDUSTRIAL ESTATE,
BONNYRIGG EH19 3JQ
Tel: 0131 220 1066
Fax: 01875 822762
E-mail: edi@citycircleuk.com
Web site: www.citycircleuk.com
Man Dir: Neil Pegg
Fin Dir: Johnson Mitchell
Ops Man: John Blair **Asst Ops Man:**
Jennifer Gibson **Eng:** James Mellon
Fleet: 15 single-deck coach.
Ops incl: excursions & tours, private hire,
continental tours.
Livery: White with Grey, Red
A subsidiary of City Circle, London

FIRST EDINBURGH LTD
See Stirling

WILLIAM HUNTER
OAKFIELD GARAGE,
LOANHEAD EH20 9AE
Tel: 0131 440 0704
Fax: 0131 448 2184
E-mail: sales@hunterscoaches.co.uk
Web Site: www.hunterscoaches.co.uk
Props: G I Hunter, W R Hunter.
Fleet: 14 - 12 single-deck coach,
2 minibus.
Chassis: 3 Toyota, 11 Volvo.
Bodies: 3 Caetano, 11 Van Hool.
Ops incl: school contracts, private hire.
Livery: Brown/Cream

LIBERTON TRAVEL
See Edinburgh, City of

McKENDRY TRAVEL
100 STRAITON ROAD, LOANHEAD
EH20 9NP
Tel: 0131 440 1013
Fax: 0131 448 2160
E-mail: dmckendry@btconnect.com

Web site: www.mckendrycoaches.co.uk
Dir: Ann McKendry
Tran Man: Stuart McCaw
Fleet: 15 - 1 double-deck bus,
12 single-deck coach, 2 minibus.
Chassis: 1 Dennis, 1 Ford Transit,
1 Freight Rover, 1 Leyland National,
4 Scania, 5 Volvo.
Bodies: 1 Caetano, 2 Jonckheere,
2 Plaxton, 5 Van Hool.
Ops incl: excursions & tours, private hire, school contracts.
Livery: White/Blue/Purple/Red vinyls

MORAY

BLUEBIRD BUSES LTD
See Aberdeenshire

CENTRAL COACHES
CENTRAL GARAGE, CHURCH ROAD, KEITH AB55 5BR
Tel: 01542 882113 **Fax:** 01542 886945
E-mail: watson@centralcoaches.co.uk
Web site: www.centralcoaches.co.uk
Partners: William Watson Smith, Veronica A Smith, William Andrew Smith
Fleet: 12 - 1 single-deck bus,
9 single-deck coach, 2 minibus.
Chassis: 1 Bova, 2 DAF, 2 Mercedes,
1 Optare, 6 Volvo.
Bodies: 1 Bova, 1 Caetano,
1 Jonckheere, 1 Leicester, 1 Mercedes,
1 Optare/Excel, 4 Plaxton, 2 Van Hool.
Ops incl: local bus services, school contracts, private hire.
Livery: White/Red

MAYNES COACHES LTD
LINKWOOD INDUSTRIAL ESTATE, ELGIN IV30 1XS
Tel: 01343 555227
E-mail: info@maynes.co.uk
Web site: www.maynes.co.uk
Dirs: Gordon Mayne, Sandra Mayne, David Mayne, Kevin Mayne
Fleet: 30 – 1 single-deck bus, 22 single-deck coach, 2 midibus, 5 midicoach.
Chassis: 12 MAN, 5 Mercedes, 1 Optare, 2 Renault, 10 Volvo.
Bodies: 2 Berkhof, 4 Marcopolo,
7 Neoplan, 1 Optare, 1 Onyx, 5 Plaxton,
8 Van Hool, 2 Other.
Ops incl: local bus services, school contracts, excursions & tours, private hire, continental tours.
Livery: Blue/Silver.
Ticket System: Setright.

NORTH AYRSHIRE

CUMBRAE COACHES
14 MARINE PARADE, MILLPORT, ISLE OF CUMBRAE KA28 0ED
Tel: 01475 530692
Web site: www.cumbraecoaches.co.uk
Fleet: 3 single-deck bus.
Chassis: 3 Alexander Dennis.
Bodies: 3 Alexander Dennis.
Ops incl: local bus services, private hire.
Livery: Red/White.

MARBILL TRAVEL
HIGH MAINS GARAGE, MAINS ROAD, BEITH KA15 2AP
Tel: 01505 503367 **Fax:** 01505 504736
E-mail: marbill@btclick.com
Web site: www.marbillcoaches.com

Man Dir: Margaret Whiteman **Eng Dir:** David Barr **Ops Dir:** Connie Barr
Fleet: 66 - 26 double-deck bus, 20 single-deck bus, 18 single-deck coach, 2 minicoach.
Chassis: 2 Bova, 34 Leyland, 2 Mercedes, 28 Volvo
Bodies: 26 Alexander, 2 Bova, 25 Plaxton, 1 Sitcar, 12 Van Hool.
Ops incl: school contracts, excursions & tours, private hire.

MILLPORT MOTORS LTD
16 BUTE TERRACE, MILLPORT, ISLE OF CUMBRAE KA28 0BA
Tel: 01475 530555
Fleet: 2 single-deck bus.
Chassis: 1 Dennis, 1 Volvo.
Bodies: 1 Plaxton, 1 Wright.
Ops incl: local bus services, private hire.
Livery: Blue/Cream.
Ticket System: Almex.

SHUTTLE BUSES LTD
CALEDONIA HOUSE, LONGFORD AVENUE, KILWINNING KA13 6EX
Tel: 01294 550757
Fax: 01294 558822
E-mail: enquiries@shuttlebuses.co.uk
Web site: www.shuttlebuses.co.uk
Man Dir: David Granger
Maintenance Supervisor: Des Bradshaw
Fleet: 31 - 6 single-deck coach,
12 midibus, 4 midicoach, 9 minibus.
Chassis: 1 AEC, 2 Dennis, 2 Ford Transit, 1 Leyland, 7 Mercedes, 8 Optare,
2 Renault, 6 Volkswagen, 2 Volvo.
Bodies: 1 Alexander Dennis, 1 Autobus,
4 Caetano, 2 Mercedes, 8 Optare,
4 Plaxton, 11 Other.
Ops incl: local bus services, school contracts, private hire.
Livery: Yellow/White.
Ticket System: Wayfarer TGX

STAGECOACH WEST SCOTLAND
See South Ayrshire

NORTH LANARKSHIRE

A&C LUXURY COACHES
4 HILLHEAD AVENUE, MOTHERWELL ML1 4AQ
Tel: 01698 252652 **Fax:** 01698 259898
E-mail: enquiries@acluxurycoaches.co.uk
Web site: www.acluxurycoaches.co.uk
Prop: Alex Grenfell
Fleet: 6 - 3 single-deck coach,
2 midicoach, 1 minicoach.
Chassis: 3 Mercedes, 1 Neoplan, 2 Volvo.
Bodies: 1 Neoplan, 1 Plaxton,
1 Van Hool
Ops incl: school contracts, private hire, excursions & tours.

CANAVAN'S COACHES
CEDAR LODGE, COACH ROAD, KILSYTH G65 0DB
Tel: 01236 822414
Prop: M., G., H., & J. Canavan.
Ops incl: local bus services.

DUNN'S COACHES
560 STIRLING ROAD, AIRDRIE ML6 7SS
Tel: 01236 722385 **Fax:** 01236 722385

Prop: Craig Dunn.
Fleet: 11 - 4 single-deck bus,
7 single-deck coach.
Chassis: 2 Alexander Dennis,
2 Dennis, 1 Mercedes, 6 Volvo.
Bodies: 1 Jonckheere, 2 Plaxton,
1 Van Hool, 6 Volvo, 1 Wright.
Ops incl: local bus services, school contracts, excursions & tours, private hire, express.
Livery: White
Ticket System: Wayfarer TGX

ESSBEE COACHES (HIGHLANDS & ISLANDS)
7 HOLLANDHURST ROAD, GARTSHERRIE ML5 2EG
Tel: 01236 423621 **Fax:** 01236 433677
Man Dir: B. Smith **Gen Man:** J. Kinnaird
Ops Man: S. Stewart.
Fleet: single-deck bus, single-deck coach, double-deck coach, midicoach, minibus.
Ops incl: School contracts, excursions & tours, private hire.
Livery: Red/Silver.
Ticket System: Wayfarer.

FIRST GLASGOW
See Glasgow, City of

GOLDEN EAGLE COACHES
MUIRHALL GARAGE, 197 MAIN STREET, SALSBURGH, BY SHOTTS ML7 4LS
Tel: 01698 870207
Fax: 01698 870217
E-mail: info@goldeneaglecoaches.com
Web site: www.goldeneaglecoaches.com
Dirs: Peter Irvine, Robert Irvine, Ishbel Irvine
Fleet: 22 - 8 double-deck bus,
14 single-deck coach.
Chassis: 1 Bova, 5 Dennis, 4 Leyland,
1 MCW, 11 Volvo.
Bodies: 2 Jonckheere, 1 MCW,
7 Van Hool, 12 Other.
Ops incl: school contracts, excursions & tours, private hire.
Livery: White, Gold & Maroon

IRVINE'S OF LAW
LAWMUIR ROAD, LAW ML8 5JB.
Tel: 01698 372452
Fax: 01698 376200
Web site: www.irvinescoaches.co.uk
Prop: Peter Irvine **Man:** Gordon Graham
Ch Eng: Scott Fisher
Fleet: 40 - 14 double-deck bus, 13 coach, 13 midibus.
Chassis incl: DAF, Dennis, Optare, Scania, Volvo.
Bodies incl: Optare, Plaxton, Van Hool
Ops incl: local bus services, excursions & tours, school contracts, private hire, express, continental tours.
Livery: Red/Cream.
Ticket System: Wayfarer.

LONG'S COACHES LTD
157 MAIN STREET, SALSBURGH, BY SHOTTS ML7 4LR
Tel: 01698 870768
Fax: 01698 870826
E-mail: info@longscoaches.co.uk
Web site: www.longscoaches.co.uk
Dir: Peter I. Long **Co Sec:** Susan Long.
Fleet: 14 - 13 single-deck coach,
1 midicoach.

Chassis: 2 Bova, 12 Volvo.
Bodies: 2 Bova, 12 Van Hool.
Ops incl: excursions & tours, private hire, express, continental tours, school contracts.
Livery: Silver/Maroon.
Ticket System: Wayfarer.

MACPHAILS COACHES
40 MAIN STREET, SALSBURGH, BY SHOTTS ML7 4LW
Tel: 01698 870768
Fax: 01698 870826
E-mail: macphail7@aol.com
Web site: www.macphailscoaches.com
Dirs: Martin MacPhail, Henry MacPhail.
Fleet incl: single-deck coach, minibus.
Chassis incl: 8 Volvo.
Bodies incl: 1 Plaxton, 7 Van Hool.
Ops incl: excursions & tours, private hire, continental tours.

M.C.T. GROUP TRAVEL LTD
NETHAN STREET DEPOT, NETHAN STREET, MOTHERWELL ML1 3TF
Tel: 01698 253091
Fax: 01698 259208
E-mail: enquiries@mctgrouptravel.com
Web site: www.mctgrouptravel.com
Man Dir: Desmond Heenan
Dir: Oswald Heenan
Fleet: 14 - 4 single-deck bus, 6 single-deck coach, 4 midicoach.
Chassis: 1 Iveco, 3 MAN, 1 Mercedes, 4 Toyota, 5 Volvo.
Bodies: 1 Esker, 1 Indcar, 4 Jonckheere, 1 Optare, 7 Other.
Ops incl: school contracts, excursions & tours, private hire, continental tours.
Livery: Turquoise/Silver

MILLER'S COACHES
22 WOODSIDE DRIVE, CALDERBANK, AIRDRIE ML6 9TN
Tel: 01236 763671
Owner: W. Miller **Tran Man:** T. Miller.
Fleet: 12 - 8 single-deck coach, 4 minicoach.
Chassis: 8 Leyland, 4 Mercedes.
Bodies: 2 Alexander, 1 Mellor, 8 Plaxton, 1 Reeve Burgess.
Ops incl: local bus services, school contracts, private hire.
Livery: Black/White/Grey.

STEPEND COACHES
92 WADDELL AVENUE, GLENMAVIS, AIRDRIE ML6 ONZ
Tel: 01236 760500
Prop: S. Chapman.
Ops incl: local bus services.

WILLIAM STOKES & SONS LTD
22 CARSTAIRS ROAD, CARSTAIRS ML11 8QD
Tel: 01555 870344
Fax: 01555 870601
E-mail: enquires@stokescoaches.co.uk
Web site: www.stokescoaches.co.uk
Dirs: John Stokes, Alex Stokes, William Stokes **Co Sec:** Walter Stokes
Ops incl: schools contracts, excursions & tours, private hire.
Livery: Red/Cream

TRAMONTANA
CHAPELKNOWE ROAD, CARFIN, MOTHERWELL ML1 5LE
Tel: 01698 861790 **Fax:** 01698 860778
E-mail: wdt@tiscali.co.uk
Prop: Douglas Telfer
Fleet: 6 single-deck coach
Chassis: 6 Volvo.
Bodies: 2 Caetano, 1 Irizar, 1 Jonckheere, 2 Plaxton.
Ops incl: excursions & tours, private hire
Livery: White

ORKNEY

M & J HARCUS
PIEROWALL, ISLE OF WESTRAY
Tel: 01857 677758
Ops incl: local bus service

J & V COACHES
VART TUN, STROMNESS KW16 3LL
Tel: 01856 851425
Web site: www.jandvcoaches.co.uk
Ops incl: excursions & tours, private hire

MAYNES COACHES LTD
ST MARGARETS HOPE KW17 2TG
Tel: 01856 831333
E-mail: inof@maynes.co.uk
Web site: www.maynes.co.uk
Dirs: Gordon Mayne, Sandra Mayne, David Mayne, Kevin Mayne
Fleet: 30 – 1 single-deck bus, 22 single-deck coach, 2 midibus, 5 midicoach.
Chassis: 12 MAN, 5 Mercedes, 1 Optare, 2 Renault, 10 Volvo.
Bodies: 2 Berkhof, 4 Marcopolo, 7 Neoplan, 1 Optare, 1 Onyx, 5 Plaxton, 8 Van Hool, 2 Other.
Ops incl: local bus services, school contracts, excursions & tours, private hire, continental tours.
Livery: Blue/Silver.
Ticket System: Setright.

STAGECOACH IN ORKNEY
6 BURNETT ROAD, LONGMAN INDUSTRIAL ESTATE, INVERNESS IV1 1TF
Tel: 01463 239292 **Fax:** 01463 251360
E-mail: highland.enquiries@stagecoachbus.com
Web site: www.stagecoachbus.com
Gen Man: Monty Smillie
Fleet: 36 – 12 single-deck bus, 12 single-deck coach, 10 midibus, 2 minibus.
Chassis: 1 Mercedes, 11 Optare, 24 Volvo.
Bodies: 9 Jonckheere, 11 Optare, 12 Plaxton, 4 Van Hool.
Ops incl: local bus services, school contracts, excursions & tours, private hire.
Livery: Stagecoach UK Bus

PERTH & KINROSS

ABERFELDY MOTOR SERVICES
BURNSIDE GARAGE, ABERFELDY PH15 2DD
Tel: 01887 820433 **Fax:** 01887 829534
E-mail: aberfeldymotors@btconnect.com
Web site: www.aberfeldycoaches.co.uk
Prop: John Stewart **Co Sec:** Lynda Stewart **Ch Eng:** David Matthew
Fleet: 8 - 6 single-deck coach, 1 midicoach, 1 minicoach.
Chassis: 2 Bova, 2 Mercedes, 4 Volvo.
Bodies: 2 Bova, 1 Plaxton, 1 Sitcar, 3 Volvo, 1 Other.
Ops incl: excursions & tours, private hire, continental tours, school contracts.
Livery: Blue

CABER COACHES LTD
CHAPEL STREET GARAGE, ABERFELDY PH15 2AS
Tel: 01887 870090
Fax: 01887 829352
E-mail: cabercoaches@btinternet.com
Man Dir: Kenneth Carey
Sec: Alexander Carey
Fleet: 8 - 2 single-deck coach, 2 midicoach, 4 minibus.
Chassis: 2 Ford Transit, 2 LDV, 2 Mercedes.
Ops incl: local bus services, school contracts, private hire.
Livery: White
Ticket system: Almex

CRIEFF TRAVEL
GLENHEATH, LODGE STREET, CRIEFF PH7 4DW
Tel: 01764 654333
Fax: 01764 654333
Recovery: 07803 591778
Owner: Dave Myles
Fleet: 14 – 7 single-deck bus, 2 single-deck coach, 3 midibus, 2 midicoach.
Chassis incl: 5 Alexander Dennis, 5 Mercedes, 2 Volvo.
Bodies incl: 5 Alexander Dennis, 5 Mercedes, 2 Plaxton.

Ops incl: local bus services, school contracts, private hire.
Livery: Black/White.
Ticket System: ERG

DOCHERTY'S MIDLAND COACHES
PRIORY PARK, AUCHTERARDER PH3 1GB
Tel: 01764 662218
Fax: 01764 664228
E-mail: info@dochertysmidlandcoaches.co.uk
Web site: www.dochertysmidlandcoaches.co.uk
Props: Jim & Edith Docherty, Colin Docherty, Neil Docherty, William Docherty
Fleet: 23 - 2 single-deck bus, 11 single-deck coach, 2 midibus, 4 midicoach, 1 minibus, 2 minicoach, 1 vintage.
Chassis: 1 Bova, 1 Leyland, 6 Mercedes, 3 Optare, 1 Renault, 6 Scania, 5 Volvo.
Bodies: 1 Bova, 4 Irizar, 2 Jonckheere, 3 Optare, 2 Plaxton, 2 UVG, 3 Van Hool, 3 Wright, 3 Other.
Ops incl: local bus services, school contracts, private hire, express.
Livery: White/Black/Grey
Ticket System: Almex

EARNSIDE COACHES
GREENBANK ROAD, GLENFARG, PERTH PH2 9NW
Tel: 01577 830360 **Fax:** 01577 830599
E-mail: info@earnside.com.
Web site: www.earnside.com
Dirs: David Rutherford, Fiona Rutherford, Gary Rutherford
Fleet: 9 - 8 single-deck coach, 1 minibus.
Chassis: 1 Ford Transit, 2 Neoplan, 1 Scania, 6 Volvo.
Bodies: 1 Berkhof, 1 Irizar, 1 Jonckheere, 2 Neoplan, 4 Plaxton.
Ops incl: local bus services, school contracts, excursions & tours, private hire, continental tours.
Livery: White
Ticket system: Almex

MEGABUS
10 DUNKELD ROAD, PERTH PH1 5TW
Tel: 01738 522456
Web site: www.megabus.com
Ops incl: express.
Livery: Stagecoach UK Bus/Megabus Blue/Yellow
Part of the Stagecoach Group

SMITH & SONS COACHES
THE COACH DEPOT, WOODSIDE, COUPAR ANGUS, BLAIRGOWRIE PH13 9LW
Tel: 01828 627310 **Fax:** 01828 628518
Recovery: 01828 626262
E-mail: info@smithandsonscoaches.co.uk
Web site: www.smithandsonscoaches.co.uk
Partners: Ian F Smith, Gordon Smith, Kenneth F Smith.
Fleet: 28 – 5 single-deck bus, 15 single-deck coach, 1 midicoach, 2 minibus, 5 minicoach.
Chassis: 5 DAF, 8 Mercedes, 5 Optare, 10 Volvo.
Bodies: 4 Bova, 1 Esker, 4 Jonckheere, 2 Marshall/MCV, 2 Mercedes, 5 Optare, 3 Sitcar, 7 Van Hool.
Ops incl: local bus services, school contracts, private hire.

Livery: White
Ticket System: Almex

STAGECOACH SCOTLAND LTD
OFFICES 47-51, EVANS BUSINESS CENTRE, JOHN SMITH BUSINESS PARK, KIRKCALDY KY2 6HD
Tel: 01738 629339 **Fax:** 01738 643264
Recovery: 01738 629339
E-mail: eastscotland@stagecoachbus.com
Web site: www.stagecoachbus.com
Fleet Name: Stagecoach in Perth
Man Dir: Doug Fleming
Ch Eng: Jim Penrose
Ops Man: Gus Beveridge
Depot Eng: John Dick
Fleet: 77 - 13 double-deck bus, 37 single-deck bus, 8 single-deck coach, 2 midibus, 17 minibus.
Chassis: 13 Alexander Dennis, 5 Dennis, 17 MAN, 17 Optare, 25 Volvo.
Bodies: 16 Alexander Dennis, 24 Alexander, 7 East Lancs, 5 Northern Counties, 17 Optare, 8 Plaxton.
Ops incl: local bus services, tram services, school contracts, excursions & tours, private hire, express.
Livery: Stagecoach UK Bus/Megabus
Ticket System: ERG

ELIZABETH YULE
STATION GARAGE, STATION ROAD, PITLOCHRY PH16 5AN
Tel: 01796 472290 **Fax:** 01796 474214
E-mail: sandra.elizabeth-yule@btconnect.com
Partners: Elizabeth Yule, Sandra Bridges
Fleet: 8 - 4 single-deck coach, 1 midibus, 2 midicoach, 1 minibus.
Chassis: 1 Ford, 3 Mercedes, 4 Volvo.
Ops incl: local bus services, school contracts, excursions & tours, private hire.
Livery: White
Ticket System: Almex

RENFREWSHIRE

ALAN ARNOTT
16 TURNHILL CRESCENT, WEST FREELANDS, ERSKINE PA8 7AX
Fleet Name: S & A Coaches, City Sprinter

ARRIVA SCOTLAND WEST
GREENOCK ROAD, INCHINNAN, PAISLEY PA4 9PG
Tel: 08700 404343 **Fax:** 0141 561 4171
Web site: www.arrivabus.co.uk
Fleet Names: Arriva, SPT
Regional Man Dir: Jonathan May
Area Man Dir: Richard Hall
Ops Man: Murray Rogers
Fleet: 185 - incl double-deck bus, single-deck bus, single-deck coach, midibus, minibus.
Chassis: DAF, Dennis, Leyland, Mercedes, Optare, Scania, VDL, Volvo.
Bodies: Alexander, East Lancs, Mercedes, Northern Counties, Plaxton, Scania, Van Hool, Wright.
Ops incl: local bus services, express.
Livery: Arriva UK Bus

GIBSON DIRECT LTD
6 NEIL STREET, RENFREW PA4 8TA
Tel: 0141 886 7772

E-mail: enquiries@gibsondirectltd.com
Web site: www.gibsondirectltd.co.uk
Operations: local bus services, private hire, school contracts.
Livery: Blue/White.

VIOLET GRAHAM COACHES
93 IVANHOE ROAD, FOXBAR, PAISLEY PA2 0LF
Tel: 01505 349758 **Fax:** 01505 349758
Owner: V. Rosike.
Fleet: 2 midicoach.
Chassis: 1 Ford Transit, 1 Freight Rover.
Ops incl: school contracts, private hire.

SHETLAND

ANDREW'S (SHETLAND) LTD
THE DYKES, WORMADALE, WHITENESS ZE2 9LJ
Tel: 01595 840292
Fax: 01595 840252
E-mail: andrews.adventures@virgin.net
Web site: www.andrewscoachhire.com
Man Dir: Morris H S Morrison
Dir: Andrew G S Morrison
Fleet: 8 - 1 single-deck bus, 2 single-deck coach, 3 midibus, 2 midicoach.
Chassis: 3 Mercedes, 1 Optare, 4 Volvo.
Bodies: 1 Caetano, 3 Mercedes, 1 Optare, 2 Plaxton, 1 Volvo.
Ops incl: local bus services, school contracts, private hire, continental tours.
Livery: Red/White
Ticket system: ERG

R G JAMIESON & SON
MOARFIELD GARAGE, CULLIVOE, YELL ZE2 9DD
Tel: 01957 744214 **Fax:** 01957 744270
E-mail: rhjamieson@hotmail.com
Partner: Robert H Jamieson
Fleet: 5 - 1 single-deck bus, 2 single-deck coach, 2 minibus, 1 midicoach.
Chassis: 1 Dennis, 2 Ford Transit, 1 MAN, 2 Mercedes.
Bodies incl: 1 Berkhof. 3 Plaxton
Ops incl: local bus services, school contracts, excursions & tours, private hire, continental tours.
Livery: White/Blue (three shades)

JOHN LEASK & SON
ESPLANADE, LERWICK ZE1 0LL
Tel: 01595 693162 **Fax:** 01595 693171
E-mail: peter.leask@leaskstravel.co.uk
Web site: www.leaskstravel.co.uk
Partners: Peter R Leask, Andrew J N Leask
Fleet: 19 - 8 single-deck bus, 6 single-deck coach, 2 midicoach, 1 minibus, 2 minicoach.
Chassis: 1 Alexander Dennis, 6 DAF, 1 Iveco, 3 Mercedes, 1 Optare, 2 Temsa, 1 VDL, 1 Volkswagen, 3 Volvo.
Bodies: 1 Alexander Dennis, 8 Ikarus, 1 Mercedes, 1 Optare, 3 Plaxton, 1 Sitcar, 2 Van Hool, 4 Wright, 1 Other.
Ops incl: local bus services, school contracts, private hire.
Livery: Ivory/Blue.
Ticket system: ERG

WHITES COACHES
ENGAMOOR, WEST BURRAFIRTH, BRIDGE OF WALLS, ZE2 9NT
Tel: 01595 809433
E-mail: john@engamoo-shetland.co.uk

Partner: John White
Fleet: 7 - 3 single-deck bus, 1 single-deck coach, 3 minibus.
Chassis: 3 Ford Transit, 3 Mercedes, Volvo.
Bodies incl: 3 Plaxton, 1 Wright
Ops incl: local bus services, school contracts, private hire.
Livery: White/Yellow/Black

SOUTH AYRSHIRE

DODDS OF TROON LTD
4 EAST ROAD, AYR KA8 9BA
Tel: 01292 288100
Fax: 01292 287700
E-mail: info@doddsoftroon.com
Web site: www.doddsoftroon.com
Man Dir: James Dodds
Ops Dir: Douglas Dodds
Admin Dir: Norma Dodds
Fleet: 23 - 2 single-deck bus, 18 single-deck coach, 3 midicoach.
Chassis: 4 Leyland, 1 Mercedes, 2 Toyota, 16 Volvo.
Bodies: 4 Alexander Dennis, 2 Caetano, 8 Jonckheere, 1 Mercedes, 2 Plaxton, 6 Van Hool.
Ops incl: school contracts, excursions & tours, express, private hire.
Livery: Green/Cream

IBT TRAVEL GROUP
CAIRN HOUSE, 15 SKYE ROAD, PRESTWICK KA9 2TA
Tel: 01292 477771 **Fax:** 01292 471770
E-mail: briant@ibtravel.com
Partner: Ian Black
Fleet: 3 single-deck coach.
Chassis: 3 Volvo
Bodies: 3 Van Hool
Ops incl: continental tours, private hire
Livery: Blue/Gold flash

KEENAN OF AYR COACH TRAVEL
DARWIN GARAGE, COALHALL, BY AYR KA6 6ND
Tel: 01292 591252 **Fax:** 01292 590980
Web site: www.keenancoaches.co.uk
Dirs: Tony Keenan, Jamie Keenan
Fleet: 20 - 2 double-deck bus, 6 single-deck bus, 10 single-deck coach, 1 midibus, 1 midicoach.
Chassis incl: 8 Leyland, 8 Volvo.
Bodies: 8 Alexander, 4 Duple, 2 Plaxton, 6 Van Hool.
Ops incl: school contracts, excursions & tours, private hire.
Livery: Red/Yellow/Orange/White

MILLIGAN'S COACH TRAVEL LTD
LOAN GARAGE, 20 THE LOAN, MAUCHLINE, KA5 6AN
Tel/Recovery: 01290 550365.
Fax: 01290 553291.
E-mail: enquiries@milliganscoachtravel.co.uk
Web site: www.milliganscoachtravel.co.uk
Dir: William J Milligan
Fleet: 20 - 18 single -deck coach, 1 midicoach, 1 minibus.
Chassis: 5 Bova, 1 DAF, 1 Ford Transit, 2 Leyland, 2 MAN, 3 Scania, 6 Volvo.
Ops incl: school contracts, excursions & tours, private hire.
Livery: Black and Silver.

STAGECOACH WEST SCOTLAND
SANDGATE, AYR KA7 1DD
Tel: 01292 613700 **Fax:** 01292 613501
Web site: www.stagecoachbus.com
Man Dir: Bryony Chamberlain
Ops Dir: Rob Jones
Eng Dir: John Harper
Fleet: 445 - 3 open-top bus, 87 double-deck bus, 140 single-deck bus, 66 single-deck coach, 86 midibus, 63 minibus.
Chassis: 82 Dennis, 26 Leyland, 1 Leyland National, 78 MAN, 23 Mercedes, 14 Neoplan, 48 Optare, 1 Scania, 172 Volvo.
Bodies: 265 Alexander Dennis, 1 ECW, 9 East Lancs, 9 Jonckheere, 11 Leyland, 14 Neoplan, 48 Optare, 84 Plaxton, 4 Wright.
Ops incl: local bus services, school contracts, private hire, express.
Livery: Stagecoach UK Bus
Ticket System: ERG

SOUTH LANARKSHIRE

ALFRA COACH HIRE
26 MACHAN ROAD, LARKHALL ML9 1HG
Tel: 01698 887581
Prop: F. Russell.
Fleet: 4 minibus.
Chassis: 2 Ford Transit, 1 Freight Rover, 1 Leyland.
Ops incl: private hire.
Livery: White.

R. & C. S. CRAIG
TOWNFOOT, ROBERTON, BY BIGGAR ML12 6RS
Tel: 01899 850655
Dirs: R. Craig, C. S. Craig
Traf Man/Ch Eng: J. Harvie
Gen Man: R. Craig.
Fleet: 3 - 2 minibus, 1 minicoach.
Chassis: Freight Rover.
Ops incl: school contracts, private hire.
Livery: White.

FIRST GLASGOW
See Glasgow, City of

HENDERSON TRAVEL
UNIT 4, WHISTLEBERRY PARK, HAMILTON ML3 0ED
Tel: 01698 710102
Fax: 01698 719110
E-mail: admin@htbuses.com
Web site: www.henderson-travel.co.uk
Ops incl: local bus services, school contracts.
Livery: Blue/White.

PARK'S OF HAMILTON LTD
14 BOTHWELL ROAD, HAMILTON ML3 0AY
Tel: 01698 281222
Fax: 01698 303731
Web site: www.parksofhamilton.co.uk
Chairman: Douglas Park
Ch Eng: Malcolm Fisher
Co Sec/Dir: Gerry Donnachie
Ops Man: Michael Andrews
Dir: Hugh McAteer.
Fleet: 100 - incl: single-deck coach, double-deck coach.
Chassis incl: Iveco, Neoplan, Volvo.
Bodies incl: Beulas, Jonckheere,
Neoplan, Plaxton, Van Hool.
Ops incl: local bus services, school contracts, excursions & tours, private hire, express, continental tours.
Livery: Black
Ticket System: Wayfarer

SILVER CHOICE
1 MILTON ROAD, EAST KILBRIDE G74 5BU
Tel: 01355 249499
Fax: 01355 265111
Recovery: 07966 315360
E-mail: enquiries@silverchoicetravel.co.uk
Web site: www.silverchoice.co.uk
Dir: David W Gardiner
Ch Eng: Jim Beaton
Fleet: 12 - 10 single-deck coach, 1 double-deck coach, 1 midicoach.
Chassis: 5 Bova, 1 Iveco, 1 Mercedes, 1 Scania, 4 Volvo.
Bodies: 1 Beulas, 5 Bova, 3 Plaxton, 3 Van Hool.
Ops incl: school contracts, excursions & tours, private hire, continental tours.
Livery: Silver

WILLIAM STOKES & SONS LTD
22 CARSTAIRS ROAD, CARSTAIRS ML11 8QD
Tel: 01555 870344 **Fax:** 01555 870601
E-mail: enquires@stokescoaches.co.uk
Web site: www.stokescoaches.co.uk
Dirs: John Stokes, Alex Stokes, William Stokes **Co Sec:** Walter Stokes
Ops incl: schools contracts, excursions & tours, private hire.
Livery: Red/Cream

STONEHOUSE COACHES
48 NEW STREET, STONEHOUSE ML9 3LT.
Tel: 01698 792145.
Prop: N. Collison
Ops incl: local bus services, school contracts, private hire.
Livery: White/Pink/Navy.

STUART'S COACHES LTD
CASTLEHILL GARAGE, AIRDRIE ROAD, CARLUKE ML8 5UF
Tel: 01555 773533
Fax: 01555 752220
E-mail: stuartscarluke@btconnect.com
Prop: Stuart Shevill **Ops Man:** Lynda Hughes **Fleet Eng:** Robert Gray
Fleet: 42 - 6 double-deck bus, 11 single-deck bus, 20 single-deck coach, 4 midicoach, 1 minibus.
Chassis: 3 Alexander Dennis, 5 Bova, 1 DAF, 1 Ford Transit, 1 Leyland, 8 Optare, 1 Scania, 17 Volvo.
Bodies: 3 Alexander, Caetano, 5 Bova, 1 Caetano, 1 Irizar, 3 Jonckheere, 8 Optare, 2 Plaxton, 4 Van Hool.
Ops incl: local bus services, school contracts, excursions and tours, private hire, express, continental tours.
Livery: Silver/Blue
Ticket system: Almex

THE RURAL DEVELOPMENT TRUST
1 POWELL STREET, DOUGLAS WATER ML11 9PP
Tel: 01555 880551
E-mail: mail@ruraldevtrust.co.uk
Web site: www.ruraldevtrust.co.uk

Man Dir: Gordon Muir.
Fleet: 10 - 1 midibus, 3 midicoach, 6 minicoach.
Chassis: 7 Mercedes, 1 Optare, 1 Toyota, 1 Other
Bodies: 1 Caetano, 6 Mercedes, 1 Optare, 1 Plaxton, 1 Other.
Ops incl: local bus services, school contracts, private hire

WHITELAWS COACHES
LOCHPARK INDUSTRIAL ESTATE, STONEHOUSE ML9 3LR
Tel: 01698 792800   **Fax:** 01698 793309
E-mail: enquiries@whitelaws.co.uk
Web site: www.whitelaws.co.uk
Man Dir/Co Sec: Sandra Whitelaw
Ginestri **Dir:** George Whitelaw
Ops Man: Lindsay McGowan
Ch Eng: Donald McGowan
Fleet: 38 - 16 single-deck bus, 11 single-deck coach, 11 midibus.
Chassis: 3 Alexander Dennis, 1 Iveco, 3 Leyland, 17 MAN, 14 Volvo.
Bodies: 6 Alexander Dennis, 9 Marshall/MCV, 2 Plaxton, 4 Van Hool, 5 Volvo, 12 Wright.
Ops incl: local bus services, school contracts, excursions & tours, private hire, continental tours.
Livery: Silver with Red/White/Blue.
Ticket System: Wayfarer TGX 150

STIRLING

ABERFOYLE COACHES LTD
MAIN STREET, ABERFOYLE FK8 3UG
Tel: 0844 567 5670
Fax: 01877 382998
E-mail: sales@aberfoylecoaches.com
Web site: www.aberfoylecoaches.com
Fleet incl: single-deck bus, single-deck coach, midicoach, minicoach.
Ops incl: local bus services, excursions & tours, private hire.
Livery: White.

BILLY DAVIES EXECUTIVE COACHES
TRANSPORT HOUSE, PLEAN INDUSTRIAL ESTATE, PLEAN, STIRLING FK7 8BJ
Tel: 01786 816627   **Fax:** 01786 811433
Web site: www.daviescoaches.com
E-mail: billy@daviescoaches.com
Prop: Billy Davies
Fleet: 11 - 4 double-deck bus, 1 single-deck bus, 5 single-deck coach, 1 midicoach.
Chassis: 1 Alexander Dennis, 1 Ayats, 2 Bova, 1 Iveco, 4 Leyland, 1 Mercedes.
Bodies incl: 1 Alexander Dennis, 1 Ayats, 1 Beulas, 2 Bova, 1 Mercedes, 1 Van Hool.
Ops incl: local bus services, school contracts, excursions & tours, private hire, continental tours.
Livery: Blue/Yellow
Ticket system: Wayfarer

BRYANS COACHES LTD
WHITEHILL FARM, DENNY FK6 5NA
Tel: 01324 824146
Ops incl: local bus services, private hire.

FERGUSON MINIBUS HIRE
33 SPEY COURT, BRAEHEAD, STIRLING FK7 7QZ
Tel/Fax: 01786 461538

E-mail: john.ferguson2@virgin.net
Ops incl: local bus services, private hire, excursions & tours.
Livery: White/Blue.

FIRST SCOTLAND EAST LTD
CARMUIRS HOUSE, 300 TIRLING ROAD, LARBERT FK5 3NJ
Tel: 01324 602200
Fax: 01324 611287
Customer Service Centre: 08708 727271
E-mail: contact.scotlandeast@firstgroup.com
Web site: www.firstgroup.com/scotlandeast
Fleet Names: First Scotland East, Midland Bluebird
Man Dir: Paul Thomas
Fleet: 419 – 155 double-deck bus, 196 single-deck bus, 10 single-deck coach, 57 midibus, 1 minicoach.
Chassis: 50 Alexander Dennis, 4 Dennis, 8 Leyland, 6 Mercedes, 167 Scania, 5 Transbus, 179 Volvo.
Bodies: 93 Alexander Dennis, 24 East Lancs, 6 Marshall/MCV, 14 Northern Counties, 5 Optare, 59 Plaxton, 4 Transbus, 214 Wright.
Ops incl: local bus services, school contracts, private hire.
Livery: FirstGroup UK Bus.
Ticket System: Almex

FITZCHARLES COACHES LTD
87 NEWHOUSE ROAD, GRANGEMOUTH FK3 8NJ
Tel: 01324 482093   **Fax:** 01324 665411
Recovery: 07753 856152
E-mail: info@fitzcharles.co.uk
Web site: www.fitzcharles.co.uk
Man Dir: George R Fitzcharles
Dir/Sec: Olive King
Ch Eng: Stewart McArthur
Fleet: 16 - 15 single-deck coach, 1 minicoach.
Chassis: 2 Ayats, 1 Mercedes, 13 Volvo.
Bodies: 2 Ayats, 4 Caetano, 6 Plaxton, 4 Sunsundegui.
Ops incl: local bus services, school contracts, excursions & tours, private hire, continental tours.
Livery: Red/Cream.
Ticket System: ERG TP5000.

HARLEQUIN COACHES LTD
8 LEEWOOD PARK, DUNBLANE FK15 ONX
Tel/Fax: 01786 822547
E-mail: harlequin@adam8.fsnet.co.uk
Web site: www.harlequincoaches-dunblane.co.uk
Man Dir: Robert Adam
Co Sec: Mrs Irene Adam
Fleet: 19 - 5 single-deck bus, 4 single-deck coach, 2 midibus, 2 midicoach, 4 minibus, 2 minicoach.
Chassis incl: 1 Bedford, 2 Iveco, 2 Mercedes, 3 Optare, 2 Toyota, 1 Volvo.
Bodies incl: 2 Caetano, 3 Optare, 1 UVG, 1 Volvo, 1 Wright.
Ops incl: local bus services, school contracts, excursions & tours, private hire, continental tours.

KELVIN VALLEY
RICHARD BRUCE HOUSE, HEAD OF MUIR, FALKIRK FK6 5NA
Tel/Fax: 01236 734883

E-mail: kvc@blueyonder.co.uk
Props: Robert B Mackenzie
Fleet: 4 midibus.
Chassis: 1 Alexander Dennis, 3 Mercedes.
Bodies: 1 Leicester, 1 Marshall/MCV, 1 Plaxton, 1 Wadham Stringer.
Ops incl: local bus services, school contracts, private hire.
Livery: Mint and Green.
Ticket System: Wayfarer TGX150.

MITCHELL'S COACHES
PRESIDENT KENNEDY DRIVE, PLEAN FK7 8AY
Tel: 01786 814319
Fax: 01786 814165
Ops incl: local bus services
Livery: White

MYLES COACHES
PLEAN INDUSTRIAL ESTATE, PLEAN FK7 8BJ
Tel: 01786 817128
E-mail: enquiries@mylescoaches.com
Web site: www.mylescoaches.com
Ops incl: local bus services, private hire.
Livery: White.

WEST DUNBARTONSHIRE

LOCHS AND GLENS HOLIDAYS
SCHOOL ROAD, GARTOCHARN G83 8RW
Tel: 01389 713713
E-mail: enquiries@lochsandglens.com
Web site: www.lochsandglens.com
Tran Man: Brian Nichols
Fleet: 23 single-deck coach
Chassis: 23 Volvo.
Bodies: 18 Jonckheere, 5 Van Hool.
Ops incl: excursions & tours
Livery: White with blue letters

McCOLL'S COACHES LTD
BALLAGAN DEPOT, STIRLING ROAD, BALLOCH G83 8IY
Tel: 01389 754321
Fax: 01389 755354
E-mail: mccolls@btconnect.com
Web site: www.mccolls.org.uk
Man Dir: William McColl
Dirs: Thomas McColl, Janet McColl
Co Sec: Ann McKinlay
Ops Man: Liam McColl
Head Mechanic: Eddie McKinley
Fleet: double-deck bus, single-deck bus, coach, minibus.
Chassis: DAF, Dennis, Ford, Ford Transit, Leyland, MCW, Mercedes, Volvo.
Bodies: MCW, Mercedes, Other.
Ops incl: local bus services, school contracts, excursions & tours, private hire.

WEST LOTHIAN

LES BROWN TRAVEL
UNIT 3, BLOCK 12, WHITESIDE INDUSTRIAL ESTATE, BATHGATE EH48 2RX
Tel: 01506 656129
Fax: 01506 656129
E-mail: les-brown@btconnect.com
Web site: www.lesbrowntravel.com
Props: Les Brown, Colin Brown
Fleet: 8 - 2 midicoach, 6 minicoach.
Chassis: 5 Ford Transit, 3 Mercedes.
Ops incl: school contracts, excursions & tours, private hire.
Livery: White with Blue, Red

BROWNINGS (WHITBURN) LTD
22 LONGRIDGE ROAD, WHITBURN EH47 0DE
Tel: 01501 740234 **Fax:** 01501 741265
E-mail: george@browningscoaches.fsnet.co.uk
Web site: www.browningscoaches.co.uk
Dirs: George Browning, Eric Browning, Gary Knox
Fleet: 15 - 3 double-deck bus, 12 single-deck coach
Chassis: 3 Alexander Dennis, 3 Leyland, 9 Volvo.
Bodies: 2 Berkhof, 1 ECW, 2 Plaxton, 5 Van Hool, 3 Wadham Stringer
Ops incl: private hire, school contracts.
Livery: Red/White/Blue.

DAVIDSON BUSES LTD
YARD 3, INCHCROSS INDUSTRIAL ESTATE, BATHGATE EH48 2HS
Tel: 01506 870226
Web Site: www.davidson-buses.com
Man Dir: Ian Davidson
Dir: Francis Gartland
Ops incl: local bus services

FIRST SCOTLAND EAST LTD
See Stirling

E & M HORSBURGH LTD
180 UPHALL STATION ROAD, PUMPHERSTON EH53 0PD
Tel: 01506 432251 **Fax:** 01506 438066
E-mail: horsburgh@btconnect.com
Web site: www.horsburghcoaches.com
Dirs: Eric Horsburgh, Mark Horsburgh
Fleet: 66 - 11 double-deck bus, 23 single-deck bus, 2 single-deck coach, 6 midibus, 4 minicoach, 22 minibus.
Chassis: 5 Dennis, 10 Ford Transit, 4 LDV, 14 Leyland, 18 Mercedes, 9 Optare.
Bodies: 4 LDV, 10 Ford, 14 Leyland, 14 Mercedes, 9 Optare, 9 Plaxton.
Ops incl: local bus services, school contracts, private hire.
Livery: Golden Yellow/White
Ticket System: Almex

McKECHNIE OF BATHGATE LTD
2 EASTON ROAD, BATHGATE EH48 2QG
Tel: 01506 654337
Fax: 01506 654337
E-mail: pmkcoach@aol.com
Dir: Peter McKechnie
Co Sec: Catherine McKechnie
Fleet: 8 - 4 single-deck coach, 2 midicoach, 2 minicoach
Chassis: 1 Leyland, 4 Mercedes, 3 Volvo.
Ops incl: school contracts, private hire.

MARTIN'S COACH TRAVEL
1 SUMMERVILLE COURT, UPHALL STATION, LIVINGSTON EH54 5QG
Tel: 01506 435968. **Fax:** 01506 435968.
E-mail: martcoach@aol.com
Web site: www.martincoaches.co.uk
Prop: Tony Martin
Fleet: 4 - 3 single-deck coach, 1 midicoach
Chassis: 1 Iveco, 1 Scania, 1 Toyota, 1 Volvo.
Bodies: 1 Beulas, 1 Caetano, 1 Irizar, 1 Other.
Ops incl: school contracts, excursions & tours, private hire.
Livery: White

PRENTICE WESTWOOD
WESTWOOD, WEST CALDER EH55 8PW
Tel/Recovery: 01506 871231
Fax: 01506 871734
E-mail: sales@prenticewestwoodcoaches.co.uk
Web site: www.prenticewestwoodcoaches.co.uk
Dirs: Robbie Prentice, David Cowen
Ops Mans: Jock Johnstone, David Reid
Fleet: 53 - 8 double-deck bus, 32 single-deck coach, 6 double-deck coach, 5 midibus, 2 midicoach.
Chassis: 9 Bova, 2 DAF, 6 Leyland, 4 MAN, 3 Mercedes, 2 Neoplan, 4 Optare, 1 Scania, 22 Volvo.
Bodies: 5 Alexander Dennis, 3 Berkhof, 9 Bova, 3 Caetano, 2 ECW, 1 Ikarus, 4 Jonckheere, 1 Mercedes, 2 Neoplan, 1 Northern Counties, 4 Optare, 12 Plaxton, 1 Sitcar, 3 Van Hool, 2 Other.
Ops incl: local bus services, school contracts, excursions & tours, private hire, continental tours.
Livery: Red/White/Blue.
Ticket System: Almex

WESTERN ISLES

COMHAIRLE NAN EILEAN SIAR
BUS COMHAIRLE, SANDWICK ROAD, STORNOWAY, ISLE OF LEWIS HS1 2BW
Tel: 01851 709728 **Fax:** 01851 709750.
Head of Service: Donald Stuart
Fleet Man: Donald Stewart
Fleet Eng: Neil McLeod
E-mail: bus@cne-siar.gov.uk
Web site: www.cne-siar.gov.uk
Fleet Name: bus na comhairle
Fleet: 13 - 7 single-deck coach, 6 midibus.
Chassis incl: 6 Mercedes
Bodies incl: 7 Plaxton.
Ops incl: local bus services, school contracts, private hire.
Livery: White/Yellow stripe

GALSON-STORNOWAY MOTOR SERVICES LTD
1 LOWER BARVAS, ISLE OF LEWIS HS2 0QZ
Tel: 01851 840269
Fax: 01851 840445
E-mail: galson@sol.co.uk
Dir: I Morrison
Ops Man: I Morrison
Fleet: 13 - 7 single-deck coach, 2 midibus, 1 midicoach, 3 minibus.
Chassis: 3 Ford Transit, 3 Mercedes, Volvo.
Bodies: 7 Plaxton, 3 Van Hool, 3 Other
Ops incl: local bus services, school contracts, excursions & tours, private hire.
Livery: White/Yellow/Brown.
Ticket System: ERG

HEBRIDEAN COACHES
HOWMORE, SOUTH UIST HS8 5SH
Tel: 01870 620345
Fax: 01870 620301
E-mail: heboc@hebrides.net
Recovery: 01870 620345
Partner: D A MacDonald
Fleet: 13 - 4 single-deck coach, 6 midibus, 3 midicoach
Chassis: 4 Dennis, 2 Ford Transit, 3 LDV, 3 Mercedes.
Bodies: 1 Duple, 2 Ford, 2 Mellor, 3 LDV, 4 Plaxton, 1 UVG
Ops incl: local bus services, school contracts, excursions & tours, private hire.
Livery: Cream/Green
Ticket System: Almex.

LOCHS MOTOR TRANSPORT LTD
CAMERON TERRACE, LEURBOST, LOCHS, ISLE OF LEWIS HS2 9PE
Tel: 01851 860288.
Fax: 01851 705857.
Dirs: C. MacDonald, R. MacDonald, S. MacDonald, A. MacDonald
Ch Eng: I. MacKinnon.
Ops incl: local bus services, school contracts, private hire.
Livery: Blue/Cream.

The Little Red Book 2011
Passenger Transport Directory for the British Isles

For information regarding advertising contact:

Graham Middleton

Tel: 01780 484632
Fax: 01780 763388

E-mail: graham.middleton@ianallanpublishing.co.uk

♿	Vehicle suitable for disabled	R24	24 hour recovery service
T	Toilet-drop facilities available		Replacement vehicle available
R	Recovery service available		Vintage Coach(es) available
	Open top vehicle(s)		
	Seat belt-fitted Vehicle		
	Coach(es) with galley facilities		
	Air-conditioned vehicle(s)		
	Coaches with toilet facilities		

The Little Red Book 2011 - in association with *tbf* Transport Benevolent Fund

ANGLESEY

ARRIVA BUSES WALES
See Conwy

CARREGLEFN COACHES
CARREGLEFN GARAGE, AMLWCH LL68 0PR
Tel: 01407 710139
Fax: 01407 710217
Prop: Alun Lewis
Fleet: 10 - 1 single-deck bus, 8 single-deck coach, 1 minicoach.
Chassis: 2 Bedford, 1 Toyota, 7 Volvo.
Bodies: 4 Caetano, 1 Duple, 5 Plaxton.
Ops incl: local bus services, school contracts, excursions & tours, private hire.
Livery: Blue/Cream

EIFION'S COACHES
MONA INDUSTRIAL PARK, GWALCHMAI LL65 4RJ
Tel: 01407 721111 **Fax:** 01407 721122
E-mail: mail@eifionscoaches.co.uk
Web site: www.eifionscoaches.co.uk
Ops incl: local bus services, school contracts, private hire, excursions & tours.
Livery: White with Red/Green/Yellow logos.

W C GOODSIR
THE GARAGE CROSS STREET, HOLYHEAD LL65 1EG
Tel: 01407 764340
Ops incl: local bus services, school contracts, private hire.
Livery: White/Black/Yellow/Orange.

GWYNFOR COACHES
ANEYLFA, 1 GREENFIELD AVENUE, LLANGEFNI LL77 7NU
Tel: 01248 722694
Prop: H. Hughes.

HDA COACHES
ARFRYN, LON GOES, GAERWEN LL60 6DR
Tel: 01248 421476
Ops incl: local bus services.

O R JONES & SONS LTD
THE BUS & COACH DEPOT, LLANFAETHLU, HOLYHEAD LL65 4NW
Tel: 01407 730204
Fax: 01407 730083
Recovery: 01407 730759
E-Mail: ioj.orj@hotmail.co.uk
Web site: www.orjones.co.uk
Ops Man: Iolo O Jones
Tran Man: Maldwyn O Jones
Fleet: 22 - 2 double-deck bus, 6 single-deck bus, 6 single-deck coach, 3 midibus, 1 midicoach, 1 minibus, 2 minicoach, 1 vintage.
Chassis: 2 Bova, 2 Bristol, 3 DAF, 1 MAN, 5 Mercedes, 5 Optare, 1 Scania, 3 Other
Bodies: 2 Bova, 1 Caetano, 2 Ikarus, 1 Irizar, 5 Mercedes, 5 Optare, 2 Plaxton, 4 Other.
Ops incl: local bus services, school contracts, excursions & tours, private hire.
Livery: Silver
Ticket system: Wayfarer

W E JONES & SON
THE GARAGE, LLANERCHYMEDD LL71 8EB
Tel: 01248 470228

Fax: 01248 852893
Props: Gwilym Evans Jones, Wyn Evans Jones
Fleet: 11 - 1 double-deck bus, 2 single-deck bus, 4 single-deck coach, 2 midibus, 2 minicoach.
Chassis: 4 DAF, 2 Dennis, 1 Ford, 1 MCW, 2 Mercedes, 2 Optare, 1 Volvo.
Bodies: 2 Alexander, 1 Carlyle, 1 Duple, 2 Mercedes, 2 Optare, 2 Plaxton, 1 Van Hool.
Ops incl: local bus services, school contracts, private hire.
Livery: Red/White

LEWIS-Y-LLAN
MADYN INDUSTRIAL ESTATE, AMLWCH LL68 9DL
Tel: 01407 832181
Fax: 01407 830112
Props: A. H. Lewis, R. M. Lewis.
Fleet: 10 - 2 double-deck bus, 4 single-deck coach, 4 midibus.
Chassis: 1 Bedford, 3 Leyland, 3 Mercedes, 2 Volvo, 1 Volkswagen.
Bodies: 1 Alexander, 1 East Lancs, 1 Jonckheere, 1 Leyland, 3 Optare, 3 Plaxton.
Livery: White/Blue.

BLAENAU GWENT

GARY'S COACHES OF TREDEGAR
42 COMMERCIAL STREET, TREDEGAR NP22 3DJ
Tel: 01495 726400
Fax: 01495 726500
Recovery: 01495 723264
E-mail: sales@garys-coaches.co.uk
Web site: www.garys-coaches.co.uk
Props: Mr & Mrs G A Lane
Ops Man: D Williams
Ch Eng: G Cresswell
Fleet: 14 - 12 single-deck coach, 1 midicoach, 1 midibus.
Chassis: 2 DAF, 1 Dennis, 1 Leyland, 2 Mercedes, 8 Volvo.
Bodies: 1 Bova, 4 Duple, 2 Mercedes, 5 Plaxton, 2 Van Hool.
Ops incl: excursions & tours, private hire, school contracts, continental tours.
Livery: White/Blue

HENLEYS BUS SERVICES LTD
HENLEYS COACH GARAGE, VICTOR ROAD, CWMTILLERY, ABERTILLERY NP13 1HU
Tel: 01495 212288
Fax: 01495 320720
E-mail: admin@henleys.org.uk
Web site: www.henleysbusservicesltd.co.uk
Dir: Martin Henley
Head Mech: Michael Henley
Sec: Daphne Henley
Fleet: 10 – 1 single-deck bus, 5 single-deck coach, 3 midibus, 1 minicoach.
Chassis: 2 Leyland, 4 Mercedes, 1 Optare, 1 Setra, 2 Volvo.
Bodies: 1 Duple, 2 Jonckheere, 1 Leicester, 1 Mercedes, 1 Optare, 3 Plaxton, 1 Setra.
Ops incl: local bus services, school contracts, excursions & tours, private hire.
Livery: White/Orange/Green
Ticket system: Wayfarer

STAGECOACH IN SOUTH WALES
See Torfaen

BRIDGEND

R & D BURROWS LTD
PENLLWYNGWENT INDUSTRIAL ESTATE, SAVILLE ROAD, OGMORE VALE CF32 7AX
Tel: 01656 840259/840345
Fax: 01656 841866
E-mail: burrowscoaches@yahoo.co.uk
Web site: www.burrowscoaches.co.uk
Man Dir & Co Sec: John G Jones
Dir: P J Jones
Fleet: 6 single-deck coach.
Chassis: 1 DAF, 1 Ford, 2 Scania, 1 Setra, 1 Volvo.
Bodies: 2 Irizar, 1 Plaxton, 1 Setra, 2 Van Hool.
Ops incl: private hire, school contracts.
Livery: Blue/Silver.

EASYWAY MINIBUS HIRE LTD
KENT ROAD, BRIDGEND INDUSTRIAL ESTATE, BRIDGEND CF31 3TU
Tel: 01656 655655
Fax: 01656 647777
E-mail: easywayminibus@aol.com
Web site: www.minicoachtravel.co.uk
Dir: R A Morris
Ops incl: local bus services.

FIRST CYMRU BUSES LTD
See City & County of Swansea

G M COACHES LTD
MOUNTAIN VIEW GARAGE, TY-FRY ROAD, CEFN CRIBWR CF32 0BB
Tel: 01656 740262 **Fax:** 01656 746040
E-mail: info@gmcoaches.com
Web site: www.gmcoaches.com
Man Dir: Carl Hookings
Dirs: Katherine Hookings, Andrea Lockwood **Co Sec:** Idris Hall
Fleet: 32 - 10 double-deck bus, 2 single-deck bus, 14 single-deck coach, 2 double-deck coach, 1 open-top bus, 1 midicoach, 1 minicoach, 1 minibus.
Chassis incl: 3 DAF, 1 Dennis, 2 MAN, 1 Mercedes, 2 Neoplan.
Bodies: 3 Alexander, 4 Berkhof, 2 ECW, 3 East Lancs, 1 Ikarus, 2 Jonckheere, 1 Marshall/MCV, 1 Mercedes, 2 Neoplan, 1 Plaxton, 10 Van Hool.
Ops incl: local bus services, school contracts, excursions & tours, private hire, continental tours.
Associated with EST Bus - see Vale of Glamorgan

GWYN JONES & SON LTD
WHITE CROFT GARAGE, BRYNCETHIN CF32 9YR
Tel: 01656 720300
Fax: 01656 725632
Recovery: 01656 720182
Chair: John Gwyn Jones
Dir: Miriam J. Jones
Fleet: single-deck coach.
Chassis: Leyland, Mercedes, Scania, Volvo.
Bodies: Berkhof, Jonckheere, Mercedes, Plaxton, Van Hool.
Ops incl: excursions & tours, private hire, continental tours, school contracts.
Livery: White/Gold/Maroon

Welsh Operators

LLYNFI COACHES
UNIT 7-9, HEOL TY GWYN INDUSTRIAL ESTATE, MAESTEG CF34 0BQ
Tel/Fax: 01656 739928
Props: David Stolzenberg, Liam Morgan
Fleet: 11 – 1 single-deck bus, 9 single-deck coach, 1 minibus.
Chassis: 4 Autosan, 1 DAF, 1 Iveco, 1 MAN, 1 Mercedes, 1 Optare, 1 Scania, 1 Volvo.
Bodies: 4 BMC, 2 Mercedes, 1 Noge, 1 Optare, 1 Plaxton, 1 Scania, 1 Van Hool.
Ops incl: local bus services, school contracts, excursions & tours, private hire.
Livery: Yellow or White

PENCOED TRAVEL LTD
18 CAER BERLLAN, PENCOED CF35 6RR
Tel: 01656 860200
Fax: 01656 864793
E-mail: info@pencoedtravel.co.uk
Web site: www.pencoedtravel.co.uk
Man Dir: Denise Cook
Ch Eng: Neil Cook **Co Sec:** Andrea Talbot
Ops: David Morris
Fleet: 10 - 2 double-deck bus, 8 single-deck coach.
Chassis: 2 Bova, 5 DAF, 3 Leyland.
Bodies: 1 Berkhof, 2 Bova, 2 Leyland, 1 Plaxton, 4 Van Hool.
Ops incl: private hire, school contracts
Livery: White/Blue

STAGECOACH IN SOUTH WALES
See Torfaen

CAERPHILLY

CASTELL COACHES LTD
UNIT 9, TRECENYDD INDUSTRIAL ESTATE, CAERPHILLY CF83 2RZ
Tel: 029 2086 1863
Fax: 029 2086 1864
Recovery: 07967 636659
E-mail: sales@castellcoaches.co.uk
Web site: www.castellcoaches.co.uk
Co Sec: Mrs S Kerslake (Tel: 07801 515119)
Dir: C Kerslake
Ops Man: B Kerslake (Tel: 07801 515117)
Fleet: 21 - 5 double-deck bus, 12 single-deck coach, 3 midicoach, 1 minibus.
Chassis: 2 Bova, 4 DAF, 6 Leyland, 4 Mercedes, 7 Volvo.
Bodies: 2 Bova, 1 Duple, 2 Jonckheere, 4 Leyland, 4 Mercedes, 6 Plaxton, 2 Van Hool.
Ops incl: excursions & tours, private hire, continental tours, school contracts.
Livery: White with multicolour

HARRIS COACHES
BRYN GWYN STREET, FLEUR-DE-LIS NP2 1RZ
Tel: 01443 832290
Man Dir: John Harris
Fleet Name: Shuttle
Ops incl: local bus services
Livery: Cream/Maroon/Red

HOWELLS COACHES LTD
UNIT 4, PENALLTA INDUSTRIAL ESTATE, HENGOED CF82 7QZ
Tel: 01443 831554
Fleet incl: double-deck bus, single-deck coach, midibus, minibus.

ISLWYN BOROUGH TRANSPORT LTD
Acquired by Stagecoach in South Wales – see Torfaen

STAGECOACH IN SOUTH WALES
See Torfaen

CARDIFF

CARDIFF BUS
SLOPER ROAD, LECKWITH, CARDIFF CF11 8TB
Tel: 029 2078 7703
Fax: 029 2078 7742
E-mail: talktous@cardiffbus.com
Web site: www.cardiffbus.com
Chairman: Cllr Joseph Carter
Man Dir: David Brown
Fin Dir/Co Sec: Cynthia Ogbonna
Dir of Service Delivery: Gareth Mole
Fleet: 233 - 13 double-deck bus, 118 single-deck bus, 19 articulated bus, 83 midibus.
Chassis: 30 Alexander Dennis, 140 Dennis, 63 Scania.
Bodies: 31 Alexander Dennis, 13 East Lancs, 139 Plaxton, 43 Scania, 7 Wright.
Ops incl: local bus services.
Livery: Blue-Green/Orange.
Ticket System: Wayfarer TGX 150.

CROESO TOURS
13 WATERLOO ROAD, PENYLAN, CARDIFF CF23 5AD
Tel: 029 2047 2313
E-mail: jmforster13@hotmail.com
Owner: John M. Forster
Fleet: 3 - 1 midicoach, 1 minibus, 1 minicoach
Chassis: 1 Iveco. 1 LDV, 1 Renault
Ops incl: private hire, school contracts.

GREYHOUND COACHES CO
COACH DEPOT, STATION TERRACE, ELY BRIDGE, CARDIFF CF5 4AA
Tel: 029 2056 1467, 2055 2767
Partners: T. James, Florence James.
Fleet: 14 - 13 single-deck coach, 1 minibus.
Chassis: 10 Bedford, 1 Ford Transit, 3 Volvo.
Ops incl: local bus services, excursions & tours, private hire.
Livery: White/Blue.

HEART OF WALES BUS & COACH LTD
YNYSFACH YARD, HEOL YR YNYS, TAFFS WELL, TONGWYNLAIS, CARDIFF CF15 7NT
Man Dir: Clayton Jones
Fleet Name: St David's Travel
Ops incl: local bus services, school contracts

NEW ADVENTURE TRAVEL LTD
UNIT 1, EXCELSIOR ROAD, EXCELSIOR INDUSTRIAL ESTATE, CARDIFF CF14 3AT
Tel: 02920 616589
Dir: Kevyn Jones
Ops incl: local bus services, private hire

STAGECOACH IN SOUTH WALES
See Torfaen

WALTONS COACHES
31 AVONDALE ROAD, GRANGETOWN CF1 7DT
Tel: 029 2039 9511
Dirs: B. J. Walton, Mrs S. F. Walton, R. J. Walton, D. McCarthy.
Fleet: 6 - 4 single-deck coach, 2 midicoach.
Chassis: Bedford, Ford, Mercedes.
Ops incl: private hire, school contracts.
Livery: Blue/White/Red.

WATTS COACHES
OLD POST GARAGE, BONVILSTON CF5 6TQ
Tel/Fax: 01446 781277
E-mail: carol.watts@eurotelonline.com
Web site: www.wattscoaches.co.uk
Prop: Clive P. Watts
Fleet: 22 - 1 double-deck bus, 15 single-deck coach, 3 double-deck coach, 3 midicoach.
Chassis: 2 Bova, 2 DAF, 2 Iveco, 2 Leyland, 2 MAN, 3 Mercedes, 6 Scania, 2 Volvo.
Bodies: 1 Ayats, 2 Beulas, 2 Berkhof, 2 Bova, 1 Duple, 1 Esker, 4 Irizar, 6 Plaxton, 1 Sitcar, 1 Van Hool.
Ops incl: school contracts, excursions & tours, private hire, continental tours.
Livery: Cream/Red/Gold.

WHEADONS GROUP TRAVEL LTD
STATION TERRACE, ELY BRIDGE, COWBRIDGE ROAD WEST, CARDIFF CF5 4AA
Tel: 029 2057 5333
Fax: 029 2057 5384
E-mail: admin@wheadons-group.co.uk
Web site: www.wheadons-group.co.uk
Chairman: E K Wheadon
Man: R Tucker
Ch Eng: S Osling
Fleet: 20 - 9 single-deck coach, 8 midicoach, 3 minibus.
Chassis: 3 LDV, 3 Mercedes, 5 Toyota, 9 Volvo.
Bodies: 1 Jonckheere, 2 Mellor, 3 Mercedes, 4 Plaxton, 4 Van Hool, 6 Other.
Ops incl: private hire, school contracts, excursions & tours.
Livery: Blue/Yellow/Silver over White.

CARMARTHENSHIRE

BYSIAU CWM TAF/TAF VALLEY COACHES
PENRHEOL, WHITLAND SA34 0NH
Tel: 01994 240908
Fax: 01994 241264
E-mail: mail@tafvalleycoaches.co.uk
Web site: www.tafvalleycoaches.co.uk
Dirs: Clive Edwards, Heather Edwards
Fleet Name: Taf Valley Coaches
Fleet: 14 - 10 single-deck coach, 2 midibus, 1 midicoach, minicoach.
Chassis: Dennis, Iveco, LDV, Leyland, Mercedes, Optare, Volvo.
Bodies: Jonckheere, Mercedes, Optare, Plaxton, Reeve Burgess, Transbus, Van Hool
Ops incl: local bus services, excursions & tours, school contracts, private hire, continental tours.
Livery: White/Silver/Blue

Welsh Operators

The Little Red Book 2011 - in association with Transport Benevolent Fund

Welsh Operators

CASTLE GARAGE LTD
BROAD STREET, LLANDOVERY
SA20 0AA
Tel: 01550 720335
Man Dir: Derek Jones
Fleet: 12 - 4 midibus, 4 midicoach, 4 minibus.
Chassis: 2 Ford Transit, 2 Freight Rover, 8 Mercedes.
Bodies: Mellor, Mercedes, Optare, Plaxton, Reeve Burgess, Wadham Stringer.
Ops incl: local bus services, school contracts, private hire.

GARETH EVANS COACHES
80 GLYN ROAD, BRYNAMMAN
SA18 1SS
Tel: 01269 823127
Fax: 01269 824533
Props: K. Davies, Mrs S. Davies.

FFOSHELIG COACHES
MAES Y PRIOR, ST PETERS, CARMARTHEN SA33 5OS
Tel: 01267 237584
Fax: 01267 236059
E-mail: ffoshelig-coaches@btconnect.com
Web site: www.ffoshelig.co.uk
Prop: Rhodri Evans
Fleet incl: single-deck coach, midibus, midicoach.
Ops incl: local bus services, private hire, excursions and tours, continental tours.
Livery: Cream with Red lettering.

FIRST CYMRU BUSES LTD
See City & County of Swansea

JONES INTERNATIONAL
STATION ROAD, LLANDEILO
SA19 6NG
Tel: 01558 822985
Fax: 01558 822984
Props: Meirion Jones, Myrddin Jones, Neil Jones **Office Man:** Carole Thompson
Ch Eng: Andrew Vale
Fleet: 7 - 2 single-deck bus, 5 single-deck coach.
Chassis: 3 DAF, 3 Leyland, 1 Volvo.
Bodies: 1 Crossley, 6 Van Hool.
Ops incl: excursions & tours, private hire, express, continental tours, school contracts.
Livery: Yellow/Blue

JONES LOGIN – TEITHIAU OSAFON/QUALITY COACH TRAVEL
LOGIN, WHITLAND SA34 0UX
Tel: 01437 563277
Fax: 01437 563393
E-mail: info@joneslogin.co.uk
Web Site: www.joneslogin.co.uk
Dirs: Endaf Jones, Arwel Jones, Ann Jones (**Co Sec**), Hannah Jones
Fleet: 16 – 1 single-deck bus, 11 single-deck coach, 1 midibus, 1 midicoach, 2 minibus.
Chassis: 6 Alexander Dennis, 2 LDV, 1 Mercedes, 1 Optare, 1 Scania, 6 Volvo.
Bodies: 1 East Lancs, 1 Irizar, 1 Optare, 12 Plaxton, 2 Other.
Ops incl: local bus services, school contracts, excursions & tours, private hire, continental tours.
Livery: Turquoise/Midnight Blue/White.
Ticket System: Setright/ERG

LEWIS COACHES WHITLAND
THE GARAGE, WHITLAND SA34 0AA
Tel: 01944 240274
E-mail: enquiries@lewiscoacheswhitland.co.uk
Web Site: www.lewiscoacheswhitland.co.uk
Dir: E Lewis
Fleet: 11 - 8 single-deck coach, 1 midibus, 2 minicoach.
Chassis: 1 Bedford, 3 Dennis, 2 LDV, 3 Leyland, 2 Volvo.
Bodies: 1 Berkhof, 1 Duple, 2 Leyland, 1 Optare, 6 Plaxton.
Livery: White with Green/Mink stripes.
Ops incl: local bus services, school contracts, private hire
Livery: White/Green with mink stripes
Ticket System: Wayfarer

MORRIS TRAVEL
ALLTYCNAP ROAD, JOHNSTOWN, CARMARTHEN SA31 3QY
Tel: 01267 235090
Fax: 01267 238183
E-mail: morristravel2000@@yahoo.co.uk
Web site: www.morristravel.co.uk
Man Dir: T J Freeman
Ops Dir: C J Freeman
Dir/Co Sec: C M Freeman
Ch Eng: P A Jones
Traffic Man: V R Shambrook
Traffic Controller: P T Davies.
Fleet: 46 - 8 single-deck bus, 31 single-deck coach, 3 midibus, 4 minibus.
Chassis: 13 Dennis, 2 LDV, 11 Leyland, 3 Mercedes, 6 Optare, 2 Renault, 9 Volvo.
Bodies: 1 Carlyle, 4 Jonckheere, 2 Marshall/MCV, 6 Optare, 16 Plaxton, 1 Reeve Burgess, 4 UVG, 12 Wadham Stringer.
Ops incl: local bus services, school contracts, private hire.
Livery: Blue/Navy/White.
Ticket System: Wayfarer

THOMAS BROS
TOWY GARAGE, LLANGADOG
SA19 9LU
Tel: 01550 777438
Fax: 01550 777807
Prop: Gareth Thomas
Fleet: 19 – single-deck coach, minibus
Ops incl: local bus services, school contracts, excursions & tours, private hire.
Livery: Cream/Green.
Ticket System: Setright.

GWYN WILLIAMS & SONS LTD
DERLWYN GARAGE, LOWER TUMBLE SA14 6HS
Tel: 01269 841312
Fax: 01269 842256
E-mail: info@gwynwilliamscoaches.com
Web site: www.gwynwilliamscoaches.com
Fleet: 27 - 3 double-deck bus, 8 single-deck bus, 17 single-deck coach, 7 minibus.
Ops incl: local bus services, school contracts, private hire, excursions & tours.
Livery: Two tone Blue/Red.

CEREDIGION

ARRIVA BUSES WALES
See Conwy

EVANS COACHES TREGARON LTD
OLD STATION YARD, TREGARON
SY25 6HX
Tel: 01974 298546
Fleet incl: single-deck coach, midibus, minibus.
Ops incl: local bus services, school contracts, private hire.

BRODYR JAMES
GLANYRAFON, LLANGEITHO, TREGARON SY25 6TT
Tel: 01974 821255 **Fax:** 01974 251618
Dirs: D E James, T M G James
Fleet: 15 - 10 single-deck coach, 2 midibus, 2 midicoach, 1 minibus.
Chassis: 5 Dennis, 1 Ford Transit, 3 Mercedes, 1 Toyota, 5 Volvo.
Bodies: 2 Caetano, 1 Jonckheere, 1 Marshall, 1 Mercedes, 8 Plaxton, 2 Reeve Burgess.
Ops incl: local bus services, school contracts, excursions & tours, private hire
Livery: White/Red/Gold.
Ticket System: Wayfarer

R J JONES TRAVEL
TYNYGRAIG, TY NANT, YSTRAD MEURIG, ABERYSTWYTH SY25 6AE
Tel: 01974 846745
Web site: www.rjjonestravelsy25.co.uk
Prop: R J Jones
Fleet incl: single-deck coach, minibus
Ops incl: school contracts, private hire.
Livery: Red & White

LEWIS COACHES
BRYNEITHIN YARD, LLANRHYSTUD
SY23 5DN
Tel/Fax: 01974 202495
E-mail: lewisgarage@btconnect.com
Prop: Gwyn R Lewis
Fleet: 18 - 2 single-deck bus, 10 single-deck coach, 1 midicoach, 2 minibus, 3 minicoach.
Chassis: 1 Bedford, 3 DAF, 1 Dennis, 1 Ford Transit, 1 Freight Rover, 3 Leyland, 2 Mercedes, 2 Optare, 3 Volvo.
Bodies: 1 Berkhof, 1 Caetano, 1 Duple, 2 Mercedes, 3 Plaxton, 3 Van Hool.
Ops incl: local bus services, private hire, excursions & tours.
Livery: White/Blue
Ticket System: Wayfarer

LEWIS-RHYDLEWIS CYF
PENRHIW-PAL GARAGE, RHYDLEWIS, LLANDYSUL SA44 5QG
Tel: 01239 851386
E-mail: post@lewis-rhydlewis.co.uk
Web site: www.lewis-rhydlewis.co.uk
Dir/Co Sec: Maldwyn Lewis
Fleet: 22 - 11 single-deck coach, 3 midibus, 5 minibus, 1 minicoach.
Chassis: 3 Bedford, 1 BMC, 3 Dennis, 5 Ford Transit, 1 Iveco, 3 Leyland, 2 Setra, 3 Volvo.
Bodies: 1 BMC, 1 Duple, 13 Plaxton, 2 Setra, 5 Other.
Ops incl: local bus services, school contracts, private hire, excursions & tours.
Livery: Cream/Red/Orange.

MID WALES TRAVEL
BRYNHYFRYD GARAGE, PENRHYNCOCH, ABERYSTWYTH SY23 3EH

Tel: 01970 828288
Fax: 01970 828940
Web: www.midwalestravel.co.uk
E-mail: enquires@midwalestravel.co.uk
Dir: J M Evans **Co Sec:** J H Morgan
Fleet: 19 - 4 single-deck bus, 14 single-deck coach, 1 midicoach.
Chassis incl: - Alexander Dennis, DAF, Dennis, Mercedes, Volvo.
Bodies incl: - Alexander Dennis, Mercedes, Plaxton, Van Hool.
Ops incl: local bus services, school contracts, excursions & tours, private hire.

RICHARDS BROS
MOYLGROVE GARAGE, PENTOOD INDUSTRIAL ESTATE,
CARDIGAN SA43 3AG
Tel: 01239 613756 **Fax:** 01239 615193
E-mail: enquiries@richardsbros.co.uk
Web site: www.richardsbros.co.uk
Gen Man: W J M Richards
Ch Eng: D N Richards
Traf Man: R M Richards
Ops Man: S M Richards
Fleet: 68 - 24 single-deck bus, 22 single-deck coach, 4 midicoach, 4 minibus, 14 midibus.
Chassis: 5 Alexander Dennis, 1 Bedford, 30 DAF, 17 Dennis, 4 LDV, 1 MAN, 8 Optare, 2 Volvo.
Bodies: 4 Alexander Dennis, 2 Autobus, 1 Caetano, 3 Carlyle, 1 Duple, 2 Ikarus, 4 LDV, 4 Marshall/MCV, 2 Northern Counties, 10 Optare, 15 Plaxton, 2 Reeve Burgess, 4 Transbus, 12 Van Hool, 3 Wright.
Ops incl: local bus services, school contracts, excursions & tours, private hire, continental tours.
Livery: Blue/White/Maroon
Ticket System: ERG

ROBERTS COACHES
UNIT 4, GLANYRAFON INDUSTRIAL ESTATE, ABERYSTWYTH SY23 3JQ
Tel: 01970 611085 **Fax:** 01970 626855
Prop: G Roberts
Fleet: 5 single-deck coach.
Chassis: 2 DAF, 3 Leyland.
Bodies: Plaxton, Duple.
Ops incl: school contracts, private hire, tours & excursions.
Livery: White or Blue

CONWY

ALPINE TRAVEL
CENTRAL COACH GARAGE,
BUILDER STREET WEST,
LLANDUDNO LL30 1HH
Tel: 01492 879133
Fax: 01492 876055
E-mail: chris@alpine-travel.co.uk
Web site: www.alpine-travel.co.uk
Dirs: Bryan Owens, Patricia Owens, Christopher Owens, Christopher Bryan Owens.
Fleet: 66 - 30 double-deck bus, 10 single-deck bus, 25 single-deck coach, 3 minicoach.
Chassis: Alexander Dennis, Autosan, Bedford, Bristol, Irisbus, Leyland, Mercedes, Volvo.
Bodies: Bova, Duple, ECW, Plaxton, Marcopolo, Mercedes.
Ops incl: local bus services, school contracts, excursions & tours, private hire, continental tours.
Livery: Red/white/Green
Ticket System: Setright.

ARRIVA BUSES WALES
IMPERIAL BUILDINGS, GLAN-Y-MOR ROAD, LLANDUDNO JUNCTION
LL31 9RU
Tel: 01492 564022 **Fax:** 01492 592968
Regional Man Dir: Phil Stone
Area Man Dir: Michael Morton
Head of Ops: Martin Robinson
Head of Eng: Nigel Cross
Business Analyst: Charys McKenzie
Fleet: 253 - 7 double-deck bus, 169 single-deck bus, 11 open-top bus, 66 midibus.
Chassis: 1 Bristol, 125 Dennis, 6 Leyland, 3 MCW, 37 Optare, 1 Scania, 64 VDL, 16 Volvo.
Bodies: 21 Alexander, 5 ECW, 6 Marshall/MCV, 3 MCW, 8 Northern Counties, 37 Optare, 102 Plaxton, 71 Wright.
Ops incl: local bus services.
Livery: Arriva UK Bus.
Ticket System: Wayfarer TGX150.

GRWP ABERCONWY
MAESDU, LLANDUDNO LL30 1HF
Tel: 01492 870870 **Fax:** 01492 860821
Fleet Name: Great Orme Tours.
Dir: I. Trevette **Tramway & Coach Man:** Rosemary Sutton.
Fleet: 4 midicoach.
Chassis: 3 Bedford, 1 Guy.
Ops incl: local bus services, excursions & tours.
Livery: Blue/Cream.
Ticket System: Almex.

LLEW JONES INTERNATIONAL
STATION YARD, LLANRWST LL26 0EH
Tel: 01492 640320 **Fax:** 01492 642040
Recovery: 07795 347476
E-mail: sales@llewjones.com
Web site: www.llewjones.com
Man Dir: Stephen Jones
Fin Dir: Eirlys Jones
Ops Man: Kevin Williams
Workshop Man: Erfyl Roberts
HR & Compliance Man: Lee Burt
Fleet: 26 - 18 single-deck coach, 6 midibus, 2 midicoach.
Chassis: 5 DAF, 2 Dennis, 1 Iveco, 1 MAN, 8 Mercedes, 4 Optare, 2 Scania, 1 Setra, 3 Volvo.

Bodies: 3 Ayats, 1 Beulas, 1 Caetano, 2 Duple, 1 Esker, 2 Irizar, 4 Mercedes, 1 Noge, 5 Optare, 4 Plaxton, 1 Setra, 2 Van Hool.
Ops incl: local bus services, school contracts, excursions & tours, private hire, continental tours.
Livery: White/Blue/Pink
Ticket system: Wayfarer TGX 150

ROBERTS MINI COACHES
RHANDIR GARAGE,
RHANDIR LL22 8BW
Tel: 01492 650449
Fleet: 4 - 3 midicoach, 1 minibus.
Chassis: 1 LDV, 3 Mercedes.
Bodies: 2 Esker, 1 Plaxton, 1 Other
Ops Inc: schools contracts, Private hire

DENBIGHSHIRE

ARRIVA BUSES WALES
See Conwy

GHA COACHES LTD
MILL GARAGE, BETWS GWERFIL GOCH, CORWEN LL21 9PU
See full entry under Wrexham

M & H COACHES
UNIT 2, BRICKWORK GARAGE,
TREFNANT, DENBIGH LL16 4UH
Tel: 01745 730700
Prop: Mrs M. Owen.
Livery: Blue/White.
Ops incl: local bus services

VOEL COACHES LTD
PENISA FILLING STATION, FFORD TALARGOCH, DYSERTH LL18 6BP
Tel: 01745 570154 **Fax:** 01745 570307
E-mail: sales@voelcoaches.com
Web site: www.voelcoaches.com
Man Dir: W M Kerfoot-Davies
Comm Man: Michelle Kerfoot Higginson.
Fleet: 25 - 7 double-deck bus, 4 single-deck bus, 12 single-deck coach, 1 minibus, 1 midicoach.
Chassis: Dennis, Mercedes, Scania, Volvo
Bodies incl: Berkhof, Van Hool.
Ops incl: local bus services, school contracts, excursions & tours, private hire, continental tours.
Livery: Orange

Welsh Operators

The Little Red Book 2011 - in association with *tbf* Transport Benevolent Fund

FLINTSHIRE

A N ANDREW COACHES
RHEWL ROAD, MOSTYN,
RUTHIN LL15 2YH
Tel: 01745 560853
Fleet: single-deck coach, midicoach.
Ops incl: school contracts, private hire.

ARRIVA BUSES WALES
See Conwy

EAGLES AND CRAWFORD
RUTHIN ROAD, MOLD CH7 5LG
Tel: 01352 700217/8 **Fax:** 01352 750211
E-mail: eaglesandcrawford@supanet.com
Partners: J. F. J. K. & W. P. Eagles.
Fleet: 15 - 6 double-deck bus,
7 single-deck coach, 2 minibus.
Chassis: 6 Bristol, 2 Dennis, 1 Freight Rover, 4 Leyland, 1 Mercedes, 1 Toyota, 1 Van Hool.
Bodies: 1 Caetano, 1 Carlyle, 3 Duple, 6 ECW, 1 Mercedes, 1 Optare, 3 Plaxton, 1 Van Hool.
Ops incl: local bus services, excursions & tours, private hire, continental tours.
Livery: White/Blue/Orange.
Ticket System: Almex.

FOUR GIRLS COACHES
THE OLD POST OFFICE YARD, CORWEN ROAD, PONTYBODKIN, MOLD CH7 4TG
Tel: 01352 770438 **Fax:** 01352 770253
E-mail: Carolyn_fg@hotmail.com
Partners: Mrs Carolyn Thomas, Mrs Elaine Williams, Gwyn Thomas, Peter Williams
Fleet: 9 - 7 single-deck coach, 1 minibus, 1 minicoach.
Chassis: 1 Mercedes, 1 Toyota, 7 Volvo.
Bodies: 1 Caetano, 1 Mercedes, 1 Van Hool, 6 Volvo.
Ops incl: school contracts, private hire.
Livery: Turquoise/Red/Yellow

H D HUTCHINSON & SON
NEWLYN, PADESWOOD ROAD, BUCKLEY CH7 2JW
Tel: 01244 543907
Ops incl: local bus services, school contracts, private hire.

JONES MOTOR SERVICES
CHESTER ROAD, FLINT CH6 5DZ
Tel: 01352 733292
Fax: 01352 763353
E-mail: tours@jonescoaches.co.uk
Web site: www.jonesholidays.co.uk
Partner: A. Jones.
Fleet: 10 - 9 single-deck coach, 1 midicoach.
Chassis: DAF, Iveco, Leyland.
Bodies: Caetano, Duple, Plaxton, Van Hool.
Ops incl: excursions & tours, private hire, express, continental tours, school contracts.
Livery: Blue.

OARE'S COACHES
TY DRAW, BRYNFORD, HOLYWELL CH8 8LP
Tel: 01352 713339 **Fax:** 01352 714871
Prop: G. A. Oare
Livery: White/Red/Silver.
Ops incl: local bus services

P. & O. LLOYD
RHYDWEN GARAGE, BAGILLT CH6 6JJ
Tel: 01352 710682
Man Dir: David Lloyd.
Fleet: 36 - 17 double-deck bus, 4 single-deck bus. 6 single-deck coach, 7 minibus.
Chassis incl: Optare, Leyland, Volvo.
Bodies incl: East Lancs, MCW, Optare, Plaxton, Van Hool.
Ops incl: local bus services, private hire, school contracts.
Livery: Cream/Red or Cream/Maroon/Gold.
Ticket System: Almex.

TOWNLYNX
CAETIA LLWYD, NORTHOP ROAD, HOLYWELL CH8 8AE
Tel: 01352 710489
Prop: S. A. Lee
Livery: White/Yellow/Blue
Ops incl: local bus services.

GWYNEDD

ARRIVA BUSES WALES
See Conwy

ARVONIA COACHES
THE SQUARE, LLANRUG LL55 4AA
Tel: 01286 675175
Fax: 01286 676406
E-mail: info@arvonia.co.uk
Web site: www.arvonia.co.uk
Prop: R. Morris.
Fleet: 4 single-deck coach
Chassis: 2 Mercedes, 1 Neoplan, 1 Setra.
Bodies: 2 Mercedes, 1 Neoplan, 1 Setra.
Ops incl: Excursions & tours, private hire, continental tours.
Livery: White/Orange/Red.
Ticket System: Almex.

CERBYDAU BERWYN COACHES
UNIT 1, TREFOR WORKSHOPS, TREFOR, CAERNARVON LL54 5LH
Tel: 01286 660315 **Fax:** 01286 660110
E-mail: berwyncoaches@aol.com
Props: Brian Japheth, Mrs Marwa Japheth.
Fleet: 20 – 3 double-deck bus, 3 single-deck bus. 6 single-deck coach, 4 midibus, 1 midicoach, 1 minibus, 2 minicoach.
Ops incl: local bus services, school contracts, private hire.
Livery: White/Yellow/Brown.

CAELLOI MOTORS (T. H. JONES & SON)
UNIT 17, GLAN Y DON INDUSTRIAL ESTATE, PWLLHELI LL53 5YT
Tel: 01758 612719
Fax: 01758 612335
E-mail: tours@caelloi.co.uk
Props: Eryl B Jones, Thomas H Jones
Fleet: 8 – 1 double-deck bus, 2 single-deck bus, 5 single-deck coach
Chassis: 1 DAF, 1 Optare, 1 Scania, 5 Volvo.
Bodies: 1 East Lancs, 1 Optare, 1 Plaxton, 4 Van Hool, 1 Wright.
Ops incl: local bus services, school contracts, excursions & tours, private hire, continental tours
Livery: Multi
Ticket System: Almex

CLYNNOG & TREFOR
TREFOR, CAERNARFON LL54 5HP
Tel: 01286 660208
Fax: 01286 660538
Dirs: D C Jones, E W Griffiths
Co Sec: I Williams
Fleet: 35 - 10 double-deck bus, 6 single-deck bus, 15 single-deck coach, 4 minibus.
Chassis: 6 Dennis, 10 Leyland, 4 Mercedes, 15 Volvo.
Bodies: 6 Alexander Dennis, 15 Jonckheere, 10 Northern Counties, 4 Plaxton.
Ops incl: local bus services, school contracts, private hire.
Livery: Red/Cream or White
Ticket system: Wayfarer TGX

EMMAS COACHES
GARTH ROAD, PENMAENPOOL, DOLGELLAU LL40 1YF
Tel/Recovery: 01341 423934
Fax: 01341 423321
E-mail: info@emmascoaches.co.uk
Web site: www.emmascoaches.co.uk
Dir: J B Thomas
Ops Man: B Thomas
Fleet: 9 - 4 single-deck coach, 3 midicoach, 2 minibus.
Ops incl: school contracts, private hire.
Livery: White/Blue, Green/Gold

EXPRESS MOTORS
THE GARAGE, LLYNFI ROAD, PENYGROES, CAERNARFON LL54 6ND
Tel: 01286 881108
Fax: 01286 882331
Recovery: 07749 844569
Web site: www.expressmotors.co.uk
E-mail: jones14@btconnect.com
Props: Eric Wyn Jones, Jean A Jones
Ops Man: Kevin Wyn Jones
Ch Eng: Ian Wyn Jones
Co Sec: Keith Jones
Fleet: 37 - 1 double-deck bus, 8 single-deck bus, 10 single-deck coach, 1 double-deck coach, 1 open-top bus, 8 midibus, 4 midicoach, 2 minicoach, 2 vintage.
Chassis: 1 Bedford OB, 2 Bristol, 3 DAF, 3 Dennis, 2 MAN, 3 Mercedes, 12 Optare, 1 Scania.
Bodies: 2 Duple, 1 ECW, 3 East Lancs, 1 Hispano, 2 Marcopolo, 2 Marshall, 3 Neoplan, 12 Optare, 1 Plaxton, 1 Scania, 3 Van Hool.
Ops incl: local bus services, school contracts, excursions & tours, private hire.
Liveries: Buses: Yellow/White; Coaches – White
Ticket System: Wayfarer 3

GRIFFITHS COACHES
3 ELIM COTTAGES, Y FELINHELI LL56 4JR
Tel: 01248 670530
Fax: 01248 671111
Prop: Hefin Griffiths
Fleet: 9 - 1 double-deck bus, 2 single-deck bus, 5 single-deck coach, 1 minibus.
Chassis: 1 Leyland, 1 Mercedes, 7 Volvo.
Bodies: 1 Jonckheere, 1 Mercedes, 4 Van Hool, 3 Other.
Ops incl: private hire, school contracts.
Livery: White

JOHN'S COACHES
NORTH WESTERN ROAD, GLAN-Y-PWLL, BLAENAU FFESTINIOG LL41 3NN
Tel: 01766 831781
Fax: 01766 831781
Prop: J R Edwards
Fleet: 6
Chassis: 1 Berkhof, 3 DAF, 2 Mercedes.
Bodies: Berkhof, Mercedes, Plaxton.
Ops incl: local bus service, school contracts, private hire.
Livery: White/Red
Ticket System: Wayfarer

NEFYN COACHES LTD
WEST END GARAGE, ST DAVIDS ROAD, NEFYN LL53 6HE
Tel: 01758 720904
Fax: 01758 720331
Dirs: B. G. Owen, M. A. Owen, A. G. Owen.
Fleet: 17 - 2 single-deck coach, 14 midibus, 1 minibus.
Chassis: 1 LDV, 11 Mercedes, 2 Optare, 1 Transbus, 2 Volvo.
Bodies: Alexander, LDV, Mellor, Optare, Plaxton, Reeve Burgess, Transbus, Van Hool.
Ops incl: local bus services, school contracts, excursions & tours, private hire.
Livery: Silver/Red/Yellow.

PADARN BUS LTD
Y GLYN INDUSTRIAL ESTATE, LLANBERIS, LL55 4EN
Tel: 01286 870880
Fax: 01286 871191
E-mail: info@padarnbus.co.uk
Web site: www.padarnbus.co.uk
Fleet Name: Padarn Bus
Man Dir: David Hulme
Ops Dir: Darren Price **Dir:** David Price
Fleet: 36 – 8 double-deck bus, 17 single-deck bus, 5 single-deck coach, 1 open top bus, 4 midibus, 1 midicoach.
Chassis: 1 Alexander Dennis, 13 Dennis, 3 Leyland, 3 MCW, 5 Mercedes, 1 Neoplan, 3 Optare, 7 Volvo.
Bodies: 9 Alexander Dennis, 1 Caetano, 2 East Lancs, 1 Jonckheere, 1 Leyland, 3 MCW, 2 Mellor, 1 Neoplan, 3 Optare, 12 Plaxton, 1 Reeve Burgess.
Ops incl: local bus services, school contracts, private hire.
Livery: Red.
Ticket System: Wayfarer 3/TGX

SILVER STAR COACH HOLIDAYS LTD
13 CASTLE SQUARE, CAERNARFON LL55 2NF
Tel: 01286 672333
Fax: 01286 678118
E-mail: enquiries@silverstarholidays.com
Web site: www.silverstarholidays.com
Man Dir: Elfyn William Thomas
Co Sec: Helen Jones **Ch Eng:** Barry Thomas **Ops Man:** Eric Wyn Thomas
Fleet: 18 - 5 single-deck bus, 9 single-deck coach, 4 midibus, 1 vintage.
Chassis: Bristol, Dennis, Leyland, Mercedes, Neoplan, Optare, Setra, Volvo.
Bodies: Alexander, Burlingham, ECW,
Neoplan, Optare, Plaxton, Setra, Van Hool.
Ops incl: local bus services, school contracts, excursions & tours, private hire, continental tours.
Livery: Green coaches/Blue buses.
Ticket System: Wayfarer 3

MERTHYR TYDFIL

SIXTY SIXTY COACHES
THE COACH DEPOT, MERTHYR INDUSTRIAL PARK, PENTREBACH CF48 4DR
Tel: 01443 692060
Fax: 01443 699061
E-mail: enquiries@sixsixty.co.uk
Web site: www.sixtysixty.co.uk
Props: G Handy, C T Handy.
Fleet: 18 - 3 single-deck bus, 9 single-deck coach, 2 double-deck coach, 3 midibus, 1 midicoach
Chassis: 6 DAF, 3 Dennis, 1 Leyland, 3 Mercedes, 2 Scania, 3 Volvo.
Bodies: 3 Alexander, 2 Caetano, 1 Duple, 3 Plaxton, 3 Reeve Burgess, 5 Van Hool, 1 LAG.
Ops incl: local bus services, school contracts, excursions & tours, private hire.
Livery: Silver
Ticket system: Wayfarer

STAGECOACH IN SOUTH WALES
See Torfaen

MONMOUTHSHIRE

CHEPSTOW CLASSIC BUSES
UNIT 6, BULWARK INDUSTRIAL ESTATE, BULWARK, CHEPSTOW NP16 5QZ
Tel/Fax: 01291 625449
E-mail: chepstowclassic@btconnect.com
Web site: www.chepstow-classic-buses.co.uk
Fleet incl: double-deck bus, single-deck bus, single-deck coach, minibus.
Ops incl: local bus services, private hire.

REES COACH TRAVEL & EUROPEAN TRAVEL
WAUNLAPRA, LLANELLY HILL, ABERGAVENNY NP7 0PW
Tel: 01873 830210
Fax: 01873 832167
Web site: reestravel@yahoo.co.uk
E-mail: info@reestravelorangehome.co.uk
Snr Partner: Neville A Rees
Partners: Nigel A Rees, Mrs Margo E Rees
Fleet: 11 - 9 single-deck coach, 1 midicoach, 1 minibus.
Chassis: 2 Alexander Dennis, 3 DAF, 1 Ford, 1 Neoplan, 1 Scania, 2 Setra, 1 Toyota.
Ops incl: local bus services, school contracts, excursions & tours, private hire, continental tours.
Livery: Green/White

STAGECOACH IN SOUTH WALES
See Torfaen

NEATH & PORT TALBOT

BLUEBIRD OF NEATH/PONTARDAWE
9-10 LONDON ROAD, NEATH SA11 1HB
Tel/Fax: 01639 643849
Fleet Name: Bluebird Coaches (Neath).
Prop: Ian S. Warren
Ch Eng: George Warren
Co Sec: Ms Melanie Evans.
Fleet: 21 - 2 double-deck bus, 18 single-deck coach, 1 midibus.
Chassis: 2 Bristol, 1 DAF, 1 Mercedes, 17 Volvo.
Bodies: 4 Jonckheere, 1 Mercedes, Leyland, 10 Plaxton, 6 Van Hool.
Ops incl: local bus services, excursions & tours, private hire, continental tours, school contracts.
Livery: White/Blue/Red.

FIRST CYMRU BUSES LTD
See City & County of Swansea

NELSON & SON (GLYNNEATH) LTD
74A HIGH STREET, GLYNNEATH SA11 5AW
Tel: 01639 720308
Fax: 01639 721949
E-Mail: nelsoncoaches@aol.com
Fleet Name: Nelson's Coaches.
Man Dir: J. L. R. Nelson
Co Sec: Mrs J Nelson
Fleet Eng: P Watkins
ran Man: G Powell
Fleet: 16 - 14 single-deck coach, 1 midicoach, 1 minicoach.
Chassis: 7 DAF, 4 Dennis, 2 Iveco, 2 Mercedes, 1 Volvo.
Bodies: 1 Berkhof, 3 Bova, 7 Plaxton, 1 Reeve Burgess, 4 Van Hool.
Ops incl: school contracts, excursions & tours, private hire.
Livery: White with Orange reliefs.

RIDGWAYS COACHES
UNIT 22, PURCELL AVENUE INDUSTRIAL ESTATE, PORT TALBOT SA12 7PT
Tel: 01639 883374

SOUTH WALES TRANSPORT (NEATH) LTD
UNIT 19, MILLAND ROAD INDUSTRIAL ESTATE, NEATH SA11 1NJ
Tel: 01639 643311
Fax: 01639 644963
E-mail: info@southwalestransport.com
Web site: www.southwalestransport.com
Ops incl: local bus services, school contracts, private hire
Livery: Green & White

	Vehicle suitable for disabled		Seat belt-fitted Vehicle	R24	24 hour recovery service
T	Toilet-drop facilities available		Coach(es) with galley facilities		Replacement vehicle available
R	Recovery service available		Air-conditioned vehicle(s)		Vintage Coach(es) available
	Open top vehicle(s)		Coaches with toilet facilities		

D J THOMAS COACHES LTD
MILLAND ROAD INDUSTRIAL ESTATE, NEATH SA11 1NJ
Tel/Fax: 01639 635502
E-mail: mail@djthomascoaches.co.uk
Web site: www.djthomascoaches.co.uk
Man Dir/Co Sec: Mrs Andrea Gibson
Man Dir: Richard Thomas
Ch Eng: Lee Gibson
Fleet: 18 - 1 single-deck bus, 9 single-deck coach, 3 minicoach, 3 midicoach, 2 minibus.
Chassis: Ford, Ford Transit Tourneo, Mercedes, Renault, Volvo.
Bodies: Berkhof, Mercedes, Plaxton, Van Hool.
Ops incl: local bus services, excursions & tours, private hire, school contracts.
Ticket system: Wayfarer

TONNA LUXURY COACHES LTD
TENNIS VIEW GARAGE, HEOL-Y-GLO, TONNA SA11 3NJ
Tel: 01639 642727
Fax: 01639 646052
Dirs: K M Hopkins, A Hopkins
Fleet: 16 single-deck coach.
Chassis: 1 DAF, 1 Dennis, 3 Mercedes, 11 Volvo.
Bodies: Alexander, Plaxton, Van Hool.
Ops incl: school contracts, private hire.
Livery: White/Blue

NEWPORT

NEWPORT TRANSPORT LTD
160 CORPORATION ROAD, NEWPORT NP19 0WF
Tel: 01633 670563
Fax: 01633 242589
Web site: www.newporttransport.co.uk
E-mail: enquiries@newporttransport.co.uk
Fleet Name: Newport Bus
Chairman: W Routley
Man Dir: C D Blyth **Fin Dir:** D Jenkins
Dir of Delivery: S Pearson
Fleet: 88 - 13 double-deck bus, 49 single-deck bus, 7 single-deck coach, 1 open-top bus, 17 midibus, 1 heritage double-deck bus.
Chassis: 17 Dennis, 1 Leyland, 6 Optare, 57 Scania, 7 Volvo.
Bodies: 36 Alexander, 7 Irizar, 1 Longwell Green, 6 Optare, 30 Scania, 8 Wright.
Ops incl: local bus services, school contracts, excursions & tours, private hire.
Livery: Green/Cream.
Ticket System: Wayfarer TGX150

STAGECOACH IN SOUTH WALES
See Torfaen

WELSH DRAGON TRAVEL
21 BEAUFORT ROAD, NEWPORT NP19 7ND
Tel: 01633 761397
E-mail: alan.smith5@ntworld.com
Prop: Alan Barrington Smith.
Fleet: 4 - 1 double-deck bus, 2 single-deck coach, 1 open-top bus.
Chassis: 1 Bedford, 1 Bristol, 2 Leyland.
Ops incl: local bus services, school contracts, private hire.
Livery: Red/Cream
Ticket System: Almex

PEMBROKESHIRE

ACORN TRAVEL LTD
SWANLEIGH, HIGH STREET, FISHGUARD SA65 9AT
Tel: 01348 874728
Fax: 01348 872797
E-mail: acorntravel@aol.com
Web site: www.acorntravel.co.uk
Ops incl: local bus services, private hire, excursions & tours.
Livery: White

W. H. COLLINS
CUFFERN GARAGE, ROCH, HAVERFORDWEST SA62 6HB
Tel: 01437 710337
Fleet Name: Collins Coaches.
Props: P. N. & M. Collins.
Fleet: 18 - 16 minibus, 2 minicoach.
Ops incl: school contracts, private hire.
Livery: Blue/Grey/White.

EDWARDS BROS
THE GARAGE, BROAD HAVEN ROAD, TIERS CROSS, HAVERFORDWEST SA62 3BZ
Tel: 01437 890230
Fax: 01437 890337
E-mail: edwardsbros@tiscali.co.uk
Prop: Robert Edwards
Fleet: 17 - 8 single-deck coach, 2 midibus, 4 midicoach, 3 minibus.
Chassis: 1 Bova, 1 Fiat, 1 LDV, 7 Mercedes, 7 Volvo.
Bodies: 1 Bova, 1 Jonckheere, 1 LDV, 1 Marshall/MCV, 3 Mercedes, 4 Plaxton, 2 Reeve Burgess, 3 Van Hool, 1 Other.
Ops incl: local bus services, school contracts, private hire.
Livery: Coaches: Gold; Contract/Service buses: White.
Ticket System: Wayfarer

FIRST CYMRU BUSES LTD
See City & County of Swansea

MIDWAY MOTORS (CRYMYCH) LTD
MIDWAY GARAGE, CRYMYCH SA41 3QU
Tel: 01239 831267
Fax: 01239 831279
E-mail: reesmidway@hotmail.com
Dirs: Elan Rees, Iwan Rees
Fleet: 15 - 3 single-deck bus, 8 single-deck coach, 2 midicoach, 1 minibus, 1 minicoach.
Chassis: 4 Dennis, 1 LDV, 4 Mercedes, 1 Setra, 1 Toyota, 4 Volvo.
Bodies: 3 Caetano, 1 LDV, 4 Mercedes, 5 Plaxton, 1 Setra, 1 Van Hool.
Ops incl: local bus services, school contracts, excursions & tours, private hire, continental tours.
Livery: Silver/Blue
Ticket system: Setright

RICHARDS BROS
MOYLGROVE GARAGE, PENTOOD INDUSTRIAL ESTATE, CARDIGAN SA43 3AG
Tel: 01239 613756
Fax: 01239 615193
E-mail: enquiries@richardsbros.co.uk
Web site: www.richardsbros.co.uk
Gen Man: W J M Richards
Ch Eng: D N Richards
Traf Man: R M Richards
Ops Man: S M Richards
Fleet: 68 - 24 single-deck bus, 22 single-deck coach, 4 midicoach, 4 minibus, 14 midibus.
Chassis: 5 Alexander Dennis, 1 Bedford, 30 DAF, 17 Dennis, 4 LDV, 1 MAN, 8 Optare, 2 Volvo.
Bodies: 4 Alexander Dennis, 2 Autobus, 1 Caetano, 3 Carlyle, 1 Duple, 2 Ikarus, 4 LDV, 4 Marshall/MCV, 2 Northern Counties, 10 Optare, 15 Plaxton, 2 Reeve Burgess, 4 Transbus, 12 Van Hool, 3 Wright.
Ops incl: local bus services, school contracts, excursions & tours, private hire, continental tours.
Livery: Blue/White/Maroon
Ticket System: ERG

SILCOX MOTOR COACH COMPANY LTD
WATERLOO GARAGE, PEMBROKE DOCK SA72 4RR
Tel: 01646 683143 **Fax:** 01646 621787
Web site: www.silcoxcoaches.co.uk
E-mail: travel@silcoxcoaches.co.uk
Man Dir: K. W. Silcox **Dir:** J Silcox
Traffic Man: H J Dix
Coach Hire Man: P Daley
Fleet: 79 - 43 single-deck bus, 20 single-deck coach, 13 midibus, 3 minibus.
Chassis: 1 Bova, 19 Dennis, 1 LDV, 31 Leyland, 1 MAN, 14 Mercedes, 5 Optare, 1 Transbus, 6 Volvo.
Bodies: 2 Berkhof, 8 Caetano, 1 Duple, 2 Marcopolo, 3 MCV, 3 Mellor, 2 Optare, 32 Plaxton, 1 Transbus, 1 UVG, 1 Van Hool, 2 Wadham Stringer, 21 Other.
Ops incl: local bus services, school contracts, excursions & tours, private hire, continental tours.
Livery: Red/Cream.
Ticket System: ERG

SUMMERDALE COACHES
SUMMERDALE GARAGE, LETTERSTON SA62 5UB
Tel: 01348 840270
Props: D. G. Davies, B. J. L. Davies, G. R. Jones.
Livery: Yellow/Blue

POWYS

A. & E. HIRE
PENYBRYN, LLANGYNIEW, WELSHPOOL SY21 0JS
Tel: 01938 810518
Dir: Arwyn P Davies
Fleet: 5 minibus
Chassis/Bodies: 4 Ford, 1 Freight Rover.
Ops incl: school contracts, private hire

A W COACHES LTD
BODAWEL GARAGE, WESLEY STREET, LLANFAIR CAEREINION SY21 0RX
Tel/Fax: 01938 810452
Dirs: A Watkins, Mrs S Watkins
Fleet: single-deck coach, minibus
Livery: Cream/Orange/Brown

ROY BROWNS COACHES
15 HIGH STREET, BUILTH WELLS LD2 3DN
Tel: 01982 552597 **Fax:** 01982 552286
E-mail: neil@rbci.fsnet.co.uk
Web site: www.roybrownscoaches.co.uk
Prop: N W Brown **Ops Man:** P H Davies

Fleet: 28 - 6 single-deck bus, 12 single-deck coach, 10 minibus.
Chassis: 4 Bedford, 5 DAF, 2 Dennis, 7 Leyland, 3 Optare, 1 Volvo
Bodies: 4 Caetano, 4 MCW, 10 Plaxton, 1 Wright, 1 other.
Ops incl: local bus services, school contracts, excursions & tours, private hire
Ticket System: Setright.

CELTIC TRAVEL
NEW STREET, LLANIDLOES SY18 6EH
Tel/Fax: 01686 412231
E-mail: info@celtictravel.net
Web site: www.celtictravel.net
Props: W P L Davies, Mrs J Davies
Ops Man: P Davies
Fleet: 22 - 15 single-deck coach, 7 minibus.
Chassis: 2 Dennis, 7 Ford Transit, 3 Leyland, 10 Volvo
Bodies: 2 Duple, 1 Jonckheere, 7 Plaxton, 3 Van Hool, 2 Wadham Stringer.
Ops incl: school contracts, excursions & tours, private hire.
Livery: Grey with green/red lettering

CENTRAL TRAVEL
OLD BULK YARD, STATION ROAD, NEWTOWN SY16 1BE
Tel: 01686 627901
Prop: R W Bowen
Fleet: 2 single-deck coach, 1 minibus
Livery: White

COOKSONS COACHES & TRAVEL
HOPE LANE, HOPE, WELSHPOOL SY21 8HF
Tel: 01938 553465
Prop: M Cookson
Fleet: single-deck coach, midicoach, minibus.
Livery: Grey with Black Lettering

R G GITTINS - COACHES
THE GARAGE, DOLANOG, WELSHPOOL SY21 0LQ
Tel/Fax: 01938 810439
E-mail: LandGGittins@aol.co.uk
Fleet: 2 midicoach
Bodies: 1 Autobus, 1 Caetano.
Ops incl: school contracts, private hire.

GOLD STAR TRAVEL
71 CLEDAN, TREOWEN, NEWTOWN SY16 1NB
Tel/Fax: 01686 628895
Web site: www.coachhirenewtown.com
Prop: H B Williams
Fleet: single-deck coach, midicoach, minibus
Livery: White with Gold & Blue Lettering

HERDMAN COACHES
HOM GARAGE, CLYRO, HAY-ON-WYE HR3 5JL
Tel: 01497 817100
Fleet: single-deck coach, minibus
Livery: Pale Blue & White

GWYN JONES (MEIFORD)
THE GARAGE, MEIFOD SY22 6DB
Tel: 01938 500249
E-mail: gwynmeifod@talk21.com
Partners: Gwyn Jones, Jean Jones, Martin Jones

Fleet: 3 - 2 single-deck bus, 1 midicoach.
Chassis/Bodies: 1 DAF, 1 Caetano, 1 Mercedes.
Ops incl: school contracts, excursions & tours, private hire, continental tours.
Livery: Green/White

LAKELINE COACHES
EBRAN-DDU, FELINDRE, KNIGHTON LD7 1YN
Tel: 01547 510234
Props: J G Reynolds, S J Reynolds
Fleet: 4 - 3 single-deck coach, 1 minibus.
Chassis: 1 Leyland, 1 LDV, 2 Volvo.
Ops incl: school contracts, private hire
Livery: Pale Blue/Dark Blue

LLOYDS COACHES
OLD CROSVILLE GARAGE, DOLL STREET, MACHYNLLETH SY20 8BH
Tel: 01654 702100
Fax: 01654 703900
E-mail: info@lloydscoaches.com
Web site: www.llyodscoaches.com
Prop: D W Lloyd
Fleet: 23 - 2 single-deck bus, 8 single-deck coach, 5 midibus. 3 midicoach, 5 minibus
Chassis: 3 Ford, 9 Mercedes, 2 Optare, 9 Volvo.
Bodies: 2 Alexander Dennis, 2 Mercedes, 2 Optare, 14 Plaxton, 3 Other.
Ops incl: local bus services, school contracts, private hire.
Livery: Silver
Ticket system: Wayfarer

OWEN'S MOTORS LTD
TEMESIDE HOUSE, STATION ROAD, KNIGHTON LD7 1DT
Tel: 01547 528303
Fax: 01547 520512
Web site: www.owensmotors.co.uk
Ops Man: D. Owen **Ch Eng:** T Owen
Sec/Dir: J Owen
Fleet: 14 - 11 single-deck coach, 3 minibus.
Chassis: 3 Dennis, 1 Ford, 2 LDV, 7 Volvo.
Bodies: 2 Duple, 1 Ford Transit, 2 LDV, 8 Plaxton, 1 Van Hool.
Ops incl: local bus services, school contracts, excursions & tours, private hire, continental tours.
Livery: Blue/Grey

RHIEW VALLEY MOTORS
TRECYNON ROAD, BERRIEW, WELSHPOOL SY21 8BG
Tel: 01686 640554
Dir: D G Haycock
Fleet: single-deck coach, midicoach, minibus
Livery: White with Gold & Blue Lettering

STAGECOACH IN SOUTH WALES
See Torfaen

STOCKHAMS COACH & TAXIS
19 PLASDERWEN, LLANGATTOCK, CRICKHOWELL NP8 1HY
Tel: 01873 810559 **Fax:** 01873 810343
Prop: Mrs Nancy Stockham
Fleet: 10- 3 single-deck coach, 3 minibus, 4 taxis.

Chassis incl: 3 Ford Transit, 3 Volvo.
Ops incl: school contracts, private hire.
Livery: Green/Cream

STRATOS TRAVEL
2 SHORTBRIDGE STREET, NEWTOWN SY16 2LW
Tel: 01686 629021
Fax: 01686 626092
E-mail: info@stratostravel.co.uk
Web site: www.stratostravel.co.uk
Prop: M Owen
Fleet: 5 - 1 single-deck bus, 3 single-deck coach, 1 midicoach.
Chassis: 1 Ayats, 1 Bova, 1 Dennis, 1 Iveco, 1 Toyota.
Bodies: 1 Ayats, 1 Beulas, 1 Bova, 1 Caetano, 1 Plaxton.
Ops incl: local bus services, excursions & tours, private hire, continental tours.
Livery: Silver/Blue
A subsidiary of Owens Coaches Ltd – see Shropshire

TANAT VALLEY COACHES
THE GARAGE, LLANRHAEDR YM MOCHNANT, OSWESTRY SY10 0AD
Tel: 01691 780212
Fax: 01691 780634
E-mail: info@tanat.co.uk
Web site: www.tanat.co.uk
Dirs: Michael Morris, Peter Morris
Ops Man: Nick Culliford
Fleet: 56 – 5 double-deck bus, 23 single-deck bus, 17 single-deck coach, 7 midibus, 1 midicoach, 2 minibus, 1 minicoach.
Chassis: 6 Alexander Dennis, 2 LDV, 10 Leyland, 9 Mercedes, 3 Neoplan, 5 Optare, 21 Volvo.
Bodies: 4 Alexander Dennis, 3 Berkhof, 1 Caetano, 2 Carlyle, 1 Duple, 1 ECW, 3 East Lancs, 3 Jonckheere, 2 LDV, 4 Leyland Lynx, 2 Mercedes, 3 Neoplan, 4 Northern Counties, 5 Optare, 8 Plaxton, 2 Reeve Burgess, 1 Sitcar, 5 UVG, 2 Wadham Stringer, 1 Wright.
Ops incl: local bus services, school contracts, excursions & tours, private hire, express.
Livery: Maroon/Mustard
Ticket System: ERG

VEOLIA TRANSPORT CYMRU PLC
See Rhondda Cynon Taf, City & County of Swansea

WEALES WHEELS
THE GRADING STATION, LLANDEWI, LLANDRINDOD WELLS, POWYS LD1 6SE
Tel: 01597 851141
Fax: 01597 850007
Prop: M Weale
Fleet: single-deck coach, minibus
Livery: White & Yellow

WILLIAMS COACHES
CAMBRIAN WAY, BRECON LD3 7BE
Tel: 01874 622223
Fax: 01874 625218
Recovery: 01874 611534
E-mail: office@williams-coaches.co.uk
Web site: www.williams-coaches.co.uk
Fleet: 30 - 17 single-deck coach, 3 midicoach, 6 minibus, 2 minicoach, 2 wheelchair accessible.
Chassis: 1 DAF, 1 Dennis, 1 Fiat, 4 Ford Transit, 1 Irisbus, 2 Iveco, 3 MAN,

9 Mercedes, 1 Neoplan, 1 Optare,
2 Renault, 5 Scania, 6 Setra,
1 Volkswagen.
Bodies inc: 1 Irizar, 1 Jonckheere,
1 Neoplan, 1 Optare, 1 Plaxton, 2 Sitcar,
5 Scania, 6 Setra, 1 Van Hool.
Ops incl: school contracts, private hire,
excursions & tours, continental tours.
Livery: Cream with Orange & Brown
Reliefs

RHONDDA CYNON TAF

EDWARDS COACHES LTD
NEWTOWN INDUSTRIAL ESTATE,
LLANTWIT FADRE CF38 2EE
Tel: 01443 202048
Fax: 01443 217583
E-mail: admin@edwardscoaches.co.uk
Web site: www.edwardscoaches.co.uk
Man Dir: Mike Edwards
Dirs: Shaun Edwards, Jason Edwards,
Kelly Edwards, Jessica Edwards
Fleet: 122 – 28 double-deck bus,
1 single-deck bus, 75 single-deck coach,
5 midibus, 3 midicoach, 10 minibus.
Chassis incl: Bova, DAF, Dennis, Ford
Transit, LDV, Leyland, MAN, MCW,
Mercedes, Scania, Setra, VDL, Volvo.
Bodies incl: Alexander, Bova, Caetano,
Duple, Ford, Irizar, Jonckheere, LDV,
MCW, Marcopolo, Marshall, Mellor,
Northern Counties, Plaxton, Setra, Sitcar,
Van Hool.
Ops incl: local bus services, school
contracts, excursions & tours, private hire,
continental tours.
Livery: White/Blue

FERRIS COACH HOLIDAYS
THE COACH HOUSE, CARDIFF ROAD,
NANTGARW CF15 7SR
Tel: 01443 844222
E-mail: sales@ferriscoachholidays.co.uk
Web site: www.ferriscoachholidays.co.uk
Dirs: J Ferris, L Ferris
Fleet: single-deck coach, double-deck
coach.
Ops incl: excursions & tours, continental
tours.

GLOBE COACHES
BROOKLANDS, FFORCHNEOL ROW,
GODREAMAN, ABERDARE CF44 6HD
Tel: 01685 873622 **Fax:** 01685 876526
E-mail:
wayne@globecoaches.entadsl.com
Web site: www.globecoaches.co.uk
Prop: Wayne Jarvis
Fleet: 18 - 16 single-deck coach,
2 midicoach.
Chassis: 2 DAF, 1 Leyland, 1 MAN,
2 Mercedes, 12 Volvo.
Bodies: 2 Berkhof, 2 Caetano, 2 Duple,
6 Jonckheere, 4 Plaxton.
Ops incl: excursions & tours, private hire,
school contracts, continental tours.
Livery: White/Blue.

MAINLINE COACHES LTD
KINGS HEAD GARAGE, GLANNANT
ROAD, EVANSTOWN CF38 8RL
Tel: 01443 670095
Fax: 01443 676695
E-mail: sales@mainlinetravel.co.uk
Web site: www.mainlinetravel.co.uk
Fleet: single-deck coach, minibus.
Ops incl: school contracts, excursions &
tours, private hire, continental tours.
Livery: Green/Yellow.

MAISEY TRAVEL
GELYNOG YARD, CASTELLAU ROAD,
BEDDAU, PONTYPRIDD CF38 2RA
Tel/Fax: 01443 205462
E-mail: info@maiseybus.co.uk
Web site: www.maiseybus.co.uk
Partners: Brian Evans, Graham Evans,
Colin Evans.
Fleet: 8 - 1 midibus, 1 minibus,
6 minicoach.
Chassis: 1 Ford Transit, 1 Iveco, 1 LDV,
5 Renault.
Bodies: 1Mellor, 7 Other.
Ops incl: school contracts, private hire.
Livery: White/Red

STAGECOACH IN SOUTH WALES
See Torfaen

THOMAS OF RHONDDA
BUS DEPOT, ABERHONDDA ROAD,
PORTH CF39 0AG
Tel: 01443 433714 **Fax:** 01443 436542
Props: W A Thomas, I G Thomas,
J E Thomas, D Thomas, T D Thomas,
A A Thomas.
Fleet: 46 - 6 double-deck bus, 3 single-
deck bus, 27 single-deck coach,
3 double-deck coach, 3 midibus,
1 midicoach, 3 minibus.
Chassis: 6 Bova, 4 BMC, 4 Dennis,
3 Ford, 1 LDV, 12 Leyland, 5 MAN,
1 Optare, 3 Scania, 7 Volvo.
Bodies: 8 Berkhof, 4 Caetano, 14 ECW,
12 East Lancs, 5 Marcopolo, 1 Mercedes,
1 Optare, 2 Van Hool.
Ops incl: local bus services, excursions
& tours, school contracts, private hire,
continental tours.
Livery: Gold
Ticket System: Almex

VEOLIA TRANSPORT CYMRU PLC
UNIT 1, HEOL CROCHENDY, PARC
NANTGARW, NANTGARW, CARDIFF
CF15 7QT
Tel: 01443 215100 **Fax:** 01443 215134
Web site: www.veolia-transport.co.uk
Chairman: John O'Brien
Man Dir: Vacant **Ch Eng:** Dave Witte
Ops incl: local bus services, school
contracts, private hire, express.
Livery: Red/White

CITY & COUNTY OF SWANSEA

DIAMOND HOLIDAYS
COACH HOLIDAY CENTRE, 22
FERRYBOAT CLOSE, SWANSEA
ENTERPRISE PARK,
SWANSEA SA6 8QN
Tel: 01792 791918
Fax: 01792 764829
E-mail:
reservations@diamondholidays.co.uk
Web site: www.diamondholidays.co.uk.
Man Dir: Chris Roberts
Ops Dir: Ryan Jones
Trans Man: Stewart Isaac
Fleet: 14 - 13 single-deck coach,
1 minibus.
Chassis: 14 DAF.
Bodies: 14 Bova.
Ops incl: excursions & tours, private hire,
express, continental tours.
Livery: Gold/Silver/Black.

FIRST CYMRU BUSES LIMITED
HEOL GWYROSYDD, PENLAN SA5 7BN
Tel: 01792 582233
Fax: 01792 561356
Web site: www.firstgroup.com
Interim Man Dir: Kevin Hart
Eng Dir: P J Davies
Fleet: 376 - 4 double-deck bus,
25 single-deck bus, 10 articulated bus,
62 single-deck coach, 266 midibus,
9 minibus.
Chassis: Alexander Dennis, BMC,
Dennis, Mercedes, Optare, Scania, Volvo.
Ops incl: local bus services, school
contracts, excursions & tours, private hire,
express.
Livery: FirstGroup UK Bus.
Ticket System: Wayfarer III

VEOLIA TRANSPORT CYMRU PLC
UNIT 41, PENCLAWDD INDUSTRIAL
ESTATE, CROFTY SA4 3RT
Tel: 01792 851430
Web site: www.veolia-transport.co.uk
Fleet: 34 - 8 single-deck bus,
25 single-deck coach, 1 minicoach.
Livery: Red/White

TORFAEN

B'S TRAVEL
13 EAST VIEW, GRIFFITHSTOWN
NP4 5DW
Tel/Fax: 01495 756889
E-mail: kay@bstravel.fsnet.co.uk
Partners: James Benning, Kay Benning.
Fleet: 4 - 1 single-deck coach,
1 midicoach, 1 minibus, 1 minicoach.
Chassis: 1 LDV, 1 MAN, 2 Mercedes.
Bodies: 1 Autobus, 1 Jonckheere,
1 Gem, 1 LDV.
Ops incl: private hire, school contracts.
Livery: White

JENSON TRAVEL
UNIT 10, PONTNEWYNDD INDUSTRIAL
ESTATE, PONTNEWYNDD,
PONTYPOOL NP4 6YW
Tel/Fax: 01495 760539
E-mail: jenson01@btconnect.com
Props: G T Jenkins, Miss N G Jenkins
Tran Man: Nicola Jenkins
Ch Eng: Peter Ryan
Fleet: 20 – 15 single-deck coach,
5 midicoach, 2 minibus.
Chassis: 6 Alexander Dennis,
9 Mercedes, 5 Volvo.
Bodies: 2 Berkhof, 1 Crest,
3 Jonckheere, 1 LDV, 3 Optare,
6 Plaxton, 1 Reeve Burgess,
3 Wadham Stringer.
Ops incl: school contracts, excursions &
tours, private hire.
Livery: Blue/White

STAGECOACH IN SOUTH WALES
1 ST DAVID'S ROAD,
CWMBRAN NP44 1PD
Tel: 01633 838856
Fax: 01633 865299
E-mail:
south.wales@stagecoachbus.com
Web site: www.stagecoachbus.com
Man Dir: John Gould
Comm Dir: Richard Davies
Eng Dir: David Howe

Fleet: 354 - 3 double-deck bus,
40 single-deck bus, 29 single-deck coach,
189 midibus, 95 minibus.
Chassis: 154 Alexander Dennis,
30 MAN, 11 Mercedes, 103 Optare,
53 Volvo.
Bodies: 153 Alexander Dennis,
7 Caetano, 110 Optare, 57 Plaxton,
14 Transbus, 10 UVG, 1 Wright, 2 Other.
Ops incl: local bus services, school contracts, express.
Livery: Stagecoach UK Bus
Ticket System: ERG

VALE OF GLAMORGAN

EST BUS LTD
UNIT 2, CROSSWAYS IND ESTATE,
LLANTWIT MAJOR ROAD,
COWBRIDGE CF71 7LJ
Tel: 01446 773333
Web site: www.estcoachbus.com
Dir: C Hookings
Ops incl: local bus services, school contracts
Livery: Maroon/Cream

HAYWARD TRAVEL (CARDIFF)
2 MURCH CRESCENT,
DINAS POWYS CF64 4RF
Tel: 029 2051 5551
Fax: 029 2051 5113
E-mail: info@haywardtravel.co.uk
Web site: www.haywardtravel.co.uk
Ops incl: private hire

WATTS COACHES
OLD POST GARAGE, BONVILSTON
CF5 6TQ
Tel/Fax: 01446 781277
E-mail: carol.watts@eurotelonline.com
Web site: www.wattscoaches.co.uk
Prop: Clive P. Watts
Fleet: 22 - 1 double-deck bus,
15 single-deck coach, 3 double-deck coach, 3 midicoach.
Chassis: 2 Bova, 2 DAF, 2 Iveco,
2 Leyland, 2 MAN, 3 Mercedes, 6 Scania,
2 Volvo.
Bodies: 1 Ayats, 2 Beulas, 2 Berkhof,
2 Bova, 1 Duple, 1 Esker, 4 Irizar,
6 Plaxton, 1 Sitcar, 1 Van Hool.
Ops incl: school contracts, excursions & tours, private hire, continental tours.
Livery: Cream/Red/Gold.

WREXHAM

ACTON COACHES
109 HERBERT JENNING AVENUE,
ACTON PARK LL12 7YA
Tel/Fax: 01978 352470
Prop: D B Evans.
Fleet: 4 - 3 single-deck coach, 1 midibus
Chassis: 1 DAF, 2 Volvo, 1 Mercedes.
Bodies: 1 Plaxton, 1 Caetano,
1 Van Hool, 1 Optare.
Livery: Blue/White
Ops incl: school contracts, private hire

ARRIVA BUSES WALES
See Conwy

GEORGE EDWARDS & SON
BERWYN, BWLCHGWYN LL11 5UE
Tel/Fax: 01978 757281
Props: G F & G Edwards.
Fleet: 4 – single-deck coaches

Ops incl: school contracts, private hire.
Livery: Red/Ivory/Maroon

GHA COACHES LTD
UNIT 11, VAUXHALL INDUSTRIAL
ESTATE, RUABON, WREXHAM
LL14 6UY
Tel: 01978 820820
E-mail: enquiries@ghacoaches.co.uk
Web site: www.ghacoaches.co.uk
Props: E G & A Lloyd Davies.
Fleet: 180 - 28 double deck bus,
26 single deck bus, 47 single-deck coach,
28 midibus, 44 minibus, 7 minicoach.
Chassis: BMC, Bova, DAF, Dennis,
Iveco, Leyland, MAN, NCW, Mercedes,
Optare, Scania, Volvo.
Bodies: Alexander, Autobus, Berkhof,
BMC, Bova, Duple, ECW, East Lancs,
Jonckheere, Marshall, MCW, Mellor,
Northern Counties, Optare, Plaxton,
Scania, UVG, Van Hool, Wright.
Ops incl: local bus services, private hire, school contracts.
Livery: Grey/Red/Maroon
Includes Bryn Melyn Motor Services,
Chaloner's, Hanmer's Coaches, Vale Travel

HAYDN'S TOURS & TRAVEL
BEVERLEY, FIELD HEAD,
CHIRK LL14 5PU.
Tel/Fax: 01691 773267
E-mail: christopherwilliams@virgin.net
Partners: M Williams, Chris Williams.
Fleet: 2 single-deck coach.
Chassis: 1 DAF, 1 Volvo.
Bodies: 1 Duple, 1 Plaxton.
Ops incl: excursions & tours, private hire, school contracts.
Livery: Red/White/Yellow/Orange
Ticket system: Wayfarer

D. JONES & SON
CENTRAL GARAGE, KING STREET,
ACREFAIR LL14 3RH
Tel: 01978 824666
Mobile: 07739 206623
Dir: David Jones
Ops Man: Gary Jones
Fleet: 12 single-deck bus
Chassis: 6 Alexander Dennis,
1 Mercedes, 5 Optare.
Bodies: 2 MCV, 5 Optare, 2 Plaxton,
3 UVG.
Ops incl: local bus services, school contracts.
Livery: Blue/White.
Ticket system: Wayfarer TGX.

E JONES & SONS
MOUNTAIN VIEW, BANK STREET,
PONCIAU LL14 1EN
Tel: 01978 841613
Props: J B & G Jones.
Fleet: 7
Livery: Blue/White/Orange.

PAT'S COACHES LTD
DERWEN HOUSE, SOUTHSEA ROAD,
SOUTHSEA, WREXHAM, LL11 6PP
Tel: 01978 720171
Fax: 01978 758459
E-mail: enquiries@patscoaches.co.uk.fsnet.co.uk
Web site: www.patscoaches.co.uk
Partners: P C Davies, J M Davies,
D K Davies
Chassis: 1 DAF, 1 LDV, 2 Mercedes,
2 Neoplan, 2 Scania, 8 Volvo.
Bodies: 1 Autobus, 4 Berkhof, 1

Jonckheere, 1 Marcopolo,
1 Marshall/MCV, 2 Mercedes, 2 Neoplan,
2 Plaxton, 1 Van Hool, 1 Wright, 1 Other.
Livery: White/Red/Yellow

PRICES COACHES
THE HAVEN, BERSHAM ROAD,
SOUTHSEA LL11 6TF
Tel/Fax: 01978 756834
Props: David Price, Terence Price
Fleet: 7 - 2 double-deck bus,
4 single-deck coach, 1 midibus
Chassis: 2 Leyland, 1 Mercedes,
1 Setra, 3 Volvo.
Bodies: 2 Leyland, 1 Kassbohrer,
1 Mercedes, 2 Plaxton, 1 Van Hool.
Ops incl: school contracts, private hire
Livery: Primrose/Green/Orange

STRAFFORDS COACHES
UNITS 7/8, FIVE CROSSES
INDUSTRIAL ESTATE, MINERA,
WREXHAM LL11 3RD
Tel: 01978 756106
Fax: 01978 722705
E-mail: info@straffordscoaches.co.uk
Web site: www.straffordscoaches.co.uk
Props: Mr & Mrs G A Strafford
Fleet: 12 - 8 single-deck coach,
4 midicoach.
Chassis incl: MAN, Mercedes, Optare, Scania.
Bodies incl: Indcar, Irizar, Van Hool
Ops incl: school contracts, private hire, excursions & tours, continental tours.
Livery: White

The Little Red Book 2011
Passenger Transport Directory for the British Isles

For information regarding advertising contact:

Graham Middleton

Tel: 01780 484632
Fax: 01780 763388

E-mail: graham.middleton@ianallanpublishing.co.uk

Ian Allan PUBLISHING

Welsh Operators

NORTHERN IRELAND

A1 COACH TRAVEL
35 NORBURGH PARK, FOYLE SPRINGS, LONDONDERRY BT48 0RG
Tel/Fax: 028 7130 9323
Prop: J. Bradshaw
Fleet: single-deck coach, midicoach
Chassis: Mercedes, VDL.
Ops incl: private hire, continental tours, school contracts.

AGNEW TRAVEL
15 TANNAGHMORE NORTH ROAD, LURGAN, Co ARMAGH BT67 9JA
Tel: 028 3832 6755
E-mail: info@agnewcoachhire.com
Web site: www.agnewcoachhire.com

AIRPORTER
QUAYSIDE SHOPPING CENTRE, STRAND ROAD, LONDONDERRY BT48 7EP
Tel: 028 7126 9996
E-mail: info@airporter.co.uk
Web site: www.airporter.co.uk
Man Dir: Niall McKeever
Dirs: Janet McKeever, Norma Smyth
Fleet: midicoach.
Chassis: Mercedes.
Ops incl: airport express.
Livery: White.

ALLEN'S TOURS
25A DONEGAL ROAD, BELFAST BT12 5JJ
Tel: 028 9091 5613
E-mail: info@allenstours.co.uk
Web site: www.allenstours.co.uk
Prop: Ben Allen
Fleet incl: open top bus, midicoach.
Ops incl: private hire, excursions & tours, sightseeing tours.

BRITTONS COACH TOURS
21 COOLERMONEY ROAD, BALLYMAGORRY, STRABANE, Co TYRONE BT82 0JX
Tel: 028 7184 1815
Web site: www.brittonscoaches.co.uk
Ops incl: excursions & tours, private hire, school contracts, continental tours.

R G J BULLICK COACH HIRE
71 NEWRY STREET, RATHFRILAND, Co DOWN BT34 5PZ
Tel: 028 4063 8006
E-mail: Ronnie@rjgbullick.co.uk
Web site: www.rjgbullick.co.uk
Fleet: single-deck coach, midicoach.
Ops incl: private hire.

CHAMBERS COACH HIRE
R24
27 HIGH STREET, MONEYMORE, MAGHERAFELT BT45 7PA
Tel: 028 8674 8152
Fax: 028 8674 8605
E-mail: mail@coachireland.com
Web site: www.coachireland.com
Chief Exec Officer: Liam Reed
Dir: Shaun Reid
Bus Dev Man: Eugene Donnelly
Fleet: 46 – 28 single-deck coach, 2 double-deck coach, 8 midicoach, 8 minicoach.
Ops incl: local bus services, school contracts, excursions & tours, private hire, continental tours.
Livery: Yellow/Black.

CROSS COUNTRY COACHES LTD
31 BALLYLINTAGH ROAD, COLERAINE BT51 3SP
Tel: 028 7086 8989
Fax: 028 7086 9191
E-mail: sales@crosscountrycoaches.com
Web site: www.crosscountrycoaches.net
Dirs: J R Telford, B Telford
Fleet: 5 - 4 single-deck coach, 1 vintage.
Chassis: 1 Bedford, 4 DAF.
Bodies: 1 Duple, 4 Van Hool.
Ops incl: school contracts, excursions & tours, private hire, continental tours.
Livery: White with Yellow/Green/Blue/Red logo

DARRAGHS COACHES
22 LISHEEGHAN ROAD, BALLYMONEY, CO ANTRIM BT53 7JY
Tel: 028 2954 0684
Fax: 028 2954 0785
Recovery: 07736 485999
E-mail: kdarragh@hotmail.co.uk
Prop: Robert Darragh
Fleet: 15 – 5 single-deck coach, 3 midicoach, 7 minibus.
Ops incl: local bus services, excursions & tours, private hire.

EUROCOACH
47 MULLAGHTEIGE ROAD, BUSH, DUNGANNON, Co TYRONE BT71 6QU
Tel: 028 8772 3031
Web site: www.eurocoachni.co.uk
Props: Sam Sinnamon, Lorna Sinnamon
Fleet: 22 – single-deck coach, midicoach, minibus.
Ops incl: school contracts, private hire, excursions & tours.
Livery: Red/Orange, White.

GILES TOURS
63 ABBEYDALE AVENUE, NEWTOWNARDS BT23 8RT
Tel/Fax: 028 9181 1099
E-mail: enquiries@gilestours.co.uk
Web site: www.gilestours.co.uk
Dirs: Neil Giles, Patricia Giles
Fleet: single-deck coach, midicoach.
Ops incl: excursions & tours, private hire, continental tours.

LAKELAND TOURS
R24
47 MAIN STREET, TEMPO, Co FERMANAGH BT94 3LU
Tel: 028 8954 1646   **Fax:** 028 8954 1424
Recovery: 07779 026597
E-mail: lakelandtours@btconnect.com
Web site: www.lakelandtour.co.uk
Prop: Ian McCutcheon
Fleet: 4 - 2 single-deck coach, 2 midicoach.
Chassis: 2 Mercedes, 2 Setra.
Bodies: 1 Autobus, 1 Esker, 2 Setra.
Ops incl: school contracts, excursions & tours, private hire.

LOGANS EXECUTIVE TRAVEL
58 GALDANAGH ROAD, DUNLOY, BALLYMENA BT44 9DB
Tel: 028 2765 7203
Fax: 028 2765 7559
E-mail: coaches@loganstravel.com
Web site: www.loganstravel.com
Prop: Sean Logan
Fleet: 40 – 21 single-deck coach, 12 midicoach, 7 minibus.
Chassis: 7 LDV, 12 Mercedes, 21 Volvo.
Ops incl: local bus services, school contracts, excursions & tours, private hire.

LYNCH COACH HIRE
80 CASTLEFIN ROAD, CASTLEDERG, Co TYRONE BT81 7EE
Tel: 028 8167 1344
Fax: 028 8167 1578
E-mail: info@lynchcoachhire.com
Web site: www.lynchcoachhire.com
Prop: Paul Lynch
Fleet: 8 – 2 single-deck coach, 4 midicoach, 2 minibus.
Chassis: 2 Ford Transit, 4 Mercedes, 2 Volvo.
Bodies: 2 Alexander Dennis, 2 Euro, 2 Van Hool.
Ops incl: school contracts, excursions & tours, private hire.

McGREAD OMAGH
110A TATTYREAGH ROAD, FINTONA, Co ARMAGH BT78 2HU
Tel: 028 8284 1731   **Fax:** 028 8284 1916
E-mail: wjdunne@lineone.net
Web site: www.mcgreadomagh.com
Props: Bill Dunne, Isabella Dunne
Fleet: 18 – single-deck coach, midibus, midicoach, minicoach.
Chassis: 1 DAF, 3 Ford Transit, 1 Iveco, 1 LDV, 9 Mercedes, 1 Renault, 1 Volkswagen, 1 Volvo.
Ops incl: excursions & tours, private hire.

ORCHARD COUNTY TRAVEL
22 ALTATURK ROAD, RICHHILL, Co ARMAGH BT61 9SG
Tel: 028 3887 9917
Fax: 028 3887 9919
Web site: www.orchardcountytravel.co.uk
Props: William Browne, Elizabeth Browne
Ops incl: school contracts, private hire, excursions & tours.

O. ROONEY COACH HIRE LTD
R24
4 DANA PLACE, HILLTOWN, NEWRY BT34 5UE
Tel: 028 4063 0825   **Fax:** 028 4063 8028
Recovery: 077721 510955
E-mail: oliver@orcoachireland.com
Web site: www.orcoachireland.com
Man Dir: Oliver Rooney
Ops Man: Aaron Rooney
Fleet: single-deck bus, single-deck coach, midibus, minibus.
Ops incl: local bus services, excursions & tours, school contracts, private hire.
Livery: White/Yellow

SLANE'S COACH & TAXI HIRE
60 DUNDALK STREET, NEWTOWNHAMILTON, Co ARMAGH BT35 0PB
Tel: 028 8308 8715
Fleet: single-deck coach, midicoach, minibus.
Ops incl: private hire.

SLOAN TRAVEL (SLO-COACHES LTD)
51 KILLOWEN OLD ROAD, ROSTREVOR, NEWRY, Co DOWN BT34 3AE
Tel: 028 4173 8568 **Fax:** 028 4173 8568
E-mail: brendanmsloan@hotmail.com
Web site: www.sloantravel.com
Dir/Ch Eng: B. M. Sloan
Sec: Ms M. Sloan
Fleet: 2 - 1 single-deck coach, 1 minibus.
Chassis/Bodies: 1 Ford, 1 Setra
Ops incl: local bus services, school contracts, excursions & tours, private hire.
Livery: Silver/Black/Red/Blue/Yellow.

SWILLY BUS SERVICE
STRAND ROAD, LONDONDERRY BT48 7PY
Tel: 00 353 74 22863
Prop: Londonderry & Lough Swilly Railway Co Ltd
Ops incl: local bus services
Livery: White (Buses)

TRANSLINK
MILEWATER ROAD, BELFAST BT3 9BG
Tel: 028 9089 9400
E-mail: feedback@translink.co.uk
Web site: www.translink.co.uk
Fleet Names: Ulsterbus, Citybus, Goldline, Metro, Ulsterbus Tours, Northern Ireland Railways
Chairman: Veronica Palmer OBE
Group Chief Exec: Catherine Mason
Chief Op Officer: Philip O'Neill
HR & Organisational Development Dir: Gordon Milligan **Fin Dir:** Stephen Armstrong **Comm & Services Dir:** David Brown **Gen Man (Bus Services):** Frank Clegg **Marketing Exec:** Ciaran Rogan
Infrastructure Exec: Clive Bradberry
Fleet: 1,382 – double-deck bus, single-deck bus, single-deck coach, double-deck coach, articulated bus, open-top bus, minibus, minicoach.
Chassis incl: Iveco, Leyland, MAN, Mercedes, Optare, Scania, Volvo.
Bodies incl: Alexander, Alexander Dennis, Ayats, Irizar, Optare, Plaxton, Sunsundegui, Van Hool, Wright.
Ops incl: local bus services, excursions & tours, school contracts, private hire, express, continental tours.
Liveries incl: Pale Blue/White (Ulsterbus), Pink/White (Citybus, Metro), Blue/Gold/White (Goldline)

TRAVELWISE COACHES
9A VICTORIA ROAD, LARNE Co ANTRIM BT40 1RY
Tel: 028 2827 8600
Fleet: single-deck coach, midicoach.

REPUBLIC OF IRELAND

AIRCOACH
AIRPORT BUSINESS PARK, DUBLIN AIRPORT, Co DUBLIN
Tel: 00 353 1 844 7118
Email: info@aircoach.ie
Web site: www.aircoach.ie
Fleet: 64 – single-deck bus, single-deck coach, open top bus, midibus.
Chassis incl: AEC, DAF, Mercedes, Optare, Scania, Setra, Volvo.
Bodies incl: East Lancs, Irizar, Jonckheere, Mercedes, Optare, Park Royal, Setra, Wright.
Ops incl: airport operations, express.
Livery: Blue
Subsidiary of First Group Plc

ALLIED COACHES
113 GRANGE WAY, BALDOYLE INDUSTRIAL ESTATE, BALDOYLE, DUBLIN D13
Tel: 00 353 1 832 8300
Fax: 00 353 1 832 8299
E-mail: info@alliedcoaches.ie
Web site: www.alliedcoaches.ie
Man Dir: Jim Nolan
Man: Seamus Nolan
Fleet: 7 - 3 single-deck coach, 2 minicoach, 2 minibus.
Chassis incl: 1 DAF, 2 Mercedes.
Bodies incl: 1 BMC, 2 Marcopolo
Ops incl: excursions & tours, private hire
Livery: Silver

ARAN TOURS LTD
14 LOWER ALBERT ROAD, SANDYCOVE, Co DUBLIN
Tel: 00 353 1 280 1899
Fax: 00 353 1 280 1799

ARDCAVAN COACH TOURS LTD
ARDCAVAN, Co WEXFORD
Tel: 00 353 53 912 2561
Fax: 00 353 53 912 3093
E-mail: info@ardcavan.com
Web site: www.ardcavan.com
Dirs: Philip O'Leary, George O'Leary
Fleet: 15 – 13 single-deck coach, 2 midicoach.
Chassis incl: Leyland, MAN, Mercedes, Setra, Van Hool, Volvo.
Bodies incl: Duple, Indcar, Jonckheere, Plaxton, Setra, Unvi, Van Hool.
Ops incl: private hire, express.
Livery: White

BARRY'S COACHES LTD
THE GLEN, MAYFIELD, CORK CITY
Tel: 00 353 21 450 5390, 450 1669 (emergencies only)
Fax: 00 353 21 450 9628
Fleet: 15 - 12 single-deck coach, 2 minibus, 1 minicoach.
Chassis: 1 AEC, 3 Bedford, 6 Leyland, 2 Mercedes, 2 Volvo.
Bodies: 7 Duple, 1 Jonckheere, 2 Mercedes, 3 Plaxton, 2 Van Hool.
Livery: Blue/White
Associated with Bernard Kavanagh & Sons, Urlingford

BARTON TRANSPORT
STRAFFAN ROAD, MAYNOOTH, Co KILDARE
Tel: 00 353 1 628 6026
Fax: 00 353 1 628 6722
E-mail: info@bartons.ie
Web site: www.bartons.ie
Man Dir: Patrick Barton
Man: Feargal Barton
Chief Eng: Brendan Barton
Fleet: 39 - 1 double-deck bus, 10 single-deck bus, 20 single-deck coach, 8 minicoach.
Chassis: 1 Autosan, 1 BMC, 23 DAF/VDL, 3 Irisbus, 1 Leyland, 2 MAN, 8 Mercedes.
Bodies: 2 Beulas, 10 Berkhof, 5 Ikarus, 12 Marcopolo, 8 Plaxton.
Ops incl: local bus services, private hire, school contracts.
Livery: Cream with Red/Blue.

BLUEBIRD COACHES LTD
72 KILBARRON DRIVE, COOLOCK, DUBLIN 5
Tel/Fax: 00 353 1 847 7896.
Dirs: Ronnie Bruen, Keith Bruen.
Fleet incl: double-deck bus, single-deck coach.
Chassis incl: Leyland, MAN, Scania.
Bodies incl: East Lancs, Irizar.
Ops incl: private hire, express, school contracts.
Livery: Cream/Red.

BUCKLEY'S TOURS LTD
WOODLANDS INDUSTRIAL ESTATE, KILLARNEY, Co KERRY
Tel: 00 353 64 663 1945
Fax: 00 353 64 663 1903
E-mail: info@buckleystours.com
Web site: www.buckleystours.com
Fleet: 41- midicoach, minicoach, minibus.
Chassis incl: Iveco, Mercedes, Volkswagen.
Ops incl: excursions & tours, private hire.
Livery: White
Associated with Kerry Coaches, Killarney

BURKE BROS (COACHES) LTD
CLARETUAM, TUAM, Co GALWAY
Tel: 00 353 93 55416
Fax: 00 353 93 55356
E-mail: burkescoaches@eircom.net
Web site: www.burkesbus.com
Dirs: P .Burke, Ms M. Burke
Ops Man: P. Steede.
Fleet: 12 - 10 single-deck coach, 2 midicoach.
Chassis incl: DAF, Mercedes, VDL.
Bodies incl: Plaxton, Van Hool.
Ops incl: local bus services, private hire, express, continental tours.
Livery: White with Blue/Orange stripes.

BUS EIREANN
BROADSTONE, PHIBSBOROUGH, DUBLIN 7
Tel: 00 353 1 703 4111
Fax: 00 353 1 830 5377
E-mail: info@buseireann.ie
Web site: www.buseireann.ie
Chairman: Dr John Lynch **Ch Exec:** Tim Hayes **Ch Op Officer:** Martin Nolan
Board Members: Dick Langford, Jim Hegarty, Mrs Tras Honan, Bill McCamley, John Moloney, John Pender, John Griffin, Susan Donohue **Co Sec:** Martin Nolan
Ch Mech Eng: Joe Neiland **Man HR:** Des Tallon **Man Sales & Marketing:** Barry Doyle
Fleet: 1300 - double-deck bus, single-deck bus, single-deck coach, double deck coach.
Chassis: Alexander Dennis, BMC, DAF, Dennis, Irisbus, Leyland, Mercedes, Optare, Scania, VDL, Volvo.
Bodies: Alexander, Alexander Dennis, BMC, Berkhof, Caetano, East Lancs, Eurocoach, Hispano, Irizar, Leicester, Leyland, Mercedes, Optare, Plaxton, Scania, Sunsundegui, Van Hool, Wright.
Ops incl: local bus services, school contracts, excursions & tours, private hire, express, continental tours.
Livery: Green/Orange/Red/White
Ticket System: Wayfarer.

BUTLERS BUSES
17 BROOKVALE, COBH, Co CORK
Tel: 00 353 21 481 1660
Fax: 00 353 21 238 0242
E-mail: ian@butlers-buses.com
Web site: www.butlers-buses.com
Prop: Ian Butler
Fleet incl: single-deck coach, midicoach, midicoach, minibus.
Chassis incl: Fiat, Mercedes, Volvo.
Ops incl: excursions & tours, private hire, continental tours.
Livery: White.

CAHALANE COACHES
UNIT 6, KILBARRY ENTERPRISE CENTRE, DUBLIN HILL, CORK
Tel: 00 353 21 430 4606
Fax: 00 353 21 430 1200
E-mail: info@cahalane-coaches.com
Web site: www.cahalane-coaches.com
Fleet incl: minicoach, midicoach, minibus.
Chassis incl: Ford Transit, Mercedes.
Ops incl: excursions & tours, private hire, continental tours.
Livery: White

CALLINAN COACHES LTD
KINISKA, GLAREGALWAY, Co GALWAY
Tel: 00 353 91 798324
Fax: 00 353 91 798962
Recovery: 00 353 87 241 3691
E-mail: info@callinancoaches.ie
Web site: www.callinancoaches.ie
Man Dir: T Callinan
Fleet: 47 - 46 single-deck coach, 1 double-deck coach.
Chassis: Scania, VDL, Volvo.
Bodies: Berkhof, Irizar, Volvo
Ops incl: excursions & tours, private hire, continental tours.
Livery: White.

CAROLAN COACH HIRE
SPIDDAL LODGE, SPIDDAL, NOBBER, Co MEATH
Tel: 00 353 46 905 2336
Fax: 00 353 46 905 2552
E-mail: info@carolancoachhire.ie
Web site: www.carolancoachhire.ie
Fleet incl: single-deck coach, midicoach, minibus, minicoach.
Ops incl: excursions & tours, private hire, continental tours.

GERRY CARROLL COACH HIRE
BALLYMAKENNY ROAD, DROGHEDA, Co LOUTH
Tel: 00 353 41 98 36074
Prop: Gerry Carroll
Dir: Patrick Carroll **Sec:** Betty Carroll
Fleet: 3 coach.
Chassis: Bedford.
Bodies: Plaxton
Ops incl: local bus services, excursions & tours, private hire.
Livery: White/Blue

CITYLINK
FORSTER STREET, GALWAY
Tel: 00 353 91 564163
E-mail: info@citylink.ie
Web site: www.citylink.ie
Man Dir: Cathy Cullen
Livery: Blue/Yellow.
A division of Metroline, part of Comfort DelGro. Service operations and fleet outsourced to Callinan Coaches Ltd.

COLLINS COACHES
DRUMCONRATH ROAD, CARRICKMACROSS, Co MONAGHAN
Tel: 00 353 42 966 1631
Fax: 00 353 42 967 2013
E-mail: info@collinscoaches.ie
Web site: www.collinscoaches.ie
Man Dir: D Collins
Fleet: 5 single-deck coach
Ops incl: excursions & tours, private hire, express.
Livery: White with Blue

CONWAY COACH AND CHAUFFEUR DRIVE LTD
RAHEEN, LIMERICK
Tel: 00 353 61 303030
Fax: 00 353 61 303202
Props: R. Conway (Gen Man), Val Conway **Prop/Ch Eng:** Patrick Conway **Prop/Sec:** Audrey Hurley
Traf Man: R. Hurley.
Fleet incl: midicoach.
Livery: White/Red.

CORCORANS EXECUTIVE TRAVEL
8 COLLEGE STREET, KILLARNEY, Co KERRY
Tel: 00 353 64 663 6666
Fax: 00 353 64 663 5666
Web site: www.corcorantours.com
Fleet incl: single-deck coach, midicoach, minibus, minicoach.
Chassis incl: MAN, Volkswagen
Ops incl: excursions & tours, private hire.
Livery: White

CORDUFF TRAVEL
ROSSPORT, BALLINA, Co MAYO
Tel: 00 353 97 88880
Fax: 00 353 97 88055
E-mail: cordufftravel@eircom.net
Web site: www.cordufftravel.ie
Ops incl: excursions & tours, private hire, express.
Incorporating Walsh's Coaches, Westport

COYLES COACHES
GWEEDORE, LETTERKENNY, Co DONEGAL
Tel: 00 353 74 953 1208
Fax: 00 353 74 953 1718

CREMIN COACHES
GEARAGH, KILKEEL, Co CORK
Tel: 00 353 86 238 5611
Fax: 00 353 27 66906
E-mail: info@cremincoaches.com
Web site: www.cremincoaches.com
Fleet incl: single-deck coach, midicoach, minibus, minicoach.
Chassis incl: DAF, Ford, Mercedes, Renault, Volvo
Ops incl: excursions & tours, private hire.
Livery: White

CRONIN'S COACHES LTD
SHANNON BUILDINGS, MALLOW ROAD, CORK
Tel: 00 353 21 430 9090
Fax: 00 353 21 430 5508
E-mail: cork@croninscoaches.com.
Web Site: www.croninscoaches.com.
Dirs: D. & Joan Cronin **Ch Eng:** Niall Cronin **Gen Man:** Nora Cronin.
Fleet: 50 - 44 single-deck coach, 3 midicoach, 3 open top bus.
Chassis: DAF, Leyland, MAN, Setra, Van Hool, Volvo.
Bodies: Jonckheere, Plaxton, Van Hool

Ops incl: private hire
Livery: Silver, White with red flash.

MARTIN CROWLEY
CLANCOOLBEG, BANDON, Co CORK
Tel/Fax: 00 353 23 42150
Fleet incl: minicoach, midicoach
Ops incl: private hire

DERO'S COACH TOURS LTD
R24
22 MAIN STREET, KILLARNEY, Co KERRY
Tel: 00 353 64 31251
Fax: 00 353 64 34077
E-mail: deroscoachtours@eircom.net
Web site: www.derostours.com
Dirs: Ms E. O'Sullivan Quille, Ms C. O'Sullivan (Sales Dir), D O'Sullivan.
Fleet incl: single-deck coach, midicoach, minicoach.
Ops incl: excursions & tours, private hire
Livery: White with multi Red/Silver/Orange.
Also relief drivers and guide agency.

DOHERTY'S COACHES
14 MAIN STREET, DUNGLOE, Co DONEGAL
Tel: 00 353 74 952 1105
Fax: 00 353 74 952 1867
E-mail: enquiries@dohertyscoaches.com
Web site: www.dohertyscoaches.com
Prop: Seamus Doherty
Fleet incl: single-deck coach, midicoach, minibus.
Chassis: Ford, Mercedes, Volkswagen.
Ops incl: local bus services, excursions & tours, private hire, express.
Livery: White

DONNELLY COACHES
46 IRISH STREET, ENNISCORTHY, Co WEXFORD
Tel: 00 353 53 923 3956
Ptnrs: James Donnelly, Mary Donnelly, Keith Donnelly
Fleet: 5- 3 midicoach, 2 minibus.
Chassis/Bodies: 2 Ford Transit, 3 Mercedes.
Ops incl: school contracts, excursions & tours, private hire.
Livery: White/Orange

DONOGHUES OF GALWAY
TARAMUID, CLARENBRIDGE, Co GALWAY
Tel: 00 353 91 776677
Fax: 00 353 91 776434
E-mail: info@donoghuesofgalway.com
Web site: www.donoghuesofgalway.com
Man Dir: Joe Donoghue
Fleet incl: single-deck coach, midicoach, minicoach.
Livery: White

DONOVAN'S COACHES LTD
HEADFORD, KILLARNEY, Co KERRY
Tel: 00 353 64 775 4041
Fax: 00 353 64 775 4041
Dirs: Joe & Maureen Donovan
Ch Eng: Joseph Donovan
Fleet: 7 - 4 single-deck coach, 1 midicoach, 2 minibus.
Chassis: 2 Ford Transit, 1 Mercedes, 4 Volvo.
Bodies: 1 Caetano, 3 Jonckheere, 1 Mercedes.
Ops incl: local bus services, school contracts, excursions & tours, private hire.

P. DOYLE LTD
ROUNDWOOD, Co WICKLOW
Tel: 00 353 1 281 8119
E-mail: willrosa@eircom.net
Web site: www.glendaloughbus.com
Fleet Name: St Kevins Bus Service
Prop/Traf Man: P. Doyle **Gen Man/Ch Eng:** J. Doyle **Sec:** John Doyle.
Fleet: 5 single-deck coach.
Chassis: DAF, Leyland, Scania, VDL.
Bodies: Plaxton, Irizar, Van Hool.
Ops incl: local bus service.
Livery: Blue/Cream.
Ticket System: Setright.

TONY DOYLE COACHES LTD
BALLYORNEY, ENNISKERRY, Co WICKLOW
Tel: 00 353 1 286 7427
Fax: 00 353 1 274 8025
E-mail: info@tonydoyle.com
Web site: www.tonydoyle.com
Dirs: Tony Doyle, Margaret Doyle
Fleet: 16 - 10 single-deck coach, 2 midicoach, 4 minicoach.
Chassis: 4 Irisbus, 3 Iveco, 5 MAN, 2 Mercedes, 2 Scania.
Bodies: 6 Beulas, 1 Esker, 4 Indcar, 2 Irizar, 3 Marcopolo.
Ops incl: excursions & tours, school contracts, private hire, continental tours.
Livery: White with Blue/Red logo.

THE DUALWAY GROUP
KEATINGS PARK, RATHCOOLE, Co DUBLIN
Tel: 00 353 1 458 0054
Fax: 00 353 1 458 0808
E-mail: info@dualwaycoaches.com
Web site: www.dualwaycoaches.com
Fleet Names: Dualway, City Sightseeing, Gray Line.
Man Dir: Anthony McConn
Gen Man: David McConn **Fin Controller:** Trish McConn **Admin Man:** Dawn Nolan
Fleet: 62 - 11 double-deck bus, 1 single-deck coach, 6 single-deck coach, 3 double-deck coach, 29 open-top bus, 4 midicoach 8 midibus.
Chassis incl: AEC, DAF, Leyland, Mercedes, VDL, Volvo.
Bodies incl: Alexander, East Lancs, Euro, Park Royal.
Ops incl: local bus services, sightseeing buses, excursions & tours, school contracts, private hire.
Livery: White, Red

DUBLIN BUS (BUS ATHA CLIATH)
59 UPPER O'CONNELL STREET, DUBLIN 1.
Tel: 00 353 1 872 0000
Fax: 00 353 1 873 1195
E-mail: info@dublinbus.ie
Web site: www.dublinbus.ie
Chairman: John Lynch
Ch Exec: Joe Meagher **Dirs:** David Egan, Bill McCamley, John Moloney, Arnold O'Byrne, Mary Mooney, Grainne Tuke, Nuala Maher **Head of Finance:** Paul O'Neill **Ch Eng:** Shane Doyle **Business Dev Man:** Paddy Doherty **Human Resources Man:** Gerry Maguire **Ops Man:** Mick Matthews
Fleet: 1,052 – 1,000 double-deck bus, 32 midibus, 20 articulated single-deck bus.
Chassis: 10 Transbus, 1,041 Volvo, 1 Wrightbus Hybrid.
Bodies: 132 Alexander, 370 Alexander Dennis, 447 Transbus, 103 Wright.

Ops incl: local bus services.
Livery: Blue/Yellow with Dublin Blue/White/Darker Blue swoosh

DUBLIN MINI COACHES & CHAUFFEUR HIRE
THE TRAVEL BANK LTD, WASDALE HOUSE, 14 CAMAC PARK, OLD NAAS ROAD, DUBLIN 12
Tel: 00 353 86 178 0049
Fax: 00 353 1 696 1001
E-mail: info.dmc@o2.ie
Web site: www.dublinminicoaches.com
Man Dir: Stephen Millar
Fleet: 12 – incl single-deck coach, midicoach, minicoach.
Chassis incl: MAN, Mercedes.
Ops incl: excursions & tours, private hire.
Livery: Blue

EIREBUS LTD
CORDUFF ROAD, BLANCHARDSTOWN, DUBLIN 15
Tel: 00 353 1 824 2626
Fax: 00 353 1 824 2627
E-mail: info@eirebus.ie
Web site: www.eirebus.ie
Man Dir: Patrick Kavanagh **Tran Man:** Derek Graham **Gen Man:** Paul Curtis
Fleet Names: Budget Bus, Flybus, Urbus
Fleet: 40 - 28 single-deck coach, 6 midibus, 6 midicoach.
Chassis incl: Irisbus, MAN, Mercedes, Optare, Scania, Toyota, Volvo.
Bodies incl: Beulas, Caetano, Euro, Indcar, Irizar, Jonckheere, Optare, Plaxton, Van Hool.
Ops incl: local bus services, excursions & tours, express, private hire.
Livery: White
A division of Bernard Kavanagh & Sons, Urlingford

ENFIELD COACHES LTD
RATHCORE, ENFIELD, Co MEATH
Tel: 00 353 46 955 5666
Fax: 00 353 46 955 5777
E-mail: info@enfield coaches.ie
Web site: www.enfieldcoaches.ie
Man Dir: J Healy
Tran Man: Ms L Healy
Fleet incl: single-deck coach, midicoach, minibus.
Ops incl: excursions & tours, private hire.
Livery: Silver

FAHERTY'S COACH HIRE
DRIMNEEN, MOYCULLEN, Co GALWAY
Tel: 00 353 91 85226
Fleet: 4 – 4 single-deck coach
Ops incl: excursions & tours, private hire.

FINEGAN COACH HIRE
29 MAIN STREET, CARRICKMACROSS, Co MONAGHAN
Tel: 00 353 42 966 1313
Fleet: 7 - 6 single-deck coach, 1 midicoach.
Ops incl: private hire.

FINLAY'S COACH HIRE
IRISH STREET, ARDEE, Co LOUTH
Tel: 00 353 41 685 6505
Fax: 00 353 41 685 7656
E-mail: finlaycoachhire@eircom.net
Web site: www.finlaybus.com
Ops incl: local bus services, school contracts, excursions & tours, private hire.
Livery: White with Blue relief.

FINNEGAN – BRAY COACH & BUS
OLDCOURT INDUSTRIAL ESTATE, BOGHALL ROAD, BRAY, Co WICKLOW
Tel: 00 353 1 286 0061
Fax: 00 353 1 286 8121
E-mail: finnegan-bray@oceanfree.net
Web site: www.finnegan-bray.ie
Dir: Eugene Finnegan
Fleet: 22 - incl double-deck bus, single-deck coach, midicoach, midibus, minibus.
Chassis incl: DAF, Dennis, MCW, Mercedes, Optare, VDL, Volvo.
Bodies incl: 1 Alexander, Ikarus, Indcar, MCW, Marcopolo, Optare, Plaxton, Van Hool.
Ops incl: local bus services, excursions & tours, school contracts, private hire.
Livery: Red

DECLAN FINNEGAN
KENMARE COACH & CAB, KENMARE, Co KERRY
Tel: 00 353 64 41491
Fax: 00 353 64 42636
E-mail: info@kenmarecoachandcab.com
Web site: www.kenmarecoachandcab.com
Fleet incl: single-deck coach, midicoach, minibus.
Ops incl: excursions & tours, private hire.

FOXHOUND TRAVEL LTD
MONAGHAN ROAD, ROCKCORRY, Co MONAGHAN
Tel: 00 353 42 974 2284
Fax: 00 353 42 974 2545
Fleet incl: single-deck coach, minibus.

MARTIN FUREY COACHES LTD
MILLTOWN, DRUMCLIFFE, Co SLIGO
Tel: 00 353 71 916 3092
Fax: 00 353 71 916 3092
E-mail: info@fureysofsligo.com
Web site: www.fureysofsligo.com
Fleet incl: single-deck coach, midicoach, minibus.
Chassis incl: Mercedes, Volvo.
Ops incl: excursions & tours, private hire.
Livery: White

GALVINS COACHES
MAIN STREET, DUNMANWAY, Co CORK
Tel: 00 353 23 45125
Fax: 00 353 23 45407
E-mail: galvinscoaches@eircom.net
Dir: R. E. Galvin
Fleet incl: single-deck coach, midicoach.
Chassis incl: Mercedes, Scania, Setra, Volvo.
Bodies incl: Euro, Irizar, Jonckheere, Setra, Unvi, Van Hool.

GALWAY CITY DIRECT LTD
MINCLOON, RAHOON ROAD, GALWAY CITY
Tel: 00 353 91 86 0814
Fax: 00 353 91 86 0815
E-mail: citydirect@eircom.net
Web site: www.citydirectgalway.com
Fleet Name: City Direct
Ops incl: local bus services
Livery: Red

GLYNNS COACHES.COM
KNOCKADERRY, TULLA ROAD, ENNIS, Co CLARE

Tel: 00 353 65 682 8234
Fax: 00 353 65 684 0678
E-mail: info@glynnscoaches.com
Web site: www.glynnscoaches.com
Dirs: Niamh Cronin, Jackie Cronin.
Fleet: 16 – 1 single-deck bus, 6 single-deck coach, 1 midibus, 2 midicoach, 1 minibus, 5 minicoach.
Chassis: 1 BMC, 3 Iveco, 4 MAN, 7 Mercedes, 1 Setra.
Bodies: 4 Beulas, 1 BMC, 4 Esker, 3 Indcar, 3 Mercedes, 1 Setra.
Ops incl: school contracts, excursions & tours, private hire.
Livery: White with Purple logo.

JAMES GLYNN
GRAIGUE NA SPIDOGUE (POST GRAIGUECULLEN), NURNEY, Co CARLOW
Tel: 00 353 503 46616
Prop/Gen Man/Traf Man: J. Glynn
Prop/Ch Eng: A. Glynn
Prop/Sec: Mrs J. Glynn.
Fleet incl: single-deck bus, single-deck coach.
Livery: Cream/Blue.

HALPENNY TRANSPORT
ASHVILLE, THE SQUARE, BLACKROCK, DUNDALK, Co LOUTH
Tel: 00 353 42 932 2023
Fax: 00 353 42 932 3742
E-mail: info@halpennytravel.com
Web site: www.halpennytravel.com
Fleet Name: Halpenny Transport
Man Dir: John Halpenny
Fleet incl: double-deck bus, single-deck bus, single-deck coach, midicoach.
Chassis: mainly Volvo.
Ops incl: local bus services, private hire, continental tours
Livery: White with Red/Blue/Green, Blue/Cream

HEALY COACHES
CASTLEGAR, GALWAY
Tel: 00 353 91 770066
Fax: 00 353 91 753335
E-mail: healybus@iol.ie
Web site: www.healytours.ie
Prop: Michael Healy, Paul Healy
Fleet incl: single-deck bus, single-deck coach, open-top bus, midicoach, midibus
Chassis incl: Dennis, Leyland, MAN, Mercedes, Scania, Volvo.
Ops incl: local bus services, excursions & tours, private hire.
Livery: White with Blue lettering

IRISH COACHES
ULSTER BANK CHAMBERS, 2-4 LOWER O'CONNELL STREET, DUBLIN 1
Tel: 00 353 1 878 8898
Fax: 00 353 1 878 8916
E-mail: dch@irishcoaches.ie
Web site: www.irishcoaches.ie
Chairman: Patrick Barton
Man Dir: D C Hughes **Dir:** Dermot Cronin
Gen Man: Ms S Curtin
Fleet incl: single-deck coach, midicoach.
Ops incl: excursions & tours, private hire, continental tours.
Livery: yellow

BERNARD KAVANAGH & SONS LTD
BRIDGE GARAGE, URLINGFORD, Co KILKENNY
Tel: 00 353 56 883 1189
Fax: 00 353 56 883 1314
E-mail: info@bkavcoaches.com
Web site: www.bkavcoaches.com.
Fleet: 50 – incl single-deck coach, midicoach, midibus, minicoach, minibus.
Chassis incl: MAN, Mercedes, Optare, Scania, Setra, Volvo.
Bodies incl: Beulas, Ikarus, Indcar, Irizar, Jonckheere, Optare, Plaxton, Setra, Sunsundegui, Van Hool.
Ops incl: local bus services, excursions & tours, private hire, express, continental tours.
Livery: White/Multi
Associated with Barry's Coaches, Eirebus, Edinburgh Coach Lines (Scotland), Matt Kavanagh Coaches

J J KAVANAGH & SONS
MAIN STREET, URLINGFORD, Co KILKENNY
Tel: 00 353 81 833 3222
Fax: 00 353 56 883 1172
E-mail: info@jjkavanagh.ie
Web site: www.jjkavanagh.ie
Joint Man Dir/Fin Cont: J. J. Kavanagh
Joint Man Dir/Ops Man: Paul Kavanagh
Maintenance Man: Edward Scully
Fleet: 90 - incl double-deck bus, single-deck bus, single-deck coach, open-top bus, midibus, midicoach.
Chassis incl: MAN, Mercedes, Optare, Setra.
Bodies incl: Indcar, Mercedes, Optare, Setra.
Ops incl: local bus services, private hire, excursions & tours, express, continental tours.
Livery: White with Blue/Green
Incorporating Kenneally's Bus Service, Waterford

MATT KAVANAGH COACHES
ROSANNA ROAD, TIPPERARY
Tel: 00 353 62 51563
Fax: 00 353 62 80808
E-mail: mattkavanagh3@aol.net
Web site: www.mattkavanagh.com
Fleet incl: single-deck coach, single-deck bus.
Ops incl: private hire, excursions & tours.
Livery: White with Blue/Yellow logo.
Associated with Bernard Kavanagh & Sons, Eirebus, Barry's Coaches

PIERCE KAVANAGH COACHES
CHURCH VIEW, URLINGFORD, Co KILKENNY
Tel: 00 353 56 883 1213
Fax: 00 353 56 883 1599
E-mail: info@kavanaghcoaches.com
Web site: www.kavanaghcoaches.com
Dirs: Pierce Kavanagh Jnr, John Kavanagh
Fleet: 32 – single-deck coach, single-deck bus, midicoach, minicoach.
Chassis incl: BMC, MAN, Mercedes, Scania, Volvo.
Bodies incl: BMC, Beulas, Indcar, Jonckheere, Sunsundegui, Van Hool.
Ops incl: private hire, excursions & tours.
Liveries: White, Red

KEENAN COMMERCIALS LTD t/a ANCHOR TOURS
BELLURGAN, DUNDALK, Co LOUTH
Tel: 00 353 42 937 1405
Fax: 00 353 42 937 1893
E-mail: bookings@anchortoursireland.com
Web site: www.anchortoursireland.com
Fleet Name: Anchor Tours
Man Dir: Seamus Keenan
Fleet: 16 - single-deck coach, midicoach, minicoach.
Ops incl: private hire, excursions & tours, continental tours.
Livery: White

KENNEDY COACHES LTD
ANNASCAUL, TRALEE, Co KERRY
Tel: 00 353 66 91 57106
Fax: 00 353 66 91 57427
E-mail: info@kennedycoaches.com
Web site: www.kennedycoaches.com
Dirs: Paddy Kennedy, Patrick Kennedy
Fleet: single-deck coach, midicoach, minicoach.
Chassis incl: Mercedes, Scania, VDL.
Bodies incl: Esker, Irizar, Unvi.
Ops incl: private hire, excursions & tours, express.

P. J. KEOGH
PK SERVICES COMPLEX, SHANNON AIRPORT, Co CLARE
Tel: 00 353 61 471111
Fax: 00 353 61 471115
E-mail: info@pktravel.com
Web site: www.pktravel.com
Fleet Name: PK Travel
Man Dir: P J Keogh
Tran Man: Mike Lawlor
Fleet: single-deck coach, midibus, midicoach, minicoach.
Ops incl: local bus services, private hire, excursions & tours, express.
Livery: White

KERRY COACHES LTD
WOODLANDS INDUSTRIAL ESTATE, KILLARNEY, Co KERRY
Tel: 00 353 64 663 1945
Fax: 00 353 64 663 1903
E-mail: info@kerrycoaches.com
Web site: www.kerrycoaches.com
Man Dir: M Buckley
Ops Man: Alan O'Connor
Fleet Names: Buckley's Tours, Kerry Tours
Fleet: 26 – single-deck coaches.
Chassis incl: MAN, Setra, Van Hool, Volvo.
Ops incl: excursions & tours, continental tours.
Livery: White

KINGDOM COACHES
2 OAKPARK DRIVE, TRALEE, Co KERRY
Tel: 00 353 64 32496
Fax: 00 353 66 718 0123
E-mail: loch@eircom.net
Web site: www.kingdomcoaches.com
Fleet Names: Kingdom Coaches, O'Shea's of Kerry
Fleet: single-deck coach, midicoach.
Chassis incl: Bova, Iveco, Mercedes.
Ops incl: excursions & tours, private hire.
Liveries: Gold, Silver.

LALLY COACHES
KINLAY HOUSE, MERCHANT'S ROAD, GALWAY
Tel: 00 353 91 562905
Fax: 00 353 91 564995

E-mail: info@lallytours.com
Web site: www.lallytours.com
Fleet: open top bus, single-deck coach, double-deck coach.
Chassis incl: Leyland, MAN, Volvo.
Ops incl: excursions & tours, private hire.
Livery: Metallic Green

DAVE LONG COACH TRAVEL LTD
CURRAGH, SKIBBEREEN, Co CORK
Tel: 00 353 28 21138

LUAS
LUAS DEPOT, RED COW ROUNDABOUT, CLONDALKIN, DUBLIN 22
Tel: 00 353 1 461 4910
Fax: 00 353 1 461 4992
E-mail: info@luas.ie **Web site:** www.luas.ie
Man Dir: Richard Dujardin
Gen Man: Brian Brennan
Fleet: 40 tram
Chassis/Bodies: Alstom Citadis
Ops: tram service
Operated by Veolia Transport Ireland Ltd

McELLIGOTT COACHES
CLARINA CROSS, CLARINA, Co LIMERICK
Tel: 00 353 61 353477
Fax: 00 353 61 353035
E-mail: McElligotts@eircom.net
Web site: www.mcelligottcoaches.com
Prop: Kevin McElligott
Transport Man: Maura Moore
Fleet: 11 – 3 single-deck coach, 4 midicoach, 4 minicoach.
Chassis: 4 Mercedes, 7 Other.
Bodies: 5 Beulas, 6 Mercedes.
Ops incl: school contracts, excursions & tours, private hire.
Livery: Silver with Red logos.

JAMES McGEE BUS HIRE
BALLINA MAIN ROAD, FALCARRAGH, LETTERKENNY, Co DONEGAL
Tel: 00 353 74 913 5174
Fleet: minibus.
Livery: White

McGEEHAN COACHES
FINTOWN, Co DONEGAL
Tel: 00 353 74 954 6150
E-mail: coaches@iol.ie
Web site: www.mcgeehancoaches.com
Fleet: 5 - single-deck coach, minibus.
Chassis incl: Mercedes, Volvo.
Ops incl: local bus services, private hire, express.
Livery: White with Black logos.

JOHN McGINLEY COACH TRAVEL
MAGHEROARTY, GORTAHORK, LETTERKENNY, Co DONEGAL
Tel: 00 353 74 913 5201
Fax: 00 353 74 913 5960
E-mail: info@johnmcginley.com
Web site: www.johnmcginley.com
Prop: James McGinley
Fleet: 21 – single-deck coach, minibus.
Chassis: Ford Transit, Mercedes, Volvo.
Bodies: Jonckheere, Plaxton, Van Hool.
Ops incl: local bus services, excursions & tours, continental tours, school contracts, private hire, express, continental tours.
Liveries: White with Blue/Orange; Black/Yellow.

J J McGONAGLE
CLAR, REDCASTLE, Co DONEGAL
Tel: 00 353 74 938 2116
Fax: 00 353 74 938 2619
E-mail: foylecoaches@eircom.net
Web site: www.foylecoaches.com
Fleet Names: Foyle Coaches, North West Busways
Fleet: single-deck coach, midibus, midicoach, minibus.
Ops incl: local bus services, private hire, excursions & tours.
Liveries: Coaches: White with Red/Orange/Yellow; Buses: Red.

MALAHIDE COACHES LTD
ST JOSEPHS, COAST ROAD, MALAHIDE, Co DUBLIN
Tel: 00 353 1 845 3809
Fax: 00 353 1 845 3099
Web site: www.malahidecoaches.com
Fleet: 18 – double-deck bus, single-deck bus, single-deck coach, midibus, midicoach.
Ops incl: private hire, excursions & tours, school contracts.
Livery: Blue

MANNING'S COACHES
CASTLE ROAD, CROOM, LIMERICK
Tel: 00 353 61 397311
Fax: 00 353 61 397931
E-mail: info@manningscoaches.com
Web site: www.manningscoaches.com
Fleet: 23 – single-deck coach, midibus, midicoach, minibus.
Ops incl: excursions & tours, private hire, continental tours.
Livery: White with logos.

ALAN MARTIN COACHES
13 ROSEMOUNT BUSINESS PARK, DUBLIN 11
Tel: 00 353 1 822 1122
Fax: 00 353 1 820 9364
E-mail: helpdesk@amconline.ie
Web site: www.amconline.ie
Dirs: A. Martin, B. C. Martin
Ch Eng: M. Reilly
Traf Man: M. Clarke.
Fleet Name: AMC Coaches
Fleet: double-deck bus, single-deck bus, single-deck coach, midibus, minibus.
Ops incl: local bus services, school contracts, excursions & tours, private hire, express.
Livery: White with Red logos.

MARTIN'S COACHES (CAVAN) LTD
CORRATILLION, CORLOUGH, BELTURBET, Co CAVAN
Tel: 00 353 49 952 6222
Fax: 00 353 49 952 3116
E-mail: jimmartin@eircom.net
Dirs: James G Martin Snr, James G Martin Jnr, Derek Martin, Alan Martin.
Fleet: 16 - 4 single-deck bus, 6 midicoach, 6 minibus.
Chassis: 4 DAF, 6 Ford Transit, 6 Mercedes.
Bodies incl: 1 Caetano, 6 Ford Transit, 2 Marcopolo, 6 Mercedes, 1 Plaxton.
Ops incl: local bus services, school contracts, private hire.

DICK MARTIN COACHES
UNIT 7, ANNACOTTY BUSINESS PARK, ANNACOTTY, Co LIMERICK

Tel: 00 353 61 333100
E-mail: martinscoachhire@gmail.com
Web site: www.martinscoachhire.com
Fleet: single-deck coach, midicoach.
Ops incl: private hire.
Livery: White

MATTHEWS COACH HIRE LTD
CALLENBERG, INNISKEEN, Co MONAGHAN
Tel: 00 353 42 937 8188
Fax: 00 353 42 937 8709
E-mail: info@matthewscoach.com
Web site: www.matthewscoach.com
Dirs: P Matthews, Mrs M Matthews
Fleet: 28 – single-deck coach, midicoach.
Chassis incl: Mercedes, Scania, Temsa, VDL, Volvo.
Bodies incl: Berkhof, Hispano, Irizar, Marcopolo, Plaxton.
Ops incl: local bus services, private hire, excursions & tours, express, continental tours.
Livery: White

MICHAEL MEERE COACH HIRE
33 CHURCH DRIVE, CLARECASTLE, ENNIS, Co CLARE
Tel: 00 353 65 682 4833
Fax: 00 353 65 684 4544
E-mail: info@michaelmeere.com
Web site: www.michaelmeere.com
Fleet: 1 minibus
Chassis: Mercedes
Ops incl: private hire
Livery: White with multi-coloured logos

MIDLAND BUS CO LTD
BLYRY INDUSTRIAL ESTATE, ATHLONE, Co WESTMEATH
Tel: 00 353 90 647 2427
Fax: 00 353 90 647 8420
E-mail: info@midlandbus.com
Web site: www.midlandbus.com
Dirs: N. Henry, A Henry, B Henry
Fleet: single-deck coach, midibus.
Chassis: DAF, MAN, Volvo.
Ops incl: local bus services, private hire, school contracts, excursions & tours, express.

JOE MORONEY
OLD COURT INDUSTRIAL ESTATE, BRAY, Co WICKLOW
Tel: 00 353 1 276 1466
E-mail: info@joemoroney.com
Web site: www.joemoroney.com
Fleet: 4 - 3 single-deck coach, 1 midicoach
Chassis: 1 MAN, 3 Volvo.
Bodies: 1 Indcar, 3 Van Hool.
Ops incl: private hire, excursions & tours, express, continental tours.
Livery: White

MORTON'S COACHES DUBLIN
TAYLOR'S LANE, BALLYBODEN, RATHFARNHAM, DUBLIN 16
Tel: 00 353 1 494 4927
Fax: 00 353 1 494 4694
E-mail: info@mortonscoaches.ie
Web site: www.mortonscoaches.ie
Prop: Paul Morton
Fleet: single-deck coach, double-deck coach, midicoach.
Chassis incl: BMC, DAF, Mercedes, Volvo.
Bodies incl: Ayats, BMC, East Lancs, Marcopolo, OVI, Wright.

Ops incl: school contracts, excursions & tours, private hire, continental tours.
Livery: White

NAUGHTON COACH TOURS LTD
SHANAGURRANE, SPIDDAL, Co GALWAY
Tel: 00 353 91 553188
Fax: 00 353 91 553302
E-mail: naugtour@iol.i.e
Web site: www.ontours.biz
Fleet Name: O'Neachtain Tours
Dir: Steve Naughton
Dir/Sec: Maureen Naughton
Fleet: single-deck coach, double-deck coach, midicoach.
Ops incl: excursions & tours, private hire

NOLAN COACHES
19 CLONSHAUGH LAWN, COOLOCK, DUBLIN 17
Tel: 00 353 1 847 3487
Fax: 00 353 1 867 8855
Mobile: 0862 592000
Prop: David Nolan
Fleet: 2 single-deck coach
Ops incl: school contracts, private hire.

O'CONNOR AUTOTOURS LTD
ROSS ROAD, KILLARNEY, Co KERRY
Tel: 00 353 64 663 1052
Fax: 00 353 64 663 1703
E-mail: oconnorautotours@eircom.net
Web site: www.oconnorautotours.ie
Dir/Gen Man: B. O'Connor
Ch Eng: R. Downing
Sec: C. Enright
Traf Man: D. Fenton
Fleet: single-deck coach, midicoach, minicoach, minibus.
Ops incl: excursions & tours, private hire.
Livery: Maroon/Yellow.

FEDA O'DONNELL COACHES
RANAFAST, Co DONEGAL
Tel/Fax: 00 353 74 954 8114
E-mail: busfeda@eircom.net
Web site: www.fedaodonnell.com
Fleet: single-deck coach, minibus.
Chassis: Ford, Volvo.
Ops incl: express

LARRY O'HARA MINI COACHES
13 SKIBBEREEN LAWN, WATERFORD CITY
Tel: 00 353 51 372232
Fax: 00 353 51 357566
E-mail: larryohara@eircom.net
Fleetname: O'Hara Autotours
Props: Larry O'Hara, Helen O'Hara
Fleet: 3 - 2 midicoach, 1minibus.
Chassis/Bodies: 3 Mercedes.

O'MALLEY COACHES
FOILDARRIG, NEWPORT, Co TIPPERARY
Tel: 00 353 61 378119
Fax: 00 353 61 378002
E-mail: info@omalleycoaches.com
Web site: www.omalleycoaches.com
Owner: E. O'Malley
Ops incl: local bus services, school contracts, excursions & tours, private hire, express.
Livery: Blue/White.

O'SULLIVANS COACHES
FARRAHY ROAD, KILDORRERY, MALLOW, CO CORK
Tel: 00 353 22 25185
Fax: 00 353 22 25731
Prop: Gerard O'Sullivan
E-mail: gosull@indigo.ie
Web site: www.osullivanscoaches.com
Fleet: 15- 10 single-deck coach, 2 midicoach, 1 minibus, 2 minicoach.
Chassis: 1 Ford Transit, 4 Mercedes, 10 Volvo.
Bodies: 1 Berkhof, 2 Mercedes, 9 Van Hool, 3 Other.
Ops incl: school contracts, excursions & tours, private hire, continental tours.

JACKY POWER TOURS
2 LOWER ROCK STREET, TRALEE, Co KERRY
Tel: 00 353 66 713 6300
Fax: 00 353 66 712 9444
Fleet: 3 midicoach.

PROBUS & CAR
KENMARE, Co KERRY
Tel: 00 353 64 43500
Fax: 00 353 64 41903
E-mail: info@probusandcar.com
Web site: www.probusandcar.com
Ops incl: private hire.

ROVER COACHES
LYNN ROAD, MULLINGAR, Co WESTMEATH
Tel: 00 353 44 934 2449
Fax: 00 353 44 938 5020
E-mail: info@rovercoaches.ie
Web site: www.rovercoaches.ie
Prop: O'Brien Bros Coaches (Mullingar) Ltd
Fleet incl: single-deck coach, midicoach.
Ops incl: private hire, excursions & tours.
Livery: White

SEALANDAIR COACHING (IRELAND) LTD
53 MIDDLE ABBEY STREET, DUBLIN 1
Tel: 00 353 1 873 3411
Fax: 00 353 1 873 2639
E-mail: info@pabtours.com
Web site: www.pabtours.com
Fleet Name: PAB Tours
Man Dir: Anthony Kelly
Fleet: 7 single-deck coach
Chassis: Volvo
Bodies: Plaxton

MATT SHANAHAN COACHES
ST MARTINS, LACKEN ROAD, KILBARRY, WATERFORD
Tel: 00 353 51 74192
Fleet: 2 - single-deck bus
Ops incl: Waterford Crystal Tour

SILLAN TOURS LTD
KINGSCOURT ROAD, SHERCOCK, Co CAVAN
Tel: 00 353 42 966 9130
Fax: 00 353 42 966 9666
E-mail: info@sillan.ie
Web site: www.sillantoursltd.ie
Fleet: 4 – 3 single-deck coach, 1 midicoach.

Chassis: 1 MAN, 3 VDL
Bodies: 1 Indcar, 3 Marcopolo.
Ops incl: express, private hire.

ST KEVIN'S BUS SERVICE
See P Doyle Ltd, above.

SUIRWAY BUS & COACH SERVICES LTD
PASSAGE EAST, Co WATERFORD
Tel: 00 353 51 382209
Fax: 00 353 51 382676
E-mail: info@suirway.com
Web site: www.suirway.com
Fleet Name: www.suirway.com
Dir: Brian Lynch
Fleet: 9 - 2 single-deck bus, 6 single-deck coach, 1 midicoach.
Chassis: 1 Alexander Dennis, 1 Mercedes, 7 Volvo.
Bodies: 1 Esker, 1 Plaxton, 5 Van Hool, 1 Volvo, 1 Wright.
Ops incl: local bus services, school contracts, excursions & tours, private hire.
Livery: White & Blue

SWILLY BUS SERVICE
BALLYRAINE ROAD, LETTERKENNY, Co DONEGAL
Tel: 00 353 74 22863
Prop: Londonderry & Lough Swilly Railway Co Ltd
Ops incl: local bus services
Livery: White (Buses)

TRAVEL DIRECT LTD
SEEFIN, CRAUGHWELL, Co GALWAY
Tel: 00 353 91 876876
Fax: 00 353 91 876555
E-mail: info@traveldirectireland.com
Web site: www.traveldirectireland.com
Man Dir: John Gavin
Fleet incl: midicoach, minicoach.
Chassis: Mercedes.
Ops incl: excursions & tours.
Livery: White/Red

TREACY COACHES
ERRIGAL, KILLALA ROAD, BALLINA, Co MAYO
Tel: 00 353 96 22563
Fax: 00 353 96 70968
E-mail: treacycoaches@eircom.net
Dirs: A. Treacy (Gen Man), M. Treacy (Sec).
Fleet: single-deck coach, midicoach.
Ops incl: excursions & tours, private hire, express.
Livery: White/Blue

WHARTONS TRAVEL LTD
CROSSDONEY, Co CAVAN
Tel: 00 353 49 433 7000
Fax: 00 353 49 433 7634
E-mail: info@whartonstravel.com
Web site: www.whartonstravel.com
Fleet: single-deck coach, midicoach.
Chassis: Mercedes, Scania.
Bodies: Irizar, Plaxton, Sitcar.
Ops incl: private hire, excursions & tours, continental tours.
Livery: Red with multi-colours.

Republic of Ireland

For information regarding advertising contact: **Graham Middleton**
Tel: 01780 484632 **Fax:** 01780 763388
E-mail: graham.middleton@ianallanpublishing.co.uk

Section 5

Indices

TRADE INDEX 2011

Several of the traders listed in this index will have more than one entry; only the first is shown here in each case.

A

ABACUS TRANSPORT PRODUCTS LTD	33
ACIS	51
ACT – APPLIED CARD TECHNOLOGIES	45
ACTIA UK LTD	26
ACTION TOURS & ACTION EUROPE	58
AD COACH SALES	14
ADG TRANSPORT PLANNING	48
ADVANCED VEHICLE BUILDERS	14
AIRCONCO	19
AIR DOOR SERVICES	24
ALBATROSS TRAVEL GROUP LTD	58
ALBION AUTOMOTIVE LTD	25
ALCOA WHEEL PRODUCTS EUROPE	47
ALEXANDER DENNIS LTD	11
IAN ALLAN PRINTING LTD	56
ALLEN & DOUGLAS CORPORATE CLOTHING LTD	46
ALLIED VEHICLES LTD	15
ALLISON TRANSMISSION	32
ALMEX UK	45
ALSTOM TRANSPORT SA	12
ALTRO TRANSFLOR	31
AMA LTD	19
ANTAL INTERNATIONAL NETWORK	50
ARDEE COACH TRIM LTD	39
ARRIVA BUS & COACH	11
ARVIN MERITOR	21
ASHTREE GLASS LTD	35
ATLANTIS INTERNATIONAL LTD	47
ATOS ORIGIN	45
AUSTIN ANALYTICS	49
AUTOGLASS COACH & BUS SERVICES	48
AUTOLIFT LTD	34
AUTOMATE WHEEL COVERS LTD	31
AUTOMOTIVE SUPPLIES DIRECT LTD	31
AUTOMOTIVE TEXTILE INDUSTRIES	31
AUTOPRO SOFTWARE	51
AUTOSAN UK	11
AUTOSOUND LTD	19
AVID VEHICLES LTD	13
AVS STEPS LTD	34
AVT SYSTEMS LTD	19
AYATS	11

B

BALFOUR BEATTY RAIL PLANT LTD	38
TERENCE BARKER TANKS	31
M BARNWELL SERVICES LTD	36
BARRONS CHARTERED ACCOUNTANTS	48
BARTONS TRANSPORT	11
BASE LTD	15
BELMONT INTERNATIONAL LTD	54
BEMROSEBOOTH LTD	45
BERNSTEIN ENGINEERING LTD	41
BESTCHART LTD	51
BEST IMPRESSIONS	49
BEULAS	12
M BISSELL DISPLAY LTD	38
BLACKPOOL COACH SERVICES	36
BLACKPOOL TRIM SHOPS LTD	47
BLUE BIRD VEHICLES LTD	13
BLUE RIBBON COACH SALES	11
BLYTHSWOOD MOTORS LTD	15
BMC PLC	11
BOMBARDIER TRANSPORTATION	12
BOMBARDIER TRANSPORTATION METROS	12
THE HENRY BOOTH GROUP	56
BORLAND NINDER DIXON LLP	54
JOHN BRADSHAW LTD	13
BRADTECH LTD	25
BRECKNELL WILLIS & CO LTD	38
BRIDGE OF WEIR LEATHER CO LTD	47
BRIGADE ELECTRONICS PLC	39
BRISTOL BUS & COACH SALES	15
BRISTOL ELECTRIC RAILBUS LTD	38
BRITAX PMG LTD	35
BRITCOM INTERNATIONAL LTD	27
BRITISH BUS PUBLISHING LTD	56
BRITISH BUS SALES – MIKE NASH	15
BRITTANY FERRIES GROUP TRAVEL	53
BROADWATER MOULDINGS LTD	45
DAVID BROWN VEHICLE TRANSMISSIONS LTD	32
BRT BEARINGS LTD	19
COLIN BUCHANAN	49
BULWARK BUS & COACH ENGINEERING LTD	20
BURNT TREE VEHICLE SOLUTIONS	14
BUS & COACH BUYER	56
BUS & COACH GLAZING	48
BUS & COACH PROFESSIONAL	57
BUSES	57
BUSES WORLDWIDE	57
BUSS BIZZ	22
BUS SHELTERS LTD	41
BUS USER	57
BUTTS OF BAWTRY GARAGE EQUIPMENT	31
BUZZLINES LTD	50

C

CAETANO (UK) LTD	12
CALEDONIAN MACBRAYNE LTD	53
CANN PRINT	45
CAPARO AP BRAKING LTD	21
CAPOCO DESIGN	49
CAREYBROOK LTD	49
CARLYLE BUS & COACH LTD	20
CARMANAH TECHNOLOGIES GROUP	41
CARRIER SUTRAK	19
CHADWELL ASSOCIATES LTD	49
CHANNEL COMMERCIALS PLC	20
CHAPMAN DRIVER SEATING	41
CHASSIS DEVELOPMENTS LTD	14
CIE TOURS INTERNATIONAL	58
CLAN TOOLS & PLANT LTD	39
CLAYTON HEATERS LTD	19
COACH & BUS WEEK	57
COACH-AID	22
COACH CARPETS	31
COACH DIRECT LTD	50
COACHFINDER LTD	51
COGENT PASSENGER SEATING LTD	41
COMPAK RAMPS LTD	34
CONCEPT COACHCRAFT	14
CONDOR FERRIES LTD	53
CONNAUGHT PSV	15
CONSERVE (UK) LTD	19
COUNTY RECRUITMENT & TRAINING LTD	50
COURTSIDE CONVERSIONS LTD	14
CRESCENT FACILITIES LTD	26
CREST COACH CONVERSIONS	20
CREWE ENGINES	28

CRONER (WOLTERS KLUWER UK LTD)	51
CROWN COACHBUILDERS LTD	20
CSM LIGHTING	35
CUBIC TRANSPORTATION SYSTEMS LTD	30
CUMMINS UK	20
CUMMINS-ALLISON LTD	22
CVI (COMMERCIAL VEHICLE INNOVATION)	14
CYBERLINE COMMUNICATIONS LTD	42

D
DAF COMPONENTS LTD	28
DATS (DAVE'S ACCIDENT & TRAINING SERVICES)	52
R L DAVISON & CO LTD	54
DAWSONRENTALS BUS & COACH LTD	15
DCA DESIGN INTERNATIONAL	51
DEANS POWERED DOORS	33
DEANS SYSTEMS (UK) LTD	24
DECKER MEDIA	56
DE LA RUE	45
DFDS SEAWAYS	53
DIESEL POWER ENGINEERING	28
DINEX EXHAUSTS LTD	27
DIRECT PARTS LTD	19
DISTINCTIVE SYSTEMS LTD	51
DRINKMASTER LTD	25
DRIVER HIRE CANTERBURY	50
DUNLOP TYRES LTD	46
DUOFLEX LTD	33

E
EASTGATE COACH TRIMMERS	20
EBERSPACHER (UK) LTD	19
KEITH EDMONDSON TICKET ROLLS	45
ELITE SERVICES LTD	40
ELLIS INTERNATIONAL TRANSPORT CONSULTING LTD	54
ELLIS TRANSPORT SERVICES	51
ELSAN LTD	25
EMISSION CONTROL LTD	27
EMINOX LTD	29
ENSIGN BUS CO LTD	15
ERENTEK LTD	36
ETMSS LTD	22
EUROTUNNEL	53
EVOBUS (UK) LTD	11
EXCEL CONVERSIONS LTD	14
EXPO MANAGEMENT LTD	53
EXPRESS COACH REPAIRS LTD	12

F
4 FARTHINGS INTERNATIONAL RECRUITMENT	52
FAST EUROPE NV	11
FCAV & CO	19
FIREMASTER EXTINGUISHER LTD	15
FLEET AUCTION GROUP	15
FORD MOTOR COMPANY	13
FREIGHT TRANSPORT ASSOCIATION	54
FTA VEHICLE INSPECTION SERVICE	27
FUEL THEFT SOLUTIONS LTD	28
FUMOTO ENGINEERING OF EUROPE LTD	29
FURROWS COMMERCIAL VEHICLES	15
FWT	49

G
GABRIEL & CO LTD	33
GARDNER PARTS LTD	32
GAUNTLET RISK MANAGEMENT (COVENTRY)	54
GEMCO EQUIPMENT LTD	31
GHE	20
GLIDERITE	42
GM COACHWORK LTD	14
IAN GORDON COMMERCIALS	15
GOSKILLS LTD	49

GRAPHIC EVOLUTION LTD	49
GREATDAYS TRAVEL GROUP	58
TONY GREAVES GRAPHICS	49
LEONARD GREEN ASSOCIATES	49
GROENEVELD UK LTD	22
JOHN GROVES TICKET SYSTEMS	22
GSM-ABBOT BROWN	20

H
HANDLEY BUS & COACH UNIFORMS	46
HANOVER DISPLAYS LTD	24
HANTS & DORSET TRIM LTD	20
HAPPICH V&I COMPONENTS LTD	30
THOMAS HARDIE COMMERCIALS LTD	15
HART BROTHERS (ENGINEERING) LTD	27
HATCHER COMPONENTS LTD	48
HATTS GARAGE & SERVICES	49
P J HAYMAN & CO LTD	54
HAYWARD TRAVEL (CARDIFF)	51
HB PUBLICATIONS LTD	56
HEATONS MOTOR CO	15
B HEPWORTH & CO LTD	48
HILTech DEVELOPMENTS LTD	27
J HIPWELL & SON	48
HISPACOLD	19
HOLDSWORTH FABRICS LTD	41
HOLLOWAY COMMERCIALS	14
B & D HOLT LTD	16

I
IBPTS	43
IMAGE 1ST CLOTHING LTD	46
IMEXPART LTD	21
IMPERIAL ENGINEERING	21
INDCAR SA	14
INDEPENDENT COACH TRAVEL (WHOLESALING) LTD	58
INDICATORS INTERNATIONAL LTD	24
INDUSTRIAL & COMMERCIAL WINDOW CO LTD	48
INIT GmbH – INNOVATION IN TRANSPORT	19
INTELLITEC LTD	26
INTERLUBE SYSTEMS LTD	31
INVERTEC LTD	20
IRISBUS (UK) LTD	11
IRISH COMMERCIALS (SALES)	16
IRISH FERRIES LTD	53
IRIZAR	12
ISLE OF MAN STEAM PACKET COMPANY	53
IVECO	28
ANDY IZATT	49

J
J & K RECOVERY LTD	50
JACOBS BABTIE GROUP LTD	52
JANES URBAN TRANSPORT SYSTEMS	57
JBF SERVICES LTD	27
JDC – JOHN DENNIS COACHBUILDERS	14
JES BUSCYCLE	20
JOURNEY PLAN LTD	38
JUBILEE AUTOMOTIVE GROUP	14
JW GLASS LTD	48

K
KAB SEATING LTD	41
KARIVE LTD	25
KCP CAR & COMMERCIAL LTD	19
KELLETT (UK) LTD	21
KERNOW ASSOCIATES	48
KING LONG UK LTD	11
KISMET GARAGE EQUIPMENT LTD	31
KNORR-BREMSE SYSTEMS FOR COMMERCIAL VEHICLES LTD	21
THOMAS KNOWLES – TRANSPORT CONSULTANT	52

The Little Red Book 2011 - in association with *tbf* Transport Benevolent Fund

Trade Index

221

L

LANCES MOBILE PAINTING	36
LANDMARK FINANCE LTD	53
LANTERN RECOVERY SPECIALISTS PLC	50
LAWTON SERVICES LTD	12
LEICESTER CARRIAGE BUILDERS	12
LEISUREWEAR DIRECT LTD	33
LEYLAND PRODUCT DEVELOPMENTS LTD	27
LH GROUP SERVICES LTD	25
LHE FINANCE LTD	53
THE LONDON BUS EXPORT CO	16
LOOK CCTV LTD	43
LOUGHSHORE AUTOS LTD	16
LVD	16

M

M A C LTD	19
MACEMAIN & AMSTAD	41
MAJORLIFT HYDRAULIC EQUIPMENT LTD	31
MAN BUS & COACH	11
MAN COACH SALES	11
MAN TRUCK & BUS UK LTD	28
MARCOPOLO	12
MARKET ENGINEERING	56
MARSHALLS COACHES LLP	27
MARTYN INDUSTRIALS LTD	20
MASS SPECIAL ENGINEERING LTD	16
MCI EXHIBITIONS LTD	53
NIGEL McCREE COACH SALES	16
McKENNA BROTHERS LTD	24
MCV BUS & COACH LTD	12
MELLOR COACHCRAFT	14
MERCEDES-BENZ	11
MIDLAND COUNTIES PUBLICATIONS	56
MIDLAND RED COACHES/WHEELS HERITAGE	53
MINIBUS OPTIONS LTD	14
MINIMISE YOUR RISK	49
MINIS TO MIDIS LTD	11
MINITRAM SYSTEMS LTD	12
MISTRAL BUS & COACH PLC	14
MOCAP LIMITED	37
MONOWASH (BRUSH REPLACEMENT SERVICE)	47
STEPHEN C MORRIS	49
MOSELEY DISTRIBUTORS	16
MOSELEY IN THE SOUTH LTD	12
MOSELEY (PCV) LTD	11
MOTIONAL MEDIA LTD	38
MOTT MACDONALD	51
J MURDOCH WIGHT LTD	31
MVA	49

N

NATIONWIDE CLEANING & SUPPORT SERVICES LTD	47
NEALINE WINDSCREEN WIPER PRODUCTS	26
NEERMAN & PARTNERS	49
NEOPLAN	11
NEXT BUS LTD	16
NOGE	13
BRIAN NOONE	11
NORBURY BLINDS LTD	24
NORFOLKLINE	53
NORTHLINK FERRIES LTD	53
NORTON FOLGATE FG PLC	54
NUTEXA FRICTIONS LTD	21
NU-TRACK LTD	14

O

OMNIBUS	51
OMNIBUS TRAINING LTD	53
OMNI WHITTINGTONS	54
OPTARE PLC (Blackburn)	11
OPTARE PLC (Leeds)	11
OPTARE PARTS DIVISION (Rotherham)	19
OPTARE PRODUCT SUPPORT LONDON	19
OPTARE PRODUCT SUPPORT ROTHERHAM	19
OPTARE PRODUCT SUPPORT SCOTLAND	19
ORVEC INTERNATIONAL LTD	33
OWENS OF OSWESTRY BMC	16

P

P & O FERRIES	53
PACET MANUFACTURING LTD	24
PARRY PEOPLE MOVERS LTD	12
PARTLINE LTD	21
PASSENGER LIFT SERVICES LTD	35
PAYPOINT PLC	45
PEAK LEGAL SERVICES LTD	49
PELLYS LLP SOLICITORS	55
PEMBRIDGE VEHICLE MANAGEMENT	16
PENTLAND FERRIES	53
PERCY LANE PRODUCTS LTD	24
PERKINS GROUP LTD	28
PETERS DOOR SYSTEMS (UK) LTD	25
PHOENIX SEATING LTD	41
H W PICKRELL	17
PINDAR PLC	55
PIONEER WESTON	34
PJA LTD	52
P.L.TRIM LTD	41
PLAXTON	13
PLAXTON COACH SALES CENTRE	11
PLAXTON PARTS	25
PLAXTON SERVICE	19
PLUM DIGITAL PRINT	50
PNEUMAX LTD	25
POLYBUSH	42
POWER BATTERIES (GB) LTD	20
PRE METRO OPERATIONS LTD	48
PRESTOLITE ELECTRIC	26
PROFESSIONAL TRANSPORT SERVICES LTD	49
PSS – STEERING & HYDRAULICS DIVISION	42
PSV GLASS	37
PSV PRODUCTS	20
PVS MANUFACTURING LTD	15

Q

Q'STRAINT	37
QUEENSBRIDGE (PSV) LTD	28
QUEENSBURY SHELTERS	41
QUICK CHANGE (UK) LTD	22

R

RAINBOW CORPORATEWEAR	46
RATCLIFF PALFINGER	35
RED FUNNEL	53
RENAULT UK LTD	14
RESCROFT LTD	35
RH BODYWORKS	21
RICON UK LTD	35
RIGTON INSURANCE SERVICES LTD	54
ROADLEASE	54
ROADLINK INTERNATIONAL LTD	22
ROBERTSON TRANSPORT CONSULTING LTD	52
ROEVILLE COMPUTER SYSTEMS	51
ROUTEMASTER BUSES LTD	37
ROUTE ONE	57

S

SAFETEX LTD	40
SALTIRE COMMUNICATIONS	49
SAMMYS GARAGE	51
SANTANDER ASSET FINANCE	11
SCAN COIN LTD	22
SCANDUS UK	41

SCANIA (GB) LTD	11
SCANIA BUS & COACH (UK) LTD	19
SCHADES LTD	45
SEA FRANCE	53
SECURON (AMERSHAM) LTD	40
SETRA	11
SHADES TECHNICS LTD	25
SHAWSON SUPPLY LTD	24
SIEMENS TRAFFIC CONTROLS LTD	38
SIEMENS VDO TRADING LTD	43
SILFLEX LTD	24
SMART CENTRAL COACH SYSTEMS	47
SMITH BROS & WEBB LTD	47
H L SMITH TRANSMISSIONS LTD	25
SNOWCHAINS EUROPRODUCTS	46
SOE	57
SOLBUS (UK) LTD	11
SOMERS TOTALKARE LTD	32
SOUTHDOWN PSV LTD	17
SPECIALIST TRAINING & CONSULTANCY SERVICES LTD	52
SSL SIMULATION SYSTEMS LTD	38
STAFFORD BUS CENTRE	17
STANFORD COACHWORKS	15
STENA LINE	53
STEPHENSONS OF ESSEX	17
STERTIL UK LTD	32
STOKE TRUCK & BUS CENTRE	17
STUART MANUFACTURING CO LTD	45
SUNSUNDEGUI	13
SUSTRACO LTD	38

T

TAGTRONICS LTD	51
TARA SUPPORT SERVICES LTD	50
TAS PARTNERSHIP LTD	52
TAYLOR COACH SALES	17
TELMA RETARDER LTD	39
TEMPLE MANUFACTURING CO LTD	39
TEMSA EUROPE	11
MARK TERRILL PSV BADGES	20
MARK TERRILL TICKET MACHINERY	22
TESLA VEHICLES LIMITED	11
THOMAS AUTOMATION LTD	22
TICKETER	22
TIFLEX LTD	31
CRAIG TILSLEY & SON LTD	28
TIME TRAVEL UK	50
TITAN BUS UK LTD	56
TMD FRICTION UK LTD	22
TOURMASTER RECOVERY	50
TOP GEARS	24
TOWERGATE CHAPMAN STEVENS	54
TOYOTA (GB) PLC	14
TRAMONTANA	12
TRAM POWER LTD	12
TRAMWAYS & URBAN TRANSIT	57
TRANMAN SOLUTIONS	51
TRANSIT MAGAZINE	57
TRANSMANCHE FERRIES	53
TRANSPORT & TRAINING SERVICES LTD	45
TRANSPORT & TRAVEL RESEARCH LTD	49
TRANSPORT CONSULTANCY – R W FAULKS	52
TRANSPORT DESIGN INTERNATIONAL	28
TRANSPORT STATIONERY SERVICES	56
TRANSPORT TICKET SERVICES LTD	45
TRAPEZE GROUP (UK) LTD	38
TRAVELGREEN COACHES	51
TRAVEL INFORMATION SYSTEMS	51
TRAVELPATH 3000	53
TREKA BUS LTD	15
TRIMPLEX SAFETY TREAD LTD	31
TRISCAN SYSTEMS LTD	31

TRUCKALIGN CO LTD	21
TRUEFORM ENGINEERING LTD	41
TTS UK	21
TUBE PRODUCTS LTD	41

U

UK BUS DISMANTLERS LTD	17
UK COACH RALLY	53
UNWIN SAFETY SYSTEMS	33
UNVI	12
USED COACH SALES	17

V

BOB VALE COACH SALES LTD	15
VAN HOOL	12
VAPOR-STONE UK LTD	25
VARLEY & GULLIVER LTD	32
VARTA AUTOMOTIVE BATTERIES LTD	20
VAUXHALL MOTORS LTD	14
VCA	52
VDL BERKHOF	13
VDL BOVA	12
VDL BUS INTERNATIONAL	12
VDL JONCKHEERE	13
VDO KIENZLE UK LTD	27
VENTURA BUS + COACH SALES	17
VETRO DESIGN	50
VICTORIA COACH STATION LTD	51
V L TEST SYSTEMS LTD	32
VOITH TURBO LTD	32
VOLKSWAGEN COMMERCIAL VEHICLES	14
VOLVO BUS	12
VOLVO BUS & COACH CENTRE (Parts/Body)	
VOLVO BUS & COACH SALES CENTRE	12
VOLVO FINANCIAL SERVICES	54
VOLVO INSURANCE SERVICES	54
VOR TRANSMISSIONS LTD	26
VOSA	53
VOSA COMMERCIAL PROJECTS UNIT	57
VULTRON INTERNATIONAL LTD	24

W

WABCO AUTOMOTIVE UK LTD	22
WACTON COACH SALES & SERVICES	17
WALLMINSTER LTD	29
WALSH'S ENGINEERING LTD	29
WARD INTERNATIONAL CONSULTING LTD	43
WAYFARER (PARKEON TRANSIT) LTD	45
WEALDEN PSV LTD	17
WEALDSTONE ENGINEERING	29
WEBASTO PRODUCT UK LTD	19
WEBB'S	52
WEDLAKE SAINT	55
WEST END TRAVEL & RUTLAND TRAVEL	52
ALAN WHITE COACH SALES	17
WHITELEY ELECTRONICS	41
WIDNEY UK LTD	39
WIGHTLINK ISLE OF WIGHT FERRIES	53
TREVOR WIGLEY & SONS BUS LTD	17
WILKINSONS VEHICLE SOLUTIONS	21
WILLIS LTD	54
DREW WILSON COACH SALES	17
WOODBRIDGE FOAM UK LTD	41
THE WRIGHT GROUP	12
WRIGHTSURE GROUP	54

Y

YORKSHIRE BUS & COACH SALES	17

Z

ZF POWERTRAIN	26

OPERATOR INDEX 2011

2ND 4TH LTD, FERNDOWN	106

A

AAA COACHES, KIRKNEWTON	192
A1 COACH TRAVEL, LONDONDERRY	212
A1 TRAVEL, YEOVIL	162
A1A LTD, BIRKENHEAD	145
A.2.B TRAVEL UK LTD, PRENTON	145
AtoB TRAVEL (LUTON) LTD, LUTON	83
A & C LUXURY COACHES, MOTHERWELL	196
A & E HIRE, WELSHPOOL	208
A & J COACHES OF WASHINGTON CO LTD, WASHINGTON, TYNE & WEAR	174
AA, KNIGHTS OF THE ROAD, SIDCUP	139
A B COACHES LTD, TOTNES	101
AM-PM TRAVEL, BIRMINGHAM	176
A R TRAVEL LTD, HEMEL HEMPSTEAD	126
A S T TEIGNBRIDGE COMMUNITY TRANSPORT, DAWLISH	101
A W COACHES LTD, LLANFAIR CAEREINION	208
AARDVARK & FIRST CHOICE COACHES, PETERBOROUGH	88
ABBEY COACHWAYS LTD, CARLTON, GOOLE	151
ABBEY TRAVEL, LEICESTER	136
G. ABBOTT & SONS, LEEMING	151
ABELLIO GROUP	82
ABELLIO LONDON LTD, LONDON SE5	139
ABELLIO WEST LONDON LTD, LONDON SE5	172
ABERFELDY MOTOR SERVICES, ABERFELDY	197
ABERFOYLE COACHES LTD, ABERFOYLE	200
ABINGDON COACHES, THATCHAM	159
ABUS LTD, BRISTOL	85
ACE TRAVEL, BURNTWOOD	168
ACKLAMS COACHES, BEVERLEY	110
ACORN TRAVEL LTD, FISHGUARD	208
ACTON COACHES, WREXHAM	211
ADAMS TOURS, BLOXWICH	176
ADAMSON'S COACHES, CRAMLINGTON	155
ADLINGTON TAXIS AND MINICOACHES, HORWICH	118
ADRAINS OF BRINKWORTH	184
AGNEW TRAVEL, LURGAN, Co ARMAGH	212
AINTREE COACHLINE, BOOTLE	145
AIRCOACH, DUBLIN	213
AIRLYNX TRAVEL, SOUTHAMPTON	122
AIRPARKS SERVICES LTD, BIRMINGHAM	176
ALAN ARNOTT, ERSKINE	198
ALDERMASTON COACHES, ALDERMASTON	84
ALEXCARS LTD, CIRENCESTER	117
ALFA COACHES LTD, STOCKTON-ON-TEES	107
ALFA TRAVEL, CHORLEY	131
ALFRA COACH HIRE, LARKHALL	199
A-LINE COACHES, COVENTRY	176
A LINE COACHES, GATESHEAD	174
ALLAN & BLACK, ABOYNE	188
ALLAN'S COACHES EDINBURGH, GOREBRIDGE	192, 195
ALLANDER COACHES LTD, MILNGAVIE	194
ALLEN'S TOURS, BELFAST	212
ALLIED COACHES, BALDOYLE, DUBLIN	213
FRANK ALLISON LTD, BROUGH	95
ALPINE TRAVEL, LLANDUDNO	205
ALS COACHES LTD, BIRKENHEAD	145
ALTONA COACH SERVICES & TRAVEL CONSULTANT, GATESHEAD	174
ALTONIAN COACHES LTD, ALTON	122
AMBASSADOR TRAVEL (ANGLIA) LTD, GREAT YARMOUTH	147
AMBER TRAVEL, TURRIFF	188
AMK CHAUFFEUR DRIVE LTD, LIPHOOK	122
GEOFF AMOS COACHES LTD, DAVENTRY	154
AMPORT & DISTRICT COACHES LTD, THRUXTON, ANDOVER	122
ANDERSON COACHES LTD, ROTHERHAM	165
ANDERSON TRAVEL GROUP, LONDON SE1	139
ANDERSON'S COACHES, FERRYBRIDGE	181
ANDERSON'S COACHES, LANGHOLM	191
A N ANDREW COACHES, MOSTYN	206
ANDREW JAMES QUALITY TRAVEL, MALMESBURY	184
ANDREW'S (SHETLAND) LTD, W£HITENESS, SHETLAND	198
ANDREW'S OF TIDESWELL LTD	97
ANDREWS COACHES, FOXTON, CAMBRIDGE	88
ANDYBUS AND COACH LTD, MALMESBURY	184
ANGEL TRAVEL, WARRINGTON	92
ANGELA COACHES LTD, BURSLEDON	122
ANGLIAN BUS & COACH LTD, BECCLES	170
ANITAS COACHES, STANSTED AIRPORT	112
ANTHONYS TRAVEL, RUNCORN	92
APL TRAVEL LTD, CRUDWELL	184
APOLLO 8 TRAVEL, KENDAL	95
APPLEBYS COACH TRAVEL, LOUTH	137, 150
APT COACHES LTD, RAYLEIGH	112
ARAN TOURS, SANDYCOVE, Co DUBLIN	213
ARDCAVAN COACH TOURS LTD, ARDCAVAN, Co WEXFORD	213
ARLEEN COACH HIRE & SERVICES LTD, PEASEDOWN ST JOHN	162
ALAN ARNOTT, ERSKINE	198
ARRIVA BUSES WALES, LLANDUDNO JUNCTION	205
ARRIVA LONDON	139
ARRIVA MIDLANDS LTD, LEICESTER	97, 135, 160, 168
ARRIVA NORTH EAST LTD, SUNDERLAND	174
ARRIVA NORTH WEST & WALES, AINTREE	92, 118, 145
ARRIVA PLC	78
ARRIVA SCOTLAND WEST, PAISLEY	198
ARRIVA SOUTHEND LTD	112
ARRIVA SOUTHERN COUNTIES, MAIDSTONE	129, 172
ARRIVA THE SHIRES LTD, LUTON	83
ARRIVA YORKSHIRE LTD, WAKEFIELD	151, 181
ARROWEBROOK COACHES LTD, CROUGHTON, CHESTER	92
ARUN COACHES/FAWLTY TOURS, HORSHAM	179
ARVONIA COACHES, CAERNARFON	206
ASHFORD LUXURY COACHES, FELTHAM	139
ASHLEY TRAVEL LTD t/a GRANT & McALLIN, SHEFFIELD	165
G. ASHTON COACHES, ST HELENS	145

ASM COACHES, WHITSTABLE	129
ASMAL COACHES, LEICESTER	135
J. & F. ASPDEN (BLACKBURN) LTD, BLACKBURN	131
ASTONS COACHES, WORCESTER	185
ATBUS LTD, FELTHAM	139
H. ATKINSON & SONS (INGLEBY) LTD, NORTHALLERTON	151
AUSDEN CLARK GROUP, LEICESTER	135
AUSTIN TRAVEL, EARLSTON	190
AUTOCAR BUS & COACH SERVICES LTD, TONBRIDGE	129
AVENSIS COACH TRAVEL LTD, ROMSEY	122
AVON COACH & BUS COMPANY, BIRKENHEAD	146
AWAYDAYS LTD t/a GEMINI TRAVEL, IPSWICH	170
AXE VALE COACHES, AXBRIDGE	162
AXE VALLEY MINI TRAVEL, SEATON	101
AYREVILLE COACHES, PLYMOUTH	101
AZTEC COACH TRAVEL, BRISTOL	85

B

B & J TRAVEL, MIDDLESTOWN	181
B B COACHES LTD, HALESOWEN	176
B M COACHES, HAYES	140
B'S TRAVEL, PONTYPOOL	210
BACK ROADS TOURING CO LTD, LONDON W4	139
BAGNALLS COACHES, SWADLINCOTE	97
BAILDON MOTORS LTD, LEEDS	181
BAILEY'S COACHES LTD, WATNALL	156
BAKERS COACHES, BIDDULPH	168
BAKER'S COACHES, DULOE, LISKEARD	94
BAKERS COACHES, MORETON-IN-MARSH	117
BAKERS COACHES, YEOVIL	162
BAKERS COMMERCIAL SERVICES, ENSTONE	159
BAKERS DOLPHIN COACH TRAVEL, WESTON-SUPER-MARE	162
BAKEWELL COACHES, BAKEWELL	98
BALDRY'S COACHES, YORK	151
BANBURYSHIRE ETA LTD, BANBURY	159
BANSTEAD COACHES LTD, BANSTEAD	172
BARCROFT TOURS & EVENTS, HASTINGS	111
BARFORDIAN COACHES LTD, BEDFORD	83
BARNARD COACHES, KIRTON LINDSEY	137
BARNARD CASTLE COACHES (BURRELLS), BARNARD CASTLE	151
BARNES COACHES LTD, SWINDON	184
BARRATT'S COACHES, ELWORTH	92
BARRY'S COACHES LTD, CORK	213
BARRY'S COACHES LTD, WEYMOUTH	104
BARTON TRANSPORT, MAYNOOTH, Co KILDARE	213
BATH BUS COMPANY	162
BATTERSBY SILVER GREY COACHES, MORECAMBE	131
BATTERSBY'S COACHES, WALKDEN	118
BEACON BUS, WINKLEIGH	101
BEACON COACHES, CHELMSLEY WOOD	176
BEAVIS HOLIDAYS, BUSSAGE	117
BEECHES TRAVEL, TWICKENHAM	139
BEECROFT COACHES, FEWSTON, NR HARROGATE	151
BEELINE (R&R) COACHES LTD, WARMINSTER	184
BEESTONS (HADLEIGH) LTD, HADLEIGH	170
BELLAMY COACHES LTD, NOTTINGHAM	156
BEN GEORGE TRAVEL LTD, BROUGHTON	150

BENNETT'S COACHES, GLOUCESTER	117
BENNETT'S TRAVEL, WARRINGTON	92
BENNETTS TRAVEL (CRANBERRY) LTD, HEATH	168
ROBERT BENSON COACHES LTD, WORKINGTON	95
BERKELEY COACH AND TRAVEL LTD, PAULTON, BRISTOL	86
BERRY'S COACHES (TAUNTON) LTD	162
BESSWAY TRAVEL LTD, GREENFORD	139
BETTER MOTORING SERVICES, STRATTON-ST MARGARET	184
JAMES BEVAN (LYDNEY) LTD, LYDNEY	117
BIBBY'S OF INGLETON LTD, INGLETON	151
BIG BUS COMPANY, LONDON SW1	139
BIRMINGHAM INTERNATIONAL COACHES LTD, TILE CROSS	176
B J S TRAVEL, GREAT WAKERING	112
BL TRAVEL, HEMSWORTH	181
BLACKPOOL TRANSPORT SERVICES LTD	131
BLACK & WHITE MOTORWAYS LTD, WINCHESTER	122
BLACK VELVET TRAVEL LTD, EASTLEIGH	122
BLAGDON LIONESS COACHES LTD, BRISTOL	162
BLAKES COACHES LTD, TIVERTON	101
MARK BLAND TRAVEL LTD, STAMFORD	137
BLUE DIAMOND COACHES, HARLOW	112
BLUE IRIS COACHES, NAILSEA	86
BLUEBIRD BUS & COACH, MIDDLETON	118
BLUEBIRD BUSES LTD, ABERDEEN	188
BLUEBIRD COACHES LTD, DUBLIN	213
BLUEBIRD COACHES (WEYMOUTH) LTD	104
BLUEBIRD OF NEATH/PONTARDAWE	207
BLUE IRIS COACHES, NAILSEA	162
BLUELINE TRAVEL, MAGHULL	146
BLUE TRIANGLE BUSES LTD, LONDON SW19	112
BLUEWAYS GUIDELINE COACHES LTD, LONDON SW11	139
BLUNSDON'S COACH TRAVEL, BLADON	159
BODMAN COACHES, DEVIZES	184
A. S. BONE & SONS LTD, HOOK	122
BORDACOACH, RAYLEIGH	112
BOSTOCK'S COACHES LTD, CONGLETON	92
BOTTERILLS MINIBUSES, THORNTON DALE	151
BOULTONS OF SHROPSHIRE, CHURCH STRETTON	160
L F BOWEN LTD, TAMWORTH	168
L F BOWEN LTD t/a JEFFS COACHES, HELMDON	154
L F BOWEN LTD t/a YORKS COACHES, COGENHOE	154
BOWERS COACHES LTD, CHAPEL-EN-LE-FRITH	98
D K & N BOWMAN, WREAY, CARLISLE	95
BOWMAN'S COACHES (MULL) LTD, CRAIGNURE	189
BOWYER'S COACHES, PETERCHURCH, HEREFORD	125
BRADSHAWS TRAVEL, KNOTT END ON SEA	131
BRAZIERS MINI COACHES, BUCKINGHAM	87
BRENTONS OF BLACKHEATH, LONDON SE6	140
BRENTWOOD COACHES	112
BRIGHTON & HOVE BUS & COACH CO LTD	111
BRIGHTONIAN COACHES, BRIGHTON	111
BRIJAN TOURS LTD, CURDRIDGE	122
BRITANNIA COACHES, DOVER	129
BRITANNIA TRAVEL, OTLEY	181
BRITTONS COACH TOURS, STRABANE, Co TYRONE	212
BRODYR JAMES, TREGARON	204
BROMYARD OMNIBUS COMPANY, BROMYARD	125

Operator index

Operator	Page
A T BROWN COACHES LTD, TELFORD	160
EDDIE BROWN TOURS LTD, YORK	151
LES BROWN TRAVEL, BATHGATE	200
BROWNINGS (WHITBURN) LTD, WHITBURN	201
S H BROWNRIGG LTD, EGREMONT	95
WILLIAM BROWNRIGG, THORNHILL	191
BROWNS COACHES (SK) LTD, PONTEFRACT	181
BROWNS COACHES, ASHFORD	129
BROWN'S OF DURHAM, DURHAM	107
ROY BROWNS COACHES, BUILTH WELLS	208
BRYANS COACHES LTD, DENNY	200
BRYANS OF ENFIELD, ENFIELD	140
BRYLAINE TRAVEL LTD, BOSTON	137
BUCKLEYS TOURS LTD, DONCASTER	165
BUCKLEY'S TOURS LTD, KILLARNEY, Co KERRY	213
BUGLERS COACHES LTD, BATH	163
R G J BULLICK COACH HIRE, RATHFRILAND, Co DOWN	212
R. BULLOCK & CO (TRANSPORT) LTD, CHEADLE	118
BURDETTS COACHES LTD, MOSBOROUGH	165
BURGHFIELD MINI COACHES LTD, READING	84
BURKE BROS (COACHES) LTD, TUAM, Co GALWAY	213
J & M BURNS, TARVES	188
BURRELLS (BARNARD CASTLE COACHES), RICHMOND	151
R & D BURROWS LTD, OGMORE VALE, BRIDGEND	202
BURTONS COACHES, HAVERHILL	88, 170
BUS EIREANN/IRISH BUS, DUBLIN	213
TERRY BUSHELL TRAVEL, BURTON-ON-TRENT	168
BUSES4U, TANDRIDGE	172
BUTLER BROTHERS COACHES, KIRKBY IN ASHFIELD	156
BUTLERS BUSES, COBH, Co CORK	214
BU-VAL BUSES LTD, LITTLEBOROUGH	119
BUZZLINES TRAVEL LTD, LYMPNE	129
BYRAN TOURS LTD, SHEFFIELD	165
BYSIAU CWM TAF/TAF VALLEY COACHES, WHITLAND	203
LES BYWATER & SONS LTD, ROCHDALE	119
BZEE BUS & TRAVEL LTD, AYLESFORD	129

C

Operator	Page
C & G COACHES, CHATTERIS	89
C & S COACH TRAVEL LTD, HEATHFIELD	111
C I LUB CLASS TRAVEL, CHELMSFORD	112
C. L. COACHES, LANCING	179
C N ENTERPRISES, ROMFORD	112
CABER COACHES LTD, ABERFELDY	197
CABIN COACHES, HAYES	140
CAELLOI MOTORS, PWLLHELI	206
CAHALANE COACHES, CORK	214
CALDEW COACHES LTD, CARLISLE	95
CALL-A-COACH, WALTON-ON-THAMES	172
CALLINAN COACHES, GLAREGALWAY	214
CANAVAN'S COACHES, KILSYTH	196
DEN CANEY COACHES LTD, BIRMINGHAM	177
CARADOC COACHES LTD, CHURCH STRETTON	160
CARADON RIVIERA TOURS, LISKEARD	94
CARAVELLE COACHES, EDGWARE	140
CARDIFF BUS, CARDIFF	203
CARMEL COACHES, OKEHAMPTON	101
J. W. CARNELL LTD, SUTTON BRIDGE	137
PETER CAROL PRESTIGE COACHING, WHITCHURCH, BRISTOL	86
CAROLAN CCOACH HIRE, SPIDDAL, Co MEATH	214
CAROUSEL BUSES, HIGH WYCOMBE	87
CARREGLEFN COACHES, AMLWCH	202
GERRY CARROLL COACH HIRE, DROGHEDA	214
CARR'S COACHES, SILLOTH	96
CARSVILLE COACHES, URMSTON	119
CARTERS COACH SERVICES, IPSWICH	170
CASTELL COACHES LTD, BEDWAS	203
CASTLE GARAGE LTD, LLANDOVERY	204
CASTLEWAYS LTD, WINCHCOMBE	117
CATHEDRAL COACHES LTD, GLOUCESTER	117
CATTERALLS COACHES, SOUTHAM	176
CAVALIER TRAVEL SERVICES, HESTON	140
CAVENDISH LINER LTD, POOLE	104
CEDAR COACHES, BEDFORD	83
CEDRIC COACHES, WIVENHOE	112
CELTIC TRAVEL, LLANIDLOES	209
CENTAUR COACHES & MINICOACHES, SIDCUP	129, 140
CENTRAL BUSES LTD, BIRMINGHAM	176
CENTRAL CONNECT, BIRMINGHAM	177
CENTRAL COACHES, KEITH	196
CENTRAL GARAGE, TODMORDEN	181
CENTRAL MINI COACHES, DOVER	129
CENTRAL TRAVEL, NEWTOWN	209
CENTRAL TRAVEL, SHEFFIELD	165
CENTREBUS GROUP	81
CENTREBUS LTD, GRANTHAM	137
CENTREBUS LTD, HARLOW	113
CENTREBUS LTD, LEICESTER	135
CENTREBUS LTD, LUTON	83
CENTREBUS LTD, STEVENAGE	126
CENTURION TRAVEL LTD, MIDSOMER NORTON	163
CERBYDAU BERWYN COACHES, TREFOR, PWLLHELI	206
CHADWELL HEATH COACHES, ROMFORD	113
CHALFONT COACHES OF HARROW LTD, SOUTHALL	140
CHALFONT LINE LTD, WEST DRAYTON	140
CHALKWELL COACH HIRE & TOURS, SITTINGBOURNE	129
CHAMBERS COACH HIRE LTD, MONEYMORE	212
CHAMBERS COACHES (STEVENAGE) LTD, STEVENAGE	126
H. C. CHAMBERS & SON LTD, BURES	171
CHANDLERS COACH TRAVEL, WESTBURY	184
CHAPEL END COACHES, NUNEATON	176
CHARIOTS OF ESSEX LTD, STANFORD-LE-HOPE	113
CHARLTON-ON-OTMOOR SERVICES, OXFORD	159
CHARTER COACH LTD, YORK	151
CHAUFFEURS OF BIRMINGHAM, EDGBASTON	177
CHEAM COACHES, CHEAM, SUTTON	172
CHENERY TRAVEL, DISS	147
CHENEY COACHES LTD, BANBURY	159
CHEPSTOW CLASSIC BUSES, CHEPSTOW	207
CHEYNE'S COACHES, INVERURIE	188
CHILTERN TRAVEL, HENLOW	83
CHIVERS COACHES LTD, WALLINGTON	172
CHOICE TRAVEL SERVICES, WOLVERHAMPTON	177
CITISTAR LTD, PAULTON, BRISTOL	86
CITY CIRCLE UK LTD, BONNYRIGG	192, 195
CITY CIRCLE (UK) LTD, HAYES	140
CITYLINK, GALWAY	214
CITY SIGHTSEEING GLASGOW, GLASGOW	194
CITY TRAVEL YORKSHIRE LTD, BRADFORD	181

Operator	Page
CLAPTON COACHES LTD, RADSTOCK	163
CLARIBEL COACHES LTD, TILE CROSS, BIRMINGHAM	177
CLARKES OF LONDON, LONDON SE26	140
CLARKSON COACHWAYS LTD, BARROW IN FURNESS	96
CLARKSONS HOLIDAYS, SOUTH ELMSALL	181
CLASSIC COACHES LTD, ANNFIELD PLAIN	107
CLEGG & BROOKING LTD, STOCKBRIDGE	122
CLIFF'S COACHES, HIGH WYCOMBE	87
CLINTONA MINICOACHES, BRENTWOOD	113
CLOWES COACHES, LONGNOR	98
CLYNNOG & TREFOR MOTORS, CAERNARFON	206
COACH COMPANIONS LTD, LEOMINSTER	125
COACHES EXCETERA, CROYDON	140
COACH HOUSE TRAVEL, DORCHESTER	104
COACHLINERS OF TYNESIDE, SOUTH SHIELDS	174
COACH OPTIONS LTD, ROCHDALE	119
COACH SERVICES LTD, THETFORD	147
COACHSTYLE LTD, CHIPPENHAM	184
COAST TO COAST PACKHORSE LTD, KIRKBY STEPHEN	96
COASTAL & COUNTRY COACHES LTD, WHITBY	151
COASTAL COACHES, NEWICK, LEWES	111
COASTAL COACHES, WARTON, PRESTON	131
COCHRANE'S, PETERLEE	107
COLEFORDIAN (WILLETS) LTD, COLEFORD	117
COLISEUM COACHES LTD, WEST END, SOUTHAMPTON	122
COLLIN'S COACHES, CARRICKAMOSS, Co MONAGHAN	214
COLLINS COACHES LTD, LONDON W7	140
COLLINS COACHES, CAMBRIDGE	89
COLLINS COACHES, SELBY	151
W. H. COLLINS, ROCH	208
COLRAY COACHES, BLACKPOOL	133
COMFORT DELGRO	82
COMHAIRLE NAN EILEAN SAR, STORNOWAY	212
COMPASS ROYSTON TRAVEL LTD, STOCKTON ON TEES	107
COMPASS TRAVEL, WORTHING	179
CONFIDENCE, LEICESTER	135
CONISTON COACHES LTD, BROMLEY	141
CONNEX TRANSPORT (JERSEY) LTD, St HELIER, JERSEY	187
CONSTABLE COACHES LTD, HADLEIGH	171
CONWAY COACH AND CHAUFFEUR DRIVE LTD, LIMERICK	214
COOKS COACHES, WESTCLIFF-ON-SEA	113
COOKSONS COACHES & TRAVEL, WELSHPOOL	209
COOMBS TRAVEL, WESTON-SUPER-MARE	163
HENRY COOPER, ANNITSFORD	174
COOPERS COACHES, WOOLSTON	122
COOPER'S TOURMASTER LTD, BEDLINGTON	155
COOPERS TOURS LTD, KILLAMARSH	165
COPELAND TOURS (STOKE-ON-TRENT) LTD, MEIR	168
DAVID CORBEL OF LONDON LTD, EDGWARE	141
CORCORANS EXECUTIVE TOURS, KILLARNEY, Co KERRY	214
CORDUFF TRAVEL, ROSSPORT, Co MAYO	214
COSGROVE'S TOURS, PRESTON	133
COTSWOLD GREEN LTD, NAILSWORTH	117
COUNTRY HOPPER, IBSTOCK	135
COUNTRY BUS, NEWTON ABBOT	101
COUNTRY LION (NORTHAMPTON) LTD, NORTHAMPTON	154
COUNTRYLINER GROUP, GUILDFORD	173
COUNTRYWIDE TRAVEL SERVICES LTD t/a DAWNEY HOLIDAYS, SHEERNESSS	129
COUNTY COACHES, BRENTWOOD	113
COUNTY MINI COACHES, LEICESTER	135
COUNTYWIDE TRAVEL, THATCHAM	123
COUNTYWIDE TRAVEL (FLEET) LTD, FARNHAM	123
COURTESY COACHES LTD, OLDHAM	119
COURTESY TRAVEL, SHREWSBURY	160 178
COURTNEY COACHES LTD, BRACKNELL	84
COX'S OF BELPER	98
COYLES COACHES, GWEEDORE, Co DONEGAL	214
COZY TRAVEL LTD, LETCHWORTH	126
R. & C. S. CRAIG, ROBERTON	199
CRAIG OF CAMPBELTOWN, CAMPBELTOWN	189
CRAIGGS TRAVEL EUROPEAN, AMBLE	155
HENRY CRAWFORD COACHES LTD, NEILSTON	192
CRAWLEY LUXURY, THREE BRIDGES	179
CREMIN COACHES, KILKEEL, Co CORK	214
CRESSWELLS COACHES (GRESLEY) LTD, SWADLINCOTE	98
N N CRESSWELL, EVESHAM	185
CRIEFF TRAVEL, CRIEFF	197
CRISTAL HIRE COACHES OF SWANWICK	98
CROESO TOURS, PENYLAN	203
CRONIN'S COACHES LTD, CORK	214
CROPLEY COACHES, FOSDYKE	137
CROPPER COACHES, TOTTINGTON	119
CROSS COUNTRY COACHES LTD, COLERAINE	212
CROSSKEYS COACHES LTD, FOLKESTONE	129
MARTIN CROWLEY, BANDON, Co CORK	214
CROWN COACHES, BICKLEY	141
CRUDGE COACHES LTD, HONITON	101
CRUISERS LTD, REDHILL	173
CRUSADE TRAVEL LTD, PENKRIDGE	169
CRUSADER COACHES, CLACTON-ON-SEA	113
CRYSTALS COACHES LTD, LONDON W10	141
CT PLUS LTD, LONDON E8	141
CUCKMERE COMMUNITY BUS, POLEGATE	111
CUMBRAE COACHES, MILLPORT	196
CUMBRIA COACHES LTD, CARLISLE	96
CUMFI-LUX COACHES, HILLINGDON	141
CUMFYBUS LTD, SOUTHPORT	146
CUNNINGHAM CARRIAGE CO, CORRINGHAM	113
CUTTINGS COACHES, BROCKLEY	171

D

Operator	Page
D & E COACHES LTD, INVERNESS	194
D & G COACH & BUS LTD, STOKE ON TRENT	169
D A C COACHES LTD, GUNNISLAKE	94
D G C BUSES, DUMFRIES	191
D H CARS OF DENSTONE LTD, UTTOXETER	169
D R M BUS & CONTRACT SERVICES, BROMYARD	125
D. R. P. TRAVEL, MILTON KEYNES	87
D-WAY TRAVEL, BUNGAY	171
DAIMLER, BIRMINGHAM	177
DAISHS TRAVEL, TORQUAY	101
DALESMAN, GUISELEY	181

Operator	Page
DAM EXPRESS, ARDWICK GREEN	119
DAMORY COACHES LTD, BLANDFORD FORUM	104
DANS LUXURY TRAVEL LTD, LONDON E18	141
DARLEY FORD TRAVEL, LISKEARD	94
DARRAGHS COACHES, BALLYMONEY, Co ANTRIM	212
DARTLINE COACHES, EXETER	101
DAVIAN COACHES LTD, LONDON N18	141
DAVID PALMER COACHES LTD, NORMANTON	182
DAVIDSON BUSES LTD, BATHGATE	201
BILLY DAVIES EXECUTIVE COACHES, STIRLING	200
DAWSON'S MINICOACHES, ALFRETON	98
TIM DEARMAN COACHES, ARDROSS	194
DECKER BUS, WHITTLESEY	89
MIKE DE COURCEY TRAVEL LTD, COVENTRY	177
DELAINE BUSES LTD, BOURNE	137
DEN CANEY COACHES LTD, BIRMINGHAM	177
DERBY COMMUNITY TRANSPORT	98
DEROS COACH TOURS LTD, KILLARNEY, Co KERRY	214
DEVERON COACHES, MACDUFF	188
DEWHIRST COACHES LTD, BRADFORD	181
RON W DEW & SONS LTD, SOMERSHAM	89
DIAMOND HOLIDAYS, SWANSEA	210
DIAMOND BUS LTD, BIRMINGHAM	177
DICKINSON'S COACHES, BOSTON	137
DIRECT COACH TOURS, BIRMINGHAM	177
DOBSON'S BUSES LTD, NORTHWICH	92
DOCHERTY'S MIDLAND COACHES, AUCHTERARDER	198
DOCKLANDS BUSES LTD, LONDON SW19	141
DODDS OF TROON LTD, AYR	199
JOHN DODSWORTH (COACHES) LTD, BOROUGHBRIDGE	151
DOHERTY'S COACHES, DUNGLOE, Co DONEGAL	214
DOIGS OF GLASGOW LTD, GLASGOW	194
DOLPHIN COACHES LTD, WIMBORNE MINSTER	105
DONNELLY COACHES, ENNISCORTHY, Co WEXFORD	214
DONOGHUES OF GALWAY, Co GALWAY	214
DONOVAN'S COACHES LTD, KILLARNEY, Co KERRY	214
DONS COACHES DUNMOW LTD, GREAT DUNMOW	113
DORSET COUNTY COUNCIL, PASSENGER TRANSPORT SECTION	105
DOUGLAS CORPORATION TRAMWAY, DOUGLAS, IoM	187
DOWN MOTORS, OTERY ST MARY	101
C J DOWN, TAVISTOCK	101
P. DOYLE LTD, ROUNDWOOD, Co WICKLOW	215
TONY DOYLE COACHES LTD, ENNISKERRY, Co WICKLOW	215
K&H DOYLE LTD, ALFRETON	98
TIM DRAPER'S GOLDEN HOLIDAYS, ALFRETON	99
DREADNOUGHT COACHES, ALNWICK	155
R DRURY COACHES, GOOLE	110
THE DUALWAY GROUP, RATHCOOLE, Co DUBLIN	215
DUBLIN BUS	215
DUBLIN MINI COACHES & CHAUFFEUR HIRE, DUBLIN	215
DUDLEY'S COACHES LTD, WORCESTER	185
DUNN'S COACHES, AIRDRIE	196
DUNN MOTOR TRACTION, HEANOR	99
DURHAM CITY COACHES LTD	107

E

Operator	Page
'E' COACHES OF ALFRETON	99
EAGLE COACHES, BRISTOL	86
EAGLE LINE TRAVEL, CHELTENHAM	117
EAGLES & CRAWFORD, MOLD	206
EAGRE COACHES LTD, MORTON	137
EARNSIDE COACHES, GLENFARG	198
EASSONS COACHES LTD, ITCHEN, SOUTHAMPTON	123
EAST LONDON BUS GROUP, LONDON E16	82, 141
EAST YORKSHIRE MOTOR SERVICES LTD, HULL	110
A. W. EASTON'S COACHES LTD, STRATTON STRAWLESS, NORWICH	148
EASTONWAYS LTD, RAMSGATE	129
EASTVILLE COACHES LTD, BRISTOL	86
EASTWARD COACHES, WINKLEIGH	102
EASYBUS LTD, LONDON NW10	141
EASYWAY MINIBUS HIRE LTD, BRIDGEND	202
EAVESWAY TRAVEL LTD, ASHTON-IN-MAKERFIELD	133
EBLEY COACHES LTD, NAILSWORTH	117
EDS MINIBUS & COACH HIRE, EAST TILBURY	113
EDINBURGH TOURS LTD, EDINBURGH	193
EDINBURGH COACH LINES, EDINBURGH	193
EDWARDS BROS, TIERS CROSS	208
EDWARDS COACHES LTD, LLANTWIT FARDRE	210
GEORGE EDWARDS & SON, BWLCHGWYN	211
L J EDWARDS COACH HIRE, HAILSHAM	111
EIFION'S COACHES, GWALCHMAI	202
EIREBUS LTD, DUBLIN	215
ELCOCK REISEN LTD, MADELEY	161
ELITE SERVICES LTD, STOCKPORT	119
ELLEN SMITH (TOURS) LTD, ROCHDALE	119
ELLENDERS COACHES, SHEFFIELD	165
ELLIE ROSE TRAVEL LTD, HULL	110
P & J ELLIS LTD, LONDON NW10	141
ELLISON'S COACHES, ASHTON KEYNES	184
ELTHAM EXECUTIVE CHARTER LTD, LONDON SE9	141
EMBLINGS COACHES, GUYHIRN	89
EMMERSON COACHES LTD, IMMINGHAM	150
EMMAS COACHES, DOLGELLAU	206
EMPRESS COACHES LTD, ST LEONARDS-ON-SEA	111
EMSWORTH & DISTRICT MOTOR SERVICES LTD, SOUTHBOURNE	123
ENDEAVOUR COACHES LTD, BIRMINGHAM	177
ENFIELD COACHES, ENFIELD, Co MEATH	215
ENSIGN BUS COMPANY, PURFLEET	113
ENTERPRISE TRAVEL, DARLINGTON	107
EPSOM COACHES GROUP, EPSOM	173
ERB SERVICES LTD, BYKER	175
ESSBEE COACHES (HIGHLANDS & ISLANDS), COATBRIDGE	196
E.S.T. BUS LTD, COWBRIDGE	211
EUROCOACH, DUNGANNON, Co TYRONE	212
EUROLINERS, REDNAL	186
EUROLINK FOLKESTONE	130
EUROSUN COACHES, CROMER	148
EUROTAXIS LTD, BRISTOL	86
EVANS COACHES TREGARON LTD	204
GARETH EVANS COACHES, BRYNAMMAN	204
EVE CARS & COACHES, DUNBAR	192
EXCALIBUR COACHES, LONDON SE15	141
EXCALIBUR COACH TRAVEL, SOUTHMINSTER	113
EXCELSIOR COACHES LTD, BOURNEMOUTH	105
EXPERT COACH SERVICES LTD, GRIMSBY	150

EXPRESS MOTORS, PENYGROES, CAERNARFON	206
EXPRESSLINES LTD, BEDFORD	83
EXPRESSWAY COACHES, ROTHERHAM	165
EYMS GROUP LTD	82

F

FAHERTY'S COACH HIRE, MOYCULLEN, Co GALWAY	215
FAIRWAY TRAVEL, EDINBURGH	193
FALCON TRAVEL, SHEPPERTON	142
FAR EAST TRAVEL, IPSWICH	171
FARELINE BUS & COACH SERVICES, EYE	171
FARESAVER BUSES, CHIPPENHAM	184
FARGO COACHLINES, BRAINTREE	113
FARLEIGH COACHES, ROCHESTER	130
FARNHAM COACHES, FARNHAM	173
FELIX BUS SERVICES LTD, STANLEY, DERBYS	99
FELIX OF LONG MELFORD, LONG MELFORD	171
FENN HOLIDAYS LTD, MARCH	89
FERGUSON MINIBUS HIRE, STIRLING	200
FERNHILL TRAVEL LTD, BRACKNELL	84
FERRERS COACHES LTD, SOUTH WOODHAM FERRERS	114
FERRIS COACH HOLIDAYS, NANTGARW	210
FERRYMAN TRAVEL, LEYBOURNE	130
FFOSHELIG COACHES, CARMARTHEN	204
DAVID FIELD, NEWENT	117
FIFE SCOTTISH OMNIBUSES LTD, KIRKCALDY	193
FILERS TRAVEL, ILFRACOMBE	102
FINEGAN COACH HIRE, CARRICKMACROSS, Co MONAGHAN	215
FINGLANDS COACHWAYS LTD, RUSHOLME	119
FINLAY'S COACH HIRE, ARDEE, Co LOUTH	215
FINNEGAN – BRAY COACH & BUS, BRAY, Co WICKLOW	215
DECLAN FINNEGAN, KENMARE, Co KERRY	215
FIRST IN ABERDEEN	188
FIRST ABERDEEN LTD, COACHING UNIT	188
FIRST BEELINE BUSES LTD, BRACKNELL	84
FIRST BRISTOL, BRISTOL	86
FIRST CYMRU BUSES LTD, SWANSEA	210
FIRST IN CHESTER & THE WIRRAL	92, 148
FIRST DEVON & CORNWALL LTD	102
FIRST EAST OF ENGLAND, CHELMSFORD	114
FIRST EAST OF ENGLAND, NORWICH	148, 171
FIRST SCOTLAND EAST LTD, LARBERT	193, 200
FIRST GLASGOW	194
FIRST HAMPSHIRE & DORSET LTD, SOUTHAMPTON	123
FIRST LONDON, LONDON W2	142
FIRST IN MANCHESTER, OLDHAM	119, 146
FIRST MIDLANDS	135, 154, 169, 186
FIRST SOMERSET & AVON LTD, WESTON-SUPER-MARE	163
FIRST SOUTH YORKSHIRE, ROTHERHAM	165
FIRST WEST YORKSHIRE, LEEDS	181
FIRST YORK	152
FIRSTGROUP PLC	79
FISHERS TOURS, DUNDEE	191
JOHN FISHWICK & SONS, LEYLAND	133
FITZCHARLES COACHES LTD, GRANGEMOUTH	200
FIVE STAR GROUP TRAVEL, PRESCOTT	146
JOHN FLANAGAN COACH TRAVEL, GRAPPENHALL, WARRINGTON	92
FLIGHTS HALLMARK LTD, BIRMINGHAM	177
FLIGHTS HALLMARK LTD, CRAWLEY	179
FLORIDA COACHES, HALSTEAD	114
FORDS COACHES, ALTHORNE	114
FORESTDALE COACHES LTD, CROYDON	142
FORGET-ME-NOT (TRAVEL) LTD, IPSWICH	171
FORMBY COACHWAYS LTD, FORMBY	146
FOUNTAIN EXECUTIVE, ABERDEEN	188
FOUR GIRLS COACHES, PONTYBODKIN	206
FOURWAY COACHES, LEEDS	181
FOWLERS TRAVEL, HOLBEACH DROVE	137
FOXHOUND TRAVEL LTD, ROCKCORRY, Co MONAGHAN	215
FREEBIRD, BURY	119
FREEDOM TRAVEL COACHES, ELY	89
FREESTONES COACHES LTD, BEETLEY, DEREHAM	148
JAMES FRENCH & SON, EYEMOUTH	190
FROME MINIBUSES LTD, FROME	163
MARTIN FUREY COACHES LTD, DRUMCLIFFE, Co SLIGO	215
L. FURNESS & SONS, HIGH GREEN	165

G

G & S TRAVEL, RAMSGATE	130
G H A COACHES LTD, RUABON	211
G. M. COACHES LTD, CEFN CRIBWR	202
G. P. D. TRAVEL, HEYWOOD	119, 133
GAIN TRAVEL EXPERIENCE LTD, BRADFORD	182
GALLEON TRAVEL LTD, HARLOW	114
GALLOWAY EUROPEAN COACHLINES LTD, MENDLESHAM	171
GALSON-STORNOWAY MOTOR SERVICES LTD, ISLE OF LEWIS	201
GALVINS COACHES, DUNMANWAY, Co CORK	215
GALWAY CITY DIRECT LTD, GALWAY	215
GANGE'S COACHES, COWES	128
GARDINERS TRAVEL, SPENNYMOOR	107
GARELOCHHEAD COACHES, GARELOCHHEAD	189
GARETH EVANS COACHES, BRYNAMMAN	204
GARNETT'S COACHES, BISHOP AUCKLAND	107
GARY'S COACHES OF TREDEGAR	202
STANLEY GATH (COACHES) LTD, DEWSBURY	182
GATWICK FLYER LTD, ROMFORD	114
GEE-VEE TRAVEL, BARNSLEY	165
GELDARD'S COACHES LTD, LEEDS	182
GEMINI TRAVEL, IPSWICH	170
GEMINI TRAVEL SOUTHAMPTON LTD, MARCHWOOD	123
GENIAL TRAVEL, STANWAY	114
BEN GEORGE TRAVEL, BRIGG	153
GIBSON DIRECT LTD, RENFREW	198
GILES TOURS, NEWTOWNARDS	212
GILLEN'S COACHES LTD, GREENOCK	195
GILL'S TRAVEL, TROWELL	156
R G GITTINS COACHES, WELSHPOOL	209
G-LINE HOLIDAYS LTD, St ANNES	133
G-LINE MINICOACHES, SWINDON	184
GLASGOW CITYBUS LTD, GLASGOW	194
GLENESK COACHES LTD, EDZELL	189
GLEN VALLEY TOURS LTD, WOOLER	155

Operator	Page
GLENVIC OF BRISTOL LTD	86
GLOBE COACHES, ABERDARE	210
GLOVERS COACHES LTD, ASHBOURNE	99
JAMES GLYNN, NURNEY, Co CARLOW	216
GLYNNS COACHES.COM, ENNIS, Co CLARE	215
GO NORTH EAST, GATESHEAD	175
GO-AHEAD GROUP PLC	80
GO-GOODWINS COACHES, ECCLES	119
J D GODSON, CROSSGATES	182
PETER GODWARD COACHES, BASILDON	114
GOLD STANDARD, THE, GREENFORD	142
GOLD STAR TRAVEL, NEWTOWN	209
GOLDEN BOY COACHES (JETSIE LTD), HODDESDON	126
GOLDEN EAGLE COACHES, SALSBURGH	196
GOLDEN GREEN TRAVEL, MACCLESFIELD	92, 169
GOLDEN PIONEER TRAVEL, HEREFORD	125
GOLDENSTAND SOUTHERN LTD, LONDON, NW10	142
GOODE COACHES, NORTHAMPTON	154
W. C. GOODSIR, HOLYHEAD	202
GOODWIN'S COACHES, BRAINTREE	114
W. GORDON & SONS, ROTHERHAM	165
GOSPEL'S COACHES, HUCKNALL	156
G. W. GOULDING, KNOTTINGLEY	182
GRAHAM URQUHART TRAVEL, INVERNESS	195
VIOLET GRAHAM COACHES, PAISLEY	198
GRAHAM'S COACHES, BRISTOL	86
GRAHAM'S COACHES LTD, KELVEDON	114
GRANT PALMER PASSENGER SERVICES, DUNSTABLE	83
GRAVES COACHES & MINIBUSES, BROXBOURNE	126
GRAYLINE COACHES, BICESTER	159
GRAYS LUXURY TRAVEL, HOYLAND COMMON	165
GRAYWAY COACHES, WIGAN	119
GRAYSCROFT BUS & COACHSERVICES LTD, MABLETHORPE	137
A GREEN COACHES LTD, WALTHAMSTOW	142
GRETTON'S COACHES, PETERBOROUGH	89
GREYHOUND COACHES CO, CARDIFF	203
GREY CARS, TORBAY	102
GREYHOUND UK LTD, LONDON W2	142
GREYS OF ELY	89
GRIERSONS COACHES, STOCKTON-ON-TEES	107
GRIFFIN BUS, LONGFIELD	130
GRIFFITHS COACHES, Y FELINHELI	206
JEFF GRIFFITHS COACHES, ST ANNES	133
GRINDLES COACHES LTD, CINDERFORD	117
GROUP TRAVEL, BODMIN	94
GROVE COACHES, HERTFORD	126
GRWP ABERCONWY, LLANDUDNO	205
GUSCOTT'S COACHES LTD, BEAWORTHY	102
GWYNFOR COACHES, LLANGEFNI	202

H

Operator	Page
HDA COACHES, GAERWEN	202
HAILSTONE TRAVEL LTD, BASILDON	114
PHIL HAINES COACHES, BOSTON	137
MIKE HALFORD COACHES, BRIDPORT	105
HALIFAX BUS COMPANY, HALIFAX	182
HALIFAX JOINT COMMITTEE, HALIFAX	182
HALPENNY TRANSPORT, BLACKROCK, DUNDALK	216
HALTON BOROUGH TRANSPORT LTD, WIDNES	92

Operator	Page
HAMILTON OF UXBRIDGE, UXBRIDGE	142
HAMILTON'S COACHES, KETTERING	154
HAMS TRAVEL, FLIMWELL	111
HANDLEY'S COACHES, MIDDLEHAM	152
HAPPY DAYS COACHES, STAFFORD	169
M & J HARCUS, WESTRAY, ORKNEY	197
HARDINGS COACHES, BETCHWORTH	173
HARDINGS INTERNATIONAL, REDDITCH	186
HARDINGS TOURS LTD, HUYTON	146
HARDY MILES COACHES LTD, SOUTHEND	114
HARGREAVES COACHES, HEBDEN, Nr SKIPTON	152
HARLEQUIN COACHES LTD, DUNBLANE	200
HARLEQUIN TRAVEL, IPSWICH	171
HARPUR'S COACHES, DERBY	99
HARRIS COACHES, BLACKWOOD	203
HARRIS EXECUTIVE TRAVEL, BROMSGROVE	186
D & H HARROD (COACHES) LTD, KING'S LYNN	148
HARROGATE COACH TRAVEL LTD	152
HARTE BUSES, GREENOCK	195
HARTWOOL LTD t/a GRAYLINE COACHES, BICESTER	159
HARVEY'S BUS LTD, MORETONHAMPSTEAD	102
HARWOOD COACHES, WEYBRIDGE	173
HATCH GREEN COACHES, TAUNTON	163
HATTONS TRAVEL, ST HELENS	146
HATTS TRAVEL, CHIPPENHAM	185
HAWKES TOURS, DERBY	99
HAYDN'S TOURS & TRAVEL, CHIRK	211
HAYTON'S EXECUTIVE TRAVEL LTD, MANCHESTER	120
HAYWARD TRAVEL (CARDIFF), DINAS POWYS	211
HAYWARDS COACHES, THATCHAM	84
HEALINGS INTERNATIONAL COACHES, OLDHAM	120
HEALY COACHES, CASTLEGAR, GALWAY	216
HEARD'S COACHES, BIDEFORD	102
HEARNS COACHES, HARROW WEALD	142
HEART OF WALES BUS & COACH LTD, CARDIFF	203
HEATON'S OF SHEFFIELD LTD	165
HEBRIDEAN COACHES, HOWMORE, SOUTH UIST	201
HEDINGHAM & DISTRICT OMNIBUSES LTD, SIBLE HEDINGHAM	114
HEMMINGS COACHES, HOLSWORTHY	102
HENDERSON TRAVEL, HAMILTON	199
HENLEYS BUS SERVICES LTD, ABERTILLERY	202
HENRY CRAWFORD COACHES LTD, NEILSTON	192
HENSHAWS COACHES LTD, JACKSDALE	99, 156
HERBERTS TRAVEL, SHEFFORD	83
HERDMAN COACHES, CLYRO	209
HERITAGE TOUR, ST MARY'S, ISLES OF SCILLY	187
HERRINGTON COACHES LTD, FORDINGBRIDGE	105
HEYFORDIAN TRAVEL LTD, BICESTER	159
HIGHLAND HERITAGE COACH TOURS, DALLMALLY	189
HIGHLAND ROVER COACHES, TAYNUILT	190
HILLS OF HERSHAM, HERSHAM	173
HILLS SERVICES LTD, TORRINGTON	102
HILLARYS COACHES, PRUDHOE	155
JOHN HOBAN TRAVEL LTD, WORKINGTON	96
HODDER MOTOR SERVICES LTD, CLITHEROE	133
HODGE'S COACHES (SANDHURST) LTD, SANDHURST	84
HODGSONS COACHES, BARNARD CASTLE	107
HODSON COACHES LTD, LINCOLN	137

Operator	Page
HOLLINSHEAD COACHES LTD, KNYPERSLEY	169
HOLLOWAY COACHES LTD, SCUNTHORPE	150
G & J HOLMES COACHES LTD, CLAY CROSS	99
HOLMES GROUP TRAVEL, NEWPORT	161
HOLMESWOOD COACHES LTD, ORMSKIRK	133
J R HOLYHEAD INTERNATIONAL, WILLENHALL	177
HOMEWARD BOUND TRAVEL, WIMBORNE	105
HOOKWAYS, EXETER	102
HOOKWAYS JENNINGS, BUDE	94
HOPLEYS COACHES LTD, TRURO	94
P & D A HOPWOOD, ASKHAM BRYAN, YORK	152
HORNSBY TRAVEL SERVICES LTD, SCUNTHORPE	150
HORROCKS BUS LTD, LYDBURY NORTH	161
E & M HORSBURGH LTD, PUMPHERSTON	201
HORSEMAN COACHES LTD, READING	85
JOHN HOUGHTON LUXURY MINI COACHES, LONDON W5	142
HOUNSLOW COMMUNITY TRANSPORT, HOUNSLOW	142
HOUNSLOW MINI COACHES, FELTHAM	142
HOUSTON'S OF LONDON, LONDON N15	142
HOUSTON'S MINICOACHES, LOCKERBIE	191
HOWELLS COACHES LTD, HENGOED	203
HOWLETTS COACHES, WINSLOW	87
HUDDERSFIELD BUS COMPANY, HUDDERSFIELD	182
JIM HUGHES COACHES LTD, SUNDERLAND	175
VIC HUGHES & SON LTD, FELTHAM	142
HULLEYS OF BASLOW, BAKEWELL	99
HULME HALL COACHES LTD, CHEADLE HULME	92
HUMBLES COACHES, SHILDON	107
F HUNT COACH HIRE LTD, ALFORD	138
HUNTER BROS LTD, TANTOBIE	107
HUNTER COACHES LTD, LEEDS	182
HUNTERS EXECUTIVE COACHES, SAUCHIE, ALLOA	190
WILLIAM HUNTER, LOANHEAD	195
H D HUTCHINSON & SON, BUCKLEY	206
HUTTON COACH HIRE, WESTON-SUPER-MARE	163
HUYTON TRAVEL LTD	146
HYTHE & WATERSIDE COACHES LTD, HYTHE	123

I

Operator	Page
IBT TRAVEL GROUP, PRESTWICK	199
IMPACT OF LONDON, GREENFORD	142
IMPERIAL BUS CO LTD, ROMFORD	115
IMPERIAL COACHES LTD, SOUTHALL	142
INDEPENDENT COACHWAYS LTD, HORSFORTH	182
INGLEBY'S LUXURY COACHES LTD, YORK	152
INTERNATIONAL COACH LINES LTD, THORNTON HEATH	143
IPSWICH BUSES LTD	171
IRISH COACHES, DUBLIN	216
IRVINE'S OF LAW, LAW	196
IRVINGS COACH HIRE LTD, CARLISLE	96
ISLAND COACHWAYS, ST PETER PORT	187
ISLAND ROVER, SCILLY ISLES	187
ISLAY COACHES, TARBERT	190
ISLE COACHES, OWSTON FERRY	166
ISLE OF MAN TRANSPORT, DOUGLAS	187
ISLE OF WIGHT COUNTY TRANSPORT DEPARTMENT, NEWPORT	128
IVYBRIDGE & DISTRICT COMMUNITY TRANSPORT, IVYBRIDGE	102

J

Operator	Page
J & C COACHES, NEWTON AYCLIFFE	107
J & D EURO TRAVEL, HARROW	143
J & L TRAVEL LTD, TRING	87
J & V COACHES, STROMNESS, ORKNEY	197
J C S COACHES, CORBY	154
J P EXECUTIVE TRAVEL, MIDDLETON	120
J P MINICOACHES, FORFAR	189
J R TRAVEL, YORK	152
J S B TRAVEL, COUNDON	108
J W COACHES LTD, BANCHORY	188
JACKSON'S COACHES, BLACKPOOL	133
ANDREW JAMES QUALITY TRAVEL, CHIPPENHAM	184
BRODYR JAMES, TREGARON	204
JAMES KING COACHES, NEWTON STEWART	191
PAUL JAMES COACHES, COALVILLE	136
R. G. JAMIESON & SON, YELL, SHETLAND	198
JANS COACHES, SOHAM, ELY	89
JAYLINE BAND SERVICES, HORDEN	108
JEFFS COACHES LTD, HELMDON	154
JEMS TRAVEL, STANNINGTON	166
JENSON TRAVEL, PONTYPOOL	210
JOHN MORROW COACHES, GLASGOW	194
JOHN'S COACHES, BLANEAU-FFESTINIOG	207
JOHNSON BROS TOURS LTD, WORKSOP	99, 156, 166
JOHNSONS COACH & BUS TRAVEL, HENLEY-IN-ARDEN	177
D JONES & SON, ACREFAIR	211
E JONES & SONS, PONCIAU	211
GWYN JONES & SON LTD, BRYNCETHIN	202
GWYN JONES (MEIFORD), MEIFOD	209
JONES EXECUTIVE COACHES LTD, WALKDEN	120
JONES INTERNATIONAL, LLANDEILO	204
JONES MOTOR SERVICES, FLINT	206
JONES LOGIN, WHITLAND	204
LLEW JONES INTERNATIONAL, LLANWRST	205
O R JONES & SONS LTD, LLANFAETHLU	202
P W JONES COACHES, HEREFORD	125
R J JONES TRAVEL, MEURIG	204
W E JONES & SON, LLANERCHYMEDD	202
JOSEPHS MINI COACHES, NEWCASTLE-UNDER-LYME	169
JOURNEYS-DESTINATION, SHEFFIELD	166
JUDGE'S MINI COACHES, CORBY	155

K

Operator	Page
K & B TRAVEL, CLIBURN, PENRITH	96
K & S COACHES, MANSFIELD	157
K LINE TRAVEL, HONLEY	182
K. M. MOTORS LTD, BARNSLEY	166
KARDAN TRAVEL, COWES, IoW	128
BERNARD KAVANAGH & SONS LTD, URLINGFORD, Co KILKENNY	216
J. J. KAVANAGH & SONS, URLINGFORD, Co KILKENNY	216
MATT KAVANAGH COACHES, TIPPERARY	216
PIERCE KAVANAGH COACHES, URLINGFORD, Co KILKENNY	216
KEENAN OF AYR COACH TRAVEL, COALHALL	199
KEENAN COMMERCIALS LTD, DUNDALK, CO LOUTH	216
KELVIN VALLEY, FALKIRK	193, 200
KENNEDY COACHES LTD, TRALEE, Co KERRY	216
KENT COACH TOURS LTD, ASHFORD	130

Operator	Page
KENT COUNTY COUNCIL, AYLESFORD	130
KENZIES COACHES LTD, ROYSTON	126
P. J. KEOGH, SHANNON AIRPORT, Co CLARE	216
KERRY COACHES LTD, KILLARNEY, Co KERRY	216
KESTREL COACHES, STOURPORT ON SEVERN	186
KETTLEWELL (RETFORD) LTD	157
KIDDLES COACHES, HUNTINGDON	89
R. KIME & CO LTD, FOLKINGHAM	138
KINCHBUS LTD, LOUGHBOROUGH	136
KINEIL COACHES LTD, FRASERBURGH	188
KING ALFRED MOTOR SERVICES LTD, ANDOVER	123
JAMES KING COACHES, NEWTON STEWART	191
KINGDOM COACHES, METHIL	193
KINGDOM COACHES, TRALEE, Co KERRY	216
KINGDOM'S TOURS LTD, TIVERTON	102
KINGFISHER MINICOACHES, READING	85
KINGS COACHES, STANWAY	115
THE KINGS FERRY LTD, GILLINGHAM	130
KINGS LUXURY COACHES, MIDDLESBROUGH	152
KINGSNORTON COACHES, BIRMINGHAM	178
KINGSLEY COACHES LTD, BIRTLEY	175
KINGSMAN INTERNATIONAL TRAVEL, FAVERSHAM	130
KINGSWINFORD COACHWAYS, BRIERLY HILL	178
KIRBYS COACHES, RAYLEIGH	115
KIRKBY LONSDALE COACH HIRE LTD, CARNFORTH	133
KIWI LUXURY TRAVEL, NEWTON STEWART	191
KONECTBUS LTD, DEREHAM	148

L

Operator	Page
L W B LIMITED, WATFORD	126
LADYLINE, RAWMARSH	166
LAGUNA HOLIDAYS, BOURNEMOUTH	105
LAINTON COACHES LTD t/a ASHALL'S COACHES, MANCHESTER	120
LAKELAND COACHES, HURST GREEN, CLITHEROE	134
LAKELAND TOURS, TEMPO, Co FERMANAGH	212
LAKELINE COACHES, KNIGHTON	209
LAKES SUPERTOURS, WINDERMERE	96
LAKESIDE COACHES LTD, ELLESMERE	161
LALLY COACHES, GALWAY	216
LAMBS COACHES, STOCKPORT	93, 120
LAMBERT'S COACHES (BECCLES) LTD	172
LANGSTON & TASKER, BUCKINGHAM	87
R S LAWMAN COACHES LTD, KETTERING	155
LAWTON'S EXECUTIVE COACHES, BOSTON	138
LEANDER COACH TRAVEL, SWADLINCOTE	99
JOHN LEASK & SON, LERWICK, SHETLAND	108
LECKS TRAVEL, ULVERSTON	96
LEE'S COACHES LTD, LANGLEY MOOR	108
LEOLINE TRAVEL, HAMPTON	143
LEONS COACH TRAVEL (STAFFORD) LTD, STAFFORD	169
LE-RAD COACHES & LIMOUSINES, WOODLEY Nr STOCKPORT	93
LEVEN VALLEY COACHES, MIDDLESBROUGH	152
LEWIS-RHYDLEWIS CYF, RHYDLEWIS	204
LEWIS COACHES, LLANDRHYSTUD	204
LEWIS TRAVEL, LONDON SE7	143
LEWIS'S COACHES, WHITLAND	204
LEWIS-Y-LLAN, AMLWCH	202
LIBERTON TRAVEL, LOANHEAD	193

Operator	Page
ARNOLD LIDDELL COACHES, BRISTOL	86
LIDDELL'S COACHES, AUCHINLECK	192
LINBURG BUS & COACH, SHEFFIELD	166
LINK LINE COACHES LTD, LONDON	143
LINKFAST LTD T/A S&M COACHES, BENFLEET	115
LINKRIDER COACHES LTD, SWANAGE	105
LITTLE BUS COMPANY, THE, ELSTREE	143
LITTLE JIM'S BUSES, BERKHAMSTED	126
LITTLE TRANSPORT LTD, ILKESTON	99
P&O LLOYD, BAGILLT	206
LLOYDS COACHES, MACHYNLLETH	209
LLYNFI COACHES, MAESTEG	203
LOCHS MOTOR TRANSPORT LTD, LEWIS	201
LOCHS & GLENS HOLIDAYS, GARTOCHAN	200
J W LODGE & SONS LTD, HIGH EASTER	115
LOGANS EXECUTIVE TRAVEL, DUNLOY, BALLYMENA	212
LOGANS TOURS LTD, NORTHFLEET GREEN	130
LONDON CENTRAL, LONDON SW19	143
LONDON GENERAL, LONDON SW19	143
LONDON SOVEREIGN, TWICKENHAM	143
LONDON TRAMLINK	143
LONDON UNITED BUS CO LTD, TWICKENHAM	143
DAVE LONG COACH TRAVEL LTD, SKIBBEREEN, Co CORK	217
LONG'S COACHES LTD, SALSBURGH	196
LONGMYND TRAVEL LTD, SHREWSBURY	161
J J LONGSTAFF & SONS LTD, DEWSBURY	182
LONGSTAFF'S COACHES, MORPETH	155
LOTHIAN BUSES PLC, EDINBURGH	193
LUAS, DUBLIN	217
LUCKETTS TRAVEL, FAREHAM	123
LUGG VALLEY PRIMROSE TRAVEL LTD, LEOMINSTER	125
A. LYLES & SON, BATLEY	182
LYNCH COACH HIRE, CASTLEDERG, Co TYRONE	212

M

Operator	Page
M LINE, ALLOA	190
M & E COACHES, HERSHAM	173
M & H COACHES, DENBIGH	205
M & J TRAVEL, CRAVEN ARMS	161
M & S COACHES OF HEREFORDSHIRE LTD, LEOMINSTER	125
M C H MINIBUSES LTD, UXBRIDGE	143
M.C.T. GROUP TRAVEL LTD, MOTHERWELL	197
M P MINICOACHES LTD, TELFORD	161
M T P CHARTER COACHES, LONDON E11	144
MacEWAN'S COACH SERVICES, AMISFIELD	191
MACKIE'S COACHES, ALLOA	190
MacPHAILS COACHES, SALSBURGH	197
MacPHERSON COACHES LTD, SWADLINCOTE	99
NICK MADDY COACHES, HEREFORD	125
MAGPIE TRAVEL, HIGH WYCOMBE	87
MAINLINE COACHES LTD, EVANSTOWN	210
MAISEY TRAVEL, PONTYPRIDD	210
MALCYS, SHEFFIELD	166
MALAHIDE COACHES LTD, MALAHIDE, Co DUBLIN	217
MANNING'S COACHES, CROOM, LIMERICK	217
MANSFIELD'S COACHES, SWINDON	185
MARBILL TRAVEL, BEITH	196
MARCHANTS COACHES, CHELTENHAM	118
MARCHWOOD MOTORWAYS, TOTTON	123

Operator	Page
MARPLE MINI COACHES	93 120
MARSHALLS COACHES LLP, LEIGHTON BUZZARD	83 126 146
MARSHALLS OF SUTTON-ON-TRENT LTD, NEWARK	157
ALAN MARTIN COACHES, DUBLIN	217
WALTER MARTIN COACHES, SHEFFIELD	166
MARTIN'S OF TYSOE, TYSOE	176
MARTIN'S COACH TRAVEL, LIVINGSTON	201
MARTINS SELF DRIVE, REDFIELD	86
MARTIN'S COACHES (CAVAN) LTD, CAVAN	217
DICK MARTIN COACHES, ANNACOTTY, Co LIMERICK	217
MASS BRIGHTBUS, ANSTON	166
MASTER TRAVEL, WELWYN GARDEN CITY	126
MATTHEWS COACH HIRE LTD, INNISKEEN, Co MONAGHAN	217
MATTHEWS COACHES, KINGS LYNN	148
MAUDES COACHES, BARNARD CASTLE	108
J A MAXFIELD & SONS LTD, SHEFFIELD	166
MAYDAY TRAVEL, CROYDON	173
MAYNE COACHES LTD, WARRINGTON	93, 121
MAYNES COACHES LTD, BUCKIE & ELGIN	188, 196
MAYNES COACHES LTD, ORKNEY	197
MAYPOLE COACHES, MELLING	147
MAYTREE TRAVEL LTD, BOLTON	121
ROY McCARTHY COACHES, MACCLESFIELD	93
McCOLLS OF ARGYLL LTD, DUNOON	190
McCOLLS COACHES LTD, BALLOCH	200
McCULLOCH AND SON, STRANRAER	191
McELLIGOTT COACHES, CLARINA, Co LIMERICK	217
McEWENS TRAVEL, MANSFIELD	157
JAMES McGEE BUS HIRE, LETTERKENNY, Co DONEGAL	217
McGEEHAN COACHES, FINTOWN, Co DONEGAL	217
McGILLS BUS SERVICE LTD, GREENOCK	195
JOHN McGINLEY COACH TRAVEL, LETTERKENNY, Co DONEGAL	217
J J McGONAGLE, REDCASTLE, Co DONEGAL	217
McGREAD OMAGH, FINTONA, Co ARMAGH	212
McKECHNIE OF BATHGATE LTD, BATHGATE	201
McKENDRY TRAVEL, LOANHEAD	195
McLEANS COACHES, WITNEY	159
MEADWAY PRIVATE HIRE LTD, BIRMINGHAM	178
MICHAEL MEERE COACH HIRE, ENNIS, Co CLARE	217
MEGABUS, PERTH	198
MEMORY LANE COACHES, OLD BOLINGBROKE	138
MEMORY LANE VINTAGE OMNIBUS SERVICES, MAIDENHEAD	85, 143, 173
MEREDITHS COACHES LTD, MALPAS	93
MERIDIAN BUS, NORTHAMPTON	155
MERIDIAN LINE TRAVEL, ROYSTON	126
MERTON COMMUNITY TRANSPORT, MITCHAM	173
MERVYN'S COACHES, MICHELDEVER	123
MESSENGERS COACHES LTD, WIGTON	96
METRO COACHES, STOCKTON-ON-TEES	108
METROBUS LTD, CRAWLEY	180
METROLINE TRAVEL LTD, HARROW	144
METROLINK, MANCHESTER	121
MID DEVON COACHES, CREDITON	102
MIDLAND BUS CO LTD, ATHLONE	217
MIDLAND CLASSIC LTD, BURTON-ON-TRENT	169
MIDLAND METRO	178
MIDLAND RED COACHES/WHEELS HERITAGE,	
BRINKLOW	176
MID WALES TRAVEL, ABERYSTWYTH	204
MIDWAY MOTORS (CRYMYCH) LTD, CRYMYCH	208
MIKES COACHES, BASILDON	115
MIL-KEN TRAVEL LTD, LITTLEPORT	89
MIL-KEN TRAVEL LTD, NEWMARKET	172
KEN MILLER TRAVEL, SHENSTONE	178
MILLER'S COACHES, AIRDRIE	197
MILLIGAN'S COACH TRAVEL LTD, MAUCHLINE	192 199
MILLMAN COACHES, GRIMSBY	150
MILLMAN'S OF WARRINGTON	93
MILLPORT MOTORS LTD, MILLPORT	196
ALEX MILNE COACHES, NEW BYTH	188
MINIBUS & COACH HIRE, EARL STONHAM	172
MINIBUS SERVICES LTD, WATFORD	127
MINSTERLEY MOTORS, SHREWSBURY	161
MITCHELL'S COACHES, PLEAN	200
MK METRO LTD, MILTON KEYNES	87
MOFFAT & WILLIAMSON LTD, NEWPORT-ON-TAY	193
MOORE'S COACHES LTD, HOLMES CHAPEL	93
JOE MORONEY, BRAY, Co WICKLOW	217
MORRIS TRAVEL, CARMARTHEN	204
JOHN MORROW COACHES, GLASGOW	194
MORTON'S COACHES, RATHFARNHAM, DUBLIN	217
MOSLEYS TOURS, DEWSBURY	166
MOTTS COACHES (AYLESBURY) LTD, AYLESBURY	87
MOUNTAIN GOAT LTD, WINDERMERE	96
MOUNTS BAY COACHES, PENZANCE	94
C. W. MOXON LTD, OLDCOTES	157
MULLANY'S COACHES, WATFORD	127
MULLEYS MOTORWAYS LTD, IXWORTH	172
MUNRO'S OF JEDBURGH LTD, JEDBURGH	190
GAVIN MURRAY & ELLISONS COACHES, ST HELENS	147
C G MYALL & SON, BASSINGBOURN	89
MYLES COACHES, PLEAN	200

N

Operator	Page
NASH COACHES LTD, SMETHWICK	178
NATIONAL EXPRESS DUNDEE	191
NATIONAL EXPRESS GROUP PLC	80
NATIONAL EXPRESS LTD, EDGBASTON	178
NATIONAL EXPRESS WEST MIDLANDS, BIRMINGHAM	178
NATIONAL HOLIDAYS, HULL	110
NAUGHTON COACH TOURS LTD, SPIDDAL, Co GALWAY	218
NBM HIRE LTD, PENRITH	96
N.C.B. MOTORS LTD, WEM	161
NEAL'S TRAVEL LTD, ISLEHAM, ELY	90
NEAVES COACHES, CATFIELD	148
NEFYN COACHES, NEFYN, PWLLHELI	207
NELSON & SON (GLYNNEATH) LTD, NEATH	207
W. H. NELSON (COACHES) LTD, WICKFORD	115
NESBIT BROS LTD, MELTON MOWBRAY	136
NETWORK COLCHESTER LTD, COLCHESTER	115
NEW ADVENTURE TRAVEL LTD, CARDIFF	203
NEW BHARAT COACHES LTD, SOUTHALL	144
NEW ENTERPRISE COACHES, TONBRIDGE	130
NEWBOURNE COACHES, LEIGHTON BUZZARD	144
NEWBURY COACHES, LEDBURY	125
NEWBURY & DISTRICT, NEWBURY	85
NEWBURY TRAVEL, OLDBURY	178

Operator	Page
NEW HORIZON TRAVEL LTD, FRATING	115
NEWPORT TRANSPORT LTD	208
M. W. NICOLL'S COACH HIRE, LAURENCEKIRK	189
NIELSEN TRAVEL SERVICES, SHEFFIELD	166
NIGEL JACKSON TRAVEL, LEICESTER	136
NOLAN COACHES, COOLOCK, DUBLIN	218
NORFOLK GREEN, KINGS LYNN	148
NORTH SOMERSET COACHES, NAILSEA	86
NORTH WEST COACHES & LIMOS, THORNTON CLEVELEYS	134
NORTON MINI TRAVEL, STOCKTON-ON-TEES	109
NOTTINGHAM CITY COACHES, SHEPSHED	136
NOTTINGHAM CITY TRANSPORT LTD	157
NOTTINGHAM EXPRESS TRANSIT	157
NOTTS & DERBY TRACTION CO LTD, HEANOR	100
NU-VENTURE COACHES LTD, AYLESFORD	130

O

Operator	Page
OFJ CONNECTIONS LTD, HEATHROW	144
OTS MINIBUS & COACH HIRE, CONSTANTINE	94
O'CONNOR AUTOTOURS LTD, KILLARNEY, Co KERRY	218
FEDA O'DONNELL COACHES, DONEGAL	218
LARRY O'HARA MINICOACHES, WATERFORD	218
O'MALLEY COACHES, NEWPORT, Co TIPPERARY	218
O'SULLIVANS COACHES, MALLOW, Co CORK	218
OARE'S COACHES, HOLYWELL	206
OBAN & DISTRICT BUSES LTD, OBAN	190
OCEAN COACHES, PORTSLADE	111
DAVID OGDEN COACHES, ST HELENS	147
OLYMPIA TRAVEL UK LTD, HINDLEY	134
OLYMPIAN COACHES LTD, HARLOW	115
OOR COACHES LTD, ANNAN	191
ORCHARD COUNTY TRAVEL, RICHHILL, Co ARMAGH	212
THE ORIGINAL LONDON TOUR, WANDSWORTH	144
OTTER COACHES, OTTERY ST MARY	101
OWEN'S MOTORS LTD, KNIGHTON	209
OWENS COACHES LTD, OSWESTRY	161
OXFORD BUS COMPANY	159

P

Operator	Page
P&M COACHES, WICKFORD	115
PADARN BUS LTD, LLANBERIS	207
DAVID PALMER COACHES LTD, NORMANTON	182
PARAGON TRAVEL LTD, UTTOXETER	169
PARAMOUNT COACHES LTD, PLYMOUTH	103
PARK'S OF HAMILTON LTD, HAMILTON	199
PARKSIDE TRAVEL, BROXBOURNE	127
PARRYS INTERNATIONAL TOURS LTD, CHESLYN HAY	169
PAT'S COACHES LTD, WREXHAM	211
PAVILION COACHES, HOVE	111
D. A. PAYNE COACH HIRE, ST NEOTS	90
PC COACHES OF LINCOLN LTD, LINCOLN	138
J D PEACE & CO ABDN LTD, ABERDEEN	189
PEARCES PRIVATE HIRE, WALLINGFORD	159
PEARSON COACHES LTD, HULL	110
PEELINGS COACHES, KING'S LYNN	149
PENCOED TRAVEL LTD, BRIDGEND	203
PENMERE MINIBUS SERVICES, FALMOUTH	94
PENNINE MOTOR SERVICES, SKIPTON	152
PEOPLES BUS LTD, LIVERPOOL	147
PERRY'S COACHES, MALTON	152
PERRYMAN'S BUSES, BERWICK UPON TWEED	155 190
PETER CAROL PRESTIGE COACHING, WHITCHURCH, BRISTOL	86
PETERBOROUGH TRAVEL CONSULTANTS, PETERBOROUGH	90
PEWSEY VALE COACHES, PEWSEY	185
PICKERING COACHES, SOUTH GODSTONE	173
PIKE'S COACHES LTD, ANDOVER	124
PLANTS LUXURY TRAVEL LTD, CHEADLE, STAFFS	169
PLASTOWS COACHES, WHEATLEY	159
DAVID PLATT COACHES & MINITRAVEL OF LEES, OLDHAM	121
PLYMOUTH CITYBUS LTD	103
JOHN POWELL TRAVEL LTD, HELLABY	166
POWELLS COACHES, CREDITON	103
POWELLS COACHES, SHERBORNE	105
JACKY POWER TOURS, TRALEE, Co KERRY	218
POYNTERS COACHES LTD, ASHFORD, KENT	130
PREMIER CONNECTIONS TRAVEL LTD, LUTON	83
PREMIER TRAVEL LTD, BRISTOL	86
PREMIERE TRAVEL LTD, NOTTINGHAM	157
PRENTICE COACHES LTD, HADDINGTON	192
PRENTICE WESTWOOD, WEST CALDER	201
PRESTON BUS LTD, PRESTON	134
PRICES COACHES, WREXHAM	211
PRIDE OF THE CLYDE COACHES LTD, GREENOCK	195
PRINCESS COACHES LTD, WEST END, SOUTHAMPTON	124
PRIORY COACH & BUS LTD, NORTH SHIELDS	175
PROBUS & CAR, KENMARE, Co KERRY	218
F PROCTER & SON LTD, FENTON	169
PROCTERS COACHES (NORTH YORKSHIRE) LTD, LEEMING BAR	152
PROSPECT COACHES (WEST) LTD, STOURBRIDGE	178
PROTOURS (ISLE OF MAN) LTD, DOUGLAS, IoM	187
PROTOURS LTD, SWADLINCOTE	100
PROVENCE PRIVATE HIRE, ST ALBANS	127
PULFREYS COACHES, GRANTHAM	138
PULHAM & SONS (COACHES) LTD, BURTON ON THE WATER	118
PULLMAN DINER, KNOTTINGLEY	182

Q

Operator	Page
QUANTOCK MOTOR SERVICES LTD, TAUNTON	164

R

Operator	Page
R & B TRAVEL, LUDLOW	161
R. & R. COACHES LTD (BEELINE), WARMINSTER	184
R B TRAVEL, PYTCHLEY	155
R H TRANSPORT SERVICES, WITNEY	159
R. K. F. TRAVEL, STROOD	131
R S TAXIS & MINICOACH HIRE, INVERURIE	189
RADLEY COACH TRAVEL, BRIGG	138 150
RADMORES TRAVEL, PLYMPTON	103
RAINHAM COACH CO, THE, GILLINGHAM	131
RAMBLER COACHES, HASTINGS	111
RAMON TRAVEL, BOSCOMBE	105
RAYLEIGH ROADWAYS LTD, WICKFORD	115
RAYS COACHES, PLYMOUTH	103
READING & WOKINGHAM COACHES, WOKINGHAM	85
READING HERITAGE TRAVEL, READING	85

Operator	Page
READING TRANSPORT LTD, READING	85
REAYS COACHES LTD, WIGTON	96
RED ARROW COACHES LTD, HUDDERSFIELD	182
RED KITE COMMERCIAL SERVICES, LEIGHTON BUZZARD	88
REDLINE BUSES, AYLESBURY	88
RED ROSE TRAVEL, AYLESBURY	88
REDROUTE BUSES LTD, NORTHFLEET	131
REDFERN TRAVEL LTD, MANSFIELD	100, 157
RED KITE COMMERCIAL SERVICES, TILSWORTH	84
REDLINE TRAVEL, LEYLAND	134
REDWING COACHES, LONDON SE24	144
REDWOODS TRAVEL, CULLOMPTON	103
REES COACH TRAVEL, LLANELLY HILL, ABERGAVENNY	207
REEVES COACH SERVICE, CHORLEY	134
REG'S COACHES LTD, WELWYN	127
REGAL BUSWAYS LTD, CHELMSFORD	115
REGENT COACHES, WHITSTABLE	131
REIDS OF RHYNIE, RHYNIE, BY HUNTLY	189
RELIANCE LUXURY COACHES, BENFLEET	115
RELIANCE MOTOR SERVICES, SUTTON-ON-FOREST, YORK	152
RENNIES OF DUNFERMLINE LTD, DUNFERMLINE	193
RENOWN COACHES, BEXHILL	111
REYNOLDS COACHES LTD, GREAT YARMOUTH	149
REYNOLDS DIPLOMAT COACHES, WATFORD	127
RHIEW VALLEY MOTORS, WELSHPOOL	209
RICHARDS BROS, CARDIGAN	205, 208
RICHARDSON'S COACHES, HARTLEPOOL	109
RICHARDSON TRAVEL LTD, MIDHURST	180
RICHMOND'S COACHES, BARLEY	90, 115, 127
RIDGWAYS COACHES, PORT TALBOT	207
RIDDLER'S COACHES LTD, ARBROATH	189
RIDLERS LTD, DULVERTON	164
RIDUNA BUSES, ALDERNEY	187
JOHN RIGBY TRAVEL, BATLEY	182
RIVER LINK, DARTMOUTH	103
RIVERSIDE COACHWAYS LTD, TELFORD	161
RIVERSIDE TRANSPORT LTD, BARRHEAD	192
ROADMARK TRAVEL LTD, ASHINGTON	180
ROBERTS COACHES, ABERYSTWYTH	205
ROBERTS COACHES LTD, HUGGLESCOTE	136
ROBERTS MINI COACHES, RHANDIR	205
ROBERTS TOURS, WINGATE	109
ROBIN HOOD TRAVEL LTD, LEEK	169
A & M A ROBINSON SEAVIEW SERVICES LTD, SANDOWN, IoW	128
ROBINSON KIMBOLTON, KIMBOLTON	90
ROBINSONS HOLIDAYS, GREAT HARWOOD	134
ROBINSONS COACHES, APPLEBY	96
RODGER'S COACHES LTD, CORBY	155
ROLLINSON SAFEWAY LTD, LEEDS	183
O. ROONEY COACH HIRE LTD, HILLTOWN	212
ELLIE ROSE TRAVEL LTD, HULL	110
ROSELYN COACHES LTD, PAR	94
ROSS TRAVEL, FEATHERSTONE	183
ROSSENDALE TRANSPORT LTD, HASLINGDEN	134
ROTALA PLC	82
ROTHBURY MOTORS, ROTHBURY	155
ROUNDABOUT BUSES, BEXLEYHEATH	144
ROUTESPEK COACH HIRE LTD, BUNGAY	172
KEN ROUTLEDGE TRAVEL, COCKERMOUTH	96
ROVER COACHES, MULLINGAR, Co WESTMEATH	218
ROVER EUROPEAN LTD, HORSLEY, STROUD	118
ROWE & TUDHOPE, DUNDONALD	192
ROWELL COACHES, LOW PRUDHOE	155
ROWLANDS GILL TAXIS & COACHES, ROWLANDS GILL	175
ROY BROWNS COACHES, BUILTH WELLS	208
ROYALE EUROPEAN COACHES, UXBRIDGE	144
ROYLES TRAVEL, SHEFFIELD	166
ROY PHILLIPS, SLEAFORD	138
RURAL DEVELOPMENT TRUST, DOUGLAS WATER	199
RUTHERFORDS TRAVEL, EASTERGATE	180

S

Operator	Page
SAFEGUARD COACHES LTD, GUILDFORD	173
SAFFORD COACHES LTD, SANDY	90
SANDERS COACHES LTD, HOLT	149
SANDGROUNDER COACHES, SOUTHPORT	134, 147
SARGEANTS BROS LTD, KINGTON	125
SCARBOROUGH & DISTRICT	153
SCARLET BAND, WEST CORNFORTH	109
SCOTBUS LTD, INVERNESS	195
SCOTLAND & BATES, APPLEDORE	131
SCOTTISH CITYLINK COACHES LTD, GLASGOW	194
SEA VIEW COACHES (POOLE) LTD	105
SEAGER'S COACHES LTD, CHIPPENHAM	185
SEALANDAIR COACHING (IRELAND), DUBLIN	218
SEATH COACHES, EAST STUDDAL, Nr DOVER	131
SELVEY'S COACHES, CAMBUSLANG	194
SELWYNS TRAVEL SERVICES, MANCHESTER AIRPORT	93, 121
H. SEMMENCE & CO LTD, WYMONDHAM	149
SERENE TRAVEL, BEDLINGTON	156
SEWARDS COACHES, AXMINSTER	103
SHAFTESBURY & DISTRICT MOTOR SERVICES LTD	105
SHAMROCK BUSES LTD, POOLE	105
MATT SHANAHAN COACHES, WATERFORD	218
SHARPE & SONS (NOTTINGHAM) LTD, NOTTINGHAM	158
HARRY SHAW, COVENTRY	178
SHAWS OF MAXEY, PETERBOROUGH	91
SHAWS OF WHITLEY, GOOLE	153
SHEARER OF HUNTLY LTD, HUNTLY	189
SHEARINGS HOLIDAYS, EXHALL	178
SHEARINGS HOLIDAYS, NORMANTON	183
SHEARINGS HOLIDAYS, TORQUAY	103
SHEARINGS HOLIDAYS, WARRINGTON	93
SHEARINGS HOLIDAYS, WIGAN	121
SHERBURN VILLAGE COACHES	109
SHERWOOD TRAVEL, IMMINGHAM	150
SHIEL BUSES, ACHARACLE	195
SHIRE TRAVEL INTERNATIONAL LTD, HEDNESFORD	169
SHORELINE BUS & COACH TRAVEL, BOURNEMOUTH	105
SHOREY'S TRAVEL, MAULDEN	84
B. R. SHREEVE & SONS LTD, LOWESTOFT	172
SHROPSHIRE COUNTY COUNCIL, SHREWSBURY	162
SHUTTLE BUSES LTD, KILWINNING	196
SIDLAW EXECUTIVE TRAVEL (SCOTLAND) LTD, AUCHTERHOUSE	189 191
SIESTA INTERNATIONAL HOLIDAYS LTD, MIDDLESBROUGH	109, 153
SILCOX MOTOR COACH CO LTD, PEMBROKE DOCK	208

Operator	Page
SILLAN TOURS LTD, SHERCOCK, Co CAVAN	218
SILVER CHOICE, EAST KILBRIDE	199
SILVER STAR COACH HOLIDAYS LTD, CAERNARFON	207
SILVERDALE LONDON LTD, HAYES	144
SILVERDALE TOURS LTD, NOTTINGHAM	158
SILVERLINE LANDFLIGHT, SOLIHULL	178
SIMS TRAVEL, BOOT	97
SIMONDS OF BOTESDALE LTD, DISS	149
SIMPSON'S COACHES, ROSEHEARTY	189
SIXTY SIXTY COACHES, PENTREBACH	207
D. W. SKELTON, BRIDGWATER	164
SKILLS MOTOR COACHES LTD, BULWELL	158
SKINNERS OF OXTED	173
SKYLINERS LTD, NUNEATON	176
SLACKS TRAVEL, MATLOCK	100
SLANE'S COACH & TAXI HIRE, NEWTOWNHAMILTON, Co ARMAGH	212
SLEAFORDIAN COACHES, SLEAFORD	138
SLEIGHTS COACHES, SWINTON	167
SLOAN TRAVEL, ROSTREVOR, Co DOWN	213
SMITH & SONS COACHES, COUPAR ANGUS	198
JOHN SMITH & SONS LTD, THIRSK	153
SMITH'S COACHES (BE & GW SMITH), SHEPTON MALLET	164
SMITH, BUNTINGFORD	127
SMITHS OF MARPLE	93
SMITHS COACHES, CORBY GLEN, Nr GRANTHAM	138
SMITHS OF TRING	127
SMITHS MOTORS (LEDBURY) LTD, LEDBURY	125
HOWARD SNAITH COACHES, OTTERBURN	156
SNOWDON COACHES, EASINGTON	109
SOLENT BLUE LINE, EASTLEIGH	124
SOLENT COACHES LTD, RINGWOOD	124
SOLID ENTERTAINMENTS, GRIMSBY	150
SOLUS COACH TRAVEL LTD, TAMWORTH	170
SOMERBUS LTD, BRISTOL	164
SOULS COACHES LTD, OLNEY	88
SOUTH GLOUCESTERSHIRE BUS & COACH COMPANY, PATCHWAY, BRISTOL	87
SOUTH LANCS TRAVEL, ATHERTON	121
SOUTH MIMMS TRAVEL LTD, NORTH MYMMS	127
SOUTH WALES TRANSPORT (NEATH) LTD, NEATH	207
SOUTH WEST COACHES LTD/SOUTH WEST TOURS LTD, WINCANTON	164
SOUTHDOWN PSV LTD, COPTHORNE	180
SOUTHERN COACHES (NM) LTD, BARRHEAD	192
SOUTHERN VECTIS OMNIBUS CO LTD, NEWPORT, IoW	128
SOUTHGATE & FINCHLEY COACHES LTD, LONDON N11	144
SOVEREIGN COACHES, LYME REGIS	106
SPA COACHES, STRATHPEFFER	195
SPEEDWELLBUS LTD, HYDE	121
SPOT HIRE TRAVEL, BEARSTED	131
SPRATTS COACHES (EAST ANGLIAN & CONTINENTAL) LTD, WRENINGHAM	149
SQUIRRELL'S COACHES, HITCHAM	172
ST ANDREWS EXECUTIVE TRAVEL, ST ANDREWS	194
STACEYS COACHES LTD, CARLISLE	97
STAGECOACH CAMBRIDGESHIRE, CAMBRIDGE	91
STAGECOACH EAST, BEDFORD	84
STAGECOACH EAST, NORTHAMPTON	158
STAGECOACH IN EAST KENT & EAST SUSSEX	112, 131
STAGECOACH EAST MIDLANDS, LINCOLN	100, 110, 138, 150, 158
STAGECOACH IN FIFE	193
STAGECOACH GROUP PLC	81
STAGECOACH IN HAMPSHIRE, BASINGSTOKE	124
STAGECOACH IN HANTS & SURREY, ALDERSHOT	124
STAGECOACH HIGHLAND	195
STAGECOACH MANCHESTER, ARDWICK, MANCHESTER	121
STAGECOACH MERSEYSIDE, LIVERPOOL	147
STAGECOACH MIDLANDS, NORTHAMPTON	155
STAGECOACH NORTH EAST, SUNDERLAND	175
STAGECOACH NORTH WEST, CARLISLE	97, 134
STAGECOACH IN ORKNEY	197
STAGECOACH IN OXFORDSHIRE	160
STAGECOACH SCOTLAND LTD, KIRKCALDY	198
STAGECOACH SHEFFIELD	167
STAGECOACH SOUTH, CHICHESTER	180
STAGECOACH IN SOUTH WALES, CWMBRAN	210
STAGECOACH SOUTH WEST, EXETER	103, 164
STAGECOACH SUPERTRAM, SHEFFIELD	167
STAGECOACH IN WARWICKSHIRE, RUGBY	176
STAGECOACH WEST, GLOUCESTER	118
STAGECOACH WEST SCOTLAND, AYR	199
STAGECOACH YORKSHIRE, BARNSLEY	167
F. W. STAINTON & SON LTD, KENDAL	97
STALLION COACHES, CHELMSFORD	116
STAN'S COACHES, MALDON	116
STANLEY TRAVEL	109
STANWAYS COACHES, STOKE-ON-TRENT	170
STAR TRAVEL, AYLESBURY	88
STEELS LUXURY COACHES, ADDINGHAM	183
STEPEND COACHES, GLENMAVIS	197
STEPHENSONS OF EASINGWOLD LTD, EASINGWOLD	153
STEPHENSONS OF ESSEX LTD, ROCHFORD	116
STEVENSONS TRAVEL, PONTEFRACT	183
STEVE STOCKDALE COACHES (VALIDFORD LTD), SELBY	153
STEWARTS OF MORTIMER LTD, READING	85
STODDARDS LTD, CHEADLE, STAFFS	170
STOCKHAMS COACH & TAXIS, CRICKHOWELL	209
WILLIAM STOKES & SONS LTD, CARSTAIRS	197 199
STONEHOUSE COACHES, STONEHOUSE	199
JIM STONES COACHES, WARRINGTON	93
STONES COACHES OF BATH	164
E STOTT & SONS LTD, MILNSBRIDGE	183
STOTT'S TOURS (OLDHAM) LTD	121
STRAFFORD'S COACHES, MINERA	211
STRATHTAY SCOTLAND OMNIBUSES LTD, KIRKCALDY	192
STRATOS TRAVEL LTD, NEWTOWN, POWYS	209
STRAWBERRY, ST HELENS	147
STREAMLINE (KENT) LTD, MAIDSTONE	131
STREETS COACHWAYS LTD, BARNSTAPLE	103
STRINGERS PONTEFRACT MOTORWAYS, PONTEFRACT	183
STUART'S COACHES LTD, CARLUKE	199
SUIRWAY BUS & COACH SERVICES LTD, PASSAGE EAST, Co WATERFORD	218
SULLIVAN BUSES LTD, POTTERS BAR	127
SUMMERCOURT TRAVEL LTD, SUMMERCOURT	94
SUMMERDALE COACHES, LETTERSTON	208
SUNBEAM COACHES LTD, NORWICH	149
SUNBURY COACHES, SHEPPERTON	144

Operator	Page
SUN FUN INTERNATIONAL, EARITH	91
SUNRAY TRAVEL LTD, EPSOM	174
SUPERTRAVEL OMNIBUS LTD, SPEKE	147
SUPREME COACHES, CHELMSFORD	116
SURELINE COACHES, WOKING	174
SURREY CONNECT, CRAWLEY	174
SUSSEX COUNTRY COACH HIRE, SHOREHAM	112, 182
SUTTON COMMUNITY TRANSPORT	174
SWALLOW COACH CO LTD, RAINHAM, ESSEX	116
SWANBROOK TRANSPORT LTD, CHELTENHAM	118
SWANS TRAVEL, CHADDERTON, OLDHAM	121
SWEYNE COACHES, GOOLE	110
SWIFTS HAPPY DAYS TRAVEL, DONCASTER	167
SWIFTSURE TRAVEL (BURTON UPON TRENT) LTD	170
SWILLY BUS SERVICE, LONDONDERRY & LETTERKENNY	213, 218

T

Operator	Page
T G M GROUP LTD, HARLOW	116
T G M GROUP LTD, HEATHROW AIRPORT	144
T L C TRAVEL LTD, BRADFORD	183
T M TRAVEL, HALFWAY	167
T N C COACHES, CASTLE BROMWICH	179
TALISMAN COACH LINES, GREAT BROMLEY, COLCHESTER	116
TALLY HO! COACHES LTD, KINGSBRIDGE	103
TAMWORTH COACH CO, TAMWORTH	170
TANAT VALLEY COACHES, LLANRHAEDR YM, OSWESTRY	209
TANTIVY BLUE COACH TOURS, ST HELIER, JERSEY	187
TAPPINS COACHES, DIDCOT	160
TOM TAPPIN LTD, OXFORD	160
TARGET TRAVEL, PLYMOUTH	104
TATES COACHES, MARKYATE	84, 127
TATE'S TRAVEL GROUP, BARNSLEY	167
TAVISTOCK COMMUNITY TRANSPORT, GUNNISLAKE	94
TAW & TORRIDGE COACHES LTD, OKEHAMPTON	104
TAYLORS COACH TRAVEL LTD, YEOVIL	164
TEEJAY TRAVEL LTD, CARNOUSTIE	189
TELFORD'S COACHES LTD, NEWCASTLETON	190
TERRYS COACH HIRE, COVENTRY	179
TERRY'S COACHES, HEMEL HEMPSTEAD	127
TEES VALLEY LUXURY COACHES LTD, EAGLESCLIFFE	109
TEES VALLEY STAGE CARRIAGE, REDCAR	153
TEST VALLEY TRAVEL LTD, WHITEPARISH	124, 185
TETLEYS MOTOR SERVICES LTD, LEEDS	183
THAMESDOWN TRANSPORT LTD, SWINDON	185
THAMES TRAVEL, WALLINGFORD	160
THIRLWELL'S COACHES, NEWCASTLE	175
THOMAS BROS, LLANGADOG	204
D J THOMAS COACHES LTD, NEATH	208
EDWARD THOMAS & SON, WEST EWELL	174
THOMAS OF RHONDDA, PORTH	210
DAVID THOMPSON TOURS LTD, CHRISTCHURCH	106
THOMSETT'S COACHES, DEAL	131
THORNES INDEPENDENT LTD, HEMINGBROUGH	153
THREE STAR COACHES.COM, LUTON	84, 88, 128
TIGER EUROPEAN, NOTTINGHAM	158
TILLEY'S COACHES, BUDE	95
TIMEBUS TRAVEL, ST ALBANS	145
TITTERINGTON COACHES LTD, BLENCOW	97
TOMORROWS TRANSPORT, ENFIELD	145
TONNA LUXURY COACHES LTD, NEATH	208
TOURIST COACHES LTD, SALISBURY	185
TOURMASTER COACHES, CROWLAND	138
TOWER COACHES, WIGTON	97
TOWLERS COACHES LTD, WISBECH	91
TOWN & COUNTRY MOTOR SERVICES LTD, HURWORTH MOOR, Nr DARLINGTON	109
TOWNLYNX, HOLYWELL	206
TRACKS VEHICLE SERVICES LTD, ROMNEY MARSH	131
TRAMONTANA, MOTHERWELL	197
TRANSDEV PLC	80
TRANSDEV BURNLEY & PENDLE	134
TRANSDEV KEIGHLEY & DISTRICT	183
TRANSDEV HARROGATE & DISTRICT	153
TRANSDEV LANCASHIRE UNITED	135
TRANSDEV YORK	153
TRANSDEV YORKSHIRE COASTLINER, MALTON	153
TRANSIT EXPRESS TRAVEL, LENTON	158
TRANSLINC, LINCOLN	138
TRANSLINK, BELFAST	213
TRATHENS TRAVEL SERVICES, PLYMOUTH	104
TRAVEL DIRECT LTD, SEEFIN, Co GALWAY	218
TRAVEL EXPRESS LTD, WOLVERHAMPTON	179
TRAVELMASTERS, SHEERNESS	131
TRAVEL WRIGHT LTD, NEWARK-ON-TRENT	158
TRAVELGREEN COACHES, DONCASTER	167
TRAVEL GUEST, BOURNEMOUTH	106
TRAVELINE, MINEHEAD	164
TRAVELLERS CHOICE, THE, CARNFORTH	135
TRAVELSURE, BELFORD	156
TRAVELWISE COACHES, LARNE, Co ANTRIM	213
TRAVEL-WRIGHT, MOUNTSORREL	136
TREACY COACHES, BALLINA, Co MAYO	218
TRELEY COACH HIRE, PENZANCE	95
TRENT BARTON, HEANOR	100
TRUEMANS COACHES (FLEET) LTD, FLEET	124
TUERS MOTORS LTD, PENRITH	97
TURNERS TOURS, CHULMLEIGH	104
TURNERS COACHWAYS (BRISTOL) LTD, BRISTOL	87
T W COACHES LTD, SOUTH MOLTON	104
TWIN VALLEY COACHES, SOWERBY BRIDGE	183
TYNE VALLEY COACHES LTD, HEXHAM	156
TYNEDALE GROUP TRAVEL, HALTWISTLE	156
R S TYRER LTD, ADLINGTON	135
TYRER TOURS LTD, NELSON	135

U

Operator	Page
UNICORN COACHES LTD, HATFIELD	128
UNITY COACHES, RETFORD	158
UNO LTD, HATFIELD	128
UPWELL & DISTRICT COACHES, UPWELL	91
GRAHAM URQUHART TRAVEL LTD, INVERNESS	195

V

Operator	Page
VALE TRAVEL, AYLESBURY	88
VEAZEY COACHES LTD, HUNTINGDON	91
VENTURE TRANSPORT (HENDON) (1965) LTD, HARROW	145
VEOLIA TRANSPORT CYMRU PLC, CARDIFF	210

Operator	Page
VEOLIA TRANSPORT ENGLAND PLC, NOTTINGHAM	158, 175
VEOLIA TRANSPORT UK LTD	82
VICEROY OF ESSEX LTD, SAFFRON WALDEN	116
VICTORIA COACHES, PETERHEAD	189
VIKING COACHES, HEYWOOD	121
VIKING MINICOACHES, BROADSTAIRS	131
VILLAGER MINIBUS, SHARNBROOK	84
VISION TRAVEL, COSHAM	124
VOEL COACHES LTD, DYSERTH	205

W

Operator	Page
W+H MOTORS, CRAWLEY	180
W+M TRAVEL, WISBECH	91
A WAIT & SON, CHIRNSIDE	190
WALDEN TRAVEL LTD, SAFFRON WALDEN	116
WALLIS COACHWAYS, BILSTHORPE, Nr NEWARK	158
WALTONS COACHES, GRANGETOWN, CARDIFF	203
WARDLE TRANSPORT, BURSLEM	170
WARRINGTON BOROUGH TRANSPORT LTD	93
WARRINGTON COACHES LTD, ILAM	100
WATERMILL COACHES, FRASERBURGH	189
WATERSIDE TOURS - see HYTHE & WATERSIDE	
PAUL WATSON TRAVEL, DARLINGTON	109
WATTS COACHES, BONVILSTON, Nr CARDIFF	203, 211
WAVERLEY COACHES LTD, ST HELIER, JERSEY	187
WEALES WHEELS, LLANDRINDOD WELLS	209
WEARDALE MOTOR SERVICES LTD, STANHOPE	109
WEAVAWAY TRAVEL, NEWBURY	85
WEBB'S PETERBOROUGH	91
WEBBER BUS, BRIDGWATER	164
WELLGLADE LTD	82
WELSH DRAGON TRAVEL, NEWPORT, MONMOUTHSHIRE	208
WELSH'S COACHES LTD, PONTEFRACT	183
WESSEX CONNECT, BRISTOL	87
WEST END TRAVEL/RUTLAND TRAVEL, MELTON MOWBRAY	136
WEST KENT BUSES, WEST KINGSDOWN	131
WEST MIDLANDS SPECIAL NEEDS TRANSPORT, BIRMINGHAM	179
WESTBUS COACH SERVICES LTD, HOUNSLOW	145
WESTERHAM COACHES, OXTED	131
WESTERN GREYHOUND LTD, NEWQUAY	95
WESTRINGS COACHES, EAST WITTERING	180
WEST'S COACHES LTD, WOODFORD GREEN	145
WESTWAY COACH SERVICES LTD, LONDON SW20	145
WHARTONS TRAVEL LTD, CROSSDONEY, Co CAVAN	218
WHEELERS TRAVEL LTD, SOUTHAMPTON	124
WHEAL BRITON TRAVEL, TRURO	95
WHINCOP'S COACHES, SAXMUNDHAM	172
WHIPPET COACHES LTD, SWAVESEY	91
WHITE BUS SERVICES, WINDSOR	85
WHITEGATE TRAVEL LTD, NORTHWICH	93
WHITELAWS COACHES, STONEHOUSE	200
WHITE ROSE BUS COMPANY LTD, BRADFORD	183
WHITES COACHES, BRIDGE OF WALLS, SHETLAND	198
WHITES COACHES, WALLINGFORD	160
WHITTLE BUS & COACH, KIDDERMINSTER	186
WHYTES COACHES LTD, NEWMACHAR	188
WICKSONS TRAVEL, BROWNHILLS	179
WIDE HORIZON, HINCKLEY	136
WIGHTROLLERS, SANDOWN, ISLE OF WIGHT	128
ALBERT WILDE COACHES, HEAGE	100
WILFREDA BEEHIVE COACHES LTD, ADWICK-LE-STREET	167
WILKINSONS TRAVEL, ROTHERHAM	168
F R WILLETTS & CO, PILLOWELL, LYDNEY	118
A C WILLIAMS LTD, ANCASTER	139
WILLIAMS COACHES, BRECON	209
WILLIAMS TRAVEL, CAMBORNE	95
GWYN WILLIAMS & SONS LTD, LOWER TUMBLE	204
WILLIAMSONS OF ROTHERHAM	168
WILLS MINI COACHES, KINGSBRIDGE	104
WILSON'S OF RHU, RHU	190
WILSON'S COACHES, ROSSINGTON	168
WILTS & DORSET BUS COMPANY LTD, POOLE	106
WINDSOR-GRAY TRAVEL, WOLVERHAMPTON	179
WINDSORIAN COACHES LTD, WINDSOR	85
WINGS LUXURY TRAVEL LTD, HAYES	145
WINN BROS, NORTHALLERTON	154
PAUL S. WINSON COACHES LTD, LOUGHBOROUGH	136
WINTS COACHES, BUTTERTON, Nr LEEK	170
WISE COACHES LTD, HAILSHAM	112
WISTONIAN COACHES, SELBY	154
MAL WITTS EXECUTIVE TRAVEL, GLOUCESTER	118
WOKING COMMUNITY TRANSPORT, WOKING	174
WOMBWELL COACH TOURS LTD, BARNSLEY	168
WOOD BROTHERS TRAVEL LTD, BUCKFASTLEIGH	104
JOHN WOODHAMS VINTAGE TOURS, RYDE, IoW	128
WOODS COACHES, BARNSLEY	168
WOODS COACHES LTD, LEICESTER	136
WOODS COACHES, TILLICOULTRY	190
P WOODS MINICOACHES, HALLGLEN	193
WOODS TRAVEL LTD, BOGNOR REGIS	180
WOODSTONES COACHES LTD, KIDDERMINSTER	186
WOODWARD'S COACHES LTD, GLOSSOP	100
WOOFS OF SEDBERGH	97
WOOTTENS, CHESHAM	88
WORTHEN MOTORS/TRAVEL, LITTLE MINSTERLEY	162
WORTHING COACHES	180
WORTHS MOTOR SERVICES LTD, ENSTONE	160
WRIGHT BROS (COACHES) LTD, NENTHEAD	97
WRIGLEY'S COACHES LTD, IRLAM	121

Y

Operator	Page
YARDLEY TRAVEL LTD, BIRMINGHAM	179
YARRANTON BROS LTD, TENBURY WELLS	186
YELLOW BUSES, BOURNEMOUTH	106
YEOMANS CANYON TRAVEL LTD, HEREFORD	125
YESTERYEAR MOTOR SERVICES, DISEWORTH, DERBY	100
YORK PULLMAN, YORK	154
YORKS COACHES, COGENHOE	154
YORKSHIRE ROSE COACHES, BARNSLEY	168
ELIZABETH YULE, PITLOCHRY	198

Z

Operator	Page
Z & S INTERNATIONAL, AYLESBURY	88